I0199367

Bastard Battalion

A History of the 83rd Chemical Mortar Battalion in World War II

"We belonged to no one ... we always supported or were attached to others ... we were a bastard battalion." — James M. Lester

By Terry Lowry
Official Historian
83rd Chemical Mortar Battalion

COPYRIGHT © 2009 TERRY LOWRY

All rights reserved. Absolutely no portion of this book may be used or reproduced in any form, including electronic or digital, without written permission of the author. Failure to comply will result in prosecution to the fullest extent of the law.

LIBRARY OF CONGRESS
CATALOG CARD NO. 2008900122

ISBN-13: 978-0-9965764-1-3
ISBN-10: 0-9965764-1-X

First Printing: June 2009
Second Printing: 2018

Cover Art: Samuel Kweskin, HQ Company, 83rd Chemical Mortar Battalion
Courtesy: Jean Siegel-Kweskin

Back Cover Photo Credits:
Top: US Army Signal Corps Collection, Carlisle Barracks, PA
Bottom: Terry Lowry Collection

Cover Design by Studio 6 Sense - www.studio6sense.com

Layout & Graphics Design: Patty Tyler
Title page photographic designer: Ian Hopkins
Photo courtesy Kenneth Hopkins, Ford Hopkins Collection

35th Star Publishing
www.35thstar.com

83rd Chemical Mortar Battalion
Col. John P. McEvoy, (Ret.)

The 83rd Chemical Mortar Battalion proved that a superior combat unit could be put together in less than a year. The components made all the difference. The men came from several areas. The initial group was largely from New York, New Jersey, and Pennsylvania while the second filler arrived a few months later and was largely from Mississippi, Alabama, Georgia, and Tennessee. A sprinkling of key people came from other states.

The officers were reserve and reserve officer university graduates as well as graduates from the newly developed officer training schools. The lone West Pointer was the commanding officer, Kenneth A. Cunin, who had transferred from the Artillery to the Chemical Corps.

The weapon they were trained to use was the 4.2 rifled mortar designed initially to fire gas-filled shells. The maximum range of only 3200 yards meant that the weapon had to be close to the enemy to work.

The men who were to fire the weapons were products of the Great Depression. Not used to an easy life they expected none in the Army. They were a fitting cross-section of America and were willing and able. Some were college graduates with technical degrees. Some were skilled in the trades. Some tried their hands as cooks. For all but a few everything about the Army was new. Even three meals a day of uncertain quality.

But the conversion moved rapidly. Close order drill was finally mastered as were the new skills needed to set up, calculate, and rapidly fire the mortar. One helped the other to learn. Field artillery methods of firing were taught by Col. Cunin. Repetitive gun drill sharpened the gun crews and they learned how to direct fire at small targets.

Less than a year after first organized and only six months after the last filler of new men, the 83rd was off to the war. The long voyage from New York to Oran, North Africa opened the adventure that was to last over two years and made the 83rd Chemical Mortar Battalion one of the most decorated units in the Army.

The chance meeting of Col. Cunin with Bill Darby, a classmate at West Point, and now commander of the Rangers, an elite Infantry unit, proved invaluable. Col. Darby quickly recognized the potential of the 4.2 mortar after a demonstration of its lethality. The 83rd would give the Rangers the bulk of firing power to hold ground once seized and quickly soften up enemy defenses. The Rangers got new firepower and the 83rd got a support mission which was to last through two hard years.

What they did during these years is the story that follows. Only a small number completed the journey from Camp Gordon back to the States but they were joined by many more who added much to a job well done.

Col. (ret.) John P. McEvoy
Major, 83rd Chemical Mortar Battalion
2009

83rd Chemical Mortar Battalion Commanders

Maj./Lt. Col. Kenneth A. Cunin
June 10, 1942 - Sept. 26, 1943
Ohio State University

Maj./Lt. Col. William S. Hutchinson, Jr.
Sept. 26, 1943 - July 7, 1944
John McEvoy

Maj./Lt. Col. Sam Efnor, Jr.
July 7, 1944 - July 23, 1945
Scott Mindrum

Maj. Gordon M. Mindrum
July 23, 1945 - Sept. 10, 1945
Scott Mindrum

Capt. Robert B. Smith
Sept. 10, 1945 - Nov. 1945
Annette Smith

Acting Battalion Commanders
(during Lt. Col. Hutchinson's absences late 1943 - early 1944.)

Maj. David W. Meyerson (left)
(Ed Trey)

Capt. Edwin G. Pike (right)
(Pike Collection)

Introduction

Often I have been asked the same question: Why, after having written a number of successful books on the American Civil War, would I wish to write a daily account of the history of one particular military organization in World War II? For some time I asked myself that same question and could not come up with a proper answer. World War II was not exactly my area of expertise. But after my mother passed away in 2003 I came across about 60 V-Mail letters written during the war between her and my father, Charlie Lowry. They were still dating at the time, but the contents showed me a side of my parents I had never known, and took me to a place in history I had only read about or seen in movies or on television. It showed me a man removed from the rural mountains and farms of Fayette County, West Virginia, to a job at a Union Carbide chemical plant in urban Charleston of the same state, then suddenly thrust into a war which took him to the battlefields of Africa and Europe. And then the return home, marriage, and the birth of two sons. Growing up we heard my father briefly speak of the war but we never paid it much mind as the family had other interests. Besides, at that time nearly everybody's dad in the neighborhood had been in World War II. It didn't seem like anything special. Even as a young boy growing up in the 1950s, with my dad asleep in his easy chair, I would play with my World War II action set and use his legs as terrain for the soldiers, never realizing those same legs had helped fight the real war which saved the world. It wasn't until many years later that the truth became quite evident.

I can yet vividly recall that day in 1981 when my father and I were sitting around the home place. Suddenly he brought out an old foot locker filled with memorabilia from his service in World War II as a soldier with the 83rd Chemical Mortar Battalion. He had recently been diagnosed with terminal colon cancer and knew his remaining days were few. Opening the trunk carefully he sifted through the various contents – two duffle bags, his uniform coat and shirt with the distinctive unit shoulder patches, his military belt and buckle, chemical warfare collar insignia, a captured German artillery officer's coat and two hats, two German helmets, a Nazi dress parade bayonet, and a host of photographs and postcards from assorted places in Sicily, Italy, France, Germany, and Austria. This was not the first time I had seen these items but this time it was different. Now he took the time to tell me various anecdotes about the war, such as the loss of many friends on an LST at Anzio and the mortal fear he had experienced riding in a glider during the invasion of southern France. At the time I was uncertain as to why he had decided upon that particular moment in time to relay this information to me although upon reflection some 25 years later the answer has become obvious.

Throughout the years I had always shown an interest in military history. Our family had a long military legacy, with ancestors in the 4th West Virginia Infantry (Union) and the 60th Virginia Infantry (Confederate) in the American Civil War. My father's two older brothers had served in World War I, and two other brothers, along with my dad, fought in World War II. Some cousins served in Korea and my brother in Vietnam. I was just about the only male member of the family never to have served in the military, having failed my physical during the Vietnam era. I was a pacifist and detested the idea of war; yet, I had always acknowledged and respected the men and women who defended our country, often sacrificing their very own lives. My interest in military history grew intense and I soon embarked on a journey of penning a number of books on the American Civil War.

With his final days drawing near, I think my father recognized my interest in the military. He knew he would not live to tell his story, but he also knew that I could convey it in some way. He was so proud of his service, and that of his comrades, and wanted their story told for posterity. It took a number of years before I came to this realization, but now I can look back and understand and thank my father and all his fellow soldiers in the 83rd Chemical Mortar Battalion, as well as all the soldiers of World War II, for their unselfish sacrifice and bravery.

I have now met and interviewed hundreds of the veterans of the battalion and their family members, read their letters and diaries, spent countless hours in various repositories such as the National Archives reading their official reports, attended numerous reunions, and, unfortunately, witnessed many of them pass on during the completion of this project. And just like my dad, each and every one was so proud of their service, openly sharing their experiences and memories. I now look back and treasure the contents of my dad's foot locker and pray and hope I have answered his final unspoken wish – to tell the complete story, day by day, of the 83rd Chemical Mortar Battalion.

It's a story of courage, endurance, comradeship, loyalty, and the ultimate sacrifice, told here, for the most part, in their own words. It's not always a perfect story nor should it be. With over 2,000 men in the battalion's ranks at one time or another, there were bound to be some flawed characters. The surviving veterans recognized this and asked that I always be truthful and not just glorify their story. Such instances were few, however, and as a whole the

83rd Chemical Mortar Battalion became one of the premier combat organizations of World War II, well exemplified in a 1946 newspaper article that stated the 83rd "was considered one of the prize battalions in the European fighting. It contributed heavily toward final victory. " But perhaps their legacy, as well as that of all World War II veterans, can be found in Ecclesiastics 44: 1-10, 13-14 of the Old Testament, which reads in part:

"There are some of them who left a name, so that men declare their praise. And there are some who have no memorial, who have perished as though they had never lived; they have become as though they had not been born, and so have their children after them. But these were men of mercy, whose righteous deeds have not been forgotten. Their posterity will continue forever, and their glory will not be blotted out. Their bodies were buried in peace, and their name lives to all generations."

In 1946 the *Army and Navy Journal* reported: "Exactly 540 days on the front lines is the record of the 83rd Chemical Mortar Battalion whose once roaring 4.2's are now encased in oil and canvas. The 83rd's operations extended over two years, two continents, five countries and six campaigns. During that time it supported 17 Infantry divisions, 3 Armored divisions, 2 Airborne divisions and numerous task forces, including Rangers and British commandos, and fought under 6 American corps, 1 French corps, 2 American armies and 1 French army. Gela, Salerno, Venafro, Minturno, Anzio, Southern France, the Vosges, Alsace, Germany and Austria saw, heard and felt their 'goon gun' fire. The Battalion participated in glider and amphibious assaults. Its members received 350 Purple Hearts and 300 posthumous awards [*actually 876 Purple Hearts*]. Ninety-eight percent of its personnel had more than 85 points when hostilities ceased. The only regret of these Combat Chemics is that they were classed as 'service' forces not entitled to wear the combat badge of the infantrymen they fought shoulder to shoulder with."

To all the members of the 83rd Chemical Mortar Battalion – this is your history – this is your legacy.

Terry Lowry
2009

Hopkins and Shields Collections

Awards & Citations

When the 83rd Chemical Mortar Battalion was deactivated on November 26th, 1945, at Camp Myles Standish, Taunton, Massachusetts, their record was even more impressive than reported in the 1946 *Army and Navy Journal*, boasting:

3 Distinguished Service Crosses (all posthumous)
5 Legions of Merit (one posthumous)
9 Soldiers Medals
39 Silver Stars
97 Bronze Stars
5 Croix de Guerre

Number of men wounded and/or killed in action: While the number of KIA/WIA is unknown, Sam Kweskin, wartime editor of *Muzzleblasts*, advised that there were 876 Purple Hearts and 91 Oak Leaf Clusters awarded to men of the 83rd during their service with the battalion in Europe during WW II. Additionally, numerous cases of men wounded were never reported.

Unit Citations
Co. B ---- For action at Anzio, Italy, 15 to 21 February 1944
Co. C ---- For action near Chiunzi Pass, Italy 10-27 September 1943
Co. D ---- For action near Vietri-Sul-Mare, Italy 9-27 September 1943

Battle Streamers
Co. B ---- Distinguished Unit Streamer embroidered ANZIO
Co. C ---- Distinguished Unit Streamer embroidered CHIUNZI PASS
Co. D ---- Distinguished Unit Streamer embroidered VIETRI PASS
Co. C & Co. D ---- Streamer in the colors of the French Croix de Guerre,
with Palm embroidered CENTRAL ITALY
Co. D ---- Streamer in the colors of the French Croix de Guerre,
with Palm embroidered VOSGES

Campaign Streamers
Sicily (with arrowhead)
Naples-Foggia
Anzio (with arrowhead)
Rome-Arno
Southern France (with arrowhead)
Rhineland
Ardennes-Alsace
Central Europe

Number of days in combat: 508 [*some sources claim as many as 540 days*]

Number of rounds fired: 500,000 (estimated)

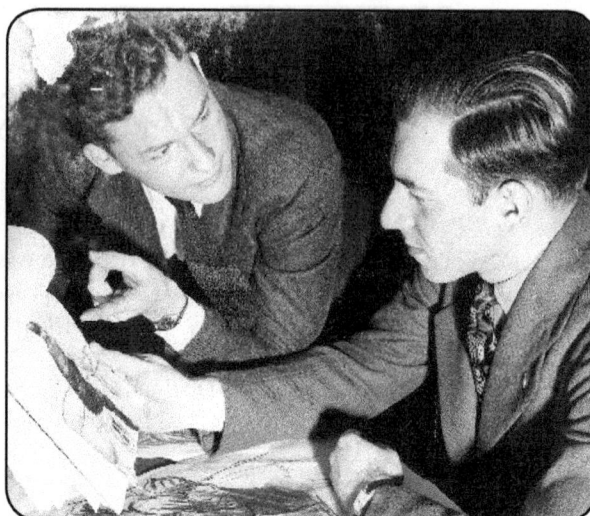

This book is dedicated to:
Samuel I. Kweskin
(1924-2005)
Co. D/HQ Co.
Premier Artist & Historian Extraordinaire
83rd Chemical Mortar Battalion
whose support and belief in me made this book possible

Painting by Sam Kweskin for the current 83rd Museum at Ft. Polk, LA. The sinking of *LST 422* is represented in the upper left, the Vosges winter in the center, the gliders in the upper right, and the Sicilian Invasion in the foreground. *Kweskin Collection*

Contents

Acknowlegdements

The following veterans of the 83rd Chemical Mortar Battalion contributed photographs, written accounts, or other material: Edward Kirk Atton, Grand Rapids, MI; George Barrett, Philadelphia, PA [deceased 2007]; Bernard Bernhardt, Pembroke, FL [deceased 2008]; Walter Bielski, Flint, MI [deceased 2008]; Clovis Birdwell, Indianapolis, IN; Robert S. Blamick, McKeesport, PA; Dale Blank, Cathedral City, CA [deceased 2005]; Fredrik M. Bockman, Nome, AK; Robert E. Bundy, Huntsville, AL; Robert J. Bush, Lake Havasu, AZ [deceased 2006]; John M. Butler, Collingswood, NJ; Joseph E. Cannetti, Lexington Park, MD; Thomas A. Cascio, West New York, NJ; Jean Pierre Combe, Loubiere, France; Edward ("Stan") Davidson, Manchester, NJ; Vicente DeLeon, San Jose, CA; Herbert Durfee, Lehigh, FL; Lawrence G. Ertzberger, Martin, GA; Robert W. Fenton, Cheboygan, MI [deceased 2008]; Lloyd L. Fiscus, Bradford, PA; James R. Fitzgerald, Louisville, KY [deceased 2008];William J. Gagliardi, Staten Island, NY; William J. Gallagher, Jr., Philadelphia, PA [deceased 2007]; James H. Gallahan, Fredericksburg, VA; Karl F. Garrett, Richmond, VA; Joseph Garsson, Los Angeles, CA [deceased 2007]; Paul S. Giles, Moultrie, GA [deceased 2008]; Alfred E. Green, Jr., Newtown, CT; William C. Gregory, New Albany, MS; John J. Hajdinyak, Easton, PA; Hale H. Hepler, Millboro, VA; Raymond W. Hoover, Milton, PA; Byron H. Jordan, Milledgeville, GA [deceased 2008]; Earl F. Kann, York, PA [deceased 2005]; Samuel I. Kweskin, Boca Raton, FL [deceased 2005]; James Marion Lester, Worthington, MN [deceased 2006]; Harry M. Lloyd, Rushville, IN; Loy J. Marshall, Griffin, GA [deceased 2006]; Nolan C. McCraine, Centreville, MS [deceased 2008]; John P. McEvoy, Arlington, VA; Carl McNabb, Jasper, TN [deceased 2007]; Gordon M. Mindrum, Cincinnati, OH [deceased 2007]; Martin J. Moloney, River Grove, IL; Jerome ("Jerry") Muschinske, St. Francis, WI; Audie W. Pierce, Kenosha, WI [deceased 2004]; Eugene A. Plassmann, Los Alamos, NM [deceased 2009]; Lawrence H. Powell, Beaver, PA [deceased 2006]; Antonio Rabaiotti, Johnston, RI; Mario Ricci, San Mateo, CA; Perry Rice, Branford, CT; Clark H. Riddle, Greensburg, PA [deceased 2008]; Kelly Seibels, Mobile, AL; William V. Slider, Moss Point, MS; Steve Snyder, Monaca, PA; Harold L. St. Gemme, Little Rock, AR; Leo ("Lee") C. Steedle, Oakdale, NY; J. T. Taunton, Opelika, AL; Kelso C. ("Red") Thompson, Corta Madera, CA; Lemuel R. Tillman, Nashville, TN; Carlos R. Trautman, Tower City, PA; Edward L. Trey, Frederick, MD; Stephen W. Vukson, Trafford, PA; Rudolph Whitt, Cedar Bluff, VA; Malcolm Doyle Wilkinson, Corpus Christi, TX; Curtis A. Williams, Memphis, TN; Lawrence L. Williams, Fulton, MS; Joseph A. Williamson, Margate City, NJ [deceased 2007].

The following families of deceased members of the 83rd Chemical Mortar Battalion contributed photographs, written accounts, or other material: Martha Anderson, Pensacola, FL (John E. Anderson); Deborah Byers Anspach (Charles L. Byers); Cpl. William J. Anspach, Camp Pendleton, CA (Charles L. Byers); Johnny Ayers, Clarksville, GA (Simeon B. Ayers); Noureen Baer, Newhall, CA (John Baer); Dr. John W. Beasley, Brooklyn, WI (James O. Beasley); Carole Beller, South Lake Tahoe, CA (Robert J. Bush); Bob & Lanie Lombardi Bencivenga (Frank Lombardi); Joyce Berry, Lebanon, TN (James Glenn Helsel); David Bishop, Princeton, WV (Melvin Bishop); Pat Blank, Rancho Mirage, CA (Dale C. Blank); Fran Borkhuis, Brooksville, FL, and Thomasina Edwards and Fred Thompson (George Borkhuis); Marcia Bunker, Camarillo, CA (Edwin "Bud" Pike); Mrs. Rupert O. Burford, Charleston, WV (Rupert O. Burford); Dick Carothers, Williamsport, PA (Edward F. Carothers); Jim Czanecki (Joseph E. Kozicki); Elizabeth Daly, Troy, MI (Kenneth K. Laundre); Sandi Daniel, Woodburn, OR (Leonard R. Kenney); Marcia Daoust and Neal & Bruton Peterson, Huntington, WV (Russell H. Peterson); Jean Decky, Deptford, NJ (Daniel J. Shields); David Dougherty, Fort Collins, CO (James F. Dougherty); Marcel R. Dubois, Irasburg, VT (Gerard L. Dubois); Anne Efnor, Salt Lake City, UT (Sam Efnor, Jr.); Daniel Else, IL (Salvatore Sapio); Brian P. Endlein (Frederick W. Endlein); Wilma S. Fisher, Calumet City, IL (James H. Fisher); Bengie Foley, New Albany, MS (Clyde McBryde); Charlie Gilles (George E. Stephenson); Warren Glossner, Lock Haven, PA (Nevin Glossner); Dr. John C. Ford, Germantown, TN (William C. Ford); Marsha Henry Goff, Lawrence, KS (Lester Lew Henry); Karen Gozur, Campbell, OH (Steve Gozur); Don Harp, Panama City Beach, FL (Carlos O. Harp); Martha Anderson Harrison, Pensacola, FL (John E. Anderson); Alice L. Hartley, Tupelo, MS (Andrew C. Leech); Francis Hodgson, Jr., Surf City, NJ (William J. Hodgson); Kenneth F. Hopkins, Hewitt, NJ (Ford E. Hopkins); Jo Ann Howell, Los Alamos, CA (Vester L. Turner); Eva M. Hughes, West Des Moines, IA (Harold Hughes); Charles W. Hulcher, Glen Allen, VA (Julius C. "Doc" Hulcher); Gary Jordan, Cumming, GA (James C. Jordan); Debby Kalk (Herbert C. Kalk); Valerie Klauscher, Crescent, PA (George Tyma); Joel Kweskin, Charlotte, NC (Samuel I. Kweskin); Mary Jane Laus, Amherst, MA (Andre Laus); Gini Lemoine, Wilmington, DE (James Jack); Sandra McCollum, Blue Mountain, MS (William C. Ford); Sara P. McLarty, Oxford, MS (Hilton McLarty); Robert L. Merrill, Bedford, NH (Leonard A. "Spike" Merrill, Jr.); Regina Dunwiddie Mueller, Pittsburgh, PA (Walter L. Dunwiddie); Robert W. Nairn, Norman, OK (William P. Nairn); Susan O'Dea, Hewitt, NJ (Frank Papaccioli); Molina and Anne Oros,

Gahanna, OH (Edward Sutlic); Richard Pirani, Rockville Centre, NY (Eugene Pirani); Gail Pizzino, Mays Landing, NJ (Joseph A. Williamson); Susannah Powell, Fletcher, NC (Richard H. Griffin); Rich Rapp, Bellmawr, NJ (Earl W. Rapp); Delores "Kitten" Rice, Pigeon Forge, TN (Jim C. Myers); Dan Robinson, Jackson, MS (Jim H. Robinson); Tom Roy, Carbondale, IL; Lorraine M. Salvi, Laconia, NH (Laurence J. Censato); Dolly Sario, Florence, SC (Carl D. Johnson); Tim Seman, Youngstown, OH (Joseph E. Kozicki); Todd A. Siefferein, Indianapolis, IN (Kenneth Thomas); Jean Siegel, Staten Island, NY (Samuel I. Kweskin); Annette Smith, Truth or Consequences, NM (Robert B. Smith); Carl Sned (Anthony J. Kowalec); Ginny Spencer, Endwell, NY (Raymond J. Knapp); Dennis & Maggie Squires, Arnold, MD (Norman C. Squires); Larry Strickler, York, PA (Clair M. Strickler); Elizabeth Taylor, Doylestown, PA (Robert S. Taylor); Ann Thorpe, Abbottstown, PA (Robert F. Thorpe); Bryan Turan, Saucier, MS (Leonard W. Turan); Betty Turner, Downington, PA (William B. McFarland); Chadd Watson, Boone, NC (Clovis J. Jones); Chris Williamson, Egg Harbor Township, NJ (Joseph A. Williamson); James Withey, Tucson, AZ (Leonard A. "Spike" Merrill, Jr.).

Additional material on the 83rd Chemical Mortar Battalion was contributed by: Col. Roy L. Bartlett, Hudson, FL (for information on the 488th Port Battalion); Gary Bedingfield, Glasgow, Scotland (for his website on Baseball in Wartime); Robert Black, Carlisle, PA (for information on the Rangers); Lt. Col. Mike Bolluyt, Commander, 83rd Chemical Battalion; Patricia Bridges, Bethlehem, GA (daughter of Loy J. Marshall and current editor of *Muzzleblasts*); LTC Eric Brigham, 83rd Chemical Battalion, Ft. Polk, LA; Marie Carpenti, National Archives, Modern Military Branch, College Park, MD; Mary B. Chapman, Deputy Clerk of Court, U.S. Army Court of Criminal Appeals, Arlington, VA (for information on Court-martials); Kathy Ciolfi, Edgewood Arsenal Archives, MD; Capt. Jeffery D. Cooper, Chemical Corps, Ft. Leonard Wood, MO; Jim Correll (Webmaster: 488th Port Battalion); Deborah Dennis, Edgewood Arsenal Archives, MD; Bonnie Duncan, Red Lion, PA (for Earl F. Kann); H. Dale Durham, Director, U.S. Army Chemical Corps Museum, Ft. Leonard Wood, MO; LTC Scott Estes, 83rd Chemical Battalion, Ft. Polk, LA; Gregg Fitzgerald, Louisville, KY (for James R. Fitzgerald); Roger Gallahan, Quinton, VA (all for James H. Gallahan); John Hajdinyak (for John J. Hajdinyak); Joe Herbert, Coaldale, PA (for George Barrett); Sally Hibma, Vicki Hibma, Molly Lester, Brewster, MN (for James Marion Lester); Maj. Adam Hilburgh, 83rd Chemical Battalion, Ft. Polk, LA; Norman Holt, Portland, OR (for information on *YMS 43*); William Hoover, Darien, CT (son of Raymond W. Hoover); Hans Houterman (for his website on the Royal Navy Officers 1939-1945); Cliff Hyatt, AHEC/USAMHI Staff, Carlisle Barracks, PA; Don Kindell, dkindell1@woh.rr.com (for information on the Royal Navy); Frank M. Kloxin, Sioux Falls, SD (veteran of *YMS*); Michelle Kruel, Lexington Park, MD (for Joseph E. Cannetti); Fawn Lamb, Logan, UT (for Kenneth Lamb & the 11th Chemical Maintenance Co.); Iris Lester, Worthington, MN (for James Marion Lester); Christy Lindberg, Historian Assistant, USACMLS, Ft. Leonard Wood, MO; Kip Lindberg, Archivist, USACMLS, Ft. Leonard Wood, MO; Capt. William D. Linn; Jim Lloyd (for Harry M. Lloyd); Lt. Heather (Morgan) McColl, 83rd Chemical Battalion, Ft. Polk, LA; Kathryn A. McKellar, Administrative Assistant, M.I.T. Alumni Association, Cambridge, MA (for William S. Doughten, Jr.); Susan Miller, Rosslyn, VA (for Dan Miller); G. Scott Mindrum, Cincinnati, OH (for Gordon M. Mindrum); Lt. Col. Claudio Morino, Anzio, Italy and Anzio Museum, Anzio, Italy; Pam Pace, Millboro, VA (for Hale H. Hepler); Tom B. Paulson, Fremont, NE (for Raymond E. Paulson); Beth Plassmann, Los Alamos, NM (information on *LST 422*); Maj. Stephen Renshaw, 83rd Chemical Battalion, Ft. Polk, LA; Kathy A. Rice, Boston, MA (for Perry Rice); Dan & Patricia Russell, Woodbridge, VA; Kelly Seibels, Jr., Mobile, AL (for Kelly Seibels, Sr.); Karen Simioni, Lehigh, FL (for Herbert Durfee); Leslie C. Smith, Woodbridge, VA (83rd Chemical Battalion); Amy Snodgrass, asnodgra24@ yahoo.com, (for information on *YMS 43*); State Historical Society of Iowa, Des Moines, IA (Harold Hughes); George Theis, National World War II Glider Pilots Association; Raymond Van Pelt, 83rd Chemical Battalion, Forest Hill, MD; Darby Watkins, darby@starstream.net (for Col. William O. Darby), Linda Whalen, Greensburg, PA (Michael J. Rebick & Richard A. Bridge Letters).

This book would not have been possible without the outstanding contributions of Patricia Tyler, Alum Creek, WV, who developed the graphics and design, worked on the manuscript and roster, data entry, proof read, and scanned photographs and other material far above the call of duty. Also invaluable to this project were Mary Johnson, Historian, and Debra Basham, Archivist, both of the West Virginia State Archives, who proof read the manuscript; Edward Trey and Lee Steedle, 83rd veterans, who also proofed the manuscript; Ed Hicks of the West Virginia State Archives for photographic assistance; Cathy Miller of the West Virginia State Archives for invaluable assistance with research; John Bowen, Silver Springs, MD, for research assistance at the National Archives; Barbara Jean Cochran, St. Albans, WV, for research assistance; Bill Steedle, St. James, NY, for photographic scanning and technical assistance; Jack and Kay Dickinson, Barboursville, WV, for technical advice; Pam Gibson, South Charleston, WV, for technical assistance; and Steve Cunningham, Sissonville, WV, for making the book a reality.

ORIGINAL BATTALION OFFICER CADRE

TENT CITY, EDGEWOOD ARSENAL, MD

MAY 10, 1942

Kenneth A. Cunin
Battalion Commander
Ed Trey

William S. Doughten, Jr.
1st Lt.
MIT Yearbook

David W. Meyerson
1st Lt.
Scott Mindrum

Rupert O. Burford
1st Lt.
Mrs. Rupert Burford

Edwin G. Pike
1st Lt.
Pike Collection

Edward L. Trey
2nd Lt.
Ed Trey

Chapter One

EDGEWOOD ARSENAL
BIRTH OF THE
83RD CHEMICAL MORTAR BATTALION

Chemical Warfare School at Edgewood Arsenal, Maryland ca. 1942
Author's Collection

Edgewood Arsenal, home of the Chemical Warfare Service [*CWS*], was located on a historic piece of peninsular property in Maryland known as "Gunpowder Neck," acquired by the U.S. government in 1917. Soon afterward an officer candidate school [*O.C.S.*] was created for the Chemical Warfare Service, quickly followed by the formation of a "Gas and Flame" unit, which became the 1st Gas Regiment. Edgewood remained a temporary facility until the close of World War I, then immediately became "a chemical warfare experimental and research center." Near the close of 1919 a permanent facility was proposed, resulting in the first graduating class from the officer candidate school in 1921. By the time of World War II, Edgewood Arsenal had become a permanent and separate branch of the U.S. Army and official home of the Chemical Warfare School.[1]

Prior to the outbreak of World War II, a number of the officers who eventually would lead the 83rd Chemical Mortar Battalion served at Edgewood Arsenal. Typical of these men and their responsibilities was Edwin G. ("Bud") Pike of Portage, Wisconsin, who graduated in 1941 from the University of Wisconsin with a degree in chemistry. Following graduation he was made a 2nd lieutenant in the Chemical Warfare Service, United States Army, and sent to Edgewood Arsenal for additional training. But he was a bit skeptical when he arrived in late June and found himself in command of Co. D, 1st CWS Training Battalion, a group of about 250 African-American recruits. Describing the living conditions at Edgewood Arsenal, Pike wrote, "We are living in wooden barracks, having barren little rooms which I have always imagined nuns or monks would live in, only on a larger scale. The walls are wood and there is no furniture, other than a chair and an army cot, and only nails to hang your clothes on. However the food is as it should be for $33.00 per month. One other pleasant thing is that we officers arise at 7:00; not 5:30. As I have been getting to bed about 11:00, it all makes for a good, healthy life … [*being*] a 'colored' company we are stuck way off on one corner of the post, about 3 miles away from everything, including the officer's club."[2]

In August of 1941, Lt. Pike took on a bit of temporary extra responsibility as Commander of the Post Guard. "For that period of 24 hours I commanded the guard personnel of the entire Edgewood Arsenal," Pike wrote in a letter home. "I was personally responsible for the keeping of 43 prisoners, guardhouse, and general property of the Post. I was quite scared, but it was interesting. There are 21 guards on the Post, guarding plants such as the Mustard Gas Plant, Toxic Gas Yards, the Reservoir which supplies the Post with its water, the Phosgene Plant, etc. I had to make an inspection of these guards between 2 and 5 in the morning and this was rather scary too. 'Halt! Who's there.' 'Commander of the Guard.' 'Advance, Commander and be recognized.' Going through this procedure in the darkness with the guard standing there pointing a loaded .45 in your general direction ain't good … Yesterday and today I was Officer of the Day for the Replacement Training Center. He handles the special guard for the training center and has a few responsibilities. Wednesday and Thursday I conducted an Automatic Rifle Range for 36 men. I had never even fired or seen fired an automatic rifle, but that doesn't mean a thing. They tell you to do something in the Army and if you don't know how you learn how in a hurry. I learned and things went off fairly well. We went out on the range at 5:00 AM and by 1:30 PM I was pretty tired and hungry and for the first time since I got here I lost my temper at some of the men and mouthed off to them. A sergeant told me later, aside, that you could not get cooperation from the men that way, so I think I have learned a very important lesson. Treat them right and they'll treat you right. I think, however, that applies generally in one's relations with all people."[3]

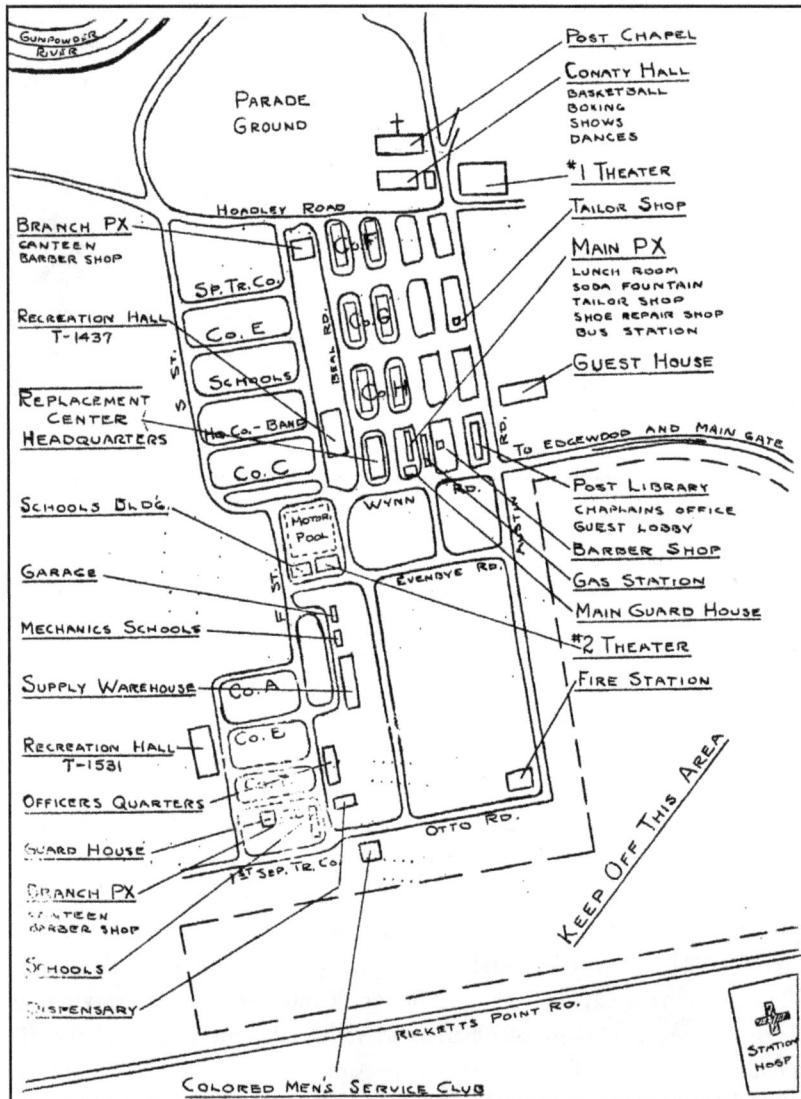

Map of Edgewood Arsenal-1942
Introducing Edgewood Arsenal

The Japanese attack on the American naval fleet at Pearl Harbor on December 7, 1941, ended the monotonous yet peaceful existence at Edgewood Arsenal. Two days later Pike vented over the attack: "Every time I think of those dirty g – d –m Japs I get madder. Here they were in Washington carrying on negotiations for peace and at the same time, back in Tokyo they were planning their surprise attack on the islands. It's enough to make one's blood boil." Describing the changes war brought to Edgewood Arsenal, Pike wrote, "No one is allowed off the post without special permission of the Commanding General. Sunday night, after hostilities had started and news reached here, all soldiers in town or anywhere outside of the post were rounded up by the Military Police and sent back to camp immediately. We had 3 special trains stop here, from New York, loaded almost completely with soldiers reporting back for duty. All officers have been ordered to dress in complete uniforms at all times. We cannot wear civilian clothes at any time. We also are to carry gas mask and revolvers at all times. Tonight at 9:00 we had a practice black-out of the entire post. Every light on the post was promptly turned out at that time, warning being sounded by a long blast of a siren. A plane flew over at that time to observe the effectiveness of the black-out. We have been given orders to 'be strict as hell with these men' and to work them hard as the devil because we

Co. E, CWS Training Battalion, Edgewood Arsenal, MD, 1942. Charlie Lowry (black circle) and Capt. Edwin Pike (black oval).
Author's Collection

don't [*know*] what we may be doing or where we may be in a week or a month."[4]

Along with war came the fear that the enemy would use chemical warfare, and Edgewood Arsenal, the center of the Chemical Warfare Service, prepared for such a possibility. In mid-December Lt. Pike discussed the subject in a letter home: "According to reports received here the Japanese are using mustard gas in China and elsewhere. And last week a boat load of about 300 tons of mustard gas was sent from here via Baltimore to an unknown destination. The opinion is prevalent that Chemical Warfare will be used extensively in our future actions."[5]

By February, Lt. Pike was Executive Officer of Co. E, 2nd CWS Training Battalion, a white company composed of many of the men who would later serve in the 83rd Chemical Mortar Battalion.[6] In fact, the organization was constituted on March 12, 1942, in the United States Army as the 83rd Chemical Battalion, listed as an inactive organization at Edgewood Arsenal, on March 18th, where the 208 enlisted men and five officers who would comprise the original cadre of the 83rd were drawn from the Chemical Warfare Service and Post Headquarters Replacement Center. The organization was formed in the old regimental style of ten companies with Headquarters and companies A through I.[7]

The routine of basic training at Edgewood was captured by Michele ("Michael"/"Mike") P. Codega, from Bristol County, Rhode Island; Russell H. Peterson, from Wisconsin via Charleston, West Virginia; and Lt. Robert Elihu Edwards, Jr., of Murphysboro, Illinois, a chemistry graduate of the University of Illinois at Urbana-Champaign. "Awakening in the morning with tears in my eyes … billeted downwind from the plant manufacturing tear gas … hikes [*with*] the leader shouting 'Gas! Gas!' - on went the gas masks as per instructions – then the dive into the ditch – then the frightening roar of a plane diving and leveling at tree tops while spraying us with tear gas – the command 'All

Karl H. McLaughlin (left) & Charlie Lowry (right) in snow at Edgewood Arsenal, MD, 1942. Lowry became one of the original cadre of the 83rd CMB. McLaughlin attended OCS and served as an instructor in the states throughout the war.
Author's Collection

Clear' – back on the road to continue the hike with masks still on," Codega wrote.[8] On March 14th Russell Peterson noted "The training period here is eight weeks … we've had 2 three-mile hikes, on the second one we were 'attacked' by an airplane and gassed (tear gas). A couple fellows didn't get their masks on in time … we had a rear guard which was to warn us of an approaching attack. They were a considerable distance behind the rest of the company, in fact, so far behind that they didn't notice that we had put on our gas masks. So, they walked right into the middle of the gassed area." Robert Edwards wrote on March 20th that " … we exercised - (3PM) sit up exercises and then a 1/2 hour of softball and then (4PM) we went down to the obstacle course. Do you get the idea? About 400 yards in length. Quite a work out." Peterson added on March 23rd "We have been practicing aiming our shooting (with no shells) the Springfield rifle." George R. Borkhuis, Co. I, 3rd CWS Training Battalion, a resident of the Bronx in New York, wrote on March 26th, "This camp covers about 26,000 acres and is devoted to gas warfare only … we live in tents and boy is it cold … whenever we leave our tents we have to carry our gas masks with us in case of an air attack which they feel will come soon … this is a brand new battalion being formed … there are four others in my tent. One is a Hungarian, one an Englishman, one a Czecko-Slovakian [*sic*], and one a Russian. They call ours the tent of all nations. Surprisingly, there are only two Jews in our camp."[9]

In late March, one of the worst snowstorms in years hit the camp. According to "Bud" Pike, "This good old unpredictable Maryland weather is holding true to form. After a nice stretch of beautiful spring weather, Saturday night it started snowing and snowed all that night and all day Sunday. The road (that main highway) was blocked between Edgewood and Baltimore and there were a lot of accidents. A lot of power lines were broken here on the post from the weight of the snow and for quite a while we were without any electricity. The snow was really deep. Then today we drilled all afternoon under a glaring sun in a morass of mud, snow, and water." George Borkhuis wrote, "We are having the worst blizzard they've ever had down here. It started last night about 9 o'clock and it's still snowing hard now. Three tents have collapsed and we've been out all day trying to put them up again. The lights all went out about twenty minutes ago … tomorrow will be our first real test, we're to have a 20-mile hike with full equipment … maybe it will be cancelled.[10] Many of the men, such as future 83rd motor pool mechanic Charlie Lowry, from the mountains of Fayette County, West Virginia, had their pictures taken in the snow.

On April 2nd, Lt. Robert Edwards wrote from Edgewood Arsenal, "Yesterday we were out inspecting a gas proof shelter and had started back -- most of us had coveralls on and those that didn't were segregated down at the tail end -- when here comes an airplane and sprays tear gas all over the segregated group and ran out before it reached the main column. Gee was it funny!" Before closing the letter he added some information on his schedule, writing, "Same routine at school. Played around with infantry tactics and rifles. Some days we have exercise and other times we get very little … There is a bill just passed to pay officers a $150 uniform bill except you can not have had your commission more than 3 years which lets me out. Ain't that terribull!" George Borkhuis wrote on the 4th, "Spring is really here. We are now wearing our summer uniform during the day as the sun gets quite hot … we had our first parade yesterday and were praised very highly by the colonel on our marching. I guess we have quite a good outfit." On April 6th Russell Peterson wrote "We were in a parade at Bel Air, Maryland, today. We carried Springfield rifles… our barracks [*Co. H, CWS Training Battalion*]

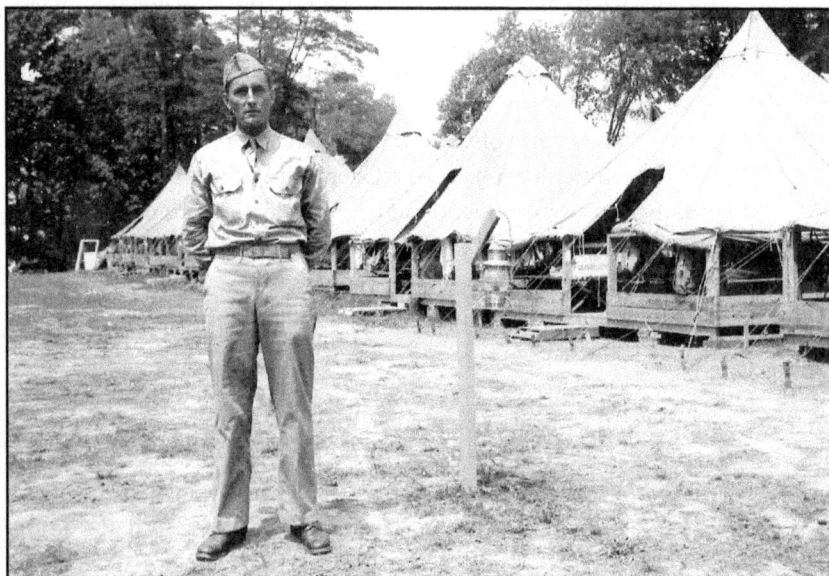

Charlie Lowry, Co. E, Training Battalion, in front of Tent City, Edgewood Arsenal, MD, 1942. *Author's Collection*

are of stucco construction."[11]

The battalion was yet inactivated on April 7th when HQ, 3rd Army, ordered the Chief of Chemical Warfare Service to activate the 81st, 82nd, and 84th chemical battalions (motorized) but to put activation of the 83rd on hold as there was not yet sufficient housing for the men.[12] An order was issued for the 83rd Chemical Battalion (Motorized) to be activated on May 1st and attached to the 2nd Army, per Headquarters Ground Forces, but the order was amended and the activation date changed to June 10th.[13] Obviously, plans were already underway for the battalion. Lt. Pike noted in a letter postmarked May 9th, "I am being transferred – to either Augusta, Georgia or to Ozark, Alabama, tentatively Georgia. We are to leave June 8 or 9. This is not definite yet but practically so. All we need now are the written orders."[14]

Those orders would not be long in coming as the original cadre of the 83rd assembled on May 10th in the Tent City area of Edgewood Arsenal, where the original officers were announced: Major Kenneth A. Cunin was designated Battalion Commander with company commanders listed as 1st Lt. William S. Doughten, Jr., 1st Lt. Edwin G. Pike, 1st Lt. Rupert O. Burford, 2nd Lt. Edward L. Trey, and 1st Lt. David W. Meyerson.[15] Veteran Jerome A. ("Jerry") Muschinske, of Milwaukee, Wisconsin, claimed the 83rd was "born in a mosquito-infested row of tents at Edgewood" where he shared a tent with Carl V. Hushen, the original 1st sergeant of the battalion.[16] This was confirmed by Trey, who, when pressed for his memories of Edgewood, stated, "About all I can remember were the damn mosquitoes."[17]

Kenneth Alonzo ("Kenny") Cunin was a more than logical choice for commanding officer, arriving with outstanding credentials. Born August 21, 1908, in Alliance, Ohio, he attended the University of Alabama for three semesters before receiving a Congressional appointment to West Point Military Academy in 1930. Cunin graduated in 1934 and immediately went into the 82nd Field Artillery at Ft. Bliss, Texas, where he learned the basic logistics and organization of artillery techniques, knowledge which would serve him well as commander of a chemical mortar battalion. He quickly developed a reputation as a sharp disciplinarian and a well-skilled field artillery officer, but he was not popular with a number of his subordinates, so much so that some referred to him as "Little Jesus." One veteran stated there were many who hated Cunin and "proffered threats." Some would claim he preferred to associate with officers of equal or higher rank, often ignoring the basic necessities of his own men. Despite such claims, John P. McEvoy, from Brookline, Massachusetts, who would later serve as major of the battalion, concluded: "He taught us field artillery forward observation procedures that were valuable when giving firing commands to 105 and 155 artillery units. Col. Cunin was a wonderful aid in teaching the basics of soldiering. He whipped into shape a willing but obstinate crew of draftees and reserve officers ... we respected him. He shaped us into a well-trained outfit. We all owe him much for our combat service."[18]

William Simpson ("Willie") Doughten, Jr., was born April 26, 1919, in Philadelphia, Pennsylvania. He graduated from Massachusetts Institute of Technology in June of 1941, where he was among the upper classmen initiated into Alpha Chi Sigma honorary chemical fraternity in 1940 and a pledge for Delta Kappa Epsilon in 1941. At Edgewood Arsenal he was a 1st lieutenant but soon afterward gained popularity with the battalion because his dad was the vice-president of the Whitman Chocolate Company and sent free candy to the men. Unfortunately, Doughten would be one of the first, if not the first, men of the 83rd Chemical Battalion to be killed in action.[19]

Edwin G. ("Bud") Pike was born October 4, 1918, in Portage, Wisconsin,

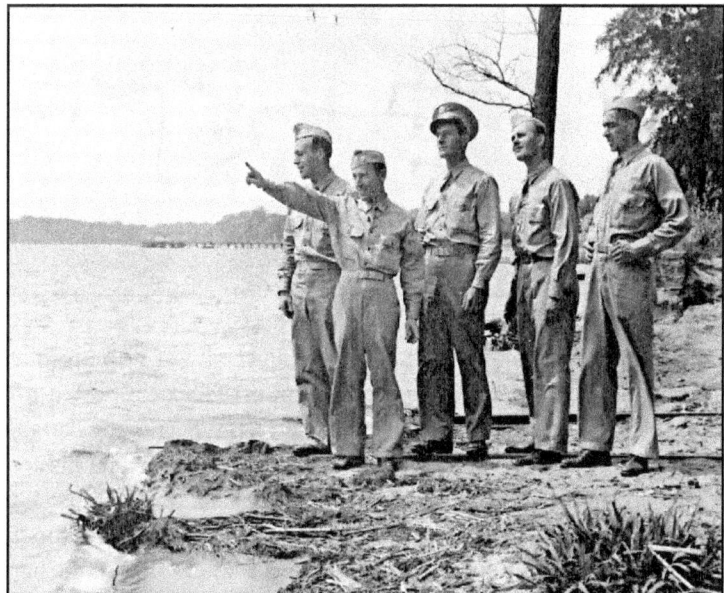

Charlie Lowry (center) & friends alongside river at Edgewood Arsenal, MD, 1942. *Author's Collection*

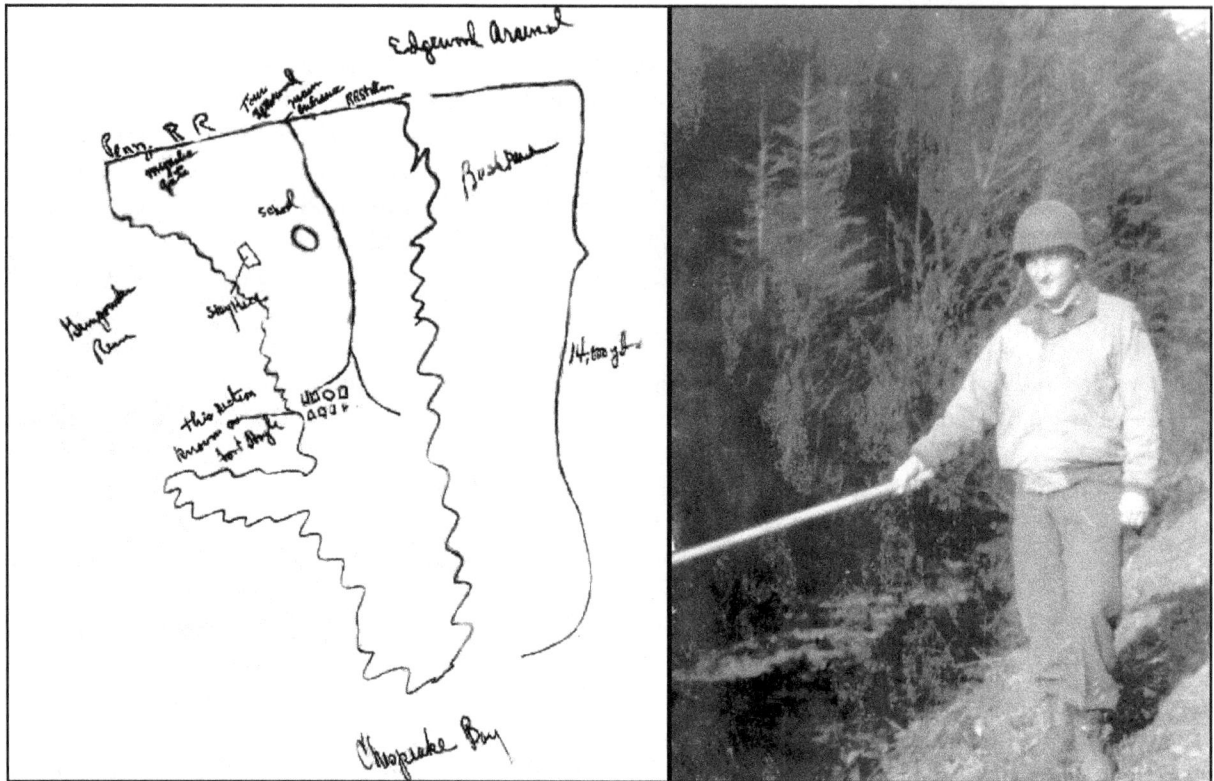

Top left: Map of Edgewood Arsenal drawn by Robert E. Edwards, Jr., 1942. *Wendy Edwards*
Top right: Robert E. Edwards Jr. *Ed Trey*
Below: Map of Edgewood Arsenal obstacle course drawn in 1942 by Lt. Robert E. Edwards, Jr. *Wendy Edwards*

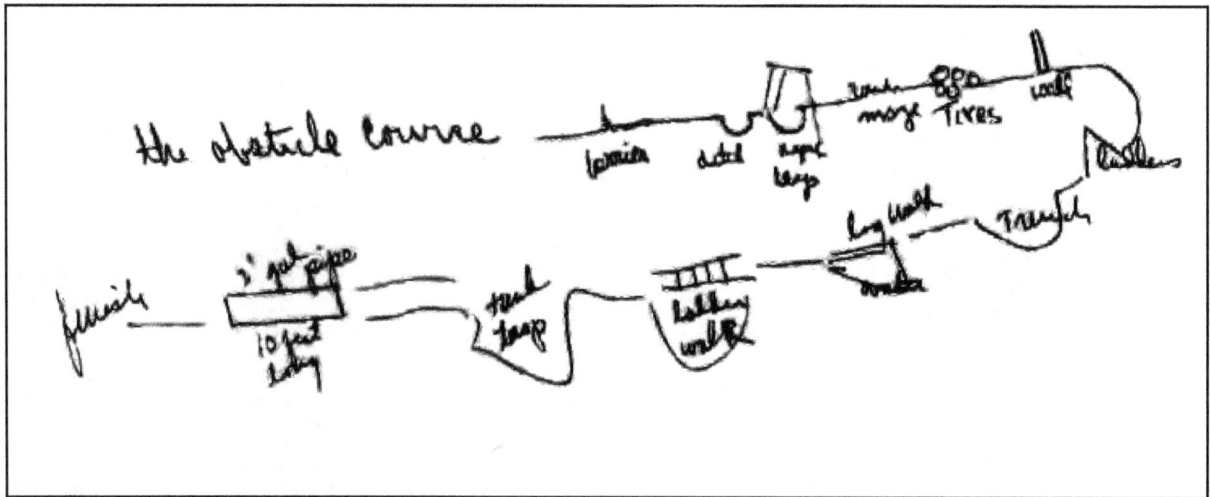

and graduated in June of 1941 from the University of Wisconsin with a degree in chemistry. A 2nd lieutenant in the Chemical Warfare Service on June 10th, 1941, he reported to Edgewood Arsenal June 25th. On July 11th, 1941, he was assigned as 2nd lieutenant, Co. D, CWS Training Battalion at Edgewood and promoted to 1st lieutenant March 7, 1942. Pike would be deeply admired by his men for his courage although he developed a great disdain for both Cunin and later battalion commander William S. Hutchinson. Ironically Cunin would later state Pike was "the outstanding one of my first cadre of five officers" and he was a "top flight" officer.[20]

Rupert Orville ("Rupe") Burford, born May 27, 1909, in Charleston, West Virginia, graduated in 1927 from Charleston High School, where he was editor-in-chief of the school newspaper and participated in chorus and boys glee club. In his high school yearbook he was labeled the teacher's pet and was described by the quote, "He is like unto a book in breeches." Burford attended West Virginia University at Morgantown, West Virginia 1932-1933, becoming a chemical engineer. He entered the service March 1, 1942 and soon afterward was a chemical warfare instructor at Edgewood Arsenal.[21]

Edward Leon ("Bulldog"/"Bulldog Drummond") Trey was born February 23, 1916, in Grand Rapids, Michigan, and attended both Grand Rapids Technical High School and Lawrence Technological University. Before entering the service in February of 1941 he worked in traffic management. Trey was considered part of the "perfect class" when he graduated from the 1st CWS Officer Candidate School class April 4, 1942, and was commissioned a 2nd lieutenant in the Chemical Warfare Reserve at Edgewood Arsenal, Maryland. He had a strong, commanding personality, which would soon earn him the nickname "Bulldog" from his subordinates. In 2007 Trey stated he believed he was the first officer of the fledgling 83rd Chemical Battalion at Edgewood to report to Cunin for duty.[22]

David W. ("Andy Jump"/"Dave") Meyerson was born January 26, 1916. He was a lieutenant in the Chemical Warfare Service and was appointed company commander, Co. D, 1st CWS Training Battalion, at Edgewood Arsenal, in March of 1942. As a 1st lieutenant he would quickly rise through the ranks of the 83rd and eventually command the 2nd Chemical Mortar Battalion overseas. Some of his comrades referred to him as a somewhat eccentric Jewish man, but very aggressive in combat, who sometimes decorated his barracks room with pink curtains and often wore white outfits in contrast to the drab military green.[23]

George Borkhuis wrote on May 15th, "We had to camp out on Wednesday night and the mosquitoes almost ate us alive. About 3 o'clock in the morning they gave us a gas attack and we all had to put our gas masks on." On the 17th he added, "I'm now in the 83rd Chemical Battalion … the boys here all feel pretty confident the war will be over soon." On the next day Borkhuis wrote, "I don't know the officers as yet so I can't say how good they are. Our Sgt. is a real German. He was born in Germany and you can cut his accent with a knife." On May 19th battalion promotions were announced. George Borkhuis added, "I met the Major [*Cunin*] today and he is a regular fellow. He said if I ever had any complaints to come directly to him, don't speak to a lot of sergeants or lieutenants first. He wanted us to feel right at home and come to him directly." Borkhuis went on to say, "We have a mosquito net over our bed and the mosquitoes were so mad that they just buzzed around outside the net all night, but they couldn't get in." The battalion also had its first court martial, an Italian boy who was late getting back to camp on a forged pass. He was sentenced to a month in prison at hard labor.

On May 28th, Lester Berry, Captain, CWS, Assistant Adjutant, by command of Brigadier General Ray L. Avery, ordered the battalion to move by rail to Camp Gordon at Augusta, Georgia, for basic training on June 8th.[24] However, according to the battalion journal, the cadre did not depart Edgewood until 4:00 p.m. on June 9th.[25] The group placed in charge of this movement consisted of 1st lieutenants Burford, Doughten, Meyerson and Pike, as well as 2nd Lt. Trey, 1st Sgt. Carl V. Hushen, and Technical Sgt. Harry B. McCloskey.[26]

Motor Vehicle Operator's Permit issued to Charlie Lowry by the U.S. Army at Edgewood Arsenal.
Author's Collection

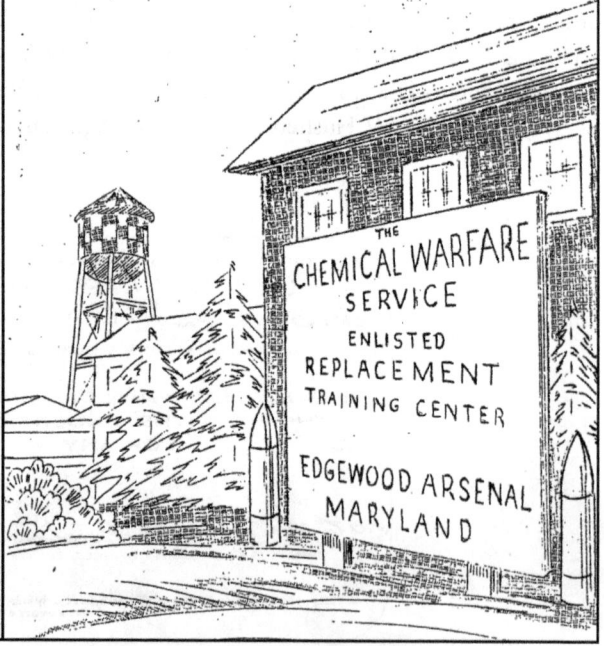

Top: Staff Officers Quarters, Edgewood Arsenal, MD, 1942 *Author's Collection*; Left: *Trainee Tribune-* official newsletter of the Chemical Warfare Training Battalion at Edgewood Arsenal, MD, 1942 *Lorraine M. Salvi*; Right: Introduction booklet for new soldiers at Edgewood Arsenal, MD, 1942 *Lorraine M. Salvi.*

Officer's Club Annex,
Edgewood Arsenal, MD.
Author's Collection

Chemical Warfare
School at Edgewood
Arsenal, MD.
Author's Collection

Commanding Officer's Quarters
at Edgewood Arsenal, MD.
Author's Collection

Post Theatre at
Edgewood Arsenal, MD.
Author's Collection

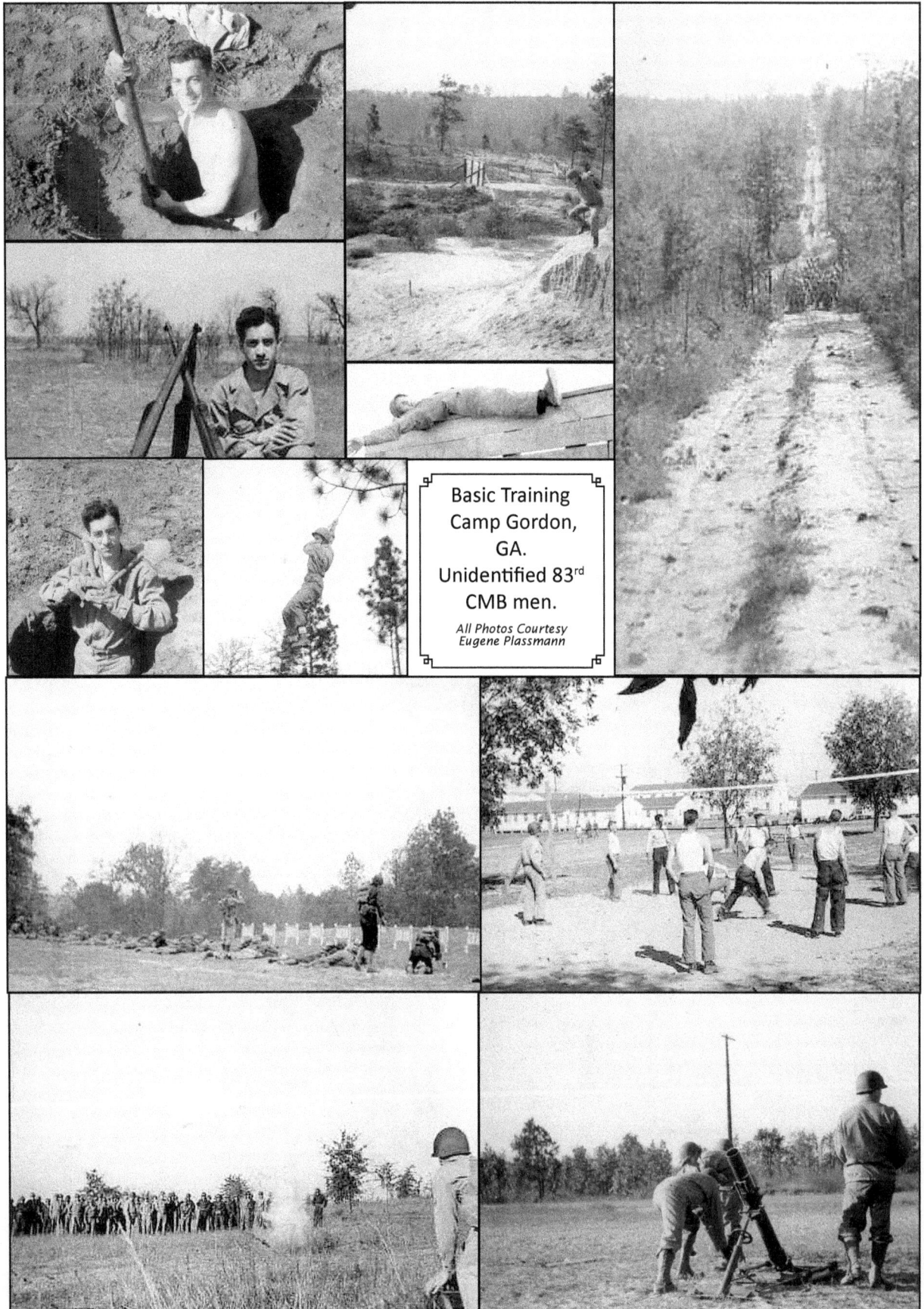

Basic Training
Camp Gordon,
GA.
Unidentified 83rd
CMB men.

*All Photos Courtesy
Eugene Plassmann*

Chapter Two
CAMP GORDON
AUGUSTA, GEORGIA
BASIC TRAINING
JUNE 10, 1942-APRIL 19, 1943

Men of the 83rd Chemical Battalion drilling at Camp Gordon, Georgia.
Ed Trey

The original cadre of 208 enlisted men and five officers of the 83rd Chemical Battalion (Motorized) arrived at Camp Gordon near Augusta, Georgia, at 2:00 p.m. on June 10th, 1942, where they were officially activated by General Order #1. Unlike at Edgewood Arsenal, where the battalion had been divided into the old regimental style of ten companies, at Camp Gordon they were broken down into five companies: Headquarters and Headquarters Co., with four weapons companies -- A through D -- and a Motor Section which serviced each company. Later a medical detachment was added. George R. Borkhuis recalled, "We left Edgewood Arsenal at 4:00 P.M. Tuesday ... the whole camp turned out and the band played ... we boarded a Pullman train and supper was at 7 P.M. in Washington, D. C. ... we arrived at Charlotte, NC, at 6:30 the next morning and arrived at Augusta at 3:00 P.M. and got to camp at 4:30".[1]

James Marion Lester, born in Minnesota and raised in Iowa, who joined the battalion as a replacement a bit later, referred to the 83rd as a "Bastard Battalion," writing, "They would break our unit down into 4 weapons companies. Then they would break them down into platoons. They would attach a platoon to an infantry regiment and we would support that regiment with mortar fire."[2] Leo C. ("Lee") Steedle, born and raised in California, but who enlisted in Pennsylvania, who would also later join the battalion as a replacement, took the description a bit further, adding, "We were bastard outfits under the wing of the Chemical Warfare Service, rather than having been Infantry heavy-weapons outfits. Our 4.2" mortar had been developed by the CWS with the potential mission of delivering gas shells as retaliation, in the event the Germans chose to reintroduce that horrible weapon. Thank God, they didn't."[3]

Kenneth Alonzo Cunin had already been appointed to command the battalion, joined by William S. Doughten,

11

Jr. as adjutant, while, according to official orders issued June 12th and 13th, the original company officers were 1st Lt. Christopher C. Cornett and 2nd Lt. James A. Loulan, Jr., (HQ Co.); 2nd Lt. Thomas M. Bolton (Co. A); 1st Lt. Joseph M. Pensack and 2nd Lt. Alfred H. Crenshaw (Co. B); 1st Lt. Robert E. Edwards (Co. C); and 2nd Lt. Gordon M. Mindrum (Co. D). In addition, 2nd Lt. Edward L. Trey was relieved from Co. B and assigned to HQ Co. as Battalion S-4 (Logistics), while Doughten was given the extra assignment at HQ Co. as Battalion Postal Officer. All of these officers were highly qualified, most having received training in chemical warfare at Edgewood Arsenal. On June 16th George Borkhuis, Co. B, said, "All the other units down here look at us like freaks in a circus. They've never seen or heard of a Chemical Battalion and have no idea what we can do. They keep asking us questions about chemistry until we feel like college professors. When you walk along the street they stop and ask us what the colors on our hat signify." On June 18th the battalion went on their first hike.[4]

George Borkhuis wrote on July 3rd, "I had my First Class Privates stripe sewed on to the shirt last night, also the battalion insignia and boy do I look swanky." On the 6th the German-speaking sergeant threatened to resign and on the 11th Christopher C. Cornett was assigned Mess Officer, 1st Lt. David W. Meyerson to Billeting Officer and 2nd Lt. James A. Loulan was made Classification and Assignment Officer. At the same time George Borkhuis transferred to Cook of Co. D.

In addition to the original cadre of the 83rd Chemical Battalion from Edgewood Arsenal, hundreds of new recruits would steadily arrive. The first batch of enlisted filler replacements, 159 from the 1229th RC [*2nd and 3rd Service Commands*], Ft. Dix, New Jersey, arrived July 23 [*according to the battalion journal July 27*].[5] According to Malcolm Doyle Wilkinson, a country boy from rural Gloster, Mississippi, "Most of the guys in my outfit were between 18 and 24 and we had a mixture of boys from the South (Mississippi, Alabama, Georgia) and then (Pennsylvania, New Jersey, New York) almost half and half …"[6] Many other states provided manpower as well, including Ohio, Virginia, West Virginia, Illinois, Texas, Iowa, California, Tennessee, and so on. George A. Barrett, Co. B, from Philadelphia, Pennsylvania, also recalled the early sectionalism, noting that when he came from Pennsylvania, "There was no one on the train that I knew … When we arrived at Camp Gordon there was hardly any fellows in our area. We sure were a homely bunch in our green fatigues which we later called Rebel Blues because all of those fellows came from southern states. It wasn't long before a lot of us got to know each other and became good friends." George Borkhuis claimed the Camp Dix men arrived July 28th and said, "I don't know why they sent us such old fellows. This group (300) all came from Camp Dix and there are some gray-haired men among them."[7]

Further describing the men who came to Camp Gordon, Malcolm Wilkinson observed, " … there were very few who I can remember who were married. Of course, later, as the Draft kicked in and the army expanded they drafted married men and some were as old as 30, but combat soldiers as a rule were very young. Aside from Cunin, who was a West Pointer, most of the officers were from university R. O. T. C. [*Reserve Officers Training Corps*] programs, " … and later there were the OCS [*Officer Candidate School*] products which we called 'ninety day wonders.' We were fortunate in our outfit as we had confidence in our officers and there were very few discipline problems."[8]

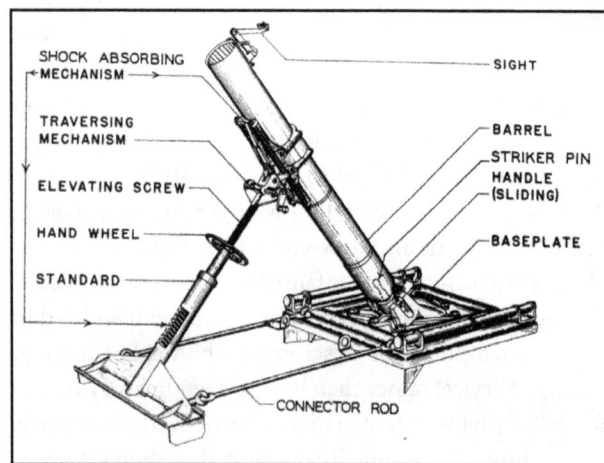

Sketch of the 4.2" mortar and mortar parts.

Basic training at Camp Gordon consisted of all the standard, required military assignments. Karl F. Garrett, HQ Co., from Richmond, Virginia, recalled the " … forced marches, over night bivouacs, target practice, crawling under live machine gun fire, and drill."[9] Loy J. Marshall, who worked in the textile mills of Georgia prior to induction into the Army, said he was attached to Co. C and was " … trained in marching skills and cadence, shooting a rifle, setting up communications posts, operating Bazookas, Browning Automatic Rifles (BAR), Mortars, and other chemical weapons. From time to time I also had the usual military assignments of Guard Duty, KP, clean-up details, etc." Harold Hughes, a Midwestern farmer with a drinking problem, who would eventually reform and become governor of Iowa and a potential presidential candidate, was also designated a BAR man, an assignment he attributed to his tall stature. He described the duties as carrying a twenty-one pound portable machine gun, with a partner that carried the ammo and handed him cartridge magazines to fire in defensive support of the mortar crews.[10] But the primary purpose of the men of the 83rd Chemical Battalion (Motorized) was to train and learn the basics of their primary weapon, the 4.2" chemical mortar.

Perhaps the most simplified description of the mortar and its ammo was given by Brig. Gen. Alden H. Waitt, CWS, U.S. Army, in the 1942 book, *Gas Warfare: The Chemical Weapon, Its Use, And Protection Against It.* As Waitt described it, "The 4.2 inch chemical mortar is a muzzle-loading, rifled, high-angle weapon which fires a high-capacity shell with the accuracy of an artillery piece at ranges from 600 to 3200 yards. For sustained fire it can deliver five rounds per minute for an indefinite period. For short periods a rate of twenty per minute can be obtained by trained crews. It is mobile and can be moved forward at the same rate as the infantry advance. It is low in silhouette, being only three and one half feet high when installed and can be concealed easily. It can be fired from small gulches, shell holes, or from behind steep ridges or buildings. Within its range it is a suitable weapon for the support of attacking troops either with smoke, gas, or explosive. The desired range is obtained by varying the elevation of the piece and the amount of propellant charge … The mortar consists of a barrel, a standard, and a base plate. Its equipment includes certain spare parts and accessories for its installation and maintenance, and a two-wheeled, rubber-tired, hand-drawn cart for transportation and combat. A sight is provided for laying the mortar to obtain the desired range and protection. When chemical troops make distant movements, the mortar, loaded on its cart, ten rounds of ammunition, an ammunition cart, and the personnel of the mortar squad are transported on a light cargo truck. The barrel complete weighs ninety-one pounds. The standard weighs fifty-three pounds. The baseplate is the heaviest part of the mortar, weighing 155 pounds … The mortar shell has thin walls and large capacity, and was designed especially for firing chemical agents. It weighs approximately twenty-five and one half pounds ready to fire and holds six to eight pounds of chemical. It is prepared for firing by inserting a cartridge into its base and placing on the cartridge container rings of powder, the number depending upon the desired range. When the shell is loaded into the muzzle of the mortar it slides down to the bottom of the barrel where the cartridge is ignited by the striker pin. The cartridge then ignites the rings. The explosion expands the plate at the base of the shell so that the shell engages in the rifling of the barrel, thereby giving the shell a rotating flight. Inside the shell is a perforated steel vane which causes the liquid filling to rotate with the shell and give the shell added stability in flight."[11] The chemical mortar battalions of World War II employed two types of shells, including white phosphorous (WP) which primarily provided smoke screens but could also cause serious burns or death. The other type shell was the high explosive (HE) which packed a strong charge of TNT.

Major John P. McEvoy of the 83rd Chemical Mortar Battalion further detailed the evolution of the 4.2" mortar, writing that during the period between the two World Wars, " … it was modified by a dedicated machine tool tinkerer who was a unique CWS officer. With a basement full of machine tools and an inventive mind, he converted the smooth bore 4" diameter mortar to a 4.2" rifled weapon. Although this mortar was intended initially to disseminate chemicals, a high explosive shell was also developed to expand the utility of the mortar. His other hobbies were rumored to be female company and alcohol … Rifling imparted a sharp spin to the round as it left the barrel. Spin prevented wobble and insured repetitive accuracy. Thrust was provided by powder rings exploded by a shotgun shell. The hollow powder rings were stacked over a short pipe at the base of the round. When the shotgun shell hit an upright metal pin on the barrel bottom the powder rings were ignited and the expanding gases pushed the departing shells throughout its short trip up the barrel. The key to imparting spin was a soft copper ring on the base of the mortar shell. This ring pushed into the rifling in the barrel when the powder blast started the shell on its trajectory. The amount of powder determined the range. Initially the range capability was 500 to 3200 yards … The barrel was aimed by putting stakes several yards in front of the barrel and by means of a sight at the end of the barrel. The sight was used to calibrate the movement right or left of the aiming stakes. By grouping 4 to 6 mortars together and by coordinating their aim to

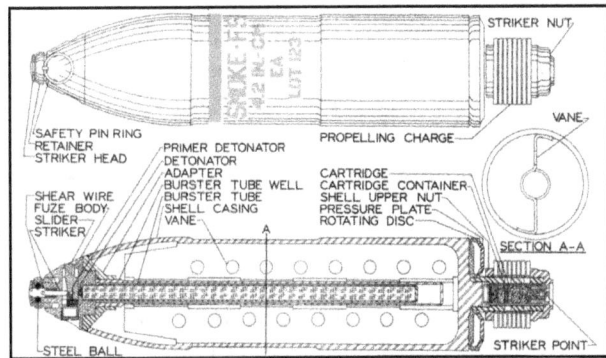

4.2"Chemical Mortar Shell

a single direction point, up to 180 shells could be landed on an area half the size of a football field ... The explosive power of each shell was enormous. About 8 pounds of TNT within a twenty-five pound shell gave a blast equivalent to a 155mm high explosive artillery shell weighing 95 pounds that fired at the rate of three to five rounds a minute. The lighter 4.2" mortar shell was not as effective as the 155mm shell in destroying fortifications but was deadly against troops in the open. A quick acting fuze exploded the 4.2" shell with 6" of the surface skinning grassy surfaces within a 25' diameter circle. Skillfully used it was dreadful to troops in the open - and kept protected troops deep in their shelter."[12]

But the enlisted men of the 83rd had their own interpretations and descriptions of the 4.2" mortar. According to James Marion Lester, Co. D Motor Pool, "The fellows called the 4.2" mortar 'stove pipe artillery.' All there was to it was a baseplate that weighed 155 lbs., a tripod, and a 90 lb. barrel. These three pieces would mount together and this was the mortar ... The shell that we used weighed about 25 lbs. The farther we wanted to fire it, the more powder rings we would put on the back of the shell. We would drop the shell in the barrel/stovepipe. When it hit the firing pin at the bottom, that would ignite the powder rings and 'poof', away it would go. The normal range it went was approximately 1400 yards. It could be shot farther, but less accuracy the further it was shot ... A mortar doesn't fire direct. It lobs it's shells. They are short range artillery."[13]

Malcolm Wilkinson, originally a member of Co. A, added, "The 4.2" mortar may not have been a secret weapon, but I think it surely was a surprise weapon. To my knowledge it had never been fired in combat until the invasion of Sicily and the Germans were very surprised. They could not figure out what it was at first because our shell carried a little more than 8 pounds of TNT or whatever explosive it was ... and that was almost as much as a 155 howitzer. Ours fired so rapidly it also surprised them ... we were so successful that today most infantry divisions have incorporated the mortar into their units. We were the pioneers though."[14] Lee Steedle added, "The artillery shell carried only 3-1/2 pounds of TNT, compared with our mortar shell's 8-1/2 pound TNT wallop. The normal rate of fire of a 105 howitzer was about four rounds per minute. Our 4.2" shell's high arcing flight time of about 30 seconds enabled us to put five or more rounds of unadjusted fire from each mortar into the air before our first shell landed."[15] Louis "Cody" Wims [*who had a brother in the 83rd*] further commented, "It [*white phosphorous*] was like a smoke shell, however the sparks and stuff would continue to burn if it hit your clothing."[16]

The mortar cart, according to Hale Hunter Hepler, Co C, " ... was a two-wheeled cart that had a pipe across the front of it. There was a soldier on each side of the cart. They hooked two chains on each side of the pipe and the soldiers would pull the cart. The weight was considerable because each shell weighed 28 pounds and the cart held 4 boxes of the shells. The mortar topped off at 250 pounds."[17] Jerry Muschinske, also of Co. C, summed up the learning experience best when he said, "Several months of training before we were indoctrinated in the use of mortars and guns ... Needless to say we all enjoyed a bottle of Hudepohl beer now and then."[18]

While the novice soldiers learned the fundamentals of the 4.2" mortar, additional men continued to arrive at Camp Gordon and adjust to their new accommodations. Stephen W. Vukson, from Torrance, Pennsylvania, recalled that when he arrived at Camp Gordon, " ... I was assigned to the 83rd Chemical Battalion and placed in a 4.2 Mortar Squad, Company B, on the first floor of the two story barracks located on 43rd Street. Camp Gordon resembled a small city with over 100,000 troops stationed there in preparation for overseas duty. There was a camp bus that would take you free of charge to the P. X., known as the Post Exchange store, with bargain prices, a Theater, Service Center or anywhere on the grounds. The camp was divided into streets and the bus was a convenience for us. There were four or five of us that would get a taxi on a Saturday evening and go into Augusta and get a good meal at one of their finer restaurants."[19] New York born Kenneth Laundre, an automobile body repairman residing in Michigan prior to the war, loved to play golf and was befriended by a Mr. Miller, a member of the Country Club of Augusta, which opened its doors to servicemen. The Miller family even invited the newly married Laundre and his bride to stay at their home so they could spend some time together.[20]

John McEvoy fondly remembered Camp Gordon, writing, " ... who that was there could forget Black Tuesday, a 15 miler in 100 degree weather wearing World War I helmets. Or forget [*William S.*] Col. Hutchinson's attempt to parade the 83rd while trying to make us sing 'This Is The Army Now Mr. Jones' - a requirement imposed by the 3rd Army commander Lt. Gen. Ben Lear ... later in Italy on a dark night when Col. Hutchinson was about, a voice could be heard -- 'If you don't know the words, sing La La La!'"[21] Mike Codega recalled with mixed emotions guard duty and the repeated showing of films relating the evils of venereal disease. On August 22nd, *The Chapel Bulletin*, the first official newsletter of the battalion debuted, primarily featuring religious news. [22]

Camp Gordon also exposed recruits to the racism particularly prevalent in the deep South, and would leave a lasting impression upon men from other areas of the country, such as New York native Eugene A. Plassmann. Assigned to Co. A for basic training, Plassmann recalled, "I quickly learned how the colored people were treated in the 'South'. We were instructed not to interfere with the local customs, and when we went to town on our occasional evening or weekend passes we were to sit in the front of the bus, and stay out of the Negro neighborhoods."[23]

According to Stephen Vukson, who soon became Battalion Parts Manager, the composition and duties of the Motor Pool of the 83rd Chemical Battalion (Motorized) were to "provide all the trucks and jeeps to transport our own troops … Headquarters and Companies 'A', 'B', 'C', and 'D' had their own trucks and jeeps which required continuous maintenance and had to be near the front lines or combat zone and available to move on short notice … [*We were*] in charge of making decisions and advice to the Company Motor Sgts. As to the mechanical problems with the trucks and jeeps … each Company Motor Pool had a Motor Sergeant in charge of maintaining their trucks and jeeps with a number of mechanics to service these vehicles." The company motor sergeant reported to the battalion parts sergeant for all parts, tires and supplies, who made out the proper requisitions and picked up the supplies at the Army Ordnance Depot. Vukson said he was given a large army troop truck known as the six-by-six and " … converted into a vehicle parts truck with cabinets loaded with an inventory of parts," towing a trailer full of spare tires.[24]

Based upon the discharge papers of West Virginian Charlie Lowry, an original member of Co. D Motor Pool, the standard duties of the mechanics were to "inspect and perform field repairs and adjustment on trucks. Examine vehicles for worn, damaged, or defective parts by visual inspection or road tests. Check steering, wheel alignment, braking efficiency, gear shift, mechanism and clutch operation. Repair axles, drive shafts, clutch and transmissions. Use hydraulic Jacks, chain hoists and various wrenches needed for repairs." In the course of the war these men would work under black-outs and shell-fire conditions.[25] John P. McEvoy summed the Motor Pool up by stating, " … driving a truck in the 83rd was tough … needless to say we had the best drivers and mechanics. They were in constant demand to support other units as well as the 83rd."[26]

September saw the arrival on the 18th of two enlisted men from the Medical RTC, Camp Pickett, Virginia. On the following day George Borkhuis, Co. D, wrote, "On Sunday the officers were playing baseball and our Lt. Pike was hit in the mouth with a baseball. They took 4 stitches in his upper lip and 5 in his lower. He also lost 5 teeth. He was pretty well banged up and I had to prepare food that he could sip through a glass tube. Mostly soups and mashed vegetables."

On the 26th [*according to the battalion journal the 28th*] the Medical Detachment of the 83rd Chemical Battalion was activated, with Capt. Everett A. Irish designated battalion surgeon and 1st Lt. Jacob Remler as assistant battalion surgeon.[27] Men of the other companies began to jokingly refer to the Medical Detachment as " … open to anyone wishing the life of Riley. All those who wish to be served chow in bed, rise at 10, and up after the lights are doused, and put on airs are eligible to apply."[28] Placing sarcasm aside, the men quickly came to respect the valor of the medical crew that often labored under the most severe battlefield conditions in order to save lives. Also on the 26th some of the battalion assisted a local farmer named Travis in picking his cotton. George Borkhuis, Co. D, also wrote, "They are going to start a battalion newspaper and I have been asked to help edit it … I won't have to print it … just be an editor. If I see it's too much trouble I won't bother."

The ranks at Camp Gordon continued to swell in October with 33 men arriving from Ft. Oglethorpe, Georgia, on the 6th, followed by 55 from Ft. McPherson, Atlanta, Georgia, the following day. Some 220 enlisted filler replacements were added to the battalion on October 8th as 45 came from Ft. McPherson and 174 from the 1301st Service Unit, RC, New Cumberland, Pennsylvania, as well as one man from Medical RTC, Camp Pickett. On that day

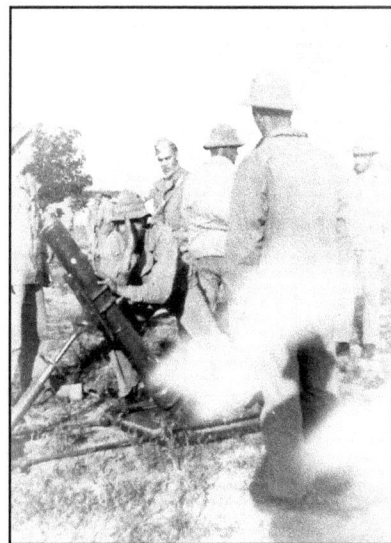

Capt. Ed Pike (center) training recruits on mortars at Camp Gordon. *Codega Collection*

George Borkhuis, Co. D, wrote, "Yesterday evening at 10:00 P.M. 175 new men arrived from Nashville, TN. Some of them can't even read or write. Today another 200 men are due and the other 250 before the end of the week. These men are to be given their training as quick as possible." He added, "All of our officers except Lt. Pike are being changed today."[29] Among the new men from Pennsylvania was James Glenn Helsel of Altoona, who remembered, "We were met by a Chinese Sgt. One boy made the remark 'a Jap Concentration Camp'

Riding the Camp Gordon Service Bus are left to right: Howard D. Bennett from PA, Herbert H. Beck from PA, Jack Bowles, Thompson from PA, & Stephen W. Vukson. *Stephen Vukson*

which the Sgt. didn't like … We also got the Chinese Sgt. and found his name to be Sgt. Kong [*possibly Russell Kwong from Kern County, California*]."[30]

On October 9th, 83 men from the 1303rd Service Unit, Camp Lee, Virginia, arrived; five more from Ft. McPherson on the 11th; 186 from Camp Shelby, Mississippi, on the 13th; 111 from the 1302nd SURC, Ft. Meade, Maryland, on the 13th; three more from Meade on the 16th and one on the 18th. Accordingly, by October 19th the battalion companies were reported at full strength. George Borkhuis confirmed, "All our men are now in and it looks like an army all by itself … today I had to make 660 pancakes."[31]

On October 29th George Borkhuis wrote, "We were issued the new Army helmets recently. They look almost like the German Army ones. They are in two pieces, one is a lightweight fabric, the other one fits on top of this one and is made of steel. They cover the back of the neck and also the ears. We call them turtle shells … we also got a brand new type of gas mask. The old one used to look funny, but this one looks worse. This is supposed to be the best one in the world. We know the enemy has nothing to compare with it. But these masks are only issued to the officers. The other men just get the regular mask. These masks are made so that you can talk while wearing them, the others are not."

A group of the 83rd traveled to Tennessee on maneuvers, returning to Camp Gordon in November. On November 5th Maj. Cunin gave a speech with the statement "It is commonly supposed that the first duty of a good soldier is to die for his country. This is a mistake. The first duty of a soldier is to make his enemy die for theirs." On the 14th of the month the first issue of *Smoke Screen*, the official newsletter of the 83rd Chemical Battalion, appeared. The paper, which contained much gossip and news of the battalion, reflected the battalion's character while at Camp Gordon. The debut issue had an introduction by Major Cunin, who said the paper "reflects the composite character of the unit it represents. As we go through our organizational life together to whatever deeds of battle will milestone our history, we must and will be remembered by this one phrase – 'the Eighty-Third Chemical Battalion, was, is, and always will be a fighting outfit.'" Shortly afterward Cunin returned to Edgewood Arsenal for a refresher course.[32]

Throughout the remainder of November Camp Gordon was full of a variety of activities involving the battalion. Harold Eisenberg, a mechanic with HQ Co., earned the nicknames "Little Corporal", as well as "Eisonboig", and 'Eisey', and displayed his musicianship by playing the chaplain's field organ. It was said he used to "wow 'em on the radio at the tender age of thirteen." Co. A had their share of talent as well, with Charles S. Levy, Harold N. Glassman, and John S. Bonarek appearing in "camouflage" with the Ballet Theater at the Civic Auditorium. Not to be outdone by the men of HQ and Co. A were the fellows of Co. D, whose home became known as the "musical barracks," with Joseph F. Huysse on trombone, Frank F. Menicola on harmonica, Pvt. Cassie Barnes on cornet, and Pat O'Toole singing Irish ballads. The Motor Pool may not have been as musically inclined as other units but Alfred E. Allinson could be found working on a vehicle nicknamed "Betsy" while immersed in oil. Co. A also had a mascot dog called "Disy" which had puppies. It would not be unusual throughout the war for the various companies to "adopt" mascots overseas, with the most well-known being "Vino," a terrier picked up in Sicily by the Motor Pool of Co. D, and "Pete," a German shepherd latched onto by Capt. Robert E. Edwards.[33]

Sports helped to develop and soothe many of the new recruits. Attempts were made to put together teams for wrestling, weight lifting, boxing, track, jujitsu, and table tennis. Touch football was a favorite and in one game Earl Rapp, Co. D, a man who knew more than a little about sports, having previously played minor league baseball, " … completed an easy pass to [*Frederick*] Sapp on the 10 yard line, then on the next play Rapp scored on an end run to give an early lead … "[34]

Late in November the big news was the completion of the new obstacle course and Carl W. Hoeth and Bernard O'Connor of HQ Co. were the unsung heroes of the Mail and Message Center. Sports remained popular. In addition to touch football and volleyball games, Albert W. Goelz (Co. C) "whipped up a basketball team," Herbert R. Quina (Co. C) got involved with boxing, and Jone O. Messer and Earl Rapp of Co. D won the ping pong tournament.[35] In addition to all of these activities five new enlisted men arrived on the 19th of the month from Sch. Det., CREI, Washington, D.C.[36]

George Borkhuis recalled that on November 20th, "Our new insignia is now being made up. It's not such a nice design, but it suits our purpose. It shows a skunk riding on a shell. I've enclosed the first issue of the battalion paper. The design is that on the front cover. It will be blue and gold with a gray shell and a black and white skunk. They'll be calling us 'Stinky' when they see us coming."

In anticipation of Thanksgiving, Pvt. Daniel J. ("Dan") Shields, Co. D, from Philadelphia, Pennsylvania, went in to Augusta on the 22nd and had a turkey dinner before taking in a movie. Thanksgiving Day fell on November 26th and wasn't a particularly exciting day for Shields, as he wrote in his diary that he arose at 6:30 in the morning, attended a lecture, practiced maneuvers in the woods, drilled, and had a big dinner before going to bed at 9:10 in the evening. The following day consisted of much the same including a ten-mile hike in full field gear.[37]

2nd Lt. Veryl R. Hays, Battalion Special Services officer, from Hutchinson, Kansas, realized some of the men were failing to bond. He recalled, "In training camp I had the worst platoon in [A] Company. Due to shifting around in the different Tables of Organization, I got the scrub that was left over. The men were all just ordinary, everyday guys. There were no outstanding soldiers. They always seemed to feel that the 2nd platoon was much better than they and,

Augusta Country Club, Augusta, GA. Kenneth Laundre is among the crowd. *Elizabeth Daly*

for that reason, they didn't try. Hence the platoon started out behind the eight-ball." Hays got the men involved in sports and other activities to bolster their confidence, and although morale improved, it would not be until he got them out on the battlefield overseas and showed them the results of their good work that they finally took pride in their platoon. Hays would later comment, "These erstwhile hillbillies stood up like veterans under the heaviest fire. Their quiet confidence and control were tops."[38]

On December 5th Maj. Cunin was promoted to lieutenant colonel and lieutenant Pike to captain. Capt. William S. Hutchinson, Jr., executive officer of the battalion, left to attend General Command and Staff School at Ft. Leavenworth, Kansas; Steve Faber (Co. B) defeated Paul E. Henke (Co. A) to become battalion table tennis champ; and George J. Funyak (HQ Co.) was in the hospital for an eye operation.[39]

An event of a more serious nature took place on December 14th when a military court composed of many officers of the 83rd was called to handle various court-martial proceedings.[40] Soon afterward an order was issued for one company of the battalion, Co. A, with attached gunners and squad leaders from other companies, to move to the Huntsville Arsenal in Alabama for a temporary two-week stay to test fire 500 of the 4.2" chemical mortars.

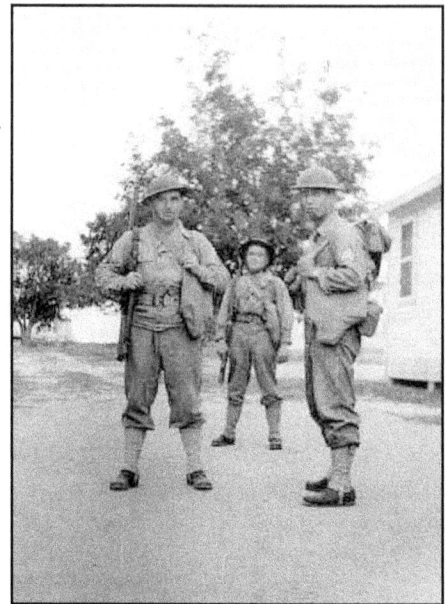

83rd men with Sgt. Russell Kwong (right).
Eugene Plassmann

James Helsel, Co. A, noted the event in his diary, writing on December 17th, " … from about two-thirds of Co. A and a few picked men from the other companies, a detail company was formed. We left Camp Gordon at about 4:30 in the morning, by truck, which was a very cold ride until the Georgia sun came out. By this time I was so cold it took until dinner time to thaw out. We stopped along the road for dinner. We passed through many of the Georgia boys' home towns. We arrived at Ft. McPherson near Atlanta, had supper and stayed in tent city over night."[41]

Helsel said the contingent left early the next morning " … to continue our trip to Huntsville, Alabama. I got a seat in the rear of the truck. The first part of the trip was cold, but after the sun came out, I began to enjoy the trip, seeing Georgia from the rear of a 6 X 6. We arrived at the Huntsville Arsenal about 5:30 [*in the*] evening. A large brick warehouse was to be our home during our stay here. Beds were already set up, and we were assigned to working squads. We learned we were to test the 4.2" Chemical Mortar. Cpl. [*Robert B.*] Bruce [*of Co. A, from South Carolina*] was my leader."[42]

By the 20th of December, Helsel and the Huntsville Arsenal detachment of the 83rd were perhaps getting too adjusted to their new locale. As Helsel wrote, "We have the warehouse in fairly good shape now. This morning Cpl. Bruce and myself made wooden crosses to put our clothes on and put them at the head of the bed. I see most everyone in the place has one made. In this one room it is so large that we have beds for the 200 men, a mess hall and a kitchen in one corner, a PX in the other corner, and also a small supply room. In the next room, which is just as large, is where we pack the mortars after they have been tested and fix the dud shells up to be fired again. The mustard plant is short of men, so the first platoon is testing the mortars and digging [*out*] shells, and the second is working in the plant making mustard shells. We are supposed to switch every week. I sort of like the plant myself. It's more like a civilian job. As for passes, for two days it was the first 50 men to get their names in, but now just so you get dressed in time to catch the last truck. It's a very nice town, it reminds me of Hollidaysburg, PA. It's about the size. The people are very friendly, of course, being the only soldiers in town might have something to do with it."[43]

Mike Codega also participated in the Huntsville expedition and wrote, "Our platoon was ordered to test fire our mortars at Huntsville … and how can one forget the cold and damp warehouse that was our quarters; the firing of the mortars with non-explosive shells; the digging [*out*] and cleaning of the shells in order to re-fire again and again. And the trips to town – giving the locals an exhibition of close order drill."[44]

Meanwhile, activities continued at Camp Gordon as Co. B held Sunday afternoon morale shows at the 472nd Field Artillery Red Hall, where among the many acts was the crowd-pleasing comedy sketches of Earl Rapp and Victor P. Barnheart. Sgt. Roberts of Co. A developed a reputation for use of the phrase, "when I was at Edgewood," and Cpl. John A. Feifer irritated others with his phrase, "the book says … "On December 24th a battalion Christmas party

New men in lineup at Camp Gordon November 7, 1942.
Codega Collection

was held at the 44[45] St. Chapel.[45] Pvt. Daniel Shields recorded his activities for the day in his diary, writing, "A.M. 5 o'clock. Rode out and fired guns, came back, lay around & wrote. Rode to Augusta. Went to Confession & Midnight Mass with [*Walter J.*] Reilly, O'Connor [*probably John A. "Pops" O'Connor*], [*Edwin H.*] Makepeace & Sapiens [*Joseph J. Sapienza*]. Took bus home. Retired 4:15."[46]

Christmas Day at Camp Gordon was rather mundane for men such as Dan Shields, as he wrote, "9.40 a.m. Lay around, wrote, scrub, drilled. Ate. Saw *Thunderbirds*. Retired 10:50."[47] Michael J. Rebick, Co. D, a man of Russian descent from Greensburg, Pennsylvania, apparently had a better holiday, writing, " ... a bunch of us fellows went out and got drunk & sobered up & found out we were still in the Army."[48] At the Huntsville Arsenal in Alabama, James Helsel " . . spent the day in the field digging [*out*] shells and what a Christmas dinner. I had two jam sandwiches and the coffee was too green to drink, and to think I had an invitation in town to a nice home for dinner. This evening I went into town and had a good meal, also took in the show."[49]

Lt. Col. Cunin, in the December 26th issue of *Smoke Screen*, while noting Co. A was still on temporary duty at Huntsville Arsenal, guardedly praised the battalion: " ... Through the efforts and actions of all concerned a high degree of military courtesy, discipline, personal appearance and hygiene has been established in our battalion. Our spirit is high. Of this you can be extremely proud. It is true that a few of our men have besmirched this record and standard. I feel such action on their part has been in most cases their failings to appreciate, respect, and reciprocate the faith, trust, and confidence which I feel we all have in one another in our present chosen or enforced profession: that of being soldiers in the fullest sense of the word. It is only by such doing can we build our unit into a fighting outfit ..."Cunin went on to make recommendations for improvement, claiming, " ... Our degree of proficiency in the technical knowledge of our service must be increased greatly," and encouraged officers and non-commissioned officers to study these subjects at every opportunity because " ... the ultimate dividends for such work will be paid only on the field of battle" and "measured by our efficiency in the use of our weapons and in the conservation of our lives and supplies." The commanding officer's statements apparently had a profound effect on Co. A, which claimed they had already been "Christmas gifted" in having Cunin and his staff as their leaders.[50]

The holiday season continued with the usual episodes in training and extra-curricular activities. Most notable was when Pvt. Bennie Liebermann (Co. D) hit Pvt. Cohen [*probably Albert Cohen of Co. D*] on the head with a hand grenade during a training exercise, and " ... the patient or casualty ran around camp with a turban bandage on his head for several days looking like a holdover from the last war." In sports a boxing tournament was started, and Co. C led the basketball league.[51]

New Year's Eve 1942 apparently was cause for little celebration at Camp Gordon, as exhibited by the entry in the diary of Daniel Shields, Co. D, which read, "6:30 a.m. Exercise. Went to movies, went to woods. Ate. Left for night problem. Retired 7:30. Up at 12:30 walked guard again 4 to 5."[52] At the Huntsville Arsenal life continued as usual for James Helsel who wrote, "Still enjoying myself at Huntsville. I believe I only missed one night being in town and I was on guard. Still testing mortars and working in the plant, they like our work. It was said the plant had a 100% better output and work while we have been here and that the General is going to try and keep us here. I am for him, for I can spend the rest of the war in this place. We have a good Company Commander and there isn't any Retreat or any of that old army ---- it's like a civilian job. The people in town still are treating us good. They give dances every Wednesday and Saturday night. I go bowling and to a show most every night. This being New Years Eve, I had a good meal, bowled a game, and took in the midnight show."[53]

Standard duties continued to be performed at Camp Gordon on New Year's Day, as represented by the entry in the diary of Dan Shields: "Rolled pack, rode back to camp. Wrote, Ate, Drill, went to movies with Bill Hoffman [*William J. Hoffman*] -- saw *For Me and My Gal* Judy Garland. Retired 9:55."[54]

Depending upon source, by the end of 1942, between 1,021 and 1,085 enlisted men had joined the 83rd, including the original cadre, as well as an undetermined number of officers, but an exact figure is difficult to determine, not only due to the discrepancy between General Orders and the battalion journal, but also because many men transferred or left for various other reasons.

1943

The new year of 1943 saw the return to Camp Gordon of the contingent of the 83rd Chemical Battalion from the Huntsville Arsenal, an event lamented by James Helsel, who wrote on January 14th, "As that old saying goes 'all good things must come to an end.' We packed up this morning and left Huntsville to return to Camp Gordon. Quite a few broken hearts, for I believe if we would have stayed here another month half

Huntsville, AL; Robert Taylor, kneeling.
Elizabeth Taylor

the outfit would have been married. We arrived in Ft. McPherson about 4:00. Passes were issued. I spent most of the night in Atlanta. We got a good meal and looked the town over until about four in the morning." The group departed Ft. McPherson on the morning of the 15th and arrived back at Camp Gordon at about 3:30 in the afternoon.[55]

Lt. Col. Cunin gave a pep talk to the men on January 16th in which he said, "If Washington calls, are we ready? My answer is YES!!" James Helsel's response was, "He sounds crazy to me, I haven't even shot a rifle yet."[56] On the 30th of the month the MPT program was completed and the unit training program initiated.[57]

During February, Lt. Veryl R. Hays, Special Services Officer of the battalion, attempted to organize a battalion orchestra, an idea which had the blessing of Lt. Col. Cunin. Possibly more intriguing to the men, though, was the long, black beard of Pvt. Americo J. Giammeria, Co. A, and the near motionless stance of Guidon Bearer Carl A. Bishop, also of Co. A. George Borkhuis, Co. D, wrote on February 9th, "Today three big Generals are coming to look us over with the idea of reorganizing the battalion. Instead of 225 men in each company they want to cut it down to 143. This means 5 cooks instead of 7."[58]

For about a week in mid-February the battalion trained in the field where "weapons companies conducted field exercises in occupation of positions, and HQ Co. stressed the practice of administrative and supply in the field. Camouflage discipline was maintained in a strict manner."[59] James Helsel recalled that during the week he " … pulled those mortar carts all day and guard all night. It was the toughest & coldest week I have yet experienced. We pulled those mortars wherever we went, up hill, down hill, even to chow one time. It took four to pull the cart and it was our misfortune to have only four in the Squad. Of course, there was [*John E.*] Briston [*of Butler County, Pennsylvania*], our Sgt., he walked along and gave us encouragement. The fellow that said 'pull' meant nothing in the Army was crazy with the heat."[60]

Further details were given by Michael Rebick, Co. D. On February 23rd he wrote, " … now they take us out for a week at a time to spend in the woods for we just got back from such a week this last Sunday & it's getting pretty tough on us & guess it's going to be a pleasure for us to go through such training so that we can save our other fellowship lives … it was tough to go out on those [*previous*] over night hikes but this was from 5:30 a.m. to 11:00 p.m. & on the move all the time & we would cover any where from 10 to 15 miles a day for six straight days & besides we were pulling a cart with this 300 lb. gun we been training with most of the time & boy some of the hills were rough & every couple of hrs. they would give us a 10 minute break & in the week we did mostly practicing in camouflaging ourselves from the enemy & going out on scouting & probability problems & that means in sneaking up on our enemy in making the least little noise & at every evening we would pitch our tents & have to dig a trench & camouflaging ourselves for in the evening we would have gas alarms & we would have to hit the hole to get our protection & going out on map & compass problems have a certain way of guarding our area when we go out on such problems & I got a chance at it from 8:00 p.m. to 6:00 a.m. & it sure is tiresome looking on all night & they sure could improve it if they would give us a woman once in awhile … "[61]

Also of interest during this period was a statement from Co. B that they were " … up to taking the 4.2" to bed. At first, when mounted on carts, this weapon seemed like a lumbering caisson. With practice, that feeling disappeared, and now we feel like spirited fillies doing our canter to martial music. With them in Co. formation at retreat we feel like fighting men dressed and ready for anything. Soon we expect them to be a part of our second nature, handled lightly as a pistol. Then we'll be one fifth of that fighting 83rd ready for the kill."[62] Following this training period the men returned to camp and participated in a regimental parade. An additional memorable event during this period was a two-day, 32-mile hike along Rt. 21 in which the men of Co. D claimed Mess Sgt. Llewellyn L. Zepp's pancakes " … make excellent shoulder pads for pack straps." Clark Riddle later confirmed this by saying, "Zepp's pancakes were five or six inches in diameter and half an inch thick and were so heavy that we referred to them as shoulder pads."[63]

February rounded out with the Medical Detachment holding a party at the Elks Lodge, basketball highlights of Earl Rapp making impossible shots, former All-American Lewis Cameron's amazing dribbling down the court, and Pvt. Donald Rugito's (Co. C) renditions on the electric "geetar" [*guitar*]. Most importantly, though, was Cunin stating the battalion had just finished a successful, crucial training period which had started during the last two weeks of January, under some of the worst possible climatic intrusions, and ended with simulated combat conditions. He told the men of the hard work ahead, the training and spring maneuvers, and wrote, "No task must be considered too tough, for success in face of adversity is the stuff of which we are made. I told you many months ago that we were going to have a fighting outfit. That statement has been fulfilled – **WE HAVE A FIGHTING OUTFIT**."[64]

The 83rd Chemical Battalion (Motorized) was assigned to the 2nd Army on March 1st, 1943, with all previous assignments and attachments revoked. On the 3rd companies A, B, and C were quarantined for measles.[65]

Michael Rebick, Co. D, wrote on March 7th that the battalion was getting ready to depart for three months of maneuvers in either Alabama or Tennessee, but apparently this did not transpire because, according to the battalion journal, on March 15th the battalion was alerted to overseas movement and "Packing of organizational equipment and requisitioning of all needed items to complete equipment of organization and individuals initiated. Enlisted replacements were requisitioned and transfer and discharge of men unfit for active field duty accelerated."[66] On the 16th [*18th according to the battalion journal*] some 73 new enlisted men came to Camp Gordon from the 552nd Engineer Battalion, HQ, 3rd Det. Sp. Trs., 2nd Army, although 22 of them were returned on March 19th as unfit for combat duty.[67]

On March 17th George Borkhuis, Co. D, wrote, "We are all quarantined for measles … we also got new steel helmets which weigh about 8 lbs. We are supposed to get guns tomorrow. Cooks will get Tommy guns like the gangsters use." Being quarantined from time to time at Camp Gordon was not unusual, as expressed by Pfc. George A. Barrett, Co. B, who said, "We were in quarantine for awhile, but the wanderlust got the best of me and off I sneaked into the theater with Mike Dobrin. When the theater lights were turned on, lo and behold I was sitting next to 1st Sgt. [*Joseph J.*] Adamski! I guess you know I got my first taste of KP."[68]

An order dated March 24th directed the battalion to leave Camp Gordon and move to the New York Port of Embarkation.[69] On the 28th Cpl. William J. Eakins, battalion motor officer & dispatcher, departed for Officer Candidate School (OCS), leaving Stephen W. Vukson as dispatcher for 130 trucks and jeeps.[70] Events followed rapidly as 21 men from the CWS RTC, Camp Sibert, Alabama, descended upon the camp on the 29th [*April 1st according to the battalion journal*] followed by 85 of the same on April 9th [*the journal claims the 10th*]; five from the 54th Chemical Impreg. Co., of Camp Sibert on the 15th; and 14 from the 7th Det. Sp. Tra. [*33rd Chemical Decontamination Center*], Camp Blanding, Florida, a day later. The same day 13 were transferred to the 552nd Engineers. The ranks of the 83rd continued to swell at Camp Gordon as a group of 17 men arrived on April 17th from the 9th Chemical Depot Co. at Camp Rucker. As early as April 14th George Borkhuis, Co. D, wrote, "Our equipment is all packed on the train and we are only awaiting the word to start … we are all restricted to camp and must even let them know where we are going when we leave the barracks."[71]

Training remained vigorous at Camp Gordon, as evidenced in a letter written by Pvt. Richard A. Bridge, Co. D, from Greensburg, Pennsylvania, who scribed on April 4th, "We've been on the range the last 2 days firing rifles. The 2 days before that we crawled 50 yards under machine gun fire from one trench to another. The bullets 18 inches from the ground. The day before that [*I*] dug a foxhole up to my shoulder & let a tank run over me. Got some dirt down my neck & a thrill as it passed over. The first part of the week we had some commando training jump[*ing*] wide

Daily lectures at Camp Gordon, L-R: Stephen Vukson, Warren Gallatin, Robert Johnston, Thompson from PA, & James O'Toole. *Stephen Vukson*

ditches 10-12 ft. deep, walked a type [*tight*] rope wire 15 ft. from the ground, broad jumped square ponds of water 3 ft. deep. And of course we came over the obstacle course every day. The only one I had trouble with was the broad jump. Well, I jumped. I made it but the other side was muddy when I landed my feet started slipping. Lost my balance & fell in all but my neck, rifle and all."[72]

Lt. Col. Cunin was emphatic about proper training. "Experience has shown that the soldier well-founded in the fundamentals of scouting, patrolling, use of camouflage, cover and concealment, and taught to move fast, will individually, live to fight many battles," Cunin later wrote. "Next to that comes teamwork, an item particularly important to our mortars. We fight as a platoon, the fire unit being the platoon. Reconnaissance, selection, and occupation of position with the greatest speed is vital. That can only be accomplished through team work and team work is only obtained first, through every individual knowing his job thoroughly and also how it fits into the team, and, second, through practice, practice, practice." Cunin felt the men of the 83rd did not have enough time to train properly before being sent overseas and added, "Dead and wounded are to be expected but these are kept to a low total by proper training. Failures in missions will be the result of poor teamwork. Failures in battle are inexcusable when such failures are a result of poor training … Training programs must be interpreted with some imagination and that should take the form of realistic, practical training. Everything practical and utmost realism injected should be the creed … ammunition … should be whistled close to the pants of … soldiers. The mortars should always be fired from actual tactical set ups; all marches, foot or motor, be tactical … In this training, the unfit must be eliminated by any and every means possible." Cunin would later remark, "Unfortunately, prior to our leaving the States, we were unable to eliminate many unfits because of slowness of administrative procedure and the fact that medical officers in station hospitals do not have a proper appreciation of the rigors of combat conditions." Once overseas Cunin would point out that, as a result of combat, the 83rd had to eliminate " … at least twenty unfit men, all of whom we knew in the States would not stand up under combat."[73]

On April 18th battalion brass was alerted to move the men by rail to Camp Myles Standish near Taunton, Massachusetts, a 1,600-acre troop staging area near Boston which had opened in October of 1942.[74] Mike Codega said the men were ordered to remove all insignia from their clothing. The officers were strictly forbidden to divulge the destination, at the risk of court martial.[75] According to Rupert Burford, however, Cunin became inebriated at a party the night before departure and released the plan to a number of other officers. As a result the wives of some of these men were able to visit them while in the Boston area. A number of other officers and men of the battalion later supported this accusation.[76]

During the early part of 1943, approximately 198 enlisted men had joined the ranks of the 83rd, and when coupled with the 1,071 men from 1942, there were 1,269 who had trained with the 83rd at Camp Gordon, as well as an undetermined number of officers. Although many did not remain the entire time with the 83rd for various reasons, this was the approximate number of men who would depart Camp Gordon for overseas service.

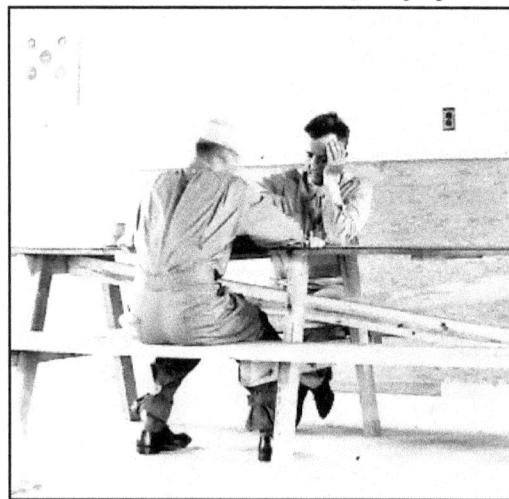

L-R: Lt. Gordon Mindrum & Mike Codega playing chess. *Codega Collection*

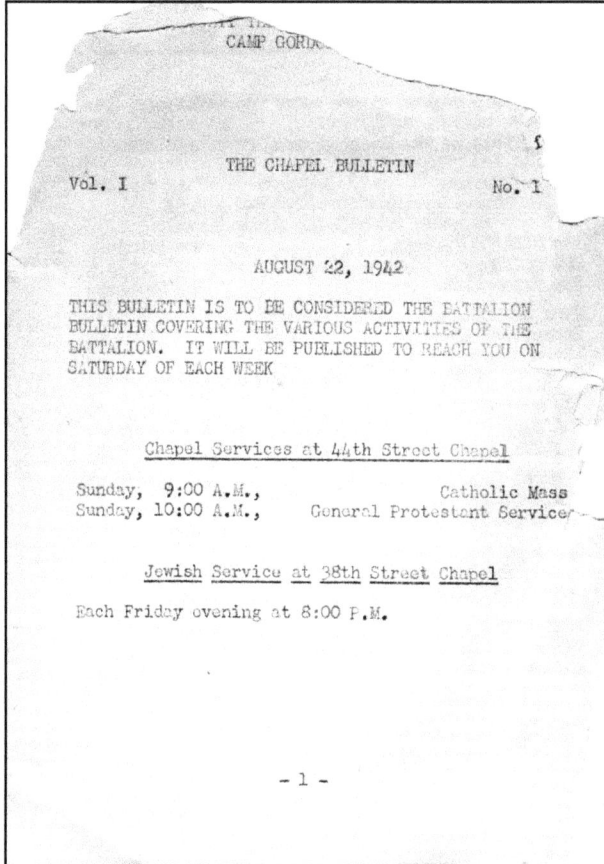

THE CHAPEL BULLETIN

Vol. I   No. 1

AUGUST 22, 1942

THIS BULLETIN IS TO BE CONSIDERED THE BATTALION
BULLETIN COVERING THE VARIOUS ACTIVITIES OF THE
BATTALION. IT WILL BE PUBLISHED TO REACH YOU ON
SATURDAY OF EACH WEEK

Chapel Services at 44th Street Chapel

Sunday, 9:00 A.M.,   Catholic Mass
Sunday, 10:00 A.M.,   General Protestant Services

Jewish Service at 38th Street Chapel

Each Friday evening at 8:00 P.M.

- 1 -

The Chapel Bulletin

First Official Newsletter of the 83rd Chemical Battalion

Two rare issues from Camp Gordon, including the August 1942 debut issue, which primarily featured battalion church news. *The Chapel Bulletin* was replaced by *Smoke Screen* in November, 1942.

Borkhuis Collection

A chapel at Camp Gordon, GA.
Borkhuis Collection

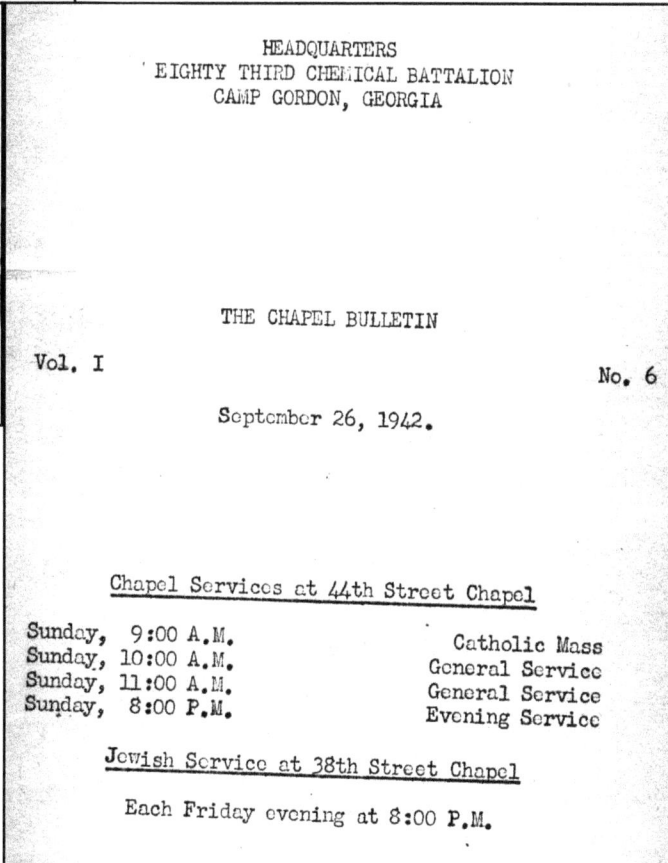

"Stinky" the unofficial mascot of the 83rd first appeared in *Smoke Screen* at Camp Gordon.
Author's Collection

HEADQUARTERS
EIGHTY THIRD CHEMICAL BATTALION
CAMP GORDON, GEORGIA

THE CHAPEL BULLETIN

Vol. I   No. 6

September 26, 1942.

Chapel Services at 44th Street Chapel

Sunday, 9:00 A.M.   Catholic Mass
Sunday, 10:00 A.M.   General Service
Sunday, 11:00 A.M.   General Service
Sunday, 8:00 P.M.   Evening Service

Jewish Service at 38th Street Chapel

Each Friday evening at 8:00 P.M.

Men of the 83rd using Livens Emplacements for mortar training at Camp Gordon.
Ed Trey

Season's Greetings
Compliments of THE MESS
Christmas Dinner
1 9 4 2

Old Gold Cigarettes

Camp Gordon Christmas mess ticket issued to George R. Borkhuis, Co. D,1942.
Fred Thompson and Thomasina Edwards

Inside the barracks at Camp Gordon. *Barrett Collection*

Left, top to bottom: Mike Codega, the Hooten brothers from IN, & Cooper from NY. *Codega Collection*

Right, L-R: Howard Merritt, Leland Rozzell, Stephen Vukson. *Stephen Vukson*

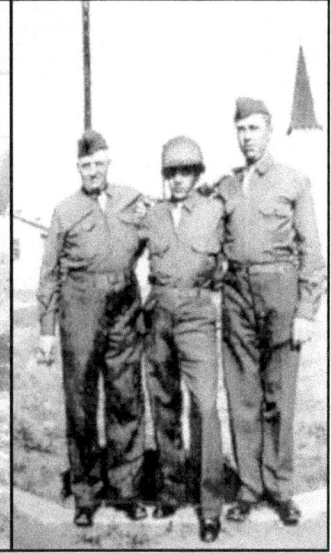

Above right, L-R: Thomas V. Bush (?), Hale H. Hepler, & Ira B. Loan. The latter suffered a heart attack at Camp Gordon. *Hale Hunter Hepler*

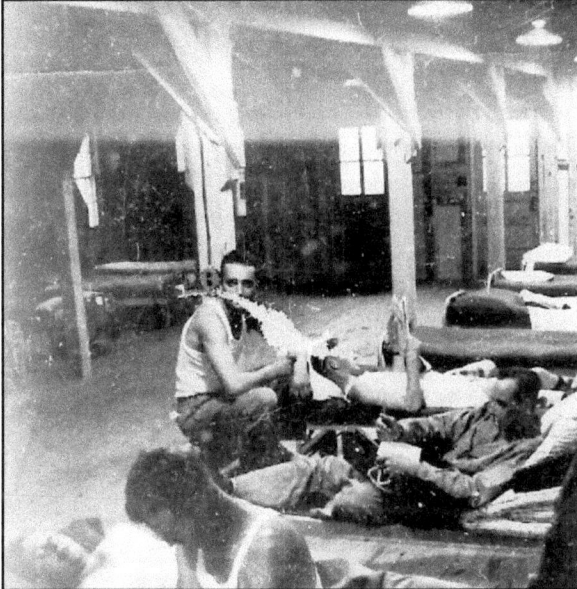

Left: Inside the barracks at Camp Gordon. *Codega Collection*

Right: George Whetsell (left) & Karl Langford (right) wearing fatigues, July 1942. *Codega Collection*

The gang from South Philly. Front row: Andy Whelan (4th on left) & James Dougherty (3rd on right). Back row: Dan Shields, (3rd on left). *Shields Collection*

William C. Ford outside the Bath & Tennis Club at Camp Gordon. *Ford Collection*

All copies of *Smoke Screen* courtesy
Ft. Leonard Wood Archives

"SMOKE SCREEN"
Newsletter of the
83rd Chemical Mortar Battalion
Camp Gordon, Georgia

Although the *CHAPEL BULLETIN* was the first official newsletter of the 83rd Chemical Battalion, the more commonly known newsletter of the battalion was *SMOKE SCREEN*, published biweekly at Camp Gordon, Georgia, 1942 – 43, the result of Special Services for the enlisted men. The first issue debuted November 14, 1942, and included an introductory salute from Maj. Kenneth A. Cunin, as well as from the newsletter staff. The first few covers featured the original coat of arms of the 83rd Chemical Battalion; a skunk nicknamed "Stinky" riding a mortar shell with the inscription underneath of "Stay Upwind". This D.I. (Distinguished Insignia) was created by Pvt. Philip J. Perlman and Lt. William S. Doughten, Jr., approved by Washington, D.C., but never placed into official use by the battalion.

A vote had been taken for the newsletter title and the winners were Pfc. Francis T. Plant, HQ Co., and Pvt. Paul Buck, Co. C. Each later received a five-day furlough as a reward. The first editor was T/4 Herbert C. Kalk and the assistant editor was Pvt. Donald I. Sparks. Art editors were Cpl. Raymond C. Walker, Pvt. Philip J. Perlman, and Pvt. Frederick L. Brooks, while sports was handled by Pvt. Darwin K. Thorne. Humor editor was Pvt. R. A. Angelone and feature editor was Pvt. Charles F. Ruff. T/5 Steve Gozur was the mimeographer.

Each company, including the motor pool and, later, the medical detachment, had a featured gossip column in which various members contributed stories. Also included was a religious column called "Chapel Chat" written by battalion Chaplain Leonard W. Boynton.

Soon afterward the newsletter fell under the auspices of Special Services Officer 2nd Lt. Veryl R. Hays, became a semi-monthly, and by February of 1943 was again a biweekly with T/5 Charles P. Cella, Jr., taking over as editor. Sparks remained as assistant editor, and T/5 John Stefanko was art contributor. By this time SMOKE SCREEN had developed a crudely drawn cartoon character appearing in each issue called Pvt. Smooch.

Ironically, in the February 27, 1943, issue, Cunin – now a colonel – wrote "We Have A Fighting Outfit", a sentiment he apparently withdrew just before the Sicilian invasion when he told the men they were not properly trained for the mission.

Herbert C. Kalk
first editor of *Smoke Screen*.
Debby Kalk

NO – NO – PVT SMOOCH – WE DON'T FIRE BACK!!

Pvt. Smooch, above, is believed to have been drawn by John Stefanko.

Chapter Three

CAMP MYLES STANDISH
TAUNTON, MASSACHUSETTS
APRIL 20-25
1943

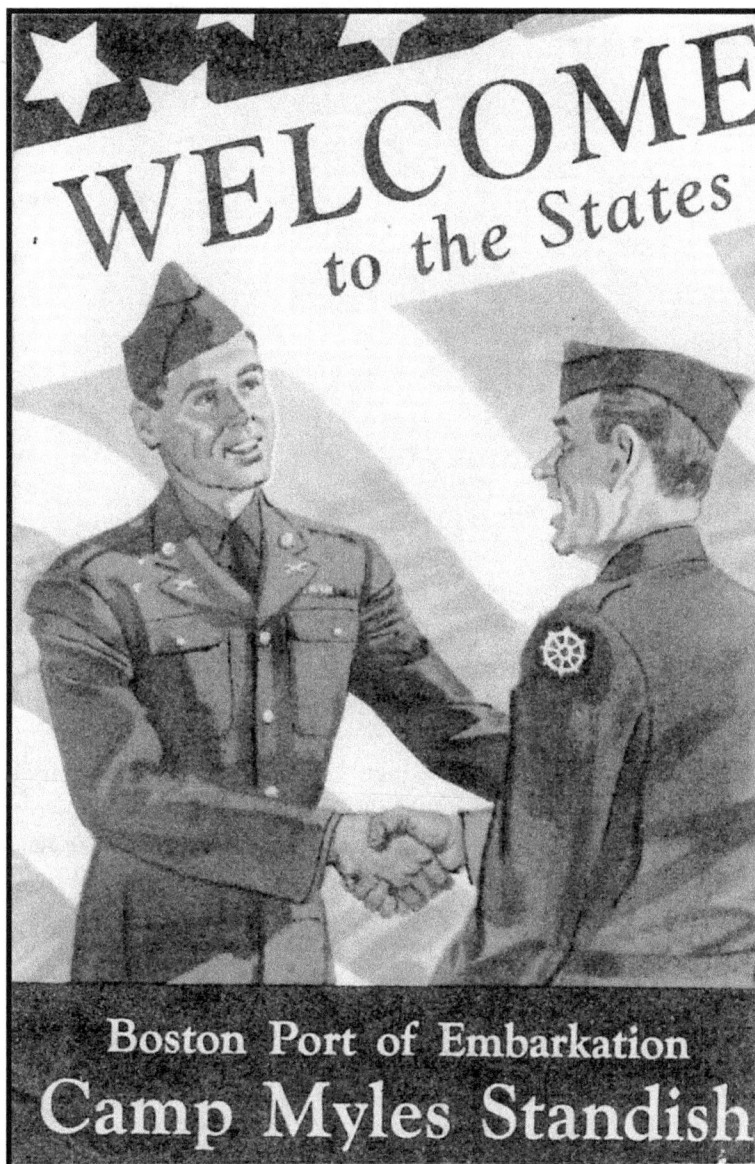

Camp Myles Standish Booklet
Author's Collection

It was a rainy day on April 19th as the men found themselves standing packed and ready to load onto the vehicles for the long journey by rail to Taunton, Massachusetts. Rupert Burford was assigned train commander of the first section, consisting of companies B and C, while Robert E. Edwards was given companies A and D. A number of other officers, including Thomas M. Bolton, Edwin G. Pike, and Edward L. Trey, had already left as an advance party. Col. Cunin, Col. Kirkwood, and other brass seeking attention came by to add to the confusion, but by 10:00 in the evening the men had entrained and settled in for the long journey north.[1] Harold Hughes remembered the train

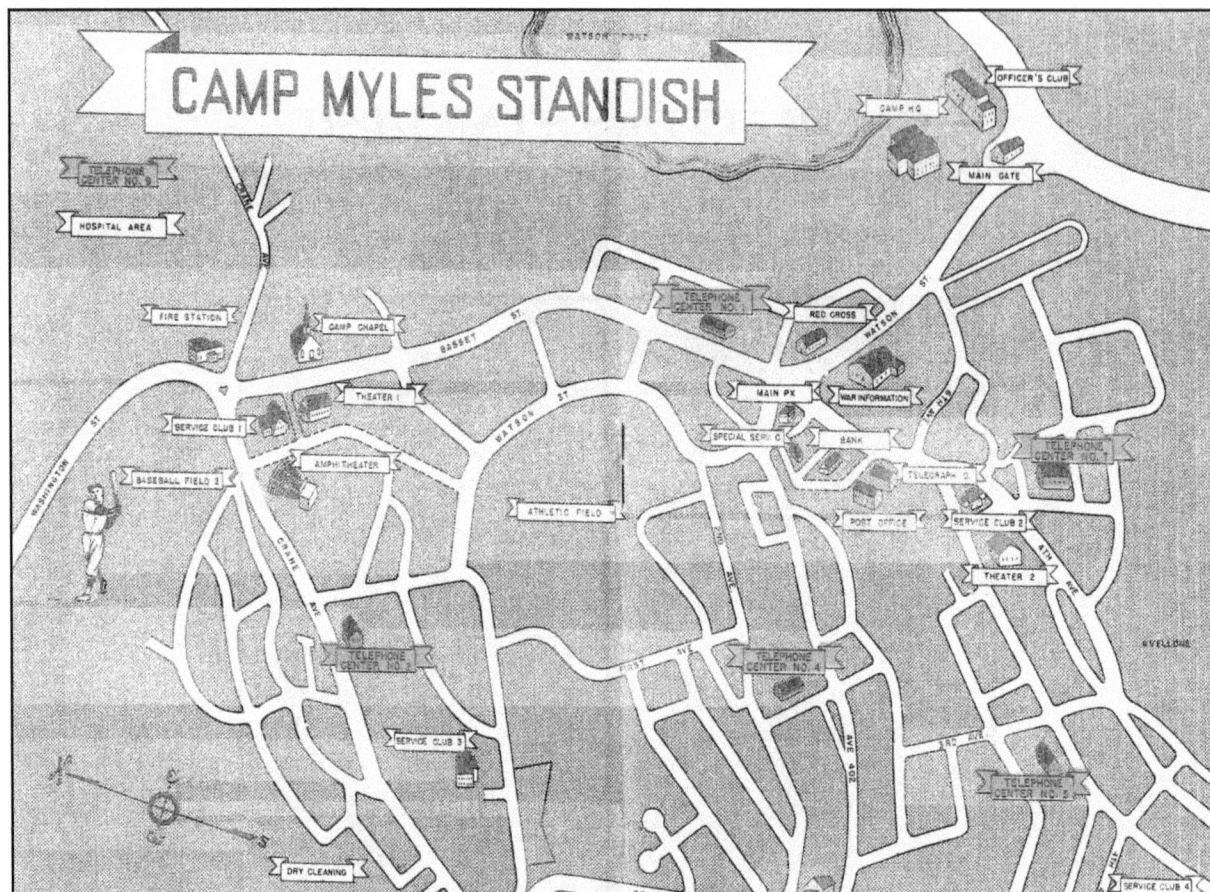

Map of Camp Myles Standish from Booklet.
Author's Collection

"chugging through the Appalachian Mountains" and meals were served in baggage cars which had been converted to temporary kitchens. George R. Borkhuis, Co. D cook, wrote, "When one tries to cook while the train is going 70 miles and hour and swaying from side to side it's no joke. As long as you can jump quick enough to avoid being splashed [*by grease*] you're okay."[2] Eugene Plassmann recalled, "… as the train slowed down or paused at small train stations along the way, girls, ladies, and older men would run alongside trying to hand us sandwiches, donuts, cake, and coffee, and clapping and cheering as we went through."[3] Karl Garrett, HQ Co., said, "En route the train stopped in Richmond [*his hometown*] for several hours. Needless to say we were under tight security for fear that our destination would be leaked. The train was locked -- no one could get off or on during this time. Here I was, approximately two miles from home and could not use a telephone to let my folks know where I was. I would not see them for 3 years -- a heart-wrenching experience."[4]

The men of companies B and C of the 83rd finally arrived at Camp Myles Standish between 9:30 and 11:00 a.m. [*depending upon source*] on the morning of April 20th, covered with perspiration and coal soot, stepping out into a cold, wintry snow. George Borkhuis wrote home, "It rained ever since we left Georgia and it's still misting."[5] Some reports imply companies A and D did not arrive at Camp Myles Standish until about 3:00 in the afternoon of April 21st, although other sources state all companies arrived the same day.[6] Despite the winter conditions the morning report of Co. D listed the weather as fair and said morale was excellent.[7]

Reflecting upon Camp Myles Standish, Rupert Burford wrote in his diary, "Upon arriving at camp we were escorted to barracks of the single story variety, each accommodating approximately 60 men. The entire camp ate meals in one huge mess hall, and showers were available, one shower room serving several barracks buildings. The officers were quartered in together in two adjacent buildings, and had showers in a nearby building, so that in order to take a bath it was necessary to first go out in the cold."[8] Jerry Muschinske, Co. C, fondly recalled the wooden sidewalks at Camp Myles Standish although James Helsel, Co. A, was more impressed by the food.[9] Lt. James O. Beasley, Co.

D, also added his impressions of the camp, writing, "All officers and men of the battalion eat in one mess hall. The mess is probably no better than previous ones but the men think it is better. The southern men are getting even with the northern ones for all the remarks made about the south. They will have to find something else to argue about if they are ever sent overseas."[10]

There was a bit of animosity at Taunton, as mentioned by Mike Codega, who supported Rupert Burford's accusation that Cunin had divulged the highly secretive destination by claiming " … there on the station platform were several wives and girlfriends of some of our officers … highly secretive? … I guess there are some privileges that should be awarded the officers."[11] Lt. Beasley would later agree with Burford, too, as he wrote, "It is very probable that several of the officers saw their wives in New England. I was fool enough to follow regulations. I believe [*Lt. Leonard A. "Spike"*] Merrill [*Jr.*] got to visit his family."[12]

Beasley also wrote home on the 21st, "We are allowed to write that we are now in New England … it is rainy weather and the sun, or rather daylight, comes too soon for it to be winter … [*Capt.*] Pike and I are rooming together now. It is practically like home. There is a coal stove … and we have to keep our own fires."[13]

The next five days, April 21st through the 25th, concentrated on preparations for overseas movement, including final physical exams, inoculations, and the issuing of equipment and clothing.[14] Samuel M. Bundy, Jr., Co. A, of Camden County, New Jersey, recorded, "Clothing was checked and we certainly have a lot of stuff to carry with us."[15] Officers and enlisted alike were restricted to camp, although an exception was made on Easter Sunday so that passes could be issued to men with relatives no farther distant than Boston. Other exceptions were Cunin and the battalion brass he had illegally informed of the movement to Taunton, reportedly when inebriated at a farewell party at Camp Gordon.[16]

As the time neared for receipt of orders for the actual overseas movement, officers were strictly forbidden to mention the impending destination. All mail was censored, and as a result rumors flew, with nearly every man convinced he knew the answer, yet the only thing actually certain among them was that they knew they were headed overseas. Practice loading onto a simulated boat was performed to help prepare the men for the maritime journey.[17]

Indeed, the big day arrived on April 25th when the battalion was alerted for a movement to the Staten Island Port of Embarkation, as a New England storm had made it unfeasible to load the ship in the Boston harbor.[18] James Helsel recalled being called out of a U.S.O. show he was attending and ordered to report to his company for departure. Lt. James Beasley, apparently yet unaware of the order, wrote, "The last few days have been real spring weather with warm sunshine and rain" and also noted that battalion surgeon Capt. Everett A. Irish had left the organization.[19] The loading of trucks with baggage was supervised by William S. Hutchinson, Jr., who marched the column to the railroad, where companies C and D boarded at midnight and into the 26th, with the remaining companies following in the next couple of days.[20] Loy Marshall, Co. C, recalled, "They made sure we were fully equipped … and that all issue equipment was in working order. We carried all essentials in our backpack and barracks bags … We removed our division sleeve patches, and our helmets were chalked with a letter and number, to give the proper marching order from the camp to the train station where we boarded railroad cars."[21]

Companies A, B, and C, which left Camp Myles Standish at 4:30 a.m., arrived at the New York Port of Embarkation at Staten Island, where they debarked, caught a ferry, and boarded the *U. S. S. Monticello* at 11:00 a.m. During this movement the train had made many stops, and the men were soaked with the smell of cigarette smoke and perspiration.[22] Sam Bundy, Co. A, said, "Loaded down with equipment and wearing long underwear and overcoats … Excited, hot, tired, and overloaded, we struggled up the steep gangplank as our names were called."[23] During the boarding Red Cross ladies handed out donuts and a brass band played "Over There" and "Give My Regards to Broadway." William Garner of Aragon, Georgia, overloaded with equipment, said, "The band was playing 'Hold That Tiger' but I couldn't even hold a little ole pussy cat!"[24]

The *U.S.S. Monticello* (AP-61) was a former Italian luxury liner built in 1928 named the *Conte Grande*. The U.S. Navy first expressed an interest in the ship in December of 1941 when it was listed as a passenger ship of an enemy country "taken over or immobilized" by Brazil and held at Santos. The U.S. Navy instructed an officer to go to Rio to negotiate a purchase and by February of 1942 the ship was valued slightly over five million dollars. The purchase was finalized April 16th, 1942, and the ship was commissioned on the same day in Brazil. Converted to a troop transport at Philadelphia with one single 5"/38 dual purpose gun mount and six single 3"/50 dual purpose gun mounts, the steam turbine *U.S.S. Monticello* departed New York to haul soldiers for the invasion of North Africa and the China-Burma-India Theater before returning to New York on April 24th, 1942.[25]

Officered by Capt. Bayard Henry Colyear of Palo Alto, California, whom Andrew C. Leech, Co. B, claimed served on a submarine in World War I, and Navigator R. E. King, the *U.S.S. Monticello* was moored starboard to the southern side of Pier #15, New York Port of Embarkation, Stapleton, Staten Island, New York, on April 28th when it commenced embarking U.S. Army troops at 3:10 a.m. Ammunition was loaded starting at 8:00 a.m. and by 11:00 a.m. the embarkation of 5,389 troops was completed, followed by the loading of naval ammunition.[26] Among the many other army troops on board was Co. A, 85th Engineer Heavy Pontoon Battalion.[27] HQ and Co. D of the 83rd left Taunton between 4:30 and 5:30 p.m. on April 27th [*Rupert Burford says this took place on the 28th as does Co. D's morning report*], arrived at Staten Island, and boarded the ship between 3:30 and 4:30 a.m.[28] Daniel Shields said he got up around 6:05 a.m., packed, and left camp about 5:30 p.m., and went to sleep on the *Monticello* about 3:30 on the morning of the 28th.[29]

Companies A, B, and C of the 83rd were assigned the task of ship guard, or military police, as they were the largest organization on board. Such duty would entail four hours on guard and eight hours off duty. This worked to the advantage of Co. A as they were placed on the top deck and were exposed to the fresh air and sunshine. No one was permitted to leave the ship and no messages could be sent to shore.[30] Due to the alphabetical listing Rupert Burford feared an unpleasant trip for himself as he was assigned to a stateroom with Cunin and two majors. He lamented, "I regret that I couldn't have had the good luck to get in with some of the more congenial officers in the battalion."[31] Rumors flew about a departure time as the ship continued to load supplies.

Letter written from Camp Myles Standish by Lt. James O. Beasley, Co. D, 83rd CMB. *John Beasley*

Chapter Four

ATLANTIC CROSSING
APRIL 29–MAY 11
1943

U.S.S. Monticello
National Archives

One medical officer and five enlisted men from Staging Area HQ, Ft. Hamilton, New York, joined the battalion as the *U.S.S. Monticello* set sail on smooth and calm waters in the early morning darkness of April 29th for a thirteen-day voyage across the Atlantic Ocean to Oran, Algeria, North Africa.[1] The departure was so abrupt that Edward Trey, seeking some supplies on dock, nearly missed the boat. He recalled, "I happened to be visiting the dock that morning and noticed the 83rd boarding ship. I boarded in my pinks and greens." Trey added, "Everything was so secret and the departure came as such a surprise I left my gun at my wife's place and had to later write and tell her to take care of it with the authorities."[2]

Lt. Comdr.. E. C. Winters, Coast Guard Reserves, had come on board to pilot the *Monticello* out of the harbor, which got underway at about 4:17 a.m., "… in accordance with Port Director, 3rd Naval District, Operation Order 19-43 of April 28th, 1943, Comtaskfor 67 in *U.S.S. Texas* Convoy."[3] The ship was in darkness due to blackout conditions but those fortunate to be on the upper deck were able to view the city of New York and the Statue of Liberty in the distance.[4] By 10:03 a.m. Lt. Comdr.. Winters had left the ship as it had cleared all vessels.[5]

The *U.S.S. Monticello* then proceeded to take its station as flagship in Convoy UGF-8 and Escort Task Force 67, a grouping of 35 ships, including troop, supply, and naval escorts. The exact composition of the grouping of Escort Task Force 67 consisted of the *U.S.S. Texas* with Capt. Roy Pfaff, U.S.N., Task Force Commander on board; the task force tanker *U.S.S. Merrimack*; destroyers *Thatcher*, *Gillispie*, *Guest*, *Brownson*, *Carmick*, *Harrison*, *Kalk*, and *Terry*; screen commander *Hobby*, and the destroyer *Greer*, which only participated for a 24-hour period. Convoy UGF-8 was comprised of *H.M.S. Tracker* with a cargo of planes; two tankers with gasoline; one merchant ship with general cargo; and, including the *Monticello*, 19 troop ships with 61,170 troops. Air coverage for the first day was provided by Commander Eastern Sea Frontier.[6]

For most of the crossing the convoy sailed in columns of five. One soldier remarked that the convoy consisted of ships in all directions as far as the eye could see, the most prominent ship being the battleship *Texas*.[7] Rupert Burford and others kidded Texans such as lieutenants Vester Lamar Turner and Thomas M. Bolton that the battleship was "hiding" in the center of the convoy. Burford also mentioned that as the sun rose it was a bright, clear day with no wind.[8]

With air coverage supplied by NAS [*Naval Air Station*] Bermuda, the convoy sailed out into the open Atlantic Ocean on April 30th, zigzagging to avoid enemy subs and radar.[9] Hale Hunter Hepler, Co. C, a former employee of the Virginia Highways Department from Millboro, Bath County, Virginia, said, "The orders for the day were to change course of direction on the ship every four minutes to avoid being sunk by the Germans. At night we would travel in a straight line."[10]

Depending upon the source, the entire trip was rather uneventful, characterized primarily by the large amount of seasickness. Charlie Lowry, a mechanic from West Virginia in Co. D's Motor Pool, wrote home to his girlfriend, "We have been at sea for days now and your little old boy has been one sick lad for about half of that time."[11] Loy Marshall, Co. C, said, "We were assigned a sling-type bunk that we were told to stay in as much as possible, and we had to keep all of our equipment there as well as sleep in it. They were stacked four deep. I was seasick for the whole trip. We were taken up on deck from time to time for calisthenics and a breath of fresh air. This didn't help much." Making matters worse, according to Marshall, "The seas were rough for almost the entire trip and many of us were seasick day after day. At first we thought we were going to die, then we were so sick we were afraid we wouldn't die. It would have been a relief."[12] Karl Garrett, HQ Co., added, " … all luxuries had been removed and troops were assigned three men per bunk. Each man had 8 hours use of the bunk and 16 hours on your feet. Seasickness not withstanding, … it was a miserable ... day trip."[13]

During the first day on the open sea a friendly aircraft was sighted, the *U.S.S. Monticello's* 20mm and 30 calibre machine guns were test fired for about nine minutes, and Pvt. Bost McKenney, attached to Army Unit #1804 TT, was confined to the brig for insubordination. The *Santa Elena* fired anti-aircraft bursts in violation of the Armed Guard discipline policy that no guns larger than machine guns would be fired without permission. The *U.S.S. George Washington* briefly fell behind, the first of repeated breakdowns for the troubled vessel. In fact, the ship, which carried over 7,000 troops requiring strong protection, had already been reported as unreliable prior to departure and in the course of the crossing would cost the convoy 11 hours and 27 minutes of time due to such complications as "low water, priming, cross-head trouble, leaky steam lines, and a disabled main feed pump." Due to these persistent problems the ship was relegated to the rear of the column, and upon the first major setback Maj. Gen. Matthew B. Ridgway, a passenger on the *George Washington* and commander of airborne troops, informed the Task Force commander that should the ship have to be left behind he wished to go overboard with his staff and be picked up by a destroyer.[14]

Other ships in the convoy would prove troublesome as well. The motor ship *John Erickson*, also previously reported as unreliable, was "a bad station keeper due to inherent qualities." The *S.S. Examiner* had repeated problems controlling speed and had to be moved to the end of a column, as did the *USAT Agwileon*, which was too slow for the convoy. The Task Force commander didn't wish to take the *Agwileon* at all, but Army authorities insisted, and when later confronted about its problems Army authorities denied knowledge of such a named ship and said it was the *A. G. Wilson*, despite evidence to the contrary. The tanker *Fort Lee*, carrying gasoline, was additionally a problem from the beginning and would soon leave the convoy with coverage from the *Terry*. Finally, *USAT E. B. Alexander*, carrying nearly 7,000 troops, was also considered unreliable and assigned last of column. The ship had numerous breakdowns due to telemeter, throttle, and other machinery problems. Worse yet, at one point she would nearly ram the *George Washington*, then swing right and almost ram *H.M.S. Tracker* due to throttle complications. The *Kalk* and *Harrison* would constantly have to provide coverage for the ship.[15]

Due to the large number of men on board the *Monticello*, recreation on the upper deck had to be scheduled, while life in the lower decks was "dull and tiring" with excessive, stifling heat. Activities below deck consisted primarily of

U.S.S. Monticello
National Archives

playing cards and musical instruments. Guard duty would actually provide the men some relief from their idleness.[16] There were a number of nurses on board with whom the single officers struck up flirtatious relationships, and a member of the 85th Engineer Heavy Pontoon Battalion later complained that the nurses continually stopped up the toilets and were extremely messy.[17]

One of the more enjoyable events of the trip for the men was a confrontation between Lt. Col. Cunin and a young 2nd lieutenant of the Air Corps. Cunin attempted to reprimand him for not wearing a necktie and was given a verbal thrashing by the lieutenant. As word of this blow to Cunin's dignity spread, "the 83rd officers chortled with glee."[18] Ed Trey also recalled an incident on the ship with Chaplain Lyle Burdick in which some of the boys got into the chaplain's communion wine. He further stated, "I also recall we had to later dismiss a chaplain for reasons I can't remember … it may have been Burdick. Chaplains suited for combat outfits were rare."[19]

Meals were served twice daily to the enlisted men and three times to the officers.[20] Capt. Edwin Pike, Co. D, gleefully wrote, "The ship on which we are riding is an old luxury liner and very nice. We officers eat like kings, even using the solid silver service which was taken over with the ship. The food is excellent and I am sleeping a great deal."[21] Capt. Rupert Burford, Co. C, also said the meals were good but lacked bulk, giving him a case of constipation. Water was considered in "critical" supply and only turned on for one hour a day.[22] Capt. Pike captured the situation, writing home, "You have heard the old phrase, 'water, water, everywhere and not a drop to drink'? Well, this old Atlantic Ocean gives you that same feeling of frustration. You can never imagine its vastness until you cross it." George R. Borkhuis, Co. D cook, wrote, "The food is fine and the crew is real swell. A lot of them are from New York City … we get two meals a day but they more than make up for the usual three we got at camp. During the daylight hours we are allowed up on deck for air. The ocean has been quite calm and we've had little rain."[23]

Not much marine life was observed during the voyage with the exception of a hammerhead shark, a couple of schools of porpoises, and a few other sea creatures. Capt. Pike noted, "So far I have seen one whale and one hammerhead shark. I hope I don't have to see them at any closer range. They looked vicious enough from here on deck."[24]

The biggest fear was an attack by an enemy submarine and precautions were taken to avoid such an incident. Not only did the convoy sail a zigzag pattern, but the men were told that in the event of an attack the large metal doors below deck would be sealed, trapping the men inside. Such a thought did not do much for the men's nerves. Capt. Burford instructed his men that should the ship be hit the non-commissioned officers and commissioned officers would handle the evacuation of the vessel.[25] Capt. Pike described the overall feeling when he wrote, " ... we are right now in that territory known as 'Torpedo Junction' [*a word play upon the popular Benny Goodman piece "Tuxedo Junction"*] or 'Sub-land.' Orders have been issued that every man sleep in all his clothes, ready for instantaneous action. It gives one an uncomfortable feeling."[26]

On the morning of May 1st, with air coverage yet provided by NAS Bermuda, a friendly ship was sighted and the *S.S. Fort Lee* fell behind due to hot bearings, eventually stopping according to the air escort. The *Fort Lee* was ordered to leave the convoy and move to Bermuda with the *Terry* as an escort. As a result, the *U.S.S. Santa Paula*, which was carrying elements of the 85th Engineer Heavy Pontoon Battalion, including HQ Co. and Service Company, assumed the position of the *Fort Lee*, the *Shawnee* assumed the station of the *Santa Paula*, and the *Mexico*, which was carrying the 167th AAA Gun Battalion among its passengers, took over for the *Shawnee*.[27]

Rain, fog, and low ceiling precluded air coverage on May 2nd although later in the day a two-minute radar contact was made with an unidentified aircraft by the Destroyer Screen Commander. The plane was apparently never visually sighted but reportedly came from the direction of Bermuda, circled the formation, and then departed. Earlier, the *U.S.S. George Washington* had again fallen behind for a brief time. Near 5:00 p.m. the convoy passed through a heavy squall and about a half hour later *Destroyer #1* made sound contact and dropped a light barrage. Shortly afterward the *U.S.S. Texas* reported receipt of enemy transmission; four minutes later *Destroyer #5* made sonar contact and dropped a depth charge.[28]

At this point in the voyage, Lt. James O. Beasley, Co. D, summed up his feelings, writing, "This life on board ship is not exactly like that on a ship in peace times, but I still like it. My appetite is tremendous and since all lights in the cabins are put out at dark it is easy to get ample sleep ... the first two days were fair and the sea was so smooth it was difficult to tell the ship was moving unless one were on deck. Yesterday was pretty rough in comparison but probably about normal. I have not had the slightest touch of sea sickness ... For some men who have never been to sea the trip is no picnic, for a number of them are seasick, and of course they are severely restricted in their movements about the ship. The officers take turns staying with the men. We are supposed to be on duty four hours and off sixteen ... last evening ... Col. Cunin came up and slapped me on the back. I do not think that any of the other officers are enjoying the trip as much as I am. I have been accused before of being too dumb to be scared ... Yesterday we received booklets giving information about where we are supposed to land. They have lessened the scope of the rumors but some people are now adding to the details."[29]

The *S.S. Parker* briefly dropped out of formation on May 3rd and the *U.S.S. Merrimack*, a Type 2 oil tanker, fell out of position to fuel the destroyer escort. During this process the *Merrimack* was "touched" by the *U.S.S. Thatcher*, which resulted in some damage to both ships and injured one man on the *Merrimack* who suffered a contusion to his right heel and ankle. Problems continued when Lt. Harry Luther Champlain, U.S.N. Reserve, from Indiana, fell off the *Brownson*, which was fueling alongside the *Merrimack*. Unsuccessful efforts were made by the *Thatcher* and *Brownson* to recover the body. This was the only fatality during the convoy's entire Atlantic crossing.[30]

Trouble also developed on the *U.S.S. Texas* during the fueling operations. The one and only plane launched by the ship during the crossing tore off a wing tip float upon landing during a heavy swell and catapulted into the sea. The plane's remains were sunk and the crew recovered. The fate of the pilot of the plane appeared unclear from the deck log of the *U.S.S. Monticello*, however, as the date is scratched out, but the official report of the convoy confirmed pilot and crew were recovered uninjured.[31] On the lighter side Capt. "Bud" Pike, aboard the *Monticello*, wrote from "somewhere in the middle of the Atlantic Ocean" that the sea " ... is a beautiful awe-inspiring sight ... the sky is so bright and clear and the water so blue. The air out here is wonderful. It is very clean and bracing and has a wonderful effect on the appetite."[32]

On Tuesday, May 4th, the *U.S.S. George Washington* again dropped behind briefly, this time due to boiler trouble, and later a periscope was sighted about 2,500 yards astern of #73 by one of the other ships. Between 2:00 p.m. and 2:27 p.m. the *U.S.S. Chateau Thierry*, the *S.S. James Parker*, and the *U.S.S. Texas* test fired their anti-aircraft guns and in the evening the Destroyer Commander reported sonar contact. The *U.S.S. Chateau Thierry* showed a light while both the *S.S. John Erickson* and *S.S. Agwileon* straggled behind.[33]

Aboard the *Monticello* Capt. "Bud" Pike, Co. D, reported, "This ship is actually a floating city, hospital, etc.," and, indeed, two appendectomy operations were performed during the day, the first on Pfc. Ulmer L. Harrison, Co. C, and the second on Pvt. Leroy A. Christiansen, Co. D. [34] This may be the event referred to by Hale H. Hepler, Co. C, who said that on the second day at sea [*although this was the sixth day at sea*] two German subs were detected at the same time that one of his squad was undergoing an appendix operation. He recalled, "During the operation, depth charges were sent to knock out the enemy subs. It seems that two emergencies can occur at the same time. Another troop ship that day had sheared off a propeller and was attacked by the Germans. My memory does not serve me as to whether the ship sank or not."[35] Ironically, neither the deck log and war diary of the *U.S.S. Monticello*, nor the task force report, reflect any such activity on May 4th.

Early on the morning of May 5th, the *S.S. E. B. Alexander*, which was carrying such troops as the 262nd Station Hospital, dropped out of formation due to a "steering gear casualty" but was able to regain position in the convoy after a short delay. The *U.S.S. George Washington* repeatedly fell behind due to engine trouble, and before the day was over the *S.S. E. B. Alexander* again dropped behind due to telemeter problems. The *U.S.S. Kalk*, a Benson style destroyer, fell back to assist the vessel, although both soon afterward resumed their positions.[36] The day closed with the sighting of an unidentified ship about five miles distant. Aboard the *Monticello* Lt. James Beasley, Co. D, wrote to his wife, "So far this is just a pleasure cruise. The weather has been mild all the way and the ship is moving so slowly that it rocks very little … My time is spent sleeping, on deck watching the other ships (I can not get close to the nurses because of the competition), or with the men which is about six hours a day. I have done more sleeping and eating than I have in a number of years."[37]

The deck log and war diary of the *U.S.S. Monticello* recorded nothing of significance for Thursday, May 6th, but during Task Force machine gun practice the following day the ever-troubled *U.S.S. George Washington*, again struggling to keep up, had a 20mm projectile strike its deck. Fortunately, the shell was a dud and did not hit anyone. It was later determined the shell came either from the *John Erickson*, the *Mexico*, or the *Shawnee*, but all three denied responsibility.[38]

Sam Bundy, William C. Ford, and James G. Helsel, all of the 83rd, claimed that a plane crash-landed while attempting to land on an aircraft carrier on the 7th, with one of the three saying the pilot drowned and one of the others stating he survived. Helsel proved democratic, saying, "Today a plane preparing to go on a patrol was shot off the aircraft carrier and went straight into the water. We couldn't see if the pilot was rescued or not." Ironically the only mention in the deck logs and official convoy report of any such incident took place as previously mentioned on May 3rd aboard the *U.S.S. Texas*.[39]

Early on May 8th planes were sighted leaving, but after dropping recognition flares they were recognized as air coverage, which was provided for the next two days as well by NAS Fort Lyautey. The *S.S. E. B. Alexander* left the convoy with the destroyers *U.S.S. Kalk* and the *U.S.S. Harrison* as escorts. About four hours later a friendly plane was sighted near the convoy but there was perhaps more excitement on board the *U.S.S. Monticello* as Pvt. Arthur Boyd, Co. B, 1804 TT, U.S. Army, apparently in conflict with others, was confined for safekeeping. Less than a half hour later the crew and passengers were exercised and participated in an abandon ship drill. A few hours after that an aircraft escort left the convoy and the *S.S. Examiner* briefly fell back, while about an hour later *Destroyer #5* made contact and dropped two depth charges. A red flare was spotted on the port side of *H.M.S. Tracker* and several explosions were heard followed by the sighting of a white flare, which apparently was the "phosphorescent display of depth charges dropped by one of the destroyer escorts." This was probably the incident in the official convoy report that the *Carmick* reported sound contact and made three attacks dropping 21 depth charges. No further contact was made and there was no evidence of a hit. Following this episode the *S.S. J. W. McAndrew* showed a white light through a porthole for about a minute, and both the *S.S. Examiner* and *U.S.S. George Washington* straggled behind the convoy.[40]

William C. Ford was a bit more detailed in his description of May 8th, stating that the convoy was attacked by ten or twelve subs and numerous depth charges were dropped throughout the day and on until the boat docked at Oran.[41] Eugene Plassmann said the battalion learned that at one point during the crossing the destroyer escorts sank at least one German U-boat.[42] The official convoy report, the ship war diaries, and the deck logs all make no claims of destroying any enemy craft during the crossing. The fear instilled in the men of the 83rd by such incidents was well illustrated by Ed Trey, who said Chaplain Lyle L. Burdick overreacted to the depth charges and nearly put the entire battalion in a panic.[43] Often the depth charges were released at night, provoking Mess Sgt. Carl W. Lepine of New York to remark, "the Lord heard some strange voices those nights."[44] The uneasiness was felt by many as noted by Capt. Pike, writing, "I almost feel sorry for [Lt. Carl K.] 'Stud' Carpenter [from Stark County, Ohio]. He is going crazy. All he ever talks about is going home and about his wife and his child and how he hates war and how he dislikes the Colonel and Captain Hutchinson, etc. He wants to swim back and turn the boat around and everything else. It's really pitiful." Pike himself reported he was "… still on the high seas. And still safe and sound, although a little jittery."[45]

Sunday, May 9th, found *Destroyer 1B* dropping depth charges, while the official convoy report states the *Hobby* made a strong submarine sound contact and dropped nine depth charges. No further contact was made and a strong fuel oil smell followed, indicating the enemy sub may have been hit. The *S.S. Mexico* fell behind and the *U.S.S. Texas* reported radar contact -- a plane was sighted and identified as friendly. Near mid-day a Portuguese merchant ship was spotted, *H.M.S. Tracker* straggled briefly, *Destroyer #2* made contact, and air coverage was provided the remainder of the day.[46] Sam Bundy wrote that land was sighted late on May 9th, with Spain on one side and Spanish Morocco on the other, although most accounts do not mention sighting land until the next day.[47] Capt. Ed Pike and James Helsel also noted in their diaries that land was first observed near Tangiers, Spanish Morocco.[48]

On the morning of May 10th, a British escort ship was spotted and the convoy began to separate into two divisions, with the *U.S.S. Monticello* designated as guide for the second division headed eastward to Oran, the first knowledge the men had of their destination, and the first division sailing south to Casablanca. Shortly afterward a friendly aircraft was seen and the second division of the convoy changed course before spotting Convoy GU-7. A Spanish trawler was soon encountered while *H.M.S. Ilex* made contact and dropped one depth charge. About an hour prior to sundown, the men were able to spot the shore of North Africa in the far distance, while near dusk, or close to 6:00 p.m., the convoy formed into three columns in order to facilitate passage through the Straits of Gibraltar.[49] Martin J. Feerick recalled, "After seeing nothing but water for almost two weeks, the first sight of land was tremendously impressive. The Rock of Gibraltar was enjoyed by the members of the 83rd … "[50] Sam Bundy, Co. A, was impressed by "a beautiful sunset tonight reflected in the Mediterranean Sea" while Dan Shields, Co. D, found the sight of land "beautiful."[51] Capt. Pike said, "We had a swell trip across the Atlantic and little of excitement happened during the journey. We had a glimpse of the Rock and it was an awe-inspiring sight."[52]

After passing though the Straits of Gibraltar, the men saw such points as Cape Spartel and Tarifa before the convoy returned to five columns in the Mediterranean Sea and passed Punta Canero. At this location, the *U.S.S. Brownson*, the *U.S.S. Guest*, and *H.M.S. Eggford* detached from the convoy, which was joined by *H.M.S. Wishart* as an escort. Following this maneuver, such points as Punta Almina and Punta Calaburras were observed.[53]

Tuesday, May 11th, found the *U.S.S. Monticello* listed in the Mediterranean Convoy Section, minus the *S.S. Fort Lee* and the *S.S. E. B. Alexander*, and accompanied by a British escort comprised of H.M.S.'s *Wishart, Calpe, Ilex, Vetch, Haydon,* and *Puckeridge*. Cape Sacratif was passed as Capt. Altieri of the *U.S.S. Pilot* came aboard to assist in docking. The tug *Jolasry* came alongside as the *U.S.S. Monticello* entered Oran harbor, passed through a submarine net, and was joined alongside by the tug *Goeland IV*. The *U.S.S. Chateau Thierry* docked shortly after 3:00 p.m. Finally, at about 3:30 p.m. the *U.S.S. Monticello* moored port side to Mole Millerand, Oran [some veterans claim they docked at 2:00 p.m., indicating they possibly did not reset their watches], or "the hell hole of Algeria" as Harold Hughes described the town.[54] Although less blunt in his description of the town, John P. McEvoy said, "You could smell Oran ten miles at sea. Native plants plus numerous if not thousands of years of history had contributed to this aroma."[55]

The tug *Goeland IV* cast off, the *S.S. Boringuen* stood in, and at about 5:40 p.m. the *U.S.S. Monticello* began to disembark the Army troops, which continued throughout the night. Due to their capacity as military police or guard, the bulk of the 83rd had to remain on board until all of the other organizations had debarked. Although the battalion began unloading at 6:00 p.m., they did not depart the ship as a whole until between 9:30 and 10:00 in the evening, and would not finish until the early morning hours of the 12th.[56] With the Atlantic voyage now behind them, Lt. Leonard A. ("Spike") Merrill, Jr., summed up the entire excursion as he wrote home "This trip has been a pleasure cruise all the way with beautiful weather and calm seas," although a number of the men probably disagreed with that assertion.[57]

The vessels reported present with the *U.S.S. Monticello* on May 12th included the *U.S.S. Chateau Thierry*, the *U.S.S. Staff*, the *U.S.S. Speed*, the *U.S.S. Study*, the *U.S.S. Orizaba*, the *U.S.S. Delta*, and the *U.S.S. Samuel Chase*. At about 3:15 a.m. the *U.S.S. Monticello* reported completion of disembarkation of 4,926 army troops, 349 officers, 71 army nurses, and one civilian employee of the army, for a total of 5,347. This was followed by the unloading of cargo.[58]

William J. Gallagher, Jr., from Philadelphia, and formerly a foreman in the Paint Division of Dupont, recalled that during the debarkation, " … one hell of an air raid was taking place. The anti-aircraft fire was terrific. One of the guys in the group said, 'Oh boy -- look at all the fireworks, I guess the war is over.' I said I guess the burning of a tanker and supply ships was accidental due to the fireworks. We soon found out the war was very much alive."[59] George A. Barrett, Co. B, also of Philadelphia, remembered the same incident: "Tony Imperato and I decided to go into town. Suddenly the whole sky lit up and I said, 'Great, Tony, they are having a celebration -- look at all the fireworks!' I urged Tony, 'Let's hurry up so we don't miss anything.' All of a sudden all this stuff was falling from the sky. As we trotted along, we asked each other what could this stuff be that was falling all around us? Never having been in an air raid, we didn't recognize that flak was raining down upon us."[60]

U.S.S. Monticello
National Archives

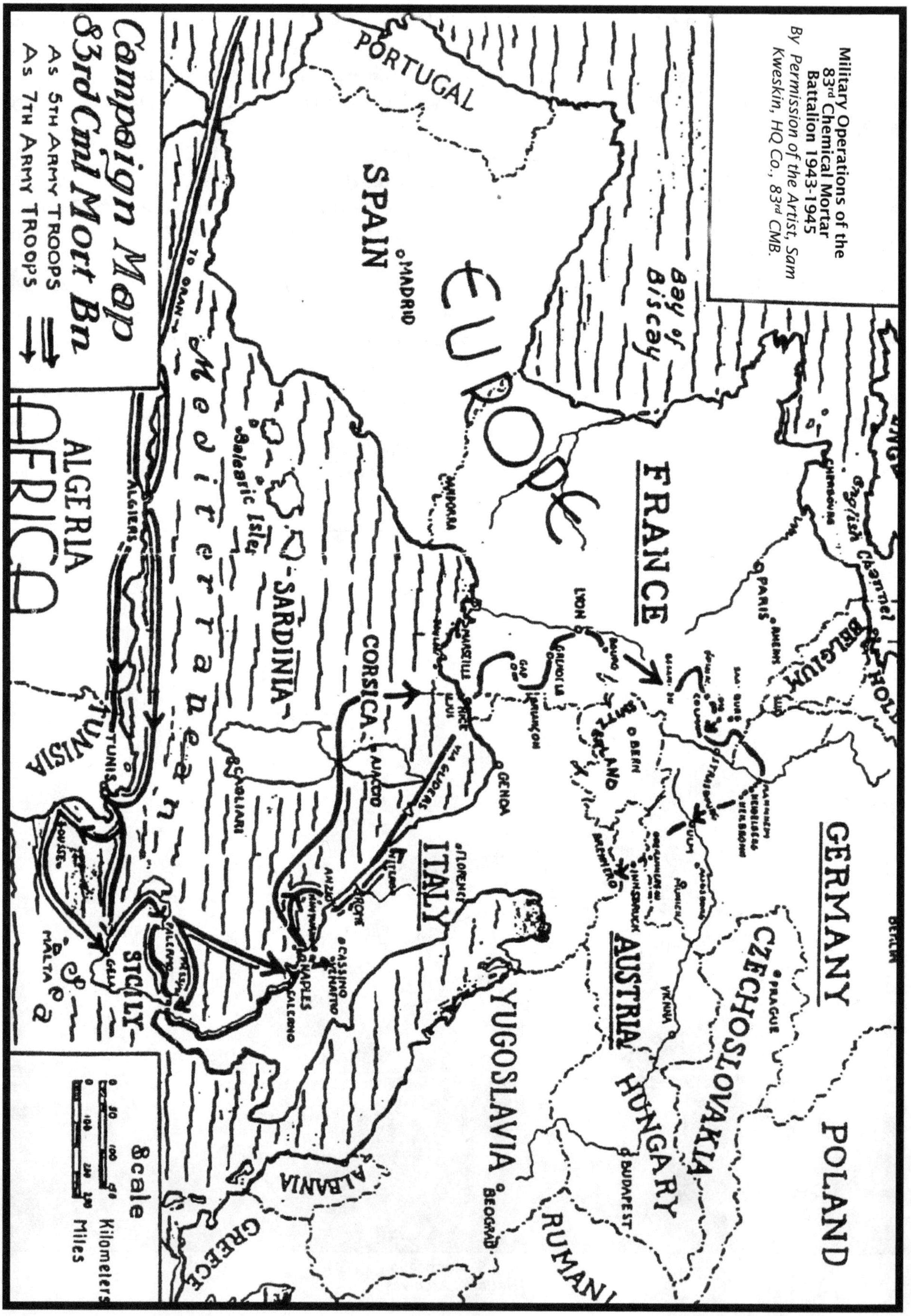
Military Operations of the 83rd Chemical Mortar Battalion 1943-1945
By Permission of the Artist, Sam Kweskin, HQ Co., 83rd CMB.
Campaign Map
83rd Cml Mort Bn
As 5th Army Troops
As 7th Army Troops
Scale
Kilometers
Miles
PORTUGAL
SPAIN
MADRID
EUROPE
Bay of Biscay
FRANCE
PARIS
LYON
English Channel
BELGIUM
GERMANY
CZECHOSLOVAKIA
PRAGUE
POLAND
AUSTRIA
HUNGARY
BUDAPEST
RUMANIA
YUGOSLAVIA
BEOGRAD
ALBANIA
GREECE
ITALY
GENOA
NICE
MARSEILLE
CORSICA
AJACCIO
SARDINIA
CAGLIARI
Balearic Isles
Mediterranean
ANZIO
CASSINO
NAPLES
SALERNO
SICILY
MALTA
AFRICA
ALGERIA
ALGIERS
TUNISIA
TUNIS
TO ORAN

Chapter Five

NORTH AFRICA INVASION TRAINING MAY 12-JULY 9 1943

Damaged photo of Port of Oran, North Africa.
Ed Trey

Following completion of disembarkation from the *U.S.S. Monticello* in the early morning hours of May 12th, the 83rd was immediately attached to the 2nd Regimental Group, Staging Area 1-G, Mediterranean Base Section, and assigned to the 1st Armored Corps, Reinforcement. Although the North African Campaign was practically over, and the 83rd would not participate, according to Capt. Pike they did arrive in time to be able to wear the North African Theater ribbon.[1]

The men, ever thankful to finally be back on land, boarded trucks and were driven to Assi-ben-Okba, a point some 11 to15 miles east-northeast of Oran, where they went into bivouac at about midnight on rocky, rugged, cactus-filled, fly- and mosquito-infested terrain known as "Goat Hill" near Fleurs.[2] James Helsel said, "We call it Goat Hill, for all that you see is Arabs [*Algerians*] and their goats."[3] A member of the 45th General Hospital, a later occupant of the site, said, "An overabundance of large stones dotted the hillside. The spot was appropriately named … One story recounted that only a goat would voluntarily live here and another more fitting version stated that goats looked at the hill with disdain and refused to reside here."[4] Since most of their equipment and supplies were still en route from the ship, all the men had were two blankets and a shelter half tent, which they carried in their packs [*although Capt. Burford claimed the men were without packs*]. The weather was warm, the ground was hard, and an eerie silence prevailed as the men attempted to sleep, only to be aroused by the flares and sounds of a nearby bombardment in Oran harbor.[5]

Writing home, Lt. James Beasley, Co. D, reported, "… we arrived safely. The weather was perfect for the trip and there were no disturbing alarms. We are now in North Africa… The rumors now are that the Germans are out of North Africa and that France has just been invaded … Our bivouac area is an interesting and scenic place. For lunch today I had a can of hash, crackers, cocoa, and candy. After eating I washed the utensils and then drank the water … There is no indication as to when we will receive mail and it may be sometime before mail will go out from here. The men feel good about the trip over and the sunshine here will soon have them well tanned."[6]

The 83rd would remain in bivouac at Assi-ben-Okba and vicinity from May 12th to the 29th in an effort to become acclimated to the environment, unpack organization equipment, and await motor transport equipment. Capt. Pike, Co. D, said "a training program was begun, emphasis being placed on a rigorous physical conditioning program. Due to the long boat ride under crowded and relatively unsanitary conditions, with little opportunity for exercise, the physical fitness of the men was low." The stay proved rather unpleasant as the sun was unbearably hot during the day, with almost no shade in sight, and the nights were cold and the ground often damp. Worse yet was the extreme poverty of the native people and the overabundance of flies, mosquitoes, and other pests.[7]

During their first morning at "Goat Hill," the boys of the 83rd woke up to the sound of French Algerians selling rich fig bars, which the men readily bought and devoured, according to Loy Marshall, Co. C, but the next morning they woke up with stomach aches and diarrhea from the rich food. On their third day they visited town and overindulged in red wine and Marshall said, "… it didn't take long for the combination of being weak from all the seasickness, the episode with the fig bars, and now the effects of the red wine to kick in. We were all sick again the next day in the worst way imaginable. So in only four days of foreign service we learned a couple of very valuable lessons. Be careful what you eat and how much you drink."[8] Co. C's Mess Sgt. Thomas A. Cute, from Steuben County, New York, did his best to locate fresh vegetables, ice, ice cream, and other non-rationed items to aid in the men's diets.[9]

Capt. Burford also described the area during this period with equally negative impressions, writing, "Flies were so numerous that we had to get under mosquito bars to avoid them. Water was scarce and a large number of the men developed dysentery." Showers were available but involved a twenty-minute walk both ways, which pretty much defeated the purpose. This situation improved late in the period when motor transportation arrived and daily showers and trips to the beach were often utilized.[10]

Sam Bundy, Co. A, echoed similar feelings when he recorded in his diary, "There are many insects around here we could well do without; I never saw so many spiders and snails before," and following a visit to nearby St. Cloud he remarked, "Boy oh boy the flies there are terrific."[11]

The rough African climate, poor food and drink, along with numerous other contributing factors, would lead to a great deal of sickness within the 83rd, primarily malaria, dysentery, and jaundice. James Helsel took note of this in his diary on May 15th as he wrote, "The flies are very plentiful and also have nerve, they crawl in your mouth and try to take it from you. A lot of dysentery has popped up, so far I've been lucky."[12] More positive in his impression was Lt. Beasley who wrote, "We are now back on regular rations. My home is also improved. It helps to dig a place in which to sleep that fits ones back. I also did the laundry and spring cleaning. All the woolen clothes, etc were packed in a separate bag for the summer." Ed Trey concurred that only woolens were to be worn in Africa, having purchased twelve sets of khakis at the New York Port of Embarkation which he had to send home. On the same day Russell H. Peterson, Cq. D, wrote "I am on dry land now. This spot has interesting and exotic (in the scientific sense of the word) flora and fauna, and the flora seemingly more so than the fauna. The geology of this spot seems worth looking in to." On the 16th Beasley added, "The past several days have been more like a vacation than anything else. The trip to North Africa was enjoyable to me because I was not sea sick and about all there was to do was eat and I developed a big appetite. The weather was good all the way and the sea comparatively smooth …We are now camping on a fairly high stony hill where there is a good breeze most of the day and night. The nights are cool and it is much easier to sleep soundly on the rocks than anyone would believe who has not tried it. I feel better than I have in months. Each man gets two cans of food per meal here. One can has meat and vegetables cooked together and the other has crackers, cocoa or coffee, sugar and candy. It is all a working man needs and it tastes good." Charlie Lowry, Co. D, wrote on the 18th "We were on the boat last pay day so I didn't get paid. They did give us $5.00 when we landed and that made me $6.00."[13]

After a visit to Oran, Capt. Pike observed, "The main points of interest were the various wine shops, the Officers Red Cross, and a few such things as Arab mosques, soldiers in the uniforms of many nations, veiled women, our first ice cream in Africa, and little else." He also visited the nearby French town of St. Cloud which he described as "…much cleaner than Oran, much smaller and the people were nicer. The principle to African cities in general is the utter filth. People do their duties in the streets, and have cows, horses, etc. living in the same room with them."[14] Sam Bundy added, "Arabians [*Algerians*], poor and shabbily clothed, roam the hills with their herds of sheep and goats. After a couple of days we began to get used to the place and we began having mortar dry-run problems and hikes."[15]

Many visits were paid to Oran to find relaxation and entertainment, often with negative results. Harold Hughes, a self-admitted alcoholic who would later reform, said the men would drink anything they could get their hands on, from warm beer to "…a foul-tasting concoction called anisette." According to Robert L. Sorensen, Medical Detachment, Hughes "…from the very first created problems with his drinking. He could always find wine and other drinks … The problem was getting him to come back to camp. The aid station would send out 3 or 4 men to bring him back. He was a very big man and it would take 4 or 5 men to bring him back but he would fight them and someone would always get hurt."[16] Michael Rebick, Co. D, took a more positive approach, writing, "Africa is not a bad country at that for we have nice scenery around here & the Arabs are very friendly & do they dress funny for they wear a towel for a hat, blanket or some kind of cloth for a coat & very few have any shoes but their wine is not bad at all."[17]

Although the date is uncertain, Carl Mac ("Skinny") McNabb of the Medical Detachment developed bleeding stomach ulcers and was sent home. His buddy, Curtis A. Williams, also of the Medical Detachment, recalled that Carl never wished to be in the service, which Carl readily admitted, as did his wife back in Tennessee, so he knew Carl would make use of the first opportunity to return home. According to Williams, Carl's wife was a nurse and never wanted him to enter the service. She told him to eat soap to create the illusion of a serious health problem. He did not have the nerve to do so prior to embarkation but, apparently, once he got to Africa and realized his predicament, he might have decided to use the soap trick. Curtis recalled that one day McNabb was deathly sick and went to the hospital. Upon returning he packed all his things and told Williams where to mail them -- to his home in the states. Whether or not Carl McNabb actually ate soap or was really sick from

Carl McNabb

Carl McNabb, nicknamed "Mac" and "Skinny", was born January 25, 1917, in Stevenson, Alabama. He played baseball in the minor leagues, including the AFL Ozarks in 1936 and for the Tyler Trojans in 1937-38. Prior to the war he was a resident of Marion County, Tennessee and enlisted in the army September 26, 1942 at Baltimore, Maryland. He was a private in Co. D, 83rd Chemical (Motorized) Battalion and was assigned to the Medical Detachment of the battalion at Camp Gordon, Georgia on November 23, 1942.

In a 2003 phone interview with the author, McNabb stated he never "took" to the military lifestyle and in North Africa developed bleeding stomach ulcers from eating C-Rations which led to a medical discharge prior to the Sicilian Campaign. Returning to the United States he entered Major League baseball on April 20, 1945, with the Detroit Tigers. According to baseball historians and trivia buffs, Carl McNabb "received all of one major-league at-bat – and struck out in his only appearance." Following the 1945 season he returned to the Minor Leagues and played for the Tyler Trojans 1947-49. He retired from baseball in 1950 and returned to Jasper, Tennessee, where he still resided in 2005. He said that during his baseball career he once played together at Hagerstown, Maryland, with Earl Rapp, another baseball alumnus of the 83rd Chemical Mortar Battalion.

Carl McNabb passed away July 16, 2007, at Jasper, Tennessee, and was buried in the Pine Grove Cemetery.

Both photos courtesy Carl McNabb

bleeding stomach ulcers is not important; he made it home and resumed his semi-professional baseball career.[18]

On May 22nd Lt. Beasley, Co. D, wrote, "All the men are writing that Rommel left as soon as he heard we were coming… Last evening I was on a detail to a nearby town to help keep the soldiers out of trouble and to see that they saluted [*and*] yesterday morning two men of the company who could leave went for a hike up a mountain. It was the hardest climb I have ever had (except to get up in the army). We were nearly exhausted and by special effort made the last ridge only to find that it was not the last but that there was a sharp decline and then the steepest climb of all. We had gotten too near to give up so we went on to the top. The men feel quite proud of themselves." Turning to another subject, Beasley wrote, "You ask what the censor would object to other than military information. I can do nothing about it but I personally object to 'I love you' being repeated more than ten times in a letter and the terms Honey, Sugar, etc. are overworked. The moon shines so bright in my tent at night that it wakes me up."[19]

Capt. Robert Edwards, Co. A, wrote home on the 23rd, "Lt. [*Veryl*] Hays just cut my hair - really short - water here is so hard it precipitates the soap and [*you*] can not get [*the*] soap off the hair. Have a mustache not so good - will remove same after I get a picture for you. Hope to get paid on the 31st. Will send you a little extra. Had to convert all U.S. money to francs. Arabs and French are peculiar. French women are very chic usually but look dirty under their make up. All rather pointed faces. Have a wine drink called half + half - 1/2 sour + 1/2 sweet with ice … Have been to main city twice including last night for M.P. duty. Very dirty and hard to keep clean here."[20] In a letter written the same day, Lt. James Beasley added, "We had a chicken dinner with string beans, good bread, canned peaches, and lemonade … I tried sleeping a while but some more men wanted passes and several flies insisted they had not had lunch. I got up and walked over a mile to get a shower and got back just in time for supper which was chili … There have been some more promotions. Lt. [*Chris*] Cornett and Lt. [*Gordon*] Mindrum were made Captains. It is expected that Captain Hutchinson will be made major any day. The only other promotions then will be some of the 2nd lieutenants to 1st lieutenants. The ones promoted are the ones I knew for a long time would be promoted."[21]

Due to the intense heat and horrid environmental conditions, training was limited to calisthenics and short marches held only during the early morning hours. In an effort to help break some of the boredom and monotony, various officers at times would take groups of men on trips to visit some of the sites. At one point Cunin took some of his officers to visit the nearby fortifications at Arzew, 22 miles east of Oran, while on the night of May 25th the 2nd Platoon of Co. C guarded some German prisoners.[22]

At 8:30 on the morning of May 29th, in preparation for future operations, Co. D of the 83rd departed the staging area at Assi-ben-Okba and was attached to the 16th Infantry, 1st Infantry Division, at St. Leu, Algeria, near Arzew. At this location Capt. Pike met with Col. Taylor, the regimental commander, and the "training program of the company was resumed with emphasis being placed on the tactics and technique of amphibious landings, service practice, and combined training with the infantry battalions supported." In addition, Co. C received orders to move by motor transport the following day, and, indeed, at 8:30 on the morning of the 30th, HQ Co. and companies A, B, and C left Assi-ben-Okba and arrived at Area "B", Invasion Training Center (I.T.C.), near the city of Georges Clemenceau, Algeria, at about 12:30 p.m. Headquarters of the I.T.C. was located at Port-Aux-Poules.[23] Sam Bundy, Co. A, remembered that "we went in trucks thru St. Cloud toward the sea and followed a narrow, winding road from above the clouds down a steep mountain thru ancient towns to a beautiful spot on the beach where we had our first dip in the Mediterranean."[24] Capt. Burford, Co. C, was not as impressed, writing, "Here we found a little more shade than we were accustomed to, although we had to camp in the middle of a stubblefield. The undergrowth was thick and the mosquitoes were numerous, so much so that in the evenings and mornings we were compelled to wear head nets for protection."[25]

On the 31st Sam Bundy said Co. A left their "worn-out area" at Georges Clemenceau and moved by truck to a point between Arzew and Mostaganem to the east, which he said "…could well have been named 'Mosquito Land' because they and they alone inhabited the rocky, thorny area."[26] James Helsel of the company supported this assessment, writing in his diary, "We got rid of the flies, but now it's mosquitoes." During the night Helsel pulled guard duty and said he " …had to bury myself in the sand to keep away from the mosquitoes. One boy said he caught one turning his dog tag over to see what type of blood he had."[27] Co. C remained at Georges Clemenceau and was attached to the 3rd Battalion, 39th Combat Engineers. Less concerned with affairs at this time was Pvt. Richard A. Bridge, with Co. D near Arzew, who tied an Easter bunny his mother had sent him to the top of his tent.[28]

Lt. Julian McKinnon, left, & Capt. Ed Trey, right, in Africa.
Ed Trey

Although most of the men excepting the officers did not know it at the time, these movements were in preparation for amphibious assault training.

On June 1st Co. A, attached to the 1st Battalion, 39th Combat Engineers, boarded the *U.S.S. Elizabeth C. Stanton* at Mostaganem for four days of amphibious training. Sam Bundy said that during the period they " … practiced climbing up and down rope nets onto barges which transported men a couple of miles to shore where they were put off onto a beach."[29] Quite often the men got off in deep water; some got seasick. After they hit the beach, they advanced inland and followed specific orders until problems were completed and they returned to the *Stanton*. Many problems arose as noted by James Helsel who said that on the second night out [*June 3rd*] " … the Higgins boat I was on got lost on the way back to the boat and we didn't get back until about nine o'clock."[30]

At St. Leu, Capt. Pike, Co. D, was involved in the usual bivouac duties. One day "I just looked out my tent and there was a man urinating in the company street. He will dig a nice deep hole in almost solid rock tomorrow for a company urinal. That is just the sort of thing that has to be dealt with summarily out here as sanitation is a big problem. The flies and mosquito are very numerous and hard to control and it is things like this that makes it thus."[31] Michael Rebick, Co. D, further added that he had to take breaks while writing letters home to chase away the flies and mosquitoes.[32] Lt. James Beasley, Co. D, more concerned with the culinary delights, wrote, "You should join the army if you want good meat. At noon we had chicken and at dinner we had fresh beef." Co. D's cook George R. Borkhuis wrote, "It's much cooler here as there is a strong wind blowing most of the time. We are restricted here and do not get passes to go to town as we did before."[33]

Co. C, yet attached to the 3rd Battalion, 39th Combat Engineers, who were commanded by Major J. C. Manning, followed up on the third day of June by boarding at Port-Aux-Poules the *U.S.S. Thurston,* a medium size troop ship manned by the U.S. Navy and commanded by Capt. Jack E. Hurf. The war diary of the *Thurston* states 35 officers and 601 enlisted men embarked under the command of Maj. Manning.[34] Their assignment would take three days, recalled Capt. Burford, who wrote, "We embarked on three LCMs (Landing Craft, Mechanized) and were taken out to the ship." He continued, "… we made three invasion landings on the shore around Arzew, supporting the 3d Bn. 39th Engineers in the simulated attack. One of the landings was in the daylight, two in darkness. The sea was extremely rough all the time and many of the men were seasick … on no one of the landings did the Navy land us on the right beach." On one attempt, Burford almost fell into the sea to be crushed by the ships, while on the final practice assault, landing at Oudja, eight miles distant from their objective, 1st Lt. Ralph T. Rankin from Oklahoma, part of the 1st Platoon, hit

Co. C group with monkey near Oran, Algeria. Raymond Risley
(behind man in white shirt); others unidentified.
Ford Collection

a false beach and received a dunking.[35] Loy Marshall, Co. C, wrote a summary of the entire practice assault: "We loaded up on big ships and were transported to a designated landing area. The ships would get as close as they could (usually a few hundred yards out) then we would transfer to a barge that would hold about thirty people and all of our equipment including our mortars and rounds, our radios and spools of communications wire. The barge would go in as far as it could and we'd jump out usually in at least chest high water by pulling our knees to our waist; once in the water we'd grab all our equipment and head for shore as fast as we could and just keep going inland until we were told to stop. It was very difficult to grab and hold all of the equipment, and we would be exhausted from the effort."[36]

This is probably the training period described by Hale H. Hepler, who wrote, "We were given the assignment to climb down a rope ladder, go out on land, dig a foxhole, and set up the gun at night while wearing a full field pack. At day break we were to get back to the boat. This training continued for several days. It was during this time that we were called to a big meeting on a hillside. There was General George Patton, giving us a 'Pep Talk'. He was telling us about making an invasion into Sicily [*there is some doubt he would have given the specific location this early*]. He used the phrase that we had to 'Kill The Bosch' [*Germans*]. He told us what was necessary to do."[37] Mike Codega was equally sharp in his description of this event, stating that an order was given for "... all non-coms and officers to journey to an air-field an hours drive distance for the purpose of listening to a pep talk by some top general -- a wait of an hour in sweltering heat -- the roar of a plane landing. General Patton on stage -- five minutes of expletives, then the journey back to camp."[38] During this three-day training period the *Thurston* reported the loss of two LCVPs.[39]

At this time Capt. "Bud" Pike, Co. D, wrote home that "We are now in a new location and still living in the field in our pup tents. It really isn't so bad..." He also said that when Ed Trey wrote home he boasted that when he got back to the States the first thing he was going to do "... was hop in a bathtub full of hot water with a cigar and a good magazine. Then on second thought that was the second thing he was going to do."[40]

On June 4th, Co. A returned from their amphibious training while Co. B, with the 1st Ranger Battalion, departed for Oudja at 7:00 in the morning for their training period. Co. C continued mortar service practice about 25 miles above Mostaganem.[41] Between June 5th and 6th Co. D, at St. Leu, boarded the *U.S.S. Chase* and practiced landings with the 16th Infantry. Capt. Pike said that "due to a lack of a sufficient number of LCVPs for training the company made the practice landings without mortars and acting as infantry to acclimate them to the water and that type of landing craft as well as for additional physical toughening. The practice mortar-infantry problem consisted of combat loading in the bivouac area; tactical motor move from bivouac area to assembly area; establishing of company ammunition dump; hand pull of mortars from assembly area to previously reconnoitered platoon positions; occupation of positions; establishing of communication nets; hand carry of ammunition from dump to mortar positions; and conduct of fire." During the operation Capt. Pike got seasick and lost a "delicious baked ham."[42] Daniel Shields, Co. D, had a much better time, writing on the 4th, the day before loading, "5:30 a.m. Ate, washed, then went out on advance party on ship *Chase*. Climbed rope ladder, ate wonderful meal, movies, listened to recordings, talked to sailors. Took a fresh shower. Retired 12:10." The next two days he was busy helping the men get aboard, practice landings and hitting the beach, not to mention he had some ice cream and coke.[43] Capt. Pike commented that "…it is so cold that I have my driver's mackinaw on. That is the way weather runs down here; one extreme to the other – hotter'n hell in the daytime, colder'n hell at night."[44]

Co. C returned from their training on the 7th while Co. B arrived from Oudja at midnight of the 8th.[45] At this time Lt. James Beasley, Co. D, wrote, "We have all received ribbons for participating in the African campaign. That is a joke and we do not consider that we should have them because we had nothing to do with it. We just happened to be on the Continent before the end came …This afternoon I had a good shower in a nearby town. Since it was unplanned I did not have soap or towel but the dirt was so thick that the shower without soap made a great improvement. Except for one pair of underwear and some handkerchiefs all my clothes are dirty. The outside clothes are so bad that the underwear gets dirty from the outside in." George Borkhuis wrote, "I'm so browned from the sun they boys have nicknamed me Arab."[46]

During this period, Co. C had one service practice and Co. B gave a demonstration of the 4.2" mortar to the Rangers.[47] Lt. Col. William Orlando Darby, a 1933 graduate of West Point, was so impressed he ordered the 83rd attached to the Ranger Task Force. This was no fluke as Darby had accidentally run into Cunin at Oran in mid-May. They were former classmates at West Point who had served together in the mid-1930's at Ft. Bliss, Texas, in the Field Artillery. In addition, when Darby was battery commander of the 99th Field Artillery at Ft. Hoyle, Maryland, he was pleased with the long range and bursting radius of the 4.2" mortars in a comparison firing to his own 75mm pack howitzers. Cunin had made it clear to Darby that several chemical battalions were set to invade Sicily, which prompted Darby, in need of such firepower as that offered by the 4.2" mortar, to immediately latch onto the 83rd, a union which would last until the demise of Darby's Rangers at Cisterna in late January of 1944. This partnership transformed Darby's Rangers "from a light, commando-like strike force into a more heavily and conventionally armed unit." The bond between the two organizations would become so close the 83rd would become known as the "Ranger's Artillery."[48]

While this union of the Rangers and the 83rd would prove most productive, it also created some distance between Cunin and his men. Apparently Cunin idolized Darby and did his best to emulate him, preferring to spend more time with the Rangers than with his own men. He became so enamored he apparently began to neglect the most basic necessities of his own command, such as food, and it did not go unnoticed. Capt. Ed "Bud" Pike observed this obsession by Cunin and wrote of Darby, "… he is a man's man and a wonderful soldier and leader. When I think of him and the Cunin I shudder at the comparison."[49] Ed Trey recalled, "Col. Darby gave me one of the original Ranger shoulder patches as I spent a lot of time in his outfit. Of course, Cunin wouldn't let me wear it."[50]

On the night before the battalion was to leave Georges Clemenceau, Lt. Col. Cunin demanded a special court martial trial be held for a number of earlier offenses, primarily drunkenness. Capt. Burford sat on this trial, which Cunin conveniently avoided to go to bed, and remarked it was the worst farce he had ever witnessed. He said David W. Meyerson was president of the court while " …[Robert M.] Schmidt was the Trial Judge Advocate, his first attempt at it, and he lost his place in the procedure several times. One of the men was being tried for drunkenness and [Christopher C.] Cornett [Jr.], sitting on the Court, was so drunk he couldn't sit up straight. Half the court, which included McEvoy, Mindrum, Edwards, Cornett, and myself were so tired from the week's strenuous activities that we couldn't stay awake. I think Mindrum and Edwards did go to sleep. All in all, I don't think justice was served by that tired, sleepy, drunk, and mosquito-harassed court."[51]

An advance party under William S. Hutchinson, along with all organizational equipment not left behind in rear echelons of weapons companies, left Georges Clemenceau on June 9th for Zeralda, located about 15 miles west of Algiers, and arrived the following day.[52] Oddly, on a photo belonging to Dan Shields, Co. D, displaying a group of men in sports uniform, is found the notation, "English Soccer Team Picked Up On Way To Algiers June 10,

1943."[53] On the 11th the Command Group, consisting of Battalion Headquarters Detachment, left their bivouac area at Georges Clemenceau by truck for Algiers at 8:00 in the morning.[54] Capt. Pike would later describe Algiers as "… full of houses of prostitution, wineries, crooks, trinket shops, filth, and little else."[55]

It was probably during this trip that Karl Garrett, HQ Co., said, "The area was mountainous and the trucks moved necessarily slowly. The Arab boys were selling fresh fruit along the roadside. While the trucks were still moving all this trading was going on. I recall one of our guys offered money to this boy who had the fruit up in one hand and reached for the money with the other. He grabbed the money and then ran down the hillside with the money and the fruit. The G.I. was so mad, he jumped out of the truck in hot pursuit. We all got a good laugh, which were few and far between. In any case, we didn't see him again until the next day. He had gotten his money back and also the fruit. The Arabs did not trust us, nor we them. They would steal anything not nailed down."[56]

Companies A, B, and C, comprising the forward echelon, went to Mers-el-Khebir, about ten miles west of Oran, on borrowed trucks as they had sent their own away earlier in the week to be water-proofed. During the forenoon they boarded the *U.S.S. Lyon* along with attached medical and ammunition train personnel and "a host of troops from the famous 1st Division." According to the war diary of the ship, 107 officers, four warrant officers, and 2,153 enlisted men embarked, for a total of 2,264 troops. Once loaded the craft remained in the harbor overnight, during which time Sam Bundy said he ate his first K-Rations.[57]

Co. D, along with attached medical and ammunition personnel, also departed St. Leu on June 11th and went by truck to Oran to board the *U.S.S. Thurston* [*the U.S.S. Chase as incorrectly stated in a Co. D report*] at 3:00 in the afternoon. The war diary of the *U.S.S. Thurston* confirms the embarkation of the 2nd Battalion, 16th Infantry, and attached units commanded by Lt. Col. J. W. Crawford, Battalion Commander. This would have included Co. D of the 83rd.[58]

On the morning of June 12th, the ships, comprising Transport Division 3, commanded by Capt. C. D. Edgar, USN, set sail for Algiers and passed along the coast of North Africa on a calm sea in good weather. During this practice "sortie" the *Thurston* fired their AA guns, expending 18 rounds of 40mm and 54 rounds of 20mm ammo.[59] Co. D, yet attached to the 16th Infantry, arrived at Algiers around noon of the 13th but did not debark until 3:00 in the afternoon due to a lack of available trucks. They went into bivouac at Staouli, about 15 miles west of Algiers. Their rear echelon remained with the rear elements of the 16th Infantry. Capt. Pike claimed this did not occur until June 10th and said that "on this move personnel went by troop ship, Oran to Algiers, and from the port of Algiers by motor vehicle to the new area; all vehicles and the company advance party went overland. Here final training and final planning were to be accomplished. The training program was continued with the aim of building up to a final dress rehearsal of the landing late in June." Capt. Pike added, "initially each platoon would take in four firing mortars, the other two mortars of each platoon coming in on D-day vehicles for use as spare parts. Eight carts were to be loaded with twelve rounds of 4.2" mortar ammunition each and each man (except communications personnel) would carry two rounds on his back to be dumped on the beach upon landing. This ammunition as well as that arriving on D-day vehicles would be in the proportion of 70% HE and 30% WP on order of the infantry battalion commanders … Uniform was woolen OD's, leggings, web belts, canteen and cup, first aid packets, combat pack, entrenching tools, steel helmet and individual weapons. Communications personnel would carry, in addition, telephones, reels of combat wire reels, radios, spare parts, and repair equipment. Mortar carts and ammunition

English soccer team picked up by Co. D on their way to Algiers, June 10, 1943. *Shields Collection*

carts deck loaded. The LCVPs aboard the transport, loaded over the side by booms, would first carry the infantry assault waves ashore and then return to the transport and carry the chemical mortar men and equipment in the fourth and fifth waves." Lastly Pike said, "As the mortar company was allotted five LCVPs for each platoon it was decided to put one mortar crew in each of four craft, splitting up the other two mortar squads among the four as additional ammunition handlers and replacements and to place platoon headquarters in the fifth craft. An officer or NCO was to be in charge of each boat group and was responsible for leading his group to the assembly area." [60]

At about 5:45 in the evening, the three weapons companies, A, B, and C, left at Mers-el-Khebir and moved to a bivouac area at Zeralda, while their rear echelon moved from Georges Clemenceau to Valmy. Co. A was placed in a nice wooded area near town where Sam Bundy said they had "daily forced marches and strenuous calisthenics ... went swimming in the sea, were issued passes to nearby towns, and had dry-run mortar problems."[61] Capt. Burford, Co. C, said that it was here that the earlier outstanding demonstration of the 4.2" mortar by Co. B and the salesmanship of Cunin paid off, as they were placed near the Rangers and attached to them for administration and tactics.[62]

A period of training for the three weapons companies at Zeralda commenced on June 14th and consisted of what Capt. Burford called night and day RSOP, or reconnaissance, selection, and occupation of position. This also involved speed marches, five miles in an hour, nicknamed the "Truscott Trot" after Gen. Lucien Truscott, who had initiated such training, and target practice, the objective being a practice maneuver of the Task Force to "attack" the beach at Zeralda-sul-Mar, held by British troops but without live ammo. The conditions were to represent the forthcoming invasion of Sicily at Gela, although only the officers had been briefed and they were held to secrecy with that information. Serving as umpires in the maneuver were British "leftenants" Lt. Vere, attached to Co. C, and Lt. Ferguson, attached to Co. B. During the practice, motor mechanic Emory G. Burgamy, Co. C, of Hancock County, Georgia, was "hit by a fragment from a 'bazooka' shell." Although not seriously injured, this first "casualty" of the 83rd was "lost for the invasion and subsequent work."[63] Lt. James Beasley, Co. D, reported, "Two days ago we had a generous serving of ice cream at our field kitchen. We have ice tea and lemonade nearly every day. Tomorrow we are to have fried chicken."[64]

Reviewing the battalion's situation on June 15th, James Helsel, Co. A, wrote, "This is a nice bivouac area, lots of shade, no flies or mosquitoes; but the training is rugged and the food is bad. Our loving Colonel sold us to the Rangers and we have been doing Ranger training; when we go on a hike now we run. Everything is done on the double."[65] At Staouli Capt. Pike added, "... my morale hit a new peak. In the morning we went on a 14 mile hike and we all dragged back in, tired, and bedraggled as heck. There awaiting us for diner [*dinner*] was fresh fried half chickens. They were delicious. We then had our own noon time siesta, in the heat of mid-day. Late in the afternoon we went for a nice cold swim. From there early to bed and a good nights sleep. What a life. I must say though that that is not a typical day. Very much to the contrary."[66] Lt. James Beasley was much in agreement with Pike as he wrote, "We have had chicken two days running now. We have a malted milk drink nearly every night for supper and for lunch lemonade or some other fruit juice. Of course for breakfast there is plenty of coffee. Most of the men say they are not doing badly, but some are trying to make heroes of themselves by trying to convince others that this company is terrible. We are better equipped, have better food, and more recreation than people ever have on regular camping trips ... This afternoon I was sleepy and slept two hours. It was disappointing to wake and find that the army had managed fairly well without me for the two hours ... The weather here has been cooler for the past few days. I doubt that the summers here are any worse than they are in Texas."[67]

This training period is probably the time mentioned by Jerome ("Jerry") Muschinske, who wrote, "While we were in a bivouac area near Zeralda several officers and enlisted men retired to an inland area to practice artillery techniques. If memory serves me correctly, among others they were Capt. [*William S.*] Hutchinson, Lt. [*Julian T.*] McKinnon, Lt. [*Harold A.*] Churchill, Sgt. [*Earl*] Shaddinger, myself and two 'C' company mortar crews. After the mortars and OP were set up the mortars were fired at a target for effect. Lt. McKinnon and Lt. Churchill were forward observers reporting the mortar shots to our command post. Sgt. Shaddinger and myself were plotting the reports on a graph and calculating the necessary corrective distance and direction to Capt. Hutchinson, who in turn gave the firing orders to the mortar crews. The forward observers communicated their observations by semaphore signals as we had no radios available. We were not told the reason for this exercise ..."[68]

The rear echelons of companies A, B, and C, and HQ Co., left Valmy for Zeralda on June 17th in a truck convoy

L-R: Sgt. Ralph Long, unidentified soldier, and William C. Ford in Africa. *Ford Collection*

with the rear echelon units of the 1st Infantry Division and, excepting Co. D, arrived at their destination at 6:00 on the evening of the 18th. A near mutiny took place in Co. A on the 20th, recalled James Helsel: "Still taking Ranger training. Still getting bad food. The fellows made quite a stink tonight after chow. We worked hard today and for supper got a slice of bread, tea, one Vienna sausage, and about two peach halves. So the boys began beating their mess kits hollering for something to eat. The Captain ran over to the kitchen and opened up a can of fruit & a can of hard candy, which a lot of fellows cut their hands on the can in the rush. Doing a lot of swimming, but it's a forced march to the beach everyday."[69] Co. D fared a bit better as Lt. Beasley wrote, "After the voyage over here [*on the Monticello*] the men's attitude towards me is almost embarrassing. I was on duty with the men much of the time when we were coming over and they think they were better taken care of than any of the other outfits. They seemed to prefer having Captain Pike or me with them rather than other officers, when depth charges were dropped or when we were in what was considered dangerous waters. Another advantage I have is that the camping commander has to handle discipline which keeps me from having to do things that make men unfriendly no matter how much they deserve to be punished. One man said a day or two ago that I could get more out of the company than anyone else. At least they do what I tell them without grumbling (in my presence) … One trouble is that they want me to try to get them out of trouble when they usually deserve more punishment than they get."[70]

In preparation for a practice amphibious landing, the 2nd Battalion, 16th Infantry, and attached units such as Co. D, 83rd Chemical Battalion, boarded the *U.S.S. Thurston* at Algiers harbor at 6:00 in the evening of the 21st. They would again be part of Transport Division 3, Task Group 81.3 and Task Force 81, commanded by Rear Admiral J. L. Hall. The *Thurston* and *Elizabeth C. Stanton* comprised Task Unit 81.3.3, led by Capt. R. A. Dierdoff, USN, which was to practice landings on beaches outside the harbor.[71] Michael Rebick, Co. D, would later write from Sicily, " … in Africa half of the time I didn't know whether I was in the Army or Navy for we sure did spend a lot of time out on the water practicing on how to jump out of the landing barges & climbing rope ladders in to one."[72]

A practice amphibious invasion with the Ranger Task force was initiated at Algiers on June 22nd consisting of companies A, B, and C, Command Group, Graves Registration Group (G.R.G.), and the Medical Detachment. All three weapons companies were to embark on LCIs (Landing Craft, Infantry). Co. A, supporting the 1st Battalion, 39th Engineers, boarded *LCI 188* [*James G. Helsel said they board LCI 17*]; Co. B, supporting the 1st Ranger Battalion embarked onto *LCI 39*; and Co. C, supporting the 4th Ranger Battalion, loaded onto *LCI 189*, which was commanded by a Lt. (jg.) Edward S. Dulcan. According to the battalion journal, the "Command group was divided, some being on the LCIs, the *U.S.S. Joseph T. Dickman*, commanded by Lt. Comdr.. C. W. Harwood, and destroyers. The Graves Registration Group, Medical Detachment, the 1st Ranger Battalion, and the 39th Engineers were on the *U.S.S. Dickman*, and the 4th Ranger Battalion on two destroyers."[73]

The task force had to practice unloading the men and equipment, both in daylight and dark, until they had it down to three minutes and 30 seconds. All three weapons companies were closely docked which meant the debarkation process had to be closely coordinated. During this practice Pvt. Edward J. Sutlic, Co. C, accidentally stumbled and dropped his BAR (Browning Automatic Rifle) into the water. An unsuccessful attempt was made to recover it with a grapnel hook.[74]

The mock invasion did not go as planned. Only the Rangers and a few other elements actually landed as the Navy was wary of the beach at Zeralda-sul-Mar and afraid of possibly beaching or damaging their LCIs. As a result, all other units basically went along for the ride and witnessed the "invasion" process. By the 24th, all weapons companies had returned to the bivouac area at Zeralda.[75]

Co. D's mission began when they left Algiers harbor at 1:00 in the afternoon of June 23rd. Debarking at 1:30

on the afternoon of the 24th, the company made a landing on a beach ten miles distant, from which point the men advanced to their position, hiked 15 miles, and returned by truck to their bivouac at 4:00 in the afternoon. Capt. Pike recalled that "the First Division D-day troops and equipment, and men and equipment (motor vehicles excluded) of Company D were loaded aboard ships in Algiers preparatory to the final practice landing. This landing was to take place west of Zeralda, Algeria, in territory almost identical with that around Gela, Sicily. The first problem encountered aboard ship was the housing and messing of troops and stowing of equipment. After this problem was settled the infantry battalion commander called a unit commanders meeting at which the battalion field order was issued." Pike concluded, "The mission of the 16th Infantry Regiment was to assault and clear 'GREEN BEACH', proceed inland and capture the [imaginary] town of 'PODUNK'. Company D to furnish fire support."[76]

The other three weapons companies spent June 25th resting and preparing in their bivouac to set out on the actual invasion the following morning, while Co. D would remain at Staouli from the 25th to the 30th performing their usual duties. During the day a group of 83rd officers was presented to " ... Gen. Alexander, British Army Chief in Africa, and two other British generals, an American general, and an American admiral." Capt. Pike, Co. D, said there were "More brass hats that you can shake a stick at." Afterwards the group adjourned to the officers' mess overlooking the Mediterranean and had a rousing party. Later in the evening Cunin gave a pep talk to the battalion in which he expressed his hopes and expectations. He wished them "good luck" but not before he told them they were not sufficiently trained, a comment which certainly could not have boosted their morale or come at a worse time.[77]

Under the command of William S. Hutchinson, the weapons companies loaded up on trucks on the morning of June 26th and moved to Algiers. By the 27th Co. A had boarded *LCI 17*; Co. B, accompanied by the Medical Detachment, was on *LCI 188*; and Co. C headed up *LCI 189*. Actually, Co. C had boarded *LCI 189* at about 9:10 on the morning of the 26th, confirmed by the craft's war diary, which read for that date, "Company 'C' of the 83rd Chemical Warfare Battalion, 187 men and four officers, Captain Rupert O. Burford, Company Commander, came aboard." The various landing craft pulled out into the harbor and remained there overnight.[78]

Co. D remained in bivouac at Staouli where Capt. Pike recalled he " ... got up for breakfast which consisted of hot coffee, sausages, and delicious raisin pancakes. It was a swell way to start the day off; full rest and a full stomach. About 9:00 church bells began to peal in the distance and aroused me to the realization that it was time for meditation. So off to look for a morning service I went. I looked all over for a Protestant Chaplain but couldn't find one so I compromised by attending a Catholic mass. It was a new experience for me and I can't say I was particularly favorably impressed. The whole thing consisted principally of the chaplain spieling off a lot of Latin which nobody could understand and bouncing up and down off your knees. What I like in a church service is to hear a man with a good logical mind and a good speaking voice get up and develop from the Scriptures a lesson of benefit to those listening, one which is applicable to every day life. To accompany this I like to hear a good chorus singing good hymns."[79]

The 83rd, minus Co. D, set sail for Tunis on the 27th for further training, passing such points as Bizerte and Cape Bon, before arriving at the small port of Tunis called La Goullette on the 29th. At one point during the voyage the craft test fired their guns and then permitted the soldiers to fire their machine guns at cans thrown overboard. *LCI 189* tied up alongside *LCI 234* at the wall just east of the entrance to Tunis harbor shortly before 3:00 in the afternoon and less than an hour later Co. C debarked the ship, leaving ten men to guard the mortars and provisions. Tunis was controlled by the British, who escorted the battalion by truck to their bivouac in the Virginia Area.[80]

The week-long stay at Tunis proved most unpleasant as there was hardly any shade to escape the blistering heat of the sun, and food and water proved insufficient. Sam Bundy, Co. A, remarked the "chow was terrible" while Capt. Burford, Co. C, said, "We were fed by a mess from the 34th Division and the meals were of very poor quality and totally inadequate." The only available drinking water was from an English lister bag which proved rusty and hot. No water was provided for washing or bathing although some men utilized the area wells against the wishes of the Arab farmers. Co. C reported one bathing expedition was permitted to Carthage but only 60 men could be accommodated. While the three weapons companies suffered at Tunis, the Headquarters Command Group, liaison and forward observer groups for the three weapons companies and the Graves Registration Group boarded the *U.S.S. Dickman* in Algiers harbor on the 30th.[81]

During this period Capt. "Bud" Pike assessed the command structure of the 83rd, writing, "There haven't been

Rare and damaged photo of a bivouac of the 83rd Chemical Battalion near Oran, North Africa, probably Goat Hill.
Ed Trey

very many changes within the Battalion lately. I guess I already told you about [*Christopher*] Cornett and Mindy [*Gordon Mindrum*] getting their promotions. Phooie to one and congratulations to the other. John Roberts is in the hospital for an operation for hemorrhoids. Stud Carpenter [*Carl Carpenter*] is still champing at the bit. We took him into town a couple weeks ago and went to a notorious hotel. 'For Officers Only'. Here we introduced him to a beautiful bawd. Stud almost went through the floor. He was tongue-tied. He just stood and stared. It was certainly funny. [*Ed*] Trey and Mindy and Sammy [*Miller*] and [*Alfred*] Forrester and [*Bernard*] Stone and Stud and I all went in together. A good clean time was had by all and we all abstained. We were all carrying a good load by the time we left for home though. That's the only time I have been high S.A. [*since Africa*]. There have been a few changes of officers within the BN but they have been of minor importance."[82]

A personal view of the African experience was also offered by Capt. Pike, as he wrote home, "Since we arrived in Africa we have changed locations a few times so that I have been able to take in new sights and have new experiences. I have visited several of the large towns of North Africa and seen many places of interest and some fame. Damn it, if the censor wasn't looking I would tell you all about them. I will say, however, that what I have seen of Africa thus far has been a pleasant surprise. As yet I still have to see my first sand dune, my first mirage, my first oasis, and I'm still looking for the Queen of Sheba and Little Egypt. What am I saying? The country along the Mediterranean is very fertile, the principal crop being grapes. From the grapes comes the wine, the wine comes to us, and there you are – a vicious circle. My college French is still taking a beating but it is fun palavering with the natives … I thought that the weather was going to remain mild around here but I am fast learning otherwise. It is getting hotter than hell around here… Not only that but the natives tell us that summer starts next month. I can hardly wait. 120° in the shade, boy oh boy."[83]

Governor Harold E. Hughes
State Historical Society of Iowa, Des Moines

HAROLD EVERETT HUGHES

Harold Everett Hughes, was born February 10, 1922, near Ida Grove, Ida County, Iowa. He attended public schools and the University of Iowa, where he developed a drinking habit that would plague him for years. He enlisted in the army September 21, 1942, at Camp Dodge, Herrold, Iowa and eventually became a member of the 83rd Chemical Mortar Battalion. Hughes served in North Africa, Sicily, and Italy and, as his alcoholism worsened, returned home to become a dairy and cattle truck driver. Unfortunately, by 1946 his drinking had become such a problem that his wife made an unsuccessful attempt to have him committed to an institution.

In 1952 Hughes was driven to the brink of suicide from his drinking, but after experiencing a spiritual revelation, declared himself an alcoholic and joined Alcoholics Anonymous. He organized independent truckers, started the Iowa Better Trucking Bureau, and served on the State Commerce Commission 1958–1962. A Democrat in the political arena, he was elected Governor of Iowa in 1962 , and re-elected twice as a reform-minded populist. Hughes also was on the executive committee, National Governors Conference 1966–1967; chairman Democratic Governors Conference 1966–1968; elected as a Democrat to the U.S. Senate in 1968 and served from 1969–1974. He made a brief attempt at the Democratic presidential nomination in 1971 but quickly withdrew.

Harold Hughes stunned his supporters in 1971 when he announced that upon completion of his term as Senator he would retire from politics to become a lay preacher and devote his time to developing programs for alcohol and substance abuse. This was the most important subject to him while in politics, having helped pass some of the most important legislation in this field. In 1979, his autobiography *The Man From Ida Grove: A Senator's Personal Story* was published by a Christian book company and told in detail of his struggle with alcoholism and his religious ministry. Also included in the book was a detailed chapter of his World War II experiences with the 83rd Chemical Mortar Battalion.

Upon leaving Washington, Hughes founded a religious retreat in Maryland and returned to Iowa in 1981, where he continued his involvement in substance abuse programs, and was founder and CEO of The Society of Americans for Recovery (SOAR). When his health began to fail from emphysema, pneumonia, and heart ailments, he moved to Glendale, Arizona, where he died October 23, 1996.

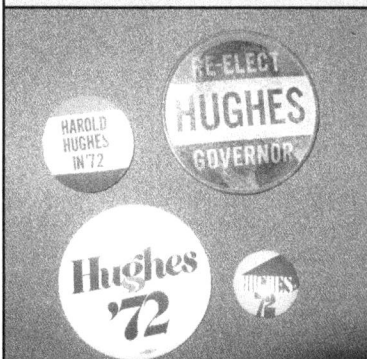

Hughes campaign buttons.
Author's Collection

Harold Hughes in military uniform, on left.

The bookcover of Senator Hughes' 1979 book, *The Man From Ida Grove*.
Chosen Books & Eva Hughes

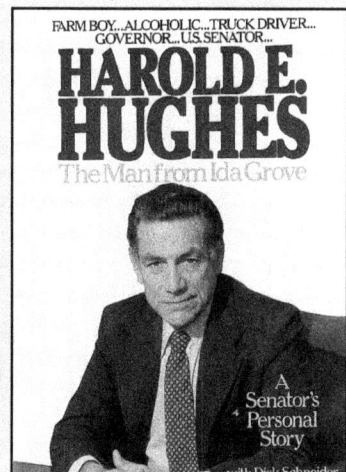

FARM BOY...ALCOHOLIC...TRUCK DRIVER... GOVERNOR...U.S. SENATOR...

HAROLD E. HUGHES
The Man from Ida Grove

A Senator's Personal Story

with Dick Schneider

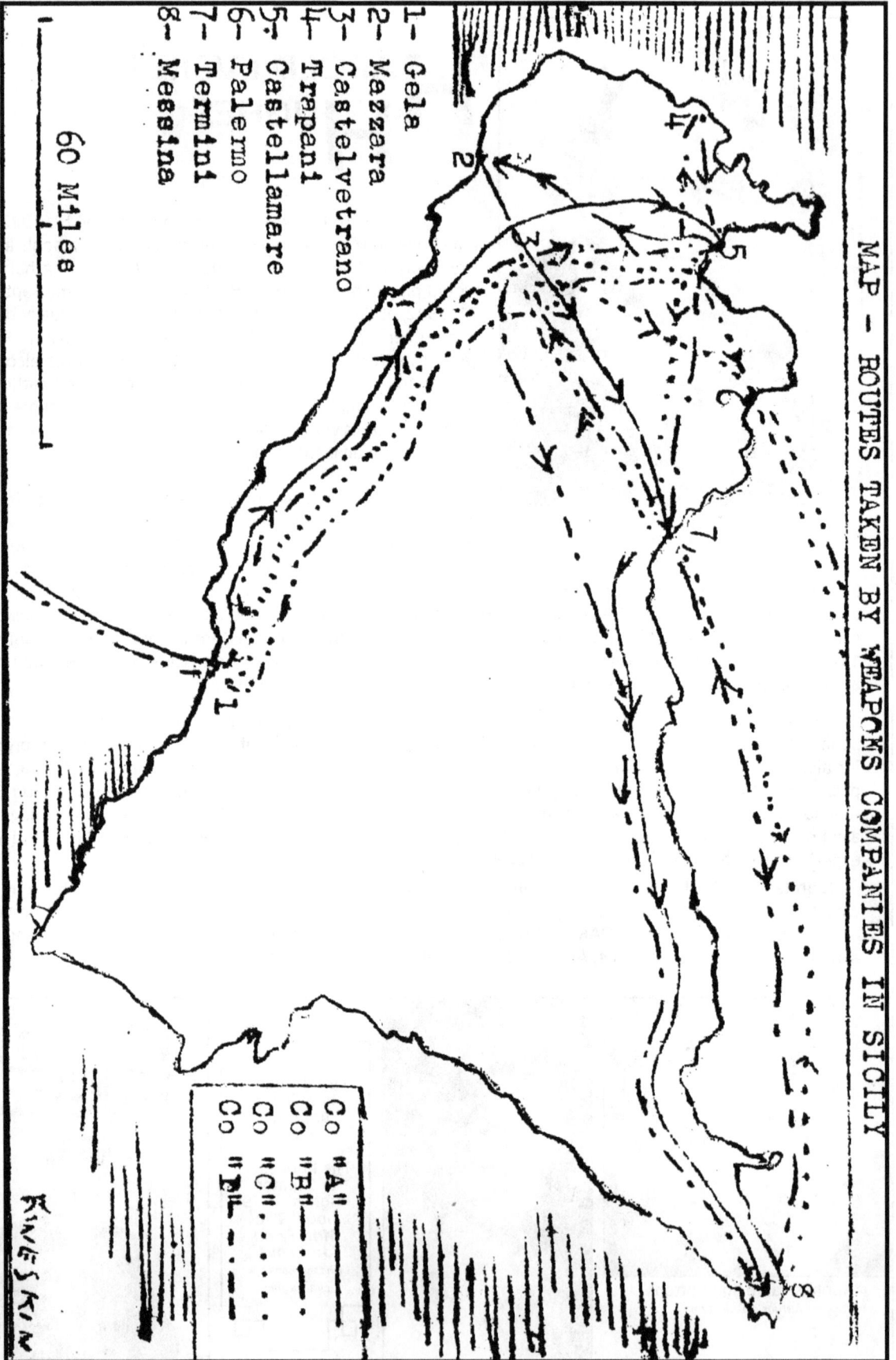

MAP — ROUTES TAKEN BY WEAPONS COMPANIES IN SICILY

1— Gela
2— Mazzara
3— Castelvetrano
4— Trapani
5— Castellamare
6— Palermo
7— Termini
8— Messina

60 Miles

Co "A" — · —
Co "B" — · · —
Co "C" · · · · · ·
Co "D" — · · —

KWESKIN

Sicilian Campaign map showing company routes of the 83rd CMB. Drawn by Sam Kweskin, HQ Co., 83rd CMB, for *Rounds Away*
Sam Kweskin

Chapter Six

OPERATION HUSKY
AND
THE SICILIAN CAMPAIGN
JULY-AUGUST
1943

U.S.S. Joseph T. Dickman
National Archives

In Operation Husky, sometimes referred to as Operation Bigot-Husky, the Allied invasion of Sicily, the mission of the Ranger Force commanded by Col. William O. Darby and attached to the 1st U.S. Infantry, which included the 83rd Chemical Battalion, was to "... land at H hour on July 10th on the beach directly in front of the town of Gela, reduce the defenses thereof together with the coastal batteries that protected the approaches from the sea and hold the town at all costs as a base for future operations." This would be no easy task as Gela was one of the most highly defensible towns in Sicily protected by pill boxes, barbed wire, coastal batteries, entrenchments, land mines, anti-personnel mines, booby and tank traps. Fortunately, intelligence was able to provide in advance a highly accurate map of the defenses.[1]

The invading Ranger Force itself would consist of the 1st and 4th Ranger Battalions; the 1st Battalion, 39th Engineer Combat Regiment; 1st Battalion, 531st Engineer Shore Regiment; and the 83rd Chemical Battalion less Co. D. Lt. Col. Cunin of the 83rd would act as executive officer of the Ranger Force "as long as the force remained intact."

During the early phases of the operation, Co. D of the 83rd was attached to the 16th Infantry, 1st Infantry Division, Lt. Col. Charles J. Denholm commanding.[2] The 1st Platoon, Co. D, of the 83rd and assorted units would embark on the *U.S.S. Elizabeth C. Stanton*, a ship officered by Capt. R. A. Dierdorff, USN, and which carried 471 officers and 7,500 men of the 16th Infantry Regimental Combat Team (RCT). Co. D's 2nd Platoon would board the *U.S.S. Thurston* at

Col. William O. Darby *National Archives*

Algiers and remain in the harbor overnight. The war diary of the ship reported the 2nd Platoon, 16th Infantry, Lt. Col. Joseph B. Crawford commanding, and attached units were aboard, comprising 70 officers and 1,209 troops. The following day the force would depart the harbor and sail along the north coast of Africa to join the convoy.[3]

On July 4th, 1943, the 83rd was alerted for movement and informed to be ready at dawn for the "main push." In the meantime, Capt. John H. Leppert, USN, commanding Task Force 81.4, arrived at Sousse, a small town on the opposite side of Cape Bon, where he found himself in command of 52 ships for the amphibious sector of the Sicilian invasion. Among the vessels at Leppert's command were those carrying the 83rd Chemical Battalion.

Co. A of the 83rd got to enjoy a rather entertaining July 4th celebration as "They had a 100 gal. barrel of wine. One boy shot all his tracers up. He told the Captain he saved the Company; that we were being attacked by the German planes. He sure was drunk."[4]

At Algiers harbor Co. D got a treat while on the *Thurston* as the Senior Officer Present Afloat (Royal Navy) presented a 21-gun national salute in honor of Independence Day. Capt. Pike said they had a big dinner, consisting of baked ham and chicken, or as he put it "fattening us up for the big kill." Pvt. Richard A. Bridge, Co. D, would later write, "This 4th we were loading up trucks & supplies to board ship to make the invasion of Sicily …last 4th I was helping eat Mom out of all her potato salad, this one helping make history, next 4th I suppose I'll be getting married." Unfortunately, Bridge would not survive to see the next 4th of July.[5]

The three weapons companies of the 83rd, A, B, and C, were escorted by truck to La Goullette at Tunis on the 5th and boarded for Sicily on the LCIs, with Co. A on *LCI 17*, Co. B and the Medical Detachment on *LCI 188*, and following a pep talk in the assembly area by Capt. Burford, Co. C embarked on *LCI 189*. The war diary of *LCI 189* confirmed Co. C's departure, stating that at 8:25 in the morning, "83rd Chemical Warfare Battalion returned aboard with two men less than formerly." Numerous men of Co. C took a quick swim in the harbor and then set sail late at night for Sousse. While rounding Cape Bon on July 6th, "… the wind increased considerably, probably force 6, and the chop was very heavy … it affected the course being made."[6]

Companies A, B, and C of the 83rd arrived at Sousse late on the night of the 7th and stopped for about two hours to take on fuel and water. All men were restricted to the various sea craft although Sam Bundy said Co. A had more dry-run loading and unloading of mortars. Also during the stop at Sousse James Helsel, Co. A, said, "The sailors rigged up a shower in a sunken boat next to us; it was cold but it was refreshing. The first shower I had overseas … toward evening we pulled out to sea a little and done swimming around the boat, which we done before just out side of Algiers." After the brief layover the convoy would set sail from Sousse on the 8th for the rendezvous, or assembly point, near Malta in fair weather, although the sea had begun to get rough. Co. D would continue their journey as well, holding various emergency boat drills.[7] Back in North Africa life continued as usual as Lt. Leonard A. ("Spike") Merrill, Jr., battalion PX officer, wrote that he "… traveled about 100 miles… for cigarettes and candy (for the PX) and passed several camels …"[8]

As a component of Task Force 81.4, the 83rd Chemical Battalion would remain on their respective LCIs. About 200 men of Co. A, under William S. Hutchinson, would stick with *LCI 17*, the flagship of the force commanded by H. G. Stender. Also aboard was Leppert and his staff and "12 two-wheeled carts bearing 4.2" mortars, 12 additional carts filled with mortar rounds, and 36 additional boxes of mortar ammunition." The Final Troop & Ship Assignment and Landing Chart (Force 343 - Beach 68B) lists give a discrepancy in Co. A's numbers -- one list states the company had three officers and 145 men while the other says six officers and 196 enlisted men. In any event, the company consisted of between 148 and 206 men in the mission. *LCI 188* held Co. B, comprised of four officers and between 190 and 199 enlisted men, totaling approximately some 194 to 203 men. Also believed to be on board was the Medical

Detachment. Additionally the two landing lists mention a detachment of three officers and five enlisted men of the 83rd on the *Princess Charlotte*. *LCI 189*, commanded by Lt. (jg) Edward S. Dulcan, contained four officers and 190 enlisted men of Co. C of the 83rd. In addition, the *U.S.S. Joseph T. Dickman* carried six officers and 19 enlisted men of the 83rd and *LST 381* held ten enlisted men (drivers) and at least eight jeeps of the battalion. Altogether companies A, B, and C, less Co. D, probably had a total of about 23 officers and 619 enlisted men in the invasion of Sicily, totaling 642 soldiers.[9]

Capt. Leppert advised his officers that during the invasion, "if any ship became high and dry it was still a fighting unit as long as it had guns and was above the surface of the water." The three LCIs containing the 83rd were to land at H + 60 followed by the detachment at H + two hours. The original landing instructions said that the three companies would be beached by the LCIs, discharged, and the LCI crews would throw off the 4.2″ ammo and the advance party of the 531st Engineers Battalion would "… endeavor to recover the ammo immediately, because … water will do the ammo no good, and … ammo boxes in the water are obstacles to other landing craft."[10]

Just prior to midnight of July 8th, Task Force 81.4 set sail from Sousse. Simultaneously, the ships with Co. D sighted Tunis and passed around the Cape Bon peninsula. Capt. Pike recalled, "… the C.O. of troops called all officers together and announced that we were on our way to Sicily. We didn't know whether to be relieved or further disheartened, having read so much about the impregnable island fortress of Sicily, but at least we now knew what we had been preparing for so long."[11]

At dawn of the 9th, the day before D-Day, the seas became extremely rough, accompanied by a strong wind from the north, forcing Capt. Leppert to increase to maximum speed in order to catch up with his transport ship, the *U.S.S. Dickman*. Once contact was made with his transport, Leppert reverted to command of the three LCIs holding the 83rd and continued to push them to their limits in order to keep up with the transport. This combination of the ravaged waters and break-neck speed created an extreme amount of seasickness among the men. As Malta was approached the convoy grew to an immense size. According to Capt. Burford, Co. C, "… looking out over the water one can see ships of all descriptions and sizes as far as the eye will reach. It is the grandest thing I have ever seen."[12]

But the sea became even worse creating an enormous amount of seasickness and fear. Burford wrote that "Our carts (mortar and ammunition) which are lashed to the deck, are taking a terrific beating as the ship tosses about. Several times I have feared we are going to lose them over the side… the LCI is not as stable in the water as a heavier or broader vessel … the ship is taking a terrific pounding, and it's a wonder her plates can take it." Nearly all the enlisted men and officers of Co. C were seasick, including lieutenants Harold A. Churchill, Donald R. Gabriel, and Julian T. McKinnon. Andrew C. Leech, Co. B, from Itawamba County, Mississippi, aboard *LCI 188*, wrote, "The old Tyrrhenian Sea was tossing and pitching us around as if she was mad. We all got seasick -- even the sailors. The sea was so rough we had to lie in our bunks and hold on to keep from being tossed out. This was a small LCI … we were on, and boy was I sick!"[13]

Sam Bundy, Co. A, riding on *LCI 17*, said the sea was "… a little rough, rougher than the sailors had ever seen it before. The poor little LCI was tossed and thrown about the water so that a person could hardly walk across the deck without holding onto something, for fear he would be hurled overboard. A constant spray washed the deck and the sides were lined with sick men – throwing up – in the sea. The Navy prepared a nice chow for us today but very few men ate anything. This is one day which most will never forget! Water was running below making much of our equipment wet. Men were vomiting all over the place; our helmets came in handy in many cases. What a mess this was." Cpl. Lawrence H. ("Larry") Powell, Co. A, from Pennsylvania, said he heard it was the roughest the sea had been in the past forty years. Ironically, a few of the men actually enjoyed the open sea; among them James Helsel, Co. A, who wrote, "The water is very rough. It is tossing the ship around like a baby. I am beginning to wish I had joined the Navy, for I sure do enjoy the sea." Despite such horrid conditions for most of the men, as well as the anticipation of going into combat for the first time, the men attempted to get their equipment in shape and get a little sleep. Ironically, Lt. Dulcan, commander of *LCI 189*, later expressed his opinion that more men actually got seasick during the invasion rehearsals.[14]

Co. D had to deal with the rough sea and resulting seasickness as well, passing Malta at about 6:00 in the evening of July 9th, followed by the island of Pantellaria [*the original destination according to Karl Garrett, but the British had already bombed the island with no resistance and Sicily had become the objective*]. The war diary of the *U.S.S. Thurston* reported that after passing Malta the ship encountered "rough seas and winds of gale strength." Capt. Pike said there was a "Hell of a windstorm, gale proportions." One LVCP was damaged by the high seas and had to be jettisoned. Pfc. Raymond W. Brinkman of Pennsylvania, on the *Thurston* with the 2nd Platoon of Co. D, came down with a case of malaria and was hospitalized. Foremost on everyone's mind, though, was their impending fate and the outcome of this great adventure.[15]

LCI 17 arrived at what was designated the DIME area for the invasion at about 9:30 in the evening. According to the commander of *LCI 189*, when it reached its "… designated station to seaward of the *Dickman*, we rigged the ramps, unlashed the mortars, and went to beaching stations."[16]

Gela, July 10

At about 2:45 a.m. in the early morning darkness of July 10th, with rough seas and hostile fire from shore, the Rangers and the mortar company observers landed at Gela, Sicily. Co. B's liaison officer and forward observers included 1st lieutenants Edward L. Trey and John P. McEvoy. Years later McEvoy recalled that, "As a Forward mission Observer with the Rangers assigned to attack and silence a coast artillery fort north of Gela, I received instructions on the timing and attack route to be followed; what I had to do to direct mortar fire on the fort in support of the attack; and when and where the mortars would probably be emplaced …" McEvoy debarked from the *Dickman* into an LCVP and made it to the beach with little trouble. Capt. James Lyle, of the Rangers, the assault leader, "was crouched by the coxswain …" McEvoy added, "The ramp fell down and we piled out across the beach … and we started up a steep path leading up to town… Then a shock. Something was choking me hard … Then the realization that the CO_2 cylinders in my life belt had released and the buckled life belt sharply expanded and punched in my stomach. A quick jab with my well prepared knife released the pressure and the belt was discarded."[17]

Lt. Trey, aboard the *Monrovia*, Gen. George S. Patton's command ship, climbed into an LCVP and went in as Co. B's forward observer in the first wave along with the 1st Ranger Battalion. The reconnaissance party of Trey, Pvt. Steven Krajcir, and Joe T. Owings landed at 3:30 a.m. under considerable enemy fire as the Rangers advanced into the city and on toward their objective. According to Trey he went in with captains Frederick J. Saams and Charles M. Shunstrom of the 1st Rangers as recon for coming mortars. "When the door of the landing craft opened I stepped out into water over my head and nearly drowned." In another account Trey added that, after landing, "We found an OP [*Observation Post*] on the second floor of a building with a translucent bathroom window facing the plains of Gela. I opened the window only wide enough to peer through it with binoculars. Because three of the cruiser *Savannah's* slow spotter planes had been shot down by Messerschmidts, fire commands for our mortars and Naval fire were transmitted for a time from our OP through a telephone line to Task Force Headquarters downtown, and then by radio."[18]

Co. B's forward observer party of Pfc. Nolan C. McCraine, Pvt. Jacob L. ("Jake") Portner, and Charles Cohen came in with the initial troops in the second wave and had little trouble crossing the beach. McCraine, a sales person in a dry goods store from Wilkinson County, Mississippi, recalled, "The Rangers had been told to not fire a shot until daylight in order to retain the element of surprise. As a result the Rangers used various edged weapons on the unsuspecting enemy, and when we later went through the streets of Gela we witnessed numerous bodies of enemy soldiers lying about with throats cut and guts ripped out."[19]

1st Lt. Thomas M. Bolton and 1st Lt. William S. Doughten, Jr., serving as Co. A's forward observer and liaison officer respectively, along with the 39th Engineers, also hit the beach on the second wave. Doughten was killed instantly as he stepped off the LCVP onto a land mine on the beach, but Capt. Burford of Co. C later said he heard Doughten had been hit in the face by a 20mm shell. Although there is no way to be absolutely certain, Doughten was probably the first man in the 83rd killed in combat. Later, at 7:00 a.m., the *Dickman* reported his body was brought aboard. In the meantime, Lt. Bolton managed to establish Co. A's OP on the second floor of a building on the south side of town.[20]

1st Lt. Ralph T. Rankin and 2nd Lt. Alvin G. Metcalfe, both of Co. C, also landed with the second wave [*although Capt. Burford claimed they came in with the first*] near a prominent jutting pier, as liaison officer and forward observer with the 4th Rangers. Accompanying this group was Capt. David W. Meyerson, Battalion S-3, as well as Sgt. Earl Shaddinger and T/5 Jerome A. ("Jerry") Muschinske, who said their group debarked from the *St. Charles*.[21]

According to Muschinske, " …when the time came for our departure we carried our rifles, grenades, extra ammunition and gas masks and we were loaded into a small landing craft with 30 Rangers. The craft was manned by a British crew who were very experienced in this type of operation. We encountered spasmodic shelling and machine gun fire on the way to our landing site, which became heavier as we neared the shore. Capt. Saams (the one of the long mustachioed fame) and Capt. [*Max*] Schneider were in the front of our craft and were the first to disembark. The British coxswain piloted our craft along the right side of the pier until we hit a sandbar. The front of the craft opened up and we plowed through waist high water toward the beach." Muschinske added that he and Shaddinger were ordered to "… fight as Rangers up to the church in town and to move out on our own to gain access to the steeple to be used as our OP."[22]

Upon landing, Muschinske continued, "We were met with machine gun fire from the right flank and made our way across the sand through a minefield in which the sappers were still digging up mines. At the end of the minefield we were sheltered by a wall where we regrouped and began our pathway through the town. We were stopped several times on our way to the church by sniper fire, machine gun fire and shell bursts. Luckily very few men were lost. It took longer to get to the church than was expected. When we arrived at the church square we were pinned down by sniper fire from the church and a two story building down the street leading to the square. After one of the Rangers was shot trying to run across the open square the sniper in the church tried to run out the front door of the church to a house across the street. Capt. Saams took care of him. After all the snipers were eliminated, Shaddinger and I entered the church and climbed the stairs to the steeple. We were soon joined by two artillery officers who were connected by radio to the *Savannah* in the harbor and directing their fire."[23]

Lt. Col. Cunin and his party came in on the third wave with a party from the 39th Engineers, while Chaplain Lyle L. Burdick and eight enlisted men of the Graves Registration Party landed later in the morning. According to the Co. C unit journal, lieutenants Ralph Rankin and Julian T. McKinnon set up an OP in the belfry of the cathedral in the center of town to conduct fire missions while Lt. Alvin Metcalfe and Lt. Col. Cunin operated from another OP.[24]

The Landing

As the Rangers and the various observers and liaison officers set about their specific assignments, the mortar companies of the 83rd approached the beach scheduled to land with the fifth wave at 3:45 a.m. An unanticipated false beach would present numerous problems for the assorted landing craft, with Co. C perhaps having the most success.

Co. A, including Maj. William S. Hutchinson, Jr., had been loaded onto *LCI 17*, flagship of the flotilla and attached to the 1st Battalion, 39th Engineers. They were to set up on the beach and provide protection for the Engineers, whose job was to secure the western edge of Gela. Co. A was also to provide fire on the coastal batteries at the western end of Gela if needed. The forward observer and reconnaissance parties had already landed at H plus 5 and now the remainder of the company was to land at H plus 45 but they received word from an Engineer boat that the initial landing party had not yet landed. In response they turned their craft around and waited. After about a half hour wait, *LCI 17* headed for shore but when the craft came within 800 yards of the beach enemy searchlights picked out the craft. The LCI crew opened with 20mm and knocked out one light and then the enemy opened fire. Lawrence H. Powell, Co. A, recalled this incident, writing, "I remember as I came up the ladder to the deck I saw a German search light shining on *LCI 17* and the search light went up the mast and showed the American flag waving. A sailor operating the machine gun on *LCI 17* shot the search light out."[25]

The LCI commander made an unsuccessful attempt to put the craft on shore in the designated area. After reversing the craft, another attempt was made 200 yards to the right and the boat was grounded on the false beach. An effort to extricate the boat caused it to turn broadside to the beach, making it an excellent target as enemy machine gun fire raked the deck. The men, yet unaware of the false beach, lowered the ramps, the port broke, and the first two squads of the 2nd Platoon, led by Lt. Andre N. Laus, stepped off into nearly ten-foot deep water, losing four mortars and ammo carts. Reno L. Toniolo, from Greensburg, Pennsylvania, said the bow of the craft was much higher than normal due to hitting the sandbar, and "We were to take the mortars on their hand-pulled carts down the ramp. [*Pfc. William M.*] Hawkins, [*from Delaware County, Pennsylvania*] had the cart's tongue in front. Hawkins weighed about 130 pounds and I about 150 pounds, both trying to keep it from running over us. When we got almost to the water the tongue broke off … and we found the water to be over our heads! I tried to hold my rifle over my head, when a

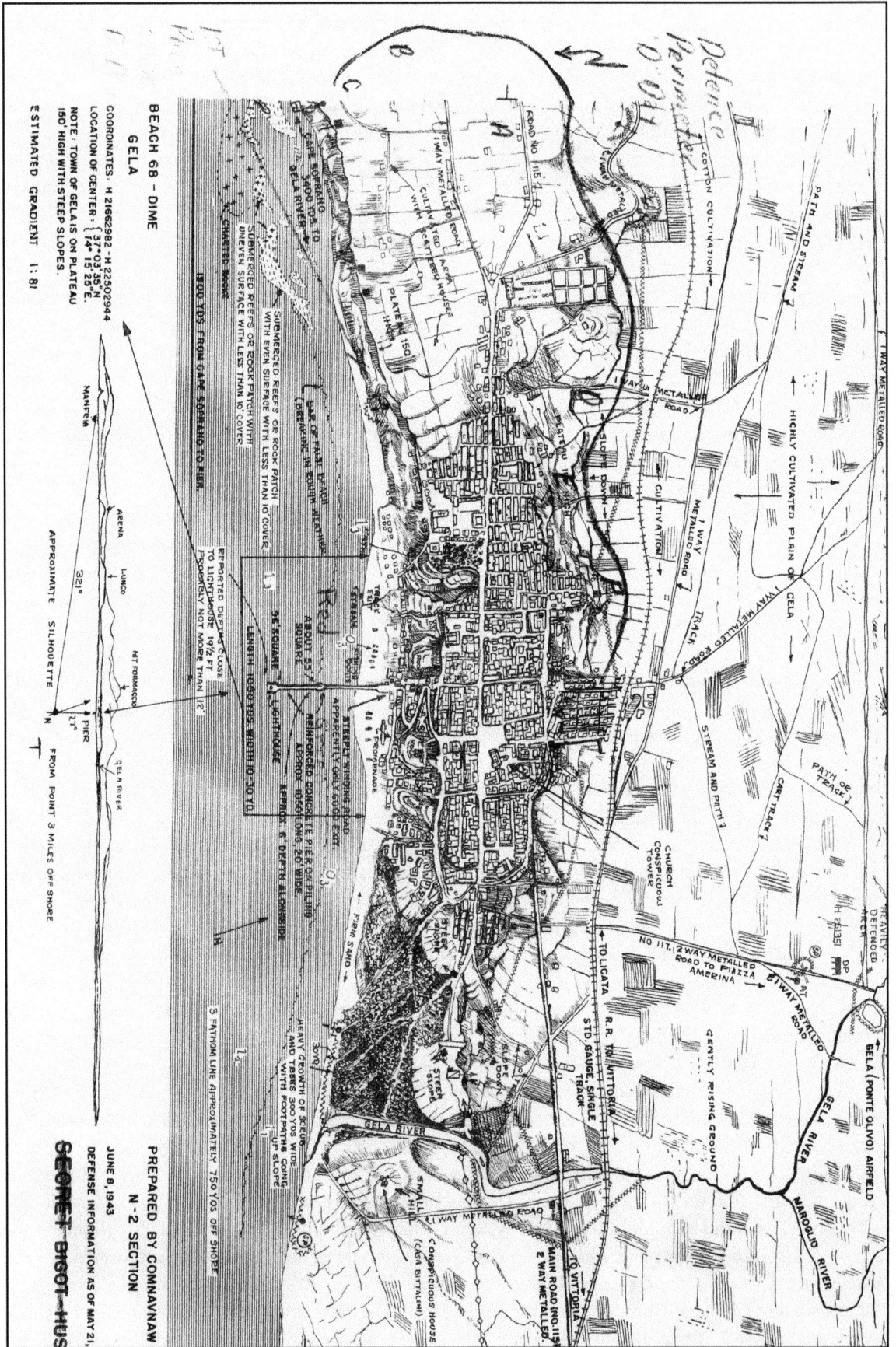

Actual map used by the Rangers for the July 10, 1943, invasion of Gela, Sicily. Note the writing on the left side which displays the defensive perimeter.
National Archives

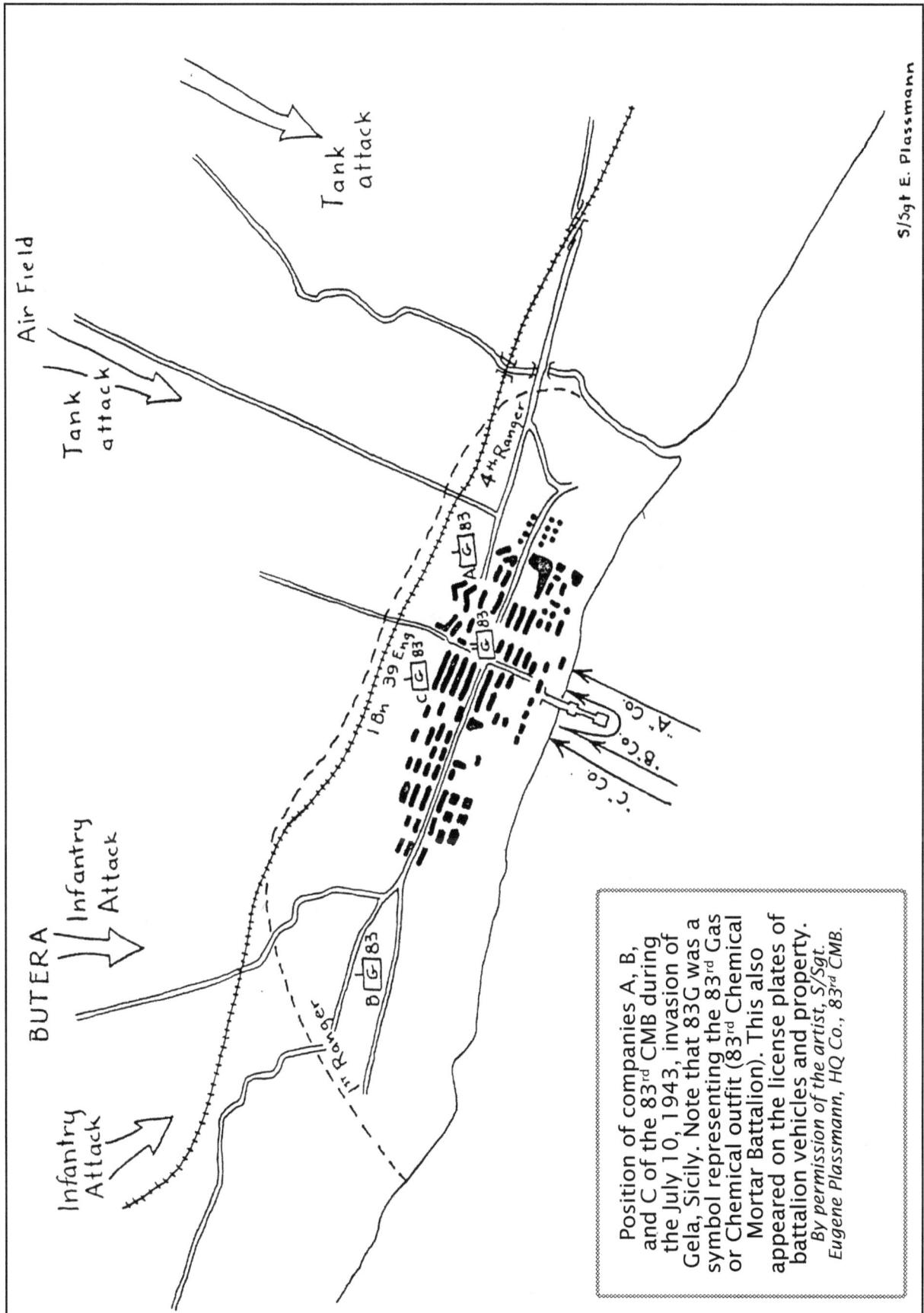

S/Sgt E. Plassmann

BUTERA

Air Field

Infantry Attack

Infantry Attack

Tank attack

Tank attack

1st Ranger

4th Ranger

1 Bn 39 Eng

A [G] 83

[G] 83

C [G] 83

B [G] 83

"C" Co.

"B" Co.

"A" Co.

Position of companies A, B, and C of the 83rd CMB during the July 10, 1943, invasion of Gela, Sicily. Note that 83G was a symbol representing the 83rd Gas or Chemical outfit (83rd Chemical Mortar Battalion). This also appeared on the license plates of battalion vehicles and property. *By permission of the artist, S/Sgt. Eugene Plassmann, HQ Co., 83rd CMB.*

great big breaker took me, and I lost my rifle. How I got to the beach is beyond me."

On board the men could hear the cries of the first group to debark. Laus and Sgt. John S. Bonarek swam to shore to assess the situation. Leaving Bonarek on the beach to assist men ashore, Laus swam back to the craft to relay the situation. James G. Helsel, Co. A, said Laus told them the "… cries for help were from the men who couldn't swim. He said he would return to help the men who were already in the water and told us to leave the boat and swim ashore. The Captain of the ship said we could rock the boat loose. By this time machine gun bullets were hitting the boat and water splashing on us from the shells that were landing near the craft." Laus was later awarded the Silver Star, the citation reading "…when the landing craft holding his company was grounded in deep water and heavy surf and was being subjected to intense enemy machine gun and coast-artillery fire, Lt. Laus swam ashore to determine the depth of water and beach conditions. He returned to his craft and, while guiding his men ashore, saved a drowning soldier's life." Sgt. Bonarek also was awarded the Silver Star in the same action and "… swam ashore with the mission of taking charge of his men as they arrived. While under fire, he quieted and reorganized his men and directed them to points of cover. During this time, he gave no thought to his personal safety."[26]

Capt. Robert E. Edwards ordered the men to leave the equipment and go overboard with life preservers to lighten the craft, to form on the beach, and to return when the LCI could make a better landing. This was accomplished with enemy artillery falling within 20 yards of the craft. According to Edward W. Krebs, Co. A, from Randallstown, Maryland, "Captain Edwards waved his pistol and shouted, 'Everybody off'! With water up to our waist, it didn't seem so bad. Wrong! We landed on a sandbar and a few beachward steps later, I was in water up to my neck." Unable to swim, Lawrence H. Powell, Co. A, later recalled that "Captain Edwards had ordered all the men to get off of the ship. Some went down the ramp. I jumped overboard with my full field pack, rifle, and helmet which was strapped to my chin … I went down twice and came back up hitting my helmet. Here is where Charles Carrullo … saved my life and I will never forget him."[27]

Karl F. Garrett, from Richmond, Virginia, added, "We assumed we were in shallow water but it was over our heads. Our guns were mounted on a two wheel cart with chains sufficient for eight men to pull them. Needless to say the guns were lost. I lost my radio and gun and consider I was lucky to survive. I am not a good swimmer … we went inland to the base of the cliff and dug fox holes with our helmets and hands." Though "a fair swimmer," James Helsel also thought himself lucky. "I almost gave my rifle up twice, but then I thought of the future and held on to it."[28]

Through the heroic actions of several men, all personnel made it ashore. Among the many who distinguished themselves by saving men from drowning were lieutenants Veryl R. Hays and Andre N. Laus, T/Sgt. Robert P. Brimm, corporals Talmadge Carter, Charles C. Carrullo, and Christian R. Ericksen, sergeants Andrew C. Connolly, Walter R. Huetson, Ralph G. Jessop, and 1st Sgt. Leonard R. Kenney, Pfc's Charles H. Dawson, William M. Hawkins, Joe L. Jones, Albert E. Sereni, William V. Slider, Rufus A. Small, Charles R. Snyder, and Leonard W. Turan, and privates Robert P. Cowan, Harry Harper, Lawrence E. McDonald, and Benjamin F. Scott. Because 24 men of the company nearly drowned, Capt. Edwards later lined the men up on the beach, and then had company calisthenics and "sink or swim" survival lessons.[29]

Co. B, including 1st Lt. William P. Tice and four enlisted men of the Medical Detachment, was aboard *LCI 188*, which was scheduled to land at H plus 90 to the left of the pier at Gela. The company was to take position in a draw 300 yards to the west and support the 1st Rangers in their initial occupation of Gela. Afterwards they were to move to a better position.[30]

The rough sea had dislodged the ramps of *LCI 188* but they had been fixed by 1:30 a.m. As the various landing ships approached the beach, a searchlight came on as earlier noted and enemy fire opened upon them, causing much confusion in the landings. An attempt was made at 3:30 to land the mortar crews but they were turned around by a pilot boat which suggested they wait due to the intense enemy fire. All the LCIs stood by at about 1,000 yards from the beach until an Italian mine blew the pier at 3:45. Lt. Ed Trey, with the forward observation party of Co. B already ashore, said he was just crossing the beach when the pier blew up and the force of the explosion knocked him to the ground nearly unconscious. The LCIs made another attempt to land to the left of the pier at 4:00 but encountered a false beach about 100 yards from shore in about seven feet of water. Andrew C. Leech, Co. B, recalled, "We tried to unload but the water was too deep. We had to stay in our compartments as the machine guns were raking our deck. We stayed hung up there for about 30 minutes and all the time were a perfect target …"[31]

To make matters worse, the starboard ramp of *LCI 188* was nearly destroyed and the port ramp had jumped the track as enemy machine gun fire was coming in to the port side and coastal fire was continuing from the west. Fortunately, the starboard ramp was leaned on, the port ramp was placed back on track, and the LCI backed out and came back in on the immediate right of the pier. Under heavy fire the ramp was lowered and the 1st Platoon, led by Lt. Carl K. ("Stud") Carpenter, crossed the beach and made contact with the reconnaissance party. According to Leech, one mortar was lost in the shoulder-high water during the 1st Platoon's debarking. Mortars were set up in the draw as two squads of the 2nd Platoon, under Capt. Gordon M. Mindrum, were able to debark before the LCI drifted back out into deep water, where enemy fire came close to hitting the craft as well as the LCI of Co. A.[32]

Under the direction of Lt. Bernard B. Stone and 1st Sgt. Joseph A. ("Flat Top") Adamski, the remainder of the men on *LCI 188* were taken out of the ship and placed on small fishing boats. The heavy surf and enemy machine gun fire made the operation difficult, and just as the last man debarked an enemy 75mm shell made a direct hit on the rear compartment of the LCI and wounded four enlisted men. Among those injured were Pfc.'s Lyndon O. Outlaw and Claud D. Kuykendall, both of Monroe County, Mississippi; Pvt. John Zukowski, of Pittsburgh, Pennsylvania; and T/5 James J. O'Toole. Zukowski was sent to the ship's hospital and evacuated, while O'Toole and Outlaw were only slightly wounded and received treatment from their aid men. Andrew C. Leech, Co. B, recalled in his memoir "… one [*shell*] came right through the side of the ship in our compartment. It blew my gun out of my hand and shook me up a bit, but no one was hurt. Then the second one came through a little higher and shrapnel flew everywhere. Kuykendall, who was standing close by me was hit -- also Outlaw, O'Toole, and Zukowski. They were carried below and we were forced out by the water filling up the compartment. When we got up on deck it was covered with people lying flat on their stomachs as the machine guns raked the deck."[33]

One navy gunner on the LCI attempted to silence the enemy coastal battery as the mortar men lined up and passed him ammunition. Unfortunately, enemy shrapnel took out the gunner, who was replaced by a fair-haired lad. As the wounded gunner was taken away he yelled to his replacement, "Give 'em hell, Blondy."[34]

Malcolm Doyle ("Wilkie") Wilkinson, Co. B, a Mississippi boy who had attended the University of Texas, later described his personal feelings about his first time under fire: "There is no way I can tell you how it felt during our first combat. Prior to the invasion of Sicily we were scared and unsure of what to expect, but when the gunfire started it was a severe shock. When you see the first guy fall, you know it is for real and your only reaction is to do as you are told. The range of emotions go from high to severe lows, and when you are being shelled and shot at there is a terror and fright that you cannot describe to anyone. The two worst things for me were the artillery shelling and the strafing by airplanes. Make no mistake about it, small arms fire was frightening but those two were overpowering. They can say what they will but you never get so hardened that you cannot be touched by seeing one of your own lying there dead or severely wounded."[35]

LCI 189, carrying Co. C, was ready at 1:30 a.m. to leave the transport area as scheduled, shortly after 2:00 a.m., but did not depart until 2:21 a.m. "We immediately left for the beach when we hit the line of departure, the *17*, *188*, and *189*," a naval officer aboard *LCI 189* reported. Approaching the shore, the LCIs turned seaward again as a searchlight fell across the whole beach. Allied craft opened fire. "A DD [*destroyer*] from the eastern side missed with four shots. A DD from the western side of the transport area knocked the stand down and the light out with its first shot. It was a very fine thing to see it go out with such workmanship, especially as we were just about to enter the area of light … On our second approach at about 0355 it came on again and was knocked out. However, just as I approached the end of the pier, parallel to it, it came on, dead on us. It was very difficult to see, and automatic weapons were firing over us to douse it. We made the turn and headed for the beach. To assure our having enough cable to allow us to hit the beach, I waited until we only used 18 fathoms. We hit the beach at approximately 0410. The phones went out and I had an extremely difficult time transmitting orders by shouting above the firing, which was intermittent, and the ramp winch engines. After five minutes of shouting I succeeded in getting the ramps lowered."[36]

While this was underway, the enemy was shooting at the LCI, "and one gun, which sounded like an 88mm seemed to like the target the conning tower offered and shells went whizzing by closely every minute or so. Fortunately his skill was not as great as his enthusiasm …" However, "Marshall D. Gardner, Flc, ASN, the port ramp winch operator was hit above his left eye by a piece of shrapnel so far as could be determined, but carried on and completed his job duty. The wound was not serious but it bled profusely. Two others were hit but in neither case was the skin broken."[37]

Hale H. Hepler, Co. C, from Millboro, Virginia, stated, "When the landing craft hit a sand bar … the pilot tried to back up twice. On the third try we were told to go down the ramps on each side of the boat and begin unloading the guns and ammunition even though we were in deep water. Germans had destroyed the ramp on the left side killing one soldier and wounding another." According to Sgt. William C. Ford, also of Co. C, from New Albany, Mississippi, "Sgt. Salvatore Sapio was the first man down the ramp, and I was the second. As we stepped off the landing ramp to head for shore, to our bewilderment and surprise, we found out that the water was over our heads." Hepler's squad was the second one down the ramp, "which was now gone. The mortar had fallen into the Mediterranean with the blast. We formed up to the right ramp. The water was deep but we continued to carry out the invasion. I swam some distance before I hit the ground. It was very dark."[38]

Loy J. Marshall, Co. C, remembered that "… we … had to jump out in water about chest deep. During this time, I was a bazooka assistant, but I also had training in use of the Browning Automatic Rifle (BAR), the loading and operation of a 4.2" mortar, the operation of telephone communications, and as a lineman who strings communications wire and makes field repairs. After struggling with my 40 pounds of regular gear (including my rifle, helmet, gas mask and suit, shelter half, blanket, rations) I also carried eight bandoliers of ammo for the bazooka. I somehow managed to get to shore by catching a swell and being carried in. My teammate had our bazooka and four bandoliers of ammo. He was really struggling because he was caught in the crest of a wave that kept smashing into him, but he finally made it."[39]

"All our practice and care in planning the debarkation was worthless as it turned out," Capt. Burford observed. "The starboard ramp broke before the first cart could be taken off. In fact, it dumped that cart, mortar and all, into the sea. This meant that all carts and personnel had to debark by the port ramp and this required 20 minutes instead of three-and-a-half minutes we had performed in practice. All this time we were under fire from shore. In fact, one 20mm shell struck the side of the vessel so close to me that I felt the hot blast from the explosion in my face and thought for a moment that I was hit … The ship beached some 50 yards from shore, so we had to wade ashore through

Co. C soldiers in Sicily. Front, L-R: William E. Johnson, William C. Ford, & Audie W. Pierce.
Back Row, L-R: Floyd L. Grissom, Louis R. Grisham, and William Curtis Gregory.
Ford Collection

three-and-a-half feet of water with a heavy surf rolling and under fire all the time."[40]

Accounts of the landing indicate the water was between 3½ and 5 feet deep at the point of debarkation, which was reported between 100 and more than 200 feet from shore. The official battle report states 4 feet deep and 100 feet from shore. According to the Co. C unit journal, no one was killed, but three men suffered shrapnel wounds. Among the wounded were Pvt. Earle L. Jones from Polk County, Georgia, and Pvt. Bernard B. Zambrano, of New Haven County, Connecticut, both by shell fragments. Pvt. Donald ("Spider") Rugito, from Greensburg, Pennsylvania, was hit by fragments from a 4.2" mortar shell at the OP.[41]

Following the landing of the three mortar companies, the mortars of Co. C were immediately set up on the beach and radio contact established with the forward observers, who had landed with the first wave. Communications wire was laid to OPs on the eastern side of Gela which overlooked the wide coastal plains behind town. The company history further elaborated, "Arriving on shore we had to cover 100 yards of beach and then proceed 150 yards through streets from which sniping was still going on to a vineyard, where we set up our guns."[42]

Capt. Burford added, "When everybody got ashore Cunin and Darby were there to meet us. Two guns were emplaced on the sand [on the beach next to the customhouse] and fire commenced on one of the shore batteries." Lt. Col. Cunin would later claim, "I believe, the first round of 4.2" ammunition was fired in World War II at 0525 the morning of 10 July. It was fired by Co. 'C' and was a round of WP on the left flank defenses of the town. Purpose was to permit our forward observer to pick up the round and proceed to adjust fire on the coastal defenses of that flank. All companies were in position soon thereafter…" According to the official battle report, there were actually two rounds of WP fired in an effort to gain the attention of the forward observer or Col. Darby, who had already advanced as an observer, and to regain contact with Ranger elements. The rest of the guns were set up in the position planned in a vegetable garden on the slope leading up into town.[43]

Jerry Muschinske, yet at the original OP of Co. C, said, "In a short time, Herb Quina [Herbert R. Quina] came up with our telephone and informed us that the mortars had been firing from the beach and were presently moving up to a new location. We were told to join the Rangers and find a different OP. We ended up with the Rangers in a search party in a large cactus patch above … [a] … 37mm gun being fired by Col. Darby and Lt. Col. Cunin."[44]

Loy Marshall remembered, "… we began to cross the long, sandy beach to reach a six foot high stone wall. This area was suddenly lit up by searchlights. The Navy ships opened fire and shot out the lights. In the dark you could see the shells from the shore batteries streaking through the air. Red tracer bullets from enemy machine guns filled the air. Our mortar team set up their mortars close to the stone wall and began firing into the city and destroyed the buildings that the red tracer bullets were coming from." William C. Ford also took note of the wall, writing, "Just as we reached the high seawall, suddenly three large searchlights came on as bright as daylight. These searchlights were shining directly at our landing craft. I believe we got across the beach before the enemy realized we had come ashore, because when the searchlights came on, all of their gun emplacements began to fire… Our Squad (First Squad) dove for the sandy beach at the base of the seawall when the searchlights came on and the firing started … Some of our men in the third and fourth squads got caught in the cross-fire … We started setting up our mortars on the beach close to the seawall and began firing at close range into the city." Capt. Burford continued, "After unsuccessfully trying to get in touch with our Forward Observer, Metcalfe, we fired a round over our previously indicated base point to let him know we were in position. We still couldn't reach him so Rankin and I went up into town to look for possible OP positions. We had to move carefully because some sniping was still going on in the town … OP's were established and the mortars were kept busy firing on targets of opportunity."[45]

At about 6:30 the Rangers were continuing their advance on the coastal guns, but radio contact was lost with the forward observer of Co. B and the naval guns unknowingly fired on the Rangers, causing casualties and forcing them to withdraw. A guide from the forward observer was contacted, communications were restored, and the naval guns forced the enemy batteries to surrender. Lt. John McEvoy recalled that as he and the Ranger group eventually worked their way to the fort he was unable to contact Co. B, unaware their radio had been lost in the sea during the landing. McEvoy would later add, "Captain Lyle reacted with resignation. The attack would go on. His radios were in contact with the lead assault elements who again advanced on the fort when the navy fires stopped. The attack on the fort from the rear succeeded easily." McEvoy continued, "Our observation post was put up on the roof of a two-story house on the north edge of the town. The roof had a stone railing surrounding the roof and stairways from the ground level to the roof. The mortars were deployed by platoon to the northeast of the house. Other houses and barns surrounded the observation post." Italian soldiers began to surrender in droves and even the cooks rounded up a few. By 7:30 the Rangers had silenced all resistance and set up their perimeters around Gela. The mortars of Co. B were emplaced in an orchard on the west side of town.[46]

Capt. Robert Edwards, Co. A, was crawling under a truck for protection when someone stepped on a land mine behind him. Shrapnel hit him in the buttocks and produced a hole in the seat of his pants along with an "impressive bloody bruise," but he was "too humiliated to apply for a Purple Heart."[47]

Platoon officers of Co. A looked for mortar positions and a CP and outpost systems were established as sniping continued in the streets and the Company Headquarters men were kept busy with the numerous prisoners. James Helsel wrote, "Buck [*Martin "Buck" Brown*] and myself dug into the bank of a 20mm gun emplacement to await future orders. While waiting Lt. [*Veryl R.*] Hays & Pvt. [*Albert E.*] Sereni from the 1st Platoon came up from the rear of the emplacement and got two Dagos out from behind the gun." Small fishing boats were located to find the lost equipment and *LCI 17*, having been cleared of the troops, was able to be extricated and landed farther down shore. But the effort with the fishing boats failed because the LCI was too far out and the surf was too rough. Two additional mortars were lost in an attempt to unload them but eventually all the submerged mortars were retrieved with ropes from the LCI. Among the many men who swam back to the LCI to help retrieve the equipment was Edward Krebs who said, "Later, in daylight, Capt. Edwards ordered us back to our shelled and disabled LCI that was still hung up on the sandbar. We unloaded equipment and while half-swimming our way back to dry beach, we saw a couple of Rangers marching some Italian prisoners who'd surrendered from a pillbox right in front of us. We suddenly realized that we'd been directly in their sights and they easily could have killed us had they wanted to open fire." James Helsel added, "We laid along a bank until daylight, then about fourteen of us went down to the beach to try and get our mortars. Half way across the beach a machine gun opened up, the 'Beach Master' ordered us back. In a few minutes it became a little secluded, we went out into the water after our guns. Martin 'Buck' Brown and myself pulled one on shore by a long rope which was completely submerged. Martin found it by diving for it." Pfc. Carl A. Bishop earned a Silver Star for his participation in the retrieval of the mortars, his citation reading, "... While his company unloaded from its landing craft under heavy enemy machine-gun and artillery fire from strongly fortified beach defenses, six 4.2 inch mortars were lost to deep water. Pvt. Bishop, after swimming ashore, learned of this fact. Despite the unusually rough surf and the heavy gun fire to which he was subjected, Pvt. Bishop voluntarily returned at least four times to the point where the mortars had sunk and exerted every effort to retrieve them."[48]

The remaining equipment was disembarked onto an LCVP and Co. A went into their assigned position three hours after daylight. During the landing, Pvt. William C. Kilpatrick of Pennsylvania received a severe face wound from an exploding land mine while unloading a DUKW and had to be evacuated to a hospital in Africa. Later, in a December 13th, 1943, letter, Robert Edwards would write home, "Almost have the cigarette habit - perhaps I forgot to tell you but at Gela after the landing and things (we thought) had quieted down and we were back on the boat getting our mortars off a sniper got a man even then - my first sergeant said 'Here have one - do you good'. Have burnt hundreds up before but this is the first one I ever really smoked. It was a Chesterfield and that's my brand." One platoon took position to fire on the coastal batteries but found it unnecessary as they had already been taken out.[49]

Following Co. A's disastrous landing it became apparent to authorities that the LCI was not suitable to landings for 4.2" chemical mortar companies where there could be a false beach. It was concluded the LCA (Landing Craft Assault) or LCVP would fare as a better craft in future operations due to their shallow draft.[50]

The Landing—Co. D

Co. D, with the 1st Platoon on the *Elizabeth Stanton* and the 2nd Platoon aboard the *Thurston*, would operate separately during the invasion. The 1st Platoon was attached to the 1st Battalion, 16th Infantry, and the 2nd Platoon to the 2nd Battalion, 16th Infantry. The mission was to land, establish a beachhead, and to take the high ground at Niscemi. The 26th Infantry would land and operate on the left and the 45th Division would land and operate on the right.

The 2nd Platoon of Co. D, led by Capt. Edwin G. Pike, consisted of three officers and 94 enlisted men. Shortly before debarkation the men were given coffee and sandwiches or, as Capt. Pike said, "fatted calves again." The War Diary of the *Thurston* stated the ship was lying in the assault area of Gela at thirty minutes after midnight, lowered their boats and LCVPs at 12:55 p.m. and all troops had debarked by 3:52 a.m. Three minutes later they commenced unloading all troop equipment and cargo. Pvt. Herbert Sullivan, from Spotsylvania County, Virginia, was injured when he fell from the debarking net into the LCVP and was returned to the ship's hospital. Harold E. Hughes, from Iowa, wrote of this in his book *The Man from Ida Grove*, stating, "The disembark signal was given. As I swung my leg over the rail, I looked down to see the landing barge on the foaming ocean leap at me, and quickly drop. I knew I must step on the barge at the peak of its surge. As I scrambled down the sagging net, I heard a hoarse scream and looked to see a soldier fall between the side of the ship and a barge. Loaded with mortar shells and a rifle, he disappeared into the raging waters like a stone." The 2nd Platoon managed to land at Red Beach II, about two miles southeast of Gela, at 3:00 a.m. [*another official source says 4:30 a.m.*], but during the approach to the beach their LCVPs came under enemy machine gun fire. One casualty resulted.[51]

Capt. Pike attempted to describe the action: "Friday night about 2300 hours the whole ship was alerted and given orders to, 'Prepare to disembark'. What a feeling! It was black as pitch and not a one of us knew what awaited us, but we expected the worst. Finally the time arrived and over the side we went into our landing boats. By this time searchlights were flashing, bullets were splattering about, and fires dotted the landscape. The invasion had arrived. We hit the shore OK and struck out from landing boats – waist deep in water. My outfit was among the first to hit the shore … We went across the sand beach and on to the plain bordering the beach … We went past a nice watermelon patch so we stopped off and started eating … So far it was just like a field problem at Camp Gordon, everything was going smoothly … Wham! Boom! An artillery shell whammed a short distance away. Wham went the whole platoon heading for the hills … fun was over and the business began … [*Co. D's 2nd Platoon*] was among the first to come under enemy shelling. The first time an enemy artillery shell hits 10 or 15 yd. from you and you hit the dirt or the first time an enemy rifle bullet zings over your head by inches are experiences which you will never forget. And they are experiences which everyone in the company have undergone. I must say that every man in the company was wonderful and considering the fact that it was the first time under fire for all of them they did a marvelous job … We moved into our first position and before we set a gun up or had a fox-hole dug the artillery laid in on us. I dug a fox-hole with about 2 scoops of my shovel and stuck my nose and hind-end so deep in the dirt … Finally the barrage lifted and I lifted with it, being badly in need of fresh air. That was it – our first firing had arrived and we had all lived through it. That initial fear was gone. We moved forward from that position and dug in again with nothing happening. I dug a new hole and fell asleep with helmet, pack, and everything else still on and my rifle within arm's reach. The hell with the war. I was just too damn tired to do anything. I would have slept through anything. (Total sleep 45 minutes)."[52]

Several men were wounded while crossing the wide, open beach under additional artillery and mortar fire. However, all of the wounded refused to be evacuated until the enemy had been contacted and the mortars placed in position. Among the wounded on the beach were 2nd Lt. Joseph C. Stiefvater, by a shell fragment, and 1st Sgt. Peter J. Kiedrowski, a shell fragment through his right arm. Kiedrowski "…continued to help his men pull their heavy carts across the deep sand, giving advice and orders as though nothing was wrong. Weakened by the loss of blood, 'Pete' was forced to give in to the pleas of the aid men. He was evacuated and returned to the States with a useless arm." Wofford L. Jackson recalled, "I was just a few feet from 1st Sgt. Kiedrowski when he got hit, his arm nearly blown off." Kiedrowski's loss provoked Capt. Pike to state that he should have had at least two men trained for every job.[53]

Harold Hughes also recalled the turmoil of the 2nd Platoon crossing the beach, writing, "It was a nightmare of fiery explosions, screaming shells and crack of bullets. Bending low, my assistant gunner and I ran across the soft sand to escape the brilliant light from the burning ships and buildings. Another man running before me staggered, then fell backwards. I knew he was dead, but as we were instructed to do, we pushed on; the ground exploded near me and I fell flat, my face buried in the sand. Shrapnel rattled off my helmet. Then I crawled forward on my elbows and knees." Hughes and his gunner finally made it through some barbed wire and "A man screamed next to me; I glanced to see him face down, the sand dark red under his helmet." The sand also damaged the BAR of Hughes, and as another shell exploded nearby he and his gunner, along with the 2nd Platoon, proceeded to move inland to a hill about two miles from the beach. At this location they supported the advance of the 2nd Battalion, 16th Infantry. Unfortunately, the enemy had a good view of the original mortar position. Enemy artillery opened upon them and wounded Pfc. Herbert S. Goldstein, from Pittsburgh, Pennsylvania, with a shell fragment in the right leg. The enemy barrage was lifted but the

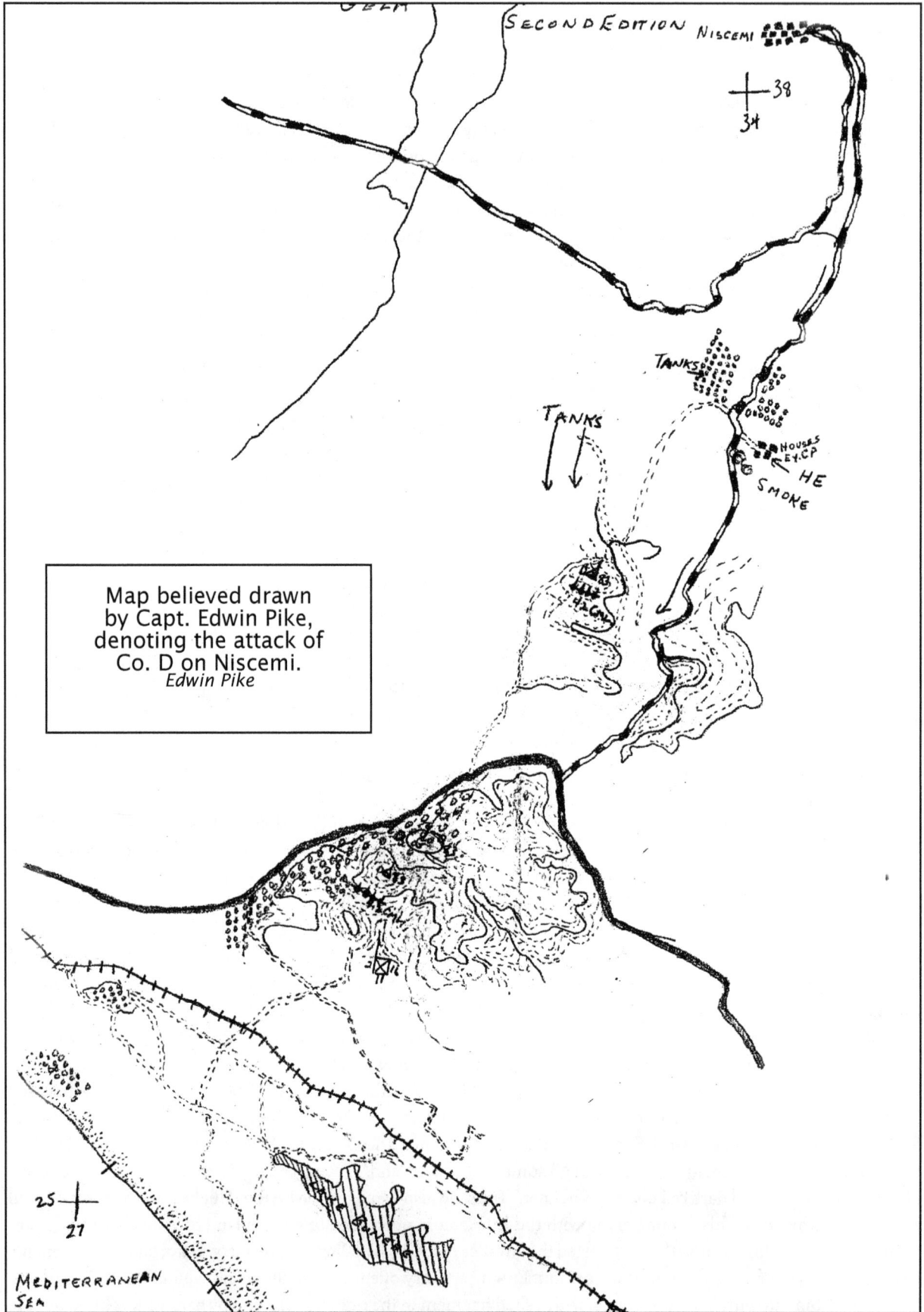

Map believed drawn
by Capt. Edwin Pike,
denoting the attack of
Co. D on Niscemi.
Edwin Pike

platoon remained in position until 10:00 p.m. when they moved to a bivouac near the ammo dump of Co. H, 2nd Battalion, 16th Infantry.[54]

Co. D's 1st Platoon, under command of 1st Lt. James O. Beasley and consisting of three officers and 93 enlisted men, encountered a false beach during the landing near Gela at 5:00 a.m. and was unable to get within 50 feet of shore, creating much difficulty in unloading the equipment. In spite of this obstacle, as well as a heavily mined beach, the platoon set up in a position not far from the beach, about a mile inland, and was able to cover all of the fields of fire supporting the 1st Battalion. A short enemy artillery barrage ensued in which the mortars did not fire. Afterwards the platoon advanced about another two miles and provided mortar fire until late in the evening. Lt. Beasley would later reflect, "I came in with the 4th wave of landing boats. A few rifle shots were fired at the boat and just as we got away from the beach the artillery started shelling it. There were a few hits on the beach but they were either poor shots or didn't want to hit anyone. A little artillery fire was all the resistance during the remainder of the day."[55]

James H. ("Banjo Eyes") Gallahan, Co. D, a former milk truck driver from Fredericksburg, Virginia, recalled he went in with the third wave and lost his rifle when he jumped from the landing

Co. D soldiers in Sicily. Front, L-R: Porter R. Davis and Willie R. Tanner; back, L-R: Charlie Lowry and Nevin L. Glossner.
Author's Collection

craft into the water. He continued on to shore with his comrades, "picked up the rifle of a fallen soldier and continued the advance. He said he [*Gallahan*] was out in the open while the enemy were in trenches and could have decimated them. However, the force of the shells from the battle ships at sea hitting those trenches caused the Italian troops to abandon their defensive positions and surrender."[56]

Pvt. Richard A. Bridge, Co. D, from Greensburg, Pennsylvania, simply described the landing by saying, "… at the break of dawn I leaped from the barge and stepped onto the Island of Sicily."[57]

Tank Attack

At daybreak of the 10th, enemy tank and infantry were spotted assembling for the first counter-attack in a small wooded area three kilometers from Gela. Before companies A and B were able to get into position, Co. C laid fire on the force attacking from the direction of the Ponte Olive Airport, dispersing the infantry and causing withdrawal of the tanks. Co. C's mortars were then displaced a platoon at a time to the south end of Gela to meet any attack from the south or northeast. Companies A and B eventually were engaged as well in helping to repulse three separate tank attacks, including one around noon in which German tanks attacked from the southeast but were forced to withdraw out of mortar range. Co. A's participation in the tank attack took place after contact was made with the forward observer party and an OP had been set up in the forward edge of town, where the company's mortar fire knocked out one tank and possibly another. James Helsel, Co. A, wrote that "The second platoon had three guns set up in a grape vineyard next to a large house, in which our Co. Medic helped an Italian woman give birth to a child. Our gun wasn't set up so I was around the platoon 'CP' when I heard Lt. Bolton's voice over the radio say 'Stand by, hell!' There are a lot of tanks coming with enough infantry to take the town back." Mortar observers passed word to naval observers who placed the tanks under fire. During the second of the three attacks, nine light Italian tanks broke through the mortars, but a 37mm gun, fired by Col. Darby and Lt. Col. Cunin, and several bazookas halted the assault. The anti-tank gun got one and a bazooka team knocked out another, which the Rangers proceeded to blow up with a pole charge. A separate pole charge dropped from a building took care of another tank, forcing the remainder to withdraw. Lawrence H. Powell, Co. A, confirmed that one tank entered town but was disabled by the bazooka fire of Pvt. William J. Golding, Co. A, from New Jersey.[58]

Sgt. William C. Ford, Co. C, remembered that during the attack, "To our right we saw a German tank coming slowly down the cobblestone road. We got the bazookas ready to blast the tank when it was in range. As the tank came closer there was someone standing on top of it. Sgt. Sapio yelled at us to hold our fire because the man standing on top of the tank was Col. [*his rank was actually Major*] Hutchinson. He had captured the tank and crew intact."[59]

Co. B also wrote of the enemy tank attack, stating that at approximately 10:30 a.m., 15 to 20 enemy tanks attacked down the Ponte Olive Airport Road. According to Edward L. Trey, Co. B, "A concentration of about 25 tanks from the Herman Goering Armored Division came so close to our perimeter that Sgt. Wofford L. ('Woof Woof') Jackson wrote that our mortar crews escaped their machine gun fire by running into a ditch." Lt. Vester L. Turner directed the fire of the mortars at ranges between 3,600 to 3,800 yards. Several tanks broke through but at noon withdrew to a heavily wooded assembly area, where they fell under heavy mortar fire. Several trucks were destroyed and four tanks were immobilized. During the afternoon the Rangers, utilizing the captured coastal guns west of Gela, knocked out all four of the immobilized tanks. 1st Sgt. Vincent Egan of the Rangers said, "It was the first time those 4.2 mortars were in action, and they did damn well."[60]

Capt. Pike, with the 2nd Platoon, Co. D, recalled the tank attack during the day as he wrote home, " … one of our platoons was on Hill 41 in support of the 2nd Battalion, 16th Infantry. 45 men and six officers, yours truly, was one of the 6 officers. [*A*] young captain … heroically … did a marvelous job. (Not I) You probably recall my telling about the lack of anti-tank guns on the hill but the yeomen service done by the one whole one which was left. The difference in number of tanks quoted came in that about 8 actually pierced thru to our front lines while 20 to 40 enemy tanks came under our fire at a greater range." Dan Shields, Co. D, summed up the day, writing, "Left ship at 2:10. Landed in Sicily at 3:35. Walked all day. Retired 10:15."[61]

Co. A did no firing throughout the night although the company remained on alert and a few enemy bombs fell nearby. Co. B reported enemy air activity transpired throughout the day with but little damage, although at 9:00 p.m. an intense air raid took place with bombs falling in Co. B's mortar positions, but no casualties occurred. A few pesky enemy patrols took place throughout the night. Co. B also took 14 prisoners whom they turned over to Force HQ in Gela. Lt. John McEvoy, Co. B, added, "At the end of the first day defensive preparations began. Individuals dug foxholes for night time protection. Some improved the comforts of their foxholes by adding any straw available. A bad decision. The fleas in the straw quickly abandoned it for the warmth and food provided by the occupant." Capt. Gordon Mindrum, Co. B, recalled "Gen. George Patton came to the OP as the action was ending. He borrowed my field glasses and failed to return them … I saw him again in the Colmar Pocket in December of 1944 and he still did not return my field glasses."[62]

Summoned to the OP at 5:00 p.m., Capt. Burford, Co. C, received orders for his company to support the 26th Infantry in an attack on the airfield north of Gela. By 9:30, Co. C met up with the 26th Infantry at a crossroads, where they were ordered to march with the heavy weapons company. Burford designated Lt. Ralph Rankin as liaison officer for the regimental commander and the column marched for about two hours. At 11:00 the column was halted as information had been received that the head of the column had walked into a trap and was pinned down by machine gun fire. Numerous retreating and disorganized infantry men came back with no useful knowledge of the enemy position until Lt. Rankin returned with sufficient information to place mortars. This account conflicted with that of Capt. Burford, who went on to say, "Finally Ralph came back to join us … and [*he*] knew less than I did about the situation. We noticed the heavy weapons company was in full retreat. Seizing an opportunity to commandeer a jeep, we rode up forward as far as we could go. We located an officer who gave us an approximate situation but couldn't tell us where the enemy was or how far away. I tried to get in touch with the infantry CO by radio and succeeded. His directions were to send an officer and communications to join a battalion commander at I Company. So Ralph set out with Sgt. [*Stephen*] Morse and some wire and telephones."[63]

Co. C set their mortars up as far forward as possible in the dark, behind a huge drainage ditch, "the spoil from which was thrown up in front of it and made excellent concealment, but not much cover." Hale Hepler, Co. C, recalled, "Little did we know that safety would be found in a sewer line. While it was very unpleasant our lives were saved. Hours later a lieutenant came along and wondered why we were so smelly …" Ammunition Sgt. Harold ("Eisey") Eisenberg, with two ammo trucks, was ordered by Burford to leave 200 rounds with the guns and move the remainder in the trucks 300 yards to the rear and conceal them. Unable to do anything else until communications were established with Rankin, the men curled up and went to sleep, although Burford said he, " … was too cold and too nervous from anticipation to be able to sleep. So I shivered, watched, and waited until something should develop."[64]

July 11—Companies A, B, and C

The body of Lt. William S. Doughten, Jr., was transferred from the *Dickman* to shore sometime between 8:00 a.m. and noon of July 11th as Co. A spent the day fighting off a small number of enemy tank attacks. James Helsel wrote in his diary, "The 3rd Squad was told to set up their mortar, which we did right after breakfast. We fired about five rounds and was given a new compass reading that turned our gun to left flank; we learned of a small tank attack about to begin. Soon we saw General Patton ride by in his command car toward that sector. It was soon beaten off for we didn't fire many rounds." One tank was hit by mortar fire and burned, while the remainder of the day saw much air activity. Sam Bundy, Co. A, wrote of the threat from above in his diary, recording, "As planes strafed our CP, Capt. Edwards and his Co. HQ personnel tumbled into their dugouts, which was previously occupied by chickens, or into the CP building – a hay loft which housed many big rats and mice. This routine was constant, especially … [*at night*] … when tracers and flares … [*lit*] … the sky. Four enemy planes flew very low over our position, and did we hug the ground! Fortunately we were neither bombed nor strafed." On the other hand, the communications men had much difficulty laying wire in the streets because vehicles were constantly running over it and destroying the wire.[65]

Co. B was kept quite busy on the 11th, as early in the morning one platoon fired on a 15-man Italian reconnaissance patrol approaching Gela from the north and drove them from one draw to another, and eventually to a haystack. One volley of HE ended the chase. Information had also been received of a counter-attack by a Panzer Division to the immediate right, east of Gela. In conjunction a company of Mark IV tanks struck from the northeast, while at 10:00 a.m. enemy infantry advanced down the Butera Road. The enemy, previously assembled behind small hills, poured into the open plains of Gela. Lt. Carl K. ("Stud") Carpenter and Lt. Vester L. Turner directed heavy mortar fire at a distance of 3,200 to 3,800 yards. At the same time the cruiser *Savannah* opened its naval guns on the area the mortars could not reach.[66]

Lt. John McEvoy recalled, "When it was clear they would come within range preparations were made to fire a single round as close to their formations as estimation would permit … the plan was to fire one round and sense its relation to the target; then take corrective action and fire two rounds from each of the four mortars in one platoon. At the same time the first platoon fired, the second platoon would fire a sensing round; then make corrections and fire a supporting volley … at last … the initial round was on its way. When it splashed close to the nearest troops they stopped initially, then sporadically resumed their advance. Then disaster. Four more rounds landed in their midst, followed seconds apart by a second, third, and fourth ripple. Panic and retreat were immediate."[67]

Ed Trey also remembered the day: "Along with [*Charles M.*] Shunstrom [*of the Rangers*], we stumbled upon an abandoned Italian 75 with a stack of ammo which we turned around and fired toward the plains of Gela and Butera." With but little cover in the open plains the enemy, unable to get within machine gun range, took heavy casualties and broke and ran in all directions. The few who did not break took cover in the lee of a high railroad right-of-way, where, for some unknown reason, fire was not directed. A few high velocity shells, believed to be 47mm anti-tank fire, forced the 1st Platoon's OP to move. Stunned and demoralized enemy survivors, some 200 in total, many of them wounded, were rounded up by the half-tracks of the 39th Combat Engineers. At 3:00 p.m. the area was strafed by two ME 109s, and at 4:00 p.m. the enemy initiated another battalion strength infantry attack from northwest of Gela along the railroad tracks. Mortar fire was placed on the near side of the enemy while cruiser fire was directed at the far side, putting a quick end to the assault. The few survivors sought refuge in the grain fields, only to be hit by WP, something they had come to fear intensely. The few remaining survivors were picked up by four tanks of the 2nd Armored Division, which had landed during the day. Another report stated the survivors were rounded up by two medium tanks and two half-tracks. Andrew Leech recalled the assorted infantry attacks, as he wrote, "We … were reported to have inflicted over one thousand casualties. Once a whole company came out of their foxholes waving a white flag, but just too bad the command had already been given to fire and three rounds were in the air. They landed right in the middle of the group and it was just too bad. We captured one major and he said that he and three others that were with him were all that were left out of his company." Reportedly, there were over 400 prisoners. Before the end of July 11th, Pfc.'s Michael J. ("Cookie") Kelly and Wilbert E, Till, Pvt. Johnny Goodwin, Jr., and T/5 Rudolph H. ("Rudy") Engel arrived to Co. B from the rear echelon. [68]

The 26th Infantry, supported by Co. C of the 83rd, had been in position at daylight on high ground just shy of their objective, the Ponte Olive Airport. Forward observer Lt. Ralph Rankin, radio operator Stephen A. Morse, both of Co. C of the 83rd, and a Pvt. Murphy of the 26th Infantry manned a machine gun in a foxhole just in front of the outpost line. Also ready for action were the mortars, placed in company front formation in the defilade of an anti-tank trap. Once visibility had become clear the Germans counter-attacked through a sloping valley. Lt. Rankin ordered the mortars to continuously sweep the valley with HE and WP. In spite of heavy losses the Germans continued to advance until Co. C ran out of ammo. According to Capt. Burford, he looked around for his ammo man, Harold ("Eisey") Eisenberg, but could not find him. Then Burford requested his jeep driver, Earl Shaddinger, to find someone connected to the ammo but he not only could not find any such person, he also couldn't locate the ammo trucks. Later it would be discovered that Eisenberg, against Burford's orders, had taken the trucks back to town during the night and upon attempting to return was stopped by an officer who would not let him proceed. Reluctantly, Burford had to inform Rankin there would be no more ammo. [69]

The 26th Infantry was forced to withdraw due to a Mark IV tank on the other flank and the advancing enemy. In order not to draw attention to the OP, Pvt. Murphy had held his fire upon Lt. Rankin's order, but as the infantry broke through he opened upon them and cleared the hill. Lt. Rankin returned to his post but Burford noticed the enemy was about to detect their position as a shell burst about 200 yards to their left. This prompted Burford at 9:00 a.m. to order Lt. Alvin Metcalfe with the 1st Platoon and Lt. Julian McKinnon with the 2nd to conceal themselves to the right in some undergrowth. Apparently, through some slip or misunderstanding, Metcalfe's men raced back toward town. Metcalfe had to commandeer a mule or horse grazing on the side of the road and pursue his men all the way to the northeast outskirts of Gela. According to Hale Hepler, as Metcalfe's platoon approached town they were met by the battalion major, who said, "Dig in. You can't win a war going that way." [70]

By 10:30 a.m. Lt. Metcalfe's 1st Platoon was posted in Gela covering the road to the Ponte Olive Airport. Three mortars were fired at some tanks in a field while anti-tank guns covering the road to the coast opened upon nine Mark IV tanks, which halted 1,000 yards short of the mortars and well out of anti-tank range. Two mortars were placed on the shoulders of the coastal road as Maj. Hutchinson went to the tower of a brewery at the crossroads and voice relayed firing commands of HE and WP. But, due to not digging or using aiming stakes, the mortars were ineffective and no tanks were hit. However, the Germans did not wish to enter the WP and HE screen and withdrew about 4,000 yards, where all nine were knocked out by tank and naval fire. [71]

In the meantime, Lt. McKinnon had led his men into the undergrowth and Burford said the remaining men were frightened and wanted to leave the equipment behind. But he insisted on an orderly withdrawal from Co. C's original position, and he was the last to leave as shells began to fall dangerously close. After arriving at the designated position, Burford and the men soon realized they were caught in the middle of the battle. He collected the men and moved downstream where he encountered McKinnon, who told him they had hidden the unwieldy carts upstream in some bushes. Burford concurred with this decision and opted to move his men to town, but when two miles from Gela they received word they were cut off by a counter-attack from the right. Burford wrote, "Soon after this all hell broke loose." Burford and his men, along with a large group from the 26th Infantry, found themselves in the center of the line of fire, even dodging mortar shells from Co. A of the 83rd. [72]

The situation began to quiet down around 3:30 and Burford rounded up all the men he could locate and moved back to Gela, where he met a highly upset Lt. Col. Cunin and joined up with Metcalfe's platoon. Burford said in the meantime Lt. Rankin had rejoined him. Later in the evening, Cunin met with Rankin and Burford and praised Rankin but belittled Burford. He charged Burford with not maintaining proper liaison, although that was actually the fault of the 26th Infantry officer, and blasted him for leaving the equipment behind. Burford felt Cunin would have court-martialed him on the spot had he not convinced him the mortar equipment was safe and could be retrieved since the enemy never advanced to that point. Burford felt Cunin was trying to find a scapegoat for his own failure to take the airport, but Burford had no control over the infantry bolting. Maj. Hutchinson, who was also present, told Burford he should be commended rather than censured, and, although this helped Burford's ego a bit, "... the attitude of Cunin still rankled."[73]

July 11–Co. D

At dawn on July 11th, the 1st Platoon of Co. D moved toward Niscemi along Highway #115 and came under enemy mortar fire. During the all-out assault by the Herman Goering Division, the 1st Platoon of Co. D was the only artillery support present. The platoon attempted to give maximum fire but was shelled mercilessly in return, once for nearly an hour. One shell landed near the 2nd squad's mortar, and shrapnel struck the barrel rendering the mortar useless. The 1st squad was ordered to a new position behind a house near two abandoned pillboxes. Although under direct tank and machine gun fire, the platoon managed to hold its position and around noon fired three rounds which eliminated several machine guns that had pinned down 14 infantrymen, even though the enemy came within 30 yards of the mortars. The bazookas of both the infantry and mortar crews helped repel the attack. At one point

Capt. Edwin G. Pike in Sicily, August 1943.
(Al Forrester is just visible at far left)
Pike Collection

during the attack the enemy made several direct hits on the CP of the unit being supported, resulting in casualties of all in command. Co. D's 1st Platoon received orders to "remain in position and hope for the best." Luckily the 3rd Battalion, 16th Infantry, soon came to reinforce the 1st Battalion and Co. D's 1st Platoon was attached to them.[74]

The 3rd Battalion, 16th Infantry, was attacked by tanks as bazooka crews, including those of Co. D's 1st Platoon, went forward and assisted in capturing three tank crews. The 3rd Battalion proceeded to attack the high ground in the area, which placed the supporting 1st Platoon of Co. D in an exposed position. The platoon fell under a heavy bombardment and enemy tanks cut their rear lines of communications. The platoon found it necessary to move to the front lines further exposing them to small arms fire. Nevertheless, the platoon managed to support the successful attack and enemy attempts to retake the high ground. This put an end to the enemy effort to push them off the beachhead. Dan Shields, Co. D, summarized the day by writing in his diary, "5:50 a.m. Up with infantry, shelled pretty heavy. Hot weather. Saw tanks felt good. Retired 10:55."[75]

Lt. James O. Beasley, Co. D, later related in detail his personal experiences that day: "... Early the second day I followed forward to find where we could be used. There was considerable artillery fire and they wanted us up at once. I went looking for the men but by the time they were assembled the road I intended for them to go up was under heavy artillery fire so they were not sent up. I went forward to find another route and found that the infantry had been forced to withdraw. The platoon was attached to another unit and I went to the beach to get our jeeps and the trucks that had arrived. On the way back the artillery started shelling the road and all the bad drivers could think to do was stop – my profanity is better than most people would give me credit for. On the way back an officer said we were badly needed in another place. When I was at the beach about thirty German bombers came over to bomb the ships and supply dumps. They did little damage because barrage balloons and anti aircraft fire kept them pretty high. When I reached the platoon they were instructed to follow and I went on ahead with a driver and a lineman in a jeep. We were supposed to turn off the paved road just before we crossed a bridge but I did not tell the driver in time and he stopped on the bridge. It was then that a machine gun opened up on us. I made an estimate of the situation, drew up a plan of action and issued orders. All this took considerably less than a second. The estimate of the situation was that the bridge was no place to be with a machine gun firing at you. My plan of action was a STRATEGIC retreat. The orders were 'get the Hell out of here' ... Unfortunately there was no official timer around or I would have the world's record for the two hundred dash which was off the bridge, through a cactus plant and into a vineyard. Some more men were coming down the road so we formed a patrol to investigate. It was all for nothing. We had just been mistaken for Germans and it was an American machine gun. It was a few minutes later that someone noticed and called my attention to the hole in my rifle stock. We went on to the gun position which was under artillery fire and was soon firing ourselves. No one was hit by the artillery fire. It was soon dark so I started back for ammunition in a jeep. The driver turned it on its side so I had to walk to where the ammunition truck was supposed to be. It was not there so I slept until daylight and then went back to the guns."[76]

The 2nd Platoon of Co. D opened July 11th by arriving at the ammo dump of Co. H, 2nd Battalion, 16th Infantry, where they delivered sporadic fire until noon. At 10:00 a.m., six to eight enemy tanks broke through the front lines and shortly before 11:30 the S-1 journal of the 16th Infantry reported commander Crawford of the 16th Infantry had been cut off by three tanks. Radio contact between the 83rd Chemical Battalion and other units was erratic. To counter the enemy attack the anti-tank weapons of two 37mm guns and several rocket launchers were employed. Mortars were also used effectively as anti-tank weapons. One tank broke through the lines and was destroyed in the rear, as the tank attack was driven off with the destruction of four enemy tanks. But it came at a high cost to the 2nd Platoon, Co. D, of the 83rd, as privates Elbert E. Phillips and James B. Scott were killed and 2nd Lt. Joseph C. Stiefvater, T/5 George J. Glockner, and Pfc's Ralph D'Antuono, Salvatore J. Guarracino, and John Verfin were wounded. This was Lt. Stiefvater's second wound in two days. Pvt. James T. Beasley, from Union County, Mississippi, was missing in action. Privates Albert Cohen and Bennie Lieberman distinguished themselves by maintaining communications while under fire. Each won the Silver Star, their citation stating that "... in the vicinity of Niscemi ... when communications to the rear failed during a period when [*they were*] under direct enemy tank and artillery fire, [*the two telephone operators*], re-established telephone communications by using radios [*they*] had found abandoned nearby. Twice while manning these radios [*Cohen and Lieberman*] were subjected to enemy tank fire, but persisted in their operation."[77]

Writing of his second day in Sicily, Capt. Pike scribed, "Come the dawn and Steve [*Stiefvater*] and I moved forward to reconnoiter a new position. We found what we wanted and moved back to the platoon and took them forward to this new position. We set our guns up and started digging our fox-holes again – just started though, for at that time the infantry was forced to withdraw – and they withdrew right into our position where they set up to make a stand. The platoon and the infantry were dug in on the reverse slope of a hill with the enemy about 2000 yd. to our direct front with another hill intervening. My OP (Observation Post) was on the crest of our hill along with the infantry OPs. In an orchard slightly to the rear of the enemy's front lines I could observe several enemy tanks maneuvering around. We delivered some fire on them not doing much good and kept an eye open for opportunity targets. Suddenly about 800 yd. to our left front an opportunity target presented itself."[78]

Harold Hughes, recalling the tanks breaking through, wrote, "In fearful fascination I watched the squat monsters lumber toward us, their machine guns pounding and 88-millimeter cannons flashing. My assistant [*Elbert E. Phillips from Virginia*] yelled he was going back ...'Stay put!' I called, but he scrambled out of his foxhole and began running. A burst of machine-gun fire cut him in half ... A tank loomed over my foxhole and I crouched deep. As it roared over I was choked by acrid exhaust fumes. When I emerged, oddly enough no German infantry followed. That fact saved many of us."[79]

Capt. Pike was in the thick of action as well: "That tank went past me no farther than 10 yards away, knocking over trees and everything else in its way. I'm telling you it's a horrible feeling when a tank goes by like that. I didn't know whether to run, dive in a fox-hole, just stand there or what to do. So I did the best I could by standing up and firing my rifle at the thing. It was just like using a pea-shooter on a bear but it sure helped my morale." Pike continued, "Anyway, the tanks pierced right through our lines, throwing a hail of lead. We then turned our anti-tank weapon around and fired at the tank and hit it with direct hits and set it afire. It continued on a short distance, then stopped, and the whole crew burned to death inside the tank. And no one felt a bit sorry for any of them, I assure you. By this time one of the other tanks had flanked us on the left and was sitting there laying fire on us from that side. The gun was turned in that direction and we took care of him in fine fashion. The gun was turned back on the tanks to our direct front and we were firing point-blank at them and knocked out two more. The rest of them decided they had had enough and pulled back to their own lines, badly beaten. I can't say just what happened to us, but we didn't exactly get off without a scratch ... although yours truly was untouched. The whole action took about 2 hours but I never want to go through another 2 hours like that, rest assured." Capt. Pike would claim July 11th was the "most exciting and horrible day" of the entire Sicilian campaign for him personally.[80]

Later, as he watched the burial details gathering bodies, Harold Hughes noted, "And it was then I saw my friend, [James B.] Scott, from Virginia [*actually he was from Tennessee*]. He had been hit by an 88. Sand encrusted entrails protruded from his torso. However on one arm I could still make out the tattooed heart and the word MOTHER. I stood there, torn with grief and nausea."[81]

But perhaps the most daring individual feat of the day for Co. D came from their aid man from the Medical Detachment, Pvt. Curtis A. Williams from Tennessee. While tending to the wounded in some cane brush Williams noticed a jeep apparently abandoned by the engineers when his group retreated through a culvert under the road. He noticed some additional wounded men who needed assistance to walk and decided to go back to get the jeep to help carry the men. His fellow soldiers advised him against this as he would get killed yet he went anyway, and in the process saw more soldiers who told him not to go. Yet undeterred, Williams made it to the jeep but suspected the engineers may have booby-trapped it so he made a quick inspection. Miraculously, he managed to get the jeep started and roared away at full speed and made it to the wounded, although in the process bullets hit everything but him and the tires and gas tank. Under this hail of enemy fire, he got the wounded to the nearest doctor. For this action, Williams was awarded the Silver Star. His citation stated that "… in the vicinity of Niscemi … despite heavy enemy tank and artillery fire, Pvt. Williams left a place of cover and crept to the aid of a severely wounded man. He then proceeded to the rear, obtained a vehicle, and, although inexperienced as a driver, drove the wounded soldier to the aid station." Sporadic enemy fire was received by the platoon throughout the remainder of the day.[82]

Capt. Pike concluded, "The rest of the day was comparatively peaceful, consisting only of German 88's laying their fire into our positions at very frequent intervals and German Messerschmidts flying over at an altitude of what seemed about 2 feet. I could have reached up and shook hands with the pilot, but I couldn't think of any good reasons for shaking hands with any German pilots at the time. And, besides, how could I shake hands while I was flat on my face in a hole about 4 feet deep." Shortly after 6:00 p.m. the 83rd reported they were low on ammunition.[83]

At 11:00 p.m., Co. A was ordered to support an attack on the Italian strong-point northwest of Gela in the vicinity of Mount della Lapa. The force would consist of three companies of the 1st Rangers; a company of half-tracks from the 1st Battalion, 39th Combat Engineers; two companies from the 1st Battalion, 41st Armored Infantry; Co. A of the 83rd; and five medium tanks from the 2nd Armored Division. Co. A would be completely motorized in four two-and-a-half ton amphibious trucks and three one-half ton jeeps. The attack would not take place until the morning of the 12th.[84]

July 12–Companies A, B, and C

Shortly before daybreak of July 12th, Co. A, via three DUKWs and three Peeps [*small jeep-like vehicles*], reached their assigned position north, along the Gela-Butera road in the Plains of Gela, in a "very shallow defilade immediately south of the strong-point where the road first bends toward the west after running straight northwest from Gela." The company immediately prepared to dig in alongside the infantry and fire, but the order was countermanded and the forward group of the company advanced west to some small hills straddling the road. Half-tracks were atop the hills firing machine guns. Capt. Edwards and Maj. Hutchinson established an OP and FDC [*Fire Direction Center*] atop the right ridge in front of the 1st Platoon. The attack began at daybreak as enemy small arms, machine gun, and small mortar fire was received, followed by 55mm shells.[85]

James Helsel gave an extended account, writing, "When the sun came up we were told to go into position on the left side of the road, which was a cotton patch. The Infantry were digging in, we were given a compass reading and started setting up the gun. Just as 'Buck' [*Martin*] and I was about to connect the barrel to the standard, a shell hit on the road just a few feet away. We took cover, I found an empty Infantry hole which I could just get my head in, for the ground was very hard, it was almost impossible to dig in. Buck and myself got up to finish putting the gun together and found it already fixed. He said he didn't do it & I am sure I didn't stay to finish it. While [*Pfc. Frank W.*] Boutyard [*of Fredericksburg, Virginia*] was out putting in the stakes for me a machine gun cut up some dirt pretty close which was followed by a very heavy barrage of '88' shells. They were so close one hit next to our mortar and covered it with dirt. One of the boys broad jumped from where he was laying right into the hole with the remark, 'I fooled them, I let them dig a hole for me.'"[86]

Mount del Zai, east of the pass behind the strong-point, had been the objective of the Rangers, and they reached

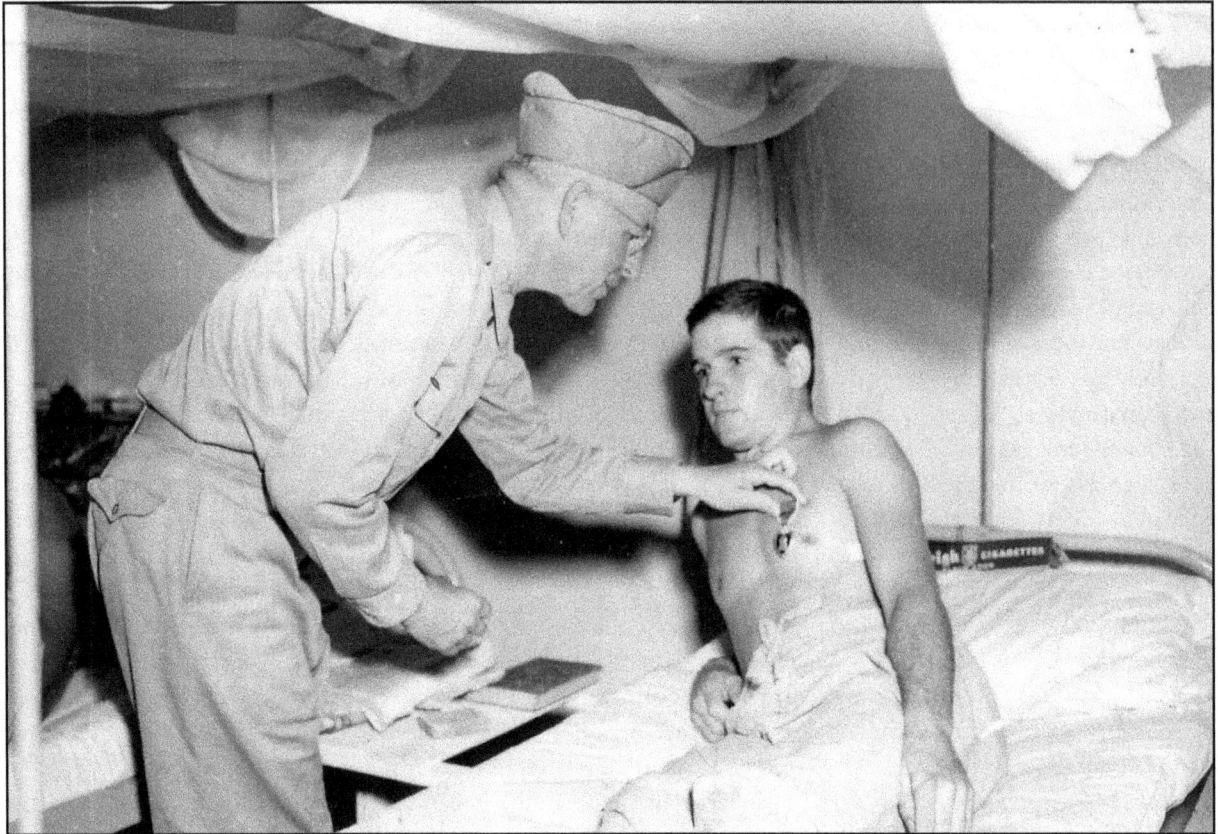

Earl Kann, Co. D, receives Purple Heart while in hospital in North Africa. *Earl Kann*

it by daylight, the Italians still controlling the strong-point, however. Unoccupied Mount della Lapa was the objective of the 41st Armored Infantry, but they were not able to advance before daylight. It would be necessary for them to cross a flat, wide open area to gain the foot of the mountain, easily exposing them to the enemy's automatic weapons. Realizing this they had to wait while the mortars, one half-track, five medium tanks, and the *Savannah* softened the position with preparatory fire throughout the day.

At 8:00 a.m., the five medium tanks of the 41st Armored Infantry advanced and blasted the enemy position, then pulled back behind the hill on which Co. A's OP was located. This move drew enemy artillery fire. At 9:00 a.m., a corporal of the 1st Rangers reported some Ranger squads pinned down on the right hill, Mount del Zai, and requested assistance. Indeed, after the mortars had opened fire from the OP of Co. A, from which the enemy defenses were plainly visible, there was fear some Rangers were still in the area and had advanced so rapidly they were out of radio range with their forward observer. Once contact had been restored it was confirmed some Rangers were still pinned down in the strong-point area to the right flank, preventing any mortar fire. Aware the enemy left flank and Mount della Lapa remained unoccupied since the 41st Armored were still deploying in the defilade to their left, heavy mortar concentrations were laid on the position.[87]

To assist the Rangers on Mount del Zai, Co. A laid down a smoke screen until 4:00 p.m. using extra powder charges due to excess ranges, although heavy breakage meant only one mortar of six in the 1st Platoon and three in the 2nd Platoon were effective. Another report stated the 1st Platoon had only two guns left and they consisted of borrowed parts. Soon after Co. A opened fire the Italians struck back with 75mm shells. Heavy enemy artillery fell in the mortar positions although five rounds were duds. Shrapnel broke one mortar and two men were injured. Sgt. Jerome Dickstein from New York and his gunner, Pvt. James C. ("J. C.") Jordan from Athens, Georgia, as well as cannoneer Hilmon R. Valentine from McGee, Mississippi, distinguished themselves by remaining loyal to their mortar as shells fell around them, splattering them with dirt. Large chunks of dirt also hit Sgt. John F. Crehan from Camden County, New Jersey, and his man, Pvt. Walter J. Franklin from Huron County, Ohio. Franklin suffered a bruised leg when dirt thrown up by a nearby exploding shell hit him for a second time. Suspecting he was out of action, Franklin temporarily forgot about his injury and "led the race to a better position." The battle report stated, "The value of deep slit trenches cannot be overemphasized." Three duds also fell in the area, two directly among the mortars and one near the ammo.[88]

Following the enemy barrage, Co. A resumed firing as the Italian artillery continued to sweep the entire valley in an effort to locate the 83[rd's] mortar positions. Excepting interdictory fire, the position was only located once, but no casualties resulted. During all of this activity, Maj. William S. Hutchinson, Jr., won the Silver Star for gallantry while serving as a forward observer at Co. A's OP. His citation read in part, "... while in a forward observation post Maj. Hutchinson was subject to heavy artillery fire and intense small arms fire holding up the advance of our troops. Maj. Hutchinson with complete disregard of his own personal safety remained in his OP and continued accurately to direct his own 4.2" mortar fire. His outstanding courage, coolness and professional skill resulted in the destruction of one enemy battery ..." Co. A fired about an equal amount of WP and HE as numerous Italian prisoners expressed their fear of the 83[rd's] "lightning guns". A flank attack of the outposts was anticipated but a few rounds from a BAR resulted in a white flag and 50 Italian prisoners. Lt. Col. Cunin would later remark, "As long as the Italian is well emplaced, as long as he can see you and knows where you are, he will fight like hell. But once you surprise him and get the jump on him or get behind him, he folds up like that."[89]

At 10:00 a.m., utilizing information provided by a 1st Ranger officer on Mount del Zai, the *Savannah* provided counter-battery fire against the Italian artillery located about 4,000 yards behind the strong-point beyond the second ridge. The firefight continued until 1:00 p.m. when the five medium tanks, along with the engineer half-tracks, returned and advanced to a high point just shy of the crest of Mount della Lapa, where they were stalled by enemy artillery, but still spurred the Italians to continue to surrender in large numbers. With hulls down the tanks covered the 41st Armored Infantry.[90]

In the afternoon, Co. A moved to a new position to support the Rangers and the 2nd Platoon eliminated two or three machine gun nests and an ammo dump. Tanks also arrived and attracted enemy fire but advanced to a point where Co. A's shells were falling. The forward OP of Edwards and Hutchinson was forced to move at 2:00 p.m. and three minutes later their old position was leveled by enemy shells. At 5:00 p.m., the 2nd Platoon moved behind the 41st Armored Infantry beneath Mount della Lapa and knocked out an enemy 75mm gun with WP. By 5:30, the Italian artillery had been crushed. James Helsel graphically recalled that "... just before sundown, under the fire of the first platoon we moved ahead. It was here I got my first real glimpse of the horror of war, for passing over the field we just fired upon was too pitiful to describe, seeing an arm here, a leg there, later on a body minus a leg or arm. Men still not yet dead crying for water or a bloated blood stained body beyond recognition. I believe if it would have been American blood I would have passed out." The 2nd Platoon moved their mortars to the rear of the 41st Armored ready to give defensive support of Mount della Lapa while the 1st Platoon moved to a position to support the Rangers on Mount del Zai.[91]

The official history of Co. B said they "fired on enemy troops & tanks" on the 12th while the official history of Co. C stated they "moved from [*their*] initial position near the beach to the places where the 1st Platoon had installed its mortars ... things were quiet, except for one air attack in which two enemy planes were brought down." Capt. Burford noted that early in the morning a portion of the 2nd Platoon retrieved their mortars from the stream bed while another group recovered the mortar and cart which had been lost during the landing. Hale Hepler, among this latter group, said, "This gave us the opportunity to bathe in the wonderful waters of the Mediterranean plus wash our smelly clothes ... We found the mortar cart with the gun intact. The ammunition cart had already been taken on land. While we were bringing it across the beach we saw a ship unloading two new Caterpillar tractors. When they came off the ship, one tractor hit a land mine on the beach and blew off the tracks. We were walking alongside the second cat and it too hit a land mine and lost its tracks. I felt lucky to be alive after the close call of the landing craft and now two missed land mines on the beach." Afterwards, the 2nd Platoon joined the 1st on the eastern edge of Gela and, departing the building they had occupied on the beach, moved inland. Hale Hepler added, "That evening we marched out six miles up a valley and set up the guns and dug foxholes. The ground was so hard that you had to chop it out to make a safe place to stay."[92]

July 12—Co. D

July 12th was also a relatively quiet day for the 1st Platoon of Co. D as equipment was brought ashore and mortars went into positions; however, at about 7:00 a.m. the #1 gun of Co. D's 1st Platoon suffered a horrible tragedy when one of their shells hit a tree limb, fell back on them and exploded. Pvt. Edmund B. Rea and Pfc's James W. Ramsey and Frank J. Murphy were killed, while the wounded included S/Sgt. Edward D. Guinness, Pvt. Charles F. Ruff, Pvt. William W. Ridenour, Sgt. James J. Finore, Pvt. Verne E. Hiltz, Pvt. Earl F. Kann, Pvt. Joseph W. Mondok, and 2nd Lt. Samuel W. Miller. Earl F. Kann said he was hit in the leg, back, and foot by shrapnel and was sent back to North Africa and presented a Purple Heart. Reportedly, Lt. Miller was a novice officer with limited knowledge of mortars who insisted on placing the mortar near the tree against the advice of the experienced enlisted men. Obviously, the episode did not endear Miller to the men. Despite this, the 2nd and 3rd squads, located near the road, continued to fire throughout the day, while a tank battle 300 yards to the front along with heavy shelling caused the 4th, 5th, and 6th squads to leave their position with the 3rd Rangers and to move to that of the 2nd and 3rd squads, where the platoon would spend the night. The mobile infantry were able to attack and seize Niscemi and the 1st Platoon of Co. D was relieved and rejoined the battalion at Gela.[93]

The 2nd Platoon of Co. D had also been active near daybreak of the 12th as the 3rd Battalion, 16th Infantry, reinforced their 2nd Battalion in anticipation of an enemy counter-attack. The 2nd Platoon of Co. D advanced to cover the two infantry battalions but the enemy failed to counter-attack, although they were subjected to enemy artillery fire throughout the morning. The 3rd Battalion was flanked on the right by tanks, but two mortars, along with cannon and tanks, were turned to fire on them. The tanks were knocked out, even though the mortars failed to hit them, because they caused the tanks to move into a vulnerable position. Dan Shields, Co. D, wrote in his diary, "6:40 a.m. Caught it again. Caught in tank battle. Lay in ditch. Got out, dig in. Retired 10:10."[94]

Once again, Capt. Pike gave a detailed description of the action: "In the morning the day was begun properly with a German machine gun opening firing on us from the left flank again. One of the tank crews had gotten out of its tank with a machine gun and set up during the night. The machine gun and crew were taken care of that morning and

Co. D Motor Pool in Sicily. Top L-R: Lovell Shoults, Willie Tanner, James Dudley, George Worrall, & James Lester. Bottom L-R: Charlie Lowry (back turned), Arthur Bilton, Ernest Hooten, & Nevin Glossner.
Author's Collection

we settled down again doing a lot of firing and being on the receiving end of German 88's again. By noon American tanks had come up and also American artillery and [*a*] Cannon Company. About 2 o'clock more German tanks attempted a break through on our right flank but were knocked out by our tanks and artillery. We too did some firing on these tanks. By evening of this day the infantry had moved well forward and we moved forward with them and the successful campaign in Sicily was on the march."[95]

July 13–August 17

Throughout the night of July 12th and the early morning darkness of July 13th, the Ranger Task Force, facing stiff opposition, attempted to take the town of Butera. Companies A and B of the 83rd moved up from their positions around Gela ready to give fire support to the Rangers when called upon. James Helsel, Co. A, wrote, "We loaded our carts, took ammo, bed rolls, and started advancing by foot again, pulling the mortars. We were to support the Rangers in their attack on Butera … We got into position about 12:30, after a long, hard pull. I finished digging in about 4 o'clock in the morning. Still no flare, which was our signal to fire, so I went to bed."[96]

Capt. Burford, Co. C, said his men were bivouacked on the western edge of Gela near a huge spaghetti factory and had spent the night in nearby homes where they were devoured by fleas and lice. The company's CP was in an upper-story window of the factory. The body of a dead civilian, killed by the Rangers for sniping, had lain in the road nearby for three days, creating a foul odor, but it was finally removed by the Graves Registration people. Co. C proceeded to move to a position one and a half miles west of Gela. Capt. Burford continued, stating his company was attached to the 4th Rangers, under Capt. Roy A. Murray, and he was ordered to join them at Monte Lungo, a hill about five miles west of Gela. He further stated they arrived after dark via a column of carts and went into bivouac on the south slope of the hill, below the Ranger position. Co. B reported marching to Mount della Lapa and going into bivouac. However, the 1st Ranger Battalion went through Butera and the assistance of the mortar companies was not needed. During this time the 78th Armored Field Artillery Battalion had been added to the command although the entire Ranger Force had been detached from the 1st U.S. Infantry Division and attached to the 2nd Armored Division.[97]

During the afternoon of July 13th, the 1st Platoon of Co. D moved to a road to await transport to a position where they could give support to the advancing 1st Battalion, 16th Infantry. However, the infantry had already taken their objective, Niscemi, and the platoon moved to the previously occupied position of the 2nd Platoon of the company near Niscemi, where there was some night shelling. Having accomplished their mission, Co. D was detached from the 16th Infantry and ordered to report to Lt. Col. Cunin at the position previously occupied by Co. B on the western end of Gela. After requesting three trucks for transportation, Co. D arrived on the western side of Gela during the early morning of July 14th. Companies C and D then joined together and moved via truck to a bivouac about 15 miles north of Gela and about two miles south of Butera, a town Capt. Pike called "old, smelly, and filthy." They were to be held as a reserve for the Rangers, who were then striking the enemy strong points along the highway and the hills to the north of town. Co. C noted no transportation had been provided for them; therefore, the 4th Rangers had to shuttle them and their equipment by truck to Butera. Throughout the trip they witnessed evidence of the effectiveness of their mortars and the heavy guns of the cruiser *Savannah*. At one point during the day Capt. Burford, jeep driver Earl Shaddinger, radio operator Roy Carroll and Angelo Simone, all of Co. C, along with Capt. Roy Murray of the Rangers, made a reconnaissance to Butera and back to Monte Lungo, during which time the jeep had a flat tire and the group experienced a number of other inconveniences.[98]

According to James Helsel of Co. A, "After eating we started advancing again, and again by foot. The march was long and hard, most of it up hill, for Butera set high on a hill and the road sure was twisted. We could see along the road that the enemy was on the run. Most of the men were shot in the back and every little bridge or culvert was blown up. Just at the foot of the hill was a Dago gun position with a direct hit. It sure was a horrible sight and I never smelled anything any worse than this, I was forced to hold my nose. We got into Butera and found that they lost contact with the enemy, so we pulled back to an olive grove to await further orders and of all places, right next to that Dago gun position. I hope the wind blows the right way." [99]

The day was not without casualties for the 83rd Chemical Battalion, however, as Pvt. Warren R. Norris and Pvt. Harry W. Woodin, Jr., both of Co. C, were injured when they fell into a tank trap. In addition, Pvt. Chester Lynch, Co. D, was treated for shell shock. Co. B reported moving through Butera and bivouacked below the west side of town. The mission of the Ranger Task Force had been accomplished by the fall of Butera and as a result the force was dissolved.[100]

In their bivouac near Butera, the 83rd initiated a program of reorganization of personnel and repair of equipment on the 15th, at which time the mess trucks of companies A, B, and C and the battalion motor maintenance arrived from the rear. In addition, the battalion's ammo, gas, and ration dumps were established in the area. Co. C complained about the scarcity of water, and of fleas nearly as bad as at Gela. On July 16th, the 83rd was attached to the 82nd Airborne Division and, as the CP at Butera closed on the 17th, moved west to link up with the paratroopers. James Helsel wrote in his diary: "Had a paratrooper scare, but it turned out that 'Pop' Bush [*probably William Bush*], the Captain's orderly, was just drunk." Co. B moved to a bivouac three miles south of Agrigento and Co. C traveled via truck several miles west of Palma. Co. B also managed to haul in 11 prisoners. Capt. Burford, Co. C, recalled, "We left Butera at 0700 hours, motored back to Gela, then turned eastward, toward Licata. We went through Licata and stopped just outside of Palma. Company C led the convoy and, upon arriving, sent the trucks back to pick up the other companies." Co. D moved by truck to an area adjacent to Co. B on the 18th and in the afternoon the two companies advanced on foot, pulling their mortar carts some nine miles to a bivouac two miles west of Porto Empedocle, just outside Agrigento, to which point Co. A had advanced from Butera. "About 1:00 in the afternoon we loaded on trucks …," James Helsel of Co. A wrote. "I thought we had it made, moving by trucks, until we unloaded and started pulling them again. We got into an olive grove about 3:00 in the morning and laid down." At Palma Co. C managed to get two Italian priests to come to their camp to hold services for their Catholic members.[101]

At 3:00 a.m., July 19th, companies A and B, supporting the advance of the 82nd Airborne to the west, moved along the coastal road hauling their mortar and ammunition carts by hand except on the steep hills, where jeeps were used to pull them. The advance of the 82nd Airborne was so rapid the two mortar companies could not keep up, although they did march 16 miles in eight hours over mountainous terrain without one man falling out. Andrew Leech, Co. B, said, "We all had blisters on our feet and were so tired." Some men of Co. A got into a fight amongst themselves and told Capt. Edwards they refused to continue until trucks were brought to their assistance. At a point near Montallegro two German Messerschmidt 109s strafed Co. A without inflicting any casualties, then turned on Maj. William S. Hutchinson's jeep, which was carrying 'Hutch', Lt. Veryl R. Hays, Sgt. Robert B. Brimm, and Privates Ross J. Naccarato and John C. Fortune. Sgt. Brimm fired at the two planes with his tommy gun while Lt. Hays, taking cover, was injured when the jeep ran over his foot. Realizing they could not keep pace with the paratroopers of the 82nd, the two companies bivouacked at Montallegro, while Co. C departed Palma and moved via truck to Porto Empedocle. Co. D remained near Porto Empedocle where morale was reported as good.[102]

It was at Porto Empedocle on the 19th that battalion commander Cunin again made a spectacle of himself, according to Capt. Burford. The men of Co. C were able to acquire a cow and, with the assistance of Mess Sgt. Thomas A. Cute from Steuben County, New York, who provided onions and potatoes, were able to have a steak dinner. But, "… while the mess line was forming he [*Cunin*] proceeded to take a bath nearby, cleaned his feet, and urinated within 50 feet of the mess area; some of the NCO's asked me later how they were expected to enforce sanitation discipline when he set such an example. He also hung aloof while everybody else got in line for the steak and was too late to get a steak after he found that nobody was going to wait on him. He raised a squawk at having to eat liver, so in order to avoid friction Ralph Rankin gave up his steak to Cunin and ate liver instead."[103]

By this time many of the 83rd were furious with Cunin, particularly his subordinate officers, who claimed he spent all of his time with the 82nd Airborne, with William S. Hutchinson serving as liaison between the battalion and Dave Meyerson, who had been left behind at Gela to catch the battalion's follow-up vehicles as they arrived. Capt. Burford said, "We hear some tall tales of Meyerson's existence in Gela, and knowing him as I do I know Dave is making himself comfortable. Sgt. [*Edward T.*] Dundon made the remark that he intended to write his Congressman about the Bn. Commander and Executive running up and down the island trying to find a war for us to get into."[104]

On the 20th, Co. A bivouacked at Montallegro and companies C and D were at Porto Empedocle. Pvt. Polk A. Carter, Co. D, was slightly wounded when a rocket launcher blew up during a test firing. Co. B advanced by truck north of Ribera in the morning, a distance of 21 miles, and then covered an additional 24 miles in the afternoon to the enemy strong point between Sciacca and Santa Margherita. Although most of the Italian soldiers had already fled the area, a few snipers were left behind who attempted to blow up the 83rd's transportation by electrically detonating a mine field. However, only a civilian cart was in the field at the time, which was destroyed, killing two civilians. Co. B took out any further resistance by placing several rounds of HE on some enemy pill-boxes. The following day Co. B moved up to a position three miles east of Santa Margherita where they emplaced their mortars to protect the line of the Fiume Belice. The company did snag three prisoners whom they turned over to the 82nd Airborne. Co. D remained at Porto Empedocle where the weather was reported as fine, morale was good, and Pvt. Michael W. Walsh was sent to the hospital with a broken leg.[105]

Companies C and D advanced by truck from Port Empedocle to Santa Margherita on July 22nd, where they dug in, and Capt. Pike said Co. D took four prisoners. Capt. Burford claimed his men remained on alert, ready to move on ten minutes notice. Co. A moved in the direction of Santa Margherita to a point near Montallegro. Co. B bivouacked at Montavago, where their rear echelon caught up with them, and then came under fire on the 23rd as they moved by truck to Trapani to support the 505th Combat Team. Ed Trey recalled that prior to the fight for the important air and harbor facilities of Trapani he and Gen. Ridgway of the 82nd Airborne were walking toward the town when an enemy shell landed and exploded nearby, prompting both to hug the ground. Ridgway then

Group of Co. D 83rd CMB soldiers in Sicily.
L-R: Unidentified, Ralph A. Goins, Byron H. Jordan and Jack Pimento; front: Joseph Kulick.
Byron Jordan

told Trey to go up on a hill and see what it was all about, to which Trey responded, "Who, me?" Soon after emplacing their mortars in an orchard, Co. B fired three or four rounds during a two to three hour engagement with the enemy. T/5 Michael J. Kelley and Pfc. Johnny Goodwin, Jr., " ... distinguished themselves by shuttling the company through heavy artillery and small arms fire in their jeeps for a distance of two thousand yards, each ... making several trips." Capt. Gordon Mindrum suffered a slight leg wound in the action.[106]

Andrew C. Leech, Co. B, recalled the fight at Trapani, writing, "As we advanced our convoy to the outskirts of Trapani the Germans opened fire on us from pillboxes and artillery pieces on the side of the mountain. We stopped the convoy, unloaded our equipment and set up and went into action. We had some 75's and 105's behind us so an artillery duel took place which lasted about two hours with our artillery gradually taking the initiative ... We moved on up into the airport and had a little small arms battle before they surrendered. We slept in the airport that night ..." Karl F. Garrett, HQ Co., recalled that while at Trapani "We had a bunch of meat eaters in our unit ... One ... day we were outside ... of Trapani. We saw a bull or cow or something that looked edible in a field. Several guys went over to liberate the animal. The farmer came running out yelling in Italian. One of the men took out a piece of paper, wrote on it - 'I.O.U. for 1 bull, signed U.S. Army'. The farmer seemed satisfied, so the bull was shot then and there. A weapons carrier towed the bull away and most of us had a bit of steak that night."[107]

Companies A, C, and D moved up on the 24th via truck from Santa Margherita to a location about two miles northwest of Castellammare del Golfo. Recalling the movement, James Helsel, Co. A, wrote, "Again we loaded up trucks to move up. This is the way to fight a war. At least we are riding. I was beginning to think they might even make us walk to our grave." Capt. Burford said Co. C bivouacked " ... at the foot of a high mountain on a bluff overlooking the sea." He added that all of his company's recent moves had been purely administrative and they were just following the front without doing any fighting.[108]

On the 25th, Lt. James Beasley, Co. D, observed that "This country is very hilly, and it is now dry and brown except for olive and almond orchards and an occasional field of cotton. There are also a number of vineyards with the grapes just getting ripe. The almonds are mature but not dry; they taste good however. In some places there are

James G. Helsel of Co. A on
August 19, 1943, in Sicily.
Joyce Berry

watermelons, cantaloupes and tomatoes. We are now bivouacked on a hill that slopes steeply down to the sea about five hundred yards in front of us." They remained at Castellammare four days, occasionally going for a swim in the sea.[109]

Co. B left the Trapani airport on the 26th and also went into bivouac at Castellammare. At these locations the companies trained as well as repaired and replaced equipment, and endured a windy rain storm on the 27th. Michael Rebick, Co. D, wrote that "the people here sure do like us, like the other day there were three of us went out on a little walk & the first thing we knew we were invited in for a spaghetti dinner & then to top the meal off we killed a gallon of wine and don't think we didn't sleep good that evening."[110]

Several of the men reflected on the Sicilian Campaign at this time. According to Rebick, " ... we hit the beach ... plenty fast & strong & we push[ed] our way for four days & nights & meeting a lot of opposition we saw them die and seen them injured but at the end we were way ahead for boy our tanks were starting to come in & boy I give my thanks to them for I think they are the ones that saved my neck. And once you asked me why we had to dig a trench ... when them bombs start[ed] hitting there [sic] target there is nothing better than [being] between the earth ..." Capt. Robert E. Edwards, Co. A, noted that *Life* magazine photographers had been present: "Supposed to have taken pictures of one of our platoon positions, also again out on the road which should have Tom [*Thomas Bolton*] in it. We have taken fire now and have passed the hardest test. Willie [*William S. Doughten, Jr.*] is no longer with us - land mine. Ole Man above has got his eye on us." On a lighter note, Michael Rebick recalled that "first fun came one afternoon when we were still going on our march, we came across a watermelon patch and don't you think we didn't make a dash for them even though we were tired as hell ... my two pals and I sat down and ate 9 of them ... "[111]

Lt. James Beasley described the campaign as "a sight-seeing trip at government expense ... I did not feel that every artillery shell that came down was going to land on me. The closest thing that came to me was a machine gun bullet that went through my rifle stock. That was an absurd, and now funny, situation ... There are all kinds of absurdities in this invasion. During the last few days there have been many Italian soldiers in the towns and along the roads waiting to be captured. Yesterday we passed many of them and did not bother with stopping. Sometimes they would salute us and the men would give them cigarettes. They would probably be good soldiers if they just had something for which to fight ... "[112]

The battalion moved to a new bivouac two miles south of Salemi on July 28th, where they remained until August 2nd, continuing to train, re-equip, repair, and also furnish transportation for the 504th Combat Team. At this location Lt. Eric H. ("Pete") Peterson, Jr., along with four new replacements and the remainder of the company's rear echelon, joined up with Co. A.

On July 31st, Lt. Beasley, Co. D, wrote home that "Supplies enough have arrived that I now have a complete change of clothing. Until this week it was necessary to wash the clothes and put them on wet or take a sun bath until they were dry. My things were in four separate lots for the invasion. The bed roll and canvas bag that reached the island were lost, and the blanket roll never landed, my blouse and overcoat, and light pants are stored somewhere in North Africa."[113]

The period at Salemi was not pleasant to many of the 83rd, however. According to Capt. Burford, "It was here that Cunin began to collect his personal staff, starting out in a modest way with a valet, a cook, and an interpreter. Of course he already had a chauffeur ... While here the 82nd Division turned us into a QM truck battalion. They commandeered our trucks, ordered them for all hours of the day and night, kept them for days at a time, and allowed no time for maintenance to the vehicles. They permitted the drivers no chance for rest, and stripped everything from the trucks that wasn't bolted on. They also felt insulted if <u>we</u> wanted to use the trucks for our own needs such as hauling rations, water or supplies. To add insult to injury the men from the 504th Paratroop Regiment committed several breaches of discipline in Salemi such as robbing civilians, breaking and entering houses, and shooting a priest; these were blamed on our men with the result that the towns were all placed off limits … especially to us."[114]

To make matters worse, while at Salemi a malaria epidemic broke out, attributed to the bite of sand fleas, and the men were ordered to remain in camp. Many of them were sent to the 120th Collecting Battalion and the 56th Medical, Trapani, for treatment. The overall medical situation in Sicily for the 120th Medical Battalion alone was clearly illustrated in their unit history, which stated, "The Second Platoon of the Clearing Company was finding diseased patients (malarial fever and dysentery) outnumbering battle casualties for the first time." According to that report, describing the 83rd as well as all troops in Sicily, 1,732 of 2,856 patients admitted by the 1st and 2nd platoons over a 37-day period were suffering from disease. Fortunately, on August 1st the health restrictions on the 83rd were lifted and the men were permitted to visit Salemi.[115]

On August 1st, James G. Helsel, Co. A, "Received a pass and went into Salemi. Not much of a time. Two of the boys had a time, [*Michael*] Kenyock & [*Reatus M.*] Graham, two from our squad, came back under arrest. They got drunk & shot a few radios and the bell in the steeple … Three extra medics have been added, quite a number in the hospital. Sgt. [*Robert S.*] Taylor, the ammo Sgt., went with 105 temperature." For James Beasley, August 1st was "just another day of hard army life. Breakfast at eight, then about three hours of censoring letters with blankets folded at my back to substitute for an easy chair. After lunch I took a helmet bath and washed some clothes. A sergeant and I spent some time discussing invasion tactics. As yet neither the British or Americans have requested our advice. My olive trees are conveniently arranged. I sit in one place all day [*long*] get about an hours sun. In most other places it was necessary to move about every half hour to stay in the shade. I got to sleep at dark and sleep until after sun up. Sleeping on the ground does not bother me at all."[116]

The remainder of the rear echelon arrived from North Africa on the 2nd, bringing four officers and 30 enlisted men as replacements, who were divided among the companies. Byron H. Jordan of Georgia was apparently among this group, although he later thought the group consisted of as many as 50 replacements.[117]

Companies B and C departed Salemi on August 3rd to go to an area two miles west of Termini Imerese, where they were attached to the 157th Infantry, 45th Infantry Division, to prepare for an amphibious operation to cut off the German retreat at Messina. Capt. "Bud" Pike, acting battalion commander in the absence of Cunin and Hutchinson, gave the order. After recalling as many of their trucks as possible from the 504th, the two companies took the coastal road through Palermo and arrived at their destination, only to find Cunin already there "bitching" about them being late. At this point Capt. Burford displayed his disgust for Cunin, writing, "Cunin is rapidly losing 'face' with his officers and men. His living with the Rangers

William C. Ford, Co. C, with German flag. Mt. Etna can be seen in the background.
William Ford

in Africa may have been called for by his position as Executive of the Force, but that should not have precluded his visiting the battalion occasionally, seeing that they got the best of everything that was possible. His constant attitude of destructive criticism and abuse towards his officers, his failure to promote deserving ones to their full T/O rank, created very poor morale among them which was reflected in their attitude toward him and in the attitude of the men. Perhaps he realizes this and doesn't particularly care, or he may be too much of an egotist to even appreciate what he is doing to the esprit de corps of his unit. His attitude toward the life of his men was especially deplorable. I once heard him remark that if he killed a man in training it was all right by him. His constant failure to commend individuals for outstanding work, but to emphasize trivial errors and threaten court-martial for those errors was a matter of common talk even among the men."[118]

Lt. Leonard A. ("Spike") Merrill, HQ Co., wrote from Agrigento on the 4th, "… [*I*] just had another Mediterranean cruise and am now sightseeing in Sicily." Karl F. Garrett, HQ Co. also recalled that near Agrigento he lost the high school ring his mother had given him upon his graduation. In the meantime, the battalion trucks moved the 504th Combat Team to Castelvetrano on the 5th, followed the next day by Co. D and HQ Co. Harold Hughes, Co. D, summed up the morbid sight of the enemy casualties of war during the movement from Gela to a cool orchard at Castelvetrano, writing, "… a wave of horror swept the long line of men ahead of us. I could smell it before I saw it, the sickly sweet odor of decaying flesh … we marched for hours through smoldering columns of blackened tanks, scout cars and trucks filled with fly-covered masses of putrefying flesh, uniforms bloated to a paper smoothness. We tied handkerchiefs around our faces, but couldn't stem the nausea." Co. D would remain at Castelvetrano until September 7th training, performing usual duties, and policing the area. Capt. Pike said in his diary the company "policed the town." Co. A moved to Mazara del Vallo where they were assigned to police the city in action with the CIC [*Counter Intelligence Corps*] and AMGOT [*Allied Military Government for Occupied Territories*].[119]

On the 6th, James Helsel, Co. A, wrote, "The Company, with the exception of Co. HQ and a few guards moved by truck, we stayed, and listened to an Italian boy about 10 years old sing. It was very impressive, a full moon and his voice could be heard very clear. The Captain got him to sing 'Ave Maria', 'O Sole Mio'. It was late before I went to sleep." On the 7th Helsel added, "The trucks came early and we loaded up the bed rolls & other equipment and motored to Mazara del Vallo and joined the rest of the company. They were set up in a creamery. Our squad had outside the creamery, but the floor was smooth & we had a wall around us." Further details were added by Charles Rolling, also of Co. A, who wrote, "HQ joined the company at 'Mazara', in a creamery which we were preparing to occupy. Here we had a fair set up. Building was nice - white side walls and tile floors. We had private wash-women. A sick-bay was provided for our malaria patients. A guard was established in town, where we were in complete charge of things … City hall building made us a good head quarters. In a couple days we moved into a modern building located in the center of town. With a couple of large rooms at our disposal, we lived quite comfortably … Here in 'Mazara' we secured grain from other towns to feed the people. Several raids were made to find hoarded mdse., food and military equipment. Ammo dumps were located, reported and disposed of. Black marketing and prices were checked. Swimming, fishing and eating ice-cream and cake were favorite past times of most of the men. Guard detail included patrol duty on a fishing boat. Vitto our best Italian worker shared our daily reveille and calisthenics with us and helped in the kitchen the remains of the day. Shave and a hair cut cost six cents. Received our first Allied Military currency here. Jewelry shops did a bang up business and could Capt. Edwards keep prices down. We will always remember 'Mazara.'"[120]

At Castelvetrano on the 7th, "Captain [*Pike*] and I [*Lt. James Beasley*] went in town to see an American movie 'Magnificent Obsession.' It was the original movie but the speech had been changed to Italian. I had never seen the picture and could not get anything out of it … It is almost dark so the bed must be made. First take a shovel and make a place in the ground somewhat like a hammock but much shallower. If it is not made properly it is worse than level ground. Second, spread a shelter half over it, third fold two blankets lengthwise and put them on the shelter half; fourth dust insect powder around the edges. To prepare to go to bed all I do is take my shoes off. I sleep between the folds of the blanket which gives three thicknesses of blankets underneath. It is comfortable sleeping and it will be difficult to get used to only 8 hours again.'"[121]

The somewhat equally tranquil period for Co. D at Castelvetrano was further described by Capt. Pike, who wrote on the 8th, "Sunday is a lazy day in these parts. We have a late breakfast, 0800 hours, and then there usually is a Catholic mass and a Protestant service for those who care to attend … Then comes the relaxation period before dinner. The entire afternoon is a siesta period. Comes a light supper, more relaxation and then on to bed and pleasant dreams. As Rup Burford says our training schedule for Sunday is, sleep at night and rest during the day. This morning I got up about eight, ate a breakfast of bacon, cereal, stewed apricots, and hot coffee and hard tack. We also received our daily ration of cigarettes, Luckies. We are issued a package a day at one of the meals and we are also issued a pack of candy every day." The Catholics in Co. D were permitted to attend Mass in a very old church in Castelvetrano built in 1500. Pike continued: "Just think, that was only 8 years after the discovery of America. In this church there is also a small museum which was begun in 1620 and which has been closed for the last 50 years. They are planning to open the museum to the public as soon as possible. The church itself was damaged slightly by bombing." Lt. Beasley added, "There is a touch of fall in the air these mornings. There has been no rain, but the rainy season is supposed to start later this month. This is Sunday morning so we were allowed to sleep another hour which was easy to do since it was just cool enough to make one want to stay under a blanket." Another member of Co. D, Michael Rebick, sat under an olive tree in the hot weather and wrote home reflecting upon his time in Africa, stating, " … it was no place to talk about for it was really a dirty place with all the diseases you could ever think of …" On a more light hearted note Lt. James Beasley added, "There is an epidemic in the company now of men trying to learn to play accordions. They have two and they are making noise from sun up until midnight."[122]

James Helsel, Co. A, wrote from Mazara on the 9th that "… the company moved into a large school house just around the corner from the courthouse, which was in the center of town. We were given charge of the town, under Mayor Hilderbard… Our Captain was Chief of Police. We were to secure grain and other foods that was stored away and give to those who had none, in other words crack down on the black market. We kept prices down, made raids. The school house was a good home. A kitchen was set up. Showers installed. Each squad had a room. The floor was hard to sleep on, but it was clean."[123]

Lt. Beasley, Co. D, was concerned about the management of his men during training. "The biggest problem is to tell when there is something wrong with a man physically or if he is just trying to get out of something. Before this men were commenting to me that Captain Pike was being too hard on them … yesterday one went to Captain Pike and said I was being too hard on him. He did not get any sympathy … We have been having some fun this week. I have a group of about twenty five each day to train. We will start out from camp and go across country three or four miles and then I will pick out some … lazier men and also one who gripes most about things not being done right to lead us back to camp. One of the men said he did not think he could ever live down his leading… Yesterday did not work so well the leader got lost and we walked about five extra miles. It is a problem to keep interesting training schedules now."[124]

In another letter, Lt. Beasley added, "We are not allowed to wear cotton pants here but short cotton pants are permitted so this morning I took a razor blade and shortened a pair of regular pants. They look terrible but they are cooler than woolen clothes. Captain Pike … then altered a pair of his cotton trousers." In a separate letter he wrote, "We are having a very easy time now with a light training schedule, but it is getting tiresome. I would like to be doing what must be done so the end would come more quickly. I realize, however, that proper planning and preparation are necessary to insure success and to take fewer lives." George R. Borkhuis, Co. D cook, composed a letter using grape juice as he ran out of ink, in which he stated, "The weather is quite warm but a cool breeze tends to keep it comfortable … we have bathing facilities nearby and cool off if we wish."[125]

For the next eight days Co. A continued to police Mazara del Vallo. HQ Co. and Co. D trained, and companies B and C prepared for an amphibious assault with the objective of landing behind enemy lines at the coastal town of Castroreale and to hold the area until contact was made with the 3rd U.S. Infantry Division. But the enemy withdrew so rapidly that the 3rd Infantry had already taken the town before the landing was completed; therefore, a new landing site for the invasion was selected at Spodofora, where Co. B would directly support the combat and Co. C would be held in reserve. This planned invasion was stalled on August 13th when it was found there was not enough mortar ammo in the 7th Army dump, so Lt. Ralph Rankin, Co. C, led a convoy of 10 trucks each from companies A and B to Gela, the nearest supply depot, and back. Cunin gave a pep talk to the men which consisted of the statement, "Well, keep your noses clean, and I hope <u>most</u> of you come back."[126]

On August 15th, Co. B placed one platoon each on *LCI 24* and *LCI 210* at San Stefano and the 3rd Platoon on *LCI 215* at Termini Imerese. Co. C also loaded up at Termini Imerese on *LCI 209*. Capt. Burford said the LCIs were

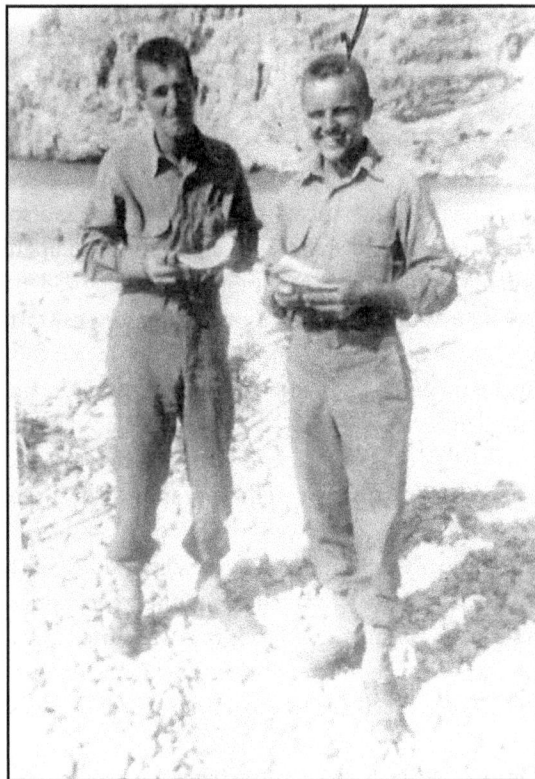

Kenneth Laundre, left, and Stephen Vukson, right, eating cantaloupe in Sicily.
Stephen Vukson

docked in an awkward manner; therefore, all of the infantry had to board before realigning the LCIs to accommodate proper loading of the mortars and carts. As a result, the mortar men of the 83rd were the last to load and were very tired from the long wait. Upon sailing, three German planes dropped bombs on the convoy but there were no casualties as no direct hits were made. At about 6:00 in the evening, word was received that the rapidly advancing American infantry had already taken Spodofora so it was decided to land at the original beach at Castroreale, where companies B and C debarked on the 18th into a heavily mined beach near Falconi that was in friendly hands. The engineers cleared a path through the minefield and the two companies moved about one mile inland and bivouacked. Capt. Burford recalled, "So at 0130 hours we landed at Castroreale. It was a bright moonlit night and would have been a massacre if it had been a real invasion. The ships were able to land in close and we didn't get wet as at Gela. I got in touch with the staff and received orders to go to a certain spot and put up for the night, so I guided the company there and we all went to sleep, except for guards posted for security … then ensued three days of misery." Burford said their K-rations had been tainted by gasoline and were inedible, water was limited to drinking only, and they were restricted from going into town. He did, however, note that from a high vantage point in camp he could see the volcano Mt. Etna in the far distance. In spite of all these handicaps, their services would not be needed as Messina fell to American troops on August 17th, ending the fighting in Sicily.[127]

During the Sicilian Campaign, the 83rd Chemical Battalion suffered at least six killed, 28 wounded, one accidental wound, one injury, one shell shock, and one missing in action, for a total loss of 38. Undoubtedly many other injuries were not reported. At the conclusion of the campaign, the battalion strength entailed 36 officers and 793 enlisted men, for a total strength of 829. Lt. James O. Beasley, Co. D, summed up his personal feelings about the campaign as he wrote, "From the accounts different men are telling I certainly missed a lot during the fighting. One lieutenant says at one time fifty more tanks than anyone else has ever reported on the island attacked their position. He was in the observation post and saw them. I am evidently almost blind and deaf for there are numerous accounts of many more enemy planes and bombs than I saw or heard. Just wait ten years and then hear the eyewitness accounts. According to some of the men it was the hardest battle of the war, but there were no men from Bataan, Guadalcanal or Stalingrad to compare the battles. It was a good training exercise anyway."[128]

The chemical mortar battalions won high praise in the Sicilian Campaign as evidenced by a report filed later that year in which various infantry officers expressed their opinions. A captain in the 179th Infantry claimed, "The chemical mortar is simply grand … they are accurate as the devil up to 3000 yards and more, and they pack a punch worth two 81mm's … A German prisoner we got referred to them as 'automatic artillery'. You can fire them at terrific speed…" A lieutenant colonel of the same regiment thought it "a magnificent and extraordinarily effective weapon" and noted that it was "most effective with white phosphorous and H.E." He added, "The Germans are very allergic to white phosphorous anyway. We would root them out of their holes with well placed rounds of phosphorous, and when [we] had them above ground, we plastered them with H.E. We killed large numbers of them in that way, and they sure dreaded the mortars." Further support was given by a lieutenant colonel of the 180th Infantry, who boasted, "The 4.2" chemical mortars are marvelous weapons … The Germans are deathly afraid of them and the prisoners told us they thought they were some kind of new secret weapon like an automatic cannon … the 4.2" is the most effective single weapon used in support of infantry I have ever seen." A lieutenant colonel of the 157th joined in the praise, adding, "The Germans fear and hate white phosphorous, especially when you deal it out to them with the 4.2" chemical mortar … the 4.2″ was one of the most powerful and effective weapons we had with us. The chemical troops did a grand job …" A captain in the 180th Infantry added, "I think it is one of the finest weapons in existence … Their effect on the Germans was tremendous. They feared them more than anything else, except our massed artillery barrages. Especially the Germans hated the WP the chemical troops rained on them. One German prisoner who spoke English is reported to have asked, 'What the hell was that new weapon that had the effect of medium artillery that blew us out of our foxholes no matter where we were and burned our tails off at the same time.' Other prisoners thought that it was another new secret cannon that fired like an automatic ack-ack gun …" Finally, a colonel of the 180th Infantry reported that letters taken from German prisoners confirmed the enemy fear of the weapon and added, "from these mortars, our fire power with the projectile was tremendous." Nearly all of the officers concurred, however, that a truck with an attached trailer should be used with the mortars for faster and more convenient transportation.[129]

In September Lt. Col. Kenneth Cunin would file a detailed report on lessons learned by the chemical mortar battalions in Sicily. He boasted "… the 4.2″ mortars have already established for themselves an excellent reputation with the units with which we have worked. The Infantry loves them; the Rangers love them; the Field Artillery thinks highly of them … the WP and HE shell have proved themselves many times over. The prevalent opinion now among the arms is that there should be some of these mortars in each division." Subjects approached were improvement of the transportation of the mortars; increasing the range; prior use of WP and HE equally for casualty effect, as the WP is so effective the Germans called the mortars "Lightning Guns"; emphasis on training and fitness; conduct of fire, gunnery; shooting classes; and material, particularly an improved sight for the mortars.[130]

On August 18th, Michael J. Rebick, Co. D, confirmed Lt. Beasley's condemnation earlier in the month of the motion pictures typically presented to the men, writing, "Our quarters are not far from a pretty large size town and there we go and have a little fun. They even have a theater here but all the words are spoken in Italian so there is not much use of … going there cause I am a Russian [descent]."[131]

Co. B, less three squads, and Co. C embarked on *LCI 33* on the 19th and moved to Palermo, and then bivouacked near Termini Imerese shortly after midnight. This episode gave Capt. Burford another opportunity to justifiably vent as he said they had to march to a beach located two miles away from the original landing beach. Upon arrival the S-3 of the 157th Infantry had failed to inform someone there were two full mortar companies to be transported. The inevitable result was that 350 men, with the mortar equipment of both companies, loaded onto *LCI 33* and caused it to beach. It took three hours to extricate the ship with the assistance of two other LCIs. By this time the men were tired, fearful of an air attack, and disgusted. But the situation only got worse as the S-3 of the 157th landed them at Palermo instead of Termini Imerese, where no arrangements had been made to either feed the men or transport them back to Termini. Lt. Alvin G. Metcalfe volunteered to go get the trucks and finally arrived with the convoy at Palermo after a six-hour delay. Capt. Burford later discovered the delay was caused by " … the trucks having been alerted for use by the 157th and were standing under orders for use by them. So not only had the 157th neglected to provide for us, but they wanted to prevent us from using our own transportation." The men finally arrived back at camp in the early morning hours of the 20th, only to find that during their absence a personal war had broken out between the mess and the drivers. The other three squads of Co. B arrived at Termini Imerese via trucks which hauled the company's mortars and equipment.[132]

Recalling this episode, Andrew C. Leech, Co. B, wrote, " … we loaded back on our ships and started back westward down the coastline to Termini from whence we had departed … We experienced an air raid during which several bombs splashed down near some of our ships, but no damaged resulted. We arrived back at Palermo and unloaded. We marched down the street with full packs and stopped to wait for our trucks to come and pick us up. We were so tired we just sprawled out on the sidewalks with our full field packs and slept until past midnight when our trucks arrived and carried us back to our area."[133]

At this time Capt. Pike, Co. D, gave his views on some battalion friends and the locale of his company. "Bill Hutchinson is now a Major … Whiskey Red [*Christopher C. Cornett, Jr.*] is staying drunk on the native wines as he did on Scotch at Camp Gordon. And things are about as harmonious as they were before…" He continued, "now that peace has descended on this island I have been swimming in the Mediterranean, from Sicilian shores and I like it better here than in Africa. The people are more friendly and there are an awful lot who have been in the States." Lt. Beasley added, "We are still camped in an olive orchard and the grapes, almonds, figs and melons are now ripe. The vineyards here are as common as cotton fields at home, but I think they have to be picked before they are good to eat. We have had good rations here, but it is good to get some things fresh. Then when we go hiking we have grapes and almonds in that period. We hike just enough to keep in good physical condition … It is still very dry here and it is about as hot as it is at home. It always gets cold at night because we are close to the sea. We can go swimming any time we want to go."[134]

Word was also received on the 20th that the battalion was detached from the 82nd Airborne Division and attached to the 3rd U.S. Infantry Division. More concerned with military discipline, Lt. James Beasley, Co. D, wrote, "Part of my evening work is done. It was inspecting latrines I had men digging for failing to make a formation on time. They were given special warning to be on time but five of them came a few minutes late. We now have three new latrines. I have had charge of some men that are attached to us from another company – they were a spoiled bunch and would gripe about everything they were told to do the least thing and would use all the ruses such as going on sick call to get out of a short hike. If they went on hikes they would drop behind … To start with four of them had to dig a sizable latrine for being behind on a hike. One started arguing that it was entirely too severe punishment. I was well fed up with them because I had let them off for something else just the day before with a reprimand. When the fellow started arguing I suddenly lost my temper and shocked one of our own sergeants. The latrines were dug with no further argument. The next day or two I had more latrines dug and restricted the men from having passes for the least infraction of rules. If they went on a sick call they were mocked … they had to dig latrines. The turnout for hikes is now very good, and they keep up. There are no arguments when they are told to do something. Probably tomorrow the whole bunch will do something worse than they have ever done and I will learn not to brag. One remarked the other day that I never joke. One of our sergeants said he 'felt sorry for my family'. It seems that the most important thing with men is that they are all treated equally and no favoritism is shown."[135]

On the 21st, Beasley and Capt. Pike "went to visit an airfield that had been used by the Germans. There were two or three million dollars worth of destroyed planes around it. There were nearly all types of German planes and some Italian. Pike saw some ammunition he wanted for a souvenir and wondered whether it was booby trapped." Beasley said, "I assured him it was not but when he started to pick it up I said 'wait until I get out of the way.' He did not pick it up. Most of the roads and beaches were mined but they are cleared by engineers before we use them."[136]

During this time, Capt. "Bud" Pike wrote an extended account of Co. D's period of relaxation. "Yesterday I took the entire company on a hike down to the beach. We arrived at the beach tired, hungry, thirsty, and sweaty so first of all we undressed and went for a dip in ye olde Mediterranean. Very refreshing. Then we went down the beach a way and participated in a fish fry accompanied by native Italian bread and wine. Also very refreshing. After that we sat around on the sand taking life easy. While we were sitting there a boat came gliding up filled with young Italian

Pfc. Edward J. Sutlic, from Pittsburgh, PA drowned August 23, 1944 at Castelveltrano, Sicily, reportedly the first death in the war for Co. C.
Molino Oros

men and women all singing. One man in the boat was playing an accordion in accompaniment to the music. They were singing beautiful old Italian love songs and all of them had fine voices and the accordionist was excellent. It was like something out of the movies and was very nice. When they saw us they brought the boat up on the beach and sang some more. Some of the men told them that I was 'el Capitano.' Immediately they had to sing a special love song for 'el Capitano' and I was hoping you could feel it in your heart as they sang. When we left we gave them all a lot of cigarettes for which they were very grateful. The Italians love to sing and their songs are very beautiful. They all are singing more freely now that the war is over for them. Lucky people. I envy them … It so happens that one of the men in the company [*James I. Bellomo*], an Italian, has several relatives living here in Sicily and his cousin lives in a town near our bivouac area. He is a fisherman and he provided the fish and bread and wine for our siesta on the beach. He is just bubbling over with pride about having his Americano cousin as a soldier in the U.S. Army … Please don't get the idea that we're having a good time all of the time."[137]

Karl F. Garrett, HQ Co. later remembered very different experiences in Sicily: "My memories of Sicily were the intense heat, dust, flies, marching, the starving civilians, and the grapes and peaches. Scarcity of water was always a problem … Food was a constant concern. We had plenty of it, but it was so monotonous - canned beans, spam, pork and eggs and hard tack …I vividly recall the starving children -- distended stomachs, hollow eyes, and sad, sad faces. They were everywhere begging for food. When we were in rest areas, we had to fence the area to keep them out. Even then they hung on the fences holding out their hands. It was difficult to swallow our food when this was going on. Many of us filled our mess kits and just handed it to them. They all carried little sand buckets to put the food in."[138]

Companies B and C were relieved of attachment to the 45th Infantry Division and rejoined the battalion via motor convoy at Castelvetrano on the 22nd. Capt. Burford, Co. C, said they got the order to move to Castelvetrano late in the evening of the 21st and were to leave before daylight. But Burford and McEvoy decided to wait until after breakfast. Burford noted, "We could have been court-martialed for this disobedience, but as far as we could see we were being relieved from our attachment to the 45th so the move was just administrative. Co. B preceded us by one-half hour, and we left Termini at 0830." During the drive through Palermo, Burford, Metcalfe, and McKinnon all got lost but eventually found their way to Castelvetrano, where Cunin told them they had two days to rest before resuming training.[139]

From August 23rd through August 31st, the 83rd Chemical Battalion, bivouacked at Castelvetrano, policed areas to the east such as Menfi and Marinella, patrolling and guarding enemy equipment. A tragedy occurred at Castelvetrano on the 23rd when Pfc. Edward J. Sutlic, Co. C, of Pittsburgh, Pennsylvania, drowned, the first death in the war for Co. C. His buddy, Loy Marshall, remembered, "Sutlic [*Marshall mistakenly called him David Sutlic in his memoir*] was the gunner of our Browning Automatic rifle (BAR) team, and I was the assistant who carried the ammo, which consisted of 20 shells in a clip, six clips to a bandolier, three bandoliers at a time. That was 18 clips at a time, which could get pretty heavy. The person who carried the BAR had to be big and strong. Sutlic was stocky and strong and at the time I weighed about 135 pounds. I was also trained in the use of the BAR. We were teamed for about six months and became very good friends. Sutlic loved to get in water and several times he had to be helped out because he couldn't swim and would get in too deep and then get in trouble. One day we were camped somewhere in Italy [*Sicily*]. Sutlic said he'd found a great pool of water in the rocks where we could wash our clothes. I told him that I needed to finish a letter and would come down soon. What seemed like only a few minutes later some guys came by and wanted to know why I wasn't down at the pool to help Sutlic. I dropped everything and went running down to see what happened. He had jumped in the pool of water and either drowned or went into shock because the water was so cold. The Medic said he was dead. I lost a good friend. Pop Hoover was his replacement, but Hoover had his own assistant, so I was then assigned to Communications because I had trained in that field also."[140]

Stephen Vukson, left, and other soldiers (unidentified) with a captured German truck in Sicily.
Stephen Vukson

Capt. Rupert Burford also wrote of the loss, jotting in his diary, "At about 1000 this morning [*John J.*] Mathews came running in to tell me that Sutlic had gone in swimming in one of the small pools nearby and had drowned. I marshaled the medics and some swimmers and rushed to the scene of the disaster. When I reached the spot they had just dragged his body out and were beginning to work on it. We worked on him over two hours until rigor mortis began to set in then he was pronounced dead. Cunin conducted an investigation and wanted to blame me for the death of Sutlic, for allowing him to go in swimming during training hours. I reminded him that he himself had told us we were to have two days for rest and clean-up, and the men were not restricted to the area." Due to the condition of the body a funeral, conducted by Chaplain Lyle L. Burdick, was held for Edward J. Sutlic on the morning of the 24th. Capt. Burford bought a casket out of the company funds and the body was prepared by two men from HQ Co. experienced in mortuary work. A salute of three rifle volleys was fired followed with the body being taken to the cemetery at Gela for burial. Company training began on the 25th and, in order to prevent any further drowning, Cunin posted guards at all area pools and streams and "ordered life guards present at all swimming parties."[141]

Co. A was yet at Mazara on the 23rd and "Still … in the school house," according to James Helsel. "Some fellows have to pull guard on a boat fifteen miles out at sea. We have made quite a few raids and got a lot of wheat, cheese. One detail went clear back to Gela on a raid. There is plenty of Vino here. One man said in answer to the question 'How long have you been drunk?' 'How long have I been in Sicily?'"[142]

Lt. Leonard A. ("Spike") Merrill, Jr., wrote a letter home in late August boasting that "… the island is completely taken," and Co. A moved to an olive grove outside Castelvetrano on the 25th. This move was confirmed on the 26th when word was received from the 3rd Division that the 83rd was assigned to patrol the area around Castelvetrano so as to preserve order and to collect arms and munitions. Each squad was given a map with a 10-mile area to police. Co. C was given the area between Santa Ninfa and Partanna, while Lt. Col. Cunin was appointed mayor of Castelvetrano, which made his appearance with the battalion rare unless he wished to issue some orders. A photo and article on Cunin had also appeared in the newspapers back in the states, which brought about Capt. Pike's reaction that "If Col. Cunin knew he had his picture in the paper and a quote he would swell up like a banty rooster. He thinks he's the cock of the walk now. Hutchinson is about as bad. He is a Major now."[143]

According to Lt. James Beasley, Co. D, "We were ordered to thoroughly check over an area including some towns for enemy materials. It was the most interesting thing we have done in several days for it required going all around the country and looking at all places where guns, ammunition, mine fields, gasoline, motor vehicles, etc. might be. The friendly civilians were a great help. For example we were examining a mine field when a civilian came along and pointed to my gun and made signs for me to follow him. He guided the Captain and I to two strongly built concrete pill boxes. There was a machine gun in each with a large quantity of ammunition. There were also several dozen hand grenades. We celebrated the fourth a little late by throwing the grenades. I went through a third pill box that had already been located and reported that there was no ammunition [*in*] it. Later just for the fun of it, I threw a grenade in the place which set some straw afire. Then ammunition began exploding and the place was lively for a minute or so. The ammunition was some scattered round in the straw. We went through several more pill boxes during the day but they had already been examined. We located some artillery pieces and ammunition, and mines that no one had reported … Where we got the machine guns, the man gave us some large delicious grapes and fresh baked bread and some very good wine and said he would be glad for us to come back at any time. The house had large shade trees around it and it would have been a pleasure to spend the afternoon there. All of the men had been in America. You guessed it—he wants the U.S. to keep the island … Late in the afternoon a British lieutenant brought a machine gun and lots of ammunition into a dump for such things. He was very much impressed with himself for his cleverness in discovering the pill box. We have several men in the company who did much more during this day. The civilians are anxious to have all such things picked up because some of them have been killed and others injured. One civilian reported the other day that there was an unexploded bomb near his place. We sent two men out to dispose of it by blowing it up with TNT. The men found the 'bomb' to be a hand grenade." In a companion letter he reflected upon his Sicilian Campaign experience as he wrote, "I was within four hundred yards of some of the German M6 tanks (the largest ones the Germans have) when they were knocked out by naval fire. The shrapnel from some of the shells fell around the observation post I was at. Anti-tank guns and artillery were also firing on the tanks."[144]

Co. D's cook, George Borkhuis wrote, "Most of the boys have some musical instruments to pass the time so I got one too. An Italian accordion. One never knows that when the war is over I might be without a job. This way I can get a monkey and go up and down Fifth Avenue collecting pennies."

It was during this time that 1st Lt. George D. Gould, Assistant Chemical Officer, HQ, 7th Army, informed authorities that Capt. Burford of the 83rd had called his attention to a new field modification of the 4.2" mortar sight, using a captured Italian mortar sight of unknown origin and model. The sight was "mounted in a vertical position on the arm and tightening screw of the standard 4.2" Chemical Mortar Sight MII" resulting in a number of improvements. Burford said Lt. Col. Cunin had recommended this particular type sight for the battalion while they were still in the States. They were made and forwarded to them while there, but nothing was done and the battalion moved overseas. The men of Co. C, who had five of the sights, voiced high praise for the sight and treasured it highly. Authorities expressed a strong desire to obtain others.[145]

Also at this time, Lt. Col. William C. Hammond, Jr., Chemical Officer of the 45th Infantry Division, wrote of the tactical use of chemical munitions in the Sicilian Campaign, stating that a "… Report received from the 83rd Chemical Battalion indicates that approximately a 25% ratio of all shells fired was WP filled and 75% HE filled. This appears … out of proportion. It is my understanding that the 83rd fired no smoke screens. If they had done so more WP would possibly have been used. It is the opinion … this shell should be divided 50% HE and 50% WP."[146]

A conference of all chemical warfare officers from each unit under the 7th Army was held at Palermo August 28-29 and included all Army, Corps and Division chemical officers; three chemical battalion commanders; the commanders of the Decontaminating, Maintenance, Depot, and two Smoke Generator companies; chemical officers from the Base Section and a representative from G-3 Office, 7th Army. Among this group could be found Lt. Col. Kenneth Cunin and Capt. (S-3) David Meyerson from the 83rd. Subjects discussed were Supply, Employment of Chemical Battalions, Employment of Service Units, suggested changes in T/O's and T/BA's, suggested improvements in equipment; liaison, training and captured enemy CWS equipment. Experience and knowledge gained in the Sicilian Campaign were used as a basis for most topics. Among Lt. Col. Cunin's and Capt. Meyerson's contributions to the discussion was Cunin's belief that most defective shells were caused by improper packaging and poor inspection. He felt they needed waterproofing, as water in the shells caused wobbling, and that cosmolene and rust on shells was a problem which could be eliminated by placing the shells in waterproof containers. Capt. Meyerson claimed there had been no consolidation of ammo dumps in Sicily and said, "We used our entire train to take care of them." Cunin added that amphibious operations must work with the Engineer Shore outfit and said, "For several days my company operated with only three peeps, hauled ammunition, rifles, and everything else … you have to fight for boats. We were over a period of three weeks getting our transportation." Regarding units of fire Cunin stated he was personally told 100 rounds, but 60 was it, adding, "Under the current set up of transportation, we can carry 60 rounds or more in a truck, that is 60 rounds per platoon, that is one unit of fire… We figured out our operation. I wanted seven or eight units of fire on the basis of 100 rounds. We figured it out on that basis. It ended up with our getting four and a half and the reason we didn't get more was the lack of shipping lift."[147]

Lt. Col. Cunin also favored luminous markings on shells to distinguish WP from HE, as well as other types of shells, and also noted the lack of replacement mortar parts during the campaign, particularly elevating screws and springs, concluding the reason for this was that there were not enough mortars in Sicily for authorities to justify spare parts. He said, "We brought our own with us," and suggested keeping mortar parts on their own trucks as it was not feasible to travel 40 or 50 miles to the rear to obtain a parts kit. Cunin also pointed out that the firing pins were different lengths and he had no idea as to the cause; all baseplates needed to be welded; and decontamination equipment need to be kept in the depot until needed. Capt. Meyerson injected that the 83rd never received administrative orders and said, "Right now we don't know where a signal and chemical maintenance depot is located." Cunin proposed that in the future all 4.2" ammo should be at or adjacent to the division dump, with Meyerson saying there was no need for a 4.2" ammo company as "a chemical ammunition company would be extravagant."[148]

As the conference continued Lt. Col. Cunin explained that in Sicily the 83rd had shot about 50-50 as far as WP and HE, and that they only shot one smoke screen in their operation, favoring the WP and HE as casualty shells. He repeatedly complained about the boats being a problem but noted rations were fine, although he did suggest bypassing HQ would solve many personnel problems and said, "I don't mind the trucks, but when they steal the drivers and personal equipment, I get excited." But Cunin got most animated over the lack of the top brass to develop a new mortar sight like the one Capt. Burford had captured from the Italians in Sicily. He fumed, "It's a good sight. I tried to get some more down in Gela, but the officer wouldn't give them out… There is nobody back at Edgewood Arsenal that knows anything about the sight, and they won't ask the Field Artillery about it." Meyerson and Cunin also suggested increasing the range of the mortar ammo to 4,500 yards, because, as Cunin noted, "We can't get the powder for the present shell. The Germans can just sit back at 5,000 yards and you can't touch them."[149]

Although Capt. "Bud" Pike was very unimpressed by his superior officers, he did enjoy the sites of Sicily, writing on the 30th, "I went on a wonderful trip yesterday and today. We drove right through the heart of a huge mountain range with all its hairpin curves, precipitous drop-offs, and stately peaks. Throughout the mountains were numerous pretty little towns – filthy and dirty as they might be. This country could be very nice to live in if they would ever clean up the towns, establish sewer systems, maintain a good pure water supply, etc. All it needs is a few more of the modern conveniences. Most of these towns are built on high hills. They are all centuries old and were purposely built on high places as defense against invaders. Thank God the defenses weren't sufficient this time." The 30th did not pass without injury as Pvt. Thomas Harrigle, Co. A, from Lehigh County, Pennsylvania, was sent to the hospital with serious burns of the face and hands when he lit a match to destroy a house filled with captured powder.[150]

At a company commander's meeting on the 31st, Cunin announced the forthcoming invasion of Italy and requested two battalion companies to participate. Companies A and D were the logical choices, but Co. A was eliminated due to the high rate of illness. Co. B was the next logical choice, and even appeared on the original boat loading plan of September 1st, but Capt. John P. McEvoy also claimed his company was not yet ready to go. So, by default, Co. C would join Co. D in the planned invasion of Italy, while companies A and B would remain in Sicily until further notice.[151]

Business continued as usual with Lt. Beasley, Co. D, as he noted, "The past few days have sounded as if a battle were on around here. After the enemy ammunition dumps were located army personnel have been blowing them up. The ammunition ranges from the heavier bombs, through artillery shells of all sizes mortar shells, mines, hand grenades, to rifle cartridges with wooden bullets. Some of our men have been firing signal (Italian) rockets today for the fun of it and also to destroy them. Throughout the day an explosion has been set off about every fifteen minutes that is close enough that we can feel a fairly strong concussion. They are destroying a nearby ammunition dump." Capt. Pike summed up the Sicilian Campaign by stating, "The Italian soldiers surrendered by the thousands. Every one I have talked to, through my jeep-driver, who speaks Italian very fluently says they hate Mussolini and are glad the Americans came. In fact, they have been waiting for the Americans for a long time. Just heard that Mussolini abdicated. Well, when Company D hit Africa, Rommel ran out. Now we hit Sicily and Mussolini runs out. Just give us a chance at Germany now and watch Hitler go. But come to think of it who would take him."[152]

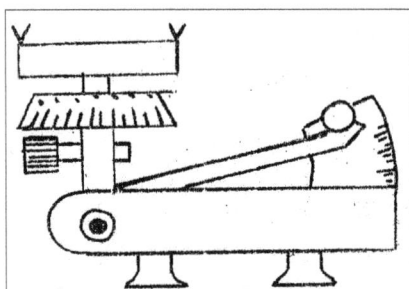

FIELD MODIFICATION OF CAPTURED ITALIAN SIGHT, 4.2" CHEMICAL MORTAR

An Italian artillery sight, of unknown make or model, is mounted in a vertical position on the arm tightening screw of the Standard 4.2" Chemical Mortar Sight MII. This sight has a 360-degree traversing screw, with a circular horizontal graduated scale. The actual sight itself consists of a rectangular tube approximately 3" x 1/2" x 1/2" sealed with lenses at each end and containing an optically illuminated vertical hair line. Two sighting notches are located on top of the tube. One sights on the aiming point thru these notches with one eye, while lining up the hair line of the sight with the other eye. The sight has also its own level bubble.

This addition to the standard mortar sight allows the following advantages:
a. Two or more mortars may be lined up on the same parallel line and use the same range.
b. The aiming stake need no longer be placed directly in front of the mortar, but may be spotted anywhere to the right of left or even to the rear of the line of fire.
c. More than one mortar can use the same aiming stake as their reference point.
d. This attachment does not in any way interfere with the normal operation of the MII sight itself.

Co. C found 5 of these Italian sights and used them as standard operating equipment. All men using this sight voiced high praise of it and treasured it highly.

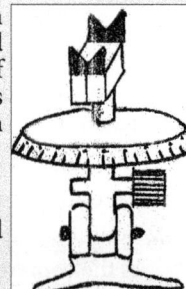

Side (left) and front (right) views of the mortar sight.
National Archives

Chapter Seven

OPERATION AVALANCHE
AND
THE ITALIAN CAMPAIGN
SEPTEMBER-DECEMBER 1943

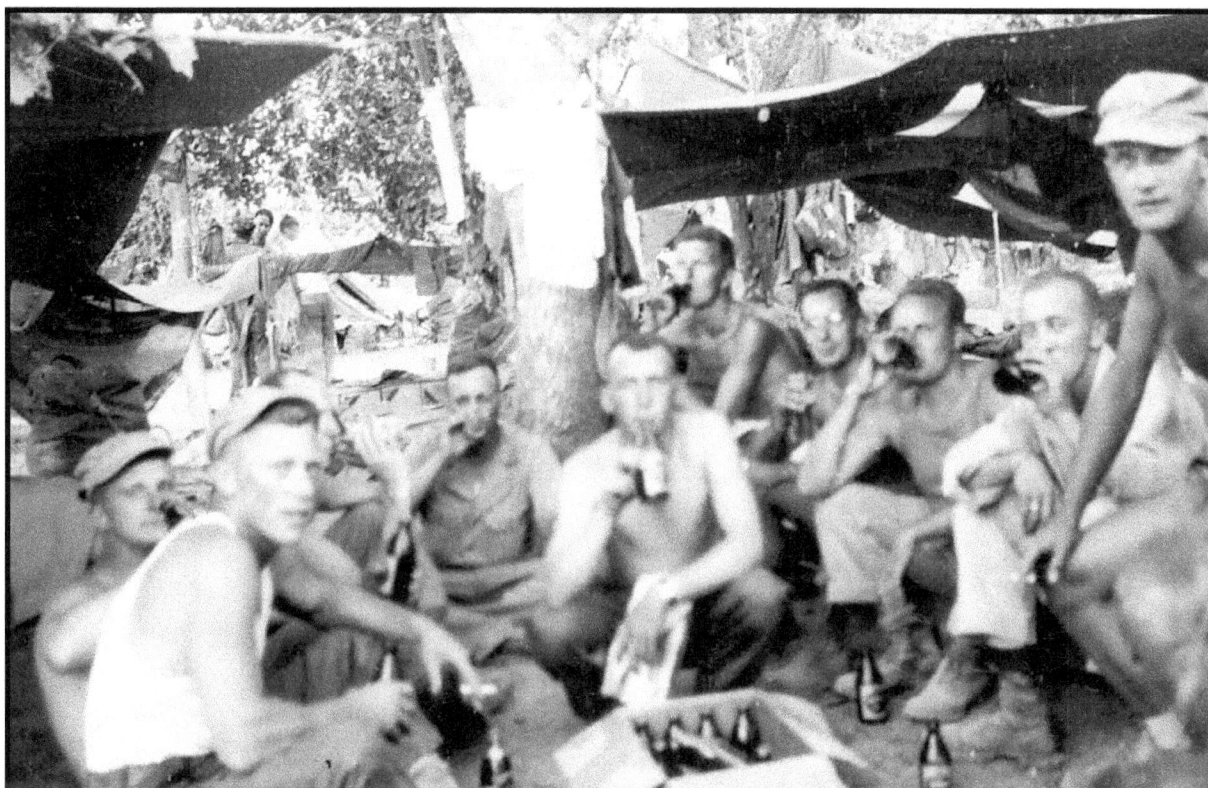

Unidentified 83rd men en route to Salerno.
Karl Garrett

Salerno & Maiori (Chiunzi Pass)

The month of September opened with the battalion at Castelvetrano, Sicily, and companies C and D "… relieved from assignment to 7th Army, assigned to 5th Army, and attached to 7th Army pending call to 5th Army." Regardless of the confusion in that order, the two companies were also alerted to prepare for an amphibious operation. Companies A and B continued to police the area known as Sub-sector #3 until they were relieved of that duty by the 7th Infantry, 3rd Infantry Division, on September 2nd. This was all part of the preparations for Operation Avalanche, the Allied invasion of Italy, in which Co. C of the 83rd, along with the 1st and 3rd Ranger battalions, were attached to the British X Corps. Their mission was to take control of the area around Salerno or, as Loy Marshall stated, to "… go ashore at Maiori, near Amalfi and about twenty miles west of Salerno, take the town, destroy nearby coastal defenses, seize Chiunzi Pass, and secure the left flank of the 5th Army." Co. D would go ashore at Vietri-sul-Mare, a little seaside town just southwest of Salerno, with the 2nd and 41st British Commandos. Harold Hughes said Co. D's assignment was to "secure the coastal highway and railroad, cutting off German reinforcements." Russell H. Peterson, Co. D, wrote, "I'm [*still*] in Sicily and have been in action but have come through without a scratch. At present I am going nuts and dodging flies and bambinos …"[1]

Throughout the next few days, companies A and B continued to perform normal training activities while companies

C and D engaged in training for the forthcoming amphibious operation, which they completed on the 6th. Rupert Burford recalled that he, Cunin, and Pike went to the Ranger CP at Corleone on September 1st. Although Col. Darby was not present, Lt. Col. Herman W. Dammer and Capt. Frederick Saams of the Rangers instructed the assembly about the forthcoming invasion and told Burford that Co. C would make their effort at Maiori. During the subsequent training period from September 2nd through the 6th, companies B and C were relieved from patrol duties to concentrate on invasion training. Burford said it was a horrendous time as "… living conditions became terrible in our area. The days were extremely hot, flies were so numerous that one had to fight them (literally) for his food. Actually, from the time a spoonful of food was taken from the meat can until the time it was near the mouth, it literally became covered with flies. Practically all the men in the company had dysentery. Here I decided to shave off my mustache because it served as a fly-trap." Despite these conditions the men prepared a towing device for the mortar carts and altered the arrangement of ammo on the carts in order to increase the load. This modification would prove most beneficial. Another meeting of officers was held at Corleone but Cunin failed to show. The officers slept on the ground and in their jeeps until the next morning, when they were informed Cunin was back at Castelvetrano.[2]

The Ranger journals reported that at Palermo on September 5th, Co. B of the 83rd loaded onto an LCT 540 K-rations but no vehicles. Another LCT was loaded with three one-fourth ton vehicles along with 800 rounds of 4.2 mortar ammo, half WP and half HE, to be placed in available space. A follow-up craft was to be loaded on the 9th at Milazzo with 4,000 rounds of ammo, in addition to all vehicles, and landed one hour after the planned invasion.[3]

Co. D was "… still in an olive orchard and also getting an occasional swim. The salt water really feels good after a day or two of being in the dust around here. The rain should start sometime this month …" Lt. James Beasley noted, "We are using our own command post tent now. It was made for use under blackout conditions and is very useful because it gets dark earlier and there is not time during the day to do the work, censor letters, and get to write once

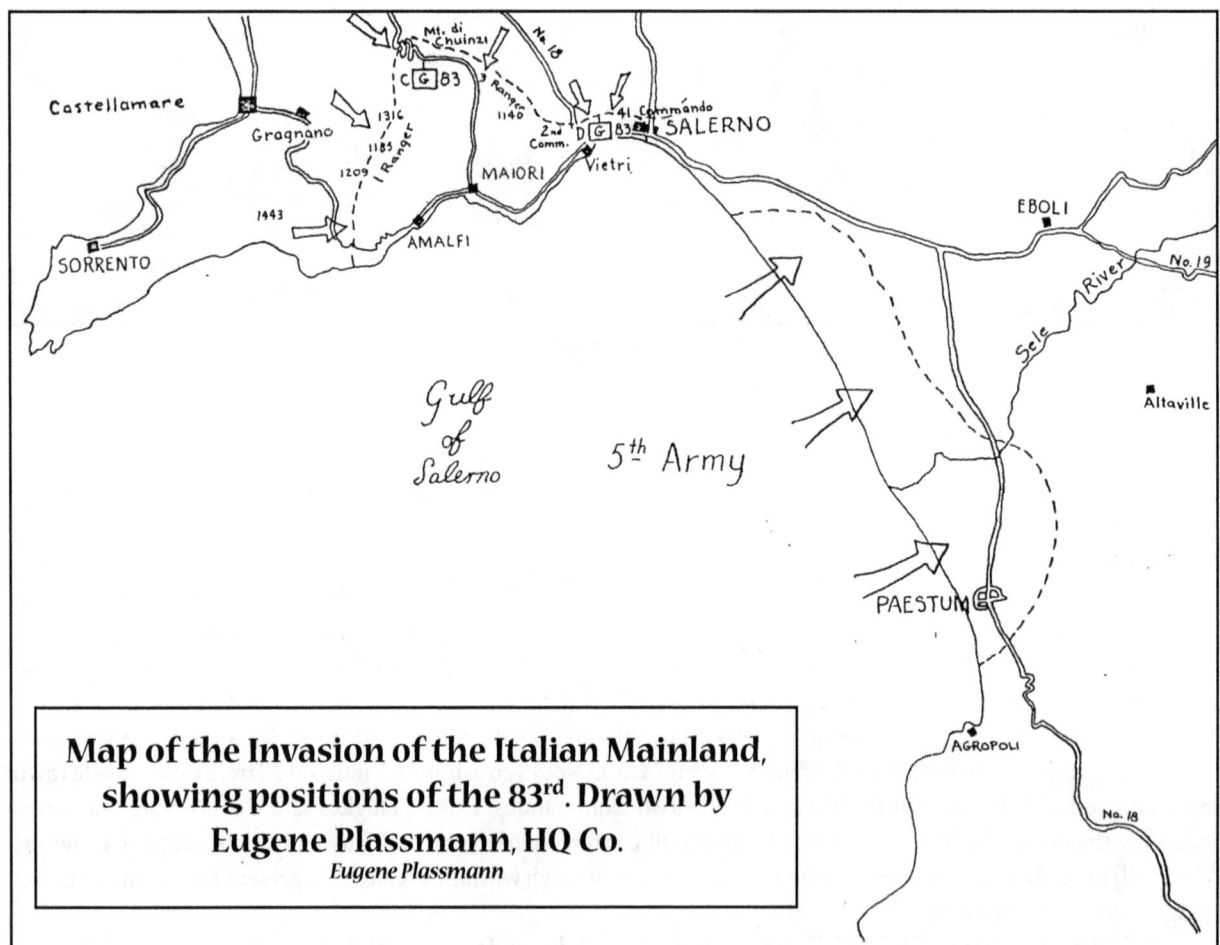

Map of the Invasion of the Italian Mainland, showing positions of the 83rd. Drawn by Eugene Plassmann, HQ Co.
Eugene Plassmann

ALBERT, THE ITALIAN COOK OF CO. A, AND OTHER SPECIAL FRIENDS

Albert Sabatino
L. Lew Henry Collection

Although he is fondly remembered by many veterans of the 83rd, very little is known about Albert, the Italian prisoner of war, reportedly a medic, who became a sort of honorary member of Co. A. What is known with certainty is that Albert, or Alberto as he was also known, first became associated with the company in Sicily and remained with them as a cook until after the surrender of Germany.

Perhaps the origins of Albert can be found in the recollections of Joseph Cannetti, Co. A, who recalled, "Pete Tranchitella was a good mess sergeant, he always fed us on the line with his two Italian prisoners. They came from Venice and told him they would stay and help him until we reached Venice. Unfortunately, they got caught in a barrage and one lost a leg. We all chipped in and got him a wooden leg." Undoubtedly, one of these two men was Albert, and, as there is no record of Albert ever having lost a leg, perhaps the other man is the person mentioned in the August 17, 1943, entry in the Co. A diary of Pfc. Charles Rolling. Co. A was assigned to police the area around Mazara, Sicily, where Rolling stated, "Vitts, our best Italian worker, shared our daily reveille and calisthenics with us and helped in the kitchen the remains of the day." Sgt. Sam Bundy, writing of the same incident, called the man Vitto and referred to him as a Sicilian worker.

No additional information has been located on Vitts/Vitto but Albert was among the Co. A survivors of LST 422 at Anzio on January 26, 1944. His full name, Albert Sabatino, appears on a list of 87 survivors of the 83rd picked up by various minesweepers and escort vessels and transferred to LST 383 on January 27. Additional survivors were placed on other craft.

Albert is mentioned again in the Co. A diaries of Bundy and Rolling on August 17, 1944, about fifteen miles from St. Maxime, France. Apparently, late at night and during a rain storm, Albert's mammoth appetite got the best of him and he went out to look for rabbits armed with only a flashlight. He entered a house and stumbled upon two German soldiers bathing. He called for someone to bring a rifle and the men were taken prisoner. Albert and Pvt. Frank Boduck each got a watch, shaving set, and German currency out of the clothing of the prisoners.

Albert Sabatino was injured on August 27, 1944, when the truck of Herschel T. Stutts hit a mountainside while attempting to negotiate a narrow, rocky mountain road in the Alps during blackout driving conditions.

Lt. Robert Bundy, Co. A, [not to be confused with Sam Bundy] recalled taking Albert home to Venice in either July or late August of 1945, writing, "Albert was a young Italian boy who traveled with the 1st Platoon of Co. A. He sure could make a great dish of spaghetti. Lt. Charles J. DeCesare and I took him home to Italy. Gordon Mindrum didn't think we could get through the Brenner Pass. However, when we got there we were greeted by a Sgt. from a sister mortar battalion. We chatted for a short time bringing him up to date as to where the 83rd went after leaving Italy. He called to his men to open the gate and let us through and we took the young man home somewhere in northern Italy."

Although the names of most other human "mascots" have faded into memory some photographic images yet exist. Additionally the exploits of Jean Pierre Combe, the young French lad who gallantly rescued a number of Co. C men at Ft. Dauphin near Briançon, France, on August 29, 1944, and became an honorary member of the battalion, is well chronicled in the narrative.

Top: Raymond Knapp with Italian boy.
Knapp Collection

Center: A group of Sicilian orphans.
Byron Jordan

Right: Italian boy "Mascot".
Knapp Collection

There are also such episodes as mentioned in the September 1st, 1943, letter written by Capt. Edwin "Bud" Pike at Castelvetrano, Sicily. According to Pike, "almost every day we have about 20 Italian kids around at noon meal time. We then have them put on the boxing gloves and fight exhibition matches. We then give them left-overs from the meal as a reward. It's a lot of fun and they really put on some good fun. One other thing; some of the men in the company have trained the kids to sing 'The Yanks Are Coming' and they sing that for us at meals also."

every two or three days …"[4]

Michael J. Rebick, also of Co. D, describing the training period, stated, "[*We've*] been [*working*] our guns [*so they*] don't get rusty sitting around [*and*] we go out every day to have some more practice so our job will be well done right when called upon … and also we go out on a hike now and then, and when time permits we go out for a swim. Then when we go out on these hikes, we start to curse from the time we start, but as we march we think of our love and the ones we left behind to build our Army, so that our bodies can run right over the dead of the [*enemy*] … " On September 3rd, Beasley sarcastically lamented, "Our ego was severely damaged this morning when we learned that Italy had been invaded without our assistance. Perhaps the 83rd will take Czechoslovakia."[5]

Two days later Beasley was a bit more animated about his activities. "We have been kidding Captain Pike about the trip to shore on the invasion of Sicily. When the artillery started shelling the landing boats he said 'Men, you are now under fire.' So far he has failed to give a good reason for doing it. After all, it might have scared them." Beasley related a second "amusing incident" involving two Italian-American sergeants. According to Beasley, the two were on a patrol when "They were halted by someone out of sight who wanted to know who they were. Thinking they were being halted by men from their own company they answered sergeant [*Mike*] Codega and sergeant [*Frank*] Lombardi. The fellow who challenged them yelled 'Throw down your arms. Come and help me Joe, I've got two dago prisoners!' The sergeants said that after this they will use the countersign. The man who challenged them was from another organization …" Less amusing was an incident involving one of Beasley's "reformed" men. Ordered to dig two latrines as punishment for missing class, the man had paid two locals to do the work instead. He then was ordered "to dig two more himself that day and one on each of the following six days after duty hours." When he failed to do that, court-martial charges were placed, "the first charges I ever filed," Beasley wrote. "One of his pals is a member of the CIO. Perhaps John L. will do something about a man having to work an hour after he had been sitting around guarding the bivouac area eight hours during the day." Back at Castelvetrano the battalion gained a special member as Albert ("Alberto") Sabatino, an Italian POW medic, "joined" up as a cook with Co. A. He would serve faithfully with them until the end of the war.[6]

During the early morning hours of September 7th, around 3:30 a.m., companies C and D departed Castelvetrano for Palermo, where Co. C boarded *LCI 35* at about 10:30. The deck log of *LCI 35* confirmed this, stating, "Loaded troops which are detached to the Rangers, they have about 30 small carriages [*the ship's Action Report stated 26 carriages and eight mortars*] which include both mortars and ammunition." Loy Marshall, as well as *LCI 35's* Action Report, stated Co. C consisted of 177 enlisted men and six officers, along with 26 carts holding eight mortars and ammunition. Co. D, comprised of six officers and 188 enlisted men with eight mortars and 18 carts of mortar ammo, embarked on *LCI 216* and also moved out into the bay. Capt. Pike noted Co. D broke camp, moved via convoy to Palermo, arriving at nine o'clock. Pike recalled that after embarking he was confronted with the usual problem of obtaining maps and field orders. The movement from Castelvetrano to Palermo did not go smoothly according to Capt. Burford, who wrote, "We arrived just outside Palermo at 0800 and had a wait of two hours before we could proceed to the harbor. While waiting here, the men visited all the wine shops in the neighborhood, and before we pushed on into Palermo, several were feeling no pain. Finally [*Executive Officer David W.*] Meyerson (who was supposed to guide us to the dock) showed up and went immediately to the harbor where we loaded … then the trucks were sent to be loaded with ammunition, and from there they were to be led by Meyerson to Corleone to join the follow-up convoy."[7]

Little seasickness was encountered since the two LCI's set out on a relatively calm sea at 3:00 a.m. the next morning, joining with a convoy of LST's and larger ships at about 9:30. The day did not go well as the two companies were subjected to two air attacks of major proportions, the heaviest yet witnessed by the men. Capt. Burford, Co. C, reported, "Several of the bombs were close enough to our little ship that we felt them, but no one was hurt." The deck log of *LCI 35* stated the first attack came at about 4:30 in the afternoon, recording, "A plane has come in on the starboard side of the convoy and dropped bombs but no damage was noted."[8]

The second attack, lasting about an hour, came at about 9:30 p.m. "Flares were dropped by enemy planes and a large air raid followed, a few planes were seen to have been shot down." J. D. Parker, Jr., commander of *LCI 216* carrying the Commandos and Co. D of the 83rd, noted the second attack, writing, "Flares and heavy bombs dropped all about us; smoke was successfully used by [*the*] British escort and our convoy was unharmed. One heavy bomb dropped 200 yards astern of this ship, lifting entire stern out of water. There was heavy anti-aircraft fire all about us. At about

Map of Vietri-sul-Mare area showing positions of the 83rd and the enemy.
Believed drawn by Capt. Edwin G. "Bud" Pike, Co. D.
Pike Collection

11:00 p.m., 20mm tracer fire was seen on port bow of convoy close to water and something - believe it was E-boat - burst into flames on water. This ship did not open fire at all as no planes were seen within range although many were heard to pass low on either hand." Recalling the two episodes Loy Marshall wrote, "During the afternoon the convoy came under enemy attack by German planes that dropped bombs. Something got hit. The convoy proceeded and was attacked again late that night when a large formation of planes attacked with bombs and flares. Smoke screens had been laid out and our LCI broke away from the main convoy and headed for Maiori." Actually, the deck logs make no mention of any LCI breaking away from the convoy. Despite such inconveniences the morale of the men was reported as good at the end of the day.[9]

Back at Castelvetrano companies A and B, HQ Co., and the Medical Detachment prepared to move the next day to a new bivouac four miles southeast of Termini Imerese, where they would be attached to Island Base Section staging area. Before departing they also saw their first movie shown expressly for the battalion since coming overseas. But the most important event of the day was news of the surrender of Italy.[10]

Action at Vietri-sul-Mare Sept. 9 - 20 & Action at Chiunzi Pass Sept. 9 - 29

September 9th was "D-Day for the companies of the 83rd as Co. C landed at Maiori and Co. D at Vietri-sul-Mare, both in the vicinity of Salerno, Italy, around four in the morning. The deck log of *LCI 35*, carrying Co. C, recorded that, at 4:05, "Have beached and the troops on board are going ashore with the carriages they had brought on board both mortars and ammunition ... the men were put ashore without getting their feet wet." Co. C encountered no opposition and quickly moved through the town behind the 1st, 3rd, and 4th Ranger Battalions. Next followed an eight-mile trek up a long, winding mountain road to Chiunzi Pass, where Pagani, Nocera, and even Mt. Vesuvius in the far distance could be viewed. The company immediately took up positions, the 1st Platoon to the right of the road and the 2nd Platoon to the left, and opened fire on the plains below. William C. Ford, Co. C, said they were told to hold the pass for three days until the 5th Army could break out of the beachhead and connect with the British 8th Army, but both got bogged down and the men had to hold Chiunzi Pass for "eighteen days of hell."[11]

Capt. Rupert Burford, Co. C, confirmed that the men landed successfully without meeting any opposition and then waited a few minutes for the Rangers to reorganize and move out. "Then we assumed an approach march formation and began to move up the Pass toward our objective. I marched at the head of the column with Earl Shaddinger (my IMG Sergeant) and some of the company headquarters men. I was a little apprehensive we were heading for trouble and kept expecting a machine gun to open up on us. As we passed a doorway, an Italian civilian came out and started to go somewhere. I roughly told him to go home, and when he protested I slapped his face to emphasize my command.

James Dougherty, Co. D, in Salerno.
Dougherty Collection

I was afraid he wanted to go rouse some Germans ..." Burford said they soon came to a tank the Rangers had blown with several demoralized Germans inside. He added, "It was a tough up-hill climb, particularly for the men who were hauling mortar carts." Lt. Ralph Rankin, ahead of the column, sent a captured German command car back by Sgt. William H. Barber. Burford continued, "Our foresight in preparing tow handles for the carts stood us in good stead and the vehicle proved a God-send. We attached the carts to the car and gradually worked our way up the hill ... the position was a splendid one for the mortars ... We had good defilade from enemy ground observation and flat-trajectory fire ... The day seemed more like a Service Practice to us than a battle, our only limiting factor being that we couldn't use too much ammunition because we didn't have much and had to conserve it ... We had to use some of our squads to fill in the gaps in the Rangers' lines."

This was probably the period described by Pvt. Loy J. Marshall, Co. C, who wrote, "We had to load all our gear, ammo, communications equipment, etc. onto two-wheel carts and pull them up the mountain ourselves. The terrain was very rough, steep, and muddy, and it was taking a while to get into a position to support the troops with our mortars and bazookas. A captain came down raising hell that his soldiers were getting killed and they needed our help and what the hell was taking us so long to get up there. Our commander told him we were doing the best we could under the conditions and that we were working as hard and as fast as we could to get up there to help and explained that we were having to push, pull, and move everything by hand. Within a week or so after this incident, each of our companies had trucks, jeeps or other vehicles assigned to pull the equipment."[12]

Co. D encountered a bit of resistance at Vietri-sul-Mare. The 1st Platoon of the company was to support the 2nd (British) Commando Battalion, and the 2nd Platoon the 41st (British) Commando Battalion. Due to the British LCIs going in late, *LCI 216* did not beach until 4:16. Actually, Capt. Pike said they were supposed to hit off shore near Capri during the early morning darkness, but turned around and came back later in broad daylight. The craft successfully landed on X-Ray Beach and disembarked the troops in ankle-deep water. The LCI did have a little trouble going in as it lost it's stern anchor and cable. As the beach was small with a high cliff the distance was misjudged by about 50 feet. Also, as the craft came in enemy shells landed within 200 yards of the stern. The port ramp cables had also become fouled so that during debarkation the ramps had to be pushed out manually. At no time during the entire operation did *LCI 216* open fire, and the only casualties were two men of Co. D who were injured " ... during the unloading process when carts going down the ramp overran the men who were hauling them." The LCI commander later gave an opinion that " ... chemical mortar companies could be more successfully landed by LCTs, as it was hard to land the heavy carts due to steep decline of ramps, and also the narrowness of the ramps."[13]

Upon landing, the 1st Platoon of Co. D was held in reserve but the 2nd Platoon immediately engaged and fired about 100 rounds, destroying one machine gun nest and routing two mortars and several vehicles. The enemy did not put up much of a fight and the morale of the men was fair, although Sgt. James V. Lauro was slightly wounded by a shell fragment and evacuated. He would not return to duty until December 11th. Lt. Alfred Crenshaw recalled, "It was an easy landing but from daylight on we were constantly under artillery and mortar fire ... while I was at an OP post, [Lt.] Sam [Miller] took one mortar to a separate position and with that mortar he knocked out a heavy machine gun." Harold Hughes claimed his men crossed the beach virtually unopposed and walked up the cobblestone streets of town while it was yet dark. Later in the day they encountered some slight resistance. Daniel Shields noted the hot weather throughout prior to his having to stand guard in a house against a tank from nine to eleven in the evening. He recalled, "Heard big guns all night."[14]

Back in Sicily, Co. A moved through Palermo to a new bivouac at Termini Imerese where they received four new officers and 50 enlisted men from the 1st Division. The only original officer remaining with the company was Lt.

James Otis Beasley

James Otis Beasley,
R. O. T. C. ca. 1928
John Beasley

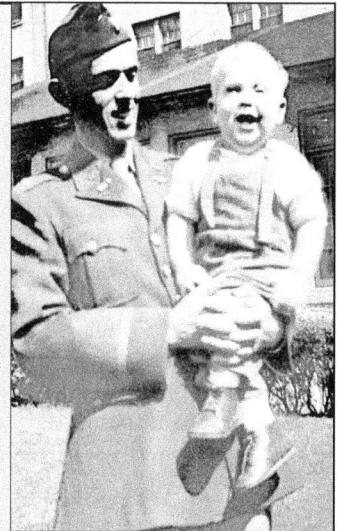

James Otis Beasley with
son, John "Jack" Beasley.
John Beasley

James Otis Beasley was born September 7, 1909, at Wells, Texas; was educated in the Texas public schools; and graduated from Lufkin High School in 1928. In 1932 he graduated from the Agricultural and Mechanical College of Texas (Texas A&M) and that same year won a traveling scholarship to visit the primary cotton growing areas in the U.S. and the important cotton merchandising and manufacturing centers of Europe. After receiving his master's degree from Texas A&M in 1934, he spent the next two years as an assistant in the Texas Agricultural Experiment Station studying the morphology of the cotton seed. Beasley entered Harvard College in 1936 as a graduate student, earning his doctorate in 1939.

While at Harvard he immersed himself in the study of genetics and the cytology of Gossypium species, yet in spite of the difficulty in growing cotton species in the Boston area, even in the greenhouse, he made quick progress in a short time. P. C. Mangelsdorf of the Botanical Museum of Harvard in 1944 wrote that Beasley, "By the use of mixed pollinations to prevent the bolls from shedding prematurely and by employing embryo culture techniques, he succeeded in producing species-hybrids not obtainable by ordinary methods. He was one of the first to utilize colchicine extensively by doubling the chromosome number of sterile hybrids to produce fertile allopolyploids." Beasley made numerous other advances in the study of cotton genetics.

Throughout parts of 1938 and 1939 he was employed by the U.S. Department of Agriculture in genetic investigations of cotton at Raleigh, North Carolina. From 1939 until he entered the military, he was agronomist and cytogeneticist on the staff of the Texas Agricultural and Experiment Station, one of only three people in the U.S. to hold such position during that period.

Utilizing his ROTC scholarship Beasley entered active military service as a 1st lieutenant in the infantry March 5, 1942, and quickly requested transfer to the Chemical Warfare Service branch, where he felt his knowledge and ability would be best served. He was soon afterward taking classes at the Chemical Warfare School, Edgewood Arsenal, Maryland. On October 23, 1942, he was assigned as 1st Lt., Co. D, 83rd Chemical Battalion, at Camp Gordon, Georgia, and transferred to HQ & HQ Co. November 26. During the Sicilian Campaign of July - August 1943, he commanded the 1st Platoon of Co. D, but was caught in an ambush and killed at Vietri-sul-Mare, Italy, on September 12, 1943, the fourth day of the Salerno invasion. Beasley's body was later recovered and buried at Avellino. He was posthumously awarded the Purple Heart for "military merit" and was recommended for an additional citation for "continuous devotion to duty." Beasley Laboratory on the campus of Texas A&M is named after him as is a street on the grounds of the U.S. Army chemical warfare compound at Ft. Detrick, Frederick, Maryland.

James Beasley in the Texas
A & M laboratory, circa 1941.
John Beasley

James and Elizabeth Beasley
on their wedding day.
John Beasley

James J. O'Connor, as Capt. Edwards left to become S-3 with HQ Co. and John P. McEvoy became the new company commander.[15]

At Chiunzi Pass on the 10th, Co. C came under severe fire in the morning from 88mm and, according to official sources, 105mm guns, although there is some conjecture as to whether or not the Germans actually had 105s. The company had an excellent view of enemy activity in the plains and returned fire, often at maximum range, but their ammo supply became critical because the follow-up convoy and Co. D had met stiffer resistance at Salerno and Vietri-sul-Mare. Capt. Burford mentioned that the Germans soon discovered that Co. C couldn't shoot much beyond 3,200 yards without causing damage to the baseplates and standards and moved their installations beyond that range. Indeed, Co. D was engaged with enemy gun positions, tanks, and motor vehicles and was under a severe fire the entire day, although they did silence one machine gun. Sgt. Max E. ("General") Nestler took a light wound by shell fragments as did Sgt. Alvin A. Cupp, his second of the war, and Pvt. Norman L. Baker. More seriously wounded was Pvt. George O. Weatherford, also injured by a shell fragment.[16]

Capt. Pike may have been describing this event when he wrote, "I had one particularly close call with death again this time. While with the Commandos our position commanding the pass was threatened by tank attack from Salerno. I went with a Commando Colonel to a position overlooking Salerno where an anti-tank gun was located. The tank came towards us at a distance of about 1500 yds. Our gun opened fire and got a near miss. It fired again and the tank stopped. The tank opened fire and the first thing I knew I was flat on my stomach, not knowing how I got there. There had been a tremendous crack directly overhead and a hell of shower of twigs, leaves, dirt, and stone. I looked around and there was a wounded Tommy with blood pouring out of his arm. I slapped a bandage and sulfa powder on him. Beside him was one of my sergeants with shrapnel in his back. To my right about 5 feet away was another of my sergeants [James V. Lauro] with one finger blown off. About 10 feet behind me was a British Captain with the top of his head blown off. Beside him was another Tommy with several big shrapnel wounds in the arms and legs and with blood pouring out of him. And I didn't have a mark on me. I believe the good Lord has been listening to my prayers and hope that he will continue to do so. I got up and went over to help the Captain but saw that it was a waste of time to do anything so [I] went over and helped the other Tommy with tourniquets and bandages. I then went and saw the British Captain die and heard his last death rattle. And … it wasn't pretty I assure you. Ten minutes before I had been talking with him and at the time the shell hit was no more than 10 ft. away from him. I say again 'C'est la guerre'. The shell had hit in the limbs of a tree directly overhead and had spattered its shrapnel directly down on us. Your old man really feels like a leather-necked, battle-scarred veteran now, and with due cause I believe."[17]

Wofford L. Jackson recalled the same incident as he wrote, "Sgt. James Lauro was directing fire onto two tanks that were attacking from the south. One German shell made a direct hit on a Commando there with him. It blew blood, guts, and everything else all over Lauro. The only thing it did to him, it blew the end of his trigger finger off."[18]

Harold Hughes, Co. D, gave a somewhat more detailed account of his platoon's encounter on the 10th, although he may have been mistaken about the date and the number of casualties. In his book, *The Man from Ida Grove*, he wrote his platoon was huddled under a railroad trestle distributing rations when an enemy mortar barrage fell amongst them. Hughes saw a blue flash and fell to the ground, nearly shell shocked. "I rolled over and found myself looking into a man's head whose skull had been blown open. His brains glistening gray and I began retching … Medics rushed about and I staggered out of their way. I hadn't been hit but was still dazed. And then I saw Steve, the boy from Illinois, on the ground. He looked as if he were resting, bright blue eyes staring into the Italian sky, blond hair hardly mussed … I turned away and began vomiting again. He and six other men died in that one mortar attack." The official casualty list does not support such a figure for that day or for any other day immediately following, but it was never unusual for many casualties not to be reported. However, at the close of the day, Co. D did report their morale as low.[19]

The position of Co. C remained virtually unchanged on the 11th and according to Capt. Burford, "From our OP on the forward slope of Mt. Chiunzi, we could see the towns of Pagani and Nocera, and Route 18 leading to Vietri and Salerno. We could locate enemy vehicular bivouacs along the road, the railroad in the two towns made an excellent target, and vehicles moving along the road afforded good shooting. The OP, however, was in unoccupied territory in front of our lines." This OP, manned by Lt. Julian McKinnon, became prime real estate as a German patrol took advantage of the heavy foliage, which obstructed the view of Co. C, and used ropes to climb up the mountain and attack the OP. Although the Rangers forced the enemy back Pvt. Joseph M. Cocco of the 83rd and a Ranger were killed, and the position had to be evacuated by McKinnon and others without retrieval of the bodies. Ironically, Cocco, the first man killed in action in Co. C, was of Italian birth and died on Italian soil. William Ford, Co. C, claimed Cocco had relatives in Naples he had planned to visit when he reached that city. Capt. Burford also reported this episode but claimed it happened on the 12th. Col. Darby reported the arrival of 300 rounds of ammo although a number of baseplates and standards were rendered useless by firing at the extreme range often required.[20]

At Vietri-sul-Mare, Co. D did not fire the entire day, but they moved six squads to the southeast section of town, leaving two squads in town to deliver fire when necessary. Despite not being engaged on the 11th, lieutenants Sammy Miller and Alfred Crenshaw captured five Germans in a house near the beach. Enemy shells fell in town, often hitting tops of buildings and producing shell fragments that seriously wounded and hospitalized Pfc.'s Theron F. Jones, Michael J. Rebick, and Eugene R. Latimer. Rebick was evacuated to Africa for treatment, where he later wrote he was recovering well and wanted " … to get back soon to get them rats."[21]

The situation at Chiunzi Pass was bolstered on September 12th when a fresh supply of ammo arrived, along with two batteries of howitzers, which assisted Co. C in engaging the enemy throughout the day. Although no enemy shell had landed near Co. C's position up to this time, a shell did find the target and wounded Pvt. Anthony T. Bonady.[22]

At some point Co. C moved their mortars 500 yards to the right of the pass to avoid enemy mortar fire, but, as Loy Marshall stated, "There was a problem of getting ammunition to this gun position. Some of the gun crews had to take positions as riflemen or carry ammunition from the road to the gun. We had a backpack that would carry two 25-pound shells at a time and we took turns going from rifleman to ammunition carrier. We were ordered to hold this position at all costs … Our water and food supply was short so we'd take only one sip of water because we didn't know when we might get more. Our food was C-rations of dried eggs for breakfast, one can of beans for lunch, and one can of hash for supper. Our emergency K-rations consisted of one can of cheese and one of dried eggs."[23]

Co. C also suffered the loss of Carlos O. Harp of Tennessee, who was accidentally shot and killed by his best friend. Hale Hepler recalled that he had shared a pup tent with Harp, who often jokingly performed a gun duel with his buddy, imitating gunslingers of the Old West. One day Harp's friend was inebriated and forgot his gun was loaded. Harp was killed as a result and, Hepler added, the last he saw of Harp's buddy he was being led away by the MPs.[24]

At Vietri-sul-Mare, Co. D's 2nd Platoon moved two mortars under a railroad in the north part of town where 49 rounds were fired. The 1st Platoon of Co. D, led by lieutenants James Otis Beasley, Samuel W. Miller, and Alfred H. Crenshaw, patrolled north of town where some Germans were reported to be in a house. The results of the patrol proved tragic and confusing. According to Crenshaw, "About 4:30 Sunday afternoon our platoon was ordered to go to another house where several Germans wanted to surrender to the Americans. Sam, Lt. Beasley (the platoon executive) and I got the platoon together … the platoon moved out towards the outskirts of town. Beasley was to go ahead and contact the supporting unit and let them know what we were going to do. He moved ahead about 75 yards, Sam and a runner [*Claude T. Burkett of Bassfield, Mississippi*] following closely behind him. I held the platoon back until contact was made. The runner came back to get an interpreter who could talk to the Italian guide. As he was returning we heard machine gun and rifle fire. Sam and Beasley were out of sight around a corner about 100 yards ahead of me. When the runner and interpreter went back they called out but got no answer, so they came back. I kept five men with me and sent the rest of the platoon back to their gun positions. I kept a bazooka man, an automatic rifle man and three riflemen. We waited for dark so that we could go out on a patrol to look for our friends. About dark we were joined by a British officer. Together we worked our way to a position above

Co. C's William C. Ford, Ralph Long, and Joseph Williamson in Salerno.
Chris Williamson

the spot where they were last seen. The British officer went ahead, returning in about an hour. He told us he had been all over the ground and could find no trace of the officers …" and assumed they had been captured.[25]

Details of the episode did not emerge until 15 days later when the ground could safely be investigated. Crenshaw reportedly found the graves of lieutenants Miller and Beasley. Some Italians told him that they had not suffered and had been buried by the Germans with military honors. Apparently a Graves Registration unit later removed the bodies to an American military cemetery. Unfortunately, due to this belated occupation of the ground, as well as to the movement of troops and Lt. Col. Cunin, much confusion developed over the exact details of the episode, with Cunin somewhat unfairly accused of giving the two men's widows false hope that the lieutenants had been captured.[26]

"Bud" Pike, who was not present but did have close access to information, gave his account of the deaths of Beasley and Miller. "Jim [*Beasley*] was out forward as an observer for the mortar fire of his platoon and he did an excellent job. He was under almost continuous fire of German artillery and still stayed there and performed his job. When this first firing mission of his was completed, he returned to the Company CP and I went out to a new observation post to observe fire for the other platoon." When he returned two days later, Pike was informed the two lieutenants were missing and launched an investigation. "In the early evening of the first day that I had gone to the OP an Italian civilian had come into Vietri-sul-Mare from the next town about 1 mile away which was occupied by the Germans and he claimed that there was a group of Germans in a house a short way down the road who wanted to surrender but could not come into our lines. He said that if some of our soldiers went down there that they could bring them in. Jim and Sammy Miller heard this and got the idea that they should go down & try to take these Germans. Accordingly they organized a patrol of about ten men out of our company [*among this group was Clark Riddle*] and started down the road. After going down the road a short distance they came to a blind turn around which they could not see. Rather than risk the lives of their men, Jim and Sammy decided to go around the curve alone first and check to see if it would be all right to bring the men forward. When they made the turn that was the last the men saw of them. They heard a few bursts of machine guns (Germans) around the corner and were not able to get around themselves to help Jim & Sammy as the turn was covered by the machine guns."[27]

When he later became commanding officer of the battalion, William S. Hutchinson, who was not present during the events either, also looked into the matter and concluded, "Jim and Sam went forward with one squad. They marched straight up the road. As they rounded a bend and came out from the protection of overhanging rocks a sniper in a house fired a machine pistol from a window evidently killing Sam and fatally wounding Jim. I believe that Jim made cover behind a small wall which ran along the road on the left side away from the hill … Without their officers the squad returned to the mortar position. They did not know that their officers were dead. Machine pistol and machine gun fire was covering the bend in the road with deadly fire. There was no possible way to flank the Germans because of the cliffs on either side. They could not call to Sam or Jim and could not get out to bring them back." Hutchinson went on to state that when the British reached the site days later, "… they found a very neat grave with Jim's dog tags on the traditional German military cross. The Germans evidently buried him with full military honors. Sam's body was still lying by the side of the road with his dog tags as identification. The Germans do not bury Jews. The British buried Sam." He later added that Crenshaw had seen Beasley's grave "… with his name written on the cross overhead and his helmet hung on the cross arm." Crenshaw also mentioned there was a small picture of the Virgin Mary with a baby in her arms tacked to the grave. Beasley's son would later find this ironic because his dad, "Like his father, [*had*] little use for religion and when he was issued his dog-tags he wanted them to be labeled 'Atheist'. The military wouldn't do that, so he settled for 'Non-Hebrew', a wise choice considering where he was going."[28]

Lt. James Otis Beasley had graduated from Texas A&M and Harvard Graduate School and was a pioneer in cotton genetics before the war. The men considered him somewhat of a mentor and word of his and Miller's deaths quickly spread through the ranks. James Marion Lester of Co. D's Motor Pool remembered that he and mechanic Charlie Lowry had been out on an assignment in their truck and when they returned to camp the men came running out to tell them the sad news. Clark Riddle recalled that Lt. Beasley was a bit "nuts" or "gung-ho" and that the men were somewhat intimidated by him because he was a college graduate and about ten years older than the average soldier. Beasley did not care for the typical drinking and partying, which made him feel like he did not "belong" to the group. But he was noted for his devotion to duty and to accomplishing the mission whatever the cost. Al Crenshaw said Beasley was "… the bravest man I ever knew - or he just didn't have any imagination and think he could get hit." Ed Trey added, "He wouldn't have survived the war in any case - he just took too many chances." An unknown source would comment, "We just couldn't figure out what he was doing out there in front of our lines - way out in 'Indian country.'" "Bud" Pike said Beasley "... was the best officer in 'D' Company, as good an officer as we had in the battalion ... he showed absolutely no signs of fear and had the respect and admiration of us all. He always had the welfare and best interests of the men under him at heart and they liked him for it ... Jim did a man's job in a man's way."[29]

Although the remainder of the 12th was rather uneventful, with no significant fighting, Dan Shields did mention there was plenty of shelling throughout the day and Lt. Col. Cunin sent a report to Brig. Gen. Alden H. Waitt, Chief of the CWS, at Gravelly Point, Virginia, detailing the lessons learned by the chemical mortar battalions in the Sicilian Campaign.[30]

Samuel Wapnitsky, Co. D, (second from right) with unidentified 83rd men in Salerno.
Dougherty Collection

On the 13th, the Germans moved their guns to a point where they could fire through Chiunzi Pass, sent out patrols to attack behind the lines, and produced continual small arms and machine gun fire. The battalion journal stated that all men of Co. C excepting those in communications and ammo details were posted in positions around the mortars. Two casualties were sustained as Corp. Mitchell C. ("Kid") Holloway of Pennsylvania, the company clerk, and Pvt. Fitzhugh Dye of Mississippi were both seriously wounded by shell fragments and evacuated. Dye later passed away from the effects of his wounds. At one point, an RAF plane dropped some bombs on the Germans using parachute flares for light. Despite the situation, the morale of Co. C was high in anticipation of a breakthrough of the pass by the 5th Army. South of Vietri the 1st Platoon of Co. D fired all four mortars while the 2nd Platoon threw 308 rounds at a tank, which made three attempts to break through the outer lines, and at a machine gun position. Daniel Shields said he slept in "a stable" during the night.[31]

The 1st Platoon of Co. C was divided on the 14th, when one section of two guns under Lt. Ralph T. Rankin moved about two miles down the road from Chiunzi Pass and attached to the 505th Parachute Infantry, 82nd Airborne Division. At this location on the right flank, they could fire on targets around Camarelle. Lt. Alvin G. Metcalfe took the other section of two guns via truck, under the cover of darkness, to Agerola on the left flank, some 20 miles from Maiori, in order to support the 4th Rangers. Targets in the vicinity of Castellammare became their priority. The 2nd Platoon remained at Chiunzi Pass under the command of Lt. Julian T. ("Mac") McKinnon.[32]

Around 10:00 p.m., Col. Darby called upon Capt. Burford to fire on some targets "just for the hell of it." Burford recalled, "He went out through the Pass with me and my communications man until we reached a position from which we could see the targets. I began to fire, but the mortars were having difficulty due to the excessive ranges being fired, the yielding soil upon which the baseplates were emplaced, lack of night lights for sighting, and other factors. After about an hour, Darby turned to me and said, 'Captain Burford, I am by no means pleased with this shooting tonight. I don't know what your troubles are, but you do. I expect you to iron out those troubles and be prepared to shoot at any time, day or night, and at any target which I designate. Now I want you to continue shooting until you have placed a concentration on that crossing (pointing). Is that clear?' I felt provoked and angry at the thought of my men working and sweating their hearts out to please him and getting no more consideration than that ... we finished the shooting at 1:00 a.m. and went to bed." Suffering through hot weather Co. D remained in their positions at Vietri where they were shelled with little effect by the enemy. Their morale was reported as fair.[33]

Companies A and B continued their usual bivouac and training duties at Termini Imerese on the 15th while the 2nd Platoon of Co. C held fast at Chiunzi Pass. Col. Darby requested Lt. Metcalfe's section of the 1st Platoon set up on the right flank to cover a half-mile tunnel where an enemy counterattack was anticipated. Lt. Rankin's section of the

1st Platoon "manhandled their mortars to the top of Mt. San Angelo di Cava" and hired Italian citizens to carry the ammo. According to Capt. Burford, the movement involved "… carrying the mortars up the side of a steep mountain with no paths, roads, or footholds. It took seven hours to get two mortars up there. Italian natives were hired to carry the ammunition, water, rations up the hill and it required two and one half hours for a man carrying two rounds of ammunition on his back to make the trip." Rankin served as observer while Lt. Donald R. Gabriel stayed with the guns, which remained in position for a week, fired at extreme ranges of 5,000 yards, and helped to silence the enemy 88mm batteries and troop concentrations beyond the range of the Allied artillery. Capt. Saams of the Rangers was so impressed by Rankin's performance he cited him for the Silver Star.[34]

Co. C was under fire throughout the day as Capt. Rupert O. Burford of Charleston, West Virginia, was slightly wounded by a shell fragment. In his diary Burford wrote a detailed account of his wounding, stating that he had been at the pass observing the improved foundations for the mortars when shells began to fall. "One landed about twenty yards away, detonated, and I stepped behind a big tree for protection. I felt a stinging sensation in my thigh, as though someone had thrown a handful of sand at me. Thinking to myself: 'Boy, that was close, I almost got hit', I looked around for a foxhole to get in. Then I felt something wet trickling down my leg, looked down and saw a hole in my trousers that hadn't been there before. So I said to myself: 'Close hell! I am hit'. After the shelling subsided I called [*Henry D.*] Bufkin, our aid man to come and look at my Purple Heart. Examination disclosed that a fragment had entered my thigh and opened up a hole about the size of a half-dollar." Burford went to the aid station, took a tetanus shot, and was advised to go to the hospital, located in the auditorium of a local church in Maiori. After turning company command over to Lt. Ralph Rankin, he gathered together his driver, Angelo Simone, and orderly, Morris R. Richards, and prepared to leave for the hospital. Then, "While standing near the jeep I heard a hail and looked around to see [*Lt. Harold A.*] Churchill who, hearing that I had been killed, had come in from the OP. I started toward him, and at that instant an explosion occurred just a few feet behind me. I looked around to see a large hole in the road where a shell had struck. Of course everybody had cleared out. Churchill gave a startled gasp: 'My God, Captain, you certainly bear a charmed life'. No more shells came in …" and Burford made it safely to the hospital where he was advised to keep the fragment in his leg.[35]

At Vietri, Co. D received and delivered fire without any serious damage although the battalion journal reported the morale of Co. D was only fair. Staff Sgt. Mike Codega, serving as an observer, earned a Bronze Star for gallantry. Apparently Codega went to the OP, which was under heavy incoming artillery fire, and remained there for twenty-four hours helping the platoon knock out some machine gun nests and a mortar emplacement, and directing some good firing on roads. Daniel Shields, a devout Catholic, noted the shelling and hot weather as he "said Rosary with Italians in an air raid shelter." After a meal of spaghetti he spent the night sleeping on some steps.[36]

The Germans attacked all three positions of Co. C on the 16th but each effort was repulsed, although the Germans got within 1,000 yards of the base of Co. C. Luckily, air support in the form of four A-36 Invaders arrived and blasted the enemy position marked by the WP smoke of the 83rd. A Ranger patrol investigated the position and located about 200 dead Germans. Unfortunately, later in the day an enemy shell fell in Co. C's gun position, killing Pvt. Thomas E. Hamilton and wounding Pvt. Chester E. Pultorak, Pvt. Edward W. Hawkins, and Pfc. Carmen Marzulli. It was learned that Hamilton, from Lafayette County, Mississippi, apparently died from the concussion as there was not a scratch on him. Hale Hepler said Hawkins did not smoke or drink and was one of the nicest men he knew.[37]

Another problem at Chiunzi Pass was an outbreak of malaria. Jerome ("Jerry") Muschinske, Co. C, came down with the infection and "was sent back to the beach where a first aid station was set up in the town church," where two British surgeons and a local nurse attended the sick and wounded. "The emergency operations were performed on the altar. My bed was a flea infested bed and mattress in the adjacent nunnery." Two days later, Muschinske was moved to Salerno, where he "stayed on the beach sand overnight while the beachhead was being bombed by German planes." Eventually, Muschinske made it to Canastel and was reassigned to the 602nd Base Ordnance Battalion for the remainder of the war.[38]

Worse yet, at about 8:00 in the evening the enemy shelled the gun position of the 2nd Platoon of Co. D at Vietri, causing numerous casualties. Among the killed were Pfc. Dillard E. Gulley, Pvt. Corbet Whittaker, and Pvt. George E. Egan, Jr. Gulley had grown a goatee in emulation of some of the British Commandos, and the shell blew his head off down to his lower lip and goatee. The wounded included Sgt. Frank P. ("Francis") Lombardi, whose right lung was pierced by shrapnel, Corp. Joseph J. Sapienza, Pfc. Arthur LeRoy, Pfc. William J. Hofmann, and privates Philip J. Turco, Fredrik M. Bockman, James H. Leonard, and John H. Winkler. Harold Hughes of the company noted that all of Vietri had become a battleground and said one man reported on his walkie-talkie that "We're holding the kitchen, the Germans are in the living room and the bathroom is unoccupied." The company stood by throughout the night awaiting instructions to move yet their morale remained fair.[39]

The battalion got a boost on the 17th at Termini Imerese with the arrival of 31 enlisted replacements from the 9th Infantry Division and 67 from the 1st Infantry Division. Additionally, Lt. Col. Cunin apparently decided to join his troops, so along with his chauffeur and interpreter, he embarked on an LST to join companies C and D in Italy. Indeed, the sections of Co. C at St. Angelo di Cava and Agerola were heavily engaged throughout the day, while Lt. McKinnon's section at Chiunzi Pass successfully repelled a number of German patrols. At Vietri, Co. D dug in at a new position about three miles north of Salerno, although Daniel Shields claimed in his diary that this took place three miles south of town.[40]

The men of Co. C knocked out a self-propelled 88mm gun on the 18th at St. Angelo di Cava. This is probably the episode mentioned by Maj. William S. Hutchinson, who would later state, "Not even a foot path led up to this peak. We paid Italian civilians 50 cents a trip to take two shells each to the gun position." In an interview Hutchinson added, "Our positions in the mountains overlooked the German main supply route from Naples to Salerno. The artillery dead space, because of the mask provided by the precipitous Sorrento Mountain peninsula, ran up to 3000 yards from our mortar positions. At the time only M5 powder was available, so that our maximum range was 3200 yards. However, because of the importance of the targets in the dead space between 3200 and 3000 yards, mortars were fired with excessive powder charges." He added the mortars held up fairly well with the excessive charges, but with the 18 ring powder charge, "the mortar failed after one round. The base cap cup locked over lugs of the base cap and the traversing screw bent and locked the mortar in place. One sample of the luckiest shot was fired with 18 rings and the aim range was approximately 4700 yards and a direct hit was scored on the 88mm gun … we emplaced those mortars on the top of Mt. St. Angelo to take advantage of the site and that 4700 yards was the horizontal distance from the crest of Mt. St. Angelo to [the target] … approximately all the firing was above 3200." In an article he wrote for the *Chemical Warfare Bulletin*, Hutchinson added, "The crew used 18 rings of M5A1 powder to get the distance, the three of the rings were simply dropped down the barrel."[41]

Co. C also fired on Germans repairing a bridge at Agerola and supported an attack of the Rangers on a knoll at Chiunzi Pass. In the latter effort, the company covered the knoll with HE and WP for eight hours. The morale of the men was also boosted as Capt. Burford returned from the hospital to Chiunzi Pass, nicknamed "Shrapnel Pass" by the men. Various troops also referred to the area as "88 Pass" and "Hellfire Pass" due to the heavy barrage of German 88mm shells. Co. D successfully engaged the enemy in support of an attack of the 2nd Commando Battalion on Pimple Hill and White Cross Hill near Salerno and then returned to Vietri under the cover of darkness. Daniel Shields slept "on ground in water."[42]

Lt. Col. Cunin arrived via LCI at a southern beach at Salerno on September 19th and moved to the Ranger headquarters, while the sections of Co. C held their three different positions at and near Chiunzi Pass. Co. D, yet attached to the Rangers and under occasional artillery fire, awaited orders as their morale improved from fair to good.[43]

Heavy fighting continued around Chiunzi Pass on the 20th as the enemy heavily shelled the Agerola area and a patrol of the 43rd Infantry "slugged it out" with the enemy less than 1,000 yards from Co. C's position at the pass. Late in the day, Co. D departed Vietri for Ferriera. During the movement they crossed a bridge under machine gun fire. Harold Hughes wrote, "We filed out of Vietri seventeen days after we landed, a decimated, dazed bunch of men. After marching eight miles we were finally given permission to sleep. Someone pointed out a small stone church that had been hit by shell fire. It looked like heaven and we straggled into it. One man hauled his sleeping buddy into the building by the heels." The next day Hughes came down with malaria and was shipped to a hospital in North Africa, unable to return to the battalion until after the Anzio invasion the following year.[44]

Lt. Ralph Rankin, serving as forward observer with Co. C, directed fire on numerous targets on the 21st, breaking up an effort by the enemy to regroup, while the Germans attempted to circle the flank at Agerola, which forced the company to establish additional guards on a 24-hour alert. Enemy shells fell throughout the day at Chiunzi Pass and Pvt. Sylvan M. Rosenfeld was slightly wounded by shell fragments. The 2nd Platoon of Co. D went into bivouac at

Ferriera, where many of the men would have their pictures taken in a local photo studio, while the 1st Platoon moved near Pietre to support an action of the 4th Ranger Battalion, where they could fire on targets in the town of Sala.[45]

Little combat activity took place at the three positions of Co. C on the 22nd, although enemy long range guns were spotted in the vicinity of Mt. Vesuvius but out of range of 105mm howitzers. The 1st Platoon of Co. D was engaged at Pietre while the 2nd Platoon remained in bivouac and reserve at Ferriera.[46]

The mortars of Co. C at San Angelo di Cava rejoined the company on the 23rd and the section at Agerola took notice of the withdrawal of the enemy in the direction of Naples. At the pass, the men reported the gathering of British armor between the pass and Maiori, indicating it was near time for the long anticipated Allied advance through the pass. Some German shells fell in the gun position and ignited "some of the propellant charges already affixed to the rounds." Capt. Burford added, "Two shells, duds, lit within a few feet of my slit trench … luckily I didn't have dysentery or my trousers would have been wet again, and this time it wouldn't have been blood."[47]

A meeting of unit commanders was held that evening, during which the planned breakthrough was explained in detail. According to Capt. Burford, "A company of engineers was to go down the road from the Pass, sweeping mines and clearing obstacles, repair the bridge at Sala and remain to defend the bridge; a battalion of infantry was to go down the forward slope of Mt. Chiunzi, enter and hold the small town of San Egidio, guarding the approach to Sala; prior to this, the mortars of Co. D were to shell Sala and Co. C was to shell San Egidio; then Co. C was instructed to create a diversion by firing on Pagani and Nocera; following these preparations … the next morning the armored brigade would proceed down the Pass and debouch upon the Plains of Naples across the bridge at Sala." In accordance with this plan, and in anticipation of a breakthrough by the British X Corps, the two platoons of Co. D moved three miles northeast of Ferriera and took up a position adjacent to Co. C at Chiunzi Pass, where they remained under heavy artillery fire. The 1st Platoon would support the attack from prepared positions at the Pass, while the 2nd Platoon would move forward with the attack and set up on the Plains of Naples. The attack would be delayed three times in a period of 72 hours due to the late arrival of the British. The morale of the men of Co. D was again reported as being fair.[48]

At Agerola the mortar section of Co. C held their position on the 24th while the men at Chiunzi Pass received an early morning report of a possible enemy parachute drop behind their lines. The guard was increased but the threat never materialized, although the position was shelled continually during the day. Casualties did occur, including two mules used for carrying ammo killed and five men wounded. Among the latter were Lt. Harold A. Churchill, Sgt. George W. Wolfe, Sgt. William L. Holmes, Pfc. Parks H. Durham, and Pvt. Arnold J. Dailey. The 1st Platoon of Co. D fired 244 rounds at a machine gun nest as well as at mortar positions, enemy troop positions, and a gasoline dump. Small arms fire prevailed throughout the night as fire was exchanged with a sniper. Pvt. Claude F. Hall of the company sustained a slight wound from a shell fragment.[49]

Lt. Col. Cunin departed the combat area and returned to the bivouac at Termini Imerese on the 25th, where companies A and B continued training activities. The section of Co. C at Agerola, detecting no enemy activity, pulled in their flank guards. Regular enemy barrages continued to fall on the 2nd Platoon of Co. C at Chiunzi Pass, which provoked forward observer Lt. McKinnon, unable to spot the enemy, to lay down a sweeping fire on every possible enemy position. Sgt. Earl Shaddinger of Philadelphia, Pennsylvania, was hit by a shell fragment, which took him out of commission for a few days. The weather was cloudy and rainy as the 1st Platoon of Co. D, yet posted about three miles northeast of Ferriera, fired about 210 rounds, while the 2nd Platoon hauled ammo and supplies to gun positions, often under enemy barrages. During one such shelling, both T/5 L. D. Whittaker of Tennessee and

Co. D's John A. Feifer standing, wearing glasses. Others unidentified.
Codega Collection

Pvt. Richard A. Bridge of Pennsylvania were wounded and hospitalized. At the end of the day the morale of Co. D was reported as fair.[50]

A major change took place for the 83rd Chemical Battalion on September 26th when Lt. Col. Cunin permanently left the battalion, having been transferred to the 1st U.S. Infantry Division to help coordinate chemical warfare units for the planned invasion of France the following year. As Cunin departed Termini Imerese for Agrigento, Maj. William S. Hutchinson, Jr., took command of the 83rd with David W. Meyerson as battalion executive officer. When word of Cunin's departure reached Rupert Burford, he happily exclaimed, "The Reign of Terror is over and maybe [*now*] we can have a pleasant outfit to work in."[51]

Maj. William Seely ("Hutch") Hutchinson, Jr., was certainly the logical successor to Cunin. Born in Washington, D.C., in 1914, the short, red-haired man attended schools in New York City before earning a BS in chemical engineering at Lehigh University and a MS in the same subject from Massachusetts Institute of Technology. After entering the service in 1940, he served as a 1st lieutenant in Procurement and Planning in the Chemical Warfare Service in 1942 before quickly achieving a captaincy in the same department in June. He was soon afterward assigned to HQ and HQ Co. of the 83rd Chemical Battalion, where he was designated executive officer of the battalion at Camp Gordon, Georgia, on September 15th, 1942. A few days later he briefly served as battalion adjutant before returning to his position as executive officer on October 10th. "Hutch" also spent time on the Summary Court at Camp Gordon and later earned a Silver Star for his July 12th, 1943, performance at Gela, Sicily. Richard Tregaskis, war correspondent with the International News Service and author of such books as *Guadalcanal Diary*, spent time near a foxhole and in a hospital tent with Hutchinson. He described Hutchinson as a great conversationalist who had statistics to prove the 4.2" mortar was the most effective weapon of the war. Additionally, "Hutch" was "… loud in praise of his men. He insisted that Purple Hearts were as common as campaign ribbons in the chemical mortar battalion." In *Invasion Diary*, his book on the Italian campaign, Tregaskis claimed that Hutchinson "was a staunch advocate of Lehigh University" and that when such subjects as chemical mortar medals and Lehigh were exhausted as topics of conversation, "… he would sing. He had a fine tenor voice, and sometimes would harmonize …" with others around him. John P. McEvoy remembered "Hutch" as "… dedicated to the U.S. Army, the Rangers, and the 83rd. He enjoyed combat operations but tended to be a bit too enthusiastic for some men … He was an effective collaborator with Darby to use the 83rd to best help the Rangers. He would heed the advice of his company commanders."[52]

Hutchinson, though, much like Cunin, was a self-centered glory seeker, strict on military discipline and authority. Although an obvious favorite with Lt. Col. Cunin, at least some of his subordinate officers and enlisted men were not enamored with him as the new commanding officer of the battalion. This attitude was best expressed through the correspondence of Capt. Edwin "Bud" Pike, Co. D, who said that, if Cunin was bad, Hutchinson was even worse. As early as May 25th, 1943, Pike had written, "Thank God Hutchinson is not yet a Major," followed on August 19th when he sadly relayed, "Bill Hutchinson is now a Major and the same opinion prevails of him as before." In a letter dated August 28th, he declared Hutchinson was "about as bad" as Cunin at attracting personal praise and attention. When Hutchinson left the battalion in 1944, Pike best summed up his feelings when he wrote, "He is a damn good BN CO and has a lot of guts, but he is still a horse's ass."[53]

The change in the top brass of the battalion had no particular effect on the men fighting it out at Maiori. The colonel of the 505th Parachute Infantry praised the work of Co. C at Agerola and was shocked to learn that only one mortar section had been used on the bridge and tunnel. The two platoons of Co. D continued their work of the previous day near Ferriera in more cloudy, rainy, damp, and cold weather, although their reported company morale improved from fair to good. One man of Co. D's 1st Platoon was wounded by enemy shell fire.[54]

Companies A and B witnessed the presentation of several awards at Termini Imerese on the 27th as Silver Stars were handed out to S/Sgt. John S. Bonarek and Pfc. Carl A. Bishop. Purple Hearts were given to 2nd Lt. Joseph C. Stiefvater (Co. D), Pfc. Claud C. Kuykendall (Co. A), and Pvt. Donald ("Spider") Rugito (Co. C). Co. C's section at Agerola prepared to move to Castellammare while the men at Chiunzi Pass again came under severe enemy fire yet managed to successfully cover the "big push," the long-anticipated Allied advance through the pass. Casualties did occur, such as Sgt. Joseph F. Naczyskio, who was killed when an enemy mortar shell hit an ammo dump. Near Ferriera the two platoons of Co. D supported the advancing troops as well, covering a combined Ranger and infantry attack. Pvt. Karl M. Langford was slightly wounded. However, the weather and the morale of the company were reported as fair.[55]

Having assumed command of the battalion, Lt. Col. Hutchinson decided to join his men in Italy and on September 28th embarked on an LST at Termini Imerese accompanied by lieutenants Joseph C. Stiefvater, Robert W. Smith, Justin G. Woomer, and Silverino V. DeMarco; Sgt. Robert P. Brimm; and 18 enlisted men culled from the Medical Detachment, HQ Co., and companies C and D. In the meantime, back in Italy the section of Co. C at Agerola moved to Castellammare while the force at Chiunzi Pass took the Plains of Naples against slight resistance, despite the fact that enemy long range guns at Mt. Vesuvius knocked out a number of Allied tanks at the pass. During the afternoon a hailstorm and heavy downpour flooded the foxholes of companies C and D. Daniel Shields, Co. D, said his foxhole filled up with rain water which prevented him from getting any sleep. To keep himself occupied he decided to sing, which caught the attention of his buddy Russell S. Doster of Maryland, who was located nearby. Doster thought perhaps Shields had lost his mind and went to see if he could help. Upon arrival at Daniel's abode he realized the predicament and offered to share his foxhole, which Shields declined. Doster returned to his hole glad to avoid his friend's singing. These were considered minor problems, though, as the stalemate at Chiunzi Pass was over.[56]

Rest and relaxation were finally realized by Co. C on the 29th as the men moved to an abandoned paper factory about two miles from Maiori. Capt. Burford summed up his company's action during the previous few weeks, stating, "Nineteen days continuous fighting, 3 men killed, 25 wounded, 10 evacuated because of malaria and other illness, total of 5240 rounds of 4.2" ammunition fired." Co. D moved to Ferriera to rest, noted the enemy was on the run, and received confirmation at Ferriera that lieutenants James O. Beasley and Samuel W. Miller had been killed in action earlier in the month. The following day Maj. Hutchinson arrived in Italy and joined Co. C at Maiori. Co. D also continued to rest at Ferriera while companies A and B remained at Termini Imerese in Sicily. It was at this time that Lt. Col. W. G. Caldwell, HQ, 7th Army, sent a letter to the commanding general of the Allied Forces, making various recommendations regarding the 4.2" chemical mortar as an organic infantry weapon, based upon lessons learned in Sicily. Among the numerous recommendations was for a "tractor drawn mount" to make the mortar more mobile, the need for "illuminating the site for night firing" as the "Germans have a small flashlight strapped around the forehead under the helmet," and a new TO consisting of the total strength of a battalion as 24 officers, 564 enlisted men, and 32 mortars.[57]

The recent action at Vietri-sul-Mare between September 9th and 20th also brought forth knowledge that mortars must be emplaced on firm soil or notable damage will occur and that proper plans regarding ammo supply must be ensured because during the operation, a misunderstanding had led to improper ammo being issued, resulting in the loss of several favorable targets of opportunity. Maj. Hutchinson also noted, "Failure of the mortars throughout the 19 day period was very heavy. At the end of the period there were approximately three mortars in action in 'C' Company and six mortars in action in 'D' Company out of the twelve in each; that is, with constant maintenance of both truck and welding crews of the Mortar Maintenance Company. The rest of the mortars were temporarily out of action due to failure. That does not mean there were only nine failures in 'C' Company. Everything was constantly being repaired," although maintenance crews were usually seven miles down the hill to the rear, and then it was "… about a six hour walk to the most remote gun position after you went the seven miles."[58]

During the 19-day engagement at Chiunzi Pass, Co. C had fired 2,127 rounds of WP and 3,287 of HE, for a total of 5,414. Total casualties were three killed, 13 wounded and evacuated, 10 wounded not evacuated, and eight evacuated for sickness. There was a high degree of damage to the mortars, principally fractured baseplates and broken standards, caused primarily by the nature of the soil. Additionally, the type of terrain required firing mortars far beyond the maximum required range and there was a lack of a proper sight for night firing. For their outstanding performance in protecting the right flank of the 5th Army at Chiunzi Pass, Co. C was awarded a Unit Citation.[59]

From October 1st through the 22nd, companies A and B continued normal training activities at Termini Imerese, Sicily. On the first of the month, Co. C was ordered to move the following day to Castellammare, Italy, and Co. D, in bivouac at Ferriera, was informed that Pfc. George E. Egan, Jr. had died on September 17th of wounds received in action. On the 2nd, Co. C arrived at Castellammare by truck convoy and sheltered in a railroad workshop, while Co. D departed Ferriera at 11:00 a.m. and arrived at Castellammare at 9:00 in the evening, where the company remained in the rain until later bivouacked in the same abandoned building as Co. C, which Daniel Shields also indicated was a railroad station. According to Capt. Robert E. Edwards, Jr., "Had a little rain storm this morning and the wind played havoc with plenty of tents. Had to hold mine up for a short period." C and D departed Castellammare by truck convoy at 7:30 on the morning of October 3rd and arrived at Naples at 10:30 a.m., where they bivouacked in the northern section of the city in the Royal Palace Capodimonte, former residence of the Duke of Acosta, late commander of the Italian forces in Ethiopia. Capt. Pike called it the "palace of [*the*] Duchess of D'Astor … beautiful estate." Ironically, within one day's time the weather had become fair and morale was reported as good.[60]

Action at Volturno River October 5 – 8

Co. C was alerted on October 4th that they were to move to the front to support the 505th Parachute Infantry in an effort to push the Germans from the south bank of the Volturno River. The company departed Naples by truck at 5:00 in the morning and advanced to Marinelle, where they remained in readiness in their trucks throughout the night awaiting further orders from the 505th. Co. D held fast at the Palace Capodimonte. The following morning Co. C moved to Villa Literno where the CO of the 505th decided to hold them in mobile reserve.[61]

On the 6th, the 1st Platoon, Co. C, moved to a position about one mile north of Villa Literno, near the Volturno River, where British Engineers were busy constructing a bridge, as all bridges were previously destroyed by the retreating enemy. In addition, the roads had been heavily mined forcing the platoon of Co. C to move by a circuitous route under the cover of darkness. The plan called for a brigade of armored vehicles to cross the river, after which Co. C would revert back to the Ranger Force. Meanwhile, in the afternoon Co. D moved out of the palace at Naples, which was taken over by 5th Army HQ, to the Botanical Gardens in the central area of the city, where they reported the weather as rainy and morale as fair.[62]

The Germans counterattacked the Volturno River crossing on the 7th but were repulsed by the infantry and the effective mortar fire of Co. C, which included two rounds of WP and 172 of HE. By five in the evening Co. C had received word that their attachment to the 505th Parachute was terminated. During the engagement at Volturno River, Co. C employed interdictory fire along enemy supply routes, precision fire on enemy installations, and concentrated fire against enemy personnel and patrols. According to the battalion journal, some problems arose. The "… terrain afforded little or no defilade, hence strict observance of camouflage discipline was necessary. The mortar fire was found to be more accurate and more effective than that of light artillery," and notice was taken of the lack of mine sweeping equipment, which caused delays in firing mortars. About the only item mentioned for the day by Co. D was rain.[63]

During October 8th, Co. C moved back to Naples by truck convoy and bivouacked in a barracks north of Naples formerly occupied by Italian soldiers. Capt. Burford said he also moved Co. D to the barracks as there was not enough room at the Botanical Gardens for both companies C and D, as well as the Rangers. Back in Sicily Gen. Matthew B. Ridgway of the 82nd Airborne Division presented Silver Stars for distinguished action to 1st Lt. Ralph T. Rankin, Co. C, of Oklahoma and Pfc. Bennie Lieberman of Washington, D.C., and Pfc. Albert Cohen, both of Co. D.

Companies C and D remained in Naples throughout the 9th and reported the weather fair and morale good. But a rash of time bombs exploding in the city brought about a decision to move Co. C out of the city and one platoon of Co. D moved to a new bivouac at San Lazzaro, where they occupied a building known as the Colonial Montana. Capt. Pike said they bivouacked in an orphanage which was on a mountain overlooking the sea. The 2nd Platoon of Co. D remained behind in Naples, although they departed the city in rainy weather, but with good morale, and rejoined the 1st Platoon at San Lazzaro the next day. Charlie Lowry, Co. D Motor Pool, confirmed the weather, writing on the 10th: "At last we are getting rain. Day and night, and it isn't good." It was also during this period that Capt. Pike displayed his emotions in reference to the fighting at Salerno, writing, "Company D did a marvelous job and further added to its excellent reputation for combat proficiency … We have seen more combat than any other company in the battalion and, I think, have done the best job. I'm proud of my men and love every one of them."[64]

Co. C was alerted for a movement to the front to be attached to the 3rd Infantry Division on October 12th, but the order was canceled the following day as the company was ordered instead to move to Sorrento and join the Ranger Force. At Sorrento, Co. C found themselves quartered with the Rangers in a hotel apartment which overlooked Mt. Vesuvius and the Isle of Capri. Capt. Burford wrote, "We 'shacked up' with the Rangers in a sanitarium building overlooking the Bay of Naples." The stay was short-lived, though, as on the 15th they were ordered to evacuate the building because it was to be used as a hospital. At 4:00 p.m. they received orders to return to Naples but at 8:00 p.m. received further orders to occupy a school building at Sorrento, which they accomplished on the 16th, the same day

Co. D left San Lazzaro and moved to a bivouac in the Colonial Permanentel building at Amalfi. Capt. Pike said the company stayed in an orphanage and he lived at the Allegro Cappuccini hotel, which he described as "marvelous." The two companies remained in their respective positions at Sorrento and Amalfi until the 19th when Co. C moved by truck convoy to Amalfi via Castellammare, Scafati, Chiunzi Pass, and Maiori. Companies C and D remained at Amalfi for the remainder of October where they performed the usual bivouac duties and instituted training programs. Capt. Burford confirmed the two companies occupied the "orphan asylum" while the officers quartered in the hotel.[65]

During this period Maj. Hutchinson wrote a letter to former battalion commander Cunin detailing the status of the men. He noted on the 18th of October that he was with Darby, as were companies C (Burford) and D (Pike). Col. Maurice Barker, CWS officer, had suggested that once the remainder of the battalion joined them the entire unit should remain with Darby's Rangers. "Hutch" also said Darby's outfit was regrouping and retraining badly needed replacements, while the 83rd planned to train alongside them, but he felt the 83rd needed "...to work in firing map data, night firing, maintaining fire charts, some simple survey, unobserved fire in general, plus plain Ranger infantry tactics." He added that he hoped "... to set up two sided problems both night and day starting with just two men and gradually increasing the size of the units until we finally have one company opposing the remainder of the battalion in which two of the Cos. will operate as infantry ... I am also told that we must be prepared to fire as a battalion."[66]

In the same letter, Hutchinson spoke of the location of the companies and the new Table of Organization, writing, "We are well situated near the Rangers in a small fishing village. Three Cos. are in a vacant orphan asylum, or rather, will be when they get here. HQ and the officers will be in a beautiful hotel overlooking the sea, and the fourth line company will be in an abandoned hospital about five miles away ... We have started battalion formations in the morning, daily inspections of all installations, a weekly Retreat Parade, and a weekly Bn hike with carts. Much the same as the old routine at Gordon, as it would have been if we had had more time for training ..." According to Hutchinson, the War Department had approved a new Table of Organization, which he expected would be implemented soon. At that time the 83rd Chemical battalion had "622 men and officers, 134 jeeps, 131 ¼ T trailers, and only 16 GMCs. HQ has no mess. Messes take up 4 GMCs and the remaining 12 are in the Bn Amm. train." Continuing, Hutchinson

Hale H. Hepler's Co. C squad at a rest area in Pozzuoli after 38 days on the front, during 35 of which it rained, creating much mud. First row L-R: Carlos Harp, Hale Hunter Hepler, and, Elmer Harris. Second row L-R: Willie Johnson, Albert Kubas, Floyd Grissom, and Arnold Porterfield. Standing is Sgt. Walter Gaiski.
Hale Hunter Hepler

wrote, "I intend to give two of these to each company and keep four in HQ The Ex. and S-3 are Majors, S-2 and 4 Captains; Adj. a 1st Lt. There are eight officers in each Co. [*and*] 3 are 2d Lts. We have not seen the detailed break down for the Cos., but expect to be able to continue as two four gun platoons. Col. Barker agrees that we need 15% over strength. We both feel that we could then operate eight guns per Co. satisfactorily. There is always much that is wrong with every T/O but I feel that the advantage of the jeeps outweighs everything else … There is a strong movement afoot to put one battalion in every division and, if this T/O is adopted, they will continue to be Cml. Bns. Otherwise anything can happen … I also understand that the Ranger Force is still under discussion. If established, we will be a part of it."[67]

Hutchinson expressed a desire to make Capt. Edwin "Bud" Pike his executive officer, Dave Meyerson the S-3, Robert E. Edwards his S-2, and Ed Trey both S-4 and detachment commander. In addition, he desired either Christopher C. Cornett or Perry Rice as S-1, Robert M. Schmidt and Leonard A. ("Spike") Merrill, Jr., were to be given "excess in grade," and John P. McEvoy, Gordon M. Mindrum, Rupert Burford, and Alfred Crenshaw would command the four weapons companies. In naming these possible appointments, he said he "… picked Pike as 2d [*in*] command on the basis of actual battle experience and leadership. Somehow I feel that Dave would have trouble carrying the whole load alone, particularly since he does not have actual combat experience. However, I will be able to promote him and we could never find a better staff officer. I expect, also, to get our staff and most of HQ into action in the next operation. When that happens, I feel, that Edwards will have plenty to do as S-2, and will be a good one. There is no chaplain in the new set up. The doctor presents another problem. We get only one. I think I'll let [*Dr. William P.*] Tice take his choice. [*Dr. George B.*] Glazier, of course, will have to go."[68]

Hutchinson "… also hope[*d*] to avoid operating without a staff. The detailed work is piling up shamefully and the whole outfit suffers for it. We have citations, promotions, and appointments galore waiting for typewriters. I am going to recommend Sgts [*John D.*] Barber and [*James L.*] Doyle for commissions, (Rudolph has gone) but I can't do it all myself in longhand … As you know, you left me a very famous battalion. We are known as the Rangers mortar battalion from General Eisenhauer [*sic*] on down. We also did some good work here with the 82nd [*Airborne*] that I managed to get in on and the whole battalion has distinctly made an excellent name for itself … All the men know this and they are just as proud as they can be. We have ordered our own distinctive shoulder patch with 83rd Chemical Bn emblazoned across it. I will send you one as

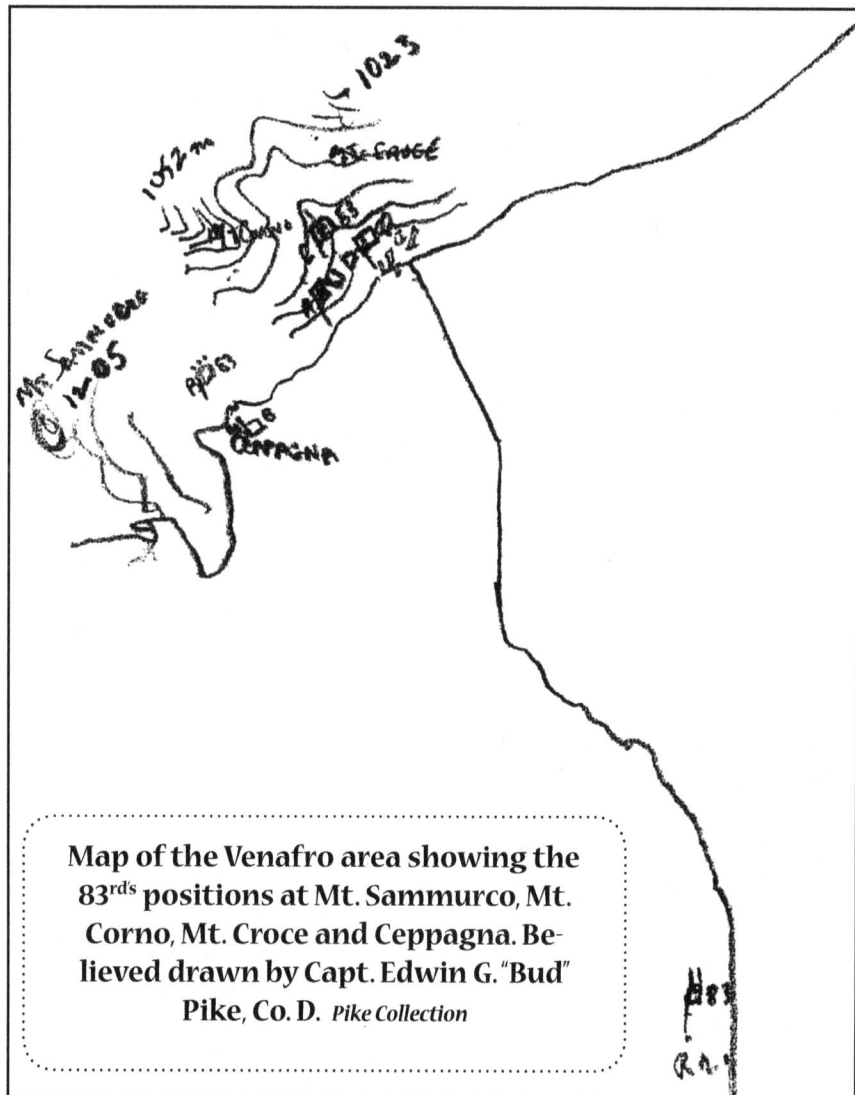

Map of the Venafro area showing the 83rd's positions at Mt. Sammurco, Mt. Corno, Mt. Croce and Ceppagna. Believed drawn by Capt. Edwin G. "Bud" Pike, Co. D. *Pike Collection*

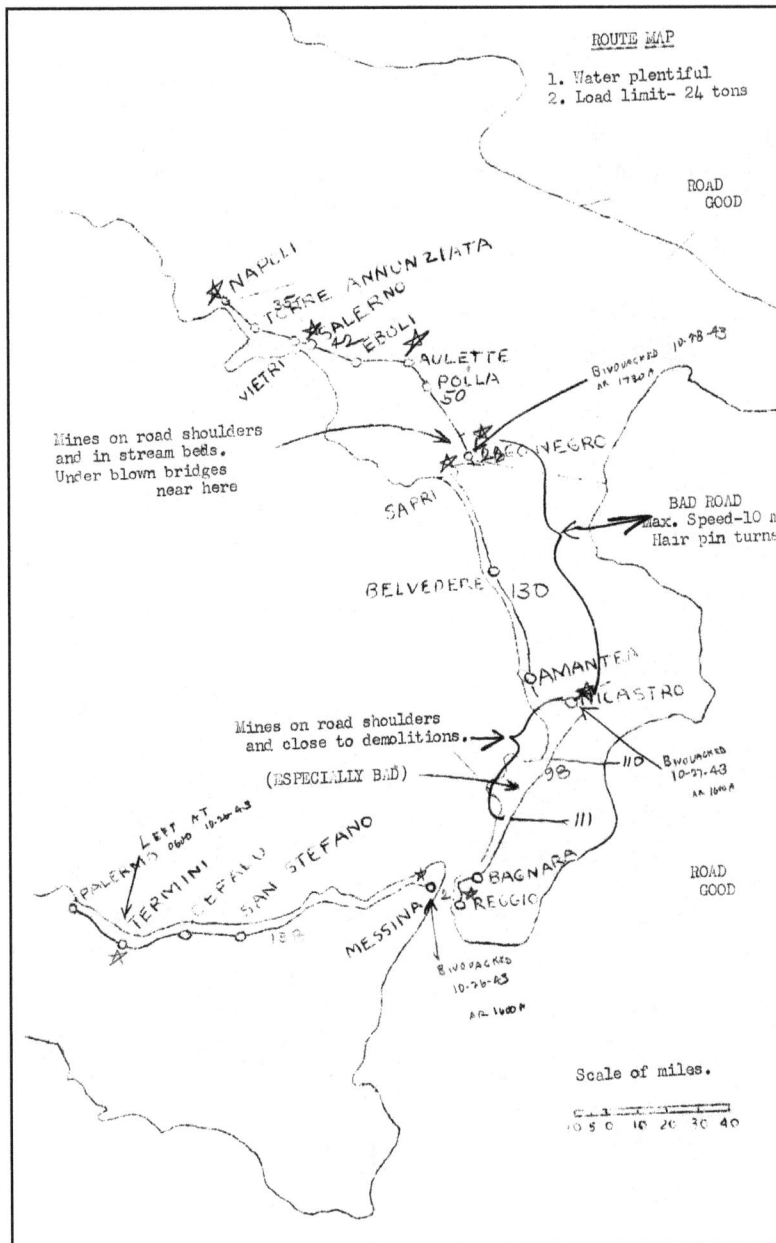

Rangers' map of the 83rd Chemical Battalion convoy
from Palermo to Naples in late October 1943.
National Archives

soon as they are ready."[69]

Further details regarding the battalion were given by Hutchinson. "Col. Barker hopes to get authority to activate one or two new Bns here in order to have one per division and one per Ranger Force. If so, I will recommend Burford for an Ex job and Edwards for an S-3. We could also furnish a top notch cadre, a considerable filler, and several more officers such as [*Alvin G.*] Metcalfe, [*Julian T.*] McKinnon, etc. as Co Comdrs. I would likewise try to dispose of Cornett, Merrill, and Schmidt. Incidentally, Burford and Metcalfe have developed into as fine a pair of officers as we have to offer." Also at this time Jim Carr Myers, a new member of the 83rd, having served previously in Battery C, 34th Field Artillery in North Africa and Sicily wrote "This outfit is just a small mortar battalion. It's not connected with any Division or Army. That's all there is to it."[70]

At Termini Imerese, Sicily, companies A and B, as well as HQ Co. and the Medical Detachment, began preparations on October 23rd for a move to Naples. Three truckloads of supplies were moved to the docks, where they were placed under a detail commanded by S/Sgt. William T. Ulmer of HQ Co., from Kentucky. By the 25th, Maj. William S. Hutchinson, Sgt. Robert P. Brimm, and a jeep driver had reached Termini Imerese via an overland route by Messina as the command completed preparations for movement to Naples and Salerno. James Helsel, Co. A, wrote in his diary, "I hear we are to move. That 'C' & 'D' Company are still having rough going. I sort of hate to leave, although we had very hard training in the morning, the afternoons were so hot that we either went to town, or go down swimming … About two days ago the rains came and I mean came. We were on the hillside and the water just ran down and we didn't do anything but eat and sleep. The first its rained since we have been in Sicily."[71]

On the 26th the command, led by the company kitchen trucks, moved near Messina and crossed the Straits of Messina via a ferry of British-operated LCTs to Reggio on the rainy morning of the 27th. Andrew C. Leech, Co. B, recalled, "It took us a day in convoy to reach Messina where we spent the night … The next morning we loaded on landing barges and crossed the Strait of Messina and continued on up the coast of Italy." The command advanced toward Naples and spent the night at Nicastro. The movement continued on the 28th as the command reached a bivouac about ten miles north of Lago Negro and advanced to Maiori on the 29th, where Co. A occupied an evacuated orphanage. HQ Co. and the Medical Detachment continued west on the Sorrento peninsula to Amalfi.[72]

Capt. Ed "Bud" Pike had previously written home relaying command structure news of the battalion, although most of the information was dated. Among the items he stated were, "Col. Cunin is no longer with the 83rd, having transferred to another outfit. Don't ask me which … Bill H. is now BN CO and is proving to be all right. How about that? … Chaplain Burdick has been transferred having turned out no good. Mindy was in the hospital in Africa for a long time with malaria, but he is all right now. I have Crenshaw, Steve [*Lt. Joseph C. Stiefvater*], Forrester, and a new 2nd Lt. Jim Woomer [*his name was actually Justin Gerald Woomer*], who is very good in D Company now and we are coming along fine"[73]

Capt. Pike continued to describe the latest news of the battalion in his various letters home. On the 29th he wrote, "Chris C. [*Cornett*] was in the hospital with hemorrhoids (that is about as romantic an ailment as he is capable of having); [*Alvin*] Metcalfe and [*Vester Lamar*] Turner have finally been promoted to 1st Lt. after over a year (Steve [*Stiefvater*] is still bucking); Tom Bolton, Andre Laus, [*Julian*] McKinnon, and [*Walter*] Hauser are all in the hospital now; Bob Schmidt is in the best of health and now is in HQ Co … The last few days I have been running over obstacle courses built by the Rangers and my gosh are they ever rugged. You climb up and down cliffs, jump out of trees, and go up rope climbs until you're blue in the face. I have also been constructing a few for the company and running them too, so that I have been tired as a dog lately (with my tail dragging between my legs) and stiff as a board (but not my tail) … we are now in the 5th Army, not the 7th. That is the prime disadvantage of having a separate battalion. You flit from army to army, whichever one happens to be fighting at the time." Russell H. Peterson, Co. D, also took this time to write home to his brother Roland, in Charleston, West Virginia, and state, "I'm sending you a check … the yellow color on it comes from carrying it in my pocket for a couple weeks with some Atrebrine tablets, or should I say Atebrin since they are German."[74]

On October 30th, Co. A was still at Maiori while the remainder of the command moved to Amalfi, where battalion headquarters, including HQ Co. and the Medical Detachment, were quartered in the Hotel Capuccini, where they remained throughout the following day. Capt. Burford said the balance of the other companies was "squeezed" into the orphanage with companies C and D. Capt. Pike gave a description of the food offerings for the men as " … supper in the company mess and was it ever delicious: chicken, potatoes and gravy, bread, butter, marmalade, canned corn, coffee, and a delicious fresh fruit salad for dessert. The cooks did a swell job."[75] At this time, George R. Borkhuis, Co. D cook, summed up the previous months writing, "I have seen some horrible things happen and have had my share of narrow escapes. I have also seen some wonderful acts of courage, self-sacrifice and loyalty. Prayer was a wonderful solace during our combat days … we are now resting and it's doing us all a lot of good. Most of us were pretty well battle-weary and this relaxation is wonderful."

During October, only Co. C had seen any combat, having fired 2,127 WP and 3,287 HE, for a total of 5,414 rounds during the Volturno River action. The battalion reported no casualties during the month but had been plagued by poor terrain and a lack of mine-sweeping equipment.[76]

November of 1943 opened with the battalion at Amalfi alerted at noon of the 1st for movement on the following day, but before departing the Ranger officers held a party that night at a hotel at Ravello which was attended by Burford, Pike, and Hutchinson. Burford said it was a most enjoyable party until it came time to depart. He explained, "I had arranged to go back to Amalfi with Hutchinson, but when he was ready to go I had some trouble. The cause of my dilemma was that Col. Darby was locked in his room with one of the nurses and my cap and flashlight were locked up with him. So, after a considerable delay and an embarrassed entrance into the room, I was able to get away with Hutchinson." The day also marked the promotion of Burford to Battalion S-2 and Rankin to captain of Co. C.[77]

On the 2nd, HQ Co., the Medical Detachment, and companies A, B, and D moved via Pompeii and Naples to a bivouac two miles south of Caiazzo. Co. C remained at Amalfi due to a lack of transportation and on the 3rd was informed that Pvt. Fitzhugh Dye of Mississippi had died on September 18th at the 104th General Hospital in Tunisia from wounds received in action September 13th at Maiori. Co. C arrived at Caiazzo by motor convoy on the 4th as companies A, B, D, and the battalion CO and staff participated in a battalion field exercise which included a 12-mile hike. On the 5th, Capt. "Bud" Pike, complaining of the extremely cold weather, again wrote home stating the current status of some of the battalion officers, writing, "I am not with 'D' Company anymore, although I don't know how long this new job will last. I am now BN S-3. This is one of those detested staff jobs which I used to gripe about so much back at Camp Gordon. I'm getting so I hate even myself as a staff man but you know the Army, 'orders is orders.'

You can address my letters to HQ and HQ Co. from now till future notice. Rup Burford has also been transferred from 'C' Company to the staff as S-2. Hutchinson figures that we have proved ourselves in combat and wants to give the junior officers a crack [*at*] commanding the companies. More power to them. I'm glad to give Crenshaw and Rankin a chance."[78]

Action at Venafro November 8 - December 14 & Ceppagna November 10 - 14

The 83rd Chemical Battalion spent the 5th to the 7th of November engaged in the usual bivouac duties. On the 8th Hutchinson, his staff, and the weapons company commanders were given a two-hour notice to make a reconnaissance from Caiazzo while the battalion had been attached to the Ranger Force and the 45th Infantry Division. James Helsel, Co. A, sensed something was astir as he wrote in his diary, "They sent all the 1st Division men as replacements to D & C companies, a few stayed with Co. 'A.' We also had cherry pie for supper, which means something. The last time it was just before the invasion of Sicily." Capt. Pike, Co. D, was more concerned with the weather, as "… the rainy season is coordinating with the cold and making life completely miserable … this drizzly, damp, cold weather is definitely 'non buono.'" During the night the 1st Ranger Battalion, with the 83rd attached, was to relieve the 180th Infantry from their position at the southern slopes of Mt. Corno and Mt. Croce [*meaning Mountain of the Cross*], two hills in the Apennine mountain range reportedly held by a Panzer Grenadier battalion, which commanded the plains of Venafro.[79]

The next day, November 9th, companies A, B, and D, along with the Medical Detachment, moved to a position 1.5 miles northeast of Presenzano, where the rear echelons of each company and the motor pool were established. The Battalion CP was set up in an olive grove at the foot of the mountain, just to the west of Venafro. Although no one in the battalion knew it at the time, it was later discovered the property was owned by an uncle of Pvt. Charles C. Carrullo of Co. A. S-2 Burford said the position was partially concealed by olive trees, with the mountains, still held by the Germans, to their front and left and the Volturno River valley to their left and rear. During the evening darkness, the three weapons companies continued to move by moonlight to an area west of Venafro where much friendly artillery fire and German interdictory fire was encountered throughout the night. Companies A and D, in position near the southern base of Mt. Corno, were to support the 1st Ranger Battalion and one battalion of the 509th Parachute Infantry, relieving one company of the 84th Chemical Battalion and a battalion of the 180th Infantry.[80]

James Helsel, Co. A, recalled the day, writing, "Toward afternoon we got orders to pack up. By two we were waiting on the trucks, the convoy already formed. We traveled until dark. Then we lost the rest of the convoy, but we kept on going until a few shells landed near the road in the field on our left side. We jumped out and unhitched the trailer and turned it around until the truck turned around. We hitched up again and started back, which was alright with me. In as far as I was concerned we went far enough. On the way back we met the BN liaison officer. He made us turn around and he took us to our Co. position. It was in an olive grove just outside of Venafro. The ammo Sgt. told us that the Germans were on the same side of the mountain and whoever got up first that's whose day it was. So I helped clean ammo and carry it to the gun positions until about two in the morning. Being new in the ammo section and not doing that kind of work, I was somewhat tired, so I just crawled in my hole and covered up with an overcoat."[81]

Co. B was attached to the 4th Ranger Battalion to take the high ground south and west of Ceppagna, and Co. C moved near Presenzano as a reserve. HQ Co., excepting the Battalion S-1 and the enlisted headquarters administrative section, which remained at Caiazzo, moved to the Presenzano area as the Battalion Aid Station was established in an annex next to a church in the west end of Venafro.[82]

With enemy shells hitting near the OP 2nd Lt. Frank P. Roan of Co. D was wounded seriously enough to take him out of action as companies A and D were heavily engaged with the enemy near Venafro on the 10th. Co. A's James Helsel wrote, "We moved up Graveyard Hill, for up in the very top stood two black crosses … One prisoner said they had orders to hold out to spring. Mike Janosz kiddingly took a few ammo boxes and said he was going to build a winter home." Daniel Shields recalled Co. D was heavily shelled and strafed twice. By the evening Co. B, implementing their part of the mission, had moved to a position 200 yards east of Ceppagna, where their gun positions were under heavy enemy artillery fire. According to Andrew C. Leech, Co. B, "We moved out and marched on up to the center of the mountain, which was in the shape of a horseshoe, and went into position. We were almost surrounded by the enemy with only one way of escape. The Jerries on the high mountains could observe us from all sides. We had to stay mighty low in our holes during the daytime."[83]

The fighting heated up on the 11th as companies A and D laid down a rolling barrage to support an attack of the 2nd Battalion, 509th Parachute Infantry, which resulted in the successful occupation of Mt. Corno and Mt. Croce by evening. William S. Hutchinson later wrote, "This was massed mortar fire, and it is the most effective killer on the battlefield. Our chemical battalions are the only units in the American Army that deliver massed mortar fire." 2nd Lt. Robert M. Schmidt, HQ Co., of Illinois, was killed while acting as a forward observer. In the meantime Co. C displaced to a position well forward in the draw between the two mountains. Once situated in these positions at Mt. Corno and Mt. Croce, with the draw between them, the 83rd would accomplish their mission of holding these points against all enemy aggression, until relieved on December 14th by the 3rd Battalion, 180th Infantry. Hutchinson added, "When you get a good gun position and a good OP overlooking the Germans, such as we had at Venafro, there is an enormous satisfaction in killing them, and you can kill a lot with the 4.2." From the draw, or defensive bowl as Hutchinson called it, companies A and D fired WP in an effort to start fires behind German lines, but the vegetation at that time of the year was too wet, "and only temporary illumination was obtained."[84]

Near Ceppagna the 4th Ranger Battalion attacked Hill 670, was repulsed, but, with some mortar support from Co. B of the 83rd, was able to renew the attack and take the hill. The Rangers continued to advance 1,000 yards beyond their objective and took hills 630 and 570. The effective mortar fire of a platoon of Co. B beyond Hill 570 forced the enemy to retreat from their forward OP. 2nd Lt. Robert W. Brasel of Randolph County, Illinois, was recommended for a Silver Star for gallantry in action as he advanced 1,000 yards into enemy territory to direct mortar fire. Later in the day, Pvt. Lloyd Foster was buried alive in his foxhole by an exploding enemy shell but was successfully extricated under intense enemy artillery fire by Capt. Gordon M. Mindrum, Pvt. Cornelius ("Neil") McCarthy, and six other men, all of whom were cited for gallantry.[85]

The battalion companies remained in position on the 12th while the enemy drove the Rangers from Hill 630, but the mortar fire of the Blue Platoon, Co. B of the 83rd, drove off the threat and the Rangers were able to reoccupy the hill. The enemy renewed their efforts to take the hills on the 13th during which at least three men of Co. B were wounded: S/Sgt. Lewis Cameron, Pfc. Paul C. George, and Pvt. Stephen C. Bullock, although George was the only one hospitalized. Hills 630 and 670 continued to exchange hands back and forth during the enemy counterattack and at one point the ammo dump of the Red Platoon of Co. B was hit and set ablaze but extinguished through the heroic efforts of Capt. Mindrum, Sgt. Denver E. Shanafelt, and Sgt. Joseph A. ("Flat Top") Adamski. All three were recommended for the Silver Star. About 45 minutes later the same ammo dump was hit and set afire again. Capt. Mindrum, Sgt. Aubrey R. Parrish, and Pvt. Donald J. Mack [or Mach] were recommended for the Silver Star for helping to extinguish the fire. A few hours afterward the company ammo dump caught fire, and despite the heroic efforts of Capt. Mindrum, T/5 Arthur Collins, and T/5 William M. Henrie, 1,000 rounds of ammo were lost. Mindrum was slightly wounded in the legs by white phosphorous and a small shell fragment, earning a second Purple Heart. All three men were recommended for the Silver Star. During one counterattack one mortar of Co. B was fired so rapidly the firing pin became fused. Andrew Leech, Co. B, said, "We shot our mortars so fast we melted the firing pins on some of them and almost melted the barrels." A total of 3,605 HE and 163 WP were fired by Co. B.

Co. C also took some casualties on the 13th, including Sgt. Wayne W. Anderson of Indiana, Pvt. Henry Goss of Mississippi, and Mack L. Dees, Jr., also of Mississippi, all of whom were killed in action.[86] William C. Ford, Co. C, recalled that during this period, "A GI in our squad was badly wounded. I helped a medic put him on a stretcher. Blood was all over his body; his clothes were cut to shreds from shrapnel. He came in as a replacement after we took Naples and had only been with us for about a month … As he wiped blood off his face he remarked that the Germans had really messed him up. Then he said, 'I am going to die'. The medic told him, 'No, I'm going to take

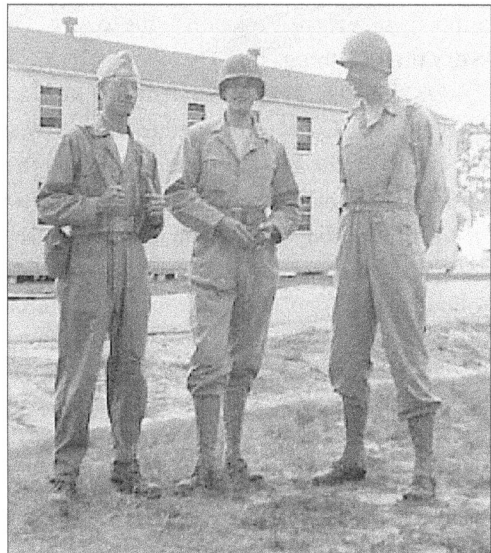

Gordon Mindrum, Andre Laus, and Julian McKinnon at Camp Gordon, GA. All three officers distinguished themselves in Sicily and Italy. *Scott Mindrum*

Capt. Edwin Pike, unidentified, Executive Officer David Meyerson, and unidentified. *Scott Mindrum*

care of you. You will soon be in a hospital and well taken care of.'" Also recalling such gruesome scenes was Vicente De Leon, a medic who later joined Co. C, who stated, "When we would get replacements, I never paid attention to their last names. I didn't want to get too close. When you're in combat you don't want to remember … If an artery was severed you had five minutes to get there because of the loss of blood. When there were more than three bullet holes, there was usually nothing you can do, so you give them a shot of morphine and tried to comfort them. You talked to them. Usually they would ask, 'Why me?' Sometimes they wanted you to tell their loved ones that they didn't suffer. And once you held them in your arms, they finally would relax and let go."[87]

Although Co. B was relieved on the 14th and returned to the rear near Presenzano, the fighting in the vicinity of Venafro continued for the next few days, with such points as Concacasle and Mt. Lonoci receiving battalion fire. Maj. Hutchinson said Venafro was the first operation in which all four companies operated as a battalion. Daniel Shields, Co. D, said it rained so much he could not stay in his foxhole and eventually sought shelter in a church. This was further confirmed by Capt. Pike, who wrote on the 16th, "The rainy season has started in earnest now as it has rained without let-up for the last 72 hours and threatens to continue doing do for quite some time. Combined with extremely cold weather this life has been anything but enjoyable of late." Indeed, the rain did continue for the next few days. Noting the onset of the Italian rainy season, Hutchinson observed that it "constituted a major problem in maintaining the health of the men. The mortars fired 24 hours a day and there was no shelter from the elements available at the mortar positions. The solution was to place a skeleton crew on duty throughout the relatively quiet hours of the night and to emplace the company kitchens on the company mortar positions so that all men could have a minimum of two hot meals daily … Winter clothing had not yet been issued to all individuals. The maximum use had to be made of blankets and shelter halves and of side wall tents available to provide shelter for the men. Each company set up a rear echelon in the town of Venafro to which men were sent periodically for rest and an opportunity to dry their clothing."[88]

On the 17th, shrapnel destroyed a mortar barrel of Co. D and wounded Pvt. Clay Tuck, while S/Sgt. George W. Wolfe, Co. C, was wounded in the leg by shrapnel. Both men were from Pennsylvania. The enemy focused on Mt. Corno on the 18th and briefly breached the line of the 509th Parachute before being repulsed. During this attack on the right flank it was decided to shift the position of Co. C to the right in order to present defensive mortar fire for the 509th. Maj. Hutchinson and Col. Darby visited the OPs and discussed various possibilities for fields of fire, such as placing mortars on the heights of Mt. Corno, but decided it was not necessary and issued no specific orders. Following their departure Lt. Harold A. Churchill, Co. C, directed the fire of some 155mm howitzers on the reported headquarters of a company of Grenadiers opposing the 157th Infantry.[89]

By the 19th, a company of enemy infantry had dug in on the reverse slope of Mt. Corno but they were driven back to two other positions by the directed fire of Lt. Julian T. McKinnon and posed no further immediate threat. Col. Darby, Maj. Hutchinson, and Capt. Edwin Pike visited the battalion OP on the 20th as the Ranger outposts exchanged grenades with the opposing enemy outposts and four S-mines, one pressure, and one trip wire mine were located nearby. Throughout the day companies A and D fired on the enemy position southwest of Concacasle and Co. B remained near Presenzano.[90]

Companies A, C, and D of the 83rd Chemical Battalion fired heavy concentrations on the 21st in support of a Ranger attack on the enemy position on the razor back in the area of Mt. Corno. The mission was a success and cleared the enemy from the immediate front from whence they had been in grenade exchange position for the previous two days. Pvt. Paul R. Wheeler, from Itawamba County, Mississippi, was wounded when some shells fell near the company's mortar position. A strong German force yet held the razor back running east from Mt. Corno on the 22nd of the month so Col. Darby called Maj. Hutchinson to the OP to adjust the fire of companies A and D on the position. The fire of Co. A, adjusted by Lt. John P. McEvoy and Lt. Eric H. Peterson, Jr., and that of Co. D fell continually on the enemy position, which held strong. Firing was continued throughout the night and Col. William P. Yarborough of the 509th Parachute presented a German mortar sight to the 83rd which his paratroopers had captured from the Germans on the ridge now held by the 83rd.[91]

A German soldier taken prisoner on the 23rd told his captors he had been in the area in September and that his abode had not been bombed and the residents had divided opinions on the war, although the soldiers had no opinions and only did as they were ordered. He also informed the 83rd members that the Germans in the area actually had no observation posts focused on their positions and "the rock" on the left flank which had been "so hotly contested for the last four days constituted nothing more than their foremost outposts." He also verified that mortar fire of the 83rd had fallen on his company but none fell near him. Soon afterward the enemy launched another attack, which was again halted, although a strong head wind caused the mortar fire of the battalion to fall short. The day did not pass without casualties as 2nd Lt. Francis A. Sloma, Co. C, was shot in the leg by a sniper, while Pfc. Luis F. Garcia and Pvt. James Hurt, both of Co. D, were admitted to the hospital for exhaustion.[92]

During the 24th, the battalion fell under a severe enemy shell barrage, sometimes by 170mm shells. Although a number of the shells that landed were duds two men of Co. D went to the hospital with shell shock. During one barrage, a shell burst and ignited four rounds of WP in the ammo dump, while another barrage ignited one WP shell and set fire to several cases, although Sgt. William T. Ulmer, ammunition officer, successfully saved the shells. At one point during the day Pvt. Troy Donald of Scott County, Mississippi, and Pvt. Verne E. Hiltz, of Washington County, Maine, both of Co. D, were slightly wounded. Additionally, Pfc. Lawrence L. Williams, of Itawamba County, Mississippi, and a Pvt. Conatser, both of Co. D, were sent to the hospital for exhaustion. This may be the period James Marion Lester, Co. D, was referring to when he wrote, "I remember ... they were shelling ... and we were holed up in a house. Somebody's living quarters ... the shells started coming in and the next morning we went out and there was a dud laying out in the street. It hadn't exploded. If that had gone off, it would have been the end of that house. However, there it laid. It bounced along and laid out in the street. Somebody was out there defusing the thing." Jim C. Myers, Co. C added "It rains here all the time. Sure is miserable."[93]

The left center of the battalion was attacked on a rainy 25th, but the effort was repulsed after nearly two and a half hours of continual mortar fire. A prisoner was taken who said his company had suffered 50 percent casualties in the past four days and attributed most of it to the mortar fire of the 83rd. Co. A of the 83rd was alerted to future operations with the 3rd Ranger Battalion while Co. B of the 84th Chemical Battalion received orders they were to be attached to the 1st Ranger Battalion and sub-attached to the 83rd Chemical Battalion. This union between the 83rd and one company of the 84th would last until December 12th.[94]

Of more amusing interest was Capt. "Bud" Pike's venture to church services. "I was sitting ... in my CP tent ... when I heard the strains of an organ floating through the air to my ears. Aha! Thanksgiving Day and the Chaplains Thanksgiving service was starting in the little chapel a short distance up the hill from the tent. So I laid aside my pen but didn't lay aside the love in my heart and went to the chapel to give my Thanks to the Lord. It was a nice service but the soldiers (and my) attempts at singing the hymns – even with the aid of the organ – were rather ludicrous. And while I always thought my singing (I Don't Want to Set the World on Fire) was bad, I now feel like Caruso after hearing the Chaplain lead the singing. I had my first aid packet out and open and ready to use on him before I realized he wasn't seriously wounded."[95]

Officer conferences were also held on the 25th to discuss moving the rear echelon of the 83rd into the town of Venafro the following day, while Capt. Pike again relayed home the current battalion command changes, stating, "Hutchinson is CO, Meyerson Exec. O., myself S-3, Burford S-2, Trey S-4 and Whiskey Red [Cornett] S-1. What a staff! Eh? McEvoy is CO of A Co., Rankin CO of C Co., Crenshaw CO of D Co., and Mindrum CO of B Co. Edwards was in the hospital with yellow jaundice but is out again now. Merrill is still quite sick with yellow jaundice and is still in the hospital. Johnny Roberts is now with the 84th Cml BN here in Italy ... C.K. [Carl Carpenter] is coming along fine ..."[96]

George Borkhuis, Co. D cook, wrote on the 26th "Yesterday was Thanksgiving but we didn't eat any turkey, not because we didn't have any, but because it arrived too late to be cleaned and dressed in time. We are going to have it for dinner today instead. I never would have believed the men in the front lines would get real turkey and now I've seen everything … the weather is cleared up but the roads and fields are still a sea of mud which makes things quite tough."

Co. B, 84th Chemical Battalion, left their bivouac known as "Mike's Place" at Roccapipirozzi, a hill village on the western rim of the Venafro Valley, to join with the 83rd in the vicinity of Venafro. The 84th men pulled their guns out of the mud, loaded up, and departed in the evening but an enemy patrol was mistaken for a counterattack and the move was delayed. Upon arrival at Venafro on the 27th, Co. B, 84th Chemical Battalion, found the 83rd was in position on the terraces of a mountainside olive grove. The remaining unoccupied position was half way up the hill, nearly 500 yards above the last installation of the 83rd. This highest position of the 83rd could be reached by truck, but only jeeps could negotiate the steep and narrow grade to the position assigned to the 84th. Sgt. Dean O. Haley, historian of Co. B of the 84th, wrote in the official battalion history, "At Venafro, there was less trouble from broken mortar parts than before, but the OP parties had a much harder time of it. When the telephone line was laid to the forward observers, a roll of wire had to be carried to the top of the mountain and rolled down over the cliffs, the end of the wire to be picked up from below. A litter team … from the OP, spent all day making the trip of only a few thousand yards. The jeep drivers never rested at Venafro. After they had spent two or three hours a day getting hot food up to the platoons, from the kitchen at the bottom of the hill; they spent the remaining daylight hours shuttling ammunition from the highest point the trucks could reach."[97]

Near dusk on the 27th the enemy attacked the 1st Rangers and 509th Parachute, including the OP at the bottom of the hill. During this engagement some shells fell in town and one burst directly over two slit trenches, which caused shrapnel wounds to four men of Co. A, 83rd Chemical Battalion, including Sgt. Joe L. Jones, as well as three of Co. B, 84th Chemical Battalion. The Field Journal of the 84th Chemical Battalion stated they actually sustained one enlisted man killed, T/4 Edward R. Glass, one seriously wounded, and one slightly wounded. The two wounded were a Corp. Norton and a Pfc. Morrison, both injured so badly they were evacuated and never returned.[98]

Action at San Pietro November 28 – December 1

During the intermittent shell fire of November 28th, Maj. William S. Hutchinson of the 83rd was wounded in the left ankle by shrapnel. The wound was not serious but did require temporary hospitalization. Hutchinson's jeep driver, Pfc. Anthony G. Nitz, transported the major seven miles down the mountain from the OP for medical aid. In Hutchinson's absence Executive Officer Dave Meyerson commanded the battalion. Michael Rebick, Co. D, having returned to the battalion from his wound in September, expressed the stark reality of the war as he wrote, "… [you] would be in a heck of a fix if you could only see us fellows now for [we] don't know how many months [since] we have taken a bath or when we [have] taken our shoes off - we don't know whether we will get them back on again or not, for we have been going though hell." Co. B of the battalion was attached to the 3rd Ranger Battalion and the 36th Infantry Division with the mission of a reconnaissance of the San Pietro valley, which was accomplished on the 29th as they took position under heavy shell fire on the southeast slope of Mt. Rotundo near Mignano. An OP was established at Cannavinelle and the "… intended plan of the Rangers was to proceed through the valley, occupy the town of San Pietro if possible, and gain all possible information concerning size, location, etc. of the enemy forces." The Rangers moved to Vallecupa, then west 2,000 yards, then southwest to Mt. Rotundo, and then northwest to San Pietro. Upon gaining the road the Rangers moved east. This situation was confirmed by Robert P. Brimm, who would write in 2004, "… the Rangers jumped off, infiltrating and fighting the well-organized enemy positions and mined areas. 83rd's Company B, supported the operation from positions to the rear of Mt. Rotundo." The weather was cloudy and turned to rain in the evening.[99]

The Rangers attempted to demolish "the rock" on the 30th, a strong point in the enemy outpost, which was followed by an unsuccessful enemy counterattack. Capt. Ed "Bud" Pike briefly served as battalion executive officer, while Co. B laid a day-long smoke screen on Mt. Lungo and Mt. Sammurco in order to screen the withdrawal of the Rangers to Ceppagna. In the course of the day's fighting three direct hits were made by light artillery on a building housing the 83rd Chemical Battalion Headquarters, wounding eleven men. Among the seriously wounded was Sgt.

Bernard O'Connor, who would die from his wounds. Less seriously wounded were Sgt. Karl F. Garrett, Corp. Joseph J. Genovese, Pfc.'s Isadore J. Reichman, Edward W. Quimby, Frank E. Cole, Austin L. Brown, Warren E. Collins, and Pvt. Gerado DiLucchio. Also among the wounded were one Italian with HQ group and Pvt. Issac A. Mansfield, who was wounded in the afternoon near the battalion ammo dump. Sgt. Garrett, who was wounded in both legs, remembered that after he was injured he was "… sent to an evacuation hospital in the rear area where surgery was performed. This was done in a tent with lamps for light and the doctor and nurses wore galoshes due to about 4 inches of mud on the floor. Eventually, I was sent to a hospital in Naples. It was worth the wound to get into a dry warm place for awhile." Co. B, 84th Chemical Battalion, continued to fire on targets of opportunity and also received fire, with one enlisted man slightly wounded by shrapnel. Undoubtedly, such incidents prompted Michael Rebick, Co. D of the 83rd, to write a letter home stating that from what he had seen, the war was not ending any time soon.[100]

Fortunately, to help cope with the high casualties and low morale of the 83rd, this day marked the official arrival of the new battalion medical officer, Lt. Julius Charles ("Doc"/"Sonny") Hulcher, reportedly the first man from the 45th General Hospital to join a combat unit. "Doc," who had received his transfer orders on November 23rd "… toured the battlegrounds before finally finding [*his*] outfit." Hulcher added, "It's too much to write but I'll never forget it. Station is in a wine cellar - not bad, in town of Venafro." Ed Trey remembered Hulcher's first entry to the 83rd a bit differently, stating in 2006, "Even with my fading memory I can remember his arrival as if it were yesterday, attired in pinks and greens without the faintest idea of what the hell he was getting into. Apparently, upon queries along the way about the 83rd he received comments like, 'Must be some kind of mess kit rear outfit', but jolly old Hulcher meshed into the outfit quickly." In actuality, Hulcher was victim of one of the running gags among chemical mortar units, which took advantage of the fact that so many, even much of the military, had no idea of the duties of the novice organization. Often they would tell new men they were joining a "water purification" unit, which is exactly what they told Hulcher, who was suckered right into the misnomer.[101]

During the month of November, the 83rd Chemical Battalion had fired a total of 15,402 rounds of HE and 7,768 WP, for a grand total of 23,170 rounds. Casualties included four killed, 19 wounded, and at least two hospitalized for shell shock.[102]

December opened fairly quietly. Julius "Doc" Hulcher, the new officer of the Medical Detachment of the 83rd, said that despite the cold, rain, and continuous shelling he slept well the previous night, there was a large sick call lasting until noon, and an enemy bomb was dropped nearby around lunch time. A Ranger patrol to Concacasle met no resistance even though there were 15 to 20 Germans dressed as civilians. Co. A of the 83rd, along with the Ranger Cannon Co., checked for enemy presence by firing a few rounds on the northwest slope of Mt. Corno, and Co. C fired on some pack trains entering Concacasle. Co. B shot at targets of opportunity throughout the day, then was relieved and ordered to withdraw from Mt. Rotundo to the rear near Ceppagna and to perform usual bivouac duties. Co. B was relieved from their position under heavy enemy fire on December 1st. Andrew C. Leech, Co. B, wrote, "The night we pulled out the Jerries were laying in a heavy barrage … It was dark and muddy and occasionally when a shell landed too close we hit the mud, so you can imagine what a mess we were in. Finally we reached the road where our trucks were to meet us. We were so tired we fell down on the side of the road to wait. A few Jerry shells kept us from falling asleep."[103]

On the administrative side of affairs, Capt. David W. Meyerson was appointed acting commanding officer of the battalion, apparently because of Hutchinson's hospital stay for his recent wound. Meyerson, given the nickname "Andy Jump" by the men due to his physical profile, was an adequate choice to temporarily command the battalion. Born January 26, 1918, he served as part of the original cadre of officers of the 83rd Chemical Battalion from Edgewood Arsenal and had assumed numerous positions at Camp Gordon including Billeting Officer, Plans and Training Officer, Operations and Training Officer, and Temporary Executive Officer. In addition he was on the Summary Court. At Gela, Sicily, he had served as captain and battalion S-3. Ed Trey remembered him as a "quirky little Jewish guy who had pink curtains in his barracks windows at Camp Gordon" and often wore light-colored clothing whenever everyone else wore dark. John P. McEvoy said Meyerson was "a quiet, scholarly man who was equally calm in camp or under fire." As early as October of 1943 Hutchinson had expressed his desire to advance Capt. Edwin "Bud" Pike to second in command, based primarily upon battle experience and leadership, and to designate Meyerson battalion S-3. He remarked in a letter to Cunin, "I somehow feel that Dave would have trouble carrying the whole load alone, particularly since he does not have any actual combat experience. However, I will be able to promote him and we could never find a better staff officer." Soon afterward Hutchinson had a change of mind and made Meyerson his second in command and Pike his S-3.[104]

When he was later "swapped" to command the 2nd Chemical Mortar Battalion, Meyerson was described as an extremely aggressive and fearless man, and "… wanted to kill Germans." In his book on the 2nd Chemical, Walter J. Eldredge quoted Bob Ladson of the 2nd as saying Meyerson "… carried a rifle in his jeep and he drove his drivers crazy by taking them so far forward. We had to rotate a new man into the job every few weeks. If you wanted to get somebody to shape up, you'd just threaten to make him Meyerson's driver. One night a German bomber came over and dropped a bunch of small anti-personnel mines we called 'butterfly bombs'. Everybody else was finding holes or hiding behind trees, but Meyerson just stayed in the command tent with a flashlight and a book he was reading."[105]

Eight air force bombers strafed Concacasle on a clear and pretty 2nd as companies A, C, and D of the 83rd, along with Co. B, 84th Chemical Battalion, fired heavy concentrations. George Borkhuis, Co. D cook wrote, "Still at the front and dodging occasional shells." Co. B remained in bivouac. A cold, rainy December 3rd passed with companies A and C supporting various Ranger patrols while Co. B, 84th Chemical Battalion, suffered one enlisted man injured by an exploding shell cartridge. Activities were limited on the fourth day of the month due to an all-day rain, which added to the muddy landscape, although Co. B, 84th Chemical Battalion, fired on an enemy detail laying mines in conjunction with 81mm mortars and suspected they killed or wounded at least six of the enemy. Also on the 4th, Maj. Hutchinson, in a hospital recovering from his recent foot wound, wrote another letter to Cunin describing the current status of the battalion. "Today is our twenty something day in the line, still with Bill. We are firing as a battalion and have burned up more than 30,000 rounds in the present position. It's a plenty hot spot. I was wrong about Pike as Exec. and have recommended Dave for promotion, also McEvoy and DeMarco. Pike is S-3, Burford is S-2, Edwards Asst. S-[*illegible*] & … McEvoy has A, Rankin has C, Crenshaw has D. Mindrum has done a marvelous job with B and has been recommended for a Silver Star. Burford has been recommended for rotation. I plan to make Mindrum S-3 and give B to Metcalfe, McKinnon, or Laus. Rankin is doing an excellent job. Crenshaw is not as good. McEvoy, of course, is tops. Our old munitions officer was killed acting as a forward observer with the Rangers in an attack. Casualties here have not been too heavy, but we have worn out the German regiments in front of us. One prisoner said that his company had actually been in the attacks on our lines … [*and*] had … suffered over 50% casualties, mostly from mortar fire. Sgts Barber and Doyle have been commissioned and Barber has been ordered back to the States on rotation. On the whole that is the picture. We have found your gunnery to be priceless … They are learning how to mass their fires for the first time. Dave, Bud, and Burf have been operating a Bn FDC with concentration number, nominal barrages, fire plans, etc. Without it we would have been lost because communication has been very difficult … "[106]

Co. D's John A. Feifer, D. E. Frazier, and Mike Codega.
Codega Collection

Other events of the day included visits by a Lt. Col. Merriett, British representative of the Chemical Section, and a Maj. Merrill of the 5th Army Chemical Section, who toured company positions and gave a discussion on the personalities and activities of the Chemical Warfare Service. This was followed on a rainy 5th by an inspection of the observation posts and Ranger positions by Capt. David W. Meyerson. "Doc" Hulcher reported there were few battle casualties.[107]

The 509th Parachute Infantry reported on the 6th, another rainy day, that the fire of a company of the 83rd on an enemy pack train had killed three mules, three chickens, and liberated several other chickens being transported to the enemy. Venafro received some heavy shelling during the day which killed one enlisted man, Sgt. David D. Miller, and seriously wounded two others of Co. B, 84th Chemical Battalion.[108]

Action at Ceppagna December 7 - 21

As the rains continued, an enemy shell burst at the OP of Co. C on December 7th, killing lieutenants Dick DeAngelis and Harold A. Churchill. A shell fragment struck Churchill's jugular vein which proved a mortal wound despite an emergency attempt by the medics to save him. A piece of the same fragment struck 2nd Lt. Alvin G. Metcalfe, cut on the face and leg. "Doc" Hulcher, Medical Detachment, wrote of the episode: "Had my first B.C. [*battle casualty*] today. Mortar shell fragment struck him & killed two Lts." 2nd Lt. Donald R. Gabriel took over command and continued operations. Co. A persisted in their mission in the vicinity of Mt. Corno, and Co. B, supporting the 3rd Rangers in their attempt to occupy Hill 950, moved into a position near Ceppagna. Michael Rebick, Co. D, nonchalantly wrote, "While we sit here looking at the enemy we keep on firing shells at each other." Charlie Lowry, also of Co. D, wrote, "It is very wet and muddy here."[109]

Although there was a heavy morning sick call, the fighting in the vicinity of Venafro and Ceppagna continued on the 8th. In the struggle by the Rangers for Hill 950, the Blue Platoon of Co. B was under such heavy enemy fire it was put out of action, sustaining 15 casualties, including Sgt. Angelo L. Possenti and Pvt. William C. Stewart killed. Among the seriously wounded were Pfc. Joseph M. Mackowiak and Pvt. Edmund W. Hill, while less serious were 2nd Lt. Bernard B. Stone, Sgt. Joseph A. ("Flat Top") Adamski, Sgt. Joseph E. Ferrance, Pfc. Calvin L. Langley, and Pvt.'s Cecil A. Marks, Hiram L. May, Sidney L. McAlister, Clovis J. Jones, Louis L. Lancaster, George A. Roberts, and George J. Straka. The company history created some confusion by increasing that number, stating there was one sergeant killed, one officer killed, and 22 enlisted men wounded, of which number 13 enlisted men and one officer were evacuated. Additionally, the company ammo dump came under enemy fire and one private was killed. Robert P. Brimm probably overstated the results when he said, "Enemy fire was intense, and one platoon of B Company received over 50% casualties." S/Sgt. Duane H. Reck and Pfc. Henry E. Fajkowski were recommended for the Silver Star for gallantry and administering first aid while under enemy shell fire, while a Sgt. Brown, Corp. Howard J. Merritt, Corp. James H. Fisher, and Sgt. Joseph E. Ferrance, the last two also lightly wounded, were cited for gallantry in the action at San Pietro. With such casualties mounting in the battalion, it was a relief that on the same day 187 replacements arrived at Battalion HQ at Venafro, although they were new to the theater, inexperienced, and were limited to 13 weeks training at Ft. Jackson, South Carolina. Thirty-three of the replacements went to Co. B and 49 to Co. D. "Doc" Hulcher noted that he witnessed his first aerial dogfight and the German plane went down in flames.[110]

Companies A, C, and D of the 83rd fired heavy concentrations on points near Mt. Corno and Concacasle on a cloudy, but rainless 9th, as the Rangers, assisted by Co. B of the 83rd, occupied Hill 950 but were forced to withdraw under heavy fire. It was a rude awakening for James Helsel, who had just returned from a three-day pass to Naples where he had heard a rumor that the war was over. All four companies of the 83rd gave fire support to a patrol in the vicinity of Concacasle on the 10th, and Co. C reported firing three mortars at one round per minute for 15 minutes. But disaster struck when an HE shell exploded in the barrel of Co. B, 84th Chemical Battalion, killing Pvt. Louis J. Lombardo and Sgt. Ernest E. Lowe, who actually died two days later, and wounding four others. The Field Journal of the 84th was more precise, stating two enlisted men were killed, two slightly wounded and evacuated, one slightly wounded and not evacuated, and one evacuated due to exhaustion. It was believed the shell "… was armed when the safety ring was pulled and the inertia of the shell impacted by the propelling charge sent the striker home and the shell exploded," blowing off the upper half of the barrel and permanently damaging the standard.[111]

Additionally, Co. A of the 83rd reported a shell they fired left a black puff of smoke about 100 yards after leaving the barrel. An investigation into the episode was begun and Col. Maurice Barker and a Col. Giles arrived at the position of the 83rd to determine the quantity and condition of the ammunition. It was announced there was a critical shortage of the 4.2" ammo in the Italian theater but the 83rd had an adequate supply. But it was also found that 50 per cent of the powder charges, an extremely limited item, had been damaged by moisture due to poor packing. This was just the beginning of the 83rd's long running problem with defective shells and parts. Despite such distractions, Co. B supported two companies of the Rangers who again took Hill 950 and were reinforced by two companies of the 504th Infantry. The Medical Detachment was less optimistic, reporting a heavy sick call and numerous battle casualties. Fortunately, the very competent Capt. (Dr.) Silverino V. DeMarco, a 1936 graduate of the Boston School of Medicine, and 1st Lt. (Dr.) George B. Glazier, battalion dentist, arrived back from a three-day visit to Naples to assist Hulcher.[112]

William C. Ford, Co. C, would later give a morbid description of the combat in and around Venafro, stating, "It was cold and blustery, with high winds constantly blowing into our faces. The lack of good visibility created problems for our forward observers, as we were firing at short range in support of attacking Rangers … It was difficult to get supplies of food and ammunition to our mortar positions high on those rocky slopes. They could be carried by Jeeps only a short distance up the narrow, muddy road, after which they would be transported the rest of the way up to us on the backs of mules … We had to rely on Italian muleskinners, because their animals would only respond to commands in that language. The mule train would usually come up after dark, and although we were hungry for the chow and mail, this made us uneasy in spite of the fact that the mules were sure-footed, their hooves clicked loudly on the rocky trail, and might easily be heard by infiltrating German patrols … Almost every night the worst trip was back down the mountain, with the mule train carrying the stiff, frozen bodies of soldiers, who had been killed during that day … It saddened me to see those bodies being loaded on mules' backs, but that was the only way we could get them off the mountain. The thought often came to me that it was good their mothers were spared the sight of seeing their sons that way. I wondered, as others in our platoon must have also, whether my turn would come to be strapped onto a mule's back for that sad ride down the mountain."[113]

Karl F. Garrett, HQ Co., supported Ford's claims, writing, "We had to resort to donkeys or mules to transport food and ammunition up the mountains. They were Italian animals and didn't understand English cursing. The most obstinate animals ever. If you wanted them to go forward, they would go backwards and vice-versa. They were also used to bring down the wounded and the dead … war is not an adventure, it is a daily sacrifice."[114]

The 83rd continued to give supporting fire to various units in the vicinity of Concacasle on December 11th and Co. B assisted in repulsing an enemy effort to retake Hill 950. During the activity, enemy planes made their first appearance in two weeks, and twelve ME 109s strafed Co. B but failed to inflict any casualties. This may have been disputed by "Doc" Hulcher who said there were four air raids during the clear weather day and during one of the raids he performed some minor surgery on a soldier injured in one of the raids.[115]

There was also an investigation conducted December 11-15 at Peninsular Base Section and 5th Army by an officer of Headquarters, Service of Supply, North African Theater of Operations, into the supply and replacement of the 4.2" chemical mortar, mortar parts, and ammunition. A number of problems were approached, and it was stated that, "Depending upon the mission to which it is assigned, each [*chemical mortar*] battalion keeps between 2,000 and 6,000 shells in the battalion area and on the firing positions." The investigation concluded that the reason for the critical situation occurring in the supply of 4.2" mortar ammo was that battalions were firing them at an unanticipated rate; battalions were firing them at distances beyond that for which they were designed; maintenance factors were based upon laboratory field test and not realistic combat and terrain situations; improperly packed or waterproofed charges; improperly designed parts; a lack of spare parts; improper manufacturer inspection of parts and shells; and lack of re-supply through normal wear and tear.[116]

Firing on points around Concacasle continued on the 12th as a public address system placed atop Mt. Corno weakly blared out a message in German to the enemy for them to surrender to the American lines, but not one enemy soldier responded. Word was also received that the 83rd and the Ranger force would be relieved on the 14th by the 3rd Battalion, 180th Infantry, and Co. B, 84th Chemical Battalion, which was relieved from their "sub-attachment" to the 83rd. The Rangers and 83rd would remain in the vicinity of Venafro. Some battle casualties were noted by "Doc" Hulcher, who met 1st Lt. (Dr.) William P. Tice, the man he replaced in the Medical Detachment. Tice, former assistant battalion surgeon at Camp Gordon, was not legally a doctor according to Curtis Williams, being a pre-med student working as a doctor for the coal mines before the war. This earned him the moniker of "Coal Doctor." He also reportedly was a bit fond of alcohol but despite any negatives he reportedly became an accomplished neuro-surgeon after the war. Williams noted that, once while operating on an Italian patient with an Italian doctor, Tice cut open the lower body and yelled, "Look, Curtis, a goiter." Curtis replied, "I don't think that's where a goiter is located," to which Tice responded, "Oh! - must be the gall bladder."[117]

The firing on points in and around Concacasle continued on the 13th. Capt. Gordon M. Mindrum, Co. B, informed Capt. David W. Meyerson, temporarily in command of the battalion, that Co. B had four officers present and needed another but could manage two or three more days without any new officers. Orders were also received attaching Co. B to the 143rd Infantry for future operations. Col. Darby returned from 5th Army HQ and brought information that his force of the 509th Parachute, 1st Ranger Battalion, and 83rd Chemical Battalion had been relieved, and he asked that his praise and appreciation of the 83rd for their performance in the recent actions be passed along to the men. James Helsel summed up the recent events as he heard this news, writing, "We learned we are to leave tomorrow for the rear. During the 35 days here over 10,000 rounds of ammo were expended. It rained 30 days. The chow was good, for they moved it right into our area. We fired day and night most of the time, by rotating shifts."[118]

Co. B went into action on the 14th attached to the 504th Parachute Regiment. Their mission was to give direct support in the consolidation of hills 1205 and 950 and to seize Hill 987 and the high ground north and west of Hill 950. Co. B gave direct support to the 3rd Battalion, 504th Parachute, as they occupied Hill 950. Soon afterwards the position was strafed by 12 ME 109s which lightly injured Pvt. Raymond A. Di Lello of Pennsylvania. Companies A, C, and D, as well as the Medical Detachment, began to move out en route to bivouac in pyramidal tents at Pozzuoli, arriving in the afternoon, to be followed by the rear echelon the next day. S-2 Burford said the battalion bivouacked in a wheat field about two miles from town and added, "Of course, the wheat wasn't growing yet, but we were told that is what it was." James Helsel, Co. A, said he had a fine, and apparently early, Christmas dinner in town.[119]

From November 8th through December 14th, the mission of the 83rd Chemical Mortar Battalion at Venafro had been to hold the position until relieved by the 180th Infantry. The battalion journal stated this was accomplished "… successfully in spite of heavy artillery and mortar fire and numerous attacks by enemy forces estimated to be from one to two Panzer Grenadier Battalions." Once again, though, problems were encountered with the mortars, which usually were fired at medium range, but "… great difficulty was experienced in keeping the mortars in operation. Due to the rocky nature of the ground the baseplates were repeatedly broken. The elevating mechanism of the standard was found to be entirely too weak and the eyes of the tie-rods had to be rewelded continually. The packing of the 4.2" ammunition … [was] … entirely unsatisfactory and due to the rain and dampness most of the powder charges had to be replaced. Other equipment was generally satisfactory. However, operations in cold, damp, mountainous country combat suits and heavier wool socks would serve to a great advantage."[120]

Co. B remained in position on the 15th but received word they would be relieved in two to four days. Six ME 109s strafed their position and wounded one man, not seriously enough to be evacuated. Meanwhile, Lt. Ed Trey arrived at Pozzuoli with several truck loads of battalion equipment and information that the personnel and motor maintenance sections were scheduled to arrive on the 16th. The battalion was reported to be "in the process of cleaning and repairing equipment, and in recreation and reorganization." On a cold 16th of the month, a truck convoy of the rear echelon of Battalion HQ left Venafro at 15-minute intervals, while the motor maintenance section remained behind to work on deadline trucks.[121]

On the 17th, the battalion's motor maintenance and ammo section arrived at Pozzuoli, where equipment was surveyed and re-equipped. Co. B remained in the vicinity of Hill 950 at Venafro but saw little action. The following day the battalion continued the repair and re-equipping of equipment at Pozzuoli as Co. B received notice they were relieved from the 504th Combat Team and were to revert to the 83rd Chemical Battalion on the 21st. Col. Barker visited the battalion at Pozzuoli on the 19th to discuss the equipment status and possible reorganization of the battalion. Co. B remained in their position near Venafro as enemy aircraft strafed around Ceppagna.[122]

December 20th proved a tragic day for Co. B as 1st Lt. Vester Lamar Turner was killed and Sgt. Denver E. Shanafelt horribly wounded by a minefield. Although the battalion journal gives little details and states Turner's remains were not recovered, Capt. Gordon M. Mindrum gave a much more informative account of the incident in a 2006 phone interview, which brought him to tears as he recalled the loss of his friend. Mindrum stated Lt. Turner called him by radio to tell him he was going to remove a mine from a minefield in order to use it as a sort of "show and tell" for the men. He said he felt confident he could extract it without any harm, to which Mindrum told him, "Vester, don't do that. I don't think that's a good idea." Turner remained convinced he could succeed and a few minutes later Mindrum, only a few hundred yards away, heard a loud explosion and his heart sank as he knew what had happened. Rushing to the scene, just over a hill, Mindrum came upon the ghastly view of his friend Lt. Turner, his head nearly blown off by the mine, and Sgt. Shanafelt, bleeding profusely from a hole in his chest, or what Mindrum described as a "sucking wound." Nolan McCraine recalled, "I was nearby when Lt. Turner, an Indian and one of the nicest men you would ever meet, picked up the mine to see how it worked and it exploded. It was a horrible sight." According to Mindrum the remains of Lt. Turner were recovered, while Sgt. Shanafelt survived his wound and eventually returned to duty in early

Vester Lamar Turner, Co. B, tragically killed near Ceppagna.
Jo Ann Howell

1944. Sgt. Hubert A. Burghart, 2nd Lt. Ewart O'Neil, Pfc. Cornelius ("Neil") McCarthy, and Capt. Mindrum were all recommended for the Silver Star for entering the minefield to render first aid. In lighter matters, some men of Co. D, including Daniel Shields, Andrew ("Andy") J. Whelan, and John H. Adams, were able to go on a sightseeing tour of the ancient city of Pompeii, where an orphan kissed Shields.[123]

Co. B was relieved of attachment to the 36th Infantry Division, reverted to control of the 83rd, and ordered to move to the rear on the 21st. "Doc" Hulcher and Capt. DeMarco, Medical Detachment, operated on the leg of an Italian boy but were more concerned about Dr. Glazier, who had been critically ill in the 23rd General Hospital for a number of days. Steve Vukson, Battalion Motor Section, Parts & Supplies, HQ Co., stationed at Pozzuoli, recalled it was both the first day of winter and a "swell day" but was shocked to return from dinner and find his tent "… with eight men's equipment in it burned to the ground. I lost all my clothing, [*and*] personal belongings … We were given all new equipment the following week."[124]

On the 22nd, the men of the other companies of the battalion already at Pozzuoli were given passes to enjoy a rest at Naples, exemplified by Charlie Lowry, Co. D Motor Pool, who wrote, "I am in a rest area at present. You can really appreciate a break after being at bat for a spell." Maj. Hutchinson, yet in the hospital recovering from his wound, sent Cunin another update on the status of the battalion. "You certainly left an efficient organization behind you. Dave has developed tremendously and took the Bn through in great shape after I left. They are out of the line now and are preparing to go on the new T/O. It will be relatively painless. We furnish one complete company to a new outfit. We are trying to get to send one Capt to the staff and to send only three officers in the company. They can't expect to get a completely veteran outfit. After all we have a war of our own to fight. None of the officers want to go except if it means promotion. That covers one 1st Lt and possibly the Capt for the staff. We can promote all our 2d Lts now regardless of vacancy. I see no point in sending a lot of good officers whom we have trained to shoot our way. [*James O.*] Beasley, [*Samuel W.*] Miller, [*Robert M.*] Schmidt, [*Vester L.*] Turner, [*Harold A.*] Churchill, and a new man named De Angelo [*actual name was Dick De Angelis*] are all in Doughtens category [*killed in action*]. Metcalfe has been wounded again. [*Bernard B.*] Stone got a fragment in the arm. [*Frank P.*] Roan and [*Francis M.*] Sloma are wounded. Its a pretty rugged war. Right now most every soldier in Italy feels lonely, but will be all right as soon as the main show starts. We haven't a crowbait in the outfit now. As long as we can prevent an epidemic of lead poisoning everybody is happy and damn proud to be in the organization."[125]

Following the arrival of Co. B at Pozzuoli on a cloudy and rainy 23rd, Christmas Eve 1943 arrived the following day. James Helsel, Co. A, recorded in his diary, "Still at Pozzuoli. Pyramidal tents have been set up with all kinds of home made stoves, for it has been quite cold. The fellows have things fixed up fairly well. Brown and myself have a good set up, we took seven shell halves, some poles, and built ourselves a small pyramidal tent. We made a stove out of a five gallon coffee can. The first night it smoked us out, the second threw so much soot we had to leave, but it's working like a furnace now." "Bud" Pike wrote home, "The sun is shining outside and the temperature is high – and it is still raining; a nice little sun shower, but all in all it is very nice. Everything is nice except for that feeling of aloneness, a desire of something more to make Christmas complete, to share the Christmas spirit with one you love. If things could only be the way we desire them instead of the way God and war decree – how wonderful it would be!" Co. B spent the day settling in to bivouac while much of the remainder of the battalion continued to enjoy their passes to Naples. A group of officers consisting of David W. Meyerson, Chrstopher C. ("Whiskey Red") Cornett, Jr., Capt. Silverino V. DeMarco, and Lt. Julius C. ("Doc") Hulcher, the latter two of the Medical Detachment, attended a Christmas Eve dance at the 45th General Hospital. Another party was attended at a nearby officer's club by Pike, Mindrum, McEvoy, Forrester, McKinnon, Crenshaw, Hauser, and a few other officers. Pike said of the event, "A merry time was had by all. We started out drinking cognac and when they ran out of that we ended up by drinking dry gin (which I hated before and hate more now). The 83rd really got drunk that night and we all paid for it the next morning with terrific hangovers." Less enthusiastic about the holidays was Steve Vukson, Motor Pool, HQ Co, who wrote in his diary, "I spent Christmas Eve by talking about the past year and thinking of what is going on at home. We were at Pozzuoli, Italy near Naples, Company B men and wine by the gallons. I drank a glass, somehow it didn't seem as if it was the great 'Eve' we always looked forward to."[126]

On Christmas Day, "Doc" Hulcher tended to an Italian kid suffering from fireworks burns, and an awards ceremony was held at 5th Army HQ at Caserta, where Gen. Mark Clark presented a battlefield promotion of lieutenant colonel to Maj. Hutchinson, or as he described it, he went from "soup to nuts." Capt. Edwin "Bud" Pike said this advancement made Hutchinson "a changed man" and that he only got the promotion due to the distinguished work of the 83rd at Venafro, claiming, "That was the higher-ups way of rewarding the BN - by promoting its commanding officer." Hutchinson viewed it a bit differently, writing, "I think Col. Bill [Darby] put me in to prevent C. W. S. sending us a Lieutenant Colonel out of a clear sky. That he was able to make it stick was due to the fine works the outfit has done." Gen. Clark also gave out Silver Stars to Sgt. Harry Cohen and Corp. Paul E. Weikel, both of Co. C. Cohen's citation read that in September "On the high ground overlooking the plain Sgt. Cohen was in charge of a gun crew when one of his men became wounded. After aiding in the evacuation of the injured man, he returned to his gun position and found it under heavy shell fire. Slightly forward of this location in an area where British armored equipment had been parked, Sgt. Cohen perceived two British soldiers lying wounded, under constant, terrific fire, unable to move. With utter disregard for his own personal safety, Sgt. Cohen moved forward under the intense artillery barrage and carried the two wounded men to a place of safety." Also in September on the high ground overlooking the plain Weikel "was stationed at an observation post with the forward observer for his platoon, a British officer, and two communications personnel. The position was subjected to heavy enemy artillery fire, forcing the evacuation of the area. Upon reaching a place of safety, the group discovered that material and documents containing important military information had been left behind. Weikel volunteered to return to the evacuated position. While the shelling was still in progress, unmindful of great danger, he made his way to the area and recovered the equipment and documents which might have been otherwise lost or captured." "Hutch" described the entire awards affair, writing, "Troops, bands, flags, newsreel cameras, news photographers, and General Clark himself to present the order … It was a very ceremonious Christmas. I was very favorably impressed by the General, just like all the good Regular officers I have known, quiet, efficient, businesslike, and very human. He put us all at ease … Incidentally, we have now fired over sixty thousand rounds, more than twice as much as all the other Bns combined … McEvoy and DeMarco are Captains."[127]

All companies celebrated the holiday and were given "old fashioned turkey dinners," after which it began to rain. James Helsel, Co. A, wrote, "The kitchen went into town and took over a restaurant. We went in by trucks and they served us a very good Christmas Dinner, much better than the jam sandwich at Huntsville, AL last year. They had turkey, mashed potatoes, gravy, filling, peas, pickles, wine, etc. An ex-bilingual comedian from 'B' Company was MC, he had quite a few good jokes; we sang; our Captain gave a talk and the evening was enjoyed by all." S-2 Rupert Burford said, "Everybody had received packages from home and the QM saw to it that we had turkey and other good things to eat, as well as an abundance of smokes. Our Medics celebrated more than any others, carousing until late Christmas morning." Shields, Co. D, fondly recalled serving Mass at 12 a.m. Christmas morning in the Rangers Area, writing, "On the trip back we sang carols, and believe it or not, I was in better spirits than during the Christmas of 1942 in the States." Charlie Lowry, Co. D Motor Pool, told his girlfriend, "had a very nice Xmas and we had turkey. I bet a lot of the people in the states didn't have turkey so after all I guess we over here are lucky." Robert P. Brimm mused, "Christmas was very enjoyable with all the trimmings. Everyone had packages from home with plenty of tidbits to munch. The chief beverage was the Christmas punch concocted from grapefruit juice, vino, and medic alcohol -- the results in some cases were disastrous." Once again, Steve Vukson, Motor Pool, HQ Co., mused, "The Great Holiday was here with very little activity going on except for our meals were exceptionally good. We had turkey and a lot of other food."[128]

The day after Christmas 50 men of the battalion were sent to the 5th Army rest camp at Naples, and a four-hour officers meeting was held in the afternoon at Venafro to discuss operations and plans for a battalion reorganization. This may be the meeting in which Capt. Pike said Hutchinson " … gave a famous speech to all the BN officers after his promotion which ranks with some of Col. Cunin's. Quote, 'I am Colonel Hutchinson. I have received a very high honor. I - I - I ' etc. in the same vein. It didn't strike a very responsive chord." During the day "Doc" Hulcher treated another Italian kid suffering from fireworks burns.[129]

Col. Maurice Barker, Chemical Officer, 5th Army, made an inspection of the battalion on a cold but clear 27th and presented a total of 45 Purple Hearts to officers and enlisted men. Leaflets, the same ones that had been previously dropped over the lines, were dropped on the troops and "Doc" Hulcher sewed up a man's hand. The remainder of the month was spent by the companies performing usual bivouac duties, replacing shortages, and checking the condition of their equipment. During the four days, the weather remained fair and cold and the morale of the men was reported as excellent. During one of the days, "Doc" Hulcher operated on an ingrown toenail and performed a circumcision. On the 30th Charlie Lowry, Co. D, wrote home, "As bad as all us boys would like to get home we still feel we have a little score to settle with some guys over here and are proud to be able to serve the ones back home. People, places, and things I have seen gives us a feeling of pride when we can say we are helping to keep such conditions from the U. S. A."[130]

Holiday celebrations were held by many on New Year's Eve, with one such incident well-described by S-3 "Bud" Pike, who wrote, "Company B hired a building in town and had a company party at which Trey and I were guests … Mindy is still CO of B Co., thus the invitation … The party started at 7:30 P.M. so I ate regular supper at HQ Co. at 5:00 consisting of turkey, dressing, cranberry sauce, etc. just to whet my appetite. Then at 7:30 I ate dinner with B Co. consisting of steak, gravy, string beans, apple pie, etc. The next day, New Years Day, our HQ Co. mess Sgt had turkey left so I had to eat another nasty old turkey dinner with all the trimmings … At the party B Co. had plenty of cognac, sherry brandy, vino, wine, gin, whiskey, champagne to drink at midnight …"[131]

During the month of December 1943, rounds fired by companies A, C, and D of the 83rd, and Co. B, 84th Chemical Battalion, included a total of 7,231 HE and 7,393 WP, for a grand total of 14,624 rounds, while Co. B, 83rd Chemical Battalion, from December 1st to 22nd, fired 2,895 HE and 606 WP, making 3,501 rounds. When placed together the sums of the 83rd Chemical Battalion, along with Co. B of the 84th, added up to 18,125 rounds fired in December. Casualties for the 83rd Chemical Battalion in December included at least four killed and 15 wounded, for a total of 19 casualties, although at least 187 replacements were received.[132]

Co. C, 2nd Platoon (Longbow Charlie White) on steps at Amalfi, Italy. For a companion view refer to the Company C photo section. *Dolly Sarrio*
Row 1 L-R: Alex Kimble, Jessie O'Berry, Daniel A. Johnson, Lemuel Russell Tillman, Orrie L. Jennings, Jerome G. Leap, Sullivan John Africano. Row 2 L-R: Philip J. Libossi, Charlie W. or Roy Carroll, Peter Mignella, Clifton E. Chancellor, William B. Jackson, Bennie Hill, Joseph C. Dickerson, Jr. Row 3 L-R: William C. Young, Isaac A. Mansfield, Italo Brash, Mack L. Dees, Sylvan M. Rosenfeld, Nathaniel L. Urso. Row 4 L-R: Alphonse Anthony Pagano, Fred Tombolini, Edward F. Carothers, Jack L. Billig, Millard O. Bond, Alfred F. Cramer, Theodore Beley. Row 5 L-R: William Thomas, Girard Dubois, Cecil S. Link, Maxie L. Knight, John A. Wojtyna, William M. Hawkins, Henry D. Bufkin. Row 6 L-R: Stanley Pokorsky, Carl D. Johnson, Cohen R. Upchurch, Earl Johnson, Rudolph Whitt, John F. Lucas, William Moore, Troy B. McLean, Lloyd S. Baker, Stephen C. Bullock. Row 7 L-R: Herbert L. Quina, Raymond W. Hoover, Wayne W. Anderson, Frederick L. Brooks, Henry or Vernal C. Goss, Claudie L. Hyde. Row 8 L-R: William L. Holmes, George W. Wolfe, James L. Doyle, Arlin E. Hilt, Peter L. Girone, "Slim" Frank R. Wilson, Thomas A. Keane, Charles Demarteliere. Missing from photo are William C. Ramsey and Norman Wahosky who were on detail in Naples, Italy, per Rudolph Whitt.

Italy   1943-1944

83rd
CHEMICAL
Bn.

Seasons
Greetings

Charlie

V-MAIL

V-MAIL

Gerald "Jerry" Johnson,
Co. D. Byron Jordan
claimed Johnson was
the artist for many of
the 83rd V-Mail greetings
until killed on the LST
at Anzio in 1944.

Byron Jordan

Italy

1943-
44

83rd
CHEMICAL
Bn.

Seasons
Greetings

V-MAIL

Various 83rd V-Mail Christmas
Greetings for 1943:
From Charlie Lowry (above
left), Russell H. Peterson
(above right), and Byron
Jordan (bottom).

*Courtesy of Author, Marcia
Daoust, and Byron Jordan.*

THE ANZIO BEACHEAD

Enemy attack
to destroy the
beach head 15-21 Feb.'44

Caroceto

B G 83

B G 83

G 83

A G 83

Line on 15 Feb.'44

ANZIO
Landing 22 Jan.'44

Nettuno

A G 83

Carano

A G 83
B G 83

4 Rangers
3 Rangers
1 Rangers

Battle of
Cisterna
29 Jan.'44

Cisterna

MILES
0   1   2   3   4   5
KILOMETERS
0   1   2   3   4   5

S/Sgt. E. Plassmann

Map drawn by S/Sgt Eugene Plassmann HQ Co., showing the positions of the 83rd Chemical Battalion on the Anzio Beachhead.
Eugene Plassmann

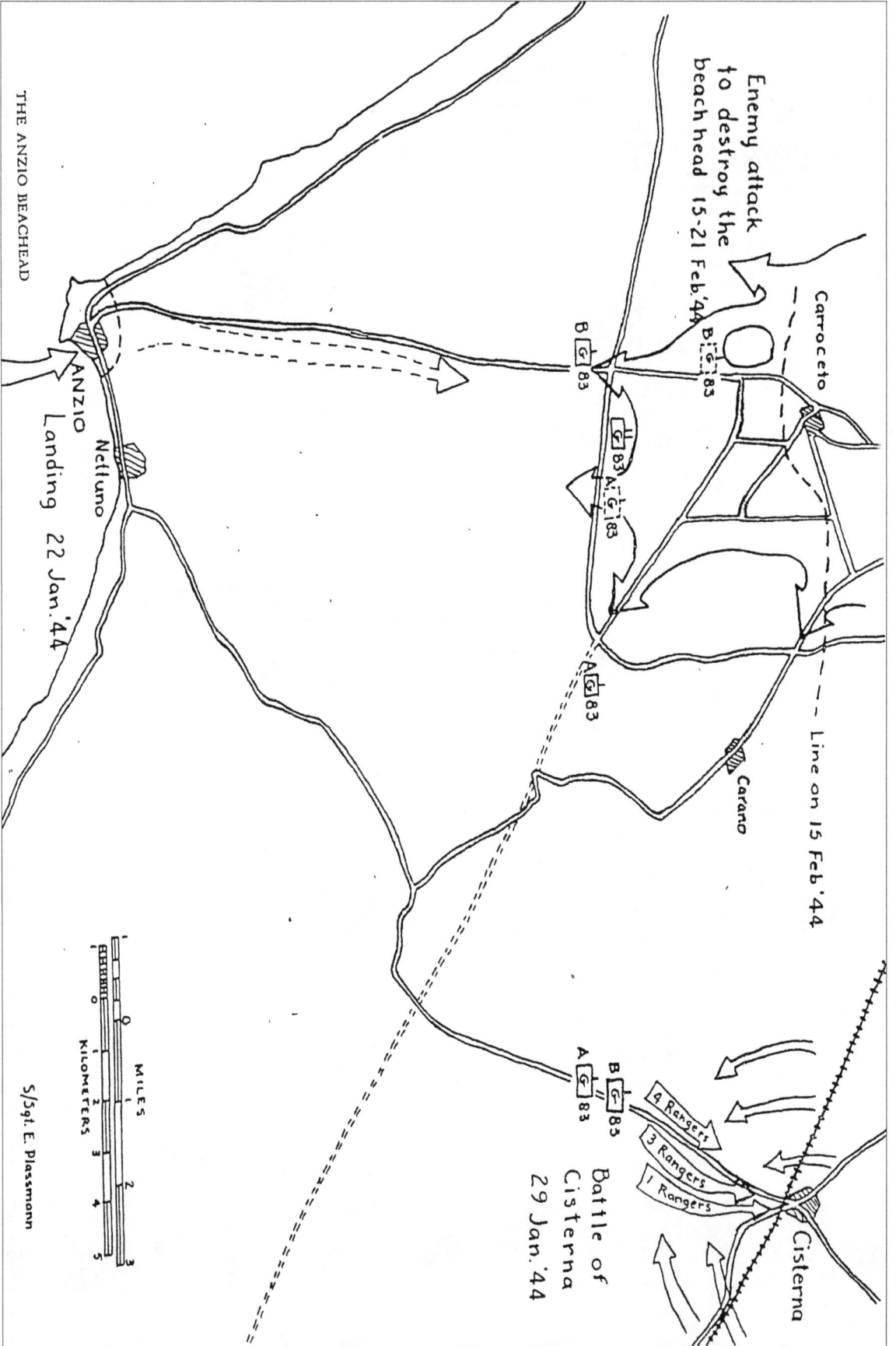

Chapter Eight

OPERATION SHINGLE
ANZIO AND THE SINKING OF LST 422
"WIN THE WAR IN '44"

Photo believed to be *LST 422* exploding at Anzio on January 26th, 1944. The image was taken from the destroyer *U.S.S. Herbert C. Jones*, one of the numerous rescue vessels. The craft in the lower left fits the description of an LST, the time clock barely visible in the lower right corner does indicate the correct time, and naval experts agree the explosions appear to be white phosphorous and high explosives.

National Archives

During the first part of January 1944, the 83rd Chemical Battalion remained stationed in the vicinity of Pozzuoli, Italy, performing usual bivouac duties and preparing for the next amphibious landing. The weather was typical of winter with cold, wind, and rain alternating with an occasional clear period. Morale was described for the most part as being excellent. The first day of the month was characterized by the typical wind and rain while 30 DUKWs from Co. D, 52nd Quartermaster ("Duck") Battalion, were attached to the Ranger Force and the crews were attached to HQ Co. for rations. Daniel Shields, Co. D, celebrated New Year's Day with a turkey dinner, as did Michael Rebick of the company, who said he had a turkey dinner with corn, beans, gravy, coffee, and peaches. "Doc" Hulcher, Medical Detachment, also talked of having a turkey dinner, as did most of the other men. Robert P. Brimm added, "The mud from the mountains of Venafro was gone and we were living royally in tents with homemade stoves. It was an amphibious training center, but Anzio was weeks away and Naples was only a few minutes drive."[1]

Following a sick call of 124 men, the battalion marched from bivouac to Pozzuoli on the 4th to hear a lecture given by the battalion chaplain and the battalion commanding officer on "What We Are Fighting For." Some of the men saw the movie *Sahara* which was cut short by a rainstorm. Another large sick call was reported on January 5th and a long officers meeting was held, followed by a review parade.[2]

But another movement was afoot as word came of the planned invasion of Anzio to help break the Cassino stalemate. S-2 Rupert Burford wrote, "A task force, composed of a reinforced corps, was assigned the mission of making another 'end-run', landing at Anzio. The Rangers were part of this task force and we were to go with them. Only two of our companies were required, and A and B companies were selected, since C & D had done most of the fighting for the battalion up to this time … We set up an Operations Tent in our area, under my supervision as S-2, procured maps and photographs of Anzio and began planning and training for the operation."[3]

The battalion attached to the VI Corps and, in spite of the cold, frozen ground, companies A and B began practicing with the DUKWs on the 6th. "Doc" Hulcher performed a partial hemorrhoidectomy on the 7th, and on the 8th companies A and B moved off the Isle of Nisida and spent two days, January 10th and 11th, in wet, foggy, freezing weather in the Gulf of Gaeta rehearsing with the DUKWs from *LST 379*. S-2 Burford said these landings were made at Baia and proved a success. This would be the first of two "undress rehearsals" for the invasion of Anzio.[4]

During the preparatory invasion activities daily soldier life continued as usual, with one rather amusing incident reported by S-3 "Bud" Pike, who wrote home, "While I can't get a Purple Heart for being wounded in action I thought I was going to get one the other day here in the bivouac area. I was calmly sitting on our fresh air "two holer" enjoying the beauties of nature and using the hole for what it was intended. Overhead a limb from a tree was holding up the canvas roof. I finished my job, stood up to put on my pants (what am I saying), and WHAM there was that tree limb square in my eye. For a minute I thought I'd put my eye out. But fortunately everything turned out OK. Doc DeMarco bandaged it up and washed it out. I looked very cute for several days with a big white bandage over my eye and adhesive all over my face. You know how people are – no one believed my story about how it happened. I couldn't even blame it on bumping into a door as we don't have any doors in our tents. Such is life." Russell H. Peterson, Co. D, lamented, "Christmas and New Years day have come and gone … [the war] is certainly no picnic, but it is not as bad as I had imagined before I saw action." Charlie Lowry, also of Co. D, added, "I am in a rest area at present, and I can say it isn't near as bad here now as it was at first. I was in the invasion of Sicily and Italy both and I can tell this much about them. They weren't any fun … Nairn (one of the boys) says hello."[5]

The battalion, minus companies C and D, was attached to the 1st Ranger Battalion on the 13th, reporting good morale and fair and cold weather. This was followed the next day by a lecture to the battalion by Lt. Col. Hutchinson, Capt. Silverino V. DeMarco of the Medical Detachment, and Chaplain George E. Gaiser, on sex hygiene. Later in the day a dress parade was held where Silver Stars were presented to 1st Lt. Andre N. Laus and Pfc. Curtis A. Williams. Additionally, nine Purple Hearts were awarded to the battalion.[6]

Michael Rebick, Co. D, wrote home on the 15th that the previous night he and his friends all went to "… a G.I. stage show & was it ever good, the band was good, the actors were perfect … the actors all came out dressed as dancers as the band played the Rhumba, tap dancers, hillbilly music & they sang the song 'Pistol Pack M.' [*"Pistol Packing Mama"*], and it didn't sound bad …" Rebick also reflected on the recent past, writing, " … we sure did have rain and mud the last time we were at the front."[7]

OPERATION SHINGLE

On January 17th, 1944, Col. William O. Darby, commanding the Ranger Task Force, issued orders for Operation Shingle, the amphibious invasion of the beaches of Anzio and Nettuno, Italy, just south of Rome, in order to break the stalemate along the Gustav Line at Cassino. The plan called for the VI Corps to land at 2:00 a.m. on the beaches in the vicinity of Anzio on a date to be announced, to seize and secure the beachhead, and to advance in the direction of Colli Laziali. This would involve the 3rd Infantry Division (reinforced) landing at the beaches between Nettuno and La Banca, seizing and establishing a beachhead, contacting the 504th Parachute Infantry regiment on the high ground north of Anzio, contacting the Ranger Force on the left, protecting the Corps right flank, and preparing to advance in the direction of Velletri on Corps orders. At the same time, the British 1st Infantry Division (reinforced) would land on the beaches northwest of Anzio, secure and establish a beachhead, protect the left flank of the Corps, contact the 504th Parachute Infantry Regiment within the British 1st Infantry's sector, and maintain contact with the 3rd Infantry Division on the right.[8]

As a component of this overall plan, the Ranger Force, which consisted of the 1st Ranger Battalion, with attachments of the 3rd and 4th Ranger Battalions, 509th Parachute Infantry Battalion, the 83rd Chemical Battalion (minus companies C and D), and Co. H of the 36th Engineer Combat Regiment, was to land at Anzio and in order of priority: (1) seize the Anzio port facilities and protect them from sabotage; (2) destroy any existing defensive batteries at Anzio; (3) clear the beach area between Anzio and Nettuno; (4) secure and establish a beachhead; and (5) contact the British 1st Infantry Division on the left, the 3rd Infantry Division on the right, and the 504th Parachute regiment to the north. To accomplish their goal, the 1st Ranger Battalion would land at 2:00 a.m. on the right half of Yellow Beach at Anzio and destroy enemy installations within its sector, establish a beachhead, make contact with the 4th Ranger Battalion on their left, and prepare to advance north upon order. Landing at the same time on the left half of Yellow Beach, the 4th Ranger Battalion would also destroy enemy installations within its sector, establish a beachhead, make contact with the 1st Ranger Battalion on their right, and, upon arrival, with the 3rd Ranger Battalion on the left, remaining available to move north when ordered. The 83rd Chemical Battalion (minus companies C and D) would land an hour after the 1st and 4th Rangers on Yellow Beach and take up positions prepared to fire concentrations.[9]

According to the Loading and Landing Table in the Ranger journal, the two companies of the 83rd (A and B) would land approximately 454 men, along with 16 mortars, 6,000 rounds of ammo, communications and welding equipment, baggage, and 13 trucks. The two companies would be placed on *LST 410* and then land in a large group of DUKWs.[10]

The 3rd Ranger Battalion would land on Yellow Beach an hour after the 83rd Chemical Battalion and pass through the 4th Ranger Battalion, then clear the town of Anzio of the enemy, seize and protect the port of Anzio from

Aboard *LST 410*. Top L-R: Stephen Vukson and Robert Bell. Right L-R: Roscoe D. Adamson, Stephen Vukson, and John Simurda, Jr. Bottom: Stephen Vukson and unidentified soldier.

All photos courtesy Stephen Vukson

Isle of Ischia off the Port of Bagnolia. Note the LST on the left of picture. *Codega Collection*

sabotage, destroy enemy installations within their sector, establish a beachhead, and make contact with the 4th Ranger Battalion on the right with preparations to advance north. The 509th Parachute Infantry Regiment would land at Yellow Beach the same time as the 3rd Rangers, clear the beach area between Anzio and Nettuno, and attack Nettuno upon order. Co. H of the 36th Engineer Combat regiment would land, clear the beach of mines, wires, and other obstacles, prepare exits from the beach, establish roadblocks, and operate the beach until relieved. Upon the initial landing by the Ranger Force the Navy and artillery guns would remain on standby and, once the Ranger Force made contact with the 3rd Infantry Division on their right, become attached to them.[11]

For the 83rd Chemical Battalion, amphibious invasion preparations continued on the 17th as companies A, B, and HQ boarded *LST 410* and departed for two days to a position off Isle de Nisida in the Gulf of Salerno, while companies C and D each provided 23 guards for the areas of the 1st, 3rd, and 4th Ranger Battalions. In the early morning darkness, under the additional cover of smoke, companies A and B landed at the beach next to the Ranger bivouac area at Baia for an invasion rehearsal. One Ranger battalion impersonated enemy forces while the other two represented the invaders. The DUKWs had to make two trips in order to land all men and equipment. The rehearsal resulted in one Ranger "killed and one man wounded from machine gun fire." Afterwards the force returned to Pozzuoli where it was announced the 83rd Chemical Battalion, excepting companies C and D, were relieved from the 1st Ranger Battalion and attached to the 6615th Ranger Force (Provisional). Once again, James Helsel, Co. A, cleverly perceived something was astir, as he wrote, "The past few days we have been taking dukw training … We have been alerted the past few days, we are attached to the Rangers and the 509 AB and have had a few amphibious dry runs with them, I guess they are just waiting on the cherry pie."[12]

Writing home on the 17th, S-3 Ed "Bud" Pike discussed the elements, stating, "Tonight it is very cold again but I am sitting in my tent with a nice fire going and with a good sized wood pile in front of me so things aren't too bad. The men in the motor pool fixed up stoves for us, made out of old 5 gallon oil cans which help out considerably on cold nights. The days lately have been very nice. Although somewhat brisk. The mountains are all capped with snow." Michael Rebick, Co. D, used a baseball analogy as he wrote home and said, "I am on a good Yankee team & hope that soon we should play our final game to decide the winner of this war." Charlie Lowry, Co. D, wrote, "My outfit is in a rest area now but you know we can't stay here too long and miss the big show." James Helsel added, "We spent last night out on the water again, we got in about five this morning. Old Mt. Vesuvius was spitting a little fire, I guess she has a little life in her yet. I might add we had our cherry pie, so I guess it won't be long."[13]

The battalion was unable to load 4,000 rounds of ammo for the forthcoming invasion on the British operated *LST 410* when the ship failed to dock on the 19th. In the midst of all the invasion preparations, additional medals were awarded with Silver Stars going to 1st Lt. Bernard B. Stone, 2nd Lt. Robert L. Brasel, and Sgt. Joseph J. Karcauskas, and a posthumous Silver Star was awarded to 1st Lt. Vester L. Turner, killed in action near Ceppagna, Italy, on December 20, 1943. Lt. Col. Hutchinson noted this made a total of 15 Silver Stars for the battalion, and Ammunition Sgt. William T. Ulmer, HQ & HQ Co., was under consideration for the award for helping to put out a fire in the battalion ammo dump. According to S-3 "Bud" Pike the medals were awarded at a "retreat ceremony" held after a court-martial session in which a man was found guilty of being AWOL at Gela. Commenting on the Silver Stars, Pike observed, "The sergeant was very deserving of his decoration."[14]

All the waiting for the impending mission ended shortly after three in the afternoon of January 20th as companies A, B, and 30 enlisted men and 7 officers from a HQ detachment boarded *LST 410* at Baia, the ship having finally docked and loaded the ammo that could not be loaded the previous day. The strength of the battalion at the beginning of the

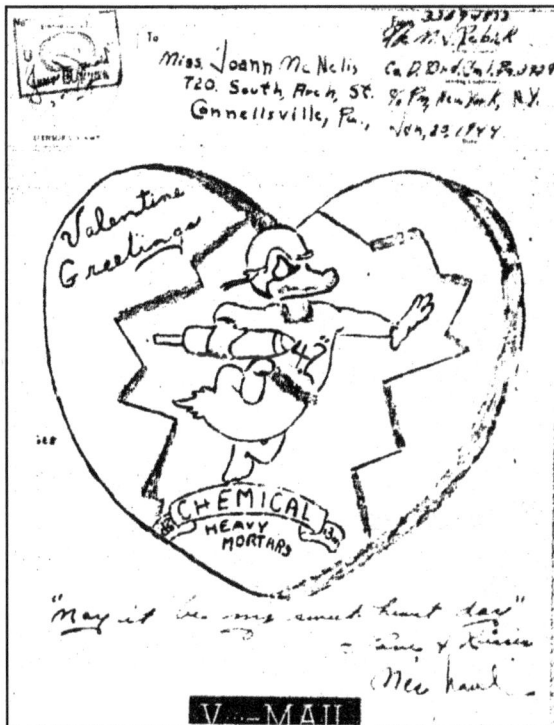

Valentine sent by Michael Rebick, Co. D,
before embarking on *LST 422*. *Linda Whalen*

operation was listed in the battalion journal as 38 officers and 1,031 enlisted men, for a total of 1,069. Stephen W. Vukson, HQ Co., Battalion Motor Section, said the ship set sail for the Port of Bagnoli, Italy, and after the evening meal he slept on the top deck in his truck. Julius "Doc" Hulcher said the LST "… was loaded down with everything on every square inch. You had an awful hard time walking on deck from one end of the boat to the other … An Italian in [*a*] row boat came alongside [*the*] boat selling oranges and I bought a few. Men continued coming aboard. While we were eating C rations we began moving out … I went out on deck until it was so cold and black I couldn't see or feel a thing."[15]

The sea was calm, a perfect blue, and the weather beautiful on January 21st at 8:00 as *LST 410* joined a large convoy, comprised of LCIs, LSTs, destroyers, and small craft, and sailed in a northwesterly direction. The mainland and islands could be seen off the starboard side and "Doc" Hulcher said the sight of all the ships gave him a sense of pride and security. The men ate breakfast and were issued life preservers. The day proved uneventful as the mission was explained to the men, who were given maps and pictures. Afterwards, "Doc" Hulcher called his men together to inform them of the destination, but they already knew. Steve Vukson said they were told the invasion would take place at 1:00 a.m. on the 22nd. The morale of the men was high and later a British destroyer sailed by with loudspeakers blaring, " … God speed and best wishes from all the kings, presidents, and high military officials." In the evening Chaplain George Gaiser held a short service for the men.[16]

While companies A and B moved closer to Anzio the weather was reported clear and cold at Pozzuoli. Co. C and the rear echelons of companies A and B of the 83rd moved to a staging area operated by the PBS, arriving about five miles south of Caserta on the Naples-Caserta Highway at about 1:00 in the afternoon. Co. D's drivers and kitchen personnel had previously moved to Capodimonte Palace in Naples for waterproofing and would move to the staging area the following day.[17]

ANZIO
January 22

At approximately 2:15 on the clear and cool morning of January 22, 1944, the 1st and 4th Ranger battalions, in addition to the 509th Parachute Battalion, hit the beaches of Anzio and were surprised to encounter hardly any enemy resistance. Within a short time the town was in Ranger hands. Just as rehearsed, companies A and B of the 83rd Chemical Battalion landed in two waves, the first with Lt. Col. Hutchinson and Meyerson at the helm, at H plus 60, after which Hutchinson set up a CP in the northwest wing of a casino. Meyerson directed the DUKWs back to the LST and got the second group, consisting of Burford and Pike and comprising the remainder of companies A and B. They landed at H plus 180, as did the 3rd Ranger Battalion. Both chemical battalion companies set up near the Battalion Command Post, Co. A just south of the casino and Co. B slightly to the north. A battalion aid station was also placed near the casino, mortar ammo was shuttled to shore in DUKWs throughout the morning, and the 3rd Ranger Battalion extended and consolidated the Ranger line.[18]

Stephen W. Vukson, HQ Co. and dispatcher for the Motor Pool, remembered the men had been given their evening meal, and got their equipment together before dark of the 21st. During the 1:00 a.m. invasion he watched the rocket shells explode on the beach and felt the concussion. "We stood on the deck of our LST in pitch blackness and watched the 'softening-up' process in the distance," S-2 Rupert Burford recalled. "This was the first time I had seen a rocket ship at work and I was amazed at the speed with which thousands of pounds of high-speed explosive and steel were thrown on the beach. I don't see how there could be any living thing left there to impede our advance."[19]

Joseph Edward Cannetti, Co. A, a former office boy from Long Island, New York, and an 83rd replacement in November of 1943, recalled "being up on the deck of our LST and watching the barge rocket launchers plaster the beach in front of us. We then went over the side down a cargo net into waiting DUKWs. I remember landing on the beach and being told to dig in. We left the beach and went up a long flight of stairs to a railroad track, where I saw my first dead Ranger and a dead German next to him." Sam Bundy, also of Co. A, added, "We loaded up on the dukws down on the crowded tank deck and waited for the doors to open and see the ramp lowered into the water … One by one the dukws left the boat and got into formation. We hit the beach at 3AM, one hour after 2 BN's of Rangers had landed. The company was taken ashore in two waves, met no resistance, and had no casualties … Lt. Hauser, our forward observer, reported enemy vehicles approaching town, but communications were incomplete, so we could not fire upon them. His OP was ahead of our troops, but he met no opposition."[20]

From the ship's deck Stephen Vukson saw "the first wave of landing craft with infantry divisions and the Ranger battalions starting towards the shore. Companies A and B of our battalion went in on the second wave. It was breaking day when [John] Simurda [Jr.], Adamson, and I went to shore. We went in on an amphibious DUKW. The Germans didn't expect us to land there and [we met with] only some small arms fire." Vukson added, "Our companies didn't fire at all. We supported the Rangers with our 4.2 mortar. We pulled a cart with oxygen and acetylene … Simurda & I were chased off the beach a few times by shells as we were working on an amphibious G.M.C. (duck as we call them)."[21]

James Helsel, Co. A, noted that, after he landed, " … we unloaded and pulled the mortars and carried the ammo across the beach, which was about 100 yards, to a very high wall. Here we waited to see where we were to go into position. Only once in crossing a German burp gun opened up, but it didn't last long. At sunup we moved into the court yard of some Prince and Princess Palace. Just a little before sunup the first platoon came in with the second wave with the Paratroopers. They took us for Germans. The first platoon set up at the casino, the paratroopers went down to Nettuno. We done very little firing. There was a lot of air activity, but our air support was very good and a lot of interesting dog fights. We spent the night here."[22]

Around 9:50 in the morning, the 83rd Chemical requested to superiors to register their mortars but were told to register them only with the Rangers, while at 9:55 the prematurely gray Lt. Walter E. Hauser, as well as Capt. Burford and Capt. Charles M. Shunstrum of the Rangers HQ, all reported sighting enemy tanks on the road north of Anzio. Three scout cars, probably for the tanks, were also observed. But the first sign of resistance came at 10:30 a.m. when enemy planes began to bomb the ships in the harbor followed at 10:55 by air-bursts over the beach. An intense artillery barrage was also received in the Anzio vicinity at the same time and the 83rd was requested to check into the source. As a result, Co. B of the 83rd fired unsuccessfully at what was believed to be a self-propelled gun.[23]

According to Andrew Leech, Co. B, "We followed behind them [the Rangers] and set up in the streets once before moving on up into the town to an old Facist college and set up on the lawn and started firing … to my surprise a shell burst right over my head and the shrapnel riddled a building right by me. I knew then it was Jerry shells, so I took cover."[24]

Lt. Veryl R. Hays, Co. A, was impressed with the relative ease of the invasion, writing, "As the landing craft carrying my men moved in for a landing it was very quiet. There was no noise at all, except for rocket shells bursting on the beach. There wasn't another shot fired. We surprised the Germans having a gay party in a large villa, and resistance was weak and unorganized. The Krauts were well likkered up and reeling around in their bare feet. We took them like Washington took the Hessians."[25]

Pvt. William J. Golding, Co. A, captured a prisoner at the OP at 2:00 in the afternoon, while the only reported casualty of the day for the 83rd was Pfc. Anthony G. Nitz of Lucas County, Ohio, who was wounded by an enemy shell burst. In the same explosion that injured Nitz, five other men, none of the 83rd, were hit - one killed and four wounded. The day concluded with harassing enemy artillery fire throughout the night.[26]

Joseph Cannetti recalled his section of Co. A spent the first night at Anzio in a wine cellar. Andrew Leech said part of Co. B spent the night in an air raid shelter while the other platoon moved to the outskirts of town. Pvt. Morton Gorowsky, Co. B, said, "Capt. Mindrum told a BAR man and me to go to the left flank and dig in, so maybe it was not going to be so peaceful as it had seemed at first."[27]

Stephen Vukson said that he and his comrades from the Motor Pool " … slept in a church near the beach which was also our Command Post. Many enemy shells started to hit the beach. One of the ships was hit by enemy fire -- also a few of our men were wounded."[28]

By the end of the day, the Ranger Task Force had taken Anzio and Nettuno and the beaches had been cleared of mines and put in operation, as was the port. Ships entered the port for unloading and the Rangers reported 18 Russian internees, prisoners used by the Germans in labor gangs, had been taken, 32 prisoners had been captured, and 40 of the enemy had been killed. Late in the afternoon the 83rd's CP had been moved forward to a bramble thicket, behind a slight knoll. S-2 Burford said, "We had a little defilade but no cover or concealment … no building to serve as wind-break and no roof over us … we were very uncomfortable and suffered a great deal from cold." Back at Pozzuoli Co. D and HQ Co. departed for the staging area five miles south of Caserta. Daniel Shields, Co. D, said the day was very cold and he "really felt it."[29]

"Doc" Hulcher summed up the day's events in his diary, writing, "… the bell rang calling for the first wave. I leaped out of bed and watch[ed] the fellows leave, wishing them good luck as they passed by loaded down with equipment. This was a little before 1 AM … When they left I went out on deck. The rocket bombardment went off at 1 AM and such noise I've never heard. Long will I remember that and the rest of this morning. We could hear the 'duck's' heading off to shore 4 miles away. All was quite [quiet] again and listen as I did I heard nothing and could see only the stars it was a black night. After a while I went back inside. Still no shooting. About 2:30 … report came thru [through] that all was well. Later heard that Green Beach (5th Inf.) was unopposed and still later Red Beach (British) report landing and advancing. About 3:30 report that little small arms fire on Red Beach and no mine casualty as yet. I felt better was dreading putting my foot on the beach. I was scared of mines [more] than anything else … Then 2nd wave bell, ours, and on went the equipment and off to the port aft deck I headed. It was truly dark. Our 'duck' came alongside and over the rails and down the side I went. On the way in 4 AM landing about 5 AM. Everything fairly quiet. Took our time going across beach. Got bunch together went up side of casino and set up aid station in basement of 6 story building. Few small arm shots every once in a while, a few prisoners passed by every so often. Planes began zooming overhead and occasion shell whizzed by overhead. Piece of shrapnel came in window into room we were sitting in and so I slept in the other room that night. I only had a few stray patients, about 3 wounded. Spent day straightening things up and I didn't venture too far from the house. Troops & supplies continued to pour in. Town was like a ghost town. I know of only 3 dead and about 3 wounded U. S. boys and about 26 P.W. and quite some Jerries killed during the first day on the beach. Engineers picked up a few mines on the beach but no one was hurt."[30]

On a cloudy and cold morning of the 23rd, Co. A was engaged with an enemy self-propelled gun on the right flank at Anzio and word was received that British and American forces had made contact on the front. Co. B moved into a new position about 2,000 yards north of Anzio to support the advancing Rangers. Later in the day, at about 3:00 p.m., Co. A, Headquarters Detachment, and the Medical Detachment advanced to a position about 10,000 yards north of Anzio on the east side of the Anzio-Rome Highway, although various members of Co. A said this transpired at noon as they were picked up by DUKWs and moved to a wooded area on the plains, where they erected a tank defense. "Doc" Hulcher, Medical Detachment, said there was a very small sick call and, "About noon Sorenson, Malm, and I moved forward about 4 miles into some woods and set up an aid station." Lt. Robert W. Fenton, Dispatcher Stephen W. Vukson, Roscoe D. Adamson, William A. Davison, John Simurda, Jr., and Robert H. Bell of the Motor Pool took up quarters in a modern house with a built-in garage located in the upper end of town and away from the beach. The men located some potatoes which they fried and later shared with Lt. Col. Hutchinson when he paid them a visit. The Rangers reported that by the end of the day they had cleaned up the port of Anzio to permit Peter shipping [a reference to the ships they employed for the invasion as part of Task Force Peter], had established contact with the 2nd S.S. Brigade and the 1st Battalion, 7th Infantry, and had made physical contact with the Scots Guards.[31]

In spite of drizzling rain, activity also continued back at Caserta where, at about 7:00 in the evening, companies C and D, sections of the Medical and Headquarters detachments, and the kitchen and supply sections of companies A and B departed the staging area for Naples harbor via trucks provided by the PBS. Although expecting to immediately load on to a LST for transport to Anzio, they were instead moved to an assembly area to await the vessel. Daniel Shields, Co. D, one of the soldiers awaiting embarkation on the LST, said he went to the Duchess of Acosta's palace and pitched a tent with Andy Whelan. Pvt. Byron H. Jordan, Co. B, already ashore at Anzio on January 22nd, said the men heard reports that C and D companies had to use the LST as there was a shortage of DUKWs due to most being sent to England for the D-Day invasion in June.[32]

Co. B, already at Anzio, remained in position on the Anzio-Rome Highway on a clear and warm January 24th. At one point in the afternoon, an officer of the 83rd called the Ranger Task Force regarding a radio lost the previous day, while shortly after 7 p.m., at the request of the Rangers, two guns of the 2nd Platoon, Co. A, were moved behind a dairy farm, where they were able to make several direct hits on a white house occupied by the enemy. Later, the company laid a smoke screen for a Ranger patrol before engaging the enemy at factory buildings in Carroceto, and continued to support the Rangers in their attack on Carroceto until the 28th. The poor "nature of the ground" caused many mortars to fail after firing only a few rounds although each platoon managed to keep at least one mortar in operation at all times. Sam Bundy, Co. A, described the movement, writing, "Late in the afternoon, from a forward OP, Lt. [*James J.*] O'Connor noticed enemy activity which was out of range of our mortars. He borrowed a jeep and returned to the company, where he loaded two squads, two comm. men and 100 rounds of ammo into two trucks, and moved to a position 200 yds ahead of the MLR [*Main Line of Resistance*]. Two mortars were set up behind a barn and comm. laid to the roof of another building 100 yds forward, where an OP was established. Sgt. [*Andrew J.*] Connolly was Platoon Exec. during the operation. First a smoke screen was laid down with 10 rounds of WP for an advancing patrol. Then Lt. O'Connor registered in on a house that contained enemy infantry and machine guns. 35 rounds of HE were fired and all were effective, either landing on the house, its outbuildings, or in the yard. At least 3 direct hits were scored."[33]

Stephen Vukson, along with his group from the Motor Pool, left their house and garage and moved to the front line on the left flank, where their mortar men fired a number of rounds and then moved to another location. According to Vukson, "The Germans hit us with a heavy concentration of shells. It was God's will that we moved into woods as that same evening the Germans bombed that block and area and where we stayed the previous evening. We dug our fox holes and slept in them ..." The Medical Detachment remained at their aid station for a couple of days where they witnessed a number of air raids, spent time pushing trucks in the mud, and at one point some shrapnel landed near "Doc" Hulcher, apparently motivating him to dig his first foxhole. At about 9:45 p.m., Lt. Col. Hutchinson reported to Col. Darby "for orders concerning the step off at daylight," to which Darby responded, "You will be ready to give support to the units I put into action tomorrow morning."[34]

Meanwhile, Capt. Robert E. Edwards had made a trip back to Caserta to bring rations to the men at Naples, where a company kitchen was established. Ten trucks also arrived from Caserta to convey the men to the docks, although embarkation was delayed for a couple of hours by a smoke screen over the Naples area. Daniel Shields said the men nearly choked on the smoke pots. Soon afterwards, on the night of the 24th, 479 enlisted men and 16 officers of the 83rd Chemical Battalion, comprising 495 men, along with 53 battalion vehicles, finally loaded onto *LST 422*.[35]

The ship had been laid down on November 12, 1942, at Bethlehem Fairfield Co., Baltimore, Maryland, and launched December 10, 1942. The ship was commissioned *U.S.S. LST 422* February 4, 1943, and transferred to the British Navy the same day. The vessel had a displacement of 1,780 t. (lt), 3,880 (fl) and was 328 feet long and 50 feet wide. The draft unloaded was bow 2'4" stern 7'6" while loaded the bow was 8'2" stern 14'1". The ship's speed of 12k was propelled by two General Motors 12-567 diesel engines, two shafts, and two twin rudders. *LST 422* complemented 8-10 officers, 100-115 enlisted crew and a troop capacity of approximately 140 officers and enlisted men. Weaponry consisted of one single 3"/50 gun mount, five 40mm gun mounts, six 20mm gun mounts, two .50 caliber machine guns, and four .30 caliber machine guns. Ironically, there were only 2 to 6 emergency boats, or LCVPs. Lt. Commander Colin Lowe Broadhurst, Royal Navy Reserves (RNR), would be the British executive officer in charge of *LST 422* at Anzio, along with 65 British officers and crew. Born circa 1904 in Hayfield District, Cheshire / Devonshire, Broadhurst was in the Royal Navy Reserves as early as 1929. Prior to his assignment to *LST 422* in June of 1943 he had served as an officer on *H.M.S. Unicorn II* in 1940. Subsequently, he served as the commanding officer on *H.M.S. Gadfly*, which was a mine-sweeping trawler, *H.M.S. Equerry*, also a mine-sweeping trawler, and *H.M. LST 39*.[36]

Lt. Commander Broadhurst ordered life belts be worn at all times during the entire voyage of *LST 422*. T/5 Claude J. Shaw, HQ Co., born in Montana but raised in Oregon, said he was assigned as assistant to the transport quartermaster and it was his job to provide a life jacket for each man, as well as 3 days emergency rations and a full compliment of ammo. Shaw added, "Well, I ran my tail off to get this done before departure time. Now, I am unable to

Assault convoy of LSTs en route to Anzio in January of 1944. Note the barrage balloons. *LST 422* is probably among this group. National Archives

explain why I did not get a life jacket for myself." The 83rd's Capt. Robert Edwards also confirmed the men were issued life belts as they embarked, although following a check it was revealed some had been missed, the remainder to be issued the following morning. Pvt. Rudolph Whitt, Co. C, a coal miner from Buchanan County, Virginia, contradicted this as he recalled the men boarded alphabetically, " … with all the 'W's' coming so near the end of the line, there were no life belts for those of us in that group." He added, "It was so cold and rainy and windy on the weather deck that I went down to the lower deck to try to get some sleep." On the way down Whitt happened upon a safety belt hanging in a cranny on a hook and buckled it around him as he lay down near the stairway to go to sleep, using his backpack as a pillow. Daniel Shields, Co. D, would later write in his diary, "Went for life belt & it was broken. Limey sailor told me they were only a mere formality, but I had him fix it, thank God." Ed Trey, HQ Co., also later recalled the men complaining and making such comments as, "Capt. Trey is a chicken making us wear these silly life jackets," and, "That God damned Trey is afraid, we gotta wear these life preservers."[37]

Also on board were 20 enlisted men and one officer of the 2nd Battalion, 68th Coastal Artillery, an anti-aircraft unit, accompanied by their 10 vehicular units, as well as 65 British officers and crew. It is also known that at least one man, and possibly others, of the 488th Port Battalion, was aboard, assuring there would be at least 582 men on the craft. Little did any of the passengers or crew realize they were soon to be involved in the worst tragedy of the entire war for the 83rd Chemical Mortar Battalion.[38]

Additionally, placed on the ship were 1,484 highly volatile rounds of 4.2" ammo belonging to the 83rd and numerous cases of .50 caliber and 40mm ammo of the 68th Coastal Artillery. Lt. Robert W. Fenton later said he personally witnessed Billy C. Rhoads, Co. C, assist in loading the ammo, but as Fenton was actually already on the Anzio Beachhead at this time he must have meant Rhoads helped load *LST 410* for the initial invasion on January 22nd. Fortunately, a number of men scheduled for the trip failed to make the journey. Typical of these were Kenneth

L-R: Charles Dial, Max Nestler, Joseph Karcauskas, Rudolph Fichtler, and Edward Guinness, all men of Co. D, in Pozzuoli, Italy. All but Dial perished on *LST 422*. *Codega Collection*

E. Laundre, who fell from a truck and broke his wrist; Charlie Lowry, Co. D Motor Pool, with an infected cut on his arm; and James Marion ("Les") Lester, also Co. D Motor Pool, in the hospital with yellow jaundice.[39]

LST 422 departed Naples on the morning of the 25th in TG [*Task Group*] 81.5, First Follow-Up Group, a convoy comprised of 39 British LSTs, 20 LCIs, and 6 LCTs, accompanied by various escorts and minesweepers. Lt. Commander Broadhurst, Royal Navy, commanding the LST, deliberately took a course south toward Messina in hopes of deceiving the enemy, then swung north toward Anzio. Broadhurst wrote, " … the weather was deteriorating all the time the ships were in convoy."[40]

In the meantime, companies A and B of the 83rd continued in action on what they described as a cloudy and misty day along the Anzio-Rome Highway, north of Anzio. Forward observers advanced with the 4th Ranger Battalion and the 509th Parachute at 7:30 a.m., but as the battalion journal recorded, "The rapidity with which assault battalions moved placed our mortars out of range of enemy targets." The Rangers established their position and sent patrols to Ficoccia Creek. A platoon of 4.2" mortars supported the Ranger operation. Lt. Col. Hutchinson visited the Ranger Force CP at 3:48 p.m. seeking Col. Darby, stated Co. B of the 83rd could be moved that night, then left the CP at 7:50 in the evening. Steve Vukson, HQ Co., noted the foxholes that he and his buddies had dug the previous day " … were a convenience when the enemy thought of throwing in a few more rounds." Additionally, Vukson was ordered to draw rations for companies A, B, and HQ in addition to his regular duties with Motor Pool parts supply. Following this directive, he started making daily runs into Anzio for rations and vehicle parts. He later wrote in his diary, "It was a dangerous run as shells kept landing along the road and in the town of Anzio. My driver and I were caught in a number of air raids." Later in the day the Ranger Task Force reported the extension of the Anzio bridgehead.[41]

Air raids also hit the Naples area throughout the day but did not deter resumption of the HQ Co. kitchen, the men having previously messed with a QM company of black soldiers assigned to the staging area. *LST 422* reached Porto D'Anzio, the Anzio harbor, sometime between 10:00 and 11:00 p.m., although Hale H. Hepler, Co. C, recalled the ship was to debark at 9:00 p.m. but failed to do so for reasons unknown to him. The ship would not actually anchor until after midnight. Depending upon source, various references have given the ship's location as being anywhere from two to 12 miles offshore, with the two to four mile range probably the most accurate. At this point Lt. Commander Broadhurst reportedly told the 83rd they most likely would not dock until the next afternoon, apparently due to the poor weather conditions, including an extremely rough sea and a strong wind blowing off shore. The Royal Navy officer requested all men be cleared from the tank deck, and as the ship was already heavily crowded, Capt. Edwards said, "many men were sleeping on the top deck, around and under vehicles." 1st Lt. Justin G. ("Jerry") Woomer, HQ Co., a former schoolteacher from Yeagerstown, Pennsylvania, informed his men of their destination and at 11:00 p.m. retired to the officers' quarters, which were located on "the deck level in the stern, rear, part of the ship." Before settling in he noticed his life jacket was missing, which he later found out had been confiscated, along with other life jackets, by an officer in the adjoining quarters to use to soften his bunk. Woomer gave it little thought and put his carbine and steel helmet on the floor as he got into the upper bunk fully clothed.[42]

THE SINKING OF LST 422
January 26

At about midnight in the port of Anzio, *YMS 226*, a yard minesweeper, the type ship that generally held a crew of four officers and 24 enlisted men, reported "strong winds, moderate seas, with intermittent rain and poor visibility," while the *U.S.S. Pilot* (AM 104), an Allied minesweeper headed by Lt. Commander S. B. Wetmore, listed winds gradually increasing to Force 5 after midnight. *LCI 196* reported the "wind increased to 35 knots" and "moderate swells." Lt. Commander Colin Broadhurst, commanding *LST 422*, reported his ship, along with the LST convoy, anchored at fifteen minutes after midnight in the Transport Area off Anzio, at which time he recorded, "Six shackles of bow anchor in 25 fathoms of water. Full sea watches were kept throughout the night. The wind was Force 6 from West and moderate to rough sea running."[43]

By three in the morning, *H.M.S. Ulster Queen*, providing air raid warnings for Operation Shingle, also reported the wind as West, Force 6, creating a high wind and rough sea, which caused *LCI 32*, the staff or flagship of the Return Convoy 81.14, to lose its anchor cable. This resulted in an order to cruise back and forth in the point "William" (Transport Area), as the ship got underway at one third speed in the mine swept channel area west of Point Charlie, using a column of anchored LSTs as a guide. The weather conditions further deteriorated by 4:00 when Rear Admiral Frank J. Lowry, commander of Task Force 81, listed the wind as West, Force 6, Sea 5.[44]

The adverse weather conditions continued to worsen at 4:08 as *SC 649*, a sub chaser anchored off Green Beach, recorded, "two sections of beach pontoon causeway were sighted drifting down on ship. Efforts to raise anchor by hand winch failed, the pontoons parting anchor chain at hawse pipe. Engines were backed down at high speed in time to prevent further damage. At this time the wind was blowing a near gale. Course was set to seaward of transport area … " At about 4:30 *YMS 62* reported, "… [the] sea becoming high with wind squalls," while the commander of the mine squadron wrote, "… [the] wind began to increase soon after midnight reaching Force 7 by 5:00." Ironically, the men of the 83rd already on shore at Anzio stated the weather was clear and warm.[45]

The events which soon followed in relation to *LST 422* are a bit confusing because reports of the exact sequence of events often conflict. Probably the most accurate reports came from Capt. Robert Edwards of the 83rd and Lt. Commander Broadhurst, Royal Navy. Broadhurst claimed that at about 5:20 a.m. on Wednesday, January 26th, strong winds blew *LST 422* into a known minefield about 12 miles offshore where it struck a mine. At this time the LST's position was fixed at 41-24-55 N. 12-44-45 E., about 400 yards outside the limits of the safe zone as designated to CTF 81. S/Sgt. Eugene A. Plassmann, HQ Co., claimed it was his understanding the British officer dropped anchor but it "apparently slipped or something," and the rough sea and wind sent the LST into a minefield. Broadhurst recalled he was resting in his bunk, next to the ship's magnetic compass, when a flash was followed by a terrific explosion, which threw the compass onto him. He slid from underneath it and made his way to the bridge, where he discovered the exploding mine had blown a huge hole in the bottom and starboard side of the LST, immediately igniting the ship's oil supply. He could see 20-foot flames emanating from the tank deck ventilators, and "The vehicles in the tank deck space had begun to explode, which had set fire to the ship's diesel fuel oil, much of which had been sprayed out the moment *LST 422* hit the mine. The explosion had ripped a massive 50 foot hole on the starboard side between the main and auxiliary engine rooms." Authorities originally thought the ship had been torpedoed, but after some survivors reported smelling sulphur in the immediate aftermath of the explosion, the brass changed the cause to striking a mine. Broadhurst would later conclude, "The loss of life will be heavy … the majority … were sleeping in vehicles on the upper deck (none was allowed in the tank space) which was ablaze in a matter of two or three minutes, and this would

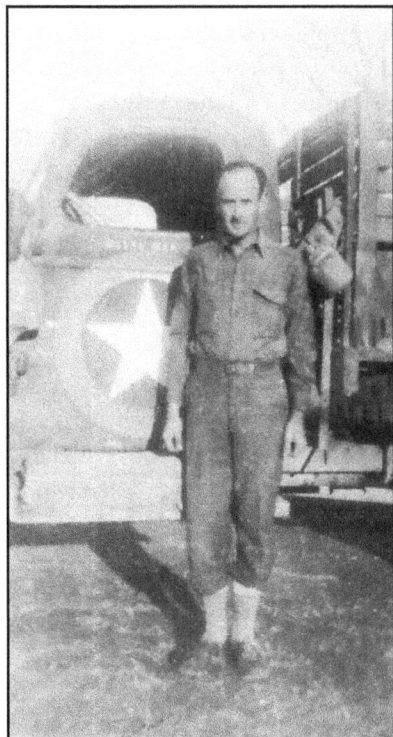

James J. Dudley, Co. D, and his truck Daisy Mae were both casualties of *LST 422*. *Lester Collection*

not give them time to get clear. Also a great many were killed by blast."[46]

In his official report filed the following day, Broadhurst went into more specific detail. The " … ship was struck by mine or torpedo on starboard side at about the bulkhead separating the Main Auxiliary Engine Rooms. I submit that it was a torpedo as the explosion curled the ship side plates outboard making a hole about 50 feet long … the [*Army*] vehicles on board were heavily loaded with phosphorous shells, rockets, smoke canisters and fireworks and ammunition of all kinds, together with the several tins of petrol on each vehicle. The ammunition started to explode as soon as the ship was hit. The upper deck and tank space were sprayed fore and aft with ship's fuel oil as a result of the explosion and the tank space was ablaze fore and aft immediately. Most of the vehicles on the upper deck were also blazing furiously two minutes after the explosion, caused by the explosion of fireworks which by this time were exploding continuously from vehicles and setting fire to every object upon which they fell. For example, the upper bridge was afire from its full length five minutes after the torpedo struck. At 0525 the L.C.P. was ablaze and dropped off the falls [*davits*] at about 0540."[47]

Broadhurst further added, "As soon as the ship was struck she became a sheet of flame fore and aft with very heavy thick smoke over everything, and all power went off. It was found impossible to approach the mess decks and tiller flat where the smoke helmet and asbestos suit were kept. Attempt was made to start the auxiliary fire foam motor, but during the attempt this was damaged by shrapnel from explosions on fore deck. It was then attempted to approach fore deck with buckets of water but the flames were blown aft by the force of the wind and the smoke coming from burning smoke canisters was suffocating."[48]

Capt. Edwards agreed on the exact time of the explosion and added, "The wooden hatch cover on the aft top deck was destroyed and flames came up from the opening. A truck was saved from falling through the hatchway by the chains used to stow the vehicle. Dense smoke permeated the entire ship immediately. Water and power facilities were destroyed by the blast. On the top deck numerous vehicles were tossed about by the blast. It is presumed that several men were killed and others, injured or pinned down by the trucks, were unable to make an effort to save themselves. Shortly after the fire started it had gained much headway because of the strong wind blowing from bow to stern. It was at that time that a series of explosions started with much white phosphorous and shell fragments being thrown around." Indeed, once the after hatch had collapsed flames reached the mortar and Coast Artillery ammo, along with rockets and other combustible materials, resulting in explosions which caused fiery debris to fall back on the men and vehicles on the upper deck. Gasoline tanks were fractured by shrapnel and within two minutes most of the upper deck was aflame. 1st Sgt. Mike P. Codega, Co. D, wrote that there was so much deadly flying shrapnel and debris that many of the men literally had to crawl along the deck.[49]

Various acts of bravery and heroism took place almost from the time of the initial explosion. Pvt. Grady Lawless, Co. C, from Jones County, Mississippi, went into the tank compartment in an effort to save men who were pinned down by blazing vehicles and managed to get two to safety. He would later be awarded the Soldier's Medal. His citation read, "As a result of the ensuing explosion a fire was started, and ammunition on board detonated, throwing shell fragments and burning white phosphorous on the deck. Trucks on the wooden hatch cover fell through to the tank compartment below. Pvt. Lawless released one of his companions pinned beneath a vehicle and lifted him to the top deck. After carrying the injured soldier to the bow, he returned to the tank compartment to attempt to release another trapped man. The fire and heat became so intense that Pvt. Lawless was forced to leave the compartment. Returning to the bow and finding several men without life preservers, he went below to the troop compartment and secured several. He distributed the preservers and then lowered his injured companion over the side of the ship with a rope. Pvt. Lawless' act of courage and selflessness saved a fellow soldier's life and aided others in saving their own lives." Pvt. Carl Nelson, also of Co. C, of Kings County, New York, helped to quiet men " … in the starboard

James M. Lester, Co. D, and his truck named after his wife, Iris. Lester did not embark on the LST but his truck went down with the ship. *Lester Collection*

passenger compartment who had become panic-stricken, and directed their evacuation of the compartment until he himself was overcome by the fumes at the foot of the forward starboard hatchway" and perished. An injured S/Sgt. Thomas A. Cute, Co. C, from Steuben County, New York, went into the compartments several times, where some of the men had been sleeping, in an attempt to persuade them to come to the top deck. Unfortunately, many preferred to remain below deck, where they probably were overcome by fumes, rather than risk the shell fragments and flames on deck. Pvt. Leonard E. Hall from Nashville, Tennessee, and 1st Sgt. Harry Cohen of Peoria, Illinois, both members of Co. C, "distinguished themselves by administering first aid to the injured and remaining on the LST until all the wounded had been transferred to the LCI [*probably LCI 209*]." Both were presented the Soldier's Medal for their actions. Cohen's citation stated he "made his way to the bow of the vessel, and seeing the confusion existing among the soldiers, took command and restored order. He administered first aid to several wounded men and placed them under cover to avoid the shell fragments and white phosphorous. He remained on the sinking ship and assisted in removing the wounded to another vessel." Hall's citation basically mirrored that of Cohen's. Another recipient of the Soldier's Medal was T/5 Glen C. Thompson, from Monona County, Iowa, a truck mechanic who "... braved fragments and phosphorous to carry a wounded companion to safety. Then he returned through the exploding ammo to the hatchway, carried another seriously wounded soldier to the bow of the craft and applied a tourniquet to save his life."[50]

T/5 Clyde E. McBryde, Co. B, from Union County, Mississippi, found himself trapped between two trucks although not injured. Unable to extricate himself with the assistance of another soldier he resigned himself to his fate and told the soldier giving aid to save himself. Clyde would never be seen again. In later years a relative would say, "I guess the fishies ate him." Reportedly, McBryde was an only child and could have been deferred, but he felt it was his patriotic duty to serve.[51]

Capt. Edwards said efforts were made to cut down life rafts, " ... but much of this work was stopped by the flames and the exploding ammunition." Due to the power outage, Lt. Edward L. Trey, HQ Co., put on a gas mask and life preserver and attempted to lower the life rafts. Trey's efforts were unsuccessful yet he did manage to loosen several rafts by cutting the cables with his trench knife. Unable to traverse the ship's bow due to the fire in midship, Trey lowered Lt. Leonard A. ("Spike") Merrill, Jr., HQ Co., from Haverhill, Massachusetts, onto the anchor cable. Merrill held onto the cable briefly before entering the water, never to be seen again. Lt. Merrill had earned a chemical engineering degree at Massachusetts Institute of Technology and had served as the battalion intelligence and meteorological officer. Battalion Executive Officer David W. Meyerson, who was not involved in the tragedy, confirmed Trey's story when he later wrote Merrill's wife and stated, "the last anyone saw Spike was on the stern of the ship where men were lowering themselves into the water." Trey, thinking he could possibly swim to Sardinia, jumped into the water where he spent several hours praying before being rescued by a British LST. The crew hoisted a ladder over the side and as he hung on they pulled the ladder up, filled him full of Scotch, and later put him ashore, where he spent some time with a British 25-pounder gun crew.[52]

Following the mostly unsuccessful efforts to cut rafts loose from *LST 422*, British officers and crew ordered all Army personnel to abandon ship. This took place at 5:25, only five minutes after the initial explosion according to Lt. Commander Broadhurst, who said the American troops were also told to take " ... all available Carly floats (No.'s 5, 6, 7, and 8 were the only ones not on fire). All floatable material such as loose timber, smoke floats, oil drums, etc., were thrown overboard to assist them." Pfc. William C. Ford, Co. C, disputed Broadhurst and claimed, "The powerful explosion had knocked out the communication system. We did not receive any orders to abandon ship because the system had been destroyed." Ford and some comrades lowered a rope ladder over the port side and dropped into the freezing water off the end of the ladder, which was too short to reach the water. Many men had lost their life jackets

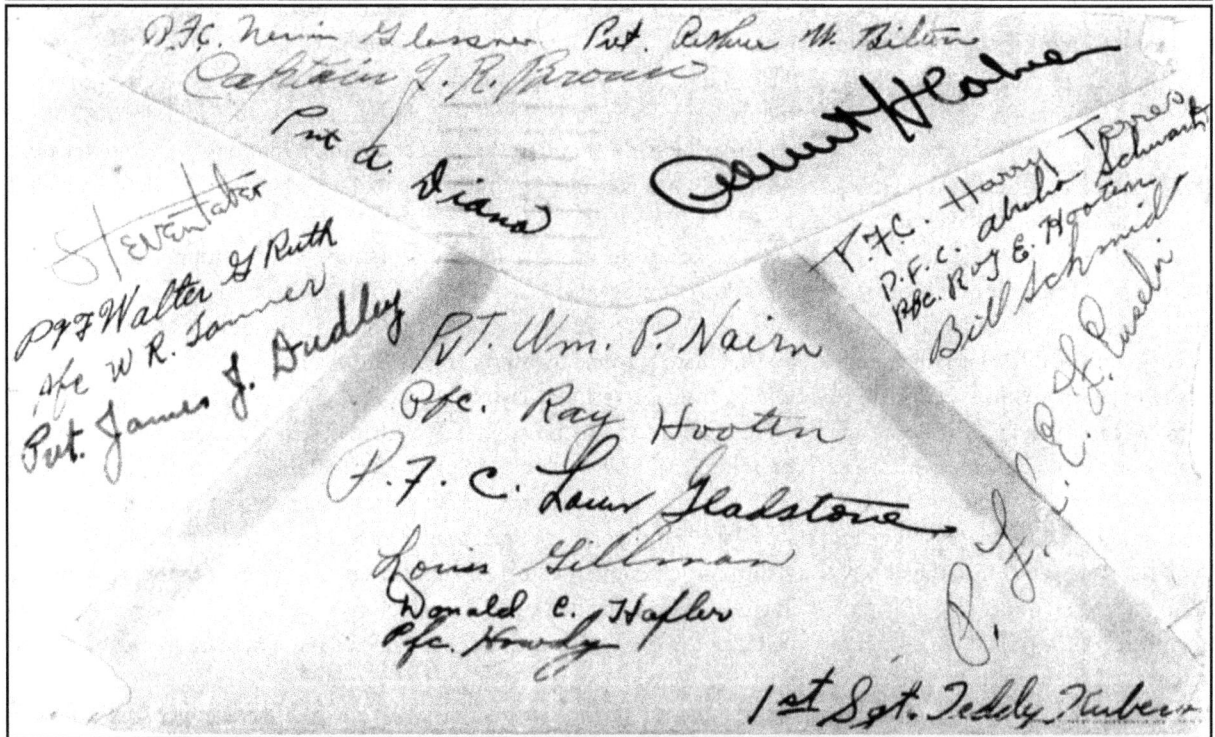

Envelope sent from Camp Gordon, GA, March 20, 1943 by Charlie Lowry, Co. D, and signed by 21 members of the 83rd Chemical Mortar Battalion, including Capt. J. R. Brown, James J. Dudley*, Willie R. Tanner, Anthony Diana, Roy E. Hooten, Teddy Kubera, Donald C. Hafler, Walter G. Ruth*, Steven Faber*, Nevin Glossner*, Arthur W. Bilton*, Albert H. Cohen*, William P. Nairn*, Louis Gladstone*, Bill Schmidt, Euro F. Eusebi, Louis Gillman, Harry Terres, Howard Bolam ("Pvt. Howdy"), Raymond W. Hooten, and Lowry. An asterisk indicates they died on *LST 422*. *Author's Collection*

in the confusion and relied upon improvised items to assist them in staying afloat. Capt. Edwards said many of the men went overboard in the next few minutes but, unfortunately, later reports indicated " … that many of the doors between the passenger compartments were closed at the time of the explosion and were jammed by the concussion, undoubtedly trapping many men below decks. It was also reported that many men were asphyxiated by the fumes of the burning paint on the bulkheads, which were heated to a cherry red by the heat of the fires raging in the tank compartment."[53]

Rescue efforts were launched by a variety of naval vessels immediately following *LST 422* hitting the mine, but times given for the incident by the rescue craft greatly contradict each other, ranging from as early as 3:00 to as late as 5:25, with the latter time probably the most accurate. *YMS 226* reported a heavy explosion seaward as early as 4:50 although the time is probably a bit premature, followed by heavy smoke and additional strong explosions. They suspected *LST 422* had struck a moored mine, but some later reports indicated to them it might have been an internal blast caused by the explosion of gasoline. Another of the premature reports came from *YMS 69*, which placed the LST in the unloading area and claimed that around 5:00 a.m. while remaining anchored in some 13 to 17 fathoms of water with a mud bottom south of Point Astura, they observed fire followed by explosions.[54]

According to his diary, Norm Holt, USN, a crewman aboard *YMS 43*, " … went on watch at 0345 and all went well until about 0500 when the wind came up and we had heavy seas … Just about then an explosion and [*I*] saw a flash of light. It was an LST hit by a mine. Explosions lasted over an hour and we thought that it was an ammunition ship. You never saw anything like it with sheets of flame and flashes of light high above the ship." In a 2004 interview, he supplemented his observations, stating, "… we knew something was wrong after we saw the explosion in the water, and I was on the flying bridge and we saw a lot of debris in the water and the officers were deciding what to do." Motor Machinist's Mate John Wittright added, "I was on duty down in the generator room when I heard the terrible noise that didn't sound just like the ordinary bomb going off, and I hit the ladder and looked through the hatch. The first thing I could see was that cargo of magnesium and phosphorous going off, it shot flames into the sky for I don't know how high … "[55]

1st Lt. Justin G. Woomer, HQ Co., said the initial explosion " … tossed my helmet up against the ceiling which deflected it into my bunk! We all knew we were in trouble! I grabbed my rifle and helmet and hurried through the smoke which was quickly filtering into our quarters … to the outside. On deck there was great excitement. The middle of the ship was a mass of high-reaching flames. Our rear end of the ship was cut off from the front end. We could not reach those up front … I had no life jacket! I returned to the quarters to see if I could be of any assistance. After returning to the open spaces a first lieutenant [*the same officer that had confiscated Woomer's life jacket earlier*] handed me a fire extinguisher, rather, he tried to do so. An impractical idea and so I told him to use it himself … We released the cork life rafts nearby and let them fall into the rough cold sea attached by a single rope line to the railing. I decided that my only chance was to get into a raft. I discarded my equipment, climbed over the rail and started down the rope to an empty raft tied to it. I had traveled about half the distance to the floating raft, I'd judge about twenty feet, when I, for some reason, looked down and saw the raft loaded with fellows who had struggled out of the sea into it. I grasped the rope tightly and stopped my descent. I looked up to the rail and wondered if I could make it back up. However, before trying to do so I looked back to the loaded raft and saw a large wave slam raft and men against the side of the partially burning ship. The raft upset and floated back away from the ship empty! Down the rope I went and crawled in; soon we had another load almost sufficient to swamp us. We cut the rope line which was still attached to the rail and floated without incident or injury around the screw propeller on out to sea a short but safe distance from the LST."[56]

Pfc. Earl F. Kann, Co. D, from York, Pennsylvania, wrote in his memoir that he slept in his clothes in the hold adjacent to the cargo hold and didn't hear the explosion. "Someone telling us the ship was on fire awakened us. We started out of the hold without life jackets. Told my friend, Pvt. Francis A. Mesaris, Co. D, of Exetor, Pennsylvania, that I was going back for the life jacket. He said you probably won't even need it, but I went back anyway. Mesaris was 15 when he enlisted. He had lied about his age. He died that night … A lot of guys had gone to sleep on the trucks and were killed when the shells exploded. We then went to the bow of the ship and jumped off. At some point I had been hit in the leg with white phosphorous from the exploding shells. Not sure if this happened before we jumped off, or after …" Kann would survive although his injury proved serious enough to eventually send him home.[57]

T/5 Claude J. Shaw, HQ Co., said during a 2004 oral interview, "The compartment next to us was the latrine in which there was a ladder on the wall that went up through a trap door to the deck. However, the door between our compartment and the latrine was closed, and the handles to open it were covered up by a huge air duct that had been blown across it." Shaw, who was fully clothed but in his stocking feet, along with his buddy, S/Sgt. Eugene A. ("Gene") Plassmann, HQ Co., from the Bronx of New York, and others, " … got under the air duct and pushed up with our backs enough to get the door handles turned and the door open. We crawled through the space and through the door, climbed the ladder and got on deck. We discovered chaos like you'd never believe. There was a large cargo hole that had been covered with planks. One of our ambulances had been sitting on the planks and the medics were sleeping in the ambulance … the explosion had blown the ambulance and planks clear over the side. There was debris everywhere. Fire was running through the hole and the flames allowed us to see a little bit. It was sleeting and the wind was blowing. We had a tremendous amount of ammunition aboard and it was blowing up all over the place. Gene and I realized the only chance we had was hitting the water. I had already been hit in the leg with something that barely broke the skin, and was hit on the back of one hand enough to cause a mild amount of bleeding. We were located on the side, just back of the center of the ship. We were close to a superstructure near the rear of the ship. We decided to go behind the superstructure for temporary safety."[58]

As Claude Shaw, Eugene Plassmann, and the others worked their way to the rear of the ship, Shaw miraculously stumbled over a life jacket in the debris. The group spotted a framework, possibly the anchor, and headed for it. "As we were climbing down this thing we noted an empty life ring drifting by," Shaw added. "It appeared to be about 12 to 15 feet long and about 8 feet wide. We decided to go for it. As I remember, Gene jumped first and then I slid down and jumped when I thought a wave had come in, however it was a valley instead, and I went down so far that I didn't think I would ever come to the surface. I saw that Gene had made it to the life ring and I headed there. The water was so cold it just numbed the body and mind both. Gene kept yelling at me to keep trying, which I did and finally got hold of the rope on the life ring. Well, before long we had a lot of guys on the raft or hanging on ropes."[59]

Pfc. Raymond W. Hoover, Co. C, who came up from the lower deck only to have his helmet blown off by an explosion, believed he had been hit by the burning battalion ammo. He suffered a shrapnel wound to the head and was later told the shrapnel could not be removed or he would die. Hoover added, "I'm the … one that didn't duck." After jumping off the boat he said he didn't remember much. A friend from Northumberland County, Pennsylvania, in the 45th Division, later saw him toe-tagged on the beach and presumed he was dead, but a heartbeat was found.[60]

Pfc. James F. ("Doc") Dougherty, Co. D, from Philadelphia, Pennsylvania, wounded in the leg by flying shrapnel, later told his son he hurried onto the ice-covered anchor chain where he observed " … life rafts or boats with men in them trying to get away from the LST but big waves smacked them back into the sides of the LST and he couldn't see any survivors, thinking they were hurt from the impact and drowned." Dougherty also claimed he was later rescued from the water by a British destroyer and said as a British sailor was hauling him in with a rope the sea shifted and slammed him into the side of the destroyer, nearly knocking him out, before a sailor helped him aboard.[61]

Pfc. Curtis A. Williams, Medical Detachment, from the vicinity of Nashville, Tennessee, said he ran around the deck telling the men to take off their helmets before diving into the water because they were breaking their necks upon impact. Curtis went down the anchor chain and slid into the water, where he witnessed large waves smashing men up against the ship. He said the waves were so high that every other one would wash over the deck, and at one point he saw a man swept off the anchor chain by a massive wave. Curtis claimed he spent about two hours in the water.[62]

Pfc. Robert M. ("John") Chamblee, Co. D, from Fulton, Itawamba County, Mississippi, remembered he was asleep below deck near his sergeant, Clark H. Riddle, and his squad sergeant, Elwood J. Keightly, during the initial explosion. The ship's sleeping quarters, which were three or four bunks high, came loose and the ship immediately plunged into darkness. As the men found themselves in an entangled mess Chamblee said, "I smell fuel. I hope nobody don't strike a match." Riddle, from Greensburg, Westmoreland County, Pennsylvania, quickly responded, "Nobody strike a match." Riddle yelled, "Don't panic, get a flashlight." Somehow Riddle and Keightly found a flashlight and located a hatch to open. The men put on their life jackets although some did not inflate. Riddle said only one tube of his inflated. S/Sgt. Edward D. Guinness, Co. D, from Queens, New York, was at the stairwell directing the men, who filed out without panicking. Guinness had two men on guard duty in the hold and, pointing a Tommy gun at Riddle's face, told him his orders were to keep the bulkhead closed. Riddle said these were his first two men lost.[63]

Despite some locked doors, Sgt. Clark Riddle, Robert Chamblee, and others found their way to the top deck and located a British sailor who told them, "You see them lights? That's the beach. And we're getting a signal that we can't pull in, cause we're in a minefield. So everybody is on his own." The sailor proceeded to jump overboard minus a life jacket and the group did not see any other sailors afterwards. One of Riddle's men panicked when his life jacket failed to inflate and jumped into the sea. Riddle and his men stood behind the stairwell housing along with the men of squad leader Claude T. Burkett, Co. D, of Bassfield, Jefferson Davis County, Mississippi, for awhile and discussed the situation. It was decided that each man would make his own choice whether or not to jump. Riddle opted to jump although only half of his life jacket inflated. Due to the intense fire on deck Chamblee and his friends also decided to jump overboard from the hot anchor chain, with a soldier he called Swifton [*possibly Cpl. James L. Swift, Co. D*] going first. The next to jump was Pvt. Arlander F. Benson, Co. D, from Itawamba County, Mississippi, whom Chamblee said had a different style life belt, followed by Chamblee. Benson would never be seen again.[64]

Co. C's Hale H. Hepler, from Millboro, Virginia, said, "As I looked over the sides I could see young men jumping off the ship without their life belts. The stern was no place to jump because it was a long way down to the water. My nerve would not let me jump there. I went to the bow of the ship and there I watched a mine sweeper circle the ship. My best chance for survival was to go down one of the lines attached to the ship. From there I could drop a much shorter distance to the water. My plan was to swim to the anchor chain and there wait for the mine sweeper to pick me up. When I got hold of the anchor chain a big wave hit the side of the boat and the motion caused the boat to roll so that the chain was many feet above the water and I was holding on for dear life. Another wave caused the anchor and me to drop down into the sea so deep I thought I would not get a breath of fresh air for a long time. The ship rolled again and this time the chain was pulled so hard I was flung off like a gnat into the water. When I came up I saw another danger. I tried to stay away from a gaping hole in the side of the ship that was made by the explosions. It was sucking the helpless soldiers back into the ship only to be drowned. I paddled as hard as I could away from that danger. I guess I was in the water for 3 or more hours."[65]

Miraculously, there were a few men who never even got their feet wet. Among these was Pvt. Daniel Alfred Miller, Co. D, from Virginia, who recalled he was awakened by the explosion with resulting flickering of lights and the strong smell of gasoline and cordite. Soldiers scrambled to the upper deck where he said there was chaos but little panic. Miller grabbed his waist-type, squeeze-inflated life preserver, but it fell around his feet as the metal snap on the buckle had broken in two. Although the preserver inflated he could not wear it and decided to hold onto it as a flotation device. When everyone began jumping into the water, Miller gave the preserver to a soldier to hold until he could climb down the anchor chain to get it. He took off his shoes ready to jump, but the soldier with his preserver jumped first and Miller lost track of him in the rough water. Minus a preserver, Miller said he had no alternative but to stay with the ship and remained with two or three British sailors who hid behind a metal shield around one of the anti-aircraft guns to protect themselves from the flying shrapnel and phosphorous. The sailors had flashlights which they used to signal rescue vessels. With fear the ship would blow up at any minute, Miller said a rescue ship, probably *LCI 209*, eventually pulled alongside and they were able to jump aboard. Miller recalled, "I could see people everywhere in the water being tossed around by the waves. Many were dead, floating face down in the water. Others were struggling … Some of the sailors on the rescue ship jumped into the water to save several who were too weak and too exhausted to help themselves." Miller credited his busted life preserver with saving his life for, had it not broken, he would have jumped into the water.[66]

Sgt. Lemuel R. Tillman, Co. C, who had worked for a milk company in Nashville, Tennessee, before the war, recalled, "I was in my bunk, jumped up and ran to the deck of the ship. In doing so - forgot my life preserver and couldn't go back to get it … I also could not swim, so I along with 3 or 4 more men - I don't know - got down on the anchor rim and stood there until we were picked up." In a 1999 interview, Tillman said he " … survived by hanging onto the ship's anchor, which was on the deck, even as waves swept over him and the others who clung to the anchor." In an additional interview he said a tugboat picked him up.[67]

At least three other men are known to have remained with *LST 422* until rescued. Robert ("John") Chamblee remembered that one of them was Pfc. Robert J. Wehrheim, Co. D, from Wright County, Iowa; an unidentified member of Co. D; and S/Sgt. John R. Holley, Co. C, of Oxford, Mississippi. These three were plucked off the LST but not before Holley had jumped off the LST and got back on the ship three to eight times. According to one source,

"He'd jump off toward the beach and the waves would just push him right back to the boat, and he'd climb back up the anchor chain." Finally, he made a successful jump to the deck of a rescue ship. Pfc. Robert J. Wehrheim had a heavy jacket that had been given to him by his buddy, James M. Lester, which he hung over the side of the LST, and " … the jacket had holes all over from the phosphorous shells that went off."[68]

T/5 George R. Borkhuis, mess sergeant of Co. D, from the Bronx of New York, remembered that prior to hitting the mine the wind, sleet, and hail made it nearly impossible to walk on the top deck so the driver of his mess truck, who complained of being cold, said he was retiring to the lower deck for warmth and sleep. Borkhuis remained with the truck under a tarp in the rear where he had just about fallen asleep. The first explosion immediately followed and as George peered from under the tarp he witnessed huge flames emanating from the elevator shaft beside his truck. He sprang to action and found S/Sgt. Max E. ("General") Nestler, Co. D, from Miffingtown, Somerset County, New Jersey, who had already been wounded twice in September of 1943, and the two grabbed a fire hose only to discover it did not work due to the power outage. Nestler departed to locate an escape route and Borkhuis began to slide toward the port side as the ship listed. George knew he couldn't swim but preferred drowning to a fiery death, so when he reached the ship's rail he found a rope attached to it and used it to slide into the water.[69]

Pvt. Rudolph Whitt, a radio operator in Co. C, recalled, "I was abruptly awakened by a loud explosion and realized the ship was on fire. Flames were fueled by all the gasoline and ammunition aboard and continued explosions were deafening. People were shouting as men began jumping off the ship." With hands burning, Whitt orally inflated his life belt, thinking he might need the air cartridge for later, and proceeded to jump into the frigid waters, where he would spend several hours and pass out from shock and exposure.[70]

Sgt. Wofford L. ("Woof-Woof") Jackson, Co. D, an admitted hard drinker from Manchester, Meriwether County, Georgia, had just been to the toilet when the LST hit the mine and the power was lost. With flashlight already in hand, he located an inflatable life preserver on the floor which he partially inflated. Following a series of explosions, Jackson told his friend, Pvt. Seth W. Strickland, Co. D, from Fair Bluff in Columbus County, North Carolina, that they should locate an escape route. Strickland responded, "Oh hell, what's the use." Standing only a short distance from his pack which contained some whiskey he wished to retrieve, Jackson changed his mind following a series of explosions and found his way to the top deck, where pandemonium reigned. A fire began in the area he had just left which led him to incorrectly suspect Strickland was dead. Jackson said, "The deck was strewn with dead, dying, and wounded." He immediately spotted S/Sgt. D. E. Frazier, Co. D, from Harris County, Texas, whom he said, " … was really broken up. His foot was behind his neck like a pillow." Reportedly, Frazier had been thrown 30 feet into the air by an explosion. Jackson knew he had some morphine in his pack below deck which he had confiscated from a medic's abandoned pack on a battlefield, but to retrieve it would be impossible, so he did what he could to help Frazier and others before leaving them. He said the LST was temporarily lit by the fire of a hydrogen-filled barrage balloon tied to the LST as he spoke briefly with S/Sgt. Edward D. Guinness, Co. D, from Queens, New York. Guinness grabbed a fire hose and ran to extinguish some burning equipment, which exploded and blew him "to pieces." After another explosion Jackson opted to abandon ship and jumped off the front of the vessel, the highest point. As he hit the water another man fell on his back, nearly breaking it.[71]

Those who escaped the ship into the extremely rough and frigid sea found themselves fighting a race for survival, a race the majority lost. Yet numerous heroics continued in the water, such as 1st Sgt. Mike Codega, Co. D, who threw a piece of timber overboard and then assisted the badly injured S/Sgt. D. E. Frazier, Co. D, by lowering him into the water via a rope and then jumping into the water himself, swimming to a life raft with Frazier in tow. He would aid the injured man in the water for three to four hours by clinging to the raft before being rescued. Codega's citation read, "A soldier [*Frazier*] was thrown approximately 30 feet by the initial explosion and was seriously wounded. 1st Sgt. Codega rushed to the injured man's aid and found the man had lost his life belt. Unable to secure another life belt, 1st Sgt. Codega threw a piece of timber overboard, lowered the injured soldier to the water by a rope, jumped overboard, and swam to support the man. After towing the soldier to the timber, 1st Sgt. Codega succeeded in reaching a life raft where he transferred the injured man to safety." Pfc. Earl F. Kann, Co. D, also recalled this as he wrote, "A long time after daylight I came upon a float of some kind with about six guys on it. I stayed with it by hanging onto the float. I believe that the cook of Co. D, Sgt. Frazier was on that float and had a broken leg. Not long after this, a minesweeper or sub chaser picked us up. After boarding, I collapsed …" 1st Lt. Julian T. McKinnon, Co. D, supported a struggling, "out of his head" Capt. Silverino V. DeMarco, Medical Detachment, in the water for about three hours until picked up by a rescue vessel. Before jumping off the LST, the two had agreed to stay together. McKinnon's citation read, "After abandoning ship, he observed another officer who had lost consciousness and was in danger of drowning in the rough sea. Although his own life preserver failed to function properly, 1st Lt. McKinnon for a period of three hours supported the stricken officer until a rescue ship arrived." Pvt. Audie W. Pierce, Co. C, of Smithville, Itawamba County, Mississippi, wrote that he threw a rope over the side of the ship and jumped in.[72]

Most of the men in the water were more concerned with just surviving rather than with individual acts of bravery. Pvt. Loy J. Marshall, Co. C, recalled, "Some metal rafts had been lowered into the water for us to climb on, but the rough seas and swells made this very difficult. Some soldiers were trapped between the metal rafts and the ship's hull and were crushed and killed."[73]

Pfc. James H. ("Banjo Eyes") Gallahan, Co. D, a milk truck driver from Fredericksburg, Virginia, had to be consoled by Pvt. Daniel J. Shields before he was thrown into the water by an explosion and suffered injuries from shrapnel and burns. He remembered, " … seeing fire all around him from oil on top of the water. Fortunately, he wore a life jacket and was eventually picked up by a PT boat" and taken to a Naples hospital. Following Gallahan's entry into the water Shields told Pvt. Horst R. Zickler, Co. D, a German by birth, to jump and then entered the water himself.[74]

Unable to swim, T/5 George R. Borkhuis, Co. D, panicked upon entering the water and kicked against the side of the ship fearing he would be sucked into the propellers, forgetting there was no power. His head hit against a gas can which he latched onto at about the same time as two other 83rd men and a British sailor. While they floated alongside the ship, an ambulance fell off the sloping vessel into the water only a few yards from them. After floating for awhile, George discovered the three other men had frozen to death, the two GIs because they had obeyed Army rules and removed their clothing before entering the water, while Borkhuis had kept on his overcoat and other clothing. The British sailor was wearing a Mae West life jacket but was apparently overcome by the cold. George was alone in the dark as the LST gradually drifted out of sight.[75]

Sgt. Wofford L. Jackson, Co. D, managed to swim around to the side of the LST and locate a group of men who were utilizing anything they could find as improvised flotation devices. Jackson found some wool beanie caps and put one on as S/Sgt. Rudolph M. Fichtler, Co. D, from Bergen County, New Jersey, appeared. Jackson attempted to get Fichtler, suffering from a bad wound on one side of his head and face, to don one of the caps, but he refused and wouldn't talk to Jackson. Fichtler was never seen again. Caught in a current, Jackson lost sight of the LST and soon observed only an occasional soldier, all on the verge of giving up their struggle. Eventually he heard S/Sgt. Max E. Nestler, Co. D, repeatedly yelling, "Lord save me!" Jackson grabbed him by his shirt collar and attempted to reason with him but it proved useless as Nestler continued to repeat the phrase. Wofford held onto him until his own left arm became numb and then had no choice but to let him slip under to his death. Jackson heard a few other men cry out, "I just can't stay any longer," and they went under as well.[76]

After hitting the water, Sgt. Clark Riddle, Co. D, located a life belt and bedroll which he placed under each arm to keep afloat. About the time he felt fairly secure, a burning ammo truck broke loose and fell overboard toward him, convincing him to get away from the LST. He looked back and saw Pfc. Bennie Lieberman, Co. D, from Washington, D. C., climbing back up the anchor chain and onto the deck of the LST. Soon afterward a man by the name of Haggerty, with only his head above water, came floating by and calmly asked Riddle if he could hold onto him as his life jacket had gone down. Clark gave him the bedroll and they remained together until Riddle's legs became numb and he told Haggerty they had better get moving or die. Haggerty responded by asking Riddle, "Do you mind if I pray?," to which Clark readily consented and also asked him to pray some for him. Clark began to think about his family as they spotted a life raft and swam to it, only to find one man inside it begging others not to get on it. With men in the water three deep around the raft Riddle and Haggerty decided it would be better to leave the raft and head out to sea in search of a ship. Some time after that Haggerty was lost.[77]

Every survivor of the disaster had his own story, including men such as Pfc. Robert M. Chamblee, Co. D, who said he was in the water for at least three hours with only the thoughts of his family keeping him alive. He stated he did spot a sailor high on the LST still giving signals as he floated away from the ship. Pvt. Audie W. Pierce, Co. C, felt he survived in the icy waters for five hours with waves going over his head because he kept on his regular pants, shirt, long underwear, and a tanker suit. Pierce wrote, "My fellow soldiers were giving up and took off their life jackets

U.S.S. Pilot

National Archives

because they felt they would never be found." According to Cpl. Norman A. Wahosky, Co. C, a survivor from Shamokin, Pennsylvania, "One man was able to swim to shore. No one knows how he was able to swim against the tide as it was going out at the time." Wahosky also incorrectly claimed a destroyer arrived the next day and sank the still burning LST, although James Marion Lester, Co. D, who was not on the ship, also later wrote, "The boat didn't sink, but it was wiped out. The Navy had to sink it." Edward Kirk Atton, Co. A, from Michigan, who joined the 83rd following the Sicilian Campaign, stated, "my camera and 3 rolls of 35 ml. [*film*] are in Anzio Bay aboard *LST 422*."[78]

THE RESCUE

U.S.S. Pilot reported at 5:25 that they were about three miles distant from *LST 422*, with the first explosion occurring approximately one mile southwest of Point Astura (Tre Astura). Visible were searchlights of small vessels that had been ordered by radio to pick up survivors. *Pilot* confirmed "various escort craft [*had been*] ordered to pick up survivors and the situation was considered to be well in hand." *YMS 3* also confirmed the explosion of *LST 422* at 5:25, as did the commander of the mine squadron and *YMS 207*, which gave the bearing of the LST as 300 (T), 650 yards from their position. Additionally, *YMS 83* recorded the explosion at this time and said the LST was " … in waters northeast of Astura … soon after, a second, third and a fourth explosion …"[79]

Many other craft were engaged in rescue operations almost from the initial explosion, among them *YMS 226*, which noticed the burning *LST 422* appeared to be drifting toward it, prompting discussions of slipping the cable if

YMS 226
National Archives

the injured craft came too close. *YMS 226* had received orders that all YMS craft "not dragging anchor" were to stay at anchor, but, according to the ship's action report, " … our anchor, then at the shortstay, was so nearly aweigh, that it was felt it might not hold if we paid out the chain again, so it was decided to weigh anchor and lie to until daylight. Also, the lights and cries for help from survivors who were coming toward us, made it seem favorable to get underway and try to rescue as many as we could." *YMS 226* was underway within minutes after the first explosion and shortly afterward another explosion was heard seaward. This sequence was confirmed by *LCI 32* which reported at this time that " … there was an explosion on *HMS LST 422* some 3500 to 4000 yards abeam of *LCI 32*. A sheet of flame immediately covered the stern half of the LST. It was thought that the LST had been hit by a torpedo and General Quarters was sounded. Shortly thereafter the crew was secured with orders to stand by and look for and pick up any survivors from the LST … *LCI 32* then searched the area on the starboard quarter of the LST with its lights and, finding nothing there, maneuvered to the port quarter. There was a second big explosion on the LST." By this time *YMS 226* had begun a search to pick up survivors from out of the water and rafts.[80]

LCI 209 reported observation of a violent explosion south of Point Charlie and pulled anchor off Red Beach to assist in rescue operations. It was reported the LST " … was dragging anchor in the Force 6 wind blowing at the time. It had been carried into the minefield south of the anchorage." *YMS 36* reported viewing *LST 422* on fire with many explosions, as did *YMS 62*, which added, "Several explosions followed the first one. Her position could not be accurately given because of darkness." Also at this time *SC 649* reported from a position 6 miles bearing 216 degrees True from the center of Green Beach that they spotted an unidentified ship explode and drift in a southerly direction.[81]

LST 16 reported at 5:30, ten minutes after the initial explosion, that *LST 422* was on fire and they were warming their engines in case they were called to assist in the rescue. Additionally, they were ordered not to fire at any attacking planes so as to not give away positions. On board *LST 422*, Lt. Commander Broadhurst recorded, "The winds increased to Force 7 … and sea and swell increased." Also at 5:30, *YMS 226* brought aboard their first rescued survivor although "poor visibility, heavy seas, rain and light draft of ship, made maneuvering difficult." Despite such complications the rescue crew, under direction of a Mr. McLaughlin, executive officer, continued to aid survivors. This may have been the point when Navy Gunner's Mate First Class Howard Dempsey Chamness "promptly and with complete disregard of his own safety, left his ship by way of a cargo net and swam with a line to a life raft and when it was brought alongside the rolling and pitching ship, he assisted untiringly, and at the great risk of being crushed against the side, in the removal of survivors from the raft to safety. His persistent and selfless efforts contributed materially to the saving of several lives." He would receive the Navy and Marine Corps Medal for his actions. *YMS 3*, which had been called to battle stations at this time, had begun anchor recovery to assist in the rescue but, during a later ensuing heavy gale, "the anchor winch burned out due to excessive strain and high seas." In order to participate they had to jettison their anchor and 90 fathoms of chain.[82]

About 5:35 volunteers were called for upon *LST 16* to man the #1 running boat to aid in the rescue, although wind had deteriorated to Force 6 and Condition 6 heavy seas. Lt. (jg.) Wilson K. Long, EM2c Robert Dunne, Coxswain John E. Patterson, F.1c William E. Seamon, Sea.1c Walter L. Palmer, and Sea.1c Robert Sagas, all of the United States Coast Guard Reserve, readily consented and departed at 5:40, despite difficulty with the heavy sea during the launch. Oddly, the deck log of the ship gives a conflicting launch time of 7:30. Long, from California, and Palmer, of New Jersey, were later awarded the Silver Star, while Seamon (Indiana), Dunne (Massachusetts), Patterson (Pennsylvania) and Sagas (Michigan) were all presented the Navy and Marine Corps Medal. Their citations were for heroism in assisting "in taking the small boat through a heavily mined area alongside the blazing *LST 422*, which was pitching and rolling in a dangerous manner and whose ammunition was exploding … in an effort to rescue personnel trapped below deck … and aided in the rescue of a soldier trapped in a lower compartment by removing him through a hole in the side of the ship … "[83]

The commander of the mine squadron also reported that at 5:40 "CTF 81 requested by voice radio that any ships of TG 81.7 available assist the burning ship," but after learning numerous other vessels were already engaged in rescue operations CTG 81.7 decided against sending any additional YMSs or AMs into the area because they would just be in the way. Probably typical of this was *YMS 13*, which claimed no participation in the rescue as they had no information on the swept or dangerous areas. Another minesweeper not involved in the rescue operations was *YMS 28* which reported that, despite the strong wind, rough sea, rain and hail near daylight their starboard anchor held although later recovery found the stock had been broken, which they would retrieve at 4:05 p.m.[84]

THE SINKING OF LCI 32

The rescue operations became more involved at 5:43 a.m. when *LCI 32*, the staff ship or flagship of Return Convoy 81.14, turned to port to bring the ship into the wind and also hit a mine. The Task and Salvage Group Commander confirmed that just as *LCI 32* approached *LST 422* to search for survivors the LCI hit a mine, which disputes modern researchers who claim *LCI 32* had picked up some survivors of the LST. John Finnerty, a crewman on *LCI 35*, said his ship was originally slated to enter the area of *LST 422* but the captain of *LCI 32* "pulled rank" and went in first, and soon afterward "all hell broke loose" as it hit a mine. Lt. (jg.) Maynes C. Fitzgerald, USNR, commanding *LCI 32*, wrote, "The explosion occurred on the starboard side aft, about 40 feet from the stern. The ship developed a heavy list to port at once and then began to list even further to port. The order to abandon ship was given when it was apparent that the ship was going to turn over. The life rafts were cut loose and an orderly abandonment of the ship was made. The ship then turned completely over and floated bow up and stern slightly under the water … As the time between hitting the mine and the capsizing of the ship was about two minutes - at the most, three minutes - there was no chance to make any recovery of either government or personal property." The ship sank much lower in the water about two hours later, showing only a small portion of the bow, and reportedly sank out of sight at a later time.[85]

Among those on *LCI 32* was Radioman 1st Class Arnott Simon who recalled that he and his buddy, Ralph DiMeola, " … were on radio watch in the command hole below deck. They were blown all the way across the beam of the ship to the port side bulkhead," knocking Ralph's thick-lensed glasses off and plunging the ship into darkness. The two men held onto each other as they were able to locate the ladder leading to the top deck. Since Ralph could not see without his glasses, Simon had him hold on to his life jacket while the two worked their way topside only to discover the ship listing dangerously to port. The two terrified men slowly crawled along the deck in an effort to reach the bow. Reportedly, DiMeola kept yelling, "Come on Si … you can make it." Unfortunately, Simon lacked the strength to pull both of them over the starboard gunwale as the ship began to flip over, the force tearing the men apart. DiMeola would not be seen again, one of the numerous casualties of the ship. Simon was flipped off the ship into the water, where he briefly lost consciousness before locating a raft full of men, as well as a number of men in the water holding onto the raft. With no room on the raft Simon held onto one of the men encircling the raft while *LCI 32* turned completely upside down but continued to float. Realizing they could be sucked under when the ship went

U.S.S. Strive

National Archives

down, someone yelled, "the 32 is sinking … kick like hell." Everyone made an effort to get the raft away from the LCI, but the man Simon was holding onto kept kicking him as he swam. Eventually Simon could no longer stand the pain from the kicking and spotted another raft with only two men aboard. Just as he let go to swim to the raft, the man he had been clinging to kicked him in the testicles, causing him to double over and go underwater. After recovering he resumed his swim toward the raft, but a sudden explosion caused him to briefly go underwater and resurface to find the raft gone. Luckily, the raft soon reappeared and the two men helped him aboard. Simon looked back and saw what appeared to be a dead man floating in the water, but the two men on the raft also pulled him aboard only to discover it was the badly injured and unconscious Commander Edward Webster Wilson, USNR, commander of Flotilla 2, who had been aboard *LCI 32*. Luckily they were able to revive him. He was diagnosed with a laceration of the left temple and a back abrasion, but in good condition.[86]

The sinking of *LCI 32* was also recalled by Walter A. Bielski of the 83rd, from Northumberland County, Pennsylvania, who said that as he floated between towering waves he saw the mine and feared he would be pushed against it, although he knew it would require metal against metal to detonate. Spotting *LCI 32* approaching, he swam away from the mine as the vessel struck it and exploded, destroying the craft and sending bodies flying high into the air.[87]

Initial reports indicated *LCI 32*, comprised of 12 officers and 50 crewmen, lost one officer killed, one hospitalized, and two missing, as well as 4 crewmen killed, one hospitalized, and 23 missing. Eventually it was determined the ship lost a total of 41, including 30 dead and 11 wounded, although current research indicates there were 31 killed, 17 wounded, and 16 known to have survived. This would suggest the LCI had at least 64 men on board.[88]

The sinking of *LCI 32*, along with the earlier order forbidding additional craft from entering the danger area, is probably the basis for the conclusion by some modern researchers that these delays contributed to the fear that other rescue vessels might meet the same fate and, therefore, led authorities to delay rescue and recovery efforts, leaving many of the survivors of both craft, the majority of whom were already injured or in shock, helpless in the frigid waters for some two to five hours. Although a logical conclusion, there does not appear to be any valid evidence to support this theory.[89]

YMS 226 completed a turn to the starboard side of rescue vessel *YMS 43*, from which point what appeared to be the bow of the stricken *LCI 32* was visible and sinking, so it was decided to "stand out" at that point for further rescue. The minesweeper continued to rapidly bring in survivors, "favoring those in [*the*] water to those on rafts." Included was Lt. (jg) Marcus Wilson Arthur of *LCI 32*, who received a painful and crippling wound to his leg when his ship was hit. In spite of his injury, he immediately began assisting dazed and injured crewmen, even remaining aboard as the ship lay on its side and the order to abandon ship had been given. Arthur continued to help his men off the ship and was among the last to leave the sinking vessel. While in the cold water and heavy sea, he held together a group of men, boosted their morale, and helped speed their rescue through the use of a flashlight to attract rescue craft. For his actions he was recommended for the Navy Cross. Also from *LCI 32* and rescued by *YMS 226* and recommended for a Navy Cross was CPhm Sidney Senter, who returned to his gear to get a waterproof flashlight after the order to abandon ship had been given and kept a group of men together in the cold and rough sea for nearly two hours. Immediately following his rescue and change to dry clothes, he spent two hours assisting the pharmacist's mate of *YMS 226* with the other rescued men.[90]

YMS 226 also reported, "The water is quite cold and weather conditions are not favorable for rescue work. All but two of the survivors rescued are so weak that they have to be dragged from the water, up and over the side. At least five men are required to haul one survivor up on cargo net, rigged portside about midship. Two men at bottom of cargo net at water's edge to lift man clear of water or raft, and at least three men to haul survivor over side, are needed. In some cases, a line has to be passed around [*a*] survivors' waist for hauling him up. The heavy preponderance of winter clothing, particularly on soldiers, combined with near exhaustion of many, makes a very heavy weight to lift over the side, particularly in rough seas, combined with rain and cold and darkness." At one point during the rescue operation Coxswain Charles J. McCarron, USN, of *YMS 226*, heroically attached a line to himself and dove off the ship's bow to assist a very weak survivor, but it was too late and McCarron made it back aboard safely to continue his work. The crew fed and clothed the survivors with their own clothing and blankets, and bedded them down in their own bunks in the wardroom. Most of the survivors were reported "in good condition in view of the circumstances" and any medical aid necessary was administered to them by CPhm C. C. Mink, USNR, and CPhm Sidney Senter, also USNR, who had been rescued from *LCI 32*.[91]

Tragically, one survivor of *LST 422* was killed as the nearby *LST 301* came to give assistance and picked him out of the water, but due to the heavy rolling vessels he fell to his death between the two craft. The official British report claimed *LST 301* rescued one stoker and one U.S. Army officer. The report also stated *PC 638* rescued six men and *LCT 609* landed 40 survivors at Anzio.[92]

PC 1227, a subchaser commanded by Lt. Richard P. Lovejoy, Jr., proceeded at standard speed at 5:45 to pick up survivors, while *LCI 209* approached *LST 422* at about the same time but found it difficult to get alongside due to Force 6 winds and heavy swells. Eventually they laid across bow, " … where many men were congested to escape explosions and flame which enveloped the mid and after section of the ship. Both vessels were pitching and rolling heavily in the wind and heavy seas." The Action Report of *LCI 209* states 44 men of the 83rd and one C.P.O. [*Chief Petty Officer*] were saved although the official Casualty Report of the ship claims 46 men were rescued. Lt. Kenneth E. Leake, USNR, commander of *LCI 209*, was later recommended for both the Bronze Star and the Silver Life Saving Medal for maneuvering the ship in the rescue, while Lt. (jg) Gordon S. Brown and Coxswain Carl E. Cumby, both of whom jumped into the heavy sea to save men, were also recommended for decorations.[93]

LCI 209 is possibly the vessel that saved Pfc. Robert M. ("John") Chamblee, Co. D, who said he spotted an LCI but thought it was a mirage - an island or a log. Once the boat became obvious Chamblee said he saw an officer with a billed cap in the conning tower just as a huge wave carried Chamblee away from the LCI. The naval officer took note and threw him a line with some coveralls tied to it, which hit him in the stomach. Chamblee grabbed the line with his left hand and hugged it toward him as the sailors pulled him up on deck. He passed out for three hours and when he awoke sailors were pouring brandy down him to rid him of the salt water he had swallowed. Also at this time the *U.S.S. Dextrous* (AM 341) reported they had received orders from CTG 81.6 to move to the burning LST, located in Fire Support Area #1, and upon arrival received further orders to send in a SC [*subchaser*] to assist in the rescue. *YMS 83* was also notified by *Pilot* to get underway due to potential " … danger of dragging anchor into unswept waters" because the wind was near gale force and the sea was heavy. Their report further stated, "Start heaving in on anchor. Recover 40 of 80 fathoms of chain out when anchor windlass fails. Despite use of engines to ease up on chain, strain on windlass tremendous because of heavy pitching from seas. Windlass blows two fuses and circuit breaker, danger of armature burning out in anchor windlass motor." Additionally at 5:45, the *U.S.S. Herbert C. Jones* (DE 137), a destroyer escort that had been patrolling the outer half of the right hand side of the swept channel to the beach south of Anzio port, was called to battle stations. By 5:50, the ship was assisting in the rescue, with the captain at the conning tower and the navigator on the bridge. *LCI 196* also immediately got underway, noting the LST was on fire "3 miles south of Green Beach."[94]

Norm Holt, USN, aboard *YMS 43*, claimed that at 6:00 the explosions aboard *LST 422* died down, as did the storm, although at the very same time *YMS 58* got underway in a heavy sea to assist in the rescue. At 6:02, *YMS 34* received orders from *U.S.S. Strive* (AM 117) to pick up only those drifting from *LST 422*, which was located about two miles distant from them bearing 320 degrees. By 6:05, *U.S.S. Pilot* (AM 104) notified *YMS 83* their position was secure if they did not drag. Confident the anchor was holding well, the crew again veered the chain to 80 fathoms and repaired the anchor windlass.[95]

At 6:07, *PC 1227* maneuvered around the burning LST, while, at 6:10, *YMS 83* spotted survivors of both *LST 422* and *LCI 32* northwest of them toward the beach and also heard their cries for help. In response the minesweeper started heaving in their chain and notified YMSs *36* and *43* of the survivors near to their ships. Following recovery of 40 fathoms of chain using the engines to ease up on the chain of *YMS 83*, the anchor windlass blew a fuse again.[96]

Around 6:15, *LCI 196* noted a "heavy gale struck," while Lt. Commander Broadhurst of *LST 422* reported, " … it was realized the ship had started to drag her anchor and attempt was made to lower the stern anchor but after another had been lowered two or three feet, the after winch could not be revolved any more by hand and was thought to have seized with the heat." Broadhurst and his crew were yet on board at 6:25 as he recalled, " … very heavy explosions were occurring at the after end of the tank space, the ship's company were ordered to abandon ship, leaving Sub. Lieutenant Unwin, Ldg. Seaman Castello, Ldg. Seaman White, A. P. Buy, A. B. Holt, A. B. Hayes with the Commanding Officer on board. Lieutenants Dennis and Meredith requested permission to remain on board as well and I approved."[97]

The diary of the 1st Battalion, 68th Coastal Artillery, recorded that, at 6:30, "Rain began falling … soon changing to hail, some of the hail stones being a half inch thick … an LST [422] was seen afire about ten miles off shore. It was later learned this ship exploded and went down with some of the 2nd Battalion, 68th Coastal Artillery aboard." Between 12 and 14 members perished. Also, at 6:30, as the horizon became lighter, many YMSs saw scattered groups of men struggling in the water to shoreward of their anchorage. As a result all YMSs got underway to assist as did *Pilot*. The *Strive* "remained anchored as a reference vessel to keep the smaller ships out of the minefield."[98]

According to Lt. Commander Broadhurst aboard *LST 422*, at 6:45, "Fire Tug ATR 1 arrived and the Tug Commander considered that nothing could be done to save the ship. It was therefore decided to abandon ship as the ship's back appeared to be broken and she was settling down." Ed Trey of the 83rd later reported to authorities that he personally witnessed Broadhurst abandoning ship much earlier. In February, Broadhurst would be recommended for a decoration for " … gallantry and great fortitude in staying for 2 and 1/2 hours in *LST 422* after she had been mined and was on fire from end to end, only abandoning the ship when any possibility of saving the ship was gone." This is believed to be the Royal Navy Reserve Decoration (pre-1941 model) presented on February 18th. He also was awarded the Distinguished Service Cross on August 1, 1944, for the January 22, 1944, Anzio landing.[99]

Also at about 6:45, *YMS 58* spotted a raft inshore from them containing 12 survivors of *LCI 32*, requested permission by radio telephone to help, and initiated assistance, while three minutes later *PC 1227* sounded General Quarters for all hands to assist in the rescue of the LST survivors. By 6:50, they were moving at different speeds and courses while reporting their "sound gear secured due to hazardous navigation and shallow water." At the same time, the commanding officer of *YMS 62* reported they heard voices in the water ahead of them and started moving out to assist, but before getting started some of the bodies began to drift among their anchorage. Their report added, "We fastened heaving lines to life rings and threw to some of the men while we were still trying to weigh anchor." *YMS 62* would continue to rescue survivors until 10:00 a.m., during which time they saved 15 men and lost their wherry. The commander added, "During the rescue work three of my own men were lost overboard trying to help someone over the side, but they were all recovered without injury." Also, at this time, at least some of the 83rd on shore heard news of the disaster.[100]

Additionally, *YMS 3* picked up 12 survivors, including 11 American and one British, with two in critical condition. Among those rescued were 1st Lt. Julian T. McKinnon, Co. D, and Capt. Silverino V. DeMarco, Medical Detachment, both of the 83rd. McKinnon said they were fairly confident they would be rescued at daylight as they had spotted rescue vessel searchlights earlier in the dark. Following two life ring tosses by the sailors aboard *YMS 3*, the two were pulled to a chain ladder with wooden rungs hanging at midship on the port side. Due to the heavy sea, the ship was rolling 37 degrees and each time the two grabbed the ladder the ship rolled starboard and pulled the men out of the sea. Weak with exhaustion, the two were unable to hold on and fell back into the water. Following two such attempts, some sailors came down the ladder and helped the men aboard. The ship's Action Report confirmed that, "Due to heavy seas it was necessary for several of our men to go over the side and assist survivors aboard. During one of these attempts John E. Hanway, SoM2c, USNR, while assisting a survivor, was carried away by a heavy swell." He was later picked up by *YMS 226*. Eight men of the crew, William P. Stechmann, Frank J. Kelly, John E. Langdon, Stacy A. Douglass, Henry A. Holdgrun, William J. Dempster, Chester A. Poliskoy, and Hanway, were singled out for their bravery and recommended for decorations.[101]

Another survivor rescued by *YMS 3* was Sgt. Wofford L. Jackson, Co. D, who said he was about to give up when at daylight a minesweeper appeared and threw him a rope, which he was barely able to touch with his good hand. The minesweeper sailed by but another soon appeared with a net hanging over the side. Jackson unsuccessfully attempted to climb the net as two sailors came down and assisted him. Once aboard he saw dead men lying all over the deck, except for Sgt. Joseph J. Karcauskas, Co. D, from Hudson County, New Jersey, with whom he briefly spoke. However, Karcauskas did not survive, while Jackson hallucinated and heard voices which made him fear he was going to be buried at sea alive. Fortunately, such an incident never materialized. Upon recovery on the minesweeper, Jackson saw Cpl. George G. Young, Co. D, of Mobile, Alabama, a survivor, and Pvt. Seth W. Strickland, Co. D, whom he thought had died on the LST.[102]

At 6:55, *U.S.S. Strive* reported spotting several life rafts and survivors off the starboard bow and *YMS 43* heard cries of survivors. In his diary, crewman Norm Holt of *YMS 43* claimed this actually happened at 6:15, and confirmed the cries came from the starboard side. He went on to say, "It was still dark and I was on the flying bridge and could see several life rafts through the binoculars. They kept calling for help but our Captain [*Lt. J. J. Wiedemann, USNR*] was undecided about going after them. When a higher officer on another ship finally ordered him to, it was too late and they had gone out of sight." Norm Holt later said Lt. Wiedemann was a pre-war lawyer and a "90 day wonder" and felt Wiedemann was responsible for the loss of many of the men in the water, although he was undoubtedly just following orders. Jules Nemes of *YMS 43* said, " … we couldn't see anyone but we heard a lot of voices screaming for help … and we just couldn't do anything about it for a while, but then as daylight broke, we started seeing them." But daylight did not necessarily aid the Navy, as evidenced by *YMS 27*, which did not participate in the rescue operations but did note the weather conditions caused their starboard anchor to part "due to the increased velocity of the rising storm." The remaining chain was recovered and the craft proceeded to patrol outside the anchorage area.[103]

It was probably during this period that 1st Lt. Justin G. Woomer, HQ Co., was rescued by *YMS 226*. He would later write, "We were seated in the partially submerged raft in the water chest deep! The paddles were on the underside of the raft. We could not get them. We had to wait for others to help us. We were at the mercy of the sea drifting aimlessly! … about two hours later, before daylight arrived, we gained the attention of a minesweeper by waving a lighted flashlight." During the rescue Woomer, weak and nearly frozen, almost fell back into the sea but was caught by Sgt. Theodore D. Haddock, Co. D, from Avoca, Pennsylvania. Woomer added, "Numerous bodies were recovered that morning and placed on deck by the minesweeper's crew."[104]

Weather conditions became critical at 7:00, as evidenced when *YMS 29* reported their starboard anchor had been carried away by the extremely heavy seas, and winds from the northwest. A YMS anchored near the *U.S.S. Pilot* and about 2.5 miles from *LST 422* visually spotted some survivors. The *Pilot* reported that at daylight they were surprised to see numerous survivors and bodies about a mile inshore of the swept channel. The ship got underway immediately to assist in the rescue. *LCI 10* also received a message at 7:00 from the Salvage Group to search for survivors.[105]

SC 638 reported that when *LST 422* was struck its location was in the "minefield QBB 190, 100 degrees true, 7 miles" from their anchorage. At dawn the subchaser noted chemicals exploding aboard the LST and rescued six survivors before returning to patrol. Later Lt.

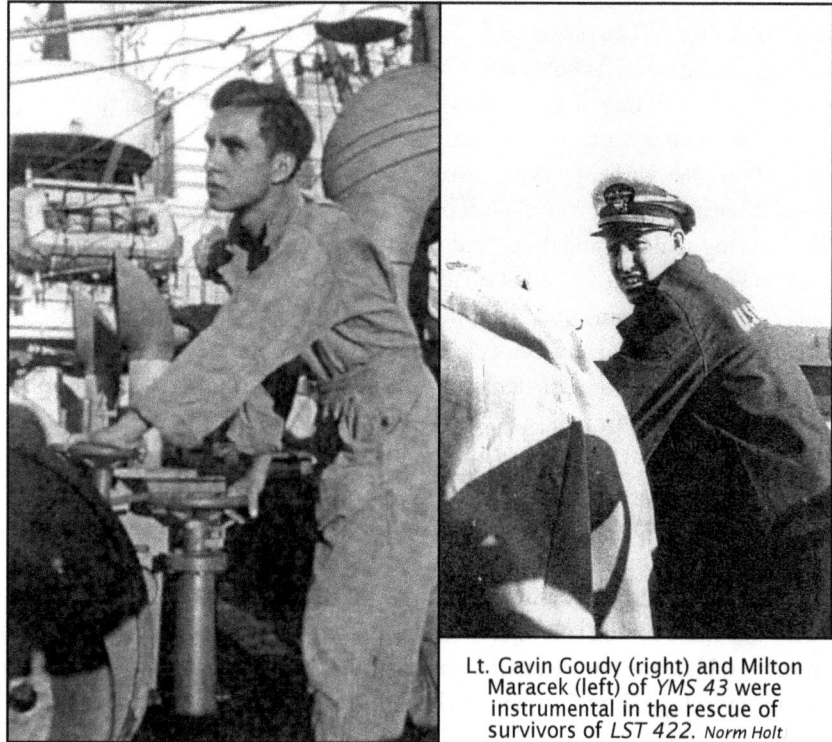

Lt. Gavin Goudy (right) and Milton Maracek (left) of *YMS 43* were instrumental in the rescue of survivors of *LST 422*. *Norm Holt*

Col. Hutchinson of the 83rd would send a letter of appreciation to the captain and crew of *SC 638* and probably all of the other rescue craft as well. CTG 81-4, in charge of most of the LCIs, also mentioned that at daylight "all pontoons on the beach were broached, one British LCI was broached, two British and ten U.S. LCT were broached. There was no unloading over X Ray Beach this day due to the weather. Many ships had got out of the swept area during the night and all were notified to get back in the area immediately and warned of the dangers outside the swept area."[106]

YMS 43 also moved out, at which time they lost their port anchor, and soon encountered the same problems with the weather and rough sea. According to crewman Norm Holt, "We got underway again while still dark and could hear the cries for help from the water. I manned the searchlight and the rest of the fellows went on deck to throw lines, life preservers, etc. over. I picked one fellow up in the light and we managed to get him aboard even though we had heavy seas which made it difficult. We picked several others that were floating around and when it got light enough to see, we could see many more. We got one life raft full aboard … " Holt added in another account, "We turned on the searchlights, twelve-inch searchlights, to pick up people in the water to see what we could find," and recalled, "We saw, besides the 83rd, other people in the water, and the debris. And at that time, I believe, Julius Nemes, or somebody else, said they needed me on the bridge and I went down on the deck to see what I could do down there. Most of us had lines out in the water trying to throw them to the survivors in the water, whatever you could find." It was difficult to maneuver alongside the survivors and, as reported in the ship's War Diary, "Most men were either too cold or too nearly drowned to help themselves. It was usually necessary for one or two men to go down the Jacobs ladder to the waters edge and lift the survivors aboard. Using the boat hook was the best method except many of the life belts tore under the strain. Survivors were drowning all around us as we were picking up some of their shipmates." The ship's Action Report added, "We found the air life belts used by the survivors inadequate. Many of the men were struggling through the water with them uninflated. The water was extremely cold causing shock to the majority of the men picked up." *YMS 43* eventually retrieved 18 survivors and applied artificial respiration to those in need. Only one died. Comprising the survivors were six men of the 83rd, 10 of the Royal Navy, and two from *LCI 32*, which included the one man, RM2c George L. Marsh, who died following life saving efforts. In addition, the ship picked up M. V. Costello of *YMS 62*, who had been out in a small boat attempting to rescue survivors.[107]

The six men of the 83rd picked up by *YMS 43* were 1st Lt. Alfred L. Forrester (Co. D), S/Sgt. Eugene A. Plassmann (HQ Co.), T/5 Claude J. Shaw (HQ Co.), Pvt. Daniel J. Shields (Co. D), Pvt. Porter R. Davis (Co. D), and Pfc. Max

C. Webb (Co. C). Plassmann and Shaw emphasized the life preserver ring " ... was something we could hold on to ... During the time we were in the water there maybe would have been 3, 4, or 6 of us on this thing while we were near the LST. As we were swept out, we were being swept out to sea apparently, and we got farther and farther away we kept picking up other guys, so by the time [*YMS 43*] picked us up, there must have been 20 of us trying to ... Well, they were dying, dying so fast, freezing to death and dying and slipping off ... Trying to get these guys to hold on was not ... just couldn't do it, there were only 6 of us [*remaining*]."[108]

YMS 43's Holt lamented, "It was a night if you've gone through it, you'll never forget it. I had a line on one, I don't know who, which outfit he was from, bringing him towards the boat and I had him almost aboard and he just let go. He just plain let go, and I never saw him again." Holt also said crewman Milton Maracek "... went over the side of the ship and hung on the ship from the outside trying to haul somebody aboard -- and Lt. Gavin Goudy who was also on the outside of the ship trying to bring people aboard." Gunner's Mate Herman Martinez said his most vivid memory of the event was of an individual called Morris from his home state of Colorado. "I didn't have anything to do with picking him up. But I had one guy on the line that I couldn't move, he must have weighed over 300 lbs., I did leave for a moment, I had the line tied to the stanchion, and when I got back a few seconds later he had let go. He wasn't there, so his face stayed with me for many years after that because it was a pleading face ... " When pressed for further details, Martinez said the man weighed so much because he was wet and fully clothed with backpack and full equipment.[109]

Frank Kloxin of *YMS 36* was awarded one of the Navy's highest medals for his part in the rescue of *LST 422* survivors. *Frank Kloxin*

Jules Nemes of *YMS 43* said his first recollection of a survivor was the one "...that we picked up ... hanging onto a 55 gallon drum ... Just keeping himself afloat. We got him up to the cargo net and set down and somebody was trying to get his fingers off the drum and he just wouldn't let go. Finally, we really yanked them off and we brought him aboard." Claude Shaw remembered the ordeal of attempting to climb up the cargo net. "I don't think it was so much that we were trying to climb. We didn't have strength enough to beat our way out of a paper bag, but we were being pushed against the ship by the waves, and it [*barnacles on the ship's hull*] tore up our faces and our arms."[110]

Motor Machinist John Wittright said the most difficult part of the ordeal for him was that, "... up until that period of time when we could start looking [*for survivors*] all we could do was stand there looking out in the dark and hear [*survivors*] hollering for help. We couldn't do a thing about it. We finally got our orders to start picking up survivors. Fortunately for us, we didn't have to pick up the dead ones ... I had to go over the side after one of those myself." Upon being brought aboard, survivors were taken below deck where "Our cook was trying to cook up a big pot of soup to get something warm in [*the survivors*], but it was so rough he had to stand on the stove and hold the pot on the stove to keep it from sliding across the stove."[111]

Frank Kloxin of *YMS 36* receiving his Navy and Marine Corps Life Saving Medal. *Frank Kloxin*

Pvt. Daniel J. Shields, Co. D, claimed he was the last man saved by *YMS 43* after surviving in the water for more than three hours. Shields recalled, "They threw a line to me and I was unable to hold on to it and fortunately for me one of their sailors reached down and grabbed me by the back of my shirt and pulled me in over top of their deck. My uniform was so twisted they had to cut it off me to get it off."[112]

YMS 69 got underway at 7:20 with a special sea detail to pick up survivors near their anchor who were being carried by sea and wind while at the same time *LCI 10* reported the wind increasing in force and sea conditions up to 7 as a hailstorm began. At 7:25,

U.S.S. Strive noted word was passed for all hands to standby and pick up survivors. At 7:30, *YMS 36* got underway in a heavy sea and rescued 12 men and retrieved one body. During the rescue Ensign Stuart Clement and Frank Maurice Kloxin, Seaman first class, heroically went overboard to assist survivors clinging to a life raft. In a 2008 interview, Kloxin recalled that at the time he was a signalman third class and loved to swim. He jumped overboard to assist in the rescue and then was brought back on the ship, only to return to the water to continue in the rescue effort. As his ship launched a small life raft, the commanding officer told him to help survivors brought to the raft, but they drifted away and were lost for an hour or two before being found again by *YMS 36*. Afterwards the crew continued to search for more survivors. Kloxin was later awarded the Navy and Marine Corps Life Saving Medal, promoted, and served out the remainder of the war on a subchaser. His citation read in part, " … Kloxin promptly and in complete disregard of his own safety dove into the water and swam to a life raft to which twelve men in an exhausted condition were clinging. He exerted extreme efforts to assist them in every possible way to remain afloat even to the extent of lashing and holding several of those survivors in the most weakened condition to the raft until they were recovered by rescue vessels." Kloxin also mentioned that later in the morning a red-headed sailor from the Royal Navy gave him his knife in appreciation of his participation in his rescue.[113]

LCI 196 also sent LCIs to the aid of *LST 422* and *LCI 32*. The *U.S.S. Dextrous* left the dangerous area, as did the *Herbert C. Jones*, which reported that "because of high seas and close quarters the rescue work had to be done by smaller ships." The *Pilot* immediately moved to the disaster site but was hindered by hail flurries, a force wind 4 - 7 west by northwest, which blew in gusts. Additionally, huge swells hampered maneuverability. This was confirmed by the commander of the mine squadron who wrote the combination of Force 7 winds, Force 6 seas, and heavy sleet and rain made it inadvisable to lower power boats for the rescue. The *Pilot* came alongside a group of survivors and soon learned that, having been in the frigid, cold water for over two hours, the survivors were too exhausted to climb up the cargo net. Many were in a state of shock or too tired to secure a line around themselves. The wind soon changed to Force 6-7 with a swell, causing the ship to roll 25 to 32 degrees, which, as noted, made lowering a boat to the survivors unfeasible. The ship maneuvered so as to drift down on survivors. It was determined the only way to rescue these men was to "send a man over the side with a line around his waist, with a line which he secured around the waist …" of the man in the water. One sailor, Arthur J. Freid, SoM2c, actually went over the side without a line secured to himself and was lost in the sea. Fortunately, he was rescued a short time later by *YMS 69*. Since the survivors were too weak to get inside a life ring or climb up the cargo net, many of the vessel's crew went over the side to help but were dipped underwater due to excessive rolling. According to the ship's Action Report, "The wooden floats were first high on the side and then the whole net submerged as the ship rolled in the heavy sea." A number of men were struck on the head by this wooden float and pushed beneath the water's surface.[114]

One man rescued by *Pilot*, Pfc. William C. Ford, Co. C, from New Albany, Union County, Mississippi, said that when he entered the water from the burning LST he attempted to avoid the burning fuel on the water's surface and also put his feet against the ship's hull so he could push away from it. He said that despite having a life jacket it was impossible to swim because the waves would continually roll him over. Ford added, "As I got further away from the LST I could see men everywhere, and most of them were dead … the tide was going out, and soon I could no longer see the burning LST." Consuming dangerous amounts of salt water, with thoughts of his family, Ford passed out but regained consciousness in time to spot the *Pilot*. Some sailors threw him a rope but he was too weak to hold on. Spotting a loop in the rope, he put his arm through it as the sailors slowly pulled him to the ship. A rope ladder was thrown over the side and two sailors came down to assist, and he passed out again. Ford suffered from severe memory loss and later had to have his family send him pictures because he could not recall their images. Ford said he was the only man from his squad to survive.[115]

Another survivor saved by the *Pilot* was Pfc. Curtis A. Williams, Medical Detachment, who said he witnessed one man holding onto an ammo crate as a flotation device who would not let go when rescued. His fingers had to be pried off the crate by the sailors. Pvt. Rudolph Whitt, Co. C, also rescued by the *Pilot*, said that after being unconscious in the water for several hours, he woke up surrounded by sailors covering him with warm blankets and offering him a drink of whiskey. He was eventually sent to Pozzuoli to recover, where he spent 21 days in the hospital.[116]

Survivors brought aboard *Pilot* during the next hour and forty minutes, would amount to 28, including 22 reported in good physical condition from *LST 422* and 6 in an unconscious, drowned state. Artificial respiration was immediately applied to these six men by the first aid party of Ensign R. I. Brueckbauer, USNR; A. S. Tilka, MoM2c, USNR; D. L. Boase, MoM3c, USN; and J. B. Clark, Jr., MoM3c, USNR. One of the six unconscious men would be up and about in six hours but the other five, despite the administration of artificial respiration for four hours, passed away. Four crew men, Elmer Posick, Robert G. Kern, Edward C. Denmark, Jr., and Edward K. Lucas, were commended for their outstanding performance in the rescue operation.[117]

Additionally, at 7:30, the life raft containing five officers and 7 enlisted men from *LCI 32* pulled up portside of *YMS 58* and rescue commenced despite difficulties encountered holding the raft alongside due to the rough sea. *SC 625* picked up some survivors at 7:40 as *LCI 10* stood by for further instructions. A line was also passed at 7.55 by *U.S.S. Strive* to another seven survivors of *LCI 32*, Commander Edward Webster Wilson of Flotilla 2 and Lt. (jg.) Maynes C. Fitzgerald, commanding the LCI. This last rescue was recalled by Radioman Arnott Simon of *LCI 32* who said the men on the raft were unable to comprehend why ships they could see in the distance were making no effort to come to them, so they started paddling with their hands toward the ships. Simon added, "Suddenly the sea became so rough it tried to dislodge the men from the life raft." They had to hang on for dear life as well as to keep the commander from being washed overboard. They finally drifted to a small American ship and the sailors on deck threw a couple of lines to the men. At this point in time, the sea was rising and falling 20 to 30 feet and the ropes were not enough for a successful rescue. The sailors on deck quickly realized this and threw over a boarding net. The problem was judging when to grab onto the net as the ship rolled. Simon grabbed a rung on the net as the ship rolled down only to discover there was no rung below for his feet. He was hanging there by the sheer strength of his arms. The sailors on deck were yelling for him to hang on as one of them, very aware that Simon could fall to his death, swiftly climbed down the net to assist him.[118]

Also apparently among this group of *LCI 32* survivors rescued by *Strive* was Coxswain Joseph Theodore Marcey, who helped his dazed and confused fellow crewmen fasten and inflate their life belts immediately after his ship was hit. When ordered to abandon ship, he almost single-handedly got both life rafts into the water and assisted the injured over the life lines and wreckage. As the LCI lay on its side, he continued to search the deck for anyone needing aid, and while in the water he was spotted at least twice leaving the comparative safety of the raft to aid others, and to investigate objects which might be survivors. Marcey spent nearly two and one-half hours in the water afloat on the raft and continually guided the raft toward the rescue craft. At least two officers recommended him for the Navy Cross.[119]

PC 1227 completed taking on 51 survivors of *LST 422* at 7:59, including the C.O. and three badly burned men. Admiral Frank J. Lowry, Commander Eighth Amphibious Force for the Anzio invasion, later commended the crew, including Radarman 3rd Class Robert E. Wilson, among the men who went overboard to assist the survivors. One of those probably rescued by *PC 1227* was T/5 George Borkhuis, Co. D, who stated he was saved by a subchaser. He recalled that, as the hail beat down on the gas can he used as a floating device, and as his life flashed before him, a huge wave lifted him up to where he was able to spot a rescue vessel. He attempted to wave with his free hand but the ship turned away. Later he saw another ship and waved only to hear a voice, followed by the ship coming to a stop. Suddenly a voice cried out, "Hold on, we see you!" Coming within a few yards of Borkhuis, the sailors threw him a life ring but he couldn't hold on to it with his frozen hand. One of the sailors tied a rope around himself, jumped overboard, swam to George, grabbed him by the coat collar, and pulled him to the ship. George lost consciousness and when he awoke the sailors were performing artificial respiration on him. They gave him black coffee, which caused him to throw up the salt water he had ingested, followed by a good cup of coffee with milk and no sugar. Eventually he was taken to Naples and placed in a former German officer's building nicknamed "The Survivors House," which contained five survivors of *LCI 32* and a badly burned dog. Borkhuis wrote home, "My personal belongings were all lost a few days ago due to some ones carelessness. I can't explain the story any better as censorship prohibits it. But I haven't anything left at all. The Red Cross has been very helpful and has given me a toilet kit containing the usual articles, also some writing paper and envelopes … I am now back in a beautiful rest area."[120]

Possibly another man rescued by *PC 1227* was Sgt. Clark Riddle, Co. D, who said the last thing he remembered seeing was a PC boat go past as he said, "God, help me." A life raft came and Riddle hooked his elbows over the side. A sailor from Boston named Salvatore dove overboard to assist him. He told Clark the sailors were having a contest to see how many stripes they could save, and Riddle had three, making him a good catch. On deck he saw survivors Lt.

Alfred H. Crenshaw and Lt. James V. Lauro, who asked of Riddle's well-being prior to his being given large amounts of coffee to bring up the salt water.[121]

Other vessels joined in the rescue operations, including *YMS 207*, which got underway at 7:50. By 7:55, *YMS 83* had replaced their blown fuses and, by carefully manipulating the windlass and engines, got underway in what they referred to as a heavy sleet and snow storm. They immediately moved to the area where survivors were last seen but found none, but did note that YMSs *34, 36, 43, 207*, along with *Strive*, were searching an area farther east of them.[122]

Unfortunately for those survivors yet in the water, the terrible weather and sea conditions got even worse as an intense storm arrived at about 8:00, with large hail, sleet, rain, winds of Force 7 (some ships reported Force 8), and swells often higher than the ships. *YMS 43*, which made note of this at the time and reported an extremely heavy hail storm, felt any other survivors had perished, although *YMS 34* got underway to join in the rescue at this time. The *Ulster Queen* reported winds at West Northwest, Force 7, accompanied by low clouds, sleet, and rain squalls, while Rear Admiral Lowry gave the wind as North West, Force 7, Sea 5. Sgt. Lemuel R. Tillman, Co. C, said, "It was storming rain, sleet, and snow and waves must have been 30 feet or higher." Despite the weather, ships such as *LCI 10* continued the search. Five minutes later *YMS 226* also reported a "heavy sleet and hail storm from northeast driven by high winds … and it is all one can do to stand the exposure of his face and hands to the slanting sheets of hail." At the same time *U.S.S. Strive* finally brought aboard from a raft the seven survivors *LCI 32* had located, while *YMS 58* also took on 12 survivors of *LCI 32*, including Lt. Commander Thompson Black.[123]

The crew of *Strive* also retrieved two bodies of 83rd men, Pvt. Robert A. Fullagar, Co. C, from New Jersey, and Pfc. William W. Ridenour, Co. D, from Campbell County, Tennessee. The Action Report of *Strive* described the rescue of the *LCI 32* men, stating, "Bearings taken on the raft were shown to be steady and it was decided that the operation could be carried out more successfully with the ship headed into the wind otherwise there would have been a heavy roll due to the wind and sea. Twenty fathoms of chain was heaved in order to decrease the yaw. As the raft approached the ship the engines were used to get the bow as close to the raft as possible. Heaving lines were used and made fast to the raft which was then led down the port side to the cargo net. The sea was heavy and the line to the raft had to be tended constantly. Executive Officer, Lt. E. B. Knowlton, USNR, and Seaman Second Class, Paul R. Varble, USNR, descended the cargo net and helped the survivors of *LCI 32* aboard." Varble also dove overboard and brought aboard the body of one soldier. This U.S. soldier and the body of another, Fullagar and Ridenour of the 83rd, had been recovered and, although obviously dead, were administered artificial respiration for a full half hour by Yeoman First Class Vincent D. Tyron, USN, and Gunner's Mate Third Class Donald H. Waid until rigor mortis set in.[124]

Hale H. Hepler, Co. C, added, "I experienced a cold rain and hail that can happen in that time of year. The white caps and swells in the water made my time there a very unpleasant experience. The worst sight was the swells would raise me up and I could see many men in the water. The next swell would show me fewer men alive. The later swells showed almost no one left. It was a terrible part of my war experience, watching those young soldiers die. The minesweeper found me in spite of the fact my life belt had been burned by phosphorous and was not holding air very well. I would have to inflate it many times. I can still see the sailor who threw the life ring with the attached doughnut on it to me three times. Each time I was not able to swim and get it. He dove into the water and wrapped my arms around the doughnut. I was pulled aboard. I immediately vomited the sea water I had swallowed. I couldn't keep down the whiskey that was offered to me. It was then I lost consciousness." He was taken to Pozzuoli the next day where he said he never received treatment for his burns.[125]

Although *LCI 196* reported a heavy gale and hail storm struck at 8:05, which they rode out in the swept channel before sending all LCTs to the Anzio harbor, *YMS 58* had completed their rescue of 12 *LCI 32* survivors. The commander of the mine squadron was informed at 8:30 by CTU 81.7.2 that CTG 81.14 (Commander Edward Webster Wilson) was among the survivors of *LCI 32* picked up by *Strive* and CTG 81.14 had "advised *LCI 32* had also been sunk by what he termed an 'underwater explosion'. This report, along with the location of the LST, convinced CTG 81.7 that the two ships had indeed been mined."[126]

Although the wind was officially reported at 50 knots by 8:31, the futility experienced by the naval rescue groups was evidenced when the Action Report of *YMS 226* stated that at 8:32, "Squall abated but that squall cost the lives of many potential survivors. They faded fast after that, and it began to become difficult to distinguish the living from the dead in the water. It was most painful to spot a living man struggling in the water with weak shouts for help, and before the ship could be brought close enough to him for rescue, to see him collapse, too far gone to reach for life preserver drifted down to him." At least one man saved was Pvt. Audie W. Pierce, Co. C, who said that after being pulled aboard *YMS 226* he was hypothermic and couldn't talk, and the crew thought he was British because of his light hair and the loss of his dog-tags. Another man brought in by *YMS 226* was Pfc. Antonio ("Tony") Rabaiotti, Co. D, from Providence, Rhode Island, who said he jumped into the water suffering from shrapnel wounds and was temporarily paralyzed in both arms. Rabaiotti recalled, "George Yakubisin and I were sleeping on the top deck and I was wearing my life belt. Following the explosion shrapnel and white phosphorous were everywhere and I was hit. Burned and with both arms temporarily paralyzed I opted to jump in the water, and I'm pretty sure I hit the bottom of the sea before resurfacing and spotting a raft. I yelled at them for help and soon we were on a minesweeper."[127]

Crewman Norm Holt of *YMS 43* wrote, "We could have saved at least 30 or 40 more ourselves but ... a severe storm came up accompanied by the worst hail storm I've ever seen. You couldn't see a thing and the waves were higher than the ship. It lasted about an hour and when it passed, all trace of the men had vanished. There were over 300 around that could have been saved if the storm hadn't come up. There were about 25 ships in the area picking up men, the same as us and they all had to stop because of the storm." In a much later interview, Holt added, " ... there were many men out there, and then this sudden squall came up. A vicious one, high waves and sleet and it lasted a very short time. I can't recall how long but when it was over, there wasn't a soul out there. Nothing more we could do." *YMS 29* reported at 8:45 they were cruising in a severe storm although by that time the storm had actually ceased. *YMS 43* stopped their search at the same time, claiming there were no more floating bodies visible, yet they renewed their search almost immediately. Holt of *YMS 43* added the rescued survivors "... were numb and sick and cold and were dried and put below in our bunks. What got me was the fellows we saw drown right before our eyes. Some had hold of lines and were being pulled aboard but lost strength within 5 to 10 feet of the ship and went under. Others just gave out while we were trying to throw lines to them. I lost count of all that I saw go down. I didn't want to look but it was fascinating and yet horrible at the same time. I'll come home a changed man and you can't blame me or any of the fellows either. One of our men almost drowned when he went down the ladder after a fellow. The man grabbed him and pulled him under and all that saved him was the fact that he had hold of a line. His hands were all cut where he had his grip." *YMS 58* made a radio report of the condition of their rescued survivors at 9:00 and commenced first aid to the seriously injured.[128]

YMS 226 brought in their last survivor at 9:18, "after a stirring struggle on his part to stay alive until we could reach him. His fine physique saved his life. He had to be dragged aboard. A total of 39 living survivors were rescued and soon [we] it began the grim task of bringing in the dead bodies still afloat." The sky began clearing at 9:25 while the commander of the mine squadron reported at 9:30, "The swept channel area for more than seven miles east of the burning ship was thoroughly covered and CTG 81.7 was convinced that nearly all, if not all, survivors in the area were recovered. It also appeared impossible for any to have drifted beyond the eastern limit of the channel and none were observed in the mined area to shoreward of the channel." Also at 9:30 *LCI 196* recorded the storm had subsided. Yet, at 9:45, the storm still apparently affected *YMS 83*, which reported, "Visibility close to zero with heavy sleet squalls and northwest winds of gale force." The ship searched downwind for survivors from *LST 422* without success and discontinued the search. At 9:50, *YMS 226* reported, "Now begins [the] task of bringing in bodies, 18 in all, which occupied our whole morning. While the weather cleared, the seas were still running heavily and a strong wind blowing. There were more dead bodies floating by than the rescue ships could possibly recover before they drifted out of range." Mr. McLaughlin, executive officer of *YMS 226*, had become too sick with yellow jaundice to continue directing operations on deck and was replaced by Mr. Batty, engineering and medical officer. From this time until 11:25, *YMS 207* reported the recovery of 10 bodies.[129]

A preliminary check of the rescue vessels by the commander of the mine squadron at 10:00 indicated the *Pilot*, *Strive*, and YMSs in the swept channel area had recovered approximately 100 survivors, with 20 in need of immediate medical attention. Information was also requested as to the disposal of 10 or 12 recovered bodies. Following this, all YMSs were ordered to follow *Pilot* into the anchorage area to await further instruction on transferal of survivors. Also around 10:00, *YMS 34* picked up the floating body of Billy C. Rhoads, Co. C. Lt. (jg) C. J. Schuh of the ship said the process involved in recovering such dead bodies included removing one dog tag for identification and leaving the other on the soldier, then placing the body in a canvas bag and weighing it down with 40mm AA shells before returning it to the sea.[130]

Many survivors had dramatic stories of rescue, such as Pvt. Loy Marshall, Co. C, who said, "I was able to get a hold on a railing on the edge of the deck of the ship and was trying to pull myself up, but the weight of all the gear I was wearing and the sheer effort to keep my head above the frigid water had exhausted me. I was about to fall back into the water when a sailor on board the ship realized what was happening and stomped on my hand to keep me from falling back. I was pulled onto the deck and my hand was injured and bleeding."[131]

Due to strict mail censorship, Capt. Robert E. Edwards, HQ Co., would later write his wife about the incident and refer to himself as someone else, although he was actually the censor of his own letters. "Had a very interesting talk with a man who was on a ship that hit a mine some time ago," Edwards wrote. "He described his floating about on big waves and how he helped some men to hang on and finally be rescued. He said he was a happy bird to get back on dry land. Said it was colder than the windy winter streets of Chicago."[132]

Pfc. Leopold Sama, 68th Coastal Artillery, rescued by *PC 1227*, died from exposure and shock at 10:15 as the vessel sailed for Naples. By 10:30, *YMS 69* had successfully rescued nine men from *LST 422*, including seven from the 83rd, one from the Royal Navy, and Arthur J. Freid of *Pilot*, who had gone overboard and then been swept away during rescue operations. At 10:46, *YMS 43* finally called off their search for survivors or bodies.[133]

YMS 36 was underway at 11:15 to the transport area to get medical aid for casualties and came alongside *LCI 19* to take aboard Lt. H. V. Coes, USN, Medical Corps, attached to *LCI 19* and on the staff of Commander Floyd (CTG 81.3), and transfer him to *YMS 226*. Five YMSs, including *3, 36, 58, 62,* and *226,* reported at 11:50 survivors were in need of medical attention; therefore, the commander of the mine squadron ordered the vessels to follow *Pilot* into anchorage, "where several LCIs with medical officers aboard were finally directed to the YMSs needing them. A great deal of confusion and some delay resulted in continuous efforts of all LCIs to put the medical officers aboard the *Pilot* and *Strive,* but eventually all serious cases received medical attention." The total number of recoveries reported by the craft of CTG 81.7 at this time included 20 living and five dead on *Pilot,* five survivors on *Strive,* 12 living and two dead on *YMS 3,* nine dead on *YMS 34,* 11 survivors and one dead on *YMS 36,* 17 living on *YMS 43,* 15 survivors on *YMS 58,* 14 living and one dead on *YMS 62,* seven living on *YMS 69,* 12 survivors on *YMS 83,* six dead on *YMS 207,* and 11 living and one dead on *YMS 226.* Information was also requested as to the disposal of bodies.[134]

At noon, just as the wind was listed at North West North, Force 6, Sea 2, *YMS 34* reported the successful recovery of 21 bodies, all but three identified. It was felt that possibly two of them could be identified by their clothes and markings only. Although most were from the 83rd, at least one

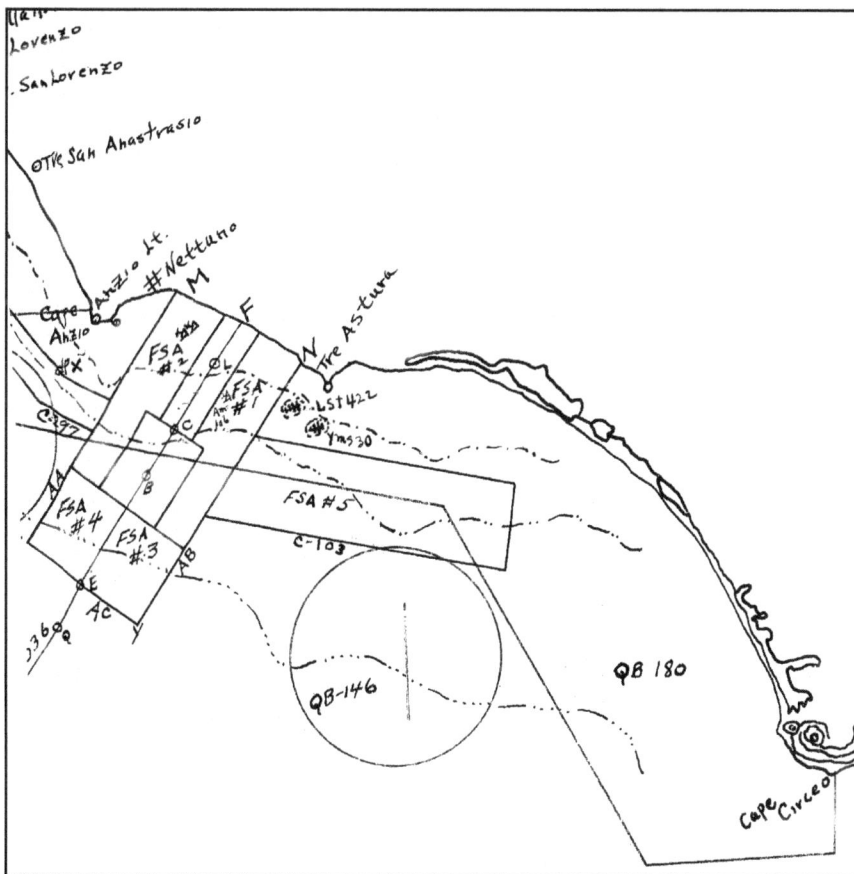

Map from the records of *U.S.S. Pilot* designating the exact location (just south of Tre Astura) where *LST 422* sank. *National Archives*

belonged to the 68th Coastal Artillery, and the three unidentified were discovered to include one from the Royal Navy and two from *LCI 32*, including an African American radioman. *YMS 207* brought in their eleventh body at 12:05, and nine minutes later *YMS 34* was ordered to stop picking up bodies. *YMS 62* moved into the anchorage area at 12:20 to locate a doctor for T/5 Warren R. Runkle of the 83rd, from Philadelphia, who was on the verge of death from drowning and shock.[135]

YMS 226 was also ordered to stop bringing in bodies at 12:30 and to stand in the transport area. Their final official count included 39 survivors and 18 dead, for a total of 57. The ship's officer wrote, "Wet clothes of survivors were piled high in passage ways, and every available bunk was in use with all necessary clothes and blankets from members of the crew. All day, M. C. Cosgrove, CCS, kept hot coffee and sandwiches available wherever needed, on deck, in galley, or below." Also at 12:30, *LCI 10* received orders from the *Biscayne* to transfer a doctor to *Pilot* to aid survivors and "… then directed us to transfer to *YMS 62* and *YMS 59*." *YMS 226* received a message from *YMS 69* at 12:45 to move to the transport area and pick up a doctor from one of three YMSs to provide medical attention for the survivors.[136]

LCI 10 made contact with *YMS 62* at 1:10 and attempted to come along the starboard side, but due to the rough sea she rammed the starboard 20mm platform of *YMS 62*. Six stanchions were broken, along with one Mark 14 gun sight and 11 crossbeams which supported the starboard 20mm gun. A second attempt proved successful. Lt. H. V. Coes, USNR medical officer, was transferred from *LCI 19* to *YMS 36* at 1:25.[137]

According to Lt. Commander Broadhurst, while he and his crew remained on Fire Tug ATR 1, *LST 422* broke in two and sank at 2:30 "in position 2 miles 200 deg. Torre Asturia," although a number of veterans claimed the ship never entirely sank. One man later even insisted the ship's remains washed ashore the following day. At 2:45, *YMS 36*, as previously directed, transferred Lt. H. V. Coes, to *YMS 226* to treat survivors.[138]

At 3:18 p.m., *YMS 34* was awaiting orders for disposal of bodies. *YMS 58* stood in at Nettuno between 3:19 and 3:21 to take aboard a medical officer from *LCI 196*. At 3:50 medical officer Coes, on *YMS 226*, reported all survivors on board were in fair condition and that his services were no longer required. He also recommended the transfer of Mr. McLaughlin to a station hospital in Naples for treatment of his yellow jaundice. Also at this time, 3:21 p.m., and contradicting the earlier report of Lt. Commander Broadhurst, *H. M. LST 425* reported observing *LST 422* overturn and flounder.[139]

By 4:00, the wind and sea began to moderate and the sky cleared, with winds North West North, Force 3, Sea 3. This was soon followed by an enemy air attack directed at *YMS 3* at 4:10, resulting in two near misses on their port bow and beam. By 4:11, *YMS 58* had pulled up alongside *LST 327* to attempt to transfer survivors but found it impossible due to the still somewhat rough seas. During this procedure the starboard 20mm anti-aircraft gun was put out of action. Afterward, the medical officer ordered the ship to move into the Anzio harbor. Elsewhere, the six volunteers in the #1 running boat of *LST 16* arrived back at their ship at 4:24 p.m. following their dramatic rescue efforts, while, at 4:30, *YMS 62* pronounced Pvt. Warren K. Runkle of the 83rd dead from drowning following six hours of artificial respiration. And at 4:50 *YMS 58* moored alongside the breakwater in Anzio harbor and transferred the medical officer and 12 survivors of *LCI 32* to a base hospital.[140]

CTF 81 issued orders at 4:55 to the commander of the mine squadron for all minesweepers to transfer survivors to *LST 327* before dark in the outer transport area and to bury all bodies at sea beyond the 50-fathom mark. It was soon afterward learned *LST 327* was already out to sea, changing orders to the transferal of survivors to any LSTs that could be located. Indeed, *YMS 34* received body disposal orders at 5:00 p.m., directing them to bury the dead at sea beyond the 50-fathom line either that night or the next day. By 5:09, *YMS 207*, in response to orders from CTG 81.7, got underway to effect burial of the 11 bodies they recovered. Around 5:20, *YMS 226* was moored near the port side of *YMS 58* at the outer end of the Anzio port breakwater and began landing survivors, as did *YMS 58*. Two minutes later, Mr. Batty and Lt. Coes went ashore to make arrangements for the survivors.[141]

Although the *LST 422* disaster was the primary center of attention on January 26th activity did not decrease on shore, where the balance of the 83rd had no idea what was happening to their comrades aboard the LST. By 6:30 a.m., one platoon of Co. B had moved into a light scrub prepared to fire their mortars but found the soft soil necessitated digging out the baseplates and repositioning the mortars after every fire mission. At the same time, the MLR [*Main Line of Resistance*] of the Ranger Force lay some 200 yards to the rear of the mortars, along the Carroceto Road.[142]

At 10:00, Co. A was ordered to emplace their mortars in the moist scrub just north of Camp di Carno Road, while Co. B emplaced their remaining mortars in their previously occupied position. In this location Co. B fired 77 HE and 20 WP intermittently throughout the remainder of the day. It was also during this period that the Battalion CP moved to a haystack and Sgt. Harry Cohen, Co. C, a survivor of *LST 422* already brought to shore, arrived at Battalion CP with news of the LST tragedy and information that at least 50 survivors were ashore at Anzio and others were being picked up by rescue vessels.[143]

The first injury of the day among the 83rd men already fighting on the Anzio beachhead took place at 5:30 as Pfc. James L. Brannan [*or Brennen*], HQ Co., from Philadelphia, was lightly wounded by "flak" while laying communication wire between Co. B and the battalion switchboard. James Helsel, Co. A, wrote in his diary, "Late in the evening we moved to a cross road by trucks. Here we unloaded and pulled them by hand up a stony road bed. The 'Rangers' were breaking along the road in one spot and they sure did ride us. We got into position just about dusk. The move was made so we could fire upon the 'factory' better. It was very swampy so a few of us decided no use digging in."[144]

Enemy planes also began to attack the Anzio port at 5:45, during which time the Battalion CP witnessed five enemy planes crash in flames, believed to be downed by AA fire, and four others damaged. One of the attacking enemy planes was shot down at about 6:00 in the evening [*Hutchinson reported the incident at 1:16 p.m.*], confirmed in the report of *YMS 226*, and crashed on the position of Co. A, directly on top of Pvt. Robert I. Crutz, killing him and wounding three others, none seriously. Joseph Cannetti, Co. A, recalled the incident, writing, "I remember seeing a German plane in flames heading straight for us. It crashed about two football fields from our position and I did not hear a loud explosion, but saw everyone running towards the crash … " Pfc. Charles Rolling, Co. A, wrote in his diary, "This evening a plane fell over the 2nd Platoon and Crutz was buried beneath earth which the explosion threw up. He was found two days later." "Doc" Hulcher, Medical Detachment, contradicted Rolling and said Crutz's body wasn't found until four days later. James Helsel, Co. A, also an eyewitness, probably best described the incident when he wrote, " … while watching a few planes battle it out in the air we heard a swish, looked up and saw a ball of fire headed for our area. It landed near the first squad … Brown said 'HHHelsel, my hole is only seventeen steps away'. Some say it was an airplane, some say it was a buzz bomb, but I say it was too damn close, whatever it was, for it made a very large hole and threw up lumps of dirt as big as the dining room table." Reno Toniolo added, "I watched two large German planes flying over, with a very small plane to their right rear. I saw the little plane peel off and head right for us. It hit about thirty or forty feet to the right of the First Mortar Squad position, and buried Crutz alive. It made a hole big enough to bury a house in, and it wounded four other men. If it had landed fifty feet more to the left, it would have wiped out our entire platoon of about fifty men." Toniolo claimed the brass later discovered it was a radio-controlled glider bomb.[145]

By 6:15 p.m., *YMS 207* had performed burial at sea services for their *LST 422* casualties and *PC 1227* had reached Nisada, where they discharged 50 survivors and one body. Yet the struggle in Anzio harbor continued at 6:19 as two near misses by German glider bombs caused the men of the *S.S. John Banvard* to abandon ship, leaving numerous members of the 488th Port Battalion in the water for as much as two hours. Luckily *YMS 29* quickly retrieved some 22 to 26 of the crew, and *YMS 83* later recovered 13 men, one with a broken arm. Additionally, while laying smoke, *SC 638* had observed the attack and rushed to pick up 90 survivors from the water and life rafts, whom they returned to the ship.[146]

Most of the men of the 83rd who had arrived at Anzio on January 22nd remained completely unaware of the disaster that had befallen their comrades out to sea and continued business as usual. At 6:30 p.m., Lt. Col. Hutchinson reported to Darby that Co. A had eight mortars and Co. B one, and said, "Sandbag butt plates. Will have 15 mortars to fire in the morning. Will be casualties on account of soft soil. Put timber down, then sandbag." At the same time this was transpiring, the 12 survivors of *LCI 32* aboard *YMS 226* went ashore at Anzio with orders to report to Commander Floyd for transport to Naples via a British LST, and at 6:35 *YMS 27* ironically reported the storm had subsided.[147]

Back out at sea, Navy Medical Officer Lt. H. V. Coes returned to *LCI 19* at 7:30 while *YMS 34* decided to immediately bury the 21 bodies they had recovered, reaching the 50-fathom line at 7:40 in the evening. Engines were stopped, the flag placed at half mast, a burial service was read, and the burial began. All men excepting the burial party of five and the captain were at General Quarters Station. *Pilot* could not transfer their 22 survivors until the next day due to the rough weather but did bury five bodies at sea in the assault area after dark. Also at 7:40, *YMS 226*, which had been under a number of nearby enemy air attacks in the previous hours, decided for the safety of the crew and the survivors not yet landed to clear port and unload in the morning under better circumstances, although Mr. Batty had not yet returned to the ship.[148]

Lt. Commander S. B. Wetmore, commanding officer, *Pilot*, officiated over a burial at sea ceremony in the assault area at 8:05 for Pvt. Ross J. Jones, Co. C; Sgt. Joseph J. Karcauskas, Co. D; Pvt. Duncan M. Kennedy, Co. C; Pvt. Howard E. Routledge, Co. D; all of the 83rd; and Shipt/Pmx S. H. Hicks of the Royal Navy. Such activities did not deter the enemy and another air attack was sustained by *YMS 3* at 10 p.m., also involving another near miss on their port beam. Luckily for all the survivors of *LST 422* and the subsequent rescue operations, the wind and sea moderated at night.[149]

1st Lt. Robert W. Fenton, HQ Co., from Michigan, recalled that on the night of the 26th, as about 40 or 50 survivors of *LST 422* stood in a field at Anzio, he and Maj. David W. Meyerson, along with a weapons carrier driver, were sent to Nettuno to retrieve some blankets from the Quartermaster supply for the survivors. During the trip, they experienced a near miss during a German air raid, and drove their vehicle into a huge bomb crater from which they had to be pulled out by a British DUKW.[150]

The total cost in life and equipment would not be known for weeks but once it was finally submitted the 83rd Chemical Battalion could list 303 dead and approximately 188 survivors [*at least 4 names unaccounted for - also conflicts with the 202 survivors & 293 killed*]; the 68th Coastal Artillery between 13 to 15 dead and six to eight survivors [*only 1 accounted for*]; and the Royal Navy, at least 29 known dead and only 10 named survivors positively identified [*apparently 36 survived*]. There was also the one known survivor of the 488th Port Battalion, assuming he actually was on the ship. This added up to a total loss of life on *LST 422* of approximately 347 and between 232 to 233 survivors. The *LCI 32* lost 31 men and had 17 wounded. *LCI 32* also reported the loss of various registered publications, commissary reports, the Purple Heart medal of Coxswain Victor Dale Saunders, which had been kept in the ship's safe, and other materials.[151]

Although it came at a high cost, and certainly not by intent, the 83rd had once again led the way in innovations, this time impacting future naval rescues. Air life belts and jackets, as previously noted by *YMS 43*, were quite inadequate, and added to the report that "Many of the men were struggling through the water with them uninflated." Additionally, following observation of hundreds of bodies in the water, Lt. Elliott B. Knowlton, executive officer, USNR, of *U.S.S. Strive*, supported this claim when he reported, "Kapok life jackets (Navy Issue) on the bodies of men floating in the water on the morning of 26 January were seen to have completely ridden up over the heads of many of them. The collars of the jackets were above the surface, but the heads were beneath. Contributory causes may have been the result of too loosely tied drawstrings, especially on the collars. However, it is the consensus of nearly all those who noted these facts that the addition of a broad crotch strap might solve the problem. Such a device is in use ... and has been tested to satisfaction by this vessel. The strap in question (canvas or leather) is on the order of a saddle cinch sewn to the hem on the waist of the jacket-back, passed under the crotch, and then secured by tie-ties or buttons in the front. Snaps are considered too insecure from concussion." In sending recommendations to the brass he suggested, "the oral inflated life belt may be helpful as long as the wearer has the strength to control his motion, but when he tires the life belt keeps his waist up and allows his head to go under water. Those wearing kapok jackets were noted to have slipped through them which allowed the head to go under water. All drawstrings should be tied tightly. A canvas band is attached to all kapok jackets on this vessel and is secured under the crotch to prevent the jacket from riding up over the wearers head. This procedure was amply demonstrated as being sound by the positions of the life jackets on the bodies. Lastly it was concluded that in a rough and cold sea rescue operations must be carried out very quickly to save the personnel in the water. Hanging on to a raft or piece of wreckage would appear to be the most likely means of survival." Admiral F. J. Lowry liked the recommendation regarding the kapok life belts but noted, "if all ties are drawn, especially the collar tie, the [*crotch*] strap should be unnecessary."[152]

The other lesson learned from the disaster, as previously noted by the *U.S.S. Pilot*, concerned the wooden floats on the cargo nets. The ship's commander stated, " ... proper equipment for life saving purposes, made up for immediate use, is needed. Short lengths of line with a hook on one end for securing about a man's waist, as well as blocks rigged on deck to aid in hauling a man aboard, are needed for this type of work. The present type of cargo net, with its wooden float on the outboard end, which bobbed up and down as the ship rolled in the trough of the sea, was more of a menace than an aid. More than one person was struck on the head and pushed beneath the surface of the water by this wooden float. Instead of a cargo net, a wide ladder made up of chain with wooden rungs is suggested. This type of ladder will remain against the ship's side no matter how much the ship may roll. The foolishness of a person going over the side with no line secured to him was witnessed by all … "[153]

A number of officers from the various rescue craft also reported their crews needed additional and better training in first aid and in administering artificial respiration. Ironically, companies C and D of the 83rd, the hardest hit in the tragedy, reverted back to battalion control during the day. Perhaps one of the most ironic statements came from Acting Commander C. M. Dalrymple-Hay, Royal Navy, commander of 2nd LST Flotilla and *H.M. LST 425*, that " … ships loaded with ammunition should also not be loaded with petrol. Had this not been the case, it is possible that 422 might have been saved." Undoubtedly, all of these lessons learned would be taken into consideration the next time the 83rd, or anyone else familiar with the *LST 422*, participated in any type of amphibious or naval operation.[154]

The morning hours of January 27th found many of the rescue vessels of the previous day transferring survivors to other ships or medical facilities, including *LCI 209*, which transferred their men to an Army hospital at Anzio harbor. *YMS 43* got underway at 7:10 to locate an LST to take their survivors to Naples while at 7:45 the bodies of Fullagar and Ridenour of the 83rd were given a burial at sea by *Strive*. At 7:55, *YMS 3* came alongside *YMS 226* to pick up their crewman, John Hanway, who fell overboard the previous day during rescue operations. *LST 383* reported at 8:10 various minesweepers and escort vessels alongside transferring survivors for transport to Naples, including *YMS 62*, which transferred their remaining 14 survivors to *SC 506*, and *YMS 43*, which transferred their survivors to *LST 383* at 8:14.[155]

YMS 3, while at the entrance to Anzio harbor at 8:40 waiting to transfer survivors, came under another enemy air attack, which dropped a bomb within 30 feet of the port bow. By 9:00, *YMS 36* was moored alongside *LST 383* transferring survivors and a casualty and, at 9:07, at the request of *Pilot*, the *SC 522* came alongside the ship to receive 22 survivors to be transported to *LST 383*. Between 9:20 and 9:30, *YMS 226* debarked all their survivors, including 21 from the 83rd, who were evacuated to the 93rd Evacuation Hospital via truck and ambulance, and five members of the Royal Navy, who were ordered to report to Capt. Turner, Royal Navy, on *HMS LST 315*. Among these 83rd survivors were T/5 Edward J. Buchanan, Co. A, from Camden County, New Jersey, who had injuries of the left wrist and ankle, and T/5 William C. Domyon, Co. C, of Passaic County, New Jersey, who suffered a head abrasion.[156]

YMS 3 tied up alongside *LST 383* around 9:25 transferring survivors, and at 9:30 *YMS 62* held burial services for Pvt. Warren K. Runkle of the 83rd. At 9:35, *YMS 43* held a burial at sea ceremony for George L. Marsh, RM2c, USNR, of *LCI 32*. After the service was read his body was committed to the sea at the 50-fathom curve. Crewman Jules Nemes said, "It was the first burial at sea that I had ever witnessed and I hope to God it will be the last. The boatswain sewed up the body in a canvas his usual way and our skipper said a short prayer and his body was committed to the deep." Also at 9:35, *LCI 10* went alongside *Strive* and took aboard the survivors of *LCI 32*, each of whom had been treated for shock, and put them ashore. Eventually all *LCI 32* survivors were transferred to Bizerte, Tunisia, for further transfer to the U.S., the officers going independently and the enlisted men under the charge of BM1c Harry Humphries. At 9:40, the crew of *YMS 226*, under direction of Lt. Coes, Medical Corps, USNR, debarked the 18 dead bodies via the fantail and laid them out on the beach to be picked up by ambulances or trucks from the U.S. Army Graves Registration. *SC 522* pulled alongside *LST 383* at 10:15 to transfer survivors, as did *YMS 69*, including their own MoMM2c J. W. Gwyn, who had been wounded by shrapnel during an enemy glider bomb attack on the ship the previous evening. Daniel Shields, who had been rescued by *YMS 43*, was among the survivors transferred to *LST 383*, which unloaded 39 British trucks at Anzio before sailing to Naples. Shields recalled the irony of being surrounded by lifejackets on the trip. *LST 16* reported five survivors aboard at 12:10, including three Navy men from *LCI 32*, for transport to Naples, and later in the day, at 3:05 p.m., *LST 16* was reported underway to Naples transporting 86 casualties [*possibly survivors*]. At 5:11 p.m., *YMS 69* came alongside *Pilot* and transferred A. J. Freid, lost overboard from *Pilot* the previous day.[157]

While such activity continued to transpire in the harbor area of Anzio, operations persisted on land, where many of the 83rd continued to be unaware of the fate of their comrades. Exceptions included Lawrence H. Powell, Co. A, from Ambridge, Pennsylvania, who said he was among a group sent to the shore to assist any survivors. While walking the beach he spotted two dog-tags on a chain glistening in the surf and upon inspection found them to be those of Pvt. Theodore ("Teddy") Beley, Co. C, a boyhood friend from Pennsylvania. Powell lamented, "Tears filled my eyes when I read the name."[158]

Lt. Andre N. Laus, Co. A, stayed with the CO of the 509th Parachute Battalion, and Col. Darby of the Ranger Force told Lt. Col. Hutchinson that when moving to the crossroads the following day his Ranger operation would not concern the 83rd very much but to be careful not to fire mortars on friendly troops. Col. Darby also requested Lt. Col. Hutchinson have the mortars of Co. B remain in position and support his forces in a short advance. Throughout the day the various platoons of the two companies would be relieved and move to alternate positions a number of times. James Helsel, Co. A, gave an overview of the day as he wrote, "We got up early again, after breakfast we started digging for Pvt. Crutz again, also looking for some idea that would give us an idea what it was, but all that could be found was pieces of aluminum. Toward dinner we fired a few rounds on the 'factory'. It was flat plains and we could see our shells hitting the building. Also a half track carrying the Ace of Spades belonging to one of the Rangers BN pulled in right next to our gun. They had a 75mm gun mounted on it. They could fire 10 rounds while we were getting ours ready … "[159]

Good news arrived at about 11:30 a.m. when Cpl. Talmadge Carter reported spotting Lt. Ed Trey at Anzio, apparently having survived the *LST 422* tragedy, and later reports arrived that lieutenants Justin G. ("Jerry") Woomer, of Yeagerstown, Pennsylvania, and Robert W. Smith had also survived. Co. A's James Helsel added, "A little after noon the third and fourth squads loaded up in jeeps with our ammo and mortars and we moved into position back of a German hospital about three miles beyond the main Line of Resistance, in support of a Paratroop Patrol. We fired upon enemy position in a house, reports were it was very effective … Our mortar came loose from the jeep when we pulled up out of a deep canal … "[160]

Around 6:30 p.m., Lt. Col. Hutchinson told Darby the only activity in his area was one man had been trampled by a bull, confirmed by "Doc" Hulcher, who said his first casualty of the 83rd at Anzio had been brought to his station, " … a soldier hit by a bull while digging a foxhole." He actually wrote this in his diary entry for the 26th although the entry is in general terms covering a period of time. In a separate incident Hulcher also repaired a laceration on the hand of a German prisoner. Lt. Col. Hutchinson also said he had moved his two mortar companies into the 509th Parachute Infantry sector. Additionally, Hutchinson received a message from Darby at 7:16 p.m. that at daylight he wanted the mortars to "fire like hell. I want noise; lots of it." Late in the evening, Darby requested the 83rd sweep a

ARTHUR H. SINCLAIR

Arthur H. Sinclair

Gary Bedingfield

Arthur H. ("Art") Sinclair was born in 1918 at Haddonfield, New Jersey, was a star athlete at Haddonfield Memorial High School, and was signed by the New York Giants after graduation. By 1936 he was pitching and playing outfield in the independent leagues in Camden County with the Lucas Athletic Association in the Lower County League and the New York Shipbuilding Corporation team in the South Jersey League. Sinclair was one of the leading hitters in the Camden County League and led the league in hitting in 1942 with a .491 average.

Arthur was inducted into the Army July 9, 1942, at Camden, New Jersey, and served as a private in Co. C, 83rd Chemical (Motorized) Battalion at Camp Gordon, Georgia during 1942 and was promoted to Private First Class, Co. C, Motor Pool January 25, 1943. By 1944 he had risen to the rank of Technician Fifth Grade and died in the LST 422 tragedy at Anzio, Italy, January 26, 1944. His name appears alongside his many battalion comrades on the Tablets of the Missing in the Sicily-Rome American Cemetery at Nettuno, Italy.

Special thanks to Gary Bedingfield and his Baseball in Wartime website.

The Lucas Athletic Association team, Lower County League champions in 1934. Art Sinclair is circled. *Gary Bedingfield*

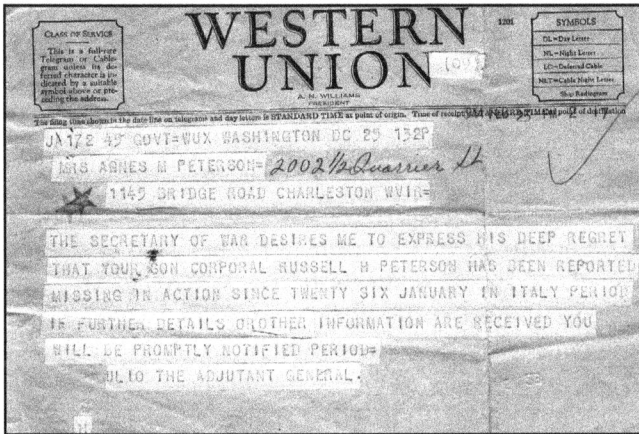

Telegrams announcing the loss of Russell
H. Peterson, Co. D. *Peterson Collection*

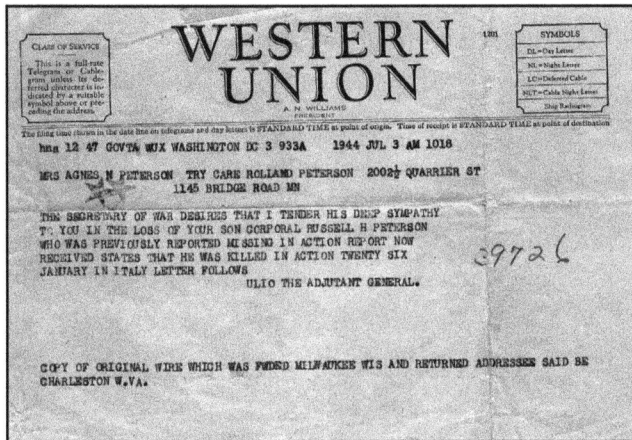

Russell H. Peterson, Co. D.

Peterson Collection

Personal effects of Russell H. Peterson, Co. D, killed
in the *LST 422* disaster, including his eye glasses
and case, General Headquarters Reserve patch, brass
Chemical Warfare Service disc, supplemental shoulder
stripes, Purple Heart, and hat. *Peterson Collection*

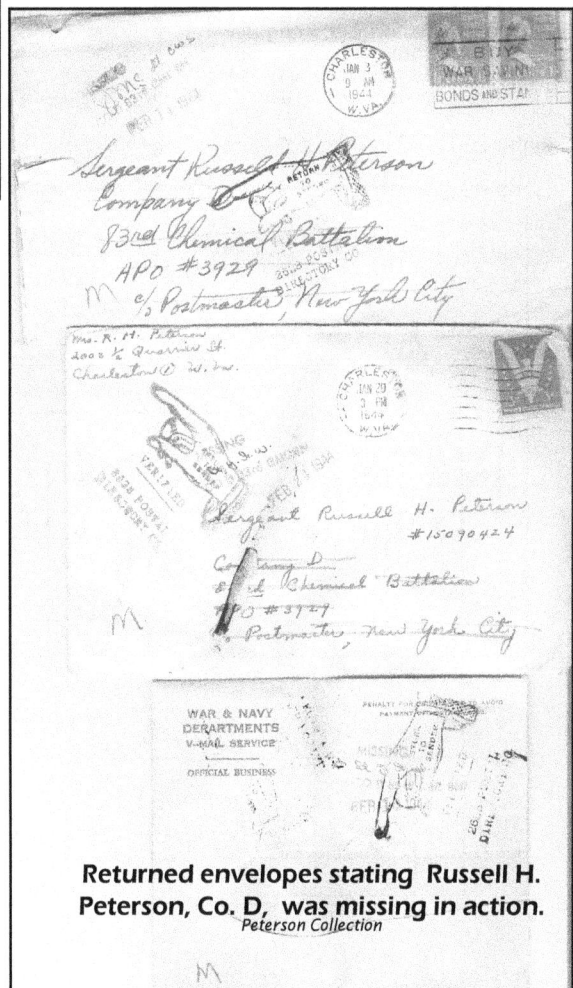

**Returned envelopes stating Russell H.
Peterson, Co. D, was missing in action.**
Peterson Collection

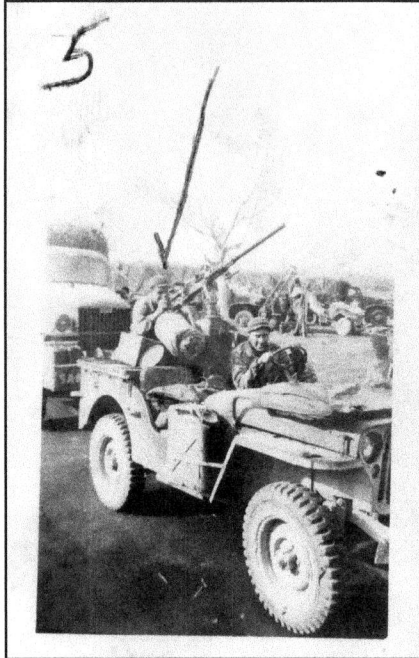

designated patch of woods with mortar fire. Also during the day the battalion CP had moved forward to a haystack and the room of a nearby residence was used as an aid station.[161]

At Naples, Lt. Perry A. Rice and T/Sgt. Arthur J. Usher checked the hospitals for *LST 422* survivors, many of whom had spent from three to five hours in the water before being rescued by minesweepers and other small naval boats, which had transferred them to a landing craft to be taken to Naples. Three officers and 42 enlisted survivors were found, as would be a number of others throughout the ensuing days. The Ranger Force at Anzio had also received a message that companies C and D of the 83rd had reverted to parent unit control on the 26th.[162]

Above: John Simurda, Jr., a jeep driver, and Stephen Vukson. Clyde L. Thorson, a survivor of *LST 422*, saved the photo from going down with the ship. As a result, the photo turned pink from exposure to salt water. *Stephen Vukson*

Right: *LST 422* in port. *British Archives*

"ALL SHIPS" AVERAGE REVOLUTIONS	BY REVS.		BY LOG		COURSE (P. C.) Gyro __ Mag. __ (Indicate which)	WIND		BAROMETER		TEMPERATURE			WEATHER, BY SYMBOLS	CLOUDS			VISIBILITY	SEA	
	NAUTICAL MILES	TENTHS	NAUTICAL MILES	TENTHS		DIRECTION	FORCE	HEIGHT IN INCHES	READING AT. THER.	AIR, DRY BULB	AIR, WET BULB	WATER AT SURFACE		FORM	MOVING FROM—	AMOUNT		CONDITION	SWELLS FROM—
1	2	3	4	5	6	7	8	9	10	11	12	13	14	15	16	17	18	19	20
—					Anchor	WSW	4	29.92		56	54		BC	a Cu	WSW	3	5	2	WSW
—					"	WSW	3	29.92		56	54		BC	a Cu	WSW	3	10	2	WSW
—					"	WSW	3	29.92		55	53		BC	a Cu	WSW	3	10	2	WSW
—					"	W	6	29.90		55	53		C-L	a Cu	W	6	10	2	W
—					"	WNW	7	29.86		54	52		C-L	H Cu	WNW	7	10	4	WNW
—					"	WNW	7	29.85		49	47		C-L	H Cu	WNW	8	10	4	WNW
—					"	WNW	4	29.90		47	47		C	H Cu	WNW	8	10	4	WNW
—					Var.	WNW	4	29.91		52	50	5	C	Cu nb	WNW	9	10	6	WNW
69.4					280	WNW	3	29.92		52	50	58	C	Cu nb	WNW	8	4	6	WNW
66.6					300	WNW	3	29.93		53	50	58	C	H Cu	WNW	8	10	6	WNW
24.3					270	NW	2	29.94		52	50	58	BC	H Cu	NW	5	15	4	W
84.1					Var.	NW	3	29.93		52	50	58	BC	a Cu	NW	5	30	4	W

THE UNITED STATES SHIP ___PILOT___ (Name) ___AM 104___ (Identification Number)

WEDNESDAY 26 (Day) JANUARY (Date), 1944 (Month)

ription ___-1___ S.B. WETMORE LT. COMDR , ___ U. S. Navy, Commanding.

Section of the log book of rescue ship *U.S.S. Pilot* for January 26, 1944. Note the decreasing weather conditions during the morning. *National Archives*

Casualties of LST 422
83rd Chemical (Motorized) Battalion

Headquarters & Headquarters Company

MERRILL, Leonard A., Jr., 1st. Lt., NH

JONES, Marion F., T/Sgt, MD

MORELAND, Henry A., Cpl., NJ

BENNETT, Carlton A., T/4, VA

TOALDO, Arthur C., T/5, NJ

BAUER, Carl J., Pfc., MI

BUSH, William, Pfc., PA

Medical Detachment

HEATH, William S., T/4, PA

BLOUNT, James G., T/5, MS

GIBBS, Charles J., T/5, VA

CUMMING, Arthur G., Pfc., NJ

MILLER, Moses, Pvt., NY

Company A

HUBBS, Joshua B., S/Sgt., IL

CUMMINGS, Robert S., T/5, RI

HOTKO, Leo W., T/5, PA

SMALL, Rufus A., T/5, GA

CLINE, William L., Pfc., TN

HALL, Arvel H., Pfc., TN

SCHLEGEL, James M., Pfc., PA

SOLEY, Andrew, Pfc., PA

PRICE, John N., Pvt., PA

Company B

NICHOLS, Jean B., S/Sgt., CA

DYER, Lester J., T/4, NJ

HOFFMAN, Stanley W., T/4, PA

SOLERO, Casildo M., T/4, NY

McBRYDE, Clyde E., T/5, MS

CHILDRESS, Albert D., Pfc., AL

CULPEPPER, Joel B., Pfc., GA

JONES, James E., Pfc., AL

KUYKENDALL, John L., Pfc., MS

LE DOYEN, Charles J., Pvt., MD

MASON, Roger B., Pvt., MS

STEPHENSON, George E., Pvt., IN

Company C

GABRIEL, Donald R., 1st. Lt., NY

RANKIN, Ralph T., 1st. Lt., OK

FINLAY, James M., 1st. Sgt., NY

CRAMER, Alfred F., S/Sgt., NJ

KINNETZ, Harry C., S/Sgt., NY

SAPIO, Salvatore, S/Sgt., PA

SHADDINGER, Earl, S/Sgt., PA

BILLIG, Jack L., Sgt., PA

CHANCELLOR, Clifton E., Sgt., MS

DE VITA, Joseph C., Sgt., NY

DUNDON, Edward T., Sgt., MA

GAISKI, Walter, Sgt., KY

HARDIN, James E., Sgt., MS

HEADLAND, Charles B., Sgt., PA

WOODIN, Harry W., Jr., Sgt., MA

HAMPTON, James R., Cpl., VA

PUTNAM, Elmer E., Pfc., PA

RIVELLO, Carmen M., Pfc., PA

RUGITO, Donald, Pfc., PA

THOMAS, Kenneth N., Pfc., KY

THOMSEN, Walter P. H., Pfc., IA

WILSON, Frank R., Pfc., VA

WOJTYNA, John A., Pfc., PA

ABBOTT, John R., Pvt. IL

AFRICANO, Sullivan John, Pvt., WV

BALTZER, Robert R., Pvt., MI

BROOKS, Frederick L., Pvt., PA

BUCK, Paul, Pvt., VA

CASSELS, Richard I., Pvt., MS

DAVIADOFF, Alexander, Pvt., NJ

DE MARTELEIRE, Charles, Pvt., PA

DE MATTEO, Jospeh, Pvt., CT

Company C (continued)

MARTINO, Bertram G., Cpl., PA	EARLEY, James D., Pvt., MS
MOORE, Robert M., Jr., Cpl., TN	FULLAGAR, Robert L., Pvt., NJ
PAGANO, Alphonse A., Cpl., NJ	GENTRY, Hershel E., Pvt., MS
POKORSKY, Stanley, Cpl., NJ	GRECZKKOWSKI, John R., Pvt., NY
WEIKEL, Paul E., Cpl., OH	HAWKINS, Edward W., Pvt., VA
FRAIND, Andrew J., T/4, PA	JACKSON, Lawrence A., Pvt., TN
McGOVERN, John F., T/4, RI	JAMES, Grady, Pvt. AL
CARROLL, Charles W., Pfc., MD	JOHNSON, Daniel G., Jr., Pvt., PA
HRABIK, George, T/5, PA	JONES, George C., Pvt., VA
LYNCH, John W., T/5, NJ	JONES, Ross J., Pvt., MO
MATHEWS, John J., T/5, NJ	KALEDA, Charles A., Pvt., PA
PHENEGER, William W., T/5, NJ	KAPRUSAK, Michael J., Pvt., CT
RUNKLE, Warren R., T/5, PA	KENNEDY, Duncan M., Pvt., GA
SINCLAIR, Arthur H., T/5, NJ	KRZECKOWER, Sam, Pvt., NY
BELEY, Theodore, Pfc., PA	LACY, Hudson M., Pvt., VA
BRASH, Italo A., Pfc., PA	LEWIS, Jack, Pvt., KY
CAROTHERS, Edward F., Pfc., PA	LIBASSI, Philip J., Pvt., NY
CARROLL, Roy, T/5, GA	LOEB, Bruno, Pvt., NY
CARVER, William D., Pfc., GA	LOVE, Emmet C., Jr., Pvt., IN
DICKERSON, Joseph (Joe) C., Jr., Pfc., MS	LUCAS, John F., Pvt., PA
DONOGHUE, Joseph M., Pfc., PA	LUGO, Filemon, R., Pvt., NY
DUDENICH, Peter, Pfc., PA	MAKOWSKI, Stephen V., Pvt., PA
DUNLAP, Winfred L., Pfc., MS	MASTERSON, Lawrence, Pvt., OH
DUNWIDDIE, Walter L. Jr., Pfc., PA	McAULEY, Thomas L., Pvt., MA
DURHAM, Parks H., Jr., Pfc., GA	MEADE, Edward J., Pvt.
ELLISON, Luther L., Pfc., MS	MERRITT, Herman L., Pvt., NC
FORTUNE, John C., Pfc., MS	METTRICK, William J., Pvt., PA
GAY, William H., Pfc., MS	MYERS, Jim C., Pvt., TN
GEIGER, William J., Pfc., PA	NACCARATO, Ross J., Pvt., PA
HALE, Olen J., Pfc., MS	NELSON, Carl, Pvt., NY
HILL, Richard K., Pfc., PA	NICHOLS, Theron E., Pvt., GA
HILT, Arlin E., Pfc., PA	NICKENS, Bynum H., Pvt., TN
HUGHES, John T., Pfc., VA	NIZIOLEK, Edmund S., Pvt., OH
JACKSON, William B., Pfc., AL	O REAR, Lecil E., Pvt., AL
JACKSON, Zelmer L., Pfc., MS	ORTLIEB, Elwood L., Pvt., KY
JENNINGS, Orie (Orrie) L., Pfc., MS	PACHINSKI, Walter, Pvt., PA
JOHNSON, Daniel A., Pfc., AL	PAGE, DeWitt T., Jr., Pvt., IL
KNIGHT, Maxie L., Pfc., MS	PALIOTTA, John S., Pvt., RI
KOELLING, Harold A., Pfc., MO	PALMER, James F., Pvt., SC
LAMBERT, Dennis B., Pfc., IN	PARKS, James F., Pvt., NJ
LE BLANC, Wilfred E., Pfc., MA	PAYNE, R. V. (Rio V.), Pvt., GA
LEAP, Jerome G., Pfc., PA	PEYTON, Joe P., Pvt., TN

Company C (continued)

LUKUS, Michael J., Pfc., PA

MANSFIELD, Isaac A., Pfc., TN

MCDANIEL, Edgar W., Pfc., GA

MIGNELLA, Peter, Pfc., OH

NEELD, Robert E., Pfc., PA

OCHABA, Martin, Pfc., PA

Company D

CLUBB, Guy L., Jr., 2nd. Lt., IA

DONALD, James M., 2nd. Lt., NJ

FICHTLER, Rudolph M., S/Sgt., NJ

GUINNESS, Edward D., S/Sgt., NY

NESTLER, Max E., S/Sgt., NJ

WHITE, Woodrow W., S/Sgt., MA

FEIFER, John A., Sgt., RI

JOHNSON, Edwin I., Sgt., RI

JOHNSON, Leo W., Sgt., UT

KARCAUSKAS, Joseph J., Sgt., NJ

METCALF, Raymond O., Sgt., GA

STANLEY, Edward R., Sgt., TN

FABER, Stephen, Cpl., NJ

LATIMER, Eugene R., Cpl., NJ

PETERSON, Russell H., Cpl., WV

SIRMONS, Henry J., Cpl., GA

SWIFT, James L., Cpl., MN

NOLAN, James H., Jr., T/4, NY

STEFANKO, John, T/4, PA

BERRYHILL, Murray H., T/5, MS

DUDLEY, James J., T/5, VA

GLOSSNER, Nevin L., T/5, PA

ALDRIDGE, Ervin C., Pfc., MS

ALLEN, Paul H., Pfc.,MS

BARILE, Bernard J., Pvt., NY

BAXTER, Fletcher C., Pfc.,MS

BOWEN, James H. (N.), Pfc., TX

BREWER, Luther M., Pfc., MS

BRIDGE, Richard A., Pfc., PA

BRINKMAN, Raymond W., Pfc., PA

CAMP, Howard, Pfc., MS

CINNAJINNY, Frank B.,Pfc., AZ

CLAYTON, James H., Pfc., MS

CURTIS, Leon, Pfc., MO

GARCIA, Louis F., Pfc., NY

REVAK, John W., Pvt., PA

RHOADS, Billy C., Pvt., IA

SMALLWOOD, Kenneth B., Pvt., TN

URSO, Nathaniel L., Pvt., DC

VITELO, Giro, Pvt., CT

WATERS, David L., Pvt., MS

WORRALL, George E., Pfc., PA

YEAGER, Robert H., Pfc., PA

ALTSCHULER, Jack, Pvt., NY

ANDERSON, John E., Pvt., TN

ATKINS, William M., Pvt., TN

AUBLE, Louis P., Pvt., IN

BARCLAY, Kenneth R., Pvt., PA

BENSON, Arlander F., Pvt., MS

BILTON, Arthur W., Pvt., PA

BOEHMER, Stephen J., Pvt., MO

BRUNOW, Robert, Pvt., MO

CANNON, Willis L., Pvt., MS

ENDSLEY. Robert W., Pvt., IL

FANNIN, Robert F., Pvt., PA

GESSNER, John C., Pvt., NJ

HALL, Coy, Pvt., MS

HITT, James W., Pvt., SC

HOLDEN, Homer G., Pvt., NC

JOHNSON, Gerald E., Pvt., MO

KIMBLER, James H., Pvt., WV

KNIGHT, Robert D., Pvt., AL

KUYKENDALL, George C., Pvt.

LEONARD, James E., Pvt., TX

LINKO, Michael, Pvt., PA

MESARIS, Francis A., Pvt., PA

MILLER, Marcus D., Pvt.,

MLYNIEC, Michael J., Pvt., IL

MONGIARDO, Dante, Pvt., NY

MOODY, Calvin D., Pvt., GA

MYERS, John F., Pvt., TN

NAIRN, William P., Pvt., PA

PERKOWSKI, John J., Pvt., IL

PHILLIPS, Viron H., Pvt., MS

PINK, Saul, Pvt., NY

PLEASANTS, Thomas M., Pvt., VA

Company D (continued)

GORDON, Thomas B., Pfc., MS

HARTGROVE, Loranza E., Pfc., VA

HOFMANN, William J., Pfc., PA

HOUGH, Carl R., Pfc.,MS

JONES, Roy E., Pfc., TN

OBENSHAIN, Raymond E., Pfc., VA

POTTER, Mabry L., Pfc., TX

PRICE, Charlie M., Pfc., GA

REBICK, Michael J., Pfc., PA

REILLY, Walter J., Pfc., NJ

RIDENOUR, William W., Pfc., TN

RUSY, Albert, Pfc., NY

RUTH, Walter G., Pfc., MD

SILVERT, Edwin S., Pfc., PA

SMITH, Marvin W., Pfc., NC

SORKEN, Nathan, Pfc., NY

STANGANELLI, Saverio, Pfc., MA

STANTON, John J., Pfc., MD

STEPANOVICH, Peter, Pfc., PA

STRAUSSER, Edwin C., Pfc., PA

STROCK, Zachariah W., Jr., Pfc., VA

SWEETING, George R., Pfc., MD

SWETLAND, George L., Pfc., OR

TUCK, Clay, Pfc., PA

UCCELLO, Salvatore M., Pfc., ME

VANCE, Charles, Pfc., PA

WHEELER, Paul R. (F.), Pfc., MS

WHEELER, Wiley B., Pfc., MS

WHELAN, Andrew J., Pfc., PA

WILLIAMS, Duvard H., Pfc., GA

POIRIER, Joseph M., Pvt., MI

PORCHI, Joseph J., Pvt., NY

PUGH, Lewis D., Pvt., PA

RHODES,Robert L., Pvt., SC

ROGERS, Howard M., Pvt., TN

ROUTLEDGE, Howard E., Pvt., MO

SCOTT, James U. L., Pvt., TN

SEDGWICK, William P., Pvt., OH

SHAIRA, Charles A., Pvt., NJ

SHARKIS, Frank A.,Pvt., MA

SHOAF, Carl S., Pvt., PA

SIMS, Shannon, Pvt., GA

SNEED, Charles M., Jr., Pvt., VA

SNYDER, Wilbur A., Pvt., NJ

STABILE, Alfonso P., Pvt., MA

SULLIVAN, William E., Pvt., NY

SWAIN, Robert H., Pvt., OR

TEAL, Edward F., Pvt., NY

TEWELL, Orville D., Pvt., OH

THORNTON, Herman L., Pvt., OK

TICHENOR, Sinclair J., Pvt., NJ

VIRGEN, Isidro P., Pvt., TX

WACLAWSKI, Joseph S., Pvt., PA

WEBSTER, Walter R., Pvt., SC

WHEELER, L. H., Pvt., TX

WIGGINS, Thomas W., Pvt., MS

WILLARD, (Williard), Tillmon, Pvt., TN

WILSON, Harry W., Pvt., PA

WIX, Robert N., Pvt., TN

Survivors of LST 422
83rd Chemical (Motorized) Battalion

Headquarters & Headquarters Company

EDWARDS, Robert E., Capt., Murphysboro, IL (HQ Co.)

CRENSHAW, Alfred H., 1st Lt., Houston, TX

FORRESTER, Alfred L., 1st Lt., Quincy, IL (Co. D)

MCKINNON, Julian T., 1st Lt., Wyoming, OH (Co. D)

TREY, Edward L., 1st Lt., Grand Rapids, MI

ALEXANDER, John E., 2nd Lt., MI (Co. C)

DOYLE, James L., 2nd Lt., Philadelphia, PA (Co. C)

WOOMER, Justin G., 2nd Lt.,Yeagertown, PA

THORSON, Clyde L., M/Sgt., Morris, IL

PLASSMAN, Eugene A., S/Sgt., Bronx, NY

HALL, Harold C., T/5, New Albany, MS

SHAW, Claude J., T/5, Milwaukie, OR

ADAIR, Kenneth C., Pfc., Ephrata, PA

FREET, Douglas W., Pfc., Hanover, PA

Headquarters & Headquarters Company (continued)

KULAGA, Fred J., 2nd Lt., Lawrence, MS

SMITH, Robert W., 2nd Lt. (Co. C)

MERRILL, Stillwell A., Pfc., Collinsville, IL

Medical Detachment

DEMARCO, Silverino V., Capt., Jersey City, NJ

BUFKIN, Henry D., Pfc, Port Gibson, MS

WILLIAMS, Curtis A., Pfc., Marks, MS

Company A

TRANCHITELLA, Peter A., S/Sgt., Wildwood Villa, NJ

BOSKO, Joesph A., T/4, Camden Co., NJ

BUCHANAN, Edward J., T/5, Camden Co., NJ

BOUTYARD, Frank W., Pfc., Fredericksburg, VA

DOUGHERTY, James F., Pfc., Philadelphia, PA

GRIMM, Henry D., Pfc., Beaver Falls, PA

KREBS, Edward W., Pfc., Randallstown, MD

BLUE, Maxwell L., Pvt., Moore Co., NC

ATTON, Edward Kirk, Highland Park, MI

SABATINO, "Albert"/Alberto, Italian POW Cook

Company B

COLLINS, Arthur, T/5, Montgomery Co., GA

HILL, B. C., Pfc., Aberdeen, MS

MCMURRY, John S., Pfc., Hattiesburg, MS

DI RIENZO, John A., Pvt., PA

LAWLESS, Grady, Pvt., Laurel, MS

Company C

COHEN, Harry, 1st Sgt., Peoria, IL

CUTE, Thomas A., S/Sgt., Hornell, NY

HOLLEY, John R., S/Sgt., Oxford, MS

WIDING, Howard B., S/Sgt., St. Paul, MN

BONO, Millard O., Sgt., Perkinston, MS

EISENBERG, Harold, Sgt., Chicago, IL

GIRONE, Peter L., Sgt., Philadelphia, PA

JOHNSON, William E., Sgt., Davidson Co., TN

KROUS, Stanley J., Sgt., Douglas, MA

TILLMAN, Leonard R., Sgt., Donelson, TN

DEFEO, Anthony J., Cpl., Philadelphia, PA

LINK, Cecil S., Cpl., Cottontown, TN

LONG, Ralph L., Cpl., Shamokin, PA

ROSENFELD, Sylven M., Cpl., Wildwood, NJ

TOMBOLINI, Fred, Cpl., San Anselmo, CA

VOGEL, Julius D., Cpl., Sewickley, PA

WAHOSKY, Norman A., Cpl., Shamokin, PA

DOMYON, William G., T/5, Passaic Co., NJ

THOMPSON, Glenn C., T/5, Onawa, IA

WIGGINS, L. W., T/5, Millen, GA

LYONS, Rex E., T/4, Suffolk, VA

BRANDECKER, Elmer O., Pfc., Philadelphia, PA

FORD, William C., Pfc., New Albany, MS

GREGORY, William C., Pfc., New Albany, MS

HAJDINYAK, John J., Pfc., Bethlehem, PA

WEBB, Mack C., Pfc., Demorest, GA

YEATS, Carroll V., Pfc., Pittsylvania Co., VA

AGURKIS, Albert S., Pvt., PA

CHURCHILL, David H., Pvt., Detroit, MI

CLAGETT, Richard C., Pvt., Clarion, IA

DOWNEY, William H., Pvt., Newark, NJ

DUBOIS, Gerrad L., Pvt., Newport Center, VT

DUNAEFF, Alex J., Pvt., New York, NY

FOSTER, Herbert L., Pvt., Wilson Co., NC

GRISHAM, Louis, Pvt., New Albany, MS

GRISSOM, Floyd L., Pvt., Guntown, MS

HALL, Leonard E., Pvt., Nashville, TN

JEAN, L. V., Pvt., Condova, AL

JORDAN, William L., Pvt., Laurel, MS

KAADY, Abraham S., Pvt., Multnomah Co., OR

KENNEDY, John J., Pvt., Westfield, MA

KIMBLE, Alex, Pvt., Clover Gap, WV

KINDIG, Robert L., Pvt., Des Moines Co., IA

LAWING, Robert L., Pvt., Atlanta, GA

LICATA, Joseph L., Pvt., Leroy, NY

LOVELAND, Donald R., Pvt., Milwaukee, WI

MAGDZIAK, John J., Pvt., Ft. Calhoun, NE

MAHONEY, James P., Pvt., Carthage, NY

MARSHALL, Loy J., Pvt., Griffin, GA

MCLEAN, Troy V., Pvt., Upton, NC

Company C (continued)

HAMPTON, Ralph B., Pfc., Ooltewah, TN

HEPLER, Hale H., Pfc., Millboro Springs, VA

HILL, Bennie, Pfc., North Birmingham, AL

HOOVER, Raymond W., Pfc., PA

HUDAK, Albert G., Pfc., Wallington, NJ

HYDE, Claudy L., Pfc., Foxworth, MS

JACKSON, Edward L., Pfc., Lindale, GA

JOHNSON, Carl D., Pfc., Effingham, SC

JOHNSON, Ervin E., Pfc., Brainerd, MN

KUBAS, Albert J., Pfc., Wallington, NJ

MCCLAFFERTY, William T., Pfc., Pittsburgh, PA

RISLEY, Raymond N., Pfc., Camden, NJ

SALISBURY, Carl L., Pfc., Howison, VA

SIMONE, Angolo, Pfc., Merchantville, NJ

STANTON, John A., Pfc., Carmel, PA

UPCHURCH, Cohen R., Pfc., Little Crab, TN

MEANS, James J., Pvt., Jefferson Co., OH

MORONEY, James B., Pvt., Carthage, NY

NEMETH, Joseph A., Pvt., Chicago, IL

NESSERALLA, Edward A., Pvt., Brockton, MA

O'BERRY, Jesse J., Pvt., Isle of Wight Co., VA

O'SALLE, Samuel L., Pvt., Hendersonville, TN

OKERMAN, Gregory, Pvt.

PETERS, Donald W., Pvt., PA

PIERCE, Audie W., Pvt., Smithville, MS

PORTERFIELD, Arnold J., Pvt., Murfreesboro, TN

PRUIETT, Charles C., Pvt., Caruthersville, MO

ROLL, Irving, Pvt., Bronx, NY

SHAFER, Kenneth E., Pvt., Cuyahoga Falls, OH

WAGGY, Stanly W., Pvt., Fayetteville, PA

WHITT, Rudolph, Pvt., Bear Wallow, VA

Company D

CODEGA, Michelle P., 1st Sgt., Barrington, RI

LAURO, James V., S/Sgt., Ozone Park, NYA

FRAZIER, D. E., S/Sgt., Harris Co., TX

HADDOCK, Theodore D., Sgt., Avoca, PA

HOLSTEIN, Seymour A., Sgt., Newwark, NJ

JACKSON, Wofford L., Sgt., Manchester, GA

KEIGHTLY, Elwood J., Sgt., Philadelphia, PA

PARRA, William F., Sgt., Ridgefield Park, NJ

POSLUSZNY, Frank C., Sgt., Wellington, NJ

QUINA, Herbert R., Sgt., Washington, DC

RIDDLE, Clark H., Sgt., Greensburg, PA

BORKHUIS, George R., T/4, Bronx, NY

BURKETT, Claude T., Cpl., Bassfield, MS

DEIST, Leo C., Cpl., Meyersdale, PA

GRANT, Robert D., Cpl., Hollidaysburg, PA

GUTHRIE, Elwood, Cpl., Portsmouth, VA

HERRING, Dannie L., Cpl., Andrews, SC

SHIRLEY, George N., Cpl., Shubuta, MS

WAPNITSKY, Samuel, Cpl., NY

YAKUBISIN, George S., Cpl., Greensburg, PA

YOUNG, George G., Cpl., Mobile, AL

DEAN, Harold O., T/5, Aliquippa, PA

DIANA, Anthony, T/5, Swissvale, PA

HOOTEN, Ernest R., T/5, Depauw, IN

BELL, Orville P., Pfc., Union Co., MS

PIRANI, Eugene E., Pfc., Brooklyn, NY

PITTMAN, James H., Pfc., Buckeye, AZ

PUCKETT, Roland K., Pfc., Wauzeka, WI

RABAIOTTI, Antonia, Pfc., Providence, RI

RAMSEY, George W., Pfc., Lyons, CO

REGA, Michael A., Pfc., Detroit, MI

RENFROE, Tom. W., Pfc., Johnson Co., GA

RUBY, Paul H., Pfc., Detroit, MI

SALWACH, Frank, Pfc., Rivergrove, IL

SCHMIDT, George, Pfc., Lorain, OH

SCIASCI, Frank, Pfc., Ozone Park, NY

SHECKLER, Abraham E., Pfc., Venango, PA

SHIVELY, Clayton C., Pfc., Ludington, MI

SMITH, Murray, Pfc., Brooklyn, NY

TARASEK, George E., Pfc., Wilkes-Barre, PA

TAYLOR, Rollin E., Pfc., Union Point, GA

TURMELLE, Roland E., Pfc., Rochester, NH

VICKERS, James W., Pfc., Wadley, AL

WAUFLE, Gordon D., Pfc., Ilion, NY

WEHREIM, Robert J., Pfc., Clarion, IA

ZICKLER, Horst R., Pfc., St. Louis, MO

CARTWRIGHT, James A., Pvt., NY

COMBEST, James L., Pvt., Rantoul, IL

DUKE, Ralph A., Pvt., Bridgeport, AL

FREER, Robert H., Pvt., Vandercook Lake, MI

Company D (continued)

BEAVERS, Victor R., Pfc., Mize, MS

BELLOMO, James I., Pfc., Fairview, NJ

BLYSTONE, Leonard G., Pfc., Fairfield, TX

CHAMBLEE, Robert M., Pfc., Fulton, MS

CYGAN, William V., Pfc., Springfield, MS

GALLAHAN, James H., Pfc., Fredericksburg, VA

HILTZ, Verne E., Pfc., New Brunswick, Canada

JAMES, Jack L., Pfc., Millington, TN

JONES, Marvin C., Pfc., Hiram, GA

KANN, Earl F., Pfc., York, PA

KILLEBREW, Delmer, Pfc., DeKalb, TX

KUBERA, Teddy W., Pfc., PA

LIEBERMAN, Bennie, Pfc. Washington, DC

MCCULLEY, Lester H., Pfc., Painton, MO

MILLER, Daniel A., Pfc., Green, SC

PALMER, Joseph H., Pfc., Camilla, GA

PIMENTO, Jack, Pfc., Highland Falls, NY

PINCINCE, Leo P., Pfc., Woonsocket, RI

FUNYAK, George J., Pvt., Homestead, PA

HUGO, John L., Pvt., Osage, WV

KEEDY, Harlan V., Pvt., Auburn, NE

LA GRECA, Joseph A., Pvt., New York, NY

MAY, James, Pvt., Pontotoc, MS

ROSENBURG, Lawrence J., Pvt., New York, NY

SATTERFIELD, Ikey, Pvt., Armuchee, GA

SCHMIDT, William J., Jr., Pvt.

SHIELDS, Daniel J., Pvt., Philadelphia, PA

SLATE, Charles A., Pfc., Fulton Co. GA

STRICKLAND, Seth W., Pvt., Fair Bluff, NC

TRAFICONTE, Biagrio J., Pvt., Warwick, RI

ULIZIO, Bramo A., Pvt., Ambridge, PA

ZOLLER, Louis J., Pvt., Aliquippa, PA

BIELSKI, Walter A., PA

DAVIS, Porter R., Dalonega, GA

JOHNSON, Dexter L., Itwamba Co., MS

BOCELLA, Eugene R., Pfc., Philadelphia, PA. Company undetermined. Misidentified as member of Royal Navy when rescued.

Casulties of the 68th Coast Artillery

CHADWELL, Henry E., Pvt., Battery H, KY

CHARLES, Herbert C., Pvt., MA*

DERMID, Jefferson D. J., Battery H, Sgt., NC

DESROCHERS, Arthur J., Pvt., Battery E, ME

EDWARDS, Blane, T/5, Battery F, KY**

FARLEY, Edgar J., Pvt., Battery G, WV

FLANICK, John, Pfc., Battery F, PA

FRANKOFF, Michael, T/5, Battery G, PA

GIROUARD, Joseph O. C., T/5, Battery E, RI

MOSLEY, Hubert E., Pvt., Battery E, MS

PACHECO, Manuel, Pfc., Battery E, RI

RAZSA, Frank J., Pvt., HQ Battery, MA

ROYBAL, Esquipula, Pfc., NM

SAMA, Leopold, Pfc., Battery E, PA

WERTZ, Harry J., Pvt., Battery E, PA

All are on the Tablets of the Missing at Sicily-Rome American Cemetery, Nettuno, Italy.

(*) - Indicates ABMC says died Jan. 29, 1944 & does not appear on Unit Journal list.

(**) - Indicates ABMC says died Jan. 30, 1944 but does appear in Unit Journal list.

Survivors of 68th Coast Artillery

WEHDE, Henry C., 1st Lt., Battery E, NE

CAPLAN, Charles, Cpl., Battery E, MA

STATUS UNKOWN :

DiSANTO, Frank J., Pvt., HQ Battery, NY

NOVACENSKI, Joseph S., T/5, Battery E, MA

Known Casualties of the Royal Navy

BIRKS, Leonard, Able Seaman, Age: 27.

BOWMER, Stephen, Electrical Artificer 4c, Age: 33

CAMPBELL, Vivian George Martin, Petty Officer Motor Mechanic, Egham Surrey, Age: 34*

CLARK, Edward William, Stoker 2c, Westham, Weymouth Dorsetshire, Age: 29.

CROWTHER, Richard H., Act/Able Seaman, Sheffield, Age: 21.

DAVIES, John Richard, Sick Berth Attendant, Liverpool, Age: 19**

DRINKWATER, Frank W., Ordinary Signalman, Age: 20.

EMERY, Reginald, Steward, Uttoxeter, Staffordshire.

FRIEL, Arthur, Able Seaman, Shettleston, Glasgow, Age: 22.

HICKS, Stanley H., Shipwright 4c, Strood, Kent, Age: 27, (USS Pilot)

HOMEWOOD, Arthur C., Able Seaman.

HOTCHEN, Leslie Gordon, Act/Able Seaman, Finsburg, London, Age: 19*

HUNT, Arnold, Able Seaman, Barnsley, Yorkshire, Age: 19.

JAMES, Harry A., Chief Petty Officer, Chiswick, Middlesex, Age: 38.

KING, Graham Brooks Hibbert, Petty Officer Motor Mechanic**

KNOWLES, Alan, Act/Engine Room Artificer 4c, Flixton, Lancashire, Age: 23**

LOCK, James, Able Seaman, Grimsby, Lincolnshire, Age: 21***

MORGAN, Emrys, Stoker 1c, Epsom, Surrey, Age: 33.

MULLINS, Ronald H. J., Leading Stoker, Landford, Wiltshire, Age: 23.

NICOLSON, Archibald G., Steward, Garalopin-by-Portree, Isle of Skye, Inverness-shire, Age: 29

NORRIS, George U., Leading Stoker, Brighton, Sussex, Age: 31.

PAYNE, John H., Petty Officer Cook.

PENGELLY, Alfred, Able Seaman, Charlton, London, Age: 20, (YMS 226)

RHODES, Albert W., Leading Stores Assistant, Old Lenton, Nottingham, Age: 28.

SHEPPARD, Reginald E., Able Seaman, Newfoundland.

SMITH, Raymond, Signalman, Shoreham-by-Sea, Sussex, Age: 22.

TAYLOR, Vernon F., Able Seaman.

WALKER, Arthur F., Steward.

WHITE, Jack B., Signalman, Chiswick, Middlesex, Age: 26.

(*) - Indicates at the Beach Head War Cemetery, Anzio, Italy.

(**) - Indicates names appears on the Chatham Naval Memorial.

(***) - Indicates at the Naples War Cemetery, Naples, Italy.

All names with no asterisk are on the Portsmouth Naval Memorial.

The bodies of Campbell & Pengelly were recovered by *YMS 226*.

The body of Hicks was recovered by *Pilot*.

The body of Emery was recovered by *YMS 34* [identified by clothing marks]

Known Survivors of Royal Navy

ALLEN, Kenneth E. - rescued by YMS 43.

AUSTIN, C. - rescued by YMS 43.

BIONARD, F. S. - rescued by YMS 43.

BLANFORD, S. G. - rescued by YMS 43.

BROADHURST, Colin Lowe, Lt. Cmdr., RNR.

CHALLIS, (?) - rescued by YMS 43.

DICKIE, J. - rescued by YMS 43.

GREEN, H. H. - rescued by YMS 43.

HIGHAM, J. - rescued by YMS 43.

JOY, I. - rescued by YMS 43.

KENNEY, John Cox, A.S. - rescued by YMS 226.

MESSEDER, Leonard J., Stkr1c - rescued by YMS 226.

Known Survivors of Royal Navy (continued)

MORRIS, Benjamin E., A.S. - rescued by YMS 226.
RIDLEY, Joseph - rescued by YMS 43.
ROBERTS, Guy R. F., Tele. - rescued by YMS 226.
WHITTAKER, J., S.B.A.R. - rescued by YMS 69.

YMS 3 - rescued 1 unnamed Royal Navy
LCI 209 - rescued 1 unnamed Chief Petty Officer.

All men rescued by YMS 226 in satisfactory condition were landed at the Anzio port at 9:30 a.m., January 27, 1944 and ordered to report to Capt. Turner, Royal Navy, in *HMS LCI 315* for further orders.

Casualties of LCI 32

RUBENS, Earl Wesley., Ens., NY - missing - SR Cem
MARTELLO, Olindo Paul, Ens., MA - missing - SR Cem.
BROWN, Thomas Joseph, CK3, MD - missing - SR Cem.
GUETHLEIN, John Earl, F1c, MD - missing - SR Cem.
JACKSON, Robert Harry, MOMM1c, CA - reported as deceased - SR Cem.
PURCELL, David Andrew, GM2c, NJ - missing - SR Cem.
SALES, Eugene Levi, MOMM2c, WI - reported as deceased - SR Cem.
STAKE, Herbert, Jr., S1c, MA - missing - SR Cem.
CABANA, George Armand, SK2c, RI - missing - SR Cem.
FINCK, John William, SC2c, NY - missing - SR Cem.
HARDING, Ralph, MOMM2c, IN **** - drowned - bur. at sea and/or SR Cem.
CAMPBELL, John Eugene, EM3c, CT - missing - SR Cem.
KENNEDY, Lawrence Matthew, SC2c, ND - SR Cem.
RICHARDSON, Hamp Lee, STM3c, AL **** - injuries - multiple extreme - at sea and/or SR Cem.
MARSH, George L., RM2c, CO** - reported as deceased - bur. at sea and/or SR Cem.
MALLAMS, Dilbert Bevsn, Lt. (Navy Med. Corps)* drowned - bur. Anzio by Graves Registration
ELKIN(S), Jack, RM3c, MA**** - drowned - bur. at sea and/or SR Cem.
NARDELLA, Paul Lewis, Cox.* drowned - bur. Anzio by Graves Registration
NISBET, William Leslie, MoMM2c* - reported as deceased
SEAVEY, Charles Wilford, MoMM1c* - injuries - multiple extreme
JOHNSON, Warren George, S2c - missing
GILBRIDE, Charles Joseph, GM3c* - injuries - multiple extreme
DEMEOLA [Di Meola], Ralph Sebastian, RM2c, CT - missing - SR Cem.
KENNEDY, D. W., RT2c*** - missing
CROWE, John William, CSM (AA) - reported as deceased - NA Cem., Tunisia
HORRY, Joseph, St3c - missing - SR Cem.
KRUSELL, Godfrey Richard, SM3c - missing - SR Cem.
LAWSON, Donald Alexander, SM2c - missing - SR Cem.
MANNING, William J., RM1c - missing - SR Cem.
MESTAS, John Ignacious, RM3c - missing - SR Cem.
MISH, Stanley Thomas, RM3c - missing - SR Cem

(*) - Indicates body was recovered by YMS 226 and brought to Anzio port at 9:40 a.m., January 27, 1944, to be called for and disposed of by the U.S. Army Graves registration.
(**) - Indicates body was recovered by YMS 43.
(***) - Indicates body was recovered by U.S.S. Pilot.
(****) - Indicates body was recovered by YMS 34. [identified by clothing marks].

<u>*Survivors of LCI 32*</u>

WILSON, Edward Webster, Flotilla Cmdr. - wounded - Strive
FITZGERALD, Maynes C., Lt. Cmdr. - Strive
BIRD, O. J., Y1c. - Strive
MARCEY, Joseph Theodore, Cox. - wounded - Strive.
MILLER, Elmer M., MoMM2c - wounded - Strive
BROWN, Leonard R., Cox - wounded - Strive
SIMON. A. A., RM2c - Strive
BENCE, Roy, QM3c - Strive
BLACK, Thompson, Lt. Cmdr. (Staff) - wounded -YMS 58
WEISBROD, William, Lt. (Staff) - wounded -YMS 58
KALB, Floyd, Lt. (Staff) - wounded - YMS 58
GILMORE, Horace W., Lt. (jg.) (Staff) - YMS 58
CARLTON, Pritchard, Ens. - YMS 58
PERKINS, Clarence, SK1c. (Staff) - wounded - YMS 58
GROSE, Blaine, Y1C. (Staff) - wounded - YMS 58
LUBER, Howard, MM1c. (Staff) - wounded - YMS 58
BUTTERFIELD, Lawrence, MM2c - YMS 58
WELLE, Raymond, QM1c - YMS 58
SKELLY, Francis Joseph, RM2c - wounded - YMS 58
CARLSON, Richard, BM2c - YMS 58
BOYSEN, M. H., Lt. (jg.) - wounded -YMS 226
SAUNDERS, Victor Dale, Cox. - YMS 226
ARTHUR, Marcus Wilson., Lt. (jg.) - wounded (leg) - YMS 226
CORDES, H. H., RM3c - YMS 226
HUMPHRIES, James Harry, BM1c - wounded - YMS 225
SENTER, Sidney, CPhM - YMS 226
DIXON, A. L., SM3c - wounded - YMS 226
McDONOUGH, Gerald T., SM3c - wounded - YMS 226
FAIRCHILD, James E. - YMS 226
McDONOUGH, Pat J., SM1c - wounded - YMS 226
MEGERLE, Ralph S., RT1c - YMS 226
RUTOWSKI, Joseph A., CRM - YMS 226
McCLURE, Willie Lawrence, OS3c

Those rescued by YMS 226 in satisfactory condition were landed at Anzio port at 18:30 January 26, 1944 and verbally ordered by Commander Floyd, CTG 81.3 (Red Beach Group) to report to any British LST for transport to Naples, and to report to senior naval officer present for further orders.

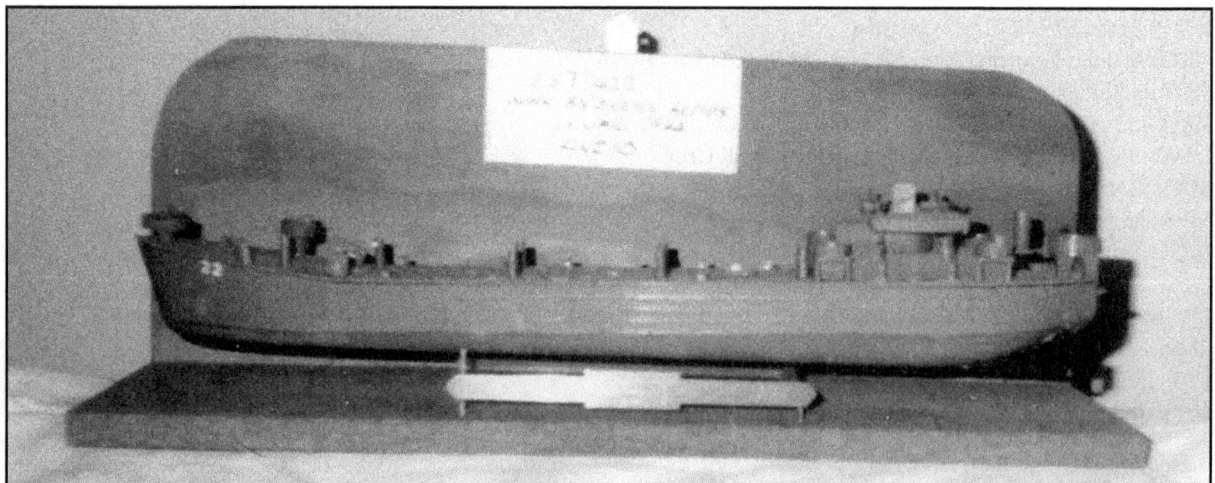

Model of *LST 422* built by Capt. Edward Trey, a survivor of the disaster. *Ed Trey*

Chapter Nine
"ANZIO TO ROME"
JANUARY-JULY
1944

Anzio Annie, also known as the Anzio Express, was a German railway gun which had a 70-foot long barrel, weighed 230 tons, and fired 550-pound shells approximately 31 miles. *Stephen Vukson*

Both platoons of Co. B of the 83rd Chemical Battalion were heavily engaged at Anzio on the clear and warm morning of January 28th, firing 154 rounds and breaking eight standards, five baseplates, and one tube, yet they managed to keep two guns in action. At 1:30 p.m., the battalion helped to stop an enemy counterattack on the Ranger front. Lt. Col. Hutchinson reported to the Ranger Force CP at 4:34 p.m. for instructions on when and how to move the 83rd from the left flank to the right flank for a planned attack on Cisterna di Littoria. The battalion had already been ordered to assemble, yet to be capable of firing. Word was also received that 33 additional survivors of *LST 422* had arrived at Naples, including Capt. Robert E. Edwards and Lt. Alfred H. Crenshaw. Contributing to the good news was the arrival at Anzio from Naples of an LST carrying Lt. Julian T. McKinnon, Co. D, along with 70 fellow officers and men who had been picked up by *YMS 3* following the marine disaster. Soon afterward, a tank shelled the Rangers and enemy shells landed in the 83rd Chemical Battalion CP.

Late in the evening of the 28th a company commanders meeting was held in which orders were issued to have the battalion moved by motor transport the following day to cover the assault on Cisterna di Littoria by the Rangers. Again, the men had no way of knowing that another tragedy was about to transpire which would directly affect the 83rd, although the Rangers would suffer the heaviest this time. James Helsel, Co. A, noted, "We fired very little … and late that night we moved back to the wooded area where we were a few days before with the first platoon. Here we got some news from our Captain. He told us they found [*Robert I.*] Crutz, that he was covered up right where he was digging his hole. That there was only about four foot of dirt on him. I also asked him about Bill Heath [*killed in the LST disaster*] of Headquarters Company, a buddy of mine from Phillipsburg, PA, and he informed me his body was just discovered … He was washed ashore."[1]

On the 29th, the plan to take Cisterna di Littoria evolved to one in which it was hoped the Ranger Force would take the town, cut Highway #7, and set up a defensive line which would deny the enemy use of this vital route. In preparation for this mission, all available elements of the 83rd evacuated their previous positions and moved by truck to a position about six miles, or 16,000 yards, southwest from their objective. Hutchinson conferred with Darby on the plan, scheduled for implementation the following morning, which was listed in the battalion journal as follows: "At 0100 [1 a.m.] hours the 7th Infantry on the left, the 15th Infantry on the right, and the 1st, 3rd, and 4th Rangers in the center were to jump off with the mission to seize, clear, occupy, and hold Cisterna di Littoria. The 1st and 3rd Ranger Battalions were ordered to jump off at 0100 hours from the line of departure marked by the road … and proceed overland between the Isola Bella-Cisterna road and the Borgo Podgora Cisterna road with Cisterna as their objective. The 4th Ranger Battalion was ordered to jump off from the same line of departure at 0200 [2:00 a.m.] hours using the Isola Bella-Cisterna road as an axis of advance clearing all opposition along the way and clearing the road of mines. The 83rd Chemical Battalion was ordered to remain on its trucks … prepared to move forward to occupy positions in support of this attack on call," or more specifically, "The 83rd Chemical Battalion (less one platoon Co. A, and companies C and D) will assemble in march order on road south of bridge prepared to move forward to positions from which support can be given on order …" Lt. Col. Hutchinson, Sgt. Roy E. Cadwalader, Sgt. Warren C. Sharp, and Pvt. Roscoe D. Adamson reported as an advance party to the Ranger Force CP at 4:20 p.m. Sgt. Sharp carried a 609 radio which would be the only means of communications with the Rangers other than messengers. At 4:31, Hutchinson left the Ranger Force CP with orders to return at 6:00 p.m. for final instructions. James Helsel, Co. A, scribed in his diary, "The whole company moved over to the right side, up the beach head. We passed through Nettuno … We went into position along the Mussolini Canal banks, the first platoon on one side of the road, us on another."[2]

Since the men of the 83rd were being held in mobile reserve, they failed to dig slit trenches. S-2 Rupert Burford said this caused a bit of a problem when an enemy plane flew over during the night and they were caught in the glare of a parachute flare. Burford added, "For some of the medics this was a novel and terrifying experience. They started scurrying for cover under our trucks, forgetting that their safest bet was to remain motionless in the strong light. I had to threaten to shoot them in order to quiet their nerves."[3]

The impending Ranger mission was not the only activity of the day. At Caserta Capt. Christopher C. Cornett, Jr., back from brief duty as 5th Army chemical officer, departed for Anzio with 49 enlisted men, comprising the rear echelons of companies A and B and a HQ Co. detachment. All did not go well as Pvt. Thomas D. Stout, Co. B, was killed when he fell stepping out of his truck while the convoy was halted prior to entering the assembly area. Despite this tragic accident the trucks began loading on to an LST at Nisida at 10:00 p.m. To close the day out the VI Corps released an official statement that six officers and 294 men had been listed as lost on *LST 422*.[4]

The plan to take Cisterna di Littoria on the early morning of the 30th did not go as planned because the enemy was well prepared and the 7th and 15th infantry regiments failed to make contact with the Rangers. By daylight, the 1st and 3rd Rangers had advanced to the southern outskirts of town, where they were pinned down and cut apart by the fire of enemy small arms, automatic weapons, tanks, artillery, and infantry. Eventually, Maj. Alvah H. Miller, commanding the 3rd Rangers, was killed and Maj. John W. Dobson, heading the 1st Rangers, suffered a severe wound. At 8:15 a.m., Col. Darby requested one company of the 83rd advance on the Isola Bella-Cisterna Road to support the attack of the 4th Rangers, who were also bogged down by enemy fire. His exact request was, "Hutch, get a couple of co.'s up here right away. Drive them as far as the [*Mussolini*] canal and put them on carts with plenty of ammo. I'll deploy them after they get here." Honoring that request, one platoon of Co. A of the 83rd was moved forward to a position 9,000 yards from Cisterna on the Isola Bella-Cisterna highway, with the other held in reserve, and opened fire alternating with HE and WP. The mortars fired continually although the soft soil kept the recoil mechanism from performing properly and the baseplates and standards often failed. Sam Bundy, Co. A, wrote of the day, "Moved up to support an attack on Cisterna di Littoria. 1st Platoon set up along the road and fired 204 HE and 47 WP; 2nd Platoon stood by."[5]

At 4:00 p.m., Lt. Col. Roy A. Murray, 4th Rangers, requested that Lt. Eric H. Peterson, Jr. of the 83rd have the mortars fire on an enemy machine gun, which was accomplished after some adjustments. As requested, Co. A moved into positions along the Mussolini Canal and manned the four outposts guarding the Ranger Force CP. Sam Bundy noted, "In the evening they set up to support our B Company, which had gone ahead to form a defensive infantry. Both platoons had dug into the bank of [the] Mussolini Canal. HQ operated from a centrally located farmhouse. 2nd Platoon did not fire." Joseph Cannetti, Co. A, also recalled, "We ... proceeded to the Mussolini Canal where we set up our mortars. We were told to dig our slit trenches deep because the Germans were firing some heavy shells. This is when we heard the Rangers were trapped. Our Sgt. said we would become riflemen and see if we could help the Rangers, but it was too late."[6]

Malcolm D. Wilkinson, also of Co. A, was told to investigate. About one-fourth mile up the road he found some men. "As I got near them I saw it was Col. Darby and 4 or 5 other men and about that time I heard my name called ... 'Wilkie! ... I turned and on the other side of the road in a small shack ... I saw Raymond Pullen [of Monroe County, Mississippi] and he motioned for me to come over there ... I began to walk over to where he was and he shouted, 'Get over here quick.' So I ran over to where he was and he said, 'Hit the floor ... someone has been shooting at me all morning' ... About that time a shot came in through a window ... he said, 'See what I mean.' he then told me that the Rangers were cut off and they were trying to get them out." After awhile, Wilkinson decided to attempt a return to his company. "There was a small window in the back of the shack and I decided to go through that and I hit the ground and with my elbows and knees I slithered about 20 or 30 yards to a shallow ditch. In training it was slow going, but I am sure I got there in record time. I lay there and caught my breath then continued down the shallow ditch for about a hundred yards then I got up and took off. By the time I got to the company area the news had been received that the Rangers were trapped and we could not get them out."[7]

As noted, Co. B had been ordered to act in the capacity of infantry and take up a defensive position guarding the line of communications between the Rangers and the 3rd Division units, which they accomplished under heavy fire without any casualties. Andrew C. Leech recalled "[that] night we marched up past the 45th Infantry Division which was coming up to strengthen the line. We passed on by and had one company to set up mortars to support us as we advanced on up to where the Rangers were. There were dead lying everywhere and equipment was strewn all around ... Machine guns opened on us and snipers shot at us from houses along the road, but we moved on up and set up a defensive line."[8]

On the 31st, Co. A covered a mine-clearing detail from enemy machine gun fire and Co. B continued to operate

Andrew Leech holding the Co. B guidon on the Anzio beachhead. *Alice L. Hartley*

as infantry supporting the 4th Rangers. A contact mission led by Lt. Ewart O'Neill, Co. B, comprised of a five-man patrol and a fifteen-man ration detail from the 4th Rangers, set out to locate Lt. Col. Murray. The enemy had infiltrated between Lt. Col. Murray's position and the Ranger Force HQ and laid down high-angle machine gun fire. At 11:22 a.m., Murray pleaded with Hutchinson to provide smoke, to which "Hutch" consented and also promised "… a little H.E." This was followed by Hutchinson being told, "… as soon as you give them the WP I want you to pour on WP until I tell you to stop; then give me 10 rounds of H.E." By 11:45, Hutchinson was told his WP was landing on friendly troops across the mined area, and Murray requested "Hutch" give him a 300-yard left deflection as he had just spotted three Germans running to a new position. Charles Rolling, Co. A, noted, "Fired upon enemy troops, and laid a smoke screen for our advancing troops. In late afternoon a counter attack was staged, and again we fired upon enemy infantry. Houses and road intersections were fired upon."[9]

The contact detail also came under fire resulting in the serious wounding of three Rangers while another was slightly wounded by a concussion grenade. Luckily the detail was able to return to the Ranger Force HQ. Andrew C. Leech, Co. B, who was among the volunteers for this patrol, recalled, "We marched past the Ranger command post and out into enemy territory. Snipers began to shoot at us and machine guns were firing across the road every few minutes. Bullets whizzed by us but we marched on. The first thing we knew we had run head-on into an enemy machine gun nest. The Germans threw a couple of hand grenades among us and got two Rangers and wounded the third one. Then they opened up with a machine gun down the road. We fell flat on the side of the road and lay there flat as a snake while the bullets whizzed not more than a few inches above our heads with tracers lighting up a bit … When the gunner let up we ran down the road and when the machine gun would open up we would hit the side of the road again. We kept this up, running at intervals, until we got back to our own lines … " Soon an enemy patrol firing one machine pistol reached the Ranger Force CP but Lt. Col. Hutchinson ordered his men to not fire until an actual attack developed, and then to hold their positions at all costs until the 6th Corps reached Camarelle.[10]

Lt. O'Neill led another five-man patrol, followed by a number of other patrols by the battalion. Word was also received that rear elements of the rear echelon of the 83rd had landed at Nettuno. But, sadly, it was confirmed that, although the 4th Rangers managed to escape, the remainder of the Ranger Force was almost completely annihilated in the attack upon Cisterna. Fewer than a handful of men got away. The situation was such that the last entry in the Ranger Force journal, handwritten rather than typed, reported, "Shelling of CP resulted in killing of Major William E. Martin & 5 enlisted men - demolishing CP." The Rangers, so long associated with the 83rd Chemical Battalion, were no more. Shortly after the debacle at Cisterna, "Axis Sally" broadcast, "Now that the Rangers are finished, the 83rd Chemical Battalion is next." The threat never materialized. Ironically, also on the 31st the Bureau of Ships, apparently yet unaware of the *LST 422* disaster, requested the ship submit a list of all radio, radar, and underwater sound equipment installed in the vessel for inspection.[11]

The month of January had been devastating to the 83rd. When they reported at the end of the month, there were 280 men missing in action, 13 known dead, and 202 survivors of *LST 422*, making a total of 495 casualties. In addition to the demise of the Rangers and the LST disaster, between the 22nd and 31st of the month the battalion lost one man killed, two wounded or injured, and seven sick in the hospital for a loss of ten. During the same period companies A and B had fired 810 rounds of HE and 170 of WP, for a total of 980 rounds.[12]

The battalion journal did note that the use of DUKWs in the amphibious landing at Anzio proved far superior to the LCIs used at Sicily and Salerno and, in the early phase of the operation, quickly made available the "inherent high fire-power" of the 4.2" mortar. On the other hand, it was discovered that the 4.2" mortar was better suited to mountain warfare than on the open plains at Anzio, where protective cover could rarely be found. It was felt that after the first two days of the invasion regular artillery would have better served the mission. Another problem was that "The murky soil in which the mortars were emplaced necessitated that the baseplates be dug up after each fire mission, and breakage of baseplates and standards occurred quite frequently. The gravelly soils found in positions at Chiunzi Pass, Salerno, and Venafro, while causing many breakages, were greatly superior to the mucky, ill-drained soil of the Anzio beachhead. The use of the new M6 propellant no doubt prevented a much higher incidence of breakage of mortar parts."[13]

February arrived with companies A and B and the battalion CP located on the Conca-Cisterna highway about five miles southwest of Cisterna. Co. A had emplaced their mortars west of the Fosse de Femmina Morta and Co. B

Mike Codega and Wofford Jackson, both of Co. D, in Pozzuoli. *Codega Collection*

just forward of the ditch where they served in the capacity of infantry, guarding the line of communications to the 4th Rangers and other forward elements. Their mission was defensive and no rounds were fired for the first ten days of the month as the enemy was out of range. According to "Doc" Hulcher, Medical Detachment, "Here we had a good spot. The aid station was in the main part of a house right out on the main highway in the broad valley. We stayed here about 2 weeks during which time I saw many things. Many lines of prisoners on the way back, wounded men. Mat Booker ran into me and I saw him for a couple of days before he moved position. One day [*Donald C.*] Herr, [*Robert M.*] Malm, and I went up on the real battle field to get an Italian who had both arms blown off and no one else would pick him up. The pictures I saw that day will linger in my mind for many moons."[14]

The first day of the month was typical of the activity for the early period, illustrated by a five-man patrol, led by Co. B's Lt. Carl K. ("Stud") Carpenter, which made contact with enemy tanks near the left flank, and Capt. Gordon Mindrum, also of Co. B, reporting an enemy buildup for a possible counterattack. Co. A remained in position without firing while the battalion rear echelon moved from Caserta to the former bivouac near Pozzuoli.[15]

With little combat activity transpiring the survivors of *LST 422*, too dazed to be effective combatants, were the focus on February 2nd as they were moved from their position on the Anzio-Albano highway and sent to the battalion CP to handle local security. With a void of officers due to the marine disaster, Lt. Robert W. Smith was assigned acting commander of Co. C and Lt. Justin G. Woomer of Co. D, with Ed Trey continuing as battalion S-4. At Pozzuoli, Lt. Julian T. McKinnon was designated acting supply officer for the rear echelon. Robert E. Edwards, Jr., wrote home, "Mindy [*Mindrum*] still in B. There is some mystery about a Purple Heart he awarded himself. McKinnon is fine. I mentioned that [*Vester*] Turner [*isn't*] with us anymore … Kenny [*Cunin*] is in England."[16]

On the 3rd, the remaining men of companies C and D set up their camouflaged pup tents near the battalion CP on the Anzio beachhead, while at Pozzuoli efforts continued to replace equipment lost in the LST disaster. Battalion S-3 "Bud" Pike wrote home of the strong enemy opposition, claiming, "The fighting is very bitter now and the Germans are proving again to be very stubborn and efficient soldiers fighting for every inch of ground … remarkable thing about this operation has been the marvelous work of our Air Corps. They have really given the Luftwaffe a going over and we have seen numerous dog-fights overhead in which the Luftwaffe always gets the worst of it, with many of their planes crashing near us. Sadistic as it may sound it is beautiful to see their Messerschmidt's & Fock-Wulfes crash and go up in a burst of flame and smoke."[17]

By the 4th, the magnitude of the situation with the LST survivors had become obvious, and the battalion CP area was shelled without any casualties. Most of the LST survivors were clearly still shell-shocked and, upon the recommendation of Lt. Col. Hutchinson, the Corps Surgeon, and Corps HQ, were ordered to return to Naples to recover and reorganize. In the meantime, the 3rd Division to the front of the 83rd regrouped into three defensive lines, the rear line immediately to the rear of Fossa de Femmina Morta.[18]

During the next few days, the weather was windy, cold, and wet as the battalion occasionally became a target for air attacks, while Cisterna di Littoria received heavy shelling. Capt. Gordon Mindrum, Co. B, wrote a letter on the 6th to Ed Trey's wife confirming Ed's survival of the LST disaster. He added, "You should see my present command post. A beautiful 8 room house with every modern convenience, even a wine cellar."[19]

Battalion S-3 Ed "Bud" Pike gave a much more detailed description of his abode. "We now have our BN CP set up in one of the numerous Italian farmhouses dotting the landscape. The section we are now in is much more prosperous and 'civilized' and this farmhouse is much neater and cleaner and more comfortable than those to which we have been accustomed. Mussolini, in his heyday, reclaimed the Pontine marshes which are included in the bridgehead area and also carried on a housing project so that all these houses look the same, somewhat like the housing projects in the states. The building has a large room downstairs, the living room & dining room, with a little store room off this one large room. To the rear of the house is the barn where they keep their oxen and also a shed for the wagon. Now we have several of the men sleeping with the oxen and our BN Aid Station set up in the wagon shed. Upstairs there are five small rooms, all bed rooms (which of course explain the high birth rate in Italy), in which the officers and a few enlisted men sleep. We go to bed about 9:00 o'clock each evening and arise about 8:00 o'clock in the morning. During the day we carry on the business of helping to win the war and during the evening we either read or play cards. We do our own cooking in the large room downstairs and all in all life is not too disagreeable – without our wives who are uppermost in all of our minds. At first we ate K rations, which are terrible, then C rations, which are a little better than terrible, and now we are eating our 10 in 1 rations, which are rations for 10 men for one day condensed in one medium-sized cardboard box and almost everything in them is dehydrated. We take turns cooking and have a terrible time trying to get a little variety into our meals … Tonight for supper we had lima beans, dehydrated corned beef hash, rice, rice pudding, grapeade, cocoa, and hardtack. Appetizing, eh? And (I guess I can tell you now) we are forming a band of guerillas which will go into action when the war is over. Its purpose is to destroy every Vienna sausage in the United States. We have had so many of the critters that they are coming out our ears."[20]

On February 9th, the 83rd Chemical Battalion was relieved from attachment to the 6615th Ranger Force and attached to the 7th Infantry [*although some accounts have them attached as early as February 2nd*], which was held in division reserve. Lt. Col. Hutchinson, Capt. Rupert O. Burford, Lt. Harlan Reynolds, and T/5 Charles P. Cella, Jr., took two officers and 49 enlisted survivors of *LST 422* from the battalion CP to Anzio to board an LST for Naples, and on the return to the battalion CP two jeep drivers were wounded, one seriously. The period from early February to the 9th was well described by "Doc" Hulcher who recalled, "From the farm house we [*Medical Detachment*] were in here we saw many planes again. About 300 bombers went over one day & dropped their bundles just a few miles ahead of us. I saw one bomber hit, burst into flames and while turning back explode in the air. Dive bombers & other bombers went over frequently. Once a Jerry strafed the road just a few yards from us. Fairly frequently the Jerries laid a barrage down just across the road from us but no one was ever injured. Spent a lot of time talking to Vino Joe and drinking his wine. Many nights you could see the infantry & tanks fighting just up ahead from us over the canal."[21]

S-2 Rupert Burford took note of the situation, writing, "The battle for the Anzio beachhead has settled into a situation of two opposing forces sitting, glaring at each other and exchanging artillery shellings and plane attacks. It has been impossible for us to break out, and the Germans have found it impossible to kick us out of here. They now have 17 divisions opposing about 5 of ours, among theirs is the famous Herman Goerring Panzer Division."[22]

The new attachment of the battalion took place on February 10th when companies A and B moved to the 45th Division sector in defense of the beachhead line in reserve, with Co. A supporting the 1st Battalion, 180th Infantry, and Co. B supporting the 2nd Battalion, 179th Infantry, while the battalion CP moved to a dairy. James Helsel, Co. A, again wrote in his diary, "It has been raining the past three days and it was very muddy and rained 'cats and dogs' all the time we were loading, until we arrived on the other side of the beach head. It was very dark and miserable." Andrew C. Leech, Co. B, stated, "We … pulled back up to the edge of the coast and set up a defensive position there. We spent about a week here with headquarters being in an Italian home. We slept all about the house and some in hay stacks and others in the dog house, barn and anywhere available. We were shelled and bombed constantly." The Medical Detachment was " … moved back again to the central sector opposite The Factory [*near Carroceto*] on the same highway we were previously on, but this time we were easily under observation of the Germans. We moved late at night so we wouldn't be seen and spent the first night with the British in a house packed like sardines and very uncomfortable."[23]

These new positions found Co. A under enemy shelling at about 10 p.m. on a rainy 11th, which killed Pvt. James R. Simmons of Lee County, Mississippi, and wounded privates Ralph H. Reddoch, also of Mississippi, and Paul Ruby of Bergen County, New Jersey. James Helsel, Co. A, said, "While first aid was being administered a dud came in and hit in the same hole, knocking the men down." This may be the period described by Joseph Cannetti, Co. A, who wrote, "The Germans … laid down a thunderous barrage. I remember bringing a wounded 83rder to the aid station - I believe his name was Texas - about a mile back. The going was difficult with all those shells coming in but we finally made it."[24]

While the official reorganization of companies C and D commenced back at Pozzuoli the Medical Detachment moved to the dairy and took over a barn, which according to "Doc" Hulcher was "… cold, damp & very uncomfortable." Over the ensuing days the detachment "kept on the lookout for a better place and found some British leaving [*an*] adjacent building that afternoon and … moved in before they moved out." Hulcher said they "Had [*a*] fine place, dry and was perfect. We operated smoothly here and could see everything going on. Many air raids, bombers over the factory & rest of the enemy. Tank battle, oh it was a swell spot for a movie."[25]

A new culinary delight was experienced at this time, as noted by "Bud" Pike, who wrote, " … a cow was killed by shrapnel out in the back-yard and of course the Italians living here and the GI's immediately went to work on it. Result – excellent steaks fried by Oscar of the Waldorf Pike and were they ever delicious for a change from beans, beans, rice, rice and beans and rice. We are going to see to it that another cow happens to wander into a shell again in a few days. Accidents will happen you know – just so they keep on happening to the cows it will be all right."[26]

Carroceto and The Factory area became the scenes of much bombing and activity for the next couple of days and one of two planes strafing Co. B was shot down. Chester D. McCann of Co. A was wounded by a shell burst at Anzio while Lt. Col. Hutchinson, Lt. Reynolds, and Cpl. Steve Gozur departed Pozzuoli for Anzio.[27]

A typical air raid transpired on the 12th, "… in the evening around 9:30 PM [*when*] Jerry bombers came over our area," according to Steve Vukson, Motor Pool, HQ Co. "They always start by sending a second plane to drop flares. The planes came over one at a time with thirty second intervals between them. They dive bombed our area and surroundings with large bombs & personnel bombs. The two of us just lay in our trench – thinking it was the end. It lasted about thirty minutes. A bomb hit an English truck and disrupted communications. We can thank God we are alive."[28]

The mortars of companies A and B were fired for the first time in February on Valentine's Day, the 14th, when Co. B moved one platoon forward about 1,500 yards and fired on positions east of Carroceto and The Factory, then fell back to the beachhead line, although in the action they broke three baseplates and one standard. S-3 "Bud" Pike reported of the battalion, " … we have moved our CP to a new location. We are now located in a large dairy – so that some of the boys are still sleeping with the cows and in addition some are now sleeping in a chicken house." Yet at the very moment Pike wrote these lines he added, "Three German Messerschmidts just zoomed over the house and dropped three bombs on a road intersection about 500 yards away. Our room is on the top floor of the main building of this dairy and the planes were about 200 feet above it. I heard the planes coming and also the ack-ack going up at them. Grabbing my field glasses I rushed out onto the balcony just in time to see a bomb come tumbling out of one of the planes and it appeared to be heading straight for the building. I really should go out to the latrine and finish the job I started up here. What am I saying? No kidding, my heart leaped right up into my mouth. Thank God that is over with."[29]

Steve Vukson also found himself under intense fire on Valentine's Day as he stated, "The weather was lovely which meant air-raids all day. Everyone got wise and started to cover our holes by putting a roof on them. [*Vukson and a buddy from the 84th Chemical Battalion*] cut timbers and put a layer of sand bags, a few inches of sand, and camouflaged it. The thoughts of evening scared us, Jerry came over again with quite a load of personnel bombs which he dumped in our area and the larger elsewhere. My raincoat was punctured with shrapnel which was on the ground, a truck & trailer had four flats, plus small holes where the bombs landed. One personnel bomb went thru the supply tent in the back of us. It missed a man's hole by a foot." Back at Pozzuoli, Charlie Lowry, Co. D, wrote, "It has been raining for three or four days but this morning the sun is shining real nice and it will be a grand day to go some place." Regarding the command structure of the battalion at this time, Robert E. Edwards, Jr., wrote, "Chris [*Cornett*] is definitely not coming back. Rupe [*Burford*] is waiting to go home."[30]

Enemy dive bombers and poor aim by friendly air attacks threatened the battalion on the 15th as enemy artillery made four direct hits on CP buildings, killing one British soldier and seriously wounding three others in addition to one American. Lt. Col. Hutchinson, having returned to Anzio, departed for Pozzuoli again along with Lt. Andre Laus, T/4 Warren C. Sharp, T/5 Steve Gozur, and the wounded Pvt. Chester D. McCann. It seemed as if Hutchinson was spending more time away from Anzio than at the scene of activity, although his presence was undoubtedly required to help reorganize companies C and D.[31]

A major enemy infantry and tank counterattack was launched along the Anzio-Albano road on February 16th. The battalion CP fell under heavy artillery fire killing one Italian civilian and one British soldier. Additionally, another British soldier and Pvt. Mike Saterello, HQ Co., a man of Italian descent from Marion County, West Virginia, were lightly wounded. The area became too dangerous and the CP was moved to the same farmhouse Co. B had used on January 26th. Co. B, under Capt. Mindrum's direction, moved up the road through intense hostile fire to a position previously occupied by an 81mm mortar section and a British mortar company but found it to be untenable, being under heavy fire. Mindrum described the position as poor because superior enemy forces had infiltrated the area. The company exhibited "great determination" in maintaining the position but were forced to evacuate within an hour.[32]

The 179th Infantry, with the 1st Platoon of Co. A, 83rd Chemical Battalion, attached, also fell back and the 157th Infantry suffered heavily on the left. Meanwhile the 180th Infantry, supported by the 2nd Platoon, Co. A, 83rd Chemical, halted some enemy efforts but also was additionally forced back in order to maintain contact with the 179th Infantry on their left. In a stirring account of the fight, James Helsel, Co. A, 2nd Platoon, wrote, "We were awakened early and given a stand by, and started firing right away. The noise of the battle ahead was clear and loud. It sounded like a continuous rumble of thunder. We fired all day fast and as long as the mortars were in action. It was very hard to keep in action due to the muddy ground. We backed the base plate up against trees and staked them down, we tried everything, but the fast firing that we were doing was too much for them. By noon I could tell the enemy had advanced somewhat. Being a gunner in Sicily I kept listening to the elevation which went from 800 up to 1000 and the number of powder rings on the shells dropped from 21 to 16. MP's were on duty keeping the men on the lines. For by now Infantry men were straggling through our area without helmets, rifles, etc. I asked one what was up there, he said 'German tanks and fifty men to our one'. Which started me thinking it's a long swim back to Naples. About two in the afternoon we received direct fire from German tanks, their shells kept us in and out of the holes for quite some time. More men were straggling back, it was so bad that MP's stopped me when I went across the fire break to bring ammo to the gun position … We continued to fire upon the tanks. Soon we received reports our firing was effective, that we chased five away and left the sixth one burning. Toward evening the noise of the battle sounded very close, but it also seemed slowed down a little, we fired very late into the night. I hope we don't do too much night firing, for ole Jerry can look down our throats."[33]

Lt. Ewart O'Neill, Co. B, of the 83rd, directed fire of a 155mm artillery battery during the engagement and knocked out one Mark VI tank. Andrew Leech, Co. B, vividly recalled this struggle: "They came riding at us in large numbers on Tiger tanks 'all wined up' ready to mop up. Some of the Germans were even doped. We were forced to give some ground, but we had some tanks dug in with the turrets sticking out. They ran into these and were mowed down by the hundreds. Then, on came the foot troopers shouting and running recklessly into death. We did a good job of mowing them down and stopping the advance …"[34]

The attack continued on the 17th as Pvt. Mitchell L. Daniels, Co. B, heroically used "a haystack as an observation point, remaining in this undefended position for ten hours directing mortar fire which destroyed and disorganized the enemy, thereby permitting the regrouping of infantry units. Disregarding heavy enemy small arms and mortar fire, he succeeded in reaching a ditch and crawling safely to his platoon." For this action Daniels was later awarded the Bronze Star. During the day Pvt. Ray D. Meek, Co. B, was lightly wounded and two of the company's mortars were abandoned after being destroyed by enemy fire. Co. B moved both platoons to a position supporting the 3rd Battalion, 157th Infantry, but had difficulty finding the regiment. Co. A supported the 179th Infantry. But the most tragic incident of the day for the 83rd transpired when twelve enemy Focke-Wulfe 190 dive bombers made a direct hit on Co. B's CP in an abandoned house about a mile back from their earlier line. Lt. Carl Carpenter was killed as was Pvt. Alvin P. Gentry, reportedly a jeep driver. Lt. Col. Hutchinson said a bomb fragment killed Carpenter. Ed "Bud" Pike noted that Carpenter had a premonition that he wasn't going to make it through the war and added, "He furnished a lot of life to the outfit and was really a swell guy. We certainly have a lot to repay the Germans and by gosh we'll do it." Among the wounded were Pvt. Arnold

Lt. Carl K. "Stud" Carpenter, Co. B, killed by an enemy dive bomber at Anzio February 17, 1944, *Ed Trey*

M. Cobb from Oklahoma and Pfc. Frederick L. LeFever of New Columbia, Pennsylvania. Capt. Gordon Mindrum was beside Carpenter during the episode and recalled, "I saw the bomb coming and the explosion perforated my ear drum and left me dazed and confused for two days. I was extremely lucky to survive." Nolan McCraine, Co. B, from Wilkinson County, Mississippi, a communications man who often served as forward observer, said he was only about four feet from Carpenter when the bomb exploded. He added, "It knocked me down and dazed me for a brief period. When I stood up in the smoke and regained my senses I saw Carpenter and Gentry, blood gushing out of the nose and mouth of each. The upper story of the house was on fire so I attempted to grab Carpenter by the feet and drag him out but a lieutenant came in and told me to get the hell out as I was still alive and Carpenter wasn't. I followed him to his jeep. In the vehicle was Arnold Cobb with a horrible fragment wound of his leg. I assume they headed for the aid station." One jeep and a large amount of communications equipment were also destroyed, and another jeep was badly damaged.[35]

A witness to this episode, Andrew C. Leech, Co. B, " … had just walked out of the house and was in a foxhole near the house." Leech continued, "The explosives almost knocked me out for a minute and I [*awoke*] to find that the bombs had set off one of our ammunition dumps nearby and shrapnel was flying all around me. I knew I had to get out of there so I crawled to a chicken house where there were two jeeps parked nearby which had been hit by shrapnel and were burning … I ran into the house and it was a wreck. There lay the bodies of two comrades. Three others had been carried to the hospital. The men that were left had run across the road to some scrubby brushes." Co. B spent the night in the woods, soaked in mud and constantly under enemy fire.[36]

Because the infantry line had nearly fallen back to the beachhead line, and because of heavy enemy tank fire, the battalion CP and aid station were moved to the motor pool and ammo dump area. Although Co. A's 1st Platoon did no firing, the 2nd Platoon supported an attack by the 179th Infantry. But the battalion journal best summed up the performance of the 83rd, writing, "The inability of our battalion to serve to the best when operating as separate platoons and with strange organizations became very apparent."[37]

The situation improved on the 18th as Lt. James J. O'Connor, Co. A, gave a credible performance at the OP directing fire on enemy tanks and infantry until pinned down by six Mark VI tanks. Eventually unable to return fire, his platoon fell back. Sam Bundy, Co. A, described the action in his diary, writing, "Representing the second Platoon was Lt. O'Connor, who fired upon enemy infantry and tanks until he was pinned down at 0230 hrs by direct fire from M-6 tanks. Out of communications, his platoon was unable to fire, so he returned to his platoon area. WP was fired upon infantry entrenched in canal position – effective. WP and HE were fired upon enemy infantry in the woods. To add to the discomfort of being pinned down under tank fire, planes strafed and bombed the surrounding areas. An AT gun close by the OP fired upon the tanks and disabled one. Remaining 5 fired back and scored a direct hit on the emplacement. Ammo exploded and it seemed 'all hell had broke loose', quoting Lt. O'Connor."[38]

Lt. Veryl R. Hays of the company advanced to make contact with the CO of the 179th Infantry but found an extreme state of confusion and was unable to locate the 2nd Battalion. Hays assisted the withdrawal of the 179th Infantry by firing at the advancing enemy. Quickly he found himself surrounded so he destroyed his 511 radio for communications and crawled over one and a half miles through enemy territory to reach the 1st Platoon of Co. A. The platoon itself was under heavy small arms fire and was forced to abandon one mortar and leave all but the barrel of another before Lt. Hays was able to take the platoon by a circuitous route to a safer position.[39]

Lt. Hays, who was awarded a Silver Star for his actions, wrote of the episode, "I was forward observer and ordered to stay at an advance OP and cover the infantry's withdrawal. My radio operator remained with me until the infantry had pulled out. Then we destroyed the radio … Soon after, the mortar position with which I had broken radio contact was overrun by the Germans. I had absolutely no contact with my men, and consequently could not give the order for them to retire. The two mortar squads elected to stay at the position with the BAR team until they could fire no more. Instead of high-tailing it out of there, they paused long enough to drop incendiary grenades down the barrels of their mortars. Then they made their way to the other two squads, still firing on the Germans, and helped them until I could get back and give orders to move out."[40]

1st Sgt. Leonard R. Kenney distinguished himself by directing the fire of both platoons of Co. A throughout the day, "repulsing numerous tank advances as well as pinning down and repelling infantry assaults." According to Sam Bundy, Co. A, "The only observed fire on the beachhead line from 1400 until 1800 hours was the mortar fire directed by Sgt. Kenney from an OP under direct fire from tanks." Lt. Col. Hutchinson added, "He set up shop in a building with personnel from other units. Ten Mark VI tanks moved up and began firing at the building, having spotted the Americans, because we are careless about camouflage until forced to be otherwise. The tanks hit every room in the building but one, the room from which the sergeant was observing. The room above him took a shell, the room on his left, on his right, and the one below him, but Kenney didn't budge from his post … There is some doubt as to whether he actually beat off the tanks with mortar fire. A Mark VI tank is a big damn thing and takes a lot of pounding. But the sergeant gets credit for a personal victory. The tanks went away, and he stayed."[41]

Co. A also took casualties in men and equipment. By the end of the day they reported five serviceable mortars, six non-serviceable, and one destroyed. Pfc. Adam G. Turek was lightly wounded and hospitalized while Pfc. George E. Hughes received a light wound.[42]

Co. B came under the fire of what was believed to be 240mm shells, which made a direct hit on the No. 4 squad, killing Sgt. Michael Teeno, Jr., and Pvt. William E. Barrett, both of Pennsylvania, and Pvt. Horace D. Hutcherson of Spartanburg, South Carolina. Andrew Leech, Co. B, writing of the incident, said, "We took a beating and had many casualties. One foxhole suffered a direct hit with three of our boys in it. We never found them, and quite a few went to the hospital with shrapnel wounds." The east-west road along the 29th Northing became the front line and Co. B fired against seven Mark IV tanks, knocking out three as the four remaining left the field. Lt. Col. Hutchinson noted that an artillery observer reported Lt. Francis J. ("Frank") Schleifer " … directed mortar fire that immobilized seven Nazi tanks." Infantry assaults were also held back despite poor radio communications to observers. Among Co. B's seriously wounded by a shell burst and evacuated were Sgt. Joseph E. Ferrence, his second wound of the war, and Sgt. George E. DeLucas. Lightly wounded were privates Tal McPeak, Paul O. Harvey, Leo L. Kurtenbach, Morton Gorowsky, and a soldier named Henderson [*possibly James Henderson Robinson*].[43]

Communications to forward observers were knocked out and fighting centered on an area known as the Overhead Pass, where a battalion of British Royalists defended each side and the rear of the pass, soon afterward supported by a battalion of Gordons and Co. B of the 83rd. The enemy pressed hard with infantry, artillery, tanks, small arms fire, and snipers, as hand-to-hand fighting broke out on the Overhead Pass. Every available man, including cooks and truck drivers, were thrown into the line. Co. B reported, "Situation looked a bit thick." James G. Helsel, Co. A, 2nd Platoon, added, "Fired a good bit again today, the elevation is now 1050 and twelve rings are being used … the Germans are quite close. I understand [*we*] have cooks, truck drivers, etc. of other outfits on the front lines. I do know all day yesterday and today [*we*] have been stretching barb wire and digging holes a few hundred yards in back of our position."[44]

The Medical Detachment was not excepted from the hell of February 18th, based upon the diary of "Doc" Hulcher, who recorded, " … they had hit every building around us and bombs and shells were hitting all around us. We were really scared nearly to death. I was sitting on the floor with Herr when the window pane broke over our heads from the shells. I could picture everything happening and I prayed a little harder often enough. About 3 PM I walked or crawled down to [*the*] CP about 400 yds to get permission to move. I couldn't call for [*the*] telephone lines were out. They told me I could move out when it got dark. I thought along with the boys that it would never get dark. But it finally came. We were already packed and out we went. Spent [*the*] night sleeping on [*the*] ground in our motor pool. Next day we pitched tents and started doing our work there."[45]

Four Mark IV tanks were fired upon by Co. B on the 19th and reportedly put out of action. The 3rd Battalion, 157th Infantry, also reported that Co. B's fire had helped to capture approximately 200 of the enemy. Co. A saw little action, as the 2nd Platoon fired only two rounds and the 1st Platoon did no firing. Back at Pozzuoli, a select group of men from Co. C and a platoon of 49 men from Co. D went to Piedmonte to give a two-day demonstration of the 4.2" mortar to the 88th Infantry Division.[46]

On the 20th, anti-personnel bombs were dropped on the battalion CP at Anzio, creating numerous holes in the tents and lightly wounding Pvt. Thomas A. Keane [*or Keene*]. About two dozen enemy shells fell in the vicinity of Co. A, including one that fell between the tent of Pfc. Earl C. Koring of Greensburg, Pennsylvania, and his slit trench. Koring was in the trench and was not injured. Another shell hit and destroyed the jeep of Sgt. William E. Gregory. Later, one platoon of Co. B was detached from the 157th Infantry and attached to the 179th Infantry, as was one platoon of Co. A. At about nine in the evening, an enemy attack of company strength was directed at the center of the 179[47] Infantry line but repulsed with the assistance of a few WP shells from Co. B.[47]

Enemy tanks advanced on the road 600 yards north of the Overhead Pass on the 21st but the fire from a platoon of Co. B forced them to withdraw. Soon afterward, Co. A was placed in support of the 180th Infantry and Co. B in support of the 179th Infantry. As a result of subsequent shifting of positions, Eldon Harris of Co. A was lightly wounded by shell fire. Various other attempts were made against the front line of the 180th Infantry without success. While such action raged at Anzio, back at Pozzuoli, HQ and D companies, in conjunction with the Rangers' rear echelon, held a dance featuring the WACs from the PBS as the guests of honor.[48]

By February 22nd, the two mortar companies of the 83rd at Anzio had managed to successfully help defend the consolidation of the 45th Infantry Division on the beachhead line. That day Co. A's Pvt. Vincent M. Pleskac of Ulysses County, Nebraska, was lightly wounded by a shell fragment. Co. B would later receive an official Unit Citation for their outstanding performance against the enemy during the period of February 15-21. On the 23rd, Charlie Lowry, Co. D, wrote from Pozzuoli, "This isn't such a nice day. It rains every little while and there is a cold wind."[49] George R. Borkhuis, Co. D cook also wrote home, "In the picture of some of the boys that I enclosed in my last letter, the fellow standing up without the hat, is an Italian prisoner of war that we brought with us from Sicily. He has washed pots and pans and repaired our stoves. He can now talk English quite well. His home is in Northern Italy but he doesn't want to go home, he hopes to be able to go to the states when the war is over. The other day the colonel [*Hutchinson*] came into our tent on an inspection tour. He saw "Al" [*Albert Sabatino*] and tried to correct his posture a little. After a few minutes of no success he said, 'How long have you been in our outfit?' Al didn't understand and only looked at the colonel. We were all standing at attention and trying to keep from laughing. Then one of the boys told the colonel that Al wasn't an American soldier. The colonel burst out laughing and then we all followed suit. He admitted he had been fooled by the American uniform Al was wearing, but he said it was O.K. with him."

During the next five days the two mortar companies at Anzio did not fire any rounds except for registration purposes, despite being under intermittent fire from the enemy every day. On a bright, sunshiny 24th, Pvt. Leondus Steptoe, Co. B, of Johnson County, Georgia, was lightly wounded, his second of the war. S-3 "Bud" Pike commented on the clear weather and repeated enemy air attacks, writing, "The weather today is … wonderful for air activity both Jerry and ours, yesterday was cloudy, rainy, and generally miserable, forcing all planes to stay on the ground. We have a heck of a time trying to decide whether we prefer the good weather or the lack of bombing and strafing. I think though that I would rather live longer in bad weather. It will always clear up at the right time." Pike also made reference to other recent enemy attacks, adding, "We were shelled out of our dairy CP so we moved to another farmhouse where we stayed one day before we were shelled out of it also. We then moved to the rear a couple of miles where we had to contend with German planes coming over every night and dropping fragmentation bombs (about 2 lbs.) by the hundreds. We woke up one morning to find our tent full of shrapnel holes. One bomb had dropped through the roof of one tent and exploded right inside of it. That tent was just one big hole although, luckily, no one was hurt. We have moved again and are now living in a hole in the ground, with our tent pitched in the hole. None of the comforts of home …"[50]

Lt. Col. Hutchinson and Capt. Burford also began their return trips to Anzio from Pozzuoli during this period, and six shells, including five duds, fell among the battalion CP personnel at Anzio on the 26th. Robert E. Edwards, Jr., wrote a letter home in which he noted Lt. Andre Laus had been given command of Co. C, while during the last two days of the month Co. A engaged the enemy again in an effort to halt an attack on the 180th Infantry line. In addition, HQ Co.'s Pfc. Warren E. Collins, of Sunflower County, Mississippi, was seriously wounded while driving his jeep on the 28th. Also on the 28th Lt. Col. Hutchinson and Capt. Burford arrived at Anzio with a list of five men who were to return to the rear echelon at Pozzuoli. Among the five was Stephen Vukson, who was to replace Kenneth Laundre, who was to replace the battalion supply sergeant lost on *LST 422*. At Pozzuoli Charlie Lowry, Co. D, reflected on an injury which kept him off the *LST 422*, writing to his girlfriend, "The wrist is O. K. Some day I'll tell you a story about the wrist which may have meant the difference in us fulfilling our plans someday or not." Lowry added, "Is this one nasty day? Rain, rain, all day long … this is Sunday, not much doing except sitting around in the tent trying to keep warm and waiting for chow time."[51]

The last day of the month found Co. A's OP moved from Padiglione to the CP of the 3rd Battalion, 180th Infantry. James Helsel, Co. A, wrote, "We are back in the rear on the right flank of the beach head in a little white house. I don't know if it was worth the trip or not, we had to walk about one mile to where our trucks were hidden, through mud about knee deep, carrying our bed rolls and to make things more comfortable, Jerry threw about two shells fairly close."[52]

Co. B remained relatively inactive. S-2 Burford, along with Steve Vukson and four other men, went to the Anzio harbor but could not get a ship to Naples as the sea was too rough. The group returned to their bunkers where Lt. Robert Warren Fenton, HQ Co., Supply, requested Vukson remain at Anzio; however, Lt. Col. Hutchinson's order prevailed due to the large amount of work required because of the many vehicles lost in the LST tragedy. The companies at Pozzuoli were also relatively inactive on the 29th.[53]

While at Anzio during the month of February companies A and B of the 83rd fired 1,011 rounds of HE and 393 WP, for a total of 1,404. The battalion suffered seventeen battle casualties: six men killed in action and eleven seriously wounded and evacuated. Calculating the *LST 422* loss at 495 (including 202 survivors), the assigned total strength of the 83rd at the close of February 1944 was 806 men. Equipment continued to be a serious problem, according to the battalion journal, which reported that mortar parts breakages "were frequent due to the soft moisture-filled poorly drained soil. It was usually found necessary to re-emplace the mortars after firing about five rounds. When the situation permitted, attempts were made to provide a better base for the mortar, by filling an excavation with pieces of trees, gravel, and rocks, depending upon what material was available, with a top layer of filled sandbags several thicknesses deep. This prepared emplacement was only slightly more satisfactory than the regular method of emplacing the mortar."[54]

Lt. Veryl R. Hays, Co. A, said that during February his camp was in a cave infested with lice. This created a health hazard for the men, so in order to resolve the situation he took a psychological approach. "It was logical for the men to shave their hair, but it did not seem advisable to come right out with an arbitrary order. So I took two of the huskier men in the platoon aside, persuaded them to shave their heads and then go around together. I made another suggestion, too. If anyone smiled at them they would bear down on him and shave a deep slice out of his hair. The victim would then have to shave off the rest in order not to look like a circus freak or aboriginal savage. Before long the bald ones outnumbered the hairy ones and, in time, we had a whole platoon of cue balls. The lice had been routed, and everybody was happy about it."[55]

As the month of March rolled in, companies A and B of the 83rd remained in action at Anzio and companies C and D continued their usual bivouac and training duties at Pozzuoli. Casualties mounted on the sunny first day of the month when Pvt. Max Peck, Co. B, was lightly wounded and hospitalized by a shell fragment in the knee, while Georgia boy Pvt. Leondus Steptoe, also of Co. B, received his third wound of the war by a shell fragment to the shoulder, which did not require hospitalization. The small group consisting of S-2 Burford, Steve Vukson, and four other men finally made it to the docks and waited several hours while ships unloaded supplies. Vukson wrote, "The enemy shells were hitting out in the water and certain sections of the town. We got on the ship about 1 p.m. and started to sail about 2:30 p.m. There were two air raid signals within one hour but it all turned out alright for us."[56]

Vukson also took the time to reflect upon his forty days on the Anzio beachhead. "A Jerry could throw a shell anywhere and was most likely to hit something. We were losing quite a bit of men and equipment, so were the Jerries. The dead were hauled in 2 ½ ton trucks to the 3rd & 45th Div. cemetery and the English had quite a few killed. They filled up one cemetery and started on another, Italians dug the graves and buried the dead. It's a sight to see, a person's morale drops to rock-bottom, especially when one sees so many of our men dead. Our 83rd Cml. suffered a loss in casualties and vehicles. During my forty days on the beach – Co. 'A' lost 4 men and 1 officer and Co. 'B' had one man killed by a shell and a man was killed by a Jerry bomb which crashed while he was digging a trench, two others were slightly wounded. There were a number of men wounded as the men were brought to the medics which was in the rear area with us during the large Jerry counterattack that lasted 4 days & nights. The Jerries were always counterattacking. In the four day drive they gained a thousand yards but we pushed them back after both sides lost many men. The artillery roared day and night from both ends, the Navy was firing and our planes kept bombing enemy positions everyday. It was a massacre a few times, I never thought the enemy had so much pep at this stage of the war."[57]

S-3 "Bud" Pike also summarized recent events. "Jerry is throwing artillery shells at us and we are replying in kind. We haven't gained an inch or lost an inch in the last week but to me it looks like Jerry is regrouping and reorganizing for at least one more major effort to push us into the sea. What the result may be only God knows. And he ain't talking. But that is the way the situation is shaping up. We knocked him down a notch or two on that last attempt and inflicted heavy losses on his forces. We'll sure do our best to keep on inflicting these heavy losses." Pike also mentioned that following the almost nightly games of Bridge between Hutchinson, Dave Meyerson, Chaplain George Gaiser, and himself, they "… all stepped outside and watched German planes bombing Nettuno and Anzio in the distance. It made a very impressive and beautiful (if morbid) sight. The tracers of the ack-ack making a brilliant, surrealistic pattern in the sky. The explosive bursts of the larger shells imparting an orangish hue to the clouds. The bright flashes of the bombs as they hit. The stars overhead and the drone of the planes. All contributed to a stirring scene. And we stood there watching and praying that none of our buddies were being hurt down there, and hoping like hell that the planes stayed away from where we were."[58]

Burford, Vukson, and comrades landed at Bagnoli harbor near Naples on March 2nd and moved to the rear area at Pozzuoli just in time for dinner. Vukson said, "I was welcomed by my friends who survived the ship which was sunk. It was great to get back from the continuous shelling and bombing at Anzio. There was that feeling of sadness in learning of my friends who ended up on the casualty list." Meanwhile, back at Anzio Co. B took a heavy shelling and Pvt. Frank G. Anderson, HQ Co., was hit but did not require a trip to the hospital for a light wound of his left shoulder.[59]

On March 3rd, Steve Vukson began his new assignment as battalion parts maintenance at Pozzuoli and described his activities and the camp in his diary: "I took over my duties … and started on making out a number of requisitions for parts and tools for all our new vehicles which we had drawn due to the sinking of *LST 422* … I was on the road almost daily and had my Jeep (Shrapnel) which we named when picking it at the front lines in Venafro, Italy and putting most new parts on it. Battalion Maintenance (six of us) got good use out of it. This was a swell area in Pozzuoli, Italy. We lived in pyramidal tents, the place looked like a tent city with Company 'A' & 'B' and HQ being together. We had an extension light connected to a battery for the light in our tent and had a 110 volt generator to generate light for the office tents. We had Italians doing our KP work in the kitchen. There were plenty of guards and guard mount as if in garrison. We got a bunch of new men to replace the ones that were killed in the sinking. The men in the company kept firing the 4.2 mortars every day into a hill above us."[60]

Between March 4th and April 23rd, Anzio became a near complete stalemate. March 5th marked the battalion's 44th day in action at Anzio, which Lt. Col. Hutchinson described as the "… longest stretch so far with no relief in sight." He also mentioned the battalion had amassed a total of 24 Silver Stars with more in the process, and an attempt was underway to get commissions for Leonard R. Kenney, Robert P. Brimm, Lewis Cameron, and Michael P. Codega as vacancies had made the positions available.[61]

At Pozzuoli Charlie Lowry described the weather as "rain and wind," while Mess Sgt. George Borkhuis, Co. D added, "We used to think March was a crazy month back home but you ought to see it here. It rains, snows, hails, and the sun shines, all in one hour. We've had enough rain in the last week to float Italy right off the continent … it was nice and sunny all day, but now we are having thunder showers." At the same time S/Sgt. James V. Lauro, Co. D, bragged about an Italian woman named Romilda whose affections he had supposedly won and took Charles Dial, Mike Codega, and George S. ("Yak"/"Jumbo") Yakubisin to her house. She lived in a family home on the waterfront near the Rangers' Cafe and was an accomplished pianist and singer who sold vino to the soldiers. Among her children was a nine-year old girl with a shrapnel wound on her chin, who would grow up to be international movie actress Sophia Loren. James Marion Lester, Co. D, remembered her as "a cute little girl."[62]

The situation at Anzio remained virtually unchanged until the 7th, when Co. B was relieved of their attachment to the 179th Infantry and reverted back to battalion control, supporting the 6th Armored Infantry. On the 8th, S-3 "Bud" Pike described his routine nightly games of Bridge with Hutchinson, Meyerson, and Gaiser, writing, "We are still continuing our evening Bridge sessions. It's very interesting the way human beings can easily adjust themselves to their surroundings. There we sit; Meyerson, Hutchinson, the Chaplain, and myself; in a tent pitched in the hole in the ground, a battery of guns sitting about 100 yards behind us, pounding away incessantly, shells coming into the area in rebuttal incessantly, a candle our only light. An airplane comes over and out goes the candle and we duck into our little air-raid shelter made out of sand-filled ammunition boxes. When the plane leaves we return to the table and resume the play. We sit on water cans, and since it has been raining so constantly we usually have our feet in a puddle of water. And in spite of it all we actually enjoy our little sessions. The Colonel is a very good Bridge player and I am trying to learn the rudiments of the game from him." At Pozzuoli, S-2 Burford and eight enlisted men boarded *LST 416*, manned by an unfriendly British crew, for Anzio. On the same day, some of the rear echelon of Co. A went into Pozzuoli to take showers and while there all visited Romilda as the house was located next door.[63]

Co. A took center stage on the 9th as they helped to repel an approximate 100-man enemy counterattack along a ditch in The Factory area. Pvt. Jacob Albert of Suffolk County, New York, suffered a slight wound of shrapnel to the chest. Co. B also was heavily shelled but their only problem was some lies spreading among the men, although the battalion journal failed to give any specifics regarding this claim. S-2 Burford arrived at the beach with S/Sgt. Eugene Plassmann and one man for Co. A and five for Co. B. Burford, who had been traveling back and forth between Anzio and Pozzuoli, noted, "I was amazed at the difference I found in the situation of the men on Anzio this time. Everybody was so completely submerged in well-hidden and protected foxholes that I had difficulty in finding any of them. I learned that the Germans had recently adopted the practice of raining down anti-personnel fragmentation bombs ('butterfly' bombs) from planes. Practically everything above ground, tents and all, was in holes from the flying particles, and the only way to keep a whole skin was to dig and dig deep." Burford also recalled that casualties by both combat and sickness were few.[64]

Describing the stalemate at Anzio, Malcolm Doyle Wilkinson observed, "It appeared that the Germans were not trying to advance and it appeared that neither were we. We dug in. Stalemates can be dangerous and we all came to feel that the Germans would not hesitate to fire an 88 shell at one person if he were out in the open. We lived like moles, we stayed in during the day and we came out at night. We had a saying … if you have to take a crap, be organized … loosen the belt, have paper in hand, go do the job and return at once or old Jerry would take a shot at you. I do not know if this was for real, but it would give you an idea of how edgy everyone was at all times. As time passed, a few of us would be given a few days in the rear for some sort of R and R. Mostly for clean clothes, some real meals, etc. One day my buddy and I were sitting around cleaning our rifles. We came up with a great idea … fire off a few rounds to clean off any rust in the rifle barrel (indeed if there was any). To us it seemed like a logical idea, but remember you are dealing with a bunch of 18 to 24 year olds and sometimes what seemed logical to them, was not received well to those older and wiser. We moved out of the area to a small ditch and he fired a clip and so did I. Within 30 seconds we were surrounded by 20 or 25 of our guys with rifles at the ready. A first lieutenant was screaming obscenities at us … to the effect, 'What in the hell are you doing?' I got the worst chewing out I ever had at any time during the war."[65]

The usual activity continued on the 10th as Lt. Col. Hutchinson, S-2 Burford, and nine enlisted men left on *LST 386*, operated by a very friendly American naval crew, for Pozzuoli, arriving the following day. But the good news was that the depleted ranks of the 83rd were bolstered when nine enlisted men from the 11th Chemical Maintenance Company and 198 enlisted replacements from Personnel Center #6 arrived, with 74 of them assigned to Co. D, although there was an air raid near Naples during the night in which flak fell in the battalion area damaging a tent.[66]

Heavy harassing fire fell on Co. A on the 12th and lightly wounded T/5 Herbert Schumann of Monmouth County, New Jersey, with a shell fragment to the leg. Co. B received some intermittent fire and was ordered attached to the 179th Infantry, 45th Division. Also, Mess Sgt. George Borkhuis, Co. D, said "We received our stars which go on our campaign ribbon. One star for combat in Sicily and one for Italy." On March 13th, Co. B, along with the 6th Armored Infantry and HQ, were alerted to the possible presence of enemy paratroops to their right but a check turned up nothing. At Pozzuoli, Lt. Col. Hutchinson made a speech at the regular morning formation where he welcomed the new replacements to the 83rd and gave a brief history of the battalion. Among the new men was Bernard ("Bernie") Bernhardt who remembered he "… was one of a large number of green replacements. I arrived in Italy to join the 83rd near Pozzuoli for training on 4.2's." William J. Gagliardi of New York, who had already had training with the 155mm howitzers and infantry tactics, also arrived as a replacement via Oran. He said his group of replacements "were sent up to another Repel Depot outside of Naples … and from there, some of us were sent to the 83rd in the town outside Pozzuoli, and were trained as mortar crewmen." Co. D truck driver James Marion Lester recalled, "We even had to train truck drivers. We had to practice blackout driving, with no lights. We did that all the time. They had to train the fellows [*new replacements*] how to fire the mortars." Naples was heavily bombed on the 14th.[67]

A group of men under Chaplain George E. Gaiser departed Anzio on the 15th for Pozzuoli, where a night firing service was held utilizing the hills to the rear of the bivouac as an impact area. Steve Vukson and Pvt. Mike Saterello of Marion County, West Virginia, spent a rainy evening driving to a point near Naples to retrieve two 83rd men whose jeep had been stolen. At Anzio, S-3 "Bud" Pike lamented on the tragedies of *LST 422* and Cisterna, and then described the stagnant situation, writing, "Lately we have preceded our evening Bridge game by enjoying a German propaganda program on a tiny one-lunged portable radio which one of the men has. It features Sally of the Axis, 'the bitch of Berlin,' and George, her stooge. They play good American recordings, tell corny jokes, and dish out the most unbelievable news flashes and propaganda which you would care to hear. No wonder the German people have been so deluded if they have listened to only stuff like that for years. We sit and laugh at it all and enjoy the recordings."[68]

On the 16th, a "lovely day and clear evening," Co. A dug in 1,000 yards forward of their former position in anticipation of an enemy attack which never developed. As a result several thousand rounds of 4.2" ammo had to be returned to the corps dump. On the 17th according to James Helsel, Co. A, "Skeleton crews went up after dark to a forward position 800 yards from the front lines to dig mortar emplacements for a small push that is scheduled. Soon they were very heavily shelled and didn't get much digging done."[69]

David Chapman (left) and Stephen Vukson (right) observing the hot lava from Mt. Vesuvius in March 1944. *Stephen Vukson*

"Doc" Hulcher, Medical Detachment, wrote a long, detailed description in his diary of the events between February 19th and March 17th. "Air raids at night were common occurrences and after sleeping one night in the aid tent all but two, Herr & Chapman, dug holes and slept in them. On the third night a German bomber dropped a bomb right smack thru the tent during one of its night raids. Luckily it was a dud, but the next night Herr & Chapman were sleeping in holes. During that raid our truck & ambulance (which we had picked up from Rangers) received 7 flat tires. Borowski [*Joseph J. Borowski of Baltimore, Maryland*] still doing all the cooking. Had steak from a battle casualty, a cow killed by shrapnel. Here we had air attacks. Often during the night and it's a miserable feeling to be lying in your hole with bombs bursting all around you and nothing to shoot the planes down … During the day our planes were active & dive bombers, bombers & patrols were constantly overhead. We stayed here about 10 days and then moved up about a mile past our original 2nd site in the woods. Here we stayed or are staying at the present time so we've been here about 3 weeks, using the truck for an aid station and each of us in a hole. … We haven't had a B.C. [*battle casualty*] for almost a month now but sick call runs pretty high at times. So far have seen about 650 patients, fever, colds, sore feet, sore back, etc… Had a bath

Two views of Mt. Vesuvius after the volcano had erupted, March 1944. *Both photos courtesy Codega Collection*

from a British shower after about 40 days on beachhead, and a haircut & a bath about 1 wk ago. Sure felt good … Air raids have cut down to a good extent but our planes continue to roar overhead. About 2 weeks ago a large number of bombers went over. Saw a B24 Liberator hit, circle around, men bail out & then the plane crash. Also a B26 hit & burst into flames. Likewise 1 P40 tail blown off & plane crash … Many shells hit near here occasionally. One time we had 12 to come on very near and only one went off. It was about 50 feet from my hole … Rain has been our biggest problem here. Everyone bails water out of their hole. Malm probably leads with 15-20 gal every night. At present we haven't had rain except for one night for a week so we feel much better but our holes are still wet … Only air raids seem to be in morning now and I'm still sleeping in my hole. I don't get up anymore just inch in a little closer in my hole."[70]

For the 83rd Chemical Battalion the next few days of March involved improving mortar emplacements and positions at Anzio. The 18th was a "beautiful day" and during this period "Doc" Hulcher wrote in his diary, "The big attack we were supposed to pull off this morning was called off but I don't know why. It's getting awfully disappointing & tiresome just sitting here. After sick call Borowski made steps for the truck, I shaved, and after lunch … Stopped by to see a crashed 'Spitfire' and then to U.S. Army cemetery to Heath's [*William S. Heath of Sandy Ridge, Pennsylvania*] grave (a casualty from the ship). Couldn't find any wine, then back to our area … After supper I fixed my hole up for it is now fairly dry and listening to radio for a while … I climbed on down into hole and read before going to bed."[71]

Repetitive exercise and duties were the order of the day at Pozzuoli, along with passes to town and to Pompeii. During one such visit on the 19th, Lt. Col. Hutchinson, Capt. Robert Edwards, S-2 Burford, and Chaplain Gaiser journeyed up Mt. Vesuvius, which had been showing signs of volcanic activity recently. When near the top the party was forced to make a quick exit down the slopes by the advancing lava flow. Steve Vukson also took a sightseeing trip and "visited Pompeii, the ancient ruins, and the famous Mt. Vesuvius which was erupting when we were there. The molten lava was coming down and covered part of the road. Simurda and I snapped quite a few pictures right by the flowing lava."[72]

While at Pozzuoli on March 20th, Lt. Col. Hutchinson and S-2 Burford made a 60-mile trip to Carano where they were informed by the Army chemical officer that companies C and D would be attached to the 88th Infantry Division, located at Carano. Around the 25th they were being sent to the Garigliano River front at Minturno for approximately two weeks to gradually condition the new replacements, as well as the *LST 422* survivors, to combat conditions. It was recommended that once they assumed their new position they support the 349th Infantry on the 88th Division's right flank William Gagliardi, assigned to Co. A, recalled, "We were sent up to … replace the unfortunate men who were lost in the sinking of the LST … it was difficult to be sent over as a replacement because in the months you are training you make a lot of good friends, then you get sent to another outfit, you get separated from some who were sent to other outfits and you never see or hear from them again … I was put into a company and made new friends all over again. This was not difficult to do, because for the most part, I was put in with a good bunch of guys."[73]

At Anzio the weather was warm and sunny as Co. B, attached to the 179th Infantry, was split in two, with one platoon attached to the 179th Infantry and the other to the 157th. During the day Capt. Robert E. Edwards, Jr., wrote of the medical situation on the beachhead: "Plasma is used to a great extent over here. It is a great life saver. It is not only used for those that lose blood because of wounds but also in several diseases … Spike [*Leonard Merrill*] had an infusion in Sicily when he had jaundice." Edwards closed with "Saw a good show last night 'Phantom of the Opera'. Not as scary as I remember the last one but music is good. In color."[74]

There was a large early morning sick call for the 83rd at Anzio on March 21st, and during the night the first air raid in about a week transpired. Albert Sabatino the ex-Italian POW returned from the hospital as he had cut his finger two weeks previously and didn't bother to have it bandaged. Blood poisoning set in and the doctors caught it just in time. Mt. Vesuvius was still erupting near Pozzuoli on the 22nd, the weather remained warm and spring-like at Anzio, where "Doc" Hulcher noted, "Artillery landing in pretty close right now. Think Jerry is shelling the road behind us." The 23rd was marked by an early morning rain and a small sick call. Some of the men had hamburgers for lunch. March 24th found Pennsylvanian Earl C. Koring, Co. A, lightly wounded in the head by an enemy shell fragment while visiting the OP with Lt. Walter Hauser.[75]

The nerve-wracking monotony of the situation at Anzio was well described by S-3 "Bud" Pike as he wrote, "Two days ago was our second month on this beachhead. It has gotten so that one just lives with his memories and takes each day as it comes, not caring much what happens. Sometimes I think it is better for a soldier's morale to be in full retreat or to be fighting against superior forces than to be just sitting, sitting, sitting, waiting for something to develop. While the enemy has made three all-out efforts to push us off the beachhead in February and March the ground held by us and the general situation are essentially the same as when we first arrived and consolidated our positions. As the papers tell you, the Germans can shell any spot on the beachhead as they desire and they also have observation of any spot but things could be worse. A person is constantly under a certain amount of nervous tension, wondering where the next one will land and yet we go for long periods of time

L-R: Suarez, Norman Brann, and Lloyd Fiscus of Co. C of the 83rd at Minturno, April 1944. *Lloyd Fiscus*

(4 or 5 hours) without having a shell land anywhere near us." Pike also reported the latest command changes in the battalion, writing, "Meyerson is now Exec. and a Major. He ranked me as a Captain. I am BN S-3. Edwards is BN S-1. Cornett has been transferred – to a non-combatant job. Leave it to Chris, eh? Trey is still S-4. I am also acting as S-2, temporarily. Company commanders are – A, McEvoy; B, Mindrum; C, Laus; and D, Crenshaw. Old timers still around also are – McKinnon, Forrester, Hays, Hauser, Stone, and Metcalfe. Metcalfe is next on the rotation list. It gets smaller and smaller all the time." He humorously added, "The English have moved in around our present position and as they get a weekly beer and whiskey ration … our association has been very chummy. We trade cigars, cigarettes, and candy for beer and whiskey so that everything works out fine."[76]

At Pozzuoli, an awards presentation was held in the afternoon with 135 Purple Hearts and 21 Clusters to the Purple Hearts given out to the battalion by colonels Maurice Barker and Koblenz [*possibly Col. Siegfried P. Coblentz*], and Gen. William C. Kabrich, CWS Technical Command. A demonstration was also given by the 12th Chemical Company (Maintenance) of two variations of the 4.2" mortar, both with original designs of recoil devices.[77]

An enemy shell burst near the 1st Platoon of Co. A on the 25th, killing Pvt. Frederick Pleskac and lightly wounding Pvt. Harry A. Clark of New York, although "Doc" Hulcher claimed there were two men wounded. James Helsel, Co. A, also claimed there were two men wounded and said Frederick Pleskac came under a heavy shelling near his hole and, as he ran past his twin brother Vincent's hole to reach his own, Vincent called for him to jump in with him. Helsel added, "But he kept on running to his own hole. In the next few seconds a shell landed close enough to kill him." This could be the episode recalled by Leonard W. Turan who said that after being out in the wide open after landing at Anzio "… there was nothing around except scrub oaks and the Germans were constantly shelling them … [*we*] cut down the scrub oaks and made three-sided barricades around [*our*] positions to protect [*us*] from the shrapnel … there were two twins in [*the*] outfit and they were sharing the same barricade and a round landed right on top of them." According to Helsel, Vincent Pleskac was transferred to another outfit soon afterward. Apparently such incidents prompted the Medical Detachment, as well as 15 men at the battalion CP, to move to new positions at Anzio. "Doc" Hulcher noted the Medical Detachment had been advised of the move the previous day to the same position with the motor pool they had held before their current locale. Hulcher said, "After sick call we packed up and moved in with [*the*] motor pool. It rained and we had to wait until it stopped before going to work on our fox holes. I haven't quite finished mine, but it's going to be a honey. I can even sit up in this one … All that digging has almost got me. I have about 50 sand bags over me if you can imagine how deluxe this hole is. No air raids and only a few shells coming in but they are some distance away."[78]

A group of 83rd men relaxing on the Anzio beach. *Codega Collection*

Back at Pozzuoli, Charles Dial again visited with Sophia Loren's mother and invited her to bring the young child to the outfit the following day for food and to see if the medics could fix the shrapnel scar in her daughter's chin. The invitation was accepted but, as pilfering Italian civilians had become a nuisance near the camp, a wire barricade was erected and Sophia and her mother were placed in a holding pen until Charles Dial found out about it and freed them. Charles took them to the medics who fixed the shrapnel wound in Sophia's chin to the point of non-visibility, and then Mess Sgt. George Borkhuis fed them and sent them home with a jeep loaded down with food. The kindness of the 83rd soldiers was recounted by Sophia Loren in her 1979 book *Sophia: Living and Loving*.[79]

A motor convoy of companies C and D, HQ and HQ Detachment, and the Medical Detachment, in support of the 88th Infantry Division, departed Pozzuoli for Minturno at 7:00 in the evening, with orders to drive with lights only as far as Madragalone, and from that point only "cat's eyes" were to be used. The last of the motor convoy reached Minturno at 2:00 in the morning of March 26th although the trip had been a bit marred when a 2½-ton truck overturned, lightly injuring five Co. D men, including privates Marion F. Harris, Domenica J. Giannino, Napoleon G. St. Louis, Henry Baun, and Frank R. Butler. The trucks were unloaded and either returned to the battalion motor pool near Carenola or to the rear echelon at Pozzuoli. This was probably the convoy mentioned by truck driver James Marion Lester who said he had a flat tire, and, "… he was alone in the truck and when the Minturno trucks came they told him to fix the tire and there would be someone waiting at the turnoff. He drove and drove and never saw anyone, and by then he was climbing up a mountain …" An Allied force was at the top and the commanding officer gave him a pass so he would not be AWOL when he returned to his outfit the next morning. He said his men were really glad to see him but not half as much as he was glad to see them.[80]

Hale H. Hepler, Co. C, one of the LST disaster survivors sent to Minturno, described being placed on the front line in an olive orchard for 38 days, where the weather was beautiful for the first two days only to be followed by 36 days of rain and mud. Hepler said, "This was a critical area to take because the Germans were using a monastery nearby for headquarters. The Allied forces did not want to bomb the monastery but needed to get the Germans out." Kelly Seibels, a Co. C replacement wrote in his log, "Minturno was a complete wreck & full of filth, fleas, etc. It overlooked the valley & we had an OP there. We were supporting the 1st Battalion of the 351st of the 88th Division." The position at Minturno, in the defilade of a small range of hills on the Garigliano River front, quickly turned tragic because the area, originally declared safe by the division Engineers, was found to be filled with enemy mines, primarily the standard S-mines and the wooden box type filled with HE but no shrapnel. The first victim was Pvt. Oscar W. Freeman, Co. D, who was seriously wounded when he detonated an S-mine (a "leaping lena"), which also wounded Cpl. Lee Steedle in the leg.[81]

Steedle later wrote, "My first night in combat … as a replacement … some of us had been assigned to man the machine gun, two at a time, at two hour intervals during the rainy night. When my turn came, one of the other new replacements, thinking I had stayed in my water-filled hole, walked to its edge to awaken me. I had been fast asleep on the level ground two feet away. I saw a huge yellow flash through my closed eyelids, as concussion lifted me off the ground. The man, whose name I had barely gotten to know, had stepped onto an S-mine -- a Bouncing Betty. It had been propelled about three feet into the air by a small charge, and exploded as an air burst. Since I was lying almost directly under the explosion, most of the shrapnel had blown outward rather than down, luckily only wounding me in one leg and shattering the stock of my carbine. The other man wasn't so lucky. There wasn't much the medics could do for him." In his memoir Steedle added, "Realizing there were probably other unswept mines in our position, we didn't hunt for a stretcher, but put our still-conscious man in a blanket, and four of us carried him to the battalion aid station about 500 yards back … There wasn't much the medics could do for our man, but just before

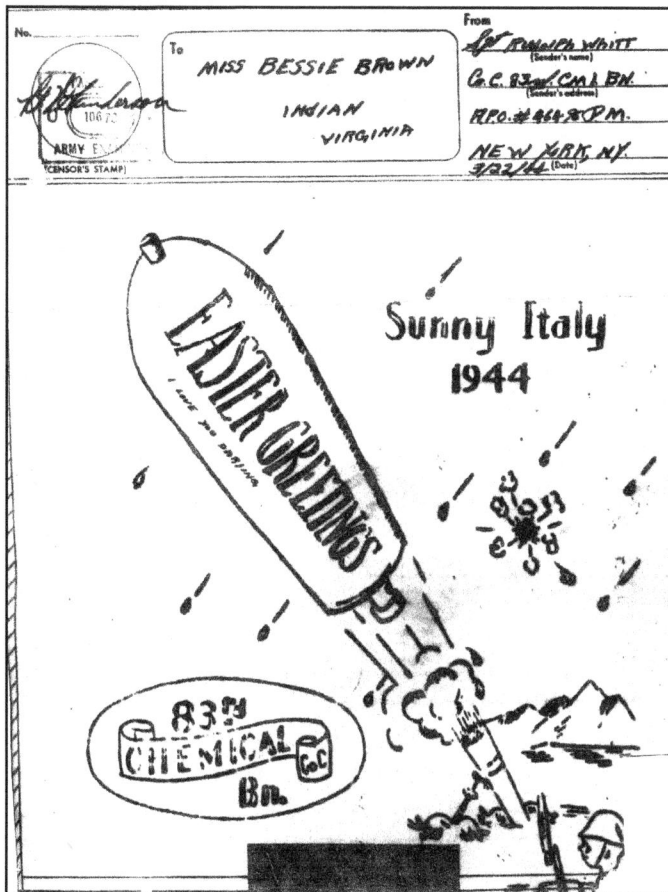

Easter Greetings V-mail sent by Rudolph Whitt
of Co. C, on March 22, 1944. *Rudolph Whitt*

we left to return to our outfit a doctor looked at me and told an aide that I'd been wounded and was in shock. I didn't believe him, until looking down, I saw that my right pants-leg and shoe were bloody. I was made to lie down, and since the wound was minor, it was an hour or two before a surgeon got around to me and dusting the wound with sulfa, extracted the shrapnel. I was able to amble back to our position before dawn."[82]

Other casualties quickly followed when an S-mine detonated in Co. C's area , killing Pvt. Thomas E. Spangenberg [*also listed as Thomas A. Pagenberg*] and seriously wounding S/Sgt. John R. Holley, who lost an arm, and 1st Lt. Victor W. Gunderson of Michigan, who died three hours later. Among the lightly wounded but not hospitalized were Cpl. Fred Tombolini, Pvt. Joseph A. Nemeth, and Pvt. Raymond N. Risley. Kelly Seibels, Co. C, wrote in his log, "We lost three men (2 dead, one arm blown off) the first morning due to an S-mine." Bernard ("Bernie") Bernhardt, also a replacement man of Co. C, recalled, " … [*we were*] camping in a field supposedly cleared of mines. I was sitting with several others when someone nearby stepped on a mine and there was a loud explosion. One of the more experienced men close to me yelled to hug the ground and stay down. It's a good thing I did, because a few seconds later (which seemed like long minutes), I heard a whizzing sound over my head. Had I given in to the impulse to get up sooner, I probably wouldn't be here now."[83]

Robert F. Thorpe, Co. C, said that during this period an S-mine popped out of the ground while he was laying a telephone line and, later Thorpe was about 50 feet from John Holley when Holley lost his arm. A few days later, when the company was tearing down tents to move, Raymond ("Pops") Hoover found one of the mines under the corner of his blanket.[84]

Also during the 26th, the battalion headquarters communications, which had set up wire connections to the 351st Infantry, about 1,000 yards west of the 83rd CP, reported two S-mines had been stepped on, flew into the air several feet, but failed to detonate. A mine sweeping platoon rechecked the 83rd area, where they found several dozen anti-personnel mines, and told the battalion that a mine sweeper had been killed in the area the previous day.[85]

Harold Hughes, Co. D, who had returned to the battalion after an extended absence due to malaria, said they supported the British 56th (Black Cat) Division, which had been making unsuccessful assaults on Monte Cassino. He added, "We existed in a no-man's land. German artillery methodically worked over our area and except for patrols we huddled in our burrows munching D-ration chocolate bars and figuring out ways to meet our personal needs such as urinating in one's helmet and pitching it up over the side … cold rains lashed the area …"[86]

Curtis A. Williams, Medical Detachment of Co. D, recalled that during this period five or six Germans had been giving them problems for some time but all but one were caught or eliminated. Curtis decided that if he went out with the Red Cross emblem on his armband he would be safe, but such philosophy proved untrue. A pesky German jumped out of the brush behind him and lunged a knife into his back. Remembering what his karate teacher had taught him, Williams mustered his strength and hit the soldier in the neck, took his knife from him, and rammed it through his throat.[87]

Back at Anzio on the 26th, "Doc" Hulcher finished digging his foxhole, which he considered a masterpiece, while S-3 Ed "Bud" Pike mentioned the rain. "We have moved our BN CP again and of course it had to start raining again immediately after all our tents were torn down and everything was exposed to the elements. Raincoats were scarce so that a few of us were soaked to the skin. That of course put everyone in a delightful mood." James Helsel, Co. A, recalled his miserable night, writing, "If there is a hell on earth, I think we have found it; a fellow can't even take a crap around here unless he camouflages it ... Jerry ... shelled our area so heavily that almost every one threw dirt and shrapnel against our hole. He had my teeth rattling like a typewriter, for I would have swore I heard one coming right through the ground toward the side of our hole. We had some very near misses, but thanks to God no one was hurt."[88]

At the beachhead on the 27th, Co. A was heavily engaged again. Three shells came into the 2nd Platoon area and seriously wounded Pvt. Benjamin F. Scott from Delaware County, Pennsylvania, in his side. Co. B, also under intense enemy shelling, forced back a Mark IV tank, and one unidentified man of the company was wounded according to "Doc" Hulcher. At Minturno, the AT company of the 351st Infantry rechecked the area for mines and Lt. Col. Hutchinson, accompanied by Lt. Justin G. Woomer, went to visit the 349th Infantry. The purpose was to check on the details of the 1st Platoon of Co. D, supporting the 349th south of Castelforte near San Lorenza that night, where the company would fire on Castelforte, Ventosa, and the draws north of the towns. Hutchinson reported he would move one platoon of four guns into position and his other platoons were in the 351st area and were registered and ready to fire upon call. Cpl. Lee Steedle, Co. D, recalled their position below Castelforte, an old village with rough stone roads, was "... well defiladed ... on the steep reverse slope of a mountain." Steedle said that during the period near Castelforte Lt. Perry Rice, acting as a forward observer, participated in a duel with a German forward observer in a stone tower, the only such known incident in which their platoon engaged. Lt. Rice eliminated his opponent.[89]

German POWs informed Co. B that they were to be the center of an attack at Anzio on the 28th, a warm day, and that the 515th Mtz. Infantry (German) had been reinforced by the 29th Panzer Grenadiers. Various assaults were made on Co. B, as well as on Co. A, but all efforts were blocked, while at Minturno ten rounds of either 88 or 105mm shells landed 35 yards south of the road near Co. C. No casualties resulted and harassing fire was placed on Ventosa and the trail between Ventosa and Castelforte. S-2 Burford received information the rear echelon was to move to Benevento but could not get confirmation, and, as he had already received his rotation orders on the 25th, he decided not to pursue the matter. Robert E. Edwards sent home his Purple Heart "from banging up received in a ship wreck ... Bill H [*William Hutchinson*] has mentioned silver cups several times, Spike [*Leonard Merrill*], Ralph [*Rankin*], [*Veryl*] Hays, [*Eric*] Peterson, besides Bill are eligible for cups." In a 2008 interview the only "cups" Ed Trey could recall included a little silver cup he was given for his work with the Rangers.[90]

The usual fire missions continued on the 29th of March. Co. C was attached to the 350th Infantry at Minturno, and six enemy shells fell near the position of HQ Co. and Co. D's Blue Platoon late in the day. Charlie Lowry, Co. D Motor Pool, wrote, "It is a very nice spring day." At Anzio there was an air raid in which some of the battalion witnessed three planes shot down. Casualties again mounted on the morning of a cloudy 30th at Anzio when a shell burst in the position of the 1st Platoon of Co. A, lightly wounding privates Frank Boduck, John H. Hopkins, Anthony J. Knapick, and Raymond S. Snyder. Lawrence Ertzberger, Co. A, a former thread manufacturing plant worker from Stephens County, Georgia, remembered the incident. "Our platoon was heavily shelled, almost a direct hit on one mortar. Raymond Snyder and Hopkins were badly wounded and never came back. I thought Snyder lost his leg as it looked like it was almost cut in two about the knee. Frank Boduck and A. J. Knapick were slightly wounded but came back." The enemy also shelled the ammo dump of the 1st Platoon, forcing the platoon to evacuate the position and return later for their equipment. Companies C and D continued to place heavy fire on the enemy at Minturno and San Lorenza, although the morning was spent "in the improvement of internal discipline."[91]

On the last day of March, as Co. D fired on positions near Mt. Ceracoli and Castelforte, companies C and D were attached to the 88th Infantry Division. On the Anzio front "Doc" Hulcher reported "26 men on sick call this AM. Lot of them breaking down from strain of battle. All was quiet until about 8 PM when [*we*] had another mild artillery barrage come in near by. Haven't had the chance to examine tent for holes and know of no other damage ... I expect to see invasion across channel within a month. Sure am disappointed in the fighting here and at Cassino." Sam Bundy, Co. A, complained the 83rd had been at Anzio so long their wine supply, previously buried for protection, was nearly exhausted.[92]

During the month of March, the 83rd had suffered 11 casualties at Anzio and 12 [*15 according to the Report of Action*] at Minturno, for a total of 23 [*or 26*], while 1,426 rounds of both HE and WP had been fired at Anzio and 1,531 by companies C and D, with 1,339 of that total at Minturno. In addition, a new type of mortar emplacement had been developed during the month at Anzio, where the soil was drier than in previous campaigns and the beachhead's flat terrain was better suited to artillery. The new emplacement used " … a foundation of four railway ties and sandbags, with two more ties planted vertically in the ground to prevent the baseplate from being driven rearwards … available mortar positions [*at Anzio*] provided little defilade, cover and concealment, but with extensive preparations, well dug in emplacements, and good use of all available means of camouflage, casualties were held to a minimum."[93]

April opened with beautiful spring weather and companies A and B holding their same positions at Anzio as a heavy enemy barrage fell on Co. B. This was also the day Pvt. Leo D. Fagan, Co. B, of Oklahoma, was given a Southern Baptism in the waters of Anzio bay by VI Corps Chaplain William E. King, purportedly the first seawater baptism at Anzio beachhead. At Minturno, the Red Platoon of Co. D fired on targets such as Castelforte and were visited by Gen. John E. Sloan of the 88th Division. One S-mine was picked up in the 83[rds] area so a jeep trail was cleared for the battalion. George Borkhuis, Co. D, wrote "The weather is getting warm … even the mosquitoes fly around like a group of bombers but they still don't like the taste of my blood." On April 2nd Co. D provided harassing fire on Hill 316 and the draw behind Ceracoli. During the action Co. D got mad when the 2nd Battalion, 349th Infantry, accused them of firing on their Co. G. Co. D claimed they were firing at Ceracoli and would fire one more smoke round for the 2nd Battalion to observe. The smoke hit west of Ceracoli which satisfied the 349th that the 83rd was not firing on them. Such activities continued at both Minturno and Anzio for the next few days and included intermittent air raids and shelling, including one shell that landed about 200 yards from "Doc" Hulcher's medical boys during the evening of the 4th.[94]

On the 5th, a German soldier surrendered to Co. B and told them he had recently arrived from Austria, belonged to the 315th Division [*German*], and that 500 replacements were on their way. "Doc" Hulcher also had to send a man from Co. B to the hospital who had passed out from malaria. But an event of more serious nature took place on the 5th. According to Veryl R. Hays, Co. A, the railroad bed and highway at Anzio formed a heavily traveled "Y," which the Germans continually shelled and which became known as Suicide Junction. "Our platoon had been emplaced at this intersection for six weeks because there was no other place available. Suicide Junction deserved its name and, as a result of wounds and combat fatigue, our platoon dwindled from 80 to 20 men … On the morning of 5 April we took a merciless shelling. Four men were seriously wounded. I ordered the rest to move back to the company command post. The men cleared out, all very badly shaken, and with their morale at a new low. The mortars were left behind." Hays continued his story, reflecting, "That evening we were told of an impending counterattack on the right flank and ordered to move the mortars to a new position to cover the danger there. The men had taken all the punishment they could absorb. They were rattled and nervous. They plainly showed it, and they said so. But we had to prevent that breakthrough on the flank. The infantry was counting on us … the Platoon Leader did not order his men to go back to the old position and get the mortars. He merely said, 'You men take it easy. We'll ask the 2nd platoon to go after the mortars.' Within five minutes every man was up on his feet and set to go. They wanted the world to know they still could take it, and furthermore they'd be damned if they'd let anyone else do their work." About 8:00 in the evening "Doc" Hulcher said the enemy launched a heavy barrage, "… and we all hit for holes, where we stayed. Some came in very close and there's quite a bit of fighting going on now. Sounds like tanks are in on it too. Lots of small arms fire. Jerry must be attacking, but I wish it were us."[95]

At Minturno, companies C and D were relieved of their

George G. Young of the 83rd Chemical Battalion in a foxhole on the Anzio beachhead. *Codega Collection*

L-R: Co. D's men named Thomas, Joseph Palmer, Abraham Sheckler, and Mike Codega living in a foxhole at Anzio. *Codega Collection*

attachment to the 88th Division, II Corps, on the 5th in preparation to join the other two companies at Anzio. During the entire Minturno action, companies C and D had expended 3,775 HE and 871 WP, for a total of 4,646 rounds.[96]

Shelling continued throughout the night at Anzio and finally stopped around 6:30 on the morning of the 6th, when "Doc" Hulcher reported six cases of malaria and feared it would present a problem throughout the summer. S-3 "Bud" Pike reported, "The anti-malaria campaign has started in earnest here now and we are eating our Atabrine every day, which helps to spoil our otherwise very good meals. We have a kitchen set up here now and they are doing a fine job." Near Minturno companies C and D departed the Garigliano River front by truck and returned to Pozzuoli to rest, repair, and reorganize for the trip to Anzio. The journal of the 349th Infantry reported companies C and D of the 83rd left the area at 4:20 in the morning and the area was cleaned. Clearance was given to a Lt. Walters of the 83rd who remained behind, not leaving until 8:05.[97]

For the next three days of April, only mild air raids transpired on the Anzio front, although by the 9th, Easter Sunday, Capt. Robert Browning Smith, nicknamed "Smitty," had arrived from the 2nd Chemical Mortar Battalion to take command of Co. C of the 83rd. Smith was born in 1906 at Bluejacket, Oklahoma Territory, but moved to New Mexico two years later and attended New Mexico A&M Preparatory School. Following graduation from Las Cruces Union High School in 1925, he attended New Mexico College of Agriculture and Mechanic Arts [*New Mexico State University*] from 1931 to 1934, majoring in civil engineering and business administration. At the outbreak of the war he was the owner/operator of a dry cleaning plant at Hot Springs, New Mexico, and entered the service August 28, 1942, as a 1st lieutenant. In May of 1943 he was promoted to captain and served in the 2nd Chemical Mortar Battalion before transfer to the 83rd. Although short on combat experience, he was well respected, liked by his men, and was quick to accept the advice of veterans. Upon his arrival, Smith wrote of the battalion, "This seems to be a good outfit but they have had a lot of tough luck so now it's time for their luck to change … Quite a lot of the men are replacements, but they have had good training and I think we'll give Jerry hell." Pvt. Byron H. Jordan, Co. B, said he spent his Easter Sunday watching the movie *The Sky's the Limit* on the Anzio beachhead.[98]

On a sunny April 10th, the 83rd's first reported casualties of the month took place as Co. B fell under a heavy barrage of what was thought to be a large caliber railroad gun, possibly the infamous "Anzio Annie," also known as the "Anzio Express." Pvt. Leland M. Rozzell of White County, Tennessee, and Pvt. Norman L. Robinson of New Castle, Pennsylvania, were lightly wounded. The battalion CP was also the focus of heavy bombardment. In the meantime, a mortar shoot was conducted at Pozzuoli wherein during one stage 16 guns concentrated on the crest of a hill to the rear of the bivouac. New replacement Lee Steedle recalled, "all eight mortars of our Company were lined up and directed at a steep, bare slope, only 300 yards away. At the Company Commander's order to fire, each crew dropped five rounds down its barrel, so rapidly that more than half the shells were in the air at the same time. Forty shells, 340 pounds of TNT, burst 300 yards from us, all within 20 seconds. We could actually feel the concussion: Awesome! More firepower by far, than a battery of artillery."[99]

Early on April 11th, "Doc" Hulcher reported there had been a battle casualty at Anzio the previous night - a wound of the chest wall. Air raids continued including a large scale air assault by the enemy on the 12th. While such activity persisted at Anzio, companies C, D, and HQ departed at 10:00 on the beautiful morning of the 12th from their bivouac area and were transported to the Texas Staging Area at Nisida in GM trucks. The men loaded on LSTs and departed Nisida for Pozzuoli en route to Anzio. Kelly Seibels, Co. C, said, "We went on an LST and the trip was uneventful." Battalion Personnel Adjutant Arthur J. Usher remained behind at Pozzuoli in charge of the rear echelon, which consisted of about 50 truck drivers and men not fully recovered from their wounds. Steve Vukson, who was left behind in charge of Rear Battalion Supply to draw parts for vehicles in the rear, noted the entire group remaining at Pozzuoli comprised 60 men, all with specific jobs. Vukson said the next two days the small group " … continued improving our new bivouac area … It was like a good sized family in comparison with the whole Battalion. There wasn't much work to do … We put our mosquito bars above the bunks as flies were getting plentiful."[100]

Shortly before the arrival of companies C, D, and HQ at Anzio on April 13th, privates George A. Caddle and Victor P. Barnheart, both of Co. B, were wounded by enemy shell fire. The medics also took care of a man with a sprained ankle. The three companies finally arrived from Pozzuoli at 7:30 a.m. and walked to the assembly area of the 45th Division, located in a British ammo dump area. Pfc. Mario Ricci, Co. C, recalled his initial impressions of Anzio, writing, "After an eerie overnight trip from Naples on a small naval craft I got my first view of Anzio-Nettuno in the early dawn. A hospital ship anchored nearby was preparing to take on the wounded. On the beach all appeared ominously still. Inland, flashes from artillery fire gave the appearance of swarms of fireflies over the dark terrain. All visible structures on the beach and port areas were in rubble … Upon disembarking I learned that, except for male volunteers employed by the Allies as dock workers, the entire civilian population had been evacuated from the Beachhead. Daylight revealed countless barrage balloons anchored by cables to ground objects. The cables served as a deterrent to low flying enemy aircraft and dive-bombers."[101]

While awaiting word on their deployment, the new replacements were rudely introduced to "Anzio Annie" or the "Anzio Express," the large German railroad gun on the southern edge of Rome, which dropped shells believed to be 280mm within 600 yards of the men. Daniel Shields, a survivor of *LST 422*, wrote in his diary, "Heard Anzio Express 1st time. It really surprised me." But by 1:30 in the afternoon they had moved by truck to the battalion motor pool where Co. D and HQ Co. set up their headquarters. Paul Simon Giles, a farmer from Moultrie County, Georgia, and a replacement cook in Co. D, recalled, "The beach area was about 7 miles deep at the widest point and 13 miles long. We occupied the beach and Germans were in the mountains. The day we arrived we were told it would be wise to get below ground level because the Germans bombed them every night. A buddy and I dug a trench about a foot deep and big enough for both to sleep in. That night, just as we had been told, the bombs fell. We quickly realized that we were vulnerable with an open top trench, so four of us worked together to dig an 'L' shaped bunker about four feet deep and big enough to sleep four. We found some railroad ties and placed them over the top of the bunker and put dirt over the ties, which made us more secure." Pfc. Mario Ricci, Co. C, added, "I was taken to the Headquarters detachment of the 83rd, which was close to its mortar units deployed behind the infantry. Making a shelter was my immediate priority. Trenches had to be shallow because of ground water. I covered the trench with branches, straw from a nearby stack, soil, and camouflaged it with brush. I placed additional straw on the moist ground. And, except when required to be at any of the mortar locations, that two by six feet burrow became my home for the next two and one half months … I was advised to stay in a shelter at all times unless required by work to be outside. One comforting feeling: the Chaplain's burrow was less than 50 feet from mine. The first night in my shelter I was suddenly awakened by lice crawling all over me. The straw was infested. The following day I dusted myself and my shelter with delousing powder." Co. C moved to a position about one mile north of the east side of the Anzio-Albano road where Bernard ("Bernie") Bernhardt of the company recalled, "The mess truck was set up in an enormous crater, where a giant shell had exploded before we arrived."[102]

Around noon Capt. Silverino V. DeMarco, Medical

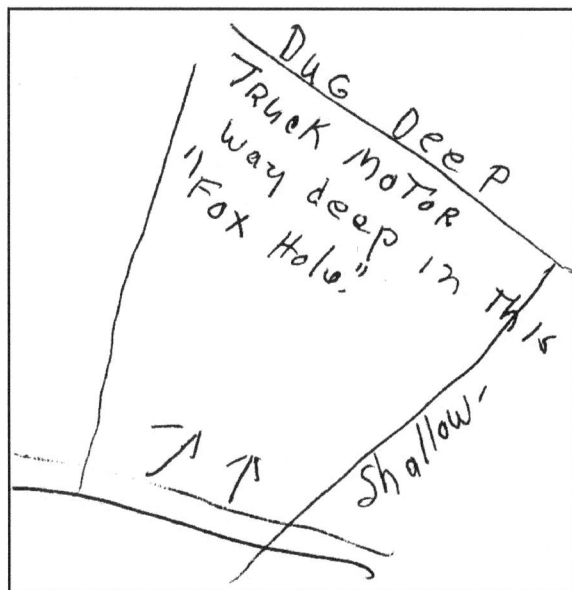

Truck foxhole at Anzio as sketched by James M. Lester, Co. D Motor Pool. *Lester Collection*

Detachment, another survivor of the *LST 422* tragedy, and the remainder of the battalion found their way to their respective positions to rejoin their comrades at Anzio. James Marion ("Les") Lester, Co. D Motor Pool, remarked that in order to protect the trucks in the motor pool they would dig a large hole, deep in the front and shallow in the back, and then drive the vehicles into the hole front end first to protect the motors and so that they could back the trucks out. Then they would put camouflage over top of the hole. Lester added, "The dirt would be mounded around it [*the truck*] so that when shells landed, if they landed nearby and exploded, the shrapnel wouldn't hit the motor. We dug holes to live in also. I lived in a hole in Anzio all the time I was there. We put branches over it, then bags filled with sand, and then more branches; for protection mostly. When the guns would fire at night we could feel that vibration in the ground." He said that every night a specific German plane came over and "Bed Check Charlie" would be yelled as a warning, but the plane never did strafe them. Finally, the commanding officer tired of this nerve-wracking nuisance and set up three mortars, which brought the plane down that night. Lester said they had no more trouble after that with "Bed Check Charlie."[103]

Pfc. Mario Ricci, Co. C, said that upon his arrival at Anzio as a radio operator he was instructed, "No radio transmissions! Enemy detection finders locked in on the sources of radio signals, and their artillery targeted the area with deadly accuracy. All communications between the various positions would be by phone or messengers ... I soon began the endless job of laying phone lines and maintaining them. These lines were frequently severed, either by enemy shell fire, or by their patrols which infiltrated our positions. This work could only be done under cover of darkness, since our entire flat beachhead was under enemy observation."[104]

Lt. Col. Hutchinson, the newly arrived Maj. Sam Efnor, and Chaplain Gaiser moved to the battalion forward CP while the battalion supply and mail and message center were placed in a house near the Army Engineer dump. This dump is probably the one referenced by James Marion Lester, who wrote, "The first time they were taking us to our gun position we had to go across from one black top road to the next one. It was probably about a mile. The engineers had just made a dirt road across it. All along, on both sides, they had gouged holes into the ground and had stored ammunition inside. The Germans knew it was there and they would fire at them. Trying to get the ammunition to burn and explode. And they did. There would be fires going on there off and on. We had just nicely started across there, an officer was leading our small convoy, when they started shelling the road. The officer stopped the convoy right out there in the middle of this assault. There we sat, of course we got out of the trucks and ran. I dived over an old barbed wire fence. I've got a scar. I tried to get a Purple Heart for it, but I couldn't. After that, we never went out in convoy. "George R. Borkhuis, Co. D wrote at this time, "If it wasn't for the shells flying and whistling overhead and the air raids, one would never know he was at the front."[105]

The following day, Co. C relieved Co. A of the 83rd and 20 enlisted men from each platoon of Co. D relieved Co. D of the 84th Chemical Battalion. There was also an air raid at battalion HQ, fondly remembered by Daniel Shields, who wrote, " ... should have seen [*Ed*] Trey getting out of [*the*] house." Upset in a different manner was "Doc" Hulcher, who was scolded by Lt. Col. Hutchinson for not having on a clean jacket. "Doc" vented that "Hutch" inspected everything, including the foxholes, protocol that Hulcher felt was "no good." More 88mm rounds fell in HQ area on the 15th along with an evening air raid. Lieutenants Veryl R. Hays and Leonard R. Kenney of Co. A were awarded Silver Stars for their performances on February 18th at Anzio. During the night and early morning "Doc" Hulcher treated a man who had shot himself in the foot and another who had cut his finger.[106]

The 83rd Chemical Battalion lost another good man, although not through combat, when David W. Meyerson, who had occasionally acted as commanding officer of the battalion during the various periods of Hutchinson's absences, left to take command of the 2nd Chemical Battalion on April 16th. Hutchinson felt Meyerson had done a fine job leading the battalion at times. Apparently Meyerson's assignment was the result of some odd exchange agreement between VI Corps and II Corps involving Sam Efnor of the 2nd Chemical Battalion and Meyerson. Reportedly both were outstanding officers but each had run afoul of authorities who found themselves with two quality officers caught in a tangled mess of problems. The entire situation remains very unclear, although the best description of affairs can be found in Walter J. Eldredge's fine book on the 2nd Chemical Mortar Battalion, *Finding My Father's War*.[107]

In any event, Eldredge states two stories have surfaced relating to Meyerson. The first story says that at Anzio Meyerson had brought the 83rd up too early for departure for a convoy, resulting in a major traffic jam which exposed the battalion to shell fire. The other story Meyerson personally relayed to Eldredge before his death, claiming that he sent his driver in his personal vehicle through an area restricted for officers only to pick up some orders. Meyerson received a letter from a very angry brigadier demanding an explanation, to which he replied the order did not state the commanding officer had to be in the vehicle to enter the restricted area. The brigadier was furious at the response and accused Meyerson of being insubordinate. This was confirmed by John P. McEvoy of the 83rd. One, or possibly both, of these incidents left VI Corps staff feeling Meyerson was unworthy of being given command of the 83rd Chemical.[108]

Efnor, likewise, was also the focus of two different stories. The first involved the 2nd Chemical Battalion going into reserve following 108 days of combat. An Inspector General (IG) appeared one day later and complained to Efnor about "equipment shortages, incomplete maintenance, and missing paperwork." According to some reports, on the second day of the inspection Efnor had had enough and told the IG the battalion did not need him telling them of their failings after 108 days of combat and to go away so they could concentrate on more important work. The other story, which took place around the same time, involved a visit by some Red Cross ladies needing a place to change. Efnor ran all the men out of one of the HQ tents, had the sides pulled down for their privacy, and then found himself in trouble when an IG came to HQ and entered the CP tent only to be surrounded by "semi-clad women." Again, one or both of these episodes left II Corps staff feeling Efnor was not worthy of being the commander of the 2nd Chemical.[109]

This mess, whatever the cause, left II and VI Corps with two high quality CWS officers with strong and aggressive personalities, but authorities were befuddled as to how to discipline them. Walter Eldredge believes that the situation was probably resolved in a series of administrative moves involving Col. Maurice Barker, 5th Army Chemical Officer, who was in charge of chemical warfare personnel in both corps. With the cooperation of Gen. William N. Porter, CWS, and Gen. Mark Clark, he found the obvious solution - place Efnor with the 83rd Chemical and Meyerson with the 2nd Chemical. It proved an excellent decision as both soon afterward commanded their new battalions with great skill and courage.[110]

Although this would prove a positive change, the stagnant situation at Anzio had caused many to develop negative feelings, as noted by "Bud" Pike, who claimed, "... I am not the only disgruntled individual in the BN. Mindy & Stone share my attitude. But I guess we'll get over it and make the best of things. A man would go crazy around here if he didn't adjust himself to the existing situation. We, some of us, have been on this damned beachhead since the day it was established and are getting plain sick and tired of the whole thing which of course doesn't improve our outlook on the world in general. I wouldn't wish something like this on my worst enemy."[111]

On the 17th, Co. A was held in reserve. Co. B and one platoon of Co. C were attached to the 7th Infantry while Co. D, plus a platoon of Co. C, were attached to the 30th Infantry. Little else transpired during the day although the lack of shelling in the Medical Detachment area, except for the occasional long range guns, struck fear in the men as they were not accustomed to such silence. Otherwise, about the only event of the day was the medics treating a man with a stomach pain. Heavy shelling persisted in the other areas into the 18th, and an enemy mortar barrage on Co. B sent T/5 Johnny Goodwin, Jr., of Virginia to the hospital and also lightly wounded Pfc. John W. Brown from California. The battalion ammunition officer reported that Co. A, yet in reserve, had, at an undetermined date, destroyed 295 HE and 300 WP at their previous forward dump.[112]

The rear area held by HQ Co., Co. D, and the Motor Pool of Co. A was hit by nearly 100 rounds of 150 or 175mm shells on the 19th. The blasts buried three of Co. A in their dugout but they were rescued without injury. Total loss from the barrage was one man slightly wounded by a shell fragment and a hole knocked in the motor block of a 2 ½-ton GMC. The day was well described by "Doc" Hulcher, who wrote in his diary that "... after lunch some of the boys went for a shower. Shortly thereafter we had an artillery barrage come in followed by 4 more barrages. I spent about 1½ to 2 hours in my hole. I judge that app. 75-100 shells came in. I really did some sweating too. The closest hit about 40 feet from me and [*the*] hole was some 8 ft. diameter – really big stuff and it looked more like bomb crater. There were holes left all over the place and only one minor casualty. We had to eat K rations because the cooks were too scared to cook anything else. All has been quiet again since about 4 PM." Co. D reported the weather as clear and warm and morale as fair.[113]

Capt. Robert B. Smith, Co. C, took the time to write home, stating the most productive part of his time had been spent digging foxholes. He added, "One very nice hole I dug filled with water immediately but this one is reasonably dry." S-3 "Bud" Pike witnessed an air action that day and "ran out of the tent just in time to see a pursuit plane falling wreathed in smoke. It had been shot down by another plane a short distance away. We couldn't tell whether it was a friendly or enemy plane because they were flying so high. It must have been Jerry though. It seems that our Air Corps claims anything as a victory – friendly or enemy."[114]

Cpl. Lee Steedle, Co. D, wrote to his father in Collegeville, Pennsylvania, that it was the first time the men were allowed to state their location in the mail and claimed the men primarily got their information on the war from the *Stars and Stripes* newspaper. Lee said, " … the closer G.I.'s get to the front, the less they know about it." He also noted the oncoming seasonal change, writing, "I guess the love lives of these mosquitoes and flies are about due to begin. We don't have many bugs now but the weather is warm and nice."[115]

The 20th was characterized with "Doc" Hulcher's summarization that during his entire time on the Anzio beachhead he had seen 1,500 patients, or about 500 each month. The persistent shelling continued as a 75 or 81mm smoke shell landed in the battalion CP area, missed one dugout by several feet, and a few minutes later two rounds of HE fell nearby. Four shells, two of which were duds, impacted in the position of the Blue Platoon of Co. C and an air burst over the company Red Platoon, followed a few minutes later by 24 medium artillery rounds. Luckily the position was not hit and there were no casualties. Lt. Col. Hutchinson reported, "I have recommended Mindrum, McEvoy, Laus, and Pike for [Ft.] Leavenworth in preparation for command of a battalion. The development of our old officers is amazing. You wouldn't recognize Hays. He's an old man. I am recommending him for rotation in May, Laus in July, and maybe MacKinnon in September. Quite a few of the old men have been sent home, Barber and Burford included. I recommended Burford for Tech Dept. to Gen. Kabrick."[116]

On the 21st, Cpl. Lee Steedle, Co. D, again wrote to his father from the Anzio beachhead describing his living conditions while sharing a deep foxhole with Sgt. Roland Puckett and Sgt. George "Jumbo" Yakubisin. "When there is nothing to do I get a lot of sleep in the daytime. Our dugout is comfortable, but at night, when we stretch the blankets over three of us, there is a lot of wrestling. Only the man in the middle can sleep sound all night. We built the dugout for protection, so the 'door' is as small as possible. On the nights when we had beans for chow, the air inside is pretty foul. But we only notice it when we move in out of the fresh air … You've heard of the heavy artillery Jerry has. We call his shells the Anzio Express." The battalion experienced artillery barrages in the morning and afternoon but no one was hurt. Capt. Robert B. Smith, Co. C, added, " … there isn't any rear here, it's all under shell fire & air attack but I don't think it's any picnic for the Jerries either."[117]

HQ Co. was heavily shelled and bombed on the 22nd. "Doc" Hulcher said there was an early morning barrage with a number of duds, followed by three heavy barrages in the afternoon. Interestingly, the battalion's telephone code name of "Longbow" changed to "Shrapnel" on the 23rd, the name previously used before being changed to "Longbow" at Chiunzi Pass in September of 1943 to correspond to the Ranger Force code. "Bud" Pike also noted, "The infantry … brought in a group of 25 Jerry prisoners and if they are true representatives of the 'Master Race' we can certainly be proud to be the people we are because we are certainly vastly superior. It is certainly good for a person's ego to see these haggard, scrawny, scared Germans." On the 24th, Charlie Lowry, Co. D, wrote his girlfriend, "I guess you read about Mt. Vesuvius blowing its top a while back. I saw it and it was really something hard to imagine. Fire, ashes, and smoke blowing up out of a mountain for thousands of feet."[118] George Borkhuis, Co. D cook added, "We have been undergoing quite some shelling in air raids. The German artillery seems to be shooting a lot of duds. In a recent attack 20 out of 27 shells were duds. As far as we're concerned we hope they all would be. The air raids have been numerous, as many as 4 in one night. They didn't bother us much with exception of keeping us awake. Our anti-aircraft guns do a good job of driving them off, or shooting them down."

On the 25th, Co. D fired on the 1st Troop, 362 Fos. Battalion, 362nd Division (German), in an operation known as "Mr. Green," an effort to gain ground in the area for field artillery observation purposes by the 3rd Battalion, 30th Infantry. This was probably the action described by "Bud" Pike, who wrote, "The company laid a smoke screen at dawn this morning for an infantry attack and it was very interesting to watch. White phosphorous makes a beautiful white cloud as the shell bursts and makes an excellent screen. Everything went off successfully." At 10:00 a.m. Brig. Gen. William C. Kabrich, CWS officer with the 45th Division, visited and gave out eleven medals, including Soldiers Medals to 1st Lt. Julian T. McKinnon, 1st Sgt. Michele P. Codega, 1st Sgt. Harry Cohen, and Pvt. Leonard E. Hall, all for heroics displayed during the sinking of *LST 422*. Bronze Stars went to 1st Lt. Julian T. McKinnon, Sgt. Hubart A. Burghart, T/5 Rudolph W. Engel, Pfc. William G. Schlachter, and Pvt. Charles W. Huffman. An additional soldier's Medal was given to Grady Lawless and two Bronze Stars were presented to men having already left the battalion, Pfc. Henry D. Bufkin and Pfc. Charles C. Engle. S-2 Rupert Burford recalled Hutchinson made him OD [*Officer of the Day*] and aide and personal escort to the general. "We had a parade in his honor and asked him to present medals to the survivors of the LST disaster. About 140 Purple Hearts, a few Silver Stars, and some soldier's medals were given out," Burford said.[119]

However, the day did not pass without a casualty as Pvt. Benedict T. ("Ben") Samulski, Co. D, of New York, was lightly wounded when six rounds of enemy fire fell in Co. D's CP position. Martin J. Moloney said, "I was with Samulski when he and I and about three others were on the road in Anzio waiting for a supply truck when Jerry sprayed the road with 88's & Samulski was hit by shrapnel." Sgt. Leo C. Deist, from Meyersdale, Pennsylvania, and Cpl. Jack L. James, of Scott County, Tennessee, were also slightly wounded. According to "Doc" Hulcher, "Artillery barrage came in while eating chow, boy did we scatter! I went into kitchen supply hole for cover. Shrapnel passed thru tent. After supper I had gone to bed, had to get up for a battle casualty."[120]

At 10:00 in the evening a shell, believed to be 81mm, made a direct hit on the rear battalion CP tent housing 1st Sgt. Thomas R. Thorp(e), Co. C, and S/Sgt. Carl W. Lepine. The two were credited with saving their own lives due to the excellent manner in which they "prepared the overhead cover for their hole." Unfortunately, HQ Co.'s service records and other materials were damaged. Daniel Shields wrote in his diary, "Bombed, hit very close, the whistle really gets a fellow going." During the latter part of the 25th and early morning hours of the 26th, "Doc" Hulcher had to attend to three battle casualties from Co. D, none serious, a soldier who sprained his ankle diving into a foxhole during the previous air raid and removal of a tick from another man's leg. More shells came in during the day but not as nearby as previously. The weather also turned rainy and cold.[121]

Shells landed about 60 yards from the battalion CP on the 27th without causing any damage, but on the 28th enemy shells found their target. "Doc" Hulcher excitedly wrote that "Jerry started shelling us along with an air raid that lasted about an hour. Plenty of close stuff came in. Shrapnel was flying all over the place. One shell landed in CP tent and tore everything to pieces but the boys were dug in and no one hurt. I heard someone yell that the tent had been hit so I went up there as [*the*] line was out. Naturally I went over to kid [*Lt. Robert W.*] Fenton a bit also. Many fires were started, one the largest I have ever seen just off to our left, it was just like day out there it was so light. Boy what excitement … Jerry really made a mess of things … in our CP tent. Supplies ruined, holes all thru tent, but no one hurt. Everyone seems to think it was an 88."[122]

Co. C was apparently not spared from the excitement either as Capt. Robert B. Smith wrote while attempting to compose a letter, "Now I am writing on a table which is shaking so hard I can hardly write … an air raid has started, and with the ack-ack and shells and bombs you can't hear yourself think, and this place shakes and trembles." Although Pvt. Dale C. Blank, Co. C, from Pennsylvania, could not remember the exact date, this was possibly the episode he graphically described when he wrote, "[*At Anzio*] Company 'C' had an entire squad knocked by an '88' artillery shell and I just happened to be the first on the scene. A squad leader was the most badly wounded with a head wound and one leg hung by a shred. Our medic was next with the calf of his left leg cut in half. I found him in a dugout bleeding to death. I made a tourniquet out of some three inch bandage and a rock to stay the bleeding and then went back to helping the lesser wounded. After we did what we could for the squad leader we put him on a stretcher and four of us started carrying him to the aid station by way of the ditches and canals to keep out of sight of the Germans. At times we had to wade in water at waist deep. The man was heavy and his severed leg kept falling off the stretcher which I would push back on. About half way to the aid station John [*name withheld*] stated that he was tired and would like to take a break. I stopped the procession and told John that if he would like a break, it would be his last, where upon I removed my .45 automatic from the holster and cocked it and told John he had a choice. Die right there or carry his share of the load. To this day I think I would have shot him. I don't know if he was a coward or just didn't care about the injured man, I never talked to John ever again." Like so many on the Anzio beachhead, John probably suffered from battle fatigue, but he remained with the company, was captured later in France, and spent months in a prisoner of war camp.[123]

Blank continued, "The squad leader later died from so much damage to his head and body … That was a bad day

203

Men of the 83rd inside the chamber and barrel of "Anzio Annie" in Rome, May 1944. *Vicente De Leon*

for me. After the shell came in and I saw the damage to all these guys, I looked for the medic and found him in the dugout. Another G.I. was sitting with him and watching him bleed to death without doing anything. I put the tourniquet on his leg and went to help the others. A couple more G.I.'s showed up and started helping. What a sorry bunch of misfits. They knew nothing about first aid or stopping bleeding wounds. My father was a coal miner and I used to go with him every Saturday and watch him and other miners practice first aid with each other. Mining is a dangerous business."[124]

The 2nd Platoon of Co. D was kept busy on the 28th as well, sending out a four-man patrol to cover an area between Co. D's position and that of Co. E, 2nd Battalion, 30th Infantry. Although they were fired upon by an enemy tank, all returned safely.[125]

Co. B was heavily assaulted on the 29th as two smoke shells fell in their position followed for the next hour by a 170mm shell every minute. Elsewhere some of the men of the battalion got their first bottle of American beer.[126]

During April, the 83rd Chemical Battalion fired 1,534 HE and 1,856 WP at the Anzio beachhead for a total of 3,390 rounds. In addition, 299 HE and 300 WP had been destroyed at Co. A's ammo dump. At Minturno the 83rd had expended 4,202 HE and 2,495 WP, which, when added to the Anzio total, reached 10,087 shells. Total casualties for the period were 14 wounded and none killed, unless the above mentioned squad leader belonged to the 83rd. Many injuries often went unreported during the Anzio period, as recalled by Paul S. Giles, a cook in Co. D, who reflected, "I had gone in to sign paperwork to receive my paycheck when the Germans began to shell. I ran and jumped head first into our 4-foot-deep trench falling on my hands. I didn't realize at the time that I had hurt my right hand. When I returned to sign for my check I could hardly write my name my hand was shaking so badly. I had apparently broken a bone or pinched a nerve. I never told anyone though." In addition, during April the battalion gave the final report on LST 422, stating the 83rd lost 80 killed and 213 missing (all of whom were dead), for a total loss of 293 men and had 202 survivors.[127]

Innovations during the month included discovering that during night firing the burning particles, believed to be from the slow-burning casing of the shells, exposed the battalion's mortar positions. Also, during an extended night firing by Co. D, the new type of emplacement utilizing a railroad tie and sandbag was employed.[128]

Every survivor of Anzio had his own personal story and feelings, such as Pfc. Mario Ricci, who wrote, "The Beachhead was a unique experience. There was no 'safe' area -- out of the reach of enemy artillery. Clean clothes and showers were a rarity; our steel helmets served as wash basins. Hot meals: never. We lived like moles in burrow systems that littered the terrain with mounds. We yearned for the day we could stand out of our shelters and not fear of becoming a casualty. A frequent expression of the GI's on the Beachhead was, 'Hitler doesn't have a shell with my name on it. It's the ones that say To Whom It May Concern that worry me.' And there were too many of those. It's difficult now to adequately express the feeling experienced on the Beachhead. You had to be there -- day after day after everlasting day to experience it. Not easily described, but unforgettable."[129]

The recollection of another Anzio survivor was provided by Bernard Bernhardt, Co. C, who said, "Before getting bogged down for months in one position, I recall we set up a gun position next to a culvert with a huge underground pipe tall enough to stand in. We all crowded in for protection as enemy fire started coming in and hit some of our

Left: Co. A, rear echelon at the "red house" CP at Anzio. L-R: John McEvoy, Walter Hauser, Sam Efnor, and Eric Peterson.
John McEvoy

Right: The "red house" that was used as Rear Command Post.
Robert Bush Collection

newly stacked ammo. There was a tremendous explosion at the entrance and we were afraid our refuge was not good enough. Actually, it turned out that it was a 5 gallon gas can that exploded from the heat. Much of our stuff caught fire and much of our personal stuff was partially destroyed. Some time later as we were cleaning up one of the men approached me with the scorched cover of a stationery kit which had framed a photograph of my wife, which he recognized as mine. That scorched photo became an even more prized possession which I carried all through the rest of my days in service."[130]

Kelso ("Red") Thompson, Co. D, said that during one stage of the Anzio stalemate he was in the second story of a house and decided to peep out the window. Unfortunately, at the same time the enemy zeroed in on the house and a WP shell landed and exploded on the roof. The acidic WP got on Thompson but luckily Sgt. George N. Shirley and another man grabbed some Burma Shave that had been left behind in the house by the previous infantry occupants and applied it to Thompson, thus saving him from any further horrid pain. Charlie Lowry, a mechanic in Co. D, said he remembered standing around talking to his buddies during a lull in the action, with his foot propped up on a tree stump. Upon conclusion of the gab fest, the men walked no further than a few yards away when a shell came down and exploded directly on the tree stump. Miraculously, no one was injured.[131]

May 1944 opened with Co. A still held in reserve resting and reorganizing; Co. B and one platoon of Co. C continuing to support the 179th Infantry; and Co. D and the other platoon of Co. C yet in support of the 180th Infantry. During the month a general buildup of troops took place in preparation for a planned breakout from the Anzio beachhead stalemate. Additionally, combat activity would increase and there was an excessive amount of counter-battery fire received by the 83rd and other units almost daily.[132]

On May 1st, "Doc" Hulcher completed a remodeling of his foxhole: "… it's really a peach. It now has an L entrance of about 12 feet before you get to my hole. A real tunnel … I'm so far in the ground I hardly hear anything anymore." S-3 "Bud" Pike wrote a letter home describing some of the recent activities, including, "A couple of weeks ago Sally, 'The Bitch of Berlin,' gave the men of the 83rd a warning on her radio propaganda program. You remember what I wrote about the Rangers. Well, Sally said, 'Watch out 83rd. We got the Rangers and we're going to get you next.' Gee, are we scared. She keeps up her usual line of BS and also is still playing her usual excellent brand of American recordings which we are more than glad to hear. Day before yesterday our morale reached new heights. Beer was issued to every man on the beachhead, one bottle per man. While it wasn't exactly the best beer in the world it certainly hit the spot. And this morning for breakfast we had the old-fashioned kind of eggs, with the shells still on them. Three eggs sunny-side up with bacon were a rare treat. All in all this added up to a marvelous week here. Can you imagine – a bottle of beer and fresh eggs all in one week." Co. D was plagued during the day by an enemy sniper.[133]

"Doc" Hulcher's foxhole adjustments proved beneficial as the enemy launched a combined air raid and shelling on the night of May 2nd, hitting a British truck about 50 yards from the Medical Detachment, sending shrapnel through the tent, one piece passing through the radio and another through the mailbox. On the lighter side, during the day Lt. Walter E. Hauser of Philadelphia had pestered Lt. Robert J. Bush, both men of Co. A, to hang pin-ups in their orderly room. In the middle of sick call on the 3rd, some of the boys saw one of their own planes go down behind their lines, the pilot bailing out. Co. A also sent skeleton squads to a position about 500 yards from the front to dig in positions in preparation for the "big push" or "breakout."[134]

Early on the morning of May 4th, "Doc" Hulcher tended to a man who had fallen off a truck during the night, and later in the day Maj. Sam Efnor visited the headquarters of the 45th Division Field Artillery to coordinate plans to use their aerial OPs to direct the fire of the 83rd's mortars, a unique experiment which went into effect the next day. In an area such as Anzio, where the bulk of the terrain was flat and not conducive to the standard OP methods, the test, in which both platoons of Co. B fired two rounds of WP and 21 HE, proved quite successful despite being marred by poor wire ground communications. Co. D also received aerial support until the enemy forced the plane to withdraw. This proved to be one of the first known instances of adjustment of the 4.2" chemical mortar by an air OP, the first having transpired March 29th when an OP for the 88th Division Artillery reported the results of the fire of Co. D at Ventosa. As was often the case, the 83rd Chemical Mortar Battalion was involved with innovations in the 4.2" chemical mortar.[135]

In a letter dated May 5th, Capt. Robert B. Smith, Co. C, declared, " ... the weather is a lot nicer and, too, I've been sleeping in a house for the past couple of weeks." Activity remained heavy and on May 6th Co. B got some well earned rest as the 1st Platoon of Co. A moved in to their relief, in direct support of the 157th Infantry. Typical of personal duties, "Doc" Hulcher and Lt. Robert W. Fenton went into the town of Anzio to use the "Anzio Maytag," an "honest-to-goodness homemade washing machine," to wash their clothes. On the 7th, the haunting memory of *LST 422* was recalled as an officer of the Graves Registration at Nettuno called to say that the body of Pfc. Luther L. Ellison, Co. C, missing in action on the LST, had been found in the Anzio harbor and brought in for burial. Co. D had success during the day using an air OP.[136]

Co. D fired on a cemetery on the 8th, probably the burial ground referred to by Lt. Perry Rice, who wrote, "One of our principal targets was a typical above ground Anzio cemetery, where the marshy land made in-ground interment impossible. The Jerries had removed bones and utilized the high tiers of narrow crypts for observation. Their heavy machine guns swept the flat of no-man's land at ground level, while their artillery and mortar observers peered at us from holes they'd made in upper crypts." Until the breakout in late May, Rice and Lt. Jerry Woomer would blanket the cemetery with WP and HE every time the Germans fired from the location. Rice added, "Even during that tough time, with death all around, we regretted the desecration of those old graves ..."[137] George Borkhuis, Co. D cook also wrote of his fellow cook, Sgt. Llewellyn Zepp, "He was sent back today to Naples for reclass. The front line is no place for him as he can't hear a shell coming. Whenever one did come close someone would have to warn him to dodge it."

Some well directed enemy shells forced the skeleton crews of Co. A's 2nd Platoon to evacuate their position at "Snake Gulch," so named due to the large number of snakes the men found in their foxholes, and moved to the position of their 1st Platoon. Herbert E. Durfee, Co. A, recalled that when they were in a foxhole and moving out he gathered up his belongings from where he'd been sleeping in a foxhole and as "he got to the blanket that he'd laid on the ground to sleep on, pulled it up, and underneath the blanket was a big old snake." Durfee said you could not put enough distance between him and a snake, so he ran out of there with whatever he had in hand and never went back. Also during the 8th a number of mortar shells fell in the gun position of Co. C's 2nd Platoon near Padiglione, wounding eight men, including Pfc. Stanley A. Silkora, who died shortly afterward, and Pvt. Herbert L. Foster, who was seriously wounded. Among the lightly wounded were Lt. Fred J. Kulaga, Pvt. David H. Churchill, Pfc. Donald R. Loveland, Pvt. George Vail, Pvt. Ralph E. Bercovici, and Pvt. Cuerino Fracassa. S/Sgt. Lemuel R. (L. R.) Tillman from Tennessee was awarded the Bronze Star for this action, in which, " ... after an intense and sustained enemy artillery barrage had wounded seven soldiers in his platoon, S/Sgt. Tillman rushed 100 yards over exposed ground through heavy enemy fire to the casualties. His rapid first aid treatment saved the lives of two of the men, and his coolness in directing the first aid treatment of the other casualties resulted in the rapid evacuation to an aid station 1300 yards distant, down a steep, narrow creek bed. He continued working in the exposed area until the casualties had been removed to the aid station." "Doc" Hulcher was apparently in another area of Anzio that day as he said he only tended to two cases: a man with a severely sprained ankle and the performance of a circumcision on another.[138]

A few of the officers got some relief from Anzio on the 9th to attend a special school. One of those who attended was "Bud" Pike, who by this time was serving as both S-2 and S-3. Pike stated, "I am going to an Orientation School. The idea of the whole thing is that the American soldier supposedly is not thinking enough about the ideals and principles for which he is fighting, if any. We officers, after attending this school, are supposed to indoctrinate our units with the 'lofty' ideals for which we are fighting. Today was our first session and so far all I have heard has been a lot of BS. A bunch of rear echelon commandos get together back in Africa and Washington and drum up a lot of swash to throw at the fighting people. But I'll do my duty and get what I can out of the course and propagate the good stuff to the troops. I know what I'm fighting for and they know what they are fighting for and I'll try to develop those thoughts." Pike also took advantage of the break to revisit some of the areas the 83rd had fought through in 1943, as well as Naples. He found that "The sexual situation in Naples is as bad as ever. Every two steps you are accosted by a pimp ranging from 4 years old to 94 yr. who says 'Bella signorina, ------- for $50.' It seems that all the Italian girls have to sell their body in order to live, times are so bad. It is actually disgusting."[139]

Companies A and B were relieved of their attachment to the 45th Infantry Division on May 10th, attached to the 1st Armored Division, and sent to a rear bivouac area to begin preparations for the impending breakout attempt. Various members of Co. A also recalled that during this period at the well-known "red house" bivouac area they nearly exhausted their company's share of wine. Capt. Robert B. Smith, Co. C, jubilant from a ride in a Cub plane the previous day, wrote, "I am now in command of Company 'C' but haven't gotten oriented well in the new company yet, but think it's a pretty good outfit, and know I'll like it … It has been commanded by a 1st Lt. from Mas. Institute of Technology who has been a 1st Lt. about sixteen months [*Lt. Andre Laus*], and he will now be my Exec. I think he's pretty good man, but of course [*he*] wanted a promotion and deserves it …"[140]

Companies C and D continued to deliver and receive fire but reported no casualties until the 14th when an enemy shell fell into the CP of Co. C's Red Platoon, lightly wounding S/Sgt. Thomas A. Cute of Steuben County, New York. At this time George Borkhuis, Co. D cook noted, "Every night the Germans shoot a big gun which we call the Anzio Express. It whistles just about half way to the target and sort of wakes one up when it arrives here." During this time companies A and B remained in the rear bivouac preparing for several alternative plans for the projected beachhead offensive.[141]

During this period George Borkhuis, Co. D, took the time to describe his abode, writing "We live in a hole in the ground big enough for four of us. The roof is made of logs and covered with sandbags. It is thick enough to protect us from small bombs and shrapnel. We have a candle holder suspended from the ceiling and it gives sufficient light. At present we are sleeping on two blankets and have one over us. We have our hole well ventilated so it doesn't get damp or musty. At night we keep our entrance door closed to keep the light from showing, but after we extinguish the candle we open the doors for fresh air and leave them open. We also have two built-in cabinets for our personal things, and an alarm clock to wake us in the morning. All in all we live like moles."

The two platoons of Co. D participated in a beachhead artillery shoot on May 15th, and on the 16th Gen. John W. O'Daniel, 3rd Infantry Division, presented a Soldier's Medal to 1st Lt. Veryl R. Hays for his actions at Gela, Sicily, July 10th, 1943. Co. D received enemy 170mm shell fire. On the 17th, a TOT shoot, held by the beachhead artillery as a whole, gave companies C and D a chance to display their abilities. None of this activity lessened the daily barrages fired by both opponents and, on the 18th, ten enemy mortar shells fell in and near the CP of Co. C's Blue Platoon. Although one shell made a direct hit on the CP there were no casualties. Capt. Smith, Co. C, praised his men, claiming, "I like the company fine and the more I see of these boys the more respect I have for them. Of course, we always have some 'louts', too, but the great majority are really just good, brave Americans who want it to be over and to go home … If I have my way every man (with very few exceptions) in this company will get the Bronze Star medal … [*they*] have my highest respect, and I think that every damn one of them are heroes. The jeep and truck drivers, the communications men, the gun crews, the cooks and all."[142]

A beer ration was issued on the 18th and an unidentified member of the 83rd got drunk on the 19th, grabbed a tommy gun, and started shooting all over the place. He was quickly subdued and locked up before any injuries occurred. Co. D reported the weather rainy and morale as good. Of much greater importance was the news that a major breakout of the Anzio beachhead, in conjunction with a breakthrough on the Cassino front, was scheduled for

May 22nd, although only some of the preparatory artillery barrage would transpire on that date.[143]

In the meantime, on the 21st, Ed "Bud" Pike had another confrontation with Lt. Col. Hutchinson. "This morning I had another run-in with our dear friend, the male half of the Hutchinson family. Boy, how I dislike that man … I went down to breakfast this morning and as I had slept a little late I had to get up, get dressed in a hurry, and get down to the kitchen or miss breakfast. In the process I did not put my leggings on. To add to the terrible way in which I had acted I then sat in His Highnesses seat at the table. Well – he then came down to breakfast himself just as I was finishing eating. He was about half an hour late. He saw me sitting in his chair so he got mad and told me that that was his place and it was reserved for him and he wanted no one else to sit there. Of course, I apologized profusely. About 2 minutes later he noticed I didn't have my leggings on. Soooooo – 'Pike, get the hell up to your tent and put your leggings on. You look like hell.' Sir, when I got up this morning I was faced with two choices. Either I left my leggings off to get to breakfast in time or else I put them on and got to breakfast late, - like you did. I didn't know which you would prefer.' Hutchinson, 'You should always be in complete uniform.' 'Yes, sir.' I then left and went to my tent and put on my leggings and then prepared to shave. Just as I was all set, shirt off, etc. the Colonel's orderly came over and told me that the Colonel wanted to see me privately in his tent. Gee, was I scared!! Like hell. I quickly put on my shirt and went over. The Duke then proceeded to chew my --- out. It seems that my remark had struck home so he proceeded to tell me that rank had its privileges and one of those was being late for breakfast and another was being the head of the table at mess, that he expected every officer to ask to be excused by him before leaving the table, that he wanted proper military courtesy to be shown him and proper respect be paid his rank of Lt. Col. He said that he wanted me in proper and complete uniform at all times. He said he wasn't much older than I was but that he was going to give me a little advice, 'If I wanted to get ahead in the army I would have to watch my dress at all times and must show proper deference to rank, etc., etc. Blah, blah, blah.' And we thought Col. Cunin was bad. Hell, he was an Angel compared to Hutchinson. I didn't tell Hutchinson what I thought about getting ahead in the army under him, how I had been screwed by him so many times, why I had no respect whatsoever for him or anything he stood for, why I wouldn't be a yes-man to him or anyone else which is what he wants. Hell, I'd rather be Captain the rest of my life than kow-tow to him … Colonel said he thought my remark was very 'impudent.'"[144]

The weather cleared and warmed on the 20th as the 21st found Steve Vukson reflecting on the rather easy and enjoyable life experienced by the 60 members of the battalion left behind at Pozzuoli. "We were bivouacking in an orchard field where there were all kinds of fruit … Most of the men in our outfit didn't have much to do as they were truck drivers, the men in the command had to do all the paper work which the BN courier brought from Anzio once a week … We cooked our own food for a few weeks, eating 10 in 1 rations, then we set up a kitchen and was much better as it takes most of the day to prepare a decent meal. Co. A Motor Pool men were our cooks … A few evenings the Germans came over and bombed Naples, but we were about fifteen miles from there. The only danger was the shrapnel from our ack-ack shells …" Of more importance, though, at Anzio Co. A's mortar men had moved to the front by truck convoy and took a position in and around a stream bed in preparation for the forthcoming mission.[145]

At this time George Borkhuis, Mess Sgt. of Co. D, wrote, "Things are quite noisy at present … [*but*] the sports calendar up here is kept very full. Baseball, soccer, cricket, beetle racing, and swimming. We even have a Sweepstakes drawing with a $2000 prize … many of the former moonshiners from the states are now back in business. They distill some kind of poison and call it liquor. I don't know what it tastes like but the effect certainly appears terrific … our kitchen seems to be the community center of the area. You can almost always see a card game or crap game in progress right in front of our door. We also have a horse-shoe pitching range and a dart board within a few feet of the kitchen. The only time the area is empty is when Jerry starts to shell us and then we dive for our holes."

Co. B of the 83rd was attached to the 1st Armored Division and put in direct support of CCB [*Combat Command B*] on the 22nd. The General Plan of the CCB was to extend the front line, break through the front line with the railroad track as the first objective, and take Highways #6 and #7. According to Lee Steedle, Co. D, "… our entire platoon displaced forward, about three hundred yards ahead of our infantry, into one of the numerous deep ditches that had drained those malaria-breeding Pontine Marshes which made Anzio's plain. We moved after midnight, so that our mortars could be sure to remain within accurate range at dawn -- H-Hour for the jump-off. Because we were crossing our own minefield, we followed a line of white tapes that had been pegged to the ground by Engineers who had swept our path some hours earlier. The problem was, however, that several white tapes criss-crossed ours, and at one point Lt. Woomer, who was leading us, chose the wrong turn. The nervous Jerries could hear muffled sounds of movements all along the line. They were expending star-shells suspended by small parachutes, at the rate of one every couple of minutes. We were in deep trouble, lost somewhere in no-man's land. Jerry Woomer had been a schoolteacher. He spoke to us in his deep, calm voice that we somehow found reassuring. Barely able to retrace our way to the right marker tape, we dropped into our forward ditch just as the sky began lightening."[146]

Company B moved into position and the general attack to effect a break-through from the Anzio beachhead and cut the two highways began at 6:25 ("H" Hour) on May 23rd. Co. C fired 1,691 rounds of WP to provide a smokescreen for the advancing infantry and also fired on targets of their own opportunity or those called upon by the infantry. Capt. Smith, Co. C, said he "… had to run some ammo up during daylight … got it through in good shape and it was something like walking out on stage, taking a truck up there in broad daylight. There were Kraut prisoners going back on all roads. In fact there were 35 in our gun positions when I got there." He also bragged Co. C had not lost a man since he had taken command on April 10th. Companies A and B laid down preparatory fire on targets designated by the 1st Armored Division, which they were supporting. Each company was the recipient of heavy mortar, artillery, and tank fire throughout the day eliminating one mortar of Co. C with a broken standard. Sgt. William C. Ford, Co. C, confirmed the hard-fought battle and said, "Dead soldiers lay all over the ground, and no one went out to recover them. Soon the odor from these dead bodies became unbearable. Seeing young men killed or wounded on a battle field was not a pretty sight. Hearing the sound of a wounded comrade cry for help eats at you every time he cries … Odor from burning bodies and tanks, smoke, and exploded ammunition added to the death and destruction that makes every part of your body sick with fear and hopelessness. There's not one of us that did not vomit at some point." Co. B broke two standards and received compliments from a Gen. Allen for their performance. Pfc. George A. Barrett, Co. B, said, "The 'Break Through' at the Anzio Beachhead is one of my fondest memories. After months of a 'living hell' it was like one of 'God's Miracles' to be freed of the confines of that unforgettable misery called Anzio. It is a memory I will cherish until I die." Lee Steedle, Co. D, described his personal close call during the action, writing, "By late morning, we were again able to displace forward along a swept lane through German minefields that the infantry had had to walk through. I cannot describe that human devastation … Hank Fajkowski [*Henry E. Fajkowski, from Baltimore, Maryland*] our platoon aid man and I got careless at one point, and climbed out of a ditch to see ahead, when a Jerry sniper who was probably exulting in having two targets at once, put a chest-high bullet right between us, as we stood only about two feet apart. Maybe the Jerry had figured he couldn't miss hitting one, if he aimed between both of us."[147]

The enemy made a strong counterattack during the 24th against the 179th Infantry sector along Spaccasassi Creek, but were forced back by the deadly fire and white phosphorous of the 83rd. Ironically, the 83rd Chemical Battalion had suffered no reported casualties during the breakout until the morning of the 24th when a jeep of Co. A, pulling a mortar cart, struck an anti-tank mine. The jeep and trailer were destroyed and Sgt. Joe L. Jones of Davidson County, Tennessee, was seriously wounded and died two hours later, while privates Harlis V. Underwood, Joseph L. ("Joe") Cuff, and Theo V. Britten were wounded seriously enough to be sent to the hospital. Privates Dominick J. DiRiemigio and Benjamin G. Weatherly were lightly wounded but did not require hospitalization. "Doc" Hulcher said all of the injuries were concussions. Later in the day a platoon of Co. B was hit by about 30 rounds of suspected 105mm shells, which injured two men, including Pvt. Randall C. Taylor, who was also hospitalized, and Pvt. Ralph W. Stoddard, lightly wounded by a shell fragment. Despite such injuries Highway #7 had been taken. At 9:30 p.m., Co. C's Blue Platoon was showered with enemy mortar and artillery shells which buried some of the foxholes but resulted in no casualties. While digging a foxhole Cpl. Louis J. Kaufman, Jr., uncovered a dead German soldier. William C. Ford said, "It was dark and we could not see very well, but the odor was terrible. We just covered him back up and moved some thirty yards away." By the close of the 24th, Co. A was attached to the 27th Field Artillery, 1st Armored Division.[148]

Good news came on the 25th when the battalion received a radio report from an air OP that II and VI Corps forces had joined on the seacoast road several miles southeast of Littoria, now occupied by friendly forces. Some shells came into the battalion CP area during the night but caused no damage. Personnel bombs were dropped during a heavy enemy air raid and one man of Co. B was lightly wounded. Co. A moved to a position in a railroad bed approximately 50 yards from some 105s. William C. Ford. Co. C, said that after his company had taken out some enemy gun and mortar positions, their rifle company advanced, "… so we started to leap frog our mortars, moving only two mortars at a time. While two mortars moved forward, the other two continued firing. Once the first two started firing, the second two would break down their mortars and move forward … we broke through the enemy's second line of defense … we had them running on their heels …"[149]

Following a fairly large battalion sick call, "Doc" Hulcher rode up to the front to retrieve the battalion jeep which had struck a mine the previous day but found it unsalvagable. During the jaunt, he "Saw prisoners, enemy machine guns, helmets, gas masks, knocked out tanks, trucks, jeeps, besides having some shells land very near to us. When we got back about 9:30 PM we were covered with dust."[150]

On May 26th, companies A and B were attached to the 36th Infantry Division to support their attack on Velletri and the hills beyond. Co. A sent out four jeeps to locate the Division CP, which, in spite of some heavy shelling en route, was located about four or five miles north of Cisterna. Co. B was attached to the 143rd Infantry and advanced along Highway #7 toward Velletri. In Co. C's area of activity, a shell hit lightly wounding Pfc. Loy J. Marshall and Pfc. Edward A. Nesseralla. Marshall recalled that the day he earned his second Purple Heart, "The lieutenant and I had been out to our Forward Observation Post to take a look at German positions and see if our mortars were hitting their marks. To get back to our unit, we used a field road, but we had to use the drainage ditches that criss-crossed the countryside as cover from bullets and bombs. About the time we got back, an officer said he needed someone to run an important message to a battalion of the 45th Infantry Division about a mile or so away. I volunteered to deliver the message. I was told to destroy the message if I was captured, even if I had to eat it, as it could not get into enemy hands. I made my way to the unit's position and handed the note to the commander. He read it and said, 'God Damn.' I asked if there was a reply to the message and he said, 'I have my orders, now you can get back to your unit.' The entire trip there and back, I had been in heavy fire fighting with bombs, mortars, and bullets flying everywhere. I was within 50 yards of my company's position when I got hit. The sole of my boot had been ripped off, and my foot was hit in several places by shrapnel and was bleeding. I'd also been hit in the face and as I reached up I got a handful of blood. I just knew that half my face had been blown off. I laid flat against the ground until the barrage was finished then managed to get back to our position where I fell into a foxhole. The medics took care of my wounds, and I stayed there until nightfall when I was put on a jeep and sent to a field hospital." He was later sent to a Naples hospital where his injuries were determined not serious enough to send him home. Against his protests an attempt to assign him to an infantry regiment was made, but fortunately, Loy's persistence paid off and he was returned to the 83rd.[151]

"Doc" Hulcher was elated with the events of May 26th, writing, "We have no more right flank now as the Southern 5th Army has met us. We have advanced way beyond Cisterna & Cori and are just 2 miles from Highway #6. Are also headed for Rome and are only 18 miles away. We could hit Rome with our artillery if we wanted to. Only few of our bombers over today but always a lot of P51 & 'Spits'. Some of the 'Anzio Express' guns have been captured & everything is just rosy. Our companies are spread all over the beachhead and we just can't take care of them all."[152] George Borkhuis, Co. D, would write of the breakout, "It was a noisy engagement but very successful."

1st Lt. Alfred L. ("Al") Forrester, Co. D, and 2nd Lt. Lemoyne W. Dilgarde were lightly wounded by an anti-personnel mine during a reconnaissance on the 27th. Co. A remained in 36th Division reserve on the 28th, while Co. C supported an attack by the 180th Infantry. Co. B also supported the attack on Velletri, placed 1,000 yards behind the line of the 143rd Infantry. Following another large battalion sick call, "Doc" Hulcher and Lt. Robert W. Fenton took a jeep ride up to Littoria, where, they said, "Italians were back in the roads, waving at us, and all seemed tremendously happy. Every building had been hit many times and most of them were flat on the ground. Saw a couple Jerry Mark IV knocked out. Also passed by a B24 bomber which had crashed this morning – some mess. On the way back we passed a Polish convoy that had come up from Southern lines. Probably one of the first to come in. Also hear we have overtaken the Factory again. This must make it at least a dozen times we had it but lost it."[153]

"Bud" Pike reflected on the past few days when he wrote home that "… the big news of the past week has been the wiping out of the beachhead – in a completely friendly fashion. It was a day of great joy here when the first elements from the Southern Front joined up with our forces. The attack is still progressing and promises to bring big results. It certainly is encouraging after these many months of sitting around waiting, waiting. The Anzio Beachhead apparently has now justified itself. Rome, here we come!!"[154]

The weather was beautiful on the 28th while Co. A was attached to the 141st Infantry and moved at night to within three miles of Velletri. Co. B reported a rash of sniper fire, and "Bud" Pike heard a rumor that "There is a possibility now that our dear Col. Hutchinson may leave the Battalion. Isn't that too bad??? He has been recommended for the Army and Navy War College which is a very good break for him if he makes it." In addition, "Doc" Hulcher and Lt. Fenton took another trip, this time to Cisterna, and "... drove about 5 – 10 miles around it. The country is beautiful but the town is just about level with the ground, just absolutely total devastation. Some craters there 30 – 40 ft. wide. Jerry graves along the road. Tanks, guns, and equipment knocked out. When I got back I had to wash completely – what dust." Pvt. Lawrence E. Yost, Co. D, ammo detail, from Des Moines, Iowa, won the Bronze Star for his heroic actions near Lanuvio. "Doc" Hulcher also reported two men of the battalion were lightly wounded on the night of the 28th. On the 29th, he noted the companies of the battalion were so spread out it was impossible to service all of them and also said the battalion lost another man killed and two injured. Possibly among those injured was Cpl. Joseph A. Williamson of Co. C., a Rutgers University graduate. He had also served as a contributing poet and correspondent to *Smokescreen* while at Camp Gordon. After the war Williamson told his son that at Anzio he was in a tree with his binoculars as a forward observer, giving coordinates to the mortars with hand signals, when an enemy shell exploded in the tree. A piece of shrapnel passed through the bottom edge of his helmet, hit him in the temple, and knocked him semi-conscious, yet he managed to remain in the tree.[155]

James Helsel, Co. A, also had an unpleasant experience on the 29th, which he recorded in his diary: "Fired just a few rounds, then about 2:00 we started to move toward a new position to fire upon Velletri and our convoy was shelled, forcing us back to our old position until dark. When dark came we again started out, I could see tracers ahead, red going one way, white the other, but I thought we were flanking the town. Our trucks pulled off the road into what was to be our area. A few of us got off the truck. It wasn't long before I heard small arms fire going over our head. So we ran around to where the trucks were to find an awful confusion. Everyone saying get on. Ours was the last truck coming out of the field. They began to drop mortar shells in on us and the driver got the front wheel in a slit trench and couldn't get it going forward or backward. I don't know who was the most excited, me or its driver, but I know I was hunting a hole in that truck among the ammo. Capt. McEvoy told us to go clear back to Reg. Rear. Here he told us that during the day the front lines had dropped back to 600 yards from what was to be mortar positions and that no one had informed us. He said 600 yards is a little close for a 6 x 6."[156]

With the rear echelon at Pozzuoli, Steve Vukson summarized the period from May 27th to May 29th, writing, "Orders came from Fifth Army HQ that all rear units will move to Anzio the following day unless rescinded for some reason or other. Everyone hated to leave Pozzuoli, Italy since getting acquainted with the people and the surroundings ... The highway was open from Naples to Anzio but we had to go by sea ... Everyone was getting their equipment together and ready to move as definite orders came that we were going to join the rest of the Battalion at Anzio. We took our pyramid tents down and packed the things in the trucks. I had my own G.M.C. 2 ½ ton truck with parts for the vehicles in it. I had the truck & trailer assigned to me, a moving supply on wheels." The rear echelon of the battalion left Pozzuoli at about 7:00 on the morning of the 30th and moved to the staging area at Bagnoli, where they proceeded to load their 35 vehicles and trailers on an LST around 4:00 in the evening. At about 6:30 p.m., the group set sail on a smooth sea under a clear sky. At the front near Velletri, the 36th Combat Engineers relieved the 143rd Infantry and Co. B of the 83rd, who were moved to an assembly area to prepare for an attack on the high ground north of Velletri.[157]

At 7:00 in the morning of the 31st, the rear echelon disembarked from their LST at Anzio, which "didn't look like the same town with most of the buildings wrecked," Steve Vukson said. "I knew where the rear command post was located and I lead the convoy. It was in the same place when I had left it three months ago. I slept in the same hole as before. We had a slight air-raid."[158]

Also during the 31st, the 143rd was relieved and the 142nd Infantry, to which Co. A had been attached the previous day, was to pass through the 141st Infantry, which was holding the Velletri-Artena road. Their mission was to occupy Hill 891 and advance southwest along Mt. Artemisio, while the 143rd was to hold Hill 891 and the high ground to the left. At 3:00 in the afternoon, a shell hit a trailer full of ammo in Co. C's Red Platoon position, resulting in the destruction of the jeep and trailer and creating a fire which lasted six hours. The explosion spread to the gun positions and ignited 425 rounds of ammo. Although no casualties were reported, Co. D's Pvt. Paul H. Ruby was

The 83rd leaving Anzio and heading to Rome on June 5th, 1944. *Kelly Seibels*

lightly wounded during the day by a bullet in the arm. Companies C and D were supporting an attack of the 45th Division in the vicinity of Lanuvio.[159]

The month of May saw the 83rd Chemical Battalion fire 7,567 HE and 3,351 WP for a total of 10,918 rounds. Casualties included two men killed and 13 wounded or injured to some degree. Several WP shells were found to be defective, "apparently the bases of the shells were damaged by the propelling charge, allowing the escape of the WP and leaving a trail of fire and smoke through the major portion of the trajectory to betray the mortar position."[160]

June of 1944 opened within the vicinity of Velletri and Lanuvio with the 83rd Chemical Battalion continuing to fire on, or be fired upon, by the enemy. Co. A was in bivouac and Co. B supporting the 143rd Infantry. Both were in the Velletri area, while Co. C, giving support to the 180th Infantry, and Co. D, supporting the 179th Infantry, were both in the Lanuvio vicinity. During the first day of the month, three of Co. B's trucks were damaged on a rough trail and several were hit by heavy sniper fire. Wisconsin native S/Sgt. Sylvester A. Romnek of the company received a slight wound, while later sniper fire lightly wounded an enlisted man of Co. B. Another native of Wisconsin, Pfc. William B. Templin, was slightly wounded by a machine gun bullet when Co. D came under heavy artillery fire. Privates Thomas C. Dudas of Pennsylvania and Warren C. White were slightly wounded although the injuries proved serious enough that they were evacuated to a hospital [*Dudas and White, listed in the June 1 casualties in the battalion journal, were listed as June 2 casualties in the Co. D morning report*]. One of Co. C's 2½-ton trucks was severely damaged when it struck an AT mine, resulting in the wounding of Pvt. Rudolph J. Stasinski and Pfc.'s Clement F. Ritch, John A. Stanton, and Louis Grisham. Co. A, which remained in the rear, escaped any serious damage.[161]

The aid station of "Doc" Hulcher packed up and moved to the front, which he described in his diary: "The ole battlefront is really a mess. All the houses we were in at one time [*are*] flat on the ground. The factory and silo are likewise flat. Knocked out tanks both ours & Jerries line the road along with other equipment. In some places shell holes are just 2 – 3 ft. apart over whole fields. We moved into a gully about 50 ft. deep with a stream running alongside just about 2000 yds behind. The front artillery shells are going over almost continuously. We had many bombers over again yesterday and the usual air raid with strafing near by."[162]

The next day, during the 143rd Infantry's attack on Hill 761, Co. B of the 83rd had two jeeps and three 2½-ton 6 x 6 trucks damaged while manipulating over a very poor mountain trail to gain a position, and Co. C suffered a major ammo loss when one of their ¾-ton trucks and a 1-ton trailer, filled with ammo, were hit by enemy artillery. The trucks were completely destroyed and 200 rounds of ammunition were lost in the vicinity of the company Red Platoon. At about 3:45 in the afternoon, the concussion of six rounds of what was believed to be either 105mm or 150mm shells impacted near the battalion CP and loosened rocks above the foxhole of three men of the Medical Detachment. Lightly wounded were Pfc. Jacob Miringoff, T/5 Robert L. Sorenson, and Pfc. Marcus L. Gentry, the latter two hospitalized. "Doc" Hulcher described the event in his diary, writing, "After lunch went to work on hole again. Heavy barrage of the Huns came in and we had to take cover. During this barrage the concussion of one of the shells caved in the rest of the medics hole and big boulders of rock pinned them in. We dug them out and sent Sorenson back with contusion of hip severe and Gentry with contusion of foot and multiple abrasions. Miringoff has contusion of shoulder but not too bad. Will finish hole tomorrow. Front line more or less stationary but our right flank is still going. Had about 4 wounded in C Co. Saw about another 100 prisoners pass by. Food has been bad." Co. D came under a heavy enemy counterattack, forcing some of the men to fight as infantry. Among the lightly wounded, but not hospitalized, were privates Royce H Waldrep, Jr., and Euro F. Eusebi.[163]

Co. B of the 83rd made contact with the 143rd Infantry near Velletri on June 3rd and fired numerous rounds on Hill 938. Velletri fell and at 8:00 p.m. Co. A moved into the bivouac of Service Co., 142nd Infantry, located in a heavily wooded chestnut forest in the hills north of Velletri. Co. A was actually in a graveyard but did not realize it until the next morning. Gunfire continued throughout the night as "… tanks, SP guns, artillery pieces, and other vehicles moved up past Bn. CP on [*the*] road to Rome."[164]

Rome was the focus of attention on the 4th as Co. A passed Lake Albano to a point about six miles from the city. Co. B advanced with the infantry through Rocca di Pappa along the Rome road and placed their headquarters in a beautiful but slightly bomb-damaged opera house. Companies C and D remained in their respective positions awaiting orders to advance, reporting the weather clear and warm and morale as fair. "Doc" Hulcher claimed that since the Anzio breakout on May 23rd casualties within the 83rd Chemical Battalion had been very slight. By 10:00 in the morning Allied tanks had reached Rome and were driving toward the Tiber River with plans to cross it. "Doc" Hulcher reported three men slightly injured when a tank hit a mine. Nolan McCraine, Co. B, summed up the previous days, stating, "The road and landscape between Anzio and Rome was littered with corpses of felled German soldiers, rotting and with maggots eating them."[165]

Roscoe D. Adamson and Stephen Vukson at the Vatican in Rome. *Stephen Vukson*

ROME
June 5

During the early morning hours of June 5th, Lt. Col. Hutchinson, along with his executive officer and the commanders of C and D companies, selected a position just north of the Tiber River. "Doc" Hulcher expressed the jubilation felt by all that day, when he wrote, "A big day. Left camp in morning and advanced about 45 miles and bivouac across the Tiber River. Saw my first view of Rome. In one place there was about 20 USA tanks knocked out. Equipment has been passing forward all day. The bridge across [*the*] Tiber River was heavily bombed. We moved into [*an*] area that had been a German CP this morning. Then after supper we drove into Rome and looked the place over. Everyone was in [*the*] streets yelling, waving, throwing flowers and it was a great thrill. It is the first time Rome had been captured from the South in history. It certainly has been a great day. We can see just about everything in Rome; St. Peters, Coliseum, World War I memorial, balcony from which Mussolini appeared, Mussolini's home and grounds, the zoo, etc. The worst part about it is my camera is broken and that breaks my heart … tonight I'm sleeping on top of the ground [*the first time*] since February. Jerry is still retreating fast and we are having a hard time keeping contact with them. Believe we will be here for some time, anyway we should after being in combat continuously since Jan. 22nd."[166]

Capt. John P. McEvoy, Co. A, also had a fond memory of that day as he recalled "… a slow trip by truck across the Tiber and up the sloping northern hills. Stopped temporarily by sniper fire in front of a convent, our trucks were surrounded by Irish nuns in their habits. Some were hauled up into the truck filled with men, mortars, and ammunition and were hugged."[167]

At 8:00 a.m., Co. B had advanced through Rome, slowed by heavy traffic, and Hilton T. McLarty got mad at Robert W. ("Curly") Knortz and Norman H. Boettcher for giving their ten and one rations away to the pretty Italian ladies. According to Andrew Leech, Co. B, "It took us all day to get through. The troops were pouring in in steady streams from all sides. It seemed like everyone wanted to get into Rome … The people thronged the street by the thousands waving and shouting, shaking our hands and passing out wine. Photographers were in evidence and cameras clicked as we drove past them. Everybody seemed to be glad, and they had turned out to greet us. Most of the city itself had been spared. It had not been touched by bombs which fell only on the outskirts where the last stand

Pep talk by Lt. Col. William S. Hutchinson (arrow) while at Tarquinia. *Codega Collection*

was made … We got permission to camp inside the Vatican that night and spent the night there."[168]

At 2:30 in the afternoon, Co. A was ordered to follow the 142nd Infantry through Rome and arrived at a point west of Vatican City a half hour later. Joseph Cannetti, Co. A, remembered, "As we continued out of Rome we ran into sniper fire and I was sent to the roof of an apartment house to see if I could locate where the fire was coming from. Much to my surprise all the people from the apartment house were up on the roof with me. I tried to explain they were in danger but they seemed to pay no attention to me. I made friends with some of them and they invited me back to have a meal with them. I finally made it back to them and enjoyed a good spaghetti dinner." Lawrence Ertzberger of the company was also riding through the streets of Rome, which "were lined with people including some Nuns and they told us their prayers had been answered. One sniper fired a few shots from a building but came down and went across the field. An officer of the infantry took him prisoner." During the night, enemy planes dropped AT bombs within 1,000 yards of Co. B.[169]

Many of the men of the 83rd Chemical Battalion heard the news of the D-Day Normandy invasion on June 6th, some of them feeling slighted by the press for neglecting their own deeds. Co. A was attached to the 141st Infantry and attempted to keep up with the fast moving column. "At a cruising speed, we toured the outskirts of Rome, and spent the night in a beautiful hilly spot with a magnificent view." Co. B loaned 10 of their trucks to the 143rd Infantry to haul men and supplies.[170]

During the late hours of June 6th and early hours of June 7th, Co. C was attacked when an enemy plane dropped a stick of five or six bombs in their motor pool. Three men were casualties in the action as they manned a .50 caliber machine gun mounted on their truck. Pfc. Ervin E. Johnson of Minnesota was killed and awarded a Bronze Star posthumously, while Pvt. Edward G. Truitt was mortally wounded and T/5 L.W. Wiggins was lightly wounded. Medic Vicente De Leon, Co. C, said one of the men was hit in both legs. "Doc" Hulcher wrote of the episode, noting, "What a night we had. About 11:30 enemy planes came over and we all ran for cover. About midnight they dropped bombs just about 50 yards from us. It killed one boy, another had traumatic amputation of rt. leg and I gave him 750 cc of plasma before [he] could be evacuated at rear at 2:30. Three other fellows injured but not seriously and one of these boys should get the Silver Star for single handed putting out ammo dump fire." Kelly Seibels, Co. C, wrote, "Our bivouac area was bombed … [at] … night. One killed, one wounded. Jerry wouldn't have dropped the eggs (small ones) if a truck driver hadn't opened up with a .50 cal. He was the wounded man." Dale C. Blank, Co. C, added, "The bombs dropped between the dispersed trucks with no direct hits, but shrapnel or concussion killed … [*Johnson*] … the trucks took quite a beating." The assault ended at about 4 a.m., but planes again continued to strafe and bomb the roads at night, with reports that a German JU-88 was shot down with anti-aircraft guns.[171]

The remainder of June 7th was relatively calm for the 83rd as Co. A moved forward and bivouacked near Manziana, and word came that the seaport town of Civitavecchia had been taken. Co. B's trucks were returned by the 143rd Infantry, and the company was attached to the 142nd Infantry, while HQ Co. and C and D continued to be held in reserve and moved to a new bivouac along Highway #1. The next day the two companies were relieved of attachment to the 45th Division and attached to the 36th Division. "Doc" Hulcher remembered that at first the 83rd thought they had been relieved but 15 minutes later were attached to the 36th Infantry Division. Co. B made contact with the 142nd Infantry and prepared for an attack for the following day. Co. A bivouacked just shy of Civitavecchia.[172]

At 9:30 on the morning of June 9th, HQ Co. had cleared a bivouac area between Civitavecchia and Tarquinia, about five miles southwest of the latter, in an olive and pine grove. Yet by 5:00 in the afternoon, officers of the VI Corps informed Lt. Col. Hutchinson to vacate the area. To remedy the situation, Maj. Sam Efnor and Capt. Edwin "Bud" Pike found a new position in a old Italian paratroop school barracks west of Tarquinia, although most of the roof had been destroyed. The movement was covered in "Doc" Hulcher's diary as he wrote, "Moved out at 9:30 AM and advanced about 50 miles. Passed many wrecked Jerry guns & trucks, all bridges were out and the railroad was a complete wreck. Arrived in our new area about 1:30 PM and everyone grabbed a Jerry Luger [*pistol*]. A Jerry battalion had just been pushed out of the area that morning. Dead Germans were lying around and one wounded one which we evacuated. Again at 9 PM we packed up and moved ahead another 10 miles. Slept in a field near a ditch in an area of destroyed Italian barracks." Capt. Pike supported Hulcher's observations at Tarquinia, stating Co. D occupied an old German CP where there were "… dead bodies, equipment, bicycle's still around." Kelly Seibels, Co. C, said, "Pyramidals [*tents*] were set up and a training program started." Co. A, in division reserve, got the opportunity during the day to view the recently captured "Anzio Annie" at Civitavecchia. Co. B had detached from the 142nd Infantry and was also placed in division reserve.[173]

Trucks from each company were sent to bring up the rear echelons from Anzio, where ammo dumps had been set ablaze by heavy raids. The battalion Mail and Message Center men had had to spend the night in their dug-outs at Anzio due to the exploding ammunition. Word was also brought that the War Department had officially changed the status of all reported as Missing In Action on *LST 422* January 26, 1944, to Killed In Action.[174]

Perhaps one of the most notable events of the period transpired on a hot and sunny June 10th when, with the arrival of the rear echelon, the entire battalion assembled as a division reserve in bivouac near Tarquinia, together for the first time since the battalion departed Pozzuoli on January 20th. Stephen W. Vukson, promoted to T/4 at Tarquinia, visited Rome with at least five other members of the 83rd, including Kenneth Laundre, William B. ("Whitey") McFarland, Kermit ("Jerky") Jorgensen, Christopher L. Ryder, and Roscoe D. Adamson from Lawrence County, Indiana. The group went to St. Peter's, where, according to Vukson, "Pope Pius XII (R. Fantuzzi) made his formal solemn entry on a portable silk covered chair that is attached to two poles and is carried by the tall Swiss Guards dressed in a colorful uniform. (The chair is called a Sedan in the American dictionary). The Pope made his entrance after we were seated. We in the 83rd were in touching distance of the Pope. The Pope's remarks were in English and thanking us for the Liberation of Rome and the country of Italy. The Pope exited in the Sedan Chair. We were on the second level of St. Peter's Basilica overlooking St. Peter's Square where all the faithful gather when being blessed by the Pope. We received a special blessing from the Pope."[175]

Although the date is uncertain, at some point after taking Rome, Martin J. ("Joe") Moloney, Co. D, was stringing communications wire in a tree when his hook came loose and he fell out of the tree, landing on a sharp, rusty metal object which caused a severe injury. Although he did not realize it at the time, this would prove to be a blessing in disguise as he was sent to the hospital and would miss the forthcoming glider mission to southern France by one day.[176]

By the 11th, the battalion had moved out of Tarquinia some 25 miles to an area near a railway station at Chiarone, about a mile from the front, where most of the men were issued carbines, "newer and better rifles," recalled James F. Dougherty of Philadelphia, Pennsylvania. He also learned never to fire his last four shots because "… if you're out of ammo and had to retreat to restock you might just need them to get back, but only fire them if you absolutely have to … to stay alive." The battalion mess also began operating, much to the delight of the local mosquitoes. A false gas attack transpired the following day, while information was received that the battalion had been detached from the 36th Infantry the previous day and placed into the 5th Army Reserve. With this new assignment the battalion began a 15-mile backward move on June 13th, yet some 60 miles north of Rome, to a wooded bivouac area with an open field about half-way between Monalto and Tarquinia and about ten miles northwest of the latter. Capt. Pike said he slept in an old Italian barracks which had been bombed and strafed. The battalion, which had had an early morning sick call, stayed at the new bivouac for the remainder of the month and engaged in the usual duties, including cleaning and repairing equipment, hikes, mortar shoots, morning and evening formations, inspections, and the like. Much to

Dan Shields of the 83rd at
Battipaglia, Italy. *Shields Collection*

the delight of the men, passes were issued to visit Rome and at various times during the period nearly one-third strength of the battalion was visiting the city.[177]

Earlier, 1st Lt. Alfred L. Forrester, Co. D, had warned his men not to go into Rome as snipers were still prevalent, but Kelso C. ("Red") Thompson, a former auto mechanic from Oklahoma, and four other members of Co. D found a hand-operated rail cart, made their way to a happy evening of drinking in Rome, and returned without getting caught, although Forrester knew his orders had been disobeyed.[178]

Some interesting events during the period included a visit on June 15th by Brig. Gen. Haig Shekerjian, commander of the Chemical Warfare Service Training Center at Camp Sibert, Alabama, and a trip into Rome by Capt. Edwin "Bud" Pike and "Doc" Hulcher. The good doctor said they "… left about 6 AM for Rome. Went to Army HQ then to St. Peter's church, saw wedding there, some type of ceremony, and climbed up to dome of church. Then had lunch at Hotel Grand eating at Gen. Devens table. After lunch we went around seeing more of town and then shopped for about 4 hours but could find nothing. Back to hotel for supper & then drove back to camp." According to Capt. Robert B. Smith, "The weather here is fine but getting hot right now. We are in a nice bivouac area now. Got here two days ago. It's far from anywhere but lots of shade and even though for the next few days we will have a vigorous training program, at least we can sleep at night without piling up sandbags …"[179]

As Allied troops continued to advance in Italy and France, the 83rd heard news on June 16th that Japan had been bombed again, and "Doc" Hulcher gave a lecture to Co. C. This was followed the next day by another speech to Co. C on field sanitation. During supper a member of the company accidentally shot himself in both legs and was sent to the hospital.[180]

June 18th opened with an early morning downpour, followed by a blazing hot sun. The rain was confirmed by "Bud" Pike, who mentioned, "… we were all sleeping in the woods here with no tents up and it rained all night. Having no place to go for cover we all slept right through it and got up in the morning half frozen and soaked through and through. It was surprising how many tents put in an appearance …" Rumors also began to circulate about the 83rd participating in another invasion, and at about 8:00 in the evening one of the men was run over by a truck and sent to the hospital.[181]

Describing the current status of the battalion, "Bud" Pike wrote, "We are resting now and we don't know just how long the rest will last although we are sure hoping that it will stretch out for some time. While supposedly resting we are carrying out a rather rugged training schedule and in between times we are being inspected by visiting firemen of varying rank. General Shekerjian last week. He is the General whose aide I was for one week back at Edgewood in 1942. Oh happy days. Strangely enough he remembered me and 'said' that he was glad to see me again. We have a nice camp area and all in all things aren't too bad. Of course the Colonel insists on having a BN officers mess with himself enthroned at the head of the table. He demands to be sirred and to be excused from the table by him. Next I think we'll be bowing to him before we seat ourselves and then start the meal with one minute's silent prayer to God (him). He can kiss my patootie. I may have told you that he has been recommended for the Army and Navy War College in Washington and of course everyone in the battalion, men and officers alike, hope he makes it – but not for the reasons he thinks. If he goes Major Efnor will become BN CO. If he remains Maj. Efnor will be transferred."[182]

The battalion had a large morning sick call on the 19th, some 75 men, and in the afternoon "Doc" Hulcher gave a sex lecture to the battalion. Capt. Robert Smith, Co. C, also reported he was able to visit Rome and take a hot bath but he still had "… a few fleas left." Another large sick call took place on the 20th as tetanus and typhoid shots were given to the entire battalion, and in the afternoon "Doc" Hulcher went to see an Italian boy thought to have malaria. "Doc" kiddingly accused him of drinking lye but the young man did not fall for the joke. During a visit to Rome, Lt. Robert J. Bush, Co. A, attended a party of the 3rd Chemical Battalion at the Apollo Club. The morning sick call grew to about 100 on the 21st, although Byron H. Jordan, Co. B, wrote home, "… we're back for a rest and part of our duties call for a swim." On the 22nd another large sick call took place after which "Doc" Hulcher gave typhus and smallpox vaccinations.

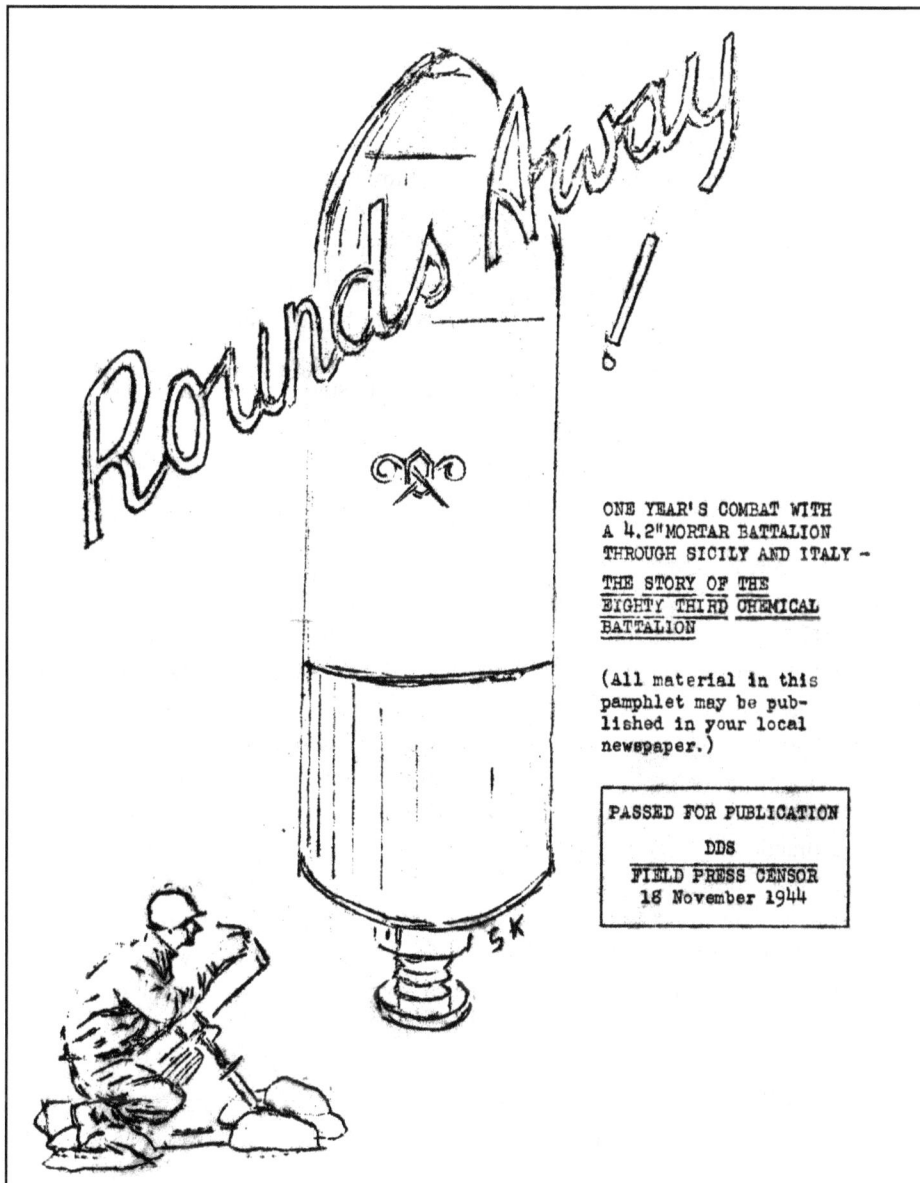

Cover of *Rounds Away*, the first written history of the 83rd Chemical Mortar Battalion, detailing their first year of combat, profusely illustrated by Sam Kweskin, and released to the public November 18, 1944. Amazingly, there is not one mention of the *LST 422* disaster. *Courtesy Lorraine M. Salvi*

Charlie Lowry, Co. D, wrote, "I am at a rest area in the woods at present."[183]

After working on a soldier's ear on the 23rd, "Doc" Hulcher "… went down and saw the Anzio Express, a 280 mm German railroad gun. Barrel is about 71 ft. long, breach better than 4 ft. in diameter, and barrel alone weighs better than 8 tons. Just think that's one of the babies that had been shelling us at Anzio." The following day, "Doc" claimed the entire battalion went to Rome and many attended a big dance at the Apollo Club. A U.S.O. show was attended by many on June 25th.[184]

June 26th brought a visit from a Capt. Frey of the 5th Army Chemical Office to announce that the battalion was to be reorganized under a new TO [*Table of Organization*]. During Frey's appearance a retreat parade was held where the posthumous award of the Legion of Merit was given to Sgt. Edwin I. Johnson, former communications sergeant of Co. D, for gallantry at Maiori, Italy, in 1943. Others recognized with Bronze Star ribbons were 2nd Lt. Ewart O'Neill and Cpl. Erskine C. Spencer.[185]

On June 27th, the company commanders of the 83rd began the reorganization process and all men not assigned to the battalion under the new arrangement were to be assigned to Personnel Center #9 and attached to the battalion. Lt. Robert Bush recalled that "Capt. Hulcher and I were lucky to be selected for a nice day visit to Rome. At the time the top floors of the Excelsior Hotel were used by Gen. Mark Clark and his staff … this was a swanky hotel. Well, after checking in, during which time our jeep was stolen by some Air Corps guys, I wanted to get cleaned up, so after taking a hot shower, I went down to the barber shop and got a haircut and a manicure, which cost me a total of 78 cents. I then went to their indoor swimming pool, took off my clothes where a huge Italian black guy just pushed me into the pool in 9 feet of water, not even knowing whether I could swim or not. That was my experience in about the first hour or two in the Excelsior. Capt. Hulcher and I had a grand visit in Rome taking in all the sights." At the time the two men probably had no idea that at 8 p.m. the battalion was alerted for a movement south. The reorganization process terminated the following day when Lt. Col. Hutchinson, noting the battalion was to go back into action soon with the 7th Army, had the reorganization indefinitely postponed.[186]

The battalion was assigned to AFHQ [*Allied Forces Headquarters*], attached SOS for supply and administration, and to the 7th Army for training and planning on the 29th followed by the announcement on June 30th that the battalion was to move south at 11:00 in the evening of July 1st. Although some of the officers already had been informed, at 1:00 p.m. on June 30th, Lt. Col. Hutchinson announced to the men that he would not be with them on the next mission as he was departing to help train the 99th and 100th Chemical Battalions, which were to be organized from two anti-aircraft battalions. The 83rd Chemical Battalion was to be attached to the 45th Infantry Division in the vicinity of Battipaglia.[187]

Pvt. Dale C. Blank, Co. C, wrote home to his mother, "Just got out of the hospital last night but I feel pretty good now although I still have my hand bandaged. My right hand at that. They told us we could visit Rome. There's nothing there but a lot of broken down buildings that you can see in any slum section of the States. I got some picture postcards that I'll send you and mark the place on one of them where I slept. Couldn't find a room so there was a lawn [*on which to sleep*]."[188]

For the men of the battalion, perhaps the most important news was the announcement of Maj. Samuel ("Sam") Efnor, Jr., as the replacement for Lt. Col. Hutchinson. Efnor was born August 29th, 1918, at Cuba, Illinois, and earned a degree in chemistry at Knox College at Galesburg, Illinois. Opting not to attend medical school he joined the service in 1940 as a lieutenant and eventually was promoted to captain, Co. B, 2nd Chemical Mortar Battalion, where he quickly established his courage and leadership in the Sicilian Campaign. At Hill 715, he was wounded in the leg by shell fragments and soon afterwards won a Silver Star for his heroic actions at Rappula River. After arousing the wrath of some top brass, he was "swapped" to the 83rd Chemical Battalion in April of 1944 for David W. Meyerson. Efnor quickly gained the respect of the battalion and was often referred to as "a man's man." John P. McEvoy described him as "A cheerful, practical leader who knew war and inspired trust in soldiers and officers alike." Hutchinson said Efnor was "the tops" and "young in years and old in experience." Ed Trey commented, "Sam was a good athlete. Spare me citing the results of our sports contests." Capt. Edwin "Bud" Pike was favorably impressed with Efnor, who "seems like a very nice fellow. He is very young, 25 yr. old and has had a lot of experience overseas with the 2nd Cml. BN … he is married and has a 4 and a half mos. old which he has never seen … he and I hit it off very well." Efnor's popularity soared quickly, evidenced in a letter Pike wrote to his wife: "Since the Colonel left, life has taken on a new zest around the battalion. Everyone in the battalion likes Major Efnor much better and the atmosphere is much smoother. The Major gives both the enlisted men and the officers much more of a break than before and does not insist on all the formality and kow-towing to which we were subjected - no BN officers mess, few parades and speeches, etc. The enlisted men get more passes and privileges so that all in all everything is much more harmonious … Hutchinson took away my initiative when I was working under him and I was getting so I didn't give a damn anymore and was loafing on the job. But things have changed." Even the beloved "Doc" Hulcher hinted at his dislike of Lt. Col. Hutchinson when he wrote in his diary, "Hutchinson is leaving us but I won't comment on that now."[189]

During the month of June, the 83rd suffered 16 casualties, including two men killed, one seriously wounded, and 13 lightly wounded, eight of those requiring hospitalization. Ammunition expended included 1,815 rounds of HE and 1,082 of WP. Most importantly, this marked the end of the first year of combat for the 83rd and the battalion journal included all the statistics, as shown in the following chart.[190]

83rd CMB 1st Year of Combat Summary		
	Ammunition Expended	
Month & Campaign	HE	WP
July 1943 Sicilian	1000	200
August 1943	0	0
September 1943 Vietri sul Mare & Salerno	3000	419
September 1943 Chiunzi Pass	3915	2385
October 1943 Crossing of Volturno	172	2
November 1943 Venafro	11275	7162
November 1943 Ceppagna	3605	163
November 1943 San Pietro	350	200
December 1943 San Pietro	130	0
December 1943 Venafro	5957	5698
December 1943 Ceppagna	2765	606
January 1944 Anzio Beachhead	810	870
February 1944 Anzio Beachhead	1011	393
March 1944 Anzio Beachhead	822	604
March 1944 Minturno	865	475
April 1944 Anzio Beachhead	1534	1856
April 1944 Minturno	2668	639
May 1944 Anzio Beachhead	7567	3351
June 1944 Lanuvio & Velletri	1815	1082
Totals	49261	26105

Medals Presented		Men KIA •	Officers	EM
Legion of Merit	1*	Sicilian Campaign	1	4
Silver Star	27	Maiori & Chiunzi Pass	0	4
Soldier's Medal	7	Vietri sul Mare	2	3
Bronze Star	9	Crossing of Volturno	0	0
Purple Heart	335	Ceppagna	1	3
1st Cluster to Purple Heart	38	Venafro	3	3
2nd Cluster to Purple Heart	1	Anzio Beachhead	1	9
Letters of Commendation**	4	Sinking of LST 422	5	288
Totals	422	Minturno	0	1
* awarded posthumously		Italy after break-thru ••	0	2
** from Higher Headquarters		Totals	13	317
• Killed in action or died from wounds during the period.			•• from Anzio Beachhead	

Note: Only 1 man was captured by the enemy during the year of combat. In addition to the battle casualties enumerated above, 3 men were accidentally killed. During the period loss replacements consisting of 28 officers, 1 warrant officer, and 547 enlisted men were assigned to the battalion.

The June 1944 report of the 83rd Chemical Battalion Unit Journal. National Archives

Charles A. ("Duke") Gargani, Co. C, near Salerno at the invasion training camp in early July 1944. *Kelly Seibels*

Lt. Col. Hutchinson summed up the 83rd's part in the Italian Campaign, stating, "The casualties in the 83rd Chemical Battalion exceeded the casualties in the other three [*chemical*] battalions combined. One reason was the ship sinking, but even discounting our losses in the ship our losses were heavier." When he left, Hutchinson noted "It really tore my heart strings. There are now only seven old officers left. Pike, Edwards, McEvoy, Mindrum, Trey, Stone, Hauser, McKinnon, Crenshaw, and Laus. That's nine isn't it [*actually ten*]? We have also appointed six officers, Barber, Doyle, Brimm, Kenney, Cameron, and [*James V.*] Lauro. It has been my only home for fourteen months. We've now chalked up 233 days of combat and fired 71,544 rounds of ammunition. Our casualties have been over 70%."[191]

The month of July was spent in preparation for the forthcoming invasion of southern France, which would be known as Operation Dragoon. As Lt. Col. Hutchinson departed for his assignment with the 5th Army at Tuscania on the first of the month, the 45th Division assigned the 83rd to a bivouac near Battipaglia. Each of the regimental combat teams were to be supported by one company of the battalion, with one company held in reserve. At 11:00 p.m., HQ and HQ Co. led a battalion convoy to the Invasion Training Center at Battipaglia via Civitavecchia, the Rome bypass, Velletri, Terrachina, Fendi, Capua, Naples, and Salerno. "Doc" Hulcher said he left at around half past midnight, riding in an ambulance. After riding all night and most of the next day, the battalion convoy reached its destination 1.6 miles southwest of Battipaglia at 3:00 in the evening of July 2nd, and Co. A went into bivouac near the 157th Infantry. Joseph Cannetti, Co. A, said the company "set up camp in a field that was a wheat field that had just been cut. Between the wheat stubs and the ashes from Mt. Vesuvius. It was a miserable camp." Sam Bundy, Co. A, added, "Pup tents were lined up in a very formal design and we were left here to roast in the sun. There are many good streams near this area which are excellent for bathing. We have a good laundry service – give clothes to wash-women one morning and get them back the next day." Riding in the rear, "Doc" Hulcher arrived around 4:30 p.m. and noted he sensed another invasion, or "boat ride" as he called it, and correctly assumed it would be southern France. Parts and supply man Steve Vukson also recalled the movement as he wrote, "We were staying in a wooded area 18 miles north of Rome, but … we moved to Salerno, a distance of 260 miles or fifteen hours of driving. It was a clear evening and we traveled at a good pace. I drove my parts truck the whole way and we got into Salerno about 5:00 PM. I was tired as all we had were about ten minute breaks several times … The weather was lovely the whole way … Our main area was out in an open field which was covered by lava dust during the great eruption of Mt. Vesuvius in March as it is about 20 miles from the volcano."[192]

Apparently before making this change of locale, Capt. Smith, Co. C, again praised his outfit, writing, "The company is coming along nicely with only the exception of the few personnel problems that are always attendant with a group of 200 men. In fact the men give me less trouble than some of the officers, but that will be straightened out, too. On the whole we have a darned good group and I'm mighty proud of them."[193]

Although the battalion lacked a July 4th celebration, and there was a large morning sick call, the men did have a turkey lunch. "Bud" Pike apparently took advantage of the holiday and wrote home that "The Colonel is now on detached service to Fifth Army HQ and the Major is running the BN. At least temporarily. The atmosphere is much clearer and congenial around here now and we are all hoping that that s.o.b. never comes back. I said the atmosphere is much clearer now but it is also hotter than hell. The sun just boils down all day and isn't exactly invigorating." During the day Pike also "presided as president of a court-martial trying three men for absence without leave. We found all three guilty and sentenced them to three months confinement at hard labor and forfeiture of $25.00 per month for a like period." Capt. Robert "Smitty" Smith, Co. C, took time to describe the area as he wrote, "It's pretty hot here but the country is really beautiful, with tall mountains around, much like parts of California."[194]

Invasion preparations began immediately and included a school on waterproofing by the 45th Infantry Division, the departure of 75 men from Co. C on July 5th for three days of practice landings with the 179th Infantry, and, under Maj. Efnor's orders, the official reorganization of the battalion began July 6th. Awards also were presented on the 6th at battalion retreat formation, including a Silver Star to 1st Lt. Francis J. Schleifer, a Soldier's Medal to Pfc. Grady Lawless of Co. B for his actions April 11th, 1944, and 24 Purple Hearts and eight First Clusters to the Purple Heart. The next few days involved continued usual bivouac duties, passes to Salerno, and the final departure of Hutchinson, having revisited the 83rd a few days prior to July 9th. Hutchinson took with him Alfred H. Crenshaw to help train the two new chemical battalions. Also, on the 8th Co. A of the battalion was attached to Co. A, 157th Infantry, 45th Infantry Division.[195]

Amphibious training and the effects of camp monotony were more than hinted at in a letter written July 8th by Capt. Smith, in which he stated, "Things have been going along pretty slowly for the past week. Have had to do a little wading coming ashore, but not too much … Some of the boys have been going AWOL occasionally, and I had a bunch of them in full field packs walking tours for a few days. Then after supper they do hard labor until dark, so am in hopes that they will feel discouraged. We have a good company, and I'll admit that I like for them to have all the fun they can, while they can, because I've seen them die. However, I also like for them to play according to the rules when I do give them a break."[196]

Sgt. Lee Steedle, Co. D, recently promoted from corporal, wrote a letter to his dad on the 9th describing the weaponry of the 83rd. "Our mortar shell has no fins. It is guided by a rotating band, and the tube is rifled like an artillery piece, so we get greater range and accuracy … We pull our mortars on a two-wheeled cart. It's damn hard work pulling cross-country in the hot sun, now I know how work horses feel."[197]

Typical cartoon circulated at Anzio and sent home by Capt. Edwin Pike, Co. D. *Pike Collection*

Under the new TO, Capt. Silverino V. DeMarco, Medical Detachment, became attached only to the 83rd, leaving "Doc" Hulcher as the only surgeon of the 83rd. Meanwhile, the battalion, minus some that had already departed for three days of pre-invasion training on *LST 174* and *LCI 48*, moved to a new bivouac near Paestum, about 2,000 yards west of Giungano, on the 11th. At this new location, Charles Rolling, Co. A, reported "getting pre-invasion food — beef, pork-chops, steak, hamburger, turkeys, chicken, ice-cream quite often and beer and cakes. Fattening us up for the kill." Personnel Adjutant Arthur J. Usher, finding some 80 enlisted men were surplus under the new organization, took them to the 2nd Replacement Depot at Caizzo. Co. A reported that about 20 of their men were among this group.[198]

On the 12th, the battalion was officially assigned to AFHQ, attached to SOS NATOUSA for supply, and attached to the 7th Army for planning, training, and administration. Andrew Leech, Co. B, wrote a letter home to his grandmother in Mississippi, expressing his gratitude for the support of the American people. "It makes our burden lighter and fills us with courage and determination to carry on under adverse conditions," Leech wrote. "We know we are fighting for a cause, such as morality and Christianity. We do not hesitate to shoulder the burden that is ours and march courageously into battle laying our lives on the altar every hour of the day, asking nothing in return but a crown in Heaven, where all can live in peace forever more. Yes, it is a great sacrifice indeed and takes more courage than one thinks; but, should we be one among the number that take our place on a lonely knoll on some distant shore, may it not have been in vain. It is for you, and posterity, we die."[199]

Maj. David Meyerson, now with the 2nd Chemical Battalion, along with Maj. Efnor and the newly arrived Capt. Raymond J. Lakey, Co. D, went to Ciampino Airport to the Airborne Training Center on the 13th as one company of the battalion was ordered to be detached from the battalion and sent to that location. They would be a part of the 1st Airborne Task Force, a conglomeration of all the Allied glider and parachute units in the Mediterranean, activated on July 11th and commanded by Gen. Robert T. Frederick, the youngest general in the U.S. Army. Co. D was selected for this assignment and ordered to move from Giungano to Lake Albano on the night of the 16th to be part of the 7th Army Provisional Airborne Division and as such would be the only company of the 83rd to fly in gliders for the invasion of southern France. Upon arrival they reported the weather clear and hot and morale good. Co. D began training with the 150th Glider Training Battalion for the mission on July 17th [*although the official report of the 1st Airborne Task Force states training began on the 20th*], with emphasis on physical conditioning. Lt. Perry Rice, Co. D, recalled, "The morning we first saw the gliders, we wondered what we had gotten into. They were little more than boxes with wings. Their floors resembled wooden industrial pallets. A blunt front end was hinged to swing upward, high enough to admit either a jeep or trailer. Looking more like bumblebees than the sleek C-47's that towed them, they were perfectly flat-sided, and constructed of doped canvas over rigid pipe frames. These primitive gliders were provided with a combination of small wheels and long skids for landing gear … Three gliders were provided per squad: one with a jeep and two men; another for the trailer with mortar, gunner, and ammo man; and the third carried the rest of the squad with ammo. There were no safety belts: each man tied himself to frame rings with rope, and was taught to inflate his Mae West at the moment of landing to cushion shock from the ropes. We learned to pile and lash the ammo in pyramids, sandwiching WP rounds snugly within the HE, to protect the phosphorous from flak."[200]

The battalion, minus Co. D, moved on the 17th and 18th to a new bivouac approximately 15 miles south of Naples, or about 2½ miles southwest of Qualiano, and continued their usual duties. The location was in a shaded orchard with ripe peaches, not so ripe pears, and apples, walnuts, and corn nearby. Kelly Seibels, Co. C, said, "We moved near Pozzuoli where the invasion troops were. We set up a company bar & reading room in a little building. It was very, very dry & dusty here." George Borkhuis wrote, "We are now at a beautiful spot. The swimming is swell and the eats are pretty good. This is an ideal place for a rest … we are going fishing tomorrow." "Bud" Pike recounted an amusing incident which took place while locating the bivouac area, writing, "McEvoy, McKinnon, Laus, Jim O'Connor, Lew Cameron, Eric Peterson, and myself made a reconnaissance for a new bivouac area and then had a few hours off while we waited to pick up our convoy to guide it into the area, so we went to a night club for a few drinks in a town which was available. When we came out there were some Air Corps officers fooling around with McEvoy's jeep. McEvoy accused them of trying to steal our jeep and one word led to another until finally McEvoy & one of the Air Corps were going at it hot and strong in the middle of the road. The rest of us stepped aside to make room for them while they fought it out. That was OK until one of the Air Corps boy's pals thought he would go out and help his buddy. As that was patently unfair (2 on 1) I stepped in and took care of him. I was cold sober and in fine fettle and took care of him very nicely. When we started we were in the middle of the road and when we finished we were across the sidewalk and up against a fence and he was trying hard to stay on his feet. He hit me just once and all I got out of it were some sore knuckles and a sore thumb from contact with his rather hard jaw."[201]

Two days later, the 20th, orders were received that Co. A would support the 157th Infantry, Co. B the 180th Infantry, and Co. C the 179th Infantry in the upcoming operations. According to various members of Co. A, a few jeeps and drivers and trucks loaded onto LSTs on the 19th and 20th. By the 23rd, "Bud" Pike had taken a group of men to the Iowa staging area to make loading preparations on the Army Liberty ship No. B-4. The same day, in hot and fair weather while boasting good morale, and in preparation for their role as a component in the Airborne Task Force in the next mission, Co. D left their rear echelon at Lake Albano and moved to Marcigliano Airfield for four days to practice loading and unloading gliders, along with several test flights to accustom them to the craft. A small rear echelon of Co. D remained behind at Lake Albano as the company was expected to return upon completion of glider training.[202]

In a letter dated July 24th, "Bud" Pike gave an extended description of some of the daily entertainment of the battalion while in bivouac, writing, "other night we enjoyed an excellent stage show put on in the bivouac area. The stars were Jack Haley and Mary Brian, of movie fame, and there was also a blonde (luscious) accordionist, a dancer (also luscious), and the girl singer from Bob Crosby's orchestra (also luscious). They put on a show consisting of humor, dancing, and music which was very amusing (darn it I started to say luscious again). The outfit was the first bunch of combat troops they had appeared before and they were rather taken aback by the reception. Every time the girls came on the stage the soldiers almost went crazy. As Jack Haley said, 'Boy, do you guys need a furlough!!' … We have been playing our usual volleyball games every evening and the officers are still undefeated. In addition pitching horseshoes is getting to be quite the fad in the battalion and between the two we have a lot of fun plus a lot of exercise. Quite often lately we've been able to have ice cream made for the company messes. We furnish all the ingredients and then have the Italians freeze it for us in town. And it is really good on the terrifically hot days, especially since we have to wear OD's all summer. Did I ever tell you that the combat troops here wear OD's the year around while the service troops wear khaki's during the summer. While the combat boys swelter with those woolen uniforms on in the summer heat they are proud to wear them as a sign of distinction. They don't want anyone to accuse them of being PBS men or any other kind of low service troops … Saturday we received a new type of beer ration – beer from the U.S. believe it or not. We were issued 4 bottles of beer and 2 bottles of coke per man, so of course I immediately traded my 2 cokes to some sucker for 2 beers and then my orderly, Abraham Lipschitz of Brooklyn, gave me a couple of bottles and altogether I had 8 bottles. Can you imagine – that was the first American beer I had tasted in 15 months. It was nectar of the angels."[203]

The same day "Bud" Pike reminisced about recent battalion entertainment, Capt. Robert Smith wrote, "Company C did some swell shooting again today [*July 24th*]. We had a Major general visit all morning at the OP. The OP was on top of a house, and we got up on an Italian ladder which is so narrow that only one foot will go on a rung at a time. Also, it lacked about four feet reaching the top of the 2nd story building and was very old and quivery. I had hoped the General would be discouraged and not try to make it, but he did, and I got him by the hand and hoisted him the last four feet. We made those guns do everything but sit up and bark like a fox and, try as he would, the General couldn't find any real fault or cross anybody up. Major Efnor, our new Bn. Commander (who came over with me from the 2nd [*Chemical Battalion*]), who was there, too, told me he was more than pleased and, incidentally I'd done a lot of miscellaneous bragging about what a show old 'C' Company could put on, and in my opinion the boys really came through."[204]

The glider training of Co. D was completed with several qualifying flights and the company returned to Lake Albano on the 27th, where they remained until August 3rd, reporting to RCT CP on the 1st. On the next to the last day of the month, Capt. Pike's rotation orders arrived and he soon afterward departed the battalion.[205]

BEACHHEAD NEWS
Sunday Supplement
This Newspaper Must Not Fall Into Enemy Hands

VOL. 1 No. 149   *Founded on the Anzio Beachhead*   Sunday, December 3, 1944

From Sicily With the 83rd

Powerful Mortars Gave Infantry Close Support

Krauts Were Surprised At Haute-Savoie

When VI Corps troops started punching the krauts around in southern France a pretty surprise package all tied up in green and yellow was handed the Germans but they weren't appreciative—in fact they didn't like it a bit.

When the surprise box was opened out jumped a detached unit of the 83rd Chemical Battalion which has been splattering its big shells in German faces for something close to 16 months now.

The surprise worked like this:

FFI forces were keeping the Germans occupied in Haute-Savoie province up near the Swiss border but they lacked big stuff—in fact, about the largest weapon they had was a captured 30 caliber machine gun. Thus, the krauts could work 'em over with their heavy weapons and they didn't have to be afraid of a reply in kind. Or, at least, they thought they knew.

That was where the 83rd detachment came in. The group was separated from the rest of the battalion soon after the August 15 landing and rushed to the aid of the Haute-Savoie French.

They set up their big mortars under the German noses and you would have to search the fatherland far and wide to find a more surprised bunch of krauts wden the HE and white phosphorous shells started falling in on them. The surprise was complete and so was the destruction.

One question guys of the 83rd always are answering is "Just what kind of an outfit you got, anyway?" The word "chemical"

proves a stumper for most of the uninitiated who immediately jump to the conclusion of gas attacks.

Truth is, the question comes up so often that it's more or less a standing joke around the battalion so that when a "rear echeloner" pops the inevitable question, some S 3rd'er probably will tell him; "we purify water" or "we repair mess kits." The answers generally are accepted too because when the uninformed get the facts they don't believe them anyhow.

It just doesn't make sense that a chemical outfit uses a mortar that throws a high velocity shell larger

The 83rd throws a high velocity shell larger than a 10%. The shell weighs almost 25 pounds, has better than 8 pounds of high explosive. 83rd's chemical mortars first barked in anger during the landing in Sicily with the Rangers, has come all the way since—including Anzio —giving close support to an appreciative infantry.

than 195. The 83rd'ers say, "why make people think you're trying to kid them when you can pull the water purification gag and everyone goes away happy?"

But, putting all gags aside, S Sgt James Jack of Company B, told an inquiring infantryman the other day—"Y'see this is really a big brother to your 81mm; except this job is rifled, has greater accuracy, increased range and"—he patted the muzzle and pointed to a stack of nearby ammunition—"those are our calling cards. Eight and a half pounds of HE in that shell and she weighs close to 25 pounds."

The 83rd, which saw its first combat in the early morning hours of July 10, 1943, when a landing was made in Sicily with the Rangers, has been moving up, always giving close support to the infantry with their powerful weapon.

The 83rd personnel now hardened to combat but, even so, they won't forget their initial target—

Beachhead News was established by the American Army on the Anzio beachhead. This particular issue, published December 3, 1944, was devoted entirely to the 83rd Chemical (Mortar) Battalion. *Author's Collection*

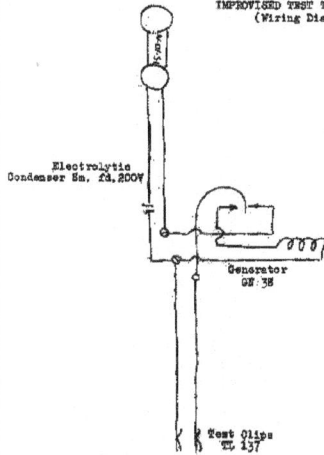

IMPROVISED AIDS IN COMMUNICATIONS
LT. ROBERT P. BRIMM

Lt. Robert P. Brimm, HQ Co. and Communications Officer of the 83rd Chemical Battalion, from Illinois, and the Communications Section of the battalion, were credited with a number of "inventions" or improvised improvements to existing communications equipment. Among these submission utilized by the 83rd were: an Improvised Test Telephone, the Four-Drop Switchboard, Cord Rack for Switchboard BD-72, Automatic Light Switch for BD-72, and an Auxiliary Telephone Receiver. According to Brimm's report these devices, "smoothed out some of the problems that have occurred in ... combat communication work ... they are offered as examples of improvisations made possible by the practical ingenuity of a communications section intent on obtaining the most efficient performance of its equipment."

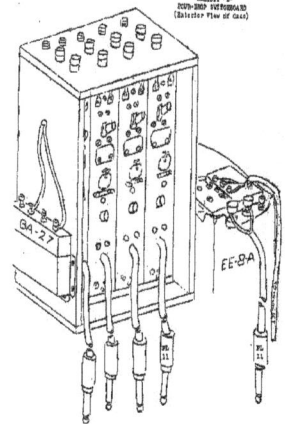

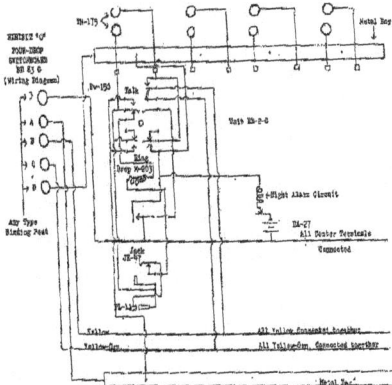

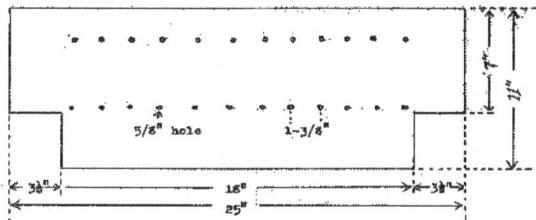

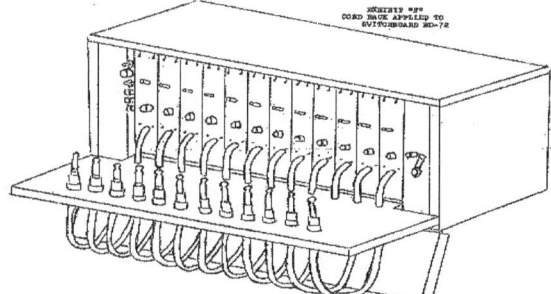

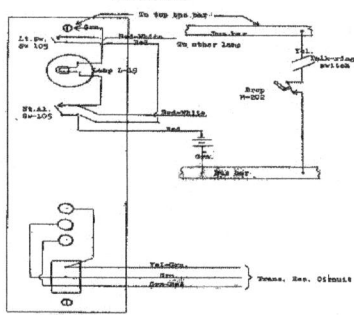

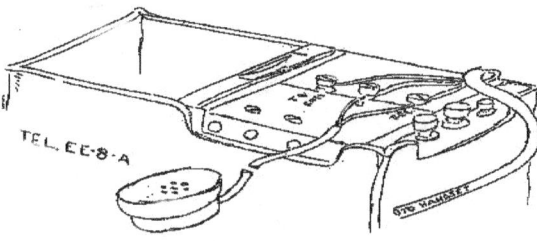

Robert P. Brimm

Eugene Plassmann

Diagrams clockwise from top left: test telephone wiring, test telephone operator, four-drop switchboard, cord rack applied to switchboard, auxiliary telephone receiver, automatic light switch, cord rack for switchboard, and four-drop switchboard wiring diagram.

National Archives

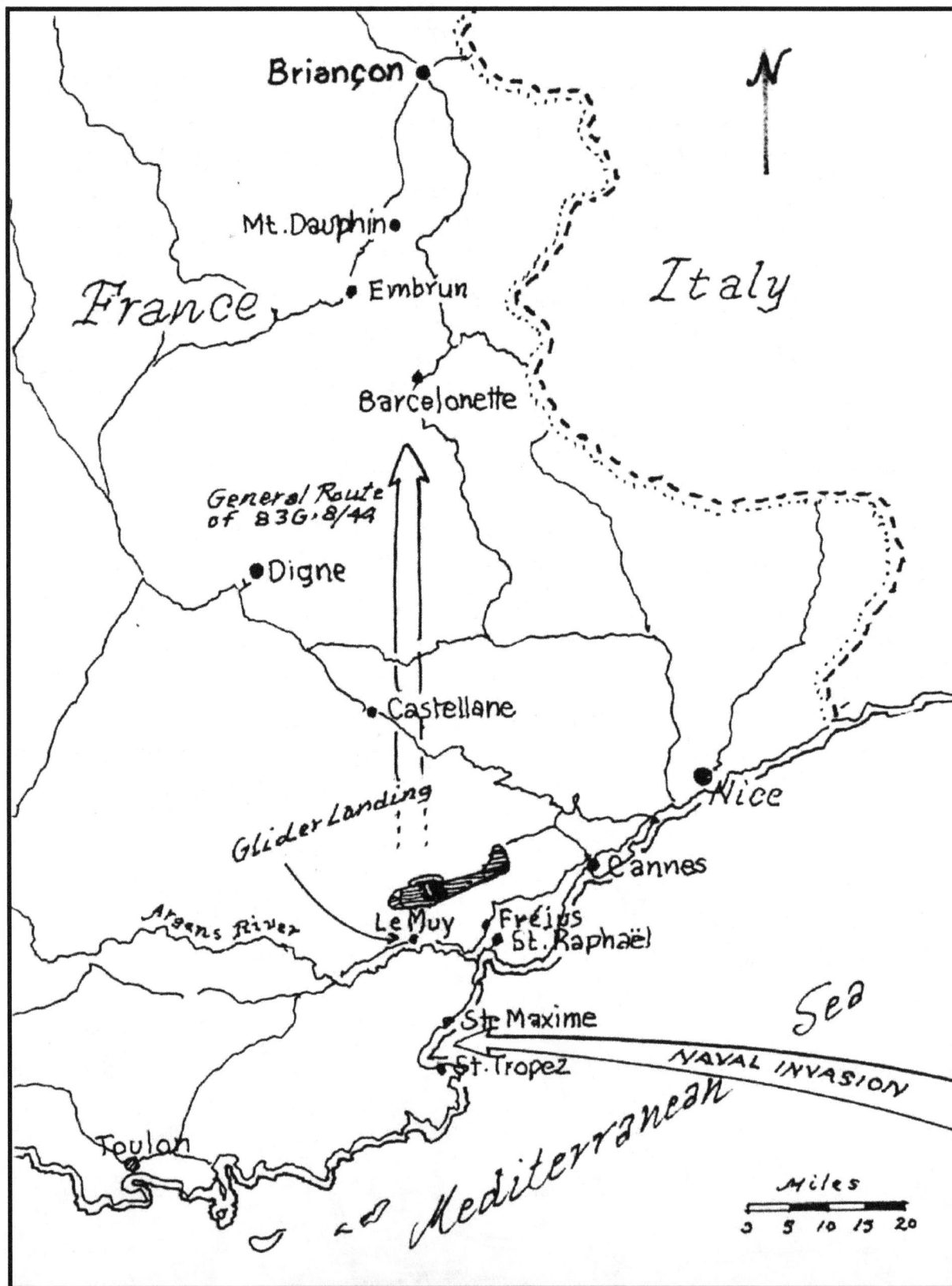

Map drawn by Sam Kweskin, Co. D, HQ Co. showing route of the 83rd during
the invasions of southern France on August 15, 1944.

Chapter Ten

INVASION OF SOUTHERN FRANCE OPERATION DRAGOON AUGUST - SEPTEMBER 1944

"We say au revoir to the Riviera" is the caption on this photo written by John Baer. The plaid, silk neckties are made from remnants of the glider parachutes. Those identified are: John Baer, far right, sitting; Frank Thomson, far left, sitting; Leonard Thomas, standing, 2nd on left; Alfred Green, standing 3rd on left; James Blackmon, standing, 4th on left; George Schmidt, standing on far right. *Noureen Baer*

During August 1st and 2nd, 1944, companies A, B, and C, of the 83rd Chemical Battalion at Qualiano and Co. D at Lake Albano, Italy, engaged in intensive training with emphasis on adjustment of rapid fire and physical fitness, target practice at Lago Di Patria, and a suspension of all passes after August 4th. On the 1st, Capt. Robert Smith, Co. C, revealed, "The company is coming along in good shape, and while we've been sort of streamlined, it enabled us to keep the best men and get rid of a couple of dozen which, of course, weeded out the ones who were problems. Haven't had a man AWOL since and have had to give company punishment to only one -- for fighting -- that is for fighting in the company. We're pretty proud of the way we get along in this company, and I don't care how much they fight on the outside, so long as they don't get in trouble."[1]

Generals Lucian K. Truscott, Jr., and William W. Eagles gave a pep talk on the 2nd as "Bud" Pike, elated with his rotation orders, said of the battalion, "Ed Trey got his Captaincy the other day and was very deserving of it. He had been a 1st lieutenant for well over 20 months. Was he ever happy. With my leaving Mindy [*Gordon Mindrum*] is going to be BN Exec. and [*John*] McEvoy S-3. Bob Edwards will remain at S-1 (he's being by-passed by Mindy and Mac) and Trey is S-4 as per usual. The Major offered me the alternative of coming home or a promotion and I took the 'coming home.' He said he didn't blame me, that he would take the same thing."[2]

On the 3rd, Co. D moved from Lake Albano to a position one mile north of Frascati where they continued their training program until the 10th. The move was probably none too soon either as Co. D had often fired shells into Lake

Albano, where Pope Pius had a nearby summer home, and upon hitting the water the shells detonated and killed the fish, bringing them to the surface of the water. This enraged many of the local citizenry. Horst R. Zickler, Co. D, a German by birth, fondly remembered his time in glider training: "The location was ideal on the shores of Lake Albano at Casto Gondolfo just outside of Rome … During the free time of training I fully enjoyed swimming and sailing a canoe which [*George W.*] Stevens and I constructed from a framework he found down by the lake and discarded German pup tent material for sails. Believe me, we had fun." George R. Borkhuis, Co. D Mess Sgt., wrote, "We have a new captain [*Raymond J. Lakey*] and he's managed to get us a moving picture projector and we have a show almost every night." Lt. Robert J. Bush, Co. A, said there was preparatory packing of equipment and James Helsel, also of Co. A, once again sensed an invasion as he wrote, "Still doing nothing. I guess they are waiting on us to get that cherry pie. I told the fellows when we got it, I was going over the hill."[3]

The initial movement of the 83rd Chemical Battalion for the invasion of southern France consisted of a "dry run" landing at Paestum, about 25 miles south of Salerno. This operation was initiated on August 4th as elements of Co. A departed Qualiano and boarded *LST 301* [*or LST 690*], followed the next day when Co. B loaded up two officers and 23 enlisted men on the *U.S.S. Lyon*, commanded by Capt. T. C. Sorenson; one officer and 17 enlisted men on *LST 312*, commanded by Lt. Charles L. Haslup; and two officers and 31 enlisted men on the *U.S.S. Stanton*, officered by William Anderson Wiedman. At about the same time, the 157th Infantry and Co. A of the 83rd placed their 1st and 2nd platoons and their HQ company, totaling five officers and 105 enlisted men, on *LST 301*, although most men said it was *LST 690*. James Helsel would reluctantly write, "Well, we had that cherry pie for dinner." For the next few days these elements of companies A and B continued practice landings with the 45th Infantry Division. Members of Co. A recalled a dry run below Salerno on the 7th and returning on *LST 664*. William C. Ford, Co. C, mentioned that on this date his company was pulled from the front and sent to Tarquinia, where the entire battalion would be attached to the 509th Parachute Battalion and the American Canadian Special Service Force, to participate in an airborne landing behind German lines in northern Italy. However, the plan was scrapped because the 5th Army continued to advance northward.[4]

The remainder of the weapons companies completed their training at Qualiano and embarked on the *S.S. Ascania* on the 9th, along with one officer and 17 enlisted men of HQ Detachment. Co. A's platoons divided, some embarking on *LST 690* [*a total of 105 men are on the boarding list but seven names are scratched*] and some on *LCI 410*. Maj. Sam Efnor, Jr., the battalion executive officer, and two enlisted men went aboard *LST 1021*, which was moored at Berth 9 at Nisada. Wooden pontoons located midship on *LST 1021* caught fire during the day but the fire was quickly extinguished. The companies remained on ship in Naples harbor and vicinity for the next two days. "Doc" Hulcher would not participate in the initial invasion due to the division of the companies and a cyst on his buttocks.[5]

Co. D, along with an AT company, of the 442nd Regimental Combat Team, participated in an exercise in which the terrain resembled as closely as possible that of the anticipated drop zone in southern France, along with the proposed time schedule and other factors.[6]

Glider training of the 83rd.

Robert Bush Collection

Howard Kelly Seibels, Co. C, said he hiked to Pozzuoli, boarded an LCI, and went to Salerno and Corsica on the 10th. Additionally, Lt. Robert J. Bush and 39 enlisted men and two officers of Co. A boarded *LCI 522* and moved near Salerno, while *LST 1021* headed for Castellammare and was anchored there on the 11th. Charles Rolling, Co. A, said his ship arrived at Corsica and Lt. Bush stated his craft was yet at Salerno. On the same day, and with their training program still in progress, the 3rd Platoon (Rear "A") of Co. D, comprised of one officer and 46 enlisted men, moved to

Qualiano, northwest of Pozzuoli. The weather was clear and hot and morale was good. The remainder of Co. D went to Ciampino on the 12th, the very same day the ships carrying the other companies of the 83rd sailed northwesterly out of Naples harbor for France.[7]

As the convoy sailed on the 13th, the men were finally briefed on the details of the operation and told the destination was the French Riviera between Toulon and Cannes. The 3rd Division was to land to the left of the 45th Division and the 36th Division to the right. On the 14th, final checks were made at sea on all vehicles and waterproofing. According to Ed Trey, the same men who had called him a coward for insisting they wear life jackets on *LST 422* "not only insisted on preservers, but inflated them in advance."[8]

At Ciampino Airfield, the 1st and 2nd Platoons of Co. D loaded gliders. The journal of the 517th Parachute Infantry states that "ammunition and other supplies [*were*] issued. Parachutes fitted and placed in Transport Planes. All bundles were packed and loaded on planes. All personnel of RCT oriented on all phases of Airborne mission. At 2300 hrs. [*11:00 p.m.*] moved to airfields to emplane." Lee Steedle, Co. D, remembered, "We were all pretty somber the night before D-Day. We'd been given a particularly good dinner, after which religious services were held." Sgt. Wofford L. Jackson also commented,

L-R: Lt. Lemoyne W. Dilgarde, Capt. Raymond J. Lakey, Lt. Justin G. Woomer, Lt. John M. Taylor, Lt. Perry B. Rice, and Lt. James V. Lauro.

Glider squads ready to take off August 15, 1944.
Top: Unidentified squad. Possibly Steedle's squad.

Left: Standing 5th from left Ford Hopkins; 6th from left standing George Yakubisin; 8th from left, standing Eugene Pirani. Front 4th from left, Mike Codega.

Bottom: Sgt. Theodore Haddock's squad.

All photos this page courtesy Codega Collection

"The evening before D-Day was hot. Jim Lauro had just been made a Second Lieutenant … I was on my way to get my platoon ready to load aboard, when Captain Lakey saw me. He said, 'Jackson, come in this tent!' I thought, oh hell, he's going to give me hell for being a little drunk before take-off. I was relieved when he said, 'How would you like a little drink first?' I said, 'Just a little one Captain, I want to have a clear head when we land.' He was about loaded himself." The 3rd Platoon of Co. D continued to perform usual bivouac duties at Qualiano.[9]

On August 15th, Operation Dragoon was in progress as an Allied naval armada consisting of over 2,500 ships carrying some 145,000 troops of the 7th Army steamed at top speed toward the beaches of the French Riviera. The force consisted of three American divisions (36th, 45th, and 3rd all of the 6th Corps, Gen. Lucian Truscott commanding) and the 1st French Army of General de Lattre de Tassigni. The entire force was under the command of Gen. Alexander Patch of the 7th Army. Opposing this force was Gen. Fredrich Weise and the German 19th Army, consisting of seven infantry divisions and one panzer division thinly stretched across the coast of southern France. Karl Garrett, HQ Co., of the 83rd recalled that "… British ships … transported us to southern France. True to form, I was sick all the way from Naples to Marseilles. However, to add insult to injury the British soldiers were cooking mutton and the odor made me doubly ill. I remained on deck the whole trip between the rows of canvas on top of the trucks."[10]

Following heavy preparatory bombardment of the beaches by the navy, the lead troops of the 7th Army hit their assigned beaches at 8:00 a.m. and met only light resistance. Only in the 45th Division area of St. Tropez did the Germans put up a good fight. The 83rd Chemical was not scheduled to land until H-Hour plus four [*around noon*], meaning this would be their first daylight landing.[11]

Co. B's Red Platoon, supporting the 180th Infantry and carrying two mortars, landed on the beach from *LST 995* at 11:30 a.m. Andrew Leech, Co. B, said, "I was on a Liberty ship and the assault wave was ahead of us for a change …

Top L-R: Wofford Jackson and Clark Riddle, August 15, 1944. Bottom: Unidentified men with Co. D preparing for gliders, August 15, 1944.
Both photos Codega Collection

we landed … near Toulon." Lt. Col. Efnor, aboard *LST 1021*, landed at approximately 2:00 p.m., and a battalion CP was established at St. Maxime at 2:30.[12]

Sam Bundy, Co. A, wrote in his diary, "We finally received word to head towards shore, so we went to within a hundred fifty yards from shore and waited for hours until pontoons were put into position for our debarkation. Tanks began unloading at 1:30, and by 3 o'clock, we had unloaded. We made a perfectly dry landing, but the 3rd Platoon got off in deep water. Ammo and pack boards were left a short distance from shore under guard, and men carried blankets and personal equipment for two or three miles. Incidentally, we landed at St. Maxime. There was no resistance on our sector of the beachhead. We spent a quiet night, with no air raids, behind a school building in St. Maxime." Being in reserve the men did not set up their mortars.[13]

The airborne phase of the invasion of southern France was directed in the vicinity of Draguignan, where there was a network of roads the Germans could utilize to strike the beachhead. Scattered enemy units had been reported in the area which made it necessary for the airborne troops to prevent them from hitting the beachhead before it was secured. With only about a week's training in loading and lashing peculiar to glider operations, two platoons of Co. D were assigned 30 CG4a gliders (towed by 30 C-47s), which permitted them to take the jeeps and trailers necessary for transporting mortars and ammo. Lee Steedle added "We had three gliders per mortar squad … there were four mortars per platoon equalling 12 gliders with squads. Plus two gliders per platoon HQ, which equals a total of 14. This accounts for 28 gliders. Maybe the two extras were HQ Co. and medics." Co. D's glider force, led by Capt. Raymond J. Lakey, consisted of 96 officers and men, 11 jeeps and trailers, eight mortars complete with carts, 1,200 rounds of mixed WP and HE, enough signal equipment to establish telephone and radio nets, and enough food and supplies to last about four

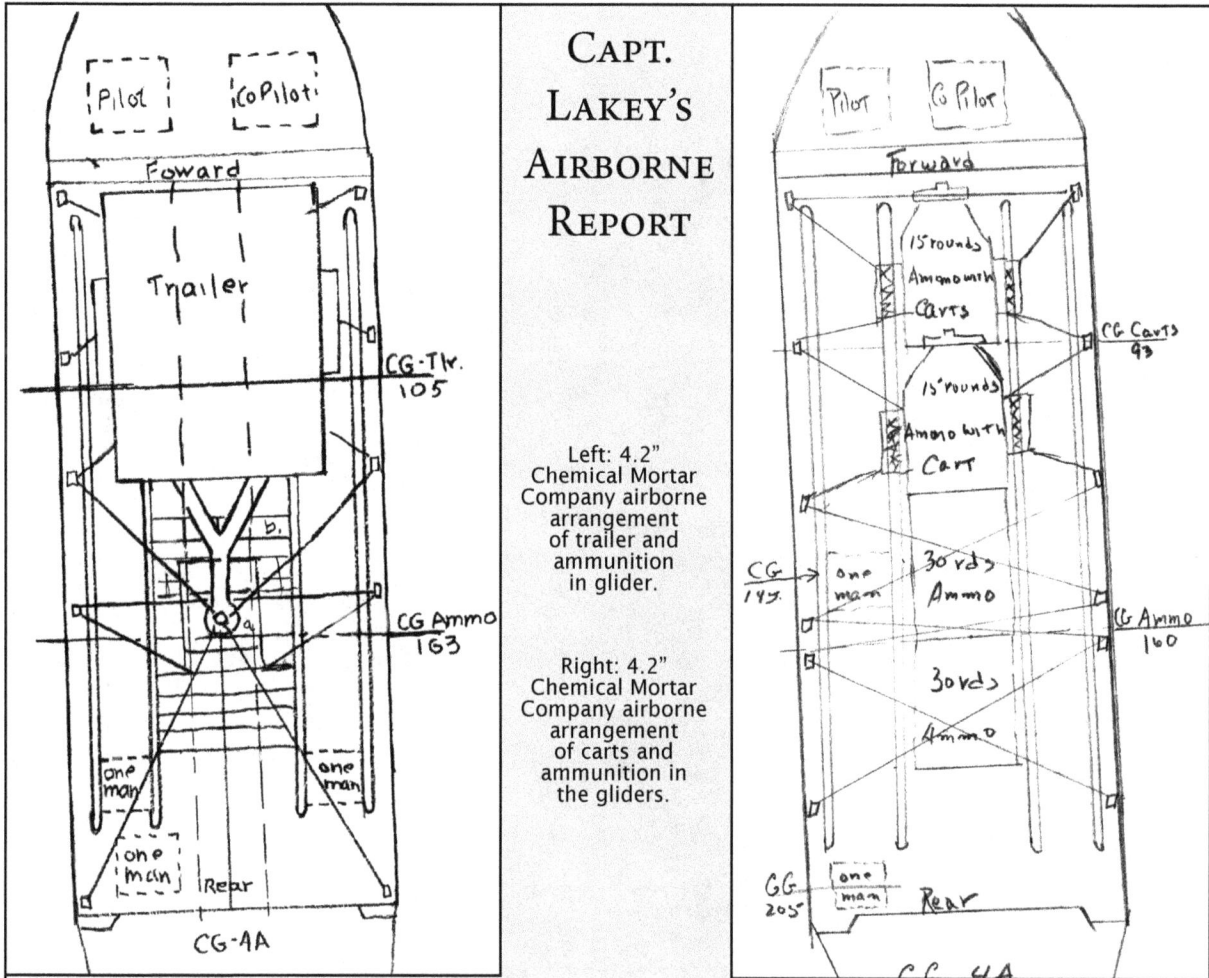

CAPT. LAKEY'S AIRBORNE REPORT

Left: 4.2"
Chemical Mortar
Company airborne
arrangement
of trailer and
ammunition
in glider.

Right: 4.2"
Chemical Mortar
Company airborne
arrangement
of carts and
ammunition in
the gliders.

On October 15, 1944, Capt. Raymond J. Lakey, Co. D, 83rd Chemical Battalion, released *4.2-Inch Mortar Airborne Report*, a 36-page written study of the methods and techniques recommended for the success of a glider-mortar operation. The report contained numerous diagrams and charts, a few of which are presented here as examples.

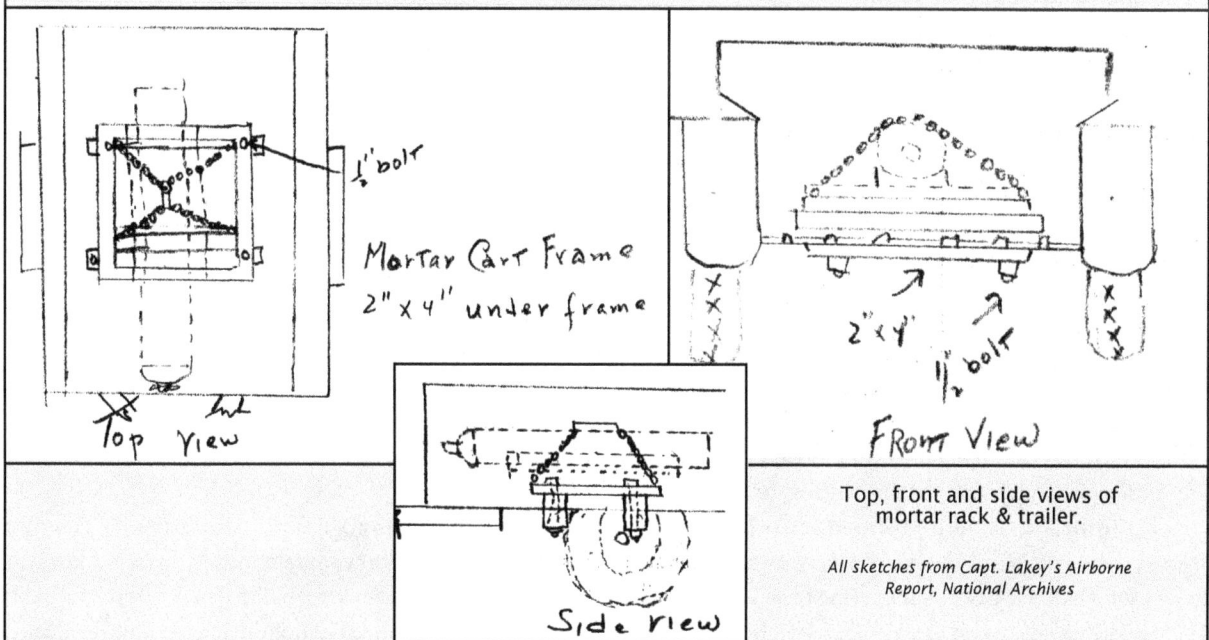

Top, front and side views of mortar rack & trailer.

All sketches from Capt. Lakey's Airborne Report, National Archives

days without resupply. The official report stated the company took in 2.5 "units of fire" [*ammo*] with the promise of more by parachute, but only about 50 rounds were received due to it being widely scattered in the drops. Lee Steedle stated "I don't know what the hell "2.5 units of fire" means, but each squad had a full trailer load of HE and WP." Co. D was attached to the 517th Parachute Infantry RCT with the mission of supporting them by all available fire.[14]

The three objectives of the 1st Airborne Task Force were: (1) a pre-dawn parachute landing; (2) a daylight glider assault landing at H-Hour; and (3) a combined parachute-glider reinforcement landing mission during the early evening hours of August 15th. Two platoons of Co. D were assigned to participate in the third, and largest, part of this mission, known as "Dove" and consisting of "348 Waco [*CG4a*] gliders loaded with 2,250 troops of the 550th Glider Infantry Battalion, the Anti-Tank Company of the 442nd Regimental Combat Team, the 596th Airborne Engineer Company, as well as Co. D, 83rd Chemical Battalion."[15]

Co. D departed Ciampino Airport in gliders at 3:00 p.m., although the official order listed departure time as 3:26. T/5 Kelso C. ("Red") Thompson from Oklahoma said, "The officers gave us pep talks in the … airport. 'No glider traps' they said, but traps were plentiful. As we got in the glider we noticed that the pilot

Crashed glider planes of the 83rd at Le Muy, France, August 15, 1944. *Dougherty Collection*

had on a parachute. He said, 'Boys, I won't leave you.' My buddy Harmon Roberts said, 'That's right, Lieutenant' as he slammed down a cartridge into his carbine." Lee Steedle noted that squad leaders were permitted to write nicknames on the sides of their gliders and he wrote "Bye Bye Baby" for his. Sgt. Wofford L. Jackson said it was his job to number the gliders prior to take-off and added, "Our two platoon HQ gliders were numbers 23 and 23J. I was to go in 23J, so I finished the 'J' out in letters as big as the side of the glider would hold, spelling out 'Jackson' on both sides. We were short an officer, so I was going in as platoon executive and Sgt. Elwood Guthrie was taking my place as platoon sergeant. That changed the seating arrangement. I had to go in number 23, and Lt. Perry Rice went in 23-JACKSON instead of me." Unfortunately, the switch would have dire consequences for Rice.[16] George Borkhuis, Co. D Mess Sgt., who stated the company kitchen would not arrive in France by boat until a few days later, wrote, "On 'D day' our company took off in the gliders and all of us left [*behind*] had tears in our eyes as we had held few hopes of ever seeing many of the boys again."

In the meantime the 3rd Platoon of Co. B arrived on the beach from *LCI 943* at 4:00 p.m., while the 2nd Platoon, aboard the *Ascania*, hit the beach thirty minutes later. At 4:45 p.m., the battalion chaplain and 17 enlisted men on the *Ascania* landed. Co. C, supporting the 179th Infantry, landed without any casualties, while Co. A, supporting the 157th Infantry, landed on the 45th Division Beach. None of the three companies fired a shot during the day. Ironically, this was disputed by Sgt. William C. Ford, Co. C, who admitted opposition was light, but stated they did encounter a number of obstacles and some stiff resistance at St. Maxime and St. Raphael: "Throughout the first night of our assault we fired constantly on enemy positions." Kelly Seibels, also of Co. C, said, "we stood offshore until about noon. Then we landed with no trouble … saw one dead G.I., a mine got him. Marched inland a ways and spent the night on a little hill."[17]

Lt. Robert J. Bush, Co. A, recalled that, during the landing, "… we disembarked off an LCI … the skipper of the LCI hit a sand bar, so we were stuck about 100 yards off the beach. When I saw the water that we had to get through, I told Robert Daniel ("Danny") Danfield, who was only about five foot or five foot four, to get in front of me on the ramp leading into the water, because I didn't know how deep the water was … and sure enough, after just a few steps, Danny went under … he was carrying two shells on his back, about 60 extra pounds. I was able to grab him … the water was up to my mouth … and somehow was able to move forward to the point that Danny could touch his feet on the bottom. That was a bit scary, but fortunately we all made it to the beach with no injuries."[18]

Fred G. Rand, Jr., added to Bush's story, stating that during the invasion Bush would take part of the platoon along with mortar, jeeps, and other equipment, while Rand would take the other part of the platoon, with most of the ammo, and the two would meet at a designated time and spot on the beachhead. Rand said, "Each of my men was to carry two shells in a backpack as he went ashore. This would insure that we'd have some ammo for initial firing, until regular supplies were offloaded." Joseph Cannetti, Co. A, confirmed, "We each had two mortar rounds strapped to our backs … "But confusion in timing during the landing from the LCI caused Rand to arrive at the location hours ahead of Bush and the mortars.[19]

At 7:07 p.m., the gliders with Co. D were released over DZ-A [*Drop Zone - A*] near Le Muy, France. According to Lt. Perry B. Rice,

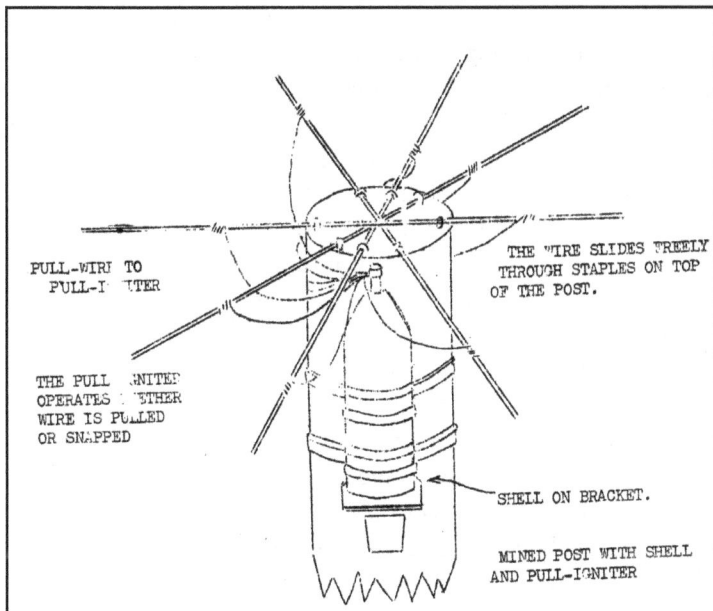

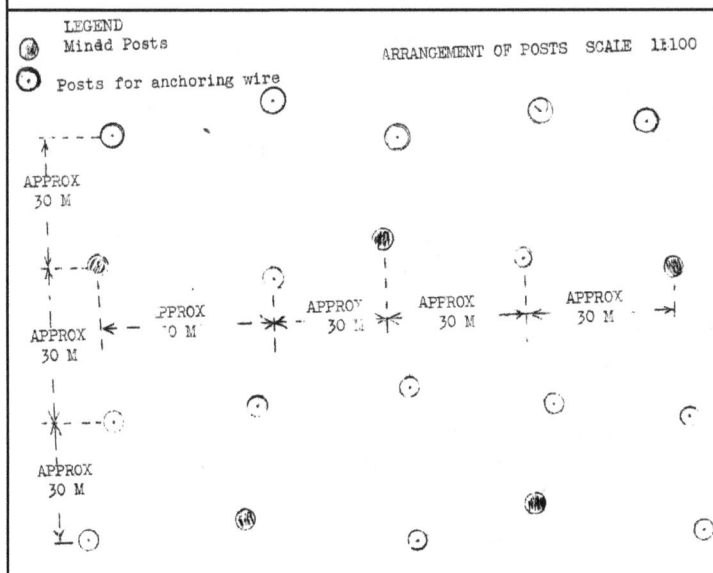

PULL-WIRE TO
PULL-IGNITER

THE WIRE SLIDES FREELY
THROUGH STAPLES ON TOP
OF THE POST.

THE PULL IGNITER
OPERATES WHETHER
WIRE IS PULLED
OR SNAPPED

SHELL ON BRACKET.

MINED POST WITH SHELL
AND PULL-IGNITER

LEGEND
Mined Posts
Posts for anchoring wire

ARRANGEMENT OF POSTS   SCALE 1:100

APPROX
30 M

APPROX
30 M

APPROX
30 M

APPROX
30 M

APPROX
30 M

APPROX
30 M

APPROX
30 M

APPROX
30 M

Left, top and bottom, are sketches of the mined posts with details of how they were arranged and wired for explosives.

National Archives

Above: Example of Rommel's Asparagus

"The C-47's cut us loose about 1,000 feet in the air over our Le Muy drop zone … The Germans had known we were coming and had loaded all fields in that area with glider traps. These were grids of 15-foot poles spaced in squares, with 5-foot piles of large stones centered in each square. In some fields they had strung wire between poles to shear off wings, and in several fields they had suspended fused shells from the wires. But a G.I. Pathfinder Team had parachuted into Le Muy … earlier to make contact with the French Forces of the Interior (FFI) partisans. Seeing the condition of the fields, they had radioed warnings and coordinates. This enabled our pilots to come down into fields that had the poles and stone piles, but not the wires and shells. Some pilots chose to crash into other gliders that had just landed seconds before, shearing off other gliders' wings and tails, but avoiding the deadly poles." These traps had been placed under the direction of Field Marshall Rommel and were known as Rommel's Asparagus.[20]

Injured in the drop were 2nd Lt. Perry B. Rice, Sgt. James H. Gallahan, Cpl. Rollin D. Taylor, T/5 George W. Stevens, T/5 Kelso C. Thompson, Cpl. Warren D. Perry, Pfc. Murray Smith, Pfc. Elvin S. Bailey, Pvt. Samuel E. Fuller, Pvt. Maynard C. Boop, Pvt. Marshall C. Coker, Pvt. William F. Biggs, Pvt. Napoleon G. St. Louis, and Pvt. Dannie L. Herring. Ironically, the journal of Co. D reported only one officer and three enlisted men as casualties.[21]

Lt. Rice, one of the more seriously injured, recalled, "Our I.M.G. [*Dannie L.*] Herring and I were lashed into jump seats behind a jeep trailer. As instructed, we pulled bolts that sent our big side doors flying away, and the in-rushing air helped slow our speed. Our pilot and co-pilot, McFarland [*probably Flight Officer Richard M. McFarland, 16th Squadron, 64th Troop Carrier Group*] and Wilcox, circled, deciding between two fields. Banking steeply to the right, they saw too late that high-tension wires ran between these fields. Our lower right wing was sheared off, and we cart-wheeled nose first into the ground … McFarland was killed outright, with Wilcox and Herring badly hurt by the loose trailer. I was thrown completely free, and was still unconscious when Staff/Sergeant Wofford Jackson found me." Jackson, who had switched planes with Rice prior to take-off, recalled, "When we were coming in for the landing, the first thing I saw was the wreckage of 23-JACKSON. It and the men were strewn over a wide area. Our glider, and some others, had rough landings and there were injuries, but the only fatalities in our platoon were in glider 23-JACKSON. I found Lt. Rice. He seemed to be broken down in his pelvis and was in a lot of pain. I gave him some morphine I'd been carrying, and tried to assure him that help would be on the way." In reality, the men suspected Rice would die, but he was later evacuated and returned to the battalion late in the year. Many years later, Rice showed up at a reunion of the 83rd, much to the astonishment of many who thought him dead.[22]

Sgt. James H. ("Banjo Eyes") Gallahan, from Fredericksburg, Virginia, recalled he was "… in a glider that carried both troops and a jeep with a 30-caliber machine gun mounted on it." His glider could not find a good landing spot and crashed as it landed. The glider split apart causing troops and equipment to be thrown from the craft. Gallahan's son said, "James was rescued by the Free French fighters in the area. He was pinned down by the jeep that had been in the glider. He had multiple injuries … As a result of these injuries he was awarded his second Purple Heart medal."[23]

T/5 Kelso C. Thompson said, "Some of the gliders hung up in trees, with the soldiers still in them, and glider traps were all over the open fields … During the landing my knee got hurt, but I didn't realize it until someone said my boot was full of blood." James Marion Lester and Charlie Lowry were in the same glider with a pilot called "Bud" who found a spot to land, but upon nearing the position another glider took the spot and "Bud" had to land the glider in a grape vineyard. The bottom of the glider was shredded and they were about a mile away from the rest of the outfit. Ford Hopkins later told his son "they had to sit on the ammo boxes in their gliders, which were only made of tubular steel and canvas with wooden wings and floors." Hopkins also told his son his glider crashed in a vineyard, and "… the wings were torn off on impact and when it stopped they all jumped out of it." He added that he "lost his M1 carbine [*and*] picked up a paratroopers model, presumably from a fallen trooper, and used it for the duration of the war."[24]

According to Gerard M. Devlin in his book *Silent Wings*, "In lives and human suffering, the cost of the Dove mission was high. Eleven pilots were killed and 32 others seriously injured in the landing crashes. The passengers, meanwhile, suffered six dead and 126 seriously injured. As usual, the cargoes of jeeps and artillery pieces, though difficult to extract from the wrecks, were nearly all in good working order."[25]

The official report of activities immediately following the glider drop stated that "… there was not too much movement and no difficulty was experienced. Jeeps and trailers were used to gather ammunition from the various gliders that had landed in the area. The defense perimeter, however, permitted limited movement … We had 11 jeeps and trailers to move everything and there was very little maintenance done on the vehicles." As the rear echelon and additional supplies were not scheduled to land on the beaches until D plus 15, the company would rely upon the 517th Parachute Infantry's supply dump. Evacuation of the wounded was also through the 517th's aid station.[26]

After assembling, Co. D departed the area at 8:15 p.m. and occupied gun positions, with all of them ready to fire by 9:00, but no fire missions were required. The official report stated, "On landing, the control was centralized. We had two platoons that were able to fire, with a company fire direction center set up in between the two for control. One OP served the two platoons, when it was in communication." Back in Italy, Rear "A" (3rd Platoon) of Co. D continued usual bivouac duties and Rear "B" prepared to move. The company journal reported the weather was clear and hot and morale was good.[27]

On the 16th, Rear "B" of Co. D, comprised of 44 enlisted men, departed their bivouac at Ciampino Airport at 8:00 a.m. and arrived at Lido di Roma 45 minutes later, while the 2nd Squad of the 3rd Platoon moved to the staging area. Meanwhile, in southern France, the battalion trucks were unloaded from the Liberty ships onto the occupied beaches.[28]

Co. A moved about six miles inland near Plan de le Tour without firing a shot; Co. B was ordered to displace their Red Platoon to support the 1st Battalion, 157th Infantry, and at 10:30 in the evening the White Platoon fired 10 HE and 7 WP at an enemy mortar convoy near a bridge. Co. C was in support of the 179th Infantry and did no firing as they moved near Les Richards. William C. Ford said Co. C took Vidauban and cleared Le Luc. The strength of the battalion at the end of the day, minus Co. D, was 28 officers and 438 enlisted men.[29]

At Les Arcs, Co. D's White Platoon fired four rounds of HE on a crossroads as the enemy returned shell fire without inflicting any casualties. Late in the evening, both the Red and White platoons fired heavy concentrations of HE to support an attack of the 517th Parachute Infantry, which reported the results as excellent. During the day, Pfc. William B. Templin, from Kenosha County, Wisconsin, was wounded by shrapnel in the forearm and elbow in a heavy enemy artillery barrage while he was laying telephone wires to the OP. This was possibly the incident described by Lee Steedle, who wrote, "Our radioman lost his arm up at the OP, as we began firing at Jerries holding a crossroad. Resistance was light, but a few hours later a German tank, belly-down, began firing directly into our position. Sgt. [*Clark*] Riddle got a paratroop radioman to relay our request to air liaison for help. Luckily, a fighter plane had been circling over Le Muy, and it knocked the tank out in a single pass."[30]

The official report of Co. D's operations read, "On D plus one we fired on enemy machine gun emplacements, counterattacks, strong points, and fired 700 rounds on enemy positions as preparation fire to a night attack (dusk)." T/5 Kelso C. Thompson added, "We expected the Germans to attack us from across the valley, in the middle of which was an oat field. Our officers had already zeroed-in. The 517th paratroopers called to report the Germans were crawling in the field and asked us for a round of smoke. That successfully accomplished, we were then asked to fire for effect. Together we completely stopped the attack and virtually destroyed the enemy that night." The combined naval and air invasion of southern France was so successful, and met with such minimal resistance, that the troops were able to advance northward with great rapidity through numerous towns. Support troops such as the 83rd had a hard time keeping up with the front the first few weeks. The operation became so leisurely it was later referred to as the "Champagne Campaign".[31]

During August 17th, Co. A, supporting the advance of the 157th Infantry, moved ten miles to a point north of Vidauban, then another ten miles to an area south of Lourges, where Albert Sabatino, the ex-Italian POW, captured two prisoners. Sam Bundy, Co. A, wrote, "Albert decided to look around for some rabbits to satisfy his mammoth appetite and ran across two Jerry's who were bathing. Upon seeing them, he called to someone to bring a rifle because all he had was a useless flashlight. Help arrived and the Jerry's were turned over to the MP's." Ironically, Charles Rolling told the story a bit differently, stating Albert "… opened a small house and what did he find but two Germans. They were taken prisoners. [*Frank*] Boduck and Albert each got a watch out of their clothing, also a shaving set and some German money." Further complicating the story was the version told by James Helsel, who said, "… two fellows from the first platoon was looking for some chickens & eggs, or some straw to sleep on and run across two German soldiers in a chicken coop and took them prisoner."[32]

Co. B, held in reserve for the 179th Infantry, did not fire a shot during the day; and Co. C, supporting the 180th Infantry, moved from Le Luc to Barjoles. The battalion CP moved near Vidauban as a truck carrying the battalion's communications section ran off a narrow mountain road during an attempt to pass a tank. Six men were lightly injured, the first casualties in that portion of the battalion attached to the 45th Division in the campaign. Among the injured were T/4 Paul James Waring, T/5 Herbert Schumann, T/5 John O'Brien, Jr., Pvt. Ralph J. Brakefield, Pvt. Ernest J. Carr [*Card?*], and Pvt. Arthur E. Emmons. Co. D remained in their same positions at Les Arcs as the enemy had pulled out of range of their mortars. Meanwhile at Quiloni, Italy, Rear "A" and Rear "B" of Co. D performed their usual bivouac duties as the 1st Squad of Rear "A" moved to the Texas Staging Area.[33]

On August 18th, Co. A moved about 20 miles to a point near Fax Amphaux after a German officer walked into camp and surrendered to Capt. McEvoy. A member of the Free French forces named Paul also linked up as McEvoy's interpreter. Co. B took position near Les Maneous; two platoons of Co. C set up near Ponteves although their company headquarters was held up for three hours at an enemy infantry strong point near Catignac; and HQ Detachment advanced from Vidauban to Sillans-la-Cascade. Co. D held a defensive position at Le Puget-sur-Argens, east of Les Arcs near Frejus. Back in Italy, the 1st Squad of the 3rd Platoon returned to the position of Rear "A" while Rear "B" left their bivouac at Lido di Roma and moved in a truck convoy of the 517th Parachute Infantry and attached units to an area three miles east of Largo-Patria.[34]

Early on the morning of the 19th, Lt. Julian T. McKinnon, Co. B, received a message from Lt. James V. Lauro, Co. D, confirming that Co. D had landed at 1700 hours (5 p.m.) and sustained 12 casualties in the landing and one man wounded by shell fire in the subsequent fighting. The company had already fired some 600 rounds and was then in a defensive position between Frejus and Les Arcs. Co. A left Fax Amphaux and moved 15 miles to Esparron; Co. B moved from Les Maneous to Rians; Co. C's Blue Platoon was at Catignac, where they helped repel a counterattack near Le Thornet; the remainder of Co. C was near Ponteves; and the battalion CP opened near Fax Amphaux. Co. D remained in the same defensive position near Le Puget-sur-Argens while rear "A" and "B" of the company awaited transport from Italy to France.[35]

The battalion CP opened about two miles east of Rians on the 20th. Co. A moved near St. Paul des Durance to support the crossing of the Durance River by the 157th Infantry. The commanding officer of the 157th "… expressed great satisfaction with the work of the mortars, giving them credit for stopping the counterattack" by firing 200 HE and 50 WP shells. The Blue Platoon of Co. B gave support to the 180th Infantry attack on Rogues where they were led into a trap in the vicinity of Peyrolles and Meyrarques. Andrew Leech recalled, "They opened up on us and threw everything they had while we sat jammed in the middle of the road. We unloaded and hit the ditches and scattered as best we could as our tanks fired back. As soon as the convoy could be straightened out and turned around we had to withdraw into the town of Peyrolles. There we went into position and fired so fast that we had to cool the barrel of the mortar with wet sacks." Frederick W. Endlein, Co. B, added, "We were firing our mortars at the shortest range possible. We fired so much that we had to wrap rags around the barrel and pour water on it to keep it cool. One shell misfired and didn't come out of the barrel. After we extracted this shell, we found that the cone at the bottom of the barrel had become so flat, it wouldn't strike the firing pin on the shell. After changing the barrel we resumed firing." Andrew Leech further explained, "The Jerries were advancing and we were under machine gun fire as well as small arms fire. We were forced to leave our guns because every time we would start to fire they would shoot at us with small arms fire. Finally the infantry withdrew. About three [*the battalion journal says two*] Mark VI tanks came down the road firing at point blank range. Everything, even our tanks, withdrew and left us out there pinned down for a while as they threw artillery all around us, shattering buildings and causing some casualties … Our forces regrouped and we laid a smoke screen and a heavy barrage of HE." The Germans held but would be driven off the next day. During the action Pvt. Melvin Bishop, Co. B, from McDowell County, West Virginia, was lightly wounded in the back of the head by an enemy shell. Bishop was "knocked unconscious when he was hit and when he opened his eyes he was lying in a ditch with lots of blood."[36]

The Red and White platoons of Co. C assembled east of Rians while the Blue Platoon went north of the Durance River to support the 179th Infantry. Lt. Norman ("Rosy") Rosenthal, Pvt. Gerard Poliquin, and Pvt. Maurice D. Lear took a German soldier dressed as a civilian prisoner at Catignac; subsequent interrogation at regimental HQ showed him to be transporting valuable military information and maps. Another six prisoners were taken near Catignac by Lt. Free, Pvt. Williams, and Pvt. Jack Vintson who turned them over to an anti-tank unit of the 7th Army. At Le Puget-sur Argens, Co. D did no firing as their trucks were used to transport infantry and equipment to a new defensive position. At Le Muy, Detachment No. 2 of the 11th Chemical Maintenance repaired six mortars brought in by Co. D of the 83rd. Ed Trey would later say of the 11th Chemical, "We couldn't have performed without them."[37]

The town of St. Eucher became the new battalion CP on the 21st, where word was received from the G-3 of the 45th Division informing Maj. Efnor that there was a possibility the 83rd would be pulled from the lines and used as service troops because supply had become critical. Co. A left St. Paul des Durance, crossed the Durance River on pontoon bridges, and advanced 12 miles to an area near Souvacanne. Co. B was active in helping the 180th Infantry defend two roadblocks; and the Red and White platoons of Co. C moved to Chateau Arnaux while the Blue Platoon supported a drive of the 179th Infantry toward Valonne. Co. D was given the mission to shell Fayence but, after encountering no opposition, entered town and prepared to defend it against any enemy approach. The S-3 of the 645th Tank Destroyer Battalion reported the 83rd had laid a smokescreen in the vicinity of Pertuis which helped to prevent the possible loss of five or six tank destroyers.[38]

Orders were issued by the 45th Division on the 22nd that a company of the 83rd establish a railhead at St. Maximin (near Uzes), an assignment Capt. Gordon M. Mindrum delegated to Co. A. Shortly afterward Maj. Efnor was informed his companies were relieved from their attachments to the infantry regiments and returned to battalion control. As a result of this order, companies B and C were to assemble in the battalion CP area and Co. A prepared to depart for St. Maximin. Co. D advanced from Fayence to Callian, while Rear "A" of the company went to bivouac at HQ of the 83rd near Aversa, Italy, and nine enlisted men (six kitchen and three motor pool) left Rear "B" and joined Rear "A".[39]

Capt. Robert B. Smith, Co. C, won the Silver Star for his actions in the fight at Briançon.
Annette Smith

At this time Capt. Robert B. Smith, Co. C, took time to write about the French people and his own injuries, penning, "The people along the way seem overjoyed at being liberated, of course, there are some who are not overjoyed too. But we never stop in a town and keep pretty well on the move. I threw my knee out of place the other night going after a group of Germans who were firing across the road and had been exposed, and then the next day I was kicking in a door looking for others and the other knee went out so [I've] been limping around like an old man but get along all right and they are both better today."[40]

The 83rd Chemical Battalion was held in division reserve on August 23rd as Co. A moved to St. Maximin, Co. B went to Mirabeau, and Co. C bivouacked at Chateau Arnaux. From Callian, elements of Co. D moved to fire on targets at St. Cezaine and advanced to St. Vallier, one platoon going to the outskirts of Vecosvire.[41]

Lt. Robert P. Brimm left for St. Maxime on the morning of August 24th in order to guide the battalion vehicles of the "D" plus 10 convoy to the battalion. Capt. John P. McEvoy departed as well in order to make contact with Co. D which was yet attached to the 7th Army Provisional Airborne Division on the right flank of the beachhead forces. Companies B and C were ordered to division CP near Aspres. One platoon of Co. D remained at St. Vallier while another supported the 3rd Battalion, 517th Parachute Infantry, in a strong fight at Le Bar [*Le Bar sur Loop*]. In the meantime, Rear "A" of Co. D departed Aversa, Italy, and embarked on a ship which remained in dock. At St. Maxime, Co. A found plans altered as the outfit that was to relieve them arrived much earlier than expected, leaving Co. A free to enjoy some leisure time, although a few men helped out at a gasoline dump a couple of hundred yards away.[42]

The town of Aspres became the battalion CP on the 25th as Co. B located at Ourines and Co. C at Aspermont. Co. C also loaned six of their 2½-ton trucks to the division quartermaster to haul prisoners and division supplies. Capt. McEvoy returned after making contact with Co. D and Lt. Brimm also returned from St. Maxime with news that no battalion trucks were on the "D" plus 10 convoy and would not be on any until the "D" plus 25 convoy carrying personnel. The Red Platoon and company headquarters of Co. D moved to Le Bar and supported the 1st Battalion, 517th Infantry at Greolieres. The White Platoon moved near Bouyon. The rear elements of Co. D were active as Rear "A" was on the boat at Naples and eight men of their 2nd Squad arrived at St. Raphael, France. Rear "B", excepting 11 enlisted men left behind at Largo-Patria, arrived at the Texas Embarkation Area.[43]

Co. A left St. Maximin for Lus-la Croix-Haute on the 26th, traveling about 116 miles via truck in the rain, to

operate a railhead for the division quartermaster. The company spent the night in a sawmill sleeping on boards. Co. B was alerted for movement to Grenoble, and Co. C remained in division reserve at Aspermont. The White Platoon of Co. D left Le Bar for Coursegaules and the Red Platoon fired a number of rounds from southeast of Bouyon.[44]

TASK FORCE BIBO
August 27 – September 2

At a conference at Aspres on the August 27th, attended by Maj. Efnor and Capt. Mindrum, the 83rd Chemical Battalion, except companies B and D, were assigned a new mission; relieved from attachment to the 45th Infantry Division, then were made a component of the VI Corps' Provisional Flank Protective Force (PFPF), known as Task Force Bibo and led by 32 year-old Lt. Col. Harold Shelton Bibo of New Mexico. The task force included two companies of the 83rd Chemical Battalion (A and C); two companies each from the 2nd and 3rd Chemical Battalions; Battery B, 171st Field Artillery; Troop A, 117th Reconnaissance Battalion; a platoon from the AT Company, 180th Infantry; a platoon from the 148th Engineers; and a signal detachment from VI Corps HQ, making a total of 1,250 American officers and enlisted men as well as some Maquis, a predominantly rural band of guerrilla French Resistance fighters. The mission of the force was to protect the right flank of the Corps from St. Paul to Albertsville, a distance of approximately 135 miles by road. This Provisional Flank Protective Force relieved the 180th Infantry, and, after Maj. Efnor and Capt. Mindrum of the 83rd learned the details of the operation, Co. A moved to St. Paul and Co. C traversed to Briançon, both under the cover of darkness.[45]

Around noon, according to Sam Bundy, Co. A, "we moved up about five miles to bivouac near Lus-la-Croix-Haute. We all moved into buildings where each man had a bed. A few men worked today loading rations at the railhead … But – plans were changed very suddenly again, and the detail was called off. At 6 o'clock we hit the road and traveled until 3 AM the next morning. On the way we passed thru Gap … beautiful scenery – into the Alps we rode. Once, very early in the morning, we had to make a back track because of a road out, so, we lost a couple hours. Extremely narrow roads and blackout driving made this trip a very difficult one. We nearly froze at this high altitude, riding in open vehicles, lightly clothed." During the trip the truck of Hershel T. Stutts hit a mountainside injuring Albert Sabatino, the former Italian POW serving in Co. A.[46]

Co. B remained with the 45th Division and operated the railhead at Grenoble, a winter resort town high in the Alps near the Swiss border. Andrew Leech, Co. B, fondly recalled, "Here they made quartermasters out of us for about three weeks and we really had a time! … Our job was to load gasoline and other supplies on train cars and send them to the troops as they advanced. We were the first soldiers to stop over in Grenoble, and the people treated us swell. They gave us dances and invited us into their homes to eat and drink with them. And the girls flocked after us and showed us a swell time. Some nights we would have as many as three dates a night and everybody had a girl. This was a soldier's paradise …" Kelly Seibels, Co. C, wrote in his log, "spent a couple of days at Grenoble while drivers and trucks were being used to haul German prisoners of war to the coast."[47]

Co. D held fast at Bouyon as one platoon fired a number of rounds at the enemy. Three non-battle casualties occurred when Cpl. James H. Pittman, Pfc. Antonio Rabaiotti, and a Pvt. Key were burned by exploding powder rings. In the meantime, eight enlisted men of the 2nd Squad of Rear "A" of Co. D reported to the company for duty while the rest of Rear "A" remained on the boat at the dock in Naples. Rear "B" departed the Texas Embarkation area and boarded *H.M.S. LST 12* at Bagnoli, Italy.[48]

On the 28th, Co. A, supported by one platoon of reconnaissance troops and one 57mm AT gun manned by 16 men, relieved Co. F of the 180th Infantry and set up a roadblock northwest of Melezen, where they sent a patrol out to St. Paul and discovered a 12-man German patrol had been in town. Afterwards they moved the AT gun above Melezen. Co. A's 3rd Platoon set up their mortars while the 1st and 2nd platoons dug in as infantry protecting the road to St. Paul. At Grenoble, Co. B continued to operate the railhead while the Red Platoon of Co. D was engaged near Bouyon by firing on a trail area and a factory building on the other side of the Le Var River near a bridge. Later in the day the White Platoon of Co. D was detached from the 517th Infantry and attached to the 550th Combat Team. Their mission was to move to St. Justin, ten miles from the Italian border, and fire on Condamine, where there had been a report of some 2,000 Germans.[49]

The Battalion CP along with the task group CP closed at Aspre-sur-Buech and moved to Briançon, a city near the Italian border at the foot of the Alps surrounded by five medieval forts. The CP of the task force took up quarters in the Grand Hotel. At 10:30 a.m., Co. C of the 83rd established a defensive position at a roadblock at Briançon and contacted Capt. Robert B. Smith, who, along with Lt. Andre N. Laus, reported on conditions at that time. By 11:25 a.m., Lt. Robert Brimm, HQ Detachment, of the 83rd reported to the Task Force Bibo CP at Briançon. A portion of Co. C had also placed their mortars and two 50 caliber machine guns in nearby Ft. Dauphin during the afternoon. Paul Bailey, of the AT Co. of the 180th Infantry, said Co. C had set up "two or three mortars near the parapet, at the east side of the terrace in front of the long building." Pvt. Dale C. Blank, Co. C, from Pennsylvania, said he believed there were no more than two mortars set up within the actual confines of the fort. Blank added, "1st Lt. James Doyle directed me to set my .50 cal. machine gun on the easternmost point of the fort facing toward Italy where the enemy was located ... Everybody was busy choosing a place to sleep and arranging all their personal equipment. No vehicles could be brought into the fort because of the small opening for a door. All vehicles along with all ammunition and fighting supplies were left outside the walls on the very narrow road leading up to the fort. The trucks had no protection where

Unidentified Co. C men with the exception of Jean Pierre Combe kneeling on far right, the young French lad who saved approximately 30 men of Co. C at Ft. Dauphin. *Jean Pierre Combe*

they were parked. There was another fort (Fort dês Tetes) to the west of us that was at a higher elevation and looked right down into Ft. Dauphin. This would have been a better choice to defend." Kelly Seibels, Co. C, said they relieved the infantry, reconnaissance was supposedly carried out, machine guns were set up and guards posted. Paul Bailey with the platoon of the AT Co. and their 57mm gun said "We found a dug road leading up the mountain to a point directly below a fort. There we located our gun pointing across the valley to cover the road coming out of Italy." Bailey added "we managed to get our 6x6 truck inside, but it was a tight fit. We parked it by the right side of the fort wall. There was a long narrow building running roughly east-west, with a level area in front of it, the strangest part of the design was a solid wall which rose in what I thought was the middle of the fort at least 30-40 feet with no loopholes or openings of any kind."[50]

Briançon had been liberated on August 22nd by the 180th Infantry of the 45th Division and "heavy weapons" had moved to nearby Ft. Dauphin. Jean Pierre Combe, a young French boy of 16 who was born in the area, had accompanied the infantry to the fort; however, upon the arrival of Co. C, 83rd Chemical Battalion, the infantry departed and refused to take Jean Pierre with them, informing him he was too young to get killed. As a result, he remained with the section of Co. C of the 83rd at Ft. Dauphin. The men of the 180th Infantry also informed the 83rd men at Ft. Dauphin the position they were setting up in was a literal paradise.[51]

Capt. Robert B. Smith, Co. C, ordered Sgt. William C. Ford, squad leader of the 1st Platoon, to take one man from each squad, along with a radio operator, and move to an outpost to observe a blown bridge on a road coming over the mountains from Italy. Leaving Cpl. Louis J. Kaufman in charge of his squad, Ford left with Cpl. Floyd L. Grissom, Pfc.'s Melvin A. Beaty and Alfred R. Sheats, along with the radio operator, and moved into some pillboxes about 500 yards up the mountain from the bridge. At this location they relieved some men of the 45th Infantry Division who warned them to move lightly and stay concealed. Ford had been ordered to listen and watch for enemy patrols and to immediately call Capt. Smith if there was any activity. With a clear view of the bridge, the men spent the entire day viewing the site through binoculars but failed to detect any enemy activity. Once darkness fell they could only listen as the bridge was no longer visible.[52]

At 5:00 p.m. Jean Pierre Combe had a conversation at Ft. Dauphin with Lt. Andre N. Laus, Co. C, and recalled, "[I] was surprised to hear him speak so well French." When Laus asked if Combe knew Miss P. Streicher, his wife's

Top left view is a diagram of Ft. Dauphin; Top right view is a modern day photo of Ft. Dauphin. Center left is a modern photo of Pont d' Asfeld, the bridge at Briançon. Center right is a modern view of the military hospital at Briançon. Bottom postcard view shows all the forts in the Briançon area, all named. *All photos on this page provided by Jean Pierre Combe.*

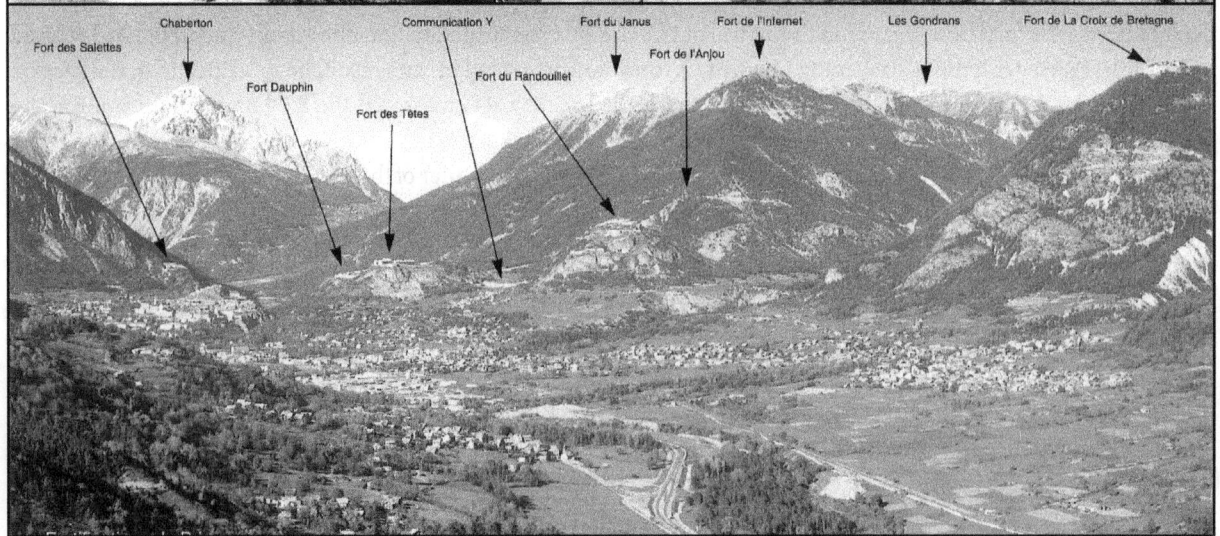

cousin, Combe answered, "Sure. She made me catechism when I was young." He agreed to take Laus to her home the next day, but, unfortunately, this proved to be their "last conversation."[53]

Laus's fluency in French soon proved invaluable to 2nd Lt. John L. Boyd, from Oregon, who had already had two bouts with malaria and suffered a recurrence at the fort. He recalled, "My fever was so high that our doctor recommended that I be sent to the nearest field hospital. Lt. Laus, who spoke fluent French, talked to some Frenchmen in Briançon and they said they could handle this right here. I was taken to the hospital located in the highest part of the town."[54]

In the meantime Capt. Smith completed a reconnaissance of the mountain north of his position around 6 p.m. and reported it as excellent for observation. At 8:00 p.m., Capt. John P. McEvoy

Some of the French resistance fighters. Though unidentified, the man in the middle may possibly be Jean Pierre Combe. *Hale Hunter Hepler*

reported that Co. A's roadblock had changed and Maj. Efnor called Capt. Smith to tell him to send a six-man patrol of FFI [*Forces Francaises d'Interior or Free French Intelligence*] under Lt. Norman ("Rosy") Rosenthal of New Jersey to investigate the forts to the right of the defensive position at Ft. Dauphin. Twenty minutes later Rosenthal returned and reported no enemy were found.[55]

That evening, Paul S. Giles, Co. C, "was sitting on a slit trench [*at Ft. Dauphin*] and heard something that sounded like a sow and pigs to this farm boy. I stood up and it stopped. It was a German patrol. I returned to the old .50 caliber and told the gunner there was a German patrol out there. He didn't think so, however, later on the sergeant informed me I was going to have to pull guard duty again that night even though I had been on guard the night before. He knew the Germans were in the area. While standing guard duty, I saw someone crawling right up to me. I waited and watched, then began to squeeze the trigger as he crawled ever closer. All at once he said, 'How's it going?' It was the new American lieutenant. I told him he didn't know how close I was to shooting him. He said he was just checking to see if anybody was sleeping. I told him nobody was sleeping here."[56]

Pvt. Lloyd L. Fiscus, Co. C, from McKean County, Pennsylvania, said movement had been detected in the hills while they were setting up mortars at the fort but it was attributed to the Free French scouting the hills. During his outpost guard duty from 3:00 to 6:00 a.m., Fiscus said it was quiet and he heard nothing. Kelly Seibels said he was on guard with a machine gun that night. Paul Bailey of the AT squad "on the night of August 28, I was on guard duty. I remember talking to a member of an observation team from the 171st Field Artillery Battalion, which had moved into Briançon that afternoon. They had four men, including a lieutenant at the fort. Late that night, I heard noises outside the wall of the fort. When I told my sergeant about it, he dismissed it as my imagination."[57]

BRIANÇON
August 29

Around midnight Sgt. William Ford and his four men of Co. C had heard enemy vehicles in the vicinity of the bridge near Ft. Dauphin at Briançon and reported the information to Capt. Smith, who ordered them to take a patrol out and investigate. Ford and Pfc. Sheats, who volunteered to accompany Ford, got close enough to the bridge to view some enemy trucks and equipment along with men working on the bridge. Ford returned to the pillbox where he called and informed Capt. Smith.[58]

Around 6:00 a.m., Mario Ricci, a Co. C forward observer radio operator, moved about ten miles east of Briançon to a flat, cleared area. By communicating with Corps HQ by International Morse Code the previous evening, Ricci had been ordered to move there and await a Piper Cub which was carrying the next seven days call letters.[59]

At 7:40, Capt. Smith reported to the task force that there were approximately 30 of the enemy working on the bridge near Briançon and requested permission to fire on them, which was granted at 7:50 by Lt. Col. Bibo, with the condition that Capt. Smith report the results by phone. Smith immediately ordered Co. C's mortars to fire on the bridge. At 8:10 Capt. Smith reported two rounds had been fired at the bridge, temporarily halting work, followed by a fired concentration resulting in an unknown number of casualties. Paul Bailey recalled "The decision was made to fire on the unidentified troops. I remember one lieutenant ordered his crew to change the charge on their mortar and got a direct hit on the target, which was a bridge the Germans were working on. Shortly after this, a Frenchman came to the fort to tell us the Germans were in the forts above and behind us, and this was soon followed by a burst of German machine gun fire." Sgt. Ford added, "We could see our shells [*from the fort*] exploding on the bridge, and soon it was destroyed again. Two German Mark IV tanks had already crossed the bridge before we destroyed it. I called back and reported the tanks to Capt. Smith. The tanks were forced to stay on the road, because it was narrow with high banks on either side. Capt. Smith put down mortar fire [*a barrage of HE*] and destroyed both tanks before they got rolling good." Pvt. Lloyd L. Fiscus confirmed this as he recalled, "As day broke the morning of the 29th, we got a fire mission. German troops were coming through the pass below us. We fired upon the bridge crossing the stream and destroyed it."[60]

In a short time the situation grew critical for Ford and his men as the enemy began firing mortar and artillery barrages on the mountainside. Ford ordered his men out of the pillbox to a position about 50 yards farther up the mountain, where they soon found themselves under an infantry attack. When Capt. Smith was informed of this development, he told Ford to hold on and return rifle fire. It was during this time that Ford learned via radio that Ft. Dauphin and Briançon were in the process of being surrounded by the enemy.[61]

Sgt. Ford vividly described the situation. "I had to make a decision which way to move, because the shells were bursting all around, and hitting big trees, spraying us with shrapnel and wood splinters. I decided to lead my men up the mountain instead of toward the road. I told the radio operator to destroy the radio so the enemy couldn't use it … We moved up a ditch under burp gun and rifle fire. Only one man was wounded, Cpl. Floyd L. Grissom, was hit. Fortunately none of his bones were broken, so we bandaged him and he was able to continue." Hit in both legs, Cpl. Grissom, from Guntown in Itawamba County, Mississippi, recalled, "We were in a ravine and the Germans were above us on a level spot, shooting away … All we could do was run. I was running so fast that the same bullet hit the front of my knee on one leg and the back of my knee on the other leg." Summarizing the situation, Pvt. Dale C. Blank wrote, "During the night the Germans infiltrated thru our lines past any outposts we may have had and occupied Fort dês Tetes. They set up machine guns at strategic points and basically had us dead to rights."[62]

Indeed, at 8:00 a.m. [*Blank said 7:00 a.m.*], the Germans, utilizing heavy gun, mortar, and artillery fire, counterattacked Co. C at Ft. Dauphin. This attacking enemy force consisted of men from the 5th Mountain Division, which had been moving west from Italy to relieve the 90th Panzer Grenadier Division. Mario Ricci claimed the attackers were Mongolian volunteers who had surrendered to Germany on the Russian Front and volunteered to serve with the German army on the Western Front. In the ensuing fight, Co. C fired 90 WP and 75 HE, as well as the majority of their small arms ammo. Kelly Seibels said he had been relieved from guard duty and was "walking back to get breakfast and sleep, stopped to help fire the mortars. Then I walked on and was about to go in the building, when I listened to a Frenchman tell Lt. Laus (Co. Exec.) that there were 31 Jerries in the fort above and behind us! Lt. Laus began to stand there in the open and watch the fort through his field glasses. I went on up to our room and cooked breakfast. Laus' continuous scouting at the other fort must have aroused Jerrie's suspicions that we might have detected them, for in a very few minutes a jerry machine gun opened up and the battle was on." According to Paul Bailey of the AT squad "the mortar crews started firing shells into the area behind the fort where the majority of the Germans appeared to be. However, they had to fire almost straight up into the air to get over the high walls and then couldn't see the effects of their attack. They soon quit for fear of the shells coming back in on us. Since almost all of us in the fort belonged to gun crews, we were armed with only 45 cal. pistols and a few carbines. Someone borrowed an M-1 rifle and tried to shoot back from somewhere up near the roof, but the German fire drove him back down. We did have a bazooka and rifles but the ammunition was in the truck, which we were cut off from by now. Rifle fire was coming as though from nowhere. I think there must have been snipers up in trees; I can't see how they could have shot down in there otherwise. What we really needed, anyway, was back-up from rifle companies, but that wasn't to be."[63]

Pvt. Robert F. Thorpe, a former newspaper boy from Mt. Savage, Maryland, who served as a radio man and forward observer with Co. C, said, "I called fire on Germans and Italians who were clearing a roadblock. Later everything broke loose at the fort. We spotted Germans coming through the woods. I stayed back and fired several rounds at them. When I got back to the road, the jeep was gone, and I made my way back to town under heavy fire. I hid all night in a wood and coal shed behind a house, hearing the screams of the women in town as the patriots were being shot by the Germans."[64]

Sgt. Ford said that at his outpost "The Germans began firing burp guns and other automatic weapons at our position. We returned fire on the Germans. This lasted about three hours. We were limited on ammunition. When we ran out of ammunition I called Capt. Smith and reported this to him. He ordered me to try to pull back to our lines. The Germans had control of the road we came in on. I would try to make it to a ditch coming down the mountain."[65]

At the fort, "Lieutenant [*Andre N.*] Laus climbed, through intense machine gun fire, to an exposed position from which he directed effective mortar fire on the enemy troops, temporarily halting their advance. Taking advantage of this situation, Lieutenant Laus secured a light machine gun and crawled back to his observation post where, despite intense enemy

Lt. Andre Laus, Co. C, killed in action at Ft. Dauphin, Briançon, France, August 29, 1944. He was awarded the Distinguished Service Cross posthumously. *Mary Jane Laus*

machine gun and mortar fire, he succeeded in destroying twenty of the hostile force. When enemy fire finally hit his ammunition belt causing a jam in the gun, Lieutenant Laus, displaying outstanding bravery, seized a rifle and inflicted additional casualties among the advancing enemy. Ordered by the Force Commander to withdraw along a road which was under heavy machine gun fire, Lieutenant Laus volunteered to make the initial advance to determine the safety of the road. After advancing about two hundred yards he was killed by enemy machine gun fire." For his actions he would be awarded posthumously the Distinguished Service Cross, one of only three men of the battalion to receive this honor. Pvt. Dale C. Blank, who would be captured, said that before Laus died the two of them destroyed two mortars in the fort with grenades after running out of ammo. Capt. Smith also later attempted, unsuccessfully, to get Laus the Congressional Medal of Honor.[66]

Smith won a Silver Star for his gallantry in the action, the citation reading, "While his company was defending a roadblock against a strong enemy force Captain Smith moved through machine gun and artillery fire to check gun positions and encourage and aid his men. To direct mortar fire he climbed to an exposed OP and succeeded in inflicting many casualties on the enemy. His gallantry was an important factor in the defense of our positions." Smith later said it was one of the "blackest days" of his life but added, "I was never actually afraid for my own life … although I'll admit my mouth got dry and there wasn't much I could do about that." Smith also noted that one of his sergeants killed four Germans by himself and the officer who would replace Laus "… got nicked in the leg by a machine gun bullet … it brought the blood barely through the skin, so he didn't mention it for a day or two." Another recipient of the Silver Star for the action was platoon leader Lt. Thomas A. Cute, Co. C, from Steuben County, New York, who "… faced heavy enemy fire and aided his men in repulsing an attack by greatly superior enemy [*numbers*]." Paul Bailey added "There was another guy, a member of the 83rd that had been wounded a couple of times before and thought the Germans couldn't possibly kill him, so the other guys told me. He found out he was wrong, when he fired from an unprotected position."[67]

Around 8:55 a firefight broke out just outside the town of Briançon and enemy machine gun fire struck trees near the Grand Hotel, while Co. B, 2nd Chemical Battalion, also came under enemy mortar fire near Briançon. At the hospital in Briançon Lt. John L. Boyd had recuperated from his malaria and was preparing to return to the fort when a nurse reported the situation to a doctor. The physician told Boyd it was not safe to leave as the fort was under attack as was the town. Boyd added, "The Germans shelled the town. One shell barely missed coming through the window of the ward that I was in with about 15 other patients. Glass and wood from the window showered everyone in the ward, some suffered severe injuries. I escaped with a few cuts and bruises. I was then transferred down the hill, 5 or 6 blocks, to another hospital."[68]

M. Daerrebe, solicitor voluntary administrator of Briançon, reported that "… the town was … subjected from the morning to a severe artillery bombing. Infantry fires were bursting a little everywhere around Fort Dauphin and Fort dês Tetes at first, then on the ramps of Fort dês Tetes, and afterwards, at Fontehuistere, and on the wooded hill overlooking the park of le Scheffe … from 8 a.m., Champ de Mars and the surroundings of the Pont d'Asfeld were swept by gusts of machine gun fire, without one knowing precisely where from the fires were coming … the people of Briançon started to go to the shelters."[69]

The situation grew more critical at 9:40 when enemy artillery and mortar fire fell near the Provisional Flank Protective Force CP in Briançon. Lt. Col. Bibo called Capt. Smith at Ft. Dauphin and told him he would place artillery fire on the fort southwest of Co. C, as Smith told him he was receiving enemy shell fire. By 10:00, Co. C had reported three casualties at the fort while enemy mortars fell in the positions of the 3rd Chemical Battalion and Detachment Number Two, 11th Chemical Maintenance Company, located about one and a half miles south of Briançon. Orders were given to withdraw from Briançon to Col du Lautaret, "… leaving behind all equipment and personal belongings, carrying only carbines, belts, and canteens of water." At 10:30, Capt. Smith called Maj. Efnor and requested the Engineers blow the bridge, and at 10:45 Smith reported it had become necessary to slightly draw back his outpost and an enemy S/P was seen coming down the road.[70]

Many of the survivors of the fight at Ft. Dauphin told of their personal experiences. Pvt. Dale C. Blank said, "I happened to be on the second floor and ran down the stairs to the first floor and ran into 1st Lt. James Doyle and a 2nd Lt. I did not know. The Lt. said to me that I looked like a good BAR man and handed me a BAR and a sack of clips of ammo. Then he told me to go out the back of the fort and he would send a squad of men with me. I exited the building and turned back to see my squad and it was non-existent. The young 2nd Lt. and a private from GA named Goins [*in another account he says the man's name was Loins/Lyons - possibly Rex E. Lyons of Co. C*] with a rifle was my squad. We worked our way up the incline back of the fort to a short wall that would give us protection. The Germans hadn't noticed we were there yet. The young Lt. acted as my observer and would point at targets for me to fire at and I would comply. We moved along the wall changing positions to throw the Germans off and it worked for a while. We started taking a lot of incoming fire and the rifleman moved out of my sight. The Lt. decided he was needed elsewhere and I was left alone to face the Germans across the way. My ammo was getting very low by this time and a bullet had lodged in the front of my leg. So I decided to move back to the fort and see what was going on there. When I got inside the fort, there was nobody in sight. I ran up the stairs to where my belongings were and looked [*at*] my leg. There was a bullet sticking out of my leg, so I pulled it out and put some sulfa on the wound and a bandage. It had to be a ricochet or it would have done more damage." The young French boy, Jean Pierre Combe, speaking in broken English, remembered, "We fought with lots of courage but at first after noon we did not have any more ammunition inside the fort, plenty inside G.M.C.'s but outside, truck could not get in because too heavy and too big for pass on the fort's drawbridge, and each time we tried to join them for get some ammunition Germans shoot us. Lt. Laus got killed trying."[71]

Pvt. Lloyd L. Fiscus said that Co. C's HQ, stationed in the town of Briançon, ordered them to hold the enemy at the fort until they could evacuate and then to evacuate themselves. "During that time, Dale Blank, Ralph Biel, Howard [*Kelly*] Seibels, and I had been at an outside wall firing at the advancing Krauts," Fiscus added. "We had destroyed three machine gun squads, killed two more as they attempted to set up, and caused many more killed or wounded as they moved in to surround us. We all ran out of ammo. Things were quite confusing as everyone was trying to decide the best way to retreat from the fort. The Germans now had all our escape routes covered by machine gun fire. Two of our officers had been killed. I heard the men say that one of the officers had run to a lower outside wall, said 'follow me' and went over and was gone. A German machine gun later covered that escape route. Apparently a lot of our men left early because only about 40 of the Company remained to be captured."[72]

Howard Kelly Seibels confirmed the account by Fiscus, stating, "We turned our mortars around and fired on the [*enemy*] fort, which was firing on us also. Ralph Biel [*who was born in Germany*], Lloyd Fiscus, and Norman A. Wahosky, and I were the only ones who fired the mortars, some of the others busy but most of them yellow. The Jerries closed in. Biel, Fiscus, and I dashed out to give [*Glen*] Thompson a hand with his machine gun and to get in a few good shots at the Germans. The machine gun kept jamming. I fired a clip of tommy gun bullets and I think I got one. I went back for more ammo and, luckily, was thus able to find out that the order to retreat had been given.

I went back to get Biel, Fiscus, Thompson, and Wahosky and what arms I could carry. When we tried to get out of the fort we were just too late. Jerry had moved a machine gun to a place where he covered our exit on the only side from which it was possible to escape." Unknown to Seibels and his buddies, many of their comrades had escaped out the downhill side of the fort. "The fort was soon surrounded and the downhill route cut off. The Germans were killing every man who ran out." T/5 Glen C. Thompson, Co. C, received a Silver Star for his part in the battle for "… manning a .50 caliber machine gun protecting the right flank of his company against which a heavy enemy attack was directed. His accurate fire served to temporarily disrupt the attack and inflict stinging casualties …" on the enemy.[73]

By 11:00 a.m., the enemy were within the fort and the force commander ordered Co. C to withdraw from Ft. Dauphin, which some did via the town and north on the highway to Le Casset, while under heavy machine gun and small arms fire. Loy Marshall recalled, "We were given orders to get out of there in a hurry taking only our small arms and ammo and leave the heavy weapons, but try to break them so the Germans couldn't

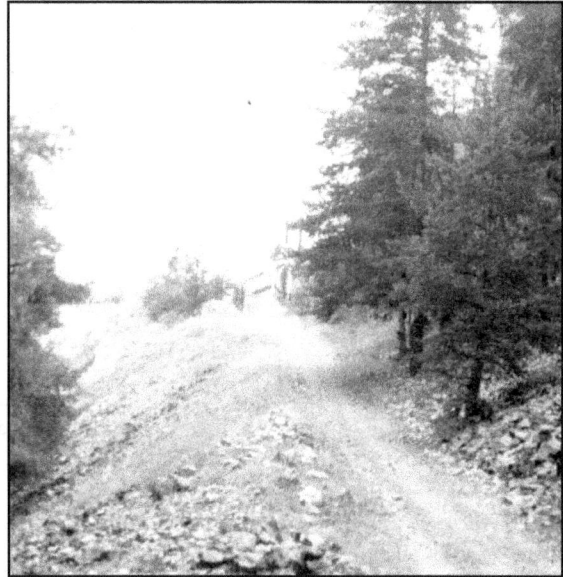

The narrow road from Ft. Dauphin showing area where 2nd Lt. Bernard Eisenberg and another man from the 171st Field Artillery Battalion were killed when trying to escape from the fort. *Paul Bailey*

get them and use them on us. I was finally able to damage and disable the .50 caliber machine gun that I was on that day by kicking it, filling the barrel with dirt, and hitting the firing mechanism with a rock." Paul Bailey said "The four men from the 171st Field Artillery Battalion decided to try to make a break for it. They drove out the gate and down the narrow road, right into the fire of German machine guns. 2nd Lt. Bernard Eisenberg and the other man I had talked to when I was on guard duty the night before were both killed. The other two jumped out of the jeep into a shallow ditch and tried to find something white to surrender with. Eventually they were both captured."[74]

Also at 11:00 a.m., M. Daerrebe of Briançon said that "… an American detachment coming from Asfeld bridge was crossing the Square de la Paix and falling back in utter confusion. They were showing their empty cartridge belts to Capt. Ambrosi, the district chief, who was trying to get them back to fight and also to various civilians, who asked them for their guns … it seems established that the Germans had not left Fort Randouillet," a fortification at an even higher elevation than Fort dês Tetes.[75]

At 11:20, the sergeant of the Engineers was ordered to blow the bridge between Briançon and La Vachette far enough north so as not to cut off the men from Ft. Dauphin. Additionally intense enemy artillery fire was laid on the Provisional Flank Protective Force CP at Briançon at 11:35, forcing Battery B, 171st Field Artillery to move north of town. Roger W. Knight of the field artillery battery recalled "The observation team [*in the fort*] reported enemy fire and the battery responded, but the targets were too elusive and close to the fort. Eventually we lost radio contact with the team and the battery began to receive mortar fire and our position was not tenable. A decision was made to hook up our guns and ford the river. The battery was fortunate and able to make a hasty retreat by fording the river. To the best of my recollection there were no casualties. Three of us decided to ford the river on foot and be picked up on the other side. As we did so the mortar fire increased and we hit the dirt. The truck drivers were anxious to get out of there. We soon found ourselves alone and everything became very quiet." Luckily the FFI found the three men and guided them to safety. At 11:50 Lt. Col. Bibo called Capt. Smith and told him to move Co. C two or three miles west of Briançon on the road to Grenoble. He asked if Smith needed assistance and said, "Why can't you move with vehicles? Shall we put FORT under fire to aid you to evacuate? I will attempt to get fire on your withdrawal. Will expect you to withdraw as soon as possible. Move to west of Briançon immediately. Will cover your withdrawal over FORT." Following this Bibo ordered Co. D, 2nd Chemical Battalion, to fire their mortars over Ft. Rondette to cover the withdrawal of Co. C of the 83rd. Afterward the battalion staff and force CP evacuated Briançon at noon in the face of mortar and small arms fire from enemy snipers who had infiltrated the town. The CP of the task force moved out of town at 12:05 and

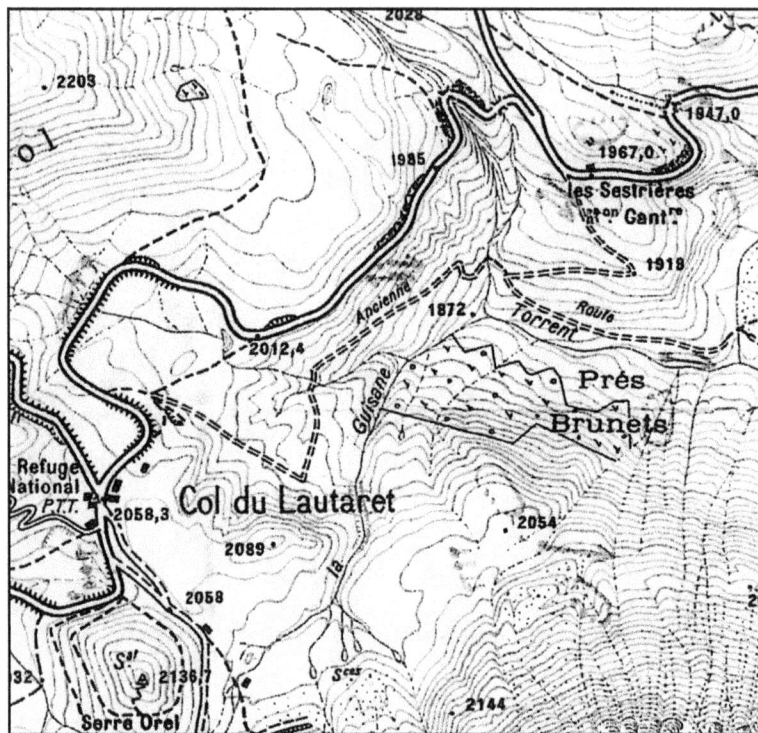

Map carried by Capt. Gordon Mindrum showing penciled in defensive mortar positions of the 83rd around Col du Lautaret following the fight at Briançon. *Gordon Mindrum*

by 12:45 a temporary defensive position had been set up on Highway 91 between Le Monettier and Col du Lautaret, where Lt. Robert Brimm, HQ Detachment of the 83rd, placed radios on both sides of the road high on the slope. Additionally, a 30 caliber machine gun was set up in the bend of the highway, with an OP to the rear of the roadblock.[76]

Lt. Col. Bibo finally decided to withdraw all troops from Briançon at 1:00 p.m. along Rt. N-91 northwest about 15 miles to Lautaret Pass. Thirty minutes later Maj. Efnor of the 83rd reported that Co. C had blown up their mortars and ammo at Ft. Dauphin since they were surrounded and some of the men had infiltrated out. Bibo rushed off a message to his superiors: "Request liaison plane notify Co. A, 83rd Chemical Battalion, in vicinity of St. Paul to move north to St. Clement to establish road block and blow bridge. Major Efnor en route to St. Clement to meet Co. A and supervise block. Defense position is being established at Le Casset on Grenoble-Briançon road. Gas supply critical. Have been forced out of Briançon. AT, infantry and artillery support needed." At 2:05 news was received that Capt. Smith and part of Co. C had escaped to the task force CP from Ft. Dauphin and at 2:30 they were placed in the assembly area to reorganize. Co. C was shuttled to Col du Lautaret, where a strong point was established.[77]

Back at Ft. Dauphin, Jean Pierre Combe remembered, "We had a jeep inside the fort, the driver was J. Haynes [*James R. (Jimmy) Haynes*]. Lt. Norman ("Rosy") Rosenthal got on [*the jeep*] with a white flag and told me to come with them. I did not understand what that meant. I came on. We got out of the fort, we rolled 30 or 50 yards after the drawbridge then Germans shoot us with a machine gun, but missed us [*then we moved*] back instantly inside the fort … he saved my life. My uniform was FFI and in that time Germans did not like us, and killed us each time they took some of us. After we got back inside the fort Lt. Rosenthal told me: We do not have a chance now, we must surrender. I replied to him, surrender if you want but me, I got way from here. If Germans take me I do not have a chance to survive, and Lt. N. Rosenthal say: You know a way to get out of here? Sure I do, it's my native country. OK, we follow you then, 35 or 45 men, I do not know exactly, follow me, and then 3 or 4 soldiers very wounded, which we must bear, not very easy in that situation, getting down the mountain, across the woods." On the narrow path down the mountains the men had to cross the d'Asfeld Bridge, nicknamed by the French people as the "devil bridge" as it was the choice for suicide. Jean Pierre Combe said, "The Germans shot us once more, they missed us and after the bridge, all along the road was a little wall which protected us all along the trip."[78]

Recalling his escape from his outpost outside the fort, Sgt. William Ford noted, "Some of the men wanted to surrender. I told them to stay with me. I did not want to be a prisoner of war … We continued to move up and over the mountain." At the top of the mountain the men ran into a man from the FFI who couldn't speak English and they could barely speak any French, but after some time they convinced the man to lead them over the rough terrain to their unit at Col du Lautaret, instead of Briançon. Had they not run into the FFI man they would have gone to Briançon and been captured.[79]

According to Lemuel R. Tillman, "Our escape route was cut off & no way to go but down the side of the Alps.

Jean Pierre Combe led us out down a very steep part of the Alps & so we escaped 30 or 40 of our men." Loy Marshall remembered that "We grabbed the ammo and had to make our way down the mountain using steep paths which zig-zagged through the rough terrain and rocks down the side of the mountain. Several times we had to crawl over stone walls or embankments that the Germans were strafing with machine gun fire. We were able to crawl over one or two at the time by watching the dirt fly on the wall and timing the length of time it took for them to shoot from one end of the wall to the other. Sometimes there was quite a drop on the other side of the wall, but we knew we had to get out of there or be captured or killed."[80]

Once down the mountain with his group, Jean Pierre Combe said, "we found the road to Briançon & I said to Lt. Rosenthal: I think we are safe now." Rosenthal asked him to return to Ft. Dauphin, but Cpl. Gilbert W. Basset from Essex County, New Jersey, objected, fearing Combe would be killed. "After that Lt. N. Rosenthal asked me the way to go to Grenoble, a big and nice town … 119 km. from Briançon. OK, follow me. And during 6 or 7 hours we walked to 30 km. There we were to the pass of Lautaret (2000 meters high). And there someone could have information by phone or radio, I do not know exactly, and told us to not move any more. Grenoble

Paul Bailey, AT Co., 180th Infantry. Captured at Ft. Dauphin *Paul Bailey*

was already occupied by German troops. We had chance that the Lautaret Pass there were … a big hotel. So we got in but always without ammunition. And nothing to eat. We stayed 4 days with empty belly … the hotel was empty. The proprietor had been killed, also his brother, owner himself of a hotel in Briançon, by Germans 12 or 15 days before, with 20 or 30 other resistants. Among them some good young friends of mine … During that time Grenoble was liberated and the 83rd came to get us with GMC and bring us to Bourgoin, a town near Grenoble where Co. C had been formed again. Officers of Co. C, 83rd Chemical were satisfied of my job and told me, if you will stay with us, you can."[81]

Vicente De Leon, a medic with Co. C, recalled that "all morning long and into the afternoon, the company medics [*at Ft. Dauphin*] were kept busy. I had some KIA's, also a number of men who needed my attention … in the afternoon we were told that we could no longer stop the Germans any more and that we needed to find a way out. Suddenly, a boy from the French Underground [*Jean Pierre Combe*] was trying to get our attention by scraping the wall. When we grew near, we found there was a staircase. My two friends scaled the top of the wall, jumping to the other side. I tried to tell them that they should not go because they needed medical attention. As they went over, I followed by throwing myself over the wall. I heard gunfire and felt hot steel burning my legs. My legs were exposed when I went over the wall. The fall seemed to be miles long when I finally hit the ground. I called for the men who needed my help." De Leon continued, "I started toward the location where I told them we would meet (the cross-bridge to the city). As I got there, one of the fellows noticed that I was wounded [*in the right leg*]. I told them that I was aware of this but did not have time to take care of myself. He, in turn, took care of me. By this time the second person showed up and he was in real need of hospital care. I knew where the hospital was and we started in that direction. I told them that this man needed immediate attention and the two of us ran into the street before the medics could stop us. We were running down the street when we were suddenly stopped by a jeep. There were two German prisoners in the jeep and the driver said that he needed us to help him. Shortly afterward, we came upon a medical field hospital where the two of us were placed for care."[82]

Radio operator Mario Ricci, awaiting the Piper Cub ten miles away, apparently got word that his company had been overrun and he met up with six other men who had escaped. They remained behind enemy lines for eleven days until they met up with a company of Free French soldiers. Ricci, who was also an accomplished artist who often drew portraits and scenes on V-Mail for the men, lost all but a few of his sketches in the disaster at Briançon. Only three scenes that he later drew in the Vosges Mountains survived the war. Raymond W. Hoover lost his wedding ring during the hasty retreat but found it in his old foxhole when the company later returned to the site.[83]

Yet at the fort, Paul Bailey of the AT squad recalled "I thought we'd be shelled, and there was a chimney that I was afraid the Germans would drop a mortar down. So I went looking for a safer place, and found a well-protected room like an arsenal. I came out when someone hollered that we'd been ordered to leave. It seemed like late in the afternoon, the order to withdraw came by radio from a colonel in Briançon. We went under two walls to a lower elevation where some steps led to the top of a low spot in the outside wall. Many of the troops had already escaped by that route, but the German machine guns had zeroed in on the spot by the time we arrived. We would have been cut in two had we gone over. At that point, about 30 of us were trapped between the lower walls. Almost everyone dismantled their weapons, because we knew that capture was imminent. However, I kept my 45 pistol intact and loaded, thinking instinctively that as long as there was a chance, I'd keep hold of it. All the others thought we'd be shot, so they told me later. We were waiting in a tunnel, and I was scared the enemy would throw in a grenade. After what seemed like an hour, the 10-12 Germans came to the top of the lower wall. At least two of them had MG-34 machine guns. As we marched out with our hands up, their lieutenant spotted my pistol, pointed at me and said something about 'pistole'. I dropped my hands and unbuckled that pistol belt in record time. It was a miracle I wasn't shot." Dale C. Blank added to the story, "I started looking for the rest of the Company. I went down thru a tunnel in the wall and there were the guys that would become prisoners of the Germans. We were all gathered in this open space surrounded by high walls. It had already been decided that we would give up because we were out of ammo and had no means of getting more because it was all in the trucks which were under German machine gun fire. The trucks should have been destroyed along with the contents but nobody thought of it. Somebody found a T shirt and put it on a stick and waved it over a wall. It wasn't long before we were herded into a line with our backs to a wall, facing two machine guns. That was scary enough, but when one of their officers gave a command and all the German soldiers moved away from us, we really got worried. But we hadn't been searched yet, so the officer started a soldier at each end and thoroughly searched each American. By noon all firing had stopped, both from the Germans and our fort. Some of us expected the rest of our company to attempt a rescue but this was not to be. Our commander, Capt. Robert Smith, his staff and the rest of the company decided that we were not worth saving, so they made no effort." Kelly Seibels added, "There were about 30 of us trapped in a covered stairway leading to the wall which was now inaccessible due to Jerry's fire. Lt. [*James L.*] Doyle, I think, was the first to mention surrender. Biel and I argued a little with him but maybe he was right. I took off my white undershirt and tied it to my carbine and upon his orders waved it out the door."[84]

Pvt. Lloyd L. Fiscus, among the group with Blank, supported Blank's description of their capture although he added, "We were very fortunate that this German officer was a good soldier. Other Germans wanted to kill us all, and others wanted to kill those of us who spoke German or French, as traitors or spies. Finally, they set up two machine guns on the wall behind us. They were manned by young soldiers who appeared to be fifteen or sixteen years old. They were shaking so bad, the guns were moving." With the exception of Pvt. Paul A. Bailey, 180th Infantry, all the men thought they were going to be executed but instead they were searched and then marched down the mountain to the bridge they had destroyed. The German engineer, a major, was furious and wanted to kill them but opted to make them help carry timber to assist in repairing the bridge. Afterwards they were all marched off as prisoners of war, most being sent to Stalag 7A at Moosburg, Bavaria, or to various work camps elsewhere. Apparently, all survived their time as POWs and were liberated near the end of the war.[85]

Pvt. Robert F. Thorpe would be taken prisoner on the 30th, having been found in the wood and coal shed at Briançon. He was taken to Italy, where he spent nine days marching with a group of 30 German soldiers, and a lieutenant who even made him dig his own grave for refusing to divulge information on the southern France landing. Following additional rough treatment by Gestapo agents, he eventually was moved to the prison at Torino, joining the other prisoners. Also among the captured, as noted, was Pvt. Paul A. Bailey of Pennsylvania, a member of the 180th Infantry AT outfit, whose squad had been left at Ft. Dauphin to support the 83rd with their 57mm anti-tank gun.[86]

Lt. Col. Bibo ordered a general withdrawal to Col du Lautaret at 4 p.m. while thirty minutes afterward an officer reported the FFI held Briançon and the road was clear to Col du Lautaret. According to M. Daerrebe of Briançon, "Until 4 p.m. the artillery fires were increasing, and the infantry fires got near to the town and burst up to the streets. The infiltration had been done by the batteries of La Lenie Etned le Fonteil and from there, by le Champ de Mars on one side, and Fort dês Tetes and Pont de Cenieres on the other … There were about 12 of the town's people killed by the Germans coming into town. There were about 10 people wounded. The losses of the FFI amounted to about 10 men."[87]

In an attempt to defend his previous actions, at 8:00 p.m. Capt. Smith reported to the task force CP and said that, upon occupation of Ft. Dauphin, Co. C of the 83rd had made certain the surrounding forts were all occupied by the French, who apparently were overrun by the Germans who then attacked Ft. Dauphin. At the hospital in Briançon, Lt. John L. Boyd was informed by his doctor of the German victory and was told to tell the German commanding officer that he had come to the hospital from the fort suffering from shell shock. Boyd and three other American soldiers would have to keep up this ruse until the town was liberated nearly a week later.[88]

Losses in the fight in and around Ft. Dauphin and Briançon were reported at a staff meeting on the evening of the 29th. The 83rd Chemical Battalion reported one enlisted man killed, one enlisted man wounded, and three officers and 48 enlisted men missing in action. The battalion also reported the loss of 12 mortars, one 2½-ton truck, nine ¼-ton trucks, three 1-ton trailers, 10 ¼-ton trailers, and two ¾-ton weapons carriers. The 2nd Chemical Battalion listed one enlisted man killed, six

L-R: Frank Thomson, Leonard R. Thomas, and Alfred E. Green, Jr., all of Co. D, at Nice on the French Riviera on September 20, 1944. *Alfred Green*

enlisted men wounded, and three enlisted men missing in action. Losses to the 3rd Chemical Battalion included one officer and seven enlisted men missing, and eight mortars lost. Battery B, 171st Field Artillery, reported one officer and three enlisted men missing, although the 83rd Chemical claimed the officer was killed [*this was probably 2nd Lt. Bernard Eisenberg from California*]. The 48th Engineer Platoon claimed they had 14 enlisted men missing, as well as one truck and mess equipment including rifles for the remaining squad. The 117th Reconnaissance had yet to file a report while the AT squad from the 180th Infantry listed 10 men lost in addition to one six-pound AT gun.[89]

The above losses were all preliminary reports and were vastly adjusted in the ensuing days when it was determined more accurately that the casualties of Co. C, 83rd Chemical Battalion, in the fight at Ft. Dauphin included 1st Lt. Andre N. Laus and Cpl. Leonard E. Hall, both killed; the wounded consisted of Pfc. Edward L. Jackson, Cpl. Floyd J. Grissom, Pvt. Vicente De Leon, Pfc. John J. Hajdinyak, and Pvt. Audie L. Pierce. Jackson had been placed in a French hospital and it was suspected he had been captured, as was the thought concerning Lt. John L. Boyd, who had been sent to a hospital the previous day. At least 50 men were reported missing in action although a number of those would return in the ensuing days.[90]

Eventually it was determined that at least 35 men from Ft. Dauphin, including one member of the 180th Infantry AT squad, were captured and made prisoners of war. All equipment was lost except for one jeep, five heavy trucks, and any personal equipment the men were able to carry out on their backs. Also lost were some 150 rounds of ammo, one truck, seven mortars, and some signal equipment which was destroyed to prevent capture. Reportedly, a number of Germans were killed or wounded, and three were captured. Late in the evening of August 29th, some 68 men of Co C of the 83rd were reported present at Col du Lautaret and the 1st Platoon, Co. A, 83rd Chemical Battalion, had established a road block at St. Crespin.[91]

Sam Bundy, Co. A, described the situation as he wrote, "French in Guillestre, 14 miles from our CP are trying to stop them from going any further, but they are few and need reinforcements. Tonight the AT men above us alarmed and alerted the company when they reported that Germans had surrounded their gun. They evacuated their position and some of them went in as far as Guillestre. We patrolled the surrounding area and found nothing. Fortunately no one fired a shot; if someone had, undoubtedly some of their own men would have been killed because the patrol is very poorly organized. Tonight our motor pool located above our CP a mile or two on the top the hill. Had a little excitement. Someone captured a French policeman who they believed to be a German. He escaped, minus his cap and dispatch case, to Guillestre and reported that we were surrounded by Germans. All night long, telephone calls came thru calling about the situation." According to James Helsel, Co. A, "The anti-tank gun crew which was attached to us alerted us and told us we were being surrounded. We all got out with our guns, but after a careful study by [*Frank C.*] Besser with his glasses we found it to be the trees moving between the moon, and clouds passing between also gave it the motion effect. But we did discover how helpless we would have been, for no one had any grenades, there was no machine guns, and I believe I had more ammo for my carbine than anyone in the platoon, and that was only thirty rounds. So we got some equipment sent up …"[92]

Pvt. Dale C. Blank, among the prisoners taken at the fort, bitterly concluded that Ft. Dauphin "… was the most indefensible fort in the entire area. I don't know who made that decision, but it was certainly the wrong one. The entrance to this more than 300 year old fort was too small to get a truck through, so all of our supplies of ammo, food and everything else had to be left in the trucks outside the fort on the narrow and only road." In another statement Blank added, "This whole fiasco was caused by the leader of 'C' Company, Officers from Headquarters Co. choosing the wrong fort and location to set up a defense of our part of the line. These officers should have been court-martialed for their part in getting 35 soldiers captured and letting the Germans take three forts from us." In a 2005 telephone interview, Gordon Mindrum supported Blank's assertion, stating, "Smith did not reconnoiter Briançon." Quite to the contrary, though, evidence suggests Smith did reconnoiter the position, and he was awarded the Silver Star for his part in the action. Paul Bailey of the 180th AT squad, also taken prisoner, vented as well, writing "I now believe that our capture was the fault of our commanders - whoever they were. I have no idea who ordered such a small handful of men into this system of huge forts. [*The*] Commanding officer was Capt. Smith and it may have been his first time in combat, or so I have heard from his troops. I realize now that the fort itself should have been better explored - before from my 1980 visit to it, I know that I only saw part of it, and there were many strategic positions ideally located for defense. Had we had machine guns and adequate infantry, it could have been defended much better, but even given our strength as it was, we could have been better organized. Looking back, I wonder why the officers didn't try to organize a defense."[93]

A Capt. Schneider, commanding the victorious German troops in Briançon, had a Dr. Erhart post notices in town informing the residents not to leave and for all men between the ages of 7 and 45, excepting doctors, to meet at the Arsenal the following day at 9 a.m. [*August 30th*]. From this time until the liberation of Briançon on September 6th, the people of Briançon were terrorized, threatened, looted, or even killed by a succession of German officers and troops, beginning with Capt. Schneider, followed by an SS troop and an Afrika Corps command.[94]

As Lt. Col. Hutchinson was no longer with the battalion, he was unaware of the Briançon fiasco when he wrote Cunin at this time praising the battalion. "The 83rd has now made five assault landings and wears three battle stars and has more than 250 days of combat. We have fired more than 100,000 rounds of ammunition, taken 75% total casualties, and killed many thousand Germans. --- Trey is a Capt. thanks to the new T/O. Mindrum is Exec. Mac will be S-3 as soon as he can leave A Co. The only old officers are Mindrum, McEvoy, Trey, Edwards, Hauser, McKinnon who has B Co., Stone, Laus, Forrester. Crenshaw and I are still assigned but we are on TD here--- We have an old Ranger, Lt. John Davis formerly of the 4th who was sold down the river to the SSF [*Special Service Force*] when all the originals went home. He applied for transfer and now has a platoon in A Co. --- D Co. went into France in gliders. I have heard that the entire battalion is doing very well and has not been hurt again yet. At least not badly--- They are attached to the Thunderbirds [*45th Infantry Division*] and getting along beautifully. This attachment has lasted with only brief interruptions since Col. Bill [*Darby*] went home. I don't know that the idea ever came to you but I wouldn't advise doing anything to disturb their present partnership."[95]

During the various activities of the day at Briançon Co. D's Red Platoon moved about three miles from Levens and the 2nd Platoon remained in support of the 550th Infantry. Back at Naples harbor the 15 men moving battalion vehicles spent the day, with the assistance of Italians, getting their vehicles loaded onto Liberty ship #251. Afterwards, they returned to the Iowa Staging Area and spent the night.[96]

At Col du Lautaret on August 30th Co. C was in reserve near the force CP and short on equipment. They were "… in extreme need of firearms, field jackets, helmets, and much other equipment before it could be used as infantry" following the Briançon debacle. Additionally, none of the men listed as missing in action at Briançon had yet returned. About mid-day Capt. Smith of Co. C was appointed assistant to Maj. Ramsey, 3rd Chemical Battalion, to defend the position. Co. C was split into two platoons and "… [*remained*] badly in need of various items of equipment. Defense setup was explained to Capt. Smith and he was asked to check the positions." The battalion CP operated as part of the force CP and mortar companies and Battery B, 171st Field Artillery, registered on the road to Briançon and the tunnel and bridge, which were prepared for demolition.[97]

At Briançon, M. Daerrebe reported the German occupation troops used the captured American equipment, which briefly led townsfolk to believe they were U.S. soldiers, costing the life of one man, M. Guerre from Chaibonhages. He also said some 250 male civilians had been rounded up "... to walk to the Arsenal ... The ground was littered with fragments of all sorts. Metal sheets from the roofs, shelters, lumps of plaster torn off by the explosions, houses smashed open by the shells, telephone wires entangled, pieces of shrapnel, bullets, etc., all the horror of war was to be seen."[98]

Co. A, at St. Paul, moved their roadblock to a position overlooking the town and the road to Condamine, while

Epinal, France. *Hopkins Collection*

Co. B, having operated the Grenoble railhead, prepared to move to Bourgoin. Co. D was yet in a position southeast of Levens when one officer and ten enlisted men from Rear "A" arrived. The remainder of Co. D also finally made it to southern France as Rear "A" landed at St. Raphael and Rear "B" disembarked *LST 12* at St. Tropez and marched three miles to a bivouac. With the weather beautiful at Naples harbor the 15 men of the rear echelon, which included Steve Vukson, awaited orders to sail, their vehicles already loaded, but such orders failed to arrive.[99]

On the last day of August, in the cold and rain, Co. C reported from Col du Lautaret as an infantry reserve at the CP of the North Provisional Flank Protective Force. No new equipment had arrived and the company rested as seven men previously reported missing in action at Briançon returned. The seven were Maurice D. Lear, Joseph A. Nemeth, John J. Magdziaz, Thomas E. Yates, Julius D. Vogel, Walter H. Bickel, and a McLeary. Maj. David Meyerson, 2nd Chemical Battalion, ordered Lt. Norman Rosenthal, Co. C of the 83rd, to "... reconnoiter the Pass to obtain information as to whether or not the enemy can use it to flank our position. Other passes to be reconnoitered were suggested by Capt. Smith." Around noon Smith took a small party to check a foot trail over the mountain on the right flank. He proceeded along the trail to Col de Arsine and returned around 6 p.m. to report it was a good observation area and it would be possible for the enemy to bring up pack howitzers with the infantry.[100]

Co. A, having been joined by Maj. Efnor and Capt. John P. McEvoy, continued their mobile roadblocks along with other units in order to contain the enemy south of Briançon. Lt. Robert F. Jackson, Co. A, who had led a patrol the previous day, again set out with five enlisted men and five Maquis in an effort to make contact with an Allied patrol from the south near Condamine. The route chosen by the Maquis proved impassable although the Maquis advanced a bit farther and were able to view Condamine in flames, apparently absent of the enemy. Meanwhile, Co. B completed the movement to Bourgoin, a town a bit smaller than Grenoble, where they also worked the rail station and whose civilians were, according to Andrew Leech, Co. B, equally as friendly as those at Grenoble. Co. D held their positions southeast of Levens and Bouyon. The rear echelon of Co. D remained in bivouac near the ports of southern France.[101]

During the month of August, the 83rd Chemical Battalion had fired 1,177 HE and 185 WP, for a total of 1,962 rounds. Casualties incurred included 33 men wounded to some degree, one killed, and 37 missing in action. This amounted to five officers and 66 enlisted men, making a total of 71 casualties for the month. The list of killed would grow in the coming days as more details arrived on the Briançon participants.[102]

The situation on September 1st found the 83rd Chemical Battalion, less companies A and C, returned to control of the 45th Infantry Division. Co. A, in position near St. Paul, was relieved by the 4 DIM [*French Forces*] and moved about 180 miles to a point near Grenoble, only to receive orders to return to a point near St. Paul. Co. B remained at Bourgoin running a railhead under the 45th Division; while Co. C and HQ Detachment were at Col du Lautaret, where Co. C served as an infantry reserve and HQ Detachment operated as a portion of Force HQ. Around 2:00 in the afternoon, Co. C reported three civilians spotted on the road to Col du Lautaret. Co. D, yet operating with the Airborne Task Force, had their CP at Levens, their Red Platoon about two miles east of town, and the White Platoon supporting the 550th Infantry A/B Battalion. Two squads of the White Platoon were called out to support the FFI who were attempting to retake a fort the Germans had taken from them on August 31st.[103]

Co. A moved to Sisteron, an unfriendly town, on a rainy September 2nd in order to operate the "midnight shift" at a railroad under VI Corps control and remained there until the 5th. Co. B continued to operate the railhead at Bourgoin; Co. C and HQ Detachment were relieved from the North Provisional Flank Protective Force by the FFI, returned to control of the 45th Division, and moved from Col du Lautaret to Bourgoin. At Bourgoin Co. C re-equipped from losses sustained at Briançon and assisted Co. B in operating the railhead. The situation of Co. D in the Levens vicinity remained the same as the White Platoon continued to assist the FFI in their effort of the previous day.[104]

September 2nd also saw the departure of the company rear echelons from Italy to rejoin the battalion. Daniel Shields recalled boarding the ship around 8:05 a.m. and sailing until about 6:10 in the evening. During the trip Shields was able to observe the eating habits of some French colonials who were aboard. On the 3rd, a large storm developed, which provoked Shields to write, "Big wave hit ship & I thought I was going for another swim. Wet to the knees. Everyone sick." Also in the rear echelon, recovered from his cyst operation, was "Doc" Hulcher, who mentioned the rough sea made nearly everyone seasick, providing him with plenty of work as the only doctor on board.[105]

Companies A, B, and C continued to operate the railheads at Sisteron and Bourgoin for the next few days, reorganize and re-equip, while HQ Detachment performed administrative duties. The CP of Co. D remained at Levens on the 4th while the Red Platoon, supporting the 2nd Battalion, 517th Parachute Infantry, moved near Lucerarul, where they were fired upon but did not return fire. The Blue Platoon, which had reported for duty on the 3rd, was attached to the 1st Battalion, 517th Parachute Infantry, and began movement to St. Jean.[106]

September 4th was also the first opportunity Capt. Smith, Co. C, had to write home detailing the recent disaster at Briançon. "My company distinguished itself and I received a verbal commendation only today from the Corps Chemical Officer in behalf of the Corps for the Company … I have lost everything I own except for the clothes I have on and the khakis and heavy overcoat which I left in Italy … however … we killed many, many Germans both by hand and with our mortars … it's a page in my life I would really like to forget. The men in this Company were wonderful, for the most part, and I am going to try to get the Congressional Medal of Honor for my Company Executive [*Lt. Andre N. Laus*], if it can be done. He was a real officer and a brave man, and many of the men were the same calibre. One Sgt. killed four Germans by himself and the other officers were tops, as well as non-coms."[107]

The railheads at Sisteron and Bourgoin continued to be operated by companies A, B, and C on September 5th, and Detachment No. 3 of the 11th Chemical Maintenance Company, which had been attached to the battalion before the departure from Italy to repair and maintain mortars, rejoined the battalion at Bourgoin. They bivouacked in a schoolhouse with HQ of the 83rd. Co. D's CP moved to a position about four miles south of L'Escarene while the Red Platoon engaged the enemy west of Lucerne and the Blue Platoon moved about a mile north of L'Escarene.[108]

Also on the 5th the company rear echelons from Naples landed via LCVP's on the 3rd Division beach near St. Maxime. Among this group was Steve Vukson who wrote, "It was real clear and at 11:00 AM land could be seen. It was about 2:30 PM when we docked and waited till the LCT came to take us into shore. My parts truck, wrecker, and [a] couple [of] others were the first to get ashore. They were unloading all evening … Most of the other personnel landed at a different port and rode another Liberty Ship."[109]

Co. A moved from Sisteron to Bourgoin in the rain on the afternoon of the 6th, part by train and the remainder by truck, where they were joined by the company rear echelons, which had landed at St. Maxime on the 4th. Daniel Shields, with the rear echelon, wrote, "Moved 258 miles to Bourgoin. Scenery through Alps was beautiful, especially sunset. Lyons was [a] very nice town." Also describing the journey which passed through Arne and Grenoble was "Doc" Hulcher, who wrote, "A grand trip, most beautiful country & the people lined the highways & streets to wave, throw kisses, give fruits etc. to us. Arrived at Bourgoin about 9 PM and here met up with our outfit … set up in school house…" Co. A returned to battalion and 45th Division control while companies B and C still operated the railhead for the 45th Division Quartermaster. The CP of Co. D moved two miles east of Contes and the White Platoon to a position named Camp Des Tourches, located in the Alps about 30 kilometers southwest of Jansiens. The Blue Platoon, covering the evacuation of wounded, fell under heavy enemy fire but suffered no casualties. Although the 83rd had moved on, friendly forces had retaken Briançon; during the liberating combat a nun was struck by a stray bullet and killed, French forces lost four Moroccan skirmishers and one FFI in an attack on the Chateau, and two skirmishers were killed during the capture of Fort dês Tetes.[110]

For the next two days companies A, B, C and HQ Detachment remained at Bourgoin performing railroad assignments, resting, re-equipping, and re-organizing. All companies and HQ were brought to full strength on the 7th as the rear echelon of the battalion from Italy had arrived at Bourgoin, where the FFI was rounding up spies. During the day the White Platoon of Co. D got into a skirmish in which their machine guns, BAR and small arms were utilized, which resulted in two Germans killed and one, severely wounded, who died two hours later. Two prisoners were also taken in the fight. Detachment No. 3, 11th Chemical Maintenance, traveled via motor transport to a field about two miles south of Lyons. The battalion CP moved to L'Escarene on the 8th as the Red Platoon moved south of Pierra Cava, while the White and Blue platoons heavily engaged the enemy without taking any casualties. Detachment No. 3, 11th Chemical Maintenance, again utilized motor transport to a point about one-half mile south of the area of Aissey and Quigney.[111]

Companies B and C retained their status at Bourgoin on a very cold 9th while the battalion CP was moved from Bourgoin about 167 miles to a field and wooded area near Aissey, about 5 to 10 miles from the actual front lines. On the way they passed through some beautiful rural country and near the home of Louis Pasteur. The location was about 15 miles from Switzerland and 50 from Germany. Co. A was attached to the 180th Infantry and moved some 155 to 165 miles to a point near Etalaus, where they were ordered to bivouac north of a river and be prepared to cross the following day at Besançon to support the infantry north of Baume. Co. D's CP remained at L'Escarene, with the Red Platoon engaged near Pierra Cava, the White Platoon knocking out two enemy machine guns, and the Blue Platoon firing on enemy infantry. Lee Steedle, Co. D, recalled "Had it easy chasing a couple German companies up that mountainous cul-de-sac. They knew that were trapped, without any chance of ration and ammo resupply, it was only a matter of time before they'd have to surrender, so they would just lob occasional shells to slow us down as they retreated. That's why, with overnight passes to Nice, it was truly our champaign war."[112]

On September 10th, companies B and C continued to work the railhead at Bourgoin. Co. A, which moved about 23 miles to the vicinity of Vergranne, was released from the 180th Infantry and held in division reserve. The three platoons of Co. D remained in action, and some prisoners taken by the White Platoon admitted that the mortar fire of the Co. D platoon had killed five of their fellow soldiers and emphatically stated the 4.2" mortar fire was deadly.[113]

Capt. Robert E. Edwards, Jr., in a letter home on September 11th describing the countryside and the battalion, stated, "Have decided that the most of France that I have seen looks like one of our well groomed parks. Must remark that the women are very neat in their attire. There are miles of blue grass meadow which looks like a well groomed front yard. Saw one farmer cutting it with a hand scythe. Did as good a job that I might have done with a lawn mower. They use the cuttings for hay. They have very good cheese around here. Also secured some milk - first fresh milk that I have had since I left the states … Mindy became a major this morning … Trey was made a Capt some time ago … The FFI are really doing a good job over here. Rather tough on the Jerries."[114]

Throughout the 11th and a moderately cold 12th, Co. A moved near Uzelle as a division reserve, with many of the men staying in a schoolhouse. HQ Detachment, along with Detachment No. 3, 11th Chemical Maintenance, moved from Aissey to Mesandans [*"Doc" Hulcher called it Romani*]. The Red Platoon of Co. D fired on enemy troops at Moulinet as the other two platoons also continued activity. The situation on a rainy 13th found Co. A in division reserve at Uzelle; Co. B moving via motor convoy from Bourgoin to Baumes Les Dames; Co. C held in division reserve at Bourgoin; and HQ Detachment yet at Mesandans. "Doc" Hulcher said a German soldier, originally from Toulon, was taken prisoner right in the HQ bivouac area, a possible reference to two prisoners brought in to the battalion CO and turned over to the 179th Infantry MPs mentioned in the battalion journal. Co. D held relatively the same positions although the White Platoon gave protective fire cover to the zones on "Petite Colval," "Les Pas Colval," and on the road south of the two areas.[115]

On a clear September 14th, Co. A, still in division reserve, was ordered by the 45th Division to search the woods east of Condenans and the north slopes of Hill 460 for the enemy, but a patrol of 20 men under the newly-appointed Capt. Joseph Garsson failed to detect any opposition. Co. B moved via motor convoy to Abbenans; Co. C was held in division reserve at Bourgoin; and HQ Detachment moved from Mesandans to Cubrial. The journal of Detachment No. 3, 11th Chemical Maintenance, states they traveled from Mesandans to Cuse, which "Doc" Hulcher called Cous. With their CP yet at L'Escarene, Co. D's three platoons of the 83rd continued to engage the enemy with the Red

Platoon firing in the vicinity of Moulinet.[116]

Co. A closed their bivouac at Uzelle on a rainy 15th, as did Co. C at Bourgoin, and both companies opened new bivouacs about two miles north of Rougemont. Chaplain George E. Gaiser, with representatives of the VI Corps Graves Registration, left for Briançon, where they found the bodies of Lt. Andre Laus and Cpl. Leonard E. Hall. Five bodies were disinterred and taken to the army cemetery at Montelimar. Co. D, although shelled nearly every day, had yet to suffer a casualty during the month.[117]

Co. B, after capturing four German prisoners, joined companies A and C near Rougemont on a rainy 16th. With continuing rain, companies A, B, C, and HQ Detachment moved to Mersuay on the 17th. "Doc" Hulcher referred to this location as "near Vesoul," where he stayed in a house and his medics took over a barn. Co. B captured seven prisoners [*"Doc" Hulcher said 10 prisoners*] before departing Rougement. The three platoons of Co. D and the CP maintained positions, although the Red Platoon had to move their guns about to cover the areas at Pierra Cava and northeast of L'Escarene. Detachment No. 3, 11th Chemical Maintenance, yet attached to the 83rd for mortar repair, moved from Cuse to Bourguignon on the 18th, where the town mayor insisted they stay in a chateau. Chaplain Gaiser returned from Briançon and gave the official casualty list for the battalion in the August 29th fight as three killed, 32 missing, and two wounded, for a total of 37. For the next three days, companies A, B, and C were held in reserve at Mersuay. Co. D continually engaged the enemy with little change and no casualties until the 22nd, although Alfred E. Green, Jr., claimed the men were brought back outside of Nice, France, on the 20th to regroup.[118]

While at Mersuay, Lawrence G. Ertzberger, Co. B, said they slept in a barn. "A blonde girl lived there and she baked us a pie every day. Three of us went down to the next town two miles away. No other soldiers in the town. An old lady came by, she was glad to see us so she came, caught me, hugged and kissed me on the cheek. We met a young girl that could speak English. She told us that this lady had been telling everyone that she was going to hug and kiss the first American soldier she saw, and I was the one."[119]

A strong letter-writing campaign was initiated on a rainy September 19th by Maj. Sam Efnor, Jr., to have the 83rd, as well as all 4.2" chemical mortar battalions, officially listed as Combat Ground Forces and privilege to all honors bestowed upon the infantry including the Expert Infantry and Combat Infantry badges. Efnor provided concrete evidence to support his claim, since the 83rd had often acted in the capacity of infantry, but despite a positive review by many high officials, the War Department was not receptive to the idea and would drag it along for months.[120]

Looking back on recent days, Capt. Robert Smith observed that Co. C "had to stop for a while to train new replacements and to re-equip, since we lost most of our equipment, but have it all back now and are ready to go … [*I*] have a few more grey hairs and a few more hurts in my heart when I think of some of the men and officers who are not here now. But we saved most of them and still have the same old 'C' Company in spirit." Capt Smith also felt compelled to relate the cohesiveness of his command as he added, "There are about 50 Krauts hiding in a woods about a mile from here, so yesterday we took a patrol out to try and locate them. After we got things pretty well lined up I sent one lieutenant back to get a couple of squads. When I got back to the woods where I was to meet them, the whole damn company was there. They had all volunteered, so you can see what 'C' Company is like. We never did find the Krauts, however, and they may have drifted on but will probably be picked up in a day or two. We did find an ammunition dump and destroyed that. So we didn't take a total loss on our day's work."[121]

As earlier noted Pfc. Alfred E. Green, Jr., Co. D, said a number of men were sent to Nice on a sunny 20th to regroup, while Sgt. Seymour A. Holstein, Co. A, of Newark, New Jersey, earned a Bronze Star for gallantry near Camp Des Tourches. Companies A, B, and C were alerted for movement on the 21st and put into motion the following day with the three companies moving from Mersuay to Xertigny, about 30 miles beyond Bains les Bains, where they bivouacked in a park. Some of Co. A recalled they bivouacked near a lake. Capt. Smith, Co. C, said his men were bivouacked in a wooded area where he complained about the rain and mud and his tent leaked. S-1 Robert E. Edwards, Jr., was more optimistic, writing, "Sitting in my tent at present listening to Jerry music (Sgt's radio). They have good music." The mortar repair men of Detachment No. 3, 11th Chemical Maintenance, left Bourguignon and traveled by motor vehicle to Dounoux, where they stayed in a hall adjoining a church.[122]

Following a brief round of fire, the Red Platoon of Co. D was relieved by the 2nd Chemical Battalion. Orders had been issued as early as September 14th that, upon arrival of the 2nd Chemical Battalion, Co. D of the 83rd would move to the VI Corps area near Sorans Les Breure, be relieved of attachment to the 1st Airborne Task Force, and revert to battalion control. During the period from September 1st to September 22nd, Co. D had fired 4,648 HE and 320 WP for a total of 4,968 rounds. Also noteworthy is that during this time one platoon of Co. D was attached to the 550th Parachute Infantry at Barcellonette, where they provided constant support fire. During the day the entire company moved from L'Escarene to a new bivouac at Drap.[123]

Although the entire stay at Xertigny was marred by rain, the men found it a nice town. According to "Doc" Hulcher, the town had "a brewery … nearby where the boys bought beer, had movies, and drunk [sic] wines. The owner did not want us to move in but we did and later she was very pleasant." The battalion was held in division reserve on the 23rd and Lt. James J. O'Connor of Co. A left for Grenoble to accompany five new officers for the battalion from the Replacement Depot. This is also the day Sam Irving Kweskin was transferred in from the 3rd Chemical Battalion, joining Co. D but eventually moving to HQ Co. as battalion combat artist.[124]

An alert for movement was issued to the three companies in the Xertigny vicinity on the 24th, followed the next day by Co. A moving from Vieux St. Laurent to Fort du Bambois, part of the Maginot Line south of Epinal, while Co. C closed at Epinal, "Gateway to the Vosges." Detachment No. 3, 11th Chemical Maintenance, also was sent to Epinal, where they bivouacked in a quarry at Rue de Faubourg. Lt. O'Connor of the 83rd returned from Grenoble with the five new officers for the battalion. Reflecting on this period, Andrew Leech, Co. B, wrote, "The old Moselle Line was a place of bitter fighting … The Germans blew up all the bridges and our infantry crossed on ropes, waded, or used amphibious ducks … We first moved into an old fort on the side of the [Moselle] river. The structure, built many years ago, was an underground fortress of stone covered with several feet of dirt." Co. D left their bivouac at Drap by motor convoy to rejoin the battalion, spending the night at Serres.[125]

On the 26th, a meeting was held of all COs in which they were notified that a platoon (reinforced) from each company would support a regiment. As a result, the 1st Platoon of Co. A was attached to the 157th Infantry, moved to a defensive position near the front, and fired 50 rounds, the first rounds fired by Co. A in the French Campaign according to Sam Bundy. The 1st Platoon of Co. B was attached to the 3rd Battalion, 180th Infantry, and the 2nd Platoon of Co. C was attached to the 179th Infantry, while the remainder of the company continued training. Despite such organizational activity the enemy was still a constant threat and Lt. Ewart O'Neill was lightly wounded in the thigh by shell fire. Co. D departed their bivouac at Serres but had to stop at Amberieo as the gas dump located there was nearly empty. With gasoline in such short supply the company had to send a truck out to locate some fuel.[126]

Companies A, B, and C were all back in action on the 27th. Members of Co. A recalled they left the Maginot Line fort, crossed the Moselle River, and advanced about seven miles to Longchamp. Lt. Charles W. O'Day and Pvt. George T. Campbell, both of Co. B, were lightly wounded by shell fire. William Ford, Co. C, said the battalion provided a barrage and smokescreen for troops crossing the Moselle, which was swollen from rain and sleet. He added, "The ground was soft and muddy, which didn't help our efforts. Another obstacle in crossing the Moselle was a twenty foot vertical concrete wall built by the Germans along the river." The Medical Detachment also arrived at Epinal, where they, along with HQ Co., bivouacked in a textile school or factory.[127]

Epinal was lauded by "Doc" Hulcher. "Here we had a wonderful set-up. Epinal is right on the Moselle River and is very picturesque. The town was almost ruined but will be back in shape. It's [the] first real destruction I've seen in France. We moved into this town the day after it was taken & snipers were still present." Despite such an optimistic view it was usually cold and raining during the entire period at Epinal. S-1 Robert E. Edwards, Jr., wrote, "The newest addition as of about four o'clock this evening was a four months old mostly German shepherd pup. They called [the dog] Tijon so we'll call [him] Jon. Have [the dog] with me and [it] is whimpering a little. All the other officers took over [the dog] like a bunch of women to a baby … not many of the [original] officers … around any more … Mindy, McEvoy, Hauser, Forrester, McKinnon, Trey + myself. In a building for the present trying to keep dry. I get exasperated at some of these Frenchmen. Some understand so readily and others either can't or don't want to." Co. D left their bivouac at Amberieo and moved outside of Vesoul as Capt. Lakey and Lt. Alfred Forrester went ahead to find the battalion CP.[128]

Capt. Raymond J. Lakey finally arrived at Epinal from Nice with Co. D on the 28th and set up quarters in a school building while the company was relieved from attachment to the 1st Airborne Task Force and reverted back to battalion control. The 1st Platoon of Co. A moved to Vomecourt as the 1st Platoon of Co. B zeroed in on areas near Destord and Pierrepont. At this time Capt. Smith, Co. C, gave an account of the earlier re-occupation of Briançon, writing, "We re-took the place where we went into position there later … I found my Company Exec's grave there, too [*Andre Laus*]. He was a brave man and a damn good soldier and officer. I have a new Company Exec now. He is also a damn good soldier and officer." Smith also expressed optimism as he added, "It has rained for the past several days now and it is getting cold, too… But the sun came out today and it sure did look good."[129]

Co. B's 2nd Platoon relieved the 1st Platoon at Destord on the 29th and moved to Nouzeville, and later fired in the vicinity of Granvillers. Lt. Robert J. Bush, Co. A, made a reconnaissance of Rambervillers and afterwards talked the commanding officers out of moving. Co. C advanced from Ferenay to Vimenil, where they fired on the woods east of town to support an infantry attack. On the 30th, Co. A fired in support of the 2nd Battalion, 157th Infantry, on the town of Bru and near Jeanmenil; the 2nd Platoon of Co. B was relieved of attachment to the 2nd Battalion, 180th Infantry, and attached to the 3rd Battalion; and Co. C's 3rd Platoon supported the 1st Battalion, 179th Infantry. Sgt. William E. Johnson, Co. C, from Davidson County, Tennessee, was slightly wounded when a jeep from the 179th Infantry detonated a mine near the gun position. Co. D was held in division reserve.[130]

During the month of September, companies A, B, and C of the 83rd Chemical Battalion had fired 620 HE and 353 WP for a total of 973. When added to the total of Co. D the battalion fired a grand total of 5,941 rounds during the month. Detachment No. 3, 11th Chemical Maintenance Company, working primarily with the 83rd Chemical Battalion, stated that for the three-day period of September 28 to 30 they repaired five baseplates, standards, and sights each, as well as five barrels. It was also discovered by the 83rd that, during the phase when one platoon per company was assigned to a regiment, "Especially good results were obtained by tree bursts of HE and WP on enemy strong points located in dense woods." Casualties were extremely light for the month with only four men wounded, and only two of those had to be hospitalized.[131]

[*It is interesting to note that at this point the battalion journal began to often report events as they transpired between noon of the previous day to the current, yet sometimes retained the method of reporting incidents from the beginning of the stated date through the end of the day. This method in the time-line, although accurate, is often confusing to those not familiar with military time. As a result, some of the events reported from the beginning of October 1944 until the return of the 83rd to the States in 1945 might have actually transpired between noon of the previous day through noon of the day reported, or with a similar time difference.*]

Joseph A. Bova

Joseph A. Bova was born May 25, 1924 [*listed as 1922 according to his military record*], in Cleveland, Ohio, where he began an acting career at the age of 12 on the local radio and stage. He was yet a resident of Cleveland, Cuyahoga County, Ohio, when he enlisted in the army on September 25, 1942, and became a Pfc. in Co. C, 83rd Chemical Mortar Battalion. Near the end of the war he was mentioned as a potential cook in Co. C of a new cadre considered for the 83rd, and was yet a Pfc., Co. C, 83rd Chemical Mortar Battalion on June 22, 1945.

Bova graduated from Northwestern University in Chicago and returned to Cleveland, where he continued as a broadcaster, program director, and entertainer in local radio and television. In the early 1950s he was the popular bumbling host of the local kiddie show "Tip Top Clubhouse", along with an unknown Dom Deluise. An attempt by the two to move the show to New York City failed. Instead he became the second host of the kiddie show "Time for Fun" as 'Uncle Joe' Bova. Between 1957 and 1960 Joe appeared in the New York based "Little Rascals Show" where he portrayed Professor Golly in a popular segment of the show called "Animaland". In the 1960s he returned to the legitimate theater, appearing opposite Carol Burnett in the musical *Once Upon A Mattress*, and was nominated for a Tony in 1970 for Best Supporting Actor (Dramatic) for *The Chinese and Dr. Fish*.

Joe Bova also appeared in a number of motion pictures, primarily B movies, and television shows. He appeared in such productions as *The Young Doctors* (1961), *Serpico* (1973), and television shows ranging from "Starsky and Hutch" to "Kojak" to "Happy Days." In 1990 he returned to kid's TV in the Disney Channel production of "Back to Hannibal: The Return of Tom Sawyer and Huckleberry Finn."

Joseph A. Bova passed away from complications from emphysema at the Actor's Fund Home, Englewood, New Jersey, on March 12, 2006.

John W. Baer

John W. Baer ca. 1944, possibly in Italy.

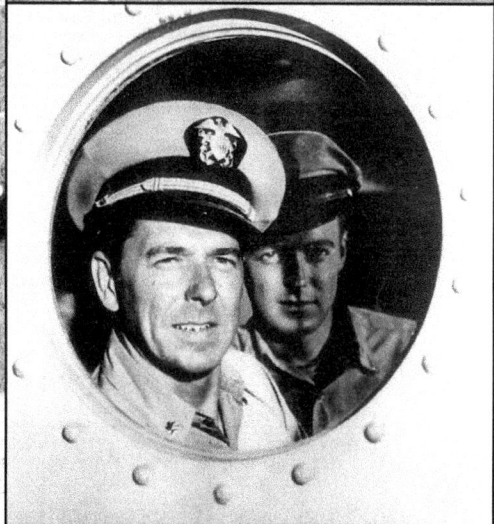

John William Baer was born June 6, 1923, in Bryn Mawr, Pennsylvania, and attended William Penn High School. Prior to the war he worked as a milling machine operator in a defense plant and attended the Pasadena College of Theatre Arts in California. Baer entered the service in March of 1943 and joined Co. D (later Co. A) of the 83rd Chemical Mortar Battalion at Anzio in 1944, where he served as a squad leader; his military record states his highest rank achieved was corporal.

Following the war John Baer went on to a highly successful movie career, primarily as a character actor in B movies. His celluloid history began in 1951 with roles in *Arizona Manhunt* and *Superman and the Mole People*. He met his wife Noureen in 1952 at the Pasadena Playhouse, where she worked in costuming. Between 1952 and 1954 he starred in the *Terry and the Pirates* TV movies, based upon the popular comic book character. In 1955 he had a lead role in the popular movie *We're No Angels* with Humphrey Bogart, Peter Ustinov, and Basil Rathbone, and also appeared in *Mississippi Gambler* with Tyrone Power. Baer was in other movies including *Night of the Blood Beast* (1958), *Bikini Paradise* (1967), and *As Good As it Gets* (1997), and made guest appearances on the TV shows "The Beverly Hillbillies" and "Mission Impossible". He also composed the musical score for *Weekend Pass* (1984). [See roster for a more detailed listing of John Baer's movies.]

In a 2006 interview Noureen said John suffered from post-traumatic syndrome as a result of the war and often had severe headaches. John Baer, one of Hollywood's leading character actors and proud veteran of the 83rd Chemical Mortar Battalion, passed away January 7, 2006, at Newhall, Los Angeles, California, and was cremated.

Clockwise above: Scene from *Terry and the Pirates*; publicity photo; clowning around in wartime photo; scene from *Beneath These Waters*, a made for TV movie with Ronald Reagan; at home with his wife, Noureen, in Placerita Canyon, Newhall, CA.

All photos courtesy Noureen Baer

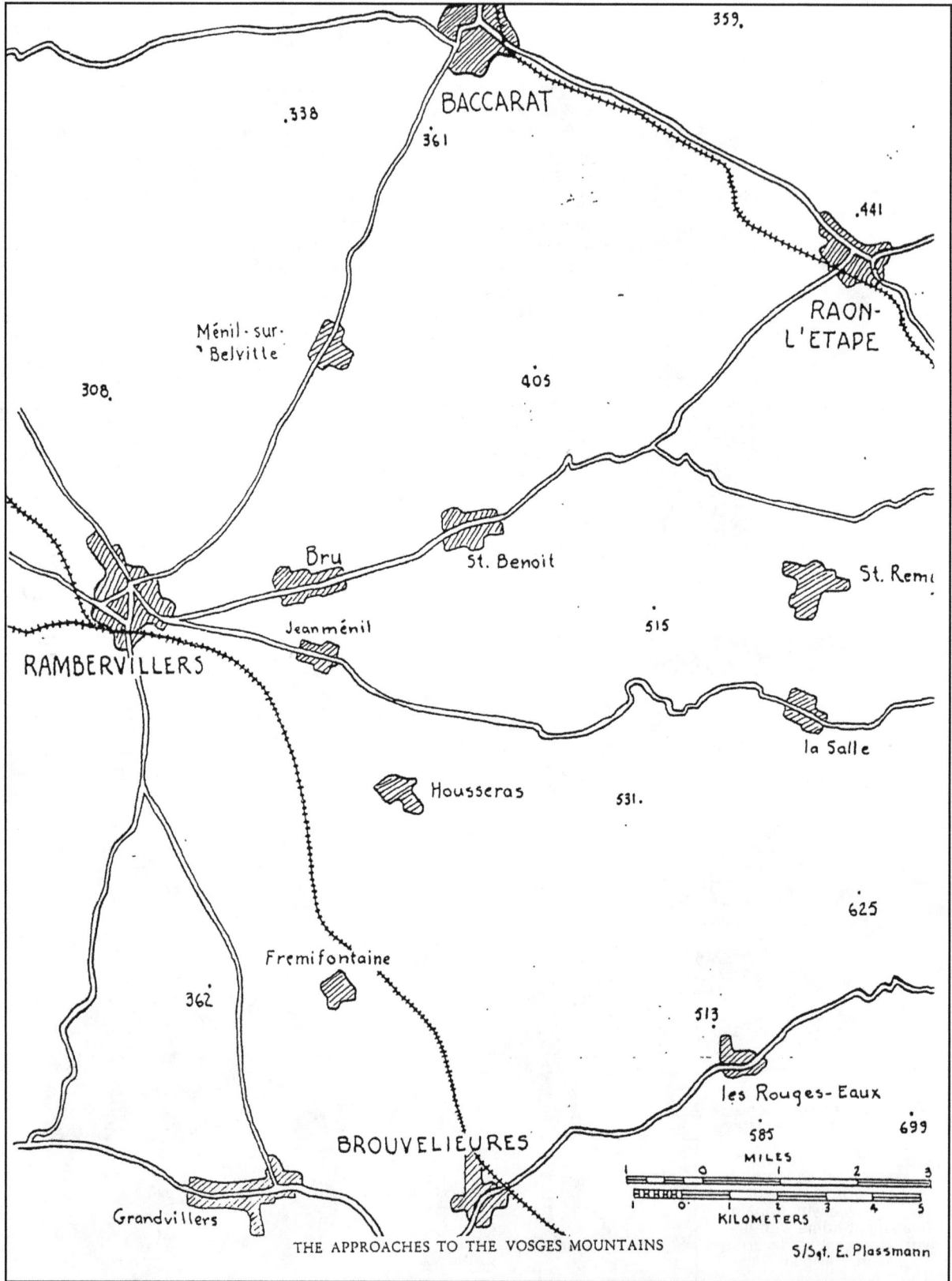

THE APPROACHES TO THE VOSGES MOUNTAINS

S/Sgt. E. Plassmann

The approaches to the Vosges Mountains drawn by S/Sgt Eugene Plassmann, HQ Co. *Eugene Plassmann*

Chapter Eleven

THE VOSGES MOUNTAINS CAMPAIGN
OCTOBER 1944 - JANUARY 1945

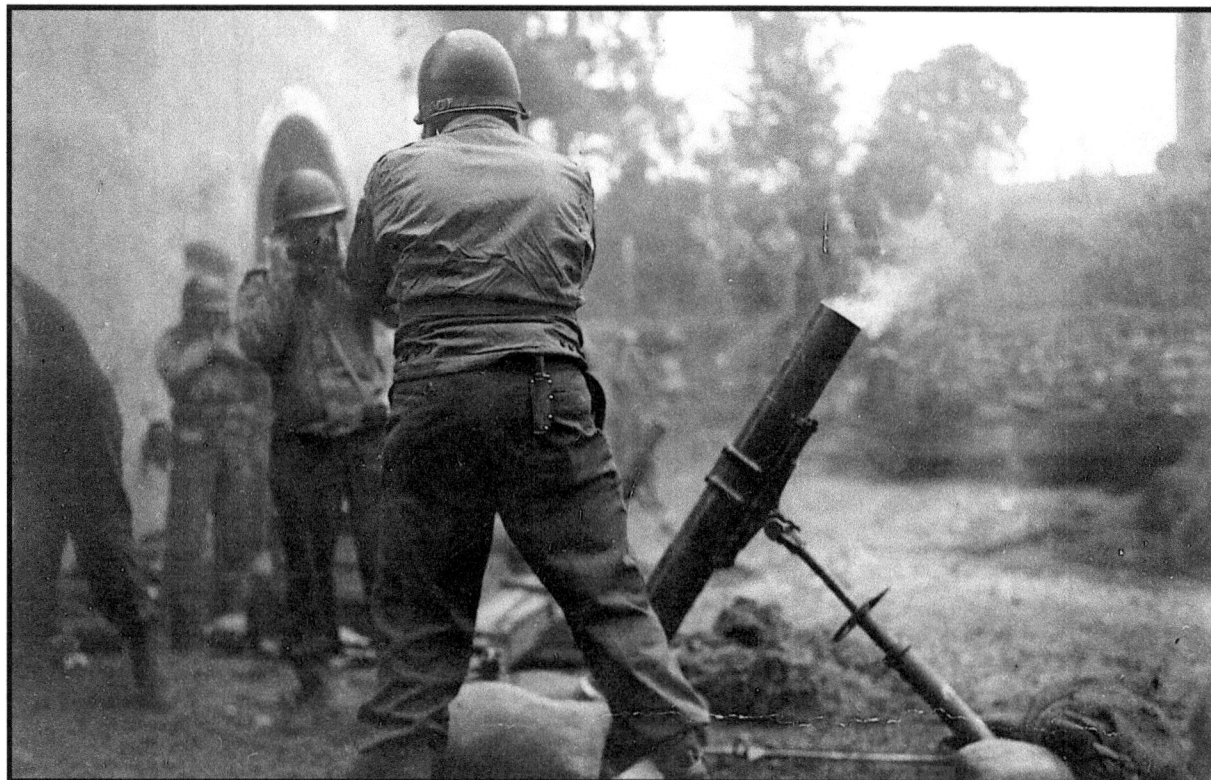

Co. C, 83rd Chemical Mortar Battalion, 45th Infantry Div., 7th Army, at Grandvillers, France, October 9, 1944, firing on the enemy in the woods. *Signal Corps Collection, National Archives*

At the beginning of October 1944 the mortar platoons of the 83rd Chemical Battalion were placed in "relatively fixed positions" with two platoons per company deployed to support the infantry. Attachments during this early period included Co. A with the 157th Infantry, Co. B the 180th Infantry, Co. C the 179th, which were all components of the 45th Infantry Division, and Co. D attached to the 141st Infantry, 36th Infantry Division.

On the first of the month, Capt. John P. McEvoy departed for the 120th Engineers to receive booby trap and mine instructions. The same day Lt. Walter E. Hauser reported the 3rd Platoon of Co. A had moved east of Rambervillers, and Charles Rolling, Co. A, said they moved into a naval barracks there and fired 200 rounds at Jeanmenil. In the previous 24-hour period, noon to noon, the 3rd Platoon had fired on positions at Bru and east of Jeanmenil in support of the 2nd Battalion, 157th Infantry, before moving to a new position to support the 1st Battalion, 157th Infantry. Co. B also covered various infantry action, while Co. C, based at Epinal, saw their 3rd Platoon, having relieved the 2nd Platoon, give strong support to the 1st Battalion, 179th Infantry.[1]

Following visitation from a couple of military brass on the 2nd, Capt. Joseph H. Garsson, Co. A, arrived at battalion CP. Co. A reported they had moved to Vomecourt via Longchamp following the placement of more firepower on Jeanmenil by the 3rd Platoon, which was then relieved by the 2nd Platoon at Rambervillers. The 2nd Platoon of Co. B had been engaged in supporting companies K and L of the 3rd Battalion, 180th Infantry, against the town of Sur L'Arentel, resulting in the capture of 50 prisoners. The 3rd Platoon of Co. C supported the 1st Battalion,

179th Infantry, and at one stage during the activity found that, as earlier noted, when firing upon heavy woods, "tree bursts were effected, thereby affording the enemy no respite from the effects of the bursting WP." In administrative affairs, Capt. Robert E. Edwards, Jr., wrote, "The latest news is that Chris [*Cornett*] is a Major - everyone including the enlisted men laugh about that. He must have really sobered up to get it."[2]

New orders arrived for the 83rd Chemical Battalion on October 3rd when the commanding general of the 45th Infantry Division ordered Major Efnor to have companies A, B, and C, minus one platoon each, committed to three infantry regiments. Co. A would commit to the 157th, Co. B to the 180th, and Co. C to the 179th. Capt. Smith reported Co. C would move to Vaudeville the following day. Meanwhile, Co. D would be held in division reserve.[3]

During the heavy shelling of the previous 24 hours, Cpl. William M. Hawkins of Pennsylvania and Pvt. Peter F. O'Reilly of New York, both of Co. A, were killed. Reno L. Toniolo recalled that early in the day, at the four mortar positions in the woods at Bischweiler, an Italian civilian came by, telling him he was going to butcher and asked if the platoon wanted any meat. Reno took orders and the man returned later with his wife and plenty of fresh meat. About this time the Germans opened up with "ladder fire," a tactic to seek out positions, and the shells soon began to fall in the position. In a matter of minutes, the barrage fell directly on the position and the men sought protection in their foxholes, while the civilian's wife jumped in the largest foxhole, followed closely by nearly the entire squad. Reno noted that Hawkins and O'Reilly had been close by, at their foxholes, sitting on their helmets frying meat with their Coleman stoves when a shell exploded nearby and killed them. William Gallagher gave a slightly varied account of these events, asserting, "Believe me, there was no Italian [*civilians*] or fresh meat or orders for meat. Hawkins dug a deep hole and O'Reilly's hole wasn't so deep. Hawkins said, 'Get in here with me, my foxhole is deeper'. O'Reilly did and there was a direct hit on the hole killing both of them. I know, because I was only about twenty feet from them. An old Frenchman told an officer in a rifle company there was a German in a hay loft directing fire and the officer killed the German. And that is what happened."[4]

The division called on 12 of the battalion's trucks to report to the Vesoul railroad station, but one of the trucks broke down at Vesoul and would remain there with an ordnance outfit until the following day. None of this had any immediate effect on the weapons companies as they continued their various combat activity at such places as Sur L'Arentel. Ironically a letter arrived from the HQ of the 7th Army stating that effective August 18, 1944, the 83rd was

Sgt. Wofford L. Jackson's Co. D squad in action. *Codega Collection*

relieved from prior assignment to the AFHQ and attachment to SOS NATOUSA for Supply, and was assigned to the 7th Army.[5]

October 4th proved a sad day for the 83rd as Chaplain George Gaiser was transferred to the 421st Field Artillery of the Airborne Task Force. This did not set well with Gaiser who had developed a strong attachment to the men of the 83rd. According to numerous veterans, the chaplain "cussed and stomped" as he departed his beloved 83rd. Ed Trey recalled, "When Gaiser received transfer orders he slammed the orders on his cot and yelled, 'I'll be an SOB, I don't want to leave this outfit.'"[6]

As the division moved to Girecourt, Co. A of the 83rd fired more upon Jeanmenil and moved back to Vomecourt by the 5th. The 1st Platoon, Co. B, supporting the 1st Battalion, 180th Infantry, fired upon Housseras, or "horses ass" as the men preferred to call it, while Co. C continued their support of the 179th Infantry. Col. Bruce T. Humphreville, chief chemical officer of the 7th Army, paid a visit to the battalion CP.[7]

The three weapons companies continued to give support to the various infantry units on the 5th while the 1st Platoon of Co. B moved to Autrey and stayed in an old Catholic mission. The battalion received orders on the 6th that Corps was attaching Co. D to the 36th Infantry Division, whose CP was in the vicinity of Docelles. Maj. Efnor apparently desired some clarification of this order and, accompanied by Capt. Lakey of Co. D, visited the 36th Division. He was told to move Co. D to the vicinity of Malanrupt, where they would be attached to the 141st Infantry and would start drawing rations the same day. Companies A, B, and C continued their various assignments, with Co. A directing all firepower upon Jeanmenil as did Co. C upon Brouvelleurs.[8]

While the Medical Detachment was stationed at Epinal in early October, a bomb blew up in one of the bomb disposal trucks. "Doc" Hulcher was called to the scene, but the aid men had already done all that could be done; two were killed and seven wounded, two of them seriously.[9]

The battalion CP, along with Communications, Kitchen Detachment, and the Medics moved across the river and about five miles to the vicinity of Deyvilliers in the Vosges Mountains on the 7th, while HQ, Supply, Motor Pool, and apparently a portion of the Kitchen Detachment, remained at Epinal. Once communications were established with the division a message was received from HQ, VI Corp, that Co. D of the 83rd and Co. C of the 3rd Chemical Battalion were detached from the 45th Infantry Division and officially attached to the 36th Infantry Division. Co. D was attached to the 141st Infantry and moved their Rear CP to La Baffe as the various platoons returned to action firing on the Laval vicinity. During the previous 24 hours, companies A and B at Housseras and C of the 83rd continued to be heavily engaged with the enemy.[10]

On this same day, a rather unusual letter was sent by W. G. Caldwell to the commanding general of the 7th Army, stating that it had been learned by the 2nd Chemical Battalion that Free French forces north of St. Paul, about 30 miles south of Briançon, had in their possession 4.2" mortars and ammo taken from the battleground of Briançon. The 83rd's commander had previously visited the site after its re-capture and, thinking all the equipment they had to abandon there had been destroyed by the enemy, had ordered new equipment. When the Free French were discovered to be in possession of that equipment, it was ordered to be returned immediately.[11]

Heavy fighting continued on the 8th with the assigned platoons of Co. A registering on Bru and Jeanmenil, while Co. B zeroed in on Villaume and Les Angeles. At one point the 179th Infantry reported Co. B had apparently knocked out a Mark V tank and many bloody enemy bandages were located in the same area. A captured German soldier reported many casualties resulting from mortar and shell fire had taken place in the towns east of Autrey. Meanwhile, Co. C took a beating and at one point the enemy made a direct hit on their CP but no casualties resulted. Later enemy artillery interdicted into the position subjecting the CP to shrapnel. The situation was partially brought under control when the 2nd Platoon's forward observer realized that, due to the close proximity to the enemy line, "it was necessary to bring the mortar fire to within 100 yards of his OP and the infantry lines. Procedure such as this … enabled the infantry to occupy the contested ground with little difficulty." Maj. Efnor also returned with information that Co. D had successfully engaged the enemy at Beaumenil, and that following one particular barrage "a German came in and gave himself up. When [the] prisoner was questioned and asked about his company he said that when our mortar barrage was laid in on his area the company left their positions, leaving him, so that he thought it best to surrender."[12]

Maj. Efnor also reported that due to a critical shortage of 4.2" ammunition, starting the following day, only

Mortar men at Grandvillers, France, placing powder rings on WP shells, October 9, 1944. *Signal Corps Collection, National Archives*

150 rounds would be allotted per battalion company per day until further notified. In addition, due to trouble with sinking baseplates, the battalion requested Detachment No. 3, 11th Chemical Maintenance, led by 1st Lt. Rollin W. Kapp, build two "A" type baseplate supports, which would not be completed until the 15th. In actuality, they began work on three wooden baseplate supports for use in soft soil, "… made in accordance with a new design drawn up by Capt. Albert Gallagher and approved by the 83rd Chemical Battalion." Capt. Gallagher claimed the new design would be more efficient and overcome any problems encountered by the original. Plans were made for the Engineers to acquire the proper 6 x 6 lumber [*listed as 8 x 8 in other records of the 11th Chemical journal*] and eventually to build 10 of the baseplate supports. Ed Trey recalled, "The ordnance corporal took over the 4.2" and redesigned the baseplate, substituting a round configuration. No feedback on any success." A recommendation was also made to keep Lt. Kapp's detachment of the 11th Chemical Maintenance in its present location with the 83rd, unless the battalion should move a great distance, as the facilities were superior to any he might find in the immediate east. Lastly, Capt. Gallagher requested all chemical mortar battalions quit "borrowing" tools and spare parts from their accompanying maintenance detachments and acquire them from the appropriate depot.[13]

The ammo situation was further addressed on a rainy 9th as Capt. Ed Trey announced that 75 per cent of the ammunition in the ammo dump that day would be issued to the 83rd and the 3rd Chemical Battalion. Thereafter 75 per cent of what arrived daily would be issued daily to the 83rd, and 25 per cent would be held in reserve. Ten battalion trucks were also sent to division at St. Loup to pick up replacements. Companies A, B, C, and D continued to heavily engage the enemy in their various positions. Co. D, in particular, centered their fire in the vicinity of Beaumenil.[14]

Fighting raged on during October 10th. Co. B fired on areas such as Villaume Fontaine and Housseras, and, in one area Co. B targeted, a Graves Registration party recorded they had removed about 50 dead Germans and there was evidence of heavy German casualties throughout the vicinity. Co. C also pounded the enemy, and a German prisoner said that on the night of October 8th the mortar fire of Co. C had killed eight Germans and wounded 32. He went on to state that "the continuous barrages of mortar fire not only inflicted physical wounds but had caused

Unidentified 83rd gunner relays mortar on target after a three-round concentration, at Grandvillers, France, October 9, 1944. *Signal Corps Collection, National Archives*

a mental state verging on hysteria of the troops subjected to the shell fire." Co. D, supporting the 141st Infantry, also added to the enemy fear at Beaumenil as their battalion CP reported that one of the company's shells had passed through the window of a house and killed a German captain. In addition, the 2nd Battalion commander of the 141st Infantry praised the good firing of Co. D.[15]

The situation of all four companies of the 83rd remained virtually unchanged on the 11th although two companies of the 180th Infantry were relieved by three companies of the 36th Engineer Regiment, to be supported by Co. B of the 83rd. Meanwhile, Sgt. William J. Hodgson of Co. D reported Capt. Raymond J. Lakey's jeep hit an enemy mine near Charmois. The jeep was destroyed and Capt. Lakey and his driver were wounded. Later in the day, Lt. Walter Hauser confirmed the report. This was followed on the 12th by another jeep accident when Lt. Bernard Stone, Co. B, collided with another jeep near Pierrepont, slightly injuring himself and his driver. Such accidents were not uncommon considering the heavy rains made the roads quite muddy, but the men did benefit from their waterproof shoes and few got wet feet. All four companies remained in action and Capt. Smith of Co. C was forced to call Maj. Efnor to report they had exceeded their quota of ammo allotted due to defensive concentrations laid on an enemy counterattack. Capt. Smith also wrote in a letter home, "The sun came out for a while yesterday, and it sure was a relief. But it's cold and wet again today. We are fighting in the woods, and our own gun is doing it's share. We plow it into the Krauts … We've been pretty lucky in this company lately, although we've worked pretty hard and done quite a bit of shooting. We haven't had a man killed or even badly wounded since August 29. I pray every night that it will keep up."[16]

News was received on October 13th that Capt. Lakey would not return to Co. D because his injuries in the mine explosion had proved too severe. Co. D was also detached from the 141st Infantry and attached to the 442nd Combat Team. Charlie Lowry, Co. D, wrote, "We are having nasty weather and plenty of mud." All four companies remained engaged with the enemy. Co. C had to send a barrel and standard for their #2 gun back to the rear for repairs. During one stage of the fighting near Grandvillers, Lt. John L. Boyd and Pvt. Robert L. Brummage received superficial shrapnel wounds while pinned down during an effort to get to their forward observation post, but both

Capt. Raymond Lakey's jeep "Golden Bobcat" that was hit by a mine near Charmois, France on October 11, 1944. *Codega Collection*

were able to make it to the position, where Lt. Boyd continued to direct fire. William Ford, Co. C, recalled the 2nd Platoon's OP was hit hard. "Lt. Boyd was badly wounded and needed hospital attention. A jeep came up as close as it could to our front line without being spotted or hit by shell fire. It waited for medics who carried Lt. Boyd from the OP to the jeep. The medics lashed him onto the jeep, and he was taken back to the field hospital." Lt. William L. Trapnell of the company gave supporting fire to the 2nd Battalion, 179th Infantry, from the forward observation post but was forced to direct his fire to within 60 yards of his OP which enabled him to "knock out" an enemy machine gun.[17]

Good news arrived on the 14th with Maj. Efnor lifting the restrictions on the 4.2" ammo as the supply had "built up somewhat." Co. B fired six WP with an experimental baseplate. A soldier of Co. G, 2nd Battalion, 179th Infantry, who had been captured by the enemy on October 8th, claimed that "his escape was made possible by a 4.2" mortar barrage which forced his captors to take cover. Seizing his opportunity he escaped and returned to his unit. Having been in a position to observe results," he said the 4.2" mortars had inflicted heavy casualties on the enemy. Co. D was detached from the 442nd Combat team and re-attached to the 141st Infantry.[18]

Word was received on the 15th that all enlisted men and officers of the 83rd on temporary duty would be called to the replacement depot. This was followed by a call to Maj. Gordon Mindrum that the allotment of ammo would now be 400 HE and 500 WP per day until further notice. A discussion was also held concerning the return of assigned men. Co. A persisted in their battering of such places as Jeanmenil and Co. D struck the town of Laval although their commanding officer had not yet returned from a reconnaissance with the 1st Battalion, 141st Infantry . The two newly-constructed "A" type baseplate supports were taken by Detachment No. 3, 11th Chemical Maintenance, to the mortar position of Co. B of the 83rd and tested. The result was, "The frame split after six rounds were fired (4000 yard - 23 powder rings). Timber used was not hard or heavy enough."[19]

The fighting continued on all fronts throughout the 16th. Although no longer present or in command of the 83rd, Lt. Col. Hutchinson kept abreast of the battalion's situation and wrote Cunin, "The 83rd now has about a total of 295 days of action out of the 463 days that have elapsed since July 10, 1943 … We never got panoramic sights until just now because despite the fact that you were not in action last spring, your priority was tops and ours was bottoms, which is only as it should be. However we fired our first rolling barrage in front of 509 Paratroopers in November 1943 with the old sight in all of the four firing platoons except Crenshaw's, which had the old Wop [*derogatory slang for Italian*] jobs. It was A and D that fired. The attack was successful, though only local … MacKinnon has been rotated. Stone commands B Co. with Davis former 4th Rangers, as Exec. I am now assigned to the 100th giving Sam Efnor undisputed title to the Bn. This means a step up all along the line." Co. D was in the vicinity of Le Boulay.[20]

On the 17th, Capt. Ed Trey called HQ regarding strengthening the weak points of the wooden baseplate and acquiring shock absorbers for the mortars. Co. A continued to support the 157th Infantry on Bru. James G. Helsel, Co. A, wrote, "Jerry is pretty well dug in here, in what is the beginning of the Vosges. All platoons have been called to the front. We take turns individually going back to Vomecourt for a two day rest." Co. B supported the 36th Engineers and 180th Infantry, Co. C the 179th, and Co. D the 141st. Lt. Norman ("Rosy") Rosenthal, Co. C, called Capt. Smith and informed him that he lacked M-16 charges with which to hit several excellent targets. Capt. Smith relayed he would

CAPTAIN EDWARD TREY
INVENTOR & INNOVATOR

Captain Edward Trey

Ed Trey

Captain and S-4 of HQ Co., Edward L. Trey, a native of Michigan, repeatedly displayed his keen eye and creativity in efforts to make improvements in the mortar equipment of the chemical mortar battalions. It remains questionable as to how many ideas he submitted and as to how many were actually accepted and employed, but there is no doubt of his involvement in the following three:

AIMING STAKE LIGHT

Prior to late 1944 the chemical mortar crews were unable to receive needed night operational materials. This led to the invention of the Aiming Stake Light by Capt. Edward L. Trey, Battalion S-4, 83rd Chemical Mortar Battalion. Known as "TL-83G" this device, a simple light, was officially approved for the Chemical Warfare Service November 11, 1944.

The description provided by the U.S. Army reads: "The light is made from readily available supplies. A flashlight bulb and reflection assembly is mounted in a tin cylinder. This fits tightly over another cylinder which contains one BA 30. In operation, the light is placed on the top of the Aiming Stake. The light is turned on by pushing the bulb reflector assembly cylinder down so that the bulb makes contact with the BA 30. The light is turned off by pulling the top cylinder up, thus breaking the contact. Both the bulb and battery can be easily replaced. The light itself is compact and rugged and can be carried in the mortar cart toolbox."

In a 2004 letter to the author, Edward Trey jokingly remarked, "I think the guys hated me for having to fire at night."

Actually, there is some conjecture as to how much impact Capt. Trey's invention had on the battalion. Lee Steedle, Co. B, wrote, "I was in combat from March 1944 through war's end, and I never once saw a light placed on an aiming stake. We used fluorescent discs about 1 – ½ inches wide that we hung on the stake. Even then we were very careful that they pointed directly at the gun, and could not be seen from the side. That was plenty bright. I would have felt spooked for sure, if we used anything brighter than that, which a Kraut patrol might have been able to see." Steedle added an additional humorous incident, stating, "We were somewhere in France, in fairly flat terrain, and when digging to fill sandbags for our baseplates we uncovered some luminous tree roots (I believe this may have been caused by a fungus of some kind). Their luminosity was so great that we became uneasy about their brightness and hastened to cover the shining roots with dirt. However, we took small glowing root pieces and fastened them to our aiming stakes where they served us very well for just one night, after which they stopped glowing."

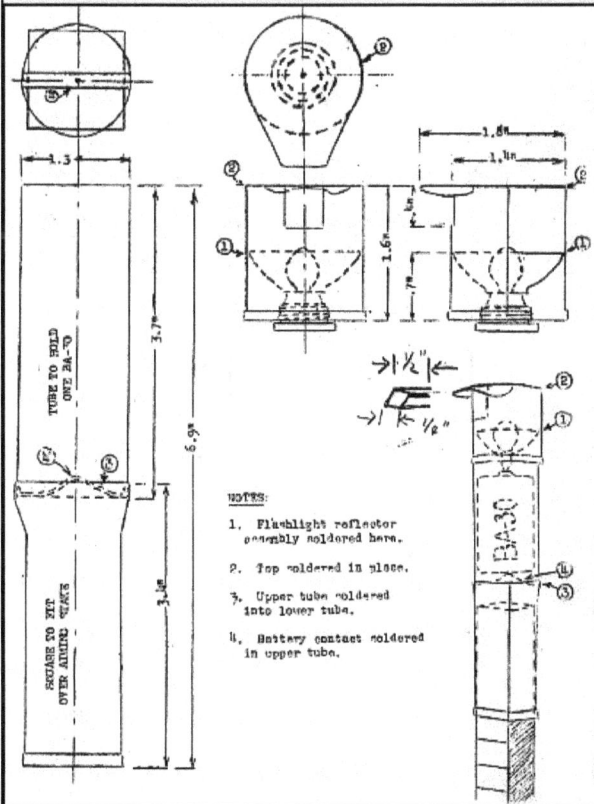

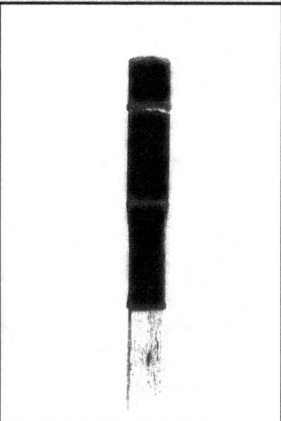

Aiming stake light diagram (left); aiming light stake with lighting attachment (center); close-up of lighting attachment (right) *National Archives*

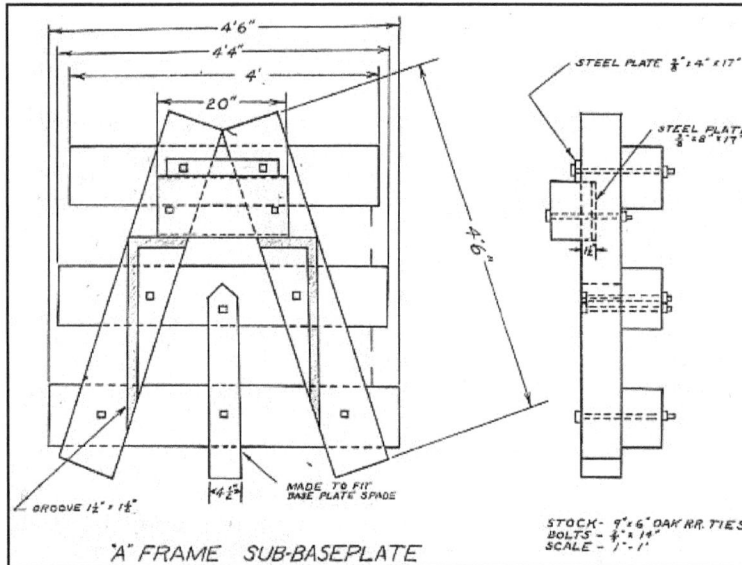

A-Frame sub-baseplate diagram. *National Archives*

Wooden baseplate support (center) and the baseplate
on the wooden sub-baseplate support (bottom).

National Archives

WOODEN SUB-BASEPLATES

Capt. Ed Trey, S-4, was also involved in Project #6, an experiment involving the use of wooden sub-baseplates for the mortars. Company commanders of the 83rd Chemical Mortar Battalion had complained that the mortar baseplates of the 4.2" chemical mortar sank too deep in the soft, muddy soil. From this originated the idea of a wooden sub-baseplate, and a drawing of such an innovation was submitted by Capt. Trey on October 14, 1944. On the 20th the Chemical Officer of the 7th Army gave the 11th Chemical Maintenance Company the nod to create five experimental models.

The models were completed on October 23rd and presented to Co. B, 83rd Chemical Mortar Battalion, for testing the following week. Their reports concluded the wood used in the baseplates was too soft and and broke easily. As a result the Engineers created eight more and replaced the soft wood with railroad ties.

A report was received on December 2nd from Co. B that the new wooden sub-baseplates had been successfully employed for five days and performed satisfactorily, except they were too heavy to move from one position to another. On the 28th Capt. Trey requested six of the sub-baseplates be sent to Co. A and work was begun on them at Battalion HQ.

Trey submitted his finding on January 4th, 1945, that the sub-baseplates had seen constant usage when the mortars were in a stationary position but nearly impossible to move after a period of time "due to the depth it sinks into the ground and the fact that the soil freezes over it."

MORTAR CART CHAIN COUPLING

Capt. Ed Trey also submitted a request, with four drawings, on November 27th, 1944, to change the chain coupling for the 4.2" chemical mortar cart from bronze to steel. Not only would this strengthen it but it would also improve the lock-in as well as make the component more available from locally manufactured material. Authorities took the suggestion under consideration but rejected it on February 28th, 1945.

In 2004 Ed Trey recalled, "I also re-designed the locking device that affixed the mortar components to the cart to allow for more rapid removal from cart into action. I don't know what the Chemical Corps or Ordnance did with it."

Photo taken December 5th, 1944, of a Co. D soldier with S/Sgt Wofford L. Jackson "who likes his schnapps" in Alsace. *Squires Collection*

attempt to send him 50 and obtain some additional ones.[21]

Word was received on the 18th that Maj. Efnor had officially been promoted to lieutenant colonel of the 83rd Chemical Battalion the previous day. Capt. Smith, Co. C, reported the total rounds fired by his company "since on line and since in Granvilliers" was 602 HE and 309 WP from September 28th through October 5th and 4,048 HE and 1,336 WP from October 6th to October 17th. This made for a grand total of 4,650 HE and 1,654 WP - a full total of 6,295 for the two periods. During the day a shell struck Capt. Smith's jeep but no one was injured. Smith, after complaining of the rain, said of the incident, "One came through the windshield between me and my driver yesterday, and nobody got a scratch."[22]

Colonels Humphreville and Benjamin F. Mattingly, chemical officers of the 7th and 6th Army respectively, along with Efnor, visited the battalion CP in the rain and mud on the 19th, as well as Co. A's position, where Jeanmenil remained a target. The following day information was received relieving Co. D from the 141st Infantry and placing them in support of the 442nd Combat Team, where they also gave some support to the 100th Battalion. The reason for this was the 3rd Division, having been relieved by the French, moved into the 179th Infantry sector and began an attack southeast of Bruyeres in conjunction with the 442nd, with Co. D in close support. This attack on Bruyeres was in conjunction with an attack of the 179th Infantry and the 157th Infantry east toward Brouvelieures, with Co. C of the 83rd in close support.[23]

Firing continued on all fronts on the 21st including Brouvelieures, where Co. C struck an apparent German escape route. Companies A, B, and C further pounded the enemy. The White Platoon of Co. D moved to La Baffe while the company's CP was established at Bruyeres on the 22nd, where Sam Kweskin said he and Paul Troia took position in an upstairs bedroom with the baseplate of their mortar placed directly against the wall in readiness. But perhaps the strangest event of the day involved 1st Lt. John M. Taylor of Co. D, "... a brave officer, but a real character, because he constantly wore a fur-lined black Air Corps jacket, even when he was up at an observation post, where there was always a possibility of being seen by the Jerries." Apparently, against all regulations, he had married a French woman who received his support allotment. When he learned of her profuse unfaithfulness he became depressed. Lee Steedle, Co. D, described Taylor as "... a bit odd, but a damn good officer. Very approachable, and he played poker with us enlisted men while we were in combat [*zones*], which was unusual. He had a high, almost feminine voice, but Taylor was gutsy and we all respected him ..." According to Steedle, "One day, returning down the mountain from the OP with our radioman [*Cpl. Marion E. "Blackie" Bailey from Ohio*], they came to a fork in the trail. Our man said, 'Hey, Lieutenant Taylor, you're taking the wrong fork!' This was the same seasoned radioman whom had been wounded four times in the past. He'd been to the OP before, and knew the trail well. Lt. Taylor replied, 'Are you sure you know the way? Then see you later', and disappeared along the wrong fork, while our worried man returned to the platoon and told us about it. We never saw Taylor alive again." Sam Kweskin wrote that a search party was sent out and found Taylor shot in the head but events of the next few days proved that untrue. After the war Lee Steedle would read Audie Murphy's classic book on the war in which he mentioned an officer in an Air Corps jacket

1st Squad, 2nd Platoon, Co. A, in Alsace, France. *Tyma Collection*

walked up to his outpost and he warned him not to go farther as only the enemy were ahead. The officer ignored Murphy and went on, only to be found dead the next morning. Lee Steedle suspected this was Taylor and attributed his death to depressive behavior.[24]

On the 23rd, Lt. Col. Humphreville called to inform the 83rd "that a detail would clean our ammo, inspect it, oil it, and put it in cardboard tubes. Tubes will be marked and we will return all tubes after firing." Co. D was relieved from the 442nd and sent back to battalion control, then attached to the 141st Infantry, then was relieved from the 36th Infantry Division, attached to the 3rd Infantry Division, and again attached to the 442nd Infantry. Co. A struck Bru again and Co. C came under the fire of the "10 barreled Nebelwerfer."[25]

Orders were issued on the 24th to detach Co. B from the 45th Infantry Division and attach them to the 36th Engineers at Rambervillers, thereby relieving Co. A to work with the 157th Infantry on a planned attack. The 1st and 2nd platoons of Co. A moved to a church area at Autrey and their 3rd Platoon was "busted up." The battalion was also informed the ammo allotment per day had been changed to 600 HE and 750 WP. Meanwhile Co. C took up positions in the vicinity of Hill 513 and the battalion Motor Pool & Supply moved to Deyvillers. Co. D was held in reserve awaiting further orders.[26]

The battalion CP at Deyvillers closed on the 25th [*although "Doc" Hulcher claimed it was the 23rd*] and moved to Fremifontaine, leaving the Medics, Motor Pool, and Supply at Deyvillers. Lt. Col. Efnor was also instructed to send six trucks, with two drivers per truck to Marseilles to convoy division troops. Co. A, supporting the 157th Infantry with a smoke screen, reported their CP at Autrey, and Charles Rolling, Co. A, said he slept in a barn where there were six dead cows. Co. B gave support to the 36th Engineers, and baseplate supports improved by solid oak timber (8" x 8") at HQ Co. of the 11th Chemical Maintenance were tested at the mortar position of Co. B of the 83rd, with the result, "Twenty-six rounds were fired at rapid fire. Only ten mill deviation was noted and a small splinter had been chipped from the rear of the frame. A steel plate bolted to the rear support would keep that support from splintering." Co. C worked with the 179th Infantry, and Co. D remained with the 442nd Combat Team and their 1st Platoon attached to the 143rd Infantry. Ironically, the medics of the 143rd found the body of Lt. John M. Taylor, Co. D, in a French coffin in the no man's land of Les Poulieres. Lee Steedle stated, "A French farmer came to our outfit and said that he had the body of a lieutenant in his barn. The weather was chilly and wet at the time, maybe even freezing at night, and Taylor's body might have been held in the barn a couple of days before we learned about it." Detachment No. 1 of the 11th Chemical Maintenance received an example of an aiming stake with light from their HQ on the 26th and were required to make six for the 83rd Chemical Battalion.[27]

Between October 26th and the 30th, Co. D of the 83rd supported the 442nd RCT in their valiant rescue of the 1st Battalion, 141st Infantry, known as the "Lost Battalion" because they had become surrounded by the enemy on a ridge above Biffontaine near Bruyeres. In the five-day battle the Japanese-American 442nd suffered over 800 casualties and rescued 211 men. The 442nd became the most decorated American unit of World War II.[28]

Capt. Joseph H. Garsson, Co. A, was instructed on the 27th to detach a platoon on the following day to support the 180th Infantry and to keep the remaining platoons in support of the 157th. All companies remained engaged with the enemy with Co. D reporting their CP at Bruyeres and their 1st Platoon at La Baffe. Sam Kweskin would later recall that at La Baffe, a town about 11 miles northeast of Epinal, "D Company lived within the houses that fronted the unpaved road that ran through the village, and daily made their short walks to the huge barn at the edge of the village, mess kits clattering, where the cooks had set up their continental cuisine." Lt. Col. Efnor visited the 180th Infantry on the 28th and returned once the 2nd Platoon of Co. A was in place at Housseras, where Lt. Robert J. Bush said a rat crawled on his face while he attempted to sleep. Co. B's 1st Platoon supported the 117th Cavalry Reconnaissance Squad against Jeanmenil.[29]

Lt. Col. Efnor left for HQ, XV Corps, at Luneville on the 29th while Co. A held their support of the 157th Infantry and Co. C supported the 179th in the vicinity of La Salle. Co. B, following more rounds laid on Jeanmenil, received instructions to be relieved from the 117th Cavalry Reconnaissance Battalion, attach themselves to the 15th Corps in support of the 44th Division, and move to Luneville. The Medical Detachment of the battalion also moved from Deyvillers to Fremifontaine, although once again "Doc" Hulcher disputed this date and said they "… moved up to Fremifontaine in a large barn. Had our aid station in a house some 100 yards down the road. Lots of children and quite a civilian practice. New 100 Div moved in and we were quite amused by their newness." During the day the White Platoon of Co. D was heavily shelled by 170 and 105mm artillery but suffered no casualties.[30]

James McGrann and John O'Brien, Jr., of HQ Co., at Rambervillers, France. *Eugene Plassmann*

While companies A, C, and D engaged the enemy on the 30th, Co. B began their motor convoy movement from Rambervillers to an assembly area near Luneville, with the company rear occupying a dairy east of Luneville. On the last day of the month, the 31st, Co. A still supported the 157th and had some shells fall in their area but no one was hurt. Co. B was near Luneville with the 44th Division, Co. C still supported the 179th, and Co. D still gave support in the Bruyeres and La Baffe area. George Borkhuis, Co. D, wrote "There has been frost for the past 3 days. Winter is definitely settling in."[31]

The month of October 1944 saw the 83rd Chemical Battalion expend 15,742 HE and 6,165 WP for a total of 21,907 rounds of 4.2" ammo. Casualties remained light with a reported three killed in action, and three lightly wounded or injured who were hospitalized, for a total of six, an exceptionally light casualty rate for a unit engaged almost daily.[32]

November opened with "the 45th Infantry Division line extended from the vicinity of St. Benoit southeast to the vicinity of La Salle. The mission of the Division was to attack northeast, clear Foret St. Barbe, and in conjunction with the 3rd and 36th infantry divisions on the right, establish the Baccarat-Raon L'Etape-St. Die line." The 1st Platoon of Co. A, 83rd Chemical Battalion, was in direct support of the 157th Infantry and the 2nd Platoon in direct support of the 180th Infantry, 45th Infantry Division; the 1st Platoon of Co. B was in support of the 156th Field Artillery Battalion, 44th Infantry Division, and the 2nd Platoon supported the 220th Field Artillery Battalion; Co. C of the battalion was in direct support of the 179th Infantry; and Co. D supported the 143rd Infantry, 36th Infantry Division.[33]

The forward CP of Co. A moved to St. Benoit on November 1st and Co. D, yet posted at Bruyeres and La Baffe, got some relief when a platoon of the 3rd Chemical Battalion relieved the 1st Platoon of Co. D. The battalion Motor & Supply moved from Deyvillers to Fremifontaine. Detachment No. 3, 11th Chemical Maintenance, attached to the 83rd Chemical and moved from Epinal to Rambervillers, where their personnel billeted in an empty house and set up a work shop in an adjoining garage. Lt. Col. Efnor was also informed that the six battalion trucks hauling division troops would get one day off. Ironically, the following day orders came through for the battalion to provide six trucks to go to Marseilles to pick up more men. During the day Co. C contributed to the action at Hill 380 and the town of St. Remy. As rain fell throughout the evening of the 1st and all day of the 2nd, Co. A's 2nd Platoon took position in a cemetery and the company's CP was firmly established at St. Benoit.[34]

The 100th Infantry Division began relieving the 45th Infantry Division on the 3rd with the 1st Platoon of Co.

The 83rd Chemical Battalion in action in the Vosges mountains as sketched by Mario Ricci, Co. C. Ricci drew numerous other sketches which were lost in the Briançon debacle. *Mario Ricci*

C at Housseras, while the company participated in many strikes in and around St. Remy, including a smoke screen enabling the safe return of two of three infantry patrol scouts. James Helsel, Co. A, recorded in his diary, "The book says mortars should set up in a defiladed position, but not this platoon. They set it up on top of a hill and fire down." The battalion CP at Fremifontaine closed on the 4th and opened in the area of Housseras, a trip in which Daniel Shields observed many dead animals due to mine fields. This same observation was made by "Doc" Hulcher who remarked he "Saw whole herds of cattle lying dead along [*the*] road." Robert J. Bush, Co. A, wrote, "… lots of mines & booby traps. One [*man*] killed, six lost legs."[35]

At Housseras the battalion was informed their ammo allotment from November 1st to November 20th would be 5,000 HE and 7,343 WP, the amount determined for the 45th Division sector. Soon afterward each company was instructed they would be issued 2,500 HE and 3,671 WP for the period stated. Companies A, B, and C were actively engaged with Co. B firing on Remoncourt and Co. C, supporting the 399th Infantry, caused havoc around Housseras, Basses Pierres, and La Salle. The weather also continued to grow colder with little sunshine. Co. D did no firing in the Bruyeres and La Baffe sector.[36]

All four battalion companies were again engaged on the 5th, including Co. A at Thiaville, and on the 6th Co. A received compliments from the colonel of the 2nd Battalion, 179th Infantry, for their performance. Meanwhile, Co. C assisted the 399th Infantry in their effort to establish a forward observation post at St. Remy and also fired on the town of Etival. The Red Platoon of Co. D was in support of the 1st Battalion, 143rd Infantry; the White Platoon was attached to the 2nd Battalion of the 143rd, and the Blue Platoon was at La Baffe. As all four companies continued to harass the enemy in any way possible for the next few days, the 2nd Platoon of Co. A supported the 3rd Battalion, 398th Infantry, on the 7th and Co. B captured a prisoner near one of their gun positions.[37]

SECURING THE BACCARAT–RAON–L'ETAPE–ST. DIE LINE
AND
MOYENMONTIER – SENONES
November 8 – 26

On November 8th, the 1st Platoon of Co. A, which had been supporting the 1st and 3rd Battalions, 157th Infantry, was relieved by the 1st Platoon of Co. C. The 2nd Platoon of Co. C engaged with the enemy at Etival and Pajaille. In the actions that followed, companies A and C constantly struggled in locating favorable gun positions due to the heavily wooded terrain. Baseplates were often supported by timbers, and trees were periodically cleared to make paths for shells. Lt. Eric H. ("Pete") Peterson, Jr., served as observer while Co. A successfully shelled a factory.[38]

All copies of *Muzzleblasts* courtesy Ed Trey

"MUZZLE BLASTS"
Official Newsletter of the 83rd Chemical Mortar Battalion

According to a 1949 issue, *Muzzleblasts* originated in November or December of 1944 at St. Marie-aux-Mines, France. As would become a war-time tradition, nearly every issue was printed on captured enemy paper, and combat artist Sam Kweskin, now transferred from Company D to HQ Co., 83rd Chemical Mortar Battalion, "armed with a typewriter and mimeograph, did most of the work." The newsletter, containing information on the war in general and the 83rd Chemical Mortar Battalion in particular, was printed each week until the battalion broke up at Innsbruck, Austria, in the summer of 1945.

In addition to the regular features in *Muzzleblasts*, Kweskin created a lovable cartoon character called "Misfire", represented as a soldier with big ears and a huge smile. Reportedly, "Misfire", representing the 83rd "Sad Sack" (but whose features owed more to Dopey of Snow White and the Seven Dwarfs), appeared on every cover, but a check of old issues has shown this not to be true. Coincidentally, Kweskin followed George Baker as cartoonist for their high school newspaper in Chicago. Baker later developed "Sad Sack". Additionally, some of the original covers (which did not feature "Misfire") were a bit risque for the times, and instructions ran in each issue, until the April 29, 1945, edition, to destroy the paper after reading.

In a 2005 interview Sam Kweskin recalled, "As far as I can REMEMBER, Gordon Mindrum sent notes to all the companies seeking photos, drawings, etc. to include in a battalion history back in October 1944. He thought the war would end next week. I had been filling sketchbooks since Italy so I sent one on . . . he was so impressed he had Cpl. Storey jeep over to our village of La Baffe to pick me up. I happened to be on the front for ten days, so Storey returned when I got back safely. Took me to HQ where I was ASSIGNED (no longer with a weapons company) to assist Bob Brimm in printing a battalion newsletter of 4 pp. every week. I don't know if Bob or another officer thought of the name of it – I don't think I did. Mindrum was even more thrilled when I told him I had worked for the *Chicago Tribune* before coming to the service."

The first postwar edition of *Muzzleblasts* (a single page spread) appeared in December of 1948, which stirred interest in holding a reunion. *Muzzleblasts* has continued on an irregular basis ever since, with fluctuating degrees of quality. Recently, veteran Lee Steedle and his son Bill took over the helm for two issues and returned the newsletter to its former focus on the 83rd veterans and their experiences. It has also remained the primary outlet for reunion information.

"Misfire" (right)

Sam Kweskin at work for the *Chicago Tribune*, early 1940s. *Jean Siegel*

Co. A received the official order to support the 398th Infantry on the 9th and engaged the enemy at a factory and enemy machine gunners in some houses. Col. Staten of the 3rd Battalion, 398th Infantry, complimented the firing of Co. A's 2nd Platoon. Some firing was performed during the day by Co. B while attached to the 156th Field Artillery Battalion. Co. C was ordered to support the 399th Infantry and fired in and around Pajaille and Hill 528.9. Later in the day, they provided smoke to assist an attack on Etival by the 15th Regiment, 3rd Division. The CO of the 15th commended Co. C on the effectiveness of the smoke screen. No firing was done by Co. D with positions held at Bruyeres and La Baffe. This was also the day Sam Kweskin was assigned to HQ Co. by Gordon Mindrum, who thought the war would soon end, to help illustrate a battalion history in conjunction with the author, Lt. Robert Brimm, HQ Communications. As Kweskin jumped in the jeep dispatched for him, his fellow mortar men of Co. D jokingly harassed him with such remarks as "What's this? Your own private jeep?," and "What? You're going to Headquarters? Whydaya want to join that chicken outfit? They're all a bunch of rear echelon blowhards. Stick around."39

The battalion CP closed at Housseras and moved to Menil-sur-Belvitte between Rambervillers and Bescanot on the 10th, where Lt. Brimm and Sam Kweskin decided to postpone the battalion history and put out a weekly newspaper, which became *Muzzleblasts*. "Doc" Hulcher, Medical Detachment, said that at the new location the medics set up in an old mill which had a generator to propel electric lights. Snow also began to fall. Co. A shelled some houses in Thiaville; Co. B was with the 156th and 220th Field Artillery battalions but did no firing; all of Co. C was at rest in the rear, and elements of Co. D were at Bruyeres and La Baffe. The 11th found Co. C supporting the 397th Infantry, where Capt. Smith reported, "We keep gradually moving, but it isn't fun or glorious, and it's colder than the hinges of Hades and getting colder. Two of my platoons had to be in a new position before daylight this morning, and I'm waiting for ammunition to be loaded to guide them up to the new dump."40

A number of changes took place on the 12th. Co. A was relieved from supporting the 398th Infantry and ordered to the rear to be held in division reserve and to re-equip and reorganize. Co. B was released from attachment to the 156th and 220th Field Artillery battalions and attached to the 71st Infantry, 44th Infantry Division. The goal of the 71st was to attack enemy positions on the Blamont-Gondrexange line the next morning and to protect the right flank of the division, the main objective of the 44th being to secure the high ground north of Saarbourg. Meanwhile, Co. C supported the 397th Infantry, 100th Infantry Division, in various actions around Bertrichamps. Information was also received that Co. D of the 83rd and one company of the 3rd Chemical Battalion would be attached to the 103rd Infantry Division on or about November 14th. Lt. Col. Efnor also requested an additional 3,500 rounds of ammo although he was informed only 2,500 were available and not to fire the allotment until after November 20th unless given clearance.41

Sgt. Woodson T. Kimbrough, Co. B, from Monroe County, Mississippi, acting as a liaison at the infantry CP, was killed in an attack on the 13th. Also that day a fire of undetermined origin in the 2nd Platoon CP of Co. C at Bertichamps caused the loss of 346 HE, 135 WP, and three mortars, putting the position temporarily out of action. Capt. Robert B. ("Smitty") Smith earned a Bronze Star in this action in which, according to the citation, the fire was caused by a direct hit on the dump during an enemy artillery barrage. The fire spread debris and shell fragments over a nearby main supply route and, "... while shells continued to explode, Captain Smith directed his men to a safe area and assisted in the removal of the debris. He then aided in displacing four mortars. His leadership and courage enabled ambulances and supply vehicles to continue their missions and the platoon to resume its supporting fire." This supported the complimentary remarks of the commander of the 397th on November 13th, who reported the mortar fire of Co. C during an action on the previous day "resulted in 70 casualties from an enemy company of 120 men, 31 casualties from [an] enemy platoon of 43 men, and 10 men left from a platoon en route to reinforce." More praise was given the company on the 14th when the Engineers reported "... that enemy entrenchments in the vicinity of Le Chique had been thoroughly swept" by Co. C's mortars. The report added, "Many graves observed in vicinity." Co. B performed admirably as well, while Co. A rested and re-equipped in the St. Benoit vicinity, and Co. D was still relatively inactive at Bruyeres and La Baffe. George Borkhuis, Co. D, said that during this time a lot of snow had fallen and he recently "saw a pasture in which were at least 50 dead cows. It seems the farmer let his herd into a German minefield and they were all killed. A costly mistake."42

On November 15th, Lt. Alfred H. Crenshaw returned to the battalion from his detached duty in Italy with Lt.

Col. Hutchinson training two new chemical units. Co. B assisted in an attack on Avricourt and Co. C had one man slightly injured in the fight for Thiaville. The journal of the 397th Infantry stated Co. C, of the 83rd fired smoke to obscure enemy observation. William Ford, Co. C, wrote, "As we prepared to make our advance on and into Thiaville, the enemy mounted an all out counterattack. They unloaded on us with 88mm artillery and mortar fire, directly into our rifle companies, and even into our mortar pit positions. Their shelling had zeroed-in on us." Co. D's 2nd Platoon moved to Luoux and then bivouacked at La Baffe. Only Co. C remained in action in the rain on the 16th as they hit points around Thiaville and Raon L' Etape. Co. B did no firing, and companies A and D were held in division reserve.[43]

HQ Co. was at Rambervillers on the 17th while some confusion developed as Capt. Smith, Co. C, had to check with Lt. Col. Efnor regarding the assignment of the company to either the 397th or 398th Infantry regiments. None of the four companies did any firing and Co. D's rear moved from La Baffe to Belmont while the platoons remained at La Baffe. As Co. A remained in division reserve on the 18th, Co. B moved along a railroad via Avricourt to Rechicourt; Co. C assisted the 398th Infantry around Hill 515 and St. Blaise; and Co. D, supporting the 143rd Infantry, advanced their remaining platoons and HQ from La Baffe to Belmont.[44]

Three enlisted men of Co. B, including S/Sgt. James Jack of Cape May County, New Jersey, and T/5 William G. ("Bill") Schlachter of Pennsylvania, were lightly wounded and evacuated on the 19th as Rechicourt received heavy shelling. Co. C maintained their fire around St. Blaise and fired 320 rounds of smoke at targets and 330 HE for the 397th Infantry at Raon L' Etape. Capt. Lakey, Co. D, returned and reported to the battalion CP. George Borkhuis, Co. D, wrote home, "The weather is warming ... snow is only on the slopes ... U.S. planes are having a field day bombing Jerry." On the 20th, Co. B screened troops crossing the Marne Canal and moved to Neufmolines while Co. D located near La Cato and southeast of Anould. During one stage in the movements they received a direct hit from a 20mm gun mounted on a flak wagon but no casualties resulted. Lt. Col. Efnor wrote Col. Maurice Barker at Edgewood Arsenal, "Lakey is now back with the outfit, but gun-fire gives him severe headaches. He would make a good officer for you back at the School. If 7th Army were to be asked if he would be available, the answer would be yes." An awards ceremony was held at Rambervillers where Brig. Gen. John S. Winn, Jr., of the 100th Infantry Division presented the 83rd Chemical Battalion with four Silver Stars, two Soldier's Medals, 17 Bronze Stars, and nine Purple Hearts. Among the Silver Star recipients was Lt. Justin G. Woomer, a platoon leader in Co. D, who "... crossed 1,500 yards of open ground under kraut fire to repair a broken communication line from a gun position to a CP." Pvt. Mack C. Webb, Co. C, from Habersham County, Georgia, was presented a Soldier's Medal for "... his action when Co. C's bivouac was bombed. Ammunition and mortar equipment were hit and one case of white phosphorous was set afire. At the risk of his life and ignoring his own burns, Webb removed a smoldering shell from an ammo dump, submerged it in water - thus preventing further explosions and probably high casualties among his company."[45]

Among those awarded the Bronze Star for various previous actions were: Capt. Edward L. Trey, Lt. Lewis Cameron, Lt. Robert D. Danfield, Lt. Andrew J. Connolly, 1st Sgt. Michele ("Mike") Codega, S/Sgt. Wofford Jackson, Sgt. Stephen A. Morse, Pfc. Leonard G. Blystone, T/5 William L. Jordan, T/5 L. W. Wiggins, T/5 Henry E. Fajkowski, Corp. Jacob L. Portner, Pvt. William L. Garner, Pvt. Robert W. Baldwin, Sgt. Seymour A. Holstein, Pvt. Lawrence E. Yost, and Pfc. Marion E. Bailey. This was also the day George Borkhuis, Co. D, said the men finally were issued sleeping bags.[46]

The battalion CP moved from the Rambervillers and Menil-sur-Belvitte area to Raon L'Etape on the 21st, where it rained nearly every day. Writing in his diary, "Doc" Hulcher described the town and accommodations for himself and his medics, stating, "... a beautiful town of about 15,000 but which had seen lots of war. It was a Jerry strong point. But the front was breaking and advance was moving nicely. We [*the medical staff*] stayed in a beautiful home here ... the medics set up in a house across the street and were given [*a*] royal welcome by the civilians. This is the home of little John, a cute little fellow of 5 or 6 years who took the G. I.'s completely and when we left he cried hard. Had our Thanksgiving dinner here [*Nov. 23rd*] and it was good."[47]

While Co. A remained in division reserve, Cpl. Lawrence G. Ertzberger, from Martin County, Georgia, had a somewhat humorous experience, recalled by Sam Bundy. According to Bundy, "Cpl. Ertzberger seems to have made a furlough out of his one-day pass which he got last Saturday morning. He returned this evening, had been picked up by MP's for not wearing a helmet, and put in the stockade. His pass had expired when they vgot him and he was carrying a pistol which a friend gave him (concealed). Poor Ertzy says they put him in a small dark room and fed K-Rations to him thru a tiny window." Bundy also said this was the date the men turned in two blankets in exchange for sleeping bags. Co. B moved to Bebing and was also placed in division reserve, although shortly afterward they were ordered to advance as part of the RCT, 324th Infantry. Co. C supported the 397th Infantry but did no firing while Co. D registered a total of 200 HE and 496 WP.[48]

The next day, November 22nd, the chemical officer of the VI Corps told Maj. Mindrum to attach the 1st Platoon of Co. A to the 191st Infantry, 36th Infantry Division, and to send them to the vicinity of St. Die, although the remainder of the company continued to be held in reserve. Co. B, supporting the 324th Infantry, 44th Division, moved behind a cannon company through Sarrelltroff to Hilbesheim, Lixeim, and bivouacked at Metting. Co. C remained mobile with the 397th Infantry and Co. D gave strong supporting fire to the 143rd Infantry. The company's White Platoon moved to St. Leonard. The G-4 of the 36th Infantry Division reported Co. D of the 83rd had 3,000 rounds of 4.2 ammo at present and felt that would be sufficient to replace any ammo supply deficiencies of the platoon that was to be attached that night. Battalion HQ moved to Baccarat, a town known for its glassware. Detachment No. 3, 11th Chemical Maintenance, traveled from Rambervillers to Raon L'Etape, where they billeted in an empty house and set up shop in a nearby garage.[49]

On November 23rd at Baccarat, Daniel Shields, HQ Co., said he had a huge Thanksgiving meal, while Sam Kweskin, with his trousers outside his leggings, said he was approached by Capt. Robert Edwards, who angrily told Company Clerk Miles Storey, "Write up court martial proceedings against this man." Edwards scolded Kweskin for the sloppy apparel and stomped from the room, whereupon Storey told Sam, "He's nuts," and nothing more was ever said or heard of the incident. Co. A was in the vicinity of St. Benoit enjoying their Thanksgiving, recalled by Charles Rolling, who wrote, "Fairly good meal but I have had better," and James Helsel added, "We had a very nice Thanksgiving dinner; chicken with all the trimmings and we eat it with all the comforts of home." On the other hand, Lt. Robert J. Bush, with the company's 1st Platoon sent to St. Die, said it was a "miserable Thanksgiving." Co. B departed Metting, moved through Eschbourg, the Eschbourg-Dossenheim Pass, and arrived at Saarbourg. Co. C continued in mobile capacity and Co. D took up positions north of Anould and outside St. Leonard, as well as the town of Mandray.[50]

St. Benoit, France, November 1944. Sitting, L-R: William P. Bailey, Albert E. Sereni, and Joseph M. Comaty. Standing, L-R: Samuel M. Bundy, Charles L. Plumly, Leonard W. Turan, and Paul Oplinger. *Turan Collection*

The battalion CP closed at Raon L'Etape on the 24th and moved to Le Hercholet, about 15 miles deep into the Vosges Mountains. "Doc" Hulcher described the location and populace, writing, "Still lots of rain. Again we [*the medical staff*] set up in a beautiful chateau in which I have a private area. We were the first Americans [*to enter*] this town and what a reception. All the people came out and wanted officers to stay in their homes. Germans had likewise been here days ago. C Co. & A Co. were relieved. The town gave big receptions & celebrations for them including a dance. Everyone is happy. The advance has moved rapidly and much equipment & supplies captured. All land this side of Rhine has practically been liberated. Then it will be on into Germany. The people here are grand. They have continuously brought out their best liquor and entertained us every evening." All four companies held their basic positions and did no firing, although this would be the official date given for the beginning of Co. D's part in the eventual victory of Alsace in the Vosges. 1st Lt. Fred G. Rand, Jr., recalled, "The Germans were burning the towns of Alsace. They told the people of St. Marie-aux-Mines their town would be burned 25 November. We moved into the town 24 November and saved their town. My platoon moved into a three-story book bindery and printing plant. The wife of the owner (she spoke English) welcomed us but warned us of danger of fire with the paper, etc. We stayed there a few days …" To the pleasure of Lt. Robert J. Bush, Co. A, the 1st Platoon was relieved from the 36th Division and returned to St. Benoit from St. Die.[51]

Co. A moved from St. Benoit to a chateau in Moyenmoutier on the 25th, and then advanced and relieved Co. C at St. Blaise le Roche, staying in a textile factory. Co. C then moved to Le Petite Raon and went into division reserve. Detachment No. 3, 11th Chemical Maintenance, also moved to Le Petite Raon, billeting in an empty house and setting up a repair shop in a cellar. Co. B moved from Dossenheim to Newviller and Co. D held their position with the 143rd. HQ Co. moved to Moussey.[52]

The 100th Infantry Division was relieved from the sector on the 26th while Co. A assembled near Moyenmoutier at a large cotton mill and Co. C at Le Petite Raon. Co. C's Capt. Smith reported, "We have been doing a pretty good job for these people and have built quite a reputation for the Division." Co. B kept with the 324th Infantry and was posted at Newviller as their rear moved from Saarbourg to Saverne. The rear of Co. D moved from Belmont to St. Marie-aux-Mines while the remainder of the company was in the Raumont area. With both Co. A at Moyenmoutier and Co. C at La Petite Raon in Corps Reserve on the 27th, Co. B moved to St. Marie-aux-Mines while Co. D was ordered to the regimental assembly area at Brouvillers. Numerous Allied bombers also flew over the battalion CP during the night.[53]

The situation for companies A, C, and D saw little change on the 28th, but Co. B was released from the 324th Infantry and attached to the 114th Infantry, 44th Infantry Division. Afterward they moved into the town of Struth where they received heavy enemy mortar fire, which killed T/5 Arthur Collins of Montgomery County, Georgia [*although he had also been reported killed on LST 422 at Anzio*], and wounded T/5 Frederick L. LeFever of New Columbia, Pennsylvania, and T/5 James D. Thomas, Jr., of Tennessee, both of whom were evacuated. The shelling also destroyed some battalion vehicles. Lt. Col. Efnor returned from VI Corps and 36th Infantry Division with orders to attach the 83rd Chemical Battalion, minus companies B and D, to the 36th Infantry Division and to assemble near Wisembach the next day.[54]

Battalion CP moved south in the Vosges Mountains to Wisembach on the 29th as did Detachment No. 3, 11th Chemical Maintenance, which quartered in an old school house and set up their repair shop in a nearby empty garage. The Medical Detachment was included in the move, which "Doc" Hulcher described as "… back thru St. Die to area around St. Mancie. HQ set up in Wisembach. Set up our aid station in 'Fricks Café', St. Die was some place. The Germans had practically destroyed everything east of [*the*] river. I walked down one street on [*the*] west side of [*the*] river and every house and store on one side of [*the*] street had been gutted while all houses on [*the*] other side of [*the*] street were undamaged … I had a big civilian practice at Wisembach, as many as 10 pts. [*patients*] at one time ranging in age from 3 or 4 yrs. to 60 and received for services lots of food & 'schnapps'. Had few casualties among our own men."[55]

Co. A was at Verpelliere, although some members said they were at a town called Le Hohwald, and Co. C was stationed at Fraize, both in division reserve, 36th Infantry Division. Capt. Smith, Co. C, received a message from the commanding officer of the 397th Infantry commending "… the aggressive and effective work of your company … on all occasions you have been well forward and anxious to fire on all appropriate targets, and that you have done so

Chateau de Moussey, where a time bomb exploded and injured a few men of HQ Co., on November 30, 1944. *Codega Collection*

most effectively." Smith later wrote that such an award " … helps morale and makes the boys more willing to work hard and risk their necks. Funny how human nature is, but a pat on the back sometimes makes people do strange things. I guess that's why they give medals, and that, too, keeps people doing foolish things." Orders came through to attach Co. A to the 142nd Infantry and Co. C to the 141st Infantry. Co. B, with the 114th Infantry, 44th Division, received some shelling but no casualties or damage resulted.

Co. D, with the 143rd Infantry, stood ready to move if needed.[56]

In an attempt to place HQ and HQ Co. in close proximity to the weapons companies on the 30th, an isolated location was found about twenty miles north of St. Die in the Vosges called Moussey. Two officers from HQ, Capt. Ed Trey and Maj. John P. McEvoy, went out in a drizzling rain to investigate an elaborate chateau at the edge of the town for any booby-traps or bombs in order to set up battalion CP. The Maison Laederich, Chateau de Moussey, a large mansion owned by an absentee utilities magnate, was approached from a long, gravel driveway which led from an iron gate. The house was located about a block or two, depending upon source, from the gate and was surrounded by forest. Trey and McEvoy made a thorough search of the premises, including the coal bin, and declared the house safe. Most of HQ had never seen such an estate and jumped at the opportunity to sleep in warm beds. The house was also furnished with the finest furniture, art, porcelain, and a library of rare first edition books. Maj. Gordon Mindrum ordered the men not to "liberate" any of these items and to respect private property.[57]

Sam Kweskin, HQ Co. and official artist of the battalion, who wrote two slightly differing accounts of his experience at Moussey, slept in an upstairs bedroom in a huge bed he shared with Cpl. Dave Chapman, the chaplain's assistant, the chaplain no longer being a part of the battalion. Sometime between one and five in the morning, probably the latter, [*Sam Kweskin gives both times*] of the 30th a timed, approximately 100 lb. dynamite land mine, hidden behind the pantry wall in a coal bin in the basement, detonated and wounded Charles P. Cella, Jr., of Pennsylvania, who was on guard, and Cpl. Paul Cuva of Essex County, New Jersey, on break in the kitchen, both members of HQ and HQ Co. Cuva had just come off guard duty and was walking into the kitchen for some hot coffee served by Sgt. George Borkhuis. The two injured men were eventually sent stateside and recovered. Sam Kweskin vividly remembered the incident, writing, "… a terrifying blast awoke us. I jumped out of bed wearing only a sweat shirt and olive drab shorts, grabbed my carbine, threw my feet into my shoes, and ran out into the hall. There was the smell of dust and plaster and concrete in the air, and as I looked down to the first floor I could see that the ornate winding staircase was now a jumble of wood and stone. Plaster and broken sticks stood out from where the staircase had been. Dust still rose in the air as others gathered below us. Somehow we were able to cautiously make our way over the rubble, and when we were satisfied that this had not been a prelude to an armed attack, Chapman and I made it back up the topsy-turvey stone and brick and wood to our room where we gathered our gear and came down again."[58]

In a slightly varied account, Kweskin said that after he and Chapman slipped on their boots and grabbed their carbines and ran out of their room to investigate, "Doug Swayze and Jake Miringoff [*Douglas A. Swayze and Jacob Miringoff, both of the Medical Detachment*] ran by, both having been knocked out of bed. The whole center of the Chateau was demolished -- Captain Robert Edwards said when he looked out the door on the second floor, he could see all the way to the basement." After struggling to the first floor, Kweskin and Chapman "... ran out into the cold, and saw Sergeant Kermit ["*Jerky*"] Jorgensen throwing a blanket over the body of Paul Cuva, who had a head and hand injury."[59]

Although not mentioned in the official journals it is believed that Lt. Lester L. Henry, Co. A, was also injured in the explosion and was treated for concussion and temporary blindness, including hazy vision in his right eye. One man who managed to avoid the incident was radioman Mario Ricci who had opted to sleep on the ground outdoors. He said he had become accustomed to roughing it and did not want to get spoiled by sleeping in luxury, which proved to be a wise decision on his part.[60]

Miraculously, there were no fatalities or other injuries at the Chateau at Moussey, but the brass decided it was not a secure place and had the men evacuate the premises. Sam Kweskin also noted that within the next few days HQ Co. moved to a large house in the town of Lusse.[61]

In other events of the day, Co. A provided some WP for the 142nd RCT, although it was rumored the 1st Platoon, which was not engaged, got drunk. Co. B was the recipient of a large enemy barrage which wounded four men, forcing two to be evacuated. Among the wounded were Pvt. Richard Watson of Adams County, Illinois, and Pfc. Hugel Willard of East Rutherford County, Tennessee. Additionally, three vehicles were badly damaged. Co. C supported the 141st Infantry in a reconnaissance of road blocks near La Bonhomme and Co. D held ready to move.[62]

During November, the 83rd Chemical Battalion fired 8,997 HE and 4,146 WP for a total of 13,143 rounds. Casualties included six wounded or injured requiring hospitalization, two seriously wounded, and two killed, for a total of 10. Detachment No. 1, 11th Chemical Maintenance, made nine aiming stake lights for the battalion during the month and Detachment No. 3 repaired a total of 23 barrels, 49 standards, and 27 baseplate assemblies, along with 47 stakes and one light. They also salvaged three baseplates and three stakes.[63]

December 1944 opened with the line of the 36th Infantry Division "... extended roughly from Selestat south and west to a point about 6 kilometers southeast of Ribeauville; thence due west to join the left flank of the First French Army." The mission was simply stated to "... seize Colmar and drive the enemy across the Rhine." On the first day of the month, Co. A of the 83rd was attached to the 142nd RCT Infantry, 36th Infantry Division. James Helsel, of the 2nd Platoon, wrote, "... early this morning we moved into a position about 300 yards from the front lines. We had to be very quiet in setting up our guns ... we were out of range and the right section is with us now. The Germans sure left here in a hurry, for a lot of their equipment was left, including rations and their sardines aren't bad. I had myself about three cans. This evening we moved up this road and set up beside a saw mill. We are staying in a cellar of a house just across the road and the wine is about two feet deep on the floor." Co. B, attached to the 114th Infantry, 44th Infantry Division, continued shelling Struth. During the action it was discovered and reported that civilians hidden in a building near a gun position were intercepting radio messages and relaying them to the enemy. The G-2 also informed the company that civilian sniper groups intent on harassing the rear were posted in towns north and northeast. Soon afterward the company rear moved to Bickenholtz. Co. C, attached to the 141st RCT, 36th Infantry Division, remained heavily engaged while Co. D, attached to the 143rd Infantry, moved to a new position without firing.[64]

Co. A advanced on December 2nd to the vicinity of Selestat, where the 2nd Platoon set up in the yard of a former German ordnance plant, while their forward CP located at Chatenois and the company's rear elements were at Lievpre. Co. B was relieved from the 44th Infantry Division,15th Corps, then departed Struth and arrived at the company rear at Bickenholtz. At this location repairs were made on their damaged vehicles. Co. C continued to engage the enemy while Capt. Smith said, "... we are in a nice place for our company CP so I am making the most of it while I can. We have hot and cold running water, a wash basin in each room, and an indoor latrine. In fact, we have taken over a hotel for the company rear in a town that we were fighting for less than a week ago, and it isn't touched. We don't have electric lights but do have a Coleman lantern which does just about as well. The people here are fairly friendly, and some of them are beginning to come back into town now, although nearly all of them speak German as well as French, and of course you can't be sure of any of them. The owner of the hotel was in custody of the Free French as a possible collaborator but got out yesterday, but still appears to be a little bit sullen ... it is quite something to be quartered in a hotel when it's so darn cold outside ... the platoons are not so well situated, and it has been my wont to spend most of my time with them, anyway." Capt. Smith correctly assumed his stay at the hotel would be of short duration as orders arrived to move out in the morning. This provoked him to write, "... maybe we'll capture another town by and by that we beat the other people into and can get the hotel or at least a school house. Damn these Krauts anyway. There's one lying just up the street with both his arms, part of his chest, and part of his head blown off. He let one of his own mines go off in his face, and as far as I'm concerned, he's just another rung in the ladder home. Yes, it's a pretty dirty business; we didn't get that commendation for playing Ring Around the Rosy."[65]

The 1st Platoon of Co. D had five rounds of 150mm shells land in their gun positions but suffered no casualties. The 2nd Platoon of the company, while firing on Aubure, had Sgt. Louis W. Slagle of Tennessee injured as he fired the mortar and was evacuated. More importantly, later the French government would award the French Croix De Guerre With Palm to Co. D for their performance in France from their landing at Le Muy, but with particular emphasis on the period from November 24th to December 2nd. The citation read, in part, "Executing a daring maneuver, it seized by surprise attack, the pass and town of St.-Marie-aux-Mines, in spite of a very difficult terrain and the savage resistance of the enemy. Following up immediately, it occupied Ste-Croix-aux-Mines, Rombac-Le-Franc, and Haru-Koenigsburg, broke into the place of Alsace and seized Selestat ... this established a wide breach in the German defense system ..."[66]

THE COLMAR POCKET
December 3 – 20

The battalion CP, along with Detachment No. 3, 11th Chemical Maintenance, moved from Wisembach to St. Marie-aux-Mines, a distance of 4.5 miles, on the 3rd. A fort and ditch observed by Lt. Robert D. Danfield of Laurel Springs, New Jersey, a man who according to Clovis Birdwell did not like to wear his lieutenant bars, came under the mortar fire of Co. A. Reorganization and repairs continued with Co. B prior to being alerted for a movement. Elements of Co. C saw action in the vicinity of St. Marie-aux-Mines and the 2nd Platoon was displaced to Aubere. Co. D's 1st Platoon was also engaged at Aubere while a 2nd Platoon's gun position came under enemy shell fire while setting up to fire on Ribeauville.[67]

A bit of good news arrived on the 4th when the 7th Army called with an allotment of passes to Paris for the battalion, limited to a quota of 15 enlisted men and two officers, the battalion required to furnish their own transportation. The ordnance department of the 36th Infantry Division at St. Croix-aux-Mines reported a lieutenant from the 83rd had come to see Col. Green about drawing some jeep tires and tubes. He said he needed them bad and the 46th Ordnance could not help him. Co. A supported an attack of the 142nd Infantry on Hirtesgerten; Co. B moved by convoy from Bickenholtz to bivouac at Wisembach; Co. C gave continued fire support to the 141st Infantry; and Co. D performed likewise with the 143rd Infantry at Ribeauville.[68]

ZELLENBERG
December 5 – 11

On the fifth day of the month the rear CP of HQ Detachment opened a new CP in the area of St. Croix-aux-Mines. Sam Kweskin, HQ Co., said they quartered in "... a palatial baroque building that had recently housed the Swiss legation." Co. A kept up their heavy support of the 142nd Infantry; Co. B continued their reorganization and repairs at Wisembach; and Co. C fired numerous rounds in support of the 141st Infantry. At Ribeauville, the 1st Platoon of Co. D fired on the road south of Aubere then moved to Zellenberg, where they came under heavy enemy fire while positioned in a town square surrounded by some stone houses. Lt. Alfred Forrester reported five men wounded, including S/Sgt. Clark H. Riddle of Greensburg, Pennsylvania, whose leg had to be amputated following evacuation; Cpl. Antonio ("Tony") Rabaiotti of Providence, Rhode Island; Pfc. Lawrence E. ("Larry") Yost; Pfc. Alfred E. Green, Jr., of Fairfield County, Connecticut, who was also evacuated; and Pvt. John J. Pohorellec.[69]

Alfred E. Green, Jr., remembered the horrific day as he wrote, "On the morning of December 5th, 1944 we moved in the early A.M. into the town of Zellenberg. As best as I can recall it was about 5:00 or 7:00 A.M. and snowing very heavy. As we were positioning our mortars and equipment the Germans shelled the village ... Several of our group were hit with shrapnel, of which Sgt. Clark Riddle and I were two of them. From there out I was treated by medics, and then Sgt. Clark Riddle and I were loaded on the top two racks on a jeep. There was another G.I. located on a

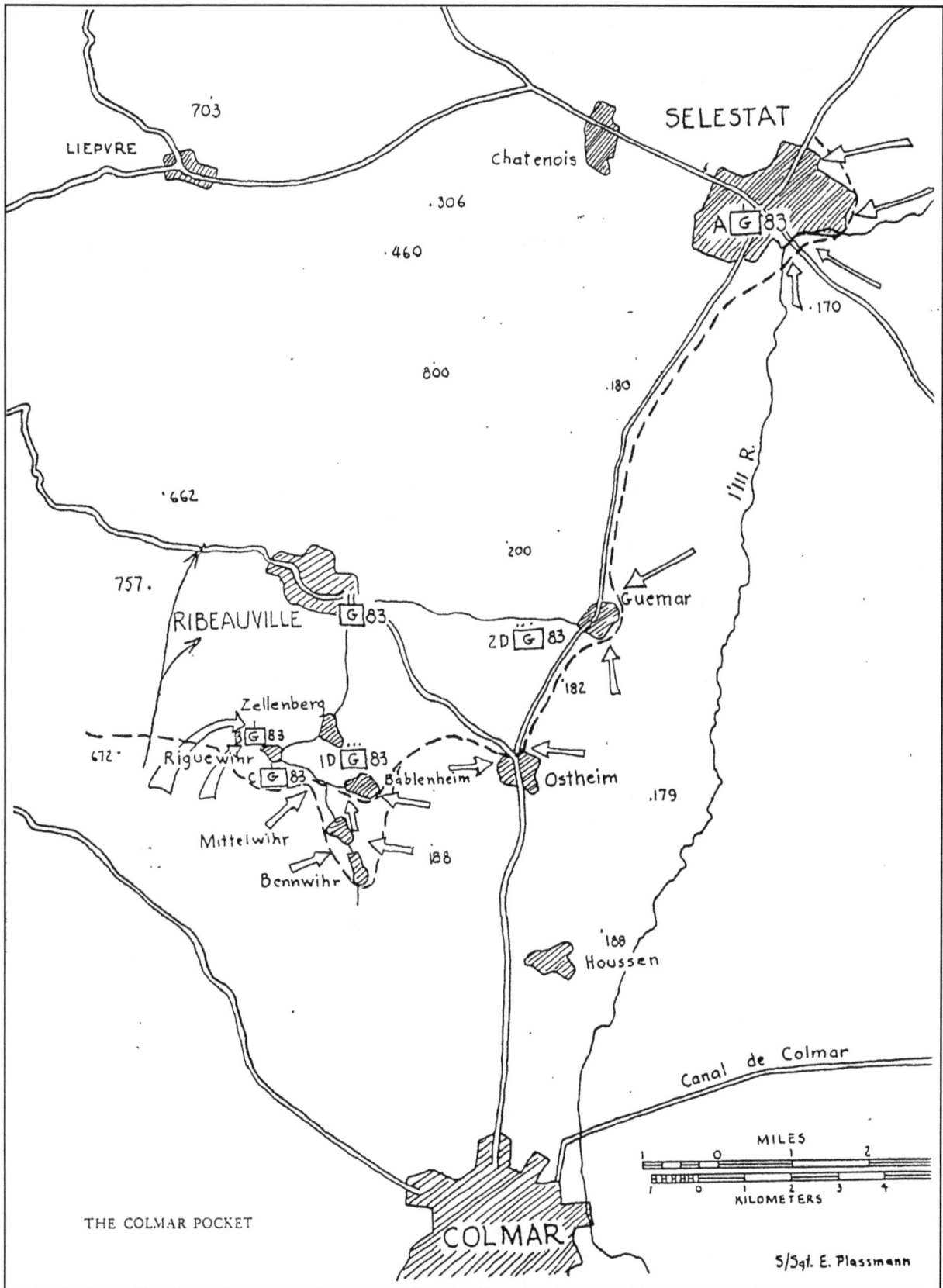

THE COLMAR POCKET

Colmar Pocket showing positions of the 83rd drawn by S/Sgt Eugene Plassmann, HQ Co. *Eugene Plassmann*

Sgt. Clark Riddle, Co. D, seriously wounded and evacuated at Zellenberg. His leg was later amputated.

Clark Riddle

stretcher alongside the jeep driver. We proceeded down the mountain roads (snowing like hell) to a medic station. At the medic station I lost track of Clark Riddle ... I was shipped to a tent hospital in Epinal. As I was hit with 24 pieces of shrapnel, they operated and removed many of the larger pieces. I still have several small pieces of shrapnel that remain in both legs, arm, and hand."[70]

Lee Steedle also recalled the episode, writing, "Ammo had come up under cover of darkness, and we were firing constantly. The counter-fire came in accurately, and toward morning Clark Riddle, our Platoon Sergeant, received a gaping leg wound. The field ambulance having already been warned away by German artillery rounds, our casualties were being evacuated by gutsy jeep drivers. Clark was tied to a jeep hood, and they raced down the totally exposed Zellenberg road, chased by kraut machine-gun fire ... A week later we heard the leg had become gangrenous and had to be amputated." Steedle also noted, "All but one man was indoors when we were slammed by a heavy concussion that rocked the very walls. We heard the shutters crack from shrapnel as our man cried out. Our own shell had exploded as an air burst. We pulled him into the house, and then saw how lucky he had been. Just one big fragment in his ass... He'd bent over to drop a shell down the barrel, and it hit a wire just over the eave of our house. He'd forgotten to check the elevation every few rounds."[71]

The 1st Platoon of Co. D, along with two tanks, would spend six days under direct enemy fire, unaware for a time their position was being relayed to the Germans via radio by a 70-year old civilian hiding in one of the houses. Lee Steedle stated, "Accurate incoming mortar fire continued to cost us casualties ... Sometimes before we'd even send the first shell on its way, the incoming rounds would come softly fluffing and then blasting into our square, which was littered by loose cobbles, empty ammo tubes, chunks of masonry and tiles from wall and roofs. We were needed on our guns. The krauts by now had established their forward line somewhere in the vines just below us. We were now firing with only a half powder ring, barely enough to propel the shell away, and it traveled only about 300 yards. No one had slept. The squad leaders and gunners particularly, were reaching the edge of exhaustion ... Each of our four mortars was set on a slightly different heading, and its barrel never cooled. As each of our 25-pound shells arched into the sky, you could follow its arc with your eyes and hear its nine pounds of TNT blast among the thick rows of grapevines just below us." At the end of the nerve-wracking six days at Zellenberg, the 1st Platoon of Co. D had 11 casualties out of 34 men, consisting of nine wounded and two men suffering from shell shock and battle fatigue. Steedle said, "Zellenberg was by far the worst position I experienced in the entire war."[72]

V-Mail sketch of Alfred Green, Co. D, made by an unknown artist while recovering in England from his Zellenberg wounds. *Alfred Green*

The 2nd Platoon of Co. D helped to break up an enemy counterattack on the 5th in which it was reported that "70% of the attacking enemy forces were casualties from mortar fire. The other 30% were taken prisoner and were dazed by [the] terrible concussion of our heavy barrage."[73]

The two platoons of Co. A fired a total of 142 HE and 16 WP on the 6th. Co. B's two platoons at Wisembach moved to Ribeauville where the forward CP was established. The 1st Platoon moved to Zellenberg; the 2nd Platoon 500 yards north of Riquewihr. At St. Marie-aux-Mines both platoons of Co. C bivouacked and were relieved from supporting the 141st Infantry, 36th Infantry Division. Co. D maintained fire on such areas as Beblenheim, Hill 251, Mittelwihr, Guemar, and Ostheim.[74]

Orders were received on December 7th relieving the 83rd Chemical Battalion from VI Corps and placing the organization under control of the First French Army. Co. A fired 59 HE and 10 WP. Company lieutenants Robert J. Bush and Leonard R. Kenney visited the OP and were nearly hit by large shells the Germans began throwing in the area.

Charles Rolling, Co. A, wrote, "Tried out new base-plate. Works very well." Co. B, with elements at Ribeauville, Zellenberg, and Wisembach gave strong support to the infantry. The 2nd Platoon was relieved from the 143rd Infantry and attached to the 141st Infantry, and the rear CP of the company moved from Wisembach to HQ rear at St. Croix-aux-Mines. Co. C was at Val-de-Ville in division reserve, although Capt. Robert B. Smith brought in two German prisoners to the battalion CP. With the company CP at St. Marie-aux-Mines, Co. D's 1st Platoon blasted away at tanks and machine guns in the strong enemy positions at Mittelwihr and Bennwihr. During one action, Lt. Justin G. Woomer "… observed several direct hits on a group of Germans, one of which flew 5

L-R: Byron Jordan, John Sawyer, unidentified, Laurence Fagan, and Leo Kurtenbach, all from Co. B. Sawyer was killed and Fagan wounded at Riquewihr. *Byron Jordan*

or 6 feet into the air." The 2nd Platoon of Co. D registered on such places as Ostheim and Guemar. At one stage, however, after successfully firing two rounds of HE, the third shell burst in the barrel, killing Sgt. George G. Young of Mobile, Alabama, and seriously wounding Pvt. John C. Shaffner. This would prove to be an ominous omen of events to come.[75]

Co. A, attached to the 142nd Infantry, remained in the Selestat area and fired on numerous targets on the 8th while Co. B, with their rear CP at St. Croix-aux-Mines, shelled available targets. Co. C rested in division reserve at Val-de-Ville, and Co. D's 1st Platoon again spent the day silencing tanks, machine guns, and other targets of interest at Mittelwihr, Hill 251, and Bennwihr. The 2nd Platoon received information from a prisoner of a planned German attack which never materialized. Lt. Col. Efnor sent a letter to the chemical officer of the 7th Army regarding the M-II rapid fire sights and said it was "necessary to have more aiming stake lights." On the 9th of the month, Co. A was engaged at Selestat; Co. B fired on Kientzheim; Co. C continued in division reserve at Val-de-Ville; and Co. D shelled tanks and other targets in support of attacks of the 143rd Infantry on Mittelwihr and Bennwihr. According to "Doc" Hulcher, part of the Medical Detachment moved to Ribeauville in the Rhine Valley, where he said he got his first glimpse of Germany across the valley. He added, "We set up in a nice home but this was the nicest place I'd been in in France. We had lots of artillery come into town. My view reminded me of days at Anzio for we could see the whole valley and the shells bursting out there. Colmar could be seen off to our left … While up there at Ribeauville we saw lots of action day & night along with lots of live bombing."[76]

Lt. Col. Efnor informed the G-4 of the 36th Infantry Division that the battalion could not continue at the "present rate of expenditure of 4.2" ammo without increased allocation." He stated that the allocation for the period November 20-December 20 of 300 HE and 300 WP per battalion per day would not suffice because for the past three days the 83rd had fired about 1,600-2,000 rounds of HE and 50 rounds of WP per day. Withdrawals had nearly depleted the accumulated credits. Further complicating the situation, Captain and S-4 Ed Trey reported that for the past three days the 83rd had fired 2,651 rounds of HE. Soon afterward Efnor would clarify that Trey's figures represented a smaller time segment. As a result, the G-4 of the 36th Infantry Division informed the 83rd on the 10th that they would be issued 1,000 HE and 750 WP per day until December 31st.[77]

Also on the 10th, Co. A sustained their fire with 107 HE and 25 WP; Co. B fired on Kientzheim again, and their rear CP moved from St. Croix-aux-Mines to Ribeauville, thence to the northeast end of Riquewihr; Co. C was still in division reserve at Val-de-Ville; and the 2nd Platoon of Co. D received a direct hit from a tank but no casualties resulted.[78]

Lt. Col. Efnor departed on December 11th for the 7th Army in the vicinity of Saverne as the battalion CP moved, along with Detachment No. 3, 11th Chemical Maintenance, from St. Marie-aux-Mines to Ribeauville, a distance of

Earl Wellington Rapp

Earl Rapp, Co. B, in France.

Rich Rapp

Earl Wellington Rapp, nicknamed "Rappy", was born May 20, 1921 in Corunna, Michigan, the son of a plant inspector. Rapp first garnered athletic notice in high school at Swedesboro, New Jersey lettering in baseball, basketball, football, and track. His prowess at baseball, though, launched a career in the sport, starting with five seasons in the minor leagues. He signed his first professional baseball contract with the Philadelphia Phillies in 1940 and played for teams in the Canadian-American League and the Northern League.

Earl enlisted in the U.S. Army September 20, 1942 at Baltimore, Maryland and was soon undergoing basic training with the 83rd Chemical (Motorized) Battalion at Camp Gordon, Augusta, Georgia. While at Camp Gordon, from 1942 – 1943, he once again displayed his multi-athletic abilities, not only in baseball, but in basketball, football, track, boxing, and table tennis. When the 83rd went overseas to fight the Axis powers Earl proved himself a more than capable soldier, earning a Silver Star and Purple Heart. Veteran Sam Kweskin recalled his first encounter with Rapp, who had just escaped capture by hiding under a bridge, writing, "I was already with HQ when Rapp was jeeped in, exhausted and wet, to tell of that December night that a B company platoon was overrun near Riquewihr. We lost about 6 men and another few captured by an SS 'graduating class'. That was the day that Lt.[*Walter*] Hauser asked ME (!) behind him riding shotgun in a jeep where we should go for his liaison first – B company or D, and I just said D 'cause I had served with them. What a lucky decision – since at that moment they (Co. B) were being overrun."

Rapp was wounded during the war in the tendons behind the knee, which would hamper his running ability and affect his baseball career. At the close of the war he was a Sergeant in Co. B and returned to civilian life to play baseball in the minor leagues. He noted that his greatest moment in the minors was a home run during the 16th inning in 1947 to win a game for Buffalo of the International League. The following year he joined the Seattle Raniers where he hit .298 with 26 doubles, 17 homers, and 96 rbi's. He advanced to the majors in 1949, where he assisted the Detroit Tigers and Chicago White Sox, hitting .259 in 20 games.

In 1950 Earl Rapp returned to the Pacific Coast League as center fielder and in mid-season of 1951 returned to the majors with the New York Giants, and later, the St. Louis Browns and the Washington Senators. Recalling his pro-ball career he stated, "I struck out my first four times at bat." He came back to the minors in 1953 and in 1957 finished out his baseball career with the San Diego Padres of the Pacific Coast League, delivering five consecutive seasons of 100 rbi's and was elected to the San Diego Baseball Hall of Fame. Rapp coached for a minor league team in Tennessee in 1958 and was hired as a baseball scout for Houston from 1960 to 1977. For the next five years Earl Rapp scouted for the Kansas City Royals and for the Montreal Expos from 1983 to 1987, and the Cincinnati Reds the following two years. He retired after undergoing heart surgery. Sam Kweskin reflected, "I used to see Earl at [83rd Chemical] reunions – after his baseball career ended – and when he was a scout with the Padres (I think). In 1952 I lived in Chicago and went early to a game at Wrigley Field between the Giants and the Cubs – he played center field, I think, next to Willie Mays – within a year I saw him again now with the defunct St. Louis Browns – he walloped a home run into the upper right field stands at Comisky Park against the White Sox." Earl Wellington Rapp, who primarily played outfield and pinch hitter during his baseball career, died February 13, 1992, at Swedesboro, New Jersey.

EARL RAPP

A selection of Earl Rapp baseball cards.

Author's Collection

EARL RAPP

Oaks Outfielder

Richard H. Griffin,
Co. B, killed in
action at Riquewihr,
France, December
12, 1944. Awarded the
Distinguished Service
Cross (posthumously).
Susannah Powell

13 miles. Co. A kept up a relentless fire on various targets and made a direct hit on a building which sent the Germans "scurrying." Co. B maintained a severe fire as well and at one stage provided a smokescreen for a mission to rescue Co. A, 1st Battalion, 141st Infantry, who were surrounded by the enemy. Co. C was yet at Val-de-Ville and Co. D provided harassing fire on Bennwihr.[79]

Although Lt. Col. Efnor returned to the battalion CP on the 12th, bad news began to arrive. Word was received that the road north of Chatenois leading to the battalion's ammo supply dump had been cut by a German counterattack and efforts were being made to stop the battalion's ammo supply trucks. Worse yet, although Co. A held their position at Selestat, Co. B suffered a major setback at Riquewihr, where the enemy managed to infiltrate the position during the morning.[80]

RIQUEWIHR
December 12

Both platoons of Co. B, supporting the 141st Infantry, were posted on the hill on the northwest end of Riquewihr, where all three battalion CPs and regimental CP of the 141st Infantry were also located. The night had been unusually quiet until about nine in the morning when the 141st Infantry reported the enemy moving toward Riquewihr from the northwest. The outpost of Co. B's White (2nd) Platoon, on the right flank, spotted an enemy infantry column of about 40 Germans in single file approaching from the high ground, or mountainside, to their right. At 9:29 Co. B reported Germans infiltrating their position from the south. Alerted by the outpost, the platoon opened fire on the unsuspecting Germans and inflicted casualties with the initial round. By 9:30 Co. B called the commanding officer of the 1st Battalion, 141st Infantry to report the Germans were in their position with small arms. Pfc. Andrew Leech, a BAR man from Itawamba County, Mississippi, recalled, "They moved right into our mortar positions before we knew it and had our second platoon surrounded. They opened up all around us with machine pistols, machine guns, hand grenades and the like. We had one outpost with four men on a machine gun and Browning automatic rifle. Our outpost opened up and mowed down quite a few of the onrushing Jerries before they killed our gunner and finally wiped out our outpost with the exception of a couple of our boys that got away."[81]

The slain gunner was probably Pfc. Richard H. ("Dick") Griffin of Asheville, North Carolina, who rushed 200 yards in advance of his squad's position in order to man a machine gun outpost. "He calmly waited until the enemy column was within 100 yards range, then opened fire, killing ten of the enemy with the initial burst of fire. Despite intense small arms, automatic weapons and light mortar fire which were directed at him, he clung to his position and continued firing. When hit by small arms fire in the right side of his body he rolled over and fired his machine gun with his left hand. Although hit a second time Dick continued firing until his position was finally overrun by the enemy and he was killed. By his stubborn courage and unselfish sacrifice, he, in giving his life, saved the lives of many of his comrades, and was instrumental in blunting the drive of superior enemy forces which threatened the security of a large sector of the front near Riquewihr." Griffin would be awarded the Distinguished Service Cross posthumously for his actions. Pfc. Victor P. Barnheart, born in West Virginia but raised in Baltimore, Maryland, also was seriously wounded manning a machine gun. Pfc. Martin J. Feerick, Co. B, would later claim, "It was due to his [*Barnheart's*] courage that the attacking members of the SS Elite Guard were stopped at the town of Riquewihr."[82]

At the same time as the attack on Griffin, the Red (1st) Platoon of Co. B also came under fire. It soon became apparent the opponent consisted of at least three full companies of infantry and "… were of much higher level, both mentally and physically than had been encountered for some time previous by our own infantry." One writer would later claim they were the elite SS troops known as Schutzstaffel. A German POW would later state the force consisted of two battalions of 750 men each of officer candidates. By 9:34 Co. B reported the enemy in the position at both platoons and were unable to stop them after having nearly exhausted their ammo.[83]

The White (2nd) Platoon outpost held out for nearly an hour before the survivors were forced to fall back to the main platoon position. The situation grew more critical as the enemy deployed into two columns and enveloped the platoon, resulting in many casualties on both sides. At 9:46 Co. B reported more Germans were coming into their position. Cut off from aid and the Red (1st) Platoon, the men were ordered at 10:08 to fall back to the high ground on their left flank following exhaustion of their small arms ammo, but the intense small arms and 50mm mortar fire of the enemy prevented this order from being carried out. Andrew Leech remembered, "They next overran our position and began shooting our boys in their foxholes and throwing hand grenades in with them. They killed several of our men including our lieutenant and the remainder were taken prisoner except for eight or ten that managed to get away and I was among that number."[84]

The officer killed during this attack was 1st Lt. Harlan Reynolds of New York, who, after placing his men in position, completely disregarded the intense fire of the enemy and ran to each man shouting encouragement and directions. As a second company of German infantry pressed his left flank, he realized the precariousness of his position and, spotting an American tank, he attempted to make contact for assistance. Running through a hail of bullets to the tank, he directed its fire until the enemy shot him in the head, killing him. Communications man Nolan McCraine said he saw Reynolds soon after he was killed, and he had been shot directly between the eyes and had blood streaming out of his mouth. McCraine said, "I don't know how the enemy managed to do that." Cpl. Edward Stanley ("Stan") Davidson said he was standing next to Reynolds when the lieutenant was hit, uttering his last words, "Malone [*possibly Kary M. Malone of Monroe County, Mississippi*], get that BAR up here." Reynolds, too, was awarded the Distinguished Service Cross posthumously. At 10:18 Co. B informed the 141st Infantry one mortar position was overrun and captured.[85]

Out of a platoon of 48, the ten enlisted men who escaped fled through the town and made contact with their command. Among them was Sgt. Earl ("Rappy") Wellington Rapp, who would gain some fame after the war as a pro baseball player. In a 1946 interview with *The Sporting News*, he recalled that Lt. Reynolds ordered the men to dig foxholes and to remain in them until dawn and make a break for friendly lines. But a German SS sharpshooter put a bullet through Lt. Reynolds' temple a few seconds later, leaving Sgt. Rapp in command. "The only way we had a chance was to jump out of our holes, one man at a time, run like mad for ten yards, then hit the ground before the SS sharpshooters got the range." Rapp witnessed his buddies fall one by one as they attempted escape, cover unsuccessfully provided by their comrades. With no one left to cover him, Rapp was the last to leave his foxhole. Rapp concluded, "I never ran so hard in my life … You never know how hard you can run until your life is at stake. I thought that night that I'd never play baseball again … and that's what I thought mostly about … I said 'Rapper', if you ever get through this you'll play baseball like you never played it … hustle … fight every pitcher … and learn to hit lefthanders."[86]

After successfully crossing the open area, Rapp, along with William P. Heelan of New York, sought cover in a nearby culvert. Cpl. "Stan" Davidson, also from New York, said, "Malone and I crawled into a vineyard next to the road running over that culvert. When we finally crept close enough to a B Company house a couple of our own men thought we were Jerries and began firing at us by mistake. We stayed among those vines and kept shouting at them for a long time. Finally we took a chance, stood up straight, and they recognized us." Davidson later amended the account and said it was Malone who stood up and said, "Don't shoot, we're G.I.'s." Sam Kweskin recalled witnessing the long, horse-faced Rapp turning up wet and exhausted because "… he hid in a drainage culvert for hours as he heard Germans running back and forth above him." He also suffered a wound or injury of the

George Barrett, Co. B, 83rd Chemical Mortar Battalion with German Nebelwerfer. *Barrett Collection*

tendons behind his knee which would later contribute to his retirement from pro ball. Additionally, Rapp was awarded the Silver Star.[87]

In the meantime, the Red (1st) Platoon, posted in some houses which faced a draw west of Bois De Kientzheim, which the enemy used as their "main axis of attack," thwarted the initial advance thrown at their position with 30 caliber machine gun and small arms fire. Initially, they were successful in inflicting heavy casualties and preventing the enemy from entering Riquewihr. According to Pfc. Andrew Leech, "The Germans … advanced across an open field toward the town … Our platoon had had time to get ready for them and opened up on them with everything they had. Our men mowed down quite a few, stopping the attack before they could get into town …" But as they ran out of small arms ammo, the regimental S-3 ordered them to fall back to the company CP and reorganize. Twenty-two men, along with Capt. Bernard Stone and lieutenants Charles W. O'Day and James K. Davis, a former Ranger, assembled in town and prepared to meet the advancing foe. While Capt. Stone was at the regimental CP and Lt. Lewis ("Kokomo") Cameron was at the OP, approximately three companies of the enemy struck with machine guns and light mortars. The 141st Infantry reported, "… Fighting from windows, doorways, towers and roof tops, our cooks, drivers and clerks picked up carbines and rifles and fired into the advancing forces." Co. B's Red (1st) Platoon saw one of their own medics, Cpl. Fred C. Weaver, and some radiomen captured, all eight mortars overrun with no chance to destroy them, and 30 rounds of ammo for both platoons lost. At

Co. C's Leonard Turan and Bill Young, Christmas Day 1944 in Bitche, France. Turan wrote on the photo: "This is where I spent Christmas day…not a house for miles." *Turan Collection*

battalion CP at Ribeauville, Daniel Shields wrote in his diary that they were "… shelled very heavy. Things look black. Roads out & one platoon practically wiped out." Reportedly, orders were issued to set the ammo trucks on fire if a retreat necessitated it.[88]

Luckily, the enemy attack was broken because the town had been alerted and elements of the 141st and 143rd infantry regiments sent reinforcements and a re-supply of ammo. Some of the infantrymen were replacements who received their baptism of fire carrying ammo to the riflemen and machine gunners. At 1 p.m. in the afternoon the Red (1st) Platoon of the 83rds Co. B regrouped and returned to their original position "by whatever means necessary." However, beyond some sniper fire, very little resistance was encountered. A mortar was set up and fired 90 HE into the draw which apparently killed at least 50 of the enemy and wounded an undetermined amount, " … evidenced by equipment and blood left behind." Due to Co. B's heavy losses only one firing platoon could be mustered to fire from its original position in the afternoon, then moved to a new area in Riquewihr. This was fortunate as the enemy had pinpointed their old position and opened counterbattery fire. By midday the German attack on Riquewihr had dissipated.[89]

A volunteer patrol was sent to the original White (2nd) Platoon position to check for wounded and found two injured enlisted men, one of whom expired. Total casualties for Co. B at the conclusion of the fight at Riquewihr were one officer [*Lt. Harlan Reynolds*] and seven enlisted men killed, one officer [*Lt. James K. Davis*] and two enlisted men seriously wounded, and 11 missing in action. Particularly tragic was the death of Sgt. Henry L. Francis, Jr., of Camden, New Jersey, who, Ed "Stan" Davidson suspected, was accidentally killed by friendly fire. Sam Kweskin said that also among the killed was a new replacement who had been in the Metropolitan Opera Ballet Company. "Doc" Hulcher claimed there were about 15 men wounded. Among the missing was Pvt. Thomas A. Cascio, a former lab tech from Hoboken, New Jersey, who had joined the 83rd at Epinal in November as a replacement. Cascio later wrote, "I was a shell bearer. I would supply the mortar with shells … in the early morning we were completely surrounded by the SS troops. We had been hitting their supply lines. Four or five men were taken as prisoners. I don't know what happened to the rest of the company. They were ready to shoot me but because one of their men was wounded, I and one of my buddies was forced to carry this German soldier back to his lines. It took us nine whole days to carry him up the mountain and stay put at night because the whole area was mined with explosives." Cascio spent numerous months afterwards in various German transit work camps, during which time assignments included filling in the bomb craters in Munich, and two weeks in a German hospital with spastic colitis, where he lost a lot of blood. Eventually he reached his base prison camp, Stalag 7A, on March 15th, 1945, and was liberated April 29th, 1945.[90]

During the engagement at Riquewihr, Co. B fired a total of 390 HE and 82 WP, for a total of 472 rounds. General John E. Dahlquist, 36th Infantry Division, credited Co. B with "… having stopped the enemy from capturing Riquewihr, disorganizing the entire 141st Infantry Regiment and possibly from creating a more serious situation." Malcolm Doyle Wilkinson, Co. B, bluntly stated, "Riquewihr was a horror story from the beginning and no one can be sure of how we survived that." For their performance at Riquewihr, the 36th Infantry Division awarded Co. B of the 83rd a Unit Citation, which read, in part, "The members of Co. B, whose mortars were located in the narrow space between the woods and the town, immediately directed heavy small arms fire at the onrushing enemy from their inferior downhill position, and fought with such valor and determination that they delayed the attackers, providing sufficient time for the deployment of reserve units …" The journal of the 141st Infantry reported "the slopes up to the wooded sector northwest, west, and southwest of town were dotted with the bodies of Germans killed in the attack. It was estimated that between 200-300 enemy dead lay throughout the regimental area."[91]

Also during the day, Lt. Alfred Crenshaw called with information the enemy had cut the road over the mountain between Ribeauville and St. Marie. With Co. C held in division reserve at Val-de-Ville, Co. D supported an attack of the 143rd Infantry. But undoubtedly the most humorous incident of the day took place in Co. A, according to Sam Bundy, who wrote that when Cpl. Lawrence Ertzberger "… entered a dark room, the first platoon thought a Christmas tree was walking thru the door, for Ertzy was sprinkled by WP when a shell left a luminous trail as it left mortar. Particles fell on all parts of our Corporal and he glowed like a Christmas tree. Infantry and Artillery observers who observed the shell called our switchboard to see if we were firing tracer shells or flares."[92]

According to "Doc" Hulcher, there was a truck accident early on the morning of the 13th which injured an additional 12 men, but there is no mention of the incident in the battalion journal. In other matters of the day, operational instructions were received ordering the 142nd RCT (Infantry) with attachments (Co. A, 83rd Chemical Battalion, at Selestat) to maintain their present mission, and the 143rd RCT (Infantry) with attachments (companies B and D of the 83rd) to relieve part of the 141st RCT (Infantry) on Hill 351. The 141st RCT (Infantry) with attachments (Co. C, 83rd Chemical Battalion, in division reserve at Val-de-Ville) was to relieve the 143rd RCT (Infantry) at Riquewihr. In response Lt. Col. Efnor ordered a platoon to the 141st and a company to the 143rd and Maj. Mindrum noted that Co. B would remain "… in position detached from the 141st … and attached to the 143rd … in direct support of the 1st Battalion… 1st Platoon of Co. B to be attached to D Co." Capt. Smith, Co. C, made the most ironic statement at this time, writing home, "If the people back home will just furnish the ammo we'll put it where it will do the most good." This promise would soon come back to haunt him in 1945 when the battalion was plagued by defective shells produced in the states. Also during this time Capt. Smith returned from a 48-hour pass to Paris, a trip the battalion had allotted 19 men and two officers, with Smith in charge, to make.[93]

Co. B continued the action around Riquewihr and their radio sergeant found an operational German radio in a Riquewihr attic and destroyed it. The 1st Platoon and the forward CP of the company located a new position and set up five guns. At Bennwihr, the two platoons of Co. D received heavy enemy shelling throughout the day and one enemy 81mm shell fell in one of the 1st Platoon's gun positions, slightly wounding Pvt. Euro F. Eusebi of Brooklyn, New York, and badly damaging his jeep. Shortly afterward one of the company's own HE shells exploded after hitting an overhead wire. Sgt. Marvin C. Jones of Georgia was slightly wounded and three jeeps were lightly damaged. Numerous enemy 170mm mortar shells soon fell in the gun position and three direct hits were made on the platoon CP. Total vehicular damage to the platoon throughout the 24-hour period included two jeeps slightly damaged, one jeep badly damaged, and three trailers slightly damaged.[94]

2nd Lt. Andrew J. ("Dick") Connolly, disputing official reports, remembered the day for a different reason. "I recall very well the day the 83rd was recognized as a combat unit. I believe Mark W. Clark really went into his shell that day. My memory brings to mind the day the 36th Division deleted the word 'attached' and added 'in support'. That happened on December 13 at Selestat. With Able Company (Co. A) in SUPPORT."[95]

December 14th opened with Co. A yet at Selestat supplying strong fire support to the 142nd and Co. C, minus kitchen and supply personnel, moving via motor transport to a new position in the vicinity of Riquewihr. Co. D, with the 1st Platoon of Co. B attached, reported the 1st Platoon of Co. D was under a constant barrage of enemy mortars, 170mm artillery, and direct tank fire. The battalion journal stated, "Platoon CP was hit three times and several shells hit in the gun position." The 2nd Platoon spent time firing on a Nebelwerfer, an enemy smoke or rocket launcher with six 150mm barrels. In the Sicilian Campaign the Allies had nicknamed this weapon the "Screaming Mimi" and "Moaning Minnie."[96]

The situation remained fairly stable on all fronts concerning the 83rd on the 15th as the battalion CP moved to St. Croix and set up in the Embassy. Capt. Smith, Co. C, reported there had been a slight enemy breakthrough at Mittelwihr the previous night but it had been resolved. Co. C was requested to provide a smokescreen at Kayserberg the following day, but the mission was called off once Co. C reported they were too far away to provide such cover. Perhaps the best news for the battalion was the arrival of the major of the 99th Chemical Battalion and his advance party with news that his battalion might relieve the 83rd. Lt. Col. Efnor also reported that 2,600 rounds of 4.2 ammo had been received, "drawn on certificates of necessity," which left the battalion 3,000 rounds in excess of their daily allocation of 1,000 rounds. He added the 83rd fired an average of 1,210 rounds for the period December 9th - December 14th and said the ammo on hand at present included 1,200 - 1,500 rounds per company, plus 2,600 rounds in the battalion dump. He clarified the basic load per company was 750 rounds. Sgt. Roy E. Cadwalader, HQ Co., added the 83rd had just expended 926 HE and 16 WP, with 1,500 HE and 1,450 WP yet in the ammo dump.[97]

A lieutenant of the Service Company of the 143rd Infantry reported locating four more bodies of Co. B men on the 16th, lost in the tragedy at Riquewihr. Despite such bad news the companies of the battalion kept up the fight in their respective sectors: Co. A was at Selestat; Co. C's 1st Platoon targeted an enemy supply route from Kayserberg east to Kientzheim, while the 2nd Platoon hit Sigolsheim; and Co. D with the 1st Platoon of Co. B shelled a variety of targets in the vicinity of Bennwihr.[98]

Between noon of the 16th and noon of the 17th, Co. A was at Selestat; Co. C fired 298 HE and 242 WP in their position; and Co. D with the 1st Platoon of Co. B struck assorted targets in Sigolsheim, Mittelwihr, and Bennwihr, including Hill 351. T/5 George F. Tucker, Co. D, at Zellenberg, was awarded a Bronze Star "during an intense enemy artillery barrage, several direct hits ignited the loft and roof of a building containing one thousand rounds of HE and WP ammunition. Disregarding the enemy artillery fire, as well as the possibility of the ammunition in the house being ignited, Technician Fifth Grade Tucker climbed to the roof of the burning building and working quickly and

Co. C men at Alsace, France, Christmas Day, 1944. Back L-R: Raymond N. Risley, Charles C. Pruiett, Samuel C. Preston, Julius D. Vogel, and Robert W. Simon. Bernard Bernhardt in front. *Bernard Bernhardt*

Assorted views of Co. C men on Christmas Day, 1944, near Phillipsburg, France. On the front row in bottom photo Cornelius McCarthy is 5th from the right and Leonard Turan is 4th from right.

All photos Vicente De Leon

Co. C men on Christmas Day 1944, near Phillipsburg, France. Written on
photo: "Carroll Vincent Yeatts and C. H." *Vicente De Leon*

efficiently, extinguished the fire." The earlier news reached the battalion that by "dark" of the 17th all components of the 83rd would be relieved by the 99th Chemical Battalion. Indeed, by 9:30 p.m. the 99th, the battalion trained by Lt. Col. Hutchinson, had assumed all mortar positions, ammunition, and tactical assignments of the 83rd. By 10:00 p.m., the 83rd Chemical had closed the battalion CP at Ribeauville as enemy artillery fire had made the area untenable and set up at St. Croix-aux-Mines along with Detachment No. 3, 11th Chemical Maintenance. Co. A rejoiced when they heard they were relieved and moved back to Liepvre from Selestat.[99]

The Germans also launched their Ardennes offensive on the 16th and 17th, better known as the Battle of the Bulge, in which they drove their armor deep into the American lines and retook miles of forest land and surrounded some Allied troops. To counter this, some components of the 7th Army were moved north to support Gen. George S. Patton's 3rd Army, leaving the lines in the south stretched to the limit. This included positions held by the 83rd, which would come under attack on the last day of the year.[100]

On December 18th, Lt. Col. Efnor held a discussion with all company officers at St. Croix-aux-Mines concerning reorganization of the battalion. Co. D would be "broken up" and transferred to companies A, B, and C, which would make possible the establishment of three platoons in each weapons company instead of two. The service records of Co. D would be turned over to Co. A. In addition, one platoon of Co. A was to be taken by Co. B, and Co. C would remain the same with any additions coming from replacements or other companies. Charles Rolling, Co. A, confirmed this as he wrote in his diary, "Heard some bad news. First platoon is being sent to 'B' Company in a few days. The second platoon is staying." All of this would go into effect on December 22nd. Following the meeting, Efnor, Maj. Mindrum, and one officer from each company left to make preparations to move the battalion to Hagenau, about 20 miles north of Strasbourg, on December 20th. In the meantime, Co. A, supporting the 142nd RCT (Infantry), returned to their rear at Liepvre while Co. C returned to Chatenois and Co. D, with the 1st Platoon of Co. B attached, wrapped up their fire on Mittelwihr and Bennwihr after being relieved and moved to the rear at St. Croix-aux-Mines.[101]

A report filed on the 19th listed all 4.2" mortar ammunition turned over to the 99th Chemical Battalion by the 83rd Chemical Battalion and included 108 HE plus 211 WP from Co. A; 358 HE and 306 WP by Co. B; some 948

HE and 652 WP by Co. C; 2,440 HE and 600 WP from Co. D; and 506 HE and 1,190 WP by HQ Battalion Dump. This amounted to a battalion total of 4,360 HE and 2,959 WP rounds. The 83rd also received operation instructions from the VI Corps to complete their move to Hagenau by the 20th, to complete battalion reorganization between the 21st and 23rd, prepare for attack on Corps orders on the 24th, and to relieve the 3rd Chemical Battalion, with one company each going to the 45th and 103rd infantry divisions.[102]

As ordered the battalion moved from St. Croix-aux-Mines to Hagenau, Alsace, France, a distance of 56 miles, between the 19th and 20th in a convoy of march groups, beginning with Co. C, followed by companies A, HQ, B and D. Also included in the move was Detachment No. 3, 11th Chemical Maintenance, which used a civilian's house as a bivouac. The weather was freezing cold as the convoy passed through Strasbourg to Hagenau, where the men bivouacked in a German barracks which had most of its windows broken out. Upon arrival the company commander and staff discussed battalion reorganization, including supply and transfer of personnel. The following day final preparations were made for the reorganization, and on December 22nd the battalion was officially reorganized and re-designated as the 83rd Chemical Mortar Battalion. Paul S. Giles, a cook in Co. D, recalled, "They dissolved 'D' Company and I was put in a squad in 'C' Company. I was no longer a cook. I went to the Captain and told him I didn't know anything about shooting mortars. He said not to worry, you'll learn in a few days. I really enjoyed being out of the kitchen." In addition, the battalion received orders from the VI Corps to provide one company as a reserve for the 79th Infantry, if needed, in Task Force Harris, a grouping of the 63rd Infantry Division led by Brig. Gen. Frederick M. Harris and designed to protect open terrain in the Vosges.[103]

Lt. Col. Efnor and the platoon officers of companies A and C made a reconnaissance for mortar positions north of Wissembourg on the 23rd, positions the companies moved into on Christmas Eve to support by attachment, the 45th Infantry Division and Task Force Hudelson respectively. Led by Col. Daniel Hudelson of Combat Command R, this mechanized task force was assigned the most easily defensible positions in the low Vosges. The remainder of the battalion was placed under Corps control. Capt. Smith, Co. C, knew all too well what the immediate future held and wrote home, "I'll be living in a damn foxhole and it's colder than blue blazes, but my hole will be a deep one and I'll fix it so it's warm inside … I … am now part of a Task Force. Wherever the fighting is that's where we are. These mortars don't get much credit except from the front line boys who know them, most people think we are service troops … [we] are now called the 83rd Chemical Mortar Bn."[104]

Lee Steedle, Co. B, believed he was in Niederbronn on Christmas Eve attending a Mass held by a local priest in a bombed out church. Steedle recalled, "That was a memorable Mass with men in overcoats, rifles slung from shoulders, flickering candlelight, and foggy breaths visible in the chilly air from scarcely remembered carols. The sound of a single shot could have changed everything, but it never came. A blessedly silent night, but not totally dark. Occasional wary star shells from both sides starkly illuminated the streets and rooftops. Jerry stayed peacefully on his side of the thin, quiet stream separating us. It was a night to realize Jerry was mortal and human, just like us."[105]

Co. A was back in action on Christmas Day with the 1st Platoon attached to the 180th Infantry, the 2nd Platoon the 157th Infantry, and the 3rd Platoon the 179th Infantry. In the period from noon of Christmas Eve to noon of Christmas Day, the company expended 272 HE and 295 WP. Those who were able attended church and listened to the chaplain of the 45th Division, some had special meals or just cooked their own, and many got drunk. Lee Steedle, Co. B, said Christmas was "… a day without gunfire … There was the rumbling of trucks and whining of jeep

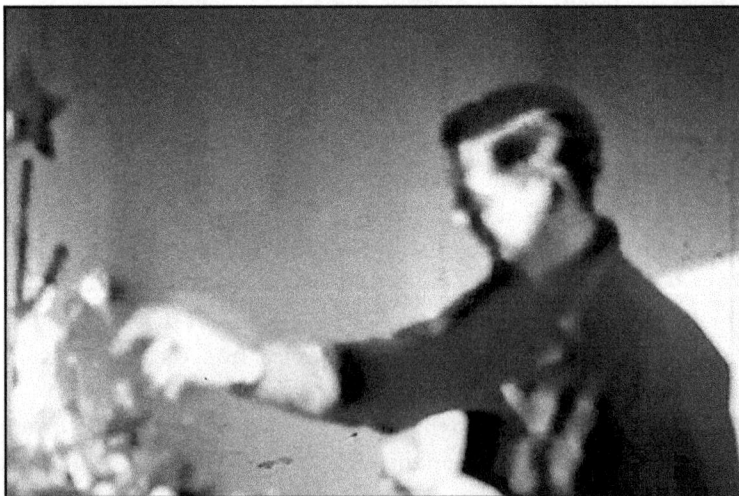

Movie still of Capt. Julius C. "Doc" Hulcher, Medical Detachment, decorating his Christmas tree, 1944. *Charles Hulcher*

engines, the sounds of resupply. Both sides breathing and waiting." Co. C, relieving the 106th Cavalry Group in Task Force Hudelson, had the 1st and 3rd platoons of Co. C support the 62nd Armored Infantry Battalion while the 2nd Platoon effected local security in support of the 94th and 117th Cavalry Reconnaissance. No firing was performed by the company. The holiday was not entirely without celebration, however, as evidenced by Catholic Daniel Shields at the battalion CP at Hagenau, who recorded in his diary, "Went to Confession [*on Christmas Eve*] in the Rectory, then Mass & Communion. All darkness except two candles on altar because Germans were just across the river. No windows in church & I almost froze, will never forget it." After a short nap he awoke and had a big Christmas dinner and saw the movie *Seven Days Ashore*. Relating to the holiday, "Doc" Hulcher, whose Medical Detachment was set up in a school building, added, "Celebrated Xmas here and made the most of it with Xmas tree, presents, grand dinner, etc… Gave immunization shots to whole outfit while here. Companies went back into line just before Xmas. Again lots of air activity overhead – day and night. A Company was set up just over the German border." Charlie Lowry, Co. D, wrote "Christmas was just another day."[106]

The shelling continued on the 26th with Co. A firing 669 HE and nine WP while Co. C also set off a few rounds in their sector. The process of reorganization continued with Detachment No. 3, 11th Chemical Maintenance, changing their title to Detachment B. Both companies A, at such places as Niedersteinbach and Niederbronn, and C were heavily engaged on December 27th and 28th, with Co. C throwing about 3,500 lbs. of TNT at two enemy positions on the 27th, according to Capt. Smith. Additionally, a rather unusual order was issued on the 28th requiring that gas masks be carried on individuals rather than on unit trains. Apparently there had been some threat the enemy would use gas warfare although this never materialized.[107]

Capt. Smith, Co. C, boasted, "My CP is in a cave like we used to dig when we were kids … it's way down deep and now I know how a gopher looks at the world. It really isn't bad, though; have a stove going full blast to try to keep the darn place warm. And it's so darned cold outside that the stove just has to do its best to keep one end warm. The switchboard is in one end … if things work out right, this company will get 7 days out of the line January 1. I sure will be glad to get in out of the cold, and for all the men, too. They're a swell bunch and can out shoot anything …"[108]

The rear of Co. A moved to Niederbronn on the 29th while the three platoons maintained strong fire on the enemy. Elements of Co. C were in the vicinity of Neudverfel, and during one stage of combat a new mortar barrel with an air recoil mechanism was tested, with the result of nine rounds reacting favorably and breakage on the tenth. Capt. Smith, Co. C, took the time to describe his duties as company commander, stating. "My work is all administration, and I am inside most of the time, though a great deal of the time our headquarters is in tents in fields with mud up to our knees … At the present we have our HQ in a nice building. The building was a school for nuns before the war, but has since been used for a hospital. The building has steam heat and electric lights … We usually stay a few miles behind the lines, but are nearly always within enemy artillery range and, of course, bombing distance, both of which we have had our share, especially at Anzio. One morning after a shelling attack our HQ tent had 53 holes in it …"[109]

While companies A and C continued in their respective actions on the 30th, operational instructions from VI Corps ordered Co. C be relieved by the 31st. Co. B was given this assignment as the company's officers made a reconnaissance of Co. C's position.[110]

On December 31st, a white New Year's Eve, Co. A was yet heavily engaged with the enemy while Co. C fired 105 HE before being relieved by Co. B and moving in convoy to Hagenau, where they reverted to company control. The Adjutant General of VI Corps issued strict orders forbidding any type of New Year's celebrations, placing all security personnel and installations on high alert. However, before any alert was issued, Daniel Shields, at the battalion CP, saw the Humphrey Bogart movie *Conflict*. "Doc" Hulcher said, "… celebrated New Year's Eve here along with a grand turkey dinner again. No parties or celebration were allowed. However everyone had a drink." One unsolicited celebration did take place, though, as recorded by James Helsel, Co. A, who wrote, "Some crazy colonel got the silly idea to celebrate New Year's last night, so at 12:00 each gun fired 2 rounds and a lot of small arms were fired toward Jerry. Luckily for us he didn't return the compliment." Capt. Joseph Garsson, Co. A, confirmed Helsel's account stating the unidentified colonel requested officers fire their guns at midnight in celebration of New Year's Eve. Unknown to them, the Germans were launching an attack at that very moment and the celebration firing halted the attack. As a result, Garsson and others were awarded the Bronze Star for stopping the German assault.[111]

BITCHE
December 31

New Year's Eve proved to be quite unpleasant for Co. B, as they moved into the defenses of the Maginot Line in front of Bitche, on the border of Germany. Lawrence G. Ertzberger, Co. B, recalled, "New Year's Eve we went up and relieved C company. It was snowing a little bit that day, and just before daylight, they called us out to fire the mortars. We had been shooting a mile or two, and the number of powder rings tells how far, usually 15-20. This time was five powder rings so that was just over a little patch of woods. Then our planes were coming over that morning and diving down at German tanks … that afternoon we went back to a little town about two miles away …"[112]

Lee Steedle, Co. B, was a bit more detailed, as he wrote, "We had been deployed so thinly that immediately in front of our platoon, there was only a strong-point in the forest road ahead of us, held by a stretched-out infantry company of the 45th Division and by some lightly-armored Cavalry recon cars." Suddenly the enemy launched a large scale attack from the vicinity of Bitche. Co. B fired heavy concentrations for about two hours, but the superior numbers of the enemy broke through on the right flank and forced the infantry to fall back. Under small arms fire and unable to extricate their mortars due to the baseplates digging into the ground, they were forced to fall back 1,000 yards while abandoning and destroying their mortars to keep them from falling into enemy hands. Lee Steedle said that each squad always carried a thermite incendiary grenade to eliminate their own mortars when necessary, and as the squad leader, Sgt. Samuel J. Romeo, had not heard the order, Steedle grabbed the sergeant's thermite grenade and burned both his and Romeo's guns.[113]

Further describing the action Steedle said, "Beyond the edge of our clearing, our Browning Automatic Rifle (BAR) man turned, set his tripod, and fired into our big ammunition pile that was stacked just off the road." Before long the shells were exploding and the white phosphorous provided cover for Co. B to withdraw down the road 1,000 yards to a shallow ditch at a dirt crossroads. Unable to use the road, the enemy pursuit was slowed by six to eight inches of snow. A new replacement 2nd lieutenant without combat experience was in command of their platoon and selected a man at random to operate a 50 calibre machine gun "… on an isolated, knocked out halftrack vehicle 30 yards away …" Apparently, Lee Steedle and Byron Jordan went to man the gun, and, according to Steedle, "Byron and I realized neither of us had ever been trained on that gun, didn't know how to arm it, and what was worse, it was separated on the left by quite a few yards from the others in our platoon. We climbed down after a few minutes of fiddling with it, and rejoined the others."[114]

Following consultation with an infantry officer on their left, the new 2nd lieutenant returned and told the platoon sergeant and squad leaders to go back up the slope and make contact with the enemy. With the full moon illuminating the bright snowy ground, spaces between the trees could be seen over a hundred yards away. Realizing this was a suicidal order Steedle commented, "The Lieutenant had accepted an order from a Major outside our chain of command just because he was outranked, and hadn't protested. We decided to disobey." The platoon sergeant and his four squad leaders told their men to leave, while all five non-coms plus their unarmed platoon aid man, T/5 Henry "Doc" Fajkowski returned to the lieutenant and told him they were ready for him to lead them on the patrol, realizing the officer would never attempt such a mission with an under-strength group. The non-coms were ordered to rejoin their men in the next village to the rear.[115]

Steedle later elaborated on the new officer: "The 'greenhorn lieutenant' was a new replacement who had just joined us a couple of days before. He'd somehow never discerned his anus from his elbow, and none of us had any respect for him. Clearly our 83rd superior officers didn't either, and he fortunately was never seen by us again after that night. I've no idea what his name was."[116]

The month of December had been a particularly difficult one for the 83rd Chemical Mortar Battalion. The total number of HE fired was 18,932 and 1,970 WP, for a total of 20,902 rounds. Detachment B (formerly No. 3), 11th Chemical Maintenance, had repaired a total of 51 baseplates, 78 standards, and 40 barrels. Casualties reported included 12 lightly wounded or injured and hospitalized, three seriously wounded, nine killed in action, and 11 missing in action, for a total of 35 casualties. This statistic did not include the New Year's Eve fight at Bitche, which would appear on the January report.[117]

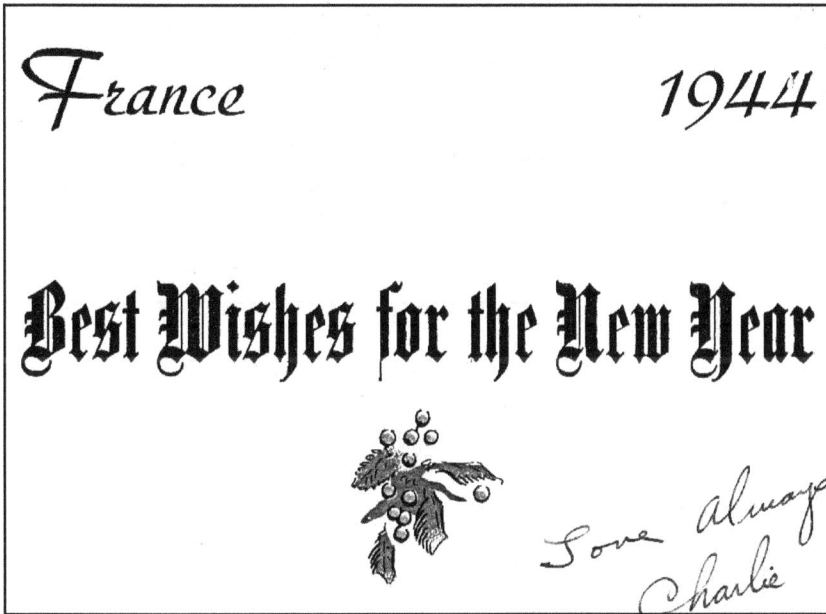

France 1944

Best Wishes for the New Year

Love Always Charlie

Holiday wishes card from Charlie Lowry, Co. D, 83rd
Chemical Mortar Battalion. *Author's Collection*

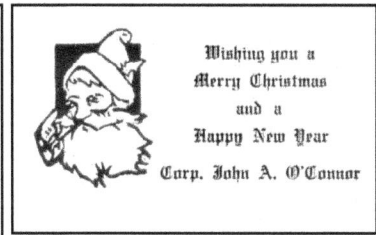

Wishing you a
Merry Christmas
and a
Happy New Year
Corp. John A. O'Connor

Christmas and New Years greeting
card sent to George R. Borkhuis
from Corp. John A. O'Connor who
was with the 83rd at Camp Gordon,
GA, but did not go overseas.
Fred Thompson and Thomasina Edwards

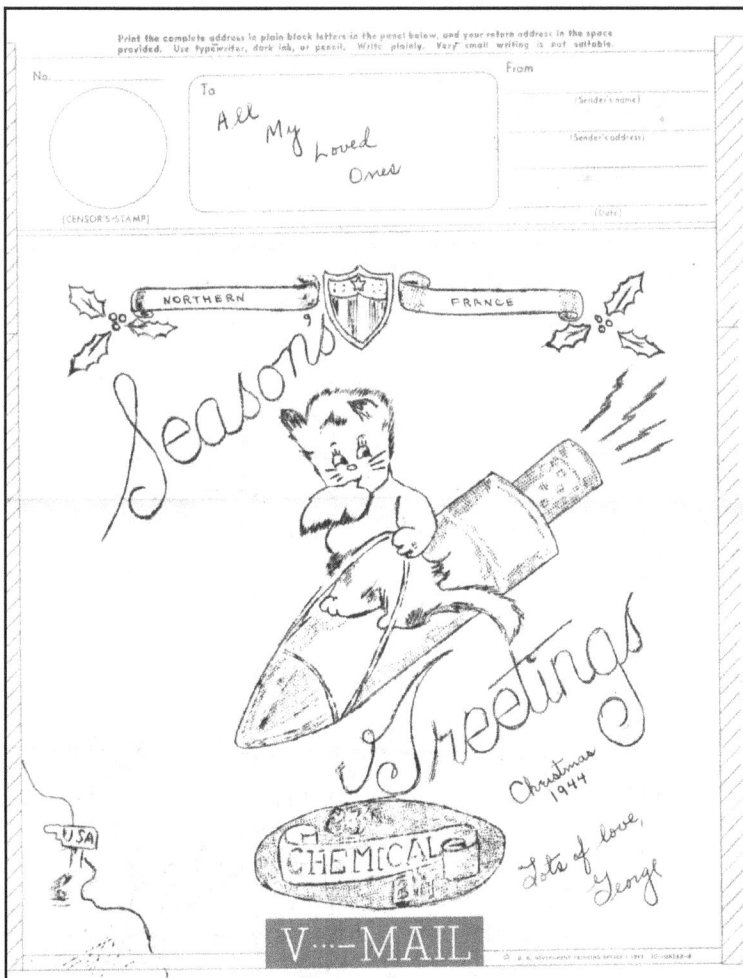

Season's Greetings V-mail sent by George R. Borkhuis from Northern
France to family at home. *Fred Thompson and Thomasina Edwards*

83rd Holiday Greetings V-mail drawn
by Sam Kweskin, HQ Co. *Jean Siegal*

Passes

Left: Medical Detachment exam "pass" signed by Julius C. Hulcher stating George Borkhuis, HQ Co., was free from lice, scabies, and veneral disease.

Fred Thompson and Thomasina Edwards

6725th Staging Company meal certificate for the Casual mess. *Fred Thompson and Thomasina Edwards*

Left: Front and back of pass to Paris, France for S/Sgt George R. Borkhuis, "103rd Quota", and signed by Capt. Robert E. Edwards.

Fred Thompson and Thomasina Edwards

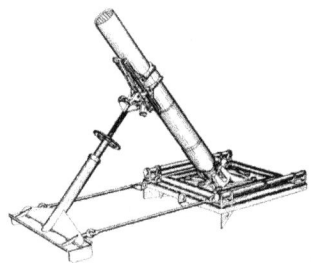

Left: George R. Borkhuis, Co. D, Liberty Pass to Nice, France, signed by Capt. Raymond J. Lakey

Fred Thompson and Thomasina Edwards

Chapter Twelve

STAY ALIVE IN '45
JANUARY-MAY
1945

Some 83rd men playing cards while waiting on a fire mission at Wimmenau, France, March 18, 1945. *Squires Collection*

The new year of 1945 opened with the line of the 45th Division extending "from a point approximately five kilometers north of Wissembourg to the 48th parallel with Task Force Hudelson on the left flank. Task Force Hudelson's line extended approximately southwest from the point of contact with the 45th Infantry Division to the 46th parallel; thence northwest to its junction with XV Corps about three kilometers south of Bitche." The mission for the period was designated as defensive.[1]

The situation was well described in the battalion journal, which recorded: "... period was characterized by repeated enemy attacks with penetrations which forced a withdrawal of the infantry to the Maginot Line, and in a short time a general withdrawal to previously prepared positions on the switch-back just north of the Hagenau Line. Mortar positions were so chosen that the sector could be thoroughly covered with mortar fire if the enemy counterattacked ... A shortage of artillery ammunition necessitated an increased amount of mortar fire. Fields of fire were so planned that the entire 45th Division sector could be thoroughly covered ..."[2]

On the opening day of the month, 1st Sgt. Joseph A. Adamski called the battalion CP to report that the enemy had overrun Co. B's platoon gun positions near Bitche on the evening of December 31st, and, after destroying their mortars while under small arms fire, were forced to withdraw 1,000 yards to a new position south of Philipsbourg, where they acted as infantry with the 117th Reconnaissance Squad, which was establishing a new defensive position. Miraculously, there were no casualties. Early in the day, 1st Lt. Francis J. Schleifer and a Lt. Price, both of Co. B, were ordered to reorganize and re-equip the platoons and move from Hagenau and meet at Wimmenau. While this transpired, the 3rd Platoon of Co. B inflicted heavy casualties on the enemy. In reference to Wimmenau, Andrew Leech, Co. B, wrote, "… we moved over past Wimmenau and set up in the woods and spent most of the winter here on the defensive. It was 'some cold' but the fighting was limited to patrolling. We even went deer hunting in the snow behind our lines in the forest and killed several deer."[3]

Lee Steedle, Co. B, injected that during the morning Co. B had been ordered to reassemble and the inexperienced 2nd lieutenant involved in the fight at Bitche never appeared nor was ever seen again by the men. Steedle added, "Our guess was that he had been reassigned. Our battalion officers didn't reproach our platoon, but Lt. Col. Sam Efnor, our battalion commander, stood silently while a full Colonel from the infantry furiously upbraided us, called us non-coms cowards, and ordered us all back into the line. He ended by saying that we sergeants would all be court-martialed. By afternoon we had replacement mortars and ammunition, and were back up front firing effectively. That's the last we heard of any court-martial." In another account, Steedle supplemented his story, stating, "At Bitche, if we had known how many S.S. Candidates would assault us, and from what direction, we might have dug in our .30 calibre machine gun on our right. It wouldn't have bought us much more time, but we at least might have been able to dig out our baseplates before we were overrun. I had to drop thermite grenades down two of our barrels and burn our guns so Jerry couldn't use them against us. But surprise is a big element in war, and surprise was on Jerry's side that night. Not incidentally, all five of us platoon non-coms were threatened with a court-martial by a Colonel for our telling our men to take off, even though we five remained. That was the only time in our war that we deliberately disobeyed an order. If we had it to do all over again I would not change a thing. We saved our men that night against a stupid order."[4]

The first day of the new year, in which at least some of the men had turkey, closed with the battalion being ordered to move, minus companies A and B, to the vicinity of Saverne the following day. Sam Bundy, Co. A, wrote of the withdrawal on the 1st, stating, "This morning we were alerted – everyone packed his equipment and trucks were loaded. For the past few days many outfits have been moving back, so finally we are following suit. Companies on line are remaining there, except for their rear elements." Ironically, Co. C had just begun their seven-day break from the front.[5]

The orders of the previous day were followed on January 2nd as the battalion CP at Hagenau, along with Detachment B, 11th Chemical Maintenance Company, closed and moved, along with Co. C, to the area of Saverne, a distance of some 20 to 25 miles, with HQ taking over a billet of the 12th Chemical Maintenance Company in an old factory building. Elements of Co. B also moved from Hagenau to Saverne. Wayne M. Moser said, "I'll always remember the few weeks I stayed with a French family during the winter of 1944 at Saverne … They were extremely good to me. The lady of the house often made delicious pastries while her husband provided the wine." Andrew Leech, Co. B, added, "We moved back to Saverne where our rear was and spent a few days. While there we killed lots of deer." Charles Rolling, Co. A, wrote, "This whole sector is pulling back. Something big is coming up," while other members of his company said they fell back to a town called Offwiller.[6]

According to Sam Kweskin, HQ Co., "It was about this time that the 'small Bulge' occurred down around our 7th Army area. General Alexander Patch, however, was wise enough to have some forward units retreat calmly, which meant that we took only our necessary material with us as we left Hagenau … Patch had the army pull back atop the Vosges Mountains where they retained the advantage of looking down the throats – as it were – of the Germans attacking south of the Bulge." Daniel Shields, also of HQ, described the retreat as disheartening. Lt. Robert Bush of Co. A was more concise as he wrote in his diary, "Talk of withdrawal." Capt. Smith, Co. C, possibly best described the German counterattack and Allied withdrawal as he implied that "… America may have had a little overdose of overconfidence." Morale might have received a slight boost as the 62nd Armored Division issued a commendation to the two platoons of Co. B which had been attached to the organization during the actions of January 1st and 2nd.[7]

During the third day of the month, the battalion CP, along with Detachment B, 11th Chemical Maintenance, was moved to the two-hotel village of Stambach, about 4.5 miles southwest of Saverne. HQ and HQ Co. took up residence in the Goetzmann Hotel, a four-story structure with the Marne Canal to its rear, and also occupied the smaller hotel next door. During their stay at Stambach, Sam Kweskin and Eugene Plassmann got the opportunity to go boar hunting. "Doc" Hulcher, like many of the men, often went trout fishing and attempted to learn to ski until the sun and rain melted the snow. Co. A's 2nd Platoon was in the vicinity of Rothbach where Cpl. Erskine C. Spencer was accidentally wounded and evacuated. The remainder of Co. A moved from Offwiller to Lichtenberg, where James Helsel said they took over a house where he "… found a nice accordion … and played it with one finger till the boys got sick of it." Co. B's platoons covered such areas as Wimmenau, Ingwiller, and Saverne, while Co. C remained in Saverne. At Stambach Sam Kweskin feared the army might pull back farther: "Our lines were falling back from points as far up as the Rhine Valley; the Battle of the Bulge was at its hottest, and in our sector there was talk of retreating further west into the Vosges. How awful that would have been. All the dead, all the carnage, the maiming, the blood spilled to no avail?"[8]

Lt. Col. Efnor, Capt. Alfred H. Crenshaw, and T/Sgt. Roy E. Cadwalader departed on January 4th to establish the battalion forward CP at Mulhausen. The 1st and 2nd platoons of Co. B left Saverne and made contact with the 17th Infantry CP at Zinntersheim, while the 1st Platoon advanced to Wingen but was driven out by the enemy. Andrew Leech, Co. B, recalled that "… one morning just before daybreak we moved into the town of Wingen. Before we had time to unload anything and set up anything we were attacked from the mountains surrounding the town. The Jerries opened up with machine guns and burp guns all around us … They came running down off the mountain yelling and hollering and shooting … We were ordered to evacuate the town as we had not unloaded our vehicles. We jumped on them and raced through the town with bullets flying everywhere. They had the road leading out of town under direct fire, as we had to run through a stream of tracer bullets as we left town. We lost one man and one or two wounded and one was captured." Elements of Co. A were at Lichtenberg where Charles Rolling remembered moving into the house of a French girl called Marie Louise who cooked great meals and was "Not a bad looker either."[9]

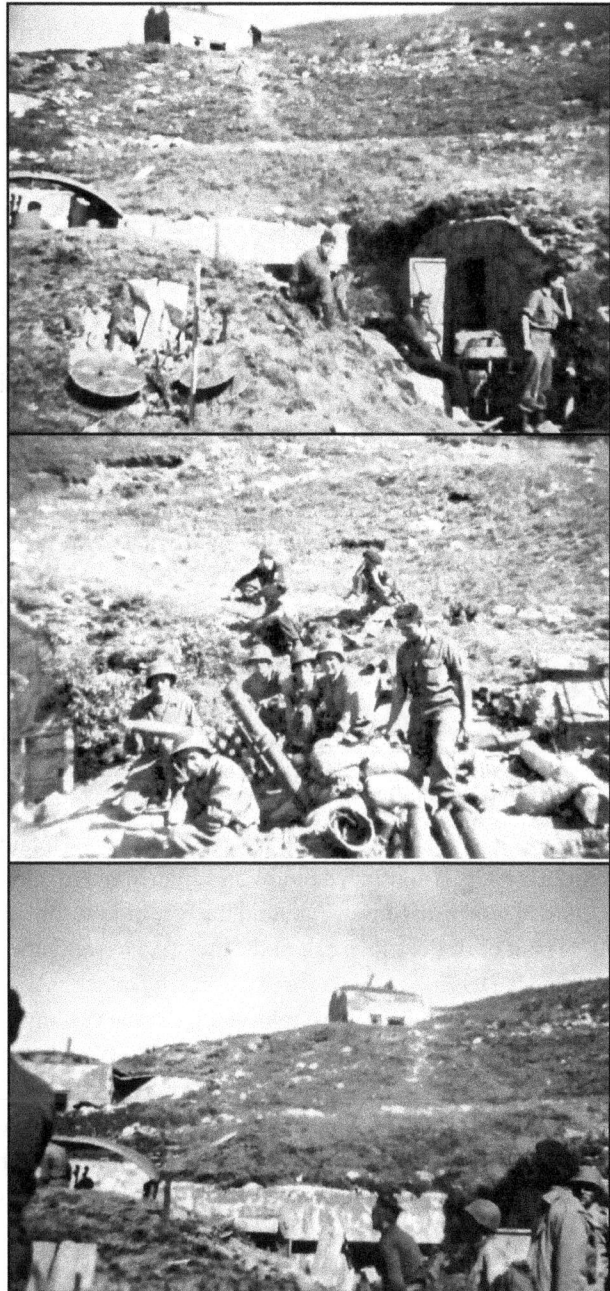

Three views of an 83rd mortar squad in action with the FFI, positioned in German pillboxes at Wimmenau, France. *Codega Collection*

Capt. Joseph H. Garsson, nicknamed "Gat" after a Buck Rogers character, officially took over Co. A on the 5th. There were some rumblings that Garsson's father, who was involved in industrial war production, had political connections and influenced military authorities to place his son in a non-combat outfit. After the war, Garsson himself claimed that the company commanders of the 83rd had been ordered by "higher headquarters" to take care of him. Lt. Col. Efnor vehemently denied the receipt of any such orders and said that he had never shown any preferential treatment to Garsson, who was "just another company commander" and "did a good job in France." Whether or not there was any truth to the accusations against Garsson, he had already served with distinction in Sicily and Italy, and the 83rd was a far cry from being a non-combat outfit. Yet Garsson was youthful and cocky, an attitude prevalent

Jean Pierre Combe, honorary member of Co. C, firing the mortar. *Jean Pierre Combe*

in many young men, but one which would later come back to haunt him. John McEvoy described him as "… a hellraiser, but militarily he knew what he was doing." Sam Kweskin, HQ Co., said, "… he was a maverick in a lot of ways, and we enjoyed his irreverence." Lt. Robert Bush recalled Garsson displayed great concern for the welfare of his men, checking with them every day, and he could always be seen eating a D bar, a Hershey-like chocolate treat.[10]

Also on the 5th, Capt. Robert Smith, Co. C, wrote a "Commendation of Volunteer Personnel" for honorary member Jean Pierre Combe. He noted Combe's heroic actions at Briançon, performance as a squad mortar man since, and his "outstanding fidelity to duties, courage, and initiative." Apparently facing the loss of Combe from the company, Smith stated, "It is with deepest regret that we would have a man of this type leave the company and it is felt by this officer that his type exemplifies the highest tradition of the French nation." Combe would remain until the last man of the battalion left for home.[11]

One man who did leave the battalion was Maj. Gordon M. Mindrum, who departed amidst snow flurries on January 6th due to a minor injury sustained in late 1944 to assume his new duties as transportation/chemical officer the 100th Infantry Division, 3rd Army. His loss to the battalion would be temporary. Co. B continued to fire on Wingen; one of Co. A's men named "Domonick" [*probably Pfc. Dominic J. Di Riemigio*] was bruised by a dud; and the rear of John Butler's truck was blown off as the enemy shelled Lichtenberg. As a result of Butler's loss, half of the men had to walk under shell fire to Reipertswiller.[12]

James Helsel, Co. A, wrote of the enemy attack: "About dinner time the town was heavily shelled, the barrage lasted one hour and forty-five min. solid. During this my gun was given a fire command. After a little argument Sgt. Jordan and myself crawled out. He got the ammo ready while I set the gun without the sight, for it was laying in the house in a dresser drawer. I then crawled over the shed and Jordan and I ran past the gun dropping our shells and run on into the house. This was repeated about four times, soon the German gun was quiet. During the barrage a dud went through the second squads house, clear down into the cellar. Our truck had it's hind duals knocked off. Also an enemy patrol had gotten quite close to town, so we were forced to tear our guns down. Under small arm fire the jeeps took all the equipment and some of the men and the rest of us went out of town along an old mule path and got shelled once on the way. We went back to a town called Rappweiler [*Reipertswiller*] and set up our guns."[13]

By January 7th the battalion forward CP had moved to Ingwiller as Co. A inflicted heavy casualties on some enemy infantry massing for an attack, while Co. B's rear remained at Saverne. Co. A, 3rd Platoon, was relieved by Co. C, 3rd Platoon, on the 8th and moved to a school house at Saverne, although Lt. Robert J. Bush's section of Co. A had a close call with a jet propelled plane in the Ingwiller vicinity. Co. C also relieved Co. B, which moved their forward CP to Wimmenau. On the lighter side the persistent snow gave some of the southern boys of Co. D their first opportunities at snowballs and sledding. Tragedy struck again on the 9th when Lt. Fred J. Kulaga, Co. C, reported a shell, which had been checked, exploded in the middle of the barrel. Three men were wounded, the most serious being Cpl. George E. Tarasek, who lost a leg below the knee. Less serious were Cpl. Alec J. Dunaeff, with shrapnel to the leg, and Pfc. William C. Plankar, who had shrapnel rip through his helmet and cut the back of his neck. "Every man in the squad was hit by shrapnel," according to William C. Ford. "I was just in a daze and numb from the close explosion. Cpl. Tarasek was badly wounded. I could see that his leg had been blown off. I took a pill from my pouch and gave it to him with water from my canteen because everything on him was bloody and shredded. At the same time Pfc. Louis Grisham took off his belt and placed it around the injured leg to slow down the bleeding. Soon the medics came with a stretcher and carried Cpl. Tarasek away along with the other injured men … it was cold and snow lay on the ground now covered with red blood."[14]

On January 10th, Lt. Col. Efnor received orders to attend a meeting of the chief of CWS in Paris the following day and Maj. John P. McEvoy was to come to the battalion forward CP. Co. C's 3rd Platoon blasted Dambach, getting satisfactory results as they tested a new type of recoil system. But premature shell bursts again plagued the battalion as the 1st Platoon of Co. C suffered three casualties when a shell exploded in their #1 gun.[15]

At this point Lee Steedle, Co. B, summed up the situation, writing in his memoir, "We were unable to reach a standstill until January 10th. All of our moves during those [first] ten days [of January] were defensive. We grew accustomed to seeing Army Engineers taping blocks of TNT to the sides of trees lining our forest roads. I recall one morning when we were ordered to fire a heavy

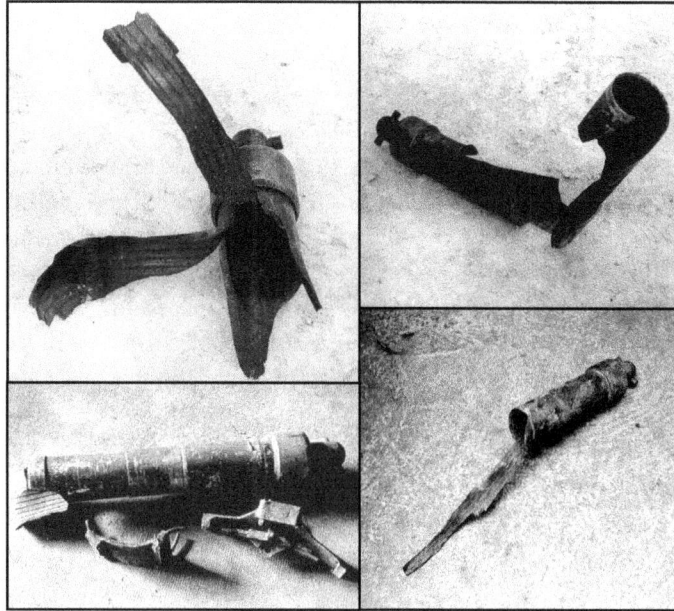

Clockwise from top left: Lower portion of burst barrel; a January 11th, 1945, effect of mortar barrel burst of HE in Co. B, of the 83rd; effect of barrel burst from HE shell; and bent slide and broken collar of mortar of the mortar barrel. *National Archives*

barrage of both HE and WP in a wide arc, not with specific targets, but just so the noise and smoke of our shelling would cover the sound of dozens of trees being blasted to form a roadblock."[16]

Defective shells continued to haunt the battalion on January 11th when, despite the fact that the ammo had been previously checked and cleaned, a premature burst in Co. B wounded five men. The group was firing HE in support of the 180th Infantry. The most seriously wounded and hospitalized was Pfc. Kary M. Malone with a broken leg, while less injured were Pfc. Eugene Overstreet, who suffered shrapnel wounds of the shoulder and arm, and Pvt. Joseph Kulick with a concussion and blast burns. Cpl. Chester P. Namiotko and Sgt. Arthur T. ("Babe") Gregory suffered concussions from the blast but were not hospitalized. According to the official report, the "shell exploded at collar; middle of barrel, barrel, standard, tie rods destroyed, locking pin gone, base plate cracked, sight still good." Lt. Kulaga reported Co. C, 2nd Platoon, also suffered two casualties during the day, Sgt. Leonard W. Turan and Pfc. Joe R. Rivera, who were slightly wounded and evacuated at an aid station when a concentrated enemy barrage impacted in the CP area.[17]

From January 11th through the 14th, the 3rd Platoon of Co. C continued to pound Dambach. By request, Co. A was attached to the 12th Armored Division on the 13th to support an attack on Herlishein about 35 miles distant, until relieved by and attached to the 36th Infantry Division. Co. A left Saverne on the 14th to establish positions for the attack but were not needed and retraced their steps to Saverne. The movement was recalled by Charles Rolling, writing, "Company moved out to go in to the lines. Big push coming soon." The battalion CP remained at Wimmenau and Co. B set their mortars loose on Barenthal on the 15th.[18]

From the 16th through the 19th, the three platoons of Co. A moved forward to support the 66th Armored, 12th Armored Division, although their services were rarely called upon. Sgt. William Ford, Co. C, recalled that his company was part of a task force attached to the 157th Infantry which also included the 158th Artillery, companies C and D of the 191st Tank Battalion, and one platoon of the 45th Reconnaissance. This force was to counterattack enemy units in the area between Mouterhouse and Barenthal that were keeping Allied forces from breaking through the Lichtenberg Forest and on into the Alsatian Plains. The ensuing battle lasted from January 14th through the 16th and was fought against the 6th SS Mountain Division from Finland in freezing weather and snow. When the battle ended there were only two prisoners and reportedly seven that escaped.[19]

Premature shell bursts were again addressed on January 17th when VI Corps called Maj. McEvoy with the defective ammo lot numbers, which information Capt. Albert H. Crenshaw relayed to Capt. Bernard Stone of Co.

B. Following this the Division G-2 requested a mobile ammo reserve as they were expecting enemy counterattacks, but they were informed of the defective ammo lot numbers. Since all rear ammo dumps had been frozen until all lots could be checked, such a move would leave the battalion with minimal ammunition. Capt. Crenshaw clarified this point to Division G-2, as Maj. McEvoy, at VI Corps, called in a directive correcting the situation from Gen. Patch: "All possible precaution will be taken when firing ammo. Recommendation that V-shaped barricades be built around the mortar with the apex of the V at the baseplate of the mortar. The man who drops in the shell is to stand outside of the barricades. All ammo in rear dumps has been released and is available." Soon afterward Lt. Col. Efnor returned from Paris and ordered all mortar positions be sandbagged to guard against future premature bursts.[20]

Due to the ammunition shortage, Lt. Col. Efnor, on the18th, instructed the G-3 to inform the men to only fire on targets within range. Col. William C. Hammond, VI Corps chemical officer, visited the battalion CP and announced there would be a demonstration in the area of Rambiersville in regard to the defective ammo.[21] Yet while the problem of defective ammunition continued to be assessed, the 3rd Platoon of Co. A came under the direct fire of German 88mm shells at Rohrwiller and Co. C supported the 157th Infantry, which had been cut off and isolated at Riepertswiller.[22]

Enemy infiltration became a problem on the 19th when a Capt. Sacks, assistant G-2 Division, called the battalion regarding "four men dressed in green uniforms, wearing little round caps, no overcoats, carrying packs, each man observed with a rifle." As this order was being issued, the 3rd Platoon of Co. A was engaged in an artillery and small arms fight with enemy infantry which had infiltrated their lines. There were no casualties but the platoon was forced to abandon 17 HE and 140 WP shells. At nearly the same time that Co. A was under fire, the 2nd Platoon of Co. C, under enemy attack while attempting to give protection to the 157th Infantry at Riepertswiller, had an enemy shell fall directly on their CP ammo dump. There were no casualties and as the position became untenable all mortars were safely removed, leaving the 2nd Platoon temporarily out of action. Sgt. William Ford, Co. C, recalled, "A shell directly hit our ammunition dump sending fire and shrapnel in all directions."[23]

The situation intensified with a heavy snow on the 20th as the 1st Platoon, Co. A, was shelled out of their position and Maj. McEvoy had the battalion trucks hauling ammo from Sarrebourg to beleaguered troops on the front that had run out of ammunition. Snow began to fall again on the 21st as the battalion CP at Ingwiller closed and moved to La Petite-Pierre. The 2nd Platoon of Co. C was relieved from supporting the 157th Infantry at Zittersheim and sent to the rear at Saverne.[24]

1st Lieutenant Francis J. Schleifer, who spoke fluent German, was lightly wounded as three inches of snow fell on the 21st. Schleifer had already demonstrated his aggressiveness in France during an incident when he served as a forward observer. One morning as the haze lifted from a village he noticed some German soldiers entering a barn at the edge of town. Schleifer ordered his radio operator, Pvt. John S. Etter, to order mortar fire on the target as a warning. The first round hit the roof and blew open the door. A soldier peered out the opening and closed the door. This happened three times until Schleifer had had enough and said to Etter, "If this is some kind of game I don't feel like playing today. Have them bring up the whole platoon of mortars." Etter requested the necessary fire and within seconds the barn was blown into a million pieces, to which Etter remarked, "The game is over."[25]

Perhaps one of the most intriguing and controversial incidents of the war involving the 83rd also took place on January 21st and occurred with the 3rd Platoon of Co. A, which was to support the 143rd Infantry in an action near Greis, France. Lt. Col. Charles J. Denholm, a young upstart officer of the 143rd Infantry, who reportedly knew little or nothing about mortars, called upon Capt. Joseph H. Garsson, Co. A, 83rd Chemical Mortar Battalion, to place his mortars in a specified position. Denholm stated he instructed Garsson to place the mortars in "Positions northwest of woods located in vicinity coordinates 080155 and somewhere northwest of the point, coordinates 0781153, but not so far back as the road going between Kurtzenhausen and Bischwiller … at Gries …" In a sequence of events that followed, Garsson, fearing for the safety of his men, refused the order, later claiming he instructed a subordinate officer not to obey the directive because it completely lacked defilade protection, thereby exposing his men to a possible massacre.[26]

The journal of the 143rd Infantry states the exact dialog exchange between the parties involved. Major Raymond Lynch of the 36th Infantry Division, serving as S-3, said to Garsson, "Lt. Col. Denholm wants you to make a rcn [*reconnaissance*] … and have your mortars in there by 1500." Garsson responded to Denholm, "I received your message and I refuse to go out there even if it means a court martial." Denholm passed Garsson's response to Gen. Robert I. Stack, assistant commander of the 36th Infantry, who told him, "Relieve him of his command and put next senior officer in command of Company."[27]

Following repeated unsuccessful efforts to get him to comply, Garsson was removed from command of the company the following day and charges eventually were brought against him in a complicated series of events. Sam Kweskin, HQ Co., in defense of Garsson, claimed that Garsson had refused to place his mortars in full view of the enemy, "... which an infantry colonel had asked him to do. The colonel, unaware that the mortar could fire just as effectively from hidden positions, could not admit he was wrong; instead he determined that Garsson refused to take orders from a superior officer, and consequently ordered him to report to the 83rd HQ."[28]

Initially, it was recommended Garsson be given an "administrative admonition" but the commanding general was not satisfied and on March 11th would order Garsson be tried by court-martial. Lt. Robert Bush remembered that the order to place the mortars fell to him once Garsson was relieved. He claimed he implored upon Garsson to follow the order, but it was all to no avail. Capt. Garsson had possibly saved the lives of an entire platoon but had refused a direct order of a superior officer, an act for which he would have to suffer the wrath of military authorities. The next day, January 22nd, Lt. Alfred L. Forrester assumed temporary command of Co. A.[29]

James Helsel, Co. A, wrote his account of the incident, which seemed to support Capt. Garsson, although he claimed it transpired on the 20th. "About 1:00 in the afternoon we moved to a little town and set our guns up along a high railroad bank. We received direct fire from German tanks once. While standing by the guns a shell came over and cut the light wires that were strung above our gun position. Capt. Garsson was relieved of his command because he refused to take us into the woods up ahead ... Captain is in jail because of refusing to move us any closer, nevertheless the first platoon fired a smoke screen using about 100 rounds of ammo while we moved up the railroad bank further. We didn't have much time to dig good holes, the ground was very loose."[30]

Co. B also got involved in an incident on January 22nd as the company commander of Co. C, 180th Infantry, out on a point, called for fire from Co. B, 83rd Chemical Mortar Battalion. According to the official report, "He adjusted the fire but pulled it too far back into his flank. 17 men were wounded by 6 WP." Capt. Bernard Stone, of battalion HQ, investigated and found Co. B was not at fault. Regimental Headquarters gave a confused account of the incident by claiming the misdirected barrage had created 17 "enemy" casualties and contributed to hindering the enemy attack, although they incorrectly gave the 23rd as the date of the episode. A prisoner supported that a direct hit on his command had routed his unit.[31]

Already during January the 83rd Chemical Battalion and the 2nd Chemical Battalion each had two barrel bursts. As a result, Lt. Col. Bruce T. Humphreville, 7th Army chemical officer, "... ordered the 6th Chemical Depot Company to remove the fuzes from the defective lot of shells and ship the fuzeless shells to [*the 11th Chemical Maintenance Company*] to rebore and rethread the shells so that Ordnance artillery fuzes could be used. Three (3) fuze wrenches were made for the 6th Chemical Depot Company to accelerate their end of the task and two (2) special boring bits for TNT, four (4) steady rests and two (2) finishing thread taps were made for the reboring and rethreading operations." This modification of the 4.2" chemical mortar shell . "... involved removal of old fuzes, reaming out the nose of the shell removing a portion of the TNT filling and rethreading the nose of the shell." These shells started coming in to the 11th Chemical Maintenance Company on the 22nd. Under the supervision of Capt. Albert Gallagher of Syracuse, New York, commanding officer of the 11th Chemical Maintenance Company, "... local machining facilities were acquired and a

11th Chemical Maintenance Co. with German mortar. *Kenneth Lamb*

production line set-up, which resulted in an [*eventual*] output of 500 to 600 completely modified shells per day," and "In spite of the acknowledged hazards of this operation no injuries were sustained … this out-put of modified shell permitted Chemical Mortar Battalions of 7th Army to meet commitments for unrestricted firing in direct support of Infantry, in addition to giving them a fuze with a delay train."[32]

On the 23rd all battalion rear installations were ordered moved west of Saverne. Co. A received a commendation from Lt. Col. Efnor for their fine shooting and a platoon of Co. C continued to fire on Rothbach. All three weapons companies remained heavily engaged with the enemy on the 24th as assorted platoons were attached to the 179th, 180th and 274th infantry regiments, as well as the 36th Engineer Regiment. It was bitter cold and the snow continued to fall, many of the men living in huts. Capt. Smith, Co. C, wrote home, "Right now all three of my platoons are living and sleeping and fighting in foxholes with a foot of snow over them." Smith said his own CP was in a wine cellar with straw on the floor. He also reported that 1st Lt. Norman ("Rosy") Rosenthal's platoon had made a direct hit on a German captain and also killed 17 other enemy soldiers with one round. Smith relayed, "They all scattered and one was taken prisoner and the prisoner said that the shell hit the captain right between the shoulders. That's one they won't have to bury."[33]

Yet once again, also on the 24th, the defective ammunition was the main topic as Lt. Col. Efnor called Col. Hammond to inform him that he was returning 300 HE shells as they had not been cleaned and the 83rd had no means to clean them in the frozen conditions. Hammond had already sent a message to Efnor dated the previous day stating assorted lots of HE and WP which had been sent were faulty and directing Efnor to return them immediately. The snow was very deep and continued to fall on the 25th. As the 26th arrived, more news of faulty ammo lots developed, a memo from the 45th Division HQ to be on the alert for enemy "penetrations, infiltrations, or parachute" attacks was received, and the 3rd Platoon of Co. A covered the movement of a patrol to Oberhoffen.[34]

Not only was the 83rd faced with such threats and bad ammo, but the inclement winter weather took its toll as well. George Borkhuis, Mess Sgt. of HQ Co., wrote on the 27th, "It has snowed continuously for the last 2 days and is still snowing." He also remarked many of the men were skiing, sledding, and that snow was good for camouflage but made the roads hazardous for jeep and tank drivers. Lt. Leonard R. Kenney of Co. A was sent to the rear with a frozen foot and Lt. Robert Bush took sick, as did many of the men. During the night of the 27th, a railroad tie used to reinforce huts erected by Co. A fell on the head of Pvt. Ralph D. Pistoia of Philadelphia, Pennsylvania. Luckily, the snow finally stopped for a while on the 28th, and Co. A moved into Bischwiller on the 30th. But the freezing temperatures and snow, which had been nearly non-stop since the beginning of January, brought operations to a near standstill. Huge snow drifts and blistering winds, as well as wet snow, created much frostbite because of wet socks and feet. James F. Dougherty, Co. A, said he used his rifle butt "… to crack the ice on streams to get drinking water after sleeping in winter time foxholes." Capt. Smith, Co. C, attempted to be optimistic: "The snow is really beautiful … I was on a reconnaissance … and ran across 8 deer. There are also wild boar in this region."[35]

Despite valiant efforts, the Allied forces were slowly forced to withdraw from various positions and on January 31st the 45th Division ordered all units to make preliminary plans to take up positions on the "Hagenau Line and Vosges Position." Capt. Smith, Co. C, noted, "Today for some reason it has turned warm and the snow has begun to melt, and it's muddy and sloshy and all, but sure nice not to be so cold … the snow is still pretty deep, but at the rate it is going it won't last too long. Sure hope it doesn't turn cold and make the roads and everything all ice, but that's probably what it will do."[36]

The month had certainly been a difficult one for the 83rd Chemical Mortar Battalion, as shown by the report of the 11th Chemical Company, Detachment "B", which had been attached to the battalion. They submitted that they had repaired 99 standard, 90 barrel, and 85 to 88 baseplate assemblies, for total repairs of between 274 and 277, which represented a turnover of about 761 per cent of the battalion's mortars. The 11th Chemical Maintenance Company also provided the 83rd Chemical Mortar Battalion with some of the new 4.2" Mortar Pneumatic Spring-Return Recoil Mechanisms due to the total inadequacy of the old shock absorbing mechanism. The new device, created by T/Sgt. Elwin A. Corrow of the 11th Chemical while in Italy, hence the name Corrow Pneumatic Shock Absorber #32, was modeled a bit like the Russian and German mortars, held up extremely well, and was believed to far surpass the old bronze slide type shock absorber. In addition, the 83rd Chemical Mortar Battalion reported a total of 39,928 shells expended for the month, along with two barrel bursts, and only 12 casualties, including none killed. The problem with the barrel bursts had already been addressed by the CWS and HQ of the 11th Chemical Maintenance Company which had reported that from January 22nd to the end of the month they had already rebored and rethreaded 278 shells for use of the artillery fuze and could have done more had more been sent.[37]

At the beginning of February, the front extended northwest approximately on the line of Hagenau, Niedermodern, Mulhausen, Reipertswiller, and Sarreinsberg. The 45th Division extended from the vicinity of Rothbach northwest to Sarreinsberg, with the 6th Corps posted on the left and the 103rd Division on the right. The mission was defined as purely defensive, although there were limited American attacks and aggressive patrols. Due to the rash of premature shell bursts the mortar crews primarily provided smokescreens with WP. Organizations that the 83rd Chemical Mortar Battalion would either be attached to or support during February included: the 141st, 142nd, 143rd, 157th, 179th, 222nd, and 232nd infantry regiments; the 36th, 42nd, and 45th infantry divisions; the 36th Engineers, RCT; and CCB - 6th Armored, 14th Armored Division.[38]

The 83rd Chemical Mortar Battalion suffered two casualties on the opening day of the month when an enemy 88mm shell from a Tiger tank landed in a Co. A position near Hagenau. Cpl. William J. Gallagher, Jr., from Philadelphia, Pennsylvania, of the 2nd Platoon, was seriously injured in the leg and evacuated while Pfc. William R. Garner from Aragon, Georgia, was lightly wounded. Gallagher recalled, "I was talking with Carlos Trautman when the first 88 shell came in and rained shrapnel all around. The fragments missed us. But a second shell came in quickly and got me in the right leg … pieces of my leg had been scattered all over the ground." Cpl. Cornelius ("Neil") McCarthy, also from Philadelphia, gave Gallagher a shot of morphine and he was eventually sent back to the States where he spent six months recovering at Ashford General Hospital, the military facility at White Sulphur Springs, West Virginia. Some time during the day, a jeep pulled into the CP of the 83rd and Cpl. McCarthy, Medical Detachment, asked, "How far are they?," questioning the Russian advance on Berlin. This was on everyone's mind at this time, including Cpl. Henry E. Fajkowski, from Baltimore, Maryland, also of the Medical Detachment, who said, "You know what the guys are saying every time some shells land in our area … They say the Russians are overshooting again."[39]

In the course of the next two days, four men of Co. A and Capt. Joe Garsson, apparently having returned to his company to await word of any charges brought against him, went to a mortar range in Sarrebourg to test the shells, which were to have the 105mm artillery fuze. Apparently there was also an experiment with a new baseplate around this time by the 83rd. At Oberhoffen on the 3rd Lt. Alfred Forrester, Co. A, was ordered by the 142nd Infantry to take the one platoon of Co. A serving with the 141st Infantry and return them to their original post at Bischwiller. Capt. Smith, Co. C, reported on the night of the 3rd, "We shot into a bunch of Krauts … and you could hear them screaming; so we threw in 20 more and that quieted things down. We also got a direct hit on a tank …"[40]

During the 36th Infantry's attack of February 4th, Lt. Lester L. Henry, a former Ranger in Co. A, serving as a forward observer, captured one German soldier. Elwood ("Long John") Guthrie noted everybody in Henry's platoon liked him and would have followed him through hell. James Helsel, Co. A, said his platoon moved up to Gambsheim to do some firing and then returned to Bischwiller. Capt. Smith, Co. C, continued to boast to his wife, "I'm a heavy mortar company commander and, according to the law of averages, if I've lived this long I'll last the rest of the war because I've learned to take care of myself and my men. We've had only five wounded since Christmas. One lost a leg and that was the worst. No killed. And if we haven't killed 300 (at least) Krauts in that time then I'm a liar." Such optimism was short-lived, though, as bad luck struck the battalion on the 5th when two rounds of 280mm shells landed in the rear CP area of Co. A at Saverne. One shell made a direct hit on a building housing personnel, slightly wounding Lt. Justin G. Woomer of Co. B and an unidentified cook.[41]

Co. C continued its good work on February 6th as the forward observer spotted some Germans standing around a fire and had the 3rd Platoon fire on them, resulting in two killed and several wounded. Rain developed as the weather began to warm, melting the snow. The ongoing problem of defective mortar shells and the employment of fuzes was addressed on the 7th when Lt. Col. William C. Hammond visited the battalion CP to discuss details of using artillery fuzes on 4.2" chemical mortars. This was followed the next day when Co. B, covering the infantry, had one round of concentrated fire fall short and kill an infantry soldier. Although their remaining rounds made a direct hit on the enemy, Col. Paul D. Adams, division commander, arrived at Saverne to lead an inquiry into the problem. The 142nd Infantry requested Lt. Col. Efnor to leave fire data and a man to stay with the incoming mortar platoon. On the 9th Motor Pool mechanic Charlie Lowry, Co. A, wrote home that "the snow was over a foot deep here a few days ago, but now it is gone and we have the mud."[42]

On February 10th, Co. A of the 83rd was busy laying a smokescreen for the 143rd Infantry, 36th Infantry Division, as they attacked Rohrwiller. The 3rd Platoon was heavily shelled and their ammo dump was hit, destroying 200 WP and 25 HE shells and causing severe WP burns to Lt. Lester L. Henry and Pvt. Fred C. Smith, who was evacuated. Additionally, the position was bombed and strafed by jet-propelled planes but no further casualties resulted. Co. A also supported Co. C, 142nd Infantry near an insane asylum. Yet, despite whatever damage the enemy inflicted on the 83rd, the enemy suffered much more as evidenced by a German SS who surrendered to the 1st Platoon of Co. C, claiming he gave up due to the "nerve wracking, incessant large mortar barrages." Co. C's 3rd Platoon fired 30 HE, eleven utilizing the delayed fuse, nine of which made a direct hit on an enemy machine gun squad positioned inside a house. The shells blew up the structure and set it on fire. At HQ Co., Mess Sgt. George Borkhuis noted the heat wave was still on and ice had melted off the canal, while Capt. Hulcher had gone out and caught 24 trout.[43]

Co. A fell back from the Rohrwiller area to Bischwiller on the 12th, and the 11th Chemical Maintenance Company placed 12 men on temporary duty at a machine shop in Vincey, France, where arrangements had been made with the 59th Ordnance Company to use six lathes to continue the reboring and rethreading process of the 4.2" shells. They began their work the following day.[44]

On a nice, clear Valentine's Day, February 14th, the mess sergeant of Co. A, Edward Blasz, along with Pfc. George W. Ramsey, Jr., and Alfred J. ("A.J.") Brown, Jr., from Nashville, Tennessee, went foraging after a cow. On the return trip, while crossing a bridge which was under enemy observation, they were fired upon, resulting in the serious wounding of Blasz and Ramsey, while Brown escaped with minor scratches to his back. The Germans also started laying in some 240mm shells on Co. A at Bischwiller and one hit the corner of the room in which "Buck" Martin and comrades were sleeping, went clear to the cellar, and exploded. On a lighter note for the day, due to the improved weather, the Air Corps "came out of hibernation" to continue their work, which inspired Capt. Smith, Co. C, to write home, "We may get a Cub for observation and fire direction in the Bn., which is what I was advocating to the hotshots at Edgewood two years ago and more. Of course the pilot comes with the Cub, but we will furnish the observer to direct fire …"[45]

The problem of defective shells was again addressed on the 16th with the receipt of a message that "premature bursts due to defective fuzes may be reduced by insuring that large brass screw plug is down when shell is dropped in to tube end by using care to avoid as much as possible imparting a rotating motion to shell on its downward course. All 4.2" mortar troops will be instructed to use ETO [*European Theater of Operations*] suggested techniques which is an additional precaution and is not a substitute for the regular inspection for missing balls [*whatever that is – ed.*]. Inspection must be continued." A letter was also received from Col. Humphreville, 7th Army, regarding the marking of ammunition boxes and containers. Such precautions apparently proved somewhat useless as the 1st Platoon of Co. A suffered a serious blow on February 17th when a defective HE shell exploded about ten to fifteen and possibly as much as twenty feet from the barrel, resulting in the death of Pvt. Richard I. Parthum. Six additional men were listed as casualties, including Cpl. Leonard G. Blystone, who was mortally wounded and passed away the next day; Cpl. Paul H. Ruby, Pvt. John J. Pehemelle, and Pvt. Edward V. Pelar (Pellar), all of whom were seriously wounded; and Pfc.'s David Goler and Ralph W. Stoddard, both lightly wounded. All were former members of old Co. D. Lamenting on Blystone's death, Lee Steedle recalled, "Bly was a small, wiry and gutsy kid my age with a constant grin and an incredible disregard for his own safety, which early on had given him a reputation in the platoon for being crazy, and which had also earned him a Bronze Star and at least one Purple Heart. I often think of my crazy Mexican-English friend, and how strange it is that while the Krauts couldn't kill him, one of our own shells did." Lt. Col. Efnor reported this was the fourth such incident the battalion had experienced, and the first that had burst outside the barrel.[46]

A number of high ranking military officials arrived at the battalion CP on the 18th and visited the platoon positions of Co. C in order to help determine the cause of the premature shell bursts; however, they probably did not witness an incident wherein an artillery forward observer, directing fire for the 3rd Platoon of Co. C, mistakenly had them fire 10 rounds of HE on Co. "E" of the 222nd Infantry, contributing to the death of two men and seriously wounding another. According to the battalion journal, "3rd Platoon of Co. C, 83G was to fire for patrol going out to recover body of man killed in a mine field. Coordinates were given to Lt. John L. Boyd, platoon commander, who figured data and fired one round of WP. This round was sensed by 'H' Co. observer, by sound, as 200 yards left. (Later investigation by Lt. Boyd showed this round to have landed 400 yards right and 300 yards short). A shift of 200 yards right was made and another WP was fired. Communications went out at this point and as time for the patrol to go out neared, the Inf. Bn. S-3, believing that the round was still over the target, ordered Lt. Boyd to fire 10 HE for effect. These were fired and landed in the right platoon of 'E' Company, killing two men and severely wounding another."[47]

With their rear CP at Eckertswiller, bad luck seemed to follow Co. A as there was another premature shell burst at their position at Bischweiler, near the house of a family named Schnell with a young grandson named Eddie. A defective HE shell fired from the #4 gun [*James G. Helsel said it was the #1 gun*] of the 2nd Platoon burst about four feet from the barrel [*Ironically, Sam Bundy claimed it to have been twenty feet from the barrel*]. Despite some inconsistencies in the reports of the tragedy, the results were horrific. Among the seriously wounded were Cpl. William E. Rushing and Pfc. Danile ("Dan") Cooper, both of whom "lost legs" according to Sam Bundy. Reno Toniolo said, "When I went to pick up Cooper's leg to put a tourniquet on it, it was blown clean off," but he did survive. Rushing died later that day in a hospital. Two corporals were slightly wounded, George T. Cairl and James G. Helsel, as was Pvt. Eustus N. Stewart. Sam Bundy wrote that the latter three men suffered "a few cuts and bruises." The worst element of this incident was that Eddie, the four-year-old [*James G. Helsel said he was three years old*] grandson of the Schnells, standing about 80 feet from the barrel, was killed by the explosion. Alfred J. Brown, Jr., attempted to give the lad first aid but found it useless as the boy's heart had been pierced by shrapnel. Toniolo said most of the men knew these defective shells were being produced by a munitions factory in the states, and "Doc" Hulcher added, "Boy it's rough. I can't see how the boys can still drop them down the barrel - but they do." Sam Bundy wrote in his diary, "Other Chemical outfits have been having more of this trouble than we – Generals from Washington are here now on an investigation. Lanyards are being used for firing mortars."[48]

By the 19th, the weather had turned very warm with sun and some fog and the battalion still subject to the Saverne Special "Jerries 380" coming in. But the defective shells remained the hot topic as Capt. Robert D. Myers, CWS, assistant chemical officer, reported to authorities the premature burst in the 83rd the previous two days and noted that the 83rd had been firing without use of a lanyard, while the 2nd and 99th chemical battalions had used the lanyard and suffered no casualties. As a result, it was recommended to use "lanyard-firing" when using the M3 fuze. Lt. Col. Hammond, VI Corps chemical officer, called the battalion on the 20th of the month regarding use of the lanyard, artillery fuze, and other related matters. Instructions were issued to all companies: "Mortar shells will be dropped into the barrel with the slide up to prevent barrel burst." Lt. Col. Hammond was more specific when he ordered, "In light of recent information from higher headquarters, it is directed that until further notice all HE filled 4.2" Cml. Mortar shells with M3 fuze be fired by use of lanyard only, with all personnel protected insofar as is practicable by revetments [*walls of sandbags erected next to the mortars*] or in dug in positions. In event rapid fire is necessary, 4.2" shell with M34A1 fuze should be used. This modified shell is available at rate of approximately 100 rounds per chemical mortar battalion per day."[49]

A Capt. Paulson of the technical staff from the States arrived on the 21st to examine the 4.2" fuzes, while the next day the 2nd Platoon of Co. C had a WP shell burst prematurely 150 yards from the barrel. Luckily no casualties resulted. Morale may have been given a slight boost on the 25th when Co. B was awarded a citation from the 36th Division for their outstanding performance in the action of December 12, 1944. Self congratulations were added by Capt. Smith, Co. C, who not only lauded his company but added, "Of course, two or three aren't worth a damn, but that's always the case. The rest are just good American boys who know their job and do it. And we can out shoot anything the Artillery has to offer. And I tell these new outfits so; then these boys back me up by doing it. So they can't get along without us and we don't get any relief." But defective ammunition remained the focus of the month when Lt. Col. Hammond informed battalion headquarters of a bad ammo lot of WP on the 26th. On the 28th the platoon leader of Co. B conferred with the colonel of the 143rd Infantry.[50]

During the month of February, the 11th Chemical Company, Detachment "B", yet attached to the 83rd, had repaired 53 standards, 51 barrels, and 68 baseplate assemblies, for a total of 172 repairs, a figure representing a turnover of 478 per cent of the mortars in the battalion. More importantly, despite the constant fear of firing defective shells, the men of the 83rd expended 21,812 HE and 12,272 WP, for a total of 34,084 shells, with only 17 casualties

Crafton Eaddy and Robert Brimm in
Stambach, France, 1945. *Eugene Plassmann*

during the month, most caused by their own shells. This problem was already being taken care of by the machine shop at Vincey where 3,252 shells had been rehabilitated since February 13th and shipped back to the ordnance depot. In addition, "… with this shell project, 167 artillery fuze wrenches were prepared by welding steel handles on the common hand wrench, to facilitate the ammunition handlers of the mortar battalions in applying the artillery fuze, and 250 boxes were constructed for the 6th Chemical Depot Company to house the M3, 4.2" mortar fuzes from the shells."[51]

March opened with the mission stated as being defensive and the front extending approximately on the Hagenau-Niedermodern-Mulhausen-Reipertswiller-Sarreinsberg line. Co. A remained in bivouac where they received orders from the 103rd Division for a 24-hour mission. Co. B, attached to the 36th Infantry Division, was engaged with various targets in direct support of the 141st and 142nd infantry regiments, while Co. C gave direct support to the 222nd and 232nd infantry regiments.[52]

The situation remained basically the same for the next few days, although on March 2nd an order was received that mortars could be fired with a lanyard "… whenever the Division Commander see's fit." This was followed on the 3rd with an order that stated, "All 4.2" Cml. Mort. HE shells will be fired with a lanyard except in cases of extreme emergency. A command decision by the Division Commander concerned is required to disregard use of the lanyard." Lt. Robert E. Bundy, newly arrived to Co. A in late February, remembered, "We had to fire using lanyards. This slowed the process down. We fired more and more WP to make up for it. Also, I might add, we were safe using time fuzes. Apparently the problem was only with the impact fuzes." Co. A also received orders to relieve Co. C, which they effectually completed on the 4th. Lt. Lester L. Henry of the company wrote home he had gone hunting and had venison for dinner. Co. C was then relieved of attachment to the 42nd Infantry, reverted to battalion control as a VI Corps reserve, and moved to the company rear echelon near Schaeferhoff. And "Doc" Hulcher was pleased that his Medical Detachment had acquired a mobile dental unit.[53]

March 4th also saw Lt. Col. Bruce T. Humpreville, chemical officer, submit to HQ, 7th Army, chemical advisor, a paper written by Lt. Col. Efnor called *Employment of 4.2" Mortars in Close Support of Infantry*, which Efnor had recently written at the request of a new division commander. Humpreville stated the instructions in the paper would continue to be used by the 83rd until any further directive was issued.[54]

HQ Co. remained at Stambach as companies A and B continued to engage the enemy for the next few days. On March 7th, near Bischwiller, Pvt. Carlos R. Trautman, Co. A, distinguished himself in action. "During an intense and sustained enemy barrage of artillery, self-propelled gun and mortar fire, Pvt. Trautman remained at a forward observation post directing the fire of mortars which aided in the repulse of an enemy counter-attack and destroyed much enemy material." Also during the day, one platoon of Co. A had a premature burst of a WP shell, which exploded about 50 feet from the gun but caused no casualties. Less than an hour later another WP shell burst about 30 feet from the gun causing one light casualty. Capt. Robert E. Edwards, Adjutant, 83rd Chemical Mortar Battalion, reported both episodes to the chemical officer of the 7th Army, stating that both mortars were fired from soggy ground, with logs and sandbags under the baseplates, and firing with 24 rings at a range of 4,000 yards. Capt. Smith, Co. C, wrote home, "My company has been supporting the Rainbow Division, and we have made quite a reputation with them …" George Borkhuis, HQ Co., wrote, "Today we received our little silver star to go on our campaign ribbon. It represents five major campaigns – Sicily, Salerno, Rome, Southern France, and Germany. It replaces the little bronze star we received up until now."[55]

Pvt. Carlos Trautman, Co. A, again displayed his courage on March 8th. "When friendly artillery fire was falling among our troops and communications could not be established, Pvt. Trautman, disregarding enemy artillery and mortar fire as well as our barrage, made his way to the rear and succeeded in lifting the friendly fire." For this action and his gallantry of the previous day, Trautman was awarded the Bronze Star.[56]

The problem with premature shell bursts was addressed again on the 10th when Co. A reported that five per cent of their HE and WP shells fired that day were "tumblers" or duds. The battalion journal reported that "... a total of 21 HE and 3 WP duds were fired. High percentage of duds due to defective ammo. Rounds did not have true rotating flight and resulted in 'tumblers' which did not detonate on striking the ground. Extremely short range also resulted." Capt. Alfred H. Crenshaw, battalion S-3, suggested segregating the ammo by lot numbers to help find the cause. Further addressing the "tumblers" Crenshaw sent one of the WP shells to Lt. Rollin W. Kapp of the 11th Chemical Maintenance Company to inspect and show to authorities. Eventually it was determined the "tumblers" were caused by "the base of the WP shell ... tearing loose, and not causing the shell to rotate ... [and] the shell disintegrating." In addition to this problem everyone was alerted to the possibility of an enemy parachute attack that night.[57]

Some Dragon's Teeth on the Siegfried line.
Tyma Collection

Co. A was busy supporting the 232nd and 242nd Infantry regiments on March 12th, while Co. B was relieved and joined Co. C in bivouac in the rear. Excepting Co. A, the 83rd Chemical Mortar Battalion was attached to the 103rd Infantry Division on the 13th, and the company and platoon leaders of B and C met at battalion CP to discuss and prepare for a reconnaissance for mortar positions. The movement was part of a planned concentrated attack by VI Corps in conjunction with a full fledged assault along the entire 7th Army front, the objective being to "... smash the Moder River defenses, breach the Siegfried Line, and help clear the west bank of the Rhine River." Instrumental in this assault, particularly on the Siegfried Line, was the 614th TD [*Tank Destroyer*] Battalion, composed entirely of African-American soldiers.[58]

For the massive operation to be launched the following day, the 103rd Infantry Division issued orders, received on the 14th, for Co. B to be attached to the 410th Infantry and Co. C to the 411th Infantry, while Co. A, yet attached to the 42nd Infantry Division, would support the attack of the 222nd and 242nd Infantry regiments. The battalion forward CP had already moved to Weinbourg, established communications, and received extensive information on enemy and friendly minefields. Co. B was ordered "to smoke Neiffern, Uhrwiller, [*and*] Kindwiller ..."[59]

During this time, Capt. Smith, Co. C, wrote home about an earlier side trip he and Lt. Norman Rosenthal had made to Lyons to procure shoulder patches for the battalion. Lt. Col. Efnor also stated that during a shoot a "4.2" shell body ruptured" and a portion of it was recovered for inspection. According to Efnor, "It was thought at first that a premature burst occurred about 100 yds. out, but upon inspection of the recovered round it was established that premature detonation did not occur." He claimed this was proof as the burster tube was still intact and eyewitnesses said there was no streamer when the shell, fired with 21 rings, left the barrel. Efnor felt this was a result of "poor production and careless inspection."[60]

On March 15th, the VI Corps attack began with Co. A of the 83rd giving the required support to the two infantry regiments of the 42nd Division to which they had been assigned as well as to other attacking units. Co. B, with their CP at Obermodern, gave close support to the 410th Infantry, 103rd Division, providing smokescreens for Neiffern and Kindwiller, but the smoke caused poor visibility which delayed the capture of Uhrwiller. In order to support the eastward attack of the 411th Infantry, 103rd Division, Co. C provided smokescreens on the hills and high ground east of Mulhausen and the high ground south and east of Rothbach and Offwiller. Capt. Smith, Co. C, personally took a prisoner who was hiding in a house being checked for a CP. "Smitty" said it was no big deal as the soldier wanted to surrender anyway.[61]

Co. A, having delivered supporting fire on the 16th, had their advance delayed by demolition and minefields. The rear CP of Co. B moved to Bouxwiller, while the forward CP moved to Uhrwiller from Obermodern and the 2nd Platoon advanced to Mietsheim. Co. C maintained direct support of the 411th Infantry. The attack continued on the 17th as the platoons of Co. A continued their support of the 222nd and 242nd infantry regiments near Offwiller; Co.

Sidney Kirschner, Co. B, at Rohrbach.
Turan Collection

B received orders to support the 409th Infantry, 3rd Division, and moved from Gundershoffen to Engwiller; and Co. C remained in mobile support of the 411th Infantry. No rounds were fired by any of the three companies during the day. Capt. Smith, Co. C, described the wholesale destruction the battalion was witnessing, writing, "… there isn't an undamaged house in the town I am now in, and most of them are completely destroyed. There is one burning 10 yards from here now that we set on fire yesterday morning. I believe that it is our work because our shell fragments are here. In fact, I guess that the other half dozen that are burning were set by us, too, since we used mostly that kind of shell."[62]

The attack progressed, and on the 18th the battalion rear CP closed at Stambach and moved, along with Detachment B, 11th Chemical Maintenance, to a wooded area near Ingwiller, Alsace, France, a distance of 26 miles, while the battalion forward CP changed locations from Weinberg to the Froeschwiller vicinity. Co. A continued to give support to the leading elements of the infantry as they moved to Niederstanbach and, during a reconnaissance led by lieutenants Leonard R. Kenney and Nicholas P. Bash, killed one German and captured another. Co. B, supporting the 409th Infantry, moved rapidly through Engwiller, Woerth, Climbach, Gundershoffen, Lembach, and Goersdorf. Co. C, attached to the 410th Infantry, supported the 411th Infantry. This latest push was described by "Doc" Hulcher, who wrote, "Many bombers overhead and during the day lots of fighters along with bombers … Lots of artillery going off and beaucoup bombers & fighters overhead all day long … Front is moving fast and most trouble coming from mines. Hope we can trap large force between us & Third Army. We have only had a few casualties from shrapnel."[63]

A VI Corps officer contacted the 83rd on the 19th to warn that a specific lot of ammo was defective and there had been a muzzle burst in the 99th Chemical Mortar Battalion. The information was undoubtedly taken under consideration as the three weapons companies continued to move, the rear CP of Co. B departing Bouxwiller for Elsasshausen. The battalion advanced farther on the 20th with the rear CP and Detachment B, 11th Chemical Maintenance, closing at Ingwiller and moving a distance of 25 miles to Merkwiller, a place described as "really beat up." The 11th Chemical said they bivouacked in an abandoned oil refinery. The forward CP moved from Froeschwiller to Lembach. Co. A departed Niederstanbach and moved to Petersbachel. One platoon of Co. B went through Climbach and Wissembourg supporting the 36th Infantry Division. Co. C, yet supporting the 410th and 411th Infantry regiments, and with one platoon held mobile at Lembach, successfully fired 20 HE utilizing the delayed action fuze against enemy bunkers. George Borkhuis, HQ Co., remarked, "We have left our nice hotel and moved into tents."[64]

While in the vicinity of Fischbach, an outpost of the Siegfried Line, on March 22nd, Co. A made a direct hit on enemy personnel and vehicles causing numerous casualties. Co. C, attached to the 410th Infantry, remained in the vicinity of Lembach. On the 23rd, Co. A moved into a German shoe factory at Dahn, where they were held in division reserve, while elements of Co. B moved through such towns as Birkenhordt and Silg. Twelve men of the 11th Chemical Maintenance Company, temporarily placed at the machine shop of the 59th Ordnance Company at Vincey, had rebored and rethreaded an additional 3,465 shells since the first of the month and an additional machine shop had been set up by eight men during the period March 18th to March 30th, "… for future use by a Base Chemical Unit, for modification of the 4.2" chemical mortar shell." The report of the maintenance company concluded, "The rethreading and reboring of the shells for the Artillery fuze has permitted several thousand rounds of Condemned Ammunition to be put back into service. Two distinct advantages have been gained by this modification, first; a delayed action in detonating and secondly due to the great decrease in the number of barrel bursts it has permitted firing the 4.2 inch Chemical Mortar without the use of a lanyard."[65]

Crossing the Rhine River.
Ed Trey

On March 24th, orders were received for all companies of the 83rd, minus Co. A, to assemble at Klingen and be held in mobile reserve. Lt. Col. Efnor gave orders to all company officers regarding fraternization with the Germans, and "… guards were posted and a roving patrol of four men patrolled streets during the night." Co. A moved into the 42nd Division reserve in the vicinity of Bruschweiller and one platoon took 52 prisoners while another bagged three more.[66]

The entire 83rd Chemical Mortar Battalion was attached to the 36th Infantry Division on March 25th and ordered to move to the vicinity of Herxheim. As the day progressed the assembly point became Steinweiler, where they would be held in division reserve. Men of Co. A recalled moving through the "dragon's teeth" of the Siegfried Line. Co. C was attached to the 71st Infantry Division and prepared to leave for Speyer. Companies A and B were set up in the vicinity of Germersheim prepared "to cover the area across the Rhine between 67 and 71st grid line."[67]

The battalion rear CP and Detachment B, 11th Chemical Maintenance, closed at Merkwiller and traveled 25 miles by motor transport to a wooded area at Herxheim, Germany, in the vicinity of Rohrbach, on the 26th, the point from which Daniel Shields and Steve Vukson, both of HQ Co., said they entered Germany. The battalion forward CP moved from Klingen to Bellheim. The 36th Infantry Division ordered the 83rd, minus Co. C and detachments, to be held in division reserve and attached Co. A to the 143rd RCT and Co. B to the 141st RCT. Co. A moved to Lambscheim, about 1,000 yards from the Rhine River, and sank some German barges that were yet afloat. The rear of Co. B moved from Klingen to Neiderhochstadt and Co. C laid smokescreens for patrols across the Rhine River near Germersheim as a feint for 36th Division troops making the primary crossing. In addition, the company fired delayed action HE on the enemy.[68]

Orders were received on March 27th for the entire 83rd Chemical Mortar Battalion to be relieved and go into VI Corps reserve in the vicinity of Rohrbach. Companies A and B immediately made the move as the battalion forward CP closed at Bellheim and also moved to Rohrbach. James Helsel, Co. A, wrote in his diary, "Some captured German liquor was issued to the men and the town was full of drunks this night." Co. C, following some more support at the Rhine River, moved to Steinweiller. The following day the battalion rear CP and Detachment B, 11th Chemical Maintenance, closed at the Herxheim-Rohrbach area and moved 10 miles by motor vehicles to Steinweiller, Germany, going into bivouac in empty buildings. "Doc" Hulcher said his men set up in a school and city hall, and the civilians had been ordered to clean up the picturesque town with their brooms. Orders had also been issued that upon arrival at the various destinations companies A and B would be relieved from attachment to the 36th Infantry Division to Corps control and Co. C would revert back to battalion control. All companies bivouacked, reorganized, and re-equipped.[69]

All of the battalion companies began a training program on the 29th, "… with particular emphasis on cleaning of equipment and military courtesy and discipline." The battalion rear CP and Detachment B, 11th Chemical Maintenance, closed at Steinweiller, where Daniel Shields and medic Douglas Swayze visited Blessed Sacrament, and moved two kilometers by motor transport to Rohrbach. Companies A and B were posted in the center of town. The 11th Chemical Maintenance Detachment stated they bivouacked in a construction factory. "Doc" Hulcher took up residency in the former home of a high ranking Nazi. The training program continued on the 30th, Good Friday, the same day Pfc. Mario Ricci, Co. A, killed a fawn which was

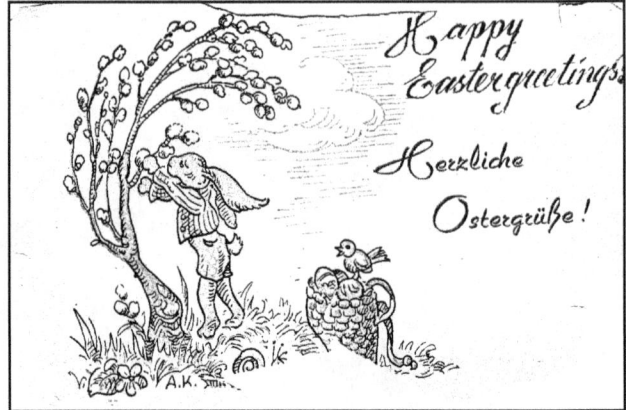

German Easter card sent home by Charlie Lowry, Co. A, Motor Pool. *Author's Collection*

prepared for Easter dinner by HQ cook T/5 Gum Q. Lee. On a beautiful 31st, the VI Corps issued orders attaching Co. A to the 63rd Infantry Division and Co. C to the 100th Infantry Division. Later in the day, the two companies were briefed on their next mission, convoy clearance secured, and convoy number R224 was assigned to Co. A and R225 to Co. C. Yet at Rohrbach, Daniel Shields attended church, of which he wrote, "First G.I. in church, people really gave me a looking over."[70]

During the month of March, the 83rd Chemical Mortar Battalion had fired 4,474 HE rounds and 12,564 of WP, for a total of 17,038 rounds. The 11th Chemical Company, Detachment B, attached to the 83rd, reported the repair of 35 standards, 29 to 30 barrels, and 18 to19 baseplate assemblies, a turnover rate of about 233 per cent of the battalion's mortars. Despite the ongoing problems of defective shells, the battalion reported only two men lightly wounded and hospitalized during the entire month.[71]

The 83rd crossing the Neckar River.
Jordan Collection

Sam Kweskin, HQ Co., took time to reflect on the past. "Looking back, there was enough sadness to go around for men of the battalion as well as people back home. My old squad sergeant, 'Alabama' Brown was dead from a muzzle blast, another squad leader had his thumb shot off when he didn't remove his hand quickly enough from a round drop; a buddy who had come overseas with me was dead (I can still see him standing across from me the day he joined with the 83rd from the 2nd); the ballet dancer was dead or captured; Charlie Cella was hospitalized back home … and names I can no longer remember were lying in temporary graves, eventually to be shipped home or rest forever in the cemetery outside Epinal."[72]

The mission for the month of April was to destroy the German 1st and 19th Armies. With the Rhine River having been crossed by some elements of the Allied forces, the main front extended primarily along the line of Lindenfels, Weinheim, and Heidelberg. During this period, Co. A of the 83rd Chemical Mortar Battalion was attached to the 863rd Field Artillery Battalion, 63rd Infantry Division, stationed in the vicinity of Rohrbach, and moved to Leiman. Co. B, in the VI Corps reserve, was also at Rohrbach, prepared to advance, as Co. C, supporting the 397th Infantry, 100th Infantry Division, advanced toward Friedrichfeld.[73]

April 1st was Easter Sunday and Protestant services

were conducted by a full colonel in the battalion CP. "Doc" Hulcher described Easter as "quiet and peaceful." Capt. Smith, Co. C, who was briefly considered for promotion to major, emphatically stated the only trouble he had at the current time was "… some of the do-nothings in Hdqrtrs are jealous because they know 'C' Company is the best that has ever been in the Bn and I have a lot of fun telling them about it, which makes them mad."[74]

Following the morning religious ceremony of April 1st, a portion of the battalion, including Co. A, moved out in convoy through cities such as Speyer, crossed the Rhine River on pontoon bridges at Ludwigshafen, and passed through Mannheim to a town they called "Kerchargimund." HQ Co. followed on the 2nd and crossed the Rhine at noon, during an enemy air raid, into Mannheim. Both Ludwigshafen and Mannheim had been nearly destroyed by war and much evidence of forced labor began to appear. Detachment B, 11th Chemical Maintenance, moved with the battalion rear CP from Rohrbach to Freidrichfeld, Germany. The battalion's forward elements moved on to towns they called "Neckarbischofsheim" and "Mauer," where two or three Gestapo soldiers were taken prisoner. They put up some resistance and were quickly subdued after a good beating from a few of the big boys in the 83rd. Elsewhere on the 2nd, the court-martial of Capt. Joseph Garsson, Co. A, convened at Augsberg, where he was defended by Maj. Gordon Mindrum. Sam Kweskin, combat artist of the 83rd, accompanied Garsson to the trial in a jeep and wished him good luck. The trial would last through the 7th.[75]

T/5 Kenneth J. Lamb, Detachment B, 11th Chemical Maintenance Co., earned a Bronze Star assisting the 83rd Chemical Mortar Battalion.
Kenneth Lamb Collection

Although the three weapons companies did not fire a single round during the first three days of April, and Co. A moved to Bad Rappenau on the 3rd, action resumed on April 4th as Co. A moved to "Lubberstadt" and Co. C provided a smokescreen for troops to establish a bridgehead and cross the Neckar River at Heilbronn. Ironically, when it came time for HQ Co. of the battalion to cross the pontoon bridge on the 5th, they had to wait hours in rain and mud as an armored outfit [*believed to be the all African-American 614th Tank Destroyer Battalion, 103rd Division*] outranked them in the crossing sequence. Due to the inclement weather and blackout conditions late at night, Pvt. Roscoe D. Adamson's jeep wrecked during the river crossing and he was seriously wounded and hospitalized. Adamson's buddy, Stephen W. Vukson, recalled the incident a bit differently, stating that during the blackout conditions Adamson's head was crushed by a jeep and that he died instantly. The official casualty list of the CWS states Adamson died a month later on May 5th, probably a misprint. Daniel Shields, of rear battalion CP, recorded in his diary that on the move to Mosbach they had to wait 12 hours to cross the bridge because of the 10th Armored Division, and "One of our fellows [*was*] killed in accident." Although no official reports have been located, Lt. Robert Bundy, Co. A, said, "This is the area in which we were strafed by a jet." Also on the 5th, a car full of quinine was found at a railway station and the battalion rear CP moved from Seckanheim to Neckarelz. Co. A was attached to the 863rd Field Artillery Battalion; Co. B went into bivouac west of Mosbach, with neither company firing any rounds, while Co. C remained in action.[76]

Detachment B, 11th Chemical Maintenance, left Freidrichfeld on April 6th and moved to Neckarelz to join with the rear CP of the 83rd. Apparently some of HQ Co. captured a German barrel of 1000 dill pickles which elated Mess. Sgt. George Borkhuis. Co. A was on the move, Co. B was ordered to relocate the recently located quinine to

Label off dill pickle barrel captured by HQ Co.
Borkhuis Collection

their bivouac area, and Co. C continued numerous fire missions, including smoke coverage for engineers building a bridge and covering a river crossing by the 1st Battalion, 397th Infantry. Co. A was back in action on the 7th supporting an attack by the 63rd Infantry Division; Co. B remained inactive; and Co. C covered various operations by infantry, engineers, and amphibious tanks. By the 8th, Co. A had passed through such towns as Oberschefflenz, with one platoon attached to the 863rd Field Artillery, and Co. B was in the vicinity of Mosbach, attached to the 398th Infantry, 100th Infantry Division. George Borkhuis of HQ added that since living in a hotel "We have been housed in tents a few times and once even stayed in an oil well for a spell. At present we are in a building." Despite such rapid movement, on April 9th a WP shell burst in a mortar barrel of Co. C, burning six men [*although only five are on the casualty list*], including Pvt. Joseph H. Runeweiz, who was severely injured, and Pfc. Donald R. Loveland, Pfc. Wilbur W. Klopp, Pfc. Kenneth E. Giesky, and Pvt. Harvey McMahon, all slightly wounded. Pfc. Steve Snyder recalled, "Runeweiz was on the #4 gun and I was on #3 when the #4 barrel burst splitting like a peeled banana. Joe was on fire and had to be tackled by a medic. The shell hit a building about 50 yards away. I was thrown about 15 feet in the air."[77]

While much of the battalion, including the forward CP, was in the area of Mosbach-Neckarelz, many of the men developed such a passion for photography that Robert L. Sorenson of the Medical Detachment, who contributed a regular photography column to the battalion newsletter *Muzzleblasts*, "could hardly get near his dark room." The colonel's trailer was put into use as a dark room to handle the extra work. Sam Kweskin, HQ Co., recalled, "Mosbach, the entire village had already been occupied by other G.I.'s. Our best hope was to pass through Heidelberg, which we knew would be a magnet for high-ranking officers, and set up HQ further down the tributary of the Rhine, the Neckar River," and consequently opened HQ at Neckarelz.[78]

In the ensuing days, the battalion rolled through various towns. Battalion CP and Detachment B, 11th Chemical Maintenance, left Neckarelz on the 10th for Bonfeld. This was the same day T/5 Kenneth J. Lamb, from Plymouth, Utah, and a member of Detachment B, 11th Chemical Maintenance Company, was awarded the Bronze Star for meritorious service assisting the 83rd Chemical Mortar Battalion from February 1, 1944, to February 28, 1945. His citation read in part, "T/5 Lamb handled the bulk of the welding repair work for his company. By his outstanding professional skill, diligence, and efficient maintenance work T/5 Lamb contributed directly to the greatly increased firepower and efficiency of the [83rd] mortar battalion which his unit serviced during this period."[79]

On the 11th, Co. A, yet attached to the 863rd Field Artillery Battalion, moved into and through Forchtenberg, encountering some stiff enemy resistance at a bridge. Co. C reported one man, Cpl. Warren D. Perry, severely wounded and two others, Pfc. Robert S. Merrington and Pvt. Russell U. Leslie, slightly wounded. "Doc" Hulcher claimed all three were wounded by shrapnel. Capt. Robert B. Smith, Co. C, wrote, "Some days this company has fired 2,200 rounds. And when you consider that an artillery battalion would consider 500 a big day you'll know that old 'Longbow Charley' has been working. I don't see why they want us to kill all of them, and knock all their houses down, and burn all their factories before they will quit. But if that's the way they want it, we'll do our best to accommodate them." At HQ Co. George Borkhuis wrote, "Enemy planes have been rather annoying these past few nights. They wake us up when they strafe the roads and it takes us a while to get back to sleep. One of my boys runs down in the cellar as soon as he hears the planes and stays there until he is sure they have gone. The boys can't understand why I'm not afraid of them, but I've had so many close calls that they don't bother me any more. I found out that as long as the lights are out while enemy planes are around, there is nothing to fear. They only strafe roads and buildings if they see a light there."[80]

Lt. Robert Bundy believed this was a photo of the Co. A mortar squad taken shortly before they accidentally shot down a friendly observation plane. *Robert Bundy*

Shocking news reached the battalion on April 12th with the announcement of President Franklin D. Roosevelt's death. Lt. Robert Bundy said he heard the news over the radio. Pfc. Mario Ricci, Co. A, added, "It was at Berchtesgaden ... that I first learned of the death of Franklin Delano Roosevelt (from a German woman, at that)," and Lt. Robert Bush claimed he was in Garmisch when he heard the announcement. This is rather odd as the latter two would probably not have been at those locations on April 12th.[81]

The battalion rear CP and Detachment B, 11th Chemical Maintenance, were at Neckarsulm on the 14th. Co. A moved into a town Charles Rolling called "Lofcheckerchback" [*probably Löschenhirschbach*], left on the 15th for "Heffothf," departed on the 16th, and confronted some enemy soldiers in a castle. In addition, between the 14th and 16th Co. B had various platoons and elements moving through Weinsberg, Bitzfeld, Rappach, and Schwabbach. "Doc" Hulcher reported he was at Orlinger. The battalion forward CP closed at Neckarelz on April 17th and moved to the vicinity of Mohrig, where communications were established with the VI Corps. Elements of Co. A moved to Schwabisch Hall while sections of Co. B were in Affaltrack, Hohenstrassen, Grab, Henberg, and Gleichenunt. The following day, Co. A was attached to the 44th Infantry, VI Corps Reserve, and was relieved by the 96th Chemical Mortar Battalion. "Doc" Hulcher was at Heilbronn, where he reported typical scenes, writing, "Was beautiful driving along the Neckar River. Any place [*there was*] any resistance, the town is flattened and when we see them they are still smoking. Still have lots of Jerry planes over at night. But boy are our bombers going over during the day – thousands of them. Saw a Jerry airplane scrap pile yesterday evening, acres of land … No casualties lately – I'm glad to say. News really good now." Sam Kweskin, HQ Co., also noted that at Heilbronn, "… the sickly pall of decaying [*enemy*] corpses pervaded the whole town." George Borkhuis remarked HQ was out in the open again.[82]

Between April 19th and 21st, companies A and B were attached to the 410th Infantry, 103rd Division. As Co. A rested near Mohrig, Co. B passed on through Mainhardt, Grab, Sechaelberg, Fronfalls, Ober-Urbach, Schorndorf, Weinsbert, and Rubersberg. William C. Ford, Co. C, remembered mopping up isolated pockets of resistance in a sector of Nurnberg on the 20th on their way toward Munich. The battalion rear CP and Detachment B, 11th Chemical Maintenance, also moved on the 20th to Sulzbach and on the 22nd joined the battalion forward CP, which had moved during a snow storm from Welzheim to Goppingen, a distance of about 20 miles, "where the weather grew cold, rained, snowed, and hailed." "Doc" Hulcher said they took up residency in a sweets factory. Capt. Smith, Co. C, said the battalion was "… getting deep into the heart of Krautland." Co. A was moving in convoy with the 410th Infantry; Co. B's CP moved to Kirschheim; and Co. C supported the 397th Infantry, where they took a total of nine German prisoners.[83]

Another tragedy for the 83rd transpired on April 23rd when the mortar crew of the Red Platoon of Co. A accidentally shot down a friendly observation plane. The battalion journal recorded, "… at 1230 hours an air artillery observation plane flew into the Red Platoon's barrage of point detonating HE. The plane was completely demolished and it's two occupants instantly killed." According to Lt. Robert Bundy, Co. A, who witnessed the event, "Toward the closing days of the war we were firing at a rapid rate when an observation plane (a two passenger Cub) was hit by one of our mortar rounds. What happened was the observers were flying in our area directing artillery fire. We did not know they were there. When they heard our rounds going off they circled back to investigate and flew right into our barrage of shells. Somebody called to me and pointed in the direction of debris. I ran to the scene of the crash, along with a couple of our troops, but the fire was so intense nobody could get near it … I was the first person to arrive at the sight of the remains … I caught hell for running out there because it was considered enemy territory … We were only able to remove the left hand of one and a foot of the second officer … I think the hand had a bracelet on it … As I recall the officers' names were Lt. Connor and a Lt. Huff. I think they might have been from the 10th Armored Division. We were working with the 10th Armored and the 103rd Infantry Divisions at the time … The Colonel commanding the task force visited our platoon and was satisfied that it was an accident." The investigation revealed the two victims as members of the 384th Field Artillery Battalion, 103rd Infantry Division, which recorded in the unit journal, "At approximately 1200 one of the battalion liaison planes was hit by a 4.2" mortar shell while in flight over Bracken, Germany … The shell was fired by friendly troops. The pilot, 1st Lt. Eugene S. Huff, and the observer, 2nd Lt. James G. Connor, were killed and the plane destroyed." Both officers were buried in the United States Military Cemetery at Bensheim, Germany [*Huff was apparently later moved to Lorraine Cemetery, St. Alvold, France*]. Lt. Huff, HQ Co., 384th Field Artillery Battalion, was from Seminole, Oklahoma, and had distinguished himself during numerous flight missions in early 1945, including the Air Medal with five Oak Leaf Clusters. Lt. Connor, of Battery B of the 384th, was from Pensacola, Florida.[84]

Charles Rolling said Co. A also ran into some serious sniper trouble at a town northeast of Blaubeuren called Zainingen. According to James Helsel, "While firing we heard some Infantry boys firing close by, also we heard the return fire. The next thing I knew Danziger [*Samuel H. Danziger, of New York*] of the fourth squad was firing his machine gun to the rear of our position. Everyone in the second platoon took off to the house. 'Tuck' Stewart and myself run up into the attic of one house. We broke the shingle out. From here we could see the sniper run along the

313

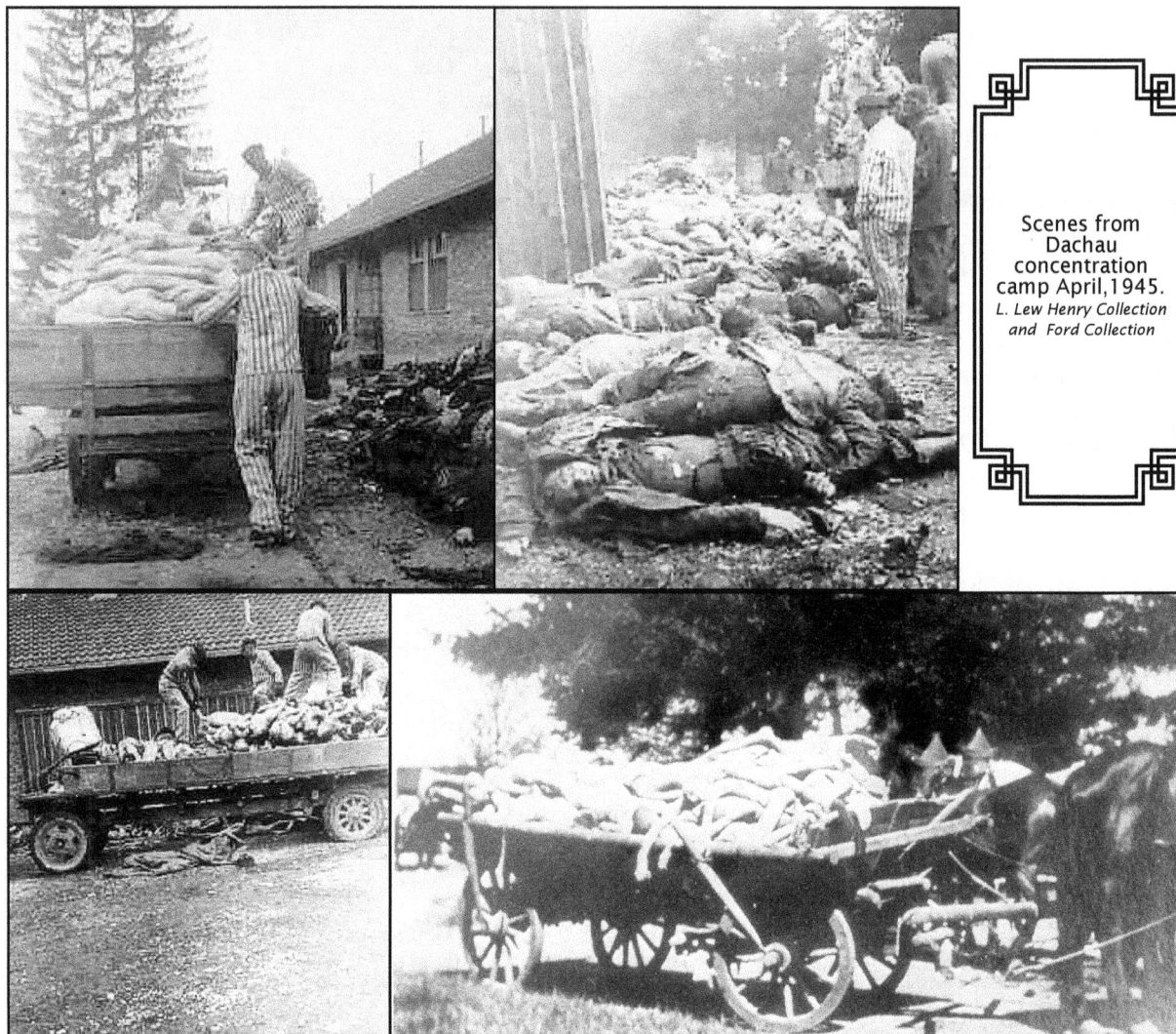

Scenes from Dachau concentration camp April, 1945. *L. Lew Henry Collection and Ford Collection*

hill. We also saw Joe Comaty, the BAR man from the first squad run along a wall at the foot of the hill. We watched when Joe came to a gate, an opening in the wall. He went into action. Results: One dead German sniper. Lt. Kenny laughed, he said he thought the way we always talked we would run if something happened, but when it did, he didn't have to say a word, he just stood and watched. We returned to our guns and took up the firing mission. The ammo and rations are about kaput …"[85]

One platoon of Co. A was at Boliningen, northwest of Zathese on the 23rd, while Co. B's CP had moved to Eningen and Co. C continued their active support of the 397th Infantry, taking 12 German prisoners who were armed with two machine guns. Also on the 23rd, Lt. Col. Bruce T. Humphreville, chemical officer, 7th Army, recommended Capt. Albert Gallagher for an award or citation for his outstanding performance with the 11th Chemical Maintenance Company, stating that, "Through his efforts a radically new type of shock-absorbing mechanism for the 4.2" Chemical Mortar, was invented, developed, tested and produced; a practical wrench for removal of damaged tube caps and base caps from 4.2" Chemical Mortar barrels was developed; a program of modifying of 4.2" Chemical Mortar shell to enable this shell to be used with a different gauge fuze was carried out."[86]

From the 23rd through the end of the month, the battalion passed through Kirscheim, Urach, Dettingen, Blaubeuren (on the 24th), Seissen, Neuhaus, Ober Elihingen, Unt-Elihingen, Nersingen, Heirligen, Babenhausen, Heiretshofen, Kissendorg, Neuberg, and Schongau. Some of the highlights of the period included the capture of 20 of the enemy, many of them wounded, on April 24th by Co. B and two by Co. A, as well as three more captured by Co. B on the 25th at Neuhaus. Also on the 25th, the battalion CP and Detachment B, 11th Chemical Maintenance,

The 83rd crossing the Danube River. *J. T. Taunton*

moved from Goppingen to Blaubeuren.[87]

This rapid movement of the battalion was vividly described by "Doc" Hulcher, who wrote in his diary, "On 24th we went to Blaubeuren another move of 74 miles. We took the wrong road and went just 4 km from Ulm where we stopped about ½ mile short of a road block where we could hear small arms fire, see air bursts and demolitions. Turned around and after another 3 hr. trip finally found our place. On the way back we picked up two prisoners who came running from the woods waving white flags. Prisoners are everywhere. We picked up 7 more in the town where we stayed."[88]

Loy Marshall said that on the 25th and 26th Co. C, with the 411th Infantry, helped liberate a satellite forced labor camp of Dachau at Landsberg. He reflected, "As we walked through the compound, we saw the bodies of hundreds of people stacked like cord wood with arms and legs sticking out this way and that. The bodies were just skin and bones. Many more naked bodies were lying in a deep pit. Some huts had been set on fire by the Nazi guards and many people were burned alive. Then we saw some survivors. They were nearly starved to death and looked like corpses and were dressed in rags. Some of the soldiers had offered them some of their food from their K Rations and in just a minute, they would be dead. They had been without food for so long that their systems could not tolerate our rations. An order was given for us not to give the liberated prisoners any food and that appropriate food and care would be arriving soon." Marshall added that, although the camp had no gas chambers and furnaces as those at Dachau, "The prisoners were forced to work in underground factories and make war materials. They lived in huts that were about the size of an American barracks building, but slept side by side on bare wooden bunks built four feet high. There were no mattresses and there were several hundred men per hut. There were about 5000 prisoners here," yet the people of Landsberg denied any knowledge of the camp.[89]

The Blue Danube was crossed via pontoon bridges by lead elements of the battalion on the 26th and HQ Co. on the 27th. The battalion was attached to the 10th Armored Division, while Co. A moved into Ulm, the perfect picture of war's horrible devastation, where a large quantity of rum was liberated. With the church the only remaining structure intact at Ulm, Sam Kweskin remembered, "… we came down what may have been main street, avoiding where we could bodies of dead German soldiers. Like a loud cry, the tower of the Ulm cathedral lunged into the sky with devastation beneath it."[90]

The battalion CP and Detachment B, 11th Chemical Maintenance, moved to Babenhausen. HQ Co. of the 11th Maintenance had been working out of a turbine factory at Frankenthal, Germany, where they hired 16 Polish lathe operators to speed up production of the rebored and rethreaded shells and "... to give the men boring out the TNT a much needed rest." Exactly 8,491 shells were processed before HQ Co. of the 11th Maintenance moved 118 miles to Goppingen on April 27th, where they set up in the buildings of the W. Speiser Machine Factory and quartered in Speiser's home. In conjunction with the shell project, the maintenance group also produced 352 boxes for the fuzes removed from the condemned shells.[91]

The period of April 26-27 was summed up by "Doc" Hulcher, who wrote, "... we moved again this time to a small town near Wissenhorn [*Wissenbourg?*] where we didn't even unpack, just spent the night. It was a 45 mile jump. On this trip we must have seen at least 10,000 prisoners being carried back. Passed thru Ulm which had large section flat to the ground from bombing, except for the beautiful cathedral which sat almost undamaged. We moved on over the Danube River which looked rather greenish, rather than blue on to our town passing all kinds of captured material. Everyone in Bn is drinking rum taken from German officer PX. People line the streets, occasionally some wave and we even saw some give the V sign. Took more prisoners here, 4 in no. [*number*]. After spending the night we moved on to Kaufbeuren about 25 miles [*north*] of Austrian border. We could see the Alps when we came to the Danube valley at Ulm. On this trip the huge Alps really stand out and are beautiful. The Swiss border is also very near by. We are heading for the Brenner Pass to cut it and trap the Germans in Italy, doing wonderful job too."[92]

Another detailed view of the rapid movement of the battalion was given by Capt. Smith, Co. C. "Today we moved about 35 miles ... Things are moving fast, and I don't see what the Germans hope to gain by prolonging it another hour. More buildings blown to hell, more men killed, more suffering and probably more hungry people ... when I look for a place for the men we just mark a group of houses, tell the people they have from 15 minutes to an hour to move, and move in. And, strange as it may seem, it doesn't seem unjust, because you know that any of them would gladly see all of us dead ... today I got caught in a column of about 1000 prisoners moving back."[93]

The battalion forward CP was established at Kaufbeuren on the 28th [*Detachment B, 11th Chemical Maintenance journal states April 29th*] where Sam Bundy of Co. A said they were quartered in two nice buildings with polished floors and the 11th Chemical and the battalion's ammunition was housed nearby. But he was most impressed that there was some good beer in town and the German women appeared to be nicer the deeper they drove into Germany. Daniel Shields was more impressed by the long lines of Germans surrendering. George Borkhuis, HQ Co., also wrote, "The number of German prisoners we see each day is enormous. It seems as if they are giving up by the hundreds." More importantly, this was the day Italian dictator Benito Mussolini was killed by partisans.[94]

According to William C. Ford, some of the battalion helped liberate the infamous Dachau prison camp. Many of the freed inmates, in their striped pajamas, were first thought to be refugees from an insane asylum, but the ghastly true reality was soon discovered. Lt. Fred G. Rand, Co. B, wrote, "Our platoon was attached to a battalion of the 103rd. To our left was Dachau where Sam Kweskin and others were (at the railroad to the ovens). Some of those poor prisoners in their striped shirts came across where we were set up. Members of our platoon opened 'C' rations and fed these starving prisoners. After not eating for a long time, some ate so fast it caused them to drop dead ... A German machine gun opened up on me. I dove behind a stack of snow and ice covered wood. When I jarred this, some of the snow fell off. It was not cord wood; it was bodies of prisoners."[95]

The rifle company of the 157th Infantry and Co. C of the 83rd Chemical Mortar Battalion were the first to reach the gates, where S/Sgt. Robert S. White of the 157th and his squad entered and either killed or captured the guards while attempting to restore order. Co. C remained outside the gates as a backup if necessary. After the camp was secured, the force took the town of Dachau and then crossed the Schleissheimer Canal toward Munich. Lt. Robert Bundy recalled, "I was liaison officer with the 45th Division and we came across the prisoners fleeing Dachau. It was a total surprise to us because we had not known of them. It was a very brief encounter." James Marion Lester, a truck driver with Co. A, wrote, "We were near Dachau. Some of those poor people who had been prisoners there and were able to walk, were coming back. They were just emaciated; their faces were gone. They had been released up ahead, I suppose." Pfc. Mario Ricci, a radio operator, recalled the horror, writing, "I ... saw hundreds of emaciated men in the blue-gray striped pajamas, survivors of the Dachau prison camp. I don't recall seeing women among them. We didn't know who they were and where they came from. Someone suggested that they had walked out of a mental hospital. They walked around aimlessly. We soon learned."[96]

Andrew Leech, Co. B, also recalled the ghastly scene of freed prisoners, writing, "… it was unbelievable to see the conditions these people were in. They were walking skeletons who had run away -- some of them that were able, to the mountains in the snow. They had no food and very little clothing which was tattering about them. They escaped because the Germans were lining them up and mowing them down with machine guns before the Americans came in. We were in one town where they had mowed down 500 of them the day before we entered … When they saw that we were Americans many of them walking skeletons wobbled down to greet us and beg food. They said they hadn't had anything to eat in about eight days … When they finished, they thanked us and wobbled off toward the road which was about a hundred yards away. Two of them fell dead by the time they reached the road."[97]

It snowed on the 29th and the 30th, as three men from HQ freed 200 Allied personnel when they walked through the gates of a German POW camp and ordered 25 guards to surrender. Additional smaller camps were liberated in the coming days. William Ford's section of Co. C moved on with the force assigned to take Munich, crossing the famed Autobahn Highway and meeting resistance on the outskirts of Cerchine. Afterwards the force crossed the Isar River into Munich, a city in chaos. "Doc" Hulcher noted his portion of the battalion was moving toward Oberammergau on the 30th, about four miles short of Austria.[98]

Co. A advanced into the Garmisch-Partenkirchen area where some of the officers later took up residence in a baron's house at Untergrainau, actually about three miles from Garmisch. According to Lt. Robert Bush, "I and my platoon had been assigned to Task Force Hudelson. Col. Hudelson had been assigned the mission of joining up with our troops in northern Italy. When we reached Garmisch, the Col. told me he wouldn't need me any further (we never had occasion to fire one round) so we occupied Garmisch-Partenkirchen and that was the end of the war for the first platoon. I took over a baron's home in Garmisch - what a place - I had blue velvet hanging over the top of my bed and while in bed I could look out on the ski jump, where the 1936 Olympics winter events were held. The baron was a Nazi who had fled to avoid capture. So that was one of my fun times of the war." Lt. Robert Bundy, Co. A, added, "I vividly recall the baron's home in Garmisch. Was he not the chief engineer of the Nuremberg Stadium? The old gal did not object to the officers staying there but she violently objected to having enlisted troops in her home. Somebody, maybe Lt. Bob Bush, told one of the soldiers to, 'Tell that bitch to go back to bed' and we moved in."[99]

Andrew Leech, Co. B, wrote in general of this period. "We drove a spearhead into Munich and one down the Lech River into Austria and up through the Austrian Alps. Here we drove three days and nights straight in a snow storm. Imagine it! It was the last of April after we had come accustomed to spring weather. It sure did hurt and some of our soldiers suffered frozen feet."[100]

Although he did not recall the exact date, Pfc. Harold St. Gemme, Co. B, a former tugboat deck hand from St. Louis, Missouri, who would become a Baptist minister after the war, said that, "… south of Garmisch, I saw lying in the road something that looked like a blackened smoking ham … it wasn't pig. Shortly afterwards, I scuffed a piece of cardboard in the road … it was not cardboard … someone had been run over by tanks. Before the day was over, we saw some men just outside of a concentration camp."[101]

At the close of April, Co. A was yet in the Garmisch-Partenkirchen area, location of the 1936 Olympics; Co. B was at Landsberg, Kaufbeuren, and Schongau; and Co. C was at Munich, attached to the 411th Infantry. No men had been killed during the month and only

Mittenwald, the town where reportedly the last shots of the 83rd were fired. *Robert Bundy*

The 83rd at Brenner Pass, the Italian-Austrian border, May 5, 1945. *McLarty Collection*

some eight to ten had been wounded, two of them seriously and six slightly but seriously enough to be hospitalized. The battalion as a whole had fired 15,794 rounds of HE and WP. Detachment B, 11th Chemical Maintenance Company, worked on 17 barrels, 13 baseplates, and 14 standard assemblies, for a total of 44 assembly repairs.[102]

Although uncertain of the exact date, Lt. Robert Bundy, Co. A, recalled that in the waning days of the war, "I served on a court martial of a fellow who was accused of rape. Lt. James J. O'Conner was the defense attorney and I was called to assist him. The accused was found not guilty of rape because of a misunderstanding between him and the victim. A German girl. But he was found guilty of a lesser crime of breaking and entering, etc. When he left the courtroom he said to O'Connor and I, 'Thanks prick.' I really thought O'Conner did a terrific job. While serving on the court-martial I was sent to gather some evidence. I believe Pfc. George J. Funyak and Pfc. James F. Kane went with me. As we were returning, and it was about one o'clock, I suggested we stop at a school house occupied by a Civil Affairs unit. They fed us, and as we were about to leave a Sgt. asked me if I cared to look around. It turned out there was a tremendous amount of the world's art. It was truly unbelievable. The rooms were set up with paintings and stain-glass windows, etc. It took us over an hour to tour the different rooms. Here was a schoolhouse full of stolen treasures. I saw a couple of hidden rooms where some Germans were retouching some of the treasures. This was highly classified for a number of reasons. As I recall the people of the town were objecting to these people receiving special attention because they were considered true Nazi. It was a touching [*touchy*] situation. When we arrived back at the jeep I thanked the Sgt. and he replied, 'Oh think nothing of it Lt., I'm expecting General Patton here in about a half an hour and I was happy to be able to practice with you.'"[103]

During the first ten days of May, there was no main line of resistance, with the exception of a few isolated pockets of the retreating German army. The companies and platoons of the battalion were scattered, attached to various organizations, and often advancing so rapidly the names of some towns faded into obscurity. On May 1st, the day after Adolf Hitler committed suicide, Co. A was attached to the 410th Infantry and moved out of Fronreiten to Farchant in the snow-covered Alps, while Co. B, with their CP at Garmisch and men at Partenkirchen, fired five rounds of WP at the enemy and advanced toward Mittenwald. Co. C, supporting the 411th Infantry, maintained their position and wire communications. Capt. Smith, Co. C, said he was "… now near the Austrian border and have never seen any more beautiful country. It's snowing right now … I am pretty high up in the mountains … the town my company rear is in is full of German soldiers and my people are the only Americans there. It's the darnedest thing you ever saw. They have turned in their arms (I hope) and have just quit fighting. And there hasn't been time to round them all up. I picked up two this evening ... And five miles away we are still shooting at each other."[104]

Demolitions became the primary opponent and prisoners, from both the field and hospitals, numbered in the thousands. Lt. Robert E. Bundy, Co. A, thought "... the final rounds of the 83rd were fired at Mittenwald. As I recall the rounds were directed at a chalet up in the hills, not into the city. I'm not sure but I think only one mortar was set up that fired at the chalet and I think it was Sgt. Roland K. Puckett, Co. A, of Wisconsin, who had the honor. We all stood around watching. That was definitely the last round fired by the 83rd. Frankly, the whole incident was not

L-R: James Marion Lester, Teddy Kubera, Charlie Lowry, and Donald Hafler, all of Co. A, on the road to Brenner Pass. *Author's Collection*

taken too seriously. That is why only one gun was set up to fire. I think only three or four of the enemy walked down with their hands on their head." Bundy added more detail later in a second accounting of the incident, stating, "I recall seeing a small group of enemy soldiers [*at Mittenwald*] taking cover in a chalet far up on the side of a mountain. Capt. [*Alfred*] Forrester was kidding with Lt. [*Leonard R.*] Kenney and made a small wager that he couldn't come close to [*hitting*] the chalet. The troops set up one mortar and Lt. Kenney called for fire. They fired three rounds and they came reasonably close considering the difference in elevation. The small group came out with their hands behind their head. Capt. Forrester said in a laughing way, 'OK, so who's going to go up after them?' No volunteers. That was the end of the firing."[105]

As two to three inches of snow fell on May 2nd, the day German troops in Italy surrendered unconditionally, Co. B's three platoons moved through Mittenwald, Muhlberg, Seefeld, and Scharmitz. On the 3rd, as another three inches of snow fell, a German general surrendered his command at Innsbruck, Austria, to elements of Co. C. Lt. Fred G. Rand, Co. B, recalled, "The Col. of the 103rd told me to get up on the barrel of a tank; he would be on the barrel behind me. We rode into Innsbruck on this gun barrel, with the Austrian people handing us flowers and wine. The Austrian people were so glad to be rid of the Germans." The following day the battalion rear also moved forward into Austria and opened the CP at Innsbruck, with the three platoons of Co. B at Zirl, Seefeld, and Buch. Sam Kweskin, HQ Co., was impressed, writing, "We rode through a fine misty rain and suddenly, having just come through a gap in the Alps, we looked down on a tremendous village. A river (the Inn) ran through it east to west, and just below us was a large town, its church spires glistening in the rain. It was Innsbruck, and we had just entered Austria." Co. B continued to advance eastward through the Innsbruck valley taking numerous prisoners.[106]

Co. C, supporting the 411th Infantry, advanced quickly to the south of Innsbruck to Brenner and the Brenner Pass, where contact was made with the 5th Army. According to Paul S. Giles, Co. C, from Moultrie, Georgia, "We went through the Brenner Pass ... on May 5, 1945, just before daylight. It was freezing outside and we were riding in open trucks. When we arrived in a little village, we bounced out of the trucks and went inside a house to get warm. There were Germans all over the house. They just picked up their guns and walked out. The Germans had surrendered. The war was over." According to "Doc" Hulcher, the battalion set up in eight buildings near an airfield which had numerous German aircraft, including jet planes.[107]

While at Innsbruck and Brenner, the 83rd Chemical Mortar Battalion received orders for all companies to be attached to the 409th Infantry and to secure and police designated areas. The battalion forward CP was established in the vicinity of Vomp, as Co. A moved about 20 miles from Innsbruck to patrol Weer and the "bucolic farm village" of Terfens. Co. B moved to Kolsass where, Lee Steedle said, they searched for SS officers who were being hunted as war criminals. Lt. Fred G. Rand, Co. B, said he believed his platoon quartered in an old school building at Kolsass.

During the day, Co. B captured 22 prisoners although two were killed in an attempted escape. Co. C occupied Pill, about 15 miles east of Innsbruck.[108]

HQ took up quarters in a castle near Vomp, a city which looked down upon another city named Schwaz. James F. ("Doc") Dougherty, Co. A, of Philadelphia, Pennsylvania, passed on the story to his son that at Vomp their commanding officer sent a German prisoner up the hill to the castle to tell the SS occupants to "… come down and surrender and if even one man does not surrender and opens fire during the process he would kill them all and turn his mortars upon the castle. They did all surrender." Doughtery was among the group ordered to secure the castle rooms and he "… and another soldier kicked open a master bedroom door … small Nazi flags were hanging all over the walls. They opened up a dresser drawer next to the bed and found two … daggers. They each stuck one down their pants … after the rooms were cleared they were ordered outside and … officers went in and scoured the place." The other soldier's dagger "… had a false tip on the handle which unscrewed and it had a few precious jewels inside." Dougherty had kept his dagger, which did not contain any jewels, hidden in his belongings through the remainder of the war.[109]

Sam Kweskin, HQ Co., recalled that while at Vomp word arrived on the outcome of Capt. Joseph Garsson's court martial at Augsberg. Garsson was found guilty of violating the 64th Article of War and sentenced to be dismissed from the service. But some fellow officers of the 83rd supported him, as did the staff Judge Advocate, and on June 15th Gen. Dwight D. Eisenhower would confirm the sentence but order that, "… owing to special circumstances in this case, the execution thereof is suspended." This decision caused some to speculate Garsson's father, through his industrial and political connections, had influenced the outcome of the case. Indeed, there was some truth to this as U.S. Representative Andrew J. May of Kentucky, a close business and personal friend of the Garsson family, wrote two letters to Eisenhower immediately following the trial requesting Eisenhower conduct an unbiased investigation. In July, generals Hugh W. Rowan and Alden H. Waitt began proceedings to return Garsson from the 51st Maj. Port., where he was then stationed, to the 83rd, pending Lt. Col. Efnor's approval. During a 2005 interview, Garsson claimed that by that time most of the chemical mortar battalions lacked any veteran officers so he was offered command of the 2nd Chemical Mortar Battalion, but the surrender of Japan put an end to that assignment before it ever got started.[110]

Sam Bundy, HQ Co., recalled moving a few miles east – past Hall – and setting up quarters in a five-story building, but Charles Rolling, Co. A, probably captured the mood best when he exclaimed on May 7th, "Well the day that every one was looking for is here, at midnight tonight, the war in Europe is over. Thank God." Indeed, May 8th, 1945, was V-E Day, described by Bundy in his diary: "VE Day is today, but no one is excited because we are not sure of our future plans. Probably a trip to the Pacific will be coming soon … Very few men celebrated. [*Douglas A.*] Swayze and a few others had a few drinks and when they grew quite mellow did a May Dance around the large pole which flies a white banner (an old sheet or pillow case I suppose) …" Capt. Smith, Co. C, writing from Pill, added, "In just a few hours now the war will be officially over here. Of course the 16,000 SS troops out in front here don't know it, but anyway people can celebrate. From now on the fight is just organized mobs and individual snipers. Of course they will all be cleaned up in due time."[111]

In his memoirs, Sam Kweskin, HQ Co., wrote, "On the 8th May, we learned that the Germans had surrendered! Oh, what a sigh of relief emanated from us! … some of our officers decided to hold a dance, inviting young women from the area." George Borkhuis claimed HQ Co. was located in a former monastery. Pvt. Wilburn A. McNeil, Co. B, from Alabama, added, "I returned from my first rest camp in Lyons, France to rejoin my company at Innsbruck, Austria to find they had just received the 'Cease Fire' order - this reunion with my buddies I will never forget."[112]

Perhaps the surrender of Germany was best put in perspective by Jean Pierre Combe, the young French boy who endeared himself to the battalion by saving many of Co. C at Briançon. On the 60th anniversary of V-E Day, he would write, "Co. C, 2nd platoon, commanded by Lt. Norman Rosenthal … we were up near Brenner Pass between Austria and Italy, near Innsbruck. We made junction with the 5th U.S. Army coming up from Italy. That was the spot where Hitler and Mussolini allied in 1937, and the same place I saw my last dead man of the war, a Captain SS from the German army, who killed himself with his own gun when we told him to surrender. This same day that was the end of a man and the end of the war."[113]

Top: 83rd baseball game at Terfens, Austria,
June 3, 1945. *Squires Collection*

Center: (L) German jet-propelled plane found at Innsbruck,
Austria. *Codega Collection*; (C) The Cathedral at Ulm, which was
one of the few buildings not destroyed in the town. *Robert
Smith Collection*; (R) Postcard of Kolsass, Austria. *Byron Jordan*

Left: Munich Beer Hall, Germany. Headquarters of the
157th Infantry, 45th Infantry Division. *Hopkins Collection*

Bottom: (L) The African-American 614th Tank Destroyer Battalion
at the crossing of the Rhine River. *Robert Bush Collection*;
(R) Postcard scene of Innsbruck, Austria. *Robert Smith Collection*

Clockwise from top left:

The 83rd crossing the Rhine River at Mannheim. *Eugene Plassmann*

Albert Sereni and Sidney Kirschner at Heilbronn. *Turan Collection*

Donald Hafler and Charlie Lowry of Co. A at Brenner Pass. *Author's Collection*

L-R: Robert Fenton, Julius "Doc" Hulcher, and Ed Trey at Brenner Pass. *Ed Trey*

Scene of destruction at Mannheim, June 1945. *Karl Garrett*

YOU ARE NOW ENTERING
AUSTRIA
THRU THE COURTESY OF THE
VI U.S. CORPS
SALERNO VOLTURNO ANZIO ROME **6** S. FRANCE ALSACE RHINE DANUBE
GERMANY

SAMUEL IRVING KWESKIN

Samuel I. Kweskin was born February 24, 1924 in Chicago, Illinois. In high school he won art scholarships and later enrolled for a summer at The Chicago Academy where a fellow student was Bill Mauldin. Upon graduation he spent a year as a copy boy at *The Chicago Tribune* before entering the military in February of 1943. He served first with the 3rd Chemical Mortar Battalion and was transferred in August of 1944 to Co. D of the 83rd Chemical Mortar Battalion. While in service he developed his natural artistic skills and in December of 1944, after being placed in HQ Co., helped launch *Muzzleblasts*, the official newsletter of the 83rd Chemical Mortar Battalion, which featured his combat artwork on a regular basis. Kweskin continued his military art in the battalion history, *Rounds Away*, published at Innsbruck, Austria, in 1945. During his service he was often called upon as an interpreter due to his fluency in numerous foreign languages.

Returning to the States at the close of the war Sam entered the Art Institute of Chicago and earned a BFA (Art Education) in 1949, having for a period shared a studio with actor Anthony Quinn. For two years he worked with Sam Singer, originator of Disney's Seven Dwarfs, on two local TV shows for children, then went on to develop his own TV show *This Is The Story* as well as another called *What's Wrong With This Picture*. This was followed by a stint drawing biblical "comic book" style stories at David Cook Publishing Company in Elgin, Illinois.

In 1952 Sam made a trip to New York and did some work for Stan Lee which led to a job with "Atlas Comics" but he, along with many other comic book artists, was soon limited in work by the new Comics Code due to risque illustrations and graphic violence. The next few years saw Kweskin as a studio artist, Art Director of an industrial film organization, Art Director for an agency of Latin American advertising, medical illustrations for the Merk Therapy Manual, and owner of a small art agency. In 1972 he met with an ailing Bill Everette of "Marvel Comics" and did some work on the *Sub-Mariner* comic in 1973, although often working under the pen name Irv (his actual first name) Wesley (as "academic" artists frowned upon comic book work). While free-lancing for "Marvel" he also worked on such favorites as *Daredevil* and *Fantastic Four*.

Sam Kweskin spent another three years as Art Director of the Ziff-Davis Publishing Company, and ten years free-lancing as a Storyboard Artist for most of the large ad agencies in New York, as well as in Chicago and Toronto. During this time he also had his paintings exhibited in Grand Central Galleries in New York, the Salmagundi Club, The Society of Illustrators, and many others. Additionally, he found time to do commissioned portraits. In 1993 Sam moved to Boca Raton, Florida, where he continued to free-lance for numerous magazines (such as *VFW: Veterans of Foreign Wars*), had his paintings displayed in galleries, and did a commissioned canvas of the 83rd for their military museum in Louisiana.

In 1997 Kweskin illustrated and contributed stories to *Mark Freedom Paid: A Combat Anthology*, a collection of memoirs of 30 men of the 83rd Chemical Mortar Battalion, and considered by many as one of the best World War II antholo-

Comic book about WW II soldiers drawn by Sam Kweskin. *Sam Kweskin*

"Self portrait" - interrogating a Nazi with a French Goumier, Castelforte May 9, 1944.

gies. This was followed by a cassette tape of additional interviews and narration by Kweskin called *Rounds Away*. Throughout the years he also continued to contribute to *Muzzleblasts*. He taught and remained one of the leading authorities on the history of the 83rd Chemical Mortar Battalion. In addition, he attended nearly every reunion of the battalion since the first in 1954 and sold his combat artwork there, donating the profits to the reunion group.

Sam Kweskin passed away at Boca Raton June 23, 2005, leaving a son (Joel) and a daughter (Jean) [Another daughter, Barbara, passed away a number of years earlier]. Sam was buried in Westlawn Cemetery, Chicago, Illinois.

Sam Kweskin aboard ship.

"Sighting In"

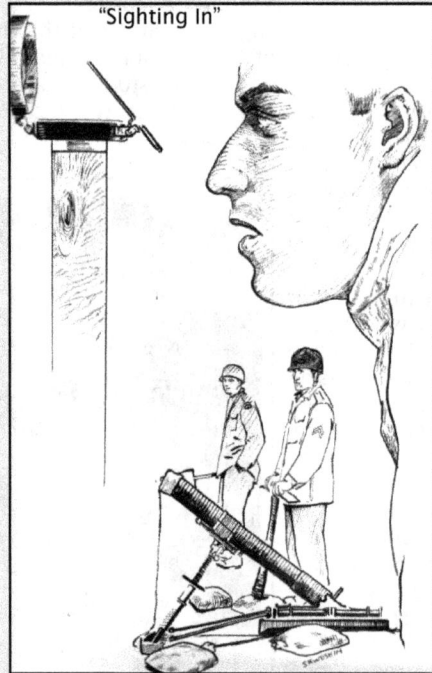
"Mortarman"

"Heilbronn 1945"

"Rounds Away"

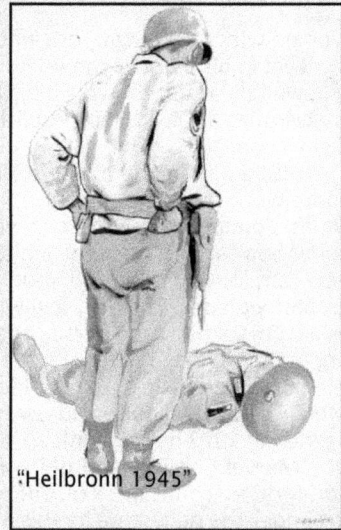
carrying the baseplate to the chemical mortar
"Carrying the baseplate"

"Powder Rings"

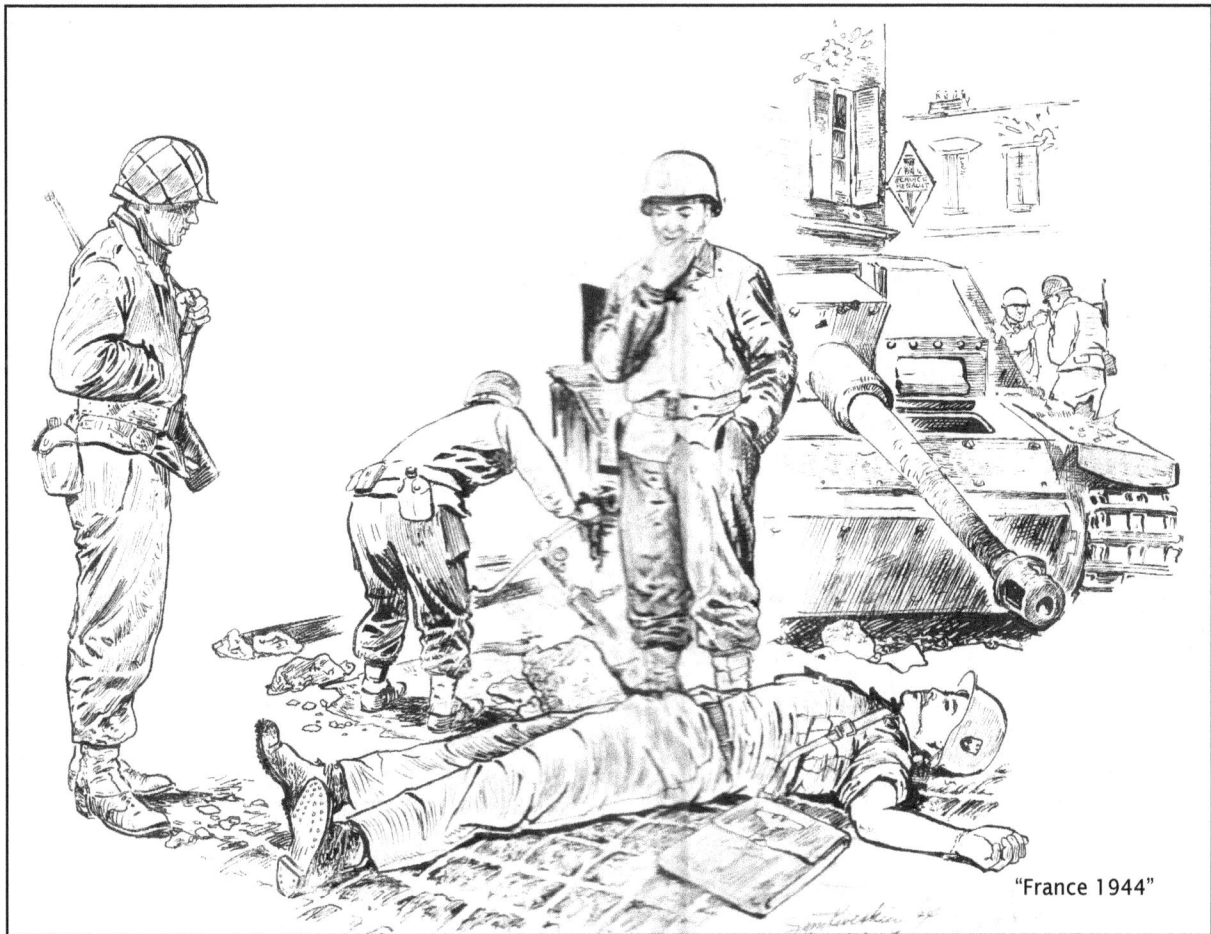

"France 1944"

"Night Firing"

"German Graves"

"Firing the mortar"

Left: Keep your a-- down

Right: Co. C dance, La Petite-Raon, November 1944. T/Sgt. Roy Cadwalader, HQ Co. (3rd from right)

All photos and sketches courtesy Sam, Jean, and Joel Kweskin

Sketches drawn by Sam Kweskin from a window overlooking the May 11, 1945 awards ceremony.
Top left: L-R Capt. Robert E. Edwards, Gen. Alden H. Waitt, and Thomas L. Cassell;
Top right: L-R: Capt. Alfred L. Forrester and Capt. Robert B. Smith.

Bottom left: L-R: Capt. Robert E. Edwards, Capt. Robert B. Smith, and Capt. Alfred L. Forrester.
Bottom right: L-R: Gen. Alden H. Waitt and Capt. Robert E. Edwards.
Sam Kweskin

Chapter Thirteen

THE FINAL DAYS
MAY - NOVEMBER
1945

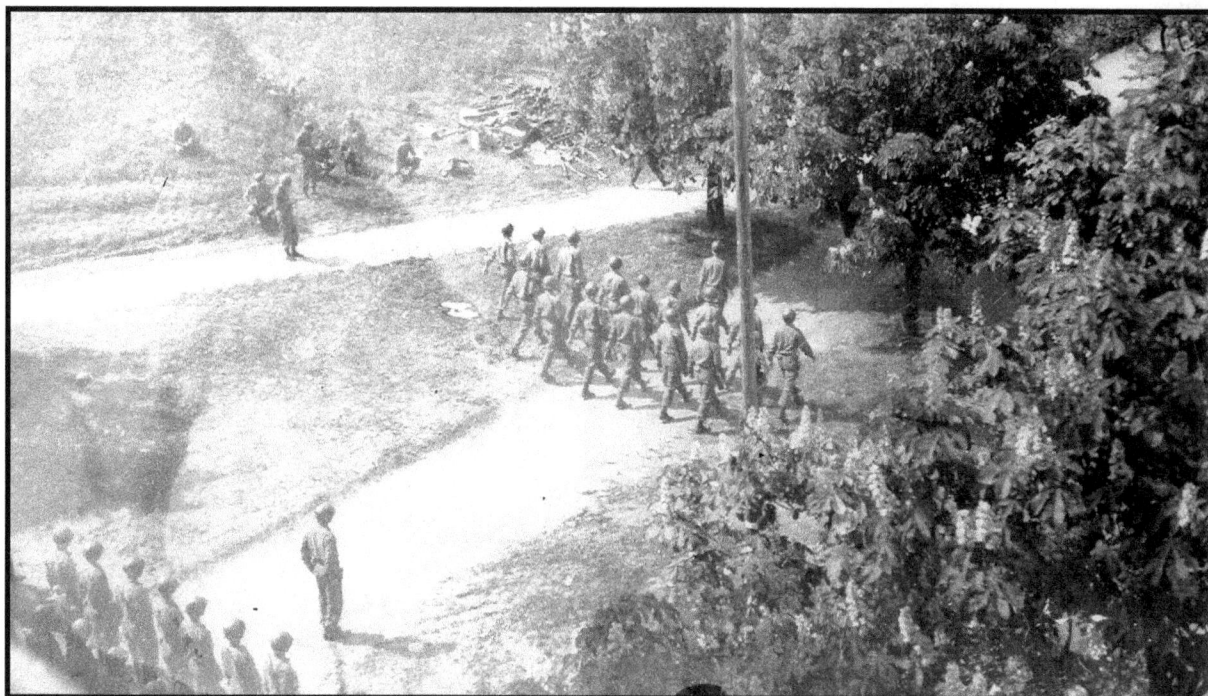

83rd Chemical Mortar Battalion awards ceremony, May 11, 1945. *Ed Trey*

The 83rd Chemical Mortar Battalion history, *Rounds Away*, published at Innsbruck, Austria, in 1945, printed a roster of 493 men present on May 8th, although an additional 184 were included on June 22nd, making an approximate total of 677 men at the close of the war with Germany. The figure may be a bit too high as a few names on the roster were duplicates. It is also misleading in that many familiar names were not on the roster due to casualties, transfers, rotation, sickness, and other circumstances throughout the war. Maj. John P. McEvoy claimed that at the end of the war there were only 7 officers and approximately 75 men of the 40 officers and 1,000 men of the 83rd who had landed at Sicily.[1]

Outside of Innsbruck an awards ceremony was held for the battalion on May 11th, with Gen. Alden H. Waitt, chief of Field Services, CWS, presenting four Silver Stars, 13 Bronze Stars (one with Oak Leaf Cluster), one Croix De Guerre, and one Unit Citation Badge. Officers attending included Lt. Col. Bruce T. Humphreville, chemical officer, 7th Army; Lt. Col. William C. Hammond, chemical officer, VI Corps; and Lt. Col. Efnor. Battalion artist Sam Kweskin recalled the event, stating, "I was at a second floor window in a building behind these guys drawing the event. Gen. Waitt, head of CWS, passing out the Bronze Stars, and a tech sergeant was handing them to him. Capt. Robert Edwards was present … this took place on a parking area outside an individual's home we had 'requisitioned' at the edge of Innsbruck."[2]

Capt. Alfred H. Crenshaw, HQ Co., was informed on May 12th that the battalion had been given its own sector to police, a duty which they continued to perform for the remainder of the month, as well as the initiation of a training program with emphasis on "supervised athletics, military courtesy and discipline, mortar drill, field sanitation, and guard duty." Each company was asked to recommend a list of men to serve as a cadre for the battalion on May 12th and names were submitted on May 17th. 1st lieutenants Fred G. Rand, Jr., William L. Trapnell, and 2nd Lt. Charles J. DeCesare were recommended for company commanders, while Capt. Robert E. Edwards got the nod for battalion commander or executive officer. In a supplemental letter Efnor suggested Capt. Robert B. Smith as battalion commander. Charles Rolling, Co. A, mentioned visiting the bombed out ruins of Munich on the 17th, but he was refused admittance to the Dachau prison camp. However, Pvt. Dale C. Blank, Co. C, a POW of Briançon returned to U.S. control on May 25th, said he did visit Dachau and realized "what we were fighting for." Blank said he saw 39 railroad carloads of dead bodies and they had all starved to death. George Borkhuis, HQ Co., wrote that they were yet at Hall on the 24th and had been awarded another battle star.[3]

Capt. Smith, Co. C, wrote, "The weather here is beautiful, and I am in the town of Pill, about 15 miles east of Innsbruck. We have the duty of maintaining road blocks and patrolling the area; and on top of that we have a training program in the mornings and an athletic program in the afternoons ... we are in the high Alps and there is snow on all the mountain peaks ... it is beautiful Spring weather, and the cold stopped all of a sudden and the clouds cleared up, and now there isn't a cloud in the sky. It has been clear for the past several days."[4]

As time passed, the routine of maintaining security and creating various forms of entertainment to pass the time became monotonous and discouraging. Capt. Robert Smith captured the feeling in his letter: "Things here are definitely the same with no change. Just waiting, trying to control civilian traffic when there is no definitely organized plan and the civilians don't know what to do and we don't either. So for the present it seems to me that we are just making asses out of ourselves. We are not allowed to fraternize with the people and go around with disdainful scorns on our pans [faces] and, in short, I think are doing our best to convince the people that they were pretty well off under the Nazi regime." Spirits were lifted a bit toward the end of the month when Lt. Norman Rosenthal threw a big party for the men, the first such since Rome the year previous.[5]

The mission of the 83rd Chemical Mortar Battalion during June of 1945 was to maintain security in the respective designated areas, while all companies continued to participate in a training program which again emphasized "supervised athletics, military courtesy and discipline, mortar drill, field sanitation, and guard duty." Lt. Col. Sam Efnor sent a letter to the chemical officer, 7th Army, giving his approval for the weight of the mortar to be increased to a total of 500 lbs. providing it would "reduce the maintenance factor to practically nil and also add range and traverse." On June 2nd the battalion received a notice from the 7th Army stating that chemical warfare units that fought in Sicily, Italy, and Europe would not be sent to the Pacific but would either be discharged on a point system or used for the Army of Occupation. Capt. Robert B. Smith, along with 1st Sgt. Thomas R. Thorpe and "driver, [T/5 Thomas V.] Bush," were in Marseilles, France, on the 6th checking on an order for battalion shoulder patches, while on the 8th the battalion was attached to the 409th Infantry and ordered to begin a movement to a new area. The battalion CP exercised this order the following day by moving from the vicinity of Vomp to Weer, Austria. Various personal diaries recorded this movement. Sam Kweskin, HQ Co., wrote, "HQ took over what may have been either a seminary or monastery in Weer. When we entered it, we found piles of German weaponry, such as bazookas, lying along the corridors. So much for privileged sanctuary." The battalion was relieved from assignment to the 7th Army and assigned to the 3rd Army effective June 9th.[6]

June 10th found the battalion again attached to the 103rd Division. Sam Bundy remembered the battalion held a dance with Austrian women on June 12th, which featured the battalion band. The outstanding reputation of the 83rd Chemical Mortar Battalion was duly noted back in the States on June 15th as the Chemical Warfare Service school at Edgewood Arsenal, Maryland, was in need of Chemical Mortar Battalion Signal Operation Instructions (SOI), and as the 83rd had an excellent SOI, requested they provide models for a "good workable set" of SOI to be taught in class. Eisenhower jackets for the men to wear home were issued on June 16th and George Borkhuis, HQ Co., had to attend a court martial for an 83rd man accused of stealing food and cigarettes from the outfit. On the 17th the 83rd, along with other units of the 103rd, was ordered to provide a detail of one officer and fifteen men, report with rations for a period of 72 hours, and guard a train transporting Russian prisoners of war back to their country. Jean Pierre Combe remembered this event, writing, "Co. C ... was cantoned in a little village between Innsbruck and Schwartz on the Inn River in Austria. At [the] middle of the month we were in charge of bring[ing] back Russian civilians, prisoners of Germany. Almost all wives and kids from a little town on the Swiss border, of which I do not remember

Proposed New Battalion Cadre
May 17, 1945

Smith, Robert B., Captain to Bn Commander or Executive Officer

Rand, Fred G., Jr., 1st Lt to Co Commander
De Cesare, Charles J., 2nd Lt to Co Commander

Trapnell, William L., 1st Lt to Co Commander

HQ & HQ Company

Tanner, Wille R., S/Sgt to Master Sgt.
Plassmann, Eugene A., S/Sgt to Sgt. Major
Benson, Tracy T., Sgt to 1st Sgt
Beach, Howell F., Jr., T/5 to Comm. Sgt.
Hughes, Elden L., Pfc to Meteorologist
Parra, William F., Sgt to Operations Sgt.
Schwab, Howard O., Cpl to Personnel Sgt.
Strickler, Claire M., Pfc to Supply Sgt.
Kozak, Andrew T., Cpl to Ammunition Sgt.
Bell, Orville P., T/4 to Mess Sgt.
Ryder, Christopher L., Pfc to Motor Sgt.
Hovland, Jacob G., T/5 to Supply Sgt.

Esterbrook, William J., Pfc to Company Clerk
Nitz, Anthony G., Pfc to Armorer Artificer
Noel, James E., Pfc to Class. Spec.
Bennett, Charles A., T/5 to Clerk Parts
Thorne, Darwin K., Pfc to Clerk Typist
Lee, Gum Q., T/5 to Cook
Bova, Joseph A., Pfc to Cook
Birt, William G., Pfc to Cook
Gregory, William E., Pvt to Mechanic Automobile
O'Brien, John Jr., Pvt to Operator Radio
Eaddy, Crafton, Pvt to Rapairman Radio

Company A

Zickler, Horst R., Sgt to 1st Sgt
Pierce, James F., T/4 to Mess Sgt.
Lester, James M., T/5 to Motor Sgt.
Gerdes, Leland S. C., Pfc to Supply Sgt.
Howe, Charles J., Pfc to Plat. Sgt.
Siepkowski, Zenon R., Pfc to Comm. Sgt.
Baer, John W., Pfc to Meteorologist
Bianchi, Emery J., Pfc to Squad Ldr.
Petro, Carl A., Pfc to Squad Ldr.
Pittman, Robert B., Pfc to Squad Ldr.

Ayers, Sim B., T/5 to Cook
Janosz, Michael, Pfc to Cook
Browne, Harry B., Jr., Pfc to Cook
Tyma, George, Pfc to Co Clerk
Barber, John D., Pvt to Gunner
Cuff, Joseph F., Pfc to Gunner
Robison, Ronald O., Pvt to Gunner
Wehrheim, Robert J., Pfc to Mechanic T/4
Bailey, Marion E., Pfc to Radio Operator T/4
Hopkins, Ford E., Pfc to Armorer & Artificer T/5

Company B

Wilt, Henry B., S/Sgt to 1st Sgt.
Tarazewski, Stanley, T/4 to Mess Sgt.
Durkee, George, T/4 to Motor Sgt.
Schoff, Elson C., Pfc to Supply Sgt.
Rozzell, Leland M., Sgt to Platoon Sgt.
Berry, Willard L., Pfc to Comm Sgt.
St Gemme, Harold L., Pfc to Meteorologist
Kattleman, Melvin J., Pfc to Squad Ldr.
Flewelling, Melvin J., Pfc to Squad Ldr.
Clark, Clyde H., Pfc to Squad Ldr.

Thompson, Edward H., Pfc to Cook T/4
Etter, John S., Pfc to Cook T/5
Hoffa, Carl L., Pfc to Cook T/4
Glanert, Paul R., Pfc to Co Clerk
Fagan, Laurence J., Pfc to Gunner
Kiester, John R., Pfc to Gunner
Green, Raymond F., Pfc to Gunner
Crone, Lawrence W., Jr., T/5 to Mechanic T/4
Giard, Clement M., Pfc to Radio Operator T/4
Norman, Robert E., Pfc to Armorer & Artificer

Company C

Tillman, Lemuel R., S/Sgt to 1st Sgt.
Lyons, Rex E., T/4 to Mess Sgt.
Reidling, Harold O., T/4 to Motor Sgt.
Harris, Howards S., Cpl to Supply Sgt.
Gargani, Charles N., Cpl to Platoon Sgt.
Drahn, Lloyd C., T/5 to Comm Sgt.
Harris, John E., Jr, Sgt to Meteorologist
Bickel, Walter H., Cpl to Squad Ldr.
Knapp, Raymond J., Pfc to Squad Ldr.
Sheats, Alfred R., Cpl to Squad Ldr.

Gregory, William G., Pfc to Cook T/4
Gorman, Oscar J., Pvt to Cook T/4
Hatfield, Arnold J., Pfc to Cook T/5
Spinti, Carl G. W., Cpl to Co Clerk
Gramo, John A., Pfc to Gunner
Hennessy, Edwin W., Jr., Pfc to Gunner
Gott, Norman D., Pfc to Gunner
Millar, Edward W., Pfc to Mechanic T/4
Brummage, Robert L., Pfc to Radio Operator T/4
Leap, Maurice D., Pfc to Armorer & Artificer

the name, to Linz, occupied by Russian troops at that time. The train which brought back those poor people was had of 27 wagons - a little one on the front after the locomotive, for 8 G.I.'s, after, 25 goods or animals wagons (for 8 more G.I. passengers). In each big good wagon 40 persons, so each time we brought back 1000 persons. But when we were inside the Russian territory, American soldiers must not go out of their wagons. If you had seen the way the Russian soldiers handled the people made prisoner by Germans, that was a shame, a big desolation. Some [*wanted*] to go back into Germany, but could not, they were prisoners once more. A truthful story about the Russians' way of treating their oppress[*ed*] people." [7]

Mortar inspection at Inn Valley, June 1945.
Jean Pierre Combe

James Helsel, Co. A, wrote on the 18th, "The Col. told us to take it easy, we had done our work, all we was to brush up on was military courtesy. We might need it before we got home."[8]

Sam Bundy was obviously agitated when he wrote on June 20th, "The 103rd is growing more chicken every day … we have grown tired of shows in Innsbruck and are bored with everything … rumors are flying wild and everyone is much concerned. It seems that men with more than 80 points may go to the 103rd." Pfc. Byron Jordan, Co. B, also reflected upon this situation as he wrote, "I now have exactly 80 points … as we were given another battle star a few days ago. My total now is six stars."[9]

Between the 19th and 21st, Co. A took about 1,000 Russians, known as D. P.'s or Displaced Persons, to Linz, Austria, and brought back some French and Italians. Maj. John McEvoy expressed his disgust at this policy as he said, "When the European war ended, we unknowingly did some unfortunate things, one of which was agreeing with the Russians that we would force the repatriation of Displaced Persons who did not want to return to Eastern Europe and Russia. Too late, we learned that the Russians shot some of them as examples for others who had involuntarily served the Germans."[10]

An awards ceremony was held for the battalion on June 25th with three Silver Stars and 46 Bronze Stars presented, with Col. Milton T. Hankins, Army Ground Forces Chemical Officer; Col. Herrold E. Brooks, personnel officer, Office of the Chief of CWS; and Lt. Col. Sam Efnor of the battalion in attendance. During the day, Sam Bundy's prediction of a few days earlier came true as orders were received to "strip" all enlisted men with 85 points or more, and all with the Italian Campaign Ribbon, and transfer them to the 103rd Infantry Division. The vacancies created in the 83rd by this order were to be filled by the low point men of the 103rd. The Medical Detachment of the battalion was to be transferred to the 326th Medical Battalion. The remaining men of the 83rd were to merge into the three regiments and artillery division of the 103rd. All of this was to take place the following day although the actual procedure did not begin until June 28th. At retreat formation on the night of the 26th, Capt. Robert Smith broke the news to his men: "I told the boys 'goodbye' last night … and now I'm having trouble trying to talk some of them out of volunteering to go with the outfit, even though it goes to the Pacific and they have earned the right to stay out of combat. Two of them just insisted, so I had to let them stay, and there will probably be others in during the day." George Borkhuis, HQ Co., said that on June 26th Capt. Robert Edwards said he would notify the men the following day of their future and they turned in their rifles and ammo. Borkhuis also said there was a rumor

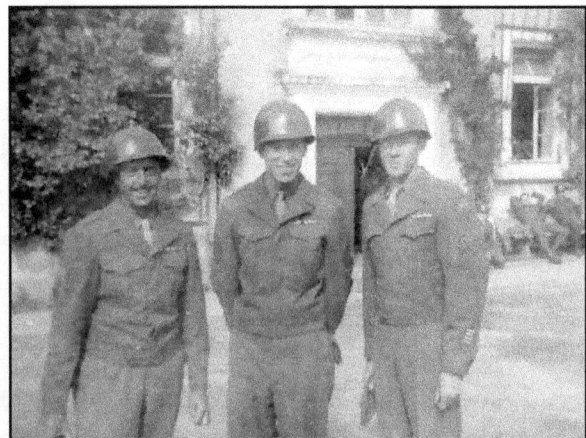

L-R: Charles L. Plumly, Douglas A. Swayze, and Samuel Bundy at Sobald Hall, Austria, June 1945.
Eugene Plassmann

L-R: Dave Meyerson, Sam Efnor, and John McEvoy at club in Public Gardens, Linz, Austria, 1945.
John McEvoy

the battalion would return to the states on the *Monticello* which the men were against because on the trip over on that ship in 1943 many had been assigned "F" Deck which was about 10 feet below the water line and the perfect spot for torpedoes to strike.[11]

Capt. Smith also described his feelings vividly on June 27th in a letter to his wife. "The last few days have been pretty sad ones, and tomorrow morning is the climax. I lose the entire company tomorrow morning, with the exception of 13 men and the officers. In other words, the old original Longbow Charley will now be no more. Of course, in its present shape even it's still not the original bunch that started overseas together, but there are some of them still here. And most of the ones here now have been with me most of the time. There have been 145 killed in action in the company since it started and, of course, many more than that wounded to varying degrees, so we couldn't expect the original bunch to all be with us."

Smith closed his letter with a morbid afternote, claiming that three nights previously two men of his outfit, normally good men and friends, got into a drunken brawl and one shot and killed the other. Lt. Robert E. Bundy vividly remembered the tragic episode, writing, "When we settled in the Inn valley we took over a couple of cafes … one evening several of the troops and some of the officers went to town. Later that night a jeep pulled up and some troops were calling for the medics. I was with Lt. Don Herr, (MSC) at the time. We ran out to the jeep and Don looked at the trooper in the back seat and immediately determined that there was nothing anybody could do. The young man was dead. Within a few minutes some of the officers returned. One of the officers was Dr. (Capt.) Julius Hulcher. He took a quick look at the dead trooper and turned away. Dr. Hulcher kept repeating something to the effect, 'If I had only been here just maybe I could have made a difference and saved him.' Don Herr tried to assure Dr. Hulcher there was nothing anybody could have done. As I recall, Dr. Hulcher cried that night, isn't anything anybody could say or do that would change his mind. It was a very emotional event. Sad as it is, it highlights the character of Dr. Hulcher. We later learned that some of the troops had too much to drink and a confrontation broke out. I think it was while they were loading back on the trucks to return to the compound. Some pushing followed and one of the soldiers pulled out his 'equalizer' and shot the other trooper." According to records the man killed was Pfc. Steve F. Briglovich, Co. C, from Youngstown, OH, on June 21st.[12]

The much dreaded dissolution of battalion veterans came as promised on June 28th. According to Sam Bundy, "At 900 hours all companies gathered in [a] field near B Company near Innsbruck where we were separated into groups to go to the 103rd Division. Quite a sad scene – everyone telling his buddies 'so-long'. We are thoroughly broken up with one man from the BN going here, two men there, and a few some other places." James Helsel, Co. A, said, "The old 83rd is being broke up and all but 28 men are being sent to the 103rd Division. The whole battalion has been drunk for the past three days, many of them still drunk. It sure is going to be hard to break up after being together this long. The 103rd trucks picked us up and took us to Innsbruck." Pfc. George A. Barrett, Co. B, said, "Some of us cried when the 83rd broke up. We in Co. B were so close that we thought that we would surely come home together … those of us fortunate enough to have enough points went home feeling sorry for those left behind, but knowing that they would soon follow." Jean Pierre Combe, the honorary member of Co. C, also recalled the disheartening dissolution, writing, "At first end of June, all ancients [*veterans*] of Battalion moved and had been replaced by new, young soldiers. A few old soldiers stayed to learn them the way to use a 4.2" mortar. I was one of them. We drilled to go fight in Japan." A battalion publicity

Top left: 83rd dissolution at Innsbruck, June 28, 1945.
John McEvoy

Top right: "Doc" Hulcher and Walter Hauser.
Robert Bush Collection

Bottom: Ralph Jessop, left of photo, at 83rd disbanding.
John P. McEvoy

history stated, "the record of the 83rd became obvious; 98% of enlisted personnel had over 85 points when they left" the battalion on this date. The battalion was placed under II Corps June 30th, with Headquarters opened at Salzburg.[13]

Lt. Robert Bundy, Co. A, also recalled the rotation system, writing, "Almost all of the troops in the 83rd were transferred to units that were heading home. Most of the troops of the 83rd had a lot more points required for rotation than called for. I think the magic number was 85. You received 1 point for every month of service, 1 point for every month overseas, 5 points for each decoration, 5 points for each battle star, I think 10 if you were married and 5 for each child [*actually 12 for each child under 18*]. I was not married at the time and had a total of 65 points. I was designated to remain in the Army of Occupation. However, I volunteered to stay with the battalion as the Bn. S-4 replacing Capt. Ed Trey, and go to the Pacific. The battalion was then filled with low point soldiers in the theater."[14]

The battalion continued to maintain security in assigned areas during July and engaged in "… training with emphasis on supervised athletics, nomenclatural functioning of mortar and the T-59 sight." Rain and cold, with snow on the nearby mountain peaks, prevailed on Independence Day, July 4th. Capt. Smith attempted to find a silver lining to the situation when he wrote, "I have had my hands pretty full for the past week, since I now have a complete new company of infantrymen. All of my old company, except 15 men, have transferred and are either going home soon to be discharged, or again will be transferred to some outfit in the Army of Occupation. We have the same officers for the time being, and then those with over 85 points <u>may</u> be transferred out and we would get new officers, and neither the new officers or the men we have now would know anything about the Mortar. So, if I stay in the company, I'll be in one hell of a fix." As Smith wrote, orders arrived for the 409th Infantry, 103rd Division, along with the 83rd, to vacate Austria by July 10th and move to the vicinity of Kaufbeuren, Germany, and he noted the roadblocks maintained in the vicinity were no longer necessary. Yet the very next day the move for the battalion was canceled as they were detached from the 103rd and attached to the 11th Armored Division in the vicinity of Steyr, Austria. Sam Bundy of Co. A wrote in his diary, "... moved in convoy to Klosterlechfeld, north of Landsberg ... a small town infested by flies." George Borkhuis, HQ Co., said he moved from Innsbruck to Issing, a point about 10 miles south of Landsberg.[15]

In the course of the next three days, the battalion was relieved from assignment to the XV Corps, cleared the roads and prepared for the July 10th movement from Weer to Losensteinleiten, Austria, and the 11th Armored Division. Capt. Smith was informed the battalion would probably sail for the States in October and be held in reserve for the Pacific Theater, a fate to which he reluctantly resigned himself. "I don't care about going to the Pacific if I don't have to ... I know that somebody has to get killed in a war, but I've already seen all of them get killed that I want to ... I don't have my old company now anymore, and most of the enlisted men out of it will probably be home before the end of this month. The new ones are shaping up well though, and I think will make a fine bunch ... this will still be a good outfit when they learn the mortar, but the outfit I slept in the same holes with and sweated out the same shell fire with, and got 'took' advantage of by at every opportunity, are gone now. And I just hate to start over, I guess I'm kinda tired."[16]

The 83rd resumed their training schedule of physical exercise, military courtesy, and basic mortar firing on July 11th and on the 12th was given the responsibility for picking up all Hungarian personnel. Gen. Willard A. Holbrook, Jr., inspected the battalion on July 14th while the 83rd continued their training focused on "Instruction and Guard Mount, military courtesy, Manual of Arms and Basic Drills for 4.2 Mortars, and organized athletics." Co. B manned roadblocks and patrolled in the vicinity of the west side of the Inn River, along the railroad south of Steyr, and searched for Hungarian personnel.[17]

On the 16th, Capt. Robert Smith noted they were in an old castle at Losensteinleiten near Steyr, about 60 miles from Vienna. He confirmed the training program to acquaint the men with the mortar was in progress and most of the old men of the 83rd were then either en route home or in the Army of Occupation. Gordon Mindrum said Steyr was where the Americans "faced-off'" against the Russians. Lt. Robert E. Bundy fondly recalled, "At Steyr I sold my watch to a Russian officer. I got a good price for an old Elgin. As a matter of fact I got enough to last me for the rest of the time I was in Austria. They were paid in script just like the rest of us. The Russians were not paid during the entire war. They were paid in a lump sum at the end but they could not take it back to Russia. So the fellow I sold my watch to rolled up his sleeve and there were at least a dozen watches on his arm. He was happy and I was happy. I'm sure the statute of limitations has run out by now. Hope so. I just wonder how many others sold watches to the Russians." Lt. Fred Kohl added, "A black market was soon thriving as the Russians were desperate for anything we had. I sold my Mickey Mouse watch for $200 and sent the money home to my wife. Lots of guys sold anything they could get their hands on. Some made thousands there."[18]

Mess Sgt. George Borkhuis stationed with the troops at Issing said that on July 17th, "A new order was issued today authorizing us to wear our 83rd Chemical insignia on our right arm and 103rd on the left. This makes us feel a lot better because we all like our original outfit the best. Previously we could only wear the 103rd insignia."

A firing test of the M3 Drawn Shell for the 4.2" chemical mortar was conducted on July 18th, apparently overseen by Lt. Col. Sam Efnor, and the conclusion was that "... there was no evidence of any mechanical failure of the drawn shell bodies for the 8 rounds which were fired at over charge (28 rings of M6 propellant) ... It appears from this very limited sample that the drawn shell are sufficiently strong mechanically to warrant the additional test which has been planned." Ironically, the results of this test were apparently not submitted to Washington until November 27, 1945.[19]

On the 19th Lt. James R. Davis, one of the former Rangers serving with the 83rd, was assigned to the 135th Chemical Company, as were many of the "old men" of the battalion, to either prepare to go to the Pacific or be shipped home.[20]

Lt. Col. Efnor inspected the battalion on July 21st as the fourth week of training began with "... emphasis on mortar drill, Platoon and Company FSC, Military Courtesy, Speed Marches and Group Athletics." More important at this time was the departure of Lt. Col. Efnor, replaced on July 23rd by Major Gordon M. Mindrum, as well as the redeployment of six first lieutenants.[21]

Gordon Melvin Mindrum was a logical successor to Efnor, having been with the battalion since its earliest stages as a first lieutenant and then as captain of Co. B. He had served with distinction in Sicily, developed an early interest in medicine while dissecting frogs at Anzio, and won two Purple Hearts, a Bronze Star and a Silver Star before becoming major of HQ Co. Maj. Mindrum recalled that while at Steyr the 83rd planned and trained for "Operation Cornet," the planned invasion of Japan. He said "there was good intelligence, contour maps, and excellent aerial photographs of our invasion site, an air-drop with 101st Airborne Division on the southern tip of the eastern peninsula of Yokohama Harbor." The atomic bomb would cancel the planned operation.[22]

Capt. Robert Smith was also detached on July 23rd to the 103rd Division to go to Kaufbeuren, Germany, for the trial of the soldier who became drunk and killed a comrade at Weer. Between the 25th and 27th, numerous officers and enlisted men were redeployed and assigned to such organizations as the 2nd Chemical Mortar Battalion, the 65th Infantry, and the 11th Armored Division. A battalion publicity history stated, "with the once-roaring 4.2 mortars now encased in oil and canvas, the 83rd is standing by. The men who comprise the battalion now may not have been at Gela and Anzio, but they know what the hell of battle is like, for wherever you go through Headquarters, A, B, and C companies, you will see the silver-and-blue Combat Infantry Badge. These ex-doughboys are proud to be in this battalion. They can recall many a time when the 4.2 mortarmen were right on line with them in France, Germany, and Austria. And even though the war is over, they still are disgusted that this battalion, with its glorious combat record is still classified in the Army Service Forces." S/Sgt. George Borkhuis now with Co. B, 409th Infantry at Munich, Germany, said his group was scheduled to move to Rheims, France, in ten days.[23]

While at Losensteinleiten a large percentage of the men suffered from dysentery. Others remained bored of the monotonous daily routine. Capt. Smith repeatedly stressed the changing structure of the battalion in his letters. "There are now only five officers of the original 44 left in the Bn.," Smith wrote on July 28th. "And, of course, all the men were changed some time ago. I, of course, am one of the five and am now Bn. Executive Officer and S-3, with Major Mindrum commanding. Col. Efnor has gone home and the other officers have been transferred to an outfit that is slated to go home and disband. The new officers are all infantry officers with low points, and so we still have a whale of a job training a completely new outfit with no cadre." The fifth week of training that began July 30th centered on "Rifle Marksmanship, Familiarization of Small Arms, and small company problems," and on the 31st the assignment of new officers of the 83rd took place. "Troop Assignment No. 127" dated July 19th, 1945, officially assigned the 83rd Chemical Mortar Battalion to U.S. Occupation Forces, Austria. Pfc. George A. Barrett, Co. B, claimed, "Occupation duty! Those were wonderful days … we really had a ball and enjoyed ourselves. But the war was over and we wanted to get home."[24]

U.S. OCCUPATION FORCES
AUSTRIA
August – November 1945

The month of August saw the battalion's continued focus on a schedule of rigid training, stressing the physical aspect, exercises, and familiarization with the firing of small arms. Capt. Robert B. Smith, HQ Co., wrote from Losensteinleiten on August 3rd that he was now the battalion executive officer and would "perhaps be promoted some day." He dejectedly reported, "All the old officers and men, except a very few, are gone now, and this is in effect a new battalion, except that we still have the same old equipment" although he did note the battalion was scheduled to return to the U.S. sometime in October.[25]

During the early part of the month, the 83rd performed mortar firing training on the range, and on August 4th Capt. Ralph A. Turner, Jr., a tall red-headed fellow from Deport, Texas, who played football at Georgia Tech, inspected battalion quarters. Two days later Capt. Smith noted, "the new outfit is coming along fine."[26]

Ford Hopkins, one of the veteran 83rd men assigned to the 135th Chemical Company, wrote from Furth, Germany, on August 6th that "Lt. Davis is trying to give all the 83rd boys a break. I don't know how we'll make out. If we can't learn the [*mortar*] sight fast enough he'll put these new fellows as gunners." He noted that experienced corporals who came into the company late, such as himself, were being "robbed" and put in as assistant gunners. Ford also was concerned about other matters, as he added, "Now there's talk going around there is to be 25 of us to be shipped out as cadre for the other four companies they're going to form. I suppose I'll be one of them. I hope not. Let them send these new guys out … I'm in the 3rd Army, 15th Corps."[27]

Meanwhile, seven new lieutenants were assigned to the 83rd Chemical Mortar Battalion from the 65th Infantry on August 9th, but undoubtedly the biggest event of the month took place at 1:03 a.m. on August 15th when many of the men heard via radio news of the surrender of Japan, although Capt. Smith had heard rumors of such five days earlier while on official business in Frankfort, Germany. James M. Lester remembered how he heard the news: "Each division had a baseball team … these different divisions would have baseball games. There was nothing else to do, so we could always go and watch the baseball games in the big stadium where Hitler made his infamous speeches. One day we were in there watching a baseball game and we weren't sure what was going to happen to us. We thought perhaps we would end up going to Japan. The war wasn't over yet in Japan. It was over in the European Theatre, but it wasn't over in Japan. They announced over the P.A. system, at the ball game, that the war was over in Japan. We knew then that we'd be getting home shortly." Lt. Robert Bundy, Co. A, added, "When VJ Day came the battalion was once again changed with people having somewhere between 70 and 85 points. I still didn't qualify."[28]

Lt. Fred Kohl said he was living in a guest house in the Alps when he heard of the Japanese surrender and added, "We'd practice shooting our mortars and then go riding or fishing when off duty. I got to be a pretty good rider. We were relieved to know we didn't have to go to the Pacific … The Japanese soldiers were incomprehensible to us." According to Jean Pierre Combe, "A morning in August during an exercise an Austrian civilian came and tell us that the war was over with Japan. A young American soldier, whom I do not remember the name, say to me: 'I think that nut is proud of himself' [*later determined as a reference to Albert Einstein*]. I asked him what do you mean, he answered, 'I'm the neighbor in U.S.A. of the man who has been working for the atomic bomb. When you cross him into the street, he always look the sky -- I tell him - Hello Mister Einstein - how do you do? After six or eight yards he looked back and said, 'Excuse me boy, I had not see you, hello!' For me that was all new, because I never hear about A. Einstein and atomic bomb before."[29]

As a result of the Japanese surrender, the battalion commander declared it a holiday for the men, and, in compliance with President Harry Truman's proclamation, the next two days were observed as a national holiday for the men. The battalion resumed their training program on August 20th but by the 22nd relaxed the program to the extent of cancellation of firing. Jean Pierre Combe was probably describing this when he wrote, "After the surrender of Japan we did not have any more exercises [*firing*]." Lt. Col. James Peale, 101st Infantry, 26th Infantry Division, formed a review of the 83rd at Steyr, Austria, on August 25th and awarded six Purple Hearts and Four Bronze Stars.[30]

A revised training program was initiated on August 27th with emphasis "placed on physical conditioning, Group Games, Orientation subjects such as GI Bill of Rights, Gasoline Engines, and Veterans Organizations & Benefits." The same day, Capt. Smith returned from a trip to Lyons, France, with shoulder patches for the men. One day later, all companies of the battalion prepared for a movement to their new quarters at Bad Hall, Austria, and were detached from the 11th Armored Division and attached to the 26th Infantry Division. The battalion completed the move to Bad Hall where for the rest of the month the training program continued with modifications. Jean Pierre Combe added, "The 83rd Bn. moved to Bad Hall. The young soldiers moved in another place too and were replaced by old soldiers, veterans. We had nothing to do, or not very much. A part take guard when that was our turn. Often we went hunting … we killed pheasants, hares, and deer. We gave some to Austrian civilians and we ate some too. That was the way to take our time."[31]

By August 30th, the remnants of the 83rd serving with the 135th Chemical Mortar Company had moved to Ottensoos, Germany, near Nurnberg. Ford Hopkins said they gave a dress parade for a visiting "big shot" and his platoon was judged the best and won a free trip to visit the notorious Dachau prison camp. Hopkins added the men had to continue to learn all about various weapons, although they had no manuals, and also to study training films.[32]

Although the exact time of the event is not certain, sometime either in July or late August, lieutenants Robert Bundy and Charles J. DeCesare, yet with the 83rd, were assigned to return Albert, the ex-Italian soldier attached to Co. A, home to Italy. Albert may also be one of the two ex-Italian soldiers remembered by Joseph Cannetti, who wrote, "Pete Tranchitella was a good mess sergeant, he always fed us on the line with his two Italian prisoners. They came from Venice and told him they would stay and help him until we reached Venice. Unfortunately, they got caught in a barrage and one lost a leg. We all chipped in and got him a wooden leg." There is no record of Albert losing a leg, although he was injured in a truck accident August 27, 1944, so the other man may be the one who was the victim.[33]

In any event, Robert Bundy remembered, "Albert was a young Italian boy who traveled with the 1st platoon of Co. A. He sure could make a great dish of spaghetti. Lt. Charles J. DeCesare and I took him home to Italy. Maj. Gordon Mindrum didn't think we could get through the Brenner Pass. However, when we got there we were greeted by a Sgt. from a sister mortar battalion. We chatted for a short time bringing him up to date as to where the 83rd went after leaving Italy. He called to his men to open the gate and let us through. When we arrived in Rome, having taken the young man home somewhere in northern Italy, we went to the Command Hqs. and met a Sgt. who immediately recognized the 83rd patch and started in by asking, 'Where did you guys go after the Volturno River?' He said, 'You guys saved my life. I was on patrol and we got cut off and I got wounded. You put down a smoke screen' and they (his unit - I think the 36th Inf.) was able to save him. He immediately called the Excelsior Hotel and made arrangements for DeCesare and me. We told him we had a driver and he assured us he would take good care of him. He did. After a week, I checked at the desk and was told there was no charge. We had a great week in Rome and it didn't cost us or our driver a cent. All because we belonged to the 83rd."[34]

From September 1st through the 8th, the battalion remained at the Occupational Zone in the vicinity of Bad Hall and continued the training program with emphasis on exercises, Group Games, and orientation conferences. Capt. Robert B. Smith wrote on Labor Day, the 3rd, a legal holiday for all troops, that he had been fishing with Maj. Mindrum and injured his right thumb in a battalion baseball game. Smith also noted "our quarters are somewhat different. We were in old German barracks buildings, but this is different. The Major and I are together in four rooms, complete with radio, running water, fine furniture, high ceilings, lots of mirrors, etc. It belonged to some rich guy. And all the other officers are also fixed up in luxury." On the 5th, the men were reviewed by Col. Lindsey of the 101st Infantry, 26th Infantry Division, who presented eight Bronze Stars, seven Purple Hearts, and two Purple Hearts with Oak Leaf Clusters, probably the last decorations given the battalion. On the 6th the 83rd was notified of a change in category classification. The same day Ford Hopkins, with the 135th Mortar Company at Ottensoos, wrote his men were being moved to the 818th Tank Destroyer Battalion to be processed to return home and said, "I tried sewing my 83rd patch

Crossing the Rhine River, September 1945.
Ed Trey

Top Left: 1st ETO (European Theater of Operations) World Series at Nurnberg Stadium. The 29th Division versus the 71st Division. *Vicente De Leon;* Scenes from the U.S. Army baseball championship games played at Nurnberg. Bottom left: Troops arriving at the games. Above: Poster for 3rd Army Baseball Championship. *Lester Collection*

on my jacket but gave it up as a bad job … I'll have to have it on when I come home. That and my corporal stripes … we all got a set of overseas stripes, too, so they'll have to be put on … I wish all the 83rd guys were going but some of them haven't 65 points yet. I don't think it will be long before they get sent home, though."[35]

Back at Steyr, the remnants of the 83rd were ordered to relieve Co. K, 101st Infantry, at their posts and camps. By September 8th, Ford Hopkins was at Altdorf, Germany, with Co. C, 818th Tank Destroyer Battalion, ready to be sent home and Capt. Robert Smith wrote from Steyr that the 83rd Chemical Mortar Battalion "may be in Category 1 now, which means occupation troops but I don't think that will change our order of going home." He also lamented, "As Battalion Executive Officer I don't do much, and feel pretty useless."[36]

Between September 9th and 15th, Maj. Gordon M. Mindrum, battalion commander, was ordered to relinquish battalion command and move to Thienville, France, in order to fly home for discharge, although in a 2006 conversation he stated he came home by boat the same as everyone else. Command of the 83rd Chemical Mortar Battalion was assumed by Capt. Robert B. Smith, who noted he now had three large rooms all to himself as though he were a general, and Capt. Anton B. Krivak, Jr., replaced Smith as battalion executive officer. On the 10th Co. K, 101st Infantry, relieved the 83rd Chemical Mortar Battalion at Steyr. Capt. Smith wrote of his "promotion" on September 12th, stating, "I am now the Battalion Commander. And it looks like it will be my job to take them home … I'm having a parade and review for a Colonel Lindsey this afternoon at 4:30." In a display of concern, Smith wrote, "I don't have any idea what may happen to the 83rd once it does get home. The men in the outfit have an average now of between 40 and 50 points, and whether it may be demobilized, re-deployed, or what, I can't say … we are now attached to the 26th Division, and they may not be on the way home until February. As you now know, we are no longer with the 103rd. That is where all our old men went in June, and I guess they are all home by now."[37]

On the 22nd of the month, the battalion was still at Bad Hall where Capt. Smith reported, "We are at present

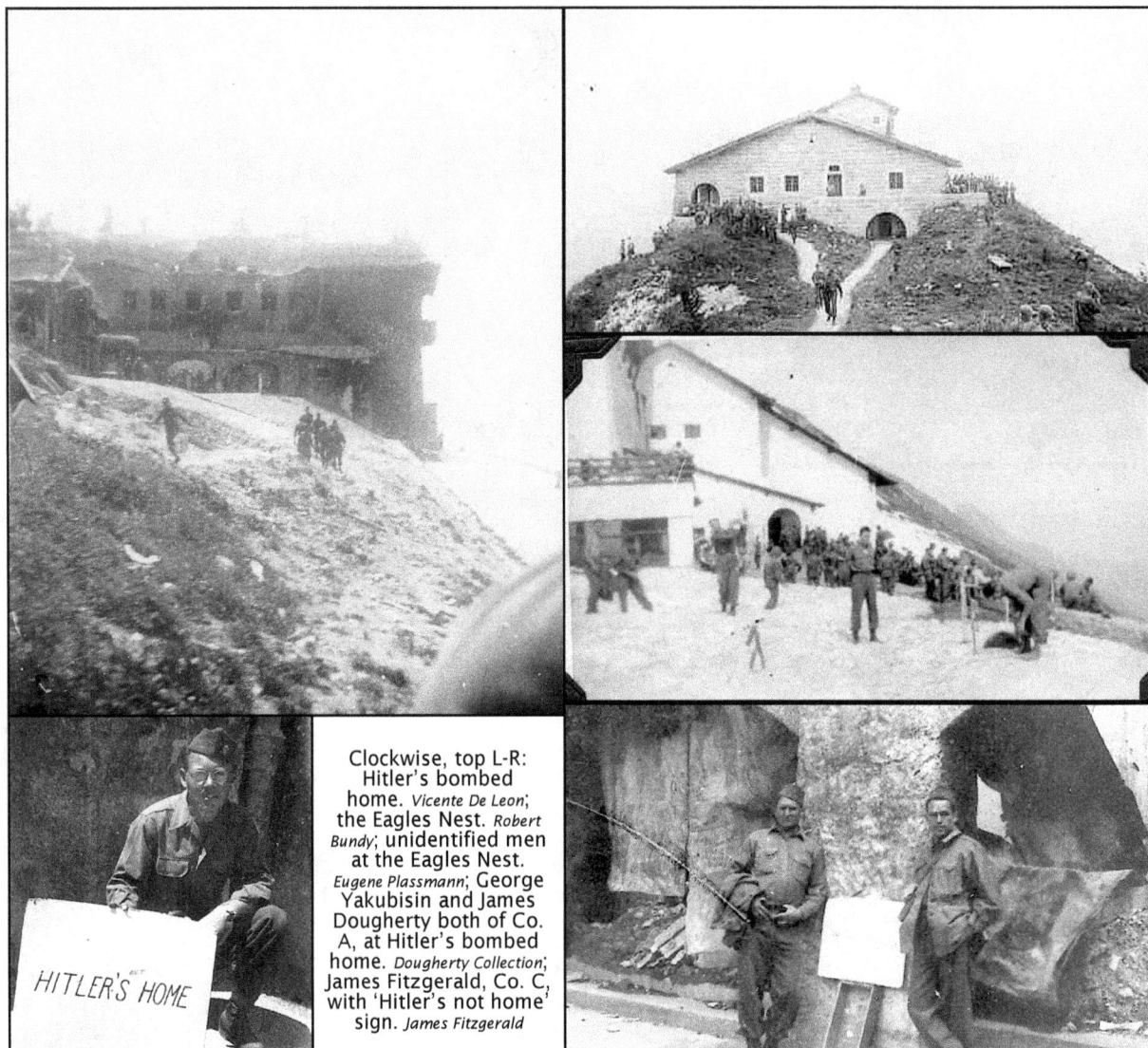

Clockwise, top L-R: Hitler's bombed home. *Vicente De Leon*; the Eagles Nest. *Robert Bundy*; unidentified men at the Eagles Nest. *Eugene Plassmann*; George Yakubisin and James Dougherty both of Co. A, at Hitler's bombed home. *Dougherty Collection*; James Fitzgerald, Co. C, with 'Hitler's not home' sign. *James Fitzgerald*

changing all the personnel again, moving out of the low point men and getting in high point men. I expect to have between 800 and 900 before we are through. And it is quite a blow to some of them to have to leave the Bn. now. We will probably go to Rheims, France early in October after we have re-organized and sail early in November for the U.S … I'm losing all but seven officers again and all but 46 men, so you can see what a personnel and re-organization problem we are going to have." Smith closed his letter noting, "Lt. Trapnell and I came into the Btn. at the same time, and are now the only two left of those that were at Anzio when we got there."[38]

The month of October found the 83rd Chemical Mortar Battalion yet in the vicinity of Bad Hall, Austria. Capt. Smith, fed up with the situation, wrote on October 11th, "We were supposed to leave here the 5th, then the 9th, now sometime between now and the 20th. I don't know now whether we will go directly to the port or to an assembly area first, but I do know that I am about crazy now." After making note of his receipt of a Bronze Star, Smith added, "We have a conglomeration of everything in this Bn and there is one officer who came to the Bn when I did and one who came last December. All the rest, officers and men, are gone."[39]

The battalion's situation remained in a quandary as of October 14th when Capt. Smith wrote, "We got orders yesterday at 2 p.m. to move to the assembly area tomorrow. Then at 3 p.m. the order was canceled. So now I don't know when we will leave, but are still supposed to start by the 20th. That may be canceled too … I'm about to lose all my patriotism." More noteworthy was Smith's announcement that an Air Corps major was now in command of the 83rd, "and he is never here. I'm supposed to be the Bn. Executive Officer, but the whole thing is so cluttered up with rear echeloners that I have no interest in the Bn anymore. It's now just a vehicle to take a group of men home and not a 4.2 Mortar Bn anymore."[40]

On October 18th, Capt. Smith said the battalion was scheduled to depart Bad Hall for home sometime between then and November 8th, but on October 27th he reported the battalion availability date was set for November 9th and the readiness order for November 24th. In the meantime, Smith had a chance to go deer hunting, visited Hitler's compound at Berchtesgaden, and went to Innsbruck to pick up some shoulder patches for the men.[41]

Capt. Smith was thoroughly disgusted with the situation of the battalion by November 8th. "I guess this is about the outfit with the lowest morale in the Army. We now have 206 men over 38 years [*points?*], 567 over 35. The rest all over 80 points, and all officers over 85 points, and they still don't send us home. The word has gotten around that the *Chicago Tribune* published an article saying that the only men left overseas who have over 80 points are those who volunteered to stay or have the gonorrhea." Despite such animosity, the following day he departed Bad Hall for home with the 83rd Chemical Mortar Battalion, scheduled to arrive at Le Havre, France, for ship transport on November 9th. Jean Pierre Combe gave a slightly different chronology of events, writing, "November 11, 1945 - We left Austria. We crossed Germany, north of France to join the Havre's harbor where a boat was waiting for bring back into U.S.A. my dear 83rd Cml. Bn. For me that was the end of a nice and good travel."[42]

According to Lt. Robert Bundy, "The battalion was ordered to take all of their equipment and vehicles by convoy to Le Havre, France and return to join the balance of the unit in Austria for transportation by train (box cars) back to Le Havre. With the Commanding Officer's permission, I went to the HQ, U.S. Forces Austria at Saltzburg and discussed the problem with a Major Herb Lauterstien and convinced him how foolish this was since we were 100% mobile. He agreed that it would be more efficient to let the battalion convoy to LeHavre and turn in their equipment and board the transport for the U.S. I did not accompany the unit, but my dog Pete [*inherited from Capt. Robert Edwards*] was aboard Lt. Trapnell's jeep ... I think Lt. Trapnell took him to Mississippi ... That was the last I saw of the battalion."[43]

Le Havre, a French harbor on the eastern side of the Bay of Siene opposite Cherbourg, had been established earlier in the war as a "tent city" for both soldiers arriving for overseas duty or departing for home. Individual camps were established and named primarily after well known American cigarette brands, hence the "Cigarette Camps," as well as American cities. Nearly all of the 83rd Chemical Mortar Battalion passed through Le Havre at one time or another to be processed for the journey home. Ironically, although no one camp was designated for the 83rd, records indicate that a large portion passed through Camp Lucky Strike, which was located between Cany and St. Valery, with the capacity to hold 58,000 soldiers.[44]

Jean Pierre Combe, the young French lad who had saved so many of the battalion at Briançon and joined Co. C as a mortar man, could not come to the States; therefore, Capt. Smith and 1st Lt. William L. Trapnell wrote him a glowing official commendation, along with travel papers, on November 10th. Jean Pierre recalled, "[*Smith and Trapnell*] gave me a good handshake and some papers to justify my passage into American Army in particular with the 83rd Cml. Mortar, Co. C. I was very proud of that battalion and all my friends. That was November 14, 1945. That day was also my anniversary, eighteen years old, and for the first time since 15 months I got back home with my family."[45]

On November 17th Capt. Smith and the boys of the 83rd embarked on the *USS George Washington*, and arrived at the New York Port of Embarkation on November 25th. The following day, at Camp Myles Standish near Boston, Massachusetts, the 83rd Chemical Mortar Battalion was officially deactivated November 26th or 28th [*depending upon source*], 1945. From Boston, Capt. Smith moved the men by rail to Ft. Bliss, Texas. Although the unit that came home was nothing more than a mere ghost of the original "Fighting 83rd," the battalion as a whole had finally ceased to exist. Elwood ("Long John") Guthrie of Co. A would later comment on his service in the 83rd: "It will be a lot to look back on. We had fun with all the hell we caught. I wouldn't have missed it for nothing but I wouldn't do it again for nothing."[46]

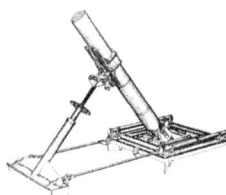

Camp Chicago near Soissons, France, December 1945. Back row: Samuel Kweskin (2nd from left), Robert Simon (4th from left), Zenon R. Siepkowski (2nd from right), and Wilbur Klopp (far right). Front: Ray Knapp (2nd from right). *Sam Kweskin*

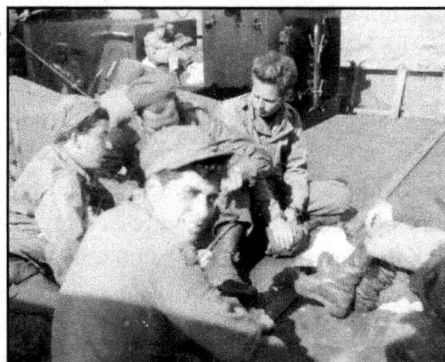

Center: (L) Byron Jordan's embarkation paper to return to the states. *Byron Jordan*; (R) Jack Pimento, facing camera, and Lee Steedle, back right, aboard ship going home. *Byron Jordan*

Bottom: (L) Ed Trey's first glimpse of Boston Harbor upon retuning to the USA. *Ed Trey*; (R) Leaving the harbor at Le Havre, France. *Ed Trey*

EPILOGUE

First reunion of the 83rd Chemical Mortar Battalion held in Baltimore, Maryland, June 3-5, 1954. *Strickler Collection*

1. Robert W. Knortz 2. Martin J. Feerick 3. George E. DeLucas 4. George A. Barrett 5. Lewis Cameron 6. Harry Browne, Jr. 7. William P. Bailey 8. Larry Giammeria 9. Steve Snyder 10. Andrew J. Connolly 11. Frederick W. Endlein 12. Grady Lawless 13. Henry B. Wilt 14. Arthur J. Usher 15. Aubrey R. Parrish 16. Justin G. Woomer 17. Edward L. Trey 18. John Montana 19. Rollin D. Taylor 20. George R. Borkhuis 21. Kenneth C. Adair 22. Kenneth K. Laundre 23. Daniel J. Shields 24. Clair M. Strickler 25. John A. O'Connor 26. Howard Bobker 27. Robert E. Bundy 28. George N. Shirley 29. Clark H. Riddle 30. Paul J. Waring 31. Howell F. Beach, Jr. 32. Clarence L. Wicks 33. Samuel H. Danziger 34. George J. Whetsell 35. John J. Babjak 36. Russell S. Doster 37. George B. Glazier 38. Raymond W. Hoover 39. Carlos R. Trautman 40. Carl W. Lepine 41. Donald C. Herr 42. Joseph J. Sapienza 43. Charles J. Dial 44. Earl F. Kann 45. Peter J. Kiedrowski 46. James V. Lauro 47. Alfred L. Forrester 48. Samuel I. Kweskin 49. William F. Parra 50. John J. Bowles 51. W. Smith 52. D. Cooper 53. Theodore D. Haddock 54. John M. Butler 55. Herbert E. Durfee 56. John J. Joyce 57. Michael Dobrin 58. Henry E. Fajkowski 59. Lawrence J. Censato 60. George Schmidt 61. C. Hall 62. Steve Gozur 63. Rudolph R. Engel 64. Wofford L. Jackson 65. Michele P. Codega 66. George S. Yakubisin 67. Frank P. Lombardi 68. James F. Dougherty

The legacy of the 83rd Chemical Mortar Battalion did not end with their deactivation. A few members of the 83rd remained or returned to the military, but most of the veterans assimilated successfully back into civilian life. It was not always an easy process, however. Malcolm Doyle Wilkinson expressed it well when he said, "The amazing part of it all was when we were brought home. We did not receive any counseling as they do today, we were simply brought home and discharged. As I look back on it, there is no question in my mind that if someone had crossed me I would have killed him without a blink. I owe my life to my wife I think. I met her the night I came home and we somehow hit it off at once. When I would react angrily to something she would put a stop to it at once and I am an example of how love can control anyone … and I mean anyone. I owe her a lot as she made a human being out of me in short order …"[1]

Some of the 83rd veterans achieved success on a national level, such as John Baer and Joe Bova, who went on to successful careers in the Hollywood film industry; Earl Rapp and Carl McNabb in professional baseball; Harold Hughes as a state governor and champion of programs against drug-addiction; and Sam Kweskin as a noted artist and illustrator, including a stint drawing the now-classic super hero characters of Marvel Comics.[2]

The 83rd Chemical Mortar Battalion was again thrown into the national spotlight in 1946 when the Mead Committee held Congressional hearings on war profiteering. Topping the list were brothers Murray and Joseph Garsson, along with U.S. Representative from Kentucky, Andrew Jackson May, who had served as chairman of the

House Committee on Military Affairs during the war. Through a series of almost unbelievable business schemes, the three, along with others, created an industrial empire based upon false premises, and managed to obtain ordnance and munitions contracts during the war which would make them wealthy men. Details of the case would fill a book unto itself, but in brief, the men were behind one of the worst cases of war profiteering ever, including ties to Chicago gangsters. To make matters worse, Murray Garsson was the father of Capt. Joseph Garsson, former captain of Co. A of the 83rd Chemical Mortar Battalion, who had been court-martialed in 1945. There was already suspicion that May and Murray Garsson had interfered with the court-martial, attempting to exert political influence. Worse yet, the Garssons and May were charged with producing the defective 4.2" chemical mortar shells which blew up and killed or maimed various members of the 83rd and other chemical mortar battalions during the war. All participants declared their innocence but the evidence against them was overwhelming, and by the time the hearings were over all had received fines and prison sentences.[3]

Capt. Joseph Garsson's reputation was further tarnished, unfortunately, although his guilt was nothing more than through family relationship. Undoubtedly, if he had had any knowledge that his father and uncle were producing defective mortar shells or fuzes he certainly would not have exposed himself, and definitely not his men, to them by accepting captaincy of a mortar company. After all, he had accepted a court-martial rather than risk the lives of his men. Capt. Garsson's undoing was due more to his brash attitude rather than to any family connections. And in spite of how justified his actions may have seemed, he did disobey a superior officer, or as his own defense counsel, Maj. Gordon Mindrum, said in a 2006 interview, "Well - he was guilty as hell of the charge." Ironically, though, in spite of Mindrum and Capt. Garsson's approval in their last interviews to release the transcript of the court-martial, which each said would contain nothing of national security or current weapon tactics or use, the Office of the Clerk of Court, U.S. Army Judiciary, continues to refuse to honor repeated Freedom of Information Act requests, citing the transcript remains "Classified," producing no explanation whatsoever. Veteran Sam Kweskin, HQ Co., said, "Just what the hell did the 83rd and Garsson do that is so secret it is still classified - who is the government trying to protect? Gen. Eisenhower maybe? Who knows?"[4]

By September of 1946, the Senate had concluded that during the war "38 officers and enlisted men had been killed and 127 wounded by faulty mortar fire; the casualties were caused by only 63 misfirings out of 4,000,000 rounds; the defects were in the fuzes, not in the shells, supplied by the Garssons." In a 2005 interview, Capt. Garsson stood by his father, who he said was an honest man caught in the middle of a bad situation, and said the defective shells were ones that had been buried in the sand in North Africa for months by the military and had deteriorated as a result. There may have been some truth to that claim, and even Sam Kweskin said the Garssons were pressured by the government to produce more shells than they were capable, resulting in shoddy workmanship. Of course, none of this excused the fact the entire company was not legitimate. Even the classic 1947 Arthur Miller play, *All My Sons*, later turned into a 1948 movie starring Edward G. Robinson and Burt Lancaster, seemed based upon the scandal. Details of the whole Garsson-May situation can be found in the *Congressional Record: Proceedings and Debates of the 79th Congress, Second Session* and in the thesis by John Hamilton-Dryden, *The Garsson-May Connection: An Account of War Profiteering In Batavia, Illinois* (Northern Illinois University, 1992).[5]

REUNIONS

As early as 1949, with the rebirth of *Muzzleblasts*, there was interest expressed in holding some type of gathering of the 83rd Chemical Mortar Battalion veterans, which led to the first official reunion in Baltimore, Maryland, on June 3-5, 1954. The event drew approximately 75 veterans and was a rousing success, despite many of them being thrown out of the hotel for drunkenness. At that reunion, Justin G. Woomer was elected president and George Shirley was voted secretary-treasurer. Reunions continued every other year, excepting an eastern regional reunion in 1957 in Philadelphia, Pennsylvania, by George Barrett and Ben Wilt (34 veterans attended) and again in 1959 (21 vets). At the end of 1968 Woomer resigned as president and turned the reins over temporarily to Ed Trey although Joe Sapienza was elected president at the next meeting. Willard Smith was elected president in 1976. The Nashville, Tennessee, reunion in 1978 attracted 86 veterans. In 1996 the reunions became yearly due to declining membership.

In 1997 there were two mini-reunions created by the wide geographic separation of the veterans.

The complete list of reunions is as follows:

2009: June 17-20, Gettysburg Hotel, Gettysburg, PA
2008: May 29-June 1, Baltimore, MD (Linthicum), Holiday Inn
2007: May 31-June 3, Fredericksburg, VA (Stafford), Days Inn
2006: June 8-11, Lancaster, PA, Lancaster Host Resort
2005: June16-19, Gettysburg, PA, The Eisenhower Inn
2004: June 16-20, Tysons Corner, VA (DC area), Holiday Inn
2003: June 18-22, Baltimore, MD, Tremont Plaza Hotel
2002: June 19-23, Williamsburg, VA, Radisson Fort Magruder
2001: June 6-10, New Orleans, LA, Royal Sonesta Hotel
2000: June 21-25, Arlington, VA, Quality Inn
1999: May 19-23, Lancaster, PA, Ramada Inn
1998: June 10-14, Dayton, OH, Ramada Inn
1997: Two Mini-Reunions – Lancaster, PA / Tupelo, MS
1996: May 15-18, Fort Bragg, NC
1994: June 1-5, Memphis, TN, The Marriott
1992: Pittsburgh, PA
1990: May 17-20, Harrisburg, PA, Sheraton Harrisburg West
1988: May 19-22, Baltimore, MD, Lord Baltimore Hotel
1986: June 19-21, Nashville, TN, Sheraton-Nashville Hotel
1984: June 21-23, Philadelphia, PA, Warwick Hotel
1982: June 24-26, Disney World, Orlando, FL
1980: June 26-28, Williamsburg, VA, The Hospitality House
1978: June 22-24, Nashville. TN, Holiday Inn
1976: June, New York, NY
1974: June 20-22, Chicago, IL, Sheraton-Chicago Hotel
1972: June 29-July 1, Philadelphia, PA, Benjamin Franklin Hotel
1970: June 25-27, Pittsburgh, PA, William Penn Hotel
1968: June 27-29, Baltimore, MD, Lord Baltimore Hotel
1966: June 23-25, New York, NY, Abbey Victoria Hotel
1964: June 25-27, Chicago, IL, Bismarck Hotel
1962: Arlington, VA (DC area)
1960: June 23-26, Baltimore, MD, Lord Baltimore Hotel
1959: June 5-7, Philadelphia, PA, Benjamin Franklin Hotel
1958: June 26-29, Baltimore, MD, Lord Baltimore Hotel
1957: Philadelphia, PA, Benjamin Franklin Hotel
1956: June 7-9, Chicago, IL, Congress Hotel
1954: June 3-5, Baltimore, MD, Lord Baltimore Hotel

In response to the 1958 83rd Chemical Mortar Battalion Reunion, Lt. Col. William S. Hutchinson wrote a letter describing his memories, which read in part: "The official history records the three Presidential Unit Citations earned by Baker, Charlie, and Dog and all the individual decorations from Andre Laus' Distinguished Service Cross down to the last Bronze Star or Purple Heart. Our memories abound in all sorts of experiences ... seasickness on the way into Gela; the confusion of the first landing; Charlie Company firing so early on the first Italian motorized infantry attack; the mess with the 26th Infantry; the nine German tanks; General Patton in Baker Companies OP; his aide swiping a pair of binoculars.

I remember the pride with which Dog Company returned to us after its baptism of fire with the 16th Infantry.

I remember Able Company on the attack toward Butera, firing during incoming fire and thus learning that this is good mortar deception that leaves the enemy uncertain as to where you really are.

The Volturno, Venafro, Anzio ... all bring memories. I remember Sgt. Holley speaking for the Charlie and Dog survivors after the ship sinking. I also remember his losing of an arm at Minturno. I remember the love we have for Andre Laus who died a hero and the love we also have for Sgt. O'Connor ... who gave his life for Uncle Sam. Turner, Miller, Beasley, Schmidt, Rankin, Reynolds, also died ... just to mention a few. We love these men as we have never any other.

I remember the one softball game the officers' team managed to win at Camp Gordon. I swear Pike put the whole Dog Company team on pass. Doc Remler played right field for the officers and never touched the ball until after the game.

I remember another softball game the officers won in bivouac after Anzio just before I was transferred. That made two in a row with a long road trip between. So we quit, so far as I know, to rest on our laurels.

I remember Meyerson and Pike trapped upstairs in the dairy building during the German push on Anzio. I remember Sgt. Cohen from Charlie Company talking on the brotherhood of man.

I remember good things, funny things, heroic things. I remember how you find strength you never knew was in you when you need it. I remember how clearly I thought I knew what was right and what was wrong."

But perhaps Hutchinson summed it best in the intro of his letter in which he proclaimed, "We were an average bunch of Americans. We fought, some of us bled, and some of us died ..."

Co. C men at a reunion. L-R: Lloyd Fiscus*, Fred Linamen*, Andrew Connolly, Hale Hepler, Dale Blank*, William L. Holmes, Lemuel R. Tillman,** Raymond Hoover, and Robert Thorpe*. * POW Briançon; **escaped from Briançon. *Bernard Bernhardt*

Top right: John McEvoy at 2005 Gettysburg reunion. Bottom right: Edward Trey at 2005 Gettysburg, PA reunion. *Bill Steedle*

Left: 2005 Gettysburg, PA, reunion. Row 1, L-R: Ed Krebs, Lawrence Powell, Kelso Thompson, Lee Steedle, Dan Miller, and John Butler. Row 2, L-R: Robert Fenton, Steve Vukson, Joseph Cannetti, Raymond Hoover, Lloyd Fiscus, Clark Riddle, Perry Rice, and Carlos Trautman. Row 3, L-R: John McEvoy, Rudolph Whitt, Earl Kann, William Gallagher, John Hajdinyak, George Barrett, Ed Trey, Eugene Plassmann, and Joseph Garsson. *Bill Steedle*

Sam Kweskin (left) Bernard Bernhardt (right) during the war at Simmelsdorf, Germany, in the summer of 1945 (left) and in later years (top). *Bernard Bernhardt*

Right: Major Edwin G. Pike Co. D, receiving a Bronze Star from Col. Maurice Barker, commanding officer of the Army Chemical Center, at Edgewood Arsenal, MD, on June 20, 1947, for meritorious service with Co. D, 83rd Chemical Mortar Battalion, June 1- July 12, 1943. *Pike Collection*

Above: Philadelphia, PA, Reunion 1972. Back row (L-R): John McEvoy, Pete Kiedrowski, Justin Gerald Woomer. Front row (L-R): Russell Doster, George Borkhuis, Kenneth Cunin, Joseph Sapienza. *John McEvoy*

Left: Lt. Col. (ret.) Kenneth Cunin at 1993 Fort Bragg, NC reactivation ceremony of the 83rd Chemical Battalion. *Earl Kann*

THE HOME FRONT

Above: Promotional ad with Marjorie Pike, wife of Capt. Edwin Pike, doing her part for the war effort. *Pike Collection*; Top right: Leonard and Dorothy Merrill with son Robert. *Robert Merrill*; Bottom right: Andre and Linnette Laus. *Mary Jane Laus*; Bottom: Camp Gordon, Georgia, visitors pass for Helen Edwards, wife of Capt. Robert Edwards. *Wendy Edwards*

The shoulder patch in use by 83rd soldiers.
Top: John Baer, who is also wearing the Glider Pin which indicates he was in Company D and on the glider mission in the invasion of Southern France, August 15, 1944. Bottom: unidentified man, probably of Company A, taken June 1945 at Innsbruck, Austria.
Both photos: L. Lew Henry Collection

83rd CHEMICAL MORTAR BATTALION SHOULDER PATCH

The shoulder patch of the 83rd Chemical Mortar Battalion went through at least four different variations during World War II. The earliest design was adopted by the 83rd in either June or July of 1943, during the Sicilian Campaign, and was approved by Col. William O. Darby, commanding officer of the Rangers, to which the battalion was attached. Some men had them hand-made and stitched by the locals in Sicily and Italy, or by family at home. An early mention of the patch can be found in a letter from Lt. Col. William S. Hutchinson, commanding the 83rd, to Lt. Col. Kenneth A. Cunin, former commander of the battalion, dated October 18, 1943. It reads in part: "We have ordered our distinctive shoulder patch with '83rd Chemical Bn.' emblazoned across it. I will send you one as soon as they are ready."

WD Circular 226 (1944) failed to give authorization to the patch so on October 10, 1944, Maj. Sam Efnor, Jr., commanding the battalion, wrote a letter to the commanding general of the 7th Army, through the 45th Infantry Division, requesting permission for the men to retain and wear the patch in spite of the restrictions in the circular. In response the request was basically denied by Col. Georges F. Doriot, Q.M.C., Assistant, on November 17, 1944, yet on December 30 of the year Maj. Gen. William N. Porter, Chief of the Chemical Warfare Service, wrote a supportive letter citing the distinguished history of the 83rd and concluding, "an exception can be made for the 83rd Chemical Battalion, and that the subject shoulder patch can be approved as an essential contribution to the esprit de corps of this battalion."

Sam Kweskin, who was transferred from Co. D to HQ Co., could not remember the exact date the patch was changed but did recall, "In December '44 I was asked to RE-design the patch. I think it read '83rd (top) CHEMICAL (middle) and Mortar Bn.' on the bottom. I can't really remember. However, the patch DID undergo variations over the years, and the very latest (since Jan. '45) is the one that I RE-designed, which reads MORTAR in the center."

(1.) Shoulder Patch, still in use today, has gold lettering with blue scroll stitching. (2.) First designed patch had blue threads with gold letters. (3.) Second patch was gray threads with gold letters. (4.) Third patch had gold letters and a blue scroll. (5.) Girard DuBois of Company C had this patch made for him by a family member, *photo from Marcel DuBois; other patch photo's from Ed Trey*

THE ORIGINAL COAT OF ARMS & D.I. OF THE
83rd CHEMICAL MORTAR BATTALION

The original Coat of Arms of the 83rd Chemical Battalion, a skunk riding a 4.2 inch mortar shell, has a somewhat confusing history. In the first issue of *Smoke Screen*, the original newsletter of the 83rd Chemical Battalion, the original design was the creation of Lt. William S. Doughten, Jr. and artist Pvt. Philip J. Perlman, both of the battalion, and included a skunk called "Stinky" riding the 4.2" mortar shell in a bonzine ring with the words "Stay Upwind" in a scroll below.

According to records, the Quartermaster General endorsed this unusual coat of arms and distinguished insignia September 13, 1942, and the Adjutant General's Office October 8, 1942, under provisions of November 20, 1931. These devices were officially approved for the 83rd Chemical Battalion December 3, 1942, although the design appears on the first four covers of the original battalion newsletter *Smoke Screen*, which debuted in November of 1942 at Camp Gordon, Georgia. The first issue said the design had been accepted by Washington, with minor alterations and the addition of color, and claimed the men of the 83rd would soon be carrying the design on their lapels and garrison caps.

Although various versions have surfaced, the original description denoted the Blazon should consist of a Shield, "or, upon a 4.2 inch chemical mortar shell in bend, nose to chief proper, a skunk statant of the last." There would be no Crest and the Motto would read "Stay Upwind". The significance of the design is that "a chemical mortar shell is used by a chemical battalion while the symbolism of the skunk" is obvious. At least five different renditions of this Coat of Arms exist, one of the earliest a crude drawing showing the words "Gas 83" written across the shell.

The Quartermaster General officially approved a version of the skunk on the shell Coat of Arms October 11, 1944, until it was rescinded February 14, 1956, as the 83rd at that time was a flexible organization and not entitled to the old Coat of Arms and Distinguished Insignia. The same memo claimed the distinguished insignia was never manufactured and there is some belief the Coat of Arms patch was never issued either, however at least one showed up on an electronic auction in 2003 although it was misrepresented as the patch of the 81st Chemical Mortar Battalion.

In reality, battalion artist Sam Kweskin created the accepted D.I. Pin of the 83rd Chemical Mortar battalion in Austria in 1945, which consists of a light blue shield, a red lightning bolt in the bend, overall a raised silver flying dragon emitting red flames from the mouth, with a silver scroll with the motto: IN OMNI ELEMENTE in black.

In January of 2003 Sam Kweskin recalled the D.I. Pin he created, stating, "When I drew it in Stambach, France - in the Vosges mountain area, just west of Saverne - it then went to the officer in charge (probably Major John McEvoy). As far as I can remember, I believe no action was taken on this until war's end, when we were billeted (HQ of HQ Co.) in a castle called Schloss Sigismundslust, in Vomp, just north of the Tyrolean town of Schwartz, on the Inn River... Innsbruck being the capital of the province, the sketch was taken to a local artisan where the pins for the men were made, based on the design I created... I honestly don't remember how that came about - was the dragon already an icon of the CWS, or did McEvoy make it up, or did I decide it was a heroic, fire-breathing entity that would represent our battalion trade - dealing out death by fire (white phosphorous) and explosive mortar rounds, or smoke shells? ...Whatever the case, the result was a pin with a fire-breathing dragon against a sky-blue background; beneath the figure was what I THOUGHT was proper Latin (Latin seemed so 'cool' to use) and as a result I wrote: In Omniae Elementae Vicimus - we conquer through all elements. This was a double-entendre, since we had attacked the enemy on land, by invasion from the sea, and (in the case of D Company) by glider... Over time, after many years that the 83rd no longer existed, there were - as expected - to be changes. However, the dragon is still being used, and new badges (pins) have come into existence."

A more modern version of this was authorized June 26, 1966, for the then current 83rd, which deactivated Dec. 20, 1966, but later reactivated and is currently on duty. This version included a dark blue hexagon, a diagonal

L-R: (1) Probably earliest known design. Crude sketch by unidentified artist with original coloring inscribed. (2) Design on cover of first issue of *Smoke Screen* Nov. 14, 1942, created by Lt. William S. Doughten and drawn by Pvt. Philip Perlman, both of the 83rd. A more detailed description is in the *Smoke Screen* sidebar. (3) Design approved and authorized Dec. 3, 1942, by the Department of the Army. Apparently the wording "83rd Chemical Mortar Bn" was added in 1944. (4) Design for the colors submitted and examined Dec. 18, 1942. Canceled Jan. 15, 1957. (5) Design approved Oct. 11, 1944, by the O.Q.M.G. *First design courtesy Ed Trey, all others Ft. Leonard Wood Archives.*

yellow lightning flash surmounted by a silver flying dragon exhaling tongues of scarlet flames, the wings extending about the hexagon, and a silver scroll with the motto CONFRONT ANY MISSION in dark blue. There is another version of this D.I. with the motto in light blue, which was made by Zadik for collectors.

The design with the skunk, although authorized Dec. 3, 1942, was rescinded Feb. 14, 1956, and was never made for the unit. In 1957 S. G. Holmes produced a collector's version of them in Wellington, Japan. Pvt. Philip J. Perlman of the original 83rd Chemical Battalion, confirmed in a 2006 interview that he drew the original skunk design, under the auspices of Major Kenneth A. Cunin, who rewarded both Perlman and Lt. William S. Doughten, Jr. for their efforts with a furlough.

Born in Galicia, Poland, Philip J. Perlman emigrated to the U.S. in 1923 and graduated from Yeshiva Rabbi Chaim Berlin and attended City College in New York. He first served with the 83rd Chemical Battalion at Camp Gordon, where he was staff artist of *Smoke Screen*, but transferred to a hospital unit before the battalion was sent overseas. Following the war he pursued a career in art and became nationally known for his works of Hebrew calligraphy, with exhibitions at Yeshiva University, Lever House, Adelphi University, and various synagogues in the New York area, where he resided in 2006.

L-R: (1) Original DI pin consisting of a light blue shield, red lightning bolt, a raised silver flying dragon emitting red flames from mouth, and a silver scroll with the motto: IN OMNI ELEMENTE in black. Maker: Piehl Klammer, Austria" (2)Authorized June 26, 1966, and unit inactivated December 20, 1966 (since reactivated). Dark blue hexagon with diagonal yellow lightning bolt surmounted by a silver flying dragon exhaling scarlet flames, scroll reading: CONFRONT ANY MISSION." (3) Same design but a light blue hexagon, made for collectors by Zadik. (4) Design authorized December 3, 1942, and rescinded February 14, 1956. Never authorized for unit. Consisted of transparent dark blue shield, 1 2.2" chemical mortar projectile in bend with skunk riding it, both silver, shaded, and detailed black. Made for collector's by S. G. Holmes in 1957. Hallmark: Wellington, Japan. (5)Variation of the skunk riding the mortar shell pin although much closer to the original Camp Gordon era design used on *Smoke Screen*.

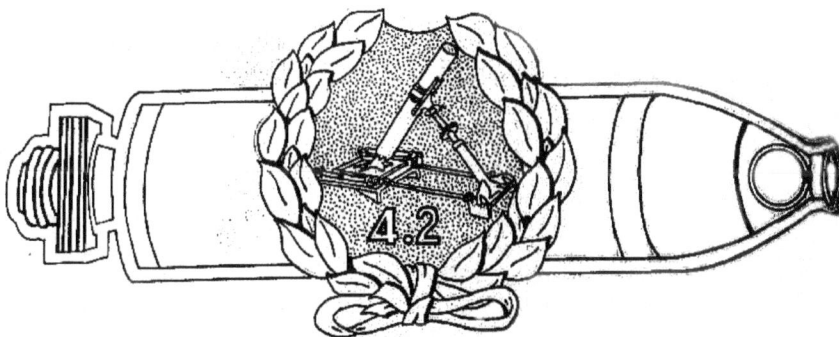

Unidentified drawing in 83rd
Chemical Mortar Battalion Files
National Archives

Battle Streamers of the 83rd
Chemical Mortar Battalion
Dale Blank

*The World War II Travels
of
Capt. Julius C. "Doc" Hulcher
Medical Detachment
83rd Chemical Mortar Battalion
May 15, 1942 to Dec. 25, 1945
Actual color film footage shot during World War II in
North Africa, Italy, France, Austria, Germany.
Running Time: 1:05:40; Color – Silent*

This rare, mostly color, amateur film footage was uncovered by Terry Lowry in 2006 while researching *Bastard Battalion*. During the 2006 reunion of the 83rd Chemical Mortar Battalion at Gettysburg, PA, Marcia Bunker loaned the letters of her father, Capt. Edwin "Bud" Pike, Co. D, to Terry for research. In a letter written July 19, 1944, Capt. Pike stated: "Doc Hulcher has an excellent camera and also a moving picture camera and he has been taking a lot of shots of us and himself. I'd sure like to visit him after the war and see the moving pictures of us." On the slim possibility the film still existed, this brief statement led Lowry on a search for the footage, although he knew Doc Hulcher had passed away in 2001. Through a series of phone calls Lowry located Doc Hulcher's son, Charles ("Chuck") Hulcher, who informed Lowry he had the film and kindly agreed to share it.

The film was apparently originally shot on 16 mm color film and displays all the flaws acquainted with vintage film, such as grainy, fuzzy images and scenes that often fade from the screen. Before his passing Doc Hulcher realized the importance of such a film and had it transferred to VHS format and placed the material in chronological order with titles. Later his son Charles transferred the movie format to DVD. And we can all be grateful to Marcia Bunker whose dad's letters gave the clue.

Doc Hulcher's entire military experiences are covered in the film. About the first five minutes cover his training at Ft. Lee, Virginia, in 1942 and his service with the 45th General Hospital at Rabat in North Africa. In late November of 1943 he was assigned to the 83rd Chemical Mortar Battalion at Venafro, Italy, the first medical officer from the 45th placed with a combat outfit. The remainder of the movie covers his time with the 83rd including Italy, Rome, Isle of Capri, France, Paris, Austria, Munich, Brenner Pass, and the voyage home.

There are no combat scenes and there is no graphic footage. The film resembles more of a travelogue, with many scenes of soldiers of the 83rd performing standard activities such as shaving, haircuts, playing cards, meals, getting inoculations, and visiting many of the famous cities and historical sites. Many of the soldiers have yet to be identified although such men as Capt. "Bud" Pike, Lt. Col. William S. Hutchinson, Capt. Robert E. Edwards, Capt. Ed Trey, and Chaplain George Gaiser have been spotted in the film. Hulcher, of course, appears in the film most often, which raises the question as to who was running the camera.

Once the film was "discovered" Charles Hulcher found two diaries kept during the war by his father, which encompass his entire military career and often mention his movie camera. Plans are currently being worked out to make copies of the movie available.

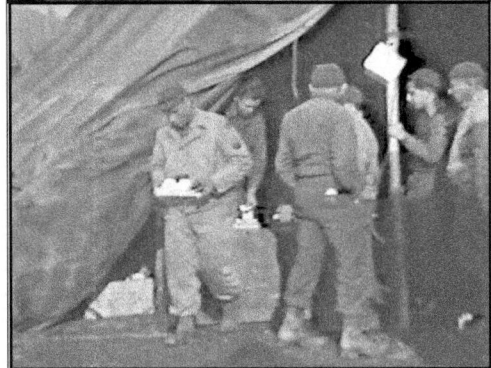

Top to bottom: Capt. Ed Pike, "Doc" Hulcher, and Capt. Gordon Mindrum (L-R); Capt. Gordon Mindrum, Silverino DeMarco, and Capt. Ed Pike (L-R); "Doc" Hulcher on left, others unidentified; unidentified 83rd men at the medic tent.
Charles Hulcher

Doughten Drive (top); Beasley and Miller Drives (bottom)
Ed Trey

STREET MEMORIALS FORT DETRICK, FREDERICK, MARYLAND

Located at Frederick, Maryland, and known for Biological Research and Development, Fort Detrick celebrated it's 25th anniversary by erecting street signs on the compound grounds christened after various soldiers of the Chemical Warfare Service. Most prominent was Doughten Drive, named after 1st Lt. William Simpson Doughten of the 83rd Chemical Mortar Battalion, who was killed in action July 9, 1943 at Gela, Sicily.

Another road sign, combined at the same intersection commemorates two other fallen heroes of the 83rd, Lts. James O. Beasley and Samuel Miller, both killed in action September 9, 1943 at Vietri, Italy.

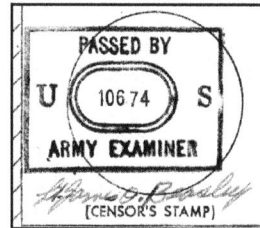

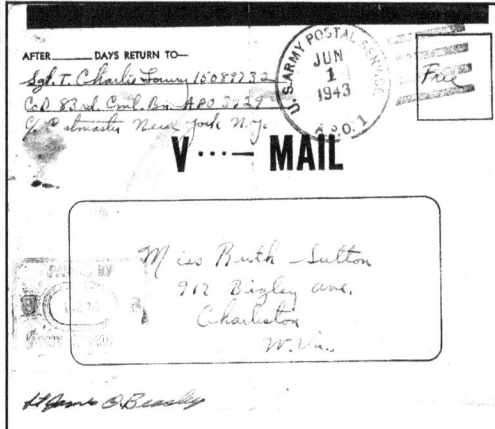

Signature of William S. Doughten, Jr., Adjutant/1st Lt., 83rd Chemical Battalion on Application for Defense Savings Bonds to T/5 Charlie Lowry, Co. A, 83rd Chemical Battalion, at Camp Gordon, GA, Sept. 10, 1942, left, with a close up of signature at right; V-mail envelope Charlie Lowry sent to his future wife showing censorship by Lt. James O. Beasley, right, with close-up of signature off the V-mail letter. *Author's Collection*

83rd Chemical Mortar Battalion Photo Gallery

Over 2,000 photos directly related to the 83rd Chemical Mortar Battalion were submitted by the many veterans and their families. Numerous images were not used due to space limitations. Identifications were either on the images, provided by the veterans, or were carefully researched by the author. We apologize for any misrepresentations. If you have additional information on any images found herein, have any questions regarding images not used, or have any new photos for possible future reprints, please contact the author.

HEADQUARTERS
&
HEADQUARTERS COMPANY

Photo taken of an 83rd mortar crew by Col. Maurice Barker, 5th Army Chemical Officer, demonstrating the need for a modified baseplate. Due to the soggy soil the mortar had to be braced to a tree. *CARLISLE BARRACKS*

L-R: Alfred Crenshaw, Sam Efnor, Gordon Mindrum, Ed Trey, and Bernard Stone
L. LEW HENRY COLLECTION

Back row, L-R: Alfred Forrester, Robert Bundy, and Doc Hulcher; front row, L-R: unidentified, Ed Trey, Arthur Usher, and Robert Edwards
L. LEW HENRY COLLECTION

353

Babjak, John J.
WILLIAM GALLAGHER

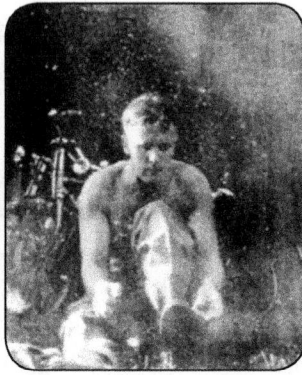

Beach, Howell F.
ED TREY

Blamick, Robert
STEPHEN VUKSON

Brimm, Robert P.
EUGENE PLASSMANN

Bundy, Samuel
STEPHEN VUKSON

Cadwalader, Roy E.
EUGENE PLASSMANN

Cocayne, Robert W.
WENDY EDWARDS

Cornett, Christopher C.
ED TREY

Crenshaw, Alfred H.
JOHN MCEVOY

Cunin, Kenneth A.
ED TREY

DeVoto, Raymond J.
SAM KWESKIN

Drugach, Nicholas
SHIELDS COLLECTION

Fenton, Robert W.
ROBERT FENTON

Garrett, Karl F.
KARL GARRETT

Gozur, Steve
KAREN GOZUR

Harper, Grady
EUGENE PLASSMANN

Hauser, Walter R.
L. Lew Henry Collection

Hoover, Raymond W.
Strickler Collection

Johnson, Judson B.
Mississippi Gulf Coast Comm. Coll.

Kohl, Fred
Fred Kohl

Kozak, Andrew
Shields Collection

Kweskin, Samuel I.
Jean Siegel

Laundre, Kenneth K.
Elizabeth Daly

Lauro, James V.
Codega Collection

McEvoy, John P.
John McEvoy

McFarland, William B.
Betty Turner

Meadows, William
World War II Memorial

Merrill, Leonard A.
Robert Merrill

Nitz, Anthony G.
Bernard Bernhardt

Plassmann, Eugene A.
Eugene Plassmann

Plumly, Charles L.
Robert Bush Collection

Ryder, Christopher L.
Shields Collection

Scovill, Claude E.
SAM KWESKIN

Shaw, Claude J.
NORM HOLT

Shields, Daniel J.
SHIELDS COLLECTION

Simon, Robert W.
KNAPP COLLECTION

Slate, Charles A.
SHIELDS COLLECTION

Stone, Bernard
SCOTT MINDRUM

Storey, Miles K.
SHIELDS COLLECTION

Strickler, Clair M.
STRICKLER COLLECTION

Taylor, Rollin D.
HOPKINS COLLECTION

Trey, Edward L.
ED TREY

Usher, Arthur J.
WENDY EDWARDS

L-R: Unidentified man and Grady Harper
KARL GARRETT

Left, L-R: Robert Fenton, Julius Hulcher, Ed Trey, and Art Usher. Note the reserved sign to left with 83rd insignia.
ED TREY

Lt. Col. William S. Hutchinson and Capt. John P. McEvoy
JOHN MCEVOY

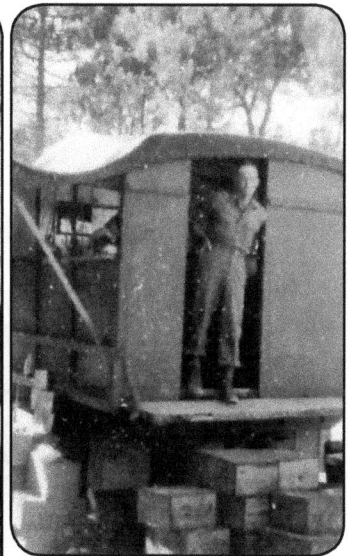

Orville P. Bell
SHIELDS COLLECTION

Standing, L-R: George E. Worrall, Jacob L. Portner, William Gallagher, John Babjak, Raymond J. Spraggins and John Fleming; kneeling, L-R: John J. Boyle, Charles A. Slate, and Clair Strickler, Camp Gordon, GA.
WILLIAM GALLAGHER

L-R: Paul Cuva, Eugene Plassmann, and Roy E. Cadwalader
EUGENE PLASSMANN

357

Alfred Crenshaw, Gordon Mindrum, and Bernard Stone. *Scott Mindrum*

Clair Strickler with truck named "Anne"
Shields Collection

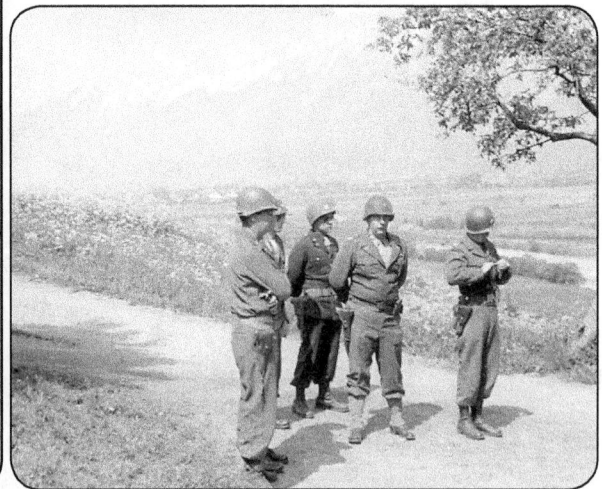

Paul Cuva & Morris Mysels
Shields Collection

"Brass" in Austria, June, 1945. Lt. Col. Sam Efnor on right
Robert Bush Collection

Kneeling, L-R: Paul J. Waring and Orlando A. Gaudino; standing, L-R: Edward W. Quimby, Miles K. Storey, Charles P. Cella, Paul Cuva, Carl W. Lepine, Kermit Jorgenson, and Arthur J. Usher.
Eugene Plassmann

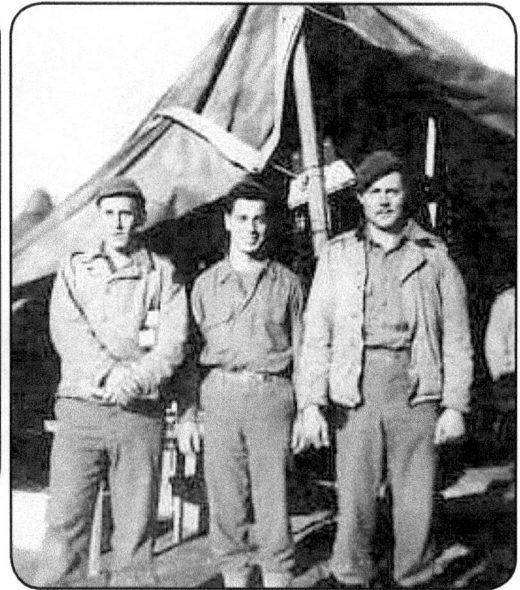

Perry Rice, Paul Cuva, and Grady Harper
Eugene Plassmann

Maj. Gordon M. Mindrum and 1st. Lt. Lester L. Henry
Robert Bush Collection

L-R: Morris Mysels, William J. Hodgson, Edward W. Quimby, Paul Cuva, and James J. McGrann
Eugene Plassmann

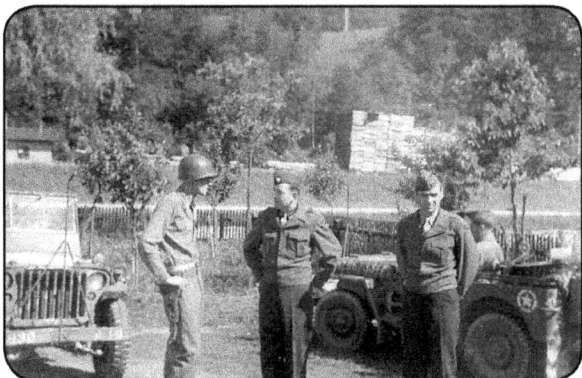

L-R: Lt. Robert J. Bush, Lt. Col. Sam Efnor, and Capt. Alfred H. Crenshaw June 16, 1945
Robert Bush Collection

Paul Cuva, Thomas Thorp, and Dale Moon
Eugene Plassmann

L-R: Lts. Leonard R. Kenney and James J. O'Connor, Capts. Bernard Stone and Alfred L. Forrester
ROBERT BUSH COLLECTION

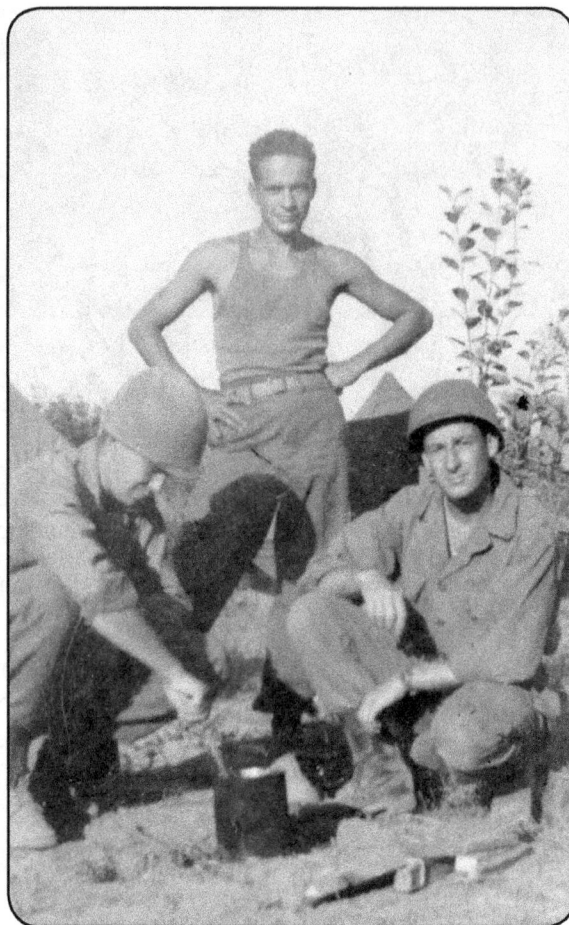

L-R: George Linck, Cecil Pate, and Paul Malot
SAM KWESKIN

Lt. Col. William S. Hutchinson (left) in the field. CARLISLE BARRACKS

Jack O'Brien and Morris Richards sitting in a slit trench under a haystack at Anzio, January 27, 1944
SIGNAL CORPS

L-R: Alfred Crenshaw, George Yakubisin, Perry Rice, Julian McKinnon, and Jim Lauro. *SHIELDS COLLECTION*

L-R: Cedric C. Speights, Sam Kweskin, and Anthony Nitz
BERNARD BERNHARDT

Frank Anderson, Charles Cleaveland, and Allen McCoy.
STEPHEN VUKSON

Back row, L-R: Charles A. Bennett, Russell S. Doster, and Miles K. Storey; front L-R: James V. Lauro and Mike Codega.
SHIELDS COLLECTION

MEDICAL DETACHMENT

Row 1: Robert Sorenson, second from left; Row 2: John Anderson on left, Douglas Swayze second from left and Cornelius McCarthy second from right; Row 3: Silverino DeMarco, third from left, Chaplain Lyle Burdick, fourth from left, and Curtis Williams, fifth from left. All others unidentified.
MARTHA ANDERSON

Vaccination line
DOC HULCHER MOVIE CLIP, CHARLES HULCHER

Wounded being treated in the Vosges Mountains.
CODEGA COLLECTION

Alexander, Peter
Sam Kweskin, Artist

Anderson, John E.
Martha Anderson

De Leon, Vicente
Vicente De Leon

DeMarco, Silverino V.
Doc Hulcher Movie Clip, Charles Hulcher

Herr, Donald C.
Shields Collection

Hulcher, Julius C.
Robert Bush Collection

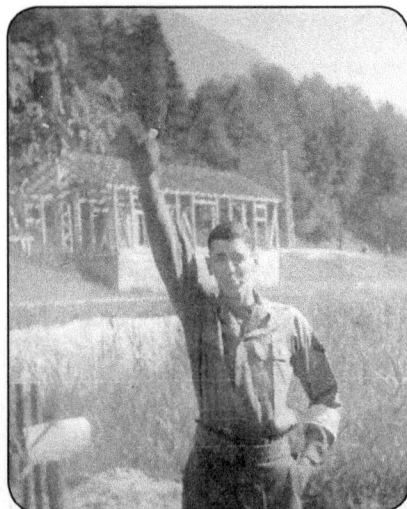

McCarthy, Cornelius
Robert Bush Collection

McNabb, Carl M.
Carl McNabb

Williams, Curtis
Doc Hulcher Movie Clip, Charles Hulcher

L-R: Douglas A. Swayze and Eldon L. Hughes, in
Stambach, Alsace. *SAM KWESKIN*

Unidentified Co. A medic on left.
TYMA COLLECTION

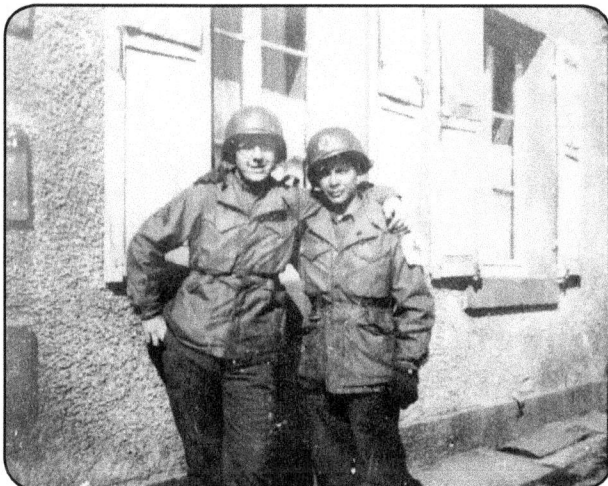

L-R: Warren D. Perry and Vicente E. De Leon
MARSHALL COLLECTION

Unidentified medic
VICENTE DE LEON

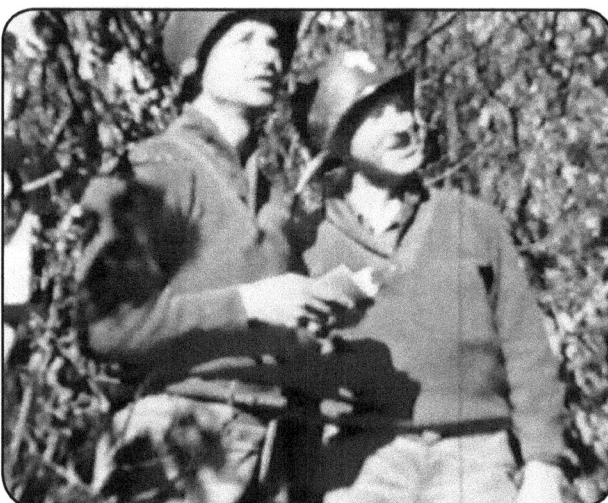

Julius "Doc" Hulcher and Chaplain George Gaiser
DOC HULCHER MOVIE CLIP, CHARLES HULCHER

Medical Detachment ambulance
DOC HULCHER MOVIE CLIP, CHARLES HULCHER

"Short Arm Inspection"
CLARK RIDDLE

Curtis Williams receiving Silver Star, Jan. 1, 1944, for gallantry at Gela, Sicily, July 11,1943. DOC HULCHER MOVIE CLIP, CHARLES HULCHER

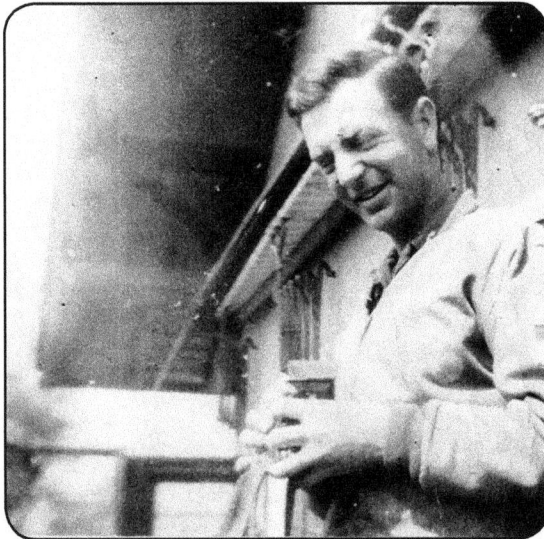

Right and left: Julius C. "Doc" Hulcher
ED TREY

"Short Arm Inspection"
STEPHEN VUKSON

COMPANY A
ABLE COMPANY

Disbanding Company A at Innsbruck, Austria, June 1945

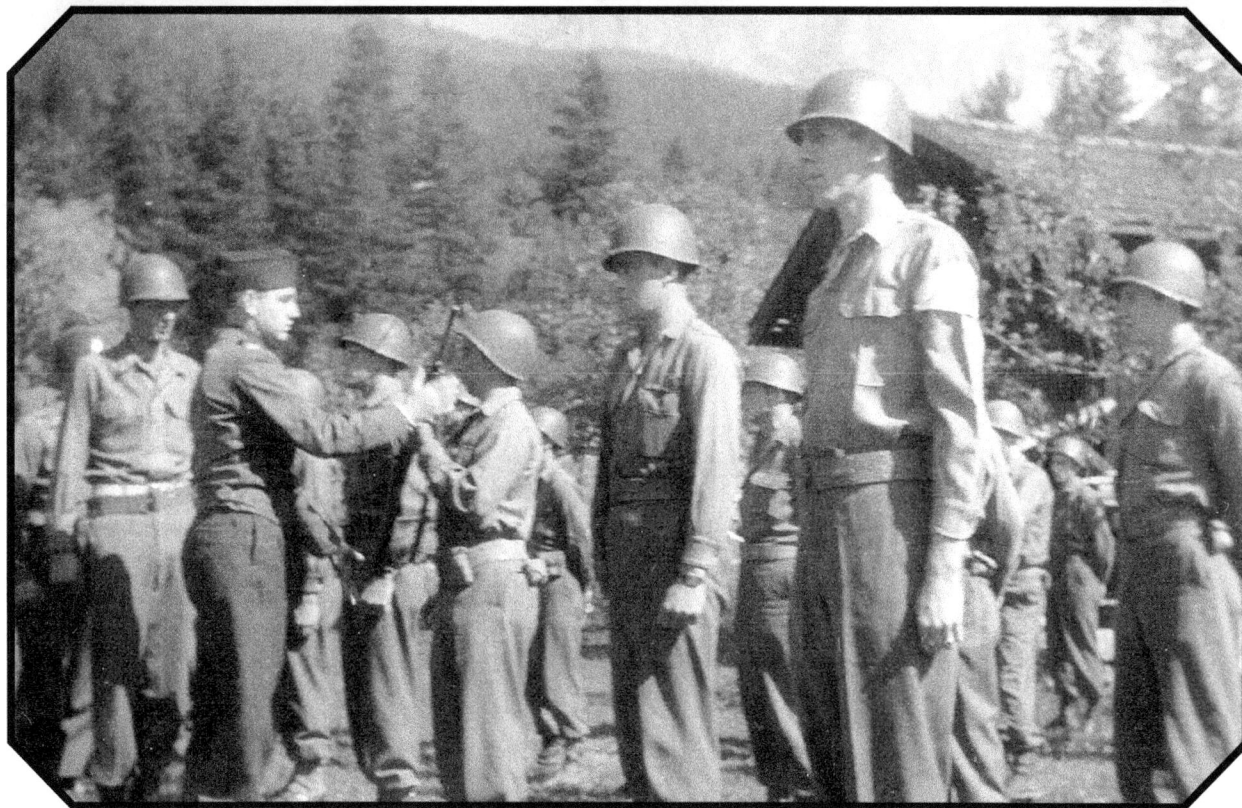

Company A inspection by Lt. Robert J. Bush (far left) and Lt. Col. Sam Efnor (2nd from left).

BOTH PHOTOS ROBERT BUSH COLLECTION

Adams, Herman
KELSO THOMPSON

Adamson, Roscoe D.
STEPHEN VUKSON

Anderson, Vincent
HOPKINS COLLECTION

Ayers, Simeon B.
JOHNNY AYERS

Baer, John W.
NOUREEN BAER

Bailey, Marion E.
L. LEW HENRY COLLECTION

Bash, Nicholas P.
PIRANI COLLECTION

Birdwell, Clovis
CLOVIS BIRDWELL

Blackmon, James
HOPKINS COLLECTION

Bobker, Howard
L. LEW HENRY COLLECTION

Bolton, Thomas M.
CODEGA COLLECTION

Bundy, Robert E.
WENDY EDWARDS

Bush, Robert J.
ROBERT BUSH COLLECTION

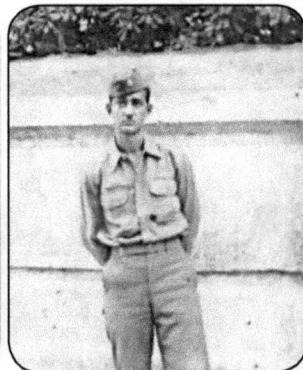

Cannetti, Joseph E.
JOSEPH CANNETTI

Cohen, Charles
L. LEW HENRY COLLECTION

Comaty, Joseph M.
TURAN COLLECTION

Davis, Leland L.
SHIELDS COLLECTION

Davison, William A.
CODEGA COLLECTION

DeCesare, Charles J.
WENDY EDWARDS

Diana, Anthony
SHIELDS COLLECTION

Dougherty, James F.
DOUGHERTY COLLECTION

Doughten, William S
MIT YEARBOOK

Dunderdale, George T.
ROBERT BUNDY

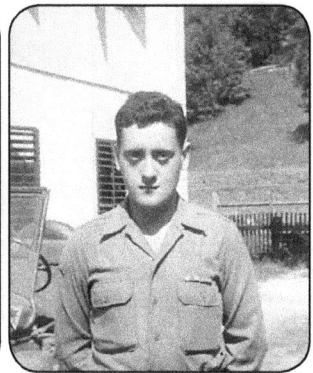

Durfee, Herbert E.
ROBERT BUSH COLLECTION

Edwards, Robert E.
WENDY EDWARDS

Effingham, Dennis H.
AMERICAN PATRIOTS

Fenster, Carl
ROBERT BUNDY

Forrester, Alfred L.
DOUGHERTY COLLECTION

Garner, William
ROBERT BUSH COLLECTION

Garsson, Joseph H.
ROBERT BUSH COLLECTION

Guthrie, Elwood
DOUGHERTY COLLECTION

Hauser, Walter R.
L. LEW HENRY COLLECTION

Hayes, Veryl R.
CWS Bulletin

Helsel, James G.
Joyce Berry

Henry, Lester Lew
L. Lew Henry Collection

Hopkins, Ford E.
Hopkins Collection

Hughes, George E.
Hopkins Collection

Jackson, Robert F.
L. Lew Henry Collection

Jackson, Wofford L.
Shields Collection

Jessop, Ralph G.
Robert Bush Collection

Johnnie
L. Lew Henry Collection

Jordan, James C.
Jordan Collection

Kenney, Leonard R.
Sandi Daniel

Kwong, Russell
Eugene Plassmann

Lester, James M.
Lester Collection

MacCollough
L. Lew Henry Collection

Mazzafer, John P.
L. Lew Henry Collection

McEvoy, John P.
John McEvoy

McLaughlin, John R.
SHIELDS COLLECTION

Minsky
L. LEW HENRY COLLECTION

O'Connor, James J.
ROBERT BUSH COLLECTION

O'Neil, Donald E.
L. LEW HENRY COLLECTION

Parthum, Richard I.
HOPKINS COLLECTION

Pass, Floyd N.
HOPKINS COLLECTION

Pierce, James F.
ROBERT BUSH COLLECTION

Pirani, Eugene
HOPKINS COLLECTION

Pistoia, Ralph D.
ROBERT BUSH COLLECTION

Porterfield, John
SIGNAL CORPS PHOTO

Powers, Byron
TURAN COLLECTION

Price, Charles A.
ROBERT BUNDY

Puckett, Roland K.
L. LEW HENRY COLLECTION

Rabaiotti, Antonio
HOPKINS COLLECTION

Ramer, Joseph A.
ROBERT BUSH COLLECTION

Ramsey, George
HOPKINS COLLECTION

Rega, Michael A.
ROBERT BUSH COLLECTION

Ricci, Mario
MARIO RICCI

Rolling, Charles F.
ROBERT BUSH COLLECTION

Schmidt, George
MARTIN MOLONEY

Shirley, George N.
SHIELDS COLLECTION

Siepkowski, Zenon
SAM KWESKIN, ARTIST

Squires, Norman C.
SQUIRES COLLECTION

Stanley, Mitchell H.
L. LEW HENRY COLLECTION

Steinbrecher
L. LEW HENRY COLLECTION

Stewart, Estus N.
ROBERT BUSH COLLECTION

St. Louis, Napoleon G.
L. LEW HENRY COLLECTION

Strack, Robert E.
L. LEW HENRY COLLECTION

Taylor, Robert S.
ELIZABETH TAYLOR

Thompson, Kelso C.
KELSO THOMPSON

Toniolo, Reno L.
L. LEW HENRY COLLECTION

Trautman, Carlos
CARLOS TRAUTMAN

Tyma, George
TYMA COLLECTION

Waldrep, Royce H., Jr.
SHIELDS COLLECTION

Wapnitsky, Samuel
L. LEW HENRY COLLECTION

Yakubisin, George S.
SHIELDS COLLECTION

Frank A. Papaccioli
SUSAN O'DEA

16
Unidentified
Men of Co. A
L. Lew Henry Collection

Top row left: Charles D. Gilliland, note the mortar shell hood ornament; right: unidentified men of Co. A; second row: left is an unidentified Captain; above, two unidentified men from Co. A. Left: Unidentified man with Reno Toniolo. Bottom: Lt. Lester L. Henry, front, with part of his platoon.
L. LEW HENRY COLLECTION

Company A cooks at Rambervillers, France, Nov. 17,1944.
Seated: Edward Blatz; standing, L-R: Sim Ayers, Sy Foley, Alvin Tobias, James Pierce, Michael Janosz, and William D. Hill LAWRENCE ERTZBERGER

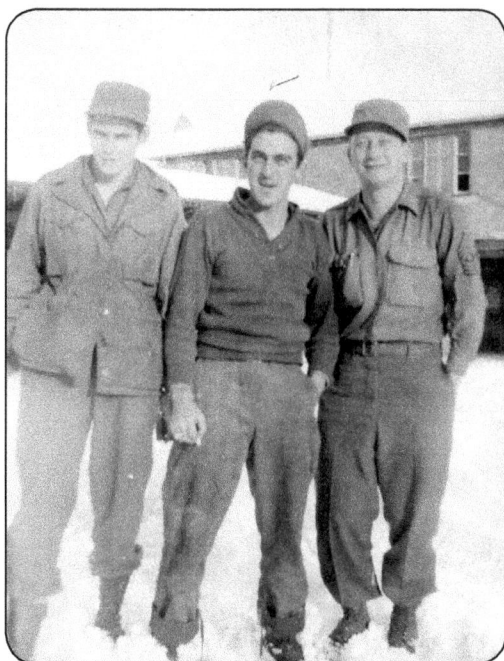

Frank C. Besser, George E. Hughes, and Ralph G. Jessop
HOPKINS COLLECTION

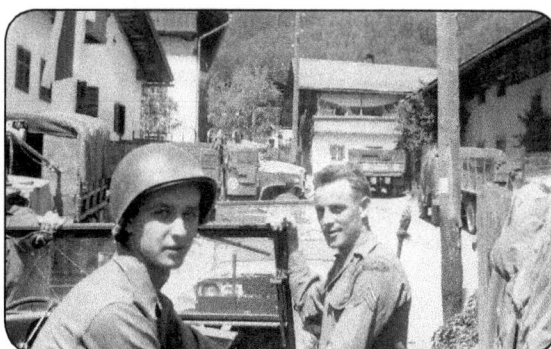

"Skip" and Sgt. Granville T. Cropp
ROBERT BUSH COLLECTION

Lt. Charles Price, Lt. Alfred Forrester, and Lt. James K. Davis ROBERT BUSH COLLECTION

James M. Lester (back row, right) and Kelso Thompson (front row right); others unidentified.
LESTER COLLECTION

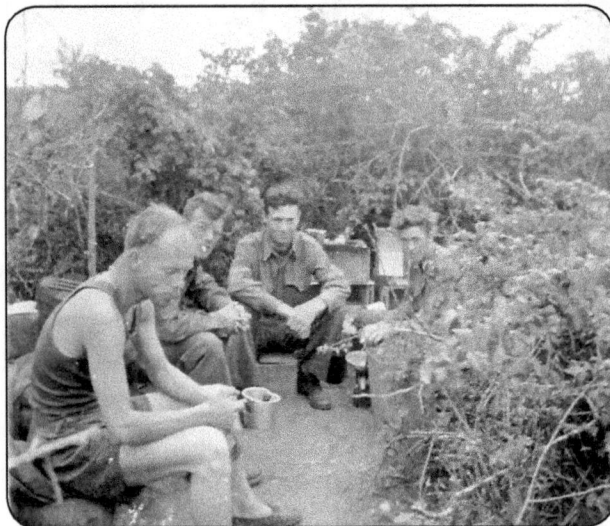

Eric Peterson (front) at Anzio; others unidentified.
ROBERT BUSH COLLECTION

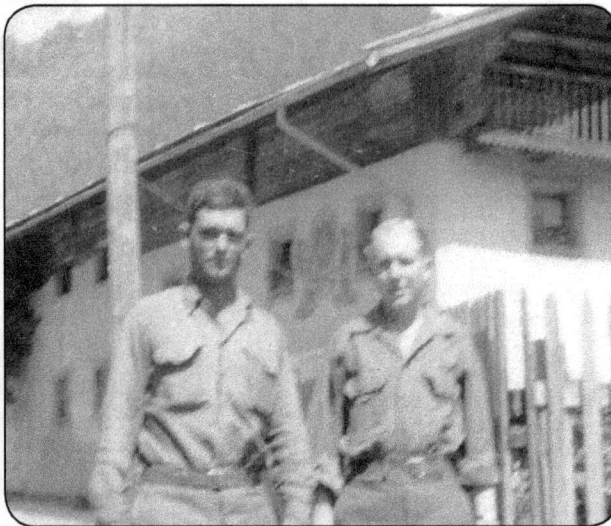

L-R: James D. Rooks and Walter W. Allen.
ROBERT BUSH COLLECTION

Left: Robert E. Bundy and unidentified soldier.
ROBERT BUNDY

Right L-R: Theodore D. Haddock, unidentified, and George J. Funyak.
ROBERT BUNDY

Above: Ford E. Hopkins, sitting (right); James Blackmon, standing (right); others are unidentified.
HOPKINS COLLECTION

Right: Standing L-R: Unidentified, Ralph Stoddard, and Ford E. Hopkins; Kneeling, L-R: Unidentified, Eugene Pirani, and unidentified.
HOPKINS COLLECTION

L-R: Unidentified, Mario Ricci and Carl A. Petro.
AUTHOR'S COLLECTION

L-R: Andy Whelan, unidentified, Lawrence Powell, and George Tyma.
TYMA COLLECTION

Back, L-R: William Gallagher, unidentified, "Beucup", and Raymond S. Dugan, Jr.; front, L-R: August T. Cappoli, Edward J. Gizey and William Borley (?). Note condom necklace worn by "Beucup".
WILLIAM GALLAGHER

"Skip", William L. Garner, Cornelius McCarthy, and George Tyma.
ROBERT BUSH COLLECTION

Left: "Didinado"
L. LEW HENRY COLLECTION

Lts. Robert Bush, John M. Taylor, and Fred Rand in Vomecourt, France, 1944. *ROBERT BUSH COLLECTION*

Above: L-R Lts. James O'Connor, Frank P. Roan, and Eric Peterson. *ROBERT BUSH COLLECTION*

Ewart O'Neill and Robert Jackson
L. LEW HENRY COLLECTION

Left: L-R, Herman Adams, George Schmidt, Kelso Thompson, and Robert Strack. *KELSO THOMPSON*

L-R: Alfred Forrester, Bernard Stone, unidentified, and Robert Danfield.
L. LEW HENRY COLLECTION

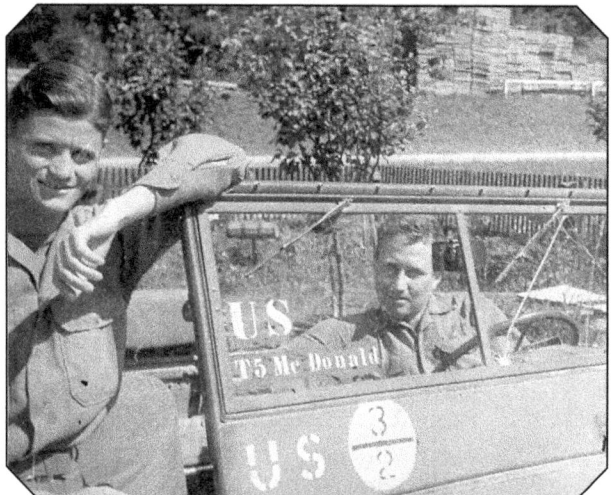

Tuck Stewart and "Eppie".
L. LEW HENRY COLLECTION

Lt. Robert J. Bush (right) with his jeep driver, Lawrence McDonald.
ROBERT BUSH COLLECTION

Mitchell Stanley and Martin J. Moloney
MARTIN MOLONEY

James C. Jordan and his squad.
JORDAN COLLECTION

L-R: Lawrence McDonald, George Hughes, Albert Sabatino, unidentified, Leonard Kenney, Frank Roan, and Robert Bush.
ROBERT BUSH COLLECTION

L-R: Alfred Forrester, unidentified, and James O'Connor.
L. LEW HENRY COLLECTION

Raymond S. Dugan, Jr., and William Gallagher
WILLIAM GALLAGHER

Lts. Nicholas P. Bash, O'Neill, Justin G. Woomer, and Eric H. Peterson.
ROBERT BUSH COLLECTION

George J. Funyak
and
Robert E. Bundy
ROBERT BUNDY

Back L-R: James Blackmon, Eugene Pirani, George Yakubisin, unidentified; front L-R: Antonio Rabaiotti, James Kane, George Tucker, Ford Hopkins. *Pirani Collection*

1. Porter Davis 2. Kelso Thompson 3. William A. Davison 4. Charlie Lowry 5. George W. Ramsey, Jr. 6. Donald C. Hafler 7. Vino 8. Willie R. Tanner 9. Marshall C. Bowes 10. Ernest R. Hooten 11. Robert J. Wehrheim 12. James M. Lester 13. Teddy Kubera. Unidentified are Park L. Smith, William P. Poole, and Glenn W. Galloway. *Author's Collection*

COMPANY B
Baker Company

Lee Steedle's squad, 2nd Platoon, Kolsass, Austria, 1945. Front, L-R: Byron Jordan, Arthur Mellen, and Jack Pimento; back, L-R: Lee Steedle, Pete Rajcevich, Larry Yost, Benedict Samulski, Ralph Goins, and Thomas Simpson.
BYRON JORDAN

Back, L-R: Grady Lawless, Arthur Collins, and Denver E. Shanafelt; front, L-R: Leland M. Rozzell, Julius S. McMurry, Arthur Gregory, B. C. Hill, and James May.
SCOTT MINDRUM

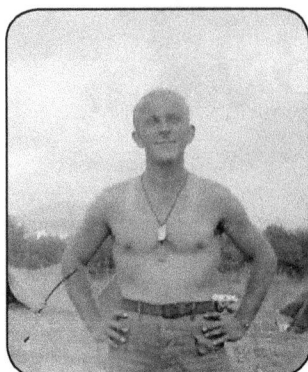

Adamski, Joseph A.
SCOTT MINDRUM

Bailey, William
TURAN COLLECTION

Barrett, George A.
BARRETT COLLECTION

Berry, Willard L.
GINI LEMOINE

Bishop, Melvin
PIKE COLLECTION

Bowles, John W.
GINI LEMOINE

Breisch, Howard W.
SAM KWESKIN, ARTIST

Cameron, Lewis
GINI LEMOINE

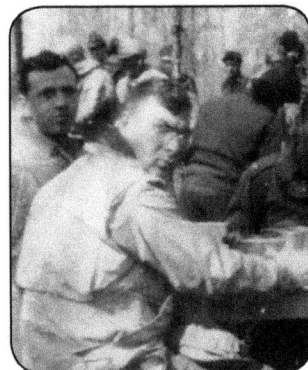

Carpenter, Carl K.
ED TREY

Cascio, Thomas A.
THOMAS CASCIO

Censato, Lawrence J.
LORRAINE SELNI

Danfield, Robert D.
L. LEW HENRY COLLECTION

Davidson, Edward S.
STAN DAVIDSON

DePalma, Pasquale
SCOTT MINDRUM

Dobrin, Michael
GINI LEMOINE

Dyer, Lester J.
NEWSPAPER ARCHIVE

Eeles, Kenneth
SAM KWESKIN, ARTIST

Endlein, Frederick W.
GARY ENDLEIN

Etter, John S.
SAM KWESKIN, ARTIST

Fagan, Laurence J.
BYRON JORDAN

Fisher, James H.
WILMA S. FISHER

Giard, Clement M.
GINI LEMOINE

Givens, Joseph V.
GINI LEMOINE

Goins, Ralph A.
BYRON JORDAN

Griffin, Richard H.
SUSANNAH POWELL

Harper, Harry
JOHN W. HARPER

Heelan, William P.
STAN DAVIDSON

Jack, James
GINI LEMOINE

Jackson, Robert F.
L. LEW HENRY COLLECTION

Johnston, Robert W.
BYRON JORDAN

Jones, Clovis J.
CHADD WATSON

Jordan, Byron H.
BYRON JORDAN

Kattelman, Melvin J.
BARRETT COLLECTION

Kirshner, Sidney
TURAN COLLECTION

Knapick, Anthony J.
SAM KWESKIN, ARTIST

Kuykendall, John L.
AUTHOR'S COLLECTION

Leech, Andrew C.
ALICE HARTLEY

McBryde, Clyde E.
NEWSPAPER ARCHIVE

McCraine, Nolan C.
SHIELDS COLLECTION

McKinnon, Julian T.
MOLLY (MCKINNON) BOYD

McLarty, Hilton T.
MCLARTY COLLECTION

Meadows, Bill
WORLD WAR II MEMORIAL

Mellen, Arthur E.
BYRON JORDAN

Mindrum, Gordon M.
SCOTT MINDRUM

Montana, John
WORLD WAR II MEMORIAL

Nichols, Jean
NEWSPAPER ARCHIVE

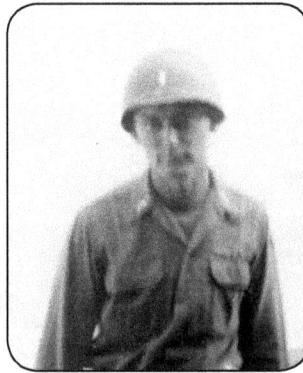

O'Day, Charles W.
ROBERT BUSH COLLECTION

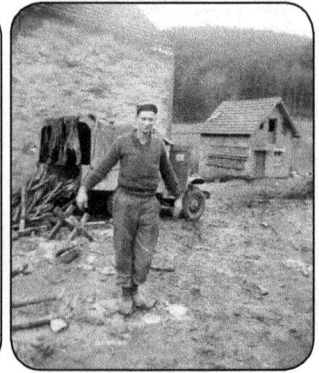

Owings, Joe T.
BARRETT COLLECTION

Paulson, Raymond E.
TOM B. PAULSON

Pimento, Jack
BYRON JORDAN

Powell, Lawrence H.
LAWRENCE POWELL

Rapp, Earl W.
RICH RAPP

Rogan, Walter
SAM KWESKIN, ARTIST

Romeo, Samuel J.
JORDAN COLLECTION

Samulski, Benedict T.
BYRON JORDAN

Sawyer, John P.
BYRON JORDAN

Sereni, Albert E.
TURAN COLLECTION

Sexton, Eugene
BYRON JORDAN

Shaw, Claude J.
EUGENE PLASSMANN

Simpson, Thomas C.
BYRON JORDAN

Slodkowski, Charles
GINI LEMOINE

Smith, James C.
TURAN COLLECTION

Socoloski, Leonard V.
GINI LEMOINE

Steedle, Lee
LEE STEEDLE

St. Gemme, Harold L.
HAROLD ST. GEMME

Teeno, Michael
BARRETT COLLECTION

Trotta, Raymond A.
BYRON JORDAN

Turner, I. B.
WORLD WAR II MEMORIAL

Turner, Vester L.
JO ANN HOWELL

Voithofer, Joseph C.
SAM KWESKIN, ARTIST

Wilkinson, Malcolm D.
MALCOLM WILKINSON

Wilt, Henry B.
GINI LEMOINE

Woomer, Justin G.
ROBERT BUSH COLLECTION

Yost, Lawrence E.
BYRON JORDAN

Unidentified, Pfc. William (last name unknown)
SAM KWESKIN, ARTIST

Left: L-R, Unidentified, unidentified, Warren K. Gallatin, Stephen Vukson, and Robert W. Johnston
STEPHEN VUKSON

Perry B. Rice and Robert D. Danfield
LAWRENCE ERTZBERGER

J. T. Taunton and Ray O. Kelsey
J. T. TAUNTON

Larry Fagan and Leo L. Kurtenbach.
BYRON JORDAN

Lawrence G. Ertzberger and Paul E. Oplinger
LAWRENCE ERTZBERGER

L-R: Preshlock, Charles Slodkowski, George Barrett, Lewis Cameron, and unidentified.
BARRETT COLLECTION

The three steps of loading the mortar. Probably L-R, Anthony Imperato, Joe Owings, and George Barrett.
BARRETT COLLECTION

L-R: Lts. Robert Danfield, Lewis Cameron, and Lee R. Ballard
BARRETT COLLECTION

Willard Smith, Art Hedjuk, Tony Imperato, and W. C. Magnos
GINI LEMOINE

Unidentified men, probably of Company B
SCOTT MINDRUM

L-R: Warren K. Gallatin, John H. Thompson, James O'Toole, Robert Johnston, and Stephen Vukson.
STEPHEN VUKSON

Above: George Barrett, far right front holding rifle, and some unidentified men of Company B
GINI LEMOINE

Sitting, L-R: Robert W. Knortz and Lloyd Foster; standing, L-R: George Cantrell, George Emerson, Hilton McLarty, and Roy Morris.
McLARTY COLLECTION

L-R: Tony Imperato and Len Socoloski
BARRETT COLLECTION

L-R: Lts. Robert Jackson, Lee Ballard, Eric Peterson, Ewart O'Neill, Justin Woomer, Perry Rice, and Lt. Col. Sam Efnor.
ROBERT BUSH COLLECTION

391

Two views of Co. B men with "liberated" champagne. Sgt. James Jack can be seen in the bottom photo on the far left. GINI LEMOINE

James Jack kneeling in center; George Barrett standing on right; others unidentified.
GINI LEMOINE

Unidentified Co. B men, man in front possibly Len Socoloski.
BARRETT COLLECTION

L-R: Unidentified, Willard Berry, George Barrett, and Anthony Imperato.
BARRETT COLLECTION

Ray Trotta on spare tire, others unidentified.
BYRON JORDAN

COMPANY C
Charlie Company

Company C, 2nd Platoon, standing on the steps at The Cathedral of Amalfi, Italy, 1943.
See companion photo on page 124.

JEAN PIERRE COMBE

Africano, Sullivan J.
AMERICAN PATRIOTS

Baker, Lloyd S., Jr.
VICENTE DE LEON

Bassett, Gilbert W.
SAM KWESIN, ARTIST

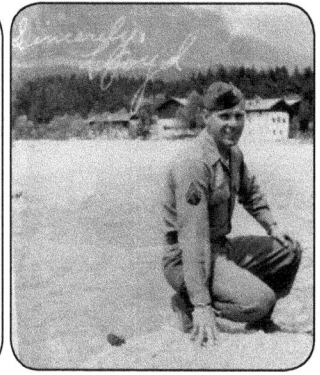

Berg, Lloyd
VICENTE DE LEON

Bernhardt, Bernard
BERNARD BERNHARDT

Blades, Homer R.
VICENTE DE LEON

Blank, Dale C.
PAT BLANK

Bova, Joseph A.
AUTHOR'S COLLECTION

Boyd, John
VICENTE DE LEON

Brash, Italio
AMERICAN PATRIOTS

Brummage, Robert L.
MARSHALL COLLECTION

Bush, Thomas V.
ROBERT SMITH COLLECTION

Carothers, Edward
DICK CAROTHERS

Connolly, Andrew J.
ROBERT BUSH COLLECTION

Cress, Claude A.
KNAPP COLLECTION

De Leon, Vicente
VICENTE DE LEON

Drahn, Lloyd C.
VICENTE DE LEON

Durham, Parks H.
HALE HEPLER

Eisenberg, Harold
KNAPP COLLECTION

Fitzgerald, James
JAMES FITZGERALD

Fortune, John Carlton
NEWSPAPER ARCHIVE

Foster, Herbert L.
WORLD WAR II MEMORIAL

Gaille, Murray
KNAPP COLLECTION

Gaiski, Walter
HALE HEPLER

Gargani, Charles A.
KNAPP COLLECTION

Giles, Paul S.
PAUL GILES

Gilmore, James C.
TURAN COLLECTION

Godlewski, Edward M.
VICENTE DE LEON

Goldenberg, Lawrence I.
KNAPP COLLECTION

Goldman, Milton
TURAN COLLECTION

Gregory, William C.
WILLIAM GREGORY

Hajdinyak, John J.
JOHN HAJDINYAK

Harp, Carlos O.
DON HARP

Harris, Howard S.
VICENTE DE LEON

Hepler, Hale H.
HALE HEPLER

Jean, L. V.
JEAN PIERRE COMBE

Johnson, Carl
DOLLY SARIO

Johnson, William E.
VICENTE DE LEON

Jones, Carl W.
MARSHALL COLLECTION

Knapp, Raymond J.
KNAPP COLLECTION

Krebs, Edward W.
MARSHALL COLLECTION

Kulaga, Fred J.
VICENTE DE LEON

Laus, Andre N.
MARY JANE LAUS

Lear, Maurice D.
ROBERT SMITH COLLECTION

Long, Ralph
VICENTE DE LEON

Lykins, William E.
KNAPP COLLECTION

Marshall, Loy J.
MARSHALL COLLECTION

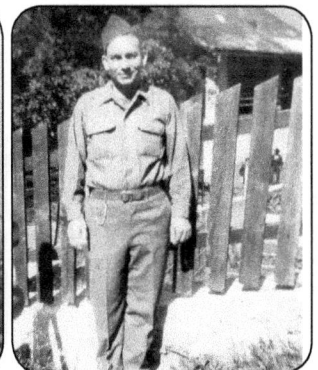

Martin, George E.
TURAN COLLECTION

Miller, Edward C.
RUDOLPH WHITT

Muschinske, Jerome A.
JEROME MUSCHINSKE

Myers, Jim Carr
DELORES RICE

Pierce, Audie W.
MARSHALL COLLECTION

Pokorsky, Stanley
WORLD WAR II MEMORIAL

Porterfield, Arnold
MARSHALL COLLECTION

Pruiett, Charles C.
KNAPP COLLECTION

Ramsey, William C.
RUDOLPH WHITT

Rhoads, Billy C.
GEORGE RHOADS

Richardson, James L.
WALTER ELDREDGE

Risley, Raymond N.
KNAPP COLLECTION

Robinson, James H.
DAN ROBINSON

Runeweiz, Joseph H.
VICENTE DE LEON

Rosenthal, Norman F.
VICENTE DE LEON

Sapio, Salvatore
DANIEL ELSE

Schleifer, Francis J.
ROBERT SMITH COLLECTION

Seibels, Kelly
KELLY SEIBELS

Sheats, Alfred
VICENTE DE LEON

Shivers, John M.
KNAPP COLLECTION

Slider, William V.
WILLIAM SLIDER

Smith, Robert B.
ANNETTE SMITH

Stasinski, Rudolph
WORLD WAR II MEMORIAL

Sutlic, Edward
MOLINA AND ANNE OROS

Thompson, Glen
SAM KWESKIN, ARTIST

Thorp, Thomas R.
ROBERT SMITH COLLECTION

Thorpe, Robert
ANN THORPE

Trapnell, William L.
VICENTE DE LEON

Turan, Leonard W.
TURAN COLLECTION

Vogel, Julius D.
ROBERT SMITH COLLECTION

Wahosky, Norman
VICENTE DE LEON

Walker, Marion A.
MARSHALL COLLECTION

Webb, Mark C.
ROBERT SMITH COLLECTION

Whitt, Rudolph
RUDOLPH WHITT

Wiggins, L. W.
ROBERT SMITH COLLECTION

Williamson, Joseph A.
JOSEPH WILLIAMSON

Yates, Thomas
VICENTE DE LEON

Unidentified Men of Company C
Vicente De Leon Collection

Unidentified men of Co. C Motor Pool.
VICENTE DE LEON

L. W. Wiggins

**Unidentified Men of
Company C
Vicente De Leon Collection**

(EXCEPT FOR L. W. WIGGINS, ABOVE)

Jean Pierre Combe,
Frenchman,
Honorary Member
of
Company C
JEAN PIERRE COMBE

Front, L-R: Bernard Bernhardt and Raymond Risley; back, L-R: Audie Pierce, William Lykins, Robert Simon, Raymond Knapp, William C. Ford, and Julius Vogel. Southern France.
WILLIAM C. FORD COLLECTION

Unidentified in Alsace, France, 1944.
JOSEPH WILLIAMSON

Back left, Raymond Risley, and back right, possibly Norman J. Brann; all others unidentified.
KNAPP COLLECTION

4th Squad, 3rd Platoon
VICENTE DE LEON

1st Squad, 3rd Platoon, reading mail.
VICENTE DE LEON

Charles Martin, front right. Others unidentified.
VICENTE DE LEON

2nd Squad, 3rd Platoon
VICENTE DE LEON

Co. C, CP, Weer, Austria, July 5, 1945.
ROBERT B. SMITH COLLECTION

3rd Squad, 3rd Platoon, France, 1945
VICENTE DE LEON

3rd Platoon Communications. Robert Brummage in front; back, L-R: Loy Marshall, Doug Perry, John Bianco, and Robert Merrington
Vicente De Leon

Back, L-R: Robert Simon, Raymond Risley, and William C. Ford; front, L-R: Norman D. Gott and Julius Vogel.
Knapp Collection

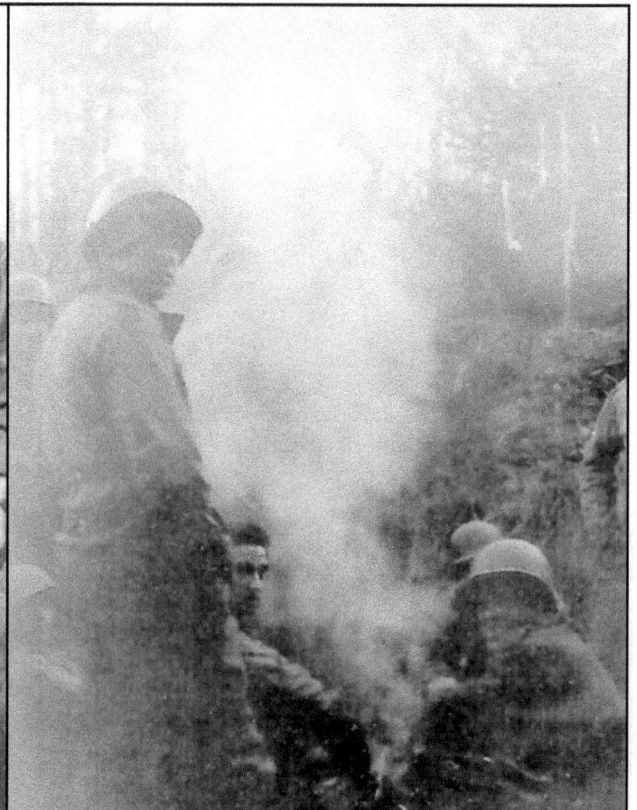

Christmas 1944, spent around a campfire.
Jean Pierre Combe

Back, L-R: Charles Pruiett, Bernard Bernhardt, Raymond Knapp, and Claude Cress; front, L-R: first two men are unidentified, Samuel Preston and Louis Kaufman.
BERNARD BERNHARDT

1. William Slider 2. Rudolph Whitt 3. Albert Agurkis 4. Alex Kimble 5. Norman Brann 6. L. W. Wiggins 7. Austin L. Brown
WILLIAM SLIDER

1. Charles A. Gargani 2. Lawrence I. Goldenberg 3. James R. Fitzgerald 4. Raymond Knapp 5. William C. Ford 6. Charles Pruiett 7. L. W. Wiggins or William Lykins 8. Alfred Sheats 9. Louis R. Grisham or Floyd L. Grissom
ROBERT SMITH COLLECTION

1. William C. Ford 2. Ralph Long 3. Charles A. Gargani 4. William Lykins 5. Julius Vogel 6. Charles Pruiett 7. Bernard Bernhardt 8. Louis R. Grisham 9. Raymond Knapp 10. Louis J. Kaufman
Among the remaining six unidentified are Bestez, Alec Dunaeff, Koody, and Williams.
WILLIAM C. FORD COLLECTION

Winter in Alsace, France. 2nd Platoon, Co. C, James Gilmore on left, others unidentified.
Jean Pierre Combe

Above & below: Co. C medals & awards presentation, Weer, Austria, 1945. *Robert Smith Collection*

Left: Unidentified Co. C men. *Knapp Collection*

Below: 3rd Platoon, Co. C, Weer, Austria. *Robert Smith Collection*

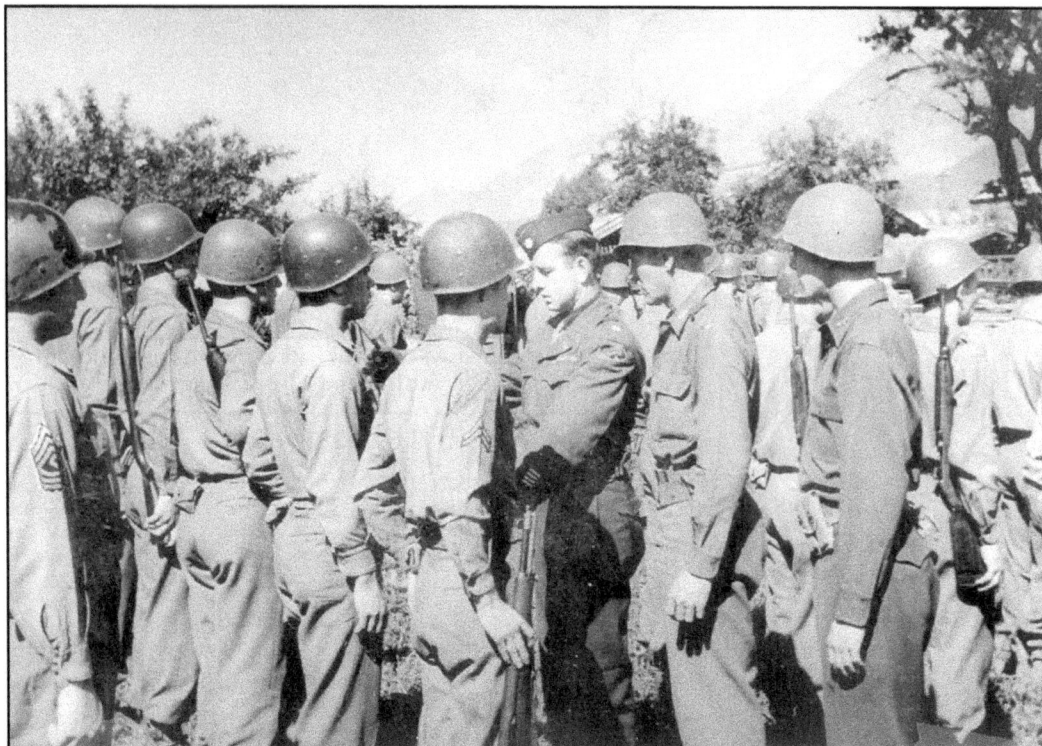

Lt. Col. Sam Efnor in center, others unidentified.
ROBERT SMITH COLLECTION

Back: Rudolph Whitt (2nd from left) and L. W. Wiggins (5th from left), front: Albert Agurkis (2nd from left) and Bennie Hill (5th from left); all others unidentified.
In Germany.
RUDOLPH WHITT

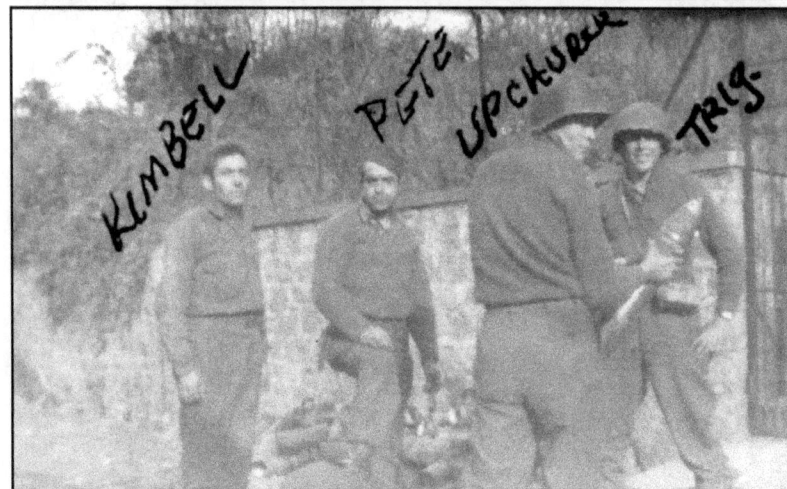

L-R: Alex Kimble, Pete Girone, Cohen R. Upchurch, and Charles A. Trego.
VICENTE DE LEON

L-R: Unidentified, William V. Slider, and possibly Rudolph Whitt.
WILLIAM SLIDER

Man in front is unidentified. Saro Martinez in far back. Others are, L-R: James Fitzgerald, Charles Gargani, Relarkie (?), Norman Gott, and Ralph Long.
JAMES FITZGERALD

L-R: Albert Agurkis, Edward F. Flory, Rudolph Whitt, Harold O. Reidling, and Bennie Hill.
RUDOLPH WHITT

Left: L-R, Lt. John Boyd, Lt. Thomas Cute, Lt. Norman Rosenthal, Lt. Andrew Connolly, and Capt. Robert Smith
ROBERT SMITH COLLECTION

Right: Christmas 1944 near Bitche, (Lorraine) France.
JEAN PIERRE COMBE

Top left: James Hampton in front, back L-R, Herbert Foster, Loy Marshall, and Joseph Williamson.
MARSHALL COLLECTION

Top right: Sitting, Gilbert Bassett, back L-R, Sylvan Rosenfeld, Lemuel Tillman, and Cecil Link.
LEMUEL R. TILLMAN

Left: L-R, front, Raymond Risley, unidentified medic from NJ, and Lawrence Goldenberg; L-R, back: Stanley S. Krous, unidentified, and William Ford.
BERNARD BERNHARDT

Bottom left: L-R: Jesse O'Berry, Austin L. Brown, Mack C. Webb, L. W. Wiggins, and Edward C. Miller.
RUDOLPH WHITT

Bottom Right: L-R, Edward W. Krebs, Loy Marshall, and Carl W. Jones.
MARSHALL COLLECTION

Company Inspection, Weer, Austria. Lt. Col. Sam Efnor (in front with back turned) and Capt. Robert Smith (holding gun); Others unidentified.
ROBERT SMITH COLLECTION

Turan's Squad in Pill, Austria, 1945. Front, L-R: Lawrence Miller and Milton Goldman; back, L-R: Leonard Turan, Vernon Kulcinski, and James Gilmore.
TURAN COLLECTION

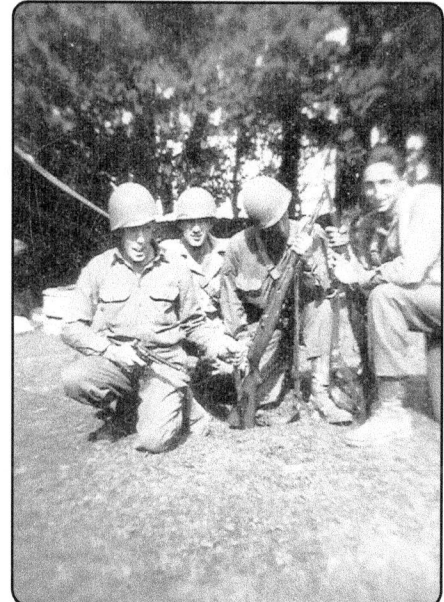

Murray Gaille on far right; others unidentified.
KNAPP COLLECTION

Left: Front, L-R: Unidentified, Raymond Knapp, and Julius Vogel; back, L-R: William C. Plankar, William Lykins, and William C. Ford.
WILLIAM C. FORD COLLECTION

Right: L-R: Herbert Sinow (?) or Snow (not on roster), Sgt. Harris, unidentified, and Kelly Seibels.
KELLY SEIBELS

COMPANY D
Dog Company

Front: Second from left, Arthur Bilton; right, Norman Squires. Back: Right, James Dougherty.
DOUGHERTY COLLECTION

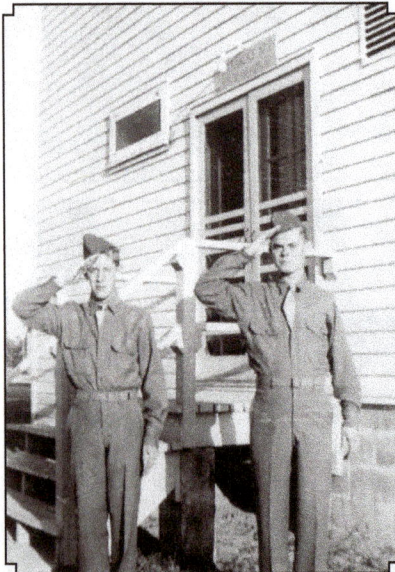

L-R: Arthur Bilton and James Hurt at Camp Gordon, GA.
SHIELDS COLLECTION

L-R: Cohen R. Upchurch and Trammel.
SHIELDS COLLECTION

L-R: Lt. Alfred Crenshaw & Capt. Edwin G. Pike
SHIELDS COLLECTION

Aldridge, Ervin C.
NEWSPAPER ARCHIVE

Baker, Norman L.
SHIELDS COLLECTION

Barclay, Kenneth B.
SHIELDS COLLECTION

Beasley, James O.
JOHN BEASLEY

Bilton, Arthur
AUTHOR'S COLLECTION

Blystone, Leonard G.
HOPKINS COLLECTION

Bolam, Howard
SHIELDS COLLECTION

Borkhuis, George R.
FRED THOMPSON & THOMASINA EDWARDS

Bridge, Richard
LINDA WHALEN

Camp, Howard
NEWSPAPER ARCHIVE

Chamblee, Robert
HOPKINS COLLECTION

Cinnajinny, Frank B.
EUGENE PLASSMANN

Clayton, James H.
NEWSPAPER ARCHIVE

Codega, Michele "Mike"
CODEGA COLLECTION

Crenshaw, Alfred H.
ROBERT BUSH COLLECTION

D'Antuono, Ralph
SHIELDS COLLECTION

413

Davis, Porter R.
AUTHOR'S COLLECTION

Donald, James M.
SHIELDS COLLECTION

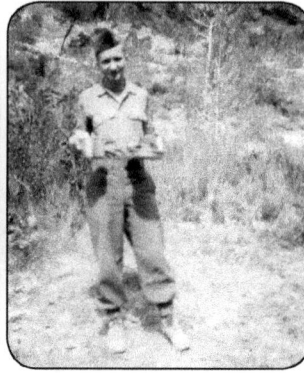

Doster, Russell S.
SHIELDS COLLECTION

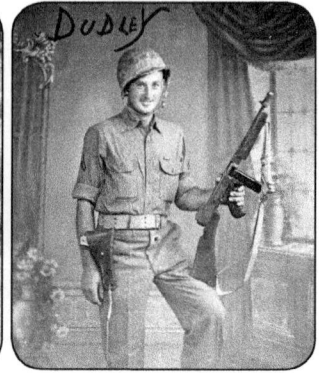

Dudley, James J.
AUTHOR'S COLLECTION

Duke, Ralph
WORLD WAR II MEMORIAL

Egans, George
SHIELDS COLLECTION

Eusebi, Euro F.
SHIELDS COLLECTION

Fannin, Robert F.
AUTHOR'S COLLECTION

Fichtler, Rudolph M.
CODEGA COLLECTION

Gallahan, James H.
JAMES GALLAHAN

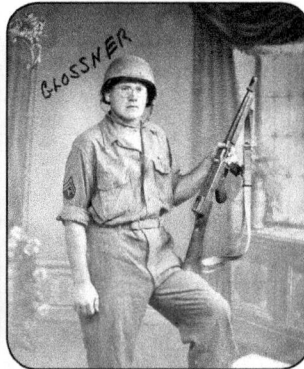

Glossner, Nevin L.
AUTHOR'S COLLECTION

Green, Alfred
ALFRED GREEN

Haddock, Theodore
HOPKINS COLLECTION

Hodgson, William J.
SAM KWESKIN, ARTIST

Hoffman, William J.
SHIELDS COLLECTION

Hughes, Harold
EVA HUGHES

Hurt, James
SHIELDS COLLECTION

Johnson, Edwin I.
NEWSPAPER ARCHIVE

Johnson, Gerald
BYRON JORDAN

Jones, Jim
AUTHOR'S COLLECTION

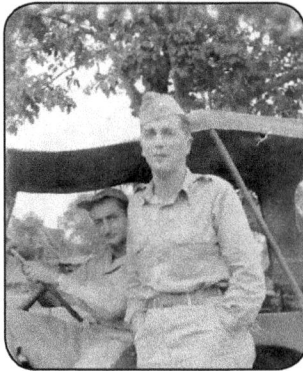

Kalk, Herbert C.
DEBBY KALK

Kann, Earl F.
EARL KANN

Kiedrowski, Peter J.
PIKE COLLECTION

Lakey, Raymond J.
PIKE COLLECTION

Lombardi, Frank
BOB & LANIE BENCIVENGA

Lowry, Charlie
AUTHOR'S COLLECTION

Makepeace, Edwin H.
SHIELDS COLLECTION

Mesaris, Francis A.
SHIELDS COLLECTION

Miller, Dan
DAN MILLER

Nairn, William P.
SHIELDS COLLECTION

O'Connor, John A.
SHIELDS COLLECTION

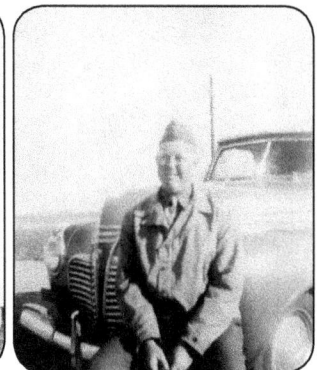

Palmer, Joseph H.
SHIELDS COLLECTION

Peterson, Russell H.
PETERSON COLLECTION

Pike, Edwin G.
MARCIA BUNKER

Rebick, Michael J.
LINDA WHALEN

Riddle, Clark H.
HOPKINS COLLECTION

Ruth, Walter G.
AUTHOR'S COLLECTION

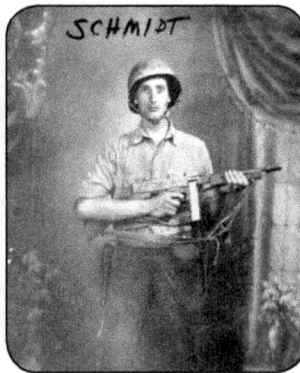

Schmidt, William J.
AUTHOR'S COLLECTION

Sheckler, Abraham E.
SHIELDS COLLECTION

Shoults, Lovell "Dutch"
SHIELDS COLLECTION

Stiefvater, Joseph C.
EARL KANN

Tanner, Willie R.
AUTHOR'S COLLECTION

Taylor, Cecil M.
SHIELDS COLLECTION

Testa, Carmen
SHIELDS COLLECTION

Thomson, Frank J.
BAER COLLECTION

Vance, Charles
SHIELDS COLLECTION

Whelan, Andrew
SHIELDS COLLECTION

Williams, Lawrence
LAWRENCE WILLIAMS

Wilson, Harry W.
DOUGHERTY COLLECTION

Yeager, Robert H.
EARL KANN

Young, George
CODEGA COLLECTION

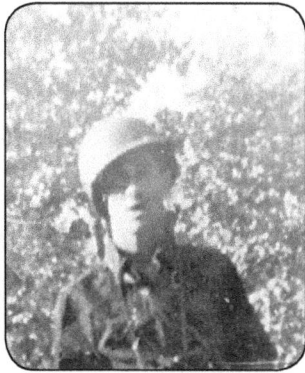

Young, George D.
CODEGA COLLECTION

Standing, L-R: [?] Bowman, Stephen Boehmer, Robert Wehrheim, and Richard Bridge; sitting, L-R: Willis Cannon, Robert Chamblee, and Clark Riddle.
CLARK RIDDLE

Left: L-R, Cpl. Harrell C. Davis and Sgt. Edwin I. Johnson
CODEGA COLLECTION

Right: L-R, Harold O. Dean and William P. Nairn
ROBERT W. NAIRN

Front, L-R: Frank J. "Jim" Murphy, Abraham Sheckler, Daniel Shields, Carmen Testa, Kenneth Barclay, and Charles F. Ruff; back row: 7. Joseph H. Palmer 8. James W. Brassfield 9. Ervin C. Aldridge 10. Elwood "Long John" Guthrie 11. Brinkerhoff (*probably Raymond Brinkman*) 12. Rollin D. Taylor. *SHIELDS COLLECTION*

Co. D squad near the Siegfried Line. Within the squad are Seymour Holstein and John Winkler. *SHIELDS COLLECTION*

Standing, left, is James Pittman and sitting on left is Leonard Blystone. *HOPKINS COLLECTION*

L-R: James Gallahan, Earl Kann, Wilson, and George Sweeting. *SHIELDS COLLECTION*

Back row, L-R: Tarver, Robert Freer, and Rollin Taylor; front row, L-R: Earl Wilkerson and Ford Hopkins.
HOPKINS COLLECTION

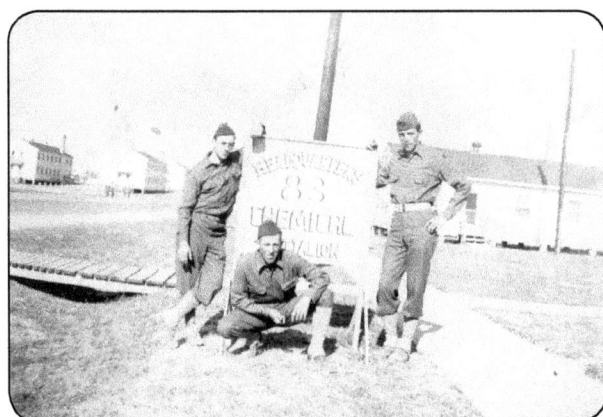

L-R: James Gallahan, Norman Baker, and Elwood Guthrie.
SHIELDS COLLECTION

L-R: Charles A. Bennett, Mike Codega, and Miles K. Storey, southern France, September 1944.
CODEGA COLLECTION

L-R: Schmidt, Bloomberg, and Charlie Lowry.
AUTHOR'S COLLECTION

Unidentified Co. D, possibly John Mazzafer kneeling on right.
SHIELDS COLLECTION

L-R: Joseph Mitchell, Clark Riddle, unidentified, and Jack Pimento.
HOPKINS COLLECTION

L-R: James Vickers, Tom Renfroe, Rudolph Fichtler, and George F. Tucker.
CODEGA COLLECTION

L-R: Robert Chamblee, Ford Hopkins, and Rollin Taylor.
HOPKINS COLLECTION

Front, L-R: Edwin S. Silvert and Harry Y. Terres; back row, L-R: Daniel Shields, Bennie Lieberman, Elwood Guthrie, and George O. Weatherford.
SHIELDS COLLECTION

Front, L-R: William J. Hoffman, Francis A. Mesaris, Earl F. Kann, Edwin S. Silvert, and Harry Y. Terres; back, L-R: Carmen Testa, Andrew Whelan, Schmidt, and Langford.
EARL KANN

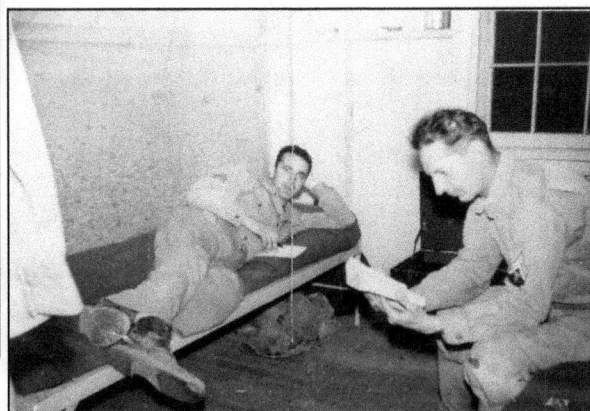

Mike Codega (left) and Theodore Wolters (right).
CODEGA COLLECTION

1. Bob Knight 2. Raymond Metcalf 3. Wofford Jackson 4. Charles Vance 5. Nevin Glossner 6. Joseph Palmer 7. George Young 8. Charles Cella 9. Clyde Decker 10. Harry Wilson 11. Unidentified 12. Cruz (*probably Robert I. Crutz*) 13. Willie Tanner 14. Robert Grant 15. Unidentified 16. Unidentified "Garry" SHIELDS COLLECTION

Back, L-R: Bernard H. McDermott, William J. Hoffman, Andy Whelan, Carmen Testa, George R. Sweeting, Harry Y. Terres, and Sullivan; front, L-R: Norman L. Baker, Kenneth Barclay, Edwin S. Silvert, and Cecil Taylor.
SHIELDS COLLECTION

Left: Clay Tuck at Camp Gordon, GA.
Right: Standing, L-R: Kenneth Barclay, Daniel Shields, Elwood Guthrie, and George W. Weatherford; kneeling, L-R: Edwin S. Silvert and Harry Y. Terres.
BOTH PHOTOS SHIELDS COLLECTION

Joseph M. Pensack and Edward Trey. *ED TREY*

L-R: Unidentified, Donald Herr, unidentified, and Russell Doster. *SHIELDS COLLECTION*

Company D men watching a movie. *SHIELDS COLLECTION*

MOTOR POOL

Front row L-R: Charlie Lowry, Harold Dean, Mike; back row L-R: William J. Schmidt, Hal, Lawrence Rosenberg, and Porter Davis, Sicily, 1943.
LESTER COLLECTION

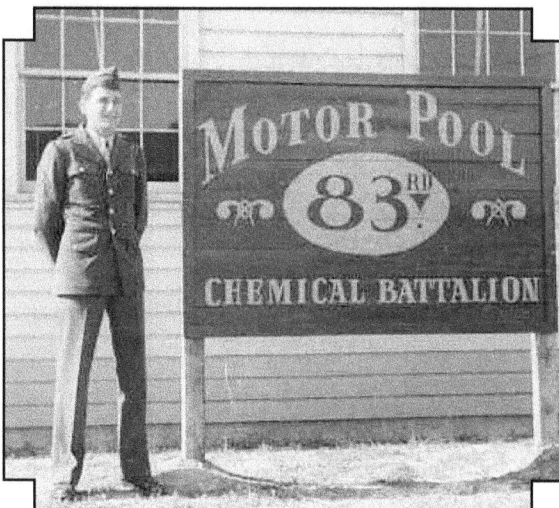

Left: Eugene Plassmann with Motor Pool sign at Camp Gordon, GA.
EUGENE PLASSMANN

Right, L-R: Charles L. Cleaveland, Allen McCoy, and Stephen Vukson
STEPHEN VUKSON

1st. Lt. Robert W. Fenton
Battalion Motor Pool Officer
WENDY EDWARDS

T/4 Stephen W. Vukson
Battalion Motor Pool/Parts & Supplies
STEPHEN VUKSON

Charles Cleaveland with jeep hit by a mine.
STEPHEN VUKSON

L-R: Charles Cleaveland, William B. McFarland, Lt. Robert Fenton, Stephen Vukson, and Clyde Thorson
STEPHEN VUKSON

1. Anderson 2. William McFarland 3. Robert Blamick 4. Stephen Vukson 5. Robert Fenton 6. Charles Cleaveland 7. Frank Russell
8. Kenneth Adair 9. Isadore Reichman 10. Clyde Thorson
STEPHEN VUKSON

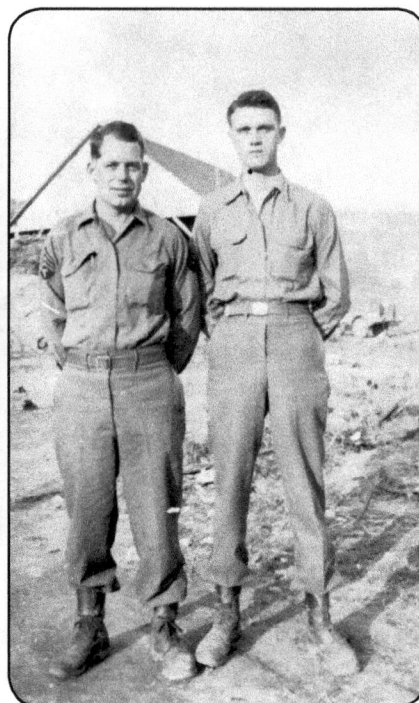

Top left: A wrecker and tank.
Hopkins Collection
Top right: Two unidentified men from the motor pool.
Vicente De Leon

Left: Unidentified man standing beside the motor pool sign at Camp Gordon, GA.
Barrett Collection

Bottom left: Co. C Motor Pool on right, Austin Brown is standing on the left, others are unidentified.
Vicente De Leon

Bottom right: Robert Bell (L) and Woodrow White (R) from Co. B Motor Pool.
Stephen Vukson

Mixed & Unknown Company Groupings

L-R: Thomas Foran, Co. B; Charles Plumly, HQ Co.; John Conicello Co. C; Robert Danfield, Co. B; and Charles Carrullo, Co. A.
ROBERT BUSH COLLECTION

Left: Unidentified.
DOUGHERTY COLLECTION

Below: Possible Co. A men.
ROBERT BUNDY

Possible Co. B men.
LAWRENCE CENSATO

Above: Unidentified men at Camp Gordon, GA.
Below: Unidentified. *Both from the Tyma Collection*

Co. B men surrounded by sand
bags.
Gini Lemoine

John Baer on right, others unidentified.
Baer Collection

Back, L-R: Cloyd Boyd and Albert Franklin; front, L-R:
George T. Cairl, Co. A, and Jay Conrow. *Turan Collection*

L-R: Joe Cutler, Jacob C. Detweiler, Co. A, and David J.
Clatterbuck, Co. B. *Turan Collection*

Top: Taylor and unidentified.
Bottom: "Our transporter".
BAER COLLECTION

Top: Possible Kelso Thompson & unidentified.
Bottom: Garry.
SHIELDS COLLECTION

Top: Unidentified. *BYRON JORDAN*
Bottom: Unidentified.
BARRETT COLLECTION

Top: Unidentified. *BAER COLLECTION* Bottom: Miller and Wade Gardner
McLARTY COLLECTION

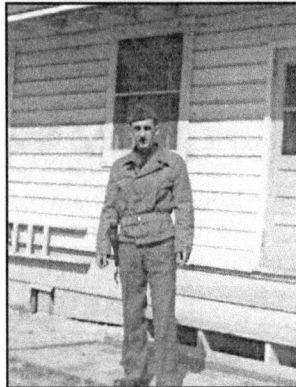

Above and below: Unidentified men at Edgewood Arsenal, MD.
BOTH AUTHOR'S COLLECTION

Above: Possibly Co. B men.
BARRETT COLLECTION

Below: Possible HQ Co. man.
KARL GARRETT

Above: Possible Co. B man.
BARRETT COLLECTION
Below: Possible Co. D man.
HOPKINS COLLECTION

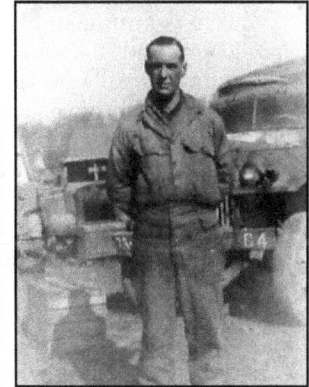

Above: Unidentified truck driver in the motor pool.
HALE HEPLER
Below: Unidentified.
BAER COLLECTION

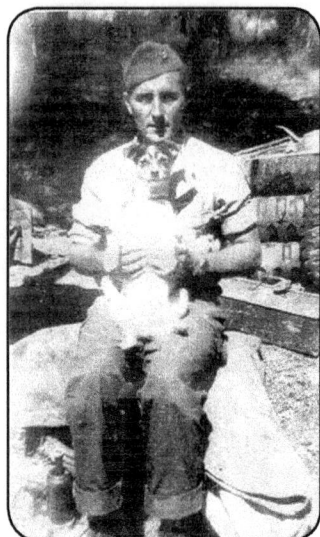

Above: Vino on stool.
AUTHOR'S COLLECTION
Left: Charlie Lowry with Vino.
LESTER COLLECTION

"Vino"
THE MASCOT DOG OF CO. D MOTOR POOL AND OTHER BATTALION MASCOTS

It has become commonplace in military history for fighting units to adopt pets as mascots. In the 83rd Chemical Mortar Battalion Loy J. Marshall remembered a pet dog in Co. C, and in the numerous photographs of the 83rd can be found an assortment of pet dogs, birds, a monkey, and even human 'mascots.' But a dog named "Vino" (Italian for wine) seems to be one of the most fondly remembered.

According to James Marion Lester (better known as Marion or Les), a truck driver for the Co. D Motor Pool in Sicily, the men noticed two puppies by the side of the road and suspected they had been dumped. Willie R. Tanner picked up the one that became "Vino". James later heard another company had picked up the other dog, although in a photo album owned by Charlie Lowry, who rode "shotgun" with Lester, there is a picture of "Vino" and another dog sitting on the hood of the truck of Nevin "Spanky" Glossner (who would later die on *LST 422*, perhaps drowning with that other dog). Lester said he thought "Vino" was a "rat terrier" or "rat terrier like" dog.

Reportedly everyone in the company loved "Vino" and looked after him, although it would appear "Vino" looked after them as well. In a V-mail letter from Charlie Lowry to his future wife Ruth Sutton dated April 4, 1944, probably writing from Minturno, Italy, he records, "One of our pets just came in (a lizard); we have another (a mouse), but they don't get much rest from Vino. That's our dog." Indeed, "Vino" was photographed with nearly every one in the company. He is held by Willie R. Tanner in a group photo taken at Terfens, Austria, in 1945. Lester claimed that Tanner, "Vino's" primary caretaker, vowed to bring the dog home with him, although it is unknown if that happened.

"Vino" was not the only mascot associated with Co. D, as evidenced in the September 1, 1943, letter written by Capt. Edwin "Bud" Pike at Castelvetrano, Sicily, stating, "We have now acquired a little puppy and a kitten as company pets and they're really cute. The dog's name is 'Chow-hound' and the kitten has no name as yet. They get along swell together and are bosom pals. Every once in a while they get playing together and then the fun begins. The pup jumps in at the kitten and the kitten stands up on its hind legs like a boxer and lets him have it right across the snout with a right hook. This usually calms the pup down somewhat but he always comes back for more."

Another well known pet in the 83rd was "Pete", a black German shepherd owned by Capt. Robert E. Edwards of HQ Co. It's not clear if this is the same dog mentioned in a September 27, 1944, letter by Capt. Edwards in which he wrote, "The newest addition as of about four o'clock this evening was a four months old mostly German shepherd pup. They called him Tijon so we'll call her Jon. Have him with me and he is whimpering a little. All the other officers took over him like a bunch of women to a baby." When Edwards left Europe to return home he gave "Pete" to Lt. Robert E. Bundy, who in turn eventually gave the dog to Lt. William L. Trapnell. Supposedly, Lt. Trapnell brought "Pete" back to the states with him.

Capt. Edward Trey could not recall the name or breed of his dog but said it was killed during an enemy artillery barrage at Anzio by a shell fragment. He said the medics attended to the dog the same as they would a human but all efforts proved fruitless.

James M. Lester on Willie Tanner's truck, left, and Porter Davis, right, both holding Vino.
LESTER COLLECTION

83rd Pets

Puppies, right and left, probably at Camp Gordon. *Eugene Plassmann*; Vino, center, standing on crate. *Kelso Thompson*

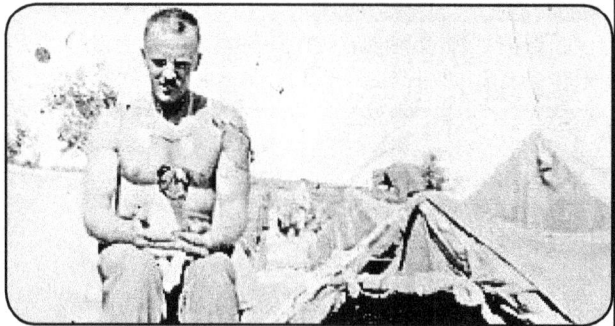

Above: top left, George Borkhuis with dog. *Shields Collection*; top right, Ed Trey and dog in North Africa. *Ed Trey*; Bottom left, Captain Robert Edwards and Pete. *Ed Trey*; bottom right, Vino and friend on Nevin Glossner's vehicle. *Author's Collection*

L-R: Arthur Mellen with puppy in a helmet. *Hopkins Collection*; Unidentified soldier with dog on HQ Co. truck. *Shields Collection*; Albert Agurkis with dog. *Rudolph Whitt*

83rd Pets

L-R: Raymond Knapp with dog. *KNAPP COLLECTION*; Capt. Robert E. Edwards with Jon. *WENDY EDWARDS*; A group of 83rd soldiers with Tijon. *WENDY EDWARDS*

L-R: George Whetsell, HQ Co., with dog. *SHIELDS COLLECTION*; Unidentified soldier with bird. *JORDAN COLLECTION*; Sgt. Walter Gaiski with dog. *HALE HEPLER*; Robert Cocayne with dog. *SHIELDS COLLECTION*

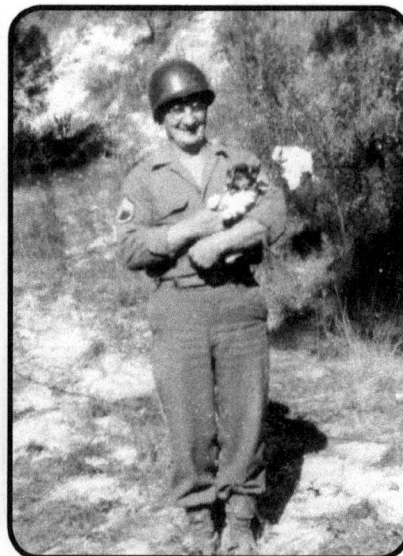

L-R: Bernie Bernhardt, Co. C, with dog; Co. C men with dog, including (L-R) Unidentified holding dog, Bernard Bernhardt and Charles Pruiett. *KNAPP COLLECTION*; Unidentified soldier holding dog. *SHIELDS COLLECTION*

Baptism at Sea

Leo D. Fagan, Co. B, first sea water baptism on the Anzio Beachhead, April 1, 1944.
SIGNAL CORPS

Time for Chow

Above left: Dinner at the Lieutenant Colonel's table. Lt. Col. Hutchinson at the head of the tables. *Hulcher Movie Clip, Charles Hulcher*; Above right: Unidentified soldiers in chow line. *Strickler Collection*

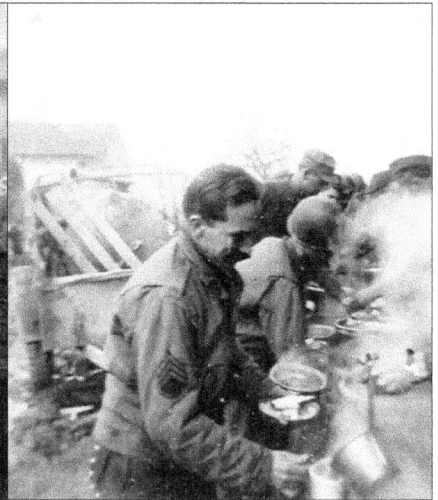

Left: Bernard Bernhardt and Raymond Risley eating chicken. *Bernie bernhardt*; Center: Lawrence Goldenberg with his chow. *Knapp Collection*; Right: Raymond Knapp in chow line. *Knapp Collection*

Left: Unidentified men in chow line. *Robert Bush Collection*
Right: L-R, Porter Davis and James Lester; those serving the chow are unidentified. *Shields Collection*

Top left: L-R, Eugene Pirani, unidentified, Ford Hopkins, unidentified, and Clark Riddle. *HOPKINS COLLECTION*

Left: Co. A chow line, all unidentified. *HOPKINS COLLECTION*

Top right: Unidentified soldiers in chow line. *BERNARD BERNHARDT*

Bottom: All unidentified except cook Carl Lepine who is wearing a white shirt and serving chow. *ED TREY*

Mail Call

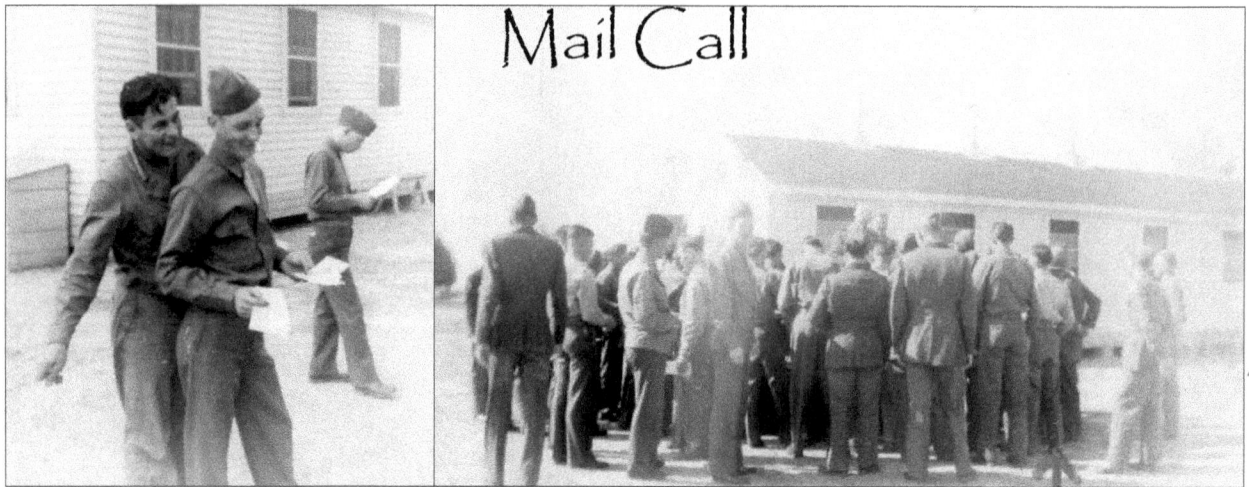

Left and right: Unidentified soldiers receiving mail from home while at Camp Gordon, GA.
Shields Collection

KP Duty

Left: Only soldier identified is Frank Lombardi, sitting in center. *Bob & Lanie Bencivenga*
Right: Unidentified soldiers peeling potatoes. *Eugene Plassmann*

Cleaning Up

Left: Edward S. Davidson holding mop, William Heelan on right, others unidentified. *Stan Davidson*
Right: L-R, Charles Vance, Harry Wilson, and James Dougherty. *Dougherty Collection*

A Shave & A Haircut

Church

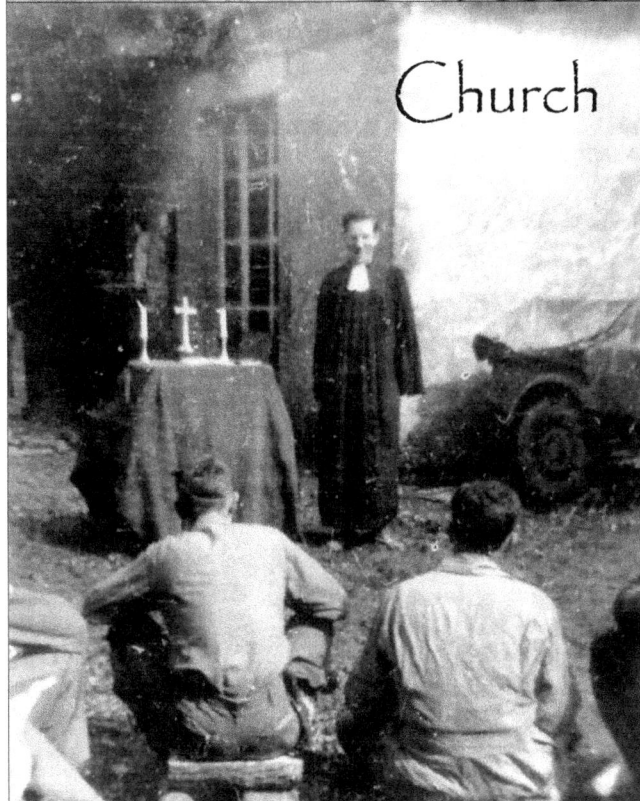

Top left: Carl Lepine getting a shave.
Top right: Capt. Edward Trey getting a haircut.
Above right: Julian McKinnon shaving.
ED TREY

Center left: Dr. Julius C. Hulcher, seated in center, gets a haircut. The others are unidentified.
HULCHER MOVIE CLIP, CHARLES HULCHER

Bottom left: Church services being held outdoors. No identification.
KNAPP COLLECTION

Camp Life

Left: Eugene Pirani camped on a hillside. HOPKINS COLLECTION; Center: The short & the tall Carl Lepine (left) and Julian McKinnon (right). ED TREY; Right: Leonard Turan in sun glasses inside foxhole, others unidentified. TURAN COLLECTION

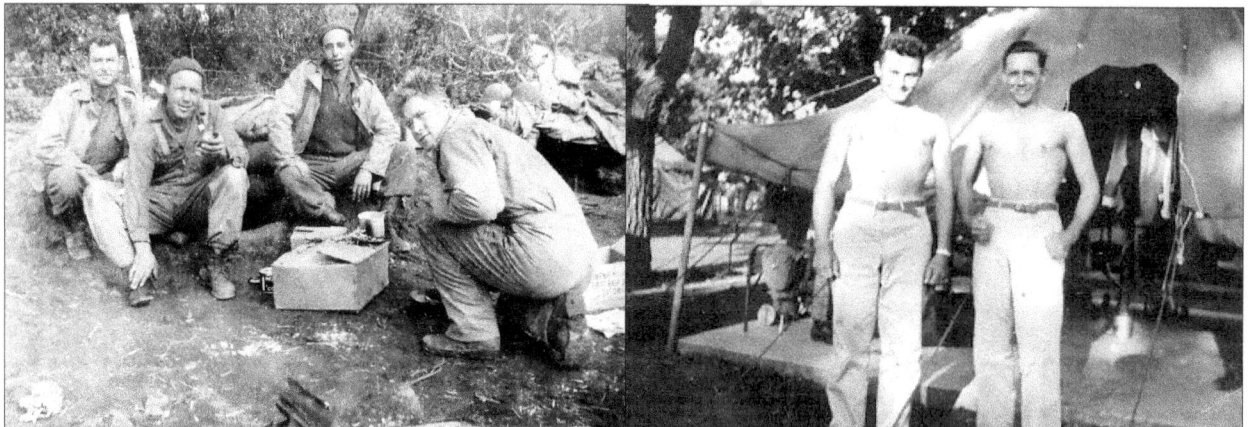

Left: L-R, Sitting around camp are Robert Chamblee, Lawrence Yost, Ford Hopkins, and Clark Riddle, all of Co. D. HOPKINS COLLECTION; Right: L-R, Unidentified and Gordon Mindrum. SCOTT MINDRUM

Left: L-R, Carl Lepine, Thomas Thorp and Clair Strickler, celebrating Thorp's birthday with cake. STRICKLER COLLECTION; Right: Unidentified soldier taking a break. EUGENE PLASSMANN

438

Goofing Off

Left: George Barrett (L) with unidentified soldiers. BARRETT COLLECTION
Right: Unidentified Co. D men shooting craps. SHIELDS COLLECTION

Left: Dave Johnson (left) Co. D and Claudie L. Kelly (right) Co. B. SHIELDS COLLECTION; Center: Dale Blank. DALE & PAT BLANK;
Right: Ford Hopkins. HOPKINS COLLECTION

Left: Laurence "One Lung" Fagan. BYRON JORDAN; Center: Eugene Pirani relaxing. HOPKINS COLLECTION; Right: Antonio
Rabaiotti takes his turn in the chair. HOPKINS COLLECTION

Clowning Around

Left: Unidentified men "fighting". SHIELDS COLLECTION; Center: Eugene Pirani in window and James Blackmon sitting. HOPKINS COLLECTION; Right: Rollin Taylor holds a gun on unidentified Mussolini impersonator. HOPKINS COLLECTION

Left: Ford Hopkins at Saverne, France. KENNETH HOPKINS; Center: George Barrett riding a "screaming mimi". BARRETT COLLECTION; Right: Mike Codega (L) and Miles K. Storey (R) "striking a pose". SHIELDS COLLECTION

Left: Unidentified men. GINI LEMOINE; Center: Raymond Risley (left) and Lawrence Goldenberg (right) all "dressed" up for Christmas December 25, 1943. BERNARD BERNHARDT; Right: Unidentified man with spring flowers on his hat. HULCHER MOVIE CLIP, CHARLES HULCHER

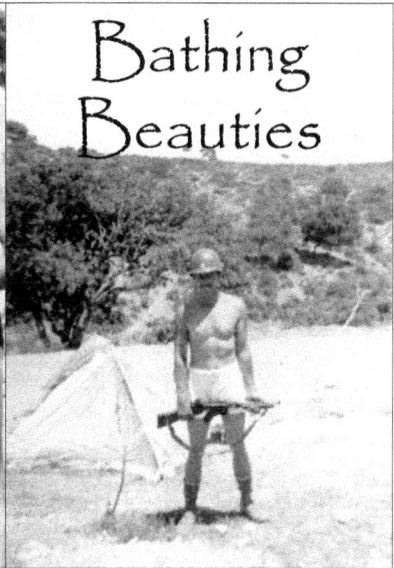

Bathing Beauties

Left: L-R, Lee Steedle, Arthur Mellen, Thomas Simpson, Ralph Goins, and Byron Jordan. BYRON JORDAN ; Center: L-R, James Jack, John Bowles, and Willard Smith. GINI LEMOINE ; Right: Capt. Edward Trey in Oran, Africa. ED TREY
Below left: George Barrett clowning around. BARRETT COLLECTION

Music

Right: Hale Hepler and the Italian boy who stayed with Co. C.
HALE HEPLER

Above center: The Red Platoon Band.
BARRETT COLLECTION

Left: Band at Camp Gordon. Front L-R: Raymond Spraggins and William Gallagher. Back L-R: Hugh Shields, Nitawick (?) and Judson Johnson.
WILLIAM GALLAGHER

Right: Charles DeCesare playing an accordion.
ROBERT BUNDY

441

Transportation

Left: Charles DeCesare riding a bicycle. *ROBERT BUNDY*; Center: Capt. Alfred Forrester driving around town in a car. *L. LEW HENRY COLLECTION*; Right: Robert Taylor with cows. *ELIZABETH TAYLOR*

Above left: Three jeeps used by the 83rd the first one is called "Rolling Ranger". *L. LEW HENRY COLLECTION*
Center: Pvt. Byron Powers. *BRYAN TURAN*
Above right: Lt. Leonard Kenney riding a horse. *ROBERT BUNDY*
Left: When you gotta go, you gotta go. Unidentified. *ROBERT BUSH*

Left: Robert Bundy in jeep, others unidentified. Center: Mortar crew convoy. Right: Driving through bombed German city. *ROBERT BUNDY*

Unidentified 83rd men.
GINI LEMOINE

Willard Smith, Co. B
GINI LEMOINE

Heavily damaged photo of some HQ men playing cards. 1. Chaplain George E. Gaiser 2. Lt. Robert W. Fenton 3. Lt. Rollin W. Kapp (of the 11th Chemical Maintenance) 4. Capt. Julius C. Hulcher 5. CWO Arthur J. Usher 6. Capt. Edward L. Trey 7. Capt. Joseph Garsson 8. Lt. James V. Lauro. *ED TREY*

McMillan 1st
Albert
~~Bailey~~ Petwiler
Canner

~~Komine~~ 2nd Bailey
Axton
Baldwin
Boyd

Helsel 3rd
Brumage
Brown A.F.
Chest.

De Vries - 1 Powder
1 Skat
1 Halozone
1 Cover

Comoty - 1 Powder
1 Skat
1 Halozone
~~1 Cover~~
4 Eye Shields

Turan 1 Cover
4 Shields

Boyd 4 Shields
1 Ointment
~~1 Ointment~~
1 Halozone
1 Cover

Right: Page from diary of Lt. Robert Bush, Co. A, listing some of his squads and his new (and illegal) mortar firing method.
ROBERT BUSH COLLECTION

Left: Leonard Turan's notebook listing some of his squad and equipment issued.
TURAN COLLECTION

Below: Mortar baseplates
SHIELDS COLLECTION

Range	WP		HE	
600	4	1030	3½	1010
650	4	915	3½	865
700	4½	1020	4	1000
750	4½	915	4	880
800	5	1020	4½	1000
850	5	935	4½	900
900	5½	1020	5	1000
950	5½	940	5	920
1000	6	1010	5½	1000
1050	6	945	5½	925
1100	6	800	6	1000
1150	6½	955	6	940
1200	6½	865	6½	945
1250	7	900	6½	
1300	7	885	6½	
1350	7½	965	7	950
1400	7½	845	7	870
1450	8	770	8	1035
1500	8	910	8	1000

Top left: "gassing up". Top right: Displaced Persons (DPs). Center left: German prisoners. Center right: Displaced Persons in Mannheim, Germany, May 1945. *ALL PHOTOS ROBERT BUSH COLLECTION*

Possibly Italian army prisoners. *LESTER COLLECTION*

Top left: Going home at Le Havre, France
Vicente De Leon

Top right: Camp Chicago PX at Le Havre
Shields Collection

Center: Le Havre, France, medical embarkation point
Doc Hulcher Movie Clip, Charles Hulcher

Below: Troop train to Le Havre, France, Sept. 1945
Ford Collection

Above: Augsburg - where Capt. Joseph Garsson, Co. A, was tried. *KWESKIN COLLECTION*

Top right, L-R: Miller, Parrish, James Jack, and Latimer, all of Co. B, at Camp Gordon, GA. *GINI LEMOINE*

Center: The 4.2 mortar. *IMPERATO COLLECTION*

Bottom right: Co. B man in rain-soaked foxhole. *IMPERATO COLLECTION*

Below: Unidentified man in an 83rd Separate Chemical Battalion T-shirt at Camp Gordon, GA *SHIELDS COLLECTION*

Newspaper clipping from the *Augusta Chronicle*, October 11, 1942, showing the model day room at Camp Gordon donated by the Rotary Club. Named are L-R, Cpl. D. E. Frazier, Pvt. Roger Moore, George Borkhuis, Sgt. Brown, Sgt. Edward Langford, Pvt. Rudolph Fichtler, Sgt. David N. Cooper, Pvt. Max Nestler, and Cpl. Harold Dean. *Borkhuis Collection*

Raymond J. DeVoto, HQ Co. *Kweskin Collection*

83rd Chemical Mortar Battalion
1942-1945
Roster

Exhausted 83rd truck driver during the Vosges Campaign
Vicente De Leon

ROSTER OF
THE 83ᴿᴰ CHEMICAL MORTAR BATTALION

This roster is an attempt to list every known soldier that served in the 83ʳᵈ Chemical Mortar Battalion in World War II, even if the soldier only served for one day. Currently this is the most extensive roster ever assembled of the 83ʳᵈ Chemical Mortar Battalion. The list contains over 2000 names and more will undoubtedly be located in the future, although a complete listing will probably never be achieved as many of the men came in later as replacements, served briefly, and then left either by wounds or for other reasons such as illness, rotation, transfer, etc., leaving very little in the way of their record of service with the 83ʳᵈ. The roster is based upon a multitude of sources and attempts to trace the soldier from birth through current status, with emphasis on the military sector. Originally spouses and parents were to be included but they have been deleted due to space limitations. Reunions are included only for the years from 1954 to 1966 and are not necessarily complete. The bulk of information came from such sources as the actual participant; the May 28, 1942, Edgewood Arsenal roster of the original cadre; Official Orders for the 83ʳᵈ Chemical Mortar Battalion, Camp Gordon, Georgia 1942-43; the two dated rosters from *Rounds Away* in 1945; official journals and casualty reports of the 83ʳᵈ Chemical Mortar Battalion, National Archives, College Park, Maryland; information extracted from the official newsletters of the 83ʳᵈ Chemical Mortar Battalion, *Smokescreen* and *Muzzleblasts*; Roll of Honor lists from *Chemical Warfare Bulletin* 1942 - 45; the American Battlefields Monuments Commission list of American soldiers buried in overseas cemeteries; Social Security Death Index; NARA List of Enlistments in World War II; NARA List of American POWs in World War II; the National World War II Memorial Registry; and lists provided by many of the veterans such as Dale Blank and Ed Trey. Most abbreviations used are standard and those for military cemeteries in foreign countries are based upon those found on the American Battlefields Monuments Commission website. If you have any questions about abbreviations, corrections, additions, etc., contact the author.

Abbreviations

Absent without leave - AWOL
Adjutant - Adj.
Artillery - Art.
Assistant - Asst.
Attended - Attd.
Born - b.
Brigade - Brig.
Brigadier General - Brig. Gen.
Buried - bur.
Captain - Capt.
Captured - capt.
Cemetery - Cem.
Colonel - Col.
Commissary - Comm.
Commissioned - Comm.
Company - Co.
Corporal - Cpl.
County - Co.
Court Martial - C.M.
Died - d.
Discharged - Dischd.
Division - Div.
Enlisted - Enl.
Exchanged - Exchd.
First Lieutenant - 1st Lt.
First Sergeant - 1st Sgt.
Fort - Ft.
General - Gen.
General Court Martial - G.C.M.
Hospital - Hosp.
Infantry - Inf.
Judge Advocate - J.A.
Killed in action - KIA
Lieutenant - Lt.

Lieutenant Colonel - Lt. Col.
Major - Maj.
Missing in action - MIA
Mortally wounded in action - MWIA
Mount or Mountain - Mt.
No further record - NFR
Orderly - Ord.
Ordnance - Ord.
Postwar record - PWR
Prisoner of war - POW
Private - Pvt.
Quartermaster - Q.M.
Reenlisted - Re-enl.
Regiment - Regt.
Released - Relsd.
Resigned - Resgnd.
Second Lieutenant - 2nd Lt.
Sergeant - Sgt.
Sergeant Major - Sgt. Maj.
Third Lieutenant - 3rd Lt.
Transferred - Transf.
United States - U.S.
Wounded in action - WIA

American Battle Monuments Commission Abbreviations

EP-Epinal France
FL-Florence, Italy
LO-Lorraine, France
NA-North Africa, Tunisia
SR, Sicily-Rome, Italy

ABBOTT, John R. b. 1918 IL. Enl. 4/20/42 Chicago, IL. Ser. No. 36332245. Pvt., Co. C, MIA, 1/26/44 Italy (Anzio), SR Cem. Body recovered 1/26/44 by YMS 34 & buried at sea same day. Next of kin: Mrs. R. A. Abbott, La Molle, IL.

ABEL, ----------. d. 2004 upstate NY. Information provided by Sam Kweskin.

ACH, Roger W. b. 10/7/1918 OH. Enl. 7/12/43 Cincinnati, OH. Ser. No. 35872133. Pvt., Co. C, MIA, 8/29/44 Briançon, France. Reported POW 9/20/44. Stalag 7A Moosburg, Bavaria. Liberated 7/18/45. d. Jan. 1978.

ACKERMAN, Richard E. b. 8/31/1924 PA. Enl. 7/27/43 Allentown, PA. Ser. No. 33830201. Pfc., Co. A, 5/8/45 Innsbruck, Austria. d. 3/5/1991 PA.

ACKLE, Nicholas J. b. 1911 MS. Hinds Co., MS. Enl. 9/24/42 Camp Shelby, MS. Ser. No. 34427019. Pvt. Co. D, 10/14/42 Camp Gordon, GA.

ADAIR, Kenneth C. b. 1924 PA. Res. Ephrate, Lancaster Co., PA. Enl. 2/11/43 Harrisburg, PA. Ser. No. 33500566. Pfc., HQ & HQ Co., LST 422 Survivor, 1/26/44 Italy (Anzio) – Purple Heart. Reported safe on 1/30/44 Morning Report. Pfc., HQ Co., 5/8/45 Innsbruck, Austria. Re-entered service 1950-51. Res. Adamstown, PA May 1954. Employee, Textile Mill, Reading, PA.

ADAMS, Herman E. b. 4/12/1925 GA. Res. Chatooga Co., GA. Enl. 8/6/43 Ft. McPherson, Atlanta, GA. Ser. No. 34826806. Pfc., Co. D, promo. T/5 (temp.), 11/1/44. T/5, Co. A, 5/8/45 Innsbruck, Austria. Res. Trion, GA May 1954. U.S. Navy, Cannes, France 1954. d. 1/23/2001 Summerville, GA.

ADAMS, John H. B. 1917 PA. Res. Philadelphia, PA. Enl. 3/20/42 Ft. George Meade, MD. Pvt. Ser. No. 33176141. Attached to Co. A 5/28/42 Edgewood Arsenal, MD. Chauffeur. Pfc., HQ & HQ Co., promo. T/5 (temp.), Camp Gordon, GA 8/3/42. T/5 (temp.), HQ & HQ Co. assigned to Post Motor Pool, Camp Gordon, GA Aug. 24, 1942. HQ & HQ Co. May 1943. Left for Sardania 3/11/44 in Daniel Shields diary.

ADAMS, Nelson G. b. 1917 MS. Res. Lowndes Co., MS. Enl. 9/18/42 Camp Shelby, MS. Ser. No. 34425793. Pvt. Co. D, 10/14/42 Camp Gordon, GA.

ADAMSKI [Adamsky], Joseph A. ("Flat Top") b. 1921 WI. Res. South Milwaukee, Milwaukee Co., WI. Enl. 3/10/42 Milwaukee, WI. Pvt., transf. Co. A to Co. B, Camp Gordon, GA 6/15/42. Pfc., (Squad Leader), promo. Cpl. (temp.), Camp Gordon, GA 7/15/42. Sgt. (temp.), promo. S/Sgt. (temp.), Camp Gordon, GA 10/20/42. Promo. 1st/Sgt. (temp.), Camp Gordon, GA 12/12/42. 1st Sgt., Co. B, sent to hospital (56th Medical, Trapani) 8/5/43. 1st Sgt., Co. B, recommended for Silver Star for action near Ceppagna, Italy 11/13/43. 1st Sgt., Co. B, WIA, 12/8/43 San Pietro, Italy – Purple Heart with Oak Leaf Cluster. 1st Sgt., Co. B on May 25, 1945 roster.

ADAMSON, Roscoe D. b. 1924 IN. Res. Lawrence Co., IN. Enl. 3/31/43 Ft. Benjamin Harrison, IN. Ser. No. 35700242. Co. A. Sgt., present at Anzio 1/29/44. HQ Co., MWIA (serious – jeep wreck crossing Neckar River), 4/5/45. Hospitalized. [Steve Vukson, an eyewitness, said he died instantly as his head was crushed by a jeep]. Official casualty list of CWS says d. 5/4/45.

ADDY, Lowell B., Jr. S/Sgt., Co. C. Present as catcher on Co. C ball team 8/4/45. Presented Purple Heart 8/25/45.

ADKINSON, Eugene. b. 1921 AL. Res. Barbour Co., AL. Enl. 9/19/42 Ft. McClellan, AL. Ser. No. 34391878. Pvt., Co. D, Camp Gordon, GA 10/8/42.

AFRICANO, Sullivan John. b. 3/8/1918 [1919 on Ser. No.] WV. Riverside Junior H. S. Catholic. Res. Granville, Monongalia Co., WV. Enl. 12/16 [or 23]/42 Clarksburg, WV. Camp Sibert, AL Pvt., Co. C, Camp Gordon, GA 4/10/43. Ser. No. 35746254. Africa. Sicily. Pvt., Co. C, MIA, 1/26/44 Italy (Anzio), SR Cem.

AGRANOFF, Abraham. b. 10/18/1917 NY. Res. Kings Co., NY. Enl. 6/20/42 Ft. Jay, Governors Island, NY. Ser. No. 32357299. Pvt., Co. A, Camp Gordon, GA 7/28/42. Transf. Co. C, Camp Gordon, GA, 12/16/42. d. Mar. 1980 NY.

AGURKIS, Albert S. b. 12/25/1908 PA. Enl. 12/11/42 Wilkes Barre, PA. Ser. No. 33457832. Pvt., Co. C, Camp Gordon, GA 4/2/43. Pvt., Co. C, LST 422 Survivor, 1/26/44 Italy (Anzio). Rescued by USS Pilot. d. 3/21/1988 Trenton, NJ.

AKEN, ----------. Pvt., assigned Co. D, 2/10/44.

AKERLY, Edgar Lorrain. Johnson, KS. Ser. No. 32390292. Pvt., Co. B, Camp Gordon, GA 7/28/42. Pfc, Co. B, transf. OCS, Signal Corps, Ft. Monmouth, NJ, Jan. 1943. Graduated Signal Officer Candidate School, Class 1943, 848th Unit.

ALBERT, Jacob. b. 3/17/1923 NY. Res. Suffolk Co., NY. Enl. 2/8/43 New York City, NY. Ser. No. 32796796. Mortar Gunner Heavy. Pvt., Co. A, WIA (light injure/wound – shrapnel in the chest), 3/8 or 9/44 Anzio, Italy. Pvt., Co A, on *LST 690* 8/9/44. Pfc., Co. B, 5/8/45 Innsbruck, Austria. Sicily, Naples-Foggia, Rome-Arno, Southern France, Rhineland, and Central Europe. d. 1/14/1994 Lindenhurst, Suffolk Co., NY.

ALBRECHT, Floyd W. Waterloo, IA. T/5, served from 1941-1945, member 951st. Field Artillery Service Battery. Pfc., Co. C, promo. Corp. (temp.) 9/15/45.

ALDERSON, Edward R. b. 1903 MS. Res. Tunica Co., MS. Enl. 9/23/42 Camp Shelby, MS. Ser. No. 34426920. Pvt. Co. D, 10/14/42 Camp Gordon, GA.

ALDRIDGE, Ervin C. b. 1912 MS. Res. Union Co., MS. Enl. Camp Shelby, MS. Ser. No. 34426830. Pvt. Co. D, 10/14/42 Camp Gordon, GA. Pfc., Co. D, KIA, 1/26/44, Italy (Anzio)

ALEXANDER, John E., Jr. Res. MI. 2nd Lt. Co. C, LST 422 Survivor, 1/26/44 Italy (Anzio). 1st. Lt. (Field Artillery), MIA, 8/29/44, Briançon, France. Ser. No. 01175922. POW Oflag 64 or 21B Schubin. Moved to Poland. Liberated 5/19/45.

ALEXANDER, Peter ("Doc"). b. 1923 NY. Enl. 9/22/42 Philadelphia, PA. Ser. No. 33335504. Pvt., Co. B, Camp Gordon, GA 10/9/42. Pvt., Co. B, assigned Med. Det., Camp Gordon, GA 11/14/42. Transf. Co. B, Camp Gordon, GA 11/17/42. Pfc., Co. B, 5/8/45 Innsbruck, Austria.

ALEXANDER, Peter. Pfc., Med. Det., 5/8/45 Innsbruck, Austria. [probably same as Peter "Doc" Alexander].

ALLEM, ----------, KIA, 1/26/44, Italy (Anzio), NFR. [Probably same as Paul H. Allen].

ALLEN, Elmore T. Pvt., HQ & HQ Co., Camp Gordon, GA 10/7/42.

ALLEN, Paul H. b. 1921 MS. Res. Hinds Co., MS. Enl. 9/24/42 Camp Shelby, MS. Ser. No. 34427055. Pvt. Co. D, 10/14/42 Camp Gordon, GA. Pfc., Co. D, MIA, 1/26/44, Italy (Anzio) SR Cem. Body recovered 1/26/44 by YMS 34 & buried at sea same day. Next of kin: Ella C. Allen, Jackson, MS.

ALLEN, Robert H. b. 1920 TN. Res. Jackson Co., TN. Enl. 9/16/42 Ft. Oglethorpe, GA. Ser. No. 34371144. Assigned from HQ 2nd Replacement Depot 11/17/44 as Pfc., Co. D.

ALLEN, Walter W. Pfc., Co. A, 5/8/45 Innsbruck, Austria.

ALLINSON, Albert B. ("Al"). b. 8/27/1897 NJ. Res. Camden Co., NJ. Enl. 7/9/42 Camden, NJ. Ser. No. 32271746. Pvt., Co. A, Camp Gordon, GA 7/28/42. Pfc. Co. A, transf. Co. B, Camp Gordon, GA, 12/16/42. Res. Fairview, NJ. d. Mar. 1966 Glendora, Camden, NJ.

ALLINSON, Alfred E., Jr. b. 1910 NY. Enl. 2/17/42 Buffalo, NY. Ser. No. 12055918. Pvt. Attached to Co. F 5/28/42 Edgewood Arsenal, MD. Mechanic Auto (Pvt.). Pfc., HQ & HQ Co., (Garage), promo. T/5 (temp.), Camp Gordon, GA 7/15/42. T/5 (temp.), HQ & HQ Co., promo. T/4 (temp.), Camp Gordon, GA 9/10/42. HQ & HQ Co. May 1943. Pfc., Co. C, 6/22/45 Innsbruck, Austria.

ALTSCHULER, Jack b. 1923 NY. Res. Bronx, NY. Enl. 7/9/42 Ft. Jay, Governor's Island, NY. Ser. No.32402280. Pvt., Co. A, Camp Gordon, GA 7/28/42. Pvt., Co. A, Camp Gordon, GA 10/20/42. In Motor Pool, Camp Gordon, GA Nov. 1942. Pvt., Co. D, MIA, 1/26/44, Italy (Anzio) SR Cem.

ANDEEN, Milford E. b. 11/17/1909 IL. Mentioned in a 1956 issue of Muzzleblasts. d. 6/22/1991 Venice, Sarasota Co., FL.

ANDERSON, Frank G. b. 1924 OH. Res. Newton Falls, Trumbull Co., OH. Enl. 4/15/43 Akron, OH. Ser. No. 35610637. T/5, HQ & HQ Co., WIA (light-left shoulder), 3/2/44 Italy – Purple Heart. Not hospitalized. T/5, HQ Co., 5/8/45 Innsbruck, Austria. Res. Lakeland, FL 1970.

ANDERSON, John E. b. 11/20/1920 Campbell Co., TN. Grew up at Oswego, TN. Oswego Grade School. Jellico High School. Champion marble player. Played basketball. Played harmonica. Caddy at Jellico Golf Club. Worked on family farm. Trapped fish & furs and sold them. CCC Camp #CC4-324236 1/4/40-6/13/41. Youth Worker Class B. Res. Campbell Co., TN. Enl. 9/18/42 Ft. Oglethorpe, GA. Ser. No. 34371843. Pvt., HQ & HQ Co., Camp Gordon, GA 10/7/42. Pvt., HQ Co., assigned Med. Det., Camp Gordon, GA 11/14/42. Medical Corps. Pvt. Co. D, KIA, 1/26/44, Italy (Anzio), SR Cem.

ANDERSON, Truman F. Pvt., Co. C, Camp Gordon, GA 10/8/42.

ANDERSON, Vincent C. b. 1918 MI. Res. Iron Co., MI. Enl. 3/20/42 Marquette, MI. Ser. No. 36195345. Pvt. Attached to Co. I 5/28/42 Edgewood Arsenal, MD. Instrument Sgt. (Sgt.). Cpl. (temp.), Co. B, promo. Sgt. (temp.), Camp Gordon, GA 11/4/42. HQ & HQ Co. May 1943. Sgt., Co. A, on LST 690 8/9/44. Sgt., Co. A, 5/8/45 Innsbruck, Austria.

ANDERSON, Wayne W. b. 1913. Res. Vigo Co., IN. Enl. 3/6/42 Ft. Benjamin Harrison, IN. Ser. No. 35041176. Pvt. Attached to Co. C 5/28/42 Edgewood Arsenal, MD. Auto Rifleman (Pvt.). Pvt., Co. B, transf. Co. C, Camp Gordon, GA 6/15/42. Pfc., Co. C, (Squad Leader), promo. Cpl. (temp.), Camp Gordon, GA 7/15/42. Cpl. (temp.), Co. C, promo. Sgt. (temp.), Camp Gordon, GA 9/3/42. Transf. HQ & HQ Co., Camp Gordon, GA 11/14/42. Sgt., Co. C, KIA, 11/13/43 Italy.

ANGELONE, Rocco A. b. 2/26/1921 PA. Enl. 9/22/42 Philadelphia, PA. Ser. No. 33335452. Pvt., Co. B, Camp Gordon, GA 10/9/42. Pvt., Humor Editor, Smokescreen, Camp Gordon, GA Nov. 1942. Pfc., Co. B, sent to hospital 7/31/43 Salemi, Sicily. d. 7/14/1990 Philadelphia, PA.

ARDREY, Albert L. b. 9/5/1916 PA. Enl. 12/12/42 Altoona, PA. Ser. No. 33567172. Pvt., Co. D, Camp Gordon, GA 4/10/43. d. 6/29/1997 Altoona, Blair Co., PA.

AREA, William R. Pfc., Co. C. Purple Heart & Oak Leaf Cluster, Sept., 1945.

ARMSTRONG, Harold L. b. 1909 OH. Res. Perry Co., IN. Enl. 3/2/42 Ft. Benjamin Harrison, IN. Ser. No. 35039469. Pvt. attached to Co. H 5/28/42 Edgewood Arsenal, MD. Supply Sgt. (Sgt.). Pvt., HQ & HQ Co., promo. Cpl. (temp.), Camp Gordon, GA 6/16/42. Cpl. (temp.), (Supply Sgt.), promo. Sgt. (temp.), Camp Gordon, GA 7/15/42. Sgt. (temp.), HQ & HQ Co., promo. S/Sgt. (temp.), Camp Gordon, GA 9/7/42.

ASTROWSKI, James B. Pvt., Co. C, Camp Gordon, GA 4/2/43.

ATKINS, William M. b. 1924 TN. Res. Rhea, TN. Enl. 2/17/43 Ft. Oglethorpe, GA. Ser. No. 34722230. Pvt., Co. D, MIA, 1/26/44, Italy (Anzio) SR Cem.

ATTON, Edward Kirk. b. 1/5/1924 Highland Park, MI. Attended school: Detroit, MI. Enl. 2/4/43. Camp Sibert, Gadson, AL. Embarked for overseas 6/10/43. Arrived at Oran 6/21/43. Joined 83rd CMB just after invasion of Sicily. Assgnd. Co. A. Radio Operator. WIA(left leg-shell fragments), Venafro, Italy 1943. Purple Heart. Pfc., Co, A, on *LST 690* 8/9/44. Served through Italy & Southern France until transf. Replacement Depot, Strasburg, France. Sent to 80th Inf. Div. Res. Grand Rapids, MI 2009.

AUBLE, Louis P. b. 1911 Boone Grove,IN. Pre-war Occupation: Indiana Steel Products Co. & painting and decorating with his father. Res. Valparoiso, IN. Enl. 12/11/42 Indianapolis, IN. Ser. No. 35573759. Pvt., Co. D, Camp Gordon, GA 4/2/43. Pvt., Co. D, MIA, 1/26/44, Italy (Anzio) SR Cem. Next of kin: Lucile Auble, wife.

AYERS, Sim (Simeon) Barton. b. 12/18/1911 GA. Res. Habersham, GA. Enl. 9/11/42 Ft. McPherson, Atlanta, GA. Ser. No. 34442503. Pvt., Co. A, Camp Gordon, GA 10/8/42. Cook in Co. A 11/17/44 photo provided by Lawrence Ertzberger. T/5, Co. A, 5/8/45 Innsbruck, Austria. Res. Clarksville, GA. d. 6/5/1990 FL.

BABEY, Joseph. b. 5/27/1922 CT. Res. Fairfield Co., CT. Enl. 2/5/43 Hartford, CT. Ser. No. 31314337. Pfc., Co. A on *LST 690* 8/9/44. d. 3/18/2007 Milford, CT.

BABJAK, John J. b. 11/23/1912 PA. Res. Philadelphia Co., PA. Enl. 9/22/42 Philadelphia, PA. Ser. No. 335517 (service record gives no middle initial). Pvt., HQ & HQ Co., Camp Gordon, GA 10/9/42. Attended 1954 & 1960 Reunions. d. 8/8/1986 Philadelphia, PA. William Gallagher says name is Bobjak.

BAER, John William. b. 6/6/1923 Bryn Mawr, Montgomery Co., PA [military record says Philadelphia, PA]. William Penn Sr. High School, York, PA. Pre-war Occupation: Milling Machine Operator / Defense Plant. Pasadena College of Theatre Arts. Res. York, PA & Los Angeles Co., CA. Enl. 3/26/43 Harrisburg, PA. Ser. No. 33505467.Departed U.S. For Africa 1/30/44. Arrived Africa 2/9/44. Military Occupation: Computer Fire Director. Joined Co. A, 83rd CMB at Anzio 1944. Rome-Arno. Southern France. Rhineland. Central Europe. Glider Badge. EAME Campaign Medal with 4 Bronze Stars. WW II Victory Medal. Good Conduct Medal. Pfc., Co. A, 5/8/45 Innsbruck, Austria. Appears to have also served with 135th Chemical Mortar Co., Germany. Departed for U.S. 12/3/45. Arrived in U.S. 12/14/45. Dischd. 12/19/45 Indiantown Gap, PA with rank of Corp. Postwar career as movie actor and builder. Appeared in such movies as Arizona Manhunt (1951), Superman and the Mole Men (1951), Saturday's Hero (1951), Indian Uprising (1951), Operation Pacific (1951), Battle at Apache Pass (1952), About Face (1952), Terry and the Pirates / Joe Palooka Story (1952), Down Among the Sheltering Palms (1953), The Mississippi Gambler (1953), Terry and the Pirates and Biff Baker U.S.A. (1953), Above and Beyond (1953), Riding Shotgun (1954), The Miami Story (1954), We're No Angels (1955), City of Shadows (1955), Huk (1956), Guns, Girls, and Gangsters (1958), Tarawa Beachhead (1958), Night of the Blood Beast (1958), Wanted Dead or Alive – Vol. 1 (1959), Fear No More (1961), The Cat Burglar (1961), The Chapman Report (1962), Bikini Paradise (1965), The Beverly Hillbillies: The Big Chicken

(1966), The Late Liz (1971), Mission Impossible: The Question (1973). Composed music for Weekend Pass (1984). Awarded World's Children Humanitarian Award 3/30/2001. d. 1/7/2006 Newhall, Los Angeles Co., CA. Cremated.

BAILEY, Elvin S. b. 1921 TN. Res. Campbell Co., TN. Enl. 9/18/42 Ft., Oglethorpe, GA. Ser. No. 34371849. Pvt., HQ & HQ Co., Camp Gordon, GA 10/7/42. Pfc. WIA (injured in glider crash) 8/15/44 Le Muy, France. Assigned from HQ 2nd Replacement Depot 11/17/44 as Pfc., Co. D. Pfc., Co. A, 5/8/45 Innsbruck, Austria.

BAILEY, Marion E. ("Blackie"). From OH. Cpl., Co. D. WIA four times. Present 10/22/44. Pfc., Bronze Star [Presented 11/20/44]. Pfc., Co. A, 5/8/45 Innsbruck, Austria.

BAILEY, William P. b. 1921 PA. Res. Philadelphia, PA. Enl. 9/22/42 Philadelphia, PA. Ser. No. 33335539. Pvt., Co. A, Camp Gordon, GA 10/9/42. Pfc., Co. A on *LST 690* 8/9/44. Pfc., Co. B, 5/8/45 Innsbruck, Austria. Attended 1954 Reunion. Deceased prior to 1979.

BAIN, Robert R. 2nd Lt., relsd. 259th Inf. & assigned 83rd CMB 8/7/45.

BAKAS, Albert J. b. 1923 IN. Res. Vermillion Co., IN. Enl. 2/8/43 Indianapolis, IN. Ser. No. 35091550. Pfc., Co. A, on *LST 690* 8/9/44. Pfc., HQ Co., 5/8/45 Innsbruck, Austria.

BAKER, John R. ("Bugler"). Pfc., Co. A, 5/8/45 Innsbruck, Austria. Mentioned in May 1954 Directory.

BAKER, John T. Pvt., Co. B, Camp Gordon, GA 4/2/43.

BAKER, Lloyd S., Jr. b. 1921 PA. Res. Westmoreland Co., PA. Enl. 9/25/42 Greensburg, PA. Ser. No. 33294887. Pvt. Co. C, 10/15/42 Camp Gordon GA. In a group photo of Co. C taken 1943 at Amalfi, Italy. T/5, Co. C, 6/22/45 Innsbruck, Austria.

BAKER, Norman L. b. 1917 NC. Res. Henry Co., VA. Enl. 9/21/42 Roanoke, VA. Ser. No. 33213349. Pvt. Co. D, 10/11/42 Camp Gordon GA. Pvt., Co. C correspondent, Smokescreen, Camp Gordon, GA Nov. 1942 & 1/9/43. Pvt., Co. D, WIA (light – shell fragment), 9/10/43 Vietre sul Mare, Italy.

BAKER, Walter A. b. 1922 PA. Res. Montgomery Co., PA. Enl. 12/14/42 Allentown, PA. Ser. No. 33485023. Pvt., HQ & HQ Co., Camp Gordon, GA 3/18/43.

BALDERSON, Clarence B. b. 1918 VA. Res. Lancaster Co., VA. Enl. 12/15/42 Richmond, VA. Pvt., HQ & HQ Co., Camp Gordon, GA 3/18/43. Ser. No. 33519624. Pvt., Co. B, KIA, 12/12/44, Riquewihr, France, EP Cem.

BALDWIN, Robert W. ("Lum") b. 2/14/1921 MS. Res. Benton Co., MS. Enl. 9/23/42 Camp Shelby, MS. Ser. No. 34426902. Pvt. Co. A, 10/14/42 Camp Gordon, GA. Accidentally shot Sgt. Byron Powers while cleaning gun. Pvt., Bronze Star [Presented 11/20/44]. Pfc., Co. B,

5/8/45 Innsbruck, Austria. d. 5/10/1991 Jefferson, Marion Co., TX.

BALLARD, George E. b. 2/5/1919 GA. Res. Laurens Co., GA. Enl. 9/19/42 Ft. McPherson, Atlanta, GA. Ser. No. 34443079. Pvt., Co. D, Camp Gordon, GA 10/9/42. d. 3/14/1990 Dublin, Laurens Co., GA.

BALLARD, Lee R. 2nd. Lt., Co. B, 5/8/45 Innsbruck, Austria. 2nd Lt. Assigned HQ 11th Armored Div. 7/23/45.

BALTZER, Robert R. b. 1920 MI. Res. Mason Co., MI. Enl. 7/14/42 Traverse City, MI. Ser. No. 36185821. Pvt., Co. C, Camp Gordon, GA 4/16/43. Pvt., Co. C, MIA, 1/26/44, Italy (Anzio) SR Cem.

BANAS, Joseph B. b. 9/16/1923. Enl. 4/28/43 Wilkes Barre, PA. Ser. No. 33604426. Pfc., Co. C, 6/22/45 Innsbruck, Austria. d. Apr. 1985 Somerset, NJ.

BARBER, John D. Pvt., Co. A, 5/8/45 Innsbruck, Austria.

BARBER, William H. b. 1909 KY. Res. Jefferson Co., KY. Enl. 3/20/42 Ft. Benjamin Harrison, IN. Pfc., Co. C, (Squad Leader), promo. Cpl. (temp.), Camp Gordon, GA 7/15/42. Ser. No. 35044066. Sgt. (temp.), Co. C, promo. S/Sgt. (temp.), Camp Gordon, GA 8/17/42. Transf. Co. A, Camp Gordon, GA, 12/16/42. Promo. 1st Sgt. 7/13/43. Promoted 2nd. Lt. Nov. 1943. Rotation orders Nov. 1943.

BARBOUR, George C. b. 1908 VA. Res. Cumberland Co., NC. Enl. 9/21/42 Roanoke, VA. Ser. No. 33213313. Pvt., Co. A, Camp Gordon, GA. 10/11/42.

BARCLAY, Kenneth B. ("Alfalfa"). b. 8/9/1922 PA. Iselin Public School & Elders Ridge Vocational School. Pre-war Occupation: Rochester-Pittsburgh Coal Co. Enl. Oct. 1942. Res. PA. Ser. No. 13084660. Pvt., Co. D, Camp Gordon, GA 10/9/42. Mentioned in the 2/21/43 entry at Camp Gordon, GA in the Daniel Shields diary. WIA Sicily 1943. Hospitalized 5 months. Pvt., Co. D, MIA, 1/26/44, Italy (Anzio). Body later found off the coast of Anzio. SR Cem. Next of kin: James M. Barclay, father.

BARILE, Bernard J. b. 1922 NY. Res. Schuyler, NY. Enl. 2/5/43 Syracuse, NY. Ser. No. 32837464. Pvt., Co. D, KIA, 1/26/44, Italy (Anzio) SR Cem.

BARKER, Charles D. Pfc., Co. C, 6/22/45 Innsbruck, Austria.

BARNES, Cassie H. b. 1921 MS. Res. Marion Co., MS. Enl. 9/21/42 Camp Shelby, MS. Ser. No. 34426309. Pvt. Co. D, 10/14/42 Camp Gordon, GA. Pvt. Co. D. Mentioned in the 11/14/42 issue of Smoke Screen.

BARNES, George H. b. 1921 MS. Res. Jones Co., MS. Enl. 9/21/42 Camp Shelby, MS. Ser. No. 34426240. Pvt. Co. D, 10/14/42 Camp Gordon, GA.

BARNHEART, Victor P. b. 4/4/1921 WV. Probably born in Cabell Co., WV as his parents reside there in 1920 census. Res. Baltimore, MD 1930 census. Enl. 9/28/42 Baltimore, MD. Ser. No. 13103958. Pvt., Co. B, Camp Gordon, GA 10/11/42. Pvt., Co. B, WIA (light – enemy shell fire), 4/12 or 13/44 Anzio, Italy. Returned to duty 6/10/44. Pfc., Co. B, WIA (serious), 12/12/44, Riquewihr, France. d. 1/28/2003 Fallston, Hartford Co., MD.

BARNETT, Robert G. b. 1920 MS. Res. Sunflower Co., MS. Enl. 9/23/42 Camp Shelby, MS. Ser. No. 34426705. Pvt. Co. D, 10/14/42 Camp Gordon, GA. Present Co. D, Camp Gordon, GA, 1/9/43.

BARRETT, George Alloysius. b. 2/19/1919 Philadelphia, PA. Res. Philadelphia, PA. Ser. No. 13124689. Pvt., Co. B, Camp Gordon, GA 10/9/42. Camp Gordon, GA. Pfc., WIA (light head – shell burst), 12/15/44 France. Pfc., Co. B, 5/8/45 Innsbruck, Austria. Re-enl. 9/13/46 at Philadelphia, PA as Pfc., CWS, for Hawaiian Dept. Res. Philadelphia, PA May 1954. Philadelphia Co. Council, VFW. Res. Philadelphia, PA 2006. d. 4/6/2007 Philadelphia, PA. Bur. S.S. Peter & Paul Cem., Philadelphia, PA.

BARRETT, George I. b. 3/20/1904 VA. Res. Westmoreland Co., VA. Enl. 9/19/42 Richmond, VA. Ser. No. 33225707. Pvt., Co. A, Camp Gordon, GA. 10/11/42. d. Dec. 1974, Washington, DC.

BARRETT, William E. b. 1922 PA. Res. Luzerne Co., PA. Enl. 10/5/42 Wilkes Barre, PA. Ser. No. 13116743. Pvt., HQ & HQ Co., Camp Gordon, GA 10/9/42. Pvt., Co. B, sick in Salemi & sent to hospital (56th Medical, Salemi) 8/6/43. Returned to duty 8/12/43. Pvt., Co. B, KIA (enemy 240mm shell), 2/18/44, Anzio, Italy.

BARTMAN, Abraham. b. 9/9/1912 Romania. Res. Kings Co., NY. Enl. 7/7/42 Ft. Jay, Governors Island, NY. Ser. No. 32406535. Pvt., Co. D, Camp Gordon, GA 7/28/42. Pvt., Co. D, transf. Co. C, Camp Gordon, GA 11/17/42. Pfc., promo. Cpl. (temp.), Camp Gordon, GA 12/15/42. d. Aug. 1982 Fresh Meadows, Queens Co., NY.

BASH, Nicholas P. b. 9/28/1914 PA. Enl. 3/21/41 Kalamazoo, MI. Ser. No. 36153144. 1st. Lt., Co. A, 5/8/45 Innsbruck, Austria. Assigned 132nd Chem. Mortar Co. 7/19/45. Practiced psychiatry for many years in Wilmington, DE & PA. d. Green Valley, Prima Co., AZ 3/29//2005.

BASSET, Gilbert W. b. MI. Res. Essex Co., NJ. Enl. 7/5/43 Newark, NJ. Ser. No. 42002017. Cpl., Co. C, present at Briançon, France 8/29/44. Cpl., Co. C, 6/22/45 Innsbruck, Austria.

BATTLES, James E. b. 2/14/1901 AL. Res. Etowah Co., AL. Enl. 9/16/42 Ft. McClellan, AL. Ser. No. 34391420. Pvt., Co. A, Camp Gordon, GA 10/8/42. Transf. Co. D, Camp Gordon, GA, 12/16/42. d. 11/15/1987 Gadsden, Etowah Co., AL.

BATTON, Orlando W. b. 2/21/1922 VA. Res. Baltimore City Co., MD. Enl. 12/11/42 Baltimore, MD. Ser. No. 33388655. Pvt., Co. A, Camp Gordon, GA 4/2/43. d. Jan. 1986 Dundalk, Baltimore Co., MD.

BAUCUM, Oree. b. 7/28/1920 MS. Res. Jones Co., MS. Enl. 9/21/42 Camp Shelby, MS. Ser. No. 34426345. Pvt. Co. D, 10/14/42 Camp Gordon, GA. d. 7/22/2008 Laurel, Jones Co., MS.

BAUER, Carl J. Res. MI. Ser. No. 36599129. Pfc., HQ Co., MIA, 1/26/44, Italy (Anzio) SR Cem.

BAUM, Robert A. b. 1915 NJ. Res. Hudson Co., NJ. Ser. No. 32389893. Pvt., Co. B, Camp Gordon, GA 7/28/42. Pvt., Co. B, Camp Gordon, GA 10/20/42. T/5, re-enl. 10/27/45, Corps of Military Police, Hawaiian Dept.

BAUN, Henry. Pvt. Co. D, WIA (light injure – truck over-turned on road between Pozzuoli & Minturno), Italy 3/25 or 26/44.

BAUS, ----------. In a group photo provided by Sam Kweskin.

BAXTER, Fletcher C. b. 1921 MS. Res. Itawamba Co., MS. Enl. 9/23/42 Camp Shelby, MS. Ser. No. 34426771. Pvt. Co. D, 10/14/42 Camp Gordon, GA. Pfc., Co. D, MIA, 1/26/44, Italy (Anzio) SR Cem.

BEACH, Howell Floyd., Jr. ("Pete"). b. ca. 1923. T/5, HQ Co., 5/8/45 Innsbruck, Austria. Res. Waterboro, SC May 1954. Attended 1954 & 1958 Reunions as Res. Waterboro, SC. d. Nov. 1958 (heart attack).

BEALL, Leroy A. b. 1903 MD. Res. Montgomery Co., MD. Enl. 9/21/42 Baltimore, MD. Ser. No. 33376452. Pvt., Co. A, Camp Gordon, GA. 10/11/42. Transf. Co. C, Camp Gordon, GA, 12/16/42.

BEARY, Melvin A. Pfc., Co. C, 6/22/45 Innsbruck, Austria.

BEASLEY, James Otis. b. 9/7/1909 Wells, TX. Wells High School. Grad. Texas A&M (ROTC scholarship) 1932. Ph.D. Harvard Graduate School ca. 1936. Made trip to England to study genetics. "His scientific work consisted of developing methods for arresting the mitosis of cotton, thereby allowing the formation of tetraploids and the development of fertile tetraploids and techniques for hybridizing Asiatic and American cottons resulting in a longer and better fiber length." Continued with genetics work at Texas A&M until the war. Present at Edgewood Arsenal Chemical School 8/24/42 & 9/19/42. 1st Lt., CWS, assigned Co. D, Camp Gordon, GA 10/23/42. Transf. HQ & HQ Co., Camp Gordon, GA 11/26/42. Asst. Supply Officer, sent to Edgewood Arsenal Command & Staff course, 1/9/43. Commanded 1st Platoon, Co. D, Sicily Invasion 1943. 1st Lt., Co. D, KIA , 9/12/43 Vietre sul Mare, Italy. Bur. Avellino. Capt. Ed Pike called him "one of the bravest and most talented men" he had ever known & "a fine man with a fine mind.". Beasley Laboratory for cotton genetics at Texas A & M, College Station, TX is named in his honor. A road is named after him on the base of Ft. Detrick, Frederick, MD chemical warfare military post.

BEASLEY, James T. b. 1913 MS. Res. Union Co., MS. Enl. 9/23/42 Camp Shelby, MS. Ser. No. 34426838. Pvt. Co. D, 10/14/42 Camp Gordon, GA. Pvt., Co. D, MIA, 7/11/43 Gela, Sicily. [also spelled Beasly].

BEASLEY, Tommy D. b. 1920 AR. Res. Hempstead Co., AR. Enl. 8/4/42 Little Rock, AR. Ser. No. 38211261. T/4, HQ Co. promo. S/Sgt. (temp.) 9/15/45.

BEATY, Melvin A. b. 1921 TN. Res. Wilson Co., TN. Enl. 8/17/42 Ft. Oglethorpe, GA. Ser. No. 34371411. Pvt., HQ & HQ Co., Camp Gordon, GA 10/7/42.

BEATY, Melvin L. Pfc. HQ Co., promo. Corp. (temp.) 9/15/45 [probably same man as Melvin A. Beaty]

BEATY, Thomas R. b. 1920 NC. Enl. 7/25/1942 Ft. Jackson, Columbia, SC. Ser. No. 34129766. Pvt., Co. D, Camp Gordon, GA 3/18/43.

BEAVERS, Victor R. b. 5/12/1915 MS. Res. Mize, Smith Co., MS. Enl. 9/21/42 Camp Shelby, MS. Ser. No. 34426314. Pfc., Co. D, LST 422 Survivor, 1/26/44 Italy (Anzio) – Purple Heart. Rescued by USS Pilot. d. Aug. 1986 Jackson, Hinds Co., MS.

BECK, Herbert H. b. 2/29/1904 PA. Res. PA. Enl. 9/25/42 Pittsburgh, PA. Pvt. Co. B, 10/15/42 Camp Gordon GA. d. Oct. 1984 Saxonburg, Butler Co., PA.

BECKER, Robert E. Sgt., Co. C. Purple Heart & Oak Leaf Cluster, Sept., 1945. Promo. S/Sgt. (temp.) 9/15/45.

BEDSORE, ----------. Mentioned in the May 1954 Directory. [Might be a fake name.]

BEISWENGER, Richard A. b. 9/12/1923 PA. Res. Cambria Co., PA. Enl. 2/4/43 Altoona. PA. Ser. No. 33572461. Served as heavy mortar crewman. Pfc., Co. C, 6/22/45 Innsbruck, Austria. Dischgd. 10/21/45. Received Good Conduct Medal, EAME Theater Ribbon with 5 Bronze Stars. Res. Amsbry, PA. d. 9/30/1991 PA.

BELCHER, William L. Pvt. HQ & HQ Co., Camp Gordon, GA 3/18/43. Ser. No. 33527113.

BELEY, Theodore ("Teddy"). b. 1922 PA. Enl. 9/25/42 Pittsburgh, PA. Ser. No. 33305614. Pvt. Co. C, 10/15/42 Camp Gordon GA. Pvt., Co. C, Camp Gordon, GA Nov. 1942. Pfc., Co. C, MIA, 1/26/44, Italy (Anzio) SR Cem.

BELL, Clifton E. b.1912 MS. Res. Union Co., MS. Enl. 9/23/42 Camp Shelby. MS. Ser. No. 34426823. Pvt., Co. D, 10/14/42 Camp Gordon, GA.

BELL, Orville P. b. 1921 MS. Res. Union Co., MS. Enl. 3/23/42 Camp Shelby, MS. Ser. No. 34426861. Pvt. Co. D, 10/14/42 Camp Gordon, GA. Pfc., Co. D, LST 422 Survivor, 1/26/44 Italy (Anzio). Rescued by YMS 69 1/26/44. T/4, HQ Co., 5/8/45 Innsbruck, Austria. Robert Chamblee said Bell was from Saltillo, MS. Res. MA 2009.

BELL, Robert H. b. 1919 MA. Res. Middlesex Co., MA. Enl. 3/4/42 Ft. Devens, MA. Pvt. Ser. No. 31071048. Attached to Co. C 5/28/42 Edgewood Arsenal, MD. Cook (Pvt.). Pfc., Co. B, (Cook), promo. T/5 (temp.), Camp Gordon, GA 7/15/42. T/5 (temp.), Co. B, promo. T/4, Camp Gordon, GA 8/10/42. T/4, Co. B, transf. HQ Co., Camp Gordon, GA 1/25/43. HQ & HQ Co. May 1943. Promo. S/Sgt. (Mechanic/Motor Section), Co. B. S/Sgt., Co. A, on *LST 690* 8/9/44. S/Sgt., Co. B, 5/8/45 Innsbruck, Austria.

BELLOMO, James I. b. 7/6/1910 or 1914 NY. Res. Fairview, Bergen Co., NJ. Enl. 4/8/42 Newark, NJ. Ser. No. 32276469. Pvt., Co. D, Camp Gordon, GA 7/28/42. Pfc., Co. D, (light injure in action), LST 422 Survivor, 1/26/44 Italy (Anzio) – Purple Heart. Returned to duty 2/2/44. Mentioned in the May 1954 Directory. Res. Fairview, NJ 1970. d. Mar. 1971 Cliffside Park, Bergen Co., NJ.

BELLUCCI, Mario R. b. 10/24/1920 NY. Enl. 7/9/42 Ft. Jay, Governors Island, NY. Ser. No. 32402455. Pvt., Co. D, Camp Gordon, GA 7/28/42. d. 12/19/1987 Brooklyn, Kings Co., NY.

BENFORD, James D. b. 1897 MD. Res. Camden Co., NJ. Enl. 7/9/42 Camden, NJ. Ser. No. 32271754. Pvt., Co. A, Camp Gordon, GA 7/28/42. Transf. Co. B, Camp Gordon, GA, 12/16/42.

BENKERT, Harry W. b. 1910 PA. Enl. 9/22/42 Philadephia, PA. Ser. No. 33335643. Pvt., Co. B, Camp Gordon, GA 10/9/42. Present Co. B, Camp Gordon, GA, 1/9/43.

BENNER, Harry R., Jr. b. 1923 PA. Enl. 1/30/43 Allentown, PA. Ser. No. 33489460. Pfc., Co. A, 5/8/45 Innsbruck, Austria.

BENNETT, Carlton A. b. 1917 VA. Enl. 9/21/42 Roanoke, VA. Ser. No. 33213350. Pvt., Co. A, Camp Gordon, GA 10/11/42. Transf. Co. D, Camp Gordon, GA, 12/16/42. Pvt., Co. A transf. HQ Co., Camp Gordon, GA 1/25/43. T/4, HQ Co., MIA, 1/26/44, Italy (Anzio) SR Cem.

BENNETT, Charles A. ("Charlie") T/5, HQ Co., 5/8/45 Innsbruck, Austria. Attended 1958 & 1962 Reunions as Res. Old Greenwich, CT. d. 9/23/1985 PA. Liver & bone cancer.

BENNETT, Howard D. b. 1921 PA. Enl. 9/25/42 Greensburg, PA. Ser. No. 33294855. Pvt. Co. B, 10/15/42 Camp Gordon GA. Pfc., Co. B, 5/8/45 Innsbruck, Austria. Res. Ligonier, PA May 1954. Machine Shop Worker. Attended 1954, 1958, 1960, 1962, & 1966 Reunions as Res. Ligonier, PA.

BENNETT, Mal M. b. 1911 NC. Res. Grainger Co., TN. Enl. 1/6/44 Ft. Oglethorpe, GA. Ser. No. 34922404. Pfc., HQ Co., presented Purple Heart 8/25/45.

BENOIT, Frances H. Pfc., Co. C. Bronze Star & Purple Heart, Sept., 1945.

BENSON, Arlander F. b. 1922 MS. Res. Itawamba Co., MS. Ser. No. 34426733. Pvt. Co. D, 10/14/42 Camp Gordon, GA. Pvt., Co. D, Camp Gordon, GA 12/19/42. Pvt., Co. D, MIA, 1/26/44, Italy (Anzio) SR Cem.

BENSON, Tracey T. b. 1915 PA. Res. Jeanette, Westmoreland Co., PA. Enl. 1/24/42 Pittsburgh. PA. Ser. No. 06851220. Sgt., Co. C, Bronze Star for action 5/8/44 Italy. Sgt., Co. C, WIA 5/9/44 Italy - Purple Heart. Sgt., HQ Co., 5/8/45 Innsbruck, Austria.

BENUSIK, John B. b. 4/3/1923 OH. Res. Cuyahoga Co., OH. Enl. 2/1/43 Cleveland, OH. Ser. No. 35533207. Pfc., Co. A, 5/8/45 Innsbruck, Austria. d. Aug. 1977 OH.

BERCOVICI, Ralph A. [or E.]. b. 1924 Romania. Res. New York Co., NY. Enl. 4/27/43 New York City, NY. Ser. No. 32898153. Pvt., Co. C, WIA (light – enemy mortar shell), 5/8/44 Anzio, Italy.

BERG, John W. Pvt., Co. B, 5/8/45 Innsbruck, Austria.

BERG, Lloyd C. Pfc., Co. C, promo. T/5 (temp.) 9/15/45.

BERNARD, Paul F. b. 7/1/1911 OH. Res. Mercer Co., OH. Enl. 3/11/42 Ft. Hayes, Columbus, OH. Ser. No. 35279082. Pvt. attached to Co. C 5/28/42 Edgewood Arsenal, MD. Gunner (Pvt.). Co. A, transf. July 1944 at reorganization. d. 2/21/1994 Bridgeton, St. Louis, MO.

BERNHARDT, Bernard. b. 9/17/1920 Rochester, NY. Pre-war Occupation: Student: State – Albany, NY. St. Bernadine of Sienna (College), Loudonville, NY. Enl. Nov. 1942 or early 1943. Joined 83rd CMB as a replacement after LST 422 disaster. Pfc., Co. C, 6/22/45 Innsbruck, Austria. Accountant – CPA until 1962. Established The Caring Connection – which seeks out sight-impaired patients. Volunteer for Talking Books for 28 years. Res. Pembroke, FL 2007. d. 3/11/2008 Hollywood, Broward Co., FL.

BERONI, Ernest P. b. 7/3/1919 IL. Res. El Paso Co., CO. Enl. 8/5/42 Pueblo, CO. 54th Chem. Impreg. Co. Ser. No. 37351378. Pvt., attached Co. B, 83rd CMB, Camp Gordon, GA 4/15/43. d. 9/17/2001 Grand Junction, Mesa Co., CO.

BERRY, John O. b. 1913 MO. Res. Los Angeles Co., CA. Enl. 2/14/42 Ft. MacArthur, San Pedro, CA. Ser. No. 39019484. Pvt. Attached to Co. F 5/28/42 Edgewood Arsenal, MD. Supply Sgt. (S/Sgt.). Pvt., Co. B, promo. T/4 (temp.), Camp Gordon, GA 6/16/42. Cpl. (temp.), (Supply), promo. Sgt. (temp.), Camp Gordon, GA 7/15/42. Sgt. (temp.), Co. B, promo. S/Sgt. (temp.), Camp Gordon, GA 9/7/42. S/Sgt., Co. B, arrived Salemi, Sicily from North Africa 8/1/43.

BERRY, Willard L. b. 1924 OR. Res. Coos Co., OR. Enl. 7/8/43 Portland, OR. Ser. No. 39335248. Present Co. B, Camp Gordon, GA 1/9/43. Pfc., Co. B, 5/8/45 Innsbruck, Austria. Attended 1962 Reunion as Res. Portland, OR.

BERRYHILL, Murray H. b. 1915 AL. Res. Monroe Co., MS. Enl. 9/23/42 Camp Shelby, MS. Ser. No. 34426724. Pvt. Co. D, 10/14/42 Camp Gordon, GA. T/5, Co. D, MIA, 1/26/44, Italy (Anzio) SR Cem.

BESSER, Frank C. b. 1921 PA. Enl. 12/22/42 Pittsburgh, PA. Ser. No. 33416573. Pvt., HQ & HQ Co., Camp Gordon, GA 3/18/43. Pvt., Co

A, on *LST 690* 8/9/44. Assigned from HQ, 2nd Replacement Depot 11/17/44 as Pvt., Co. A.

BESTEZ [Bastez], ----------. Co. C. In a group photo provided by Loy Marshall.

BEUN, Henry. Pfc., Co. C, 6/22/45 Innsbruck, Austria.

BIANCHI, Emery J. Pfc. b. 1924 MD. Res. Lawrence Co., PA. Enl. 4/30/43 Pittsburgh, PA. Ser. No. 33685500. Co. A, 5/8/45 Innsbruck, Austria. Res. Bessemer, PA.

BIANCO, John. b. 10/12/1913 MO. Res. St. Louis, MO. Enl. 11/15/43 Jefferson Barracks, MO. Ser. No. 37628776. Pfc., Co. C, 6/22/45 Innsbruck, Austria. Sgt., Co. C. Presented Purple Heart 8/25/45. d. 7/22/1996 Fallon, Saint Charles Co., MO.

BICKEL, Walter H. b. 1923 OH. Res. Hamilton Co., OH. Enl. 2/15/43 Cincinnati, OH. Ser. No. 35789313. Reported MIA 8/29/44 Briançon, France. Returned 8/31/44. Pfc., Co. C, promo. Cpl. (temp.), 11/1/44. Cpl., Co. C, 6/22/45 Innsbruck, Austria.

BIEL, Ralph. b. 1922 Danzig/Germany. Res. NY. Enl. 4/28/43 New York, NY. Ser. No. 32898305. Pvt., Co. C, MIA, 8/29/44 Briançon, France. POW Stalag 7A Moosburg, Bavaria. Liberated 6/22/45.

BIELSKI, Walter A. b. 5/9/1921 Ranshaw, PA. Res. Northumberland Co., PA. Enl. 9/15/42 Harrisburg, PA. Ser. No. 33240953. Pvt., Co. A, Camp Gordon, GA 10/9/42. Survivor LST 422, 1/26/44, Italy (Anzio). T/5 Co. A, 5/8/45 Innsbruck, Austria. Res. Flint, MI for over 50 years, retired from General Motors. d. 6/23/2008 Mountain Manor Nursing & Rehabilation Center, Kulpmont, PA.

BIGGS, William F. Pvt. WIA (injured in glider crash) 8/15/44 Le Muy, France.

BILBOW, Frank E. b. 1924 PA. Res. New Haven Co., CT. Enl. 3/16/43 Hartford, CT. Ser. No. 31328549. Pvt., Co. C, MIA, 8/29/44 Briançon, France. POW 9/24/44. POW Stalag 7A Moosburg, Bavaria. Liberated 5/23/45.

BILLIG, Jack L. b. 1921 PA. Grad. Williamsport High School. Pre-war Occupation: Reading Railroad Co. Res. Lycoming Co., PA. Enl. 9/21/42 Harrisburg, PA. Ser. No. 33240895. Pvt., Co. C, Camp Gordon, GA 10/9/42. Transf. Co. A, Camp Gordon, GA, 12/16/42. Sgt., Co. C, MIA, 1/26/44, Italy (Anzio) SR Cem. Next of kin: Newton Billig, father.

BILLINGTON, Jack E. Pvt., Purple Heart [Presented 11/20/44]. Pfc., Co. C, 6/22/45 Innsbruck, Austria.

BILTON, Arthur W. b. 1921 PA. Enl. 9/22/42 Philadelphia, PA. Ser. No. 33335596. Pvt., Co. D, Camp Gordon, GA 10/9/42. Pvt., Co. D, KIA, 1/26/44, Italy (Anzio) SR Cem. Remains reportedly recovered 6/1/44 near Caglari, Sardania.

BIRDWELL, Clovis. b. 8/24/1923 Red Bowling Springs, Clay Co., TN. Mount Vernon Grammar School. Pre-war Occupation: Farmer's Truck Driver for County & State. Res. Clay Co., TN. Enl. 4/9/43 Ft. Oglethorpe, GA. Ft. Sill, OK 4/9/43 – Aug. 1943. Ft. Leonard Wood, MO. Field Artillery. 8/12/43 – Dec. 1943 75th Division Field Artillery. Ser. No. 34729628. Overseas Embarkation: 1/30/44. Replacement for men lost on LST 422. Pvt., Co. A, on *LST 690* 8/9/44. Truck Driver Light: Drove trucks up to 2 and a half ton capacity. Hauled army personnel and equipment. Cleaned and lubricated vehicle. Made minor road repairs. Checked brakes, lights, and other operating parts. Served in European Theater of Operations. Rome-Arno. Southern France. Central Europe. EAME Theater Ribbon w/4 Bronze Stars. Good Conduct Ribbon. Bronze Arrowhead. Victory Medal. Jeep driver for Lt. Robert Danfield. Sgt. Overseas Departure: 12/3/45. Dischd. 12/19/45 Atterbury, IN. Res. Indianapolis, IN 2009.

BIRT, William G. Pfc., HQ Co., 5/8/45 Innsbruck, Austria.

BISCIOTTI, Albert. b.11/27/1904 PA. Enl. 8/29/42 Philadelphia, PA. Ser. No. 33331092. Pvt., Co. C, Camp Gordon, GA 10/9/42. d. Nov. 1961.

BISER, Caleb E. ("Whitie"). b. 6/10/1917 DE. Enl. 7/27/43 Harrisburg, PA. Ser. No. 335133856. Truck driver Co. B, Epinal France, 10/5/44. Pfc., Co. B, 5/8/45 Innsbruck, Austria. d. Nov. 1977 PA.

BISHOP, Carl A. b. 1920 PA. Res. Philadelphia, PA. Enl. 9/22/42 Philadelphia, PA. Ser. No. 33335474. Pvt., Co. A, Camp Gordon, GA 10/9/42. Guidon Bearer, Co. A, Camp Gordon, GA Feb. 1943. Pfc., Co. A, Silver Star for Gela, Sicily 7/10/43. (presented 9/27/43 in Sicily). Rotated 3/19/44.

BISHOP, Melvin. b. 3/23/1924 Maitland, McDowell Co., WV. Enl. 4/8/43 Huntington, WV. Ser. No. 35657338. Pvt., WIA (light), 8/20/44 Peyrolles, France. Pfc., Co. B, 5/8/45 Innsbruck, Austria. Retired after 44 years with the Celanese Corp. d. 7/1/2003 Lindside, Monroe Co., WV. Bur. Resthaven Mem. Cem., Princeton, Mercer Co., WV.

BLACK, Augustus W. b. 5/3/1904 TN. Res. Davidson Co., TN. Enl. 9/18/42 Ft. Oglethorpe, GA. Ser. No. 34371692. Pvt., HQ & HQ Co., Camp Gordon, GA 10/7/42. d. Jan. 1970, Nashville, Davidson Co., TN.

BLACK, Lloyd W. Pfc., Co. C, 6/22/45 Innsbruck, Austria.

BLACK, William F. b. 1923 TX. Res. Inez, Victoria Co., TX. Enl. 12/3/42 San Antonio, TX. Ser. No. 18231594. Pvt., Co. D, WIA, 3/26/44 Italy – Purple Heart.

BLACKBURN, Clarence L. b. 1913 AL. Res. Franklin Co., AL. Enl. 9/16/42 Ft. McClellan, AL. Ser. No. 34391455. Pvt., Co. B, Camp Gordon, GA 10/8/42.

BLACKMON, James C. Cpl., Co. A, 5/8/45 Innsbruck, Austria.

BLADES, Homer R. b. 1/25/1909 MO. Res New Madrid Co., MO. Enl. 12/10/42 Jefferson Barracks, MO. Ser. No. 37402900. Pvt., Co. C, Camp Gordon, GA 4/2/43. d. Nov. 1974 Malden, Dunklin Co., MO.

BLAMICK, Robert S. b. 10/31/1922, Port View, PA. Res. Allegheny Co., PA. Prewar occupation: U.S. Steel, McKeesport, PA. Railroad worker/electrician. Enl. 5/1/43 Pittsburgh, PA. Ser. No. 33685754. Joined the 83rd at Pozzuoli, Italy. Pfc., HQ Co., 5/8/45 Innsbruck, Austria. Rome-Arno, Southern France, Rhineland, and Central Europe. Good Conduct Medal, EAME Theater Ribbon with 4 Bronze Stars, and WWII Victory Medal. Postwar occupation: Railroad/Assistant Trainmaster. Res. McKeesport, PA, 2009.

BLANK, Dale Carlton. b. 11/27/1924 PA. Enl. 4/1/43. Res. PA. Ser. No. 33756843. Seven months basic artillery training. Africa. Mine sapping & demolition training. Assigned 83rd CMB at Cassino, Italy. Anzio. Pvt., Co, C (Lt. James Doyle's Platoon/Tony Defeo's Squad). MIA & WIA (bullet), 8/29/44 Briançon, France. POW 9/24/44. POW Turin, Italy to prison in Milan. Later transf. Munich (Stalag 7A). Liberated 5/24/45. Purple Heart. POW Medal. Returned home July 1945. Left service Dec. 1945. Owned own store & made horseshoes. Res. Rancho Mirage, CA 2004. Res. Cathedral City, CA 2005. Appeared in a History Channel documentary. d. 11/8/2005 Loma Linda, CA.

BLASZ, Edward. b. 11/10/1919 NY. Res. Erie Co., NY. Enl. 3/5/42 Ft. Niagara, Youngstown, NY. Ser. No. 32251972. Pvt. Attached to Co. B 5/28/42 Edgewood Arsenal, MD. Cook (Pvt.). Pfc., Co. A, (Cook), promo. T/5 (temp.), Camp Gordon, GA 7/15/42. S/Sgt., WIA (light), 2/14/45 France. Res. Eden, NY May 1954. Employee, Tennessee Transmission Co. Attended 1954 & 1962 Reunions as Res. Eden, NY. d. 8/28/1995 Eden, Erie Co., NY [also spelled Blatz].

BLAUT, Clarence J., Sr. ("Sailor") b. 3/19/1921 Bernwood, NY. Res. Bergen Co., NJ. Enl. 7/9/42 Newark, NJ. Ser. No. 32390467. Pvt., Co. C, Camp Gordon, GA 7/28/42. Pfc., Co. C transf. Motor Pool, Camp Gordon , GA 1/26/43. T/5, Co. C, on June 22, 1945 roster. Bronze Star. Carpenter. Res. Barryville, NJ. d. 4/28/2001 Hackensack Med. Center. Bur. Parish Cem., St. Anthony's Church, Yulan, NY.

BLAYLOCK, Thomas H. b. 8/23/1909 MS. Res. Monroe Co., MS. Enl. 9/23/42 Camp Shelby, MS. Ser. No. 34426922. Pvt. Co. D, 10/14/42 Camp Gordon, GA. d. May 1983 Eupora, Webster Co., MS.

BLOOMBERG, ----------. Appears in a photo in a Charlie Lowry photo album, probably Co. D.

BLOUNT, James G. b. 1920 MS. Res. LaFayette Co., MS. Enl. 9/22/42 Camp Shelby, MS. Ser. No. 34426535. Pvt. Co. C, 10/14/42 Camp Gordon, GA. Pvt., Co. C, transf. Med. Det., Camp Gordon, GA 11/17/42. Pfc., Med. Det. correspondent, Smokescreen, Camp Gordon, GA Feb. 1943. T/5, Med. Det., MIA, 1/26/44, Italy (Anzio) SR Cem. [Middle initial also given as D.]

BLUE, Maxwell L. b. 1915 NC. Res. Moore Co., NC. Enl. 10/19/40 Ft. Bragg, NC. Pvt., Quartermaster Corp. Ser. No. 14028645. Pvt., Co. A, WIA (light injure), 1/26/44 Italy (Anzio).

BLUNT, James G. T/5, MIA, 1/26/44, Italy (Anzio) [probably same as James G. Blount].

BLYSTONE, Leonard G. ("Bly"). Ser. No. 38430490. Fairfield, TX. Pfc., Co. D, LST 422 Survivor, 1/26/44 Italy (Anzio) – Purple Heart. Pfc., Bronze Star [Presented 11/20/44]. Cpl., MWIA (serious – defective shell aerial burst), 2/17/45, France (Alsace). Died in hospital. EP Cem.

BOBKER, Howard. b. 2/14/1925 NJ. Res. Essex Co., NJ. Enl. 5/15/43 Newark, NJ. Ser. No. 32922130. Cpl., Co. A, 5/8/45 Innsbruck, Austria. Postwar res. Newark, NJ. Auto Supply Business, NJ. Attended 1954 Reunion. d. 3/31/1992 Short Hills, Essex Co., NY.

BOCELLA, Eugene R. b. 1905 Italy or San Marion. Res. Philadelphia, PA. Enl. 10/31/42 Philadelphia, PA. Ser. 33343797. Pfc., LST 422 Survivor, 1/26/44 (Anzio), Italy. Rescued by YMS 226 and misidentified as member of Royal Navy.

BOCKMAN, Fredrik M. b. 1921. Enl. 2/11/43 Tacoma, WA. Ser. No. 39200501. Pvt., Co. D, WIA (enemy shell - serious), 9/16/43 Vietre sul Mare, Italy. Evacuated to the U.S. Six months in hospital. Resident Nome, AK 2009.

BOCOCK, James W. b. 1900 VA. Res. Henry Co., VA. Enl. 9/21/42 Roanoke, VA. Ser. No. 33213362. Pvt., Co. A, Camp Gordon, GA 10/11/42. Transf. Co. C, Camp Gordon, GA, 12/16/42.

BODUCK, Frank. Pvt., Co. A, WIA (light – enemy shell burst), 3/30/44 Anzio, Italy. Pfc., Co. A, on LST 690 8/9/44. Cpl., Co. B, 5/8/45 Innsbruck, Austria.

BOEHMER, Stephen J. b. 1923 MO. Res. Osage Co., MO. Enl. 2/18/43 Jefferson Barracks, MO. Ser. No. 37602741. Pvt., Co. D, KIA, 1/26/44, Italy (Anzio).

BOEHN, Robert O. b. 1922 IL. Res. Lake Co., IL. Enl. 10/23/43 Chicago, IL. Ser. No. 16153214. Pvt. Co. A 8/4/45.

BOETTCHER, Norman H. b. 1916 IL. Res. Macoupin Co., IL. Enl. 12/4/42 Peoria, IL. Ser. No. 36438466. Pvt., Co. B, Camp Gordon, GA 4/2/43. Pvt., Co. B, sent to hospital (56th Medical, Trapani) 8/5/43. Returned to duty 8/14/43. Pfc., Co. B, 5/8/45 Innsbruck, Austria.

BOLAM, Howard C., Jr. ("Howdy"). b. 11/29/1916 PA. Enl. 9/24/42 Pittsburgh, PA. Ser. No. 33305642. Pvt. Co. D, 10/15/42 Camp Gordon GA. Present at Camp Gordon, Pvt., Co. D. mentioned in the 12/12/42 issue of Smokescreen. Attended 1970 Reunion. [Also spelled Belam]. d. 1/10/1994 Butler Co., PA.

BOLTON, Thomas M. b. TX. Res. San Francisco, CA. 2nd Lt., Co. A, Camp Gordon, GA, 6/12/42. Transf. Co. A to Co. C, Camp Gordon, GA 7/27/42. Transf. Co. A, Camp Gordon, GA 10/1/42. Promo. 1st Lt., Camp Gordon, GA Nov. 1942. In hospital with a bad knee [not a wound] 1/2/44. Present in Naples with bad knee 5/21/44.

BOLTZ, Rupert W. b. 1918 TX. Res. Victoria Co., TX. Enl. 3/15/42 Ft. Sam Houston, TX. Ser. No. 38093070. Pfc., Co. B, (Gen. Mech.), promo. T/5 (temp.), Camp Gordon, GA 7/15/42. Sgt., Co. B 5/8/45 Innsbruck, Austria.

BONADY, Anthony T. b. 1921 PA. Enl. 9/21/42 Altoona, PA. Ser. No. 33253613. Pvt., Co. C, Camp Gordon, GA 10/9/42. Pvt., Art Contributor, Smokescreen, Camp Gordon, GA Feb. 1943. Pvt., Co. C, WIA (light – shell fragment), 9/12/43 Maiori, Italy.

BONAREK, John S. b. 3/28/1919 NY. Res. Erie Co., NY. Enl. 2/9/42 Ft. Niagara, Youngstown, NY. Ser. No. 32233403. Pvt. Attached to Co. F 5/28/42 Edgewood Arsenal, MD. Squad Leader (Sgt.). Pfc., Co. A promo. Cpl. (temp.), Camp Gordon, GA 7/27/42. Cpl. (temp.) promo. Sgt. (temp.), Camp Gordon, GA 8/19/42. Sgt. Co. A, transf. Co. D, Camp Gordon, GA, 12/16/42. Sgt., Co. D, Camp Gordon, GA 12/19/42. S/Sgt., Co. A, Silver Star for gallantry at Gela, Sicily 7/10/43. (presented 9/27/43 in Sicily). Rotated 3/19/44. Attended 1966 Reunion. d. 6/19/1988 NY.

BOND, Millard O. b. 5/4/1922 MS. Res. Perkinston, Stone Co., MS. Enl. 10/1/42 Ft. McClellan, AL. Ser. No. 14163364. Pvt., Co. C, Camp Gordon, GA 10/8/42. Pvt., Co. C correspondent, Smokescreen, Camp Gordon, GA Nov. 1942 & 1/9/43. Sgt., Co. C, LST 422 Survivor, 1/26/44 Italy (Anzio) – Purple Heart. d. Feb. 1959 MS.

BONDRA, Joseph E., Jr. b. 2/18/1909 PA. Res. Westmoreland Co., PA. Enl. 11/29/40 Pittsburgh, PA. Ser. No. 33030164. Pfc., Co. A, 5/8/45 Innsbruck, Austria. d. May 1976 PA.

BONSAL, Wilbur F., Jr. b. 12/17/1921 MD. Enl. 9/26/42 Baltimore, MD. Ser. No. 33377215. Pvt. HQ & HQ Co., 10/15/42 Camp Gordon GA. Cpl., HQ Co., 5/8/45 Innsbruck, Austria. d. 3/12/2000 Sykesville, Carroll Co., MD.

BOOKER, Joseph. b. 3/15/1909 IL. Res. Sangamon Co., IL. Enl. 11/30/42 Peoria, IL. Ser. No. 36437932. Pvt., Co. D, Camp Gordon, GA 4/2/43. d. 10/24/1993 Springfield, Sangamon Co., IL.

BOOP, Maynard C. Pvt. WIA (injured in glider crash) 8/15/44 Le Muy, France. Pfc., Co. A, 5/8/45 Innsbruck, Austria.

BORKHUIS, George R. b. 11/3/1912 NY. Res. Bronx, NY. Enl. 3/21/42 Camp Upton, Yaphank, NY. Pvt. Ser. No. 32231292 Attached to Co. I 5/28/42 Edgewood Arsenal, MD. Gunner (Pvt.). Pfc., Co. D (temp.), assigned assistant cook, Co. D, 7/11/42. T/5 (temp.), Camp Gordon, GA Aug. 1, 1942. Promo. T/4 (temp.), Camp Gordon, GA 9/26/42. Apptd. news editor battalion newspaper Camp Gordon, GA, 9/30/42. Mess Sgt., Co. D. T/4, Co. D, LST 422 Survivor, 1/26/44 Italy (Anzio) – Purple Heart.. S/Sgt., HQ Co., 5/8/45 Innsbruck, Austria. Dischd. Sept. 1945. Res. Bronx, NY May 1954. Head of Loan Dept., Bank of the Manhattan Co. Later employed by Foreign Exchange House and an Animal Boarding Kennel. Attended 1954, 1956, 1958, 1960, 1962, & 1966 Reunions as Res. Bronx & Cammack. Res. Duluth, MN 1997. d. 12/24/1999 Duluth, St. Louis Co., MN.

BOROWSKI, Joseph J. b. 1918 MD. Res. Baltimore City Co., MD. Enl. 9/21/42 Baltimore, MD. Ser. No. 33376335. Pvt., Co. A, Camp Gordon, GA 10/11/42. Pvt., Co. A, assigned Med. Det., Camp Gordon, GA 11/23/42. Transf. Co. B, Camp Gordon, GA, 12/16/42. Present at Anzio. Sent to work as a medical aid man for Co. A 3/28/44. Returned 3/31/44. Transf. 83rd CMB to 1984th Engr. Composite Plat.

BORST, Theodore E. b. 12/18/1910 NY. Res. Oneida Co., NY. Enl. 4/17/42 Syracuse, NY. Ser. No. 12073156. 54th Chem. Impreg. Co. Pvt., attached to Co. B, 83rd CMB, Camp Gordon, GA 4/15/43. d. Dec. 1985 Zephyrhills, Pascos Co., FL.

BOSKO, Joseph A. b. 5/7/1920 PA. Res. Camden Co., NJ. Enl. 7/9/42 Camden, NJ. Ser. No. 32271747. Pvt., Co. A, Camp Gordon, GA 7/28/42. Post Motor Pool, Camp Gordon, GA 8/24/42. T/4, Co. A, WIA (light), LST 422 Survivor, 1/26/44 Italy (Anzio). d. 3/15/1995 Clementon, Camden Co., NJ.

BOUTYARD, Frank W. Res. Fredericksburg, VA. Pvt., Co. A, Camp Gordon, GA 10/11/42. Transf. Co. B, Camp Gordon, GA, 12/16/42. Ser. No. 33225483. Pfc., Co. A, (light injure), LST 422 Survivor, 1/26/44 Italy (Anzio) – Purple Heart.

BOVA, Joseph A. ("Joe"). b. 5/25/1924 (1922 on military record), Cleveland, OH. Res. Cuyahoga Co., OH. Enl. 9/25/42 Cleveland, OH. Ser. No. 35513193. Pfc., Co. C, 6/22/45 Innsbruck, Austria. Postwar career in movies and TV, beginning in 1961 with The Young Doctors and others such as Serpico (1973). Television included "Starsky and Hutch", "Kojak", and "Happy Days" as well as "Uncle Joe" Bova on a New York City radio station.

BOWEN, James H. (or N.). Res. TX. Ser. No. 38370609. Pfc., Co. D, MIA, 1/26/44, Italy (Anzio) SR Cem.

BOWES, Marshall C. b. 6/6/1920 IL. Res. La Salle Co., IL. Enl. 3/2/42 Camp Grant, IL. Pvt. Attached to Co. H 5/28/42 Edgewood Arsenal, MD. Gunner (Pvt.). Pvt., Co. D transf. HQ & HQ Co., Camp Gordon, GA 6/15/42. Pfc., HQ & HQ Co., Camp Gordon, GA 8/26/42. Promo. Cpl. (temp.) Camp Gordon, GA 9/23/42. Promo. Sgt. (temp.), Camp Gordon, GA 12/21/42. Pfc., Co. A, 5/8/45 Innsbruck, Austria. Postwar Minister. Res. Ottawa, Illinois May 1954. Attended 1954 & 1956 Reunions. d. Nov. 1986 Rossville, Walker Co., GA.

BOWLES, Andrew J. b. 1907 VA. Enl. 12/15/42 Charlottesville, VA. Ser. No. 33446217. Pvt., Co. A, Camp Gordon, GA 3/18/43.

BOWLES, Jasper G. b. 1916 VA. Res. Bedford Co., VA. Enl. 9/21/42 Roanoke, VA. Ser. No. 33213317. Pvt., Co. A, Camp Gordon, GA 10/11/42.

BOWLES, John W. ("Jack") b. 1917 PA. Enl. 8/25/42 Pittsburgh, PA. Ser. No. 33305518. Pvt. Co. B, 10/15/42 Camp Gordon GA. Present Camp Gordon, GA 1942. Corp., Co. B, MIA, 12/12/44, Riquewihr, France. Attended 1958 Reunion. Res. Pittsburgh, PA.

BOWMAN, ----------. In a group photo provided by Clark Riddle, died during war.

BOYD, Cloyd. b. 8/12/1919 VA. Res. Buchanan Co., VA. Enl. 4/16/41 Roanoke, VA. Ser. No. 33046820. Pvt., HQ & HQ Co., Camp Gordon, GA 3/18/43. Front line foot soldier. Res. Raven, VA. d. 1/30/2002 Buchanan, VA.

BOYD, John L. Entered service at age 31. Res. OR. Attended OCS. 2nd Lt., Co. C, MIA, 8/29/44, Briançon, France. Returned to duty 9/7/44. Lt., Co. C, WIA (superficial – shrapnel), 10/13/44 near Grandvillers, France-Purple Heart. 1st. Lt., Co. C, 6/22/45 Innsbruck, Austria. Assigned 135th Chem. Mortar Co. 7/19/45. American Campaign Medal, WWII Victory Medal, EAME w/Bronze Arrowhead, 4 Bronze Stars. d. 6/2 or 28/2002.

BOYLAN, Joseph J. b. 1/21/1922 PA. Enl. 12/14/42 Philadelphia, PA. Ser. No. 33475249. Pvt., HQ & HQ Co., Camp Gordon, GA 3/18/43. d. Dec. 1984 Philadelphia, PA.

BOYLE, John J. b. 11/17/1913 PA. Enl. 9/22/42 Philadelphia, PA. Ser. No. 33335571. Pvt., HQ & HQ Co., Camp Gordon, GA 10/9/42. Pvt., HQ Co., assigned Med. Det., Camp Gordon, GA 11/14/42. d. 7/17/1992.

BOYNTON, Leonard W. Assigned to HQ & HQ Co. & designated Battalion Chaplain, Camp Gordon, GA 7/3/42.

BOZEMAN, Ullis. b. 1910 AL. Res. Dade Co., FL. Enl. 4/2/42 Camp Blanding, FL. Ser. No. 34201359. Pvt., Co. C, (light injure in action), LST 422 Survivor, 1/26/44 Italy (Anzio). Returned to duty 2/9/44.

BRADFORD, Thomas A. Pfc., Co. A, 5/8/45 Innsbruck, Austria.

BRAKEFIELD, Ralph J. b. 1923 IN. Res. Montgomery Co., IN. Enl. 3/8/43 Ft. Benjamin Harrison, IN. Ser. No. 35095955. Pvt., WIA (light injure – truck ran off road), 8/17/44 France.

BRANDECKER, Elmer O. b. 1909 PA. Res. Philadelphia, PA. Enl. 9/22/43 Philadelphia, PA. Ser. No. 33335446. Pvt., Co. C, Camp Gordon, GA 10/9/42. Pfc., Co. C, (light injure in action), LST 422 Survivor, 1/26/44 Italy (Anzio) – Purple Heart. Pfc., HQ Co., 5/8/45 Innsbruck, Austria.

BRANN, Norman J. b. 2/4/1925 WA. Res. Whatcom Co., WA. Enl. 4/13/43 Seattle, WA. Ser. No. 39206561. Pvt., Co. C, MIA, 8/29/44 Briançon, France. POW. Liberated 10/22/45. d. 11/15/1992 Burlington, Skagit Co., WA.

BRANNAN [Brennan?], James L. b. 1907 England (?). Enl. 4/12/43 Philadelphia, PA. Ser. No. 33599809. Pfc., HQ & HQ Co., WIA (light – by flak), 1/26/44 Italy (Anzio). Mentioned in the May 1954 Directory.

BRASEL, Robert W. b. 1923 IL. Res. Randolph Co., IL. Enl. 1/18/42 Jefferson Barracks, MO. Ser. No. 17035262. 2nd Lt., Co. B, recommended for Silver Star for advancing 1000 yards into enemy territory to direct mortar fire on 11/11/43. 2nd Lt Co. B, Silver Star – presented 1/19/44.

BRASH, Italo A. b. PA. Aliquippa High School. Catholic. Res. Aliquippa, PA. Enl. 9/26/42 [or 10/10/42] Pittsburgh, PA. Ser. No. 33305760. Pvt. Co. C, 10/15/42 Camp Gordon GA. Pfc., Co. C, MIA, 1/26/44, Italy (Anzio) SR Cem. Purple Heart. Campaign ribbon with four bronze stars. Presidential Unit Citation.

BRASSELL, Harry W. b. 1897 TN. Res. Davidson Co., TN. Enl. 9/18/42 Ft. Oglethorpe, GA. Ser. No. 34371701. Pvt., HQ & HQ Co., Camp Gordon, GA 10/7/42.

BRASSFIELD, James W. b. 1921 MS. Res. Union Co., MS. Enl. 9/23/42 Camp Shelby, MS. Ser. No. 34426886. Pvt. Co. D, Camp Gordon, GA 3/24/43.

BRAUNSTEIN, Max. b. 7/18/1911 NY. Res. King's Co., NY. Enl. 5/2/42 Ft. Jay, Governor's Island, NY. Ser. No. 32330132. Pvt. Attached to Co. G 5/28/42 Edgewood Arsenal, MD. Squad Leader (Sgt.). Pfc., Co. A, promo. Cpl. (temp.), Camp Gordon, GA 8/19/42. Cpl., Camp Gordon, GA 8/28/42. d. May 1971 NY.

BREISCH, Howard W. b. 6/14/1922 PA. Res. Montgomery Co., PA. Enl. 12/14/42 Allentown, PA. Ser. No. 33484976. Pvt., Co. A, Camp Gordon, GA 3/18/43. Pfc., Co. A, on *LST 690* 8/9/44. Pfc., Co. B, 5/8/45 Innsbruck, Austria. d. 5/20/1993 PA.

BREMER, Herbert H. b. 4/16/1906 IN. Res. Marion Co., IN. Enl. 4/21/43 Indianapolis, IN. Ser. No. 35142421. d. 7/10/1999 Kansas City, Platte Co., MO.

BREWER, Luther Mason. b. 1921 MS. Res. Tishumingo Co., MS. Attnd. Tippah Union High School. Enl. 9/23/42 Camp Shelby, MS. Ser. No. 34426880. Pvt. Co. D, 10/14/42 Camp Gordon, GA. Pfc., Co. D, KIA, 1/26/44, Italy (Anzio). Body recovered 1/26/44 by USS YMS 226 and turned over to Graves Registration at Anzio 1/27/44. Next of kin: Jake Brewer, New Albany, MS.

BREWSTER, Thomas A. b. 9/27/1902 VA. Res. Tazewell Co., VA. Enl. 10/3/42 Abingdon, VA. Ser. No. 33214358. Pvt., Co. A, Camp Gordon, GA 10/11/42. Transf. Co. B, Camp Gordon, GA, 12/16/42. d. July 1974 Mountain Home, Washington Co., TN.

BRICKER, Fred W. b. 1900 PA. Enl. 9/22/42 Philadelphia, PA. Ser. No. 33335580. Pvt., Co. B, Camp Gordon, GA 10/9/42. Pvt., Co. B, Camp Gordon, GA Nov. 1942.

BRIDGE, Richard A. b. 1920 PA. Res. Armbrust, PA. Enl. 9/25/42 Greensburg, PA. Ser. No. 33294876. Pvt. Co. D, 10/15/42 Camp Gordon GA. Pvt., Co. D, WIA (shell fragment), 9/25/43, Italy – Purple Heart with Oak Leaf Cluster. Hospitalized. Returned to duty 11/12//43. Pfc., Co. D, MIA, 1/26/44, Italy (Anzio) SR Cem.

BRIDGES, Orie D. b. 6/2/1921 MS. Res. Franklin Co., AL. Enl. 9/16/42 Ft. McClellan, AL. Ser. No. 34391452. Pvt., Co. B, Camp Gordon, GA 10/9/42. d. 7/19/1998 Golden, Itawamba Co., MS.

BRIGGS, Charles R. Pvt. Attached to Co. H 5/28/42 Edgewood Arsenal, MD. Communication Sgt.

BRIGLOVICH, Steve F. b. 1924 OH. Res. Mahoning Co., OH. Enl. 3/19/43 Ft. Hayes, Columbus, OH. Ser. No. 35606319. Pfc., Co. C. Killed 6/21/45.

BRIMM, Robert P. b. 6/25/1912 IL. Enl. 2/18/42 Peoria, IL. Ser. No. 16054095. Pvt. Attached to Co. H 5/28/42 Edgewood Arsenal, MD. Communication Sgt. (T/Sgt.). Pvt., HQ & HQ Co., promo. T/4 (temp.), Camp Gordon, GA 6/16/42. Cpl. (temp.), promo. Sgt. (temp.), Camp Gordon, GA 8/1/42. Sgt. (temp.), HQ Co., promo. S/Sgt. (temp.), Camp Gordon, GA 11/3/42. Promo. T/Sgt. (temp.), Camp Gordon, GA 12/5/42. T/Sgt., distinguished in action 7/10/43 Sicily. 1st. Lt., HQ Co., 5/8/45 Innsbruck, Austria. Assigned to 490th Armored Field Artillery Battalion 7/23/45. Writer of Rounds Away 1945. Attended 1956 Reunion. School teacher IL. d. Oct. 1985 Cedar Falls, Black Hawk Co., IA.

BRINKMAN, Raymond W. b. 1922 PA. Enl. 10/5/42 Philadelphia, PA. Ser. No. 13124668. Pvt., Co. D, Camp Gordon, GA 10/9/42. Malaria during Sicily Invasion, 1943. Pfc., Co. D, KIA, 1/26/44, Italy (Anzio), SR Cem.

BRISTON, John E. b. 1916 IL. Res. Butler Co., PA. Enl. 3/2/42 Pittsburgh, PA. Ser. No. 13058649. Pvt. Attached to Co. B 5/28/42 Edgewood Arsenal, MD. Telephone Lineman (Pvt.). Pfc. Co. A, transf. Co. B, Camp Gordon, GA, 12/16/42. Sgt., rotated home 6/4/44. Present as Asst. Barracks Leader, Indiantown Gap, Grantville, PA, November 1944. Released from service after brother, Paul, was killed.

BRITTEN, Theo V. b. 1919 MI. Res. Kalamazoo Co., MI. Enl. 3/23/42 Kalamazoo, MI. Ser. No. 36195473. Pvt., Co. A, WIA (serious – anti-tank mine), 5/24/44 Anzio, Italy. Hospitalized. Pvt., Co. A, on *LST 690* 8/9/44. [Also listed as Brittain].

BRONSKI, Chester J. b. 7/6/1924 PA. Res. Wayne Co., PA. Enl. 6/16/43 Pittsburgh, PA. Ser. No. 33689618. Pfc., Co. C, 6/22/45 Innsbruck, Austria. d. Mar. 1975 PA.

BROOKS, Frederick L. b. 1921 PA. Enl. 9/21/42 Altoona, PA. Pvt., HQ Co., assigned Med. Det., Camp Gordon, GA 11/14/42. Art Editor, Smokescreen, Camp Gordon, GA Nov. 1942. Ser. No. 33253579. Pvt., HQ & HQ Co., Camp Gordon, GA 10/9/42. In a group photo of Co. C taken 1943 at Amalfi, Italy. Pvt., Co. C, MIA, 1/26/44, Italy (Anzio) SR Cem.

BROWN, "Alabama". Co. D. KIA (exploding mortar barrel) Nov. 1944. Information provided by Sam Kweskin.

BROWN, Alfred J., Jr. ("A.J."). b. 1921 TN. Res. Davidson Co., TN. Enl. 9/18/42 Ft. Oglethorpe, GA. Ser. No. 34371790. Pvt., Co. A,

Camp Gordon, GA 10/7/42. Pfc., Co. A, on *LST 690* 8/9/44. WIA (back) 2/14/44 France. Cpl.,Co. A, 5/8/45 Innsbruck, Austria. Res. Nashville, TN May 1954. Rendering Business. Attended 1956, 1958, 1960, 1962 & 1966 reunions as Res. Nashville, TN. In a 2006 letter from Joyce Berry, daughter of James Glenn Helsel, she stated "A. J. Brown died many years ago."

BROWN, Austin L. b. 1918 MS. Res. Itawamba Co., MS. Enl. 9/23/42 Camp Shelby, MS. Ser. No. 34426761. Pvt. HQ & HQ Co. 10/14/42 Camp Gordon, GA. Pvt., HQ & HQ Co., WIA (light), 11/30/43 Venafro, Italy. Pfc., Co. C, 6/22/45 Innsbruck, Austria.

BROWN, Ira C. Pfc., HQ Co., 5/8/45 Innsbruck, Austria.

BROWN, James E. b. 1920 TX. Res. Mesquite, Dallas Co., TX. Enl. 1/29/41 Syracuse, NY. Infantry Service. Ser. No. 12017370. Pvt., HQ & HQ Co., WIA 2/19/43 Tunisia – Purple Heart [award probably for service prior to 83rd CMB].

BROWN, John L. b. 1906 CA. Res. Contra Costa Co., CA. Enl. 3/9/42 Presidio of Monterey, CA. Ser. No. 39091848. Pvt. Attached to Co. B 5/28/42 Edgewood Arsenal, MD. Gunner (Pvt.). Pfc., Co. B, promo. Cpl. (temp.), Camp Gordon, GA 8/24/42.

BROWN, John W. b. 1921. Enl. 9/21/42 Harrisburg, PA. Ser. No. 33240923. Pvt., Co. B, Camp Gordon, GA 10/9/42. Transf. Co. A, Camp Gordon, GA, 12/16/42. Pfc., Co. B, WIA (light – enemy shell barrage), 4/18/44 Anzio, Italy. Not hospitalized. Pfc., Co. B, 5/8/45 Innsbruck, Austria.

BROWN, Johnnie R. b. 3/6/1904 GA. Res. Randolph Co., GA. Enl. 9/23/42 Ft. McPherson, Atlanta, GA. Ser. No. 34443730. Pvt. Co. D, 10/14/42 Camp Gordon, GA. Transf. Co. A, Camp Gordon, GA, 12/16/42. d. June 1977 Edison, Calhoun Co., GA.

BROWN, Walter K., Jr. Pvt., Co. B, Camp Gordon, GA 4/10/43.

BROWN, William E. b. 9/2/1900 MS. Res. Newton Co., MS. Enl. 9/26/42 Camp Shelby, MS. Ser. No. 34427556. Pvt. Co. C, 10/14/42 Camp Gordon, GA. d. April 1964, MS.

BROWNE, Harry B., Jr. ("Brownie"). b. 9/14/1915 VA. Res. Norfolk Co., VA. Enl. 9/21/42 Richmond, VA. Ser. No. 33225286. Pvt., Co. A, Camp Gordon, GA 10/11/42. Pfc., Co. A, on *LST 690* 8/9/44. Assigned from HQ 2nd Replacement Depot 11/17/44 as Pfc., Co. A. Pfc., Co. A, 5/8/45 Innsbruck, Austria. Res. Churchland, Portsmouth, VA May 1954. Construction Co. Employee. Attended 1954, 1958 & 1960 Reunions as res. Churchland, VA. d. Jan. 1979 Portsmouth, Portsmouth City Co., VA.

BROZ, James. Pfc., Co. C, 6/22/45 Innsbruck, Austria.

BRUCE, Robert B. b. 1918 SC. Enl. 3/5/42 Ft. Jackson, Columbia, SC. Ser. No. 34213872. Pvt. Attached to Co. I 5/28/42 Edgewood Arsenal, MD. Squad Leader (Sgt.). Cpl., Co. A, Camp Gordon, GA 12/12/42.

BRUMMAGE, Robert Leslie. b. 9/26/1923 Piedmont, WV. Enl. 4/1/43 Clarksburg, WV. Ser. No. 35752295. Pvt., Co. A, on *LST 690* 8/9/44. Pvt., Co. C, WIA (superficial – shrapnel), 10/13/44 France. Radioman for Lt. John L.Boyd. Pfc., Co. C, 6/22/45 Innsbruck, Austria. 30 years in National Guard. Chief Warrant Officer CW-4 1977. National Guard Command Administrative Specialist. HHB, 1st. BN, 201st. Field Artillery, Fairmont, WV, d. 1/22/1977 Marion Co., WV. bur. Grandview Memorial Gardens, Fairmont, WV.

BRUNDY, [Robert C.?]. b. 1922 CA. Res. Ventura Co., CA. Enl. 8/28/40 Ft. MacArthur, San Pedro, CA. Coast Artillery Corps or Mine Planter. 2nd Lt., assigned 83rd CMB 2/15/45.

BRUNOW, Robert. b. 1914 MO. Res. Johnson Co., MO. Enl. 5/9/42 Ft. Francis E. Warren, Cheyenne, WY. Res. MO. Ser. No. 17054500. Pvt., Co. D, KIA, 1/26/44, Italy (Anzio) SR Cem.

BRUTON, Harry S. b. 1915 MS. Res. Sunflower Co., MS. Enl. 9/23/42 Camp Shelby, MS. Ser. No. 34426668. Pvt. Co. D, 10/14/42 Camp Gordon, GA.

BRYAN, Lawrence W. Pfc., Co. A, 5/8/45 Innsbruck, Austria.

BRYSON, George A. b. 1923 AZ. Res. Pima Co., AZ. Pvt., Co. A, Camp Gordon, GA 3/18/43. Ser. No. 38278052. Ordnance Dept. Re-enl. for Hawaiian Dept. 7/5/1946 Phoenix, AZ.

BUCHANAN, Edward J. b. 1912 PA. Res. Camden Co., NJ. Enl. 7/9/42 Camden, NJ. Ser. No. 32271718. Pvt., Co. A, Camp Gordon, GA 7/28/42. T/5, Co. A, WIA (light injure – left ankle and left wrist), LST 422 Survivor, 1/26/44 Italy (Anzio). Rescued by USS YMS 226. Taken to 93rd Evac. Hosp.

BUCHINSKY, Stanley. b. 2/17/1917 PA. Enl. 12/22/42 Greensburg, PA. Ser. No. 33413335. Pvt., Co. A, Camp Gordon, GA 3/18/43. d. 11/6/1994 Detroit, Wayne Co., MI.

BUCK, Paul. b. 1907 VA. Enl. 8/31/42 Richmond, VA. Ser. No. 33223841. Pvt., Co. C, Camp Gordon, GA 10/11/42. Pvt., Co. C, Camp Gordon, GA Nov. 1942. Pvt., Co. C, Camp Gordon, GA 12/22/42. Pvt., Co. C, MIA, 1/26/44, Italy (Anzio)

BUFKIN, Henry D. b. 11/8/1921 MS. Res. Port Gibson, Clairborne Co., MS. Enl. 9/22/42 Camp Shelby, MS. Ser. No. 34426441. Pvt. Co. C, 10/14/42 Camp Gordon, GA. Pvt., Co. C, assigned Med. Det., Camp Gordon, GA 11/14/42. In a group photo of Co. C taken 1943 at Amalfi, Italy. Pfc., Med. Det./Co. C, LST 422 Survivor, 1/26/44 Italy (Anzio) – Purple Heart. Rescued by USS Pilot. Bronze Star [presented 4/25/44 – not present having left the 83rd]. d. 5/15/1995 Jackson, Hinds Co., MS.

BUFTER, David E. b. 9/3/1916 MD. Res. Baltimore City Co., MD. Enl. 3/4/42 Camp Lee, VA. Ser. No. 33154321. Pvt. Attached to Co. H 5/28/42 Edgewood Arsenal, MD. Platoon Sgt. (S/Sgt.). Sgt.(temp.), Co. D, promo. S/Sgt. (temp.), Camp Gordon, GA 8/1/42. d. 3/10/1992 MD.

BUKOVESKY, Stephen J. b. 1921 CT. Res. Fairfield Co., CT. Enl. 4/10/43 New Haven, CT. Ser. No. 31332144. Served in North Africa, Italy, Anzio, Monte Cassino, and Southern France. Pvt., Co. C, MIA, 8/29/44 Briançon, France. POW 10/15/44. POW Stalag 7A Moosburg, Bavaria. Liberated 6/6/45. Res. Belfast, ME.

BULLARD, Jim B. b. 1914 PA. Res. Chester Co., PA. Enl. 2/17/41 Erie, PA. Ser. No. 20312780. Pvt., Co. C, 6/22/45 Innsbruck, Austria.

BULLOCK, Stephen C. b. 1919 GA. Res. Polk Co., GA. Enl. 9/21/42 Ft. McPherson, Atlanta, GA. Ser. No. 34443165. Pvt., Co. C, Camo Gordon, GA 10/9/42. In a group photo of Co. C taken 1943 at Amalfi, Italy. Pvt., Co. C, WIA (light), 11/13/43 Italy.

BUNCH, Billy J. ("Billy the Kid"). b. 3/9/1917 TX. Res. Tarrant Co., TX. Enl. 3/26/42 Dallas, TX. Ser. No. 18080571. Pvt. Attached to Co. K 5/28/42 Edgewood Arsenal, MD. Gunner (Pvt.). Cpl. (temp.), Co. B, promo. Sgt. (temp.), Camp Gordon, GA 10/20/42. Report to Commandant, CWS OCS, Edgewood Arsenal, MD 12/30/42. d. 7/8/1990 Ft. Worth, Tarrant Co., TX.

BUNDY, Robert E. b. 1/3/1923 Pittsburgh, PA. St. Andrews Elementary School. Grad. St. James High School 6/6/41. Pre-war Occupation: Dairy Products Laboratory. Enl. 7/15/42 New Cumberland Army Depot. Transf. Camp Sibert, AL ca. 8/1/42. Transf. Cadre Training Detachment Oct. 1942. Assgnd. Replacement Detachment. Promo. Cpl. 12/2/42. Transf. OCS, Army Chemical School, Edgewood Arsenal, MD Apr. 1943. Grad. 9/4/43 & Transf. Officers Replacment, Camp Sibert, AL Transf. Chemical School, Edgewood Arsenal, MD Nov. 1943 & attended Chemical Officer's Basic Course & Mortar Battalion Officers' Course. Camouflage Course, Ft. Belvoir, VA Jan. 1944. Camp Reynolds, PA ca. Feb. 1944 and departed for overseas May 1944. Arrived England ca. 6/1/44. Assgnd. 229th Chemical Base Depot Co., Wrexham, Wales & designated co. motor officer. Led advance party to Southhampton & took ship to Normandy to Rennes, France. Visited HQ, U.S. Army, Europe in Paris Dec. 1944 & requested transfer to a mortar battalion. Ordered to 83rd CMB Jan. 1945. 1st. Lt., relsd. 229th Base Depot, Normandy Base Sec. & assigned 83rd CMB 2/26/45. Joined 83rd CMB at Luneville, France Feb. 1945. Assigned Platoon E.O., Co. A, 83rd CMB 3/5/45. Promo. 4/1/45. 1st Lt./Capt., Co. A, 5/8/45 Innsbruck, Austria. Post Exchange Officer, HQ Co. 7/1/45. Battalion S-4 7/23/45. Bn. S-4, PX Officer, HQ Co. Assgnd. G-4 section, USFA 10/4/45-1/20/46. Dischd. 1946. Clarion State College 1946. Reserves 1946-48. Re-enl. Army. Army Chemical Center, Edgewood Arsenal, MD 7/15/48. Commissioned 1949. 3rd Armored Cav. 3/1/50. 2nd CMB, Korea Nov. 1950. WIA Yoji Feb. 1951 while directing fire for British Co. of Commonwealth Brig. Bronze Star & Purple Heart. Co. Commander, Co. A, 2nd CMB, Korea July 1951. Returned from Korea 12/1/51. ROTC Instructor, Conisius College, Buffalo, NY 1/1/52. Chemical Officers Advance Course, Ft. McClellan 1954-55. Res. Buffalo, NY May 1954. Assgnd. Office of the Chief Chemical Officer, Wash., D.C. July 1955. Office of Deputy Chief for Logistics July 1957. Awarded Army Commendation Medal. Undergraduate University of MD. Attended 1958 Reunion as Res. Pittsburgh, PA. Syracuse Univ. July 1959-Sept. 1960 (Masters in Business Administration). Promo. Major. Assgnd. U.S. Army Logistics Management School, Ft. Lee, VA. Assgnd. U.S. Naval

War College (student). George Washington Univ. (Masters International Affairs). Assgnd. Div. Chemical Officer, 25th Inf. Div. Sept. 1963. Transf. Vietnam Mar. 1966. Promo. Lt. Col. & Awarded Bronze Star. Transf. HQ, U.S. Military Assistance Command Vietnam (MACV), Saigon. Departed MACV Mar. 1967 & Awarded Joint Services Commendation Medal. Assgnd. Office of the Deputy Chief of Staff for Logistics June 1967. Promo. Col. Comptroller, U.S. Sentinel Command, Redstone Arsenal, AL 1968. Promo. Col. 9/25/68. Deputy Commander and Chief of Staff until retired Jan. 1973. Awarded Legion of Merit. High School teacher (business) 1973-1983. Retired June 1983. Saigon. Left MACV March 1967 & awarded Joint Services Commendation Medal. Saigon. Retired as Army Col., 1973. Res. Huntsville, AL 2009.

BUNDY, Samuel M., Jr. b. 2/28/1921 NJ. Res. Camden Co., NJ. Enl. 7/9/42 Camden, NJ. Ser. No. 32271693. Pvt., Co. A, Camp Gordon, GA 7/28/42. Sgt., Co. A on *LST 690* 8/9/44. Transf. HQ Co. Dec. 1944. Sgt., HQ Co., 5/8/45 Innsbruck, Austria. Dischd. Oct. 1945. Wanamaker's Dept. Store, Philadelphia, PA. Employee of Jimmy Swaggart. Kept a diary which he wrote a foreword to in 1984. d. 9/28/1991 Baton Rouge, Baton Rouge Co., LA.

BURDICK, Lyle L. Nebraska Wesleyan College. Pastor, Tamora, NE. Chaplain, HQ & HQ Co., Camp Gordon, GA 4/13/43. Present with Graves Registration Party in Sicily Invasion, 1943. Left 83rd CMB Sept. 1943.

BURFORD, Rupert Orville. Maj./Lt., Co. C. b. 5/27/1909 Charleston, Kanawha Co., WV. Grad. Charleston High School, Charleston, WV 1927. Editor-In-Chief of high school newspaper The Book Strap. Also in Chorus, Boy's Glee Club (second bass). Chemical Engineer: West Virginia University 1932-33. Enl. 3/1/42. Chem. Warfare Instructor, Edgewood Arsenal, MD. 1st Lt., C.W.S. 5/28/42 Edgewood Arsenal, MD May 28, 1942. Promo. Capt., Co. C, Nov. 1942. Served in Naples, Foggia, Rome-Arno, Anzio, Sicily. Capt., Co. C, WIA (shrapnel left thigh), 9/15/1943 Maiori (Chiunzi Pass), Italy. Returned to duty 9/18/43. Transf. Battalion S-2 11/1/43. Rotated 3/29/44. Purple Heart, Army Commendation Ribbon, Dist. Unit Badge, Victory Medal, Amer. Campaign Ribbon. Edgewood Arsenal, MD Sept. 1945. Ft. Benning, GA. Diamond Shamrock Chem. Co. (formerly Belle Alkali Co.) 36 years. Kept a diary of service called Foreign Service Memoirs (unpublished). d. 4/26/1989 Charleston, WV. Body donated to WVU Medical School.

BURGAMY, Emory G. b. 1919 GA. Res. Hancock Co., GA. Enl. 9/18/42 Ft. McPherson, Atlanta, GA. Ser. No. 34442833. Pvt., Co. C, Camp Gordon, GA 10/8/42. S/Sgt., Co. C, 6/22/45 Innsbruck, Austria. Res. Sparta, GA.

BURGHART, Hubert A. b. 10/10/1915 PA. Enl. 9/22/42 Philadelphia, PA. Ser. No. 33335540. Pvt., Co. B, Camp Gordon, GA 10/9/42. Sgt., Co. B, recommended for Silver Star for action 12/20/43. Sgt., Bronze Star [presented 4/25/44]. 2nd. Lt., Co. C, 6/22/45 Innsbruck, Austria. 1st Lt. Assigned 65th Inf. Div. 7/23/45. Res. Philadelphia, PA May 1954. d. 7/13/1993 Havertown, Delaware Co., PA.

BURKETT, Claude T. b. 8/21/1920 MS. Res. Bassfield, Jefferson Davis Co., MS. Enl. 9/21/1942 Camp Shelby, MS. Ser. No. 34426218. Pvt. Co. D, 10/14/42 Camp Gordon, GA. T/4, Co. D, LST 422 Survivor, 1/26/44 Italy (Anzio) – Purple Heart. Sgt. Co. A, 5/8/45 Innsbruck, Austria. d. 1/20/1990 Bassfield, Jefferson Davis Co., MS. Robert Chamblee said Burkett was from McComb, MS.

BURKS, Paul S. b. 7/4/1921 TN. Res. Davidson Co., TN. Enl. 9/18/42 Ft. Oglethorpe, GA. Ser. No. 34371789. Pvt., Co. A, Camp Gordon, GA 10/7/42. d. 7/9/1998 Dayton, Montgomery Co., OH.

BURNS, Robert A. Pfc., HQ Co., promo. S/Sgt. (temp.) 9/15/45.

BURNS, Robert L. 1st Lt., relsd. 260th Inf. & assigned 83rd CMB 8/7/45. 1st Lt., Co. C. Placed on Special Duty as Co. Executive Officer, HQ Co., 9/10/45.

BUSH, Robert Joseph ("Bob"). b. 10/15/1919 NJ. Entered service early 1942. Camp Sibert, Gadsden, AL OCS. Ft. Custer, MI training MP's. Departed U.S. 3/28/44. 2nd Replacement Depot, Naples, Italy 4/18/44. Joined Co. A, 83rd CMB at Anzio 4/30/44. Sick at Station 225 Hospital with dysentery 7/22/44-7/30/44. 2nd Lt. to 1st Lt. 9/30/44. In hospital with jaundice Feb. 1945. 1st. Lt., Co. A, 5/8/45 Innsbruck, Austria. 1st Lt. Assigned 65th Inf. Div. 7/23/45. Res. Woodland Hills, CA May 1954. Prudential Insurance Company. Res. Lake Havasu, AZ 2005. d. 1/3/2006 (cancer) Lake Havasu, Mohave Co., AZ. Cremated.

BUSH, Thomas V. b. 9/19/1918 GA. Res. Laurens Co., GA. Enl. 9/19/42 Ft. McPherson, Atlanta, GA. Ser. No. 34443073. Pvt., Co. C, Camp Gordon, GA 10/8/42. Jeep driver for Capt. Robert B. Smith. In hospital with pneumonia 5/1/45. T/5, Co. C, 6/22/45 Innsbruck, Austria. d. 4/29/1976 Fort Valley, Peach Co., GA.

BUSH, William. b. 1909 PA. Res. Three Springs, PA. Enl. 9/18/42 Altoona, PA. Ser. No. 33253373. Pvt., Co. A, Camp Gordon, GA 10/9/42. Pfc., HQ Co., KIA, 1/26/44, Italy (Anzio) SR Cem. Next of kin: Daisy Lauver, mother.

BUSNIAK, Michael ("Buzz" / "Nickle Nose" / "Noseniak"). b. 1922 NJ. Res. Hudson Co., NJ. Enl. 12/10/42 Newark, NJ. Ser. No. 32598595. Pvt., HQ & HQ CO., Camp Gordon, GA 4/2/43. Pfc., Co. B, 5/8/45 Innsbruck, Austria. Res. Jersey City, NJ May 1954. Attended 1956, 1958, 1960, 1962 & 1966 Reunions as Res. Jersey City, NJ.

BUTALLA, Stephen J. b. 12/12/1921 PA. Enl. 1/22/43 Greensburg, PA. Ser. No. 33415917. Pfc., HQ Co., 5/8/45 Innsbruck, Austria. d. 10/26/2002 Latrobe, Westmoreland Co., PA.

BUTLER, Frank R. b. 1925 PA. Enl. 7/21/43 Philadelphia, PA. Ser. No. 33791439. Pvt., Co. D, WIA (light injure – truck over-turned on road between Pozzuoli & Minturno), Italy 3/25 or 26/44.

BUTLER, John M. b. 1921 PA. Res. Camden Co., NJ. Enl. 7/9/42 Camden, NJ. Ser. No. 32271689. Pvt., Co. A, Camp Gordon, GA 7/28/42. Pvt., Co. A, Camp Gordon, GA 10/21/42. T/5, Co. A, 5/8/45 Innsbruck, Austria. Motor Pool. Dischd. 1945. Esterbrook Pen Co. Owens

Corning. Attended 1956, 1958 & 1962 Reunions as res. Somerdale, NJ. Retired 1984. Res. Collingswood, NJ 2004. Res. NJ 2006.

BUTTS, Clifford. b. 12/8/1899 MS. Res. Lafayette Co., MS. Enl. 9/22/42 Camp Shelby, MS. Ser. No. 34426529. Pvt. Co. D, 10/14/42 Camp Gordon, GA. d. Feb. 1976 Water Valley, Yalobusha Co., MS.

BYERS, Charles L. ("Rebel"). b. 7/8/1917 Davidson, NC. Attended school at Cornelius, NC. Res. Rockingham Co., VA. Enl. 2/10/1942 Washington, D.C. Ser. No. 06385183. Pvt. Co. D, 10/11/42 Camp Gordon GA. Present at Africa, Sicily, Italy. Medical dischg. late 1943 due to asthma & emphysema. Departed Naples to North Africa. Train to Casablanca. Departed Casablanca for the U.S. 12/26/43. Arrived in U.S. 1/3/44. Stationed at Portsmouth, then PA, then Ft. Monroe, VA, 2/6/45. Res. Chambersburg, PA May,1954. Owns "Family Sewing Machine Co.". Sewing Machine Mechanic. Singer Corp. Coffee Shop Operator, Lancaster, PA. d. 2/26/1997 Coatesville, PA. Bur. St. Mary's Cem., Lancaster, PA. Suffered entire life from respiratory illness from some type of wound(s) from the war.

CADDLE, George A. Pvt., Co. B, Camp Gordon, GA 4/16/43. Pvt., Co. B, WIA (serious – enemy shell fire), 4/12 or 13/44 Anzio, Italy. Res. Jersey City, NJ.

CADWALADER, Roy E. Enl. 3/21/42. Pvt. Attached to Co. K 5/28/42 Edgewood Arsenal, MD. Gunner (Pvt.). Cpl. (temp.), Co. B, Camp Gordon, GA 8/24/42. Promo. Sgt. (temp.), Camp Gordon, GA 10/20/42. Special duty to Battalion HQ Camp Gordon, GA 11/24/42. Transf. HQ & HQ Co., Camp Gordon, GA 12/15/42. S/Sgt., apptd. T/Sgt., HQ & HQ Co. 3/15/43. T/Sgt., HQ Co., 5/8/45 Innsbruck, Austria.

CAGLE, Harry B. b. 8/17/1906 OK. Res. Tulsa Co., OK. Enl. 12/8/42 Tulsa, OK. Ser. No. 38324565. Pvt., HQ & HQ Co., Camp Gordon, GA 4/2/43. d. Dec. 1983 Cushing, Payne Co., OK.

CAHILL, Gerard F. b. 9/10/1898 NY. Res. New York Co., NY. Enl. 7/9/42 Ft. Jay, Governors Island, NY. Ser. No. 32402200. Pvt., Co. A, Camp Gordon, GA 7/28/42. Pvt., Co. A, duty as S-4, Camp Gordon, GA 9/14/42. Pfc., transf. Co. A, Camp Gordon, GA 11/26/42. Promo. Cpl. (temp.), HQ Co., Camp Gordon, GA 12/21/42. d. Oct. 1964 NY.

CAHILL, Zack D. b. 1907 VA. Res. Henry Co., VA. Enl. 9/21/42 Roanoke, VA. Ser. No. 33213371. Pvt. Co. D, 10/11/42 Camp Gordon GA.

CAIRL, George T., Jr. b. 1920 PA. Res. Jackson Co., MO. Enl. 9/21/42 Ft. Myer, VA. Ser. No. 33197637. Pvt., Co. A, Camp Gordon, GA 10/11/42. Cpl., Co. A, 2nd Platoon. WIA (light – premature muzzle-burst), Bischweiler, France (Alsace) 2/18/45. Cpl., Co. A, 5/8/45 Innsbruck, Austria.

CALDRON, ----------. Present in Co. A 8/4/45.

CALLENDER, Emmit P. b. 1921 MS. Res. Wilkinson Co., MS. Enl. 9/18/42 Camp Shelby, MS. Ser. No. 34425664. Pvt. Co. D, 10/14/42 Camp Gordon, GA.

CAMERON, Lewis ("Kokomo"). b. 5/25/1918 Kokomo, IN. Kokomo High School 1937. Grad. Manchester College 1941 – BA Education. Star baseball fielder for Manchester College. Player for coach Lester Dekle's Double Cola Team of Kokomo. Res. Kokomo, Steuben Co., IN. Enl. 3/14/42 Ft. Benjamin Harrison, IN. Ser. No. 35042835. Pvt. Attached to Co. I 5/28/42 Edgewood Arsenal, MD. Gunner (Pvt.). Pfc., Co. B, (Squad Leader), promo. Cpl. (temp.), Camp Gordon, GA 7/15/42. Cpl., Co. B, Camp Gordon, GA 8/3/42. Promo. Sgt. (temp.), Camp Gordon, GA 8/26/42. Sgt., Co. B, transf. Co. A, Camp Gordon, GA, 12/16/42. S/Sgt., Co. B, WIA 11/13/43 Italy – Purple Heart. Returned to duty 12/20/43. 2nd Lt., promo. 1st Lt. 8/17/44. Bronze Star [Presented 11/20/44]. 1st Lt., WIA (light), 1/12/45 France. Battlefield commission as 1st Lt. 1st. Lt., Co. B, 5/8/45 Innsbruck, Austria. 1st Lt., assigned 65th Inf. Div. 7/23/45. Dischd. 12/6/45. Earned three Purple Heart's & one Bronze Star. Mentioned in the May 1954 Directory. Attended 1954, 1956 & 1960 Reunions Administrator Caston School Corp. Taught school & principal 32 years – most at Caston & Fulton schools. d. 12/28/2000 Logansport Memorial Hospital, IN. bur. Ever Rest Memorial Park, Logansport, IN.

CAMP, Howard. b. 1920 MS. Res. Union Co., MS. Enl. 9/23/42 Camp Shelby, MS. Ser. No. 34426839. Pvt. Co. D, 10/14/42 Camp Gordon, GA. Pfc., Co. D, MIA, 1/26/44, Italy (Anzio) SR Cem.

CAMPBELL, Donald R. b. 7/31/1922 WA. Res. Santa Clara Co., CA. Enl. 12/9/42 San Francisco, CA. Ser. No. 39116694. Pvt., Co. B, Camp Gordon, GA 4/2/43. Pfc., Co. B, 5/8/45 Innsbruck, Austria. Attended 1956 Reunion. d. 7/8/2002 Sunland, Los Angeles Co., CA.

CAMPBELL, George T. b. 1918 PA. Enl. 9/25/42 Pittsburgh, PA. Ser. No. 33305537. Pvt. Co. B, 10/15/42 Camp Gordon GA. Pvt., Co. B, WIA (light – shell fire), 9/27/44 France.

CAMPBELL, Hollis W. b. 4/19/1919 VA. Res. Bath Co., VA. Enl. 9/21/42 Roanoke, VA. Ser. No. 33213327. Pvt. Co. B, Camp Gordon, GA 10/11/42. Co. B, Camp Gordon, GA. Cpl., Co. B, 5/8/45 Innsbruck, Austria. d. 11/20/1993 Covington, VA.

CANNETTI, Joseph Edward. b. 9/13/1924 Astoria, Long Island, NY. Pre-war Occupation: Office Boy. Res. Queens Co., NY. Enl. 2/12 (or 19)/43 New York City, NY. Ser. No. 32803286. Basic Training: 82nd Inf. Div., 2/19/43-July 1943. Joined 83rd CMB Nov. 1943. Joined Co. A, early Dec. 1943 at Venafro. Pvt., Co. A, on *LST 690* 8/9/44. 192nd Chemical Depot Co., Dec. 1944-Nov. 1945. Res. Lexington Park, MD 2009.

CANNON, Willis L. b. 1921 MS. Res. Neshoba Co., MS. Enl. 9/22/42 Camp Shelby, MS. Ser. No. 34426459. Pvt. Co. D, 10/14/42 Camp Gordon, GA. Pvt., Co. D, MIA, 1/26/44, Italy (Anzio) SR Cem.

CANTRELL, Clayman. b. 1919 AL. Res. Monroe Co., MS. Enl. 9/23/42 Camp Shelby, MS. 34426901. Pvt. Co. C, 10/14/42

Camp Gordon, GA.

CANTRELL, George J. b. 10/12/1921 GA. Res. Franklin Co., GA. Enl. 9/12/42 Ft. McPherson, Atlanta, GA. Ser. No. 34441781. Pvt., Co. B, Camp Gordon, GA Nov. 1942. Pfc., Co. B, 5/8/45 Innsbruck, Austria. d. 12/6/1997 Toccoa, Stephens Co., GA.

CAPPOLI, August T. b. 1923 IN. Res. Cass Co., IN. Enl. 2/17/43 Indianapolis, IN. Ser. No. 35093499. Pvt., Co. A, on *LST 690* 8/9/44. Pfc., Co. B, 5/8/45 Innsbruck, Austria.

CARLSON. Gunnard. Res. Eveleth, MN. Enl. 1/23/42. Sgt. & Squad leader, Co. A, 83rd CMB. Served in Rhineland & Central Europe. Combat Infantryman Badge. Good Conduct Medal. EAME Campaign Service Medal. Dischd. 12/1/45.

CARNES, Eugene M. Pfc., Co. C. Purple Heart, Sept., 1945.

CARNILL, Roy R. b. 1920 PA. Res. Altoona, PA. Enl. 10/5/42 Altoona, PA. Ser. No. 13084641. Pvt., HQ & HQ Co., Camp Gordon, GA 10/9/42. Pfc., Co. B, WIA (light injure), 2/16 or 17/44 Italy – Purple Heart. Pfc. Transf. 83rd CMB to HQ Ry. Sv. 7/18/44.

CAROTHERS, Edward Frank. b. 11/9/1907 Lyons, Shomokin, PA. Grad. Coal Twp. High School, Shomokin, PA 1927. Worked in coal mines for about a year. Pre-war Occupation: Weaver in port Textile Silk Mill. Res. Lycoming Co., PA. Enl. 9/21/42 Harrisburg, PA [family says inducted 4/5/42]. Ser. No. 33240942. Pvt., Co. C, Camp Gordon, GA 10/9/42. Camp Gordon, GA. North Africa. Sicily. WIA Salerno, Italy, Sept. 1943-Purple Heart. Pfc., Co. C, KIA, 1/26/44, Italy (Anzio), SR Cem. Purple Heart with Oak Leaf Cluster. Next of kin: Cora Agnes Carothers, mother.

CARPENTER, Carl K ("C.K." / "Stud" / "Carp"). b. 1914 OH. Res. Stark Co., OH [another source says Jackson, MI]. Enl. 7/3/41 Cleveland, OH. Ser. No. 35026522. 2nd Lt., CWS, 1st CWS Troop Officers Course, Edgewood Arsenal, MD – Mar. 1942. 1st Lt., CWS, assigned Co. D, Camp Gordon, GA 6/19/42. Transf. Co. B, Camp Gordon, GA 10/1/42. Reported as battalion liasion officer 11/18/43. 1st Lt., Co. B, KIA (enemy dive bombers – bomb fragment), 2/17/44, Anzio, Italy.

CARR, Clay. b. 1927 TN. Res. Overton Co., TN. S/Sgt., Co. A 8/4/45. Re-enl.7/16/46 Ft. Oglethorpe, GA. Ser. No. 14218575.

CARR, Ernest J. b. 1924 NY. Res. Suffolk Co., NY. Enl. 7/16/43 New York City, NY. Ser. No. 32985448. Pfc., WIA (light injure – truck ran off road), 8/17/44 France.

CARRAWAY, Orange D. ("Zip"). b. 9/4/1915 MS. Res. Warren Co., MS. Enl. 10/7/42 Camp Shelby, MS. Ser. No. 14150957. Pvt. Co. D, 10/14/42 Camp Gordon, GA. Res. Vicksburg, MS May 1954. P.O. Payroll Clerk Rural Disbursing Section. d. Oct. 1975.

CARROLL, Charles W. b. 1920 MD. Res. Baltimore City Co., MD. Enl. 7/22/43 Baltimore, MD. Ser. No. 33205859. Pvt., HQ & HQ Co., Camp Gordon, GA 4/16/43. Pfc., Co. C, MIA, 1/26/44, Italy

(Anzio) SR Cem.

CARROLL, Roy. b. 1921 GA. Res. Polk Co., GA. Enl. 9/21/42 Ft. McPherson, Atlanta, GA. Pvt., HQ & HQ Co., Camp Gordon, GA 10/9/42. Ser. No. 34443227. Pfc., apptd. T/5, HQ & HQ Co., 4/15/43. Radio Operator, Co. C, 7/14/43. T/5, Co. C, MIA, 1/26/44, Italy (Anzio) SR Cem.

CARULLO, Charles C. ("Chuck") b. 1921 NJ. Res. Camden Co., NJ. Enl. 7/9/42 Camden, NJ. Ser. No. 32271737. Pvt., Co. A, Camp Gordon, GA 7/28/42. Pfc. Co. A, transf. Co. D, Camp Gordon, GA, 12/16/42. Cpl., distinguished in action 7/10/43 Sicily. Co. A, transf. July 1944 at reorganization.

CARTER, Coy H. b. 1922 TN. Res. Sumner Co., TN. Enl. 9/17/42 Ft. Oglethorpe, GA. Ser. No. 34371662. Pvt., Co. A, Camp Gordon, GA 10/7/42. Pfc., Co. A, on *LST 690* 8/9/44. Pfc., Co. B, 5/8/45 Innsbruck, Austria.

CARTER, Polk A. b. 11/12/1917 GA. Res. Bibb Co., GA. Enl. 12/15/42 Ft. McPherson, Atlanta, GA. Ser. No. 34578118. Pvt., Co. D, Camp Gordon, GA 4/10/43. Pvt., Co. D, WIA (slight – accidental due to a rocket launcher blowing up while test firing), 7/20/43 Porto Empedocle, Sicily. d. 12/15/1998 Bainbridge, Decatur Co., GA.

CARTER, Talmadge. b. 1919 GA. Res. Pierce Co., GA. Ser. No. 34263492. Pvt. Attached to Co. A 5/28/42 Edgewood Arsenal, MD. Chauffeur. Pfc., HQ & HQ Co., promo. Cpl. (temp.), Camp Gordon, GA 12/12/42. Pfc., Camp Gordon, GA 12/19/42. Cpl., distinguished in action 7/10/43, Sicily. HQ Co. driver 2/15/45. Cpl., HQ Co., 5/8/45 Innsbruck, Austria.

CARTER, Vernon Lee. Pvt. Attached to Co. I 5/28/42 Edgewood Arsenal, MD. Gunner (Pvt.). Pfc., Co. C, (Squad Leader), promo. Cpl. (temp.), Camp Gordon, GA 7/15/42.

CARTWRIGHT, James A. b. 1924 NY. Res. Cattaraugus Co., NY. Enl. 2/4/43 Buffalo, NY. Ser. No. 32831724. Pvt., Co. D, WIA (light injure), LST 422 Survivor, 1/26/44 Italy (Anzio).

CARTWRIGHT, William B. b. 1898 TN. Res. Cheatham Co., TN. Enl. 9/18/42 Ft. Oglethorpe, GA. Pvt., Co. A, Camp Gordon, GA 10/7/42. Transf. Co. D, Camp Gordon, GA, 12/16/42.

CARVER, William D. b. 1910 GA. Res. Floyd Co., GA. Enl. 10/9/42 Ft. McPherson, Atlanta, GA. Ser. No. 14139790. Pvt. Co. C, 10/14/42 Camp Gordon, GA. Pfc., Co. C, KIA, 1/26/44, Italy (Anzio), SR Cem.

CARY, ----------. Present as pitcher in Co. B ball team 8/4/45.

CASCIO, Thomas A. b. 8/19/1918 Hoboken, NJ. High School & one year NYU Extension Study. Pre-war Occupation: Lab Technician. Res. Hudson Co., NJ. Enl. 11/9/43 Newark, NJ. [12/9/43 according to Cascio]. Ser. No. 42101959. Joined 83rd CMB at Epinal, France Nov. 1944 and assigned to Co. B. Arms/Shell Bearer. Pvt., Co. B, MIA (capt.), 12/12/44, Riquewihr, France. Stalag 7A 3/15/45.. Spent time in German hospital for colitis. Liberated 4/29/45. Res. West New York, NJ 2009.

CASSELL, Thomas L. b. 12/25/1913 TX. Res. Tarrant Co., TX. Enl. 8/16/41 Ft. Sam Houston, TX. Ser. No. 38033807. Corp. Assigned to HQ & HQ Co. 5/28/42 Edgewood Arsenal, MD. Operations Sgt. (T/Sgt.). Sgt. (temp.), HQ & HQ Co., (Operations) promo. S/Sgt. (temp.), Camp Gordon, GA 7/15/42. Cpl. (temp.), HQ & HQ Co., promo. Sgt. (temp.), Camp Gordon, GA 8/16/42. S/Sgt., promo. T/Sgt. (temp.), Camp Gordon, GA 10/21/42. M/Sgt., HQ Co., 5/8/45 Innsbruck, Austria. d. 3/23/1995 TX.

CASSELS, Richard I. b. 1921 MS. Res. Wilkinson Co., MS. Enl. 9/18/42 Camp Shelby, MS. Ser. No. 34425658. Pvt. Co. D, 10/14/42 Camp Gordon, GA. Pvt., Co. D, MIA, 1/26/44, Italy (Anzio) SR Cem.

CATRON, John. b. 10/15/1920 VA. Res. Buchanan Co., VA. Enl. 12/7/42 Abingdon, VA. Ser. No. 33527123. Pvt., Co. A, Camp Gordon, GA 3/18/43. d. 3/4/1994 Grundy, Buchanan Co., VA.

CAVALIER, Harold E. b. 1922 Canada. Res. Niagara Co., NY. Enl. 1/29/44 Buffalo, NY. Ser. No. 42094140. Pfc., HQ & HQ Co., promo. T/5 (temp.) 7/24/45.

CAVENDER, Wilbur H. b. 1/30/1921 LA. Res. Macon Co., GA. Enl. 9/19/42 Ft. McPherson, Atlanta, GA. Ser. No. 34442975. Pvt., HQ & HQ Co., Camp Gordon, GA 10/8/42. d. 5/8/2004 Americus, Sumter Co., GA.

CELARDO, Salvatore. b. 9/13/1919 NY. Res. King's Co., NY. Enl. 6/16/42 Ft. Jay, Governor's Island, NY. Ser. No. 32354759. Pvt., Co. B, Camp Gordon, GA 4/16/43. Pvt., Co. B, 5/8/45 Innsbruck, Austria. d. Nov. 1973 NY.

CELLA, Charles P., Jr. b. 1918 PA. Enl. 9/21/42 Philadelphia, PA. Ser. No. 33335266. Pvt., Co. D, Camp Gordon, GA 10/9/42. Pvt., Co. D, special duty Battalion HQ, 11/24/42. Pvt., Managing and Acting Editor Smokescreen, Camp Gordon, GA 1/9/43. T/5, Editor, Smokescreen, Camp Gordon, GA Feb. 1943. Present at Anzio as T/5, 2/9/44. Sam Kweskin said he was WIA (light – German time bomb), 11/30/44 Moussey, France and sent stateside to recover.

CENSATO, Lawrence/ Laurence Joseph ("Cinci"). b. 10/28/1915 Richmond, MA. Battery D, 7th Field Artillery Feb. 1936 – April 1937. Res. Berkshire Co., MA. Enl. 2/12/42 Ft. Devens, MA. Ser. No. 31064695. Pvt. Attached to Co. C 5/28/42 Edgewood Arsenal, MD. Cook (Pvt.). Pfc., HQ & HQ Co., (Cook), promo. T/5 (temp.), Camp Gordon, GA 7/15/42. T/4, HQ & HQ Co., 1/13/44. S/Sgt., Co. B, 5/8/45 Innsbruck, Austria. Dischd. 10/5/45. Res. Richmond, MA May 1954. Attended 1954 Reunion. d. 8/9/2003.

CENTER, Guy H. b. 3/29/1917 GA. Res. Oglethorpe Co., GA. Enl. 9/21/42 Ft. McPherson, Atlanta, GA. Ser. No. 34443235. Pvt., Co. A, Camp Gordon, GA 10/9/42. Transf. Co. C, Camp Gordon, GA, 12/16/42. d. 9/3/1993 Athens, Clarke Co., GA.

CENTRERAS, Antonia H. Pfc., Co. C. Bronze Star, Sept. 1945.

CERVANTEZ, Refugio. (Cervantes) Pvt., Co. A, Camp Gordon, GA 3/18/43. Ser. No. 38222634. Later served in New Guinea, South Philippines Liberation, Asiatic-Pacific Theater. South Philippines Liberation Ribbon and Good Conduct Medal. Res. Artesia, NM.

CHAMBLEE, Robert Marlin. ("John"). b. 5/24/1915 MS. Res. Fulton, Itawamba Co., MS. Ser. No. 34426730. Enl. 9/23/42 Camp Shelby, MS. Pvt. Co. D, 10/14/42 Camp Gordon, GA. Pfc., Co. D, LST 422 Survivor, 1/26/44 Italy (Anzio) – Purple Heart. Postwar res. Fulton, Itawamba Co., MS. d. 4/17/1987 VA Hospital, Memphis, TN.

CHANCELLOR, Clifton E. b. 1920 MS. Res. Forrest Co., MS. Enl. 9/21/42 Camp Shelby, MS. Ser. No. 34426158. Pvt. Co. C, 10/14/42 Camp Gordon, GA. Transf. Co. A, Camp Gordon, GA, 12/16/42. Sgt., Co. C, MIA, 1/26/44, Italy (Anzio) SR Cem.

CHANDLER, ----------. In a group photo provided by Sam Kweskin.

CHAPMAN, David G. b. 1913 GA. Enl. 12/15/42 Ft. Myer, VA. Ser. No. 33450467. Pfc., Co. A, Camp Gordon, GA 3/18/43. T/5, assistant to the chaplain 11/30/44. T/5, Co. C, 6/22/45 Innsbruck, Austria. Attended 1962 Reunion as res. Falls Church, VA.

CHAPMAN, Franklin J. b. 1924. Res. Lancaster Co., PA. Enl. 4/21/43 Harrisburg, PA. Ser. No. 33507755. Pvt., Co. A on *LST 690* 8/9/44.

CHEST, Raymond. b. 10/26/1924 NY. Res. Montgomery Co., NY. Enl. 3/30/43 Utica, NY. Ser. No. 32854985. Pvt., Co. A, on *LST 690* 8/9/44. Pfc., Co. B, 5/8/45 Innsbruck, Austria. d. 12/2/1992 Gulfport, Harrison Co., MS.

CHICARILLA, Jack J. b. 6/12/1912 PA. Res. Middlesex Co., NJ. Enl. 6/20/42 Newark, NJ. Ser. No. 32385116. Pvt., Co. C, Camp Gordon, GA 7/28/42. Pfc., Co. C, Camp Gordon, GA 12/19/42. Pfc., promo. T/5 (temp.), Camp Gordon, GA 12/29/42. Pfc., Co. C, Camp Gordon, GA, transf. OCS, 1/9/43. d. 3/16/1997 Edison, Middlesex Co., NJ.

CHILDRESS, Albert D. b. 1920 AL. Res. Chilton Co., AL. Enl. 9/19/42 Ft. McClellan, AL. Ser. No. 34391804. Pvt., Co. B, Camp Gordon, GA 10/8/42. Pfc., Co. B, KIA, 1/26/44, Italy (Anzio), SR Cem.

CHOQUETTE, Joseph A. b. 9/17/1913 RI. Res. Providence Co., RI. Enl. 8/8/42 Providence, RI. Ser. No. 31173114. 54th Chem. Impreg. Co. Pvt., attached to Co. B, 83rd CMB, Camp Gordon, GA 4/15/43. d. Feb. 1992 Providence, Providence Co., RI.

CHRISTIANSEN, Leroy A. b. 2/21/1922 IA. Res. Crawford Co., IA. Enl. 12/21/42 Camp Dodge, Herrold, IA. Ser. No. 37651732. Pvt., Co. D, Camp Gordon, GA 4/10/43. Had an appendectomy operation on the U.S.S. Monticello 5/4/43. d. 11/13/1999 Portland, Mulmonah Co., OR.

CHURCHILL, David H. b. 1919 MI. Res. Detroit, Wayne Co., MI. Enl. 9/14/40 Detroit, MI. Ser. No. 16011563. Pvt., Co. C, LST 422 Survivor,

1/26/44 Italy (Anzio) – Purple Heart. Pvt., Co. C, WIA (light – enemy mortar shell), 5/8/44 Anzio, Italy – Purple Heart with Oak Leaf Cluster. Returned to duty 5/9/44. Pvt., Co. C, MIA, 8/29/44 Briançon, France. POW Stalag 7A Moosburg, Bavaria. Liberated 10/24/44.

CHURCHILL, Harold A. 2nd Lt., Co. C, WIA (light), 9/24/43, Italy. Returned to duty 10/18/43. 2nd Lt., Co. C, KIA, 12/7/43 Italy.

CINNAJINNY, Frank B. b. 1920 Klagetoh, AZ. Res. Apache Co., AZ. Enl. 5/5/42 Phoenix, AZ. Ser. No. 38004310. Pfc., Co. D, MIA, 1/26/44, Italy (Anzio) SR Cem. Purple Heart. Good Conduct Medal. EAME Campaign Medal.

CIOFFI, Patsy. Pvt., HQ & HQ Co., Camp Gordon, GA 10/9/42. Ser. No. 33296781.

CIULIA, Joseph F. b. 1912 Italy. Res. Passaic Co., NJ. Enl. 7/20/42 Newark, NJ. Ser. No. 32449646. Pvt., HQ & HQ Co., Camp Gordon, GA 4/16/43. [spelled CUILLA on ser. no.]

CLAGETT, Richard C. b. 1916 MD. Res. Clarion, IA. Enl. 12/2/42 Baltimore, MD. Pvt., Co. C, Camp Gordon, GA 4/10/43. Pvt., Co. C, WIA (light), LST 422 Survivor, 1/26/44 Italy (Anzio) – Purple Heart. Returned to duty 2/8/44.

CLARK, Clyde J. b. 1923. Enl. 4/7/43 Pittsburgh, PA. Ser. No. 33677410. Pvt., Co. A on *LST 690* 8/9/44. Pfc., Co. B, 5/8/45 Innsbruck, Austria.

CLARK, Harry A. b. 1923 NY. Res. Ozone Park, New York Co., NY. Enl. 3/5/43 New York City, NY. Ser. No. 32823876. Pfc., Co. A, WIA (light-enemy shell burst), 3/25 or 26/44 Anzio, Italy – Purple Heart. Returned to duty 5/1/44.

CLARK, James F. b. 1903 PA. Res. Allegheny Co., PA. Enl. 9/25/42 Pittsburgh, PA. Ser. No. 33305535. Pvt. HQ & HQ Co., 10/15/42 Camp Gordon GA.

CLARK, Loyal D. b. 1924 MI. Res. Branch Co., MI. Enl. 3/31/43 Kalamazoo, MI. Ser. No. 36459510. Pvt. Co., A on *LST 690* 8/9/44.

CLARK, Vernon. b. 1915 IN. Res Vigo Co., IN. Enl. 12/11/42 Evansville, IN. Ser. No. 35719675. Pvt., Co. A, Camp Gordon, GA 4/2/43.

CLARK, Willis J. Pvt., Co. B, Camp Gordon, GA 10/8/42.

CLATT, Colin ("Yukon"). Jeep Driver, HQ Co. Mentioned in unpublished memoir of Sam Kweskin. [possibly John K. Klatt, Co. D].

CLATTERBUCK, David J. b. 1/6/1924 VA. Enl. 4/29/43 Richmond, VA. Ser. No. 33635773. Pfc., Co. B, 5/8/45 Innsbruck, Austria. d. 4/19/2004 Port St. Lucie, St. Lucie Co., FL.

CLAYTON, James H. b. 1920 MS. Res. Union Co., MS. Enl. 9/23/42 Camp Shelby, MS. Ser. No. 34426864. Pvt. Co. D, 10/14/42 Camp Gordon, GA. Pfc., Co. D, MIA, 1/26/44, Italy (Anzio) SR Cem.

CLEAVELAND, Charles L., Jr. b. 10/30/1919 GA. Res. Troup Co., GA. Enl. 2/28/42 Ft. McPherson, Atlanta, GA. Pvt. Ser. No. 34262351. Attached to Co. A 5/28/42 Edgewood Arsenal, MD. Chauffeur. Pfc., HQ & HQ Co., promo. T/5 (temp.), Camp Gordon, GA 8/3/42. T/5 (temp.), HQ & HQ Co. assigned to Post Motor Pool, Camp Gordon, GA Aug. 24, 1942. T/5 (temp.), HQ Co. promo. T/4 (temp.), Camp Gordon, GA 1/25/43. S/Sgt., HQ Co., 5/8/45 Innsbruck, Austria. Mentioned in the May 1954 Directory. d. 4/17/1983 Lagrange, Troup Co., GA.

CLEMENS, James J. b. 1913 IN. Enl. 12/8/42 Indianapolis, IN. Ser. No. 35573096. Pvt., Co. B, MIA, 12/12/44, Riquewihr, France.

CLEMENT, Howard R. Pfc., Co. B. Bronze Star, Sept., 1945.

CLIFT, James A. b. 1913 VA. Enl. 12/15/42 Charlottesville, VA. Ser. No. 33536518. Pvt., Co. A, Camp Gordon, GA 3/18/43.

CLINE, William L. b. 1922 KY. Res. Davidson Co., TN. Enl. 9/18/42 Ft. Oglethorpe, GA. Ser. No. 34371716. Pvt., Co. A, Camp Gordon, GA 10/7/42. Transf. Co. B, Camp Gordon, GA, 12/16/42. Pfc., Co. A, MIA, 1/26/44, Italy (Anzio) SR Cem.

CLOUTIER, Charles P. b. 1911 ME. Res. Kennebec Co., ME. Enl. 1/7/42 Portland, ME. Ser. No. 11016959. Pfc., HQ Co., 5/8/45 Innsbruck, Austria.

CLUBB, Guy L., Jr. b. 1917 MO. Res. Adams Co., NE. Enl. 6/22/42 Ft. Des Moines, IA. Ser. No. 37420238. 2nd Lt., Co. D, MIA, 1/26/44, Italy (Anzio) SR Cem.

CLUSE, John R. Pvt., Co. D, Camp Gordon, GA 10/9/42. Ser. No. 33296798. Co. D. Mentioned in a letter of Dec. 1944 from John 'Pop' O'Connor to Ed Pike.

CLYMER, Levi L. b.9/6/1923. Res. Bucks Co., PA. Enl. 3/4/43 Allentown, PA. Ser. No. 33618515. Pfc., Co. B, 5/8/45 Innsbruck, Austria. d. June 1973 PA.

COBB, Arnold M. b. 1922 OK. Res. Grady Co., OK. Enl. 11/2/42 Oklahoma City, OK. Ser. No. 38273956. Pvt., Co. B, WIA (light – enemy dive bombers), 2/17/44 Anzio, Italy.

COCAYNE, Robert W. b. 10/17/1919. Enl. 4/3/42. Transf. From Camp Sibert, AL 4/9/43. S/Sgt., HQ & HQ Co., Camp Gordon, GA 4/10/43. S/Sgt., HQ Co., 5/8/45 Innsbruck, Austria. d. 4/14/1988.

COCCO, Joseph M. b. 1920 Italy or San Marino. Enl. 9/21/42 Philadelphia, PA. Pvt., Ser. No. 33335300. Pvt., Co. C, Camp Gordon, GA 10/9/42. Pvt. Co. C, KIA, 9/11 or 12/43, Maiori (Chiunzi Pass), Italy, SR Cem.

COCHRAN, Loneil O. b. 1914 AL. Res. Monroe Co., MS. Enl. 9/23/42 Camp Shelby, MS. Ser. No. 34426910. Pvt. Co. C, 10/14/42 Camp Gordon, GA.

CODEGA, Michele [Michael] P. b. 2/27/1919 RI. Res. Berrington, Bristol Co., RI. Enl. 4/3/42 Providence, RI. Ser. No. 31112470. Pvt. attached to Co. K 5/28/42 Edgewood Arsenal, MD. Telephone Lineman (Pvt.). Pfc., Co. D, promo. Cpl. (temp.), Camp Gordon, GA 9/26/42. Promo. Sgt. (temp.), Camp Gordon, GA 11/5/42. Sgt. Co. C, transf. Co. A, Camp Gordon, GA, 12/16/42. Bronze Star for mortar observer 9/15/43 near Salerno, Italy. 1st Sgt., Co. D, LST 422 Survivor, 1/26/44 Italy (Anzio) – Purple Heart. Soldier's Medal for gallantry on LST 422 [Presented 4/25/44], Purple Heart with Oak Leaf Cluster. 1st Sgt., Bronze Star [Presented 11/20/44 for action 9/15/43 near Salerno]. 1st Sgt. For 'old' Co. D. 1st. Sgt., HQ Co., 5/8/45 Innsbruck, Austria. Co. M in the 409th Infantry Reg. Dischd. Oct. 1945. Postwar res. Berrington, RI. Res. Old Forge, NY May 1954. Motel Owner. Municipal Auditor, Pittsfield, MA. Attended 1954 & 1958 Reunions as Res. Old Forge, NY. Retired Mar. 1981. d. 3/17/2001 Sarasota, Sarasota Co., FL.

COFFER, Robert O. b. 1920 MO. Res. Jackson Co., MO. Enl. 2/5/43 Hartford, CT. Ser. No. 37504133. Pfc., HQ Co., 5/8/45 Innsbruck, Austria.

COFFEY, Harley A. b. 1912 KS. Res. Oklahoma Co., OK. Enl. 3/20/41 Oklahoma City, OK. Ser. No. 38020922. HQ, 11th Armored Div., assigned 1st Lt., Co. B, 83rd CMB 7/25/45.

COHEN, Albert. b. 1921 NY. Res. Kings Co., NY. Enl. 9/21/42 Richmond, VA. Ser. No. 33225554. Pvt. Co. D, 10/11/42 Camp Gordon GA. Pvt., Co. D, distinguished in action 7/11/43 Niscemi, Sicily. Pfc., Co. D, Silver Star presented 10/8/43. Pfc., Co. D, KIA, 1/26/44, Italy (Anzio)

COHEN, Charles. Res. Mt. Vernon, NY. Pfc., Co. A, 5/8/45 Innsbruck, Austria. At one point in the war Cohen was guarding some German prisoners when one, about 50 years old, remarked, "Don't shoot me. I'm a good prisoner. I was a good prisoner in the last war too."

COHEN, Harry. b. 1919 IL. Res. Peoria, Cook Co., IL. Enl. 2/20/42 Camp Grant, IL. Ser. No. 36319938. Pvt. Attached to Co. A 5/28/42 Edgewood Arsenal, MD. Squad Leader (Sgt.). Pfc., Co. C, (Squad Leader), promo. Cpl. (temp.), Camp Gordon, GA 7/15/42. Cpl (temp.), Co. C, promo. Sgt. (temp.), Camp Gordon, GA 8/17/42. Sgt. Co. C – Silver Star [presented 12/5/43]. 1st Sgt., Co. C, LST 422 Survivor, 1/26/44 Italy (Anzio) – Purple Heart with Oak Leaf Cluster. 1st Sgt., Soldier's Medal for gallantry on LST 422 [presented 4/25/44]. Purple Heart with two Oak Leaf Clusters. ETO Ribbon with five stars. Good Conduct Medal. Rotated home prior to 1/11/45. Harry Cohen Enterprises, Habilitating Commerce Engineering, Peoria, IL 1959. d. 1976 according to Muzzleblasts.

COHEN, Milton I. b. 1907 NY. Res. Bronx Co., NY. Enl. 7/9/42 Ft. Jay, Governors Island, NY. Ser. No. 32402364. Pvt., Co. A, Camp Gordon, GA 7/28/42. Pfc. Co. A, transf. Co. B, Camp Gordon, GA, 12/16/42.

COHEN, Phillip. b. 9/16/1922 MD. Enl. 9/28/42 Baltimore, MD. Ser. No. 13103952. Pvt., Co. B, Camp Gordon, GA 10/11/42. d. 4/30/1990.

COKER, Marshall C. b. 1921 TN. Res. Sumner Co., TN. Enl. 9/17/42 Ft. Oglethorpe, GA. Ser. No. 34371508. Pvt., HQ & HQ Co., Camp Gordon, GA 10/7/42.Pvt. WIA (injured in glider crash) 8/15/44 Le Muy, France.

COLE, Frank E. b. 1920 GA. Res. Paulding Co., GA. Enl. 9/21/42 Ft. McPherson, Atlanta, GA. Ser. No. 34443198. Pvt., HQ & HQ Co., Camp Gordon, GA 10/9/42. Pfc., HQ & HQ Co., WIA (light), 11/30/43 Venafro, Italy. Returned to duty 12/1/43.

COLLIN[S], Arthur. b. 1921 GA. Res. Montgomery Co., GA. Enl. 9/19/42 Ft. McPherson, Atlanta, GA. Ser. No. 34443052. Pvt., Co. B, Camp Gordon, GA 10/8/42. Transf. Co. A, Camp Gordon, GA, 12/16/42. Pvt., Co. B transf. Motor Pool, Camp Gordon, GA 1/25/43. T/5, Co. B, recommended for Silver Star for action near Ceppagna, Italy 11/13/43. T/5, Co. B, LST 422 Survivor, 1/26/44 Italy (Anzio) although also on a list as T/4, KIA, 1/26/44, Italy (Anzio) – [also listed as T/5, Co. B, KIA 11/28/44 Struth, France].

COLLINS, Frank D. Pfc., Co. A, 5/8/45 Innsbruck, Austria.

COLLINS, Norman E. b. 1915 VA. Res. Washington Co., VA. Enl. 10/3/42 Abingdon, VA. Ser. No. 33214308. Pvt., Co. B, Camp Gordon, GA 10/11/42.

COLLINS, Warren E. b. 1921 AL. Res. Sunflower Co., MS. Enl. 9/22/42 Camp Shelby, MS. Ser. No. 34426665. Pvt. HQ & HQ Co. 10/14/42 Camp Gordon, GA. Pvt., HQ Co., assigned Med. Det., Camp Gordon, GA 11/14/42. Transf. HQ & HQ Co., Camp Gordon, GA 11/30/42. Pfc., HQ & HQ Co., WIA (light), 11/30/43 Venafro, Italy. Pfc., HQ Co., WIA (serious – while driving jeep), 2/28 or 29/44 Anzio, Italy. Mentioned in the May 1954 Directory.

COMATY, Joseph M. ("Joe"). Res. Trenton, NJ. Reported as a BAR man 4/23/45 in Helsel diary. Pfc., Co. A, 5/8/45 Innsbruck, Austria.

COMBE, Jean – Pierre E. E. Honorary Member. France. b. 11/14/1927 Briançon, France. Student – Briançon College. French youth 'adopted' by Co. C. Saved approximately 30 - 40 members of Co. C from capture 8/29/44 at Briançon, France. Entered service 8/29/44. Remained with mortar crew of Co. C until end of war. Stayed 5 days in a heavy weapons company of the 45th Division but told not to go with them as he was too young to get killed. Res. Loubiere, France 2009.

COMBEST, James L. b. 1920 KY. Res. Rantoul, Champaign Co., IL. Enl. 8/1/41 Chicago, IL. Ser. No. 36044850. Enlisted for Philippine Dept. Pvt., Co. D, LST 422 Survivor, 1/26/44 Italy (Anzio) – Purple Heart.

COMER, John D. b. 4/25/1924 VA. Enl. 4/22/43 Roanoke, VA. Ser. No. 33648809. Pvt., Co. A, on *LST 690* 8/9/44. Pfc., Co. C, 6/22/45 Innsbruck, Austria. d. 6/16/1997 White Hall, MD.

CONATSER, ----------. Pvt. Co. D, sent to hospital for exhaustion 11/24/43 Venafro, Italy.

CONICELLO, John. b. 1916 PA. Enl. 9/22/42 Philadelphia, PA. Ser. No. 33335471. Pvt., Co. A, Camp Gordon, GA 10/9/42. Transf. Co. B, Camp Gordon, GA, 12/16/42. A. J. Brown recalled "going to see Conicello in the stockade." Pvt., Co. C, 6/22/45 Innsbruck, Austria.

CONNOLLY, Andrew J. ("Dick"). b. 10/6/1918 NY. Res. New York City, New York Co., NY. Enl. 7/9/42 Ft. Jay, Governor's Island, NY. Ser. No. 32402177 Pvt., Co. A, Camp Gordon, GA 7/28/42. Pfc., Co. A, Camp Gordon, GA 10/30/42. Sgt., distinguished in action 7/10/43 Sicily. Co. C. Received battlefield commission. S/Sgt., Co. A, on *LST 690* 8/9/44. Sgt./2nd Lt., Bronze Star [Presented 11/20/44]. Bronze Star with Oak Leaf Cluster. 2nd. Lt., Co. C, 6/22/45 Innsbruck, Austria. Dischd. April 1945. 1st Lt. assigned 65th Inf. Div. 7/23/45. Employee New York Daily News. Two years (Korean War) with 477th Cml. Service Bn. Dischd. 1953. Fort McClellan, Alabama. Thirteen weeks schooling, Ft. Benning, GA (under Maj./Lt. Col. Pike). Res. Woodside, New York May 1954. Attended 1954, 1956, 1958, 1960, 1962 & 1966 Reunions as Res. Woodside, NY. Atlantic Electronic Co. Retired 1981. d. 12/30/2002 Woodside, Queens Co., NY.

CONNOLLY, Thomas M. b. 1914 NY. Res. New York Co., NY. Enl. 12/11/42 New York City, NY. Ser. No. 32681149. Pvt., Co. D, Camp Gordon, GA 4/2/43.

CONNORS, John J. b. 1904 PA. Enl. 9/26/42 Allentown, PA. Ser. No. 33368047. Pvt. Co. C, 10/15/42 Camp Gordon GA.

CONRAD, Charles A. Pvt., HQ & HQ Co., Camp Gordon, GA 10/9/42. Pvt., HQ Co., assigned Med. Det., Camp Gordon, GA 11/14/42. Ser. No. R696749.

CONROW, Jay R. b. 10/4/1923 NJ. Res. Burlington Co., NJ. Enl. 2/5/43 Camden, NJ. Ser. No. 32749854. In a group photo in Leonard W. Turan's photo album and mentioned in the scrapbook of Lt. Robert Bush. d. 8/6/1992 Iowa Park, Wichita Co., TX.

CONROY, Robert E. ("Bob" / "Grandpappy"). b. 1899 PA. Res. Allegheny Co., PA. Enl. 10/9/42 Pittsburgh, PA. Ser. No. 33305429. Pvt. Co. D, 10/15/42 Camp Gordon GA. Pvt., Co. D, assigned Med. Det., Camp Gordon, GA 11/1/42. Present, Med. Det., Camp Gordon, GA, 1/9/43. Mentioned in the May 1954 Directory.

CONSTANTINO, Dennis E. b. 1924. Enl. 4/21/43 Wilkes Barre, PA. Ser. No. 33604056. Pvt., Co. A, on *LST 690* 8/9/44. Pvt., Co. C, 6/22/45 Innsbruck, Austria.

CONTRERAS, ----------. Listed as latrine/slit trench expert, Co. C 8/4/45.

COOK, Cline. b. 1920 VA. Pvt., Co. A, Camp Gordon, GA 3/19/43. Ser. No. 33527057. Re-enl. 1/30/46 Ft. George Meade, MD for Panama Canal Service.

COOPER, Danile (" Dan."). b. 1924 NY. Res. Kings Co., NY. Enl. 3/27/43 New York City, NY. Ser. No. 32875890. Pvt., Co. A on *LST 690* 8/9/44. Pfc., Co. A, 2nd Platoon. WIA (serious – leg – by premature muzzleblast), Bischweiler, France (Alsace) 2/18/45. Res. Brooklyn, NY May 1954. Attended 1954 & 1966 Reunions.

COOPER, David N. Pvt. Attached to Co. C 5/28/42 Edgewood Arsenal, MD. Squad Leader (Sgt.).

COOPER, Richard C. Pfc., HQ Co., 5/8/45 Innsbruck, Austria.

COPELAND, Oather L. b. 1916 TX. Enl. 1/17/42 Jacksonville, FL. Ser. No. 34156130. Pvt., WIA (light), 2/19/44 Italy. Returned to duty 5/25/44.

COPPOLA, Michael. b. 1921 NY. Res. Kings Co., NY. Enl. 7/20/42 Ft. Jay, Governors Island, NY. Ser. No. 32409087. Pvt., HQ & HQ Co., Camp Gordon, GA 4/16/43.

CORNETT, Christopher C., Jr. ("Whiskey Red") 1st Lt., HQ & HQ Co., Camp Gordon, 6/12/42. Mess Officer, Camp Gordon, GA 7/11/42 Assigned Co. D, Camp Gordon, GA 8/24/42. Transf. Co. A, Camp Gordon, GA 10/1/42. Transf. HQ & HQ Co. & designated Adj. & Postal Officer, Camp Gordon, GA 12/2/42. Apptd. Life Insurance Officer, Camp Gordon, GA 12/15/42. 1st Lt./Adj. HQ, Camp Gordon, GA 1/25/43. Remained with rear echelon during Sicilian campaign and rejoined battalion at end of combat. Present as S-1 11/26/43. Chemical Officer, 5th Army 1/20 – 29/44. Reported transferred to a non-combat unit in a letter dated 3/24/44.

CORSA, Lawrence J. b. 1/28/1920 PA. Res. York Co., PA. Enl. 2/24/42 Ft. George Meade, MD. Ser. No. 33169893. Pvt. Attached to Co. G 5/28/42 Edgewood Arsenal, MD. Squad Leader (Sgt.). d. Nov. 1968 PA.

COSTELLEE, James T. Pfc., Co. C. Purple Heart, Sept., 1945.

COTTEN, Clarence J. b. 1911 MS. Res. Coahoma Co., MS. Enl. 9/23/42 Camp Shelby, MS. Ser. No. 34426914. Pvt. Co. D, 10/14/42 Camp Gordon, GA.

COURSE, William S. b. 1906 MA. Res. New York Co., NY. Enl. 7/9/42 Ft. Jay, Governors Island, NY. Ser. No. 32402257. Pvt., Co. B, Camp Gordon, GA 9/10/42. Pfc., Co. B, transf. OCS, Quartermasters, Camp Lee, VA, Jan. 1943.

COWAN, Robert P. Pvt., distinguished in action 7/10/43 Sicily.

COWAN, William R. b. 1916 VA. Res. Lee Co., VA. Enl. 12/5/42 Abingdon, VA. Ser. No. 33526913. Pvt., Co. A, Camp Gordon, GA 3/18/43. Pvt., Co. A, on *LST 690* 8/9/44. Pfc., HQ Co., 5/8/45 Innsbruck, Austria.

COX, William C. Jr. b. 9/28/1909 GA. Res. Polk Co., GA. Enl. 9/19/42 Ft. McPherson, Atlanta GA. Ser. No. 34442911. Pvt. Co. A, Camp Gordon, GA 10/9/42. d. 1/25/2004 Cartersville, Bartow Co., GA.

COX, L. M. b. 1912 TN. Res. Shelby Co., TN. Enl. 6/27/1942 Ft. Oglethorpe, GA. Ser. No. 34287793. Pvt., Co. A, Camp Gordon, GA

10/7/42.

COYLE, James A. Present at Anzio, Italy Apr. 1944. Pfc., Med. Det., 5/8/45 Innsbruck, Austria.

CRAMER, Alfred F. b. 1916 NJ. Res. Essex Co., NJ. Enl. 7/2/42 Newark, NJ. Ser. No. 32388060. Pvt., Co. C, Camp Gordon, GA 7/28/42. Pfc., Co. C, promo. Cpl. (temp.), Camp Gordon, GA 12/15/42. Cpl. Co. C, transf. Co. A, Camp Gordon, 12/16/42. In a group photo of Co. C taken 1943 at Amalfi, Italy. S/Sgt., Co. C, MIA, 1/26/44 Italy (Anzio).

CRAMER, Quentin. HQ, 11th Armored Div., assigned as Capt., HQ & HQ Co., 83rd CMB 7/23/45. Present as Bn. Surgeon 8/4/45.

CRANFORD, Robert C. b. 3/24/1921 MS. Res. Bolivar Co., MS. Enl. 9/23/42 Camp Shelby, MS. Ser. No. 34426932. Pvt. Co. D, 10/14/42 Camp Gordon, GA. d. 7/24/1989, Porum, Muskogee Co., OK.

CREHAN, John F. b. 8/9/1910 NJ. Res. Camden Co., NJ. Enl. 7/9/42 Camden, NJ. Ser. No. 32271767. Pvt., Co. A, Camp Gordon, GA 7/28/42. Pfc. Co. A, transf. Co. B, Camp Gordon, GA, 12/16/42. Sgt., Co. A, distinguished in action 7/12/43 Gela, Sicily. d. Oct. 1970 Pottstown, Montgomery Co., PA.

CRENSHAW, Alfred H. b. 4/13/1917 Genoa, TX. Grad. Milby High School 1934. Grad. Rice Institute 1940 (BA in accounting). Prewar occupation: Arthur Anderson Accounting Firm. Res. Houston, Harris Co., TX. Enl. 4/17/41 Houston, TX. Ser. No. 36055654. 2nd Lt., Co. B, Camp Gordon, GA, 6/12/42. Transf. Co. D, Camp Gordon, GA 10/12/42. Promo. 1st Lt., Camp Gordon, GA Nov. 1942. Transf. Co. A, Camp Gordon, GA, 12/16/42. Present as C.O., Co. D 11/26/43. 1st Lt., CWS, LST 422 Survivor, 1/26/44 Italy (Anzio) – Purple Heart. Present as C.O., Co. D, 3/24/44. Present as C.O., Co. D, 5/9/44. Left with Lt. Col. Hutchinson 7/9/44 to help train two new chemical battalions. 1st Lt., promo. Capt. 8/17/44. Returned from detached duty in Italy 11/15/44. Capt., HQ Co., 5/8/45 Innsbruck, Austria. Capt. Assigned 65th Inf. Div. 7/23/45. Awarded Silver Star and Bronze Star. U.S. Army Reserve (retired 1977 as Lt. Col.). Postwar occupation: U.S. Treasury Dept. (retired 1973). d. 11/23/2008 Houston, TX. bur. Forest Park Lawndale.

CRESS, Claude A. b. 1924 VA. Pvt., Co. C, 6/22/45 Innsbruck, Austria.

CREWS, Olin P. b. 1904 AL. Res. Randolph Co., AL. Enl. 9/18/42 Ft. McClellan, AL. Ser. No. 34391620. Pvt., Co. D, Camp Gordon, GA 10/8/42.

CRIESSER, Frank J. Pvt. Attached to Co. G 5/28/42 Edgewood Arsenal, MD. Platoon Sgt. (S/Sgt.).

CROCKER, Bernard, Jr. 1st Lt., CWS. Edgewood Arsenal, MD, designated Summary Court, Camp Gordon, GA 11/25/42. Transf. From Co. C to Co. A, Camp Gordon, GA 11/26/42. Apptd. Mess Officer for Battalion Officers Mess, Camp Gordon, GA 12/15/42.

CROCKER, Charles R. b. 1920 PA. Res. Butler Co., PA. Enl. 9/26/42 Pittsburgh, PA. Ser. No. 33305811. Pvt. HQ & HQ Co., 10/15/42 Camp Gordon GA. Pvt., HQ Co., assigned Med. Det., Camp Gordon, GA 11/14/42.

CRONE, Lawrence W., Jr. b. 8/27/1914 GA. Res. Rabun Co., GA. Enl. 9/23/42 Ft. McPherson, Atlanta, GA. Ser. No. 34443642. Pvt., Co. A, Camp Gordon, GA 10/12/42. T/5, Co. B, 5/8/45 Innsbruck, Austria. d. 2/4/2005 Clayton, Rabun Co., GA.

CRONK, Donald J., Jr. b. 11/20/1924 NY. Res. Westchester Co., NY. Enl. 12/14/42 New York City, NY. Ser. No. 32684087. Pvt., Co. A on *LST 690* 8/9/44. d. 4/21/1996 Delray Beach, FL.

CROOM, Cecil C. b. 4/30/1921 AL. Res. Houston Co., AL. Enl. 9/19/42 Ft. McClellan, AL. Ser. No. 34391788. Pvt., HQ & HQ Co., Camp Gordon, GA 10/8/42. Co. A, (WIA?) sent to hospital in Africa 7/14/43. d. Feb. 1978 Dothan, Houston Co., AL.

CROPP, Granville T. ("Buck"). b. 1921 VA. Res. Spotsylvania Co., VA according to NARA record [Res. Stafford Co., VA according to Cropp]. Enl. 9/21/42 Richmond, VA. Ser. No. 33225644. Pvt., Co. A, Camp Gordon, GA 10/11/42. A. J. Brown recalled Cropp "losing the guard watch at Venafro." Sgt., Co. A on *LST 690* 8/9/44. Sgt., Co. A, 5/8/45 Innsbruck, Austria. Res. Falmouth, VA May 1954. Sheet Metal Worker, U.S. Govt., Quantico, VA. Attended 1962 Reunion as Res. Falmouth, VA. Res. Fredericksburg, VA 2009.

CROSBIE, William E. b. 11/12/1911 OH. Res. Cuyahoga Co., OH. Enl. 11/30/42 Cleveland, OH. Ser. No. 35524058. Pvt., Co. D, Camp Gordon, GA 4/10/43. d. Nov. 1982, Cleveland, Cuyahoga Co., OH.

CROSS, Charles W. Assigned from 65th Inf. Division as 2nd Lt., Co. B, 7/23/45.

CROSTEN, Leonard L (or R.). b. 10/18/1922 Morton, WV. Civilian Occupation: Groundman. Pre-war res. Mill Creek, WV. Enl. 9/2/42 Clarksburg, WV. Ser. No. 35394876. T/4, Co. C. Operator Radio Telephone Fire. Naples-Foggia, Rome-Arno, Southern France, Rhineland, Central Europe. Bronze Star. Good Conduct. European African Middle Eastern Service Ribbon Appears 6/22/45 Innsbruck, Austria. Returned to U.S. 9/19/1945. Separation: 10/23/1945.

CRUMPTON, Lemuel M. b. 12/13/1911 KY. Res. Hanford, Kings Co., CA. Enl. 12/14/42 Sacramento, CA. Ser. No. 39405301. Pvt., Co. B, Camp Gordon, GA 4/10/43. Pvt., Co. B, sent to hospital (120th Collecting Bn.) 8/4/43. Returned to duty 8/8/43. Pvt., Co. B, WIA (light injure) 2/16 or 17/44 Italy – Purple Heart. d. 9/22/1992 San Jose, Santa Clara Co., CA.

CRUTZ, Robert I. b. 4/18/1924. Ser. No. 32771129. Pvt., Co. A, KIA (enemy plane shot down & fell on him), 1/26 or 27/44, Anzio, Italy. Re-interred 8/2/48 at Beverly Nat. Cem., Beverly, NJ.

CUFF, Joseph F. ("Joe"). Pvt., Co. A, WIA (serious – anti-tank mine), 5/24/44 Anzio, Italy – Purple Heart. Hospitalized. Pvt., Co. A, on *LST*

690 8/9/44. Pfc., Co. A, 5/8/45 Innsbruck, Austria. Res. Carbondale, PA May 1954. Novelty Store Manager. Attended 1966 Reunion.

CUILLA, Joseph F. [see listing under Joseph F. CIULLA].

CULMAN, William F. b. 1923 NY. Enl. 3/23/43 Ft. Hayes, Columbus, OH. Ser. No. 35606977. Pfc., HQ Co., promo. Sgt. (temp.) 9/15/45.

CULPEPPER, Joel B. b. 1920 GA. Res. Meriwether Co., GA. Enl. 9/21/42 Ft. McPherson, Atlanta, GA. Ser. No. 34443100. Pvt., Co. B, Camp Gordon, GA 10/9/42. Pfc., Co. B, KIA, 1/26/44, Italy (Anzio), SR Cem.

CULVER, Henry G. b. 1902 GA. Res. Jenkins Co., GA. Enl. 9/19/42 Ft. McPherson, Atlanta, GA. Ser. No. 34442968. Pvt., Co. C, Camp Gordon, GA 10/9/42.

CUMMING, Arthur G. b. 1921 NJ. Res. Bergen Co., NJ. Enl. 7/1/42 Newark, NJ. Ser. No. 32387658. Pvt., Med. Det., attached to HQ & HQ Co., Camp Gordon, GA 9/26/42. Pfc., Med. Det., MIA, 1/26/44, Italy (Anzio) SR Cem.

CUMMINGS, Robert S. [or R.]. b. 1907 RI. Res. Providence Co., RI. Enl. 3/5/42 Ft. Devens, MA. Pvt. Attached to Co. C 5/28/42 Edgewood Arsenal, MD. Squad leader (Sgt.). Pfc., Co. A, promo. T/5 (temp.), Camp Gordon, GA 9/23/42. Ser. No. 31071893. T/5, Co. A, KIA, 1/26/44, Italy, FL Cem.

CUNIN, Kenneth Alonzo ("Kenny"). Col./Maj. b. 8/21/08 Alliance, OH. Attended University of Alabama for 3 semesters in 1927. Congressional Appointment to West Point Military Academy 1930. West Point 1934. FA-CWS-Arty (82nd Field Artillery, Ft. Bliss, TX). Maj. 83CmlBn, Camp Gordon, GA 6/10/42 & 8/1/42. Promo. Lt. Col. 12/5/42 Camp Gordon, GA. CO 83CmlBn T-M 1943. Lt. Col., Camp Gordon, GA 1/25/43. Transf. 1st Inf. Div. 9/26/43. CmlO 1st Inf. Div T-ME 1943-44. Reassigned to England to prepare for the planning of D-Day. Member of the landing party at Omaha Beach Bronze Star 1944. CmlO Hq 1 Ar T-E 1944-45 (BSM). Pres., Chemical Warfare Board, Edgewood Arsenal, MD 1945. Pres. CmlC Bd 1945-46 (CR), Command and General Staff School, Ft. Leavenworth, KS. Remained on faculty to teach logistics and combined arms. Deputy Commander & CO Deseret Chem Dep., Tooele, UT 1951-52. Chief of Plans & Operations, Field Artillery Corps, Hq 8th Army, Korea 1953-54 (LM). Said his greatest satisfaction in that assignment was the preparation of the 8th Army plan for repatriation of POW's after Korean War ended. HQ, 2nd U.S. Army, Ft. Meade, MD 1954. Prof. Military Science Ohio State University 1956-59 (CR). Ft. Hayes. Attended 1958 & 1960 Reunions as res. Columbus, OH. Ret. 1959 as Col. Resident Hall Administrator, Ohio State University until 1968. Moved to San Antonio, TX 1971. d. 3/13/1994. Bur. Ft. Sam Houston Nat. Cem., San Antonio, TX.

CUPIT, Lawrence. b. 2/18/1902 MS. Jefferson Co., MS. Enl. 9/22/42 Camp Shelby, MS. Ser. No. 34426434. Pvt. Co. D, 10/14/42 Camp Gordon, GA. d. Nov. 1966 Natchez, Adams Co., MS.

CUPP, Alvin A. b. 1920 PA. Res. Blair Co., PA. Enl. 3/3/42 New Cumberland, PA. Ser. No. 33160337. Pvt. Attached to Co. B 5/28/42 Edgewood Arsenal, MD. Cook (Pvt.). Pvt., HQ & HQ Co. transf. Co. D, Camp Gordon, GA 6/15/42. Pfc., (Cook), promo. T/5 (temp.), Camp Gordon, GA 7/15/42. T/5, Co. D, promo. T/4 (temp.), Camp Gordon, GA 8/28/42. Reduced to Pvt., Camp Gordon, GA 11/25/42. Sgt., Co. D, WIA (slight), 7/10/43 Italy. S/Sgt., Co. D, WIA (light – shell fragment), 9/10/43 Vietre sul Mare, Italy. Returned to duty 10/15/43. Purple Heart was sent home for public display. Believed to have later served as an M.P.

CURTIS, Leon. b. 1921 MO. Res. New Madrid Co., MO. Enl. 12/10/42 Jefferson Barracks, MO. Ser. No. 37402939. Pvt., Co. D, Camp Gordon, GA 4/2/43. Pfc., Co. D, MIA, 1/26/44, Italy (Anzio) SR Cem.

CUTE, Thomas A. b. 11/7/1910 NY. Res. Hornell, Steuben Co., NY. Enl. 1/6/42 Elmira, NY. Ser. No. 12044756. T/4. Assigned to Co. B 5/28/42 Edgewood Arsenal, MD. Mess Sgt. (S/Sgt.). T/4 (temp.), Co. C, (Mess), promo. S/Sgt. (temp.), Camp Gordon, GA 7/15/42. S/Sgt., Co. C, WIA (light), LST 422 Survivor, 1/26/44 Italy (Anzio) – Purple Heart. Returned to duty 1/27/44. S/Sgt., Co. C, WIA (light), 5/14/44 Anzio, Italy. 2nd Lt., Silver Star [presented 11/20/44]. 2nd Lt., Silver Star 1945. 1st. Lt., Co. C, 6/22/45 Innsbruck, Austria. 1st Lt. Assigned 65th Inf. Div. 7/23/45. [Middle initial J. 5/28/42 Edgewood Arsenal, MD]. d. 10/22/1987 Lake Worth, Palm Beach Co., FL.

CUTLER, Joe. In a group photo in Leonard W. Turan's album and mentioned in Lt. Robert Bush's scrapbook.

CUVA, Paul. b. 1921 NJ. Res. Essex Co., NJ. Enl. 7/9/42 Newark, NJ. Ser. No. 32390232. Pvt., HQ & HQ Co., Camp Gordon, GA 7/28/42. Corp., HQ & HQ Co., WIA (light – head and hand - German time bomb), 11/30/44 Moussey, France. Sam Kweskin said he was eventually sent stateside and recovered.

CYGAN, William V. Res. Springfield, MA. Ser. No. 11018699 [does not match]. Pfc., Co. D, MIA, 1/26/44, Italy (Anzio) – possibly survivor – Purple Heart. [Probably same as William W. Cygan – b. 1918 MA. Res. Hampden Co., MA. Enl. 10/25/40 Springfield, MA. Pvt., Coast Artillery Corps. Ser. No. 11008399].

DAAR, Arnold. Sgt., Co. C. Transf. To 2nd CMB. Mentioned in the letters of Capt. Robert B. Smith.

DACIER, Raymond F. b. 1908 (4/30/1909 on SSDI) NY. Res. Jefferson Co., NY. Enl. 4/10/43 Syracuse, NY. Ser. No. 32934869. Pvt., Co. A, on *LST 690* 8/9/44. Res. Watertown, NJ May 1954. Attended 1966 Reunion. d. May 1987 Watertown, Jefferson Co., NY.

DA CUNTO, Epimaco M. Assigned from 65th Inf. Division as 2nd Lt., Co. C, 7/23/45.

DAILEY, Arnold J. b. 1910 PA. Enl. 9/22/42 Philadelphia, PA. Ser. No. 33335441. Pvt., Co. C, Camp Gordon, GA Nov. 1942. Transf. Co. A, Camp Gordon, GA, 12/16/42. Pvt., Co. C, WIA (serious), 9/24/43 Maiori, Italy. Pfc., Co. C, KIA, 1/26/44, Italy (Anzio).

D'AMATO, Rudolph. b. 4/27/1909 NY. Res. Bronx Co., NY. Enl. 3/16/42 Camp Upton, Yanphank, NY. Ser. No. 32229017. Pvt. Attached to Co. I 5/28/42 Edgewood Arsenal, MD. Gunner (Pvt.). Pfc., Co. C, (Squad Leader), promo. Cpl. (temp.), Camp Gordon, GA 7/15/42. d. 3/4/1996 Bronx, Bronx Co., NY.

DANFIELD, Robert Daniel ("Danny"). b. 9/26/1921. Res. Laurel Springs, NJ. Ser. No. 32271717. Pvt., Co. A, Camp Gordon, GA 7/28/42. S/Sgt., Co. A on *LST 690* 8/9/44. Sgt./2nd Lt., Bronze Star [Presented 11/20/44]. Earned a battlefield commission. 1st. Lt., Co. B, 5/8/45 Innsbruck, Austria. 1st Lt., assigned 65th Inf. Div. 7/23/45. d. 5/17/2005 Stratford, Camden Co., NJ. Bur. Marlton Baptist Cem. Lt. Robert Bush remembered he "was an incredibly good ballplayer despite being short and having small hands." Clovis Birdwell said he did not like to wear his Lt.'s bars.

DANIELS, Douglas H. b. 1915 Canada. Res. New York Co., NY. Enl. 7/9/42 Ft. Jay, Governors Island, NY. Ser. No. 32402157. Pvt., Co. A, Camp Gordon, GA 7/28/42. Pfc. Co. A, transf. Co. D, Camp Gordon, GA, 12/16/42.

DANIELS, Mitchell L. b. 1920 AL. Res. Emanuel Co., AL. Enl. 9/19/42 Ft. McPherson, Atlanta, GA. Ser. No. 34442855. Pvt., HQ & HQ Co., Camp Gordon, GA 10/8/42. Pfc., Co. B, distinguished in action near Anzio, Italy 2/17/44 - Bronze Star. Pfc., Co. B, 5/8/45 Innsbruck, Austria.

D'ANTUONO, Ralph. b. 10/29/1921 NY. Res. Kings Co., NY. Enl. 7/9/42 Ft. Jay, Governors Island, NY. Pvt., Co. D, Camp Gordon, GA 7/28/42. Pfc., Co. D, Camp Gordon, GA 10/21/42. Pfc., Co. D, WIA (light), 7/11/43 Gela, Sicily. Given furlough to the states December 1943. Co. C, S.C.U. 1488 A.G. & S.F., Hotel Vanderbilt, Asheville, NC 1944. John O'Connor called him the best pancake maker in the U.S. Army. d. Aug. 1972 NY. [also spelled D'Antonio].

DANZIGER, Samuel H. b. 1924 NY. Res. Kings Co., NY. Enl. 3/27/43 New York City, NY. Ser. No. 32876464. Pvt., Co. A, on *LST 690* 8/9/44. Pfc., Co. A, 5/8/45 Innsbruck, Austria. Res. Brooklyn, NY May 1954. Registered Pharmacist.

DASCENZO, Herman. b. 9/29/1916 Italy. Enl. 9/22/42 Philadelphia, PA. Ser. No. 33335548. Pvt., HQ & HQ Co., Camp Gordon, GA 10/9/42. d. Oct. 1967, PA.

DAVIADOFF, Alexander. b. 1910 NJ. Res. Hudson Co., NJ. Enl. 8/7/42 Newark, NJ. Ser. No. 32390146. Pvt., Co. C, Camp Gordon, GA 7/28/42. Pvt., Co. C, MIA, 1/26/44, Italy (Anzio) SR Cem.

DAVIDSON, Edward Stanley ("Stan"). b. 1917 NY. Res. Bronx Co., NY. Enl. 7/9/42 Ft. Jay, Governors Island, NY. Ser. No. 32402349. Pvt., Co. B, Camp Gordon, GA 7/28/42. Pfc., Co. B, Camp Gordon, GA 11/21/42. Present Co. B, Riquewhir, France, 12/12/44. Cpl., Co. B, 5/8/45 Innsbruck, Austria. Res. New York, NY May 1954. Buyer for Macy's. Contributed to Muzzleblasts 2004. Res. Manchester, NJ, 2009.

DAVIDSON, James J. T/4, Co. B, 5/8/45 Innsbruck, Austria.

DAVIES, Walter C. b. 1921 NJ. Res. Bergen Co., NJ. Enl. 7/8/42 Newark, NJ. Ser. No. 32390020. Pvt., assigned to Med. Det., Camp Gordon, GA 2/10/43.

DAVIS, Alton J. b. 1919 MI. Res. Allegan Co., MI. Enl. 11/25/42 Kalamazoo, MI. Ser. No. 36412029. Pfc., Co. B, sent to hospital (120th Collecting Bn.) 8/4/43. Returned to duty 8/7/43. Pfc., Co. B, promo. T/5 (temp.) 9/15/45.

DAVIS, Claude H. ("Boots"). b. 9/9/1921 MS. Res. Yazoo Co., MS. Enl. 9/23/42 Camp Shelby, MS. Ser. No. 34426851. Pvt. Co. A, 10/14/42 Camp Gordon, GA. Transf. Co. D, Camp Gordon, GA, 12/16/42. Pvt., Co. A on *LST 690* 8/9/44. Mentioned in the May 1954 Directory. d. 1/17/1996 Gillette, WY.

DAVIS, Curt. Co. C. Listed as running in a track meet at Berchtesgaden August 1945. [possibly Harrell C. Davis].

DAVIS, Harrell C. Pvt. Attached to Co. A 5/28/42 Edgewood Arsenal, MD. Gunner (Pvt.). Pvt., Co. C transf. Co. D, Camp Gordon, GA 6/15/42. Cpl. (temp.), Co. D, promo. Sgt. (temp.), Camp Gordon, GA 11/5/42.

DAVIS, James F. b. 1921 PA. Res. Westmoreland Co., PA. Enl. 9/25/42 Greensburg, PA. Ser. No. 33294853. Pvt. Co. B, 10/15/42 Camp Gordon GA. Attended 1960 Reunion.

DAVIS, James G. Pvt., Co. A, Camp Gordon, GA 4/10/43.

DAVIS, James K. Lt., joined Co. A, 83rd CMB July 1944 (former Darby Ranger). 1st. Lt., Co. A on *LST 690* 8/9/44. 1st Lt. (Cavalry), WIA (light) 12/12/44, Riquewihr, France.. 1st Lt., Co. A, 5/8/45 Innsbruck, Austria. Assigned 135th Chem. Mortar Co. 7/19/45.

DAVIS, Leland L. ("L.L."). b. 1922 IA. Res. Keokuk Co., IA. Ser. No. 37651536. Pvt., Co. D, Camp Gordon, GA 4/10/43. T5, Co. A, 5/8/45 Innsbruck, Austria.

DAVIS, Porter R. b. 2/19/1916 GA. Res. Dahlonega, Lumpkin Co., GA. Enl. 9/19/42 Ft. McPherson, Atlanta, GA. Ser. No. 34443032. Pvt., Co. D, Camp Gordon, GA 10/8/42. Co. D, LST 422 Survivor, 1/26/44 Italy (Anzio). Rescued by YMS 43. T/4, Co. A, 5/8/45 Innsbruck, Austria. d. 5/25/1969 GA (truck accident).

DAVISON, William A. b. 1922 PA. Res. Luzerne Co., PA. ROTC. Enl. 10/6/42 State College, PA. Ser. No. 1310169. Pfc., WIA (light), 10/11/44 France. Pfc., Co. D, promo. T/5 (temp.), 11/1/44. T/5, Co. A, 5/8/45 Innsbruck, Austria.

DAWSON, Charles H. b. 2/19/1913 Fly, OH. Res. Sistersville, Tyler Co., WV. Sistersville High School. Jefferson College, PA. Pvt. Attached to Co. G 5/28/42 Edgewood Arsenal, MD. Gunner (Pvt.). Pfc., Co. A, Camp Gordon, GA 8/28/42. Transf. Co. D, Camp Gordon, GA, 12/16/42. Pfc., Co. D, Camp Gordon, GA 12/19/42. Pfc., distinguished in action 7/10/43 Sicily. Pfc., Co. A, on *LST 690* 8/9/44. Retired production worker, American Cynamid. Attended 1958 Reunion. d. 3/22/1983. Bur. Arlington Nat. Cem.

DAY, Delos. b. 10/19/1902 MS. Res. Wilkinson Co., MS. Enl. 9/18/42 Camp Shelby, MS. Ser. No. 34425661. Pvt. Co. D, 10/14/42 Camp Gordon, GA. d. June 1974 Natchez, Adams Co., MS.

DEAN, Harold O. b. 1912 PA. Res. Aliquippa, Beaver Co., PA. Enl. 3/18/42 New Cumberland, PA. Pvt. Ser. No. 33164288. Attached to Co. A 5/28/42 Edgewood Arsenal, MD. Chauffeur. Pvt., HQ & HQ Co. transf. Co. D, Camp Gordon, GA 6/15/42. Pfc, Co. D temp. T/5 Camp Gordon, GA 8/1/42. T/5 Co. D, transf. Co. A, Camp Gordon, GA, 12/16/42. T/5, Co. D, LST 422 Survivor, 1/26/44 Italy (Anzio) – Purple Heart. T/5, Co. A, 5/8/45 Innsbruck, Austria.

DE ANGELIS, Dick. b. 1923 NY. Res. San Francisco Co., CA. Enl. 6/30/42 San Francisco, CA. Ser. No. 39045208. Ser. No. O1176596. 2nd Lt., Co. C, KIA, 12/7/43, Italy, SR Cem.

DE BERRY, James C. b. 2/26/1921 TN. Res. Robertson Co., TN. Enl. 9/17/42 Ft. Oglethorpe, GA. Ser. No. 34371528. Pvt., Co. A, Camp Gordon, GA 10/7/42. Transf. Co. C, Camp Gordon, GA, 12/16/42. d. Nov. 1983 Cross Plains, Robertson Co., TN.

DE CATO, Michael. Pvt., HQ & HQ Co., Camp Gordon, GA 4/10/43.

DeCESARE [De Cesare], Charles J. b. 1918 CT. Res. Fairfield Co., CT. Enl. 3/17/41 Hartford, CT. Ser. No. 31022961. 1st. Lt., Co. A, 5/8/45 Innsbruck, Austria.

DECKER, Clyde V. b. 1918 OH. Enl. 10/5/42 Philadelphia, PA. Ser. No. 33338231. Pvt., Co. D, Camp Gordon, GA 10/9/42. Present Co. D, Camp Gordon, GA, 1/9/43.

DECKER, Leymoyne E. b. 1911 MD. Res. Cook Co., IL. Enl. 4/3/42 Chicago, IL. Ser. No. 36328492. Pvt., Co. C transf. HQ & HQ Co., Camp Gordon, GA 6/15/42. Cpl. (temp.), HQ & HQ Co., promo. Sgt. (temp.), Camp Gordon, GA 9/1/42. Promo. S/Sgt. (temp.), Camp Gordon, GA 10/1/42. T/Sgt. (temp.), HQ Co. promo. to 1st Sgt. (temp.), Camp Gordon, GA 1/25/43. T/Sgt., HQ Co., 5/8/45 Innsbruck, Austria. EAME Theater Ribbon with 6 Bronze Stars & 1 Arrowhead, Bronze Star. Res. Chicago, IL May 1954. Chemist/Armour Co. Attended 1956 & 1958 Reunions as res. Chicago, IL. Res. San Diego, CA.

DECKER, Myles V. b. 2/6/1922 PA. Enl. 9/21/42 Greensburg, PA. Ser. No. 33294458. Pvt. Co. C, 10/15/42 Camp Gordon GA. Pvt., Co. C, MIA, 8/29/44 Briançon, France. POW Stalag 7A Moosburg, Bavaria. Liberated 7/27/45. d. Aug. 1970 East Hickory, Forest Co., PA.

DEES, Mack L., Jr. b. 1920 MS. Res. De Soto Co., MS. Enl. 9/22/42 Camp Shelby, MS. Ser. No. 34426780. Pvt. Co. C, 10/14/42 Camp Gordon, GA. Pfc., Co. C, KIA, 11/13/43, Italy, SR Cem.

DE FEO, Anthony J. b. 7/2/1921 PA. Res. Philadelphia, PA. Enl. 9/22/42 Philadelphia, PA. Ser. No. 33335454. Pvt., Co. C, Camp Gordon, GA 10/9/42. Corp., Co. C, LST 422 Survivor, 1/26/44 Italy (Anzio) – Purple Heart. Sgt., Co. C, MIA, 8/29/44 Briançon, France. POW Stalag 7A Moosburg, Bavaria. Liberated 7/21/45. d. Aug. 1987 Philadelphia, PA.

DEIHL, Earl K. b. 8/25/1918 PA. Res. Northampton, PA. Enl. 3/20/42 Ft. George Meade, MD. Ser. No. 33178652. Sgt., Co. A, Camp Gordon, GA 4/10/43. d. May 1960 PA.

DEIST, Leo C. b. 7/19/1920 PA. Res. Meyersdale, PA. Enl. 10/5/42 Altoona, PA. Ser. No. 13084657. Pvt., Co. D, Camp Gordon, GA 10/9/42. Cpl., Co. D, LST 422 Survivor, 1/26/44 Italy (Anzio) – Purple Heart. Sgt., Co. D, WIA (light), 4/26/44 Anzio, Italy. Present at Indiantown Gap, Grantville, PA late 1944. Assigned as an M.P. at Pittsburgh, PA. d. 12/15/98 Lakemore, Summit Co., OH.

DE LEON, Vicente V. Pvt., Co. C, WIA (light-shot in right leg), 8/29/44, Briançon, France. Returned to duty 9/16/44. Pfc., Purple Heart [Presented 11/20/44]. Pfc., Med. Det., 5/8/45 Innsbruck, Austria. Res. San Jose, CA, 2009.

DE LUCAS, George Emil. b. 1917 Haddonfield, NJ. Res. Camden Co., NJ. Enl. 7/9/42 Camden, NJ. Ser. No. 32271712. Pvt., Co. B, Camp Gordon, GA 7/28/42. Pfc., Co. B, promo. Cpl. (temp.), Camp Gordon, GA 12/12/42. Present in North Africa, Sicily, Italy. Sgt., Co. B, WIA (serious – shell burst) 2/18/44 Anzio, Italy - Purple Heart. Evacuated. Good Conduct Medal. WW II Victory Medal. American Theatre Ribbon. ETO Ribbon with three battle stars. Furniture Sales, Strawbridge & Clothier, Phil., PA for 35 years. Attended 1954, 1956, 1958, 1960, 1962, & 1966 Reunions as res. Haddonfield, NJ. Retired 1979. Res. Ocean City, NJ 2005. d. 8/29/2005 Somers Point, NJ. Private burial.

DeMARCO, Silverino V. b. 2/6/1913. Boston University School of Medicine 1936. Res. Jersey City, NJ. Lt., 9/28/43. Promo. Capt. 12/29/43. Capt., Medical Corps, Survivor LST 422, 1/26/44 Italy (Anzio) – Purple Heart. Transf. 83rd CMB to 95th Evac. Hosp. 7/31/44. d. 3/26/2002 Spring Lake, Monmouth Co., NJ.

DE MARTELEIRE, Charles. b. 1913 PA. Enl. 9/22/42 Philadelphia, PA. Ser. No. 33335442. Pvt., Co. C, Camp Gordon, GA 10/9/42. Pvt., Co. C, MIA, 1/26/44, Italy (Anzio) SR Cem.

DE MASI, Louis A. b. 1915 CT. Res. Fairfield Co., CT. Enl. 2/17/42 Ft. Devens, MA. Ser. No. 31065483. Pfc., Co. C, 6/22/45 Innsbruck, Austria.

DE MATTEO, Joseph. Res. CT. Ser. No. 06150715. Pvt., Co. C, MIA, 1/26/44, Italy (Anzio) SR Cem.

DEN HAESE, James A. b. 1916 PA. Enl. 12/14/42 Philadelphia, PA. Ser. No. 33475158. Pvt., Co. A, Camp Gordon, GA 3/18/43.

DENNIS, Rollo D. b. 1922 MI. Res. Jackson Co., MI. Enl. 11/23/42 Kalamazoo, MI. Ser. No. 36411389. Pfc., transf. 2nd CMB 7/25/45.

DE PALMA, Pasquale. b. 1919 CT. Res. New Haven Co., CT. Enl. 12/14/42 Hartford, CT. Ser. No. 31274305. Pvt., Co. B, Camp Gordon, GA 4/10/43. Pvt., Co. B, sent to hospital (120th Collecting Bn.) 8/4/43. Returned to duty 8/8/43. HQ Co. 1/25/45. Pfc., HQ Co., 5/8/45 Innsbruck, Austria. Jeep driver for Gordon Mindrum. Claimed that prior to the war he was a gangster.

DE SPAIN, Kenneth E. b. 1922 KY. Res. Sangamon Co., IL. Enl. 3/23/43 Peoria, IL. Ser. No. 36478392. Jeep driver for Lt. Robert J. Bush of Co. A, 5/2/44. Bush called him, "A swell fellow and a damn good guy." Pvt., Co. A, on *LST 690* 8/9/44. Pfc., Co. B, 5/8/45 Innsbruck, Austria.

DETWEILER, Jacob C. b. 6/5/1922 PA. Res. Montgomery Co., PA. Enl. 12/14/42 Allentown, PA. Ser. No. 33485004. Pvt., Co. A, Camp Gordon, GA 3/16/43. Pfc., Co. A, 5/8/45 Innsbruck, Austria. d. Jan. 1983 PA.

DEVEREAUX, Frank J. Pvt., Co. A, Camp Gordon, GA 10/9/42. Transf. Co. D, Camp Gordon, GA, 12/16/42. Ser. No. 13116749. A. J. Brown recalled Devereaux "AWOL at Anzio."

DE VITA, Joseph C. b. 1917 NY. Res. Kings Co., NY. Enl. 3/21/42 Camp Upton, Yaphank, NY. Ser. No. 32231393. Sgt., Co. C, MIA, 1/26/44, Italy (Anzio) SR Cem.

DEVLIN, John A. Pfc., Co. C, 6/22/45 Innsbruck, Austria.

DEVON, Edward B. b. 8/27/1918 MD. Res. Chester Co., PA. Enl. 3/2/42 Ft. George Meade, MD. Ser. No. 33171181. Pvt. Attached to Co. B 5/28/42 Edgewood Arsenal, MD. Squad Leader (Sgt.). d. 5/28/2000 PA.

DE VOTO, Raymond J. b. 1917 CA. Res. Alemeda Co., CA. Enl. 1/5/42 Presidio of Monterey, CA. Ser. No. 39085237. Pfc., Co. A, Camp Gordon, GA 3/18/43. Pfc., HQ Co., 5/8/45 Innsbruck, Austria.

DeVRIES, ----------. On a list of 83rd men in Lt. Robert Bush's scrapbook.

DE YOUNG, Theodore C. b. 10/16/1918 PA. Res. Camden Co., NJ. Enl. 2/27/42 Ft. Dix, NJ. Pvt. Ser. No. 32243080. Attached to Co. G 5/28/42 Edgewood Arsenal, MD. Radio Operator (Corp. & Pvt.). Pfc., HQ & HQ Co. temp. T/5 Camp Gordon, GA 8/1/42. T/5 (temp.), promo. T/4 (temp.), Camp Gordon, GA 11/4/42. T/4, HQ Co., 5/8/45 Innsbruck, Austria. d. 5/22/2002 Clementon, Camden Co., NJ.

DIAL, Charles J. b. 1916 IL. Res. Essex Co., NJ. Enl. 7/3/42 Newark, NJ. Ser. No. 32388397. Pvt., Co. C, Camp Gordon, GA 7/28/42. Pfc., Co. C, transf. Co. D, Camp Gordon, GA 10/23/42. Promo. Cpl. (temp.), Camp Gordon, GA 11/5/42. Present at Pozzuoli, Italy March 1944. Company Clerk. Transf. shortly before Anzio breakout to a non-combat unit as his 2 brothers had been KIA. Job offered to Lee Steedle who declined. Attended OCS (Co. K, 3 Pat. Q.M.O.C.S., Camp Lee, VA) after returning home. Res. Montclair, NJ May 1954. Partner in Co. that manufactures handbag frames, and small metal parts for aircraft and

communications industries. Attended 1954, 1958 & 1966 Reunions as res. Montclair, NJ. George Borkhuis said Dial was "a swell chap."

DIANA, Anthony ("Tony"). b. 1922 PA. Res. Swissvale, PA. Enl. 10/9/42 Erie, PA. Ser. No. 13110309. Pvt. Co. D, 10/15/42 Camp Gordon GA. T/5, Co. D, LST 422 Survivor, 1/26/44 Italy (Anzio) – Purple Heart. Rescued by USS Pilot. Cpl., Co. A, 5/8/45 Innsbruck, Austria. Res. Swissvale, PA May 1954. Lab Tech Westinghouse Atomic Plant.

DICKERSON, Joseph (Joe) Cepus., Jr. b. 1921 MS. Res. Sunflower Co., MS. Enl. 9/23/42 Camp Shelby, MS. Ser. No. 34426682. Pvt. Co. C, 10/14/42 Camp Gordon, GA. Transf. Co. A, Camp Gordon, GA, 12/16/42. Pfc., Co. C, MIA, 1/26/44, Italy (Anzio) SR Cem.

DICKSTEIN, Jerome. b. 8/19/1918 NY. Enl. 7/9/42 Ft. Jay, Governors Island, NY. Ser. No. 32402164. Pvt., Co. A, Camp Gordon, GA 7/28/42. Pfc. Co. A, transf. Co. C, Camp Gordon, GA, 12/16/42. Pvt., Co. A, correspondent, Smokescreen, Camp Gordon, GA 1/9/43. Sgt., Co. A, distinguished in action 7/12/43 Gela, Sicily. d. 7/10/2002 Cortland, Cortland Co., NY.

DIEHL, Jesse M. b. 1898 MD. Res. District of Columbia. Enl. 9/21/42 Ft. Myer, VA. Ser. No. 33197656. Pvt., Co. A, Camp Gordon, GA 10/11/42. Transf. Co. C, Camp Gordon, GA, 12/16/42.

DIES, ----------. Pfc. Camp Gordon, GA. In Dan Shields' photo album.

DI GIVLIO, Constantino. 2nd Lt., relsd. 261st Inf. & assigned 83rd CMB 8/7/45.

DI LELLO, Raymond A. b. 1920 PA. Enl. 9/22/42 Philadelphia, PA. Ser. No. 33335497. Pvt., Co. B, Camp Gordon, GA 10/9/42. Pvt., Co. B, WIA – (light injure by plane strafing), 12/14/43 Italy.

DILGARDE, Lemoyne W. 2nd Lt., WIA (light – anti-personnel mine), 5/27/44 Italy - Purple Heart [Presented 11/20/44]. 2nd. Lt., Co. C, 6/22/45 Innsbruck, Austria. Assigned 134th Chem. Mortar Co. 7/19/45.

DI LUCCHIO, Gerardo. ("Jerry") b. 2/22/1913 Italy or San Marino. Res. Providence Co., RI. Enl. 12/14/42 Providence, RI. Ser. No. 31246178 Pvt., HQ & HQ Co., Camp Gordon, GA 4/10/43. Pvt., HQ & HQ Co., WIA (light), 11/30/43 Venafro, Italy. Jeep driver for Lt. Walter Hauser. Present at Zellenberg, France Nov. 44. Pfc., HQ Co., 5/8/45 Innsbruck, Austria. d. 10/31/89 East Providence, Providence Co., RI.

DI PINTO, Anthony W. b. 2/7/1923 MA. Res. Middlesex Co., MA. Enl. 2/2/43 Boston, MA. Ser. No. 31294648. Pfc., Co. C, 6/22/45 Innsbruck, Austria. d. 2/21/1998 Somerville, Middlesex Co., MA.

DI RIEMIGIO, Dominic J. b. 10/2/22. Pvt., Co. A, WIA (light – anti-tank mine), 5/24/44 Anzio, Italy. Not hospitalized. Pvt., Co. A, on *LST 690* 8/9/44. Believed to be the "Dommick" that was WIA (bruised by a dud enemy shell), 1/6/45 Lichtenberg. Pfc., Co. A, 5/8/45 Innsbruck,

Austria. d. Nov. 1985 Elizabeth, Union Co., NJ.

DI RIENZO, John A. b. 1921 PA. Enl. 9/21/42 Harrisburg, PA. Ser. No. 33240932. Pvt., Co. B, Camp Gordon, GA 10/9/42. Pvt., Co. B, WIA (light injure), LST 422 Survivor, 1/26/44 Italy (Anzio).

DOBRIN, Michael. b. 2/7/1922 PA. Enl. 9/25/42 Pittsburgh, PA. Ser. No. 33305619. Pvt. Co. B, 10/15/42 Camp Gordon GA. T/5, Co. B, 5/8/45 Innsbruck, Austria. Attended 1954, 1956, 1958, 1962 & 1966 Reunions as res. Baden, PA. d. 6/23/1989 PA.

DOERFLER, Herbert A., Jr. b. 2/21/1925. Pfc., Co. A, 5/8/45 Innsbruck, Austria. U.S.A.R. 1950-51. Res. Boston, Mass. May 1954. Science & Math Teacher, Boston Trade High School. d. 3/4/1999 East Hampton, MA.

DOMYON, William G. b. 1913 NJ. Res. Passaic Co., NJ. Enl. 6/25/42 Newark, NJ. Ser. No. 32366199. Pvt., Co. C, Camp Gordon, GA 7/28/42. T/5, Co. C, WIA (light – head abrasion), LST 422 Survivor, 1/26/44 Italy (Anzio). Rescued by USS YMS 226. Taken to 93rd Evac. Hosp. Bronze Star for service 7/10/43-10/17/44 in Sicily, Italy, and France.

DONAHUE, John A. b. 1914 PA. Res. Camden Co., NJ. Enl. 2/27/42 Ft. Dix, NJ. Ser. No. 32243131. Pvt. Attached to Co. G 5/28/42 Edgewood Arsenal, MD. Gunner (Pvt.). Pfc., Co. B, Camp Gordon, GA 8/17/42.

DONALD, James M. Res. NJ. Ser. No. 01173219. Field Artillery. 2nd Lt., Co. D, MIA, 1/26/44, Italy (Anzio) SR Cem.

DONALD, Troy. b. 1916 MS. Res. Scott Co., MS. Enl. 9/23/42 Camp Shelby, MS. Ser. No. 34426651. Pvt. Co. D, 10/14/42 Camp Gordon, GA. Pfc., Co. D, WIA (light), 11/24/43 Italy.

DONNELLY, Edward J. b. 1905 PA. Enl. 12/15/1942 Philadelphia, PA. Ser. No. 33475546. Pvt., Co. A, Camp Gordon, GA 3/18/43.

DONOGHUE, Joseph M. b. 1922 PA. Res. Allegheny Co., PA. Enl. 2/23/42 Pittsburgh, PA. Pvt. Attached to Co. G 5/28/42 Edgewood Arsenal, MD. Gunner (Pvt.). Pfc., Co. C, Camp Gordon, GA 12/19/42. Ser. No. 13058400. Pfc., Co. C, MIA, 1/26/44, Italy (Anzio) SR Cem.

DOOLEY, Roy H. b. 1924 VA. Enl. 4/22/43 Roanoke, VA. Ser. No. 33648813. Pvt., Co. A, on *LST 690* 8/9/44. Pfc., Co. A, 5/8/45 Innsbruck, Austria.

DORMAN, Rufus L. b. 9/18/1904 AL. Res. Fulton Co., GA. Enl. 9/23/42 Ft. McPherson, Atlanta, GA. Ser. No. 34443555. Pvt., Co. B, Camp Gordon, GA 10/12/42. Transf. Co. A, Camp Gordon, GA, 12/16/42. d. Dec. 1968 Opp, Covington Co., AL.

DOSTER, Russell S. b. 11/30/1915 MD. Enl. 9/26/42 Baltimore, MD. Ser. No. 33377165. Pvt. Co. D, 10/15/42 Camp Gordon GA. Transf. Pfc., 548th Army Postal Unit,Southern France, 1944. Res. Sparks, MD May 1954. Cost Accountant, Crown Cork & Seal Co., Baltimore. At-

tended 1954, 1956, 1958, 1960, 1962 & 1966 Reunions as res. Sparks, MD. d. 2/23/1994 Cockeysville, Baltimore Co., MD.

DOUGHERTY, James Francis ("Doc"). b. 1/31/1919 PA. Quit school & did odd jobs. Installed boilers, Navy Yard, Philadelphia, PA. Enl. 9/22/42 Philadelphia, PA. Ser. No. 33335551. Pvt., Co. D, Camp Gordon, GA 10/9/42. Pfc., Co. D, LST 422 Survivor, WIA (light injure), 1/26/44 Italy (Anzio). Returned to duty 6/20/44. Pfc., Co. A, 5/8/45 Innsbruck, Austria. Attended 1954 Reunion as res. Philadelphia, PA. Worked for Texas Co. (Texaco), Philadelphia, PA & Westville, NJ.. Attended 1958, 1960 & 1966 Reunions as res. Glassboro, NJ. Spelled Daugherty in some sources.

DOUGHERTY, William J., Jr. b. 1914 PA. Enl. 10/5/42 Philadelphia, PA. Ser. No. 13124649. Pvt., HQ & HQ Co., Camp Gordon, GA 10/9/42. T/5, apptd. T/4, HQ & HQ Co. 4/15/43. T/4, Co. C, 6/22/45 Innsbruck, Austria.

DOUGHTEN [Doughton], William Simpson, Jr. b. 4/26/1919 Philadelphia, PA. MIT upperclassmen initiated into Alpha Chi Sigma, honorary chemical fraternity 5/11/40, Pledge for Delta Kappa Epsilon 1941, graduated MIT June 1941. 1st Lt., C.W.S. 5/28/42 Edgewood Arsenal, MD May 28, 1942. 1st. Lt./Adjutant 6/10/42, Camp Gordon, GA. Bn. Postal Officer, 6/12/42. 1st Lt./Assistant Adjutant, Camp Gordon, GA Sept. 1942. Released as Adj. & designated Asst. Adj., Camp Gordon, GA 9/25/42. Released as Asst. Adj. & designated Adj., Camp Gordon, GA 10/10/42. Released as Adj. & Postal Officer & designated Communications Officer, Camp Gordon, GA 12/2/42. 1st Lt., Co. A, KIA (stepped on a land mine), 7/10/43, Gela, Sicily. Body brought aboard the U.S.S. Joseph T. Dickman at 7:00 a.m. 7/10/43. Body transferred to shore 7/11/43. Lt. Doughten's father was VP of Whitman's Chocolates Co. and sent free candy to the battalion. At Camp Gordon Lt. Doughten made out a will witnessed by Thomas M. Bolton, David Meyerson, and Carl K. Carpenter.

DOUGLAS, Dale D. b. 9/1/1911 IA. Res. Louisa Co., IA. Enl. 12/21/42 Camp Dodge, Herrold, IA. Ser. No. 37651664. Pvt., Co. A, Camp Gordon, GA 4/10/43. d. Dec. 1966 IA.

DOUGLAS, Thomas A. Cpl., HQ Co., 5/8/45 Innsbruck, Austria. Postwar: Dentist, Louisville, KY.

DOWELL, Allen P. b. 1921 TN. Res. Davidson Co., TN. Enl. 9/18/42 Ft. Oglethorpe, GA. Ser. No. 34371724. Pvt., Co. B, Camp Gordon, GA 10/7/42. Transf. Co. A, Camp Gordon, GA, 12/16/42.

DOWNEY, William H. b. 1921 NY. Res. Newark, NJ/Wayne Co., NY. Enl. 7/11/40 Rochester, NY. Enlisted for Philippine Dept. Field Artillery. Ser. No. 12002181. Pvt., Co. C, LST 422 Survivor, 1/16/44 Italy (Anzio) – Purple Heart.

DOYLE, James L. b. 1905 PA. Res. Philadelphia Co., PA. Enl. 3/12/42 Ft. George Meade, MD. Ser. No. 33173664. Pfc., Co. C, (Squad Leader), promo. Cpl. (temp.), Camp Gordon, GA 7/15/42. In a group photo of Co. C taken 1943 at Amalfi, Italy. Promoted 2nd Lt., Co. C, Nov. 1943. LST 422 Survivor, 1/26/44 Italy (Anzio) – Purple Heart. 1st Lt., Co. C,

MIA, 8/29/44 Briançon, France. POW Stalag 7A Moosburg, Bavaria. Liberated 7/24/45.

DOYLE, Paul W. b. 1923 IL. Res. Mason Co., IL. Enl. 4/3/43 Peoria, IL. Ser. No. 36480738. Sgt., Co. B, promo. S/Sgt. (temp.) 9/15/45.

DRAHN, Lloyd C. b. 1918 IA. Res. Clayton Co., IA. Enl. 7/6/43 Camp Dodge, Herrold, IA. Ser. No. 37674415. T/5, Co. C, 6/22/45 Innsbruck, Austria.

DRUGACH, Nicholas. b. 12/7/1910 PA. Res. Bergen Co., NJ. Enl. 6/24/42 Newark, NJ. Ser. No. 32385851. Pvt., HQ & HQ Co., Camp Gordon, GA 7/28/42. Pfc., HQ Co., Camp Gordon, GA 12/19/42. d. 1/28/2004 NJ.

DRUKENMILLER, Donald E. Pvt. Attached to Co. A 5/28/42 Edgewood Arsenal, MD. Platoon Sgt. (S/Sgt.).

DUBOIS, Girard [Gerard] Laurier. b. 3/25/1922 Magog, Quebec, Canada. Moved to North Troy, VT as a young boy. Moved to Newport Center, VT. Naturalized at Lake Placid, NY. Res. Newport Center, Orleans Co., VT. Pre-war Occupation: Canadian Pacific Railroad Enl. 12/4/42 Rutland, VT. Ser. No. 312000624. Pvt., Co. C, Camp Gordon, GA 4/2/43. Pvt., Co. C, LST 422 Survivor, 1/26/44 Italy (Anzio) – Purple Heart. Corp., Co. C, MIA, 8/29/44 Briançon, France. POW, Stalag 7A Moosburg, Bavaria. Liberated 5/30/45. Dischd. Res. Newport Center, VT. [name Gezard on ser. no.] Res. North Troy, VT. Postwar Occupation: Canadian Pacific Railroad. Carpenter. Retired as a factory worker 1986. d. 7/19/1989 North Troy, VT. bur. Notre Dame Cem., North Troy, VT.

DUDAS, Thomas C. b. 1924. Enl. 4/10/43 Greensburg, PA. Ser. No. 33670695. Pvt., Co. D, WIA (light), 6/1/44 Italy. Evacuated to hospital.

DUDENICH, Peter ("Chow Hound"). b. 1921 PA. Res. Ambridge, Beaver Co., PA. Enl. 9/25/42 Pittsburgh, PA. Ser. No. 33305615. Pvt. Co. C, 10/15/42 Camp Gordon GA. Co. C, Camp Gordon, GA Nov. 1942. Pfc., Co. C, MIA, 1/26/44, Italy (Anzio) SR Cem.

DUDLEY, James J. b. 1909 VA. Res. Huddleston, Bedford Co., VA. Enl. 9/21/42 Roanoke, VA. Ser. No. 33213311. Pvt. Co. D, 10/11/42 Camp Gordon GA. Transf. Co. A, Camp Gordon, GA, 12/16/42. T/5, Co. D, KIA, 1/26/44, Italy (Anzio) SR Cem. Body recovered 1/26/44 by YMS 34 & buried at sea same day. Next of kin: Daisy C. Dudley, Huddleston, VA.

DUGAN, George. Present in HQ Co. 8/4/45.

DUGAN, Raymond S., Jr. b. 7/3/1922 PA. Enl. 10/5/42 Philadelphia, PA. Ser. No. 13124672. Pvt., Co. A, Camp Gordon, GA 10/9/42. Pfc., Co. A, on *LST 690* 8/9/44. Pfc., promo. Cpl. (temp.) 11/17/44. Cpl., Co. B, 5/8/45 Innsbruck, Austria. d. 5/24/1991 Philadelphia, Philadelphia Co., PA.

DUKE, Ralph A. b. 1921 AL. Res. Bridgeport, Jackson Co., AL. Enl. 10/8/42 Ft. McClellan, AL. Ser. No. 34394162. Pvt., Co. D, LST 422 Survivor, 1/26/44 Italy (Anzio) – Purple Heart. Rescued by USS YMS 226. Taken to 93rd Evac. Hosp.

DULANEY, Floyd. b. 3/18/1921 MS. Res. Itawamba Co., MS. Enl. 9/23/42 Camp Shelby, MS. Ser. No. 34426918. Pvt. Co. D, 10/14/42 Camp Gordon, GA. d. Jan. 1974 Fulton, Itawamba Co., MS.

DUNAEFF, Alec [Alex] J. b. 1922 NY. Res. New York, New York Co., NY. Enl. 11/30/42 New York City, NY. Ser. No. 32648693. Pvt., Co. C, Camp Gordon, GA 4/2/43. Pvt., Co. C, LST 422 Survivor, 1/26/44 Italy (Anzio) – Purple Heart. Fell ill at Anzio and spent time in a Naples hospital. Pfc., Co. C, promo. Cpl. (temp.), 11/1/44. Cpl., WIA (slight – shell burst in barrel – shrapnel in leg), 1/9/45 France. Loy Marshall nicknamed him "The Crazy Russian."

DUNDERDALE, George T. Ft. Custer, MI. Joined Lt. Robert Bush's platoon, Co. A, 9/26/44. 1st. Lt., Co. A, 5/8/45 Innsbruck, Austria. Res. Santa Monica, CA May 1954.

DUNDON, Edward T. b. 1910 MA. Res. Essex Co., MA. Enl. 2/26/42 Boston, MA. Pvt. Attached to Co. H 5/28/42 Edgewood Arsenal, MD. Squad Leader (Sgt.). Pfc., Co. C, (Squad Leader), promo. Cpl. (temp.), Camp Gordon, GA 7/15/42. Ser. No. 11048491. Sgt., Co. C, KIA, 1/26/44, Italy, FL Cem.

DUNLAP, Winfred L. b. 1920 MS. Res. De Soto Co., MS. Enl. 9/23/42 Camp Shelby, MS. Ser. No. 34426799. Pvt. Co. C, 10/14/42 Camp Gordon, GA. Pfc., Co. C, MIA, 1/26/44, Italy (Anzio) SR Cem.

DUNN, James O. Res. LA. Ser. No. 38415891. Pvt., Co. C, MIA, 8/29/44 Briançon, France. POW Stalag 7A Moosburg, Bavaria. Liberated 6/12/45.

DUNWIDDIE, Walter L. Jr. ("Dutch"). b. 1922 PA. Res. Allegheny Co., PA. Enl. 9/23/42 Pittsburgh, PA. Ser. No. 33305541. Pvt. Co. C, 10/15/42 Camp Gordon GA. Pfc., Co. C, KIA, 1/26/44, Italy (Anzio) SR Cem. [Also listed as KIA with Co. D 1/26/44].

DURFEE, Herbert E. b. 1924 MA. Res. Worcester Co., MA. Enl. 4/2/43 Springfield, MA. Ser. No. 31288046. Pvt., Co. A, on *LST 690* 8/9/44. Pfc., Co. A, 5/8/45 Innsbruck, Austria. Sgt. Dischd. 11/3/45. Accidentally mustered out as Pvt. Res. Dudley, MA. May 1954. Res. Lehigh, FL, 2009.

DURHAM, David I. b. 1918 AL. Res. Jackson Co., AL. Enl. 9/18/42 Ft. McClellan, AL. Ser. No. 34391649. Pvt., Co. A, Camp Gordon, GA 10/8/42. Sgt., Co. A, on *LST 690* 8/9/44. Sgt. Co. A, 5/8/45 Innsbruck, Austria.

DURHAM, Parks H., Jr. b. 1921 GA. Res. Polk Co., GA. Enl. 9/21/42 Ft. McPherson, Atlanta, GA. Ser. No. 34443267. Pvt., Co. C, Camp Gordon, GA 10/9/42. Pfc., Co. C, WIA (serious), 9/24/43 Maiori, Italy. Pfc., Co. C, MIA, 1/26/44, Italy (Anzio) SR Cem.

DURKEE, George E. b. 9/8/1910 NY. Res. Rensselaer Co., NY. Enl. 2/13/43 Albany, NY. Ser. No. 32748301. Pvt., Co. A, on *LST 690* 8/9/44. T/4, Co. B, 5/8/45 Innsbruck, Austria. d. 2/11/1989 Hoosick Falls, Rensselaer Co., NY.

DU ROSS, Frederick W. b. 1923 NY. Res. Essex Co., NY. Enl. 2/12/43 Albany, NY. Ser. No. 32748026. Pfc., Co. A, on *LST 690* 8/9/44. Pfc., Purple Heart [Presented 11/20/44]. Pfc., Co. C, 6/22/45 Innsbruck, Austria.

DUTY, Bernard. b. 4/20/1920 VA. Res. Buckingham Co., VA. Enl. 12/3/41 Richmond, VA. Ser. No. 33122008. d. June 1984, Buckingham Co., VA.

DUVALL, Richard E. Pvt., Co. C, 6/22/45 Innsbruck, Austria.

DYE, Fitzhugh. b. 1911 MS. Res. De Soto Co., MS. Enl. 9/23/42 Camp Shelby, MS. Pvt., Ser. No. 34426800. Pvt. Co. C, 10/14/42 Camp Gordon, GA. Co. C, (MWIA), 9/13/43, Maiori, Italy. Evacuated to Tunisia. d. at 104th Gen Hosp. 9/18/43. NA Cem. Rupert Burford lists Dye WIA 9/23/43.

DYER, Lester J. b. 1920 NJ. Grad. Camden Catholic High School, Camden, NJ. Pre-war Occupation: Kieckefer Container Co., Pennsauken, NJ. Res. Camden Co., NJ. Enl. 7/9/42 Camden, NJ. Pvt., Co. B, Camp Gordon, GA 7/28/42. Pfc., Co. B, promo. T/5 (temp.), Camp Gordon, GA 11/4/42. Ser. No. 32271784. T/4, Co. B, MIA, 1/26/44, Italy (Anzio) SR Cem.

EADDY, Crafton. b. 4/19/1924 SC. Res. Williamsburg Co., SC. Enl. 3/24/43 Ft. Jackson, Columbia, SC. Ser. No. 34649922. Pfc., HQ Co., 5/8/45 Innsbruck, Austria. d. 5/18/1996 Hemingway, burg, SC.

EADIE, James W. b. 1923 NH. Res. Wash., D.C. Enl. 12/15/42 Wash., D.C. Ser. No. 13143756. Pvt., Co. A, Camp Gordon, GA 3/18/43. Served in Africa; Gela, Sicily; fired 4.2 mortars. Received medical discharge 2/24/1944.

EAKINS, William J. b. 1916 NY. Res. Bergen Co., NJ. Enl. 7/1/42 Newark, NJ. Ser. No. 32387830. Pvt., HQ & HQ Co., Camp Gordon, GA 7/28/42. Pvt., HQ & HQ Co., assigned Battalion Motor Officer, Camp Gordon, GA 10/12/42. Motor Pool correspondent, Smokescreen, Camp Gordon, GA Nov. 1942. T/5, Motor Pool, correspondent, Smokescreen, Camp Gordon, GA, 1/9/43. Cpl., Battalion Motor Officer/Dispatcher to Officer Candidate School 3/28/43.

EARLEY, James D. b. 1913 MS. Res. Sunflower Co., MS. Enl. 9/19/42 Camp Shelby, MS. Ser. No. 34426124.Pvt. Co. C, 10/14/42 Camp Gordon, GA. Pvt., Co. C, MIA, 1/26/44, Italy (Anzio) SR Cem.

EATON, Everette E. b. 1916 MS. Res. Marion Co., MS. Enl. 5/23/41 Camp Shelby, MS. Pfc. Transf. 83rd CMB to HQ Ry. Sv. 7/18/44.

EBLEN, Glen F. b. 1906 TN. Res. Roane Co., TN. Enl. 5/29/41 Ft. Oglethorpe, GA. Ser. No. 34140097. T/5 (temp), Co. D, reduced to Pvt., 11/1/44. Pfc., HQ Co., 5/8/45 Innsbruck, Austria.

ECKEL, William C. b. 1916 TN. Res. Overton Co., TN. Enl. 4/1/43 Ft. Oglethorpe, GA. Ser. No. 34728452. Pvt., Co. C, MIA, 8/29/44 Briançon, France. POW, Stalag 7A Moosburg, Bavaria. Liberated 6/12/45.

ECKERSON, Ollie L. b. 1906 MO. Res. San Francisco Co., CA. Enl. 12/15/42 San Francisco, CA. Ser. No. 39034707. Pvt., HQ & HQ Co., Camp Gordon, GA 4/2/43. Pfc., Co. C, 6/22/45 Innsbruck, Austria.

ECKERT, George F. 2nd Lt., relsd. 260th Inf. & assigned 83rd CMB 8/7/45.

EDGE, Henry. b. 3/5/1923 SC. Res. Spartanburg, SC. Enl. 2/11/43 Ft. Jackson, Columbia, SC. Ser. No. 34645681. Pvt., Co. A on *LST 690* 8/9/44. Pvt., Co. A, on *LST 690* 8/9/44. Ammunition handler. Assigned from HQ 2nd Replacement Depot 11/17/44 as Pvt., Co. A. Pfc., Co. A, 5/8/45 Innsbruck, Austria. EAME Theater Ribbon with 5 Bronze Stars and Bronze Arrowhead. Res. Poplar Springs, SC. d. 4/17/2004 Woodruff, Spartanburg, SC.

EDMONDSON, Harold S. 2nd Lt., relsd. 261st Inf. & assigned 83rd CMB 8/7/45.

EDWARDS, Robert E. Res. Murphysboro, IL. Enl. Mar. 1942. 1st. Lt., Co. C, Camp Gordon, GA 6/13/42. Transf. Co. A, Camp Gordon, GA 7/27/42. Transf. Co. C to Co. A, Camp Gordon, GA 7/27/42. Transf. HQ & HQ Co., Camp Gordon, GA 11/26/42. Promo. Capt., Nov. 1942. Temp. released as Asst. Operations & Training Officer & designated Operations & Training Officer, Camp Gordon, GA 12/2/42. In hospital with yellow jaundice Nov. 1943. Capt., CWS, LST 422 Survivor, 1/26/44 Italy (Anzio) – Purple Heart. Present as S-1 3/24/44. Present as S-1, 5/9/44. Present as S-1 8/2/44. Capt., HQ Co., 5/8/45 Innsbruck, Austria. Purple Heart with Oak Leaf Cluster. Capt. Assigned HQ 65th Inf. Div., AC Sect. 7/23/45. Sent to 431st AAA. Remained in service until 1962. Promo. Maj. Edwards True Value Hardware Store. Attended 1966 Reunion. Retired 1973. d. 11/22/2000.

EELES, Kenneth. b. 12/30/1919. Present at Anzio, Italy 1/22/44. Pfc., Co. B, 5/8/45 Innsbruck, Austria. d. Jan. 1982 Des Plaines, Cook Co., IL.

EFFINGHAM, Dennis Harold. b. 7/1/1918 Huntington, Cabell Co., WV. Enl. 9/24/42 Huntington, WV. Ft. Bragg, NC. Rome-Arno, Southern France, Rhineland, Central Europe. American Theater Service Ribbon. European African Middle Eastern Service Ribbon. Good Conduct Medal. World War II Victory Ribbon. Six Battle Stars. Ser. No. 35446544. Pfc., Co. A, 5/8/45 Innsbruck, Austria. Cpl. Dischd. 11/2/45. Bricklayer. d. 5/11/1981 VA Hosp., Huntington, WV. Bur. Spring Hill Cem., Huntington, WV.

EFNOR, Sam/Samuel, Jr. b. 8/29/1918 Cuba, IL. Attended Knox College, Galesburg, IL: Degree in Chemistry. Entered service 1940. Lt., Dec. 1940. 2nd Chemical Mortar Battalion. Capt., Co. B, 2nd CMB, WIA (shell fragment in leg), Hill 715, Sicily. Capt., Co. B, 2nd CMB, Silver Star for Zappula River, Sicily action 8/9/43. Purple Heart 1944. Bronze Star. Replaced Meyerson in April 1944 as Maj. of 83rd. Maj. promo. Lt. Col. 10/17/44 replacing Hutchinson. Lt. Col., HQ Co.,

5/8/45 Innsbruck, Austria. Remained in service postwar – assigned Executive Officer Dugway Proving Grounds and later Post Commander. Transf. Atomic Energy Commission, Wash., D.C. Later attended Air Command and Staff School, Montgomery, AL. Deputy Commander, Rocky Mt. Arsenal, Denver, CO. Res. Denver, CO. May 1954. Rocky Mt. Arsenal. Commander, 81st Chemical Group, Ft. Bragg, NC. On staff of 7th Army, Stuttgart, Germany. Retired from military 1961 as Commanding Officer, Chemical Engineering Command, Edgewood Arsenal, MD. Moved to Salt Lake City, UT and entered second career in Civil Service. d. 8/19/2002 Salt Lake City, UT.

EGAN [S], George E., Jr. Res. Kaukauna, WI. Joined 83rd CMB in Sicily. Pvt., Co. D, KIA, 9/16 or 17/43 Vietre sul Mare, Italy.

EISENBERG, Harold ("Eisey"). Res. Chicago, IL. Ser. No. 36324398. Pvt. Attached to Co. C 5/28/42 Edgewood Arsenal, MD. Mechanic General (Pvt.). Pfc., HQ & HQ Co., (Co. Mechanic), promo. T/5 (temp.), Camp Gordon, GA 7/15/42. Cpl., HQ Co., Camp Gordon, GA 12/19/42. Promo. Sgt. (temp.), Camp Gordon, GA 12/21/42. HQ & HQ Co. May 1943. Sgt., Co. C, LST 422 Survivor, 1/26/44 Italy (Anzio) – Purple Heart. Pfc., Co. C, 6/22/45 Innsbruck, Austria. Res. Chicago, IL May 1954. Attended 1956 Reunion.

EKONEN, Tauno C. b. 1919 MI. Res. Washtenaw Co., MI. Enl. 5/5/1941 Detroit, MI. Ser. No. 36114181. Assigned from 65th Inf. Division as 2nd Lt., Co. B, 7/23/45. Res. Atlantic Mine, MI.

ELDER, Frank F. b. 10/22/1899 PA. Res. Armstrong Co., PA. Enl. 9/21/42 Pittsburgh, PA. Ser. No. 33304928. Pvt. Co. B, 10/15/42 Camp Gordon GA. d. Dec. 1973 Kittanning, Armstrong Co., PA.

ELLIOTT, Russell J. Assigned from 65th Inf. Division as 2nd Lt., Co. A, 7/23/45.

ELLIS, Herman L. b. 1917 PA. Enl. 9/22/42 Philadelphia, PA. Ser. No. 33335658. Pvt., Co. B, Camp Gordon, GA 10/9/42. Pvt., Co. B, special duty Battalion HQ, Camp Gordon, GA 12/19/42.

ELLIS, Jessie C. b. 1911 MS. Res. Itawamba Co., MS. Enl. 9/22/42 Camp Shelby, MS. Ser. No. 34426500. Pvt. Co. C, 10/14/42 Camp Gordon, GA. Re-enl. 10/18/45 Myrtle Beach AAF, SC. Pfc. Air Corps.

ELLISON, Dennis. b. 1923 GA. Res. Whitfield Co., GA. Enl. 2/27/43 Ft. McPherson, Atlanta, GA. Ser. No. 34762249. Pvt., Co. A, on *LST 690* 8/9/44. Assigned from HQ, 2nd Replacement Depot 11/17/44 as Pvt., Co. A. Pfc., Co. A, 5/8/45 Innsbruck, Austria.

ELLISON, Luther L. b. 1920. Res. Yazoo Co., MS. Enl. 9/23/42 Camp Shelby, MS. Ser. No. 34426661.Pvt. Co. C, 10/14/42 Camp Gordon, GA. Pfc., Co. C, KIA, 1/26/44, Italy (Anzio). Body found in Anzio harbor 5/7/44 and brought in for burial. SR Cem.

EMERSON, George B. b. 1918 VA. Res. Roanoke Co., VA. Enl. 10/5/42 Richmond, VA. Ser. No. 33226342. Pvt., Co. B, Camp Gordon, GA 10/11/42. Pvt., Co. B, Camp Gordon, GA Nov. 1942. Cut men's hair at Camp Gordon, GA Feb. 1943.

EMMONS, Arthur E. b. 1918 MI. Res. Chalevoix Co., MI. Enl. 12/22/42 Kalamazoo, MI. Ser. No. 36415599. Pvt., WIA (light injure – truck ran off road), 8/17/44 France. Returned to duty 10/3/44.

ENDLEIN, Frederick W. b. 2/14/1919 Haddonfield, NJ. Haddonfield High School. Res. Camden Co., NJ. Enl. 7/9/42 Camden, NJ. Ser. No. 32271697. Pvt., Co. B, Camp Gordon, GA 7/28/42. 'Joined 83rd in first filler group'. Pfc., Co. B, promo. Cpl. (temp.), Camp Gordon, GA 12/12/42. Sgt., Co. B, 5/8/45 Innsbruck, Austria. Dischd. Sept. 1945. Res. Moorestown, NJ May 1954. Electrician for Universal Rundle Co. of Camden, NJ, Wills & Stiles Electrical Contractor of Medford, NJ & Medford Leas of Medford, NJ from which he retired in 1984. d. 10/6/1999 Moorestown, Burlington Co., NJ. bur. Calvary Cemetery, Cherry Hill, NJ.

ENDSLEY. Robert W. b. 1924 IL. Res. Coles Co., IL. Enl. 2/2/43 Peoria, IL. Ser. No. 36445979. Pvt., Co. D, KIA, 1/26/44, Italy (Anzio), SR Cem.

ENGEL, Leo. Pvt. Attached to Co. I 5/28/42 Edgewood Arsenal, MD. Clerk (Corp. & Pvt.).

ENGEL, Rudolph R. ("Rudy"). b. 1906 WI. Res. Cook Co., IL. Enl. 6/29/42 Chicago, IL. Ser. No. 36355809. Pvt., HQ & HQ Co., Camp Gordon, GA 11/21/42. T/Sgt. T/5, Co. B, arrived Gela, Sicily, 7/11/43. T/S, Bronze Star [presented 4/25/44]. T/4, Co. B, 5/8/45 Innsbruck, Austria. Worked on NIKE project 1952, Allentown, PA. Res. Cicero, IL May 1954. Attended 1956, 1958 & 1966 Reunions as res. Cicero, IL.

ENGLE, Charles C. b. 9/6/1916 PA. Enl. 9/22/42 Philadelphia, PA. Ser. No. 33335601. Pvt., Co. C, Camp Gordon, GA 10/9/42. Transf., Co. A, Camp Gordon, GA, 12/16/42. Pfc., Bronze Star [presented 4/25/44 – not present having left the 83rd]. d. 3/9/1992.

ERICKSEN, Christian R. b. 10/18/1911 NJ. Res. Essex Co., NJ. Enl. 7/3/42 Newark, NJ. Ser. No. 32388566. Pvt., Co. A, Camp Gordon, GA 7/28/42. Cpl., distinguished in action 7/10/43 Gela, Sicily. Awarded Silver Star. Medic. Rotated 11/9/43. d. 6/25/2001 Jacksonville, FL.

ERICKSON, George J. b. 6/12/1911 MI. Res. Marquette Co., MI. Enl. 3/18/43 at Kalamazoo, MI.Ser. No. 36456999. Pvt., Co. A on *LST 690* 8/9/44. d. 11/19/1998.

ERSTEIN, Jonas D. b. 1918 NY. Res. Kings Co., NY. Enl. 7/6/42 Ft. Jay, Governors Island, NY. Ser. No. 32399791. Pvt., Co. A, Camp Gordon, GA 7/28/42. Pfc. Co. A, transf. Co. C, Camp Gordon, GA, 12/16/42. Served in all theaters. Received EAME Theater Ribbon and Asiatic-Pacific Campaign Medal. Served for 42 months from July 7, 1940 to December 31, 1945.

ERTZBERGER, Lawrence Glen. b. 4/9/1919 Martin, GA. Attended Franklin County High School. Pre-war Occupation: Thread Manufacturing Plant. Res. Toccoa, Stephens Co., GA. Enl. 9/24/42 Ft. McPherson, Atlanta, GA. Ser. No. 34443983. Pvt. Co. A, 10/14/42 Camp Gordon, GA. Transf. Co. B, Camp Gordon, GA, 12/16/42. Cpl., Co. A, on *LST 690* 8/9/44. Present as Cpl., Co. A, 11/16/44. Cpl., Co. B, 5/8/45

Innsbruck, Austria. After war served in Co. H, 410th Infantry, 103rd Div., until discharge. Res. Martin, GA 2009.

ESTERBROOK, William J. b. 10/24/1911. Pfc., Co. A, on *LST 690* 8/9/44. Pfc., Co. A, 5/8/45 Innsbruck, Austria. Mentioned in the May 1954 Directory. d. July 1984 Newburgh, Orange Co., NY.

ETTER, John S. Served in France as a radio operator with Lt. Francis J. Schleifer. Pfc., Co. B, 5/8/45 Innsbruck, Austria.

EUSEBI, Euro F. ("Eddie" / "Tiney"). b. 9/16/1921 NY. Res. Brooklyn, Kings Co., NY. Enl. 7/7/42 New York City, NY. Ser. No. 12090936. Pvt., Co. D, Camp Gordon, GA 7/28/42. Pvt., Co. D, Camp Gordon, GA 12/17/42. Pvt., Co. D, WIA, 9/9/43 Italy – Purple Heart. Pvt., Co. D, WIA (light), 6/2/44 Italy. Pvt., Co. D, WIA (light – enemy 81 mm mortar shell), 12/13/44 Bennwihr, France. Res. Lodi, NJ May 1954. Beater Room Engineer in Papermill. d. 5/1/1980 Long Beach, Los Angeles Co., CA.

EYERMAN, George E. b. 7/3/1901 PA. Enl. 9/22/42 Philadelphia, PA. Ser. No. 33335450. Pvt., Co. A, Camp Gordon, GA 10/9/42. d. Aug. 1975, Philadelphia, PA.

FABER, Stephen. b. 1920 NJ. Res. Union Co., NJ. Enl. 6/30/42 Newark, NJ. Pvt., Co. D, Camp Gordon, GA 7/28/42. Pvt., Co. D, special duty Communications School of 472nd Field Artillery, Camp Gordon, GA 10/12-17/42. Ser. No. 32387443. Cpl., Co. D, MIA, 1/26/44, Italy (Anzio) SR Cem.

FACCIOLO, Joseph J. b. 7/25/1918 PA. Res. Clifton Heights, PA. Enl. 10/5/42 Philadelphia, PA. Ser. No. 33338318. Pvt., Co. A, Camp Gordon, GA 10/9/42. Pfc., Co. A on *LST 690* 8/9/44. Article in 1972 Muzzleblasts. d. 10/20/2000 Royersford, PA.

FAGAN [Feagan], Laurence J. ("One Lung"/"Larry"). Res. OK. Pvt., Baptized at Anzio, Italy 4/1/44. Pvt., Co. B, WIA (light), 12/12/44, Riquewihr, France. Pfc., Co. B, 5/8/45 Innsbruck, Austria.

FAGAN, Leo Daniel. Res. OK. Reportedly first sea water baptism on Anzio Beachhead 4/1/44. Pfc., Co. B, 5/8/45 Innsbruck, Austria.

FAILE, Grady L. b. 1914 SC. Res. Mecklenburg Co., NC. Enl. 11/27/42 Camp Croft, SC. Ser. No. 34592091. T/5, Co. A, promo. T/4 (temp.) 7/24/45. Present as T/4, Co. A 8/4/45.

FAJKOWSKI, Henry E. ("Hank"). b. 1919 MD. Enl. 9/21/42 Baltimore, MD. Ser. No. 33376386. Pvt., Co. A, Camp Gordon, GA 10/11/42. Pvt., Co. A, assigned to Med. Det., Camp Gordon, GA 11/14/42. Transf. Co. B, Camp Gordon, GA, 12/16/42. Pfc., Co. B, recommended for Silver Star for gallantry & administering first aid while under shell fire 12/8/43. T/5, Bronze Star [Presented 11/20/44]. Present as Cpl., Med. Det., 2/1/45. T/5, Med. Det., 5/8/45 Innsbruck, Austria. Attended 1954 & 1958 Reunions as res. Baltimore, MD.

FANNIN, Robert F. b. 1921 PA. Res. Philadelphia Co., PA. Enl. 9/21/42 Philadelphia, PA. Ser. No. 33335324. Pvt., Co. D, Camp Gordon, GA

10/9/42. Transf. Co. A, Camp Gordon, GA, 12/16/42. Pvt., Co. D, KIA, 1/26/44, Italy (Anzio), SR Cem.

FARINA, Michael D. b. 5/71916 CT. Res. Fairfield Co., CT. Enl. 4/3/42 Hartford, CT. Ser. No. 31104226. Pvt. Attached to Co. K 5/28/42 Edgewood Arsenal, MD. Telephone Operator (Pvt.). Pfc., Co. C, detailed Supply, Camp Gordon, GA 8/3/42 Returned to Co. duty, Camp Gordon, GA 8/10/42. d. 5/25/2002 Stamford, Fairfield Co., CT..

FEERICK, Martin J. b. 1/30/1915. Pvt., Co. A, Camp Gordon, GA 7/28/42. Ser. No. 32402181. Pfc., Staff Member, Smokescreen, Camp Gordon, GA Feb. 1943. Pfc., Co. B, 5/8/45 Innsbruck, Austria. Res. Dumont, NJ May 1954. Foreign Correspondent, Chase National Bank of the City of New York. Attended 1954 & 1966 Reunions. d. Mar. 1984 Island Heights, Ocean Co., NJ.

FEIFER, John A. b. 1912 RI. Providence College 1936. Res. Providence Co., RI. Enl. 3/2/42 Providence, RI. Pvt. Attached to Co. C 5/28/42 Edgewood Arsenal, MD. Gunner (Pvt.). Pvt., Co. C transf. Co. D, Camp Gordon, GA 6/15/42. Ser. No. 11063287. Cpl. Co. D, transf. Co. A, Camp Gordon, GA, 12/16/42. Sgt., Co. D, MIA, 1/26/44, Italy (Anzio) SR Cem. Name appears on the War Memorial Grotto, Providence College.

FEITELL, Sidney. b. 7/9/1917. 1st Lt. Assigned HQ & HQ Co. & designated Dental Officer, Camp Gordon, GA 7/23/42. Transf. Med Det., Camp Gordon, GA 9/26/42. d. Oct. 1966 NY.

FELDMAN, Mike. b. 1909 Russia. Res. Hamilton Co., TN. Enl. 9/15/42 Ft. Oglethorpe, GA. Ser. No. 34371039. Pvt., Co. A, Camp Gordon, GA 10/7/42. Pfc., Co. A correspondent, Smokescreen, Camp Gordon, GA Nov. 1942. Transf. Co. D, Camp Gordon, GA, 12/16/42.

FENKNER, Elwood C. b. 4/2/1922 PA. Res. Philadelphia Co., PA. Enl. 12/14/42 Philadelphia, PA. Ser. No. 33475288. Pvt., Co. A, Camp Gordon, GA 3/18/43. d. 9/25/1991 PA.

FENSTER, Carl. b. 1919 NY. Enl. 7/9/42 Ft. Jay, Governors Island, NY. Ser. No. 32402220. Pvt., Co. A, Camp Gordon, GA 7/28/42. Pvt., assigned special duty with Battalion HQ 10/14/42 Camp Gordon, GA. T/5, Co. A, 5/8/45 Innsbruck, Austria. Company Clerk.

FENSTERMACHER, William P. b. 1921 PA. Res. Spotsylvania Co., VA. Enl. 9/21/42 Richmond, VA. Ser. No. 33225441. Pvt., Co. C, Camp Gordon, GA 10/11/42. T/5, Co. C, 6/22/45 Innsbruck, Austria.

FENTON, Robert Warren. b. 11/15/1919 Richmond, MI. Southeastern High School 1939. Detroit Eastern/Michigan State. Pre-war Occupation: Salesman-Dodge Motors. Enl. Oct. 1941. Ser. No. 01038612. QM/Truck Driver, Cheyenne, WY 10/10/41. OCS Nov. 1942 (CWS). Commissioned 3/20/43. Joined 83rd CMB July 1943. Battalion Motor Sgt., Camp Gordon, GA. 1st. Lt., HQ Co., 5/8/45 Innsbruck, Austria. Ammunition Officer. 1st Lt. Assigned 65th Inf. Div. 7/23/45. Capt. Nov. 1945. Bronze Star. Four years Agricultural College. Farmer. 27 years with Proctor & Gamble. Res. Cheboygan, MI 2006. Robert Bush said he was an excellent softball player. d. 11/6/2008 Cheboygan, MI.

bur. Oak Hill Cem., Aloha, MI.

FERRANCE [Ferrence], Joseph E. b. 1917 PA. Res. Elizabeth, Union Co., NJ. Enl. 2/21/42 Ft. Dix, NJ. Ser. No. 32240575. Pvt. Attached to Co. G 5/28/42 Edgewood Arsenal, MD. OCS, Commissioned Edgewood Arsenal, MD. Squad Leader (Sgt.). Pfc., Co. B, Camp Gordon, GA 8/3/42. Pfc., Co. B, promo. Cpl. (temp.), Camp Gordon, GA 8/19/42. Promo. Sgt. (temp.), Camp Gordon, GA 12/12/42. Sgt., Co. B, WIA (light), 12/8/43 San Pietro, Italy & cited for gallantry in action. Sgt., Co. B, WIA (light – shell burst), 2/18/44 Anzio, Italy. Evacuated. Attended 1962 Reunion as res. NY.

FERRELL, James R. Pvt. Attached to Co. C 5/28/42 Edgewood Arsenal, MD. Auto Rifleman (Pvt.). Sgt., Co. D, Camp Gordon, GA Nov. 1942.

FICHTLER, Rudolph M. b. 1919 NJ. Res. Bergen Co., NJ. Enl. 7/1/42 Newark, NJ. Pvt., Co. D, Camp Gordon, GA 7/28/42. Pfc., Co. D, promo. Cpl. (temp.), Camp Gordon, GA 11/5/42. Ser. No. 32387648. S/Sgt., Co. D, KIA, 1/26/44, Italy (Anzio) SR Cem.

FIDEOR, Charles B. b. 4/16/1919 NY. Res. Monroe Co., NY. Enl. 10/12/43 Rochester, NY. Ser. No. 42090672. Pvt., MIA, 8/29/44, France – also listed as Pvt., MIA, 12/12/44 France. d. 12/25/1994 Rochester, Monroe Co., NY.

FINEBERG, Eli D. b. 1910 OH. Res. Bronx Co., NY. Enl. 3/21/42 Camp Upton, Yaphank, NY. Ser. No. 32231296. Pfc., Co. A, (Squad Leader), promo. Cpl. (temp.), Camp Gordon, GA 7/15/42.

FINEFIELD, Edward B. Pvt. attached to Co. A 5/28/42 Edgewood Arsenal, MD. Gunner (Pvt.). Ser. No. 37116877. Pfc., Co. A, to Battalion Supply., Camp Gordon, GA 7/27/42. Transf. Co. A to HQ & HQ Co. & promo. Cpl. (temp.), Camp Gordon, GA 8/6/42. Promo. S/Sgt. (temp.), Camp Gordon, GA 11/23/42. Promo. T/Sgt., Camp Gordon, GA 12/21/42. Promo. 1st/Sgt. (temp.), Camp Gordon, GA 12/27/42.

FINLAY, James. b. 1912 NY. Res. Queens Co., NY. Enl. 3/10/42 Milwaukee, WI. Pvt. Attached to Co. C 5/28/42 Edgewood Arsenal, MD. Pvt., Co. A transf. Co. C, Camp Gordon, GA 6/15/42. Pfc., (Squad Leader), promo. Cpl. (temp.), Camp Gordon, GA 7/15/42. Squad Leader (Sgt.). Transf. Co. A, Camp Gordon, GA, 12/16/42. Ser. No. 16049753. 1st Sgt., Co. C, MIA, 1/26/44, Italy (Anzio) SR Cem.

FINORE, James J. b. 2/3/1921 NY. Res. Kings Co., NY. Enl. 7/9/42 Ft. Jay, Governors Island, NY. Ser. No. 32402374. Pvt., Co. D, Camp Gordon, GA 7/28/42. Pfc., Co. D, Camp Gordon, GA 11/14/42. Transf. Co. A, Camp Gordon, GA, 12/16/42. Sgt., Co. D, WIA (serious - from explosion of own shell hitting tree limb), 7/12/43 Gela, Sicily. Purple Heart, Bronze Star, Combat Infantryman Badge, EAME Theater Ribbon, WWII Victory Medal. Asst. Chief of Security, United Nations 1970. d. 4/4/1994 Boynton Beach, Palm Beach Co., FL.

FISCHER, Francis F. Pfc., HQ Co., presented Purple Heart 8/25/45.

FISCHER, Kenneth P. Assigned from 65th Inf. Division as 2nd Lt., Co. B, 7/23/45.

FISCUS, Lloyd L. b. 1/20/1925 Kane, PA. Res. McKean Co., PA. Enl. 4/19/43 Erie, PA. Ser. No. 33436973. 69th Division Aug. - Dec. 1943. Joined 83rd CMB Feb. 1944. Pvt., Co. C. (Norman Wahosky's Squad), MIA 8/29/44 Briançon, France. POW Stalag 7A Moosburg, Bavaria. Liberated 6/6/45. POW Medal. Dischd. Dec. 1945. Thompson College. Korean War 1950. VP, Boviard Co. Contributor MFP 1997. Res. Bradford, PA 2009.

FISHBEIN, Samuel. b. 1921 PA. Enl. 10/5/42 Philadelphia, PA. Ser. No. 13124655. Pvt., HQ & HQ Co., Camp Gordon, GA 10/9/42. Pvt., HQ & HQ Co., Camp Gordon, GA 11/21/42. Pfc., Co. B, 5/8/45 Innsbruck, Austria.

FISHER, James H. b. 3/28/1916 Linton, IN. Pre-war occupation: Inspector Refinery. Res. Newton Co., IN according to NARA Enl. record [Res. Lake Co., IN according to widow]. Enl. 3/30/42 Indianapolis, IN. Ser. No. 35350115. Pvt. Attached to Co. K 5/28/42 Edgewood Arsenal, MD. Gunner (Pvt.). Pfc., Co. B, promo. Cpl. (temp.), Camp Gordon, GA 12/12/42. Cpl., Co. B, WIA & cited for gallantry in action 12/8/43, San Pietro, Italy. T/4, Co. B, 5/8/45 Innsbruck, Austria. Embarked for U. S. 9/18/45. HQ Co. 2nd. Bn 409th Inf. Dischd. 9/25/45 Camp Atterbury, IN. EAME Theater Ribbon w/6 Bronze Stars & 1 Bronze Arrowhead. Good Conduct Medal. Purple Heart. Bronze Star. Attended 1956 & 1960 Reunions. d. 7/2/1992.

FITZGERALD, James Roger,("Doc"). b. 4/24/1921 Springfield. OH. Prewar occupation laboratory assistant. Res. Clark Co., OH. Enl. 12/2/43 Columbus, OH. Ser. No. 35296405. Started active duty at Ft. Thomas, KY 12/23/43. Basic training Ft. Sibert, AL 1/13/44. Mortar gunner. Departed for overseas 7/1/44, arrived Naples, Italy 7/15/44. Rome-Arno, So. France, Rhineland, Central Europe. Good Conduct Medal, EAME Service Medal w/4 Bronze Stars, & Victory Medal. Pfc., Co. C, 6/22/45 Innsbruck, Austria. Departed for US 11/21/45, arrived in US 11/29/45. Discharged as Cpl. 12/6/45 PA. d. 8/22/2008, Louisville, Jefferson Co., KY.

FITZPATRICK, Patrick E. b. 1921 PA. Res. Allegheny Co., PA. Enl. 5/26/44 New Cumberland, PA. Ser. No. 33940784. Pfc., Co. A, promo. T/5 (temp.) 7/24/45.

FIUMERA, Santino G. b. 1921 NY. Res. Delaware Co., NY. 4/12/43 Ft. Devens, MA. Ser. No. 11080159. Reserve Officer. Cavalry. Assigned from 65th Inf. Division as 2nd Lt., Co. A, 7/23/45.

FLANAGAN, Joseph F. HQ, 11th Armored Div., assigned 1st Lt., HQ & HQ Co., 83rd CMB 7/23/45.

FLANDERS, Herschel. b. 12/31/1924 GA. Res. Berrien Co., GA. Enl. 4/2/43 Ft. McPherson, Atlanta, GA. Ser. No. 34766577. Pfc., Co. B, 5/8/45 Innsbruck, Austria. d. June 1986 Bartow, Polk Co., FL.

FLEMING, Andrew S. Assigned from 65th Inf. Division as 2nd Lt., HQ & HQ Co. (Mtr. & Ammo Officer) 7/23/45. Assigned Co. B,

7/25/45.

FLEMING, John J. Pvt., HQ & HQ Co., Camp Gordon, GA 10/9/42. Ser. No. 33335479.

FLEWELLING, Charles L. b. 3/31/1917 NY. Res. Saratoga Co., NY. Enl. 4/8/43 Albany, NY. Ser. No. 32856076. Pfc., Co. B, 5/8/45 Innsbruck, Austria. d. May 1981 Corinth, FL.

FLONES, Melvin. Res. Ortley, SD. Pvt. Attached to Co. H 5/28/42 Edgewood Arsenal, MD. Squad Leader (Sgt.). Ser. No. 37115065. Ammunition Sgt., Co. C, LST 422 Survivor, 1/26/44 Italy (Anzio) – Purple Heart with Oak Leaf Cluster.

FLORY, Edward F. b. 9/3/1917 PA. Res. Franklin Co., PA. Enl. 7/5/43 Harrisburg, PA. Ser. No. 33512369. T/4, Co. C, 6/22/45 Innsbruck, Austria. d. 4/10/1995 Fayetteville, Franklin Co., PA.

FLOWERS, Alvin ("Screwball"). b. 1904 AL. Res. Lee Co., AL. Enl. 9/19/42. Ser. No. 34391811. Pvt., HQ & HQ Co., Camp Gordon, GA 10/9/42. HQ Co. Mentioned in the 12/12/42 issue of Smokescreen.

FLOYD, John H. b. 1914 GA. Res. Hamilton Co., TN. Enl. 9/12/42 Ft. Oglethorpe, GA. Ser. No. 34370268. Pvt., Co. B, Camp Gordon, GA 10/7/42. Pfc., Co. B, sent to hospital (120th Collecting Bn.) 8/8/43. Present at Anzio 1/22/44.

FOLEY, Sy S. b. 1906 TX. Res. Kimble Co., TX. Enl. 3/3/42 Ft. Bliss, El Paso, TX. Ser. No. 38101703. Pvt. Attached to Co. C 5/28/42 Edgewood Arsenal, MD. Cook (Pvt.). Pfc., Co. A, (Cook), promo. T/5 (temp.), Camp Gordon, GA 7/15/42. T/4 Co. A, transf. Co. D, Camp Gordon, GA, 12/16/42. T/4, Co. A, 5/8/45 Innsbruck, Austria.

FORAN, Thomas A. b. 1921 PA. Enl. 9/22/42 Philadelphia, PA. Ser. No. 33335550. Pvt., Co. A, Camp Gordon, GA 10/9/42. S/Sgt., Co. B, 5/8/45 Innsbruck, Austria.

FORD, William Clifford. b. 10/29/1921 MS. Res. New Albany, Union Co., MS. Enl. 9/23/42 Camp Shelby, MS. Ser. No. 34426824. Pvt. Co. C, 10/14/42 Camp Gordon, GA. Joined 83rd CMB Oct. 1942. Pfc., Co. C, LST 422 Survivor, 1/26/44 Italy (Anzio) – Purple Heart. Rescued by USS Pilot. Squad Leader, 1st Platoon. Bronze Star with Oak Leaf Cluster. Sgt., Co. C, 6/22/45 Innsbruck, Austria. S/Sgt. Dischd. Sept. 1945. U.S. Postal Service. Retired 1990. Contributed to MFP 1997. d. 5/6/2005.

FORMAN, Benjamin Z. b. 1924 LA. Res. Catahoula Co., LA. Enl. 6/24/43 Shreveport, LA. Ser. No. 38392401.

FORRESTER, Alfred L. ("Al"). b. 5/9/1918 IL. Res. Quincy, Adams Co., IL. Enl. 3/5/41 Quincy, IL. Ser. No. 20604279. 2nd Lt., CWS, assigned to Co. A, Camp Gordon, GA 11/26/42. Transf. Co. B, Platoon Officer, Camp Gordon, GA 12/2/42. 1st Lt., Co. D, LST 422 Survivor, 1/26/44 Italy (Anzio) – Purple Heart. Rescued by YMS 43. 1st Lt, CWS, Co. D, WIA (light – anti-personnel mine), 5/27/44 Italy – Purple Heart with Oak Leaf Cluster. Assumed Captaincy, Co. A, 1/21/45. Promo.

Capt., Co. A 3/1/45. Capt., Co. A, 5/8/45 Innsbruck, Austria. Capt. Assigned 65th Inf. Div. 7/23/45. Known for playing his accordion all day and night in bivouac. Res. Moline, IL May 1954. Employee, Eagle Signal Corp., Moline & Davenport, IA. Attended 1954, 1956 & 1966 Reunions. d. 6/24/1995 Quincy, Adams Co., IL.

FORTUNE, John Carlton. b. 1916 MS. Res. Union Co., MS. Enl. 9/28/42 Camp Shelby, MS. Ser. No.34426814. Pvt. Co. C, 10/14/42 Camp Gordon, GA. Pfc., Co. C, KIA, 1/26/44, Italy, FL Cem.

FOSTER, Herbert L. b. 1921 NC. Res. Wilson Co., NC. Enl. 9/7/40 Ft. Bragg, NC. Ser. No. 14018044. Enlisted for Philippine Dept. Pvt., Field Artillery. Pvt., Co. C, LST 422 Survivor, 1/26/44 Italy (Anzio). Pvt., Co. C, WIA (serious – enemy mortar shell), 5/8/44 Anzio, Italy. Served in 9th Infantry Div. Res. Lucama, NC.

FOSTER, Lloyd. b. 1922 MO. Res. Perry Co., MO. Enl. 12/10/42 Jefferson Barracks, MO. Ser. No. 37402998. Pvt., Co. B, Camp Gordon, GA 4/2/43.

FOSTER, Martin A. Pfc., Co. C, 6/22/45 Innsbruck, Austria.

FOWLER, Jack J. Pfc., Co. C, 6/22/45 Innsbruck, Austria.

FOX, Morris B. b. 1908 NY. Res. Philadelphia Co., PA. Enl. 12/14/42 Philadelphia, PA. Ser. No. 33475293. Pvt., Co. A, Camp Gordon, GA 3/18/43.

FRACASSA, Cuerino. Pvt., Co. C, WIA (light – enemy mortar shell), 5/8/44 Anzio, Italy.

FRAIND, Andrew J. b. 1917 PA. Res. Columbia Co., PA. Enl. 3/3/42 Ft. George Meade, MD. Pvt. Attached to Co. B 5/28/42 Edgewood Arsenal, MD. Auto Rifleman (Pvt.). Pfc., Co. C, promo. T/5 (temp.), Camp Gordon, GA 9/3/42. Pvt., Co. B transf. Co. C, Camp Gordon, GA 6/15/42. Ser. No. 33171553. T/4, Co. C, MIA, 1/26/44, Italy (Anzio) SR Cem.

FRAM, Paul E. b. 1913 PA. Enl. 5/15/42 Greensburg, PA. Ser. No. 33275320. S/Sgt., HQ Co. promo. 1st Sgt. (temp.) 9/15/45.

FRANCIS, Henry L., Jr. b. 1921 PA. Woodrow Wilson High School, Camden, NJ. Left school 1941 to work as chipper's helper, New York Shipbuilding Co. Res. Camden Co., NJ. Enl. 7/9/42 Camden, NJ. Ser. No. 32271802. Pvt., Camp Gordon, GA 7/28/42. Pvt., Co. B, Camp Gordon, GA 9/25/42. Sgt., Co. B, KIA, 12/12/44, Riquewihr, France, LO Cem.

FRANKEL, Hiram Dave. b. 5/21/1910 MN. Res. Bergen Co., NJ. Enl. 7/6/42 Newark, NJ. Ser. No. 32387648. Pvt., Co. D, Camp Gordon, GA 7/28/42. Pfc., Co. D, promo. Cpl. (temp.), Camp Gordon, GA 11/5/42. Served as a Lt. with 81st CMB in France. d. 6/17/1995 La Luz, Otero Co., NM.

FRANKLIN, Albert. In a group photo in Leonard W. Turan's photo album.

FRANKLIN, Walter J. b. 1908 OH. Res. Huron Co., OH. Enl. 12/21/42 Toledo, OH. Ser. No. 35538130. Pvt., Co. A, Camp Gordon, GA 4/10/43. Pvt., Co. A, WIA (light – leg – bruised by dirt thrown from exploding shell) 7/12/43 Gela, Sicily. Sent to hospital in Africa 7/14/43.

FRASCINO, Dom. Mentioned in the 5/7/43 entry on the Monticello in the Daniel Shields diary. [Probably Dominic J. Frascino. b. 1917 PA. Enl. 10/26/42 Philadelphia, PA. Ser. No. 33342478].

FRAZIER, D. E. b. 1918 TX. Res. Harris Co., TX. Enl. 3/4/42 Ft. Sam Houston, TX. Ser. No. 38092979. Pvt. Attached to Co. C 5/28/42 Edgewood Arsenal, MD. Squad Leader (Sgt.). Present as Assistant Cook at Camp Gordon, GA. Pfc., Camp Gordon, GA 8/6/42. Pfc., Co. D, promo. T/5 (temp.), Camp Gordon, GA 8/19/42. T/5 (temp.) Co. D, promo T/4 (temp.), Camp Gordon, GA, 12/16/42. S/Sgt., Co. D, (light injure in action), LST 422 Survivor, 1/26/44 Italy (Anzio). Sgt. Mike Codega rescued Frazier. [probably same man mentioned as Cook of Co. D who survived LST 422 with a broken leg by Earl Kann in 2005 Muzzleblasts article]. Wofford L. Jackson said Frazier's "foot was behind his head like a pillow." George Borkhuis said Frazier was "a fair cook and a willing worker."

FRAZIER, Donald J. b. 5/10/1923 MD. Res. Dorchester Co., MD. Enl. 4/22/43 Baltimore, MD. Ser. No. 33722416. Pfc., Co. C, 6/22/45 Innsbruck, Austria. d. Nov. 1980 Cambridge, Dorchester Co., MD.

FREDERICK, Byron L. b. 9/11/1906 OH. Res. Wood Co., OH. Enl. 5/3/43 Toledo, OH. Ser. No. 35554667. Pfc., Co. B, 5/8/45 Innsbruck, Austria. Res. Bloomdale, OH May 1954. Carpenter, Electric Auto Lite Co., Spark Plug Div., Fostoria, OH. d. 5/24/1988 Bloomdale, Wood Co., OH.

FREE, ----------. Lt. Co. C. Captured six prisoners near Catignac, France 8/20/44 according to battalion journal.

FREEDMAN, Morris M. b. 1913 NY. Res. Erie Co., NY. Enl. 3/6/42 Ft. Niagara, Youngstown, NY. Ser. No. 32252002. Pvt. Attached to Co. B 5/28/42 Edgewood Arsenal, MD. Cook (Pvt.). Pfc., Co. D, assigned HQ & HQ Co. & report to Classification & Assignment, clerk general, Camp Gordon, GA 7/11/42. Pfc., (Clerk, Battalion HQ), promo. T/5 (temp.), Camp Gordon, GA 7/15/42. T/5 promo. Cpl., Camp Gordon, GA 8/7/42.

FREEMAN, Oscar W. b. 1921 AL. Res. Etowah Co., AL. Enl. 10/16/42 Ft. McClellan, AL. Ser. No. Ordnance Dept. Pvt., Co. D, WIA (serious – detonated an S-mine), Minturno, Italy 3/26/44.

FREER, Robert H. b. 1920 MI. Res. Vandercook Lake, Jackson Co., MI. Enl. 12/22/42 Kalamazoo, MI. Ser. No. 36415759. Pvt., Co. D, LST 422 Survivor, 1/26/44 Italy (Anzio) – Purple Heart. Rescued by USS Pilot.

FREET (FRETT), Douglas W. b. 4/10/1922 PA. Res. Hanover, York Co., PA. Enl. 10/5/42 Harrisburg, PA. Ser. No. 13093256. Pvt., Co. D, Camp Gordon, GA 10/9/42. Pvt., HQ & HQ Co., LST 422 Survivor, 1/26/44 Italy (Anzio) – Purple Heart. Pfc., transf. HQ Ry. Sv. 7/26/44.

d. 11/2/1997 Hanover, York Co., PA.

FRIES, Alfred C. b. 7/24/1919 PA. Enl. 12/14/42 Allentown, PA. Ser. No. 33484970. Pvt., Co. A, Camp Gordon, GA 3/18/43. d. Nov. 1984 Emmaus, Lehigh Co., PA.

FRINK, Edward H. b. 1924 VT. Res. Hartford Co., CT. Enl. 3/2/43 Hartford, CT. Ser. No. 31326425. Pfc., Co. C, 6/22/45 Innsbruck, Austria.

FRITSCH, Lawrence T. b. 1913 TX. Res. Harris Co., TX. Enl. 3/4/42 Ft. Sam Houston, TX. Ser. No. 38092975. Pvt. Attached to Co. C 5/28/42 Edgewood Arsenal, MD. Squad Leader (Sgt.). Pvt., Co. A transf. Co. C, Camp Gordon, GA 6/15/42. Pfc., (Squad Leader), promo. Cpl. (temp.), Camp Gordon, GA 7/15/42. Cpl. (temp.), Co. C, promo. Sgt. (temp.), Camp Gordon, GA 9/3/42. Transf. OCS, CWS, Edgewood Arsenal, MD Dec. 1942.

FULLAGAR, Robert L. b. 1919 NJ. Res. Cape May Co., NJ. Enl. 2/27/42 Ft. Dix, NJ. Pvt. Attached to Co. G 5/28/42 Edgewood Arsenal, MD. Mechanic Auto (Pvt.). Pvt., HQ & HQ Co. transf. Co. C, Camp Gordon, GA 6/15/42. Pfc., (Auto Mech.), promo. T/5 (temp.), Camp Gordon, GA 7/15/42. Ser. No. 32243223. Pvt., Co. C., KIA, 1/26/44, Italy (Anzio). Body recovered by U.S.S. Strive 1/26/44. Buried at sea 1/27/44. Name on tablet of dead and missing at SR Cem.

FULLER, Lenord B. b. 1910 TN. Res. Trousdale Co., TN. Enl. 9/16/42 Ft. Oglethorpe, GA. Ser. No. 34371299. Pvt., HQ & HQ Co., Camp Gordon, GA 10/7/42.

FULLER, Samuel E. Pvt. WIA (injured in glider crash) 8/15/44 Le Muy, France.

FULLINGTON, Elmer T. Pfc., Co. B, sick in Salemi, Sicily & sent to hospital (56th Medical, Trapani) 8/6/43. Returned to duty 8/14/43. Pfc., HQ Co., 5/8/45 Innsbruck, Austria.

FUNYAK, George J. b. 6/12/1920 PA. Res. Homestead, Allegheny Co., PA. Enl. 10/9/42 Greensburg, PA. Ser. No. 33392455. Pvt. HQ & HQ Co., 10/15/42 Camp Gordon GA. Pvt., HQ Co., Camp Gordon, GA Nov. 1942 – in hospital for eye operation. Pvt., Co. D, LST 422 Survivor, 1/26/44. Rescued by USS YMS 226. Taken to 93rd Evac. Hosp. Pfc., Co. A, 5/8/45 Innsbruck, Austria. d. May 1973 PA.

FURIS, Nick M. b. 1921 WV. Enl. 9/25/42 Pittsburgh, PA. Ser. No. 33305594. Pvt. Co. B, 10/15/42 Camp Gordon GA. Field Lineman (Radio Operator) 36th. Infantry Div. Co. B. Radio Operator. WIA 12-8-1943. Lost hearing in right ear from enemy shell hitting nearby which also caused permanent ringing in left ear. Sent home prior to Southern France invasion. Sicily, Naples-Foggia, Rome-Arno Campaigns. Purple Heart, Good Conduct Medal, EAME Theater Ribbon. Served 757th Military Police.

GABLES, Gene G. 2nd Lt., relsd. 260th Inf. & assigned 83rd CMB 8/7/45.

GABRIEL, Donald R. 2nd Lt., CWS. Edgewood Arsenal, MD, assigned Co. D, Camp Gordon, GA 11/25/42. Res. NY. Ser. No. O1036151. 1st Lt., Co. C, KIA, 1/26/44, Italy (Anzio) SR Cem.

GAGLIARDI, William J. b. 1923 NY. Res. Richmond Co., NY. Enl. 4/26/43 New York City, NY. Ser. No. 32897233. Sent to Ft. Bragg, NC for 155 mm howitzer training. Oran, Africa Oct. 1943. Jan. 1944 Naples. Trained as mortar crewmen at Pozzuoli to Cassino and then to Anzio as replacement for 83rd CMB men lost on LST 422. Pvt., Co. A, on *LST 690* 8/9/44. During Battle of the Bulge period was sent as a replacement to 54th Armored Battalion, 10th Armored Div., at Bastogne. Sherman tank gunner. Returned home Oct. 1945. New York City Fire Dept. for 30 years. Res. Staten Island, NY 2009.

GAILE, Murray. b. ca. 1924. Mortarman in 83rd CMB, Co. C. Fought at Anzio. Res. Manhattan, NY 2009.

GAISER, George E. Chaplain. Present with the 83rd CMB at Anzio and in Southern France. Tranf. 421st Field Artillery 10/4/44. Res. & Chaplain at Ft. Myer, VA May 1954.

GAISKI, Walter. b. 1917 KY. Enl. 3/17/42 Ft. Thomas, KY. Pvt. Attached to Co. I 5/28/42 Edgewood Arsenal, MD. Gunner (Pvt.). Ser. No. 35134832. Pvt., Co. C, to Cpl. (temp.) 10/14/42 Camp Gordon, GA. Sgt. Co. C, transf. Co. A, Camp Gordon, GA, 12/16/42. Sgt., Co. C, KIA, 1/26/44, Italy (Anzio). Body recovered 1/26/44 by USS YMS 226 and turned over to Graves Registration at Anzio 1/27/44. Only identification found on body was Soc. Sec. # and he had on a paratrooper uniform. SR Cem.

GALLAGHER, William James., Jr. ("Bill"). b. 3/20/1921 Philadelphia, PA. Grammar & High School. Graduated high school 1940. Pre-war Occupation: Dog Food Factory, Power Pipeline Company & Dupont Foreman Paint Division. Enl. 10/5/42 Philadelphia, PA. Ser. No. 13124671. Pvt., HQ & HQ Co., Camp Gordon, GA 10/9/42. Cpl., WIA (serious – right leg – evacuated), 2/1/45 France. Purple Heart. Sgt., Co. A. 1st Platoon, Communications Squad. Six months recovery from wound at Ashford General Hospital, White Sulphur Springs, WV. Dischd. Apr. 1946. Res. Philadelphia, PA May 1954. Dupont Employee. Retired 1986. Contributed to MFP 1997. Res. Philadelphia 2007. d. 10/16/2007.

GALLAHAN [Gallehan], James Hunter. ("Banjo Eyes"). b. 6/5/1921 Fredericksburg, VA. Attended Fredericksburg City School. Pre-war Occupation: Milk Truck Driver / Farmer's Creamery. Res. Fredericksburg, Spotsylvania Co., VA. Enl. 9/21/42 Richmond, VA. Ser. No. 33225714. Pvt. Co. D, 10/11/42 Camp Gordon GA. Pfc., Co. D, (light injure in action – shrapnel & burns), LST 422 Survivor, 1/26/44 Italy (Anzio) – Purple Heart. Returned to duty 2/2/44. Sgt., Co. D. WIA (multiple injuries in glider operation 8/15/44 Le Muy, France – pinned by a jeep – Purple Heart. Sent to a Naples hospital. Dischd. 11/4/45 Ft. Meade, MD. Postwar Occupation: FMC. Postwar res. Spotsylvania Co., VA. Res. Fredericksburg, VA May 1954. Res. Richmond, VA 2009.

GALLATIN [Gailatin], Warren Kenyon. b. 1/11/1922 Monongalia Co., WV. Res. Beaver Co., PA. Enl. 9/28/42 Pittsburgh, PA. Ser. No.

33305749. Pvt. Co. B, 10/15/42 Camp Gordon GA. Cpl., Co. B, KIA, 12/12/44, Riquewihr, France.

GALLOWAY, Glenn W. b. 1908 NC. Res. Transylvania Co., NC. Enl. 2/13/42 Charlotte, NC. Ser. No. 14062663. Pvt., Co. A transf. Co. D, Camp Gordon, GA 6/15/42.

GANNON, Johnny. Mentioned in the 5/17/43 entry in North Africa in the Daniel Shields diary.

GANTER, William. b. 8/4/1901 PA. Res. Westmoreland Co., PA. Enl. 9/25/42 Greensburg, PA. Ser. No. 33294810. Pvt. Co. B, 10/15/42 Camp Gordon GA. d. 10/13/1994 Farmington, Fayette Co., PA.

GARBINI, Othello A. b. 10/19/ 1920 Austen, Preston Co., WV. Both parents were born in Italy. Res. Salem Co., NJ. Enl. 6/27/42 Ft. Dix, NJ. Ser. No. 32270712. Pvt., Co. D, Camp Gordon, GA 7/28/42. Pfc., Co. D, promo. Cpl. (temp.), Camp Gordon, GA 11/5/42. [Name is Ottavio on birth certificate].

GARCIA, Luis F. b. 1923. Res. New York Co., NY. Enl. 2/20/43 New York City, NY. Ser. No. 32811303. Pfc., Co. D, WIA (light), 11/23/43 Venafro, Italy. Returned to duty 12/8/43. Pfc., Co. D, MIA 1/26/44 Italy (Anzio).

GARDNER, Bruce Wade. b. 6/1/1902 VA. Res. Sullivan Co., TN. Enl. 9/21/42 Richmond, VA. Ser. No. 33225675. Pvt., Co. B, Camp Gordon, GA 10/11/42. In wartime photo from Hilton McLarty collection. d. Dec. 1980 Culpeper, Culpeper Co., VA.

GARGANI, Charles A. ("Duke") b. 1924. Enl. 3/26/43 Philadelphia, PA. Ser. No. 33596192. Co. C. In photo collections of Ray Knapp and William C. Ford.

GARGIS, Hartwell. b. 11/17/1908 AL. Res. Colbert Co., AL. Enl. 7/4/42 Ft. McClellan, AL. Ser. No. 34333253. Pfc., Co. B, 5/8/45 Innsbruck, Austria. d. 9/7/1987 Sheffield, Colbert Co., AL.

GARHART, Cyrus M., Jr. Pvt., Purple Heart, 1944. Pfc., Co. B, 5/8/45 Innsbruck, Austria.

GARNER, William L. b. 1921 GA. Res Aragon, Polk Co., GA. Enl. 9/21/42 Ft. McPherson, AL. Ser. No. 34443285. Pvt., HQ & HQ Co., Camp Gordon, GA 10/9/42. Present boarding the U.S.S. Monticello 1943. Pvt., Bronze Star [Presented 11/20/44]. WIA (light), 2/1/45 France. Pfc., Co. A, 5/8/45 Innsbruck, Austria. Believed to be same William L. Garner in 1954 directory listed as M/Sgt USAF. Killed 'in line of duty' Mar. 17, 1954 in Africa. Forwarding address Aragon, GA.

GARNETT, James M. b. 1902 District of Columbia. Res. District of Columbia. Enl. 9/21/42 Ft. Myer, VA. Ser. No. 33197705. Pvt., HQ & HQ Co., Camp Gordon, GA. 10/11/42.

GARRETT, Karl Frederick. b. 9/16/1920 Richmond, VA. Res. Henrico Co., VA. Attended Univ. of Virginia. Dupont Employee. Enl. 8/21/42 Richmond, VA. Ser. No. 33225748. Ft. Lee, VA. Pvt., HQ & HQ Co.,

Camp Gordon, GA. 10/11/42. Pvt., HQ & HQ Co., Camp Gordon, GA 11/21/42. To Radio Operators School, Ft. Benning, GA Dec. 1942. T/5, apptd. T/4, HQ & HQ Co. 4/15/43. T/4, HQ & HQ Co., WIA (light – both legs), 11/30/43 Venafro, Italy. Spent time in Naples hospital until middle of Jan. 1944. Reclassified for limited duty. Worked in a Replacement Depot. Dischd. Oct. 1945, Ft. Meade, MD. Grad. Univ. of VA. Purchasing Section for Dupont, Richmond, VA. Res. Richmond, VA 2009.

GARRETT, Owen J. b. 11/9/1912 MS. Res. Lauderdale Co., MS. Enl. 9/25/42 Camp Shelby, MS. Ser. No. 34427258. Pvt. Co. C, 10/14/42 Camp Gordon, GA. d. Sept. 1994 Toomsuba, Lauderdale Co., MS.

GARRISON, Radford. b. 1918 TN. Res. Rhea Co., TN. Enl. 9/11/42 Ft. Oglethorpe, GA. Ser. No. 34369982. Present Co. D, Camp Gordon, GA 12/1/42.

GARSSON, Joseph H. ("Gat" / "Bud"). b. 1919 NY. Res. King's Co., NY. Enl. 3/6/41 Jamaica, NY. Ser. No. 32024842. Assigned 4th Medical Battalion, Ft. Benning, GA. Transf. 1st Chemical Co., Edgewood Arsenal, MD. Attended OCS. Transf. Rocky Mt. Arsenal, Denver, CO. Promo. Capt. 11/19/43. Served with distinction in Sicily and Italy. Capt., Co. A 10/2/44. Bronze Star and Purple Heart 12/24/44. Near Gries, France on 1/20/45 refused an order from Col. Charles J. Denholm, 143rd Infantry, to post his mortars in an exposed position. Recommended "an administrative admonition" but ordered court-martialed 3/11/45. Found guilty during trial from 4/2-7/45 but given a suspended sentence 6/15/45. Ordered returned to 83rd CMB from 51st Maj. Port 7/11/45. Offered command of the 2nd CMB. Returned to U.S. 10/22/45. Relieved from active duty Jan. 1946. Offered reserve command 6/5/46. Worked in railroad department of Batavia Metals. Res. Los Angeles, CA 2005. d. 9/6/2007 Los Angeles, CA – massive heart attack.

GASIOR, Thaddeus P. Pfc., Co. C, 6/22/45 Innsbruck, Austria.

GATELY, John F. Pfc., Co. B, 5/8/45 Innsbruck, Austria.

GATTON, James F. b. 9/13/1921 MD. Enl. 9/26/42 Baltimore, MA. Ser. No. 33377220. Pvt. Co. A, 10/15/42 Camp Gordon GA. Transf. Co. C, Camp Gordon, GA, 12/16/42. d. 7/19/1995 Brooklyn, Anne Arundel Co., MD.

GAUDINO, Orlando A. b. 1912 NY. Res. Philadelphia Co., PA. Enl. 12/15/42 Ft. Myer, VA. Ser. No. 33450461. Pvt., HQ & HQ Co., Camp Gordon, GA 3/18/43.

GAUN, Thomas. b. 7/24/1924 NJ. Mentioned in 1956 Muzzleblasts. d. Feb. 1985, Trenton, Mercer Co., NJ.

GAVLAK, Edwin G. b. 1922 NJ. Res. Bergen Co., NJ. Enl. 7/9/42 Newark, NJ. Ser. No. 32390615. Pvt., HQ & HQ Co., Camp Gordon, GA 7/28/42.

GAY, Edward F. Pfc., Co. C. Purple Heart. Sept., 1945.

GAY, William H. b. 1920 MS. Res. Lafayette Co., MS. Enl. 9/22/42 Camp Shelby, MS. Ser. No. 34426537. Pvt. Co. C, 10/14/42 Camp Gordon, GA. Pfc., Co. C, KIA, 1/26/44, Italy (Anzio), SR Cem.

GEARHART, John C. Cpl., Co. C, promo. Sgt. (temp.) 9/15/45.

GEDDERT, Edward H. b. 1921 OH. Res. Mahoning Co., OH. Enl. 8/11/42 Akron, OH. Ser. No. 35335324. Pfc., Co. C, Camp Gordon, GA 4/10/43.

GEIGER, William J. b. 1921 PA. Res. Westmoreland Co., PA. Enl. 9/25/42 Greensburg, PA. Ser. No. 332948. Pvt. Co. C, 10/15/42 Camp Gordon GA. Transf. Co. A, Camp Gordon, GA, 12/16/42. Pfc., Co. C, KIA, 1/26/44, Italy (Anzio), SR Cem.

GEISEL, Leroy G. b. 1/6/1921 PA. Enl. 9/25/42 Greensburg, PA. Ser. No. 33294867. Pvt. HQ & HQ Co., 10/15/42 Camp Gordon GA. d. 6/24/1995 Arlington, Tarrant Co., TX.

GELBERG, Melvin. b. 6/30/1921 NY. Res. Kings Co., NY. Enl. 7/8/42 Ft. Jay, Governors Island, NY. Ser. No. 32402259. Pvt., Co. A, Camp Gordon, GA 7/28/42. Pvt., Co. A, special duty Communications School of 472nd Field Artillery, Camp Gordon, GA 10/12-17/42. Pvt., Co. A, relsd. SD to 4th Signal Corps, 4th Mtz Div, Camp Gordon, GA, 12/16/42. Medical Technician 409th. Served in Sicily, Naples-Foggia, and Rome-Arno Campaigns. d. Sept. 1985 Huntington, Suffolk Co., NY.

GENOVESE, Joseph J. b. 1921 NY. Res. Astoria, Long Island / Queens Co., NY. Enl. 7/7/42 New York City, NY. Ser. No. 12090928. Pvt., HQ & HQ Co., Camp Gordon, GA 7/28/42. Pfc., HQ Co., promo. T/5 (temp.), Camp Gordon, GA 12/3/42. T/5, HQ Co. Correspondent, Smokescreen, Camp Gordon, GA Feb. 1943. T/5, HQ & HQ Co., WIA, 11/30/43 Venafro, Italy – Purple Heart.

GENTRY, Allie F. b. 1921 TN. Res. Davidson Co., TN. Enl. 9/18/42 Ft. Oglethorpe, GA. Ser. No. 34371719. Pvt., Co. B, Camp Gordon, GA 10/7/42. Pfc., Co. B, sent to hospital 8/12/43. Pvt., Co. B, KIA, 1/26/44, Italy (Anzio). Official CWS casualty list says he is same man as Alvin P. Gentry and was KIA (enemy dive bombers), 2/17/44, Anzio, Italy [see entry for Alvin P. Gentry].

GENTRY, Alvin P. Pvt., Co. B, KIA (enemy dive bombers), 2/17/44 Anzio, Italy. [See entry for Allie F. Gentry].

GENTRY, Hershel E. b. 1921 MS. Res. Itawamba Co., MS. Enl. 9/23/42 Camp Shelby, MS. Ser. No. 34426727. Pvt. Co. C, 10/14/42 Camp Gordon, GA. Pvt., Co. C, MIA, 1/26/44, Italy (Anzio) SR Cem.

GENTRY, Marcus L. Pvt., Med. Det., WIA (light – contusion of foot & multiple abrasions), 6/2/44 Italy – Purple Heart. Hospitalized. Pfc., Med. Det., 5/8/45 Innsbruck, Austria.

GEORGE, Paul C. b. 1920 TN. Res. Davidson Co., TN. Enl. 9/18/42 Ft. Oglethorpe, GA. Ser. No. 34371717. Pvt., Co. B, Camp Gordon, GA 10/7/42. Transf. Co. A, Camp Gordon, 12/16/42. Pfc., Co. B, WIA (light), 11/13/43 Italy. Returned to duty 12/11/43.

GERDES, Leland S. C. Pfc., Co. A, 5/8/45 Innsbruck, Austria. Family sent him a cowhide vest to keep him warm. Res. Chickasha, OK May 1954. Manager, RC Cola & Dr. Pepper Bottling Companies, OK.

GERMAIN, Christopher. b. 1919 PA. Enl. 9/22/42 Philadelphia, PA. Ser. No. 33335585. Pvt., Co. A, Camp Gordon, GA 10/9/42. Transf. Co. D, Camp Gordon, GA, 12/16/42.

GESSLER, Ralph L. b. 3/29/1904 PA. Enl. 9/22/42 Pittsburgh, PA. Ser. No. 13111185. Pvt. Co. B, 10/15/42 Camp Gordon GA. Pvt., Features Staff, Smokescreen, Camp Gordon, GA Feb. 1943. d. Nov. 1982 PA.

GESSNER, John C. b. 1920 NJ. Res. Middlesex Co., NJ. Enl. 2/12/42 Ft. Dix, NJ. Ser. No. 32236323. Pvt., Co. D, MIA, 1/26/44, Italy (Anzio) SR Cem.

GIAMMARIA, Larry / Americo J. b. 2/3/1922 PA. Res. Ambridge, PA. Enl. 9/25/42 Pittsburgh, PA. Ser. No. 33305612. Pvt. Co. A, 10/15/42 Camp Gordon GA. Cpl., Co. B, 5/8/45 Innsbruck, Austria. [man named Larry L. Giammaria attended 1954 & 1956 Reunions – probably same man]. d. 12/7/2006 Seminole, Pinellas Co., FL.

GIANNINO, Domenica J. b. 1918 NY. Res. New York Co., NY. Enl. 2/8/40 New York City, NY. Ser. No. 12007071. Field Artillery. Pvt., Co. D, WIA (light injure – truck over-turned on road between Pozzuoli & Minturno), Italy 3/25 or 26/44.

GIARD, Clement M. b. 1924 RI. Res. Providence Co., RI. Enl. 4/23/43 Providence, RI. Ser. No. 31293226. Pfc., Co. B, 5/8/45 Innsbruck, Austria. Res. Woonsocket, RI.

GIBBS, Charles J. b. 1914 VA. Res. Bedford Co., VA. Enl. 9/21/42 Roanoke, VA. Pvt. Co. D, 10/11/42 Camp Gordon GA. Ser. No. 33213339. Pvt., Co. D, assigned Med. Det., Camp Gordon, GA 11/30/42. T/5, Med. Det., MIA, 1/26/44, Italy (Anzio) SR Cem.

GIBSON, Edward L., Jr. b. 1916 Canada. Res. Albany Co., NY. Enl. 8/29/41 Ft. Jay, Governors Island, NY. Ser. No. 32100451. Sgt., Co. C, MIA, 8/29/44 Briançon, France. POW Stalag 7A Moosburg, Bavaria. Liberated 7/21/45.

GIBSON, Ernest S. Pfc., Co. C, 6/22/45 Innsbruck, Austria.

GIBSON, Willard R. Res. Wash., D.C. Pfc., Co. B, 5/8/45 Innsbruck, Austria.

GIESEY [Giesky], Kenneth E. b. 4/28/1920. Res. Belmont Co., OH. Enl. 4/13/43 Columbus, OH. Ser. No. 35217450. Pfc., WIA (light), 4/9/45 Germany. Pfc., Co. C, 6/22/45 Innsbruck, Austria. d. 4/30/1997 Cambridge, Guernsey Co., OH.

GILES, Paul Simon. b. 2/14/1925 Moultrie, GA. Sunset Elementary School. Pre-war Occupation: Farmer. Res. Colquitt Co., GA. Enl. 3/27/43 Ft. McPherson, Atlanta, GA. Ser. No. 34765811. Trained as a

Cook, Ft. Bragg, NC. Departed Newport News, VA 10/3/43. Replacement Cook for Co. D. Injured hand at Anzio. Co. C after dissolution of Co. D and put in mortar squad. Pfc., Co. C, 6/22/45 Innsbruck, Austria. Returned home Oct. 1945. Res. Moultrie, GA 2005. d. 4/4/2008 Moultrie, GA. b. Midway Cemetery, Moultrie, GA.

GILLIAM, Lee E. b. 12/15/1911 VA. Res. Campbell Co., VA. Enl. 9/19/42 Roanoke, VA. Ser. No. 33213277. Pvt. Co. D, 10/11/42 Camp Gordon GA. d. Nov. 1987 Lynchburg, VA.

GILLILAND, Charles D. b. 5/24/1924 OH. Res. Jackson Co., OH. Enl. 7/20/43 Columbus, OH. Ser. No. 35224699. Pfc., Co. A, 5/8/45 Innsbruck, Austria. d. June 1983 Jackson, Jackson Co., OH.

GILLMAN, Louis. b. 10/28/1919 NJ. Res. Bronx Co., NY. Enl. 7/9/42 Ft. Jay, Governors Island, NY. Ser. No. 32402367. Pvt., Co. D, Camp Gordon, GA 7/28/42. Pvt., Co. D, Camp Gordon, GA 10/21/42. Present, Motor Pool, Camp Gordon, GA, 1/9/43. d. June 1963 NY.

GILMORE, James C. ("Bud"). b. 7/28/1922 Greenwood, Doddridge Co., WV. Pre-war Occupation: Forging Press Operator. Res. Cairo, Ritchie Co., WV. Enl. 12/18/43 Clarksburg, WV. Ammunition Bearer. Sicily. Naples-Foggia. Rome-Arno. Southern France. WIA 9/26/44 France. Purple Heart. Rhineland. Central Europe. Good Conduct Medal. EAME Service Ribbon with Bronze Arrowhead. WW II Victory Ribbon. American Theater Service Ribbon. Pfc., Co. C, 6/22/45 Innsbruck, Austria. Dischd. 11/2/45. Maintenance, General Services Administration at Federal Building & Bureau of Public Debt., Parkersburg, WV. d. 1/22/2000 Parkersburg, WV. Bur. IOOF Cem., Vienna, WV.

GILROY, Thomas D. b. 10/20/1921 NY. Res. Bergen Co., NJ. Enl. 7/7/42 Newark, NJ. Ser. No. 32389591. Pvt., HQ & HQ Co., Camp Gordon, GA 7/28/42. Pfc., HQ Co., Camp Gordon, GA 12/19/42. d. 11/16/1992 Cliffside Park, Bergen Co., NJ.

GIRONE, Peter L. b. 11/5/1915 PA. Enl. 9/22/42 Philadelphia, PA. Ser. No. 33335522. Pvt., Co. C, Camp Gordon, GA 10/9/42. Pvt., Co. D, WIA (light), LST 422 Survivor, 1/26/44 Italy (Anzio). [Official casualty sheet says Sgt., Co. C, WIA (light), 1/26/44 Italy (Anzio) & returned to duty 2/5/44]. Pfc., Co. C, 6/22/45 Innsbruck, Austria. d. Jan. 1985 Philadelphia, Philadelphia Co., PA.

GIVENS, Joseph V. b. 1924 OH. Res. Belmont Co., OH. Enl. 4/21/43 Columbus, OH. Ser. No. 35218179. Pfc., Co. B, 5/8/45 Innsbruck, Austria.

GIZEY, Edward J. b. 1/11/1914. Pvt., Co. A, Camp Gordon, GA 4/10/43. Pfc., Co. B, 5/8/45 Innsbruck, Austria. d. 6/11/2004 Yonkers, Westchester Co., NY.

GLADSTONE, Louis. b. 9/18/1902 NY. Res. Kings Co., NY. Enl. 7/9/42 Ft. Jay, Governors Island, NY. Ser. No. 32402380. Pvt., Co. D, Camp Gordon, GA 7/28/42. Pvt., Co. D, Camp Gordon, GA 9/25/42. Present, Motor Pool, Camp Gordon, GA, 1/9/43. John O'Connor said he was a good singer and one of the best jeep drivers in the battalion. d. June 1974 New York City, New York Co., NY.

GLADYS, Kazmar M. b. 1917 PA. Enl. 12/22/42 Greensburg, PA. Ser. No. 33413436. Pvt., Co. A, Camp Gordon, GA 3/18/43.

GLANERT, Paul Robert. b. 1919 WI. Res. Milwaukee Co., WI. Enl. 12/22/42 Milwaukee, WI. Ser. No. 36291684. Pfc., Co. B, 5/8/45 Innsbruck, Austria.

GLASS, Carl S. b. 1914 GA. Res. Spalding Co., GA. Enl. 9/21/42 Ft. McPherson, Atlanta, GA. Ser. No. 34443230. Pvt. Co. A, Camp Gordon, GA 10/9/42. Transf. Co. C, Camp Gordon, GA, 12/16/42.

GLASSMAN, Harold N. b. 9/25/1912 CT. Res. New Haven Co., CT. Enl. 3/2/42 Hartford, CT. Ser. No. 11065267. Pvt. Attached to Co. C. 5/28/42 Edgewood Arsenal, MD. Auto Rifleman (Pvt.). Cpl. (temp.), Co. A, promo. Sgt. (temp), Camp Gordon, GA 9/23/42. d. 4/21/1992.

GLAZER, Nathan W. b. 1919 KY. Res. Bronx Co., NY. Enl. 7/9/42 Ft. Jay, Governors Island, NY. Ser. No. 32402281. Pvt., Co. B, Camp Gordon, GA 7/28/42.

GLAZIER, (Dr.) George B. 1st Lt., assigned Med. Det.& designated Battalion Dental Officer, Camp Gordon, GA 4/15/43. Present in Sicily. Listed with rank of Capt. & in 23rd General Hospital 12/16/43. Mentioned in the May 1954 Directory. Attended 1954 Reunion.

GLEASON, Richard J. Pvt., Co. A, Camp Gordon, GA 4/10/43.

GLOCKNER, George J. b. 9/12/1918 NJ. Res. Hudson Co., NJ. Enl. 7/8/42 Newark, NJ. Pvt. Ser. No. 32389956. Pvt., HQ & HQ Co., Camp Gordon, GA 7/28/42. HQ & HQ Co. Post Motor Pool, Camp Gordon, GA 8/24/42. T/5, Co. D, WIA (serious), 9/11/43 Gela, Sicily. [SICILY OR SALERNO ??] d. 1/26/1994 Secaucus, Hudson Co., NJ.

GLOSSNER, Nevin L. b. 1921 PA. Res. Lock Haven, PA. Enl. 9/21/42 Altoona, PA. Ser. No. 33253578. Pvt., Co. D, Camp Gordon, GA 10/9/42. T/5, Co. D, KIA, 1/26/44, Italy (Anzio). According to his brother, Albert, he was buried at Lock Haven, PA 1949.

GODIN, George V. H. 2nd Lt., CWS, assigned Co. C, Camp Gordon, GA 9/14/42. Transf. Co. B, Camp Gordon, GA 10/1/42. Transf. HQ & HQ Co., Camp Gordon, GA 11/26/42. Asst. Intelligence Officer, assigned to 18th Chemical Co., Camp Campbell, KY, 1/9/43.

GODLEWSKI, Edward M. b. 9/15/1924 DE. Res. New Castle Co., DE. Enl. 6/21/43 Camden, NJ. Ser. No. 32952369. Pfc., Co. C, 6/22/45 Innsbruck, Austria. d. Jan. 1972 DE.

GOELZ, Albert W. b. 8/10/1902, PA. Enl. 9/22/42 Philadelphia, PA. Ser. No. 33335514. Pvt., Co. C, Camp Gordon, GA 10/9/42. Pvt., Co. C, assigned Med. Det., Camp Gordon, GA 11/14/42. Present, Pvt., Med. Det., Camp Gordon, GA, 1/9/43. d. Apr. 1984.

GOERZ, Gustave F., Jr. B. 1910 NJ. Res. Essex Co., NJ. Enl. 7/6/42 Newark, NJ. Ser. No. 32389109. Pvt., Co. C, Camp Gordon, GA 7/28/42.

GOINS, Ralph A. b. 1921 TN. Res. Rhea Co., TN. Enl. 2/17/43 Ft. Oglethorpe, GA. Ser. No. 34722362. Pvt., Co. B, 5/8/45 Innsbruck, Austria. [Steedle's Squad, 2nd Platoon, Co. B].

GOLDEN, William F. b. 1916 TN. Res. White Co., TN. Enl. 9/18/42 Ft. Oglethorpe, GA. Ser. No. 34371797. Pvt., Co. B, Camp Gordon, GA 10/7/42.

GOLDENBERG, Lawrence I. b. 1924 NY. Res. Bronx Co., NY, Enl. 4/26/43 New York City, NY. Ser. No. 32897027. Cpl., Co. C, 6/22/45 Innsbruck, Austria. Res. Boca Raton, FL 2009.

GOLDHABER, Leonard. 2nd Lt., CWS. Edgewood Arsenal, MD, assigned Co. B & designated Platoon Officer, Camp Gordon, GA 11/27/42. Replaced Godin as Asst. Intelligence Officer, Camp Gordon, GA, 1/9/43.

GOLDING, William J. b. 1922 NJ. Res Hunterdon Co., NJ. Enl. 11/20/42 Newark, NJ. Ser. No. 32592483. Pvt., Co. A, Camp Gordon, GA 4/2/43. Captured a POW at Anzio, Italy 1/22/44.

GOLDMAN, Arnold. b. 1920 Czechoslovakia. Res. Kings Island, NY. Enl. 4/24/43 New York City, NY. Ser. No. 32896506. Pvt., Co. C, MIA, 8/29/44 Briançon, France. POW Stalag 7A Moosburg, Bavaria. Liberated 7/9/45. Res. Brooklyn, NY.

GOLDMAN, Irving E. Pfc., Co. B, promo. T/5 (temp.) 9/15/45.

GOLDMAN, Milton. Res. Brooklyn, NY. Cpl., Co. C, 6/22/45 Innsbruck, Austria.

GOLDSTEIN, Herbert S. b. 1921 PA. Enl. 9/25/42 Pittsburgh, PA. Ser. No. 33305581. Pvt. Co. D, 10/15/42 Camp Gordon GA. Pvt., Co. D correspondent, Smokescreen, Camp Gordon, GA Nov. 1942. Pfc., Co. D, WIA – (light - shell fragment – right leg), 7/10 or 11/43 Gela, Sicily. Purple Heart. Award record say res. Ambridge, PA.

GOLER, David ("Red"). b. 6/16/1924 NJ. Res. New York Co., NY. Enl. 4/19/43 New York City, NY. Ser. No. 32891853. Pfc., Co. A, 1st Platoon. WIA – (slight – defective shell aerial burst), France (Alsace) 2/17/45. Pfc., Co. A, 5/8/45 Innsbruck, Austria. d. 9/6/1995.

GOMBERG, Richard. b. 3/4/1919 MA. Res. Norfolk Co., MA. Enl. 2/21/41 Boston, MA. Ser. No. 31017254. 2nd Lt., CWS. Edgewood Arsenal, MD, assigned HQ & HQ Co., Camp Gordon, GA 11/25/42. Designated Assistant Munitions Officer, Camp Gordon, GA 11/26/42. d. 3/9/1994 Lexington, Middlesex Co., MA.

GOODWIN, Johnny, Jr. b. 1919 VA. Res. Loudon Co., VA. Enl. 9/21/42 Ft. Myer, VA. Ser. No. 33197623. Pvt., Co. B, Camp Gordon, GA 10/11/42. Pvt., Co. B, Camp Gordon, GA Dec. 1942. Pvt., Co. B,, arrived Gela, Sicily, from rear echelon 7/11/43. Pfc., Co. B, distinguished in action 7/23/43 Trapani, Sicily. T/5, Co. B, WIA (light – enemy mortar barrage), 4/18/44 Anzio, Italy. Hospitalized.

GORALSKI, Edward J. b. 1916 MI. Res. New Castle, DE. Enl. 1/21/43 Camden, NJ. Ser. No. 32488421. Pfc., Co. A, apptd. T/5 (temp.) 9/10/45.

GORDON, Thomas B. b. 1922 MS. Res. Choctaw Co., MS. Enl. 2/18/43 Camp Shelby, MS. Ser. No. 34622864. Pfc., Co. D, MIA, 1/26/44, Italy (Anzio) SR Cem.

GORMAN, James J. b. 1905 PA. Enl. 9/22/42 Philadelphia, PA. Ser. No. 33335528. Pvt., Co. C, Camp Gordon, GA 10/9/42.

GORMAN, Oscar J. b. 1912 OH. Res. Cook Co., IL. Pre-war Occupation: Restaurant Cook. National Guard. Enl. 3/18/42 Chicago, IL. Ser. No. 36395507. Pvt. Attached to Co. A 5/28/42 Edgewood Arsenal, MD. Cook (Pvt.). Pvt., Co. D transf. HQ & HQ Co., Camp Gordon, GA 6/15/42. Pfc., (Cook), promo. T/5 (temp.), Camp Gordon, GA 7/15/42. T/4, HQ Co., reduced to Pvt., Camp Gordon, GA 10/21/42. Pfc., Co. C, 6/22/45 Innsbruck, Austria.

GOROWSKY, Morton. b. 6/17/1924 PA. Res. Kings Co., NY. Enl. 3/27/43 New York City, NY. Ser. No. 32876363. Joined 83rd CMB Dec. 1943. Pvt., Co. B. [Co. C?], Sgt. Kimbrough's Squad. Pvt., Co. B, WIA (light – shell burst), 2/18/44 Anzio, Italy. Later served with 88th Infantry Div. In Italy. Dischd. November 1945. Milk Industry. Retired 1987. Contributed to MFP 1997. d. 11/6/2006 Boca Raton, Palm Beach Co., FL.

GOSS, Henry. b. 1913 MS. Res. Scott Co., MS. Enl. 9/23/42 Camp Shelby, MS. Ser. No. 34426647. Pvt. Co. C, 10/14/42 Camp Gordon, GA. Pvt., Co. C, KIA, 11/13/43, Italy, SR Cem.

GOSS, Vernal C. b. 1919 ME. Res. Oxford Co., ME. Enl. 2/18/42 Ft. Devens, MA. Ser. No. 31065903. Pfc., Co. A, 5/8/45 Innsbruck, Austria.

GOSSMAN, Karl H. b. 1906 Germany. Res. Westchester Co., NY. Enl. 9/5/42 Ft. Jay, Governors Island, NY. Ser. No. 32496524. Pvt., Co. B, Camp Gordon, GA 3/18/43.

GOTHARD, Kermant B. b. 4/12/1912 AL. Res. Jackson Co., AL. Enl. 9/18/42 Ft. McClellan, AL. Ser. No. 34391652. Pvt. Co. B, Camp Gordon, GA 10/9/42. d. June 1981 Chattanooga, TN.

GOTT, Norman D. b. 1923 ME. Res. Penobscot Co., ME. Enl. 12/26/42 Bangor, ME. Ser. No. 31282623. Pfc., Co. C, 6/22/45 Innsbruck, Austria.

GOURSE, Willard S. b. 1913 MA. Res. New York Co., NY. Enl. 7/9/42 Ft. Jay, Governors Island, NY. Ser. No. 32402257. Pvt., Co. B, Camp Gordon, GA 7/28/42.

GOZUR, Steve. b. 6/7/1919 Robbins, OH. Campbell Memorial High School. Pre-war Occupation: Steel Worker. Res. Mahoning Co., OH. Enl. 3/19/42 Camp Perry, Lacarne, OH. Ser. No. 35289130. Pvt. Attached to Co. I 5/28/42 Edgewood Arsenal, MD. Chauffeur. Pvt., HQ & HQ Co. transf. Co. C, Camp Gordon, GA 6/15/42. Pfc., Co. C, promo.

T/5, Camp Gordon, GA 8/3/42. Mimeographer, Smokescreen, Camp Gordon, GA Nov. 1942 & Feb. 1943. T/5, HQ Co., Camp Gordon, GA 12/21/42. T/5, Mimeographer, Smokescreen, Camp Gordon, GA, 1/9/43. Jeep driver for Lt. Col. Kenneth Cunin. Pvt., HQ Co., 5/8/45 Innsbruck, Austria. Attended 1954 & 1960 Reunions. d. 3/15/1993 Campbell, Mahoning Co., OH.

GRADY, James. b. 1907 AL. Res. Cullman Co., AL. Enl. 5/6/42 Ft. McClellan, AL. Ser. No. 34169599. Pvt., MIA, 1/26/44, Italy (Anzio) SR Cem.

GRAHAM, Reatus M. b. 1915 GA. Res. Jeff Davis Co., GA. Enl. 9/19/42 Ft. McPherson, Atlanta, GA. Ser. No. 34443085. Pvt., Co. A, Camp Gordon, GA 10/8/42. Present in Naples and suffered from shell shock.

GRAMO, John A. b. 1924 NJ. Res. Essex Co., NJ. Enl. 7/2/43 Newark, NJ. Ser. No. 42001485. Pfc., Co. C, 6/22/45 Innsbruck, Austria.

GRANGER, John R. Pfc., HQ Co., 5/8/45 Innsbruck, Austria.

GRANT, Robert D. b. 1921 PA. Res. Hollidaysburg, PA. Enl. 10/5/42 Altoona, PA. Ser. No. 13084647. Pvt., Co. D, Camp Gordon, GA 10/9/42. Pfc., Co. D, LST 422 Survivor, 1/26/44 Italy (Anzio) – Purple Heart. Rescued by USS YMS 226. Taken to 93rd Evac. Hosp.

GRAY, Leslie M. b. 2/12/1921 AL. Res. Madison Co., AL. Enl. 9/24/42 Ft. McClellean, AL. Ser. No. 34392419. Pvt. Co. A, 10/14/42 Camp Gordon, GA. d. April 1985 Huntsville, Madison Co., AL.

GRAY, Ralph T. b. 1902 AL. Res. Jefferson Co., AL. Enl. 9/19/42 Ft. McClellan, AL. Ser. No. 34391793. Pvt., Co. C, Camp Gordon, GA 10/8/42. Transf. Co. A, Camp Gordon, GA, 12/16/42.

GRECIAN, William D. S/Sgt., Co. C promo. 1st Sgt. (temp.) 9/15/45. 410th Infantry, 103rd Div. Liberated Landsberg (Dachau). Battles included Vosges Mountains, St. Die, Schillersdorf, Sessenheim, and action in Belgium and Germany. Res. Topeka, KS.

GRECZKKOWSKI, John R. b. 1921 NY. Res. Oneida Co., NY. Enl. 9/23/40 Utica, NY. Field Artillery. Ser. No. 12003327. Pvt., Co. C, MIA, 1/26/44, Italy (Anzio) SR Cem.

GREEN, Alfred E., Jr. b. 1922 CT. Res. Fairfield Co., CT. Enl. 4/8/43 New Haven, CT. Ser. No. 31331975. Joined Co. D, 83rd CMB at end of Anzio campaign as a replacement. Gunner. Co. D. Pfc., Co. D, WIA (mortar shell - 24 fragments in arm, hand, leg), Zellenberg, France 12/5/44. Evacuated to field hospital at Epinal. Sent to 48th Gen. Hosp., Paris. Sent to hospital ship at Cherbourg to 25th Hosp., Bourne, England. Sent to Holloran Hosp., Staten Island, NY. Dischgd. after about 7 months. Res. CT 2009.

GREEN, Dempsy. b. 1900 TN. Res. Warren Co., TN. Enl. 9/16/42 Ft. Oglethorpe, GA. Ser. No. 34371246. Pvt., Co. A, Camp Gordon, GA 10/7/42.

GREEN, James. b. 1915 PA. Enl. 10/9/42 Pittsburgh, PA. Ser. No. 33307877. Pvt. Co. A, 10/15/42 Camp Gordon GA. Transf. Co. B, Camp Gordon, GA, 12/16/42.

GREEN, Raymond F. Pfc., Co. B, 5/8/45 Innsbruck, Austria.

GREER, Alfred P., Jr. b. 8/12/1918 GA. Res. Meriwether Co., MI. Enl. 12/21/42 at Ft. McPherson, Atlanta, GA. Pvt., Co. A on *LST 690* 8/9/44. d. Feb. 1984 Tifton, GA.

GREGORY, Arthur T. ("Babe"). b. 2/2/1921. Res. Nashville, TN. Pvt. Co. B, transf. Co. A, Camp Gordon, GA, 12/16/42. WIA, Italy – Purple Heart. Got malaria a few days after reaching Rome. Sgt., Co. B, WIA (slight – shell burst in barrel – blast), 1/11/45 France. Sgt., Co. B, 5/8/45 Innsbruck, Austria. Attended 1956 Reunion. d. 10/6/1987 Nashville, Davidson Co., TN.

GREGORY, William Curtis. b. 3/25/1920 (1921 on service record) Union Co., MS. Union (Grammar) School & Macedonia High School. Res. New Albany, Union Co. MS. Pre-war Occupation: Farmer. Enl. 9/23/42 Camp Shelby, MS. Pvt. Co. C, 10/14/42 Camp Gordon, GA. Sicily. Naples- Foggia. Pfc., Co. C, LST 422 Survivor, 1/26/44 Italy (Anzio) – Purple Heart. Southern France. Rhineland. Central Europe. EAMETO Medal. Good Conduct Medal. Bronze Arrowhead. Pfc., Co. C, 6/22/45 Innsbruck, Austria. Res. New Albany, MS 2009.

GREGORY, William E. b. 1918 ME. Res. Knox Co., ME. Enl. 2/12/42 Portland, ME. Ser. No. 11027898. Pvt. Attached to Co. F 5/28/42 Edgewood Arsenal, MD. Motor Sgt. (S/Sgt.). Pfc., HQ & HQ Co., (Dispatcher), promo. T/5 (temp.), Camp Gordon, GA 7/15/42. Sgt., Co. A, 1st. Platoon, jeep destroyed by enemy shell 2/20/44 Anzio, Italy. T/4, Co. A, on *LST 690* 8/9/44. Pfc., HQ Co., 5/8/45 Innsbruck, Austria.

GREY, Les. Name mentioned in Muzzleblasts. d. ca. 1980's.

GRIDER, John T. b. 1921 NJ. Res. Marion Co., IN. Enl. 2/27/42 Ft. Benjamin Harrison, IN. Ser. No. 15099745. Pvt. Attached to Co. H 5/28/42 Edgewood Arsenal, MD. Squad Leader (Sgt.).

GRIESEMER, Raymond C. b. 1918 PA. Res. Carbon Co., PA. Enl. 12/14/42 Allentown, PA. Ser. No. 33484970. Pvt., Co. A, Camp Gordon, GA 3/18/43.

GRIESSER, Frank J. b. 12/20/1919 PA. Res. Philadelphia Co., PA. Enl. 2/21/42 Ft. George Meade, MD. Ser. No. 33143930. Pfc., Co. C, (Squad Leader), promo. Cpl. (temp.), Camp Gordon, GA 7/15/42. Ser. No. 33143930. Sgt., Co. C, transf. Co. D, Camp Gordon, GA 10/21/42. Sgt., Co. D, Camp Gordon, GA 12/15/42. d. 12/19/1999 Springfield, Deleware Co., PA.

GRIFFIN, ----------. Present in Co. A 8/4/45.

GRIFFIN, Richard Hamilton. ("Dick"). b. 1925 NC. Res. Asheville, Mitchell Co., NC. Enl. 3/10/43 Camp Croft, SC. Ser. No. 34608995. Pfc., Co. B, KIA, 12/12/44, Riquewihr, France. EP Cem. Distinguished Service Cross (posthumous).

GRIMES, Albert T. b. 1920 MS. Res. Itawamba Co., MS. Enl. 9/23/42 Camp Shelby, MS. Ser. No. 34426744. Pvt. Co. C, 10/14/42 Camp Gordon, GA.

GRIMM, Henry D. b. 1922 PA. Res. Beaver Falls, PA. Enl. 9/24/42 Pittsburgh, PA. Ser. No. 33305431. Pvt. Co. A, 10/15/42 Camp Gordon GA. Pfc., Co. A, LST 422 Survivor, 1/26/44 Italy (Anzio) – Purple Heart.

GRISHAM, Louis R. b. 11/29/1919 MS. Res. New Albany, Union Co., MS. Enl. 9/23/42 Camp Shelby, MS. Ser. No. 34426907. Pvt. Co. C, 10/14/42 Camp Gordon, GA. Pvt., Co. C, LST 422 Survivor, 1/26/44 Italy (Anzio) – Purple Heart. Pfc., WIA (light) 6/1/44, Italy. Returned to duty 7/13/44. Pfc., Co. C, 6/22/45 Innsbruck, Austria. d. 3/23/2002 New Albany, Union Co., MS.

GRISSOM, Floyd L. b. 3/23/1921 MS. Res. Guntown, Itawamba Co., MS. Enl. 9/23/42 Camp Shelby, MS. Ser. No. 34426762.Pvt. Co. C, 10/14/42 Camp Gordon, GA. Pvt., Co. C, LST 422 Survivor, 1/26/44 Italy (Anzio). Rescued by YMS 69 1/26/44. Cpl., Co. C, WIA (light), Briançon, France 8/29/44. Returned to duty 9/1/44. Cpl., Co. C, 6/22/45 Innsbruck, Austria. d. 9/22/2002 Saltillo, Lee Co., MS.

GRISWOLD, Lewis Z. Pvt. Attached to Co. A 5/28/42 Edgewood Arsenal, MD. Instrument Sgt. (Sgt.).

GUARRACINO, Salvatore J. b. 1922 PA. Enl. 10/5/42 Philadelphia, PA. Ser. No. 13124621. Pvt., Co. D, Camp Gordon, GA 10/9/42.Transf. Co. A, Camp Gordon, GA, 12/16/42. Pfc., Co. D, WIA (light), 7/11/43 Gela, Sicily. Mentioned in the May 1954 Directory.

GUARRIELLO, Jerry G. b. 1920 NY. Res. Kings Co., NY. Enl. 10/22/42 New York City, NY. Ser. No. 32537860. Assigned from 65th Inf. Division as 2nd Lt., Co. C, 7/23/45.

GUINNESS, Edward D. b. 1918 NY. Res. Queens Co., NY. Enl. 2/26/42 Ft. Dix, NJ. Pvt. Attached to Co. G 5/28/42 Edgewood Arsenal, MD. Squad Leader (Sgt.). Ser. No. 32242617. Sgt. (temp.), Co. D, promo. S/ Sgt. (temp.), Camp Gordon, GA 12/2/42. S/Sgt., Co. D, WIA (serious - from explosion of own shell hitting tree limb), 7/12/43 Gela, Sicily. S/ Sgt., Co. D, KIA, 1/26/44, Italy (Anzio) - (by fire equipment explosion on LST 422). SR Cem. Body recovered 1/26/44 by YMS 34 & buried at sea same day. Next of kin: Patricia Guiness, Ozone Park, NY.

GUITIERREZ, Ramon F. Pvt. Attached to Co. K 5/28/42 Edgewood Arsenal, MD. Gunner (Pvt.).

GULLEY, Dillard E. b. 1920 TN. Res. Macon Co., TN. Enl. 9/16/42 Ft. Oglethorpe, GA. Ser. No. 34371173. Pfc., Co. C, KIA (enemy shell), 9/16/43, Vietre sul Mare, Italy, SR Cem.

GULLICK, Harold T. b. 1922 WI. Res. Iowa Co., WI. Enl. 12/5/42 Milwaukee, WI. Ser. No. 36288413. Sgt., Co. A, promo. S/Sgt. (temp.) 9/15/45.

GUNDERSON, Victor W. b. 1917 MI. Res. Wayne Co., MI. Enl. 4/2/42 Ft. Custer, MI. Ser. No. 36178422. Joined 83rd CMB from the Peninsula Base Section. 1st Lt., Co. C, MWIA (serious – S-mine), 3/26/44, Minturno, Italy. Died three hours later. [Also incorrectly listed as Cpl., KIA, 1/26/44, Italy (Anzio)].

GUNNIP, George Tracy. b. 12/22/1910 MD [Military record says 1909]. Enl. 8/3/43 Baltimore, MD. Ser. No. 33732117. Pfc., Co. B. Dischd. 11/30/45 Ft. Meade. Crane Operator American Can Co. d. 7/19/1971 Sevier, TN. bur. Pigeon Forge Baptist Cem., Pigeon Forge, TN.

GUTHRIE, Benjamin T. Enl. 8/11/39 Raeford, NC. Res. Garfield, OK. Ser. No. 06272855. Name appears in a 1970 Muzzleblasts. Martin Moloney says he was a Sgt. in Co. D.

GUTHRIE, Elwood / Edwood ("Long John"). b. 1920 NC. Res. Portsmouth, Norfolk Co., VA. Enl. 9/21/42 Richmond, VA. Ser. No. 33225548. Pvt. Co. D, 10/11/42 Camp Gordon GA. Transf. Co. A, Camp Gordon, GA, 12/16/42. Corp., Co. D, LST 422 Survivor, 1/26/44 Italy (Anzio) – Purple Heart. S/Sgt., Co. A, 5/8/45 Innsbruck, Austria. Postwar res. Portsmouth, VA. Civil Service employee.

HADDOCK, Theodore D. b. 1/10/1922 PA. Res. Avoca, PA. Enl. 10/5/42 Wilkes Barre, PA. Ser. No. 13116744. Pvt., Co. D, Camp Gordon, GA 10/9/42. Sgt., Co. D, LST 422 Survivor, 1/26/44 Italy (Anzio) – Purple Heart. Rescued by USS YMS 226. Taken to 93rd Evac. Hosp. Sgt. Co. A, 5/8/45 Innsbruck, Austria. Postwar res. Avoca, PA. Res. Pittston, PA. Lumber Yard Manager. Attended 1954, 1956, 1958, 1960, 1962 & 1966 Reunions as res. Pittsburgh, PA. d. Oct. 1975 PA.

HADLOW, Earl B. Pfc., HQ Co., promo. T/5 (temp.) 9/15/45.

HAFLER, Donald C. b. 7/4/1920 PA. Res. Bergen Co., NJ. Enl. 7/6/42 Newark, NJ. Ser. No. 32388983. Pvt., Co. D, Camp Gordon, GA 7/28/42. T/5, Co. A, 5/8/45 Innsbruck, Austria. d. Jan. 1983 Wood Ridge, Bergen Co., NJ.

HAGGERTY, ----------. Clark Riddle assisted him in the water after the sinking of LST 422 1/26/44 at Italy (Anzio). May have belonged to another unit.

HAISLIP, Norman M. b. 1917 VA. Enl. 12/15/42 Charlottesville, VA. Ser. No. 33446280. Pvt., Co. A, Camp Gordon, GA 3/18/43.

HAJDINYAK, John J. b. 1921 PA. Res. Bethlehem, Lehigh Co., PA. Enl. 8/13/42 Allentown, PA. Ser. No. 33188681. Pvt. HQ & HQ Co., Camp Gordon, GA 4/16/43. Pfc., Co. C, WIA, LST 422 Survivor, 1/26/44 Italy (Anzio) – Purple Heart. Pfc., Co. C, WIA (light), 8/29/44, Briançon, France. Returned to duty 9/16/44. Pfc., Co. C, 6/22/45 Innsbruck, Austria.

HALDEMAN, William C., Jr. b. 1913 PA. Enl. 10/4/42 Philadelphia. Ser. No. 13124627. Pvt., Co. D, Camp Gordon, GA 10/9/42.

HALE, Olen J. b. 1921 AL. Res. Itawamba Co., MS. Enl. 9/29/42 Camp Shelby, MS. Ser. No. 34426772. Pvt. Co. C, 10/14/42 Camp Gordon, GA. Pfc., Co. C, MIA, 1/26/44, Italy (Anzio) SR Cem.

HALL, Arvel H. b. 1913 TN. Res. Campbell Co., TN. Enl. 9/18/42 Ft. Oglethorpe, GA. Pvt., Co. A, Camp Gordon, GA 10/7/42. Ser. No. 34371845. Pfc., Co. A, MIA, 1/26/44, Italy (Anzio) SR Cem.

HALL, Claude E. [or F.]. Pvt., Co. D, WIA (slight-shell fragment), 9/24/43 Italy. Pfc., Co. A, 5/8/45 Innsbruck, Austria. Res. Baltimore, MD May 1954. With Gas & Electric Co. Attended 1954 & 1958 Reunions as res. Baltimore, MD.

HALL, Coy. b. 1920 MS. Res. Monroe Co., MS. Enl. 9/22/42 Camp Shelby, MS. Ser. No. 34426496. Pvt. Co. D, 10/14/42 Camp Gordon, GA. Pvt., Co. D, KIA, 1/26/44, Italy (Anzio), SR Cem. Robert Chamblee said Hall was from Amory, MS.

HALL, Frank J. Pfc., Co. B, 5/8/45 Innsbruck, Austria.

HALL, Harold C. b. 1922 MS. Res. New Albany, Union Co., MS. Enl. 9/23/42 Camp Shelby, MS. Ser. No. 34426865. Pvt. HQ & HQ Co. 10/14/42 Camp Gordon, GA. T/5, HQ & HQ Co., LST 422 Survivor, 1/26/44 Italy (Anzio) – Purple Heart. Pfc., Co. C, 6/22/45 Innsbruck, Austria.

HALL, Hobson Jr., ("Biggie"). b. 1921 TN. Res. Davidson Co., TN. Enl. 9/18/42 Ft. Oglethorpe, GA. Ser. No. 34371786. Pvt., Co. B, transf. Co. A, Camp Gordon, GA, 12/16/42. Pfc., Co. B, Camp Gordon, GA Feb. 1943.

HALL, Leonard E. b. 1921 TN. Res. Nashville, Davidson Co., TN. Enl. 9/18/42 Ft. Oglethorpe, GA. Pvt., Co. C, WIA (light injure), LST 422 Survivor, 1/26/44 Italy (Anzio) – Purple Heart with Oak Leaf Cluster. Soldier's Medal for gallantry on LST 422 [presented 4/25/44]. Pfc., Co. C, WIA, 5/30/44 Italy – Purple Heart with Oak Leaf Cluster [Battalion journal says WIA 5/26/44]. Cpl., Ser. No. 34371699. Cpl., KIA, 8/29/44, Briançon, France, RH Cem.

HALLENBECK, John P. Present in HQ Co. 8/4/45. T/Sgt., HQ Co., presented Bronze Star 8/25/45.

HALLOWELL, Westley C. b. 5/5/1897 NJ. Res. Atlantic Co., NJ. Enl. 7/9/42 Camden, NJ. Ser. No. 32271813. Pvt., Co. B, Camp Gordon, GA 7/28/42. d. Mar. 1980 Vineland, Cumberland Co., NJ.

HAMBLIN, Raymond E. b. 8/28/1921 MS. Res. Union Co., MS. Enl. 9/23/42 Camp Shelby, MS. Ser. No. 33426877. Pvt. Co. C, 10/14/42 Camp Gordon, GA. d. 8/15/2005 New Albany, Union Co., MS.

HAMILTON, James E. HQ, 11th Armored Div., assigned CWO, HQ & HQ Co., 83rd CMB 7/23/45.

HAMILTON, Luther L. b. 5/16/1900 TN. Res. Davidson Co., TN. Enl. 9/18/42 Ft. Oglethorpe, GA. Ser. No. 34371872. Pvt. Co. C, transf. Co. A, Camp Gordon, GA, 12/16/42. d. June 1978, Nashville, TN.

HAMILTON, Thomas E. b. 1920 MS. Res. Lafayette Co., MS. Enl. 9/26/42 Camp Shelby, MS. Ser. No. 34426522. Pvt. Co. C, 10/14/42 Camp Gordon, GA. Pfc., Co. C, KIA, (shell concussion), 9/16/43, Maiori, Italy, SR Cem.

HAMMERS, Herman G. b. 1920 KY. Enl. 12/21/42 Evansville, IN. Ser. No. 35720360. T/5, Co. B, promo. T/4 (temp.) 7/24/45.

HAMPTON, James R. b. 1914 NC. Res. Henry Co., VA, Enl. 9/21/42 Roanoke, VA. Ser. No. 33213378. Pvt., Co. C, Camp Gordon, GA 10/11/42. Cpl., Co. C, MIA, 1/26/44, Italy (Anzio) SR Cem.

HAMPTON, Ralph B. b. 1921 TN. Res. Ooltewah, Hamilton Co., TN. Enl. 9/14/42 Ft. Oglethorpe, GA. Ser. No. 34370717. Pfc., Co. C, LST 422 Survivor, 1/26/44 Italy (Anzio) – Purple Heart. Sgt., Co. C, 6/22/45 Innsbruck, Austria.

HANDERAHAN, James E. b. 1898 PA. Res. Northumberland Co., PA. Enl. 9/21/42 Harrisburg, PA. Ser. No. 33240939. Pvt., HQ & HQ Co., Camp Gordon, GA 10/9/42. Pvt., HQ Co. Mentioned in the 12/12/42 issue of Smokescreen.

HANFIELD, James W. Pvt. Bronze Star 1944. Pfc, Co. B, 5/8/45 Innsbruck, Austria.

HANNAN, John K. b. 1924. Enl. 4/9/43 Seattle, WA. Ser. No. 39206244. Pfc., Co. B, promo. T/5 (temp.) 9/15/45.

HANSFORD [Handsford], Russell W. b. 2/2/1921 VA. Res. Essex Co., NJ. Enl. 7/8/42 Newark, NJ. Ser. No. 32389831 Pvt., Co. A, Camp Gordon, GA 7/28/42. Pvt., Co. A, Camp Gordon, GA 10/21/42.. Pfc., Co. B, 5/8/45 Innsbruck, Austria. d. Sept. 1985.

HANZLEK, Harry R. b. 1921 NJ. Res. Bergen Co., NJ. Enl. 7/8/42 Newark, NJ. Ser. No. 32390052. Pvt., Co. D, Camp Gordon, GA 7/28/42.

HARDIN, James E. b. 1915 MS. Res. Smith Co., MS. Enl. 9/22/42 Camp Shelby, MS. Ser. No. 34426388. Pvt. Co. C, 10/14/42 Camp Gordon, GA. Sgt., Co. C, MIA, 1/26/44, Italy (Anzio) SR Cem.

HARDY, George R. Sgt. (temp.), Co. D, promo. S/Sgt. (temp.), Camp Gordon, GA 9/7/42. Promo. 1st/Sgt. (temp.), Camp Gordon, GA 10/3/42.

HARDY, William. Pfc. Co. A 8/4/45.

HARGER, Elmer F. b. 1904 PA. Res. Westmoreland Co., PA. Enl. 9/25/42 Greensburg, PA. Ser. No. 33294818. Pvt. Co. B, 10/15/42 Camp Gordon GA.

HARP, Carlos O. b. 1923 TN. Res. Robertson Co., TN. Enl. 9/17/42 Ft. Oglethorpe, GA. Ser. No. 34371540. Pvt. Co. C, transf. Co. A, Camp Gordon, GA, 12/16/42. A gunner in Co. C who was accidentally shot and killed by a fellow soldier in Italy, according to Hale Hepler. Died 9/12/43.

HARPER, Grady L. b. 8/9/1917 GA. Res. Spaulding Co., GA. Enl. 9/24/42 Ft. McPherson, Atlanta, GA. Ser. No. 34443938. Pvt., HQ & HQ Co., Camp Gordon, GA 10/12/42. S/Sgt., Battalion PX noncom. Pfc., apptd. Cpl., HQ & HQ Co. 3/20/43. S/Sgt., HQ Co., 5/8/45 Innsbruck, Austria. d. 7/5/1998 Griffin, Spaulding Co., GA.

HARPER, Harry. b. 4/19/1921 GA. Res. Jasper Co., GA. Enl. 9/19/42 Ft. McPherson, Atlanta, GA. Ser. No. 34443019. Pvt., Co. A, Camp Gordon, GA 10/8/42. Transf. Co. D, Camp Gordon, GA, 12/16/42. Pvt., distinguished in action 7/10/43 Sicily. Pvt. Purple Heart 1944. WIA, steel plate in head. Pfc., Co. A, on LST 690 8/9/44. Pfc., Co. B, 5/8/45 Innsbruck, Austria. d. 3/8/1990 Rutledge, Morgan Co., GA.

HARPER, William H. Pvt. Attached to Co. I 5/28/42 Edgewood Arsenal, MD. Squad Leader (Sgt.).

HARRELL, William C. b. 1924. Enl. 4/23/43 Greensburg, PA. Ser. No. 33671751. Cpl., LIA, 12/13/44 France. Cpl., Co. B, 5/8/45 Innsbruck, Austria.

HARRIGLE, Thomas. b. 9/24/1922 PA. Res. Lehigh Co., PA. Enl. 12/10/42 Altoona, PA. Ser. No. 33484647. Pvt., Co. A, WIA (powder burn of face), 8/30/43. Hospitalized. Pvt., Co. A, Camp Gordon, GA 3/18/43. d. 5/29/1992 Allentown, Lehigh Co., PA.

HARRIS, Eldon. Co. A. WIA (light – enemy shell fire), 2/21/44 Anzio, Italy.

HARRIS, Howard S. Cpl., Co. C, 6/22/45 Innsbruck, Austria.

HARRIS, Jeff. b. 7/5/1918 MS. Res. Monroe Co., MS. Enl. 9/22/42 Camp Shelby, MS. Ser. No. 34426635. Pvt. HQ & HQ Co. 10/14/42 Camp Gordon, GA. d. 1/13/2006 Amory, Monroe Co., MS.

HARRIS, John E., Jr. Sgt., Co. C, 6/22/45 Innsbruck, Austria.

HARRIS, Leon S. b. 1923 OK. Res. Tulsa Co., OK. Enl. 3/11/43 Oklahoma City, OK. Ser. No. 38402036. Pfc., Co. B, promo. T/5 (temp.) 9/15/45.

HARRIS, Marion F. Ser. No. 6972020. Pvt., Co. D, WIA (light injure - truck over-turned on road between Pozzuoli & Minturno), Italy 3/25 or 26/44.

HARRIS, William T. b. 1906 VA. Res. District of Columbia. Enl. 9/21/42 Ft. Myer, VA. Ser. No. 33197710. Pvt., Co. C, Camp Gordon, GA 10/11/42.

HARRISON, Ulmer L. b. 1/26/1921 MS. Res. Jones Co., MS. Enl. 9/21/42 Camp Shelby, MS. Ser. No. 34426252. Pvt. Co. C, 10/14/42 Camp Gordon, GA. Had appendectomy operation on U.S.S. Monticello 5/4/43. d. June 1976, Laurel, Jones Co., MS.

HART, Neal T. ("Parson"). b. 9/6/1911 GA. Res. Clarke Co., GA. Enl. 9/19/42 Ft. McPherson, Atlanta, GA. Ser. No. 34442924. Pvt., Co. B, Camp Gordon, GA 10/8/42. d. June 1994 Athens, Clarke Co., GA.

HARTGROVE, Loranza [Loranzo] E. b. 1921 VA. Enl. 12/9/42 Abingdon, VA. Ser. No. 33527305. Pvt., Co. D, Camp Gordon, GA 4/10/43. Pfc., Co. D, MIA, 1/26/44, Italy (Anzio) SR Cem.

HARTMAN, Clarence D. b. 1917 PA. Res. Bedford Co., PA. Enl. 12/2/42 Altoona, PA. Ser. No. 33259917. Pvt., Co. A, Camp Gordon, GA 3/18/43.

HARTMAN, Willmore K. b. 2/5/1905 IN. Res. Knox Co., IN. Enl. 3/21/42 Ft. Benjamin Harrison, IN. Ser. No. 35044414. Pvt. Attached to Co. I 5/28/42 Edgewood Arsenal, MD. Gunner (Pvt.). d. Sept. 1983.

HARTWIG, Arthur E. b. 2/18/1907 IN. Res. Huntington Co., IN. Enl. 4/20/43 Indianapolis, IN. Ser. No. 35142296. Pvt., Co. B, MIA, 12/12/44, Riquewihr, France. d. 10/25/1995 Huntington, Huntington Co., IN.

HARVEY, Paul O. b. 1924 NY. Enl. 3/23/43 Philadelphia, PA. Ser. No. 33595136. Pvt., Co. B, WIA (light – shell burst), 2/18/44 Anzio, Italy.

HASSA, Michael. b. 9/18/1914 NY. Res. Nassau Co., NY. Enl. 8/12/42 Ft. Jay, Governors Island, NY. Ser. No. 32426630. Pvt., Purple Heart, 1944. Pfc., Co. C, 6/22/45 Innsbruck, Austria. d. Nov. 1986 Washington, Nassau Co., NY.

HASTINGS, Carleton ("Hasty"). Pvt., Co. B, Camp Gordon, GA 10/11/42. Pfc., Co. B correspondent, Smokescreen, Nov. 1942. Pfc., Features Staff & Co. B correspondent, Smokescreen, Camp Gordon, GA Feb. 1943. Cpl., Co. B, arrived Salemi, Sicily from North Africa 8/1/43. Cpl., Co. B, 5/8/45 Innsbruck, Austria. Res. Milwaukee, WI May 1954. Salesman, Employer's Mutual Insurance Co.

HATCH, Millard. b. 1/22/1917 MA. Enl. 7/11/41 Detroit, MI. Ser. No. 36122833. 2nd Lt., CWS. Edgewood Arsenal, MD, assigned Co. C, Camp Gordon, GA 11/25/42. d. Aug. 1971.

HATFIELD, Arnold J. Pfc., Co. C, 6/22/45 Innsbruck, Austria.

HATLEY, Thelbert W. b. 1920 TN. Res. Benton Co., TN. Pfc., Co. C, promo. Corp. (temp.) 9/15/45. Ser. No. 34326836. Enl. For Hawaiian Dept. 9/26/46 Ft. Oglethorpe, GA. Corp. Cav.

HAUG, Elmer E. Joined Army July 1942. Served overseas. Pfc., Co. C, 6/22/45 Innsbruck, Austria. Dischgd. November 1945. Res. Windsor, WI.

HAUSER, Walter E. b. 7/22/1917 PA. Res. Philadelphia Co., PA. Enl. 8/21/41 Camp Lee, VA. Ser. No. 33073287. 2nd Lt., CWS. Edgewood Arsenal, MD, assigned Co. A, Camp Gordon, GA 11/25/42. Transf. Co. D, Camp Gordon, GA, 12/16/42. Promo. 1st Lt., Co. A, 1/14/44. 1st. Lt., Co. A, on *LST 690* 8/9/44. 1st. Lt./Capt., HQ Co., 5/8/45 Innsbruck, Austria. 1st Lt. Assigned 65th Inf. Div. 7/23/45. Res. 2nd Cml. Weapons Bn., Dug Way Proving Ground, UT May 1954. d. 3/14/1987. Lt. Robert Bundy said he was an accomplished clarinet player.

HAVER, Forrest E., Jr. b. 1915 NY. Res. Westchester Co., NY. Enl. 2/11/42 Camp Upton, Yaphank, NY. Ser. No. 32214645. Pvt. Attached to Co. I 5/28/42 Edgewood Arsenal, MD. Gunner (Pvt.). Pfc., Co. C, (Squad Leader), promo. Cpl. (temp.), Camp Gordon, GA 7/15/42.

HAWKINS, Edward W. b. 1917 VA. Res. Henrico Co., VA. Enl. 9/19/42 Richmond, VA. Ser. No. 33225639. Pvt., Co. C, Camp Gordon, GA 10/11/42. Pvt., Co. C, (WIA – light - enemy shell), 9/16/43, Maiori, Italy. Returned to duty 9/19/43. Pvt., Co. C, MIA, 1/26/44, Italy (Anzio) SR Cem.

HAWKINS, William M. b. 1922 PA. Res. Delaware Co., PA. Enl. 10/5/42 Philadelphia, PA. Ser. No. 33338150. Pvt., Co. A, Camp Gordon, GA 10/9/42. Pfc., distinguished in action 7/10/43 Sicily. Cpl., Co. A, on *LST 690* 8/9/44. Cpl., Co. A, KIA, 10/3/44, France, EP Cem.

HAY, ----------. Present as pitcher for Co. A ball team 8/4/45.

HAYNES, James R. ("Jimmy"). Present at Briançon, France 8/29/44. T/5, Co. C, 6/22/45 Innsbruck, Austria. Res. Batesville, MS. d. 3/22/2003.

HAYS , Veryl Robert. b. 6/17/1922 KS. Res. Hutchinson, Reno Co., KS. Enl. 1/6/42 Ft. Riley, KS. Ser. No. 17028356. 2nd Lt., CWS, assigned to HQ & HQ Co., & designated Battalion Special Services Officer, Camp Gordon, GA 11/26/42. Apptd. Asst. Mess Officer for Battalion Officers Mess, Camp Gordon, GA 12/15/42. Lt., distinguished in action 7/10/43 Sicily. Lt., WIA (foot ran over by Maj. Hutchinson's jeep while taking cover from attacking plane) 7/19/43 Sicily. 1st Lt., WIA 12/5/43 Italy – Purple Heart. 1st Lt., HQ Co. Platoon Leader. Promo. 1st Lt., Co. A, 1/14/44. Awarded Silver Star 4/15/44 for gallantry at Anzio 2/18/44. Presented Soldier's Medal 5/16/44 for action at Gela, Sicily 7/10/43. [Ed Trey states Hayes was in Co. A and was rotated shortly after the Anzio landing although he was actually rotated 6/4/44.]. Wrote article "Psych – A For Platoon Leaders" in Chemical Warfare Bulletin Nov.-Dec. 1944 (Vol. 30 – No. 5) issue. Also a letter in same issue about the Anzio landing. Purple Heart 1944. Postwar res. Ventura, CA. Pierpont Bay, CA bartender. d. 5/10/1967 (murdered-stabbed to death). Bur. Golden Gate Nat. Cem., San Bruno, San Mateo, CA.

HEADLAND (Headlund), Charles Bruce. Res. PA. Present at Camp Gordon, GA Nov. 1942. Ser. No. 33296809. Pvt., Co. C, Camp Gordon, GA 10/9/42. Transf. Co. A, Camp Gordon, GA, 12/16/42. Sgt., Co. C, MIA, 1/26/44, Italy (Anzio) SR Cem.

HEATH, William Sheldon. b. 10/24/1920 PA. Res. Sandy Ridge, PA. Phillipsburg High School. Penn State College. Graduate Eckels School of Embalming, Philadelphia, PA. Apprentice Undertaker with Harry Weber of Phillipsburg. Accomplished Musician. Enl. 10/5/42 Altoona, PA. Ser. No. 13084662. Pvt., Co. A, Camp Gordon, GA 10/9/42. Pvt., Co. A, assigned Med. Det., Camp Gordon, GA 11/14/42. Transf. Co. B, Camp Gordon, GA, 12/16/42. Advanced training at Lawson General Hospital, GA. T/4., Med. Det., KIA, 1/26/44, Italy (Anzio). Body recovered 1/26/44 by USS YMS 226 and turned over to Graves Registration at Anzio 1/27/44. Next of kin: John L. Heath, Sandy Ridge, PA.

HECK, Horace. Pvt. Attached to Co. A 5/28/42 Edgewood Arsenal, MD. Clerk (Corp. & Pvt.). Pfc., HQ & HQ Co., (Clerk, Battalion HQ), promo. T/5 (temp.), Camp Gordon, GA 7/15/42. T/4 (temp.), HQ & HQ Co., Camp Gordon, GA 8/24/42. Promo. S/Sgt. (temp.), Camp Gordon, GA 9/1/42. Promo. T/Sgt. (temp.), Camp Gordon, GA 10/21/42. Tranf. OCS, CWS, Edgewood Arsenal, MD Dec. 1942. Res. Spickard, MI.

HEDRICK, Harry J. Pfc., Co. A, 5/8/45 Innsbruck, Austria.

HEELAN, William P. ("Chubby Bubby Wubby"). b. 9/3/1919 NY. Res. New York City, NY. Enl. 7/9/42 Ft. Jay, Governors Island, NY. Ser. No. 32402167. Pvt., Co. B, Camp Gordon, GA 7/28/42. Pfc., Co. B, WIA 3/14/44 Italy – Purple Heart. Cpl., Co. B, 5/8/45 Innsbruck, Austria. d. Nov. 1984 New York City, New York Co., NY.

HEJDUK, Arthur E. b. 9/16/1923 OH. Res. Cuyahoga Co., OH. Enl. 4/19/43 Cleveland, OH. Ser. No. 35059752. Pfc., Co. B, 5/8/45 Innsbruck, Austria. d. 3/1/1999 Cleveland, Cuyahoga Co., OH.

HELLER, J. Pvt. Attached to Co. E 5/28/42 Edgewood Arsenal, MD. Squad Leader (Sgt.). Pfc., Co. A, (Platoon Sgt.), promo. Cpl. (temp.), Camp Gordon, GA 7/15/42. Cpl. (temp.), Co. A promo. Sgt. (temp.), Camp Gordon, GA 7/27/42. Sgt. (temp.), promo. S/Sgt. (temp.), Camp Gordon, GA 9/23/42.

HELMBOLD, William W. b. 1915 KY. Res. Campbell Co., KY. Enl. 2/14/42 Ft. Thomas, Newport, KY. Ser. No. 15090347. Pvt. Attached to Co. C 5/28/42 Edgewood Arsenal, MD. Squad Leader (Sgt.). Pfc., Co. B, (Squad Leader), promo. Cpl. (temp.), Camp Gordon, GA 7/15/42. Transf. OCS, CWS, Edgewood Arsenal, MD Dec. 1942.

HELMER, ----------. Listed in Leonard Turan's notebook, Co. C.

HELSEL, James Glenn. b. 1921 PA. Enl. 10/5/42 Altoona, PA. Ser. No. 13084650. Pvt., Co. A, Camp Gordon, GA 10/9/42. Cpl., Co. A, 2nd Platoon. Sick at 109th Clearing Station 6/8/44. Cpl., Co. A, on *LST 690* 8/9/44. WIA – (light – premature muzzleburst), Bischweiler, France (Alsace) 2/18/45. Cpl., Co. A, 5/8/45 Innsbruck, Austria. 2nd Platoon, 3rd Squad. Gunner. Purple Heart. Dischd. Sept. 1945. Mentioned in the May 1954 Directory. Attended 1958, 1960 & 1966 Reunions as res. Roaring Springs, PA. d. 2/22/2005 from complications of pneumonia, bur. Roaring Springs, PA.

HENDERSON, ----------. Pvt., Co. B, WIA (light – shell burst), 2/18/44 Anzio, Italy. [See Jim Henderson Robinson].

HENKE, Paul E. b. 2/12/1922 PA. Enl. 9/7/42 Allentown, PA. Ser. No. 33366517. Pvt. Co. A, 10/15/42 Camp Gordon GA. Co. A, reclassified Dec. 1943. d. 8/7/1989.

HENNESSY, Edwin W., Jr. Pfc., Co. C, 6/22/45 Innsbruck, Austria.

HENDRICKSON, Honest L. b. 1900 MS. Res. Humphreys Co., MS. Enl. 9/21/42 Camp Shelby, MS. Ser. No. 34426298. Pvt. Co. C, 10/14/42 Camp Gordon, GA.

HENRIE, William M. ("Hank"). b. 12/22/1916 NJ. Res. Mercer Co., NJ. Enl. 6/29/42 Ft. Dix, NJ. Ser. No. 32270825. Pvt., Co. B, Camp Gordon, GA 7/28/42. Pfc., Co. B, promo. T/5 (temp.), Camp Gordon, GA 12/15/42. T/5, Co. B, recommended for Silver Star for action near Ceppagna, Italy 11/13/43. T/4, Co. B, 5/8/45 Innsbruck, Austria. Res. Hopewell, NJ May 1954. Office Manager, Mill Supply House. d. 5/1/1992 NJ.

HENRY, Chester L. 1st Lt. Assigned HQ 11th Armored Div. 7/23/45 [probably same man as Lester L. Henry].

HENRY, Lester Lew. b. 1/13/1917 Sabetha, KS. University of Kansas. Camp Wheeler, Macon, GA. Left Camp Wheeler Jan. 1943. Joined the Rangers at Nemours. 1st and 4th Ranger Battalions. 1st Ranger Battalion Apr. 1943 – Aug. 1943. Assigned to 1st Ranger Battalion 6/3/43. Tunisia & Sicily. 1st Lt., Co. A, 1st Ranger Battalion 7/10/43 Gela, Sicily. Detached 6648 Casual Battalion Oct. 1943 – July 1944. Italy. Seriously wounded at Anzio. 1st Lt., HQ, 2nd Repl. Depot, assigned 1st Lt., Co. D, 83rd CMB 11/1/44. WIA (serious-head injury right eye, temporary blindness & concussion), Moussey, France 11/30/44. 1st Lt., Co. A, WIA (light – phosphorous burn – right hand), 2/10/45 France. Returned to duty 2/11/45. 1st. Lt., Co. A, 5/8/45 Innsbruck, Austria. Kansas State University – Law (LLB) June 1950. City Councilman. Res. Lawrence, KS May 1954. Attorney. State Representative (two terms), 12th Dist., KS. d. 10/18/1973 Topeka, KS. bur. Oak Hill Cem., Lawrence, KS. [Also see entry for Chester L. Henry].

HEPLER, Hale Hunter. b. 6/7/1917 Millboro, VA. Millboro High School. Accepted at Virginia Tech but did not attend. Pre-war Occupation: Highway Department. Res. Millboro Springs, Bath Co., VA. Enl. 9/21/42 [10/5/42 according to Hepler] Roanoke, VA. Ser. No. 33213297. Pvt., Co. C, Camp Gordon, GA 10/11/42. Co. C, Camp Gordon, GA. Pfc., Co. C, LST 422 Survivor, 1/26/44 Italy (Anzio) – Purple Heart (phosphorous burns). T/5, Co. C, 6/22/45 Innsbruck, Austria. Dischd. 10/15/45. Res. Millboro, VA 2009.

HERNACKI, Leo. Pfc., Co. A, 5/8/45 Innsbruck, Austria.

HERR, Donald C. b. 1914 PA. Enl. 9/25/42 Pittsburgh, PA. Ser. No. 33305582. Pvt. Co. D, 10/15/42 Camp Gordon GA. Pvt., Co. D correspondent, Smokescreen, Camp Gordon, GA Nov. 1942. Pvt., Co. D, assigned Med. Det., Camp Gordon, GA 11/14/42. Pvt. Med. Det., correspondent, Smokescreen, Camp Gordon, GA, 1/9/43. Received a battlefield promotion. S/Sgt., Co. B, 1/25/45. 2nd. Lt., Med. Det., 5/8/45 Innsbruck, Austria. Assigned to 22nd Tank Battalion 7/23/45. Res. Bradford Woods, PA May 1954. Attended 1954, 1956 & 1958 Reunions as res. Bradford Woods, PA.

HERRING, Dannie L. b. 1921 SC. Res. Andrews, Georgetown Co., SC. Corp., Co. D, LST 422 Survivor, 1/26/44 Italy (Anzio) – Purple Heart Rescued by YMS 69 1/26/44. Pvt. WIA (injured in glider crash) 8/15/44 Le Muy, France. Re-enl. 11/2/45 Ft. Jackson, Columbia, SC for Hawaiian Dept. Pfc., Signal Corps.

HERUDEK, John R. b. 1920 NJ. Res. Burlington Co., NJ. Enl. 8/23/42 Newark, NJ. Ser. No. 32385511. Pvt., HQ & HQ Co., Camp Gordon,

GA 7/28/42. Pvt., HQ & HQ Co., Camp Gordon, GA 9/25/42.

HIBBS, David Y. b. 1920 NJ. Enl. 9/22/42 Philadelphia, PA. Ser. No. 33335581. Pvt., Co. B, Camp Gordon, GA 10/9/42.

HIGHTOWER, Charles H. b. 1921 GA. Res. Polk Co., GA. Enl. 9/19/42 Ft. McPherson, Atlanta, GA. Ser. No. 34442912. Pvt., Co. B, Camp Gordon, GA 10/8/42. Pfc., Silver Star. Pfc., Purple Heart, 1944. T/5, Co. B, 5/8/45 Innsbruck, Austria. Silver Star.

HILL, B. C. b. 6/3/1921 MS. Res. Aberdeen, Monroe Co., MS. Enl. 9/22/42 Camp Shelby, MS. Ser. No. 34426479. Pvt. Co. B, 10/14/42 Camp Gordon, GA. Pvt./Pfc., Co. B, (light injure in action), LST 422 Survivor, 1/26/44 Italy (Anzio) – Purple Heart. T/5, Co. B, 5/8/45 Innsbruck, Austria. d. May 1982 Aberdeen, Monroe Co., MS.

HILL, Bennie. b. 1916 AL. Res. North Birmingham, Jefferson Co., AL. Ser. No. 34391659. Pvt., Co. C, Camp Gordon, GA 10/9/42. In a 1943 photo of Co. C taken at Amalfi, Italy. Pfc., Co. C, LST 422 Survivor, 1/26/44 Italy (Anzio) – Purple Heart. T/5, Co. C, 6/22/45 Innsbruck, Austria.

HILL, Edmond W. b. 10/26/1919. Res. Newcastle, AL. Pvt., Co. B, Camp Gordon, GA 10/8/42. Pfc., Co. B, WIA (serious), 12/8/43 Italy. d. 10/21/2003 Gardendale, Jefferson Co., AL.

HILL, Gordon H. b. 1920 TN. Res. Warren Co., TN. Enl. 9/16/42 Ft. Oglethorpe, GA. Ser. No. 34371267. Pvt., Co. A, Camp Gordon, GA 10/7/42. Transf. Co. D, Camp Gordon, GA, 12/16/42.

HILL, Ottis W. b. 1920 AL. Res. Jefferson Co., AL. Enl. 9/19/42 Ft. McClellan, AL. Pvt., HQ & HQ Co., Camp Gordon, GA 10/8/42. Pvt., HQ & HQ Co., assigned to duty from absent sick at 225th Station Hospital on 1/29/44 Morning Report.

HILL, Richard K. b. 1920 PA. Enl. 9/20/42 Greensburg, PA. Ser. No. 33294840. Pvt. Co. C, 10/15/42 Camp Gordon GA. Pfc., Co. C, MIA, 1/26/44, Italy (Anzio) SR Cem.

HILL, William D. b. 1921 MS. Res. Houlka, Pontotoc Co., MS. Enl. 9/22/42 Camp Shelby, MS. Ser. No. 34426639. Pvt. Co. A, 10/14/42 Camp Gordon, GA. Cook in Co. A 11/17/44 photo provided by Lawrence Ertzberger. Pfc., Co. A, 5/8/45 Innsbruck, Austria.

HILL, Wingo ("Curly"). HQ Co. Present at Camp Gordon, GA Feb. 1943.

HILT, Arlin E. b. 1922 PA. Res. York Co., PA. Enl. 10/5/42 Harrisburg, PA. Ser. No. 13093251. Pvt., HQ & HQ Co., Camp Gordon, GA 10/9/42. Pfc., Co. C, MIA, 1/26/44, Italy (Anzio) SR Cem.

HILTZ, Verne E. b. 1921 ME. Res. Washington Co., ME / Res. Union Mills, New Brunswick, Canada. Enl. 12/15/42 Bangor, ME. Ser. No. 31282325. Pvt., Co. D, Camp Gordon, GA 4/10/43. Pvt., Co. D, WIA (from explosion of own shell hitting tree limb) 7/11/43, Gela, Sicily. Pfc., Co. D, WIA, 11/24/43 Italy – Purple Heart with Oak Leaf Cluster.

Pvt., Co. D, LST 422 Survivor, 1/26/44 Italy (Anzio) – Purple Heart with Oak Leaf Cluster. Pfc., Co. D.

HISSEM, Paul Loyd b. 1921 PA. Enl. 9/25/42 Greensburg, PA. Ser. No. 33294851. Pvt., Co. A, transf. Co. C, Camp Gordon, GA, 12/16/42. Assigned to 5th base P.O., initially in Oran, N. Africa. Transported mail at night to front lines in N. Africa, Italy, and France for 38 months.

HITE, Joseph A. b. 11/27/1920 PA. Res. Blair Co., PA. Enl. 10/5/42 Altoona, PA. Ser. No. 33254523. Pvt., Co. C, Camp Gordon, GA 10/9/42. Transf. Co. A, Camp Gordon, GA, 12/16/42. Served in North Africa, Rhineland, Ardennes, Central Europe. Service Medal, Victory Medal. Postwar res. Altoona, PA. d. 9/19/1990.

HITT, James E. Res. SC. Ser. No. 07083105. Pvt., Co. D, MIA, 1/26/44, Italy (Anzio) SR Cem.

HNIDOWICH, Yulian. b. 1910 NJ. Res. Hudson Co., NJ. Enl. 7/9/42 Newark, NJ. Pvt., HQ & HQ Co., Camp Gordon, GA 7/28/42. Pvt., HQ & HQ Co., special duty Communications School of 472nd Field Artillery, Camp Gordon, GA 10/12-17/42. Pfc., Camp Gordon, GA 11/21/42. Possibly KIA.

HOCKENBERRY, Joseph P. b. 3/17/1911 OH. Res. Summit Co., OH. Enl. 3/5/42 Ft. Niagara, Youngstown, NY. Ser. No. 32251896. Pvt. Attached to Co. B 5/28/42 Edgewood Arsenal, MD. Telephone Operator (Pvt.). Pfc., Co. A, promo. T/5 (temp.), Camp Gordon, GA 9/23/42. Cpl., Camp Gordon, GA 11/21/42. Cpl., Co. A, relsd. from SD to 4th Signal Corps, 4th Mtz Div, Camp Gordon, GA, 12/16/42. S/Sgt., Co. A on *LST 690* 8/9/44. Present as Acting Sgt. 8/14/44. S/Sgt.,Co. A, 5/8/45 Innsbruck, Austria. d. Oct. 1980 Jamestown, Chatauqua NY.

HODGSON, William Joseph. b. 2/19/1920 Philadelphia, PA. Grad. LaSalle College. Enl. 9/22/42 Philadelphia, PA. Ser. No. 33335064. Pvt., HQ & HQ Co., Camp Gordon, GA 10/9/42. North Africa. Italy. Present as a Sgt., Co. D in France Oct. 1944. Res. Ship Bottom, NJ May 1954. Teaching/Business. Businessman in various liquor, restaurant, real estate & banking endeavors. Mayor, Ship Bottom, NJ. Retired Key Biscayne, FL d. 2005, Key Biscayne, FL.

HOETH, Carl W. b. 1917 WI. Res. Arlington Co., VA. Enl. 1/7/42 Baltimore, MD. Ser. No. 33069333. Pvt. Attached to Co. A 5/28/42 Edgewood Arsenal, MD. Message Center Chief (Sgt.). Pfc., HQ & HQ Co., (Message Center), promo. Cpl. (temp.), Camp Gordon, GA 7/15/42.

HOETTKER, Frank. Pvt. Attached to Co. C 5/28/42 Edgewood Arsenal, MD. Communication (Cpl.).

HOFFA, Arthur R. b. 1907 PA. Enl. 10/5/42 Philadelphia, PA. Ser. No. 13124718. Pvt., HQ & HQ Co., Camp Gordon, GA 10/9/42.

HOFFA, Carl Leroy. b. 1921 PA. Enl. 9/21/42 Harrisburg, PA. Ser. No. 33240962. Pvt., Co. B, Camp Gordon, GA 10/9/42. Pvt., Co. B, Camp Gordon, GA Dec. 1942. Pfc., Co. B, sent to hospital (120th Collecting

Bn.) 8/4/43. Returned to duty 8/7/43. Pfc., Co. B, 5/8/45 Innsbruck, Austria. Res. Tamaqua, PA May 1954. Pennsylvania Power Co.

HOFFMAN, Stanley W. b. 1919 PA. Res. Carbon Co., PA. Enl. 3/3/42 Ft. George Meade, MD. Ser. No. 33171422. Pvt. Attached to Co. B 5/28/42 Edgewood Arsenal, MD. Cook (Pvt.). Pfc., Co. B, (Cook), promo. T/5 (temp.), Camp Gordon, GA 7/15/42. T/5 (temp.), Co. B, promo. T/4 (temp.), Camp Gordon, GA 8/10/42. T/4, Co. B, MIA, 1/26/44, Italy (Anzio) SR Cem.

HOFFMANN, Oscar W. b. 8/1/1909 PA. Enl. 9/22/42 Philadelphia, PA. Ser. No. 33335602. Pvt., Co. C, Camp Gordon, GA 10/9/42.d. June 1986, Lancaster Co., PA.

HOFMANN, (HOFFMAN), William J. b. 1921 PA. Res. Blair Co., PA. Enl. 10/5/42 Altoona, PA. Ser. No. 33254454. Pvt., Co. D, Camp Gordon, GA 10/9/42. Pfc., Co. D, WIA (enemy shell - serious), 9/16/43 Vietre sul Mare, Italy. Returned to duty 10/26/43. Pfc., Co. D, MIA, 1/26/44, Italy (Anzio) SR Cem.

HOKKANEN, Vilho. Pvt., Co. A, Camp Gordon, GA 3/18/43. Ser. No. 32438646. Served in the European and Asiatic-Pacific Theaters of Operations with Co. E, 1301st Engineer Gen. Ser. Reg. as a duty soldier in Normandy and Northern France. EAME Theater Ribbon, Asiatic-Pacific Theater Ribbon, American Theater Ribbon, Good Conduct Medal, and WWII Victory Medal. Res. Canterbury, CT.

HOLDEN, Homer G. b. 1919 NC. Res. Onslow Co., NC. Enl. 11/14/40 Ft. Bragg, NC. Field Artillery. Ser. No. 14034624. Pvt., Co. D, MIA, 1/26/44, Italy (Anzio) SR Cem.

HOLDEN, John M. Pfc., HQ Co. Bronze Star & Purple Heart, Sept. 1945.

HOLLEY, John R. b. 2/24/1921 MS. Res. Oxford, Lafayette Co., MS. Enl. 9/22/42 Camp Shelby, MS. Ser. No. 34426519. Pvt. Co. C, 10/14/42 Camp Gordon, GA. Transf. Co. A, Camp Gordon, GA, 12/16/42. S/Sgt., Co. C, LST 422 Survivor, 1/26/44 Italy (Anzio) – Purple Heart. S/Sgt., Co. C, WIA (serious – lost an arm - S-mine), Minturno, Italy 3/26/44. Athletic Staff, Univ. of MS, 1981. d. Feb. 1983 Oxford, Lafayette Co., MS.

HOLLOWAY, James W. b. 1921 MS. Res. Washington Co., MS. Enl. 9/23/42 Camp Shelby, MS. Ser. No. 34426673. Pvt. Co. C, 10/14/42 Camp Gordon, GA.

HOLLOWAY, Mitchell C. ("Kid"). b. 1921 PA. Enl. 9/25/42 Pittsburgh, PA. Ser. No. 33305565. Pvt. Co. D, 10/15/42 Camp Gordon GA. Pvt., Co. D correspondent, Smokescreen, Camp Gordon, GA Nov. 1942. Pvt., Co. D, special duty Battalion HQ, Camp Gordon, GA 12/2/42.Pvt., Managing and Acting Editor Smokescreen, Camp Gordon, GA 1/9/43. Pfc., Mimeographer, Smokescreen, Camp Gordon, GA Feb. 1943. Corp., Co. C. Company Clerk. Corp., Co. C, WIA (serious – shell fragment), 9/13/43, Maiori, Italy. Evacuated. Attended 1956 Reunion.

HOLMES, William L. b. 1920 CT. Res. New London Co., CT. Enl. 2/28/42 Hartford, CT. Ser. No. 11065219. Pvt. Attached to Co. H 5/28/42 Edgewood Arsenal, MD. Gunner (Pvt.). Pfc., Co. C, promo. Cpl. (temp.), Camp Gordon, GA 9/3/42. Cpl. (temp.) Co. C, to Sgt. (temp.) Camp Gordon, GA 10/14/42. Sgt., Co. C, WIA (light), 9/24/43 Maiori, Italy. Returned to duty 10/24/43. Dischgd. October 1945. Purple Heart, 3 Bronze Stars, Distinguished Unit Citation, & French Croix De Guerre. Mentioned in the May 1954 Directory. Res. Groton, CT. d. 6/28/2003.

HOLMES, William W. b. 1901 Centerville, MD. Res. Wash., D.C. Enl. 9/21/42 Ft. Myer, VA. Ser. No. 33197690. Pvt., Co. A, Camp Gordon, GA 10/11/42. Pvt., Co. A, assigned Med. Det., Camp Gordon, GA 11/30/42. Transf. Co. D, Camp Gordon, GA, 12/16/42. d. 1970. bur. Centerville, MD.

HOLSTEIN, Seymour A. b. 1917 NJ. Res. Newark, Essex Co., NJ. Enl. 7/9/42 Newark, NJ. Ser. No. 32390424. Pvt., Co. D, Camp Gordon, GA 7/28/42. Pfc. Co. D, transf. Co. A, Camp Gordon, GA, 12/16/42. Sgt., Co. D, LST 422 Survivor, 1/25/44 Italy (Anzio) – Purple Heart. Sgt., Co. D, Bronze Star [Presented 11/20/44 for action 9/20/44 near Camp De Tourches, France]. Sgt., Co. A, 5/8/45 Innsbruck, Austria. Postwar res. Newark, NJ. Wofford Jackson called Holstein "the best squad sergeant to work under him."

HOLTERHOFF, Hans A. b. 1906 Germany. Res. Passaic Co., NJ. Enl. 6/25/42 Newark, NJ. Ser. No. 32386385. Pvt., Co. B, Camp Gordon, GA 7/28/42. Pvt., Co. B, special duty Communications School of 472nd Field Artillery, Camp Gordon, GA 10/12-17/42. Pfc., promo. Cpl. (temp.), Camp Gordon, GA 12/12/42.

HOLTZ, Rupert W. Pvt. Attached to Co. C 5/28/42 Edgewood Arsenal, MD. Mechanic General (Pvt.).

HOMER, James W. b. 1897 PA. Enl. 9/27/42 Philadelphia, PA. Ser. No. 33335604. Pvt., Co. D, Camp Gordon, GA 10/9/42. Pvt., Co. D, assigned Med. Det., Camp Gordon, GA 11/14/42.

HOMIAK, Norman. b. 1912 PA. Res. Northumberland Co., PA. Enl. 12/22/42 Harrisburg, PA. Ser. No. 33494977. Pvt., Co. A, Camp Gordon, GA 3/18/43.

HOOKANSON, Edward J. L. Assigned from 65th Inf. Division as 2nd Lt., Co. B, 7/23/45.

HOOTEN, Ernest R. b. 1913 IN. Res. De Pauw, Harrison Co., IN. Enl. 3/2/42 Ft. Benjamin Harrison, IN. Ser. No. 35112929. Pvt. Attached to Co. H 5/28/42 Edgewood Arsenal, MD. Gunner (Pvt.). Pvt., Co. C transf. Co. D, Camp Gordon, GA 6/15/42. Pfc., Co. D, transf. to Motor Pool, Camp Gordon, GA 1/25/43. T/5, Co. D, LST 422 Survivor, 1/26/44 Italy (Anzio) – Purple Heart. T/4, Co. A, 5/8/45 Innsbruck, Austria.

HOOTEN, Roy E. b. 1904 IN. Res. Harrison Co., IN. Enl. 2/3/42 Ft. Benjamin Harrison, IN. Ser. No. 35039441. Pvt. Attached to Co. H 5/28/42 Edgewood Arsenal, MD. Gunner (Pvt.).

HOOVER, Raymond W. ("Pop") b. 1910 PA. Res. Northumberland Co., PA. Pre-war: 4 years in Cavalry. Re-enl. 1941. Enl. 10/5/42 Harrisburg, PA. Ser. No. 13093269. Pvt., HQ & HQ Co., Camp Gordon, GA 10/9/42. Pfc., Co. C, WIA (light), LST 422 Survivor, 1/26/44 Italy (Anzio) – Purple Heart. Cpl., Co. B. Silver Star. Bronze Star. Pfc., HQ Co., 5/8/45 Innsbruck, Austria. Res. Milton, PA May 1954. Turkey Farm Employee. Claims to suffer from headaches from Anzio. Attended 1954 & 1956 Reunions. Res. Milton, PA 2009.

HOPKINS, Floy A. b. 1921 AL. Res. Houston Co., AL. Enl. 9/19/42 Ft. McClellan, AL. Ser. No. 34391774. Pvt., Co. B, Camp Gordon, GA 10/9/42. Pvt., Co. B, 5/8/45 Innsbruck, Austria.

HOPKINS, Ford Elwood. b. 8/16/1915 Paterson, NJ. Res. Passaic Co., NJ. Welding School/Maintenance Mechanic. Enl. 6/30/43 Newark, NJ. Ser. No. 42000999. Ft. Dix, NJ 7/14/43. Artillery Training, Ft. Bragg, NC. Algiers, North Africa 2/9/44. Italy 8/15/44. Gunner for mortar. Determined range, sight, and firing. Performed 1st echelon maintenance Italy, France, Germany, Austria. Pfc., Co. A, 5/8/45 Innsbruck, Austria. Assigned Co. C, 818th Tank Destroyer Battalion. Returned to U.S. 10/29/45. Dischd. 11/2/45 Ft. Dix, NJ. Said he lost his hearing from the 4.2" mortars. Pipefitter/Maintenace Mechanic. d. 10/22/2004 Warwick, NY. Bur. Cedar Lawn Cem., Paterson, NJ.

HOPKINS, James T. b. 1915 NY. Res. New York Co., NY. Enl. 7/17/41 Camp Upton, Yaphank, NY. Ser. No. 32161104. HQ 2nd CMB, assigned Pfc., HQ & HQ Co., 83rd CMB 7/25/45.

HOPKINS, John H. b. 1915 MD. Enl. 12/22/42 Baltimore, MD. Ser. No. 33390947. Pvt., Co. A, Camp Gordon, GA 3/18/43. Pvt., Co. A, WIA (light – enemy shell burst), 3/30/44 Anzio, Italy. Lawrence Ertzberger said the wound was serious and Hopkins never returned to the battalion.

HORN, Donald. Pvt. Attached to Co. K 5/28/42 Edgewood Arsenal, MD. Gunner (Pvt.). Pfc., Co. A, promo. T/5 (temp.), Camp Gordon, GA 8/26/42.

HOROSCHAK, Paul A. b. 1924 CT. Res. New Haven Co., CT. Enl. 3/31/43 New Haven, CT. Ser. No. 31331261. Pfc., Co. B, 5/8/45 Innsbruck, Austria.

HOTKO, Leo W. b. 1914 PA. Res. Luzerne Co., PA. Enl. 3/17/42 Ft. George Meade, MD. Ser. No. 33175224. Attached to Co. A 5/28/42 Edgewood Arsenal, MD. Chauffeur. Pvt., HQ & HQ Co. transf. Co. A, Camp Gordon, GA 6/15/42. Pfc., Co. A temp. T/5 Camp Gordon, GA 8/1/42. T/5, Co. A, MIA, 1/26/44, Italy (Anzio) SR Cem.

HOTSKO, George. b. 1924 PA. Res. Carbon Co., PA. Enl. 1/9/43 Allentown, PA. Ser. No. 33487311. Assigned from 65th Inf. Division as 2nd Lt., Co. A. 7/23/45.

HOUCHEN, Hugh E. b. 1921 KY. Res. Clark Co., IN. Enl. 12/16/42 Louisville, KY. Ser. No. 35690870. Pvt., Camp Gordon, GA 4/10/43.

HOUGH, Carl R. b. 1914 MS. Res. Smith Co., MS. Enl. 9/22/42 Camp Shelby, MS. Ser. No. 34426427. Pvt. Co. D, 10/14/42 Camp Gordon, GA. Pfc., Co. D, MIA, 1/26/44, Italy (Anzio) SR Cem.

HOVLAND, Jacob G. T/5, HQ Co., 5/8/45 Innsbruck, Austria.

HOWARD, Gus E. b. 1909 MS. Res. Union Co., MS. Enl. 9/23/42 Camp Shelby, MS. Ser. No. 34426888. Pvt. Co. C, 10/14/42 Camp Gordon, GA.

HOWE, Charles J. Pfc., Co. A, 5/8/45 Innsbruck, Austria. Postwar res. Passaic, NJ.

HOWE, George A. Pfc., Co. B, 5/8/45 Innsbruck, Austria.

HOXMEIER, John T. b. 5/25/1918. Res. Los Angeles Co., CA. Enl. 2/14/42 Ft. MacArthur, San Pedro, CA. Ser. No. 39019484. Pvt. Attached to Co. F 5/28/42 Edgewood Arsenal, MD. Supply Sgt. (S/Sgt.). Pvt., Co. C, promo. T/4 (temp.), Camp Gordon, GA 6/16/42. Cpl. (temp.), (Supply), promo. Sgt. (temp.), Camp Gordon, GA 7/15/42. Sgt. (temp.), Co. C, promo. S/Sgt. (temp.), Camp Gordon, GA 9/7/43. S/Sgt., Co. C, 6/22/45 Innsbruck, Austria. d. Dec. 1977 CA.

HRABIK, George. Res. PA. Ser. No. 13116745. Pvt., Co. C, Camp Gordon, GA 10/9/42. T/5, Co. C, MIA, 1/26/44, Italy (Anzio) SR Cem.

HUBACH, Neal A. b. 7/16/1906 NJ. Res. Hudson Co., NJ. Enl. 7/6/42 Newark, NJ. Ser. No. 32389070. Pvt., HQ & HQ Co., Camp Gordon, GA 7/28/42. d. 2/8/2003 Springfield, Union Co., NJ.

HUBBS, Joshua B. b. 1910. Res. Morgan Co., IL. Enl. 3/3/42 Peoria, IL. Pvt. Attached to Co. C 5/28/42 Edgewood Arsenal, MD. Supply Sgt. (S/Sgt.). Pvt., Co. A, promo. T/4 (temp.), Camp Gordon, GA 6/16/42. Cpl. (temp.), (Supply Sgt.), promo. Sgt. (temp.), Camp Gordon, GA 7/15/42. Sgt. (temp.), Co. A, promo. S/Sgt. (temp.), Camp Gordon, GA 9/7/42. Ser. No. 16054396. S/Sgt., Co. A, KIA, 1/26/44, Italy (Anzio), SR Cem.

HUDAK, Albert G. b. 3/5/ 1913 NJ. Res. Wallington, Bergen Co., NJ. Enl. 7/9/42 Newark, NJ. Ser. No. 32390497. Pvt., Co. C, Camp Gordon, GA 7/28/42. Pfc., Co. C, WIA 9/16/43 Italy – Purple Heart. Pfc., Co. C, LST 422 Survivor, 1/26/44 Italy (Anzio) – Purple Heart with Oak Leaf Cluster. Attended 1966 Reunion. d. Oct. 1985 Wallington, Bergen Co., NJ.

HUENKE, William P., Jr. b. 1921 PA. Enl. 9/22/42 Philadelphia, PA. Ser. No. 33335498. Pvt., Co. C, Camp Gordon, GA 10/9/42.

HUETSON, Walter R. Cpl., Co. A, Camp Gordon, GA Nov. 1942. Sgt., distinguished in action 7/10/43 Sicily.

HUETSON, Webster P. b.1/6/1908. Res. Laclede Co., MO. Enl. 3/18/42 Jefferson Barracks, MO. Ser. No. 17045734. Pvt. Attached to Co. A 5/28/42 Edgewood Arsenal, MD. Instrument Sgt. (Sgt.). Cpl. Co. A, transf. Co. D, Camp Gordon, GA, 12/16/42. d. 3/8/1988.

HUFF, Emmett M. b. 1917 VA. Res. Bedford Co., VA. Pvt., Co. C, Camp Gordon, GA 10/11/42. Re-enl. 9/26/46 Roanoke, VA. Ser. No. 33213380.

HUFFMAN, Charles W. b. 1921 PA. Enl. 7/24/42 Altoona, PA. Ser. No. 13083661. 54th Chem. Impreg. Co. Pvt., attached to Co. B, 83rd CMB, Camp Gordon, GA 4/15/43. Pvt., Bronze Star [presented 4/25/44].

HUGHES, Elden [Eldon] L. b. 9/17/1920 OK. Res. Washington, D.C. Enl. 9/21/42 Ft. Myer, VA. Ser. No. 33197639. Pvt., Co. A, Camp Gordon, GA 10/11/42. Pvt., Co. A, WIA (light injure), 2/21 or 22/44 Italy – Purple Heart. Returned to duty 2/27/44. Pfc., HQ Co., 5/8/45 Innsbruck, Austria. d. 5/17/1999 OK.

HUGHES, George E. b. 8/28/1920 PA. Res. Westmoreland, PA. Enl. 9/24/42 Greensburg, PA. Ser. No. 33294757. Pvt. Co. A, 10/15/42 Camp Gordon GA. Co. A, WIA (light), 2/18/44 Anzio, Italy. T/5, Co. A, 5/8/45 Innsbruck, Austria. d. 4/11/2006 Jeanette, Westmoreland, Co., PA.

HUGHES, Harold E. b. 2/15/1922. Res. Ida Co., IA. Appeared in the movie *The Monkey's Paw* (1933). Enl. 12/21/42 Camp Dodge, Herrold, IA. Ser. No. 37651558. Pvt., Co. D, Camp Gordon, GA 4/10/43. BAR man. North Africa. Sicily. Italy. Contracted malaria and spent over a month in hospital. Departed Italy for home 6/1/44. Military Police, Camp Butner, NC. Iowa Commerce Commission 1958-62. Iowa Governor 1962-68. U.S. Senator 1969-75. Presidential Candidate 1972 (withdrew). Portrayed himself in the movie *Born Again* (1978). Book "Harold E. Hughes: The Man From Ida Grove" (1979) contains chapter on his service with 83rd CMB. d. 10/23/1996 Glendale, Maricopa Co., AZ.

HUGHES, John T. b. 1920 VA. Res. Henrico Co., VA. Enl. 9/21/42 Richmond, VA. Ser. No. 33225730. Pvt., Co. C, Camp Gordon, GA 10/11/42. Transf. Co. A, Camp Gordon, GA, 12/16/42. Pfc., Co. C, KIA, 1/26/44, Italy (Anzio), SR Cem.

HUGO, John Lawrence. b. 3/1/1913 Meadowbrook, Monongalia Co., WV. Res., Osage, WV. Pre-war Occupation: Chemist Assistant. Enl. 3/19/42 Ft. Hayes, Columbus, OH. Ser. No. 35290328. Pvt. Attached to Co. I 5/28/42 Edgewood Arsenal, MD. Gunner (Pvt.). Pfc., Co. D, promo. Cpl. (temp.), Camp Gordon, GA 12/2/42. Cpl. Co. D, transf. Co. A, Camp Gordon, GA, 12/16/42. Squad Leader. Sicily. Naples-Foggia. Rome-Arno. North Apenndines. Po Valley. Good Conduct Medal Co. #9 - 83rd CMB (1943). Pvt., Co. D, LST 422 Survivor, 1/26/44 Italy (Anzio) - Purple Heart Medal Co. #2 HQ - 83rd CMB (1944). Rescued by USS Pilot. European African Middle Eastern Service Ribbon. Departed for U.S. 9/13/45. Arrived in U.S. 9/29/45. Dischd. 10/5/45 Ft. George Meade, MD. U.S. Postal Employee, Monongalia Co., WV. Retired 1977. d. 2/28/1996 Morgantown, WV. bur. East Oak Grove Cem., Morgantown, WV.

HULCHER, Julius Charles ("Doc" / "Sonny" / "Hungry"). b. 8/2/1915 Richmond, VA. His father, Dr. J. J. Hulcher, delivered him on the kitchen table. Virginia Tech – Class President 1937. Medical College of VA, Richmond. Medical school graduate when enlisted May 1942. Camp Lee, VA - 45th General Hospital. Rabat. Chemical Warfare Service training, Casablanca 4/26/43. Ordered by telephone to transfer to the 83rd CMB late Nov. 1943. Joined 83rd CMB 12/2/43 at Venafro, Italy. Capt., Med. Det. Italy. France. Germany. Austria. Capt., Med. Det., 5/8/45 Innsbruck, Austria. Assigned to 81st Armored Medical Battalion 7/25/45. Filmed color mm home movies of his service. Attended 1958 & 1962 Reunions as res. Richmond, VA. Res. Richmond, VA May 1954. M.D. d. 1/22/2001 Midlothian, Chesterfield Co., VA.

HULSEY, David Dorsey. Capt., assigned HQ & HQ Co., & designated Plans and Training Officer, Camp Gordon, GA 6/22/42. Designated Executive Officer, Camp Gordon, GA 7/27/42. Apptd. Summary Court, Camp Gordon, GA 8/10/42. Released as Battalion Executive Officer & designated Battalion Training & Operations Officer, Camp Gordon, GA 9/15/42. Released as Operations & Training Officer and designated Executive Officer, Camp Gordon, GA 9/25/42. Capt./ Executive Officer. Camp Gordon, GA Sept. 1942. Transf. 10/10/42. Res. Tupelo, MS.

HUNT, James M. b. 1919 MS. Res. Monroe Co., MS. Enl. 9/23/42 Camp Shelby, MS. Ser. No. 34426898. Pvt. Co. B, 10/14/42 Camp Gordon, GA.

HUNT, John E., Jr. b. 1924 PA. Res. Washington Co., PA. Enl. 10/3/42 Pittsburgh, PA. Ser. No. 13129011. Pvt. Co. A, 10/15/42 Camp Gordon GA. Pvt., Co. A, Camp Gordon, GA 11/21/42. Pvt. Co. A, relsd. SD to 4th Signal Corps, 4th Mtz Div, Camp Gordon, GA, 12/16/42. Pfc., HQ Co., 5/8/45 Innsbruck, Austria.

HUNT, Rowland H. b. 1921 TN. Res. Loudon Co., TN. Enl. 8/13/42 Ft. Oglethorpe, GA. Ser. No. 34364243. Pvt., LIA, 12/13/44 France. Pfc., Co. B, 5/8/45 Innsbruck, Austria. Res. Knoxville, TN May 1954. Bookkeeper, Royal Jewelers Co.

HURT, James. Pvt. Co. D. Admitted to hospital for exhaustion 11/23/43 Venafro, Italy. Buddy of Arthur Bilton. Photo's in Dan Shields album taken at Camp Gordon, GA.

HUSHEN, Carl V. b. 11/24/1916 PA. Res. Northampton Co., PA. Ser. No. 06891407. 1st/Sgt., C.W.S. Assigned to Military Police 5/28/42 Edgewood Arsenal, MD. 1st Sgt. 5/28/42. Present Co. C, Camp Gordon, GA, 1/9/43. Co. C. Reduced in rank 7/13/43. d. 11/11/2002 PA.

HUSTER, Charles R. b. 4/25/1925 IA. Res. Cedar Rapids, Linn Co., IA. Enl. 7/5/43 Camp Dodge, Herrold, IA. Ser. No. 37674397. Pfc., Co. C, WIA 5/26/44 Italy – Purple Heart. Pfc., Co. C, 6/22/45 Innsbruck, Austria. d. 12/30/1998 IA.

HUTCHERSON, Horace D. b. 1923 SC. Res. Spartanburg Co., SC. Enl. 4/7/43 Ft. Jackson, Columbia, SC. Ser. No. 34651952. Pvt., Co. B, KIA (enemy 240mm shell), 2/18/44, Anzio, Italy, SR Cem.

HUTCHINSON, William Seely, Jr. ("Hutch"). b. 10/30/1914 Wash., D.C. Bethlehem, PA public schools. Collegiate School, NYC. Lehigh University (BS chemical engineering). M.I.T. (MS – chemical engineering). Entered military service 10/30/40. 1st. Lt., CWS, Procurement Planning 3/27/42. Capt., CWS Procurement Planning 5/21/42 & 6/5/42. Military Command & General Staff College and National War College. Capt., CWS, assigned to HQ & HQ Co. & designated Battalion Executive Officer, Camp Gordon, GA 9/15/42. Released as Executive Officer & designated Adj., Camp Gordon, GA 9/25/42. Released as Adj. & designated Executive Officer, Camp Gordon, GA 10/10/42. Appointed Summary Court, Camp Gordon, GA 10/13/42. Silver Star for performance at Gela, Sicily 7/12/43. Took command of the 83rd CMB 9/23/43 [actually took command 9/26/43]. Major, HQ & HQ Co., WIA (shrapnel in right ankle), 11/28/43 Italy – Purple Heart. Battlefield promo. Lt. Col. 12/25/43. Reassigned 7/1/44. Lt. Col., Silver Star, 1944. Lt. Col., Legion of Merit with Oak Leaf Cluster. Military Valor Cross from Italy. Left 83rd CMB July 1944 to train 99th and 100th chemical battalions. Officially left 83rd CMB 10/7/44. Commanded 503rd Airborne Inf., Munich, Germany. Col., in service in Korea 1954 commanding 2nd Inf. Div. Chemical Co. Atomic Energy Commission. Manhattan Project. Nuclear Weapons Effects testing, Los Alamos, NM (five years). Nevada Test Site. Sandia Base, Eniwetok Atoll in Pacific. Southern Command NATO HQ, Naples, Italy. Attended 1960 Reunion. Retired 3/3/1966 at Cornell Aeronautical Laboratory, Bangkok, Thailand. Deputy Director Public Works, Jacksonville, FL. d. 2/2/1992 Jacksonville, FL. bur. Arlington Nat. Cem. Interment 2/10/1992. Service in WW II, Korea, Vietnam.

HUTKO, Joseph, Jr. b. 2/23/1921 OH. Res. Mahoning Co., OH. Enl. 12/9/42 Cleveland, OH. Ser. No. 35525310. Pfc., Co. B, 5/8/45 Innsbruck, Austria. d. Sept. 1973 Youngstown, Mahoning Co., OH.

HUYSSE, Joseph F. b. 8/19/1921 NJ. Res. Bergen Co., NJ. Enl. 7/9/42 Newark, NJ. Ser. No. 32390517. Pvt., Co. D, Camp Gordon, GA 7/28/42. Pfc., Co. D, Camp Gordon, GA 11/14/42. Transf. Co. A, Camp Gordon, GA, 12/16/42. Considered an excellent baseball player with ability to go professional. d. 12/25/1990 NJ.

HYDE, Claudy Lee. b. 8/22/1920 Bogalusa, LA. Res. Foxworth, Marion Co., MS. Enl. 9/21/42 Camp Shelby, MS. Ser. No. 34426347. Pvt. Co. C, 10/14/42 Camp Gordon, GA. Pfc., Co. C, LST 422 Survivor, 1/26/44 Italy (Anzio) – Purple Heart. Pfc., HQ Co., 5/8/45 Innsbruck, Austria. Retired after 32 years Gaylord Mill. d. 9/12/98 Bogalusa, LA. bur. Hillview Memorial Gardens.

IMPERATO, Anthony G. ("Tony"). b. 1/4/1921 NY. Res. New York Co., NY. Enl. 7/2/42 Ft. Jay, Governors Island, NY. Ser. No. 32398409. Pvt., Co. B, Camp Gordon, GA 7/28/42. Pvt., Co. B, sent to hospital 8/7/43. Cpl., Co. B, 5/8/45 Innsbruck, Austria. Called to service in Korea. Res. New York, NY May 1954. Employee, U.S. Treasury Dept. Attended 1958 Reunion as res. Woodridge, NJ. d. 8/25/2002.

INGRATE, Joseph P. b. 1918 NY. Res. Kings Co., NY. Enl. 3/21/42 Camp Upton, Yaphank, NY. Pvt. Ser. No. 32231563. Attached to Co. I 5/28/42 Edgewood Arsenal, MD. Chauffeur. Pvt., HQ & HQ Co. transf. Co. B, Camp Gordon, GA 6/15/42. Pfc, Co. B temp. T/5 Camp Gordon, GA 8/1/42. Present as Cpl., Motor Pool, Camp Gordon, GA, 1/9/43. T/5, Co. B, sent to hospital 8/14/43.

INGWERSEN, Timothy B. b. 8/17/1908 IL. Res. Bernalillo Co., NM. Enl. 3/6/42 Ft. Bliss, El Paso, TX. Ser. No. 38102312. Pvt. Attached to Co. C 5/28/42 Edgewood Arsenal, MD. Auto Rifleman (Pvt.). d. 3/11/1992 NM.

IOZZIA, Peter. b. 7/24/1924 NY. Res. Brooklyn/Kings Co., NY. Enl. 2/20/43 New York City, NY. Ser. No. 32811851. Pfc., Co. C, 6/22/45 Innsbruck, Austria. d. 10/16/2003 NY.

IRISH, Everett A. Capt. Ser. No. 0241119. Assigned Med. Det. & designated Battalion Surgeon, Camp Gordon, GA 9/29/42. In a James O. Beasley dated 4/25/43 "Capt. Irish has left the battalion."

JACK, James. b. 8/2/1919 NJ. Res. Cape May Co., NJ. Enl. 2/27/42 Ft. Dix, NJ. Ser. No. 32243200. Pvt. Attached to Co. G 5/28/42 Edgewood Arsenal, MD. Squad Leader (Sgt.). Pfc., Co. B, (Platoon Leader), promo. Cpl. (temp.), Camp Gordon, GA 7/15/42. Cpl. (temp.), Co. B promo. Sgt. (temp.), Camp Gordon, GA 7/27/42. Sent to hospital 8/14/43. S/Sgt., Co. B, WIA (light), 11/19/44 Rochicourt, France. d. 12/17/1988 Marmora, Cape May Co., NJ.

JACKSON, Clyde H. b. 1920 GA. Enl. 6/2/42 Ft. Jackson, Columbia, SC. Ser. No. 34124542. Pvt., Co. B, Camp Gordon, GA 4/16/43. Pvt., Co. B, sent to hospital (56th Medical, Trapani) 8/5/43. Returned to duty 8/14/43. Sent to hospital 8/19/43, returned to duty 8/21/43.

JACKSON, Edward L. b. 1921 GA. Res. Lindale, Floyd Co., GA. Enl. 9/17/42 Ft. McPherson, Atlanta, GA. Ser. No. 34442462. Pfc., Co. C, LST 422 Survivor, 1/26/44 Italy (Anzio) – Purple Heart. Pfc., WIA (serious) & MIA, 8/29/44, Briançon, France. Returned to U.S. control 9/7/44.

JACKSON, Lawrence A. b. 1923 TN. Res. Wayne Co., TN. Enl. 2/20/43 Ft. Oglethorpe, GA. Ser. No. 34723015. Pvt., Co. C, MIA, 1/26/44, Italy (Anzio) SR Cem.

JACKSON, Robert F. 2nd Lt., Co. A, joined 83rd CMB July 1944. 2nd Lt., Co. A, on LST 690 8/9/44. Promo. 1st Lt. 8/17/44. 1st. Lt., Co. B, 5/8/45 Innsbruck, Austria. 1st Lt. Assigned HQ, 11th Armored Div. 7/23/45.

JACKSON, William B. b. 1921 AL. Res. Madison Co., AL. Enl. 9/24/1942 Ft. McClellan, AL. Ser. No. 34392324. Pvt. Co. C, 10/14/42 Camp Gordon, GA. Pfc., Co. C, MIA, 1/26/44, Italy (Anzio) SR Cem.

JACKSON, Wofford Lee. ("Woof-Woof"). b. 9/4/1916 GA. Res. Manchester, Meriwether Co., GA. Enl. 9/21/42 Ft. McPherson, Atlanta, GA. Ser. No. 34443123. Pvt., Co. D, Camp Gordon, GA 10/9/42. Transf. Co. A, Camp Gordon, GA, 12/16/42. Sgt., Co. D, LST 422 Survivor, 1/26/44 Italy (Anzio) – Purple Heart. S/Sgt./Platoon Sgt., Co. D. S/Sgt., Bronze Star [Presented 11/20/44]. S/Sgt., Co. A, 5/8/45 Innsbruck, Austria. Dischd. Oct. 1945. Res. Manchester, GA May 1954. Two Purple Hearts & Combat Infantryman Badge. City/County Government. Church Deacon. Attended 1954, 1956, 1958, 1960 & 1962 reunions as res. Manchester, GA. Owner/50 yrs. - Western Auto

Assoc. d. 11/30/2002 Manchester, Meriwether Co., GA. bur. Meriwether Mausoleum.

JACKSON, Zelmer L. b. 1919 MS. Res. Itawamba Co., MS. Enl. 9/23/42 Camp Shelby, MS. Ser. No. 34426745. Pvt. Co. C, 10/14/42 Camp Gordon, GA. Pfc., Co. C, MIA, 1/26/44, Italy (Anzio) SR Cem.

JACOBS, Elwood N. Pfc., Co. B, promo. Cpl. (temp.) 7/24/45. Ser. No. 36715916. Promo. Sgt. (temp.) 9/15/45.

JACOBS, Marshall A. Pvt. Attached to Co. C 5/28/42 Edgewood Arsenal, MD. Squad Leader (Sgt.).

JAGIELLO, Benjamin P. b. 1921 NJ. Res. Bergen Co., NJ. Enl. 7/9/42 Newark, NJ. Ser. No. 32390529. Pvt., HQ & HQ Co., Camp Gordon, GA 7/28/42. Pfc., HQ Co., promo. Cpl. (temp.), Camp Gordon, GA 11/3/42. Transf. OCS, Infantry, Ft. Benning, GA Nov. 1942. 1st. Lt., 142nd. Inf., 36th. Inf. Div., KIA 11/5/44. EA Cemetery, Epinal, France. Bronze Star. Purple Heart w/Oak Leaf Cluster.

JAMES [Jame], Grady. b. 1907 AL. Res. Cullman Co., AL. Enl. 5/6/42 Ft. McClellan, AL. Ser. No. 34169599. Pvt., Co. C, KIA, 1/26/44, Italy (Anzio). [Listed as Jame under his serial number]. Next of kin: John H. James, father.

JAMES, Jack L. b. 1920 MS. Res. Millington, Scott Co., TN. Enl. 2/19/43 Camp Shelby, MS. Ser. No. 34623144. Pfc., Co. D, LST 422 Survivor, 1/26/44 Italy (Anzio) – Purple Heart. Sgt., Co. D, WIA 4/24/44 Italy – Purple Heart with Oak Leaf Cluster.

JAMES, Joe. Co. A. Mentioned in the 6/21/43 entry in the diary of James G. Helsel.

JAMMARON, Alfred L. b. 1902 PA. Enl. 9/25/42 Pittsburg, PA. Ser. No. 33305566. Pvt. HQ & HQ Co., 10/15/42 Camp Gordon GA.

JANOSZ, Michael. b. 6/18/1908 NH. Res. Lucas Co., OH. Enl. 3/10/42 Ft. Benjamin Harrison, IN. Ser. No. 35041881. Pvt. Attached to Co. C 5/28/42 Edgewood Arsenal, MD. Gunner (Pvt.). Pfc., Co. A, promo. T/5 (temp.), Camp Gordon, GA 10/23/42. Pfc., Co. A, on *LST 690* 8/9/44. Cook in Co. A 11/17/44 photo provided by Lawrence Ertzberger. Pfc., Co. A, 5/8/45 Innsbruck, Austria. d. Jan. 1985 Toledo, Lucas Co., OH.

JARDINE, John P. b. 1924 GA. Res. Coffee Co., GA. Enl. 5/6/43 Ft. McPherson, Atlanta, GA. Ser. No. 34820275. Pfc., Co. A, promo. Cpl. (temp.) 9/15/45.

JEAN, L. V. b. 1923 AL. Res. Condova, Walker Co., AL. Enl. 4/1/43 Ft. McClellan, AL. Ser. No. 34801566. Pvt., Co. C, LST 422 Survivor, 1/26/44, Italy (Anzio) – Purple Heart. Cpl., Co. C, 6/22/45 Innsbruck, Austria.

JENNINGS, Orie (Orrie) L. b. 1920 MS. Res. Sharkey Co., MS. Enl. 9/21/42 Camp Shelby, MS. Ser. No. 34426655. Pvt. Co. C, 10/14/42 Camp Gordon, GA. Pfc., Co. C, KIA 1/26/44, Italy (Anzio), SR Cem.

JENSEN, George R. b. 8/16/1922 NY. Enl. 10/5/42 Philadelphia, PA. Ser. No. 33338221. Pvt., Co. D, Camp Gordon, GA 10/9/42. d. Dec. 1984, Broadalbin, Fulton Co., NY.

JEROME, J. Mentioned in the 9/28/44 entry of the diary of Daniel Shields.

JESSOP, Ralph G. b. 12/13/1908 MD. Res. York, PA. Enl. 2/24/42 Ft. George Meade, MD. Ser. No. 33169897. Pvt. Attached to Co. G 5/28/42 Edgewood Arsenal, MD. Squad Leader (Sgt.). Pfc., Co. A, promo. Cpl. (temp.), Camp Gordon, GA 8/19/42. Sgt., distinguished in action 7/10/43 Sicily. Acting 1st Sgt., June 1944. Promo. 1st Sgt., Co. A July 1944. 1st Sgt., Co. A, on *LST 690* 8/9/44. 1st Sgt., Co., A, 5/8/45 Innsbruck, Austria. d. 3/1/2000.

JOHANSON, James C. b. 4/26/1921 PA. Res. Philadelphia Co., PA. Enl. 9/17/42 Philadelphia, PA. Ser. No. 33334668. Pvt., Co. A, Camp Gordon, GA 10/9/42. Transf. Co. C, Camp Gordon, GA, 12/16/42. d. 1/18/1998 Yonkers, Westchester Co., NY.

JOHNSON, Calmer T. b. 1900 KY. Res. Sumner Co., TN. Enl. 9/17/42 Ft. Oglethorpe, GA. Ser. No. 34371649. Present Co. B, Camp Gordon, GA, 12/31/42.

JOHNSON, Carl David. b. 8/16/1922 Marion Co., SC. Timmonsville Public Schools, Timmonsville, SC. Pre-war Occupation: Farmer. Res. Effingham, Florence Co., SC. Enl. 12/10/42 Ft. Jackson, Columbia, SC. Ser. No. 34517928. Sicily. Naples-Foggia. In a group photo of Co. C taken 1943 at Amalfi, Italy. Pfc., Co. C, LST 422 Survivor, 1/26/44 Italy (Anzio) – Purple Heart. Rome-Arno. Southern France. Rhineland. Central Europe. EAMET Campaign Medal with 6 Bronze Service Stars with 1 Bronze Service Arrowhead. Good Conduct Medal. Pfc., Co. C, 6/22/45 Innsbruck, Austria. SV Co., 409th Inf. Dischd. 9/26/45.

JOHNSON, Daniel A. b. 1921 AL. Res. Jefferson Co., AL. Enl. 9/19/42 Ft. McClellan, AL. Ser. No. 34391807. Pvt., Co. C, Camp Gordon, GA 10/8/42. Pfc., Co. C, MIA, 1/26/44, Italy (Anzio) SR Cem.

JOHNSON, Daniel G., Jr. b. 1925. Enl. 4/13/43 Philadelphia, PA. Ser. No. 33600106. Pvt., Co. C, MIA, 1/26/44, Italy (Anzio) SR Cem.

JOHNSON, David E. b. 1921 GA. Res. Johnson Co., GA. Enl. 9/19/42 Ft. McPherson, Atlanta, GA. Ser. No. 34443072. Pvt., Co. D, Camp Gordon, GA 10/8/42.

JOHNSON, Dexter L. b. 1922 MS. Res. Itawamba Co., MS. Enl. 2/18/43 Camp Shelby, MS. Ser. No. 34622823. Co. D, LST 422 Survivor, 1/26/44 Italy (Anzio).

JOHNSON, Edwin I. ("Blue Nose"). b. 1917 NJ. Haddon Heights High School 1935. Apprentice Electrician, New York Shipbuilding Corp. Shipyard, Camden, NJ. Res. Camden Co., NJ. Enl. 2/27/42 Ft. Dix, NJ. Ser. No. 32243125. Pvt. Attached to Co. G 5/28/42 Edgewood Arsenal, MD. Communication Sgt. (Sgt.). Cpl., Co. D, Camp Gordon,

Cem.

GA 8/6/42. Promo. Sgt. (temp.), Camp Gordon, GA 10/3/42. Sgt., Co. D, KIA, 1/26/44, Italy (Anzio). "Escaped from LST 422 but died of injuries." Legion of Merit (posthumous) 1944 for gallantry at Maiori, Italy 1943. Re-interred Arlington Nat. Cem. 4/1/49.

JOHNSON, Eli. Mentioned by Wofford L. Jackson in *Mark Freedom Paid* as being present at Gela, Sicily 7/10/44 [Eli possibly a middle name].

JOHNSON, Ervin E. b. 1922 MN. Res. Brainerd, MN. Enl. 12/19/42 Ft. Snelling, MN. Ser. No. 37543059. Pfc., Co. C, LST 422 Survivor, 1/26/44 Italy (Anzio) – Purple Heart. Pfc., Co. C, KIA, 6/6 or 7/44, Italy, SR Cem. Bronze Star (posthumous).

JOHNSON, Gerald E. b. 1923 MO. Res. St. Francois Co., MO. Enl. 2/9/43 Jefferson Barracks, MO. Ser. No. 37417502. Pvt., Co. D, KIA, 1/26/44, Italy (Anzio)

JOHNSON, John B. Pvt., Co. B, 5/8/45 Innsbruck, Austria.

JOHNSON, Judson B. b. 1921 MS. Res. Saucier, MS. HSJJC 1939-42. Res. Oktibbeha Co., MS while attending Mississippi State College, Starkville, MS when enlisted. Enl. 9/21/42 Camp Shelby, MS. Ser. No. 34426199. Pvt. HQ & HQ Co. 10/14/42 Camp Gordon, GA. Although all official casualty lists, as well as Johnson's brother, state Pfc., HQ Co., KIA, 1/26/44, Italy (Anzio), veteran William Gallagher, a personal friend of Judson's in the 83rd, states he was undeniably KIA 7/10/43 at Gela, Sicily. According to Millard Bond of the 83rd, Johnson's friend and eyewitness to his death, after the war his body was found in a grave four miles inland from the Anzio beach. bur. Blackwell Cem., Success, Harrison Co., MS.

JOHNSON, Leo W. b. 1907 UT. Res. Salt Lake Co., UT. Enl. 3/5/42 Ft. Douglas, UT. Pvt., Co. C transf. Co. D, Camp Gordon, GA 6/15/42. Pfc., Co. D, promo. Cpl. (temp.), Camp Gordon, GA 12/2/42. Cpl. Co. D, transf. Co. A, Camp Gordon, GA, 12/16/42. Ser. No. 39682429. Sgt., Co. D, MIA, 1/26/44, Italy (Anzio) SR Cem.

JOHNSON, Vonnie M. b. 2/24/1921 AL. Res. Itawamba Co., MS. Enl. 9/23/42 Camp Shelby, MS. Ser. No. 34426755. Pvt., Co. B, 10/14/42 Camp Gordon, GA. Pfc., Co. B, 5/8/45 Innsbruck, Austria. d. Oct. 1973 MS.

JOHNSON, William E. b. 1920 TN. Res. Davidson Co., TN. Enl. 9/18/42 Ft. Oglethorpe, GA. Ser. No. 34371823. Sgt., Co. C, LST 422 Survivior, 1/26/44, Italy (Anzio). Sgt., Co. C, WIA (light - 179th Infantry jeep detonated mine near gun position), 9/30/44 France. S/Sgt., Co. C, 6/22/45 Innsbruck, Austria.

JOHNSTON, Robert W. Cpl., Co. B, 5/8/45 Innsbruck, Austria. d. 11/12/1999 Chapel Hill, TN. [Also listed as Johnson].

JONES, Boy M. b. 1901 MS. Res. Coahoma Co., MS. Enl. 9/23/42 Camp Shelby, MS. Ser. No. 34426917. Pvt. HQ & HQ Co. 10/14/42 Camp Gordon, GA.

JONES, Carl W. Sgt., Co. C, 6/22/45 Innsbruck, Austria.

JONES, Clovis J. b. 1921 MS. Pre-war Occupation: Farmer. Res. Guntown, Itawamba Co., MS. Enl. 9/23/42 Camp Shelby, MS. Ser. No. 34426723. Pvt. Co. B, 10/14/42 Camp Gordon, GA. Pvt., Co. B, WIA (light), 12/8/43 San Pietro, Italy (near Hill 950) – Purple Heart. Returned to duty 3/28/44. Pfc., Co. B, 5/8/45 Innsbruck, Austria. EAMETO Medal. Good Conduct Medal. Bronze Arrowhead (on EAMATO Ribbon). Co. A, 289th Inf.

JONES, Earle L. b.1905 VT. Res. Rochmont, Polk Co., GA. Enl. 9/22/42 Ft. McPherson, Atlanta, GA. Ser. No. 34443442. Pvt., Co. C, Camp Gordon, GA 10/9/42. Pfc., Co. C, WIA (serious - shell fragment), 7/10 or 11/43 Gela, Sicily. Purple Heart.

JONES, George C. b. 1923 VA. Res. Westmoreland Co., VA. Enl. 9/19/42 Richmond, VA. Ser. No. 3322571. Pvt., Co. C, Camp Gordon, GA 10/11/42. Transf. Co. A, Camp Gordon, GA, 12/16/42. Pvt., Co. C, MIA, 1/26/44, Italy (Anzio) SR Cem. Body recovered 1/26/44 by YMS 34 & buried at sea same day. Next of kin: Bertha C. Jones, Potomac Hills, VA.

JONES, James E. b. 1918 AL. Res. Fayette Co., AL. Enl. 9/23/42 Camp Shelby, MS. Ser. No. 34426714. Pvt. Co. B, 10/14/42 Camp Gordon, GA. Transf. Co. A, Camp Gordon, GA, 12/16/42. Pfc., Co. B, MIA, 1/26/44, Italy (Anzio) SR Cem.

JONES, Jim. Res. Pendleton, IN. In a photo in the Charlie Lowry Collection. [possibly same as James E. Jones].

JONES, Joe L. b. 1921 TN. Res. Davidson Co., TN. Enl. 10/1/42 Ft. Oglethorpe, GA. Ser. No. 34327141. Pvt., Co. , Camp Gordon, GA 10/7/42. Pfc., distinguished in action 7/10/43 Sicily. Sgt., Co. A, WIA (light), 11/27/43 Italy. Sgt., MWIA (anti-tank mine), 5/24/44 Anzio, Italy. Died two hours after being wounded.

JONES, Marion F. b. 1916 IN. Res. Montgomery Co., MD. Enl. 9/10/41 Baltimore, MD. Sgt. Assigned HQ & HQ Co. 5/28/42 Edgewood Arsenal, MD. Supply Sgt. (T/Sgt.). Sgt. (temp.), HQ & HQ Co., promo. S/Sgt. (temp.), Camp Gordon, GA 6/16/43. Ser. No. 33066716. S/Sgt. (temp.), promo. T/Sgt. (temp.), Camp Gordon, GA 8/6/42. T/Sgt., HQ Co., MIA, 1/26/44, Italy (Anzio) SR Cem.

JONES, Marvin C. b. 1922 GA. Res. Hiram, Spaulding Co., GA. Enl. 12/22/1942 Ft. McPherson, Atlanta, GA. Ser. No. 34579705. Pfc., Co. D, LST 422 Survivor, 1/26/44 Italy (Anzio) – Purple Heart. Sgt., Co. D, WIA (light – injured by own shell), 12/13/44 Bennwihr, France.

JONES, Robert H. T/5, HQ Co., reduced to Private for inefficiency.

JONES, Robert R. Pfc., HQ Co., presented Bronze Star 8/25/45.

JONES, Ross J. b. 1924 MO. Res. Adair Co., MO. Enl. 2/28/43 Ft. Leavenworth, KS. Ser. No. 37512145. Pvt., Co. C, KIA, 1/26/44, Italy (Anzio). Body recovered by USS Pilot. Buried at sea 1/26/44. SR Cem.

JONES, Roy E. b. 1920 TN. Res. Davidson Co., TN. Enl. 9/18/42 Ft. Oglethorpe, GA. Ser. No. 34371722. Pfc., Co. D, MIA, 1/26/44, Italy (Anzio) SR Cem.

JONES, Sam P. b. 1919 GA. Res. Hall Co., GA. Enl. 9/17/42 Ft. McPherson, Atlanta, GA. Ser. No. 34442509. Pvt., Co. D, Camp Gordon, GA 10/8/42.

JONES, Theran [Theron] R. b. 9/19/1922 AL. Res. Jefferson Co., AL. Enl. 8/1/42 Ft. McClellan, AL. Ser. No. 14131141. Pfc., Co. D, WIA (shell fragment- serious), 9/11/43 Vietre sul Mare, Italy. Hospitalized. Res. Fountain Inn, SC May 1954. Salesman, Furniture Co. d. 4/19/1998 SC.

JONES, William S. b. 1915 VA. Res. Isle of Wight Co., VA. Enl. 12/15/42 Richmond, VA. Ser. No. 33519638. Pvt., Co. A, Camp Gordon, GA 3/18/43.

JORDAN, Byron H. b. 3/10/1923 Gadsen, AL. Pre-war Occupation: Goodyear – B-24 Fuel Cells – Republic Steel & Goodyear. Res. Etowah Co., AL. Enl 2/2/43 Ft. McClellan, AL. Ser. No. 34704542. Camp Sibert, AL. Joined as a replacement as Pvt., Co. D, 83rd CMB Aug. 1943. Present in Sicily with HQ Co. Sept. 1943. "Ammo man at Mt. Etna during the Salerno invasion." Transf. Co. B Mar. 1944. Present at Zellenberg 1944. Present as Pfc., Co. B Feb. 1945. Pfc., Co. B, 5/8/45 Innsbruck, Austria. [Steedle's Squad, 2nd Platoon, Co. B]. Present with Co. E, 16th Inf., Bamberg, Germany 7/18/45. Present with 134th Chem. Mortar Co., Germany, 7/29/45. Cpl., Co. A, 818th Tank Destroyer Battalion Oct. 1945. Embarked on ship Claymont, Marseille, France 10/18/45. Civil Service. Joined Air Force Reserve, Mobile AL. Active Duty Nov. 1950. Dec. 1951-1952 Air Force, Japan & Korea. Retired from Robbins Air Force Base and C&S Bank. Res. Milledgeville, GA 2007. d. 12/30/2008. bur. Magnolia Park Cem.

JORDAN, Cordell. b. 1921 AL. Res. Geneva Co., AL. Pvt., Co. D, Camp Gordon, GA 10/9/42. Re-enl. 1/29/46 Richmond, VA. Ser. No. 34391357. Pfc., Transportation Corps.

JORDAN, James Charlie. ("J. C."). b. 9/5/1921 Athens, GA. Danielsville High School, Danielsville, GA 1936. Pre-war Occupation: Worked with father, Oscar Clarence Jordan, in family plumbing business. Res. Madison Co., GA. Enl. 9/17/42 Ft. McPherson, Atlanta, GA. Ser. No. 34442978. Pvt., Co. A, Camp Gordon, GA 10/8/42. Distinguished in action 7/12/43 Gela, Sicily. Cpl. (temp.), Co. A promo. Sgt. (temp.), 11/17/44. Sgt. Co. A, 5/8/45 Innsbruck, Austria. Worked in family plumbing business until employed by Navy Supply Corps School 1956 as plumber & pipefitter. Retired 1977. Res. Danielsville, GA. d. 3/23/2006. bur. Friendship Baptist Church, Danielsville, GA.

JORDAN, Wilbur L. ("Bill"). b. 7/20/1922 Cedar Grove, Orange Co., NC. Enl. Nov. 1942. Pfc., Co. B, 5/8/45 Innsbruck, Austria. [also served in 81st CMB]. Dischd. Dec. 1945. Universal Leaf Tobacco Co., Richmond, VA for 40 years. Vice President, J. P. Taylor Tobacco Co. 1976. Senior Vice President, W. H. Winstead Tobacco Co. 1977. d. 2/7/2006 Goldsboro, NC. bur. Evergreen Memorial Cem., Goldsboro, NC.

JORDAN, William L. b. 1919 MS. Res. Laurel, Jones Co., MS. Enl. 9/21/42 Camp Shelby, MS. Ser. No. 34426246. Pvt. Co. C, 10/14/42 Camp Gordon, GA. Pvt., Co. C, LST 422 Survivor, 1/26/44 Italy (Anzio) – Purple Heart. T/5, Bronze Star [Presented 11/20/44]. T/5, Co. C, 6/22/45 Innsbruck, Austria.

JORGENSEN, Kermit ("Jerky"). b. 8/12/1914 CA. Res. Alameda Co., CA. Enl. 1/21/42 Presidio of Monterey, CA. Ser. No. 39087157. Pvt. Attached to Co. B 5/28/42 Edgewood Arsenal, MD. Telephone Operator (Pvt.). Pfc., HQ & HQ Co., (Co. Pers. Clerk), promo. Cpl. (temp.), Camp Gordon, GA 7/15/42. HQ & HQ Co., May 1943. Present as Sgt., Moussey, France 11/30/44. d. Nov. 1977 Los Angeles, Los Angeles Co., CA.

JOYCE, John J. b. 1910 MA. Res. Norfolk Co., MA. Enl. 3/16/42 Ft. Devens, MA. Ser. No. 31073125. Pvt., Co. C transf. HQ & HQ Co., Camp Gordon, GA 6/15/42. Pfc., HQ & HQ Co., promo. T/5 (temp.), Camp Gordon, GA 12/12/42. T/4, HQ Co., 5/8/45 Innsbruck, Austria. Attended 1954 Reunion.

JUDSON, Arnold A. b. 1898 PA. Enl. 9/25/42 Pittsburgh, PA. Ser. No. 33305682. Pvt. HQ & HQ Co., 10/15/42 Camp Gordon GA. Present Pvt., HQ Co., Camp Gordon, GA, 1/9/43.

JUNKINS, Robert A. Sgt. Assigned to Co. K 5/28/42 Edgewood Arsenal, MD. 1st Sgt. Sgt. (temp.), Co. D, promo. S/Sgt. (temp.), Camp Gordon, GA 6/16/42. S/Sgt. (temp.), promo. 1st Sgt (temp.), Camp Gordon, GA 7/15/42. Ser. No. 6964545.

JUYSEE, ----------. Mentioned in the May 1954 Directory. [Possibly John J. Joyce or Joseph F. Huysse.]

KAADY, Abraham S. b. 11/15/1921 OR. Res. Portland, Multnomah Co., OR. Enl. 12/3/42 Portland, OR. Ser. No. 34322729. Pvt., Co. C, WIA (light), LST 422 Survivor, 1/26/44 Italy (Anzio). Purple Heart. Returned to duty 2/5/44. Pfc., Co. C, 6/22/45 Innsbruck, Austria. d. 6/17/1999 OR.

KALEDA, Charles A. b. 1918. Enl. 3/25/43 Allentown, PA. Ser. No. 33621212. Pvt., Co. C, MIA, 1/26/44, Italy (Anzio) SR Cem.

KALK, Herbert Charles. b. 8/27/1918 Chicago, Cook Co., IL. Res. Cook Co., IL. Grad. University of Chicago (BA English) ca. 1939-40. University of Chicago Magazine. Enl. 3/19/42 Camp Grant, IL. Ser. No. 36325809. Pvt. Attached to Co. A 5/28/42 Edgewood Arsenal, MD. Clerk (Cpl. & Pvt.). Cpl. (temp.), Co. D, promo. T/4 (temp.) & assigned HQ & HQ Co., Camp Gordon, GA 9/10/42. Editor, Smokescreen, Camp Gordon, GA Nov. 1942. Attended OCS, Grinnell College, IA, 1/22/43. Went to the Pacific Theater with another outfit and served in New Guinea & the Philippines. Appointed head of the Army extension school in the Philippines. Achieved rank of Captain. Postwar: Professor & administrator in Chicago City Colleges for over forty years and eventually Vice-President. d. 6/8/2006 St. Louis, MO. bur. Westlawn Cem., Chicago, IL.

KANE, James F. Pfc., Co. A, 5/8/45 Innsbruck, Austria.

KANE, Patrick E. Pfc. Co. B, promo. Cpl. (temp.) 9/15/45.

KANN, Earl F. b. 9/7/1922 York, PA. Gross School. Pre-war Occupation: McCann's (made winches for ships). Res. York, York Co., PA. Enl. 10/5/42 Harrisburg, PA. Ser. No. 13093254. Pvt., Co. D, Camp Gordon, GA 10/9/42. Pvt., Co. D, WIA (serious - from explosion of own shell hitting tree limb – shrapnel in leg, back, foot), 7/12/43 Gela, Sicily - Purple Heart. Pfc., Co. D, WIA (white phosphorous on leg during sinking of LST 422) 1/26/44 Italy (Anzio) – Purple Heart with Oak Leaf Cluster. Returned to U.S. Res. York, PA May 1954. Harrisburg Auto Parts. Attended the 1954, 1956 & 1958 Reunions as res. York, PA.. d. 11/20/2005 York, PA.

KANNIKAR, Ludwig J. b. 1919 PA. Res. Cambria Co., PA. Enl. 8/12/43 Altoona, PA. Ser. No. 33764097. Pvt., Co. C, MIA, 8/29/44 Briançon, France. [also listed as Kamnlkar].

KAPRUSAK, (KAPRISAK), Michael J. Res. CT. Ser. No. 31342883. Pvt., Co. C, KIA, 1/26/44, Italy (Anzio). Body recovered 1/26/44 by USS YMS 226 and turned over to Graves Registration at Anzio 1/27/44. SR Cem. Next of kin: Mary Kaprusak, Unionville, CT.

KARCAUSKAS, [KARASUSKAS/KARCAUKUS], Joseph J. b. 1917 NY. Res. Hudson Co., NJ. Enl. 6/18/42 Newark, NJ. Pvt., Co. D, Camp Gordon, GA 7/28/42. Pfc. Co. D, transf. Co. A, Camp Gordon, GA, 12/16/42. Ser. No. 32309328. Sgt., Silver Star – presented 1/19/44. Sgt., MIA, 1/26/44, Italy (Anzio). Body recovered by USS Pilot. Buried at sea 1/26/44. SR Cem. Wofford L. Jackson said Karacauskas was still alive immediately after being rescued and he spoke with him.

KATTELMAN, Melvin John. b. 1923 OH. Res. Hamilton Co., OH. Enl. 1/27/43 Cincinnati, OH. Ser. No. 35687608. Pfc., captured by enemy, 1/4/45 France. Returned to duty 1/7/45. Pfc., Co. B, 5/8/45 Innsbruck, Austria. Res. Cincinnati, OH May 1954. Supervisor, National District Prod. Corp.

KAUFMAN, Louis J., Jr. Present at Briançon, France 8/29/44. Cpl., Co. C, 6/22/45 Innsbruck, Austria.

KAY, ----------. Present as pitcher in Co. A ball team 8/4/45.

KEANE, Thomas A. b. 1921 NJ. Res. Hudson Co., NJ. Enl. 7/22/42 Newark, NJ. Ser. No. 32450890. Pvt., HQ & HQ Co., Camp Gordon, GA 4/16/43. Pvt., WIA (light – anti-personnel bomb), 2/20/44 Anzio, Italy. Pfc., Co. B, 5/8/45 Innsbruck, Austria. [also spelled Keene].

KEARNEY, Thomas E. b. 1922 NC. Res. Franklin Co., NC. Enl. 11/23/42 Ft. Bragg, NC. Ser. No. 34464463. Pfc., Co. A, promo. T/5 (temp.) 9/15/45.

KEEDY, Harlan V. Res. Auburn, NE. Ser. No. 37122834. Pvt., Co. D, LST 422 Survivor, 1/26/44 Italy (Anzio) – Purple Heart.

KEELAN, William. Mentioned in the May 1954 Directory. [Probably William P. Heelan].

KEIGHTLY, Elwood J. b. 1915 PA. Res. Philadelphia, PA. Ser. No. 06885406. Pvt., Co. D, Camp Gordon, GA 10/9/42. Pvt., Co. D, Camp Gordon, GA Nov. 1942. Transf. Co. A, Camp Gordon, GA, 12/16/42. Sgt., Co. D, LST 422 Survivor, 1/26/44 Italy (Anzio) – Purple Heart. Re-enl. 5/17/46 Philadelphia, PA for Hawaiian Dept. T/5, Transportation Corps.

KEIL, Charles C. b. 1916 OH. Res. Allen Co., OH. Enl. 3/2/42 Camp Perry, Lacarne, OH. Ser. No. 35287088. Pvt. Attached to Co. H 5/28/42 Edgewood Arsenal, MD. Gunner (Pvt.).

KELBAUGH, Andrew J. b. 1/28/1900 MD. Enl. 9/26/42 Baltimore, MD. Ser. No. 33377153. Pvt. Co. B, 10/15/42 Camp Gordon GA. d. May 1969 Parkton, Baltimore Co., MD.

KELL [Kelly?], Michael J. b. 1922 PA. Enl. 10/15/42 Akron, OH. Ser. No. 35586119. T/5, Co. B, 5/8/45 Innsbruck, Austria. [Possibly T/5 Michael J. Kelly who was distinguished in action at Trapani, Italy 7/23/43].

KELLEY, Claudie L. b. 1921 AL. Res. Winston Co., AL. Enl. 9/15/42 Ft. McClellan, AL. Ser. No. 34391334. Pvt., Co. D, Camp Gordon, GA.

KELLEY, Jack E. b. 1915 PA. Enl. 12/12/42 Altoona, PA. Ser. No. 33567121. Pvt., Co. D, Camp Gordon, GA 4/10/43.

KELLEY, R. A. Wilson. Ser. No. 34444178. Pvt. Co. D, 10/14/42 Camp Gordon, GA.

KELLISON, William Carl. b. 11/4/1920 Jacox, Pocahontas Co., WV. Res. Pocahontas Co., WV 1930. Enl. 9/6/42 Baltimore, MD. Ser. No. 33377170. Pvt. Co. A, 10/15/42 Camp Gordon GA. T/5, Co. A, 5/8/45 Innsbruck, Austria. Postwar: Fairfield Manufacturing Co., Inc. Res. Lafayette, IN 1983. d. Lafayette, IN May 1985.

KELLY, Jack. Res. AL. Co. B, Camp Gordon, GA Feb. 1943.

KELLY, Michael J. ("Cookie"). b. 1906 Irish Free State. Res. Bronx Co., NY. Enl. 7/9/42 Ft. Jay, Governors Island, NY. Ser. No. 32402466. Pvt., Co. B, Camp Gordon, GA 7/28/42. Pfc., Co. B, Camp Gordon, GA 10/20/42. Pfc., Co. B,, arrived Gela, Sicily from rear echelon 7/11/43. T/5, Co. B, distinguished in action 7/23/43 Sicily. T/5, jeep driver for Lt. Davis 1/11/45. Res. Bronx, NY May 1954. [also spelled Kelley].

KELLY, William J. Pvt., Co. B, Camp Gordon, GA 10/9/42. Ser. No. 33296791.

KELSEY [KELSIE], Ray O. Res. KS. Present with Co. A 10/25/44. Sgt., Co. B, Squad Leader, 4th Squad. Sgt., Co. B, 5/8/45 Innsbruck, Austria. d. ca. 1980's.

KENNEDY, Duncan M. b. 1916 NC. Res. GA. Enl. 10/21/41 Ft. McPherson, Atlanta, GA. Ser. No. 34089076. Pvt., Co. C, KIA, 1/26/44, Italy (Anzio). Body recovered by USS Pilot. Buried at sea 1/26/44. SR Cem. Middle initial W on casualty list.

KENNEDY, John J. b. 1921 MA. Res. Westfield, Hampden Co., MA. Enl. 4/3/43 Springfield, MA. Ser. No. 31346010. Pvt., Co. C, LST 422 Survivor, 1/26/44 Italy (Anzio) – Purple Heart.

KENNEDY, William C. b. 1/11/1918 MS. Res. Scott Co., MA. Enl. 9/23/42 Camp Shelby, MS. Ser. No. 34426855. Pvt. Co. C, 10/14/42 Camp Gordon, GA. d. 2/20/1994. Morton, Scott Co., MS.

KENNEY, Leonard R. b. 11/19/1917. Res. WA. Pvt., attached to Co. F 5/28/42 Edgewood Arsenal, MD. Mechanic Auto (Pvt.). Pvt., HQ & HQ Co. transf. Co. A, Camp Gordon, GA 6/15/42. Pfc., (Auto Mech.), promo. T/5 (temp.), Camp Gordon, GA 7/15/42. T/4 (temp.), Co. A, promo. S/Sgt. (temp.), Camp Gordon, GA 10/6/42. 1st Sgt., distinguished in action 7/10/43 Sicily. 1st Sgt., Co. A, awarded Silver Star 4/15/44 for gallantry at Anzio 2/18/44. 2nd Lt. June 1944. 2nd Lt., CO. A, on LST 690 8/9/44. Promo. 1st Lt., 8/17/44. Sent to the rear with a frozen foot 1/26/45. Promo. 1st. Lt., Co. A, 5/8/45 Innsbruck, Austria. 1st Lt., assigned 65th Inf. Div. 7/23/45. Res. Walla Walla, WA May 1954. d. 9/24/1998 Walla Walla, Walla Walla Co., WA.

KENYOCK [Kanyock], Michael. b. 9/9/1911 PA. Res. Luzerne Co., PA. Enl. 12/14/42 Wilkes Barre, PA. Ser. No. 33458070. Pvt., Co. B, Camp Gordon, GA 3/18/43. d. Aug. 1973 PA.

KERN, Walter F. b. 1922. Res. Lehigh Co., PA. Enl. 4/10/43 Allentown, PA. Ser. No. 33623134. Pfc., Co. C, promo. S/Sgt. (temp.) 9/15/45.

KERR, William O. b. 1/26/1914 MS. Res. Union Co., MS. Enl. 9/23/42 Camp Shelby, MS. Ser. No. 34426833. Pvt HQ & HQ Co. 10/14/42 Camp Gordon, GA. d. Sept. 1985, Myrtle, Union Co., MS.

KETCHUM, Murphy R. b. 9/15/1920 MS. Res. Yazoo Co., MS. Enl. 9/23/42 Camp Shelby, MS. Ser. No. 34426750. Pvt. HQ & HQ Co. 10/14/42 Camp Gordon, GA. HQ Co. Mentioned in the 12/12/42 issue of Smokescreen. d. 12/13/1995 Benton, Yazoo Co., MS.

KEY, ----------. Pvt., Co. D, WIA (non-battle injury – burned by exploding powder rings), Bouyon, France 8/27/44.

KEYSER, Albert H. b. 4/8/1912 VA. Res. Bath Co., VA. Enl. 9/21/42 Roanoke, VA. Ser. No. 33213298. Pvt., Co. C, Camp Gordon, GA 10/11/42. According to Hale H. Hepler this soldier suffered a heart attack at Camp Gordon, GA. d. June 1983 Bacova, Bath Co., VA.

KIEDROWSKI, Peter J. ("Polak"). b. 4/11/1919 ND. Res. Hennepin Co., MN. Enl. 2/21/1942 Ft. Snelling, MN. Ser. No. 17049562. Pvt. Attached to Co. H 5/28/42 Edgewood Arsenal, MD. Supply Sgt. (S/Sgt.). Pvt., Co. D, promo. T/4 (temp.), Camp Gordon, GA 6/16/42. Cpl. (temp.), (Supply), promo. Sgt. (temp.), Camp Gordon, GA 7/15/42. Sgt. (temp.), Co. D, promo. S/Sgt. (temp.), Camp Gordon, GA 9/7/42. Promo. T/Sgt. (temp.), Camp Gordon, GA 10/21/42. Promo. 1st Sgt. (temp.), Camp Gordon, GA 11/5/42. Carl McNabb said: "Pete used to scare recruits to death with that loud voice, and such a big guy, too." 1st. Sgt., Co. D, WIA (shell fragment through right hip - serious), 7/10/43 Gela, Sicily.. Evacuated. Spent "quite a few months" at Chick General Hospital, Clinton, IA for "arm injury". Discharged July 1944. Mailman,

Minneapolis, MN. 1945. Res. Minneapolis, MN. May 1954. Postal Employee. Attended 1954, 1956, 1958, 1960, 1962 & 1966 Reunions. d. Dec.1981 Minneapolis, Hennepin Co., MN.

KIESTER, John R. b. 7/25/1920 PA. Res. Allegheny Co., PA. Enl. 8/17/43 Pittsburgh, PA. Ser. No. 33700094. Pfc., Co. B, 5/8/45 Innsbruck, Austria. d. 4/8/1992 PA.

KIEWITT, Louis F. b. 1906 MO. Res. Milwaukee Co., WI. Enl. 12/21/42 Milwaukee, WI. Ser. No. 36291143. Pvt., Co. B, Camp Gordon, GA 4/10/43. Assigned to Co. A, 2nd CMB. KIA 3/30/1945 by enemy mortar, tree-burst directly over his mortar firing position, near the city of Aschaffenburg. Purple Heart. LO Cem.

KILLEBREW, Delmer [Delmen]. b. 7/10/1922. Res. De Kalb, Bowie Co., TX. Enl. 12/14/42 Tyler, TX. Ser. No. 38305333. Pfc., Co. D, LST 422 Survivor, 1/26/44 Italy (Anzio) – Purple Heart. Rescued by YMS 69 1/26/44. d. May 1978 Texarkana, Bowie Co., TX.

KILLMER, Morris R. b. 7/18/1898 NJ. Res. Camden Co., NJ. Enl. 7/9/42 Camden, NJ. Ser. No. 32271714. Pvt., Co. B, Camp Gordon, GA 7/28/42. Pvt., Co. B, tranf. Gas Det. Sta. Compliment, Camp Gordon, GA, and attached Co. B, for rations and quarters only 10/9/42. d. Nov. 1983 NJ.

KILPATRICK, William C. b. 1918 PA. Enl. 9/22/42 Philadelphia, PA. Ser. No. 33335463. Pvt., Co. A, Camp Gordon, GA 10/9/42. Pvt., Co. A, WIA, (serious – face - land mine), 7/10/43, Gela, Sicily. Sent to hospital in Africa 7/14/43.

KIMBLE, Alex. [Alexander Kimbal on birth record] b. 6 [or 7]/25/1914 Glover Gap, Wetzel Co., WV. Pre-war Occupation: Machinist Apprentice. Enl. 12/16/42 Clarksburg, WV. Ser. No. 35746272. Pvt., Co. C, Camp Gordon, GA 4/10/43. Sicily. Pvt., Co. C, WIA (light), LST 422 Survivor, 1/26/44 Italy (Anzio) – Purple Heart. Naples-Foggia. Rome-Arno. Southern France. Rhineland. Central Europe. Sgt., Co. C, 6/22/45 Innsbruck, Austria. Sgt., Co. M, 411th Inf. Good Conduct Medal. Bronze Star Medal. EAME Service Ribbon with Bronze Arrowhead. Dischd. 10/16/45 Retired as Postmaster, Knob Fork, WV. d. 12/11/82. bur. Oak Forest Cem., Hundred, Wetzel Co., WV.

KIMBLER, James H. b. 1915 WV. Res. Logan Co., WV. Enl. 8/9/40 Ft. Thomas, Newport, KY. Field Artillery. Ser. No. 15054233. Pvt., Co. D, MIA, 1/26/44, Italy (Anzio) SR Cem.

KIMBROUGH, (KIMBOUGH), Woodson T. b. 1921 AR. Res. Monroe Co., MS. Enl. 9/22/42 Camp Shelby, MS. Ser. No. 34426561. Pvt. Co. B, 10/14/42 Camp Gordon, GA. Transf. Co. A, 12/16/42. Sgt.,Co. B. KIA, 11/13/44, France, EP Cem.

KIMMEL, Stephen. b. 1910 Austria. Res. Sacramento Co., CA. Enl. 1/22/43 Sacramento, CA. Ser. No. 39408075. Pfc., HQ Co., 5/8/45 Innsbruck, Austria.

KINDIG, Robert L. b. 1923 IA. Res. Des Moines Co., IA. Enl. 2/12/43 Camp Dodge, Herrold, IA. Ser. No. 37661041. Pfc., Co. C, WIA (light),

LST 422 Survivor, 1/26/44 Italy (Anzio). Res. Burlington, IA.

KING, ----------. On a list of 83rd men in Lt. Robert Bush's scrapbook.

KINGREA, Brainard L. b. 6/8/1913 VA. Res. Montgomery Co., VA. Enl. 2/16/42 Camp Lee, VA. Ser. No. 33132812. Pfc., Co. A, 5/8/45 Innsbruck, Austria. d. Nov. 1976 Christiansburg, Montgomery Co., VA.

KINNETZ, Harry C. Res. NY. Pvt. Attached to Co. F 5/28/42 Edgewood Arsenal, MD. Motor Sgt. (M/Sgt.). Pfc., HQ & HQ Co., (Mechanic), promo. T/5 (temp.), Camp Gordon, GA 7/15/42. T/4, HQ & HQ Co., transf. Co. C & promo. S/Sgt. (temp.), Camp Gordon, GA 10/6/42. Ser. No. 06687758. S/Sgt., Co. C, MIA, 1/26/44, Italy (Anzio) SR Cem.

KIRSCH, Murray W. 1st. Lt., CWS, assigned Med. Det., Battalion Dental Officer, Camp Gordon, GA 12/29/42.

KIRSCHBAUM, Carl E. ("Kirsch"). b. 10/22/1920 NJ. Res. Essex Co., NJ. Enl. 7/9/42 Newark, NJ. Ser. No. 32390241. Pvt., HQ & HQ Co., Camp Gordon, GA 7/28/42. Pfc., HQ Co., Camp Gordon, GA 12/19/42. Res. Windfield, NJ May 1954. Operator, Gas Station. d. 11/28/2002 Linden, Union Co., NJ.

KIRSHNER, Sidney. b. 1922 PA. Enl. 10/5/42 Wilkes-Barre, PA. Ser. No. 13116734. Pvt., Co. A, Camp Gordon, GA 10/9/42. Cpl., Co. A on *LST 690* 8/9/44. Res. Wilkes - Barre, PA. Cpl., Co. B, 5/8/45 Innsbruck, Austria.

KISH, John J. b. 1921 PA. Ser. No. 33294849. Pvt. Co. D, 10/15/42 Camp Gordon GA. Re-enl. 6/15/46. Res. Allegheny Co., PA. Sgt.

KITTLE, Robert E. Pfc., Co. C, 6/22/45 Innsbruck, Austria. Res, PA.

KLATT, John K. b. 1907 IA. Res. Enl. 6/13/42 Traverse City, MI. Ser. No. 16084720. Pfc., Co. A, 5/8/45 Innsbruck, Austria. Postwar res. Iron Mountain, MI.

KLEIN, Earle H. b. 1907 CT. Res. Suffolk Co., MA. Enl. 7/15/43 Boston, MA. Ser. No. 31367482. Pvt., Purple Heart, 1944. Pfc., Co. C, 6/22/45 Innsbruck, Austria.

KLOOCK, Arthur J., Jr. b. 7/18/1919 MI. Res. Wayne Co., MI. Enl. 2/18/42 Detroit, MI. Ser. No. 18062367. Pvt. Attached to Co. H 5/28/42 Edgewood Arsenal, MD. Squad Leader (Sgt.). d. 12/26/1993 Trenton, Wayne Co., MI.

KLOPP, Wilbur W. b. 4/11/1915 PA. Enl. 7/14/43 Harrisburg, PA. Ser. No. 33512954. Pfc., WIA (light), 4/9/45 Germany. Pfc., Co. C, 6/22/45 Innsbruck, Austria. d. Aug. 1987 Ephrata, Lancaster Co., PA.

KNAPICK, Anthony J. b. 1921 PA. Enl. 9/21/42 Harrisburg, PA. Ser. No. 33240910. Pvt., Co. A, Camp Gordon, GA 10/9/42. Pvt., Co. A,

WIA (light – enemy shell burst), 3/30/44 Anzio, Italy. Returned to duty 5/22/44. Pvt., Co. A, on *LST 690* 8/9/44. Pfc., Co. B, 5/8/45 Innsbruck, Austria.

KNAPP, Raymond James. b. 9/29/1924 Scranton, PA. Binghamton High School. Res. Broome Co., NY. Enl. 3/25/43 Binghamton, NY. Ser. No. 32848730. Pfc., Co. C, 6/22/45 Innsbruck, Austria. d. 4/24/2005.

KNAUSS, Harold L. b. 11/10/1920 PA. Res. Lehigh Co., PA. Enl. 7/9/42 Allentown, PA. Ser. No. 33185560. Pfc. Co. A. Present 8/4/45. Medic. Departed for University Grenoble, France, army education program. d. 5/16/2002 Bristol, PA.

KNICELEY, Claude E. b. 1907 VA. Enl. 12/15/42 Charlottesville, VA. Ser. No. 33446480. Pvt., Co. B, Camp Gordon, GA 3/18/43.

KNICKERBOCKER, Samuel. b. 1924 NJ. Res. Saratoga Co., NY. Enl. 3/6/43 Albany, NY. Ser. No. 32851856. Pvt., Co. C, 6/22/45 Innsbruck, Austria.

KNIGHT, Maxie L. b. 1917 MS. Res. Claiborne Co., MS. Enl. 9/22/42 Camp Shelby, MS. Ser. No. 34426431. Pvt. Co. C, 10/14/42 Camp Gordon, GA. Pfc., Co. C, MIA, 1/26/44, Italy (Anzio) SR Cem.

KNIGHT, Raymond F. Assigned from 65th Inf. Division as 1st Lt., HQ & HQ Co. (S-1) 7/23/45. 1st Lt./Adjutant 9/10/45.

KNIGHT, Robert D. b. 1906 AL. Res. Lee Co., AL. Enl. 9/19/42 Ft. McClellan, AL. Ser. No. 34391827. Pvt., Co. D, Camp Gordon, GA 10/9/42. Pvt., Co. D, MIA, 1/26/44, Italy (Anzio) SR Cem.

KNORTZ, Robert W. ("Curly") b. 6/20/1916 NJ. Res. Camden Co., NJ. Enl. 7/9/1942 Camden, NJ. Ser. No. 32271713. Pvt., Co. B, Camp Gordon, GA 7/28/42. Cpl., Co. B 5/8/45 Innsbruck, Austria. Attended 1954, 1956, 1958, 1960, 1962 & 1966 Reunions. d. 3/12/1980 Haddonfield, Camden Co., NJ.

KNOX, George H., Pvt. Attached to Co. H 5/28/42 Edgewood Arsenal, MD. Squad Leader (Sgt.).

KOBE, ----------. In a group photo provided by Sam Kweskin.

KOELLING, Harold A. Res. MO. Ser. No. 37610362. Pfc., Co. C, MIA, 1/26/44, Italy (Anzio) SR Cem.

KOHL, Fred B. ("Cabbage Head"). Kansas State Basketball Scholarship 1940. R.O.T.C. O.C.S, Ft. Benning, GA, 2nd Lt. Sent overseas late 1944. Served with 27th Inf. Div. & 65th Combat Div. & 73rd CMB. 2nd Lt., relsd. 259th Inf. & assigned 83rd CMB 8/7/45. Assigned POW guard, Linz, Austria after war ended. Junior Aide, Gen. Robert C. Macon. Returned to U.S. March 1946. Kansas State. PE & Health Teacher, Central Junior High, Kansas City, KS. Science & Math Teacher, Argentine Middle & High Schools. Director, Physical Education, Health & Safety, Kansas School District, KS. Established first Driver's Education class school district. Retired & res. Shawnee, KS 2001.

KOHN, Paul J. b. 10/25/1913 PA. Res. Allegheny Co., PA. Enl. 12/22/42 Pittsburgh, PA. Ser. No. 33416583. Pvt., Co. B, Camp Gordon, GA 3/18/43. d. 7/14/1984.

KOODY, ----------. Co. C. In a group photo provided by Loy Marshall.

KOOLLING, Harold A., Pfc., KIA, 1/26/44, Italy (Anzio). [Probably same as Harold A. Koelling]

KOOPMAN, ----------. Present as pitcher for HQ Co. 8/4/45.

KORING, Earl C. b. 10/22 or 23/1921 PA. Enl. 9/25/42 Greensburg, PA. Ser. No. 33294865. Pvt. Co. A, 10/15/42 Camp Gordon GA. Pfc., Co. A, WIA (light-head-enemy shell fragment), 3/24/44 Anzio, Italy. Rotated 7/14/44. Attended 1958 & 1962 Reunions. Res. Greensburg, PA. d. 5/19/1988 Greensburg, Westmoreland Co., PA.

KOVERCHICK, Michael J. ("Butterball"). b. 1915 NY. Res. Camden Co., NJ. Enl. 7/6/42 Camden, NJ. Ser. No. 32271468. Pvt., HQ & HQ Co., Camp Gordon, GA 7/28/42. Departed 83rd CMB Dec. 1942.

KOWALEC, Anthony J. ("Tony"). b. 11/17 or 18/1916 Wilkes Barre, PA. Res. Luzerne Co., PA. Enl. 3/17/42 Ft. George Meade, MD. Ser. No. 33175227. Pvt. Attached to Co. A 5/28/42 Edgewood Arsenal, MD. Clerk (Cpl. & Pvt.). Pfc., HQ & HQ Co., (Supply Clerk), promo. Cpl. (temp.), Camp Gordon, GA 7/15/42. Cpl. (temp.) reduced to Pvt., HQ & HQ Co., Camp Gordon, GA 7/27/42. Pfc., promo. Cpl. (temp.), Camp Gordon, GA 9/23/42. Promo. Sgt. (temp.), Camp Gordon, GA 11/3/42. Sgt. Co. B, sent to hospital 8/17/43. Served as a Courier at Anzio 1944. Sgt., WIA – Purple Heart [Presented 11/20/44]. Pfc., Co. C, 6/22/45 Innsbruck, Austria. 103rd Inf. EAMETO Ribbon. Presidential Unit Citation. With Oak Leaf. Finished college after service. Quality Control Supervisor, Tobyhannock Army Depot. d. 10/6/1994. bur. St. Mary's Cem., West Wyoming, PA.

KOZAK, Andrew T. b. 1920 PA. Enl. 9/25/42 Greensburg, PA. Ser. No. 33294826. Pvt. Co. A, 10/15/42 Camp Gordon GA. Served with Co. A in France. Transf. HQ Co., Dec. 1944. Cpl., HQ Co., 5/8/45 Innsbruck, Austria. Attended 1958 Reunion as res. Greensburg, PA.

KOZICKI, Joseph E. b. 1924 OH. Played guitar & sang. Res. Mahoning Co., OH. Enl. 3/19/43 Ft. Hayes, Columbus, OH. Ser. No. 35606296. Pvt., Co. C, KIA, 1/26/44, Italy (Anzio). bur. Youngstown, OH.

KRAJCIR, Steven. b. 1915 PA. Enl. 12/22/42 Pittsburgh, PA. Ser. No. 33416693. Pvt., Co. B, Camp Gordon, GA 3/18/43. Pvt. Co. B, present with AOU party, Gela, Sicily 7/10/43.

KRAMER, William P. b. 11/29/1901 PA. Enl. 9/21/42 Harrisburg, PA. Ser. No. 33240891. Pvt., Co. A, Camp Gordon, GA 10/9/42. Transf. Co. B, Camp Gordon, GA, 12/16/42. d. 11/20/1997, Williamsport, Lycoming Co., PA.

KREBS, Edward W. b 1921 MD. Res. Randallstown, MD. Enl. 9/26/42 Baltimore, MD. Ser. No. 33377164. Pvt. Co. A, 10/15/42 Camp Gordon GA. Transf. Co. B, Camp Gordon, GA, 12/16/42. Pfc., Co. A, WIA (light injure), LST 422 Survivor, 1/26/44 Italy (Anzio) – Purple Heart. Cpl., Co. C, 6/22/45 Innsbruck, Austria. Attended 1960, 1962 & 1966 Reunions as res. Randallstown, MD.

KRESS, Edward A. [or H.]. b. 1921 PA. Enl. 6/24/42 Pittsburgh, PA. Ser. No. 13087015. Pvt., Med. Det., attached to HQ & HQ Co., Camp Gordon, GA 9/26/42. Pvt., Med. Det., transf. HQ & HQ Co., Camp Gordon, GA 11/5/42. Sgt., Co. B 5/8/45 Innsbruck, Austria. Attended 1958 Reunion – Res. Owing Mills, MD.

KRIVAK, Anton B. b. 1913 MI. Res. Cuyahoga Co., OH. Enl. 4/23/41. Ser. No. 35022483. Transf. from 11th Armored Div. Present as Bn. S-3 HQ Co. 8/4/45.

KROUS, Stanley S. b. 11/23/1918 MA. Res. Douglas, Worcester Co., MA. Enl. 2/27/42 Ft. Devens, MA. Ser. No. 31069755. Pvt. Attached to Co. H 5/28/42 Edgewood Arsenal, MD. Gunner (Pvt.). Pfc. Co. C, transf. Co. A, Camp Gordon, GA, 12/16/42. Cpl./Sgt., Co. C, (light injure in action), LST 422 Survivor 1/26/44 Italy (Anzio) – Purple Heart. Returned to duty 3/1/44. S/Sgt., Co. C, 6/22/45 Innsbruck, Austria. d. Apr. 1986.

KRUELSKI, Edward A. b. 10/12/1914 NY. Res. Kings Co., NY. Enl. 2/28/42 Camp Upton, Yaphank, NY. Ser. No. 32220809. Pvt. Attached to Co. I 5/28/42 Edgewood Arsenal, MD. Gunner (Pvt.). d. 12/8/2000 Brooklyn, Kings Co., NY.

KRZECKOWER, Sam U. b. 1924 Poland. Res. Bronx Co., NY. Enl. 4/24/43 New York City, NY. Ser. No. 32873003. Pvt., Co. C, MIA, 1/26/44, Italy (Anzio) SR Cem. [Spelled Krezckower with no middle initial on official casualty list].

KUBAS, Albert J. b. 12/21/1919 NJ. Res. Wallington, Bergen Co., NJ. Enl. 7/9/42 Newark, NJ. Ser. No. 32390518. Pvt., Co. C, Camp Gordon, GA 7/28/42. Pfc., Co. C, LST 422 Survivor, 1/26/44 Italy (Anzio) – Purple Heart. T/5, Co. C, 6/22/45 Innsbruck, Austria. d. 9/2/1976.

KUBERA, Teddy W. b. 1922 PA. Enl. 9/26/42 Pittsburgh, PA. Ser. No. 33305765. Pvt. Co. D, 10/15/42 Camp Gordon GA. Transf. Co. A, Camp Gordon, GA, 12/16/42. Pfc., Co. D, LST 422 Survivor, 1/26/44 Italy (Anzio). T/5, Co. A, 5/8/45 Innsbruck, Austria. Mentioned in the May 1954 Directory.

KULAGA, Fred J. b. 1919 MA. Res. Lawrence, Essex Co., MA. Enl. 2/24/41 Boston, MA. Ser. No. 31017505. 2nd Lt., CWS, LST 422 Survivor, 1/26/44 Italy (Anzio) – Purple Heart. 2nd Lt., CWS, Co. C, WIA, (light – enemy mortar shell), 5/8 or 9/44 Anzio, Italy – Purple Heart with Oak Leaf Cluster. Returned to duty 6/20/44. 1st Lt., Co. C, 6/22/45 Innsbruck, Austria. 1st Lt. Assigned 65th Inf. Div. 7/23/45. Res. Lawrence, MA. May 1954.

KULCINSKI, Vernon L. b. 7/13/1922 WI. Res. La Crosse Co., WI. Enl. 12/15/42 Milwaukee, WI. Ser. No. 36289995. Pfc., Co. C, 6/22/45 Innsbruck, Austria. d. 3/6/1989 La Crosse, La Crosse Co., WI.

KULICK [Kulich], Joseph. b. 1920 PA. Enl. 12/22/42 Harrisburg, PA. Ser. No. 33494985. Pvt., Co. B, Camp Gordon, GA 3/18/43. Pvt., WIA (slight – shell burst in barrel – concussion blast burn), 1/11/45 France. Pfc., Co. B, 5/8/45 Innsbruck, Austria.

KURTENBACH, Leo L. b. 3/7/1922 IL. Res. Iroquois Co., IL. Enl. 12/7/42 Peoria, IL. Ser. No. 36438722. Pvt., Co. B, Camp Gordon, GA 4/10/43. Pvt., Co. B, WIA (light – shell burst), 2/18/44 Anzio, Italy. Pfc., Co. B, 5/8/45 Innsbruck, Austria. d. 10/22/1999 Joliet. Will Co., IL

KUYKENDALL, Claud D [or C.]. b. 1921 MS. Res. Monroe C., MS. Enl. 9/22/42 Camp Shelby, MS. Ser. No. 34426468. Pvt. Co. B, 10/14/42 Camp Gordon, GA. Transf. Co. A, Camp Gordon, GA, 12/16/42. Pfc., Co. B, WIA (serious - by 75mm shell), 7/10/43 Gela, Sicily. Purple Heart [presented 9/27/43 in Sicily]. Rotated at Anzio.

KUYKENDALL, George C. Res. Converse County, WY. Ser. No. 37458485. Pvt., Co. D, MIA, 1/26/44, Italy (Anzio)

KUYKENDALL, John Lewis. b. 2/5/1921 MS. Res. Itawamba Co., MS. Enl. 9/23/42 Camp Shelby, MS. Ser. No. 34426749. Pvt. Co. B, 10/14/42 Camp Gordon, GA. Pfc., Co. B, MIA, 1/26/44, Italy (Anzio) SR Cem.

KWESKIN, Samuel Irving. b. 2/24/1924 IL. Enl. 2/14/43 Camp Grant, IL. Shepperd Field, Wichita Falls, TX Feb. 1943. Herbert Smart Field, Macon, GA Apr. 1943. ASTP Berkeley College. 3rd CMB in Italy. 537th Replacement Co., 21st. Bn. Aug. 1944. Croix de Guerre. Transf. Pvt., Co. D, 83rd CMB Sept. 1944 Epinal, France. Assgnd. HQ Co. 11/9/44 Epinal, France. Promo Pfc. 1/11/45. Combat Artist, 83rd CMB. Artist for Muzzleblasts and Rounds Away (1945). Pfc., HQ Co., 5/8/45 Innsbruck, Austria. Transf. 410th Inf. 6/17/45. Transf. 134th Chemical Co. Transf. 648th TD BN. Dischd. 12/19/45. Art Institute of Chicago. Illustrator. Advertising Agency Art Director. TV Cartoonist. Medical Illustrator. Marvel Comics 1949-92 (Submariner, Fantastic Four, etc.). This Is My Story TV show. Left TV 1952. Res. New York, NY May 1954. Artist. U.N. World. Portrait Artist. Contributed to MFP 1997. Attended nearly every reunion. d. Boca Raton, FL 6/23/2005. bur. Westlawn Cem., Chicago, IL.

KWONG, Russell. b. 1908 CA. Res. Kern Co., CA. Enl. 3/31/42 Ft. MacArthur, San Pedro, CA. Ser. No. 39025307. Pvt. Attached to Co. K 5/28/42 Edgewood Arsenal, MD. Gunner (Pvt.). Pfc., Co. A, (Squad Leader), promo. Cpl. (temp.), Camp Gordon, GA 7/15/42. Cpl.(temp.), Co. A, promo. Sgt. (temp.), Camp Gordon, GA 8 /19/42. Transf. OCS, CWS, Edgewood Arsenal, MD Dec. 1942.

LACY, Hudson M. b. 1920 VA. Enl. 2/16/43 Roanoke, VA. Ser. No. 33532743. Pvt., Co. C, MIA, 1/26/44, Italy (Anzio) SR Cem.

LA GRECA, Joseph A. b. 1922 NY. Res. Kings Co., NY. Enl. 2/8/43 New York City. Ser. No. 32796308. Pvt., Co. D, WIA (light injure), LST 422 Survivor, 1/26/44 Italy (Anzio). Corp., Co. A, 5/8/45 Innsbruck, Austria.

LAKEY, Raymond J. ROTC, Edgewood Arsenal. Present as Capt., Co. D, 6/19/44. Commanded Co. D in Glider Mission 8/15/44. Capt., Co. D, WIA (light), 10/11/44 near Charmois, France. Battalion informed 10/13/44 Lakey was too injured to return. Returned to duty 11/6/44. Also present 11/19/44. On 11/20/44 Lt. Col. Efnor reported Lakey was back with 83rd but gunfire gave him severe headaches and recommended him as an officer for Edgewood Arsenal.

LAMBERT, Dennis B. b. 1923 IN. Res. Morgan Co., IN. Enl. 2/4/43 Indianapolis, IN. Ser. No. 35090592. Pfc., Co. C, MIA, 1/26/44, Italy (Anzio) SR Cem.

LANCASTER, Louie L. b. 5/24/1921 AL. Res. Gadsden, Etowah Co., AL. Enl. 9/16/42 Ft. McClellan, AL. Ser. No. 34391404. Pvt., Co. B, Camp Gordon, GA 10/8/42. Pvt., Co. B, WIA (light), 12/8/43 San Pietro, Italy – Purple Heart. d. 4/18/1999 Gadsden, Etowah Co., AL.

LANDERS, Woodrow M. Pfc., HQ Co., promo. T/5 (temp.) 9/15/45.

LANGDON, Ike B. b. 4/30/1900 MS. Res. Yazoo Co., MS. Enl. 9/22/42 Camp Shelby, MS. Ser. No. 34426538. Pvt. Co. B, 10/14/42 Camp Gordon, GA. d. Nov. 1979 Grady, Montgomery Co., AL.

LANGFORD, Earl H. b. 1922 GA. Pvt., Co. D, Camp Gordon, GA 10/9/42. Re-enl. 10/23/45 Phoenixville, PA. Ser. No. 33335579. Pfc., Med. Dept.

LANGFORD, Edward P. b. 1915 NY. Res. Bronx Co., NY. Enl. 3/5/42 Ft. Dix, NY. Ser. No. 32245644. Pvt. Attached to Co. I 5/28/42 Edgewood Arsenal, MD. Squad Leader (Sgt.). Transf. OCS October, 1942 Camp Gordon, GA. Was a res. Fordham, NY.

LANGFORD, Karl M. Pvt., Co. D, WIA (light), 9/27/43 Italy.

LANGLEY, Calvin L. b. 1921 NC. Res. Norfolk Co., VA. Enl. 9/21/42 Richmond, VA. Ser. No. 33225792. Pvt., Co. B, Camp Gordon, GA 10/11/42. Pfc., Co. B, WIA (light), San Pietro, Italy 12/8/43.

LANSON, Frank J. b. 8/9/1918 LA. Res. Bossier Co., LA. Enl. 6/3/42 Camp Livingston, LA. Ser. No. 38172959. Pvt., Co. B, Camp Gordon, GA 3/18/43. d. 1/20/2000 LA.

LATIMER, Eugene R. b. 1914 NJ. Res. Union Co., NJ. Enl. 6/30/42 Newark, NJ. Ser. No. 32387502. Pvt., Co. D, Camp Gordon, GA 7/28/42. Pfc/ Co. D, transf. Co. A, Camp Gordon, GA, 12/16/42. Pfc., Co. D, WIA (shell fragment – serious), 9/11/43 Vietre sul Mare, Italy. Hospitalized. Cpl., Co. D, MIA, 1/26/44, Italy (Anzio) SR Cem.

LATIMER, William M. b. 1918 CA. Res. San Francisco Co., CA. Enl. 2/11/42 Presidio of Monterey, CA. Ser. No. 39088839. Pvt. Attached to Co. F 5/28/42 Edgewood Arsenal, MD. Squad Leader (Sgt.). Pfc., Co. B, (Squad Leader), promo. Cpl. (temp.), Camp Gordon, GA 7/15/42.

LAUNDRE, Kenneth Knowlton. b. 2/3/1913 Glen Falls/Queensbury, NY. Res. Genesee Co., MI. Pre-war Occupation: Automobile body repairman (acetylene welding)/Superintendent. Quality Standards Dept., Fisher Body Parts 1933.. Enl. 2/13/42 Ft. Custer, MI. Ser. No. 36171917. Pvt. Attached to Co. F 5/28/42 Edgewood Arsenal, MD. Motor Sgt. (S/Sgt.). Pvt., HQ & HQ Co. transf. Co. C, Camp Gordon, GA 6/15/42. Pfc., (Chauff.), promo. Cpl. (temp.), Camp Gordon, GA 7/15/42. T/4, Co. C, transf. HQ & HQ Co., Camp Gordon, GA 10/6/42. Automotive Technician. Quartermaster Supply Technician. Sicily. Naples-Foggia. Rome-Arno. Southern France. Rhineland. Central Europe. T/Sgt., HQ Co., 5/8/45 Innsbruck, Austria. EAMETO Medal with six bronze stars. Resumed job Fisher Body Parts. Attended 1954, 1956, 1958 & 1960 Reunions as res. Flint, MI. d. 4/15/1967 (heart attack). bur. Crestwood Cem., Grand Blanc, MI. Prior to Anzio landing fell from truck & broke wrist which probably kept him from boarding LST 422.

LAURO, James V. b. 11/22/1920 NY. Res. Ozone Park, Queens Co., NY. Enl. 6/23/42 Ft. Jay, Governors Island, NY. Ser. No. 32358876. Pvt., Co. D, Camp Gordon, GA 7/28/42. Pfc., Co. D, promo. Cpl. (temp.), Camp Gordon, GA 11/5/42. Sgt., Co. D, WIA (light – shell fragment), 9/9/43 Vietre sul Mare, Italy. Evacuated. Returned to duty 12/11/43. S/Sgt., Co. D, LST 422 Survivor, 1/26/44 Italy (Anzio) – Purple Heart with Oak Leaf Cluster. Rescued by USS Pilot. 2nd Lt., promo. 1st Lt. 8/17/44. 1st. Lt., HQ Co., 5/8/45 Innsbruck, Austria. 1st Lt. Assigned 65th Inf. Div. 7/23/45. Married his Austrian girlfriend. Res. Long Island, NY May 1954. Attended 1954, 1958, 1960, 1962 & 1965 reunions as res. Ozone Park, NY. d. 12/11/2003 Round Top, Greene Co., NY.

LAUS, Andre N. b. circa 1915 France. Son of Abdon & Charlotte N. Laus of Alsace, France. Res. Boston, MA. 1930. M.I.T. - June 1937. Research Chemist. Reserve Officer. His father was a bassoonist in the Boston Symphony Orchestra & mother was head of the French Women's Club of Boston. 1st. Lt., Ser. No. O-353944, MA. Present at Edgewood Arsenal, MD Apr. 1942. 2nd Lt., CWS, assigned to Co. A, Camp Gordon, GA 9/17/42. Transf. HQ & HQ Co., Camp Gordon, GA 10/1/42. Transf. Co. A, Camp Gordon, GA 11/26/42. Transf. Co. B, Camp Gordon, 12/16/42. Lt., distinguished in action 7/10/43 Gela, Sicily. Silver Star – presented 1/14/44. Purple Heart. French Croix De Guerre with Gilt Star. Promo. Capt. 2/28/44. Present as CO, Co. C, 3/24/44. Present as CO, Co. C, 5/9/44. 1st Lt., Co. C, KIA, 8/29/44, Briançon, France, RH Cem. Distinguished Service Cross (Posthumous). Widow: Alline (Lynette/Linette) Perrin Laus, Little Falls, NJ 1956.

LAWING, Robert L. b. 1923 GA. Res. Atlanta, Fulton Co., GA. Enl. 2/12/43 Ft. McPherson, Atlanta, GA. Ser. No. 34689889. Pvt., Co. C, LST 422 Survivor, 1/26/44 Italy (Anzio) – Purple Heart. Rescued by USS Pilot.

LAWLER, Elwin F. b. 4/19/1922 MA. Res. Essex Co., MA. Enl. 9/28/42 Boston, MA. Ser. No. 11048488. Pvt. Attached to Co. H 5/28/42 Edgewood Arsenal, MD. Gunner (Pvt.). d. 2/9/2000.

LAWLESS, Grady. b. 1918 MS. Res. Laurel, Jones Co., MS. Enl. 9/21/42 Camp Shelby, MS. Ser. No. 344266275. Pvt. Co. B, 10/14/42 Camp Gordon, GA. Tranfs. Co. A, Camp Gordon, GA, 12/16/42. Pvt., Co. B, arrived Salemi, Sicily from North Africa 8/2/43. Pvt., Co. B, sent to hospital 8/9/43. Pvt., Co. B, LST 422 Survivor, 1/26/44 Italy (Anzio) – Purple Heart. Rescued by YMS 69 1/26/44. Pfc., awarded Soldier's Medal 7/6/44 [actual presentation 4/25/44]. Pfc., Co. B, 5/8/45 Innsbruck, Austria. Attended 1954 & 1956 reunions as L. Lawless.

LAWMASTER, John F. b. 1/14/1919 NJ. Res. Camden Co., NJ. Enl. 7/9/42 Camden, NJ. Ser. No. 32271776. Pvt., Co. B, Camp Gordon, GA 7/28/42. Pvt., Co. B, Camp Gordon, GA 10/20/42. d. 4/22/199 Williamstown, Gloucester Co., NJ.

LEAP, Jerome G. b. 1917 PA. Res. Lilly, PA. Enl. 12/7/42 Altoona, PA. Pvt., Co. B, Camp Gordon, GA 3/18/43. Ser. No. 33566855. Pfc., Co. C, MIA, 1/26/44, Italy (Anzio) SR Cem.

LEAR, Maurice D. b. 1915 Wash., D.C. Pre-war Occupation: Westinghouse Electric & Manufacturing Co., Philadelphia, PA. Res. Bronx Co., NY/Alvin, PA.. Enl. 10/7/42 Ft. Jay, Governors Island, NY. Ser. No. 32523464. Reported MIA 8/29/44 Briançon, France. Returned 8/31/44. Pfc., Co. C, 6/22/45 Innsbruck, Austria.

LEAT, ----------. Cpl. Co. A, 3rd. Platoon, 8/4/45.

LE BLANC, Wilfred E. b. 1923 MA. Res. Middlesex Co., MA. Enl. 4/8/43 Boston, MA. Ser. No. 31309478. Pfc., Co. C, MIA, 1/26/44, Italy (Anzio) SR Cem. Body recovered 1/26/44 by YMS 34 & buried at sea same day. Next of kin: Teresa Le Blanc, Wakefield, MA.

LECKLITNER, Myron D. 1st Lt. Assigned to Med. Det. & designated Assistant Battalion Surgeon, Camp Gordon, GA 2/21/43.

LEDFORD, John C. b. 1914 GA. Res. Rabun Co., GA. Enl. 9/23/42 Ft. McPherson, Atlanta, GA. Ser. No. 34443678. Pvt., Co. C, Camp Gordon, GA 10/12/42.

LE DOYEN, Charles J. b. 1922 MD. Enl. 9/28/42 Baltimore, MD. Ser. No. 13103961. Pvt., Co. B, Camp Gordon, GA 10/11/42. Pvt., Co. B, MIA, 1/26/44, Italy (Anzio) SR Cem.

LEE, Gum Q. CWS Air Operations, GA. T/5, HQ Co., 5/8/45 Innsbruck, Austria. Cook. "Could skin a deer or a boar." Chinese ancestry. [Probably Gum B. Lee. b. 1923 Asia. Res. Bronx Co., NY. Enl. 3/5/43 New York City, NY. Ser. No. 32824364]

LEECH, Andrew Candler. b. 8/2/1908 MS. Raised in Itawamba Co., MS. Smithville High School 1931. Mississippi State University one year. Jones County Junior College two semesters. Teacher, Greenwood Springs, MS. Teacher, Runnelstown High School, Perry Co., MS 1941. Res. Monroe Co., MS. Enl. 9/22/42 Camp Shelby, MS. Ser. No. 34426489. Pvt. Co. B, 10/14/42 Camp Gordon, GA. Transf. Co. A, Camp Gordon, 12/16/42. BAR-Man. Pfc., Co. B, 5/8/45 Innsbruck, Austria. After German surrender was at 98th General Hosp., Germany two months for battle fatigue. Dischd. 11/11/45 Camp Shelby, MS.. Kept a wartime diary used in the book WW II Experiences of Andrew Candler Leech. Kist Bottling Co., Hattiesburg, MS. University of Southern Mississippi (teaching certificate). Principal & Social Studies Teacher, Hamilton High School, Hamilton, MS 1948 – 51. Coach. Monroe Co.

Welfare Director 1951. Retired Aug. 1973. Res. Aberdeen, MS 1985. d. May 1990 MS.

LE FEVER, Frederick L. b. 1921 PA. Res. New Columbia, PA. Enl. 9/21/42 Harrisburg, PA. Ser. No. 33240899. Pvt., Co. B, Camp Gordon, GA 10/9/42. Pfc., Co. B, WIA (enemy dive bombers) 2/17/44 Anzio, Italy – Purple Heart. T/5, Co. B, WIA (light), 11/28/44 Struth, France. T/5, WIA (light), 1/9/45 France. Returned to duty same day. T/5, Co. B, 5/8/45 Innsbruck, Austria. Res. PA May 1954. Self-employed Carpenter. Attended 1958 Reunion as res. Mountoursville, PA.

LEGER, Andrew J. b. 1926 PA. Res. Westmoreland Co., PA. Enl. 8/30/44 Pittsburgh, PA. Ser. No. 33925071. Pfc., Co. A, 5/8/45 Innsbruck, Austria.

LENHARDT, John E. b. 1914 OH. Enl. 5/15/42 Pittsburgh, PA. Ser. No. 13061803. Pvt., Med. Det., MIA, 8/30/44, Briançon, France. Returned to duty 9/7/44. Jean Pierre Combe stated Lenhardt, while repairing a communications line with Fred Tombolini and Combe, was WIA in the Vosges by a German mortar, believed to be 81mm, which sent a splinter inside his shoulder. He spent about a month in the hospital. Res. Lowellville, OH 1946.

LEONARD, James E. Res. Wichita Falls, TX. Ser. No. 38370487. Byron Jordan said Leonard was always getting drunk and threatening to "beat his ass" but never attempted to do so. Pvt., Co. D, MIA, 1/26/44, Italy (Anzio) SR Cem.

LEONARD, James M. Pvt., Co. D, WIA (enemy shell - light), 9/16/43 Vietre sul Mare, Italy.

LEPINE, Carl W. ("Spanky"). b. 8/13/1916 NY. Res. Franklin Co., NY. Enl. 1/9/42 Camp Upton, Yaphank, NY. Ser. No. 32192239. T/5. Assigned to Co. G 5/28/42 Edgewood Arsenal, MD. Mess Sgt. (S/Sgt.). T/4 (temp.), HQ & HQ Co., (Mess), prom. S/Sgt. (temp.), Camp Gordon, GA 7/15/42. S/Sgt., HQ Co., 5/8/45 Innsbruck, Austria. Ed Trey said that Lepine hunted wild boar with a Tommy gun in Germany. Res. Malone, NY May 1954. d. 9/1/1990.

LEROY, Arthur. Pvt. Attached to Co. G 5/28/42 Edgewood Arsenal, MD. Telephone Operator (Pvt.). Pfc., Co. D, WIA (enemy shell - light), 9/16/43 Vietre sul Mare, Italy. Returned to duty 10/26/43.

LESIO, ----------. Present as pitcher on Co. C ball team 8/4/45.

LESLIE, Russell U. b. 3/18/1924 AR. Res. Tulare Co., CA. Enl. 2/22/42 Portland, OR. Ser. No. 39327523. Pvt., WIA (light – shrapnel), 4/11/45 Germany. Pfc., Co. C, 6/22/45 Innsbruck, Austria. d. 6/26/1996 Watsonville, Santa Cruz Co., CA.

LESTER, James Marion ("Les"). b. 8/12/1915 Magnolia, Rock Co., MN. Attended school at Adrian. Moved to Clarion, IA. Graduated high school 1933. Pre-war Occupation: Gas business for a few years. Men's Clothing Store [Leuthold & Hinkley]. Res. Wright Co., IA. Enl. 12/21/42 Camp Dodge, Herrold, IA. Ser. No. 37651503. Camp Sibert, AL. (basic training). Sent to 83rd CMB as a replacement. Pvt., HQ &

HQ Co., Camp Gordon, GA 4/10/43. T/5, Co. A, 5/8/45 Innsbruck, Austria. Res. Worthington, MN 2005. d. 2/20/2006 Worthington, MN. bur. Worthington Memorial Garden Cem.

LEVINE, Morris. b. 1904 Poland. Res. Bronx Co., NY. Enl. 7/9/42 Ft. Jay, Governors Island, NY. Ser. No. 32402293. Pvt., Co. B, Camp Gordon, GA 7/28/42.

LEVY, Charles S. b. 1920 OK. Res. St. Louis Co., MO. Enl. 1/31/42 Jefferson Barracks, MO. Ser. No. 17044579. Pvt. Attached to Co. G 5/28/42 Edgewood Arsenal, MD. Squad Leader (Sgt.). Cpl. (temp.), Co. A, promo. Sgt. (temp.), Camp Gordon, GA 8/19/42. Pfc., (Squad Leader), promo. Cpl. (temp.), Camp Gordon, GA 7/15/42.

LEWIS, Clarence D. b. 4/22/1921 VA. Res. Henrico Co., VA. Enl. 9/21/42 Richmond, VA. Ser. No. 33225721. Pvt., Co. B, Camp Gordon, GA 10/11/42. Pvt., Co. B, sent to hospital (120th Collecting Bn.) 8/8/43. Returned to duty 8/16/43. Pfc., Co. B, 5/8/45 Innsbruck, Austria. d. March 1986 Richmond, VA.

LEWIS, Edwin. Pvt., Co. C, Camp Gordon, GA 10/9/42. Ser. No. 33296792.

LEWIS, Jack. b. 1923 AR. Res. KY. Enl. 3/6/43 Ft. Benjamin Harrison, IN. Ser. No. 35726133. Pvt., Co. C, MIA, 1/26/44, Italy (Anzio) SR Cem.

LEWNES, Louis S. b. 1921 MD. Enl. 9/26/42 Baltimore, MD. Ser. No. 33377193. Pvt. Co. A, 10/15/42 Camp Gordon GA.

LEYS, Francis T. b. 1/24/1921 NY. Enl. 10/9/42 Pittsburgh, PA. Ser. No. 33307668. Pvt. Co. A, 10/15/42 Camp Gordon GA. Transf. Co. D, Camp Gordon, GA, 12/16/42. d. Feb. 1988 Millville, Cumberland Co., NJ.

LIBASSI, Philip J. Res. NY. Pvt., Co. C, Camp Gordon, GA 4/10/43. Ser. No. 32686857. Pvt., Co. C, KIA, 1/26/44, Italy (Anzio), SR Cem.

LICATA, Joseph L. b. 1914 NY. Res. LeRoy, Genesee Co., NY. Enl. 2/23/42 Ft. Niagara, Youngstown, NY. Ser. No. 32250199. Pvt., Co. C, (light injure in action), LST 422 Survivor, 1/26/44 Italy (Anzio) – Purple Heart. Returned to duty 3/12/44.

LIEBERMAN, Bennie. b. 1921 Wash., D.C. Res. Wash., D.C. Enl. 9/21/42 Ft. Myer, VA. Ser. No. 33197625. Pvt. Co. D, 10/11/42 Camp Gordon GA. Pvt., Co. D, distinguished in action 7/11/43 Niscemi, Sicily. Pfc., Co. D, Silver Star presented 10/8/43. Present on LST 422 at Italy (Anzio) 1/26/44 according to Clark Riddle. Purple Heart. Res. Silver Springs, MD. Stationed at Ft. Myer, VA, July 1944. Present in Washington, DC, as an M.P. February 1945.

LIEBOWITZ, Sidney L. b. 1921. Res. Bronx Co., NY. Enl. 7/9/42 Ft. Jay, Governors Island, NY. Ser. No. 32402191. Pvt., Co. B, Camp Gordon, GA 7/28/42. Pfc., Co. B, sent to hospital 8/13/43.

LINAMEN, Fred D. b. 11/6/1919 PA. Res. Chautauqua Co., NY. Enl. 3/5/42 Ft. Niagara, Youngstown, NY. Ser. No. 32251901. Pvt. Attached to Co. B 5/28/42 Edgewood Arsenal, MD. Communication (Cpl.). Pfc., Co. C, promo. Cpl. (temp.), Camp Gordon, GA 9/3/42. Sgt., Camp Gordon, GA 11/21/42. T/4, Co. C, MIA, 8/29/44 Briançon, France. POW Stalag 7A Moosburg, Bavaria. Liberated 5/25/45. d. 5/31/2004.

LINCK, George J., Jr. b. 11/22/1916 OH. Res. Stark Co., OH. Enl. 9/7/43 Akron, OH. Ser. No. 35236398. Served first in 3rd CMB with Sam Kweskin. Co. D, 83rd CMB. Pfc., Co. C, 6/22/45 Innsbruck, Austria. d. 6/27/2003 Akron, OH.

LINDSEY, Herbal B. b. 3/21/1914 MS. Res. Itawamba Co., MS. Enl. 9/23/42 Camp Shelby, MS. Ser. No. 34426736. Pvt. Co. B, 10/14/42 Camp Gordon, GA. d. 1/27/1988.

LINDSEY, James C. Pfc., Co. C, 6/22/45 Innsbruck, Austria.

LINK, Cecil S. b. 7/19/1921 TN. Res. Cottontown, Sumner Co., TN. Enl. 9/16/42 Ft. Oglethorpe, GA. Ser. No. 34371463. Cpl., Co. C, LST 422 Survivor, 1/26/44 Italy (Anzio) – Purple Heart with Oak Leaf Cluster. Rescued by USS YMS 226. Taken to 93rd Evac. Hosp. Sgt., Co. C, 6/22/45 Innsbruck, Austria. d. 8/2/2003.

LINKO, Michael. b. 1915 PA. Res. Luzerne Co., PA. Enl. 6/24/42 Wilkes Barre, PA. Ser. No. 13100027. Pvt., Co. D, KIA, 1/26/44, Italy (Anzio), SR Cem.

LIPSCHITZ, Abraham. Res. Brooklyn, NY. Orderly for Capt. Edwin Pike July 1944.

LIPSCOMB, ----------. 1st Lt., assigned to 83rd CMB 2/15/45.

LLOYD, Harry M. b. 3/16/1918 IN. Res. Rush Co., IN. Enl. 12/1/41 Ft. Benjamin Harrison, IN. Ser. No. 35250442. Pfc., Co. C, MIA, 8/29/44 Briançon, France. POW Stalag 7A Moosburg, Bavaria. Liberated 6/4/45. Res. Rushville, IN. d. 1/24/2000 Rushville, Rush Co., IN.

LOAN, Ira Brandon [Brandt]. b. 8/23/1914 VA. Res. Bath Co., VA. Enl. 9/21/42 Roanoke, VA. Ser. No. 33213302. Pvt., Co. C, Camp Gordon, GA 10/11/42. According to Hale H. Hepler this soldier suffered a heart attack at Camp Gordon, GA. d. May 1977 Millboro, Bath Co., VA.

LOEB, Bruno. b. 1914 Germany or Danzig. Res. New York Co., NY. Enl. 3/27/43 New York City, NY. Ser. No. 32875677. Pvt., Co. C, MIA, 1/26/44 Italy (Anzio), SR Cem.

LOEW, Paul H. b. 5/25/1914 NY. Res. Wash., D.C. Enl. 2/24/42 Camp Lee, VA. Ser. No. 33133749. Pvt. Attached to Co. G 5/28/42 Edgewood Arsenal, MD. Gunner (Pvt.). Pfc., Co. C, promo. Cpl. (temp.), Camp Gordon, GA 8/17/42. Cpl. (temp.) Co. C, to Sgt. (temp.) Camp Gordon, GA 10/14/42. Sgt. Co. C, Camp Gordon, GA, transf. OCS, 1/9/43. d. 11/24/2003.

LOMBARDI, Frank P. ("Francis"). b. 1921 NY. Res. Kings Co., NY. Enl. 7/9/42 Ft. Jay, Governors Island, NY. Ser. No. 32402330. Pvt., Co. D, Camp Gordon, GA 7/28/42. Pfc., Co. D, promo. Cpl. (temp.), Camp Gordon, GA 11/5/42. Cpl. Co. D, transf. Co. A, Camp Gordon, GA, 12/16/42. Sgt., Co. D, WIA (enemy shell – serious – shrapnel through right lung), 9/16/43, Vietre sul Mare, Italy. Transported to North Africa by a British outfit and sent home. Spent months recovering in Walter Reed Hospital. Dischd. Dec. 1944. Res. Rosedale, NY May 1954. Attended 1954, 1956 & 1966 Reunions. d. 6/17/2006.

LONG, Ralph L. b. 1921 PA. Res. Shamokin, PA. Enl. 9/21/42 Harrisburg, PA. Ser. No. 33240929. Pvt., Co. C, Camp Gordon, GA 10/9/42. Transf. Co. A, Camp Gordon, GA, 12/16/42. Cpl., Co. C, WIA (light), LST 422 Survivor, 1/26/44 Italy (Anzio) – Purple Heart with Oak Leaf Cluster. Sgt., Co. C, 6/22/45 Innsbruck, Austria.

LOONEY, Elster C. b. 1920 VA. Enl. 10/5/42 Richmond, VA. Ser. No. 13118170. Pvt., Co. B, Camp Gordon, GA 10/11/42. Pvt., Co. B, Camp Gordon, GA Nov. 1942.

LOTZ, ----------. Pfc., Co. B, sent to hospital (56th Medical, Trapani) 8/5/43.

LOULAN, James A., Jr. b. 9/5/1918 OH. Res. Summit Co., OH. Enl. 2/27/41 Cleveland, OH. Ser. No. 35010646. 2nd Lt., CWS. 2nd Lt., HQ & HQ Co., Camp Gordon, GA, 6/12/42. Bn. S-2. Classification & Assignment Officer, Camp Gordon, GA 7/11/42. Released as Battalion Intelligence & Meteorological officer, Camp Gordon, GA 11/10/42. Promo. 1st Lt., Camp Gordon, GA & transf. Air Corps, Maxwell Field, AL Nov. 1942. d. July 1984 New Berne, NC.

LOVE, Emmet C., Jr. b. 1924 IN. Res. Allen Co., IN. Enl. 3/6/43 Camp Perry, Lacarne, OH. Ser. No. 35766035. Pvt., Co. C, MIA, 1/26/44, Italy (Anzio) SR Cem.

LOVE, Leonard E. b. 8/28/1921 KY. Res. Jefferson Co., AL. Enl. 9/25/42 Ft. McClellan, AL. Ser. No. 34392469. Pvt. Co. B, 10/14/42 Camp Gordon, GA. Present as Pvt., Camp Gordon, GA, 1/9/43. d. 11/16/1990.

LOVELAND, Donald R. Res. Milwaukee, WI. Pvt., Co. C, LST 422 Survivor, 1/26/44 Italy (Anzio) – Purple Heart. Pfc., Co. C, WIA (light – enemy mortar shell), 5/8/44 Anzio, Italy. Cpl., WIA (light), 4/9/45 Germany. Cpl., Co. C, 6/22/45 Innsbruck, Austria.

LOVELL, Wayne F., Jr. b. 8/19/1923 TN. Res. Knox Co., TN. Enl. 2/10/43 Ft. Oglethorpe, GA. Ser. No. 34720946. Pfc., Co. C, MIA, 8/29/44 Briançon, France. POW Stalag 7A Moosburg, Bavaria. Liberated 5/18/45. d. Nov. 1974.

LOWE, Alfred A., Jr. b. 1915 MA. Res. Suffolk Co., MA. Enl. 9/25/42 Boston, MA. Ser. No. 11089876. Pvt., Co. B, Camp Gordon, GA 3/18/43.

LOWERY, Edward. b. 1918 PA. Res. Philadelphia Co., PA. Enl. 12/14/42 Philadelphia, PA. Ser. No. 33475134. Pvt., Co. B, Camp

Gordon, GA 3/18/43. Pvt., Co. B, 5/8/45 Innsbruck, Austria.

LOWMAN, Donald L. b. 1920 OK. Res. Payne Co., OK. Enl. 2/6/42 Oklahoma City, OK. Ser. Np. 18084887. Pfc., Co. C, (Pers.), promo. Cpl. (temp.), Camp Gordon, GA 7/15/42.

LOWRY, Carl B. b. 3/1/1900 MS. Res. Lee Co., MS. Enl. 9/22/42 Camp Shelby, MS. Ser. No. 34426604. Pvt. Co. B, 10/14/42 Camp Gordon, GA. d. April 1982 Verona, Lee Co., MS.

LOWRY, Charlie. b. 9/11/1911 Springdale, Fayette Co., WV. Meadow Bridge High School, Meadow Bridge, WV 1932. Pre-Med., Potomac State College, Keyser, WV. Union Carbide, South Charleston, WV 1934-1942. Res. Kanawha Co., WV. Enl. 2/3/42 Ft. Thomas, Newport, KY. Pvt. Ser. No. 15089732. Received U.S. Army Motor Vehicle Operator's Permit 5/29/42, Edgewood Arsenal, MD. Co. E, CWS Training Battalion, Edgewood Arsenal, MD. Attached to Co. E 5/28/42 Edgewood Arsenal, MD. Squad Leader (Sgt.). Pvt. Pfc., Co. A, T/5 (temp.), Camp Gordon, GA 8/1/42. T/5 (temp.), Co. A assigned to Post Motor Pool, Camp Gordon, GA 8/24/42. T/5, Co. A, 83rd CMB, Camp Gordon, GA 9/10/42. T/5 Co. A. transf. Co. B, Camp Gordon, GA, 12/16/42. Sgt., Co. D, 83rd CMB, Camp Gordon, GA 3/20/43. Sicily. Naples-Foggia. Rome-Arno. Southern France (gliders). Rhineland. Central Europe. EAME Service Ribbon with 1 Bronze Arrowhead. Good Conduct Medal. Glider Pin. T/4, HQ Co., 411th Inf. Returned to U.S. 9/18/45. Dischd. 10/17/45. Union Carbide, South Charleston, WV. d. 5/17/1981 South Charleston, Kanawha Co., WV. Body donated WVU Medical School.

LOWY, Alfred L. b. 1913 NY. Res. Bronx Co., NY. Enl. 7/9/42 Ft. Jay, Governors Island, NY. Ser. No. 32402377. Pvt., Co. B, Camp Gordon, GA 7/28/42. Pfc., Co. B, Camp Gordon, GA 10/20/42. Pfc., Co. B, 5/8/45 Innsbruck, Austria.

LOZUR, Charles. Name provided by James Marion Lester of Co. D Motor Pool/Co. A. Lester's wife, Iris, said she wrote to Lozur's wife during the war who told her he was sent home due to a "mental problem."

LUCAS, John F. b. 1921 PA. Enl. 9/21/42 Altoona, PA. Ser. No. 33253593. Pvt., Co. C, Camp Gordon, GA 10/9/42. In a group photo of Co. C taken 1943 at Amalfi, Italy. Pvt., Co. C, MIA, 1/26/44, Italy (Anzio)

LUCAS, Nicholas. Pvt., Co. B. Served from 6/6/43 - Oct. 1945. Military occupation: Heavy Mortar Crewman. North Africa. Naples-Foggia. Anzio. Rome. Southern France. Rhineland. Central Europe. Awards: Combat Infantryman Badge, Silver Star, Bronze Star, Purple Heart, 1944. Glider Badge. Pvt., Co. B, 5/8/45 Innsbruck, Austria.

LUGO, Filemon R. b. 1907. Res. Kings Co., NY. Enl. 3/20/43 New York City, NY. Ser. No. 32868980. Pvt., Co. C, MIA, 1/26/44, Italy (Anzio) SR Cem.

LUKUS (Lukas), Michael J. b. 1911 PA. Res. Luzerne Co., PA. Enl. 9/22/42 Wilkes Barre, PA. Ser. No. 33354545. Pvt., Co. C, Camp Gordon, GA 10/9/42. Pfc., Co. C, MIA, 1/26/44, Italy (Anzio) SR Cem.

LUSE, William C. b. 1920 NY. Res. New Castle, DE. Pvt. Attached to Co. C 5/28/42 Edgewood Arsenal, MD. Communication (Cpl.). Pvt., Co. B transf. Co. A, Camp Gordon, GA 6/15/42. Re-enl. Pfc., Brigham City, UT 11/24/45. Ser. No. 32243270.

LUTZ, Jacob A., Jr. b. 1913 NC. Res. Lowndes Co., MS. Enl. 9.232.42 Camp Shelby. MS. Ser. No. 34426621. Pvt. Co. B, 10/14/42 Camp Gordon, GA.

LYKINS, William E. b. 3/15/1923 KY. Res. Stark Co., IN. Enl. 2/1/43 Indianapolis, IN. Ser. No. 35090114. Pfc., Co. C, 6/22/45 Innsbruck, Austria. d. 11/9/1993.

LYNCH, Chester. Pvt., Co. D, WIA (shell shock), 7/14/43 Sicily.

LYNCH, John W. b. 1921 NJ. Res. Bergen Co., NJ. Enl. 7/9/42 Newark, NJ. Ser. No. 32390602. Pvt., HQ & HQ Co., Camp Gordon, GA 7/28/42. Pfc, HQ Co. assigned to Motor Pool, Camp Gordon, GA 1/26/43. Apptd. T/5 4/15/43. T/5, Co. C, MIA, 1/26/44, Italy (Anzio) SR Cem.

LYONS, Rex Elvin. Res. Nansemond Co., VA. Enl. 10/24/39. Ser. No. 06900111. Survivor, LST 422, 1/26/44 Italy (Anzio). Rescued by USS YMS 226. Taken to 93rd Evac. Hosp. T/4, Co. C, 6/22/45 Innsbruck, Austria. Dischgd. September 1945. Res. Suffolk, VA.

MABE, Raymond R. b. 12/15/1919 VA. Res. Carroll Co., VA. Enl. 2/14/42 Camp Lee, VA. Ser. No. 33132660. Pfc., Co. C, 6/22/45 Innsbruck, Austria. d. 8/9/1994 Grayson, VA.

MACK, Donald J. b. 10/4/1910 PA. Res. New York Co., NY. Enl. 7/9/42 Ft. Jay, Governors Island, NY. Ser. No. 32402194. Pvt., Co. B, Camp Gordon, GA 7/28/42. Pfc., Co. B, promo. Cpl. (temp.), Camp Gordon, GA 12/12/42. Pvt., Co. B, recommended for Silver Star for action near Ceppagna, Italy 11/13/43. T/5, Co. B, 5/8/45 Innsbruck, Austria. Res. New York, NY May 1954. d. Feb. 1980 Poughquag, Dutchess Co., NY. Attended 1954 Reunion. [also spelled Mach].

MacKENDER, William A., Jr. b. 1910 NY. Enl. 2/18/42 Buffalo, NY. Ser. No. 12055929. Pvt. Attached to Co. F 5/28/42 Edgewood Arsenal, MD. Motor Sgt. (S/Sgt.) Pvt., HQ & HQ Co. transf. Co. A, Camp Gordon, GA 6/15/42. Pfc., (Motor Sgt.), promo. Cpl. (temp.), Camp Gordon, GA 7/15/42. Pfc., Co. A, 5/8/45 Innsbruck, Austria.

MACKOWIAK, Joseph M. b. 1921 PA. Enl. 9/21/42 Harrisburg, PA. Ser. No. 33240943. Pvt., Co. B, Camp Gordon, GA Nov. 1942. Pfc., Co. B, WIA (serious), 12/8/43 San Pietro, Italy .

MACON, Marion E. b. 1921 MO. Res. Marion Co., KS. Enl. 2/4/41 Ft. Riley, KS. Ser. No. 17002782. Field Artillery. Res. Aptos, CA, 1988.

MAGDZIAZ, John J. Res. Fort Calhoun, NE. Pvt., Co. C, LST 422 Survivor, 1/26/44 Italy (Anzio) – Purple Heart. Rescued by USS Pilot. Reported MIA 8/29/44 Briançon, France. Returned 8/31/44. Pfc., Co. C, 6/22/45 Innsbruck, Austria.

MAGEL, John M. b. 1913 NY. Res. Bergen Co., NJ. Enl. 7/1/42 Newark, NJ. Ser. No. 32387892. Pvt., Co. C, Camp Gordon, GA 7/28/42. Pvt., Co. C, special duty Communications School of 472nd Field Artillery, Camp Gordon, GA 10/12-17/42. Pfc., promo. Cpl. (temp.), Camp Gordon, GA 10/21/42. Present, Cpl., Co. C, Camp Gordon, GA, 1/9/43.

MAGILL, Travis. b. 1920 MS. Res. Union Co., MS. Enl. 9/23/42 Camp Shelby, MS. Ser. No. 34426866. Pvt. Co. B, 10/14/42 Camp Gordon, GA. Sgt., Co. B, 5/8/45 Innsbruck, Austria.

MAGNUS, W. G. [C.?]. b. 1921 GA. Res. Haralson Co., GA. Enl. 9/18/42 Ft. McPherson, Atlanta, GA. Ser. No. 34442758. Pvt., Co. B, Camp Gordon, GA 10/8/42. Pvt., Co. B, MIA, 12/12/44, Riquewihr, France. Attended 1956 Reunion.

MAHONEY, James B. Res. Carthage, NY. Ser. No. 32287196. Pvt., Co. C, LST 422 Survivor, 1/26/44 Italy (Anzio) – Purple Heart.

MAKEPEACE, Edwin H. b. 1918 NJ. Res. Bergen Co., NJ. Enl. 7/6/42 Newark, NJ. Ser. No. 32389223. Pvt., Co. D, Camp Gordon, GA 7/28/42. Pfc., Co. D, promo. Cpl. (temp.), Camp Gordon, GA 11/5/42.

MAKOWSKI, Stephen V. Res. Oil City, PA. Catholic. Ser. No. 33432577. Pvt., Co. C, MIA, 1/26/44, Italy (Anzio) SR Cem. [Also spelled Stephan].

MALCHUSKI, Theodore J. Pvt., Co. B, Camp Gordon, GA 10/11/42. Ser. No. 6353241. Pvt., Co. B, Camp Gordon, GA Nov. 1942.

MALM, Robert M. b. 10/9/1910 Sweden. Res. Fairfield Co., CT. Enl. 7/6/42 Hartford, CT. Ser. No. 31142918. Pvt., assigned Med. Det. & attached HQ & HQ Co., Camp Gordon, GA 10/10/42. T/3, Med. Det., 5/8/45 Innsbruck, Austria. d. 8/31/1993 Fairfield, Fairfield Co., CT.

MALONE, Kary M. b. 1920 MS. Res. Monroe Co., MS. Enl. 9/23/42 Camp Shelby, MS. Ser. No. 34426836. Pvt. Co. B, 10/14/42 Camp Gordon, GA. Pfc., WIA (serious – shell burst in barrel – broken leg), 1/11/45 France.

MALOT, Paul A. b. 1910 PA. Res. Kings Co., NY. Enl. 8/28/43 New York City, NY. Ser. No. 42034182. Pvt. Co. D, 3rd CMB. In a group photo of 83rd CMB men provided by Sam Kweskin.

MALSAVAGE, Andrew C. Pfc., Co. A, 5/8/45 Innsbruck, Austria.

MANNATT, William E. b. 1924. Res. Los Angles Co., CA. Enl. 9/11/43 Los Angles, CA. Ser. No. 39709552. Assigned from 65th Inf. Division as 2nd Lt., Co. C, 7/23/45.

MANNING, Cody M. b. 10/25/1921 AR. Res. White Co., AR. Enl. 6/19/42 Camp Joseph T. Robinson, Little Rock, AR. Ser. No. 38178611. Pvt., Co. C, 6/22/45 Innsbruck, Austria. d. Feb. 1981 Rock, AR.

MANSFIELD, Isaac A. b. 1922 TN. Res. Davidson Co., TN. Enl. 9/18/42 Ft. Oglethorpe, GA. Ser. No. 34371784. Pvt., HQ & HQ Co., Camp Gordon, GA 10/7/42. Pvt., WIA, 11/30/43 Venafro, Italy. Pfc., Co. C, MIA, 1/26/44, Italy (Anzio) SR Cem.

MANZI, Reynoldi [Renoldi] L. b. 10/25/1919 NJ. Res. Hudson Co., NJ. Enl. 7/22/42 Newark, NJ. Ser. No. 32450686. Pvt., Co. A, Camp Gordon, GA 7/28/42. Pfc., Co. A correspondent, Smokescreen, Camp Gordon, GA Nov. 1942 & Feb. 1943. d. June 1983 Dumont, NJ.

MARCHE, William T. b. 4/22/1916 Wash., D.C. Res. Hyattsville, Prince Georges Co., MD. Enl. 5/22/42 Baltimore, MD. Ser. No. 33200803. Pfc., Bronze Star, 1944. Pfc., Co. C, 6/22/45 Innsbruck, Austria. d. Oct. 1978 [Muzzleblasts says 1984].

MARCILLE, James W. b. 11/1/1912 ME. Res. York Co., ME. Enl. 3/13/42 Camp Upton, Yaphank, NY. Ser. No. 32227544. Pvt. Attached to Co. I 5/28/42 Edgewood Arsenal, MD. Gunner (Pvt.). Pfc., Co. B, (Squad Leader), promo. Cpl. (temp.), Camp Gordon, GA 7/15/42. d. 2/7/1994 Pensacola, FL.

MARKHAM, Orvel L. Pvt., Co. B, Camp Gordon, GA 3/18/43. Ser. No. 38278422.

MARKIEWICZ, Chester F. b. 12/22/1917 NY. Res. Kings Co., NY. Enl. 2/11/42 Camp Upton, Yaphank, NY. Ser. No. 32214258. Pfc., Co. A, 5/8/45 Innsbruck, Austria. d. May 1980.

MARKOLA, Harold John. b. 7/6/1919 Hancock Co., WV. Both parents were born in Finland. Res. Lake Co., IN. Enl. 2/14/42 Ft. Benjamin Harrison, IN. Ser. No. 35258356. Cpl., Assigned to Co. E 5/28/42 Edgewood Arsenal, MD. Sgt. Maj. Cpl. (temp.)., HQ & HQ Co., promo. Sgt. (temp.), Camp Gordon, GA 6/16/42. (T/Sgt.). Sgt. (temp.), (Personnel), promo. S/Sgt. (temp.), Camp Gordon, GA 7/15/42. S/Sgt. (temp.), promo. T/Sgt. (temp.), Camp Gordon, GA 8/1/42. T/Sgt. (temp.), HQ & HQ Co., Camp Gordon, GA 8/24/42. Promo. M/Sgt. (temp.), Camp Gordon, GA 10/21/42. Designated Asst. Adjutant, Camp Gordon, GA 11/26/42. d. 12/22/1995 Lake, IN

MARKOSKI, Henry L. b. 1/30/1921 PA. Enl. 10/5/42 Philadelphia, PA. Ser. No. 13124670. Pvt., HQ & HQ Co., Camp Gordon, GA 10/9/42. d. 8/21/2003 Palmerton, Carbon Co., PA.

MARKS, Cecil A. b. 1921 MS. Res. Lee Co., MS. Enl. 9/22/42 Camp Shelby, MS. Ser. No. 34426618. Pvt. Co. B, 10/14/42 Camp Gordon, GA. Pvt., Co. B, WIA, (light), 12/8/43 San Pietro, Italy. Purple Heart, EAME Theater Ribbon, Good Conduct Medal. Naples & Sicily. Res. Tupelo, MS.

MARMION, John W. b. 1907 NY. Res. Philadelphia Co., PA. Enl. 12/15/42 Philadelphia, PA. Ser. No. 33475381. Pvt., Co. B, Camp Gordon, GA 3/18/43.

MARSHALL, Eugene C. b. 1915 OH. Res. Richland Co., OH. Enl. 3/18/43 Ft. Hayes, Columbus, OH. Ser. No. 35633124. Pfc., Co. A, 5/8/45 Innsbruck, Austria. Served In Army in Korea. Res. Cedar Vale,

KS May 1954.

MARSHALL, Loy Joseph. b. 12/20/1921 Forsyth, Monroe Co., GA. Attended Monroe Co., GA Public Schools. Pre-war Occupation: CCC & Cotton Mill Worker. Res. Griffin, Spalding Co., GA. Enl. 9/19/42 Ft. McPherson, Atlanta, GA. Pvt., Co. C, Camp Gordon, GA 10/8/42. BAR assistant to Edward J. Sutlic until 8/23/43 then assigned Communications. Pvt., Co. C, LST 422 Survivor, 1/26/44 Italy (Anzio) – Purple Heart. Pfc., Co. C, WIA (light - shrapnel in foot and face), 5/26/44 Anzio, Italy. Hospitalized. Purple Heart with Oak Leaf Cluster. Cpl., Co. C, 6/22/45 Innsbruck, Austria. Dischd. Sept. 1945. d. 12/21/2006 Griffin, GA bur. Griffin Memorial Gardens.

MARTIN, Charles Albert Warren. b. 8/12/1920 Haywood, Harrison Co., WV. Res. Wash., D.C. Enl. 9/21/42 Ft. Myer, VA. Ser. No. 33197664. Pvt., HQ & HQ Co., Camp Gordon, GA. 10/11/42. Pvt., HQ & HQ Co., Camp Gordon, VA 11/21/42. Pfc., apptd. T/5, HQ & HQ Co. 4/15/43. Pfc., Co. C, 6/22/45 Innsbruck, Austria.

MARTIN, Ernest F. b. 1920 GA. Res. Hall Co., GA. Enl. 9/18/42 Ft. McPherson, Atlanta, GA. Ser. No. 34442759. Pvt., HQ & HQ Co., Camp Gordon, GA 10/8/42. Res. Burford, GA May 1954. Hosiery Mill Worker.

MARTIN, Frank. b. 1920 Andorra or Portugal. Res. Newport Co., RI. Enl. 12/14/42 Providence, RI. Ser. No. 31246148. Pvt., Co. C, Camp Gordon, GA 4/10/43.

MARTIN, George E. Res. Danville, VA. Pfc., Co. C, 6/22/45 Innsbruck, Austria.

MARTINDALE, Herbert L. b. 3/21/1899 MS. Res. Shelby Co., TN. Enl. 9/19/42 Camp Shelby, MS. Ser. No. 34426081. Pvt. Co. B, 10/14/42 Camp Gordon, GA. d. Nov. 1976. Winter Park, Orange Co., FL.

MARTINEZ, Saro B. b. 1919 TX. Res. Dallas Co., TX. Enl. 6/5/42 Dallas, TX. Ser. No. 38116087. Pfc., Co. C, 6/22/45 Innsbruck, Austria.

MARTINO, Bertram G. b. 1920 PA. Enl. 9/21/42 Altoona, PA. Ser. No. 33253588. Pvt., Co. C, Camp Gordon, GA 10/9/42. Transf. Co. A, Camp Gordon, GA, 12/16/42. Cpl., Co. C, MIA, 1/26/44, Italy (Anzio) SR Cem.

MARZULLI, Carmen. b. 10/27/1921 PA. Enl. 9/22/42 Philadelphia, PA. Ser. No. 33335470. Pvt., Co. C, Camp Gordon, GA 10/9/42. Pfc., Co. C, WIA (enemy shell), 9/16/43, Mairoi, Italy. d. Oct. 1985 PA.

MASON, Roger B. b. 1921 MS. Res. De Soto Co., MS. Enl. 9/23/42 Camp Shelby, MS. Ser. No. 34426807. Pvt. Co. B, 10/14/42 Camp Gordon, GA. Pvt., Co. B, MIA, 1/26/44, Italy (Anzio) SR Cem.

MASON, Walter T. ("Pappy"). b. 1905 PA. Res. Atlantic Co., NJ. Enl. 2/23/42 Ft. Dix, NJ. Ser. No. 32240661. Pvt. Attached to Co. G 5/28/42 Edgewood Arsenal, MD. Mechanic Auto (Pvt.). Pvt., HQ & HQ Co., promo. T/4 (temp.), Camp Gordon, GA 6/16/42. T/4 (temp.), (Motor Sgt.), promo. Sgt. (temp.), Camp Gordon, GA 7/15/42. Sgt. (temp.),

HQ & HQ Co., promo. S/Sgt. (temp.), Camp Gordon, GA 9/14/42.

MASSEY, John. In a photo provided by Dale C. Blank taken at Pozzuoli, Italy 1944.

MASSEY, Otis A. b. 1922 GA. Res. Brooks Co., GA. Present as Sgt. Co. A 8/9/44. Re-enl. as Sgt. CWS 12/22/45 Ft. McPherson, Atlanta, GA. Ser. No. 34012613.

MASTERSON, Lawrence. b. 1921 OH. Res. Franklin Co., OH. Enl. 3/31/43 Ft. Benjamin Harrison, IN. Ser. No. 35635443. Pvt., Co. C, MIA, 1/26/44, Italy (Anzio) SR Cem.

MATHEWS, John J. b. 1921 NJ. Res. Burlington Co., NJ. Enl. 7/6/42 Camden, NJ. Ser. No. 32271357. Pvt., Co. C, Camp Gordon, GA 7/28/42. T/5, MIA, 1/26/44, Italy (Anzio) SR Cem.

MATTHEWS, Auvie R. b. 8/7/1920 MS. Res. Itawamba Co., MS. Enl. 9/23/42 Camp Shelby, MS. Ser. No. 34426759. Pvt. Co. B, 10/14/42 Camp Gordon, GA. Pfc., Co. B, 5/8/45 Innsbruck, Austria. d. 9/24/1994 Fulton, Itawamba Co., MS.

MATTHEWS, John T. b. 1919 PA. Enl. 8/21/42 Harrisburg, PA. Ser No. 33238833. Pvt., Co. B, Camp Gordon, GA 10/9/42. Re-enl. 6/19/46 Camp Gordon, Augusta, GA. T/Sgt., Adj. Gen. Dept.

MATTHEWS, Ralph. d. 6/16/1997.

MATZIEVSKY, Andrew ("Smitty"). b. 1916 NJ. Res. Union Co., NJ. Enl. 6/29/42 Newark, NJ. Ser. No. 32387279. Pvt., HQ & HQ Co., Camp Gordon, GA 7/28/42.

MAU, Albert A. Cpl., Co. B, promo. Sgt. (temp.) 9/15/45.

MAY, Herman L. b. 1919 MS. Res. Scott Co., MS. Enl. 9/23/42 Camp Shelby, MS. Ser. No. 34426642. Pvt. Co. B, 10/14/42 Camp Gordon, GA. Pvt., Co. B, WIA (light), 12/8/43 San Pietro, Italy.

MAY, James. b. 1919 MS. Res. Pontotoc, Pontotoc Co., MS. Enl. 4/24/41 Ft. McClellan, AL. Ser. No. 34102715. Pvt., Co. B, LST 422 survivor, 1/26/44 Italy (Anzio) - Purple Heart. Had seven campaign stars as of 1/11/45. Pfc., Co. B, 5/8/45 Innsbruck, Austria.

MAY, Leslie W. b. 1/21/1909 Detroit, MI. Pre-war Occupation: Photo engraver. Enl. 8/10/43 Detroit, MI. Res. Wayne Co., MI. Ser. No. 36869156. Pfc. HQ Co. Radio operator. Embarked overseas 7/15/44. Served in Northern France; Rhineland in Central Europe. EAME Theater Ribbon w/3 bronze stars, American Theater Ribbon, Good Conduct Medal, WWII Victory Medal. Embarked to US 11/17/45, Discharged 11/30/45 Camp Atterbury, IN.

MAYNARD, Corris. b. 1919 GA. Res. Gwinnett Co., GA. Enl. 9/17/42 Ft. McPherson, Atlanta, GA. Ser. No. 34442481. Pvt., Co. B, Camp Gordon, GA 10/8/42.

MAYNARD, Elbert J. b. 1921 TN. Res. Davidson Co., TN. Enl. 9/18/42 Ft. Oglethorpe, GA. Ser. No. 34371800. Pvt., HQ & HQ Co., Camp Gordon, GA 10/7/42. Pvt., HQ Co., correspondent, Smokescreen, Camp Gordon, GA 1/9/43.

MAYOR, Michael C. b. 9/15/1908 PA. Enl. 12/15/42 Greensburg, PA. Ser. No. 33412383. Pvt., HQ & HQ Co., Camp Gordon, GA 3/18/43. d. 3/8/1990 PA.

MAYRUND, ----------. Listed as wearing arm in sling, Co. C 8/4/45.

MAZZAFER, John P. Pfc., Co. A, 5/8/45 Innsbruck, Austria.

MAZZELLA, Carmine. b. 7/15/1924 Italy. Res. Webster Co., WV. Enl. 7/6/43 Clarksburg, WV. Ser. No. 35757592. Arrival in North Africa 3/12/44. Heavy Mortar Crewman. Naples-Foggia. Rome-Arno. Southern France Rhineland. Central Europe. Good Conduct Medal. European African Middle Eastern Theater Ribbon with Bronze Arrowhead. World War II Victory Ribbon. Pfc., Co. A, 5/8/45 Innsbruck, Austria. Returned to U.S. 12/14/45. Dischd. 12/19/45. d. 12/27/2004 Naperville, DuPage Co., IL.

McAFEE, Clifford B. ("Cliff"). b. 1916 IN. Res. Floyd Co., IN. Enl. 12/16/42 Louisville, KY. Ser. No. 35690848. Pvt., Co. A, Camp Gordon, GA 4/10/43. Pfc., HQ Co., 5/8/45 Innsbruck, Austria. Res. New Albany, IN May 1954. Auto & Heavy Equipment Construction Equipment Mechanic.

McALISTER, Sidney L. b. 1921 MS. Res. Sheffield, Union Co., MS. Enl. 9/23/42 Camp Shelby, MS. Ser. No. 34426862. Pvt. Co. B, 10/14/42 Camp Gordon, GA. Pvt., Co. B correspondent, Smokescreen, Camp Gordon, GA Nov. 1942. Pfc., Co. B, WIA (light), 12/8/43 San Pietro, Italy.

McANINCH, Alfred A. b. 1911 IN. Enl. 12/9/42 Indianapolis, IN. Ser. No. 35573239. Pfc., Co. B 1/25/45. Pfc., Co. B, 5/8/45 Innsbruck, Austria.

McAULEY, Thomas L. b. 1919 MA. Res. Bristol Co., MA. Enl. 4/8/43 Boston, MA. Ser. No. 31309523. Pvt., Co. C, MIA, 1/26/44, Italy (Anzio) SR Cem.

McBRIDE, Albert L. b. 10/3/1913 TN. Res. White Co., TN. Enl. 10/29/1940 Ft. McPherson, Atlanta, GA. Ser. No. 14032390. Infantry. Re-enl. 9/18/46 Ft. Oglethorpe, GA. Cpl., Corps of Military Police, Hawaiian Dept. Ser. No. 33471728. d. February 1982, Sparta, White Co. TN.

McBRYDE, Clyde E. b. 1915 MS. Res. Union Co., MS. Enl. 9/22/42 Camp Shelby, MS. Ser. No. 34426809. Pvt. Co. B, 10/14/42 Camp Gordon, GA. T/5, Co. B, arrived Salemi, Sicily from North Africa 8/1/44. T/5, Co. B, MIA, 1/26/44, Italy (Anzio) SR Cem.

MacCULLOUGH, ----------. In a photo belonging to L.Lew Henry, probably Co. A.

McCAFFREY, James L. b. 1902 PA. Enl. 10/9/1942 Pittsburgh, PA. Ser. No. 33307726. Pvt. Co. B, 10/15/42 Camp Gordon GA.

McCANN, Chester D. b. 1908 NY. Res. Morton, Monroe Co., NY. Enl. 2/24/42 Rochester, NY. Ser. No. 12056411. Pvt. Attached to Co. I 5/28/42 Edgewood Arsenal, MD. Gunner (Pvt.). Pfc. Co. A, transf. Co. B, Camp Gordon, GA, 12/16/42. Pfc., Co. C, Camp Gordon, GA 12/19/42. Pvt., Co. A, WIA (shell burst), 2/12 or 13/44 Anzio, Italy – Purple Heart.

McCARTHY, Cornelius [Neil]. b. 7/21/1920 PA. Res. Philadelphia Co., PA. Enl. 8/25/42 Philadelphia, PA. Ser. No. 33330058. Pvt., Co. A, Camp Gordon, GA 10/9/42. Pvt., Co. A, assigned Med. Det., Camp Gordon, GA 11/14/42. Transf. Co. D, Camp Gordon, GA, 12/16/42. Pvt., Co. B, noted for gallantry on 11/11/43. Pfc., Co. B, recommended for Silver Star for action on 12/20/43. T/5, Co. A, on *LST 690* 8/9/44. T/5, Med. Det., 5/8/45 Innsbruck, Austria. Res. Philadelphia, PA May 1954 [also listed as Co. B]. d. 12/15/2004 Philadelphia, Philadelphia Co., PA.

McCAY, John D. b. 2/1/1905 PA. Enl. 9/22/42 Philadelphia, PA. Ser. No. 33335503. Pvt., Co. A, Camp Gordon, GA 10/9/42. Transf. Co. C, Camp Gordon, GA, 12/16/42. d. July 1964 PA.

McCLAFFERTY, William T. ("Pop"). b. 1897 PA. Res. Pittsburgh, Allegheny Co., PA. Enl. 10/8/42 Pittsburgh, PA. Ser. No. 33307617. Pvt. Co. C, 10/15/42 Camp Gordon GA. Pfc., Co. C, LST 422 Survivor, 1/26/44 Italy (Anzio) – Purple Heart.

McCLOSKEY, Harry B. b. 4/13/1914 NJ. Res, Hudson Co., NJ. Enl. 9/16/40 Jersey City, NJ. National Guard. Pfc. Infantry. T/Sgt., C.W.S. Assigned HQ & HQ Co. 5/28/42 Edgewood Arsenal, MD. Sgt. Maj. (M/Sgt.). 5/28/42 T/Sgt. (temp.), HQ & HQ Co. promo. Master/Sgt. (temp.), Camp Gordon, GA 6/16/42. Mentioned in the May 1954 Directory. d. 1/25/1996.

McCLOSKEY, William J. b. 1/29/1913 PA. Enl. 9/22/42 Philadelphia, PA. Ser. No. 33335508. Pvt., HQ & HQ Co., Camp Gordon, GA 10/9/42. d. 3/13/1988 Philadelphia, PA.

MCCLURG,----------. Present as catcher for Co. B ball team 8/4/45.

McCORMACK, William F. b. 1921 NY. Res. Hudson Co., NJ. Enl. 7/8/42 Newark, NJ. Ser. No. 32390155. Pvt., Co. D, Camp Gordon, GA 7/28/42.

McCOY, Allen D. b. 1913 TN. Enl. 12/17/43 Evansville, IN. Ser. No. 35811807. Pfc., HQ Co., 5/8/45 Innsbruck, Austria. T/5, promo. T/4 (temp.) 9/15/45. Mentioned in the 1970 Muzzleblasts.

McCRAINE, Nolan Christopher. b. 4/1/1921 Wilkinson Co., MS. Grad. Boechstand High School. Pre-war Occupation: Sales Person/Dry Goods Store. Res. Wilkinson Co., MS. Enl. 9/18/42 Camp Shelby, MS. Ser. No. 34425659. Pvt. Co. B, 10/14/42 Camp Gordon, GA. Attended Communications School at Camp Gordon, GA. Pfc. Co. B, present with AOU party Gela, Sicily, 7/10/43. Head injured when hit against a truck hauling troops in France. Often used as Forward Observer. T/5, Communications 1/11/45. T/5, Co. B, 5/8/45 Innsbruck, Austria. Returned home Dec. 1945. Postmaster, Centreville, MS. Cattleman and farmer. Instrumental in re-establishing the Eastern Wild Turkey in southwest MS in the 1950s. Retired Postal Worker. Res. Centreville, Wilkinson Co., MS 2006. d. 11/8/2008, Centreville, MS. bur. Evergreen Cem., Woodville, MS.

McCULLEY, H. b. 1922 MO. Res. Painton, Stoddard Co., MO. Enl. 1/22/43 Jefferson Barracks, MO. Ser. No. 37413366. Pfc., Co. D, LST 422 Survivor, 1/26/44 Italy (Anzio) – Purple Heart with Oak Leaf Cluster. Rescued by USS YMS 226. Taken to 93rd Evac. Hosp. [listed on survivor list as Pvt.].

McDADE, Roy Eldo ("Peck"). b. 11/21/1920 Ravenswood, Jackson Co., WV. Res. Jackson Co., WV. Enl. 8/8/40 Ft. Hayes, Columbus, OH. Ser. No. 15011224. Enl. For Philippine Dept. Pvt., Field Artillery. Pvt., Co. B, WIA (light injure), 1/25/44 Italy (Anzio). Tunisian Sicilian – Naples Foggia. American Defense – American Theater – European African Middle Eastern – Bronze – Victory Medal Dischd. 2/16/47. Res. Ft. Myers, FL. d. 9/10/1974 St. Petersburg, FL. bur. Lee Memorial Park.

McDANIEL, Edgar W. b. 1922 AL. Res. Haralson Co., GA. Enl. 9/19/42 Ft. McPherson, Atlanta, GA. Ser. No. 34422999. Pvt., Co. Co, Camp Gordon, GA 10/9/42. Pfc., Co. C, KIA, 1/26/44, Italy (Anzio). Body recovered 1/26/44 by USS YMS 226 and turned over to Graves Registration at Anzio 1/27/44. Next of kin: Sally McDaniel, GA.

McDANIEL, Thomas W. ("Doc"). b. 1917 GA. Res. Jeferson Co., GA. Enl. 12/17/42 Ft. McPherson, Atlanta, GA. Ser. No. 34578650. Pvt., Co. A on *LST 690* 8/9/44. Pfc., Med. Det., 5/8/45 Innsbruck, Austria. Res. Louisville, PA May 1954. Fire Dept., Camp Gordon, Augusta, GA.

McDERMOTT, Bernard H. Pvt., Co. D, Camp Gordon, GA 10/9/42. Ser. No. 33335575. Pvt., Co. D. Mentioned in the 12/12/42 issue of Smokescreen. Present Pvt., Co. D, Camp Gordon, GA, 1/9/43. Photo in Dan Shields' album.

McDONALD, Fred. b. 1919 AL. Res. Lawrence Co., AL. Enl. 9/19/42 Ft. McClellan, AL. Ser. No. 34391773. Pvt., Co. C, Camp Gordon, GA 10/8/42. Present as Pvt., Co. C, Camp Gordon, GA, 1/9/43.

McDONALD, Lawrence E. Pvt., Co. A, Camp Gordon, GA 4/10/43. Pvt., distinguished in action 7/10/43 Sicily. T/5, Co. A, on *LST 690* 8/9/44. T/5, Co. A, 5/8/45 Innsbruck, Austria. Jeep driver assigned to Lt. Robert Bush.

McEVOY, John Patrick. b. 2/27/1919 Brookline, MA. Grad. Brookline High School 1936. Mass. Institute of Technology (MIT) 1940. Enl. Apr. 1942. Joined 83rd CMB July 1942. 2nd Lt., assigned HQ & HQ Co. & designated Motor Transportation Officer, Camp Gordon, GA 6/22/42. Designated Munitions Officer, Camp Gordon, GA 8/24/42. 1st Lt., transf. Co. A, Camp Gordon, GA, 12/16/42. Served as a Forward Observer with Rangers at Gela, Sicily. Served as Forward Observer with Co. B throughout the Sicilian Campaign and commanded the company during Capt. Mindrum's hospitalization August and in a beach landing

in Sicily of the 179th Infantry. Following Sicilian Campaign assigned commander Co. A. Present as CO, Co. A 11/26/43. Still present as CO, Co. A, 3/24/44. Present as CO, Co. A, 5/9/44. Present as CO, Co. A, 7/19/44. Present as CO, Co. A on *LST 690* 8/9/44. After Southern France invasion Aug. 1944 transf. Battalion HQ as S-3 (Operations Officer). Granted leave to England to visit cousins 4/23/45. Major/Lt. Col., HQ Co., 5/8/45 Innsbruck, Austria. Major assigned to 65th Inf. Div. 7/23/45. Rejoined Army 1947 as liaison officer to the Air Force. Masters Degree 1949. Korean War. Res. Rocky Mt. Arsenal, Denver, CO. May 1954 Industrial College. Chemical Officers Advance Course, Ft. McClellan 1954-55. Attended 1956, 1962 (res. Army Chemical Center, MD) & 1966 Reunions. Assigned with Chief of Staff at the Pentagon. Retired from Army 1966 as Col. Microbiological Associates. Retired 1982. Contributed to MFP 1997. Res. Arlington, VA 2009. Lt. Robert E. Bundy described him as "a brilliant man."

McEWEN, Leon. b. 1919 MS. Res. Scott Co., MS. Enl. 9/23/42 Camp Shelby, MS. Ser. No. 34426859. Pvt. Co. B, 10/14/42 Camp Gordon, GA.

McFARLAND, William B. ("Mac" / "Whitey"). b. 5/31/22 Pittsburgh, PA. Res. Delaware Co., PA. Enl. 10/5/42 Philadelphia, PA. Ser. No. 33338178. Pvt., HQ & HQ Co., Camp Gordon, GA 10/9/42. Pvt., HQ Co. transf. Motor Pool, Camp Gordon, GA 1/25/43. Pvt., apptd. Pfc., HQ & HQ Co. 3/3/43. Pfc., apptd. T/5, HQ & HQ Co. T/4, HQ Co., 5/8/45 Innsbruck, Austria. Res. Trenton, NJ May 1954. Attended 1956 & 1958 Reunions (res. Mayaguez, Puerto Rico). Postwar Diesel Engine School, CA. American Automobile Association, Dept. of the Army, Navy, Post and Agriculture. Narver & Holmes: U.S. Atomic Energy Proving Grounds, Eniwetok & Bikini Atolls, Marshall Islands. Atomic Energy Commission. Pan Am World Airlines: Guided Missile Range Division, Patrick AFB, FL; Electronic Test facility for U.S. Army, AZ; Nuclear Rocket Development Station NRDS), NV. USAF Facilities, Cape Kennedy, FL & down range stations. Retired from Pan Am early 1980's. Res. FL. d. 6/19/2005 Satellite Beach. bur. Florida Memorial Gardens (Garden of the Apostles), Rockledge, FL. Buried with his dog tags.

McGAHEE, David C. b. 1921 GA. Res. McIntosh Co., GA. Enl. 9/19/42 Ft. McPherson, Atlanta, GA. Ser. No. 34443061. Pvt., Co. B, Camp Gordon, GA 10/9/42.

McGAHEE, Rancy Edward. b. 1921 GA. Res. Louisville, Jefferson Co., GA. Enl. 9/18/42 Ft. McPherson, Atlanta, GA. Ser. No. 34442773. Pvt., Co. A, Camp Gordon, GA 10/8/42. Cpl., Co. A, 5/8/45 Innsbruck, Austria. Res. Ft. Lauderdale, FL May 1954. County Board of Public Instruction.

McGEE, Mike F. b. 1906 SD. Res. Lucas Co., OH. Enl. 12/21/42 Toledo, OH. Ser. No. 35538119. Pvt., Co. A, Camp Gordon, GA 4/10/43. Pfc., Co. A, on *LST 690* 8/9/44. Pfc., Co. C, 6/22/45 Innsbruck, Austria.

McGILL, Arthur H. b. 6/23/1902 PA. Enl. 9/26/42 Pittsburgh, PA. Ser. No. 33305846. Pvt. Co. C, 10/15/42 Camp Gordon GA. d. July 1976 Harrisville, Butler Co., PA.

McGLINCHEY, Edward J. b. 1907 PA. Enl. 9/22/42 Philadelphia, PA. Ser. No. 33335475. Pvt., Co. A, Camp Gordon, GA 10/9/42. Transf. Co. B, Camp Gordon, GA, 12/16/42. Present Co. A, Camp Gordon, GA, 1/9/43.

McGLINCHEY, William J. b. 1918 PA. Pvt., Co. C, Camp Gordon, GA 10/9/42. Pfc., Co. C, MIA, 8/29/44 Briançon, France. POW Stalag 7A Moosburg, Bavaria. Liberated 6/14/45. Re-enl. 11/23/45 Camp Anza, CA. Cpl. Ser. No. 33335587.

McGOVERN, John F. b. 1915 RI. Res. Providence Co., RI. Enl. 3/5/42 Ft. Devens, MA. Pvt. Attached to Co. C 5/28/42 Edgewood Arsenal, MD. Cook (Pvt.). Pfc., Co. C, (Cook), promo. T/5 (temp.), Camp Gordon, GA 7/15/42. T/5 (temp.), Co. C, promo. T/4, Camp Gordon, GA 9/3/42. Ser. No. 31071883. T/4, Co. C, MIA, 1/26/44, Italy (Anzio) SR Cem.

McGILL, William G., Jr. b. 1921 MS. Res. Union Co., MS. Enl. 9/23/42 Camp Shelby, MS. Ser. No. 34426893. Pvt. Co. B, 10/14/42 Camp Gordon, GA.

McGRANN, James J. b. 1920 Irish Free State. Enl. 10/5/42 Philadelphia, PA. Ser. No. 13124641. Pvt., HQ & HQ Co., Camp Gordon, GA 11/21/42. T/5, HQ Co., 5/8/45 Innsbruck, Austria.

McINTYRE, George M. b. 4/7/1901 PA. Res. Camden Co., NJ. Enl. 7/9/42 Camden, NJ. Ser. No. 32271723. Pvt., Co. B, Camp Gordon, GA 7/28/42. d. June 1983 Clementon, Camden Co., NJ.

McKEE, Jay W. b. 1914 PA. Res. Clarion Co., PA. Enl. 5/16/41 Pittsburgh, PA. Ser. No. 33039306. Cpl. Assigned to Co. A 5/28/42 Edgewood Arsenal, MD. 1st Sgt. Cpl. (temp.), Co. A, promo. Sgt. (temp.), Camp Gordon, GA 6/16/42. Sgt. (temp.), (1st Sgt.), promo. S/Sgt. (temp.), Camp Gordon, GA 7/15/42. S/Sgt. (temp.), promo. 1st Sgt. (temp.), Camp Gordon, GA 8/1//42. Tranf. OCS, Dec. 1942. 1st Lt., KIA 4/5/45.

McKINION, William B. b. 1901 MS. Res. Neshoba Co., MS. Enl. 9/22/42 Camp Shelby, MS. Ser. No. 34426481. Pvt. Co. B, 10/14/42 Camp Gordon, GA.

McKINNON, Julian T. ("Mac"). b. 7/16/1921 Clio, AL. Univ. of AL 1938-1942. ROTC. Enl. July 1942. Joined 83rd CMB Sept. 1942. 2nd Lt., CWS, assigned HQ & HQ Co., and designated Communications Officer, Camp Gordon, GA 10/1/42. Designated Asst. Communications Officer, Camp Gordon, GA 12/2/42. 1st Lt., Co. D, LST 422 Survivor. Designated Acting Supply Officer (rear echelon) 2/2/44. Capt./1st Lt., Co. C. 2nd Platoon. Legion of Merit (1944), Bronze Star [presented 4/25/44], Soldier's Medal for gallantry on LST 422 [presented 4/25/44], Purple Heart. In hospital with bad eyes 5/21/44. Present as CO, Co. B, 7/19/44. Ft. Leavenworth War College teacher. Stationed at Edgewood Arsenal 1945. Dischd. Mar. 1946. Proctor & Gamble Co., ca. 1947. Res. Wyoming, OH May 1954. Attended 1962 Reunion as res. Dallas, TX. Retired 1984. Contributed to MFP 1997. d. 1/22/2003 (murdered) Millbrook, Elmore Co., AL.

McLARTY, Hilton T. b. 7/21/1920 MS. Toccopola High School. Pre-war Occupation: School Bus Driver. Res. Lafayette Co., MS. Enl. 9/22/42 Camp Shelby, MS. Ser. No. 34426524. Pvt. Co. B, 10/14/42 Camp Gordon, GA. Military Occupation: Motor Assistant. Sicily. Naples-Foggia. Rome-Arno. Southern France. Rhineland. Central Europe. EAMETO Medal. Good Conduct. Bronze Arrowhead. Pfc., Co. B, 5/8/45 Innsbruck, Austria. Co. H, 409th Inf. Dischd. 9/27/45. Attended 1956 & 1958 Reunions as res. Lafayette Springs, MS. d. 12/27/1993 Oxford, MS. bur. Lafayette Springs Cem., Lafayette Co., MS.

McLAUGHLIN, John R. Pfc., Co. A, 5/8/45 Innsbruck, Austria.

McLAUGHLIN, William F., Jr. b. 1906 PA. Enl. 9/22/42 Philadelphia, PA. Ser. No. 33335509. Pvt., Co. D, Camp Gordon, GA 10/9/42.

McLEAN, Troy V. b. 2/12/1923 NC. Res. Upton, Caldwell Co., NC. Enl. 7/9/42 Ft. Jackson, Columbia, SC. Ser. No. 14123711. Pvt., Co. C, LST 422 Survivor, 1/26/44 Italy (Anzio) – Purple Heart with Oak Leaf Cluster. Rescued by USS Pilot. Pfc., Co. C, 6/22/45 Innsbruck, Austria. d. 7/25/1995 Valdese, Burke Co., NC.

McLOUGHLIN, Joseph F. b. 1911 NY. Enl. 9/22/42 Philadelphia, PA. Ser. No. 33335662. Pvt., Co. A, Camp Gordon, GA 10/9/42.

McLEARY, ----------. Co. C. Reported MIA 8/29/44 Briançon, France. Returned 8/31/44.

McMAHON, Harvey. Pvt., WIA (light), 4/9/45 Germany. Pfc., Co. C, 6/22/45 Innsbruck, Austria.

McMILLAN, Raymond D. b. 1921 VA. Res. Henry Co., VA. Enl. 9/21/42 Roanoke, VA. Ser. No. 33213399. Pvt., Co. A, Camp Gordon, GA 10/11/42. Cpl., Co. A on LST 690 8/9/44. Cpl., Co. B, 5/8/45 Innsbruck, Austria.

McMURRAY, Archie E. b. 1913 ND. Res. Res. Beltrami Co., MN. Enl. 4/16/44 Ft. Snelling, MN. Ser. No. 37592856. Pfc., HQ Co., promo. T/5 (temp.) 9/15/45.

McMURRY, Julius S. b. 1914 MS. Res. Hattiesburg, Forrest Co., MS. Enl. 10/5/42 Camp Shelby, MS. Ser. No. 14140947. Pvt. Co. B, 10/14/42 Camp Gordon, GA. Pfc., Co. B, LST 422 Survivor, 1/26/44 Italy (Anzio) – Purple Heart. Returned to duty 2/9/44.

McNABB, Carl Mac ("Skinny"). b. 1/25/1917 Stephenson, AL. Res. Marion Co., TN. Enl. 9/26/42 Baltimore, MD. Ser. No. 33377255. Pvt. Co. D, 10/15/42 Camp Gordon GA. Pvt., Co. D, assigned Med. Det., Camp Gordon, GA 11/23/42. Medic. Developed bleeding stomach ulcer in North Africa and was returned to the States and discharged.. Professional Baseball. Detroit Tigers 1945. McNabb Grocery Store. Rural Mail Carrier. Started & Coached an American Legion Baseball team in Jasper. Res. Jasper, TN May 1954. d. 7/16/2007 Jasper, TN. bur. Pine Grove Cem.

McNALLY, John J. b. 1916 PA. Res. Camden Co., NJ. Enl. 7/9/42 Camden, NJ. Ser. No. 32271721. Pvt., Co. B, Camp Gordon, GA 7/28/42.

North Africa, Naples-Foggia, Sicily, Anzio and Rome-Arno. Res. Laurel Springs, NJ.

McNIEL, Wilburn A. b. 1/19/1920 AL. Res. Monroe Co., AL. Enl. 9/23/42 Ft. McClellan, AL. Ser. No. 34392244. Pvt. Co. B, 10/14/42 Camp Gordon, GA. Pvt., Co. B, 5/8/45 Innsbruck, Austria. d. 5/5/1989 Panama City, Bay Co., FL.

McPEAK, Tal. b. 11/11/1920 TN. Res. Norene, Wilson Co., TN. Enl. 9/17/42 Ft. Oglethorpe, GA. Ser. No. 34371661. Pvt., Co. B, Camp Gordon, GA Nov. 1942. Pvt., Co. B, WIA (light – shell burst) 2/18/44 Anzio, Italy – Purple Heart. d. 9/29/1996 Nashville, Davidson Co., TN.

MEADE, Edward J. b. 1921 PA. Enl. 9/22/42 Philadelphia, PA. Ser. No. 33335620. Pvt., Co. C, Camp Gordon, GA 10/9/42. Pvt., Co. C, KIA, 1/26/44, Italy (Anzio). Body recovered 1/26/44 by USS YMS 226 and turned over to Graves Registration at Anzio 1/27/44. Only identification found on body was name and home address of 1511 W. Indiana Ave., Philadelphia, PA.

MEADOWS, Emett L. b. 1922 AL. Res. Houston Co., AL. Enl. 9/19/42 Ft. McClellan, AL. Ser. No. 34391816. Pvt., HQ & HQ Co., Camp Gordon, GA 10/8/42.

MEADOWS, William M. b. 1922 GA. Res. Polk Co., GA. Enl. 10/5/42 Ft. McPherson, Atlanta, GA. Ser. No. 14139619. Pvt., HQ & HQ Co., Camp Gordon, GA 10/9/42. Cpl., Co. B, 5/8/45 Innsbruck, Austria. Res. Cedartown, GA.

MEANS, James J. b. 1924 OH. Res. Jefferson Co., OH. Enl. 4/21/43 Akron, OH. Ser. No. 35172992. Pvt., Co. C, WIA (light), LST 422 Survivor, 1/26/44 Italy (Anzio) – Purple Heart. Returned to duty 3/4/44. Cpl., Co. C, 6/22/45 Innsbruck, Austria.

MEEK, Ray D. b. 6/16/1920 MS. Res. Panola Co., MS. Enl. 9/19/42 Camp Shelby, MS. Ser. No. 34426073. Pvt. Co. B, 10/14/42 Camp Gordon, GA. Pfc., Co. B, WIA (light), 2/16/44 Anzio, Italy. Returned to duty 6/5/44. d. 1/13/2004 Courtland, Panola Co., MS.

MEISEL, Norman. b. 1922 IL. Enl. 9/28/42 Pittsburgh, PA. Ser. No. 13128445. Air Corps. [Name appears in Leonard Turan notebook].

MEISS, John F. b. 1918 PA. Enl. 12/12/42 Altoona, PA. Ser. No. 33567129. Pvt., Co. A, Camp Gordon, GA 4/10/43.

MELBORNE, James C. Res. Mt. Pleasant, TX. [Name appears in Leonard Turan notebook].

MELENDEZ, Casildo. Pvt., Co. B, Camp Gordon, GA 7/28/42. Pvt., Co. B, promo. T/5 (temp.), Camp Gordon, GA 10/13/42. T/5 (temp.), Co. B, promo. T/4 (temp.), Camp Gordon, GA 11/4/42. T/4, Co. B, arrived Salemi, Sicily from North Africa 8/1/44. T/4, Co. B, KIA, 1/26/44, Italy (Anzio). [Possibly full name Casildo Melendez Solero].

MELLEN, Arthur E. ("Pappy"). b. 2/14/1911 MA. Res. Suffolk Co., MA. Enl. 7/7/43 Boston, MA. Ser. No. 31365759. Pfc., Co. B, 5/8/45 Innsbruck, Austria. [Steedle's Squad, 2nd Platoon, Co. B]. d. 1/15/1990 MA.

MENICOLA, Frank F. b. 6/3/1920 NJ. Res. Bergen Co., NJ. Enl. 7/9/42 Newark, NJ. Ser. No. 32390617. Pvt., Co. D, Camp Gordon, GA 7/28/42. Pvt., Co. D, Camp Gordon, GA 9/25/42. Pfc., Co. D, Camp Gordon, GA 12/19/42. Orderly, jeep driver & Italian interpreter for Capt. Ed Pike in Sicily. In hospital for hernia and undescended testicle operation 1/20/44. Sent to Replacement Center 3/1-12/44. Reported present in another CWS outfit 5/28/44. Mentioned in the May 1954 Directory. Attended 1962 & 1966 Reunions as res. East Patterson, NJ. d. Jan. 1976 NJ.

MERRILL, Leonard Abbott, Jr. ("Spike"). b. 9/22/1917 Haverhill, MA. Moved to Miami, FL at a young age & then to Peterborough, NH. Grad. Peterborough High School 6/19/34. Grad. Cushing Academy, Ashburnham, MA 6/10/1935. Grad. Massachusetts Institute of Technology (MIT) – BS in Chemical Engineering – 6/6/39. [While at MIT was in ROTC/2nd Lt. 3/23/39/ 1st Lt.-CWS 5/24/39/Ft. Devens June 1939]. Chemical Engineer/"fire: inspector for insurance co., Buffalo, NY 6/1/39 – 2/4/42. Worked on father's farm. Res. NH. Enl. 2/4/42. Ser. No. O-378222. Ft. Bliss, TX. 2nd Lt., CWS, 1st CWS Troop Officers Course, Edgewood Arsenal, MD – Mar. 1942. 2nd Lt., assigned to Co. A, Camp Gordon, GA 6/19/42. Transf. Co. C, Camp Gordon, GA 10/1/42. Transf. HQ & HQ Co. & designated Battalion Intelligence & Meteorological Officer, Camp Gordon, GA 11/10/42. Recovered from pneumonia Jan. 1943. In Sicily hospital with jaundice 11/17/43-12/17/43. Returned to Italy 12/18/43. 1st Lt., HQ Co., MIA, 1/26/44, Italy (Anzio) SR Cem. Memorial Service held 7/16/44 All Saints' Episcopal Church, Petersborough, NH.

MERRILL, Stillwell A. Res. Collinsville, IL. Pvt. Attached to Co. I 5/28/42 Edgewood Arsenal, MD. Gunner (Pvt.). Pfc., Co. A, (Squad Leader), promo. Cpl. (temp.), Camp Gordon, GA 7/15/42. Pfc., HQ & HQ Co., LST 422 Survivor, 1/26/44 Italy (Anzio) – Purple Heart. Rescued by USS YMS 226. Taken to 93rd Evacuation Hosp.

MERRINGTON, Robert S. b. 1918 NY. Res. Westchester Co., NY. Enl. 8/3/43 New York City, NY. Ser. No. 42035053. Pfc., WIA (light – shrapnel), 4/11/45 Germany. Pfc., Co. C, 6/22/45 Innsbruck, Austria.

MERRITT, Herman L. b. 1923 NC. Res. Rowan Co., NC. Enl. 3/6/43 Camp Croft, NC. Ser. No. 34608553. Pvt., Co. C, MIA, 1/26/44, Italy (Anzio) SR Cem. Body recovered 1/26/44 by YMS 34 & buried at sea same day. Next of kin: Mary V. Merritt, Salisbury, NC.

MERRITT, Howard J. b. 1916 NJ. Res. Chester Co., PA. Enl. 7/9/42 Camden, NJ. Ser. No. 32271720. Pvt., Co. B, Camp Gordon, GA 7/28/42. Cpl., Co. B, cited for gallantry in action 12/8/43. Sgt., Co. B, 5/8/45 Innsbruck, Austria.

MESARIS, Francis A. ("Frank"). b. 1924 PA. Res. Exetor, PA. Enl. 10/5/42 Wilkes Barre, PA. Ser. No. 13116736. Pvt., Co. D, Camp Gordon, GA 10/9/42. Pvt., Co. D, MIA, 1/26/44, Italy (Anzio) SR

Cem. Earl Kann said Mesaris was only 15 years old and lied about his age to enlist.

MESSER, Jone O. Pvt. Attached to Co. H 5/28/42 Edgewood Arsenal, MD. Telephone Operator (Pvt.).

MESSERALLA, Edward A. b. 1924 MA. Res. Plymouth Co., MA. Enl. 3/5/43 Boston, MA. Ser. No. 31301693. Pvt., Co. C, WIA (light injure), LST 422 Survivor, 1/26/44 Italy (Anzio).

MESSINA, Armando J. b. 1923 NJ. Res. Richmond Co., NY. Enl. 2/22/43 New York City, NY. Ser. No. 32813253. Pfc., Co. C, 6/22/45 Innsbruck, Austria.

METCALF, Raymond O. b. 1915 VT. Res. Fulton Co., GA. Enl. 10/3/42 Ft. McPherson, Atlanta, GA. Ser. No. 14139514. Pvt., Co. D, Camp Gordon, GA 10/8/42. Transf. Co. A, Camp Gordon, GA, 12/16/42. Co. C, WIA Nov. 1943 Italy. Sgt., Co. D, MIA, 1/26/44, Italy (Anzio) SR Cem.

METCALFE, Alvin G. 2nd Lt., CWS, assigned Co. C, Camp Gordon, GA 11/10/42. 2nd Lt., Co. C, Sicily, 1943. 2nd Lt., Co. C, WIA (light), 12/7/43 Italy. Promo. 1st Lt. Sept. 1943 [?].

METTRICK, William J. b. 1918 PA. Enl. 12/19/42 Pittsburgh. PA. Pvt., Co. C, Camp Gordon, GA 3/18/43. Ser. No. 33406217. Pvt., Co. C, KIA, 1/26/44, Italy (Anzio), FL Cem.

MEUWENBERG [Meeuwenberg], Chris S. b. 4/29/1933 MI. T/5, Medic. Purple Heart, Sept., 1945. d. 6/26/2005 Fremont, Newaygo Co., MI.

MEYERSON, David W. ("Andy Jump"/"Dave") b. 1/26/1916. Lt., appointed company commander, Co. D, 1st CWS Training Battalion, Edgewood Arsenal, MD, March 1942. 1st Lt., C.W.S. 5/28/42 Edgewood Arsenal, MD 5/28/42. Billeting Officer, Camp Gordon, GA 7/11/42. Designated Plans & Training Officer, Camp Gordon, GA 7/27/42. Released as Battalion Training & Operations Officer & designated Asst. Battalion Operations & Training Officer, Camp Gordon, GA 9/15/42. Released as Asst. Operations & Training Officer and designated Operations & Training Officer, Camp Gordon, GA 9/25/42. Temporary Executive Officer, Camp Gordon, GA 12/2/42. Apptd. Summary Court (temp.), Camp Gordon, GA 12/19/42. Capt., Bttn. S-3, Sicily, 1943. Present as Executive Officer 11/26/43. Acting C.O. 12/1/43. Present as Maj. 2/14/44. Present as Executive Officer & Maj. 3/24/44. Commanded 83rd at various times at Anzio. Left 83rd 4/16/44 for 2nd CMB. Promo. Lt. Col. 2nd CMB Oct., 1944. Commanding Officer, 2nd CMB 1944-45. d. 9/28/2001 Houston, TX. Bur. Beth Yeshurun Cem. - Allen Parkway.

MICKIEWICZ [MICKOWITZ], Henry J. b. 1908 NY. Res. Bronx Co., NY. Enl. 7/9/42 Ft. Jay, Governors Island, NY. Ser. No. 32402318. Pvt., Co. B, Camp Gordon, GA 7/28/42. Present as Pvt., Co. B, Camp Gordon, GA, 1/9/43. Res. New York, NY May 1954.

MIDDLETON, Laborn B. b. 8/20/1920 AL. Res. Monroe Co., MS. Enl. 9/22/42 Camp Shelby, MS. Ser. No. 34426494. Pvt. Co. B, 10/14/42 Camp Gordon, GA. Pfc., Co. B, 5/8/45 Innsbruck, Austria. d. 11/4/1995 Aliceville, Pickens Co., AL.

MIGNELLA, Peter. b. 1921 Italy. Res. Mahoning Co., OH. Enl. 12/16/42 Cleveland, OH. Ser. No. 35526218. Pvt., Co. C, Camp Gordon, GA 4/10/43. Pfc., Co. C, MIA, 1/26/44, Italy (Anzio) SR Cem.

MIKLOS, Rudolph E. Pvt., Co. C, Camp Gordon, GA 4/10/43.

MILKLE, Carlton L. Pfc., Co. C. Purple Heart, Sept., 1945.

MILLAR, Edward W. b. 1906 PA. Res. Monmouth Co., NJ. Enl. 5/19/43 Newark, NJ. Ser. No. 32922809. Pfc., Co. C, 6/22/45 Innsbruck, Austria.

MILLER, Charles C. b. 1916 OR. Res. Washington Co., OR. Enl. 2/20/42 Ft. Lewis, WA. Ser. No. 39386160. Pvt. Attached to Co. H 5/28/42 Edgewood Arsenal, MD. Communication Sgt. (Sgt.). Cpl. (temp.), Co. B, promo. Sgt. (temp.), Camp Gordon, GA 11/4/42.

MILLER, Dan Alfred. b. 8/5/1920 Greer, SC. Res. Norfolk Co., VA. Enl. 9/21/42 Petersburg, VA. Ser. No. 33225543. Pvt. Co. D, 10/11/42 Camp Gordon GA. Pvt., Co. D, LST 422 Survivor – Purple Heart. Pfc., Co. D. Detached at Epinal, France 1944 and reassigned CMZ (Missing & Deceased), Paris, France. Res. Annandale, VA 2009. [enl. record gives name as Daniel & enl. at Richmond, VA].

MILLER, Edward C. Res. IL. Pfc., Co. C, 6/22/45 Innsbruck, Austria.

MILLER, Gwin. b. 1914. Res. Fulton, MS. d. 1/19/2005. Information provided by Alice Hartley.

MILLER, James H. b. 1913 PA. Enl. 9/25/42 Pittsburgh, PA. Ser. No. 33305690. Pvt. Co. A, 10/15/42 Camp Gordon GA. Transf. Co. C, Camp Gordon, GA, 12/16/42.

MILLER, Lawrence J. Pfc., Co. C, 6/22/45 Innsbruck, Austria.

MILLER, Marcus D. Res. Wilcox Co., GA. Ser. No. 6927686. Pvt., Co. D, KIA, 1/26/44, Italy (Anzio)

MILLER, Marion G. b. 1913 AL. Res. Wayne Co., MI. Enl. 9/22/42 Camp Shelby, MS. Ser. No. 34426577. Pvt. Co. B, 10/14/42 Camp Gordon, GA.

MILLER, Moses. b. 1905 Lithuania. Res. Kings Co., NY. Enl. 3/3/42 Camp Upton, Yaphank, NY. Ser. No. 32221877. Pvt. Attached to Co. I 5/28/42 Edgewood Arsenal, MD. Gunner (Pvt.). Pfc., Co. C, to Battalion Dental Office, Camp Gordon, GA 8/10/42. Pfc., Co. A, released from Dental Office duty, Camp Gordon, GA 9/7/42. Promo. Cpl. (temp.), Camp Gordon, GA 10/23/42. Cpl. Co. A, transf. Co. C, Camp Gordon, GA, 12/16/42. Pvt., Med. Det., KIA, 1/26/44, Italy (Anzio).

MILLER, Roy L. Pvt., Co. C, Camp Gordon, GA 4/10/43.

MILLER, Samuel W. Res. Kings Co., NY. 2nd Lt., assigned Co. D, Camp Gordon, GA 11/5/42. 2nd Lt., Co. D, WIA (from explosion of own shell hitting tree limb) 7/12/43 Gela, Sicily. Returned to duty 7/17/43. 2nd Lt., Co. D, KIA 9/12/43 Vietre sul Mare, Italy. Bur. Avellino.

MILLER, Verle V. M/Sgt., HQ Co., presented Bronze Star 8/24/45.

MILLER, William H. b. 1919 NJ. Res. Hudson Co., NJ. Enl. 7/7/42 Newark, NJ. Ser. No. 32389424. Pvt., Co. C, Camp Gordon, GA 7/28/42.

MILLIGAN, John H. Assigned from 65th Inf. Division as 2nd Lt., HQ & HQ Co., 7/23/45. Assigned Executive Officer, HQ Co. 7/31/45. Placed on Special Duty as Platoon Officer, Co. C, 9/10/45.

MILLIMAN, George R. b. 1920 MI. Enl. 2/11/42 Ft. Custer, MI. Ser. No. 36171477. Pfc., Co. A, promo. Cpl. (temp.) 7/24/45.

MILNER, Virgil M. b. 1914 AL. Res. Muscogee Co., AL. Enl. 9/19/42 Ft. McClellan, AL. Ser. No. 34391814. Pvt., Co. C, Camp Gordon, GA 10/8/42.

MINDRUM, Gordon Melvin. b. 7/7/1919 Fountain, MN. Triple degree in mathematics, physics & chemistry. Enl. 6/25/41. Res. Oelwein, IA. Ser. No. 0407946. 2nd Lt., Infantry June 1941. 2nd Lt., Co. D, Camp Gordon, GA 6/13/42. Assigned HQ & HQ Co., Camp Gordon, GA 8/24/42. Transf. Co. B, Executive Officer, Camp Gordon, GA 12/2/42. Capt., Co. B, Sicily, 1943. Sent to hospital 7/30/43 Salemi, Sicily. Capt., Co. B, cited for gallantry 11/11/43. Capt., Co. B, WIA (slight - leg), near Trapani, Sicily July 1943 – Purple Heart. Hospitalized with malaria Aug. 1943. Capt., Co. B, WIA (slight - leg – white phosphorous & fragment), near Ceppagna, Italy 11/13/43 [recommended for 3 different Silver Stars for 3 different actions on same day] - Silver Star & Purple Heart. Present as Capt., Co. B 11/26/43. Capt., Co. B, recommended for Silver Star for action on 12/20/43. Capt., Co. B, WIA (ear drum perforated by bomb), 2/17/44 Anzio, Italy. Still present as CO, Co. B, 3/24/44. Present as CO, Co. B, 5/9/44. Present on staff 7/19/44. Appointed Major 9/11/44. Assigned to 100th Inf. Div. 12/6/44. Reassigned to 83rd 2/12/45. Major, HQ Co., 5/8/45 Innsbruck, Austria. Bronze Star. Legion of Merit. Commanding Officer, 83rd CMB 7/23/45. Relsd. as Battalion commander for discharge 9/10/45. Distinguished Unit Badge. American Defense Service Medal. American Theater Service Medal. Germany Occupation Medal. EAME Service Medal. Bronze Service Arrowhead. Arrived in U.S. 10/10/45. Dischd. 9/30/46 as Lt. Col. Medical Degree – University of Iowa – 1950. University of Cincinnati. Res. Cincinnati, OH May 1954. M.D. Specialist, Gastroenterology. Internist & Occupational Medicine Specialist. Lt. Col., Medical Corps, disch. 7/26/65. On staff for General Electric where he worked on the space program (responsible for the medical hygiene of the capsule). Christ Hospital. Corryville VA Hospital (addiction psychiatry program) 2001. Res. Cincinnati, OH 2006. d. 5/12/2007 Cincinnati, OH.

MINSKY, ---------. In a photo belonging to L. Lew Henry, probably Co. A.

MIRINGOFF, Jacob. b. 1915 NY. Res. Suffolk Co., MA. Enl. 6/12/42 Boston, MA. Ser. No. 31133868. Pfc., Med. Det., WIA (light – contusion of shoulder), 6/2/44 Italy. Pfc., Med. Det., 5/8/45 Innsbruck, Austria. [probably same Jacob Miringoff listed Co. B].

MIRINGOFF, Jacob. Pfc., Co. B, 5/8/45 Innsbruck, Austria. [probably same Jacob Miringoff listed Med. Det.].

MISHINSKIE, Floren F. b. 1912 PA. Enl. 9/21/42 Harrisburg, PA. Ser. No. 33240936. Pvt., Co. C, Camp Gordon, GA 10/9/42.

MITCHELL, Joseph A. Pfc., Co. A, 5/8/45 Innsbruck, Austria.

MITCHELL, Millard G. b. 1912 NY. Res. Niagara Co., NY. Enl. 3/5/42 Ft. Niagara, Youngstown, NY. Ser. No. 32251795. Pvt. Attached to Co. B 5/28/42 Edgewood Arsenal, MD. Telephone Lineman (Pvt.). T/5, Co. A, Camp Gordon, GA 10/20/42. Rescinded, Camp Gordon, GA 10/21/42. Pfc., Co. A, promo. T/5, Camp Gordon, GA 8/19/42.

MITCHELL, Orren R. HQ, 11th Armored Div., assigned 1st Lt. (Mtr. & Ammo Officer), HQ & HQ Co., 83rd CMB 7/25/45. Bronze Star for action in Battle of the Bulge. One of first officers into Mauthausen near end of war. Res. Madisonville, TN.

MLYNIEC, Michael J. b. 1917 IL. Enl. 6/10/42 Chicago, IL. Ser. No. 36347659. Pvt., Co. D, MIA, 1/26/44, Italy (Anzio) SR Cem.

MOFFA, Rudolph F. b. 8/5/1924 NJ. Res. Camden Co., NJ. Enl. 6/25/43 Camden, NJ. Ser. No. 32952796. Pfc., Co. A, 5/8/45 Innsbruck, Austria. d. 12/7/2005 Atco, Camden Co., NJ.

MOLETRESS, Michael. b. 11/15/1918 PA. Res. Montgomery Co., PA. Enl. 12/19/42 Allentown, PA. Ser. No. 33485332. Pvt., Co. C, Camp Gordon, GA 4/10/43. d. 5/14/1999 Reading, Berks Co., PA.

MOLLIS, Michael E. b. 1918 RI. Res. Providence Co., RI. Enl. 10/14/44 Providence, RI. Ser. No. 31449755. Pfc., Co. C, promo. Corp. (temp.) 9/15/45.

MOLONEY, Martin J. ("Joe"). b. 10/25/1923 Chicago, IL. Attended Schurz High School, Chicago. Pre=war Occupation: Parmalee Transfer, Chicago, IL. Entered service Feb. 1943. Ft. Sheridan. Ft. Sill. Camp Shelby, MS. North Africa. Joined 83rd CMB as replacement for men lost on LST. Injured near Rome (fell from a tree and cut on rusty metal while stringing communications wire). Sent to hospital. Rejoined battalion 8/16/44 France. T/5, Co. A, 5/8/45 Innsbruck, Austria. Dischd. 11/6/45. Attended 1956 Reunion. Parmalee Transfer, Chicago, IL for 20 years. Postal worker for 20 years. Res. River Grove, IL 2009.

MONACO, Frank S. b. 1902 Italy. Enl. 9/24/42 Pittsburgh, PA. Ser. No. 33305495. Pvt. HQ & HQ Co., 10/15/42 Camp Gordon GA.

MONDOK, Joseph W. Pvt., Co. D, Camp Gordon, GA 4/10/43. Pvt., Co. D, WIA (light), 7/12/43 Gela, Sicily.

MONGIARDO, Dante. b. 1921 Italy. Res. Kings Co., NY. Enl. 7/20/42 Ft. Jay, Governors Island, NY. Ser. No. 32409101. Pvt., Co. D, Camp Gordon, GA 4/16/43. Pvt., Co. D, KIA, 1/26/44, Italy (Anzio) SR Cem.

MONROE, Samuel T. b. 1904 NJ. Res. Camden Co., NJ. Enl. 7/9/42 Camden, NJ. Ser. No. 32271796. Pvt., Co. B, Camp Gordon, GA 7/28/42.

MONTANA, John ("Killer"). b. 1920 PA. Res. Camden Co., NJ. Enl. 7/9/42 Camden, NJ. Ser. No. 32271740. Pvt., Co. B, Camp Gordon, GA 7/28/42. Pvt., Co. B, Camp Gordon, GA 9/25/42. Pfc., Co. B, arrived Salemi, Sicily from North Africa 8/1/43. T/5, Co. B, 5/8/45 Innsbruck, Austria. Attended 1956 Reunion.

MOODY, Calvin D. Res. Fulton Co., GA. Ser. No. 07004363. Pvt., Co. D, MIA, 1/26/44, Italy (Anzio) SR Cem.

MOODY, Frank J. Pvt., Co. A. Reportedly had the longest time overseas of anyone in the battalion having landed at England 7/13/42. Present 1/11/45.

MOON, Dale L. b. 1928 KS. Res. Tulare Co., CA. T/5, HQ Co. promo. S/Sgt. (temp.) 9/15/45. Air Corps. Re-enl. for Hawaiian Dept. 5/21/46 at San Francisco, CA.

MOON, Frank H. b. 6/20/1915 AL. Res. Floyd Co., GA. Enl. 9/17/42 Ft. McPherson, Atlanta, GA. Ser. No. 34442461. Pvt., HQ & HQ Co., Camp Gordon, GA 10/9/42. d. March 1976, Lindale, Floyd Co., GA.

MOORE, Baker. b. 1908 MS. Res. Noxubee Co., MS. Enl. 9/21/42 Camp Shelby, MS. Ser. No. 34426364. Pvt. HQ & HQ Co. 10/14/42 Camp Gordon, GA. "The Company wit and humorist."

MOORE, Layton H. Pfc., Co. A, 5/8/45 Innsbruck, Austria.

MOORE, Robert M., Jr. b. 1919 TN. Res. Shelby Co., TN. Enl. 9/23/42 Camp Shelby, MS. Ser. No. 34426931. Pvt. Co. C, 10/14/42 Camp Gordon, GA. Cpl., Co. C, MIA, 1/26/44, Italy (Anzio) SR Cem.

MOORE, Roger S. b. 1912 OH. Res. Darke Co., OH. Enl. 3/5/42 Ft. Thomas, Newport, KY. Ser. No. 35132588. Pvt. Attached to Co. C 5/28/42 Edgewood Arsenal, MD. Mechanic General (Pvt.). Pfc., Co. D, (Gen. Mech.), promo. T/5 (temp.), Camp Gordon, GA 7/15/42. T/5 (temp.), HQ Co., promo. T/4 (temp.), Camp Gordon, GA 11/4/42. Promo. Sgt. (temp.), Camp Gordon, GA 12/21/42. HQ & HQ Co. May 1943.

MOORE, Wayne R. b. 1/1/1899 PA. Enl. 9/26/42 Pittsburgh, PA. Ser. No. 33305729. Pvt. Co. C, 10/15/42 Camp Gordon GA. d. Oct. 1971 FL.

MOORE, William. In a Co. C group photo taken at Amalfi, Italy.

MORELAND, Henry A. b. 1923 NJ. Res. Essex Co., NJ. Enl. 7/8/42 Newark, NJ. Pvt., HQ & HQ Co., Camp Gordon, GA 7/28/42. Pvt., HQ & HQ Co., Camp Gordon, GA 10/1/42. Ser. No. 12094445. Pfc., apptd. Cpl., HQ & HQ Co. May 1943. Cpl., HQ Co., MIA, 1/26/44, Italy (Anzio) SR Cem.

MORGAN, Frank. Pfc. KIA, Germany. [Probably same as Frank P. Morgan].

MORGAN, Frank P. b. 1920 VA. Res. Spotsylvania Co., VA. Enl. 9/21/42 Richmond, VA. Ser. No. 33225776. Pvt., Co. B, Camp Gordon, GA 10/11/42. Pfc., Co. B, MIA, 12/12/44, Riquewihr, France. POW Stalag 7A Moosburg Bavaria on 7/30/45 reported deceased.

MORRIS, Joel J. b. 1921 MS. Res. Union Co., MS. Enl. 9/23/42 Camp Shelby, MS. Ser. No. 34426858. Pvt. Co. B, 10/14/42 Camp Gordon, GA.

MORRIS, Roy ("Mac"). b. 1920 TX. Res. Rusk Co., TX. Enl. 3/26/42 Tyler, TX. Pvt., HQ & HQ Co. transf. Co. B, Camp Gordon, GA 6/15/42. Cpl. (temp.), Co. B, promo. Sgt. (temp.), Camp Gordon, GA 12/12/42. Ser. No. 18108876. Sgt., KIA, 1/4/45, France, EP Cem. (ABMC) or 1/4/44, Italy (Muzzleblasts for Dec. 12, 1960). Silver Star.

MORRISSEY, Jeremiah J. b. 1916 IL. Res. Cook Co., IL. Enl. 3/6/42 Chicago, IL. Ser. No. 16068637. Pvt. Attached to Co. C 5/28/42 Edgewood Arsenal, MD. Telephone Operator (Pvt.). Pvt., Co. A transf. Co. B, Camp Gordon, GA 6/15/42.

MORSE, Stephen A. b. 1919 IL. Res. Du Page Co., IL. Enl. 3/9/42 Camp Grant, IL. Ser. No. 36323742. Pvt. Attached to Co. C 5/28/42 Edgewood Arsenal, MD. Telephone Lineman (Pvt.). Pfc., Co. C, promo. Cpl. (temp.), Camp Gordon, GA 8/17/42. Sgt., Bronze Star [Presented 11/20/44]. Pfc., Co. C, 6/22/45 Innsbruck, Austria.

MOSARIS, Frances. Res. Exeton, PA. Enl. At age 18. Believed d. on LST 422 1/26/44. [see Muzzleblasts article by Earl Kann Oct. 2005] – [see Frances Mesaris].

MOSER, Edward. Pvt., Co. C, Camp Gordon, GA 3/18/43. Ser. No. 37209274.

MOSER, Wayne M. Present at Saverne, France Winter 1944. Pfc., HQ Co., 5/8/45 Innsbruck, Austria.

MOSSALI, John. b. 6/27/1922 MA. Res. Middlesex Co., MA. Enl. 7/7/43 Boston, MA. Ser. No. 31365936. Pvt., Co. C, MIA, 8/29/44 Briançon, France. POW Stalag 7A Moosburg, Bavaria. Liberated 6/6/45. Res. Somerville, MA. d. 4/9/2005 Middlesex Co., MA.

MROSKA, ----------. Present in Co. A 8/4/45.

MUENKS, Roy J. Present in Co. A 8/4/45. Cpl., Co. A. promo. Sgt. (temp.) 9/14/45.

MULLIGAN, James. b. 1909 PA. Res. Philadelphia Co., PA. Enl. 9/22/42 Philadelphia, PA. Ser. No. 33335520. Pvt., Co. C, Camp Gordon, GA 10/9/42.

MULLIS, Marshall M. b. 10/10/1911 NC. Res. Cabarrus Co., NC. Enl. 5/14/42 Ft. Bragg, NC. Ser. No. 34303738. Pfc., Co. A, 5/8/45 Innsbruck, Austria. d. Mar. 1982 Concord, Cabarrus Co., NC.

MULQUEEN, Arthur C. b. 1909 NJ. Enl. 9/21/42 Ft. Myer, VA. Ser. No. 33197647. Pvt., Co. C, Camp Gordon, GA 10/11/42. Pvt., Co. C. Mentioned in the 12/12/42 issue of Smokescreen.

MUNCZENSKI, Sylvester M. b. 1920 PA. Enl. 9/18/42 Greensburg, PA. Ser. No. 33294289. Pvt. Co. C, 10/15/42 Camp Gordon GA.

MURPHY, Frank J. Grad. New Castle High School 1939. Res. Lawrence Co., PA. Ser. No. 33296785. Pvt., Co. D, Camp Gordon, GA 10/9/42. Pfc., Co. D, KIA, (mortar shell during tank battle) 7/12/43, Gela, Sicily.

MURPHY, John M. b. 1904 NY. Res. Hudson Co., NJ. Enl. 7/9/42 Ft. Jay, Governors Island, NY. Ser. No. 32402345. Pvt., Co. B, Camp Gordon, GA 7/28/42.

MURRAY, William C. b. 1916 WA. Res. Multnomah Co., OR. Enl. 7/10/43 Portland, OR. Ser. No. 39335491. T/5, WIA (light), 12/13/44 France [originally reported as LIA].

MUSCHINSKE, Jerome A. ("Jerry"). b. 11/12/1919 Milwaukee, WI. Marquette University & University of Wisconsin. Pre-war Occupation: Machining Methods Planner. Res. Milwaukee Co., WI. Enl. 3/10/42 Milwaukee, WI. Ser. No. 16049792. Pvt. Attached to Co. C 5/28/42 Edgewood Arsenal, MD. Mechanic General (Pvt.). Pfc., Co. C, (Gen. Mech.), promo. T/5 (temp.), Camp Gordon, GA 7/15/42. T/5 (temp.), Co. C, to Cpl. (temp.) 10/14/42 Camp Gordon, GA. Came down with malaria at Maori, Italy and evacuated. 602nd Base Ord. Bn. Dec. 1943 – Nov. 1946. Res. St. Francis, WI 2009.

MUTH, John. b. 1/18/1900 NJ. Res. Essex Co., NJ. Enl. 7/9/42 Newark, NJ. Ser. No. 32390462. Pvt., HQ & HQ Co., Camp Gordon, GA 7/28/42. d. June 1971 Maplewood, Co., NJ.

MYERS, Ezra. 5/8/1899 MS. Res. Neshoba Co., MS. Enl. 9/22/42 Camp Shelby, MS. Ser. No. 34426487. Pvt. Co. B, 10/14/42 Camp Gordon, GA. d. March 1970.

MYERS, Jim (James) Carr. b. 1916 TN. Res. Knox Co., TN. Enl. 9/5/40 Charlotte, NC. Ser. No. 14009814. Battery C, 34th Field Artillery, Ft. Bragg, NC, 1941. Served in North Africa with Battery C, 34th Artillery. Joined Co. B, 83rd CMB September 1943. Transf. Co. C, 83rd CMB 1943. Pvt., Co. C, KIA, 1/26/44, Italy (Anzio). Body recovered 1/26/44 by YMS 34 & buried at sea same day. Next of kin: Chrystal M. Myers, Knoxville, TN.

MYERS, John F. b. 1922 TN. Res. Davidson Co., TN. Enl. 9/18/42 Ft. Oglethorpe, GA. Pvt., HQ & HQ Co., Camp Gordon, GA 10/7/42.

Pvt., HQ & HQ Co., Camp Gordon, GA 11/21/42. Ser. No. 34371765. Pvt., Co. D, MIA, 1/26/44, Italy (Anzio) SR Cem.

MYSELS, Morris. b. 1921 PA. Enl. 11/12/42 Pittsburgh, PA. Ser. No. 33400171. Pfc., HQ & HQ Co., Camp Gordon, GA 4/10/43. Pvt., HQ Co., 5/8/45 Innsbruck, Austria.

NACCARATO, Ross J. b. 1916 PA. Enl. 12/22/42 Greensburg, PA. Pvt., Co. C, Camp Gordon, GA 3/18/43. Ser. No. 33413390. Pvt., Co. C, MIA, 1/26/44, Italy (Anzio) SR Cem. Body recovered 1/26/44 by YMS 34 & buried at sea same day. Next of kin: Micklena Naccarato, Monessen, PA.

NACZYNSKI, Joseph F. b. 1917 PA. Res. Beaver Co., PA. Enl. 3/18/42 New Cumberland, PA. Pvt. Attached to Co. A 5/28/42 Edgewood Arsenal, MD. Squad Leader (Sgt.). Pfc., Co. C, (Squad Leader), promo. Cpl. (temp.), Camp Gordon, GA 7/15/42. Order rescinded 7/28/42. Ser. No. 33164177. Sgt., Co. C, KIA (shell hit ammo dump), 9/27/43, Maiori, Italy, SR Cem.

NAIRN, William P. b. 11/1/1920 MD. Moved to Aliquippa, PA in late 1920's. Res. PA. Enl. 9/26/42 Pittsburgh, PA. Ser. No. 33305764. Pvt. Co. D, 10/15/42 Camp Gordon GA. Transf. Co. A, Camp Gordon, GA, 12/16/42. Mechanic. Pvt., Co. D, KIA, 1/26/44, Italy (Anzio), SR Cem. Body recovered 1/26/44 by YMS 34 & buried at sea same day. Next of kin: A. L. Nairn, Aliquippa, PA.

NAMIOTKO, Chester P. b. 7/17/1918 PA. Res. Luzerne Co., PA. Enl. 9/22/42 Wilkes Barre, PA. Ser. No. 33354544. Pvt., Co. B, Camp Gordon, GA 10/9/42. Cpl., Co. B, WIA (slight – shell burst in barrel – blast), 1/11/45, France. Cpl., Co. B, 5/8/45 Innsbruck, Austria. d. Mar. 1982 Wilkes Barre, Luzerne Co., PA.

NAPPI, Alfred. b. 1919 CT. Res. New Haven, CT. Enl. 12/14/42 Hartford, CT. Ser. No. 31274426. Pvt., Co. D, Camp Gordon, GA 4/10/43.

NATHANSON, David. Pfc., Co. B, 5/8/45 Innsbruck, Austria.

NEELD, Robert E. (Jr.). b. 1918 PA. Res. Luzerne Co., PA. Enl. 12/19/42 Wilkes Barre, PA. Ser. No. 33458342. Pfc., Co. C, KIA, 1/26/44, Italy (Anzio). Body recovered 1/26/44 by USS YMS 226 and turned over to Graves Registration at Anzio 1/27/44. Next of kin: Margaret Neeld, Ashley, PA.

NEIGHBORS, Benjamin W. ("Bennie") Radio Operator for Capt. Robert B. Smith, Co. C, 12/25/44. Pfc., Co. C, 6/22/45 Innsbruck, Austria.

NELSON, Carl. b. 1908 NY. Res. Kings Co., NY. Enl. 7/8/42 Ft. Jay, Governors Island, NY Pvt., Co. C, Camp Gordon, GA 7/28/42.. Pvt., Co. C, Camp Gordon, GA 9/25/42. Ser. No. 32401487. Pvt., Co. C, MIA, 1/26/44, Italy (Anzio). Noted for bravery on LST 422 1/26/44. SR Cem.

NELSON, Donald H., Jr. Assigned from 65th Inf. Division as 2nd Lt., Co. C, 7/23/45.

NEMETH, Joseph A. Res. Chicago, IL. Ser. No. 36650298. Pvt. Co. C, LST Survivor, 1/26/44 Italy (Anzio). Rescued by USS Pilot. Pvt., Co. C, WIA (light - S-mine), Minturno, Italy 3/26/44 – Purple Heart. Not hospitalized. Reported MIA 8/29/44 Briançon, France. Returned 8/31/44. Pfc., Co. C, 6/22/45 Innsbruck, Austria.

NESSERALLA, Edward A. b. 1924 MA. Res. Brockton, Plymouth Co., MA. Enl. 3/5/43 Boston, MA. Ser. No. 31301693. Pvt., Co. C, LST 422 Survivor, 1/26/44, Italy (Anzio) – Purple Heart. Pvt., Co. C, WIA (light), 5/26/44 Anzio, Italy. – Purple Heart with Oak Leaf Cluster.

NESTLER, Max E. ("General"). b. 1916 PA. Res. Miffingtown, Somerset Co., NJ. Enl. 8/27/42 Newark, NJ. Pvt., Co. D, Camp Gordon, GA 7/28/42. Pfc., Co. D, promo. Cpl. (temp.), Camp Gordon, GA 11/5/42. Ser. No. 32386797. Sgt., Co. D, WIA (light – shell fragment), 9/10/43 Vietre sul Mare, Italy. Returned to duty 9/11/43. S/Sgt., Co. D, WIA, 9/24/43 Italy – Purple Heart with Oak Leaf Cluster. S/Sgt., Co. D, MIA, 1/26/44, Italy (Anzio) SR Cem. Purple Heart 1944.

NEUMAN, Richard C. b. 1922 WI. Res. Milwaukee Co., WI. Enl. 12/7/42 Milwaukee, WI. Ser. No. 36288469. T/5, Co. A, promo. T/4 (temp.) 7/24/45.

NEWBY, Malcolm M. b. 12/16/1921 VA. Res. Henrico Co., VA. Enl. 9/21/42 Richmond, VA. Ser. No. 33225763. Pvt., Co. B, Camp Gordon, GA 10/11/42. d. Nov. 1983 Hollywood, Broward Co., FL.

NICHOLAS, John H. b. 1921 AL. Res. Jefferson Co., AL. Enl. 9/19/42 Ft. McClellan, AL. Ser. No. 34391877. Pvt., HQ & HQ Co., Camp Gordon, GA 10/8/42.

NICHOLS, Jean B. b. 1919. Grad. Long Beach Poly 1938. Res. Los Angeles Co., CA. Pre-war Occupation: Cook. Enl. 12/29/41 Ft. MacArthur, San Pedro, CA. T/5. Assigned to Co. B 5/28/42 Edgewood Arsenal, MD. Mess Sgt. (S/Sgt.). T/5., Co. B, promo. T/4 (temp., Camp Gordon, GA 6/16/42. T/4, (Mess), promo. S/Sgt., Camp Gordon, GA 7/15/42. Ser. No. 39015427. S/Sgt., Co. B, MIA, 1/26/44, Italy (Anzio) SR Cem. Next of kin: Mildred Nichols, wife.

NICHOLS, Theron E. b. 1915 GA. Res. Brooks Co., GA. Enl. 10/9/40 Jacksonville, FL. Medical Dept. Ser. No. 14027256. Pvt., Co. C, MIA, 1/26/44, Italy (Anzio) SR Cem.

NICKENS, Bynum Harding. b. 6/7/1921 TN. Res. Davidson Co., TN. Enl. 9/18/42 Ft. Oglethorpe, GA. Ser. No. 34371771. Pvt., Co. C, KIA, 1/26/44, Italy (Anzio). Body recovered 1/26/44 by USS YMS 226 and turned over to Graves Registration at Anzio 1/27/44. Only identification found on body was Soc. Sec. #. Re-interred 8/12/48 at Nashville Nat. Cem., Madison, TN.

NIERODA, Tophile. b. 1917 MA. Res. Berkshire Co., MA. Enl. 2/13/42 Ft. Devens, MA. Ser. No. 31065118. Pfc., Co. B, KIA, 12/12/44, Riquewihr, France.

NILESKI, Floyd G. b. 1915 PA. Enl. 12/7/42 Altoona, PA. Ser. No. 33566833. Pvt., Co. C, Camp Gordon, GA 3/18/43.

NIPPE, Clarence B. b. 5/17/1917. Pfc., Co. A, 5/8/45 Innsbruck, Austria. d. July 1978 Cedar Rapids, Linn Co., IA.

NITAWICK [?], ----------. HQ & HQ Co., Camp Gordon, GA. In a photo provided by William Gallagher.

NITZ, Anthony G. b. 1914 OH. Res. Toledo, Lucas Co., OH. Enl. 6/29/42 Toledo, OH. Ser. No. 35329960. Jeep driver for William S. Hutchinson. Pfc., HQ Co., WIA (light – enemy shell burst), 1/22/44 Anzio, Italy – Purple Heart. Returned to duty 3/16/44. Pfc., HQ Co., 5/8/45 Innsbruck, Austria.

NIX, Wade M. b. 1921 MS. Res. Tippah Co., MS. Enl. 9/18/42 Camp Shelby, MS. Ser. No. 34425844. Pvt. Co. B, 10/14/42 Camp Gordon, GA.

NIZIOLEK, Edmund S. b. 1922 OH. Enl. 3/12/43 Ft. Hayes, Columbus, OH. Ser. No. 35051773. Pvt., Co. C, MIA, 1/26/44, Italy (Anzio) SR Cem.

NOEL, James E. Pfc., HQ Co., 5/8/45 Innsbruck, Austria.

NOLAN, James M., Jr. b. 1/18/1909 PA. Res. Allegheny Co., PA. Enl. 3/5/42 Ft. Niagara, Youngstown, NY. Pvt. Attached to Co. B 5/28/42 Edgewood Arsenal, MD. Squad Leader (Sgt.). Pfc., Co. D, promo. T/5 (temp.), Camp Gordon, GA 9/7/42. Ser. No. 32251936. T/4, Co. D, MIA, 1/26/44, Italy (Anzio) SR Cem. [Middle initial R. 5/28/42 Edgewood Arsenal, MD].

NONE, Johnnie. Mentioned in the Feb. 25, 1945 entry of Sam Bundy, Co. A, diary, writing, "Johnnie None returned to the BN. He has been over the hill since we visited Rome and that was a long time ago, he is awaiting trial." [Possibly Johnnie R. Brown, see entry].

NORMAN, Robert E. Pfc., Co. B, 5/8/45 Innsbruck, Austria.

NORRIS, Warren R. b. 1911 NJ. Res. Camden Co., NJ. Enl. 7/9/42 Camden, NJ. Ser. No. 32271739. Pvt., Co. C, Camp Gordon, GA 7/28/42. Pfc, Co. C, Camp Gordon, GA 10/20/42. Pvt., Co. C, WIA (injured by tank trap) 7/14/43 Gela, Sicily.

NORWOOD, Morris. b. 1921 MS. Res. Smith Co., MS. Enl. 9/22/42 Camp Shelby, MS. Ser. No. 34426390. Pvt. Co. B, 10/14/42 Camp Gordon, GA. Cpl., Co. B, 5/8/45 Innsbruck, Austria.

OAKLEY, Paul J. Pfc., HQ & HQ Co., Camp Gordon, GA 4/16/43. Pvt., Co. B, sent to hospital 8/7/43.

OBENSHAIN, Raymond E. b. 1915 VA. Enl. 12/19/42 Roanoke, VA. Ser. No. 33528259. Pvt., Co. D, Camp Gordon, GA 4/10/43. Pfc., Co. D, MIA, 1/26/44, Italy (Anzio) SR Cem.

O'BERRY, Jesse. b. 9/3/1918 VA. Res. Isle of Wight Co., VA. Enl. 12/15/42 Richmond, VA. Ser. No. 33519642. Pvt., Co. C, Camp Gordon, GA 3/18/43. Pvt., Co. C, WIA (light injure), LST 422 Survivor, 1/26/44 Italy (Anzio). d. 4/15/1993 Smithfield, Isle of Wight Co., VA.

O'BRIEN, Jack. Pfc., present at Anzio, Italy 1/27/44. Temple University Grad. 1948. Accounting. Res. Philadelphia, PA May 1954. d. 1998. [possibly same man as John O'Brien, Jr.].

O'BRIEN, John, Jr. b. 1922 PA. Enl. 10/5/42 Philadelphia, PA. Ser. No. 13124628. Pvt., HQ & HQ Co., Camp Gordon, GA 10/9/42. T/5, WIA (light injure – truck ran off road), 8/17/44 France. Returned to duty 8/19/44. Pfc., HQ Co., 5/8/45 Innsbruck, Austria. [see entry for Jack O'Brien].

OCHABA, Martin. b. 1913 Austria. Res. PA. Enl. 9/4/42 Pittsburgh, PA. Ser. No. 33305510. Pvt. HQ & HQ Co., 10/15/42 Camp Gordon GA. Pfc., Co. C, MIA, 1/26/44, Italy (Anzio) SR Cem.

O'CONNOR, Bernard. b. 1915 NY. Res. Queens Co., NY. Enl. 7/8/42 Ft. Jay, Governors Island, NY. Ser. No. 32401657. Pvt., HQ & HQ Co., Camp Gordon, GA 7/28/42. Pvt., HQ & HQ Co., special duty Battalion HQ, Camp Gordon, GA 8/26/42. Mail & Message Center, Camp Gordon, GA Nov. 1942. Pfc., promo. T/5 (temp.), Camp Gordon, GA 12/3/42. HQ & HQ Co. May 1943. Sgt., HQ & HQ Co., WIA (serious), 11/30/43 Venafro, Italy. Died from his wounds 3/28/44. In a 1958 letter Lt. Col. Hutchinson says O'Connor died from his wound.

O'CONNOR, James J. Entered the service from Fromberg, MT. 1st Lt., Bronze Star for service 11/8/43 – 6/10/44. Lt., Co. A, at Anzio. 1st. Lt., Co. A, 5/8/45 Innsbruck, Austria. 1st Lt. Assigned 65th Inf. Div. 7/23/45. Two Year General Merchandise Store. Math Teacher (7 years), Fromberg High School. Res. Fromberg, MT, May 1954. Partner/O'Connor Construction Co. (pipelining). Attended 1954 Reunion.

O'CONNOR, John A. ("Pops"). b. 1898 NY. Res. Kings Co., NY. Enl. 7/7/42 Ft. Jay, Governors Island, NY. Ser. No. 32400758. Part of the original Edgewood Arsenal cadre. Pvt., Co. D, Camp Gordon, GA 7/28/42. Pfc., Co. D, promo. T/5 (temp.), Camp Gordon, GA 12/3/42. Mail Clerk for Co. D. Discharged for age a few weeks before battalion went overseas. Res. Jersey City, NJ May 1954. d. 7/5/1956.

O'DAY, Charles W. 2nd Lt., WIA (light – shell fire), 9/27/44 France. Purple Heart, 1944. 1st. Lt., Co. B, 5/8/45 Innsbruck, Austria. Company Commander, Co. B, Furth July 1945. Assigned 134th Chem. Mortar Co. 7/19/45.

ODOM, Charles L. b. 1922 MS. Res. Marion Co., MS. Enl. 9/21/42 Camp Shelby, MS. Ser. No. 34426312. Pvt. Co. B, 10/14/42 Camp Gordon, GA.

OGONEK, Henry J. b. 2/18/1902 NY. Res. Philadelphia Co., PA. Enl. 9/22/42 Philadelphia, PA. Ser. No. 33335606. Pvt., Co. A, Camp Gordon, GA 10/9/42. d. 6/22/2004, Philadelphia, PA.

OKERMAN, Gregory. Res. KS. Ser. No. 37518361. Pfc., Co. C, LST 422 Survivor, 1/26/44 Italy (Anzio). Pfc., Co. C, MIA, 8/29/44 Briançon, France. POW 9/20/44. POW Stalag 7A Moosburg, Bavaria. Liberated 6/12/45.

OLSZEWSKI, ----------. Co. D. Mentioned in Sam Kweskins memoir. Transf. from an artillery unit in Vosges. Always wore a cloth overseas cap and never bathed.

O'NEIL, Donald E. Pfc., Co. A, 5/8/45 Innsbruck, Austria. Mentioned in the May 1954 Directory.

O'NEILL, Ewart. b. 8/6/1919. 2nd Lt., Co. B, recommended for Silver Star for action on 12/20/43. Lt., Co. B at Anzio, Italy. 2nd Lt., Legion of Merit, 1944. 2nd Lt., Bronze Star 1944. 1st Lt., WIA (light – thigh – shell fire), 9/26/44 France. 1st Lt., Co. B, 5/8/45 Innsbruck, Austria. 1st Lt. Assigned 65th Inf. Div. 7/23/45. Attended 1958 Reunion as res. Houston, TX. d. 1/20/2003 Lake Jackson, TX.

OPLINGER, Paul E. b. 1920 PA. Res. Westmoreland Co., PA. Enl. 9/25/42 Greensburg, PA. Ser. No. 33294821. Pvt. Co. A, 10/15/42 Camp Gordon GA. Sgt., Co. A, on *LST 690* 8/9/44. Sgt., Co. B, 5/8/45 Innsbruck, Austria.

O'REAR, Lecil Elzie. b. 1923 AL. Res. Jasper, AL. Enl. 4/1/43 Ft. McClellan, AL. Ser. No. 34801583. Pvt., Co. C, MIA, 1/26/44, Italy (Anzio) SR Cem.

O'REILLY, Peter F. b. 1907 NY. Res. New York Co., NY. Enl. 12/14/41 New York City, NY. Ser. No. 12036768. Pvt., Co. A, on *LST 690* 8/9/44. Pvt., Co. A KIA, 10/3/44 France.

ORR, Eugene M. b. 10/11/1913 IA. Res. Louisa Co., IA. Enl. 12/21/42 Camp Dodge, Herrold, IA. Ser. No. 37651650. Pvt., Co. A, Camp Gordon, GA 4/10/43. Res. Mediapolis, IA. d. May 1982 Louisa Co., IA.

ORR, Fred K. b. 1902 PA. Res. Butler Co., PA. Enl. 9/25/42 Pittsburgh, PA. Ser. No. 33305680. Pvt. Co. C, 10/15/42 Camp Gordon GA.

ORTLIEB, (ORTIEF) Elwood L. b. 1924 KY. Res. Cold Spring, KY. Grad. St. Joseph Parochial School, Cold Spring, KY. Pe-war Occupation: Bardes Range and Foundry Co., Cincinnati, OH. Enl. 3/30/43 Ft. Thomas, Newport, KY. Ser. No. 35796415. Trained at Camp Wheeler, GA & Ft. Bliss, TX [another source says Camp Swift, TX].. Pvt., Co. C, MIA, 1/26/44, Italy (Anzio) SR Cem.

O'SAILE [OSAILE], Samuel L. b. 1924 TN. Res. Hendersonville, Sumner Co., TN. Pvt., Co. C, WIA (light injure), LST 422 Survivor, 1/26/44 Italy (Anzio) – Purple Heart. Rescued by USS Pilot. Returned to duty 2/7/44. Re-enl. 10/24/45.

O'SHEA, ----------, ("Doc"). Pfc. Co. A 8/4/45.

OSBORNE, Joseph. S/Sgt., HQ Co., 5/8/45 Innsbruck, Austria.

OSTER, Enoch. b. 10/31/1899 PA. Enl. 9/21/42 Harrisburg, PA. Ser. No. 33240913. Pvt., Co. B, Camp Gordon, GA 10/9/42. d. Dec. 1967, York, York Co., PA.

O'TOOLE, James C. b. 1922 PA. Res. Westmoreland Co., PA. Enl. 9/29/42 Greensburg, PA. Ser. No. 33391593. Pvt., Co. B, Camp Gordon, GA 10/20/42. Promo. T/5 (temp.), Camp Gordon, GA 12/3/42. [possibly same man as James J. O'Toole].

O'TOOLE, James J. T/5, Co. B, WIA (by 75 mm shell), Gela, Sicily 7/10/1943. d. ca. 1987.

O'TOOLE, Patrick J. Ser. No. 13129299. Pvt. Co. D, 10/15/42 Camp Gordon GA. Co. D. Mentioned in the 1/19/42 issue of Smoke Screen. Present Co. D, Camp Gordon, GA, 1/9/43.

OUTLAW, Lyndon O. b. 1921 MS. Res. Monroe Co., MS. Enl. 9/23/42 Camp Shelby, MS. Ser. No. 34426889. Pvt. Co. B, 10/14/42 Camp Gordon, GA. Pfc., Co. B, WIA (by 75mm shell), Gela, Sicily 7/10/1943.

OVERBY, Henry S. b. 1922 NC. Res. Johnston Co., NC. Enl. 9/14/44 Ft. Bragg, NC. Ser. No. 44012363. Pfc., HQ Co., promo. T/5 (temp.) 9/15/45.

OVERDORF, Paul D. b. 5/10/1922 PA. Enl. 12/14/42 Pittsburgh, PA. Ser. No. 33405773. Pvt., Co. D, Camp Gordon, GA 4/10/43. d. 12/8/1994 Monroeville, Allegheny Co., PA.

OVERSTREET, Eugene b. 1918 VA. Res. Bedford Co., VA. Enl. 9/21/42 Roanoke, VA. Ser. No. 33213315. Pvt., Co. B, Camp Gordon, GA 10/11/42. Transf. Co. A, Camp Gordon, 12/16/42. Pfc., Co. B, sent to hospital 8/16/43. Pfc., WIA (light), 11/20/44 France. Pfc., WIA (slight – shell burst in barrel – shoulder and arm burns), 1/11/45 France. Pfc., Co. B, 5/8/45 Innsbruck, Austria.

OWEN, Neal R. b. 1921 MA. Res. Essex Co., MA. Enl. 10/1/42 Boston, MA. Ser. No. 20115389. Pfc., Co. C, 6/22/45 Innsbruck, Austria.

OWINGS, Joe T. b. 9/9/1918 MS. Res. Monroe Co., MS. Enl. 9/23/42 Camp Shelby, MS. Ser. No. 34426689. Pvt. Co. B, 10/14/42 Camp Gordon, GA. Pfc., Co. B, 5/8/45 Innsbruck, Austria. d. 3/6/2002 Hamilton, Monroe Co., MS.

PACHINSKI, Walter. b. 1924. Res. PA. Enl. 4/23/43 Greensburg, PA. Ser. No. 33671785. Pvt., Co. C, MIA, 1/26/44, Italy (Anzio) SR Cem.

PADDIE, Eli, Jr. b. 1916 LA. Pfc., HQ Co., 5/8/45 Innsbruck, Austria.

PAGANO, Alphonse Anthony. b. 1918 NJ. Res. Bergen Co., NJ. Enl. 7/9/42 Newark, NJ. Pvt., HQ & HQ Co., Camp Gordon, GA 7/28/42. Ser. No. 32390577. Cpl., Co. C, MIA, 1/26/44, Italy (Anzio) SR Cem.

PAGE, DeWitt T., Jr. b. 1918 TN. Res. Will Co., IL. Enl. 3/5/43 Ft. Oglethorpe, GA. Ser. No. 34724971. Pvt., Co. C, MIA, 1/26/44, Italy (Anzio) SR Cem.

PAGENBERG, Thomas A. Pvt., Co. C, KIA (S-mine), Minturno, Italy 3/26/44. [see entry for Thomas E. Spangenberg].

PALERMO, Salvatore. b. 1906 Italy. Res. Middlesex Co., MA. Enl. 11/3/42 Boston, MA. Ser. No. 31229484. Pvt., Co. D, Camp Gordon, GA 4/10/43.

PALIOTTA, John S. b. 1924 RI. Res. Providence Co., RI. Enl. 4/21/43 Providence, RI. Ser. No. 31293454. Pvt., KIA, 1/26/44, Italy (Anzio)

PALMER, James F. b. 1923 SC. Res. Cleveland Co., NC. Enl. 4/1/43 Ft. Jackson, Columbia, SC. Ser. No. 34651217. Pvt., Co. C, MIA, 1/26/44, Italy (Anzio) SR Cem.

PALMER, Joseph H. b. 1921 GA. Res. Camilla, Mitchell Co., GA. Enl. 9/19/42 Ft. McPherson, Atlanta, GA. Ser. No. 34442987. Pvt., Co. D, Camp Gordon, GA 10/8/42. Pfc., Co. D, LST 422 Survivor, 1/26/44 Italy (Anzio) – Purple Heart.

PANOS, ----------. Present as catcher for Co. A ball team 8/4/45.

PAPACCIOLI, Frank A. ("Pappy"). b. 4/2/23 Bethlehem, PA. Pvt., Co. A, Camp Gordon, GA 4/10/43. Pfc., Co. A, on LST 690 8/9/44. Sgt. Co. A, 5/8/45 Innsbruck, Austria. Postwar occupation: U. S. Postal Service supervisor and postal credit union, Long Island, NY. d. 2/2/2004, Long Island, NY.

PARKER, Thomas M. R. b. 1923 MS. Res. Monroe Co., MS. Enl. 9/23/42 Camp Shelby. MS. Ser. No. 34426726. Pvt. Co. B, 10/14/42 Camp Gordon, GA.

PARKS, James H., Jr. b. 1921 NJ. Res. Camden Co., NJ. Enl. 7/9/42 Camden, NJ. Ser. No. 32271804. Pvt., Co. C, Camp Gordon, GA 7/28/42. Pvt., Co. C, Camp Gordon, GA 10/21/42. T/5, Co. C, MIA, 1/26/44, Italy (Anzio) SR Cem.

PARRA, William F. b. 1920 NJ. Res. Ridgefield Park, Bergen Co., NJ. Enl. 7/8/42 Newark, NJ. Ser. No. 32390110. Pvt., Co. D, Camp Gordon, GA 7/28/42. Sgt., Co. D, LST 422 Survivor, 1/26/44 Italy (Anzio) – Purple Heart. Sgt. Co. A, 5/8/45 Innsbruck, Austria. Postwar res. Park, NJ. Mentioned in the May 1954 Directory. Attended 1954, 1956, 1958 Reunions (res. Fair Lawn, NJ) & 1962 & 1966 Reunions (res. Saddle Brook, NJ.).

PARRISH, Aubrey Richard, Jr. b. 5/17/1917 Belington, Barbour Co., WV. Res. Kanawha Co., WV. Enl. 2/10/42 Ft. Thomas, Newport, KY. Ser. No. 35266102. Pvt. Attached to Co. F 5/28/42 Edgewood Arsenal, MD. Squad Leader (Sgt.). Pfc., Co. B, (Squad Leader), promo. Cpl. (temp.), Camp Gordon, GA 7/15/42. Sgt. (temp.), Co. B, promo. S/Sgt. (temp.), Camp Gordon, GA 12/12/42. Sgt., Co. B, recommended for Silver Star for action near Ceppagna, Italy 11/13/43. Sicily, Naples Foggia, Southern France, Northern France, Central Europe. Good

Conduct Medal, European African Middle Eastern Service Ribbon. Pvt., Co. B, 5/8/45 Innsbruck, Austria. Dischd. 10/23/1945. Postwar Res. St. Albans, Kanawha Co., WV. Dupont Chemical Co. Retired from U.S. Postal Service. d. 10/18/2000 Parkersburg, Wood Co., WV. No funeral service.

PARRISH, Wilburn A., Jr. Pvt., Co. B, 5/8/45 Innsbruck, Austria.

PARTHUM, Richard I. b. 1922 MA. Res. Essex Co., MA. Enl. 3/10/43 Ft. Devens, MA. Ser. No. 11057606. Pvt., KIA, 2/17/45, France (Alsace). Battalion Journal says Pvt., Co. A, 1st Platoon - KIA 2/19/45 by defective shell aerial burst.

PASQUALE, Jerry R. b. 10/25/1917 PA. Res. Westmoreland Co., PA. Enl. 9/29/42 Greensburg, PA. Ser. No. 33391679. Pvt., Co. A, Camp Gordon, GA 10/20/42. Transf. Co. B, Camp Gordon, GA, 12/16/42. d. 5/11/1997.

PASS, Floyd N. b. 1912 GA. Res. Spalding Co., GA. Enl. 9/25/42 Ft. McPherson, Atlanta, GA. Ser. No. 34444133. Pvt., Purple Heart: 1944. Pvt., Co. A, 5/8/45 Innsbruck, Austria.

PASSENI, ----------. Corp., Co. B, Camp Gordon, GA Nov. 1942. [See Angelo L. Possenti].

PATE, Cecil A. b. 1917. Enl. 9/10/41 Jacksonville, FL. Ser. No. 34072334. T/5, HQ Co., 5/8/45 Innsbruck, Austria.

PATRIE, Noel. b. 1921 Canada or New Foundland. Res. Somerset Co., ME. Enl. 12/12/42 Bangor, ME. Ser. No. 31282245. Pvt., Co. A, Camp Gordon, GA 4/10/43.

PAULSON, Raymond Ernest b. 12/17/1907 Bloomington, NE. Bloomington High School 1927. Hastings Business School. Bank Employee. 4 Campaign Stars: Rome-Arno, Southern France, Rhineland, & Central Europe. Pfc., Co. B, 5/8/45 Innsbruck, Austria. Postwar: Owned Movie Theater. Postmaster, Wakefield, NE 1954-1974. Retired. Planted over 2000 trees in Nebraska Nat. Forest. Res. Wakefield, NE 2009.

PAYNE, R. V. (Rio V.). b. 1923 NC (grave says 2/11/1919). Res. Cherokee Co., GA. Enl. 3/27/43 Ft. McPherson, Atlanta, GA. Ser. No. 34765768. Pvt., Co. C, KIA, 1/26/44, Italy (Anzio), SR Cem. Bur. Liberty Church Cem., Ball Ground, GA.

PEACEMAKER, Ed. Lt., Co. D. With 45th Chemical Lab Co., India, Dec. 1944.

PEACOCK, Thomas B. b. 1920 NC. Res. Wayne Co., NC. Enl. 11/27/42 Ft. Bragg, NC. Ser. No. 34464904. Cpl., Co. B, promo. Sgt. (temp.) 9/15/45.

PECK, Max. Pvt., Co. B, WIA (light-shell fragment in knee), 3/1/44 Anzio, Italy. Hospitalized.

PECK, Robert D. b. 1924 KY. Enl. 10/5/42 Richmond, VA. Ser. No. 13118175. Pvt., Co. B, Camp Gordon, GA 10/11/42.

PEHEMELLE, John J. Pvt., Co. A, WIA (serious – aerial burst – defective shell) 2/17/45 France.

PELAR, Edward V. b. 1924 OH. Res. Mahoning Co., OH. Enl. 7/16/43 Akron, OH. Ser. No. 35234020. Pvt., WIA (serious – aerial burst – defective shell), 2/17/45 France. Purple Heart. Res. Youngstown, OH.

PENDLETON, Frederick. b. 1907 NY. Res. Dutchess Co., NY. Enl. 12/16/42 Albany, NY. Ser. No. 32667392. Pvt., Co. B, Camp Gordon, GA 4/10/43.

PENNEBAKER, Joe W., Jr. b. 1924 PA. Res. Mifflin Co., PA. Enl. 7/23/43 Altoona, PA. Ser. No. 33763400. Pvt., Co. A, on *LST 690* 8/9/44. Pvt., Co. B, 5/8/45 Innsbruck, Austria.

PENNINGTON, William H. b. 11/9/1909 MS. Res. Monroe Co., MS. Enl. 9/23/42 Camp Shelby, MS. Ser. No. 34426707. Pvt. Co. A, 10/14/42 Camp Gordon, GA. Transf. Co. D, Camp Gordon, GA, 12/16/42. d. 1/17/1979 Greenwood Springs, Monroe Co., MS.

PENSACK, Joseph M. 1st Lt., CWS. 2nd Sep. Chem. Bn., Ft. Bragg, NC. Assigned as CO, Co. D, 83rd CMB, Camp Gordon, GA 6/12/42 [Smokescreen says Co. B]. 1st Lt., transf. 54th Chemical Co., Camp Rucker, AL Nov. 1942.

PENTON, Ira R. ("Slim") b. 1921 MS. Res. Harrison Co., MS. Enl. 9/28/42 Camp Shelby, MS. Ser. No. 34427779. Pfc., Co. A, 5/8/45 Innsbruck, Austria.

PERKOWSKI, John J. b. 1917 IL. Res. Cook Co., IL. Enl. 8/22/40 Chicago, IL. Field Artillery. Ser. No. 16001118. Pvt., Co. D, MIA, 1/26/44, Italy (Anzio) SR Cem.

PERLMAN, Philip [Phillip] J. b. 1919 Galacia, Poland. Emigrated to U.S. 1923. Grad. Yeshiva Rabbi Chaim Berlin. City College, NY. Res. Kings Co., NY. Enl. 6/30/42 Ft. Jay, Governors Island, NY. Ser. No. 32397469. Pvt., Co. D, Camp Gordon, GA 7/28/42. Pfc., Co. D, special duty Battalion Supply, Camp Gordon, GA 9/3/42. Pvt., Art Editor, Smokescreen, Nov. 1942. Pvt., Camp Gordon, GA 12/19/42. Transf. Base Hospital, Camp Gordon, GA. Postwar: Art Director for ad agencies. Began Judaica art & calligraphy 1976. Associate member Pastel Society of America. Oil & pastel portraits. Accredited Judaica artist & calligrapher with Commission on Synagogue Administration of the Union of American Hebrew Congregation. Res. Great Neck, NY 2009.

PERRONE, Leonardo G. ("The Mole"). b. 1918 NY. Res. Bronx Co., NY. Enl. 6/26/42 Ft. Jay, Governors Island, NY. Ser. No. 32395352. Pvt., Co. A, Camp Gordon, GA 7/28/42. HQ Co., left 83rd CMB Feb. 1943 to work in labs at Huntsville, AL.

PERRY, Warren D. b. 5/12/1924 Bluefield, Mercer Co., WV. Prewar occupation: Sales-Distrubution clerk. Res. Bluefield, Tazewell Co., VA. Enl. 11/16/42 Ft. Thomas, KY. Ser. No. 13130791. Military occupation: Signal RCO. Departed for French Morrocco 11/17/43, arrived 11/27/43. Cpl. WIA (injured in glider crash) 8/15/44 Le

Muy, France. Cpl., WIA (serious – shrapnel), 4/11/45 Germany. Departed for U.S. 6/27/45, arrived 7/8/45. Dischd. 11/26/45 Ft. George Meade. Campaigns: Rome-Arno, Southern France, Rhineland. Glider Badge, Good Conduct Medal, Purple Heart, American Theater Service Ribbon, EAME Service Ribbon with Bronze Arrowhead, and WWII Victory Ribbon.

PETCAVAGE, John S. Pvt., Co. B, Camp Gordon, GA 10/9/42. Transf. Co. A, Camp Gordon, 12/16/42. Ser. No. 13116751. T/5, Co. B, 5/8/45 Innsbruck, Austria. Res. Scranton, PA.

PETERS, Donald W. b. 1924. Enl. 4/24/43 Harrisburg, PA. Ser. No. 33508068. Pvt., Co. C, WIA (light), LST 422 Survivor, 1/26/44 Italy (Anzio). Pvt., Co. C, MIA, 8/29/44, Briançon, France. POW 9/20/44. POW Stalag 7A Moosburg, Bavaria. Liberated 6/6/45.

PETERSON, Eric H., Jr. ("Pete"). b. 4/6/1915 Millville, NJ. Rutgers University School of Agriculture 1937. Pre-war Occupation: J. P. Ritters and Seabrook Farms, Bridgeport, NJ. Enl. 1941 as Pvt. Present in Africa, Sicily, Italy. Lt., present at Venafro. Lt., awarded Bronze Star 1/22/44 Anzio, Italy. Present at Anzio Co. A, 1st. Platoon. Silver Star for gallantry 2/10/45. 1st. Lt., Co. B, 5/8/45 Innsbruck, Austria. 1st Lt. Assigned 65th Inf. Div. 7/23/45. Dischd. Dec. 1945. Railroad Perishables Inspection Agency. Union County Agricultural Office 1947 - 1981. Apptd. Senior Agricultural County Agent 1950. Teacher & Professor Rutgers 1959. President NJ Agents' Association. Twenty-five years Secretary of the Somerset Union Soil Conservation District. Retired 1981. Res. Westfield, NJ until 2000. Res. Neptune, Monmouth Co., NJ. d. 7/3/2001 Tinton Falls, NJ. Private interment.

PETERSON, Russell Hamilton. b. 10/3/1920 Milwaukee, WI. Graduate Charleston High School, Charleston, WV, 1938. Attended Morris Harvey College, Charleston, WV, 1939-41. Res. Kanawha Co., WV. Enl. 2/16/42 Ft. Thomas, Newport, KY. Pvt. Attached to Co. H 5/28/42 Edgewood Arsenal, MD. Instrument Sgt. (Sgt.). Promo. Cpl. 8/1/42. Cpl. (temp.), Co. D, Camp Gordon, GA 8/24/42. Personnel Clerk, for Co. D September 1942. Dislocated thumb during calisthenics, September 1942. Cpl. (temp.) Co. D, promo. Sgt. (temp.) Sgt., Camp Gordon, GA, 12/16/42. Camp Gordon, GA 12/22/42. Ser. No. 15090424. Cpl., Co. D, MIA, 1/26/44, Italy (Anzio) SR Cem. [middle initial N. 5/28/42 Edgewood Arsenal, MD].

PETRO, Carl Andrew. b. 1925 MA. Res. Suffolk Co., MA. Enl. 6/29/43 Boston, MA. Ser. No. 31364625. Pfc., Co. A, 5/8/45 Innsbruck, Austria. Postwar res. Revere, MA.

PETTIS, Phil L. b. 1903 MS. Res. Lafayette Co., MS. Enl. 9/22/42 Camp Shelby, MS. Ser. No. 34426637. Pvt. Co. A,10/14/42 Camp Gordon, GA. Transf. Co. C, Camp Gordon, GA, 12/16/42.

PEYTON, Joe P. b. 1912 TN. Res. Maury Co., TN. Enl. 3/19/42 Ft. Oglethorpe, GA. Ser. No. 34193564. Pvt., Co. C, KIA, 1/26/44, Italy (Anzio). Body recovered 1/26/44 by USS YMS 226 and turned over to Graves Registration at Anzio 1/27/44. SR Cem. Next of kin: Jessie Dale, Mt. Pleasant, TN.

PEZZELLA, Philip U. b. 1916 NY. Res. Philadelphia Co., PA. Enl. 12/2/40 Philadelphia, PA. Ser. No. 33025197. Pfc., Co. A, 5/8/45 Innsbruck, Austria.

PHENEGER, William W. b. 1921 PA. [another source says 1920] Res. Camden Co., NJ. 1927. Enl. 7/9/42 Camden, NJ. Pvt., Co. C, Camp Gordon, GA 7/28/42. Pvt., Co. C, Camp Gordon, GA 10/21/42. Ser. No. 32271769. T/5, Co. C, MIA, 1/26/44, Italy (Anzio) SR Cem.

PHILLIPS, Due T. b. 4/21/1921 MS. Res. Lafayette Co., MS. Enl. 9/22/42 Camp Shelby, MS. Ser. No. 34426568. Pvt. Co. B, 10/14/42 Camp Gordon, GA. d. 10/22/2001 Oxford, Lafayette Co., MS.

PHILLIPS, Elbert E. b. 1920 VA. Enl. 9/26/42 Baltimore, MD. Ser. No. 33377205. Pvt. Co. D, 10/15/42 Camp Gordon GA. Pfc., Co. D, KIA, 7/11/43 Gela, Sicily

PHILLIPS, Viron H. b. 1922 MS. Res. Newton Co., MS. Enl. 2/25/43 Camp Shelby, MS. Ser. No. 34623922. Pvt., Co. D, MIA, 1/26/44, Italy (Anzio) SR Cem.

PIERCE, Audie W. b. 7/19/1920 MS. Res. Smithville, Itawamba Co., MS. Enl. 9/23/42 Camp Shelby, MS. Ser. No. 34426779. Pvt. Co. C, 10/14/42 Camp Gordon, GA. Pvt., Co. C, LST 422 Survivor, 1/26/44 Italy (Anzio) – Purple Heart with Oak Leaf Cluster. Rescued by USS YMS 226. Taken to 93rd Evac. Hosp. Cpl., Co. C, WIA (light), 8/29/44 Briançon, France. Sgt., Co. C, 6/22/45 Innsbruck, Austria. d. 4/7/2004 Kenosha, Kenosha Co., WI.

PIERCE, James F. b. 3/6/1921 MS. Res. Jefferson Co., MS. Enl. 9/22/42 Camp Shelby, MS. Ser. No. 34426432. Pvt. Co. A, 10/14/42 Camp Gordon, GA. Transf. Co. C, Camp Gordon, GA, 12/16/42. Cook in Co. A 11/17/44 photo provided by Lawrence Ertzberger. T/4, Co. A, 5/8/45 Innsbruck, Austria. d. 5/13/1998, Jackson, Hinds Co., MS.

PIERPOINT, Robert W. T/5 (temp.), HQ & HQ Co., Camp Gordon, GA 4/2/43.

PIKE, Edwin G. ("Bud"). b. 10/4/1918 WI. Res. Portage, WI. University of Wisconsin (Chemistry) June 1941. 2nd Lt., CWS 6/10/41. Reported to Edgewood Arsenal, MD 6/25/41. 2nd Lt., Co. D, 1st CWS Training Battalion, Edgewood Arsenal, MD 7/11/41. Promo. 1st Lt., 3/7/42 Edgewood Arsenal, MD. Assigned commander Co. D, 83rd CMB May 1942. 1st Lt./Lt. Col., C.W.S. 5/28/42 Edgewood Arsenal, MD 5/28/42. Promo. Capt., Co. D, Nov. 1942. Capt., Co. D, Sicily, 1943. Also served as battalion S-3. Acting Battalion Commander 8/3/43 & for a few days as battalion Executive Officer Nov. 1943. Rotation orders arrived 7/30/44. Returned home Sept. 1944. Awarded Bronze Star for "meritorious achievement in connection with military operations in the Mediterranean Theater 6/1/43 - 7/12/43." Faculty, Chemical Corps School, Edgewood Arsenal, MD 1945. Entered Regular Army 1947. Air Chemical School, U. S. Air Force, Keesler Air Force Base, Biloxi, MS 1948 – 49. Transf. Chairman, Chemical Committee of the Tactical Dept., Infantry School, Ft. Benning, GA 1949 – 52. In Sept. 1952 assigned to Korea for ten months as Executive Officer, 2nd Chemical Mortar Bn., commanding officer of a smoke battalion, and Chemical Officer, 40th

U.S. Inf. Div. Sixteen months Administrative Officer & Plans & Training Officer, HQ Army Forces, Far East, Camp Zama, Japan 1954. Assistant Chief of the Plans and Operations Branch, Office of the Chief Chemical Officer, Washington, D.C. Dec. 1954 – June 1955. Chemical Section, HQ, U.S.A.F.F.E. University of Maryland (BA – Military Science & Masters in Industrial Management) – 1957. Assigned Chief's Office, Washington, D.C. Chief of the Plans & Policies Branch & Chief of the Military Personnel Branch of the Personnel Div., Office of the Chief Chemical Officer. Command and General Staff College , Ft. Leavenworth, KS 1959. Army Language School, Presidio of Monterey , CA (French) & Strategic Intelligence School, Washington, D.C. & Assistant Army Attache, Brussels, Belgium 1960 – 64. Assistant Commandant, U.S. Army Chemical School, Ft. McClellan, AL. Promo. Col. July 1963. 1964-1968 Professor of Mil. Sci. & Commandant ROTC, UW Madison 1968-1971. Ret. 1971, Sun Prarie, WI. Commander, U.S. Army Chemical Center and School June 1965. Medals & Honors awarded in military career: Bronze Star with Oak Leaf Cluster, Army Commendation Medal with two Oak Leaf Clusters, Distinguished Unit Citation with Oak Leaf Cluster, Korean Presidential Unit Citation, Meritorious Unit Commendation. Participated in four major campaigns in Italy in WW II and three major campaigns in Korea. Four overseas bars and the bronze arrowhead for three amphibious assault landings. d. Sept. 1983 Sun Prarie, Dane Co., WI.

PIMENTO, Jack. b. 1923 MA. Res. Highland Falls, Orange Co., NY. Enl. 3/19/43 New York City, NY. Ser. No. 32867710. Pfc., Co. D, LST 422 Survivor, 1/26/44 Italy (Anzio) – Purple Heart. Pvt. Steedle's Squad, 2nd Platoon, Co. B.

PINCINCE, Leo P. b. 1924 RI. Res. Woonsocket, Providence Co., RI. Enl. 4/23/43 Providence, RI. Ser. No. 31293257. Pfc., Co. D, LST 422 Survivor, 1/26/44 Italy (Anzio) – Purple Heart.

PINK, Saul. b. 1918 NY. Res. Kings Co., NY. Enl. 3/27/43 New York City, NY. Ser. No. 32876001. Pvt., Co. D, MIA, 1/26/44, Italy (Anzio) SR Cem.

PINTO, Thomas D. b. 1905 NY. Res New York Co., NY. Enl. 3/19/42 Camp Upton, Yaphank, NY. Ser. No. 32230395. Pvt. Attached to Co. I 5/28/42 Edgewood Arsenal, MD. Gunner (Pvt.). Pfc., Co. A, (Squad Leader), promo. Cpl. (temp.), Camp Gordon, GA 7/15/42.

PIPPIN, Robert W. b. 1921 MO. Res. St. Louis City Co., MO. Enl. 11/25/42 Jefferson Barracks, MO. Ser. No. 37400535. Pfc., Co. C, promo. T/5 (temp.) 9/15/45.

PIRANI, Eugene E. b. 8/22/1924 Brooklyn, NY. Res. Brooklyn, Kings Co., NY. Enl. 3/8/1943 New York City, NY. Ser. No. 32826634. Pfc., Co. D, LST 422 Survivor, 1/26/44 Italy (Anzio) – Purple Heart. Rescued by USS YMS 226. Taken to 93rd Evac. Hosp. Pfc., Co. A, 5/8/45 Innsbruck, Austria. Postwar occupation: Draftsman, Sheet Metal Workers of America, Local 28, 35 years. d. 3/5/1994 Mineola, Nassau Co., NY. bur. Holy Rood Cemetery, Westbury, NY.

PISTOIA, Ralph D. b. 8/7/1921 PA. Enl. 9/22/42 Philadelphia, PA. Ser. No. 33335558. Pvt., Co. A, Camp Gordon, GA 10/9/42. Pfc., Co.

A, on *LST 690* 8/9/44. Pvt., Co. A, 5/8/45 Innsbruck, Austria. Res. Philadelphia, PA May 1954. B-L-H Corp. (diesels). d. 2/12/2001 Philadelphia, Philadelphia Co., PA.

PITT, Garnett. b. 1914 AL. Res. Lawrence Co., AL. Enl. 9/19/42 Ft. McClellan, AL. Ser. No. 34391754. Pvt., HQ & HQ Co., Camp Gordon, GA 10/8/42.

PITTMAN, James H. b. 1924 TX. Res. Buce, Maricopa Co., AZ. Enl. 3/16/43 Phoenix, AZ. Ser. No. 39857814. Pfc., Co. D, (light injure in action), LST 422 Survivor, 1/26/44 Italy (Anzio) – Purple Heart. Returned to duty 2/2/44. Cpl., Co. D, WIA (non-battle injury – burned by exploding powder rings), Bouyon, France 8/27/44. Cpl.,Co. A, 5/8/45 Innsbruck, Austria.

PITTMAN, Robert B. Pfc., Co. A, 5/8/45 Innsbruck, Austria.

PLANKAR, William C. Pfc., Co. C, WIA (slight – shell burst in barrel – shrapnel ripped through helmet and cut back of neck), 1/9/45 France. Pfc., Co. C, 6/22/45 Innsbruck, Austria. Ser. No. 36715304.

PLANT, Francis T. b. 10/2/1910 MA. Res. Rensselaer Co., NY. Enl. 6/18/42 Ft. Jay, Governors Island, NY. Ser. No. 32355928. Pvt., Co. A, Camp Gordon, GA 7/28/42. Pfc., Co. A, transf. HQ Co., Camp Gordon, GA 11/4/42. Pfc., HQ Co. correspondent, Smokescreen, Camp Gordon, GA Nov. 1942. d. Aug. 1984 Troy, Renessalaer Co., NY.

PLASSMANN, Eugene Adolph. b. 6/7/1921 Bronx, NY. Stuyvesant High School (1939). Westinghouse Scholar 1939 World's Fair. Cooper Union College (NYC) - chemical engineering. Res. Bronx Co., NY. Enl. (Drafted) 6/17/42 / (8/17/42) Ft. Jay, Governors Island, NY. Ser. No. 32355253. Pvt., Co. A, Camp Gordon, GA 7/28/42. S/Sgt., HQ & HQ Co., LST 422 Survivor, 1/26/44 Italy (Anzio) – Purple Heart. Rescued by YMS 43. Reported safe 1/30/44 Morning Report. S/Sgt., HQ Co., 5/8/45 Innsbruck, Austria. HQ Co., 382nd Field Artillery Bn., 103rd Inf. Div., Aug. - Sept. 1945 (to be shipped back to U.S.). Dischd. 10/1/45. Drew maps for Rounds Away. Hastings College, NE (BS-Physics). Indiana University (MS-Physics). University professor of physics & math University of Kentucky. Moved to Los Alamos, NM, 1953. Laboratory in the Critical Assembly Group at Pajarito Site. Atomic Energy Committee, NM. d. 4/3/2009, Los Alamos, NM.

PLEASANTS, Thomas M. b. 1910 VA. Enl. 12/17/42 Charlottesville, VA. Ser. No. 33446456. Pvt., Co. D, MIA, 1/26/44, Italy (Anzio) SR Cem.

PLESKAC, Frederick. Res. Ulysses, NE. Ser. No. 37072854. Pvt., Co. A, KIA (enemy shell burst), 3/25/44 Anzio, Italy. Twin brother of Vincent M. Pleskac.

PLESKAC, Vincent M. Res. Ulysses, NE. Pvt., Co. A, WIA (light – shell fragment), 2/22/44 Anzio, Italy – Purple Heart. Twin brother of Frederick Pleskac. Glenn Helsel says he was transf. to another outfit soon after his brother was killed.

PLUMLY, Charles Lincoln. b. 1906 PA. Res. Philadelphia, PA. Enl. 9/22/42 Philadelphia, PA. Ser. No. 33335456. Pvt., Co. A, Camp Gordon, GA 10/9/42. Transf. Co. D, Camp Gordon, GA, 12/16/42. Sgt., HQ Co., 5/8/45 Innsbruck, Austria.

POHORELLEC, John J. b. 1912 IL. Enl. 4/22/43 Baltimore, MD. Ser. No. 33565888. Pvt., Co. D, WIA (light), 12/5/44 Zellenberg, France. Returned to duty 2/6/45. Pvt., WIA (serious), 2/17/45 France.

POIRIER, Joseph M. Res. MI. Ser. No. 36583989. Pvt., Co. D, MIA, 1/26/44, Italy (Anzio) SR Cem.

POKORSKY, Stanley. b. 1917 PA. Polish descent. Moved NJ. ca. 1922. Cherry Hill, NJ. Pre-war Occupation: Assistant Golf Pro, Merchantville (NJ) Country Club. Res. Burlington Co., NJ. Enl. 7/9/42 Camden, NJ. Ser. No. 32271729. Pvt., Co. C, Camp Gordon, GA 7/28/42. Cpl., Co. C, MIA, 1/26/44, Italy (Anzio) SR Cem.

POLIQUIN, Gerard E. Pfc., Co. C, present 1/11/45. Pfc., Co. C, 6/22/45 Innsbruck, Austria. [Possibly Gerard A. Poliquin. b. 1925 NH. Res. Hillsborough Co., NH. Enl. 1/19/44 Manchester, NH. Ser. No. 31376317].

POLLOCK, Bernard D. b. 11/10/1916 OH. Res. Summit Co., OH. Enl. 3/9/42 Camp Perry, Lacarne, OH. Ser. No. 35287584. Pvt. Attached to Co. C 5/28/42 Edgewood Arsenal, MD. Radio Operator (Cpl. & Pvt.). Pvt., HQ & HQ Co. transf. Co. C, Camp Gordon, GA 6/15/42. d. 2/15/1988.

POLZER, Oscar A. b. 8/19/1906 PA. Enl. 12/22/42 Pittsburgh, PA. Ser. No. 33416506. Pvt., Co. C, Camp Gordon, GA 3/18/43. d. Sept. 1982, Pittsburgh, Allegheny Co., PA.

PONGRAC, Stephen G. b. 9/26/1916 PA. Res. Allegheny Co., PA. Enl. 2/11/42 New Cumberland, PA. Ser. No. 33149967. Pfc., Co. A, 5/8/45 Innsbruck, Austria. d. Dec. 1977 Pittsburgh, Allegheny Co., PA.

POOLE, William P. Pfc., Co. A, 5/8/45 Innsbruck, Austria.

PORCHI, Joseph J. b. 1923 Italy. Res. NY. Enl. 2/19/43 New York City, NY. Ser. No. 32810716. Pvt., KIA, 1/26/44, Italy (Anzio) SR Cem.

PORTERFIELD, Arnold J. b. 1922 TN. Res. Murfreesboro, Rutherford Co., TN. Enl. 9/17/42 Ft. Oglethorpe, GA. Ser. No. 34371615. Pvt., Co. C, LST 422 Survivor, 1/26/44 Italy (Anzio) – Purple Heart. Rescued by USS Pilot. Cpl., Co. C, 6/22/45 Innsbruck, Austria.

PORTERFIELD, John F. b. 1920 AL. Res. Montgomery Co., AL. Enl. 9/19/42 Ft. McClellan, AL. Ser. No. 34391786. Pvt., Co. A, Camp Gordon, GA 10/8/42. Pfc., Co. A, (Radio Operator), Anzio, Italy 1/26/44. Sgt., Co. A, evacuated from LST 690 8/9/44.

PORTNER, Jacob L. ("Jake"). b. 1922 PA. Res. York Co., PA. Enl. 10/5/42 Harrisburg, PA. Ser. No. 13093253. Pvt., HQ & HQ Co., Camp Gordon, GA 10/9/42. Pvt., Co. B, present with AOU party, Gela, Sicily, 7/10/43. Pvt., Co. B, sent to hospital 8/11/43. Pfc./Cpl.,

Bronze Star [Presented 11/20/44]. Pfc., Co. B, 5/8/45 Innsbruck, Austria. Res. Red Lion, PA May 1954. Employed by S. Morgan Smith Co. Attended 1958 Reunion as res. Red Lion, PA.

POSLUSZNY, Frank L. b. 1921 CT. Res. Wallington, Bergen Co., NJ. Enl. 7/9/42 Newark, NJ. Ser. No. 32390589. Pvt., HQ & HQ Co., Camp Gordon, GA 7/28/42. Pfc., HQ Co., promo. Cpl. (temp.), Camp Gordon, GA 12/19/42. Sgt., Co. D, LST 422 Survivor, 1/26/44 Italy (Anzio) – Purple Heart. Sgt. Co. A, 5/8/45 Innsbruck, Austria.

POSSENTI, Angelo L. b. 1917 PA. Res. Cumberland Co., NJ. Enl. 2/26/42 Ft. Dix, NJ. Ser. No. 32242270. Sgt., Co. B, sent to hospital (56th Medical, Trapani) 8/5/43. Returned to duty 8/14/43. Sgt., Co. B, KIA, 12/8/43 San Pietro, Italy. [See Passeni].

POTTER, Mabry L. b. 1921 TX. Res. Callahan Co., TX. Enl. 7/14/42 Abilene, TX. Ser. No. 38134336. Pfc., Co. D, KIA, 1/26/44, Italy (Anzio)

POUNDS, Caudell. b. 5/23/1919 AL. Res. Marshall Co., AL. Enl. 5/13/43 at Ft. McClellan, AL. Ser. No. 34806077. Pvt., Co. A on LST 690 8/9/44. d. Aug. 1983, Boaz, AL.

POUPARI, Eugene E. Cpl., Co. C, promo. T/4 (temp.) 9/15/45.

POWELL, Harmon F. b. 1917 TX. Res. Wood Co., TX. Enl. 9/12/42 Tyler, TX. Ser. No. 38202149. Pvt., Co. C, Camp Gordon, GA 3/18/43.

POWELL, Lawrence H. b. 2/5/1922 Zion, IL. Ambridge (PA) High School. Pre-war Occupation: Propeller Inspector / Curtis-Wright Enl. 9/25/42. Pvt. Co. A, 10/15/42 Camp Gordon GA. Joined 83rd CMB Oct. 1942. Co. A. Cpl., Co. B, 5/8/45 Innsbruck, Austria. Dischd. Oct. 1945. Pipefitter. Retired 1985. Contributed to MFP 1997. Res. Beaver, PA 2005. d. 4/3/2006.

POWERS, Byron. b. 1921 AR. Res. Olive Branch, De Soto Co., MS. Enl. 9/23/42 Camp Shelby, MS. Ser. No. 34426793. Pvt. Co. A, 10/14/42 Camp Gordon, GA. Sgt., Co. A, on LST 690 8/9/44. Sgt. Co. A, accidentally wounded (shot below knee, middle calf) by Radio Operator Robert Baldwin who was cleaning his gun. Sgt. Co. A, 5/8/45 Innsbruck, Austria.

POWERS, Ryland L. b. 2/22/1918 VA. Res. Norfolk Co., VA. Enl. 9/21/42 Richmond, VA. Ser. No. 33225784. Pvt., Co. A, Camp Gordon, GA 10/11/42. d. July 1983 Moyock, Currituck Co., NC.

POYNOR, Wesley L. b. 6/2/1918, TX. Res. Eastland, Eastland Co., TX. Enl. 3/18/42 Camp Wolters, TX. Pvt. Ser. No. 38099857. [In notebook carried by Leonard Turan]. d. 8/10/2000 Ranger, Eastland Co., TX.

PRATT, ----------. Present Co. D, Motor Pool, Camp Gordon, GA, 1/9/43.

PRESHLOCK, Michael. b. 1920 PA. Enl. 9/21/42 Harrisburg, PA. Ser. No. 33240925. Pvt., Co. B, Camp Gordon, GA 10/9/42. Sgt., Co. B, MIA 12/12/44, Riquewihr, France. POW Stalag 13C Hammelburg.

Liberated 6/19/45.

PRESLEY, Robert G. b. 1919 MI. Res. Bay Co., MI. Enl. 2/11/42 Ft. Custer, MI. Ser. No. 36171539. Pvt. Attached to Co. H 5/28/42 Edgewood Arsenal, MD. Gunner (Pvt.). Pvt., Co. C transf. Co. D, Camp Gordon, GA 6/15/42.

PRESTON, Samuel C. b. 1917 KY. Enl. 12/17/42 Cincinnati, OH. Ser. No. 35678326. Pfc., Co. C, 6/22/45 Innsbruck, Austria.

PRICE, Charles A., Jr. Present 1/1/45. 2nd. Lt., Co. A, 5/8/45 Innsbruck, Austria. 2nd Lt. Assigned HQ 11th Armored Div. 7/23/45.

PRICE, Charles H. b. 1918 NY. Res. Chautauqua Co., NY. Enl. 3/5/42 Ft. Niagara, Youngstown, NY. Ser. No. 32251912. Pvt. Attached to Co. B 5/28/42 Edgewood Arsenal, MD. Communication (Cpl.). Pfc., HQ & HQ Co., (Clerk, Battalion HQ), promo. T/5 (temp.), Camp Gordon, GA 7/15/42. T/5 (temp.), HQ & HQ Co., promo. Sgt. (temp.), Camp Gordon, GA 8/6/42.

PRICE, Charlie M. Res. GA. Pvt., Co. D, Camp Gordon, GA 4/10/43. Ser. No. 34585580. Pfc., Co. D, MIA, 1/26/44, Italy (Anzio) SR Cem.

PRICE, John N. b. 1920 PA. Enl. 12/12/42 Altoona, PA. Ser. No. 33567115. Pvt., Co. A, Camp Gordon, GA 4/10/43. Pvt., Co. A, MIA, 1/26/44, Italy (Anzio) SR Cem.

PRICE, Richard H. b. 1918 PA. Enl. 10/5/42 Philadelphia, PA. Ser. No. 13124664. Pvt., Co. A, Camp Gordon, GA 10/9/42. Cpl., Co. A on *LST 690* 8/9/44. T/4, Co. A, 5/8/45 Innsbruck, Austria.

PRIEST, O'Neal. b. 1911 MS. Res. Lee Co., MS. Enl. 9/22/42 Camp Shelby, MS. Ser. No. 34426598. Pvt. Co. A, transf. Co. C, Camp Gordon, GA, 12/16/42. Pvt., Co. A, 5/8/45 Innsbruck, Austria.

PRINTZ, Robert G. Pvt. Attached to Co. C 5/28/42 Edgewood Arsenal, MD. Auto Rifleman (Pvt.).

PROBST, Raymond X. b. 10/8/1914 IN. Res. Berrien Co., MI. Enl. 12/15/42 Kalamazoo, MI. Ser. No. 36414421. Pvt., Co. A, Camp Gordon, GA 4/10/43. d. 3/14/1993 Niles, Berrien Co., MI.

PRUIETT, Charles [Charlie] C. b. 5/10/1922 MO. Res. Caruthersville, Pemiscot Co., MO. Enl. 12/9/42 Jefferson Barracks, MO. Ser. No. 37402826. Pvt., Co. C, Camp Gordon, GA 4/10/43. Pvt., Co. C, LST 422 Survivor, 1/26/44 Italy (Anzio) – Purple Heart. Sgt., Co. C, 6/22/45 Innsbruck, Austria. d. 9/9/2001.

PUCKETT, Roland K. Res. Wauzeka, WI. Pfc., Co. D, LST 422 Survivor, 1/26/44 Italy (Anzio) – Purple Heart. Sgt. Co. A, 5/8/45 Innsbruck, Austria.

PUGH, Lewis D. b. 1925. Res. Swoyerville, PA. Enl. 4/15/43 Wilkes Barre, PA. Ser. No. 33603513. Pvt., Co. D, KIA, 1/26/44, Italy (Anzio). Killed on 19th birthday.

PULLEN, Raymond G. b. 1919 MS. Res. Quincy, Monroe Co., MS. Enl. 9/23/42 Camp Shelby, MS. Ser. No. 34426691. Pvt. Co. A, 10/14/42 Camp Gordon, GA. Cpl., Co. A, on *LST 690* 8/9/44. T/4, Co. A, 5/8/45 Innsbruck, Austria.

PULTORAK, Chester E. Pvt., Co. C, Camp Gordon, GA 4/10/43. Pvt., Co. C, WIA (light - enemy shell), 9/16/43, Maiori, Italy.

PUTNAM [PUTMAN], Elmer E. b. 1920 PA. Enl. 9/21/42 Altoona, PA. Ser. No. 33253619. Pvt., Co. C, Camp Gordon, GA 10/9/42. Pfc., Co. C, MIA, 1/26/44, Italy (Anzio) SR Cem.

QUIMBY, Edward W. b. 1914 PA. Enl. 10/5/42 Philadelphia, PA. Ser. No. 13124719. Pvt., HQ & HQ Co., Camp Gordon, GA 10/9/42. Pfc., HQ & HQ Co., WIA (light), 11/30/43 Venafro, Italy.

QUINA, Herbert R. b. 1915 FL. Res. Wash., D.C. Enl. 6/19/42 Ft. Jay. Governors Island, NY. Ser. No. 32356573. Pvt., Co. C, Camp Gordon, GA 7/28/42. Pfc., Co. C, promo. T/5 (temp.), Camp Gordon, GA 12/29/42. Sgt., Co. C, LST 422 Survivor, 1/26/44 Italy (Anzio) – Purple Heart.

RABAIOTTI, Antonio ("Tony"/"Rabbit"). b. 1923 RI. Res. Providence, Providence Co., RI. Enl. 4/8/43 Providence, RI. Ser. No. 31292605. Pfc., Co. D, WIA (light injure-shrapnel-temporarily paralyzed in both arms), LST 422 Survivor, 1/26/44 Italy (Anzio) – Purple Heart. Rescued by USS YMS 226. Taken to 93rd Evac. Hosp. Pfc., Co. D, WIA (non-battle injury – burned by exploding powder rings), Bouyon, France 8/27/44. Cpl., Co. D, WIA (light-shrapnel-left leg & right wrist), 12/5/44 Zellenberg, France. Cpl., Co. A, 5/8/45 Innsbruck, Austria. Dischgd. 11/3/45. Purple Heart with Oak Leaf Cluster. Res. Providence, RI May 1954. Postal Employee. Attended 1956 reunion. Res. Johnston, PA 2009.

RADTKE, Clifford J. b. 1917 WI. Res. Union Co., NJ. Enl. 6/24/42 Newark, NJ. Ser. No. 32385821. Pvt., HQ & HQ Co., Camp Gordon, GA 7/28/42. Pfc., HQ Co., promo. Cpl. (temp.), Camp Gordon, GA 11/3/42. Present, Cpl., HQ Co., Camp Gordon, GA, 1/9/43.

RAKES, Cecil. b. 1920 VA. Res. Dickerson Co., VA. Enl. 10/6/42 Abingdon, VA. Ser. No. 33214479. Pvt., Co. C, Camp Gordon, GA 10/11/42.

RAJCEVICH, Peter. Pvt., Co. B, 5/8/45 Innsbruck, Austria. [Steedle's Squad, 2nd Platoon, Co. B].

RAMER, Joseph A. b. 10/28/1921 PA. Res. Philadelphia Co., PA. Enl. 9/22/42 Philadelphia, PA. Ser. No. 33335531. Pvt., Co. A, Camp Gordon, GA 10/9/42. Cpl., Co. A, 5/8/45 Innsbruck, Austria. Company Clerk. d. 11/8/1986 PA.

RAMSEY, George W., Jr. b. 1923 CO. Res. Lyons, Boulder Co., CO. Enl. 3/12/43 Denver, CO. Ser. No. 37343225. Pfc., Co. D, LST 422 Survivor, 1/26/44 Italy (Anzio) – Purple Heart. Rescued by USS Pilot. Pfc., WIA (light), 2/14/45 France. Pfc., Co. A, 5/8/45 Innsbruck, Austria.

RAMSEY, James C. b. 1921 AL. Res. St. Clair Co., AL. Enl. 9/29/42 Ft. McClellan, AL. Ser. No. 34392782. Pvt., Co. C, Camp Gordon, GA 10/8/42.

RAMSEY, James W., Jr. b. 1921 GA. Res. Richmond Co., GA. Enl. 9/23/42 Ft. McPherson, Atlanta, GA. Pvt., Co. D, Camp Gordon, GA 10/12/42. Ser. No. 34443707. Pfc., Co. D, MWIA (from explosion of own shell hitting tree limb) 7/12/43, Gela, Sicily. d. 7/14/43, Tunisia, NA Cem. (ABMC) or 7/11/43 (Muzzleblasts for Dec. 12, 1960).

RAMSEY, William Carrington. b. 1/26/1916 VA. Res. Bedford Co. VA. Enl. 9/21/42 Roanoke, VA. Ser. No. 33213333. Pvt., Co. C, Camp Gordon, GA 10/11/42. Pfc., Co. C. d. 1/3/2007 Lynchburg, VA.

RAND, Fred Griffith, Jr. b. 7/28/1921 TX. Enl. Jan. 1943. Joined Co. A, 83rd CMB July 1944. Co.'s A & D. Promo. 2nd Lt., promo. 1st Lt. 8/17/44. 1st. Lt., Co. B, 5/8/45 Innsbruck, Austria. Purple Heart. Dischd. May 1946. Capt. Army Reserve. Retired as Col. Res. Pasadena, TX May 1954. Mathieson Chemical Corp. Chemical Engineer, Olin & Mobil Fertilizer Plant. Attended 1956 reunion. Retired 1981. Contributed to MFP 1997. d. 12/25/ 2004 Pasadena, Harris Co., TX.. bur. Houston Nat. Cem., Houston, TX.

RANDOLPH, Delise J. b. 2/17/1921 MS. Res. Monroe Co., MS. Enl. 9/22/42 Camp Shelby, MS. Ser. No. 34426331. Pvt. Co. B, 10/14/42 Camp Gordon, GA. d. 4/8/1999 Nettleton. Itawamba Co., MS.

RANKIN, Ralph T. Res. Oklahoma City, OK. 2nd Lt., CWS, assigned to HQ & HQ Co., Camp Gordon, GA 9/17/42. 1st. Lt., Co. C, Sicily, 1943. Ser. No. O-365551. Promoted Capt. 11/1/43, Co. C. Silver Star presented 10/8/43 for performance at Chiunzi Pass, Maiori, Italy. Present as CO, Co. C 11/26/43. 1st Lt., Co. C, MIA, 1/26/44, Italy (Anzio) SR Cem.

RAPP, Earl Wellington ("Rappy"). b. 5/20/1921 Corunna, MI. Five seasons Minor League Baseball prior to war. Enl. 9/20/42 Baltimore, MD. Ser. No. 33377259. Pvt. Co. B, 10/15/42 Camp Gordon GA. Transf. Co. A, Camp Gordon, 12/16/42. WIA (tendons behind the knee). Sgt., Co. B, 5/8/45 Innsbruck, Austria. Minor League Baseball 1945-48. Professional Baseball 1949 (Detroit Tigers & Chicago White Sox). Pacific Coast League 1950. Returned to Major League Baseball 1951 (New York Giants – Browns – Senators). Minor League Baseball 1953. Retired & became baseball scout. Attended 1962 & 1966 Reunions as res. Swedesboro, NJ. d. 2/13/1992 Swedesboro, NJ.

RATAJCZAK, Henry R. b. 1914 NJ. Res. Middlesex Co., NJ. Enl. 6/22/42 Newark, NJ. Ser. No. 32385275. Pvt., Co. C, Camp Gordon, GA 7/28/42.

RAUM, Elmer J. b. 1902 District of Columbia. Res. District of Columbia. Enl. 9/21/42 Ft. Myer, VA. Ser. No. 33197635. Pvt., Co. B, Camp Gordon, GA 10/11/42.

REA, Edmund Bernard. b. 1915 VA. Res. Henry Co., VA. Enl. 9/21/42 Roanoke, VA. Ser. No. 33213351. Pvt. Co. D, 10/11/42 Camp Gordon GA. Pvt., Co. D, KIA (from explosion of own shell hitting tree limb)

7/12/43 Gela, Sicily. Widow: Emily Rea at Price, NC.

REBICK, Michael J. b. 1921 PA. Enl. 9/25/42 Greensburg, PA. Ser. No. 33294873. Pvt. Co. D, 10/15/42 Camp Gordon GA. Pfc., Co. D, WIA (shell fragment – serious), 9/11/43 Vietre sul Mare, Italy. Sent to hospital in North Africa. Returned to duty 10/26/43. Pfc., Co. D, KIA, 1/26/44, Italy (Anzio), SR Cem.

RECK, Duane H. b. 1920 NE. Res. Linn Co., OR. Enl. 2/28/42 Ft. Lewis, WA. Ser. No. 39387457. Pvt. Attached to Co. H 5/28/42 Edgewood Arsenal, MD. Gunner (Pvt.). Pfc., Co. B, (Squad Leader), promo. Cpl. (temp.), Camp Gordon, GA 7/15/42. Sgt., Co. B, Camp Gordon, GA 8/10/42. S/Sgt., Co. B, recommended for Silver Star for gallantry & administering first aid while under shell fire 12/8/43.

REDDING, Alfred N. b. 3/14/1909. Enl. 10/5/42 Philadelphia, PA. Ser. No. 13124608. Pvt., Co. A, Camp Gordon, GA 10/9/42. Mentioned in the 12/12/42 issue of Smokescreen. Transf. Co. B, Camp Gordon, GA, 12/16/42. Co. A, reclassified Dec. 1943. d. May 1974 Chestertown, Kent Co., MD.

REDDOCH, Ralph H. b. 1911 MS. Res. Jones Co., MS. Enl. 9/21/42 Camp Shelby, MS. Ser. No. 34426294. Pvt. Co. A, 10/14/42 Camp Gordon, GA. Transf. Co. B, Camp Gordon, GA, 12/16/42. Pvt., Co. A, WIA (light), 2/11 or 12/44 Anzio, Italy.

REECE, Marion H. b. 11/6/1920 GA. Res. Fulton Co., GA. Enl. 9/29/42 Ft. McPherson, Atlanta, GA. Ser. No. 34444816. Pvt., Co. B, Camp Gordon, GA 4/10/43. Pvt., Co. B, returned to duty from hospital 8/10/43. Pfc., Co. B, 5/8/45 Innsbruck, Austria. d. 9/10/1996 Atlanta, Dekalb Co., GA.

REED, Harold E. b. 1909 PA. Enl. 9/26/42 Allentown, PA. Ser. No. 33368058. Pvt. HQ & HQ Co., 10/15/42 Camp Gordon GA.

REGA, Michael A. b. 5/8/1923 NY. Res. Brooklyn, Kings Co., NY. Enl. 3/9/43 New York City, NY. Ser. No. 32827847. Pfc., Co. D, LST 422 Survivor, 1/26/44 Italy (Anzio) – Purple Heart [listed as R. A. Michael on survivor list]. Pfc., Co. A, 5/8/45 Innsbruck, Austria. Officer's Orderly June 1945. d. May 1981 Woodhaven, Queens Co., NY.

REGA, Ralph. b. 6/3/1916 CT. Res. Westchester Co., NY. Enl. 8/18/1942 Ft. Jay, Governors Island, NY. Ser. No. 32431178. Mentioned in 1956 Muzzleblasts. d. Feb. 1989.

REHULA, Victor A., Jr. b. 4/3/1918 PA. Res. Washington Co., PA. Enl. 2/23/42 New Cumberland, PA. Ser. No. 33153400. Pvt. Attached to Co. G 5/28/42 Edgewood Arsenal, MD. Gunner (Pvt.). Graduated Signal OCS Class 40-44. d. 3/24/1993 Washington, Washington Co., PA.

REICHMAN, Isadore J. b. 1911 NY. Res. Kings Co., NY. Enl. 7/9/42 Ft. Jay, Governors Island, NY. Ser. No. 32402344. Pvt., HQ & HQ Co., Camp Gordon, GA 7/28/42. Pvt., HQ &Co., Camp Gordon, GA 10/20/42. Pfc., WIA, 11/30/43 Venafro, Italy.

REIDLING, Harold O. b. 8/15/1923 OH. Res. Seneca Co., OH. Enl. 1/27/43 Toledo, OH. Ser. No. 35544261. T/4, Co. C, 6/22/45 Innsbruck, Austria. d. Mar. 1985 Fostoria, Seneca Co., OH.

REILLY, Walter J. b. 1921 NJ. Res. Bergen Co., NJ. Enl. 2/8/42 Newark, NJ. Ser. No. 32390115. Pvt., Co. D, Camp Gordon, GA 7/28/42. Pfc., Co. D, MIA, 1/26/44, Italy (Anzio) SR Cem.

REIMER, ----------. Pfc., Co. B, Camp Gordon, GA Nov. 1942.

REINMUND, Otto B. Cpl. Assigned to Co. F 5/28/42 Edgewood Arsenal, MD. 1st Sgt. Cpl. (temp.), Co. B, promo. Sgt. (temp.), Camp Gordon, GA 6/16/42. Sgt. (temp.), (1st Sgt.), promo. S/Sgt. (temp.), Camp Gordon, GA 7/15/42. S/Sgt. (temp.), promo. 1st Sgt. (temp.), Camp Gordon, GA 8/1/42. 1st Sgt., Co. B, transf. HQ & HQ Co., & promo. M/Sgt. (temp.), Camp Gordon, GA 11/23/42. Promo. Sgt./Maj., Camp Gordon, GA Nov. 1942. Spoke very broken English.

REMLER, Jacob. 1st Lt. Ser. No. 0482092. Assigned to HQ & HQ Co., & designated Medical Officer, Camp Gordon, GA 7/3/42. HQ & HQ Co., transf. Med Det., Camp Gordon, GA 9/26/42. Battalion Surgeon, Medical Detachment, Camp Gordon, GA. Relesd. and designated Assistant Battalion Surgeon, Camp Gordon, GA 9/28/42. Present, Med. Det., Camp Gordon, GA, 1/9/43.

RENFROE, Tom W. b. 11/15/1921 GA. Res. Johnson Co., GA. Enl. 9/19/42 Ft. McPherson, Atlanta, GA. Ser. No. 34442881. Pvt., Co. D, Camp Gordon, GA 10/8/42. Pfc., Co. D, LST 422 Survivor, 1/26/44 Italy (Anzio). Rescued by USS Pilot. Sgt. Suffered from combat fatigue in Southern France and was placed in a Postal outfit. d. Aug. 1972 GA.

RETTINO, Edward F. b. 1899 NJ. Res. Bergen Co., NJ. Enl. 7/9/42 Newark, NJ. Ser. No. 32390580. Pvt., Co. A, Camp Gordon, GA

REVAK, John W. b. 1918 PA. Res. Allegheny Co., PA. Enl. 1/16/42 New Cumberland, PA. Ser. No. 33144592. Pvt., Co. C, MIA, 1/26/44, Italy (Anzio) SR Cem.

REYNOLDS, Harlan. Res. NY. Ser. No. 01038096. Book reviewer for Doubleday & Doran. Present as Lt., Co. B, 3/8/44. 1st. Lt., Co. B, KIA (shot in head), 12/12/44, Riquewihr, France. Distinguished Service Cross (posthumous). Purple Heart. LO Cem.

RHEA, David F. b. 7/29/1906 VA. Res. Bath Co., VA. Enl. 9/21/42 Roanoke, VA. Ser. No. 33213337. Pvt., Co. C, Camp Gordon, GA 10/11/42. Truck Driver, Co. C Motor Pool, Camp Gordon, GA. T/4, Co. C, MIA, 8/29/44 Briançon, France. POW Stalag 7A Moosburg, Bavaria. Liberated 6/12/45. d. Feb. 1973 Millboro, Bath Co., VA.

RHOADS, (RHODES), Billy C. b. 1/1/1922 Albia, IA. Res. Monroe Co., IA. Enl. 8/29[30]/40 Chicago, IL. Ft. Bragg, Fayetteville, NC. Battery A, 60th Field Artillery, 9th Div. Jeep & truck driver. Served in North Africa & Sicily with 60th Field Artillery (60th RCT). Transf. Co. C, 83rd CMB 8/27/43. Ser. No. 16001304. Dentist filled a tooth 1/15/44. Pvt., Co. C, KIA, 1/26/44, Italy (Anzio), SR Cem. Body recovered 1/26/44 by YMS 34 & buried at sea same day. Next of kin: Edwin D. Rhoads, Albia, IA.

RHODES, Robert L. b. 1922 SC. Res. Laurens Co., SC. Enl. 3/18/43 Ft. Jackson, Columbia, SC. Ser. No. 3468896. Pvt., Co. D, MIA, 1/26/44, Italy (Anzio) SR Cem.

RICCI, Mario. b. ten miles north of Cassino at Arc, Italy. Sent to the 83rd CMB Feb. 1944. Radio Operator/Forward Observer, Co. C. Escaped capture at Briançon, France 8/29/44. Combat Artist. Pfc., Co. A, 5/8/45 Innsbruck, Austria. Res. San Mateo, CA 2009.

RICE, Claude S. b. 9/9/1921 VA. Res. Halifax Co., VA. Enl. 9/22/42 Richmond, VA. Ser. No. 33225916. Pvt., Co. B, Camp Gordon, GA 10/11/42. Pfc., Co. B, MIA, 12/12/44, Riquewihr, France. d. 4/2/2003 Virgiling, Halifax Co., VA. POW Stalag 7A Moosburg Bavaria. Liberated 3/18/46.

RICE, Perry B. b. 1917 NY. Res. Kings Co., NY. Enl. 3/17/42 New York City, NY. Ser. No. 12060769. Joined 83rd CMB July 1944. Co. D. Platoon Leader. Bronze Star. 1st Lt., Co. D, WIA (light injure), 8/15/44 Le Muy, France 8/15/44 – Purple Heart.. 1st Lt., Co. B, 5/8/45 Innsbruck, Austria. 1st Lt. Assigned 65th Inf. Div. 7/23/45. Dischd. Dec. 1945. Asst. Controller/Credit Manager, Arnold Bakers, Inc. Retired Apr. 1985. Contributed to MFP 1997. Res. Branford, CT 2009.

RICHARD, Stanley G. b. 1911 NJ. Res. Middlesex Co., NJ. Enl. 7/16/42 Newark, NJ. Ser. No. 12095147. Pvt., HQ & HQ Co., Camp Gordon, GA 7/28/42. Pfc., HQ Co., promo. Cpl. (temp.), Camp Gordon, GA 11/3/42.

RICHARDS, Morris R. b. 1906 MD. Enl. 12/22/42 Baltimore, MD. Res. Brandywine, MD. Ser. No. 33390908. Pfc., Co. C, Camp Gordon, GA 3/18/43. Orderly for Capt. Rupert O. Burford 1943. Pfc., present at Anzio, Italy 1/27/44. Orderly for S-3 Ed "Bud" Pike Feb. 1944.

RICHARDSON, Donald A. b. 1912 OH. Res. Summit Co., OH. Enl. 3/9/42 Camp Perry, Lacarne, OH. Ser. No. 35287591. Pvt. Attached to Co. C 5/28/42 Edgewood Arsenal, MD. Squad Leader (Sgt.). Pfc., Co. A, (Squad Leader), promo. Cpl. (temp.), Camp Gordon, GA 7/15/42.

RICHARDSON, Emmett F. b. 3/26/1900 VA. Res. Henrico Co., VA. Enl. 9/21/42 Richmond. Ser. No. 33225762. Pvt., Co. B, Camp Gordon, GA 10/11/42. d. Jan. 1973 Richmond, VA.

RICHARDSON, James Leonard. Served in Sicily with 3rd CMB. Tranfd. to 2nd. CMB. Sent to 83rd CMB late in war. Pfc., Co. C, 6/22/45 Innsbruck, Austria. Richardson's Lawn & Garden Store, Columbus, GA.

RIDDLE, Clark H. b. 9/20/1921 Greensburg, PA. Pre-war Occupation: Billing Clerk, Wilson & Co. Res. Greensburg, Westmoreland Co., PA. Enl. 9/25/42 Greensburg, PA. Ser. No. 33294823. Pvt. Co. D, 10/15/42 Camp Gordon GA. Pvt., Co. D, Camp Gordon, GA Nov. 1942. Sgt., Co. D, LST 422 Survivor, 1/26/44 Italy (Anzio) – Purple Heart. Platoon Sgt. In 'old' Co. D. S/Sgt., Co. D, WIA (serious – leg amputated), 12/5/44 Zellenberg, France. Evacuated. Res. Greensburg, PA May 1954. Works for a Pipeline Constructor. Attended 1954, 1956, 1958, & 1962 Reunions as res. Greensburg, PA. Res. Greensburg, PA 2006. d. 9/1/2008 Greensburg, PA.

RIDENOUR, William W. b. 1920 TN. Res. Campbell Co., TN. Enl. 9/18/42 Ft. Oglethorpe, GA. Pvt., Co. D, WIA (from explosion of own shell hitting tree limb), 7/12/43 Gela, Sicily. Ser. No. 34371838. Pfc., Co. D, KIA, 1/26/44, Italy (Anzio). Body recovered by U.S.S. Strive 1/26/44. Buried at sea 1/27/44. Name on tablet of dead and missing at SR Cem.

RIEDEL, Beverly H. b. 1915 MO. Res. Marion Co., MO. Enl. 9/11/41 Los Angeles. CA. Ser. No. 39163590. Assigned from 65th Inf. Division as 1st Lt., Co. B, 7/23/45.

RIEMER, Arthur D. b. 4/15/1920 NY. Res. Kings Co., NY. Enl. 1/28/42 Camp Upton, Yaphank, NY. Ser. No. 32196123. Pvt. Attached to Co. G 5/28/42 Edgewood Arsenal, MD. Gunner (Pvt.). d. Oct. 1984 Astoria, Queens Co., NY.

RINALDO, Michael L. b. 1912 OH. Res. Bergen Co., NJ. Enl. 7/9/42 Newark, NJ. Ser. No. 32390575. Pvt., HQ & HQ Co., Camp Gordon, GA 7/28/42. Present, Camp Gordon, GA, 1/9/43.

RINGES, Vincent L. b. 4/29/1921 PA. Res. Northumberland Co., PA. Enl. 9/21/42 Harrisburg, PA. Ser. No. 33240947. Pvt., Co. B, Camp Gordon, GA 10/9/42. d. Sept. 1985, Rochester, Monore Co., NY.

RISLEY, Raymond N. b. 7/7/1921 NJ. Res. Camden Co., NJ. Enl. 7/9/42 Camden, NJ. Ser. No. 32271768. Pvt., Co. C, Camp Gordon, GA 7/28/42. Pfc., Co. C, LST 422 Survivor 1/26/44 Italy (Anzio) – Purple Heart. Pvt., Co. C, WIA (light – S-mine), Minturno, Italy 3/26/44 – Purple Heart with Oak Leaf Cluster. Not hospitalized. Cpl., Co. C, 6/22/45 Innsbruck, Austria. d. 9/28/1995 Audubon, Camden Co., NJ.

RITCH, Clement F. b. 1920 CT. Res. Stanford, Fairfield Co., CT. Enl. 2/9/42 Ft. Devens, MA. Ser. No. 31063269. Pfc., Co. C, WIA (light), 6/1/44 Italy – Purple Heart. Returned to duty 6/13/44. Pfc., Co. C, 6/22/45 Innsbruck, Austria.

RIVELLO, Carmen M. b. 1921 PA. Enl. 9/22/42 Philadelphia, PA. Ser. No. 33335605. Pvt., Co. C, Camp Gordon, GA 10/9/42. Pfc., Co. C, MIA, 1/26/44, Italy (Anzio) SR Cem.

RIVERA, Joe R. Pvt., WIA (light), 10/23/44 France. Pfc., WIA (light – enemy bullet), 1/11/45 France. Hospitalized. Pfc., Co. C, 6/22/45 Innsbruck, Austria.

ROAN, Frank P. 2nd Lt., Co. D, WIA (light), 11/10/43 Italy. Attended 1962 Reunion as res. Plymouth, PA.

ROATEN, Luther L. b. 5/11/1911 MS. Res. Tupelo, Lee Co., MS. Enl. 9/22/42 Camp Shelby. MS. Ser. No. 34426601. Pvt. Co. A, 10/14/42 Camp Gordon, GA. Transf. Co. D, Camp Gordon, GA, 12/16/42.

Pfc., Co. B, 5/8/45 Innsbruck, Austria. d. 8/15/2002 New Albany, Union Co., MS.

ROBERTO, Patrick M. b. 1917 NY. Res. Bronx Co., NY. Enl. 1/27/42 Camp Upton, Yaphank, NY. Ser. No. 32195711. Cpl. Assigned Sp. Tng. Co. 5/28/42 Edgewood Arsenal, MD. Platoon Sgt. (S/Sgt.). Pvt., Co. A transf. Co. C, Camp Gordon, GA 6/15/42. Cpl. (temp.). Co. C, Camp Gordon, GA 6/17/42. Sgt. (temp.), (Platoon Leader), promo. S/Sgt. (temp.), Camp Gordon, GA 7/15/42. Commanding Officer, Air Operation, China-Burma-India Theatre.

ROBERTS, Arvil D. b. 8/20/1900 AL. Res. Blount Co., AL. Enl. 10/2/42 Ft. McClellan, AL. 14163407. Pvt., Co. C, Camp Gordon, GA 10/9/42. d. Feb. 1964 AL.

ROBERTS, Frederick C. b. 1911 MI. Res. Wayne Co., MI. Enl. 3/16/42 Detroit, MI. Ser. No. 36145075. Pfc., Co. A, promo. Cpl. (temp.), Camp Gordon, GA 10/6/42. Promo. Sgt. (temp.), Camp Gordon, GA 11/27/42.

ROBERTS, George A. b. 1911 KY. Enl. 11/10/42 Evansville, IN. Ser. No. 35716901. Pvt., Co. B, Camp Gordon, GA 4/2/43. Pvt., Co. B, WIA (light), 12/8/43 San Pietro, Italy. Returned to duty 4/4/44.

ROBERTS, Harmon Martin. b. 7/11/1918 GA. Res. Putnam Co., FL. Enl. 4/29/43 Camp Blanding, FL. Ser. No. 34783615. North Africa Campaign, Anzio, Monte Cassino, Rome, Glider invasion of Southern France, & Liberation of Dachau. T/5, Co. A, 5/8/45 Innsbruck, Austria. Attended 1962 Reunion as res. Crescent City, FL. d. 12/21/1997. bur. Crescent City Cem., FL.

ROBERTS, John H. ("Johnny"). 2nd Lt., CWS, assigned Co. B, Camp Gordon, GA 11/10/42. In hospital for hemorrhoids 6/27/43 Africa. Missed the Sicilian campaign due to illness. Present with 84th CMB 11/26/43. Reported working in a POW camp 1/25/44. Ed Pike saw him in July 1944.

ROBERTS, John M. b. 2/24/1921 MS. Res. Scott Co., MS. Enl. 9/23/42 Camp Shelby, MS. Ser. No. 34426646. Pvt. Co. D, 10/14/42 Camp Gordon, GA. d. August 1987, Forest, Scott Co., MS.

ROBERTS, Joseph A. b. 1897 NJ. Enl. 9/21/42 Harrisburg, PA. Ser. No. 33240901. Pvt., Co. B, Camp Gordon, GA 10/9/42.

ROBINS, Clyde. b. 6/3/1914 VA. Enl. 12/7/42 Abingdon, VA. Ser. No. 33527050. Pvt., Co. C, Camp Gordon, GA 3/18/43. Sick in hospital with meningitis early Jan. 1944. d. Dec. 1977 Bristol, Bristol Co., VA.

ROBINSON, Jim Henderson. b. 9/7/1920 Taylorsville, Smith Co., MS. Pre-war Occupation: Truck Driver, State Highway Dept. Taylorville, MS 1938-1942. Res. Smith Co., MS. Enl. 9/22/42 Camp Shelby, MS. [Record Pay Book is dated 8/22/42 & signed by Capt. Robert Edwards]. Entered Service 10/6/42. Ser. No. 34426410. Pvt. Co. A, 10/14/42 Camp Gordon, GA. Transf. Co. C, Camp Gordon, GA, 12/16/42. Overseas Embarkation: 4/29/43. Arrived Overseas: 5/11/43. Sicily. Naples-Foggia. Rome-Arno. Rhineland. Military Occupation: Mortar

Crewman Heavy. WIA (bullet through stomach & came out back & landed between his back & shirt). Pfc., HQ Co., 3rd Bn., 291st Inf. 11/12/45. EAMETO Medal. Good Conduct Medal. WWII Victory Medal. Departure for US: 11/13/45. Arrived US: 11/24/45. Dischd. 12/12//45. Apparently also served on 1180th Military Police Co. Res. Taylorsville, MS. Acting Postmaster & Clerk, Post Office, Taylorsville, MS until retired. d. 4/11/1986 Hattiesburg, MS. bur. Fellowship Cem., Taylorsville, MS. Carried bullet that wounded him on a keychain for years.

ROBINSON, Norman L. Res. New Castle, PA. Ser. No. 33296797. Pvt., Co. B, Camp Gordon, GA 10/9/42. Transf. Co. A, Camp Gordon, 12.16.42. Present in Sicily. Pvt., Co. B, WIA (light – large caliber German artillery), 4/10/44 Anzio, Italy – Purple Heart. Cpl., Co. B, 5/8/45 Innsbruck, Austria.

ROBISON, Ronald O. Co. A, reclassified dec. 1943. Pfc., Co. A, 5/8/45 Innsbruck, Austria.

RODGERS, Joseph L. b. 8/12/1920 AL. Res. Madison Co., AL. Enl. 9/17/42 Ft. McClellan, AL. Ser. No. 34391509. Pvt., HQ & HQ Co., Camp Gordon, GA 10/8/42. Pfc., Co. C, MIA, 8/29/44 Briançon, France. POW Stalag 7A Moosburg, Bavaria. Liberated 5/31/45. Attended 1986 Reunion. d. 11/28/2006 New Market, Madison Co., AL.

RODGERS, Lacy L. b. 3/1/1920 MS. Res. Union Co., MS. Enl. 9/23/42 Camp Shelby, MS. Ser. No. 34426924. Pvt. Co. A, 10/14/42 Camp Gordon, GA. Transf. Co. D, Camp Gordon, GA, 12/16/42. d. 6/13/2005 Blue Springs, Union Co., MS.

RODKEY, Melvin E., Jr. b. 3/21/1925 PA. Res. Mifflin Co., PA. Enl. 7/23/43 Altoona, PA. 33763375. Pvt., Co. A, 5/8/45 Innsbruck, Austria. d. 1//4/1999 Lewistown, Mifflin Co., PA.

ROETTKER, Frank. b. 10/22/1905 OH. Res. Hamilton Co., OH. Enl. 3/5/42 Ft. Thomas, New port, KY. Pfc., Co. B. Ser. No. 6639629. Temp. T/5 Camp Gordon, GA 8/1/42. T/5 (temp.), Co. B, promo. Cpl. (temp.), Camp Gordon, GA 8/10/42. d. Apr. 1977.

ROGAN, Walter K. b. 1918 PA. Enl. 10/18/43 Philadelphia, PA. Ser. No. 33802530. In Co. B sketch drawn by Sam Kweskin.

ROGERS, Howard M. b. 1924 TN. Res. Cannon Co., TN. Enl. 4/6/43 Ft. Oglethorpe, GA. Ser. No. 34729125. Pvt., Co. D, MIA, 1/26/44, Italy (Anzio) SR Cem. Body recovered 1/26/44 by YMS 34 & buried at sea same day. Next of kin: Mamie Rogers, Readyville, TN.

ROLL, Irving. b. 1916 NY. Res. Bronx, NY. Enl. 11/13/41 Camp Upton, Yaphank, NY. Ser. No. 32191033. Pvt., Co. C, LST 422 Survivor, 1/26/44 Italy (Anzio). Rescued by USS YMS 226. Taken to 93rd Evacuation Hosp. Pfc., Co. C, WIA, 4/5/44 Italy – Purple Heart with Oak Leaf Cluster. Had seven campaign stars as of 1/11/45.

ROLLING, Charles F. b. 9/25/1917 PA. Enl. 9/22/42 Philadelphia, PA. Ser. No. 33335433. Pvt., Co. A, Camp Gordon, GA 10/9/42. Transf. Co. C, Camp Gordon, GA, 12/16/42. Pfc., Co. A, 5/8/45 Innsbruck,

Austria. d. Apr. 1989. Kept a diary of his service.

ROLLMAN, Edward C. Cpl., Co. C, promo. Sgt. (temp.) 9/15/45.

ROMEO, Samuel J. Pvt. Attached to Co. G 5/28/42 Edgewood Arsenal, MD. Squad Leader (Sgt.). Ser. No. 32238466. Pfc., Co. B, (Squad Leader), promo. Cpl. (temp.), Camp Gordon, GA 7/15/42. Cpl., Co. B, Camp Gordon, GA 8/3/42. Promo. Sgt. (temp.), Camp Gordon, GA 12/12/42. Sgt., Co. B, 5/8/45 Innsbruck, Austria.

ROMNEK, Sylvester A. b. 1908 WI. Res. Menesha, Winnebago Co., WI. Enl. 9/19/40 Milwaukee, WI. Ser. No. 16006528. Field Artillery. S/Sgt., Co. B, WIA (light), 6/1/44, Italy – Purple Heart. S/Sgt., Co. B, 1/25/45. Pfc., HQ Co., 5/8/45 Innsbruck, Austria.

RONAI, Kenneth S. b. 1922 NY. Res. Queens Co., NY. Enl. 7/8/43 New York City, NY. Ser. No. 32981064. Pfc., Co. B, 5/8/45 Innsbruck, Austria.

ROOKE, Albert William. b. 12/5/1920 PA. Res. Philadelphia Co., PA. Enl. 9/22/42 Philadelphia, PA. Ser. No. 33335489. Pvt., Co. B, Camp Gordon, GA 10/9/42. d. April 1981, Wildwood, Cape May Co., NJ.

ROOKS, James Durley. b. 5/15/1911 MS. Res. Monroe Co., MS. Enl. 9/23/42 Camp Shelby, MS. Ser. No. 34426701. Pvt. Co. A, 10/14/42 Camp Gordon, GA. Pfc., Co. A, on *LST 690* 8/9/44. Pfc., Co. A, 5/8/45 Innsbruck, Austria. d. 11/26/1988 Caledonia, Monroe Co., MS.

RORABECK, Delmas A. ("Rory"). b. 8/13/1914 WI. Res. Trempealeau Co., WI. Enl. 3/3/42 Ft. Sheridan, IL. Ser. No. 36236671. Pvt. Attached to Co. H 5/28/42 Edgewood Arsenal, MD. Communication Sgt. (Sgt.). Pfc., Co. A, promo. Cpl. (temp.), Camp Gordon, GA 8/19/42. Promo. Sgt. (temp.), Camp Gordon, GA 9/23/42. 1st Sgt., Camp Gordon, GA 11/21/42. Sgt. Co. A, relsd. from SD to the 4th Signal Co., 4th Mtz Div, Camp Gordon, GA, 12/16/42. T/4, HQ Co., 5/8/45 Innsbruck, Austria. Res. Beloit, WI, May 1954. Electrician. American Legion Post. d. 12/19/1990 WI.

ROSE, Merle A. T/4, HQ Co., presented Purple Heart 8/25/45.

ROSENBERG, Lawrence J. b. 1920 NY. Res. New York, Kings Co., NY. Enl. 6/16/42 New York City, NY. Ser. No. 12087469. Pvt., Co. D, LST 422 Survivor, 1/26/44 Italy (Anzio) – Purple Heart.

ROSENFELD, Sylvan M. b. 1915 PA. Res. Wildwood, NJ. Enl. 10/5/42 Philadelphia, PA. Ser. No. 13124615. Pvt., Co. C, Camp Gordon, GA 10/9/42. Pfc., Co. C, WIA (light – shell fragment), 9/21/43, Maiori, Italy. Returned to duty 9/28/43. Cpl., Co. C, LST 422 Survivor, 1/26/44 Italy (Anzio) – Purple Heart with Oak Leaf Cluster. Sgt., Co. C, MIA, 8/29/44 Briançon, France. POW Stalag 7A Moosburg, Bavaria. Liberated 5/31/45.

ROSENTHAL, Norman F. ("Rosy"). Enl. 6/7/42. Ser. No. 01038816. Pre-war occupation: Meat Inspector. Present in Southern France and at Briançon, France 8/29/44. 1st. Lt., Co. C, 6/22/45 Innsbruck, Austria. 1st Lt. Assigned 65th Inf. Div. 7/23/45. Dischgd. 11/30/45. Res. Pennington, NJ 1949. Res. Sheboygan, WI. d. 6/16/1998.

ROSOL, Chester. Pfc., Co. A, 5/8/45 Innsbruck, Austria.

ROSS, Joe. b. 1905 AL. Enl. 4/15/41 Ft. McClellan, AL. Ser. No. 34101904. Pvt., Co. B, Camp Gordon, GA 10/9/42.

ROSS, Michael J. b. 1914 OH. Res. Hamilton Co., OH. Enl. 3/9/42 Ft. Thomas, Newport, KY. Ser. No. 35133086. Pvt. Attached to Co. C 5/28/42 Edgewood Arsenal, MD. Gunner (Pvt.). Pvt., Co. C transf. Co. D, Camp Gordon, GA 6/15/42.

ROUTLEDGE, Howard E. Pvt., Co. D. Ser. No. 37515549. Res. MO. KIA, 1/26/44, Italy (Anzio). Body recovered by USS Pilot. Buried at sea 1/26/44. SR Cem.

ROYSE, Richard L. b. 1917. Enl. 3/9/42 Peoria, IL. Ser. No. 16054613. Pvt. Attached to Co. I 5/28/42 Edgewood Arsenal, MD. Gunner (Pvt.). Pfc., Co. A, (Squad Leader), promo. Cpl. (temp.), Camp Gordon, GA 7/15/42.

ROZZELL, Leland M. b. 5/4/1920 TN. Res. White Co., TN. Enl. 9/15/42 Ft. Oglethorpe, GA. Ser. No. 34370900. Pvt., present at Camp Gordon, GA Nov. 1942. Pvt. transf Co. A, Camp Gordon, GA, 12/16/42. Pvt., Co. B, WIA (light – large caliber German artillery), 4/10/44 Anzio, Italy. Sgt., Co. B, 5/8/45 Innsbruck, Austria. d. May 1981 Chattanooga, Hamilton Co., TN.

RUBY, Paul H. Res. Detroit/Bay Poer, MI. Ser. No. 36571341. Pfc., Co. D, LST 422 Survivor, 1/26/44 Italy (Anzio) – Purple Heart. Pvt., Co. D, WIA (light – bullet in arm), 5/31/44 Italy – Purple Heart with Oak Leaf Cluster. Cpl., Co. A, 1st Platoon. WIA (serious – defective shell aerial burst), France (Alsace) 2/17/45. Cpl., Co. A, 5/8/45 Innsbruck, Austria.

RUDOLPH, ----------. Lt. Co. D. Joined the 83rd CMB Sept. 1943. Mentioned in a letter dated 10/18/43 from Lt. Col. Hutchinson to Kenneth Cunin stating "Rudolph has gone [left the battalion].

RUFF, Charles F. ("Chuck"). b. 1920 PA. Enl. 10/9/42 Greensburg, PA. Ser. No. 33392486. Pvt., Co. D, 10/15/42 Camp Gordon GA. Pvt., Feature Editor, Smokescreen, Camp Gordon, GA Nov. 1942. Pfc., Co. D, WIA (light - from explosion of own shell hitting tree limb), 7/12/43 Gela, Sicily.

RUGITO, Donald ("Spider"). b. 1921 PA. Enl. 9/24/42 Greensburg, PA. Pvt. Co. C, 10/15/42 Camp Gordon GA. Co. C, Camp Gordon, GA Nov. 1942. Pvt., Co. C, WIA (light - shell fragment from 4.2 mortar), 7/10/43 Gela, Sicily. Ser. No. 33294807. Purple Heart [presented 9/27/43 in Sicily]. Pfc., Co. C, MIA, 1/26/44, Italy (Anzio) SR Cem.

RUIT, Paul. b. 1921 NJ. Res. Bergen Co., NJ. Enl. 7/9/42 Newark, NJ. Ser. No. 32390525. Pvt., HQ & HQ Co., Camp Gordon, GA 7/28/42. Co. A, (WIA?), left in Gela, Sicily 7/14/43. Pvt., Co. A, WIA (enemy shells), 2/11 or 12/44 Anzio, Italy.

RUNEWEIZ, Joseph H. Pvt. Co. C, WIA (severe-mortar barrel burst), 4/9/45.

RUNKLE, Warren R. b. 1916 PA. Res. Philadelphia Co., PA. Enl. 3/19/42 Camp Lee, VA. Pvt. Attached to Co. A 5/28/42 Edgewood Arsenal, MD. Squad Leader (Sgt.). Pfc., Co. C, promo. T/5 (temp.), Camp Gordon, GA 9/3/42. Ser. No. 33156388. T/5, MIA, 1/26/44, Italy (Anzio). Rescued by YMS 62 1/26/44. Died aboard YMS 62 from drowning and shock at 2:30 p.m. 1/26/44. bur. At sea at 9:30 a.m. 1/27/44 by YMS 62. SR Cem.

RUSHING, William E. b. 1921 MS. Res. Lafayette Co., MS. Enl. 9/22/42 Camp Shelby, MS. Ser. No.34426542. Pvt. Co. A, 10/14/42 Camp Gordon, GA. Cpl., Co. A on LST 690 8/9/44. Cpl., Co. A, 2nd Platoon. MWIA (serious – leg – premature muzzleburst), Bischweiler, France (Alsace) 2/18/45. Died in a hospital.

RUSPINI, Albert J. b. 4/16/1925 NY. Res. Bergen Co., NJ. Enl. 4/2/43 Newark, NJ. Ser. No. 42001697. Pfc., Co. C, MIA, 8/29/44 Briançon, France. POW Stalag 7A Moosburg, Bavaria. Liberated 5/31/45. Res. Park Ridge, NJ. d. 2/25/2004 Hillsdale, Bergen Co., NJ.

RUSSELL, Charles G. b. 1902 TX. Enl. 9/26/42 Baltimore, MD. Ser. No. 33377198. Pvt. Co. B, 10/15/42 Camp Gordon GA.

RUSSELL, Frank. b. 5/13/1921 MS. Res. Yazoo Co., MS. Enl. 9/23/42 Camp Shelby, MS. Ser. No. 34426658. Pvt. HQ & HQ Co. 10/14/42 Camp Gordon, GA. Present at Stambach 3/17/45 entry in Daniel Shields diary. Pfc., HQ Co., 5/8/45 Innsbruck, Austria. Res. Yazoo City, MS, May 1954. Cattle Dealer. d. 7/7/1998 Yazoo City, Yazoo Co., MS.

RUSSELL, Harold B. b. 1901 MS. Res. Jones Co., MS. Enl. 9/21/42 Camp Shelby, MS. Ser. No. 34426244. Pvt. Co. C, 10/14/42 Camp Gordon, GA.

RUSSELL, Robert L. 1st Lt. Appointed battalion S-2 on 9/15/45.

RUSSELL, William J., Jr. b. 1919 GA. Enl. 1/17/42 Ft. Bragg, NC. Ser. No. 34177201. Pvt. Attached to Co. A 5/28/42 Edgewood Arsenal, MD. Clerk (Cpl. & Pvt.). Pfc., Co. A, (Pers. Clerk), promo. Cpl. (temp.), Camp Gordon, GA 7/15/42.

RUSSO, Vincent R. b. 1918 NY. Res. Kings Co., NY. Enl. 7/7/42 Ft. Jay, Governors Island, NY. Ser. No. 32400838. Pvt., Co. C, Camp Gordon, GA 7/28/42.

RUSSO, William P. b. 1915 RI. Res. Providence Co., RI. Enl. 6/9/42 Providence, RI. Ser. No. 31120374. Pvt., Co. C, MIA, 8/29/44 Briançon, France. POW Stalag 7B Memmigen, Bavaria. Liberated 7/21/45.

RUSY, Albert. Res. NY. Pvt., Co. D, Camp Gordon, GA 4/10/43. Ser. No. 32685072. Pfc., Co. D, MIA, 1/26/44, Italy (Anzio) SR Cem.

RUTH, Walter G. b. 1918 MD. Res. Baltimore, MD. Enl. 8/31/42 Baltimore, MD. Ser. No. 33373670. Pvt. Co. D, 10/15/42 Camp Gordon

GA. Pfc., Co. D, MIA, 1/26/44, Italy (Anzio) SR Cem.

RYBNICK, William. b. 1920 Poland. Res. Kings Co., NY. Enl. 7/8/42 Ft. Jay, Governors Island, NY. Ser. No. 32401509. Pvt., Co. C, Camp Gordon, GA 7/28/42. Served 6 mos. with 83rd CMB, then limited service because of poor vision. Station hospital, Camp Gordon, GA.

RYE, Giles W. b. 4/16/1913 MS. Res. Monroe Co., MS. Enl. 9/23/42 Camp Shelby. MS. Ser. No. 34426715. Pvt. Co. A, 10/14/42 Camp Gordon, GA. Transf. Co. B, Camp Gordon, GA, 12/16/42. d. 4/22/1992.

RYDER, Christopher L. b. 1913 NJ. Res. Essex Co., NJ. Enl. 6/2/43 Newark, NJ. Ser. No. 32925649. T/5, HQ Co., 5/8/45 Innsbruck, Austria.

SABATINO, Albert. Honorary member. Ex- Italian soldier (medic) 'picked' up by Co. A in Italy 9/5/43. Co. A, Survivor, LST 422, 1/26/44 Italy (Anzio). Injured in truck accident 8/27/44. Remained with Co. A until brought back to Italy at wars end by Lt. Robert Bundy & Lt. Charles J. Decesare. Also referred to as Alberto .

SABATINO, Salvatore M. b. 11/1/1920 PA. Enl. 12/12/42 Altoona, PA. Ser. No. 33567173. Pvt., Co. A, Camp Gordon, GA 4/10/43. d. 7/28/1998 PA.

SACHATELLI, Joseph A. b. 11/11/1921 NY. Res. Kings Co., NY. Enl. 7/9/42 Ft. Jay, Governors Island, NY. Ser. No. 32402457. Pvt., Co. D, Camp Gordon, GA 7/28/42. d. Feb. 1964 NY.

SADLER, Glen C. b. 2/3/1903 TN. Res. Davidson Co., TN. Enl. 9/18/42 Ft. Oglethorpe, GA. Ser. No. 34371864. Present Co. B, Camp Gordon, GA 12/31/42. d. March 1967, Nashville, Davidson Co., TN.

SAILLANT, Charles J. b. 1920 PA. Res. Camden Co., NJ. Enl. 7/9/42 Camden, NJ. Ser. No. 32271773. Pvt., Co. C, Camp Gordon, GA 7/28/42. Pfc., Co. C, Camp Gordon, GA 10/20/42. T/5, Co. C, Bronze Star for service 7/10/43 – 5/23/44 Sicily & Italy.

SALE, Myron D. b. 1924 MI. Res. Allegan Co., MI. Enl. 4/5/43 Kalamazoo, MI. Ser. No. 36460173. Pfc., HQ Co., 5/8/45 Innsbruck, Austria.

SALISBURY, Carl Leo. b. 1919 VA. Res. Howison, Spotsylvania Co., VA. Enl. 9/19/42 Richmond, VA. Ser. No. 33225549. Pvt., Co. C, Camp Gordon, GA 10/11/42. Transf. Co. A, Camp Gordon, GA, 12/16/42. Heavy Machine Gunner 605, Marksman with BAR 30 and 50 caliber. Pfc., Co. C, LST 422 Survivor, 1/26/44 Italy (Anzio) – Purple Heart. Rescued by USS Pilot. T/5, Co. C, 6/22/45 Innsbruck, Austria. Purple Heart, EAME Theater Ribbon, & Good Conduct Medal. Res. Richmond, VA.

SALWACH, Frank. Res. Rivergrove, IL. Pfc., Co. D, LST 422 Survivor, 1/26/44 Italy (Anzio) – Purple Heart. Rescued by USS YMS 226. Taken to 93rd Evac. Hosp. Res. Elmwood Pk., IL May 1954. Plasterer.

SAMUELS, Irving D. b. 1925. Enl. 4/6/43 Pittsburgh, PA. Ser. No. 33677256. Pfc., Co. A, promo. T/5 (temp.) 9/15/45.

SAMULSKI, Benedict T. ("Ben"/"Sam"). b. 1923 NY. Res. Erie Co., NY. Enl. 4/25/43 Buffalo, NY. Ser. No. 32844147. Pvt., Co. D, WIA (light), 4/25/44 Anzio, Italy – Purple Heart. Pfc., Co. B, 5/8/45 Innsbruck, Austria. [Steedle's Squad, 2nd Platoon, Co. B].

SANDOVAL, Manuel H. b. 1918. Res. Fresno Co., CA. Enl. 3/10/41 Sacramento, CA. Ser. No. 39077612. HQ, 2nd CMB, assigned Pfc., HQ & HQ Co., 83rd CMB 7/25/45.

SANDERFORD, Wallace. b. 1905 MS. Res. Smith Co., MS. Enl. 9/22/42 Camp Shelby, MS. Ser. No. 34426508. Pvt. Co. A, 10/14/42 Camp Gordon, GA.Transf. Co. B, Camp Gordon, GA, 12/16/42.

SAPIENZA, Joseph J. b. 3/5/1920 NY. Res. Queens Co., NY. Enl. 6/15/42 Ft. Jay, Governors Island, NY. Ser. No. 32354133. Pvt., Co. D, Camp Gordon, GA 7/28/42. Pvt., Co. D, Camp Gordon, GA 11/21/42. Mechanic of Maintenance. Cpl., Co. D, WIA (light), 9/16/43 Vietre sul Mare, Italy. With HQ Detachment, Camp Edison (Ft. Monmouth), NJ., Dec. 1944. Res. New York, NY May 1954. Food Inspector for Army Q.M. Attended 1954, 1956, 1958, 1960, 1962 & 1966 Reunions as res. Floral, Park Co., NY. Res. Greenwich Village, NY. d. Dec. 1975 NY.

SAPIO, Salvatore. b. 3/24/1918 [military record says 1917] NJ. Raised Haddonfield, NJ. Res. Philadelphia Co., PA. Pre-war Occupation: Manager of fruit & produce department of a local chain grocery store / New York Shipbuilding Corp. Enl. 7/9/42 Camden, NJ. Ser. No. 32271748. Pvt., Co. C, Camp Gordon, GA 7/28/42. S/Sgt., Co. C, MIA, 1/26/44, Italy (Anzio) SR Cem. He was a boyhood friend of Art Sinclair.

SAPP, Frederick. b. 3/10/1919 PA. Res. Beaver Co., PA. Enl. 9/25/42 Pittsburgh, PA. Ser. No. 33305545. Pvt., Co. B, 10/15/42 Camp Gordon GA. Pfc., Co. B, arrived Salemi, Sicily from North Africa 8/1/43. Pfc., Co. B, WIA, (light), 4/22/44 Italy - Purple Heart [Presented 11/20/44]. Pfc., Co. B, 5/8/45 Innsbruck, Austria. d. 8/7/1995 Bader, Beaver Co., PA.

SAPPINGTON, Charles N. ("Sad Sack"). b. 12/26/1921 MS. Res. Union Co., MS. Enl. 9/23/42 Camp Shelby, MS. Ser. No. 34426883. Pvt., Co. A, 10/14/42 Camp Gordon, GA. Transf. Co. D, Camp Gordon, GA, 12/16/42. Cpl., Co. A, on LST 690 8/9/44. Cpl., Co. A, 5/8/45 Innsbruck, Austria. Res. Albany, MA May 1954. Owner 117 acre farm. d. 5/30/1997 New Albany, Union Co., MS.

SATERELLO, Mike. b. 9/29/1918 Monongah, Marion Co., WV. Parents were from Italy. Res. Jackson Co., MI. Enl. 12/21/42 Kalamazoo, MI. Ser. No. 36415512. Pvt., Co. A, Camp Gordon, GA 4/10/43. Pvt., HQ & HQ Co., WIA (light – enemy shell), 2/16/44 Anzio, Italy. Returned to duty 2/28/44.

SATTERFIELD, Ikey. b. 7/30/1921 GA. Res. Armuchee, Floyd Co., GA. Enl. 9/17/42 Ft. McPherson, Atlanta, GA. Ser. No. 34442477. Pvt., HQ & HQ Co., Camp Gordon, GA 10/8/42. Pvt., Co. D, LST 422 Survivor, 1/26/44 Italy (Anzio) – Purple Heart. Cpl.,HQ Co., truck driver Epinal, France, 10/5/44. Cpl., HQ Co., 5/8/45 Innsbruck, Austria. d. 12/28/1988 Rome, Floyd Co., GA.

SAUERMAN, Edward E. Karl., Jr. b. 1919 MD. Res. Ann Arundel Co., MD. Enl. 2/7/42 Ft. George Meade, MD. Ser. No. 33138897. Pfc., HQ & HQ Co., special duty with Battalion Medical Officer, Camp Gordon, GA 7/28/42. Pfc., HQ & HQ Co., transf. Med Det., Camp Gordon, GA 11/5/42. Pfc., Med. Det., correspondent, Smokescreen, Camp Gordon, GA, 1/9/43.

SAUERMAN, Howard E., Jr. Pvt. Attached to Co. E 5/28/42 Edgewood Arsenal, MD. Radio Operator (Cpl. & Pvt.).

SAWYER, John P. ("Tom"). b. 1/7/1924 NY. Res. Bronx Co., NY. Enl. 11/7/42 New York City, NY. Ser. No. 12183459. Cpl., Co. B, KIA, 12/12/44, Riquewihr, France. b. Long Island Nat. Cem., NJ. Re-interment 4/8/49.

SCALIA, Anthony F. Pfc., Co. C, 6/22/45 Innsbruck, Austria.

SCARBERRY, James L. b. 1921 VA. Pvt., Co. A, Camp Gordon, GA 10/11/42. Transf. Co. C, Camp Gordon, GA, 12/16/42. Served at Anzio and in the infantry. Re-enl. 11/20/45 Huntington, WV. Res. Pike Co., KY. Pfc., Transportation Corps. Postwar res. Paw Paw, KY.

SCHADLER, Alfred E. b. 6/22/1922 PA. Enl. 12/14/42 Allentown, PA. Ser. No. 33484944. Pvt., Co. C, Camp Gordon, GA 3/18/43. Pfc., HQ Co., 5/8/45 Innsbruck, Austria. d. 1/6/2001 Topton, Berks Co., PA.

SCHANAFELT, Denver E. Pvt. Attached to Co. H 5/28/42 Edgewood Arsenal, MD. Telephone Lineman (Pvt.). [see Denver E. Shanafelt].

SCHLACHTER, William G. ("Bill"). b. 7/29/1917 PA. Enl. 10/5/42 Philadelphia, PA. Ser. No. 12165665. Pvt., Co. B, Camp Gordon, GA 10/9/42. Pfc., Bronze Star [presented 4/25/44]. T/5, Co. B, WIA (light), 11/19/44 Rochicourt, France. Returned to duty 12/16/44. T/5, Co. B, 5/8/45 Innsbruck, Austria. Res. Pottsville, PA May 1954. Mailman. d. May 1987 Pottsville, Schuylkill Co., PA.

SCHLEGEL, (SCHELEGEL), James M. b. 1921 PA. Enl. 9/21/42 Harrisburg, PA. Ser. No. 33240907. Pvt., HQ & HQ Co., Camp Gordon, GA 10/9/42. Pfc., Co. A, MIA, 1/26/44, Italy (Anzio) SR Cem.

SCHLEIFER, Francis J. ("Frank"). Lt., HQ Co., assigned to Co. B, 8/1/43. 1st Lt., awarded Silver Star 7/6/44. 1st Lt., WIA (light), 1/21/45 France. Lt. & S-3 for Capt. Robert B. Smith 5/8/45. Relsd. 83rd. CMB & transf. HQ European Theater of Operations, USA 5/10/45 for duty with Army Exchange Service. Spoke German.

SCHLENKER, Henry W. ("Hank"). b. 1914 NJ. Res. Union Co., NJ. Enl. 4/7/41 Newark, NJ. Ser. No. 32065162. 2nd Lt., CWS, assigned HQ & HQ Co. & designated Communications Officer, Camp Gordon, GA 7/28/42. 2nd Lt., CWS, assigned HQ & HQ Co., & designated Communications Officer, Camp Gordon, GA 8/1/42. 2nd Lt., CWS, Communications Officer, released and transf. HQ &HQ Co. to Co. D. Camp Gordon, GA 10/1/42. Transf. HQ & HQ Co. & designated Asst. Communications Officer, Camp Gordon, GA 12/2/42. Attended Communications School, Ft. Benning, GA Dec. 1942.

SCHMELZINGER, William M. Pfc., Co. A, 5/8/45 Innsbruck, Austria.

SCHMIDT, Eric C. Res. NY. T/5, Co. C, 6/22/45 Innsbruck, Austria.

SCHMIDT, George. b. 1923 OH. Res. Lorain, Lorain Co., OH. Enl. 4/19/43 Cleveland, OH. Ser. No. 35059823. Pfc., Co. D, WIA (light), LST 422 Survivor, 1/26/44 Italy (Anzio) – Purple Heart. Pvt., Co. D. returned to duty 2/9/44. Pvt. Co. D, truck driver, 9/30/44, Iuxeuil. T/4, Co. A, 5/8/45 Innsbruck, Austria. Camera/Photo Business, Los Angeles, CA. Attended 1954, 1956, 1958, 1960 & 1962 Reunions as res. Elyria, OH.

SCHMIDT, Norman H. b. 7/15/1918 PA. Res. Beaver Co., PA. Enl. 9/23/42 Pittsburgh, PA. Ser. No. 33305288. Pvt. Co. A, 10/15/42 Camp Gordon GA. Transf. Co. D, Camp Gordon, GA, 12/16/42. d. 4/23/2005 Rochester, Beaver Co., PA.

SCHMIDT, Robert M. Res. IL. 2nd Lt., CWS, assigned Co. A, Camp Gordon, GA 11/10/42. 2nd. Lt., transf. Co. C, Camp Gordon, GA, 12/16/42. Ser. No. O1036011. 2nd Lt., HQ & HQ Co., KIA (while acting as a forward observer), 11/11/43, Italy, SR Cem.

SCHMIDT, William J., Jr. Res. New Castle, PA. Ser. No. 33296783. Pvt., Co. D, Camp Gordon, GA 10/9/42. Present in North Africa. Pvt., Co. D, WIA (light injure), LST 422 Survivor, 1/26/44 Italy (Anzio). Returned to duty 2/19/44. Bronze Star & 2 Purple Hearts.

SCHNITZKI, John J. b. 5/22/1905 PA. Res. Butler Co., PA. Enl. 9/25/42 Pittsburgh, PA. Ser. No. 33305663. Pvt. HQ & HQ Co., 10/15/42 Camp Gordon GA. d. Jan. 1983 Lyndora, Butler Co., PA.

SCHOFF, Alson C. b. 9/9/1920 NH. Res. Orleans Co., VT. Enl. 7/10/43 Manchester, NH. Ser. No. 31373226. Pfc., Co. B, 5/8/45 Innsbruck, Austria. Promo. Sgt. (temp.) 9/15/45. d. 7/21/2006 Jeffersonville, IN.

SCHOOLEY, Arch D. [Archie Douglas Schooley on birth record]. b. 6/7/1915 Thomas, Tucker Co., WV. Enl. 12/8/42 Abingdon, VA. Ser. No. 33527094. Pvt., Co. B, Camp Gordon, GA 4/10/43.

SCHRAMM, Henry. b. 8/30/1897 PA. Res. Allegheny Co., PA. Enl. 10/9/42 Pittsburgh, PA. Ser. No. 33307695. Pvt. Co. C, 10/15/42 Camp Gordon GA. d. Dec. 1985 Mt. Airy, Frederick Co., MD.

SCHRODER, Fritz J. Pvt., Co. C, Camp Gordon, GA 3/18/43. Ser. No. 37424814.

SCHROLL, Alfred W. b. 1/5/1914 IA. Res. Wapello Co., IA. Enl. 12/21/42 Camp Dodge, Herrold, IA. Ser. No. 37651489. Pvt., Co. C, Camp Gordon, GA 4/10/43. d. Jan. 1987 Ottumwa, Wapello Co., IA.

SCHUMANN, Herbert. b. 1918 NJ. Res. Monmouth Co., NJ. Enl. 5/22/42 Newark, NJ. Ser. No. 32303733. T/5, HQ & HQ Co., Camp Gordon, GA 11/22/42. T/5, Co. A, WIA (light-shell fragment to leg), 3/12 or13/44 Anzio, Italy. Returned to duty 4/7/44. T/5, WIA (light – injure – truck ran off road), 8/17/44 France. Returned to duty 9/27/44.

SCHUMM, Karl D. b. 12/24/1921 NJ. Res. Bergen Co., NJ. Enl. 7/10/42 Newark, NJ. Ser. No. 32390933. Pvt., HQ & HQ Co., Camp Gordon, GA 7/28/42. Pvt., HQ & HQ CO., Camp Gordon, GA 9/25.42. Pvt., HQ Co., 5/8/45 Innsbruck, Austria. d. May 1972 NJ.

SCHUTTLER, Linfred Leroy. b. 11/2/1924 Spencer, SD. Res. Hanson Co., SD. Store Clerk. Enl. 5/7/43. Basic Training: Camp Wolters, TX. Pfc., Co. F, 411th Inf., 103 Div. Sent Overseas: Oct. 1944. France, Alsace Lorraine, Brenner Pass. Hospital: Mar. - Apr. 1945 with hepatitis. Assigned to 83rd CMB after war's end. "Positioned along a line south of Steyr, Austria 2 months facing off Russians". Bronze Star, European Theater Ribbon, 3 Battle Stars, Combat Infantry Badge. Dischd. 4/13/1946. Res. Spearfish, SD 1947. Mailman. Bell, Book, and Candle Shop.

SCHWAB, Howard Charles. A classically trained pianist. His family wanted to insure his hands but couldn't because he was in the army. Clerk for Co. C, Camp Gordon, GA 1942. Cpl., Co. C, 6/22/45 Innsbruck, Austria.

SCHWARTZ, Abraham. b. 1915 NY. Res. Kings Co., NY. Enl. 7/9/42 Ft. Jay, Governors Island, NY. Ser. No. 32402423. Pvt., Co. D, Camp Gordon, GA 7/28/42. Pvt., Co. D, Camp Gordon, GA 10/21/42. Pfc., Co. C, 6/22/45 Innsbruck, Austria.

SCHWARTZ, Milton S. Assigned from 65th Inf. Division as 2nd Lt., Co. A, 7/23/45. Apptd. Investigative Officer 7/31/45.

SCHWED, Harry C. b. 1925 OH. Res. Cuyahoga Co., OH. Enl. 3/21/44 Ft. Benjamin Harrison, IN. Ser. No. 35247570. Pfc., Co. C. Purple Heart, Sept. 1945.

SCIASCIA, Frank. b. 1923 NY. Res. Ozone Park, Queens Co., NY. Enl. 2/6/43 New York City, NY. Ser. No. 32794711. Pfc., Co. D, LST 422 Survivor, 1/26/44 Italy (Anzio) – Purple Heart.

SCOTT, Benjamin F. b. 1922 PA. Res. Delaware Co., PA. Enl. 10/5/42 Philadelphia, PA. Ser. No. 33338254. Pvt., Co. A, Camp Gordon, GA 10/9/42. Pvt., distinguished in action 7/10/43 Sicily. Pvt., Co. A, WIA (shell-serious-side), 3/27/44 Italy.

SCOTT, Charles F. b. 1903 PA. Enl. 9/25/42 Pittsburgh, PA. Ser. No. 33305686. Pvt. HQ & HQ Co., 10/15/42 Camp Gordon GA.

SCOTT, James B. b. 1909 TN. Res. Davidson Co., TN. Enl. 9/18/42 Ft. Oglethorpe, GA. Ser. No. 34371910. Pvt., Co. D, KIA, 7/11/43, Gela, Sicily, FL Cem. Possibly the man referred to as 'Scott' by Harold Hughes in his book The Man From Ida Grove and noted, possibly incorrectly, as being from western Virginia.

SCOTT, James U. L. b. 1923 TN. Res. Jackson Co., TN. Enl. 3/27/43 Ft. Oglethorpe, GA. Ser. No. 34727940. Pvt., Co. D, MIA, 1/26/44, Italy (Anzio) SR Cem.

SCOTT, Marshall. Pvt., Co. C, 6/22/45 Innsbruck, Austria.

SCOVILL, Claude E. b. 1922 UT. Res. Emery Co., UT. Enl. 6/9/43 Salt Lake City, UT. Ser. No. 39916129. Ft. Douglas, Salt Lake City, UT. Joined 83rd CMB at Anzio. T/5, HQ Co., 5/8/45 Innsbruck, Austria. Res. Orangeville, UT 2003.

SEDGWICK, William P. Res. OH. Ser. No. 35409280. Pvt., Co. D, MIA, 1/26/44, Italy (Anzio) SR Cem.

SEIBELS, Howard Kelly. b. 1923 AL. Grad. Birmingham University School. University of the South, Sewanee, TN. Res. Jefferson Co., AL. Enl. 2/23/43 Ft. McClellan, AL. Ser. No. 34707209. Pfc., Co. C, MIA, 8/29/44 Briançon, France. POW 9/20/44. POW. Stalag 7A Moosburg, Bavaria. Liberated 6/12/45. Res. Homewood, AL.

SEIDL[E], Herbert C. b. 1909 PA. Enl. 12/22/42 Pittsburgh, PA. Ser. No. 33416539. Pvt., Co. C, Camp Gordon, GA 3/18/43.

SEPULVADO, Rupert. b. 10/29/1918. Enl. 4/10/41 Jacksonville, FL. Ser. No. 34072234. With the 141st Field Artillery Battery at Camp Shelby and fought at Anzio, Italy. Pfc., Co. A, 5/8/45 Innsbruck, Austria. d. 8/21/1991 LA.

SERAFIN, Walter E. b. 7/18/1909 NJ. Res. Bergen Co., NJ. Enl. 7/9/42 Newark, NJ. Ser. No. 32390557. Pvt., HQ & HQ Co., Camp Gordon, GA 7/28/42. Pvt., HQ & HQ Co., transf. Co., D 10/9/42 Camp Gordon, GA. Fought against German Panzer Divisions in the Battle of the Bulge in Ardennes Forest. Frostbitten while sleeping outside. d. 11/29/1998 Elmwood Park, Bergen Co., NJ.

SERENI, Albert E. b. 1921 PA. Res. Philadelphia, PA. Enl. 9/22/42 Philadelphia, PA. Ser. No. 33335533. Pvt., Co. A, Camp Gordon, GA 10/9/42. Pfc., distinguished in action 7/10/43 Sicily. Sgt., Co. A, on LST 690 8/9/44. Sgt., Co. B, 5/8/45 Innsbruck, Austria.

SEXTON, Eugene. Pfc., Co. B, 5/8/45 Innsbruck, Austria.

SHABESKY, Joseph J. 2nd Lt., CWS, assigned Co. C, Camp Gordon, GA 10/24/42 from HQ, 4th Service Command, Atlanta, GA.

SHADDINGER, Earl. b. 1906 PA. Res. Philadelphia Co., PA. Enl. 2/25/42 Ft. George Meade, MD. Pvt. Attached to Co. G 5/28/42 Edgewood Arsenal, MD. Gunner (Pvt.). Ser. No. 33170347. Pfc., Co. C, to Battalion Supply, Camp Gordon, GA 7/27/42. Relieved from Supply, Camp Gordon, GA 8/3/42. Promo. T/5 (temp.), Camp Gordon, GA 12/3/42. Promo. Cpl. (temp.), Camp Gordon, GA 12/29/42. Jeep driver for Capt. Rupert Burford 7/14/43. Sgt., Co. C, WIA (light), 9/25/43 Maiori, Italy. Returned to duty 10/31/43. Rotation orders Nov. 1943. S/Sgt., Co. C, MIA, 1/26/44, Italy (Anzio) SR Cem.

SHAFFER, Kenneth E. b. 1922 OH. Res. Cuyahoga Falls, Summit Co., OH. Enl. 7/4/40 Ft. Hayes, Columbus, OH. Coast Artillery Corps. Ser. No. 15010137. Pvt., Co. C, (light injure in action), LST 422 Survivor, 1/26/44 Italy (Anzio) – Purple Heart.

SHAFFNER, John C. Cpl./Pvt, Co. D, WIA (serious – shell exploded in barrel), 12/7/44 France.

SHAIRA, Charles A. b. 1919 PA. Res. Bergen Co., NJ. Enl. 7/9/42 Newark, NJ. Pvt., HQ & HQ Co., Camp Gordon, GA 7/28/42. Ser. No. 32390629. Pvt., Co. D, KIA, 1/26/44, Italy (Anzio) SR Cem.

SHANAFELT, Denver E. b. 11/18/1918 OK. Res. Skiatook, Osage Co., OK. Enl. 3/4/42 Ft. Sill, OK. Pfc., Co. B, (Squad Leader), promo. Cpl. (temp.), Camp Gordon, GA 7/15/42. Ser. No. 38088029. Cpl. (temp.), Co. B, promo. Sgt. (temp.), Camp Gordon, GA 8/26/42. Sgt., Co. B, recommended for Silver Star for action near Ceppagna, Italy 11/13/43. Sgt., Co. B, WIA (serious - minefield – chest wound), 12/20/43 Italy – Purple Heart. Returned to duty from 300th Gen. Hospital 1/31/44. d. 1/6/1994 Mcalester, Pittsburg Co., OK.

SHANEFELTER, Clair P. b. 9/10/1909 France. Res. York Co., PA. Enl. 2/24/42 Ft. George Meade, MD. Ser. No. 33169984. Pvt. Attached to Co. G 5/28/42 Edgewood Arsenal, MD. Gunner (Pvt.). d. Jan. 1981 Hanover, York Co., PA.

SHANNON, John A. b. 2/23/1909 PA. Res. Armstrong Co., PA. Enl. 12/22/42 Pittsburgh, PA. Ser. No. 33416724. Pvt., Co. D, Camp Gordon, GA 3/18/43. d. Feb. 1972 Ford City, Armstrong Co., PA.

SHARKIS, Frank A. b. 1919 MA. Res. Plymouth Co., MA. Enl. 12/8/42 Boston, MA. Ser. No. 31238346. Pvt., Co. D, MIA, 1/26/44, Italy (Anzio) SR Cem. Body recovered 1/26/44 by YMS 34 & buried at sea same day. Next of kin: Antonia Sharkis, Brockton, MA.

SHARP, James A. b. 1900 KY. Res. Campbell Co., KY. Enl. 8/14/42 Ft. Oglethorpe, GA. Ser. No. 34364494. Present Co. D, Camp Gordon, GA, 12/31/42.

SHARP, Warren C. T/5, HQ & HQ Co., Camp Gordon, GA 11/21/42. T/5, apptd. T/4, HQ & HQ Co., Camp Gordon, GA 3/4/43. T/4 at Anzio 2/15/44. T/Sgt., HQ Co., 5/8/45 Innsbruck, Austria. Res. Denver, CO, May 1954. Civil Aeronautics Adm.

SHAW, Claude J. b. 1/5/1917, Geraldine, MT. Res. Milwaukie, Tillamook Co., OR. Grad. Milwaukie High School 1935. Enl. 12/4/42 Portland, OR. Ser. No. 39322916. Pfc., HQ & HQ Co., Camp Gordon, GA 4/10/43. T/5, HQ & HQ Co., LST 422 Survivor, 1/26/44 Italy (Anzio) – Purple Heart. Rescued by YMS 43. Reported safe on 1/30/44 Morning Report. S/Sgt., Co. B, 5/8/45 Innsbruck, Austria. Oregon State Policeman 1950. Res. Vernonia, OR, 1950. Livestock theft investigator, Oregon Dept. of Agriculture, Ontario, OR. Ret. law enforcement 1974, LaGrande, OR. d. 3/28/2009. bur. Willamette National Cemetery.

SHEARS, Ralph C. ("Shorty"). b. 11/28/1919 IL. Res. Shiawassee Co., MI. Enl. 11/24/42 at Kalamazoo, MI. Ser. No. 36411554. Pfc.,

Co. A 8/4/45. d. Aug. 1984, Albuquerque, NM.

SHEATS, Alfred R. Cpl., Co. C, 6/22/45 Innsbruck, Austria.

SHECKLER, Abraham E. b. 1917 PA. Res. Venango, PA. Enl. 9/21/42 Erie, PA. Ser. No. 13110054. Pvt. Co. D, 10/15/42 Camp Gordon GA. Pfc., Co. D, LST 422 Survivor, 1/26/44 Italy (Anzio) – Purple Heart. Rescued by YMS 69 1/26/44. Present at Camp Butner, SC, August 1944.

SHEFFIELD, Thomas D. b. 3/20/1921 MS. Res. Dorsey, Itawamba Co., MS. Pvt. Co. A, 10/14/42 Camp Gordon, GA. Transf. Co. C, Camp Gordon, GA, 12/16/42. Re-enl. 6/23/46 as Pfc., for service in Hawaiian Dept. Previous service in CWS. Ser. No. 34426766. d. 8/8/1997 Tupelo, Lee Co., MS.

SHELTON, Daniel. b. 10/28/1902 VA. Res. Spotsylvania Co., VA. Enl. 9/21/42 Richmond, VA. Ser. No. 33225613. Pvt., Co. A, Camp Gordon, GA 10/11/42. Transf. Co. B, Camp Gordon, GA, 12/16/42. d. August 1974 Fredericksburg, VA.

SHERRILL, William W. b. 1900 TN. Res. Fentress Co., TN. Enl. 9/15/42 Ft. Oglethorpe, GA. Ser. No. 34370815. Pvt., Co. A, Camp Gordon, GA 10/7/42. Transf. Co. B, Camp Gordon, GA, 12/16/42.

SHERWOOD, Wilber [Wilbur] G. b. 5/12/1917 MO. Res. Los Angeles Co., CA. Enl. 11/19/41 Los Angeles, CA. Ser. No. 39169917. T/5, Co. C, Camp Gordon, GA 4/10/43. d. 2/6/1996.

SHIELDS, Daniel J. ("Dan"). b. 7/6/1918 PA. Grad. Roman Catholic High School. Res. Philadelphia Co., PA. Enl. 9/23/42 Philadelphia, PA. Ser. No. 33335825. Pvt., Co. D, Camp Gordon, GA 10/9/42. Pvt., Co. D, WIA (light injure), LST 422 Survivor, 1/26/44 Italy (Anzio). Awarded Purple Heart 3/12/44. Rescued by YMS 43. Returned to duty 3/28/44. Transf. Battalion Supply. Promo. Pfc. 8/14/44. Pfc., HQ Co., 5/8/45 Innsbruck, Austria. EAME Service Medal with six Bronze Stars. Grad. LaSalle College 1953. Res. Philadelphia, PA May 1954. Internal Revenue Agent. Attended 1954, 1956, 1958, 1960, 1962 & 1966 Reunions as res. Philadelphia, PA. Laid wreath honoring 83rd CMB at Tomb of Unknown Soldier, Washington, D.C. 1962. d. 1/5/2000.

SHIELDS, Hugh A. b. 1907 Irish Free State. Enl. 6/26/42 Camp Blanding, FL. Ser. No. 34208101. T/5, HQ & HQ Co., Camp Gordon, GA 11/21/42. T/5 apptd. Cpl., HQ & HQ Co. 4/15/43. Pfc., Co. B, 5/8/45 Innsbruck, Austria.

SHIRLEY, George Norman. b. 8/24/1915 MS. Res. Shubuta, Jones Co., MS. Enl. 9/21/42 Camp Shelby, MS. Ser. No. 34426284. Pvt. Co. D, 10/14/42 Camp Gordon, GA. Cpl., Co. D, LST 422 Survivor, 1/26/44 Italy (Anzio) – Purple Heart with Oak Leaf Cluster. Rescued by YMS 69 1/26/44. Sgt., Co. A, 5/8/45 Innsbruck, Austria. Res. Laurel, MS May 1954. Operator, Wholesale Produce Co. Attended 1954 & 1962 Reunions as res. Laurel, MS. d. Dec. 1978, Laurel, Jones Co., MS.

SHIVE, Allen F. b. 1916 NC. Res., Rowan Co., NC. Enl. 11/27/42 Camp Croft, SC. Ser. No. 34591996. S/Sgt., HQ Co. Bronze Star,

Sept., 1945.

SHIVELY, Clayton C. b. 1916 MI. Res. Ludington, Mason Co., MI. Enl. 3/31/43 Kalamazoo, MI. Ser. No. 36459366. Pfc., Co. D, WIA (light injure), LST 422 Survivor, 1/26/44 Italy (Anzio) – Purple Heart. Sgt. Co. A, 5/8/45 Innsbruck, Austria. Attended 1956 Reunion.

SHIVERS, John M. Pfc., Co. C, 6/22/45 Innsbruck, Austria.

SHOAF, Carl S. b. 1921 PA. Enl. 9/25/42 Greensburg, PA.. Ser. No. 33294816. Pvt. HQ & HQ Co., 10/15/42 Camp Gordon GA. Pvt., Co. D, MIA, 1/26/44, Italy (Anzio) SR Cem.

SHOEMAKER, Harold M. b. 4/11/1912 VA. Enl. 12/15/42 Charlottesville, VA. Ser. No. 33536501. Pvt., Co. D, Camp Gordon, GA 3/18/43. Present in North Africa. Stationed at Ft. Myer, VA, July 1944. d. 10/20/1996 Harrisonburg, Harrisonburg Co., VA.

SHORE, John H. b. 5/1/1903 GA. Res. Richmond Co., GA. Pvt. Co. A, Camp Gordon, GA 10/9/42. Re-enl. 9/20/44 Ft. McPherson, Atlanta, GA. Ser. No. 66326235. d. April 1971, Augusta, Richmond Co., GA.

SHOULTS, Lovell M. ("Dutch"). b. 9/30/1915 IN. Res. Washington Co., IN. Enl. 2/12/42 Ft. Benjamin Harrison, IN. Ser. No. 35257965. Pvt. Attached to Co. F 5/28/42 Edgewood Arsenal, MD. Mechanic Auto (Pvt.). Pvt., HQ & HQ Co. transf. Co. D, Camp Gordon, GA 6/15/42. Pfc., (Motor Mech.), promo. T/5 (temp.), Camp Gordon, GA 7/15/42. T/4 (temp.), Co. D, promo. S/Sgt. (temp.), Camp Gordon, GA 10/6/42. d. 1/4/1992 Mooresville, Morgan Co., IN.

SHOWACRE, William M. b. 7/26/1921 Baltimore, MD. Res. Marion Co., WV. Enl. 4/19/41 Ft. Benjamin Harrison, IN. Air Corps. Attended CWS & OCS. Ser. No. 20544535. Air Base Chemical Defense Operation. Chemical Warfare Unit Commander 2/20/43. Departed for overseas 6/24/43, arrived overseas 7/1/43. 1st Lt., assigned to 83rd CMB 2/15/45. 1st. Lt., Co. C, 6/22/45 Innsbruck, Austria. Assigned 132nd Chem. Mortar Co. 7/19/45. Central Europe. EAME Service Medal & WWII Victory Medal. Co. L, 315th Inf, 79th Div. departed for US 11/26/45, arrived US 12/11/45. Discharged 2/18/46 Ft. Meade, MD. Re-enl. 9/11/50 Ft. Benning, GA. Artillery School Ft. Sill, OK Sept.-Dec. 1950, Armed Forces School, Carlisle Barracks, PA March-May 1951. 17th Field Artillery Bn. UN Service Medal, Korean Service Medal. Capt. Volunteer Reservist. Res. Fairmont, WV.

SHUMAKE, Everette L. b. 1924 NC. Res. Rockingham Co., NC. Enl. 4/7/43 Camp Croft, SC. Ser. No. 34771978. Pfc., Co. C, 6/22/45 Innsbruck, Austria.

SICLARE, Joseph P. b. 1925 NY. Res. Kings Co., NY. Enl. 7/15/43 New York City, NY. Ser. No. 32984838. Pfc., Co. C, MIA, 8/29/44 Briançon, France. POW Stalag 7A Moosburg, Bavaria. Liberated 6/9/45.

SIEPKOWSKI, Zenon R. Pfc., Co. A, 5/8/45 Innsbruck, Austria. Res. Chicago, IL.

SIKORA, Stanley A. b. 1916 OH. Res. Belmont Co., OH. Enl. 8/4/43 Columbus, OH. Ser. No. 35225665. Pfc., Co. C, MWIA (enemy mortar shell), 5/8/44 Anzio, Italy. Died shortly after being wounded.

SILVERT, Edwin S. b. 1921 PA. Res. Philadelphia Co., PA. Enl. 9/22/42 Philadelphia, PA. Ser. No. 33335615. Pvt., Co. D, Camp Gordon, GA 10/9/42. Pfc., Co. D, MIA, 1/26/44, Italy (Anzio) SR Cem.

SIMMONS, James R. b. 1921 MS. Res. Lee Co., MS. Enl. 9/22/42 Camp Shelby, MS. Ser. No. 34426619. Pvt. Co. A, 10/14/42 Camp Gordon, GA. Official casualty list states: Pvt., HQ & HQ Co., KIA (enemy shells), 2/11 or 12/44 Anzio, Italy. Another list states: Pvt., KIA, 1/26/44, Italy (Anzio).

SIMON, Robert W., Pfc. HQ Co., 5/8/45 Innsbruck, Austria. Res. Pittsburgh, PA May 1954. Sales Manager, Diamond Match Co.

SIMONE, Angelo. b. 1915 PA. Res. Merchantsville, Camden Co., NJ. Enl. 7/9/42 Camden, NJ. Ser. No. 32271742. Pvt., Co. C, Camp Gordon, GA 7/28/42. Pvt., Co. C, Camp Gordon, GA 9/25/42. Pfc., Co. C, LST 422 Survivor, 1/26/44 Italy (Anzio) – Purple Heart.

SIMPSON, Thomas C. Res. Ruleville, MS. Pvt., Co. B, 5/8/45 Innsbruck, Austria.

SIMS, Shannon. b. 1921 GA. Res. Jones Co., GA. Enl. 9/19/42 Ft. McPherson, Atlanta, GA. Ser. No. 34443084. Pvt., Co. D, Camp Gordon, GA 10/9/42. Pvt., Co. D, KIA, 1/26/44, Italy (Anzio), SR Cem.

SIMS, Walter W. Pvt., Co. B, 5/8/45 Innsbruck, Austria.

SIMURDA, John, Jr. b. 1918 Czechoslovakia. Enl. 9/22/42 Philadelphia, PA. Ser. No. 33335597. Pvt., Co. A, Camp Gordon, GA 10/9/42. Transf. Co. D, Camp Gordon, GA, 12/16/42. Pvt., Co. A transf. HQ Co., Camp Gordon, GA 1/25/43. T/4, Co. B, 5/8/45 Innsbruck, Austria.

SINCLAIR, Arthur H ("Art"). b. 1917 Haddonfield, NJ [another source says b. 1918]. Haddonfield Memorial High School where he was a star athlete. Signed by the New York Giants after graduation. Minor League Baseball: Pitcher/Outfield. Lucas Athletic Association Team (Lower County League) & New York Shipbuilding Team (South Jersery League) 1936. Leading hitter in the Camden County League 1942. Res. Camden Co., NJ. Enl. 7/9/42 Camden, NJ. Pvt., Co. C, Camp Gordon, GA 7/28/42. Pvt., Co. C, Camp Gordon, GA 9/25/42. Pfc. transf. Co. A, Camp Gordon, GA, 12/16/42. Pfc., Co. C transf. to Motor Pool, Camp Gordon, GA 1/25/43. Ser. No. 32271725. T/5, Co. C, MIA, 1/26/44, Italy (Anzio) SR Cem.

SINCLARE, Joseph P. Pfc., MIA, 8/29/44, France. [See entry for Joseph P. Siclare].

SINOW, Herbert E. b. 1/3/1911 IA. Res. Carroll Co., IA. Enl. 12/21/42 Camp Dodge, Herrold, IA. Ser. No. 37651594. Pvt., Co. B, Camp Gordon, GA 4/10/43. Pvt., Co. B, sick in Salemi, Sicily & sent to hospital (56th Medical Trapani) 8/6/43. d. Mar. 1970 IA.

SIPE, William. b. 1912 PA. Res. York Co., PA. Enl. 10/4/42 Harrisburg, PA. Ser. No. 13093258. Pvt., HQ & HQ Co., Camp Gordon, GA 10/9/42.

SIRMONS, Henry J. b. 1922 GA. Res. Lanier Co., GA. Enl. 10/19/42 Ft. McPherson, Atlanta, GA. Ser. No. 34448061. Cpl., Co. D, MIA, 1/26/44, Italy (Anzio) SR Cem.

SKALLEY, Lawrence M. b. 4/27/1898 KY. Res. Davidson Co., TN. Enl. 9/18/42 Ft. Oglethorpe, GA. Ser. No. 34371739. Pvt., HQ & HQ Co., Camp Gordon, GA 10/7/42. d. July 1977 Nashville, Davidson Co., TN.

SKELLIE, Harrison R. b. 1/20/1920 PA. Enl. 10/9/42 Erie, PA. Ser. No. 13110306. Pvt. Co. C, 10/15/42 Camp Gordon GA. Pvt., Co. C, assigned Med. Det., Camp Gordon, GA 11/14/42. Pvt., Med. Det. correspondent, Smokescreen, Camp Gordon, GA Dec. 1942 & Feb. 1943. Attended 1962 Reunion as res. Erie, PA. d. July 1981 Erie, Erie Co., PA.

SKELTON, Paul R. b. 1908 AL. Res. Fulton Co., GA. Enl. 9/15/42 Ft. McPherson, Atlanta, GA. Ser. No. 34441983. Pvt., Co. D, Camp Gordon, GA 10/8/42.

SLAGLE, Lewis W. b. TN. Res. Unicoi Co., TN. Enl. 9/29/39 for Panama Canal Dept. Ser. No. 06994569. Sgt., Co. D, WIA (serious – injured while firing mortar), 12/2/44 Aubere, France. Evacuated.

SLATE, Charles A. b. 1921 GA. Res, Fulton Co., GA. Enl. 9/21/42 Ft. McPherson, Atlanta, GA. Ser. No. 34443307. Pvt., HQ & HQ Co., Camp Gordon, GA 10/9/42. Pfc., Co. D, LST 422 Survivor, 1/26/44 Italy (Anzio). Pfc., HQ Co., 5/8/45 Innsbruck, Austria.

SLATER, Herbert W., Jr. b. 1921 MD. Enl. 9/25/42 Baltimore, MD. Ser. No. 33376941. Pvt. Co. B, 10/15/42 Camp Gordon GA.

SLATT, Axel G. A. Pfc., Co. B, promo. T/5 (temp.) 9/15/45. Served overseas 4 1/2 years. Res. Brooksville, FL.

SLIDER, William Vernon. b. 1/8/1921 Wilmer, AL. Baker High School, Mobile, AL. Pre-war Occupation: Shipyard Worker. Res. Jackson Co., MS. Enl. 9/19/42 Camp Shelby, MS. Ser. No. 34425929. Pvt. Co. A, 10/14/42 Camp Gordon, GA. Pfc., distinguished in action 7/10/43 Sicily. Pfc., Co. A, on LST 690 8/9/44. T/5, Co. C, 6/22/45 Innsbruck, Austria. Dischgd. at Camp Shelby, MS. Res. Moss Point, MS 2005.

SLODKOWSKI (Slodkoski), Charles. b. 11/11/1920 PA. Enl. 9/21/42 Harrisburg, PA. Ser. No. 33240967. Pvt., Co. B, Camp Gordon, GA 10/9/42. Pfc., WIA (light), 9/29/44, France. Pfc., Co. B, 5/8/45 Innsbruck, Austria. d. 3/19/1988 Shamokin, Northumberland Co., PA.

SLOMA, Francis M. b. 1919 NJ. Res. Passaic Co., NJ. Enl. 3/26/42 Ft. Dix, NJ. Ser. No. 32263155. 2nd Lt., Co. C, WIA (light – shot in leg by sniper) , 11/23/43 Venafro, Italy. Evacuated.

SMALL, Rufus A. b. 1915 GA. Res. Bulloch Co., GA. Enl. 9/19/42 Ft. McPherson, Atlanta, GA. Pvt., Co. A Camp Gordon, GA 10/9/42. Pfc., distinguished in action 7/10/43 Sicily. Ser. No. 3444300. T/5, Co. A, MIA, 1/26/44, Italy (Anzio) SR Cem.

SMALLWOOD, Kenneth B. b. 1911 TN. Res. Washington Co., TN. Enl. 7/4/41 Ft. Oglethorpe, GA. Ser. No. 34041141. Pvt., Co. C, MIA, 1/26/44, Italy (Anzio) SR Cem.

SMETANIUK, Joe. b. 4/11/1922 PA. Res. Montgomery Co., PA. Enl. 12/14/42 Allentown, PA. Ser. No. 33485002. Pvt., Co. D, Camp Gordon, GA 3/18/43. Served in Africa, then served in France as a cook. Res. Lansdale, PA. d. Aug. 1981 Montgomery Co., PA. [Joseph on death record].

SMITH, Albert. b. 1911 AL. Res. Geneva Co., AL. Enl. 9/17/42 Ft. McClellan, AL. Ser. No. 34391481. Pvt., HQ & HQ Co., Camp Gordon, GA 10/8/42.

SMITH, Cecil B., Sr. b. 1919 NY. Res. Buncombe Co., NC Enl. 10/21/44 Camp Croft, SC. Ser. No. 44018046. Pfc., Co. B, promo. Cpl. (temp.) 9/15/45.

SMITH, Dayton M. b. 10/29/1907 TN. Res. Davidson Co., TN. Enl. 9/18/42 Ft. Oglethorpe, GA. Ser. No. 34371731. Pvt., HQ & HQ Co., Camp Gordon, GA 10/7/42. d. 6/15/1998 Murfreesboro, Rutherford Co., TN..

SMITH, Donald E. Pfc., HQ Co., 5/8/45 Innsbruck, Austria.

SMITH, Fred C. b. 1908 MI. Res. Adair Co., KY. Enl. 12/14/42 Cincinnati, OH. Ser. No. 35677674. Pvt., WIA (light – WP burns – evacuated), 2/10/45 France. Pfc., Co. A, 5/8/45 Innsbruck, Austria.

SMITH, James C. b. 1918 GA. Res. Fulton Co., GA. Enl. 12/14/42 Ft. McPherson, Atlanta, GA. Ser. No. 34578016. Pfc., Co. A, on LST 690 8/9/44. Pvt., Co. A, Camp Gordon, GA 4/10/43. Pfc., Co. B, 5/8/45 Innsbruck, Austria.

SMITH, John F. b. 1903 PA. Enl. 9/22/42 Philadeplhia, PA. Ser. No. 33335582. Pvt., Co. C, Camp Gordon, GA 10/9/42.

SMITH, John W. b. 1921 MD. Enl. 9/26/42 Baltimore, MD. Ser. No. 33377149. Pvt. Co. A, 10/15/42 Camp Gordon GA. Transf. Co. C, Camp Gordon, GA, 12/16/42.

SMITH, Leondus. Pfc., Co. B, 5/8/45 Innsbruck, Austria.

SMITH, Marvin W. b. 1911 NC. Res. Guilford Co., NC. Enl. 9/17/40 Charlotte, NC. Field Artillery. Ser. No. 14021298. Pfc., Co. D, MIA, 1/26/44, Italy (Anzio) SR Cem.

SMITH, Murray. b. 1923 NY. Res. Brooklyn, Kings Co., NY. Enl. 3/29/43 New York City, NY. Ser. No. 32677095. Pvt., Co. D, LST 422 Survivor, 1/26/44 Italy (Anzio) – Purple Heart. Cpl. WIA (injured glider crash) 8/15/44 Le Muy, France. Present at Repl. Depot 12/11/44.

Departed or U.S. on 30-day plan March 1945.

SMITH, Park L., Jr. ("Chew Tobacco") b. 1925. Enl. 4/28/43 Harrisburg, PA. Ser. No. 33508343. Pfc., Co. A, 5/8/45 Innsbruck, Austria.

SMITH, Robert Browning ("Smitty"). b. 8/27/1906 Bluejacket, Oklahoma Territory. Moved New Mexico 1908. Attended New Mexico A&M preparatory school Grad. Las Cruces Union High School 1925. New Mexico College of Agriculture and Mechanic Arts [New Mexico State University] 1931-34 – Civil Engineering & Business Administration. Owner/Operator, Dry Cleaning Plant, Hot Springs, NM 1935-42. Enl. 8/24/42 as a 1st Lt. Ser. No. 01037307. Promo. Capt. May 1943. Served in 2nd CMB. Joined Co. C, 83rd CMB 4/9/44 at Anzio. Present as Capt., Co. C, 6/19/44. Injured both knees late Aug. 1944. Bronze Star for action at Bertichamps, France 11/13/44. Silver Star [presented 11/20/44 for action at Briançon, France 8/29/44]. Capt., Co. C, 6/22/45 Innsbruck, Austria. Silver Star 1945. Capt., transf. HQ & HQ Co. 7/27/45. Assigned Battalion Executive Officer 7/31/45. Assigned Battalion Commanding Officer 9/10/45. Retired from service May 1947 as Maj. Owner/Operator Valley Motor Supply Co. Pres./Director Hot Springs National Bank. Attended 1956 Reunion. d. 2/10/1959. bur. National Cemetery at Santa Fe, NM.

SMITH, Robert W. Lt., CWS, LST 422 Survivor, 1/26/44 Italy (Anzio). Rescued by USS YMS 226. Taken to 93rd Evac. Hosp. Acting CO, Co. C, 2/2/44. 2nd Lt., assigned Co. A, March 1944. Lt., Co. A, left Co. A July 1944. Sick with dysentery at 225th Station Hosp. Returned 7/30/44. 2nd Lt. Relsd. Co. A, 83rd CMB and attached unassigned to 7th Repl. Depot for purpose of ZA. Travel by most expeditious means 8/2/44.

SMITH, Thomas E. Pfc., Co. A, 5/8/45 Innsbruck, Austria. Res. Astoria, NY May 1954. Machine Engraver.

SMITH, Willard A. b. 8/9/1920. Arrived at Camp Gordon, GA 10/9/42 & assgnd. Co. B. 2nd Platoon, Mortar Squad. Pvt., Co. B correspondent, Smokescreen, Camp Gordon, GA Nov. 1942. 2nd Platoon, Communications. Pfc., Co. B, 5/8/45 Innsbruck, Austria. 103rd Inf. Div. Res. Pittsburgh, PA May 1954. Attended 1954, 1956, 1958, 1960, 1962 & 1966 reunions as res. Pittsburgh, PA. d. 1/14/2007 Bridgeville, Allegheny Co., PA.. bur. Mt. Lebanon Cem. Mausoleum, PA.

SMITH, William W. b. 1910 PA. Res. Westmoreland Co., PA Enl. 9/29/42 Greensburg, PA. Ser. No. 33391669. Pvt., Co. C, Camp Gordon, GA 10/20/42.

SNEED, Charlie M., Jr. b. 1907 VA. Res. Bedford Co., VA. Enl. 9/21/42 Roanoke, VA. Ser. No. 33213314. Pvt. Co. D, 10/11/42 Camp Gordon GA. Pvt., Co. D, KIA, 1/26/44, Italy (Anzio). Body recovered 1/26/44 by USS YMS 226 and turned over to Graves Registration at Anzio 1/27/44. Next of kin: Sally Sneed, Bedford, VA.

SNYDER, Charles R., Jr. b. 1916 IA. Res. Wright Co., IA. Enl. 12/21/42 Camp Dodge, Herrold, IA. Ser. No. 37651601. Pvt., Co. A, Camp Gordon, GA 4/10/43. Pfc., distinguished in action 7/10/43 Sicily. Pfc., HQ Co., 5/8/45 Innsbruck, Austria.

SNYDER, Raymond S. b. 12/7/1919 PA. Enl. 12/19/42 Allentown, PA. Ser. No. 33485321. Pvt., Co. A, Camp Gordon, GA 4/10/43. Pvt., Co. A, WIA (light – enemy shell burst – leg), 3/30/44 Anzio, Italy. Lawrence Ertzberger said Snyder was seriously wounded, possibly lost his leg, and never returned to the battalion. Attended the 1982 reunion on crutches. d. 5/19/1989 Nazareth, Northampton Co., PA.

SNYDER, Steve. b. 3/14/1922, Monaca, PA. Prewar occupation: CCC worker. Steel mill worker. Res. Beaver Co., PA. Enl. 9/24/42 Pittsburgh, PA. Ser. No. 33305425. Pvt. Co. A, 10/15/42 Camp Gordon GA. Contracted malaria in Sicily. Malaria recurrence on the Anzio invasion 1/22/44. Pfc., Co. A, on *LST 690* 8/9/44. Pfc., Co. C, 6/22/45 Innsbruck, Austria. Res. Monaca, PA May 1954. Foreman, Kappers Co. Attended 1954 Reunion. Postwar occupation: Steel mill worker. Res. Monaca, PA, 2009.

SNYDER, Wilbur A. Ser. No. 32757385. Res. NJ. Pvt., Co. D, KIA, 1/26/44, Italy (Anzio), SR Cem.

SOCOLOSKI, Leonard V. b. 10/8/1921 PA. Res. Northumberland Co., PA. Enl. 9/21/42 Harrisburg, PA. Ser. No. 33240946. Pvt., Co. B, Camp Gordon, GA 10/9/42. Transf. Co. A, Camp Gordon, GA, 12/16/42. Sgt., Co. B, 5/8/45 Innsbruck, Austria. Res. Mt. Carmel, PA. d. 4/1/2005 Mt. Carmel, Northumberland Co., PA.

SOLERO, Casildo M. b. 1908 NY. Res. New York Co., NY. Enl. 7/9/42 Ft. Jay, Governors Island, NY. Ser. No. 32402170. T/4, MIA, 1/26/44, Italy (Anzio) SR Cem.

SOLEY, Andrew. b. 1921 PA. Res. Lyndora, PA. Enl. 9/25/42 Pittsburgh, PA. Ser. No. 33305658. Pvt. Co. A, 10/15/42 Camp Gordon GA. Pfc., Co. A, MIA, 1/26/44, Italy (Anzio) SR Cem. Next of kin: John Soley, father.

SOLOMON, David. b. 1903 PA. Res. Camden Co., NJ. Enl. 7/9/1942 Camden, NJ. Ser. No. 32271791. Pvt., Co. C, Camp Gordon, GA 7/28/42. Present Co. C, as a cook, Camp Gordon, GA, 1/9/43.

SORENSON, Julius J. b. 9/25/1915 TX. Res. TX. Enl. 3/3/42 Ft. Bliss, El Paso, TX. Ser. No. 38101799. Pvt. Attached to Co. C 5/28/42 Edgewood Arsenal, MD. Squad Leader (Sgt.). Pfc., Co. B, Camp Gordon, GA 8/3/42. Promo. Cpl. (temp.), Camp Gordon, GA 8/26/42. Promo. Sgt. (temp.), Camp Gordon, GA 12/12/42. S/Sgt., Co. B, 5/8/45 Innsbruck, Austria. Res. Taylor, TX May 1954. Dairy Farmer. d. 8/27/1994 Taylor, TX.

SORENSON, Robert L. Enl. Feb. 1942. Pvt. Attached to Co. G 5/28/42 Edgewood Arsenal, MD. Telephone Operator (Pvt.). Pfc., Co. B, assigned Med. Det., Camp Gordon, GA 11/30/42. Sent as medical aid to Co. A 4/4/44. Returned 4/7/44. T/5, Med. Det., WIA (light – severe contusion of hip), 6/2/44 Italy – Purple Heart. Hospitalized. T/4, wrote a column on cameras in Muzzleblasts 1944-45. T/4, Med. Det., 5/8/45 Innsbruck, Austria. Dischd. Sept. 1945 as T/3. Director, Mental Health Clinic. Contributed to MFP 1997. [also spelled Sorensen.]

SORKEN, Nathan. b. 1912 MI. Res. Erie Co., NY. Enl. 10/20/42 Buffalo, NY. Ser. No. 32553551. Pfc., Co. D, MIA, 1/26/44, Italy (Anzio) SR Cem.

SORRENTINO, John J. b. 1922 NY. Res. Hudson Co., NJ. Enl. 4/17/43 Newark, NJ. Ser. No. 32915491. Pfc., Co. A, 5/8/45 Innsbruck, Austria. Postwar bus driver, Newark, NJ.

SPANGENBERG, Thomas E. b. 1924 PA. Enl. 5/12/43 Wilkes Barre, PA. Ser. No. 33605325. Pvt., KIA, 3/26/44, Italy, SR Cem. [Probably same man listed as Pvt. Thoma A. Pagenberg, Co. C, KIA (S-mine), Minturno, Italy 3/26/44].

SPARKMAN, Thomas W. b/ 1914 AL. Res. Jefferson Co., AL. Enl. 3/10/42 Ft. McPherson, AL. Ser. No. 34263828. Pvt. Attached to Co. A 5/28/42 Edgewood Arsenal, MD. Squad Leader (Sgt.). Cpl. (temp.), Co. A, promo. Sgt. (temp.), Camp Gordon, GA 8/19/42.

SPARKS, Donald I. b. 1922 PA. Res. Delaware Co., PA. Enl. 10/5/42 Philadelphia, PA. Ser. No. 33338211. Pvt., Co. B, Camp Gordon, GA 10/9/42. Pvt., Co. B – Color Guard of Co. B & Asst. Editor, Smokescreen, Camp Gordon, GA Nov. 1942. Transf. Co. A, Camp Gordon, GA, 12/16/42. Pvt., Asst. Editor, Smokescreen, Camp Gordon, GA Feb. 1943.

SPEAL, John. b. 1/17/1917 PA. Enl. 12/22/42 Greensburg, PA. Ser. No. 33413314. Pvt., Co. D, Camp Gordon, GA 3/18/43. d. Jan. 1965.

SPEIGHTS, Cedric C. b. 1919 OK. Res. Contra Costa Co., CA. Enl. 3/6/41 San Francisco, CA. Ser. No. 39003901. T/5, HQ Co., 5/8/45 Innsbruck, Austria.

SPENCER, Erskine Clark. b. 1921 AL. Res. Cleveland, Sunflower Co., MS. Enl. 9/23/42 Camp Shelby, MS. Ser. No. 34426683. Pvt. Co. A, 10/14/42 Camp Gordon, GA. Cpl., Bronze Star ribbon 1944. Cpl., Co. A, on *LST 690* 8/9/44. Cpl., Co. A, WIA (accidental – evacuated), 1/3/45 France. Information provided in battalion journal for January 1945.

SPERANZO, Michael C. b. 1921 NJ. Enl. 9/22/42 Philadelphia, PA. Ser. No. 33335554. Pvt., Co. A, Camp Gordon, GA 10/9/42.

SPERIAN [Speiran], Patrick P. ("Paddy" / "Patty"). Entered service NY. Cpl., Co. D, Bronze Star for action 11/11/44 France. Cpl. Co. A, 5/8/45 Innsbruck, Austria. Res. New York, NY May 1954. Hotel Employee. Attended 1962 Reunion as res. New York City.

SPINTI, Carl G. W. b. 1922 WI. Res. Dane Co., WI. Enl. 12/29/42 Milwaukee, WI. Ser. No. 36293078. Cpl., Co. C, 6/22/45 Innsbruck, Austria.

SPIRA, Maurice L. 1st Lt. Assigned 65th Inf. Div. 7/23/45.

SPRAGGINS, Raymond J. Pvt., HQ & HQ Co., Camp Gordon, GA 10/9/42. Ser. No. 33335483.

SPRAGUE, Anderson. b. 1915 WV. Res. Nicholas Co., WV 1920. Enl. 8/17/40 Ft. Knox, KY. Medical. Ser. No. 06662980. Pfc., Med. Det., 5/8/45 Innsbruck, Austria.

SPRINGOWSKI, John J. T/5, HQ Co., promo. T/4 (temp.) 9/15/45.

SQUIRES, Norman Charles. b. 1/31/1913 Wash., D.C. Seat Pleasant School, MD. Pre-war Occupation: Standard Oil, Wash., D.C. For six months. Supervisor/Manager Retail Automotive Service. Res. Prince George Co., MD. Enl. 12/22/42 Baltimore, MD. Ser. No. 33390998. Pvt., Engineer Training. Pvt., Co. D, Camp Gordon, GA 3/18/43. Glider Badge. Pfc. Light Truck Driver. Served in North Africa, Sicily, Italy, France, Germany & Austria. Drove jeeps, 3/4, 1 & half, 2 & half ton vehicles. Drove in combat & during blackouts. Hauled ammunition, food, & service supplies. Did minor serving & repairing on vehicles. EAMA Service Ribbon with Bronze Arrowhead. Good Conduct Medal. Pfc., Co. A, 5/8/45 Innsbruck, Austria. Dischd. 10/18/45. Res. Seat Pleasant, MD May 1954. Sears, Roebuck & Co. d. 1/17/2000.

STABILE, Alfonso P. b. 1923 MA. Res. Middlesex Co., MA. Enl. 4/9/43 Boston, MA. Ser. No. 31309611. Pvt., Co. D, MIA, 1/26/44, Italy (Anzio) SR Cem.

STACKHOUSE, Karl E. b. 8/6/1914 IA. Res. Marshall Co., IA. Enl. 2/22/43 Camp Dodge, Herrold, IA. Ser. No. 37662664. Pfc., Co. A, 5/8/45 Innsbruck, Austria. 410th Infantry, Co. H. d. Mar. 1980.

STAEHLE, Charles L. b. 1916 NJ. Res. Bergen Co., NJ. Enl. 2/19/42 Ft. Dix, NJ. Ser. No. 32239353. Pvt. Attached to Co. G 5/28/42 Edgewood Arsenal, MD. Gunner (Pvt.). Pfc., Co. C, (Squad Leader), promo. Cpl. (temp.), Camp Gordon, GA 7/15/42. Sgt., Co. C, transf. Co. D, Camp Gordon, GA 10/21/42.

STAHL, John H. b. 1901 NJ. Res. Essex Co., NJ. Enl. 7/9/42 Newark, NJ. Ser. No. 32390380. Pvt., HQ & HQ Co., Camp Gordon, GA 7/28/42.

STAHL, Robert H. Assigned from 65th Inf. Division as 2nd Lt., Co. C, 7/23/45. 2nd Lt., Co. C. Bronze Star, Sept., 1945.

STANGANELLI, Saverio. b. 9/6/1918 MA. Res. Lawrence, MA. Enl. 3/8/43 Boston, MA. Ser. No. 31301994. Flame Thrower & Interpreter. Pfc., Co. D, MIA, 1/26/44, Italy (Anzio) SR Cem. bur. Ridgewood Cem., North Andover, MA.

STANLEY, Edward R. b. 1914 TN. Res. Haywood Co., TN. Enl. 8/28/42 Ft. Oglethorpe, GA. Ser. No. 34367238. Sgt., Co. D, MIA, 1/26/44, Italy (Anzio) SR Cem.

STANLEY, Mitchell H. Pfc., Co. A, 5/8/45 Innsbruck, Austria.

STANTON, John A. b. 1910 PA. Res. Carmel, Northampton Co., PA. Enl. 7/9/42 Ft. Jay, Governors Island, NY. [Award says entered service from Pittsburgh, PA]. Ser. No. 32402426. Pvt., Co. C, Camp Gordon, GA 7/28/42. Pfc., Co. C, Bronze Star for action 7/10/43 Sicily. Pfc.,

Co. C, LST 422 Survivor, 1/26/44 Italy (Anzio) – Purple Heart. Pfc., Co. C, WIA (light), 6/1/44 Italy.

STANTON, John J. b. 1914 NY. Res. Baltimore City Co., MD. Enl. 3/27/43 New York City, NY. Ser. No. 3287557. Pfc., Co. D, MIA, 1/26/44, Italy (Anzio) SR Cem.

STASINSKI, Rudolph J. b. 1916 NY. Res. Kings Co., NY. Enl. 5/13/43 New York City, NY. Ser. No. 32906758. Pvt., Co. C, WIA (light), 6/1/44 Italy. Wounded badly outside Limoges, France; picked up by 7th Army, Communications Div.

STECKEL, Leslie F. Pvt., Co. C, Camp Gordon, GA 10/9/42. Ser. No. 33296804.

STEEDLE, Leo Charles. ("Lee"/'Young-Un'). b. 11/12/1924 Santa Monica, CA. Res. Collegeville, Allegheny Co., PA. Enl. 11/21/42 Pittsburgh, PA. Ser. No. 13167886. Field Artillery. Joined 83rd CMB Mar. 1944. Co. D. Squad Leader. Cpl., Co. D, WIA 3/26/44 Minturno, Italy – Purple Heart. Got malaria a few days after reaching Rome. Promo. to Sgt. & Sqaud Leader after Anzio. Squad gave him his nickname. Sgt., Co. B, 5/8/45 Innsbruck, Austria. Dischd. Nov. 1945. Advertising Agency Copywriter. International Marketing Director Reader's Digest. Retired 1981. Editor & Contributor MFP 1997. Res. Oakdale, NY 2009.

STEELE, Relder O. b. 11/3/1904 MS. Res. Lee Co., MS. Enl. 9/22/42 Camp Shelby, MS. Ser. No. 34426594. Pvt. Co. A, 10/14/42 Camp Gordon, GA. Transf. Co. D, Camp Gordon, GA, 12/16/42. d. 6/21/1991.

STEELE, Robert A. b. 1902 PA. Enl. 9/24/42 Greensburg, PA. Ser. No. 33294809. Pvt. HQ & HQ Co., 10/15/42 Camp Gordon GA.

STEFANKO, (STEFANKA), John. b. 1905 PA. Res. Allegheny Co., PA. Enl. 6/8/42 Pittsburgh, PA. T/5, HQ & HQ Co., Camp Gordon, GA 11/21/42. Art Contributor, Smokescreen, Camp Gordon, GA Feb. 1943.. Ser. No. 33269394. T/5, apptd. T/4, HQ & HQ Co., Camp Gordon, GA 3/4/43. T/4, Co. D, MIA, 1/26/44, Italy (Anzio) SR Cem.

STEINBRECHER, ----------. In a photo belonging to L. Lew Henry, probably Co. A.

STEPANOVICH, Peter. b. 1908 PA. Res. Butler Co., PA. Enl. 8/25/42 Pittsburgh, PA. Ser. No. 33305677. Pvt. Co. D, 10/15/42 Camp Gordon GA. Pfc., Co. D, KIA, 1/26/44, Italy (Anzio) SR Cem.

STEPHENSON, George E. b. 1911 IN. Enl. 12/16/1942 Louisville, KY. Ser. No. 35690913. Pvt., Co. B, Camp Gordon, GA 4/10/43. Pvt., Co. B, KIA, 1/26/44, Italy (Anzio). His wallet was found on the beach near the water and returned to his mother. Had also stated to his mother he probably would not return from the war.

STEPHENSON, Harley. b. 1906 OH. Res. Muskingum Co., OH Enl. 12/16/42 Akron, OH. Ser. No. 35595044. Pvt., Co. A, Camp Gordon, GA 4/10/43.

STEPHONAC, John, Jr. b. 12/18/1912 PA. Enl. 8/29/42 Pittsburgh, PA. Ser. No. 33301371. Pvt. Co. D, 10/15/42 Camp Gordon GA. d. 4/11/1988 Washington Co., PA.

STEPTOE, Leondus. b. 1919 GA. Res. Douglas, Johnson Co., GA. Enl. 12/15/42 Ft. McPherson, Atlanta, GA. Ser. No. 34578146. Pvt., Co. B, Camp Gordon, GA 4/10/43. Pvt., Co. B, WIA (light-shell fragment in shoulder), 1/3/44 [?] Anzio, Italy. Not hospitalized. Pfc., Co. B, WIA (light – enemy shell fire), 2/24/44 Anzio, Italy – Purple Heart. Pfc., Co. B, WIA 2/28/44 Italy – Purple Heart with Oak Leaf Cluster.

STERNER, Francis E. b. 1918 PA. Enl. 10/5/42 Philadelphia, PA. Ser. No. 13124721. Pvt., Co. B, Camp Gordon, GA 10/9/42. Cpl., Co. B, KIA, 12/12/44, Riquewihr, France, LO Cem.

STETTER, Peter P. b. 1913 PA. Enl. 12/12/42 Altoona, PA. Ser. No. 33567123. Pvt., Co. B, Camp Gordon, GA 4/10/1943.

"STEVE". Co. D. Pre-med student. Res. IL. Mentioned by Harold Hughes in his book The Man from Ida Grove. KIA (mortar barrage), Sept. 1943, Vietri sul Mare, Italy.

STEVENS, George W. T/5 WIA (injured in glider crash) 8/15/44 Le Muy, France. Cpl., Purple Heart [Presented 11/20/44] Attended 1956 Reunion. Res. Richmond, VA.

STEVENSON, Edgar F. b. 1898 PA. Enl. 9/5/42 Philadelphia, PA. Ser. No. 33332678. Pvt., Co. B, Camp Gordon, GA 10/9/42.

STEWART, Estus N. ("Tuck"). b. 2/19/1919 MS. Res. Smith Co., MS. Enl. 9/22/42 Camp Shelby, MS. Ser. No. 34426386. Pvt. Co. A, 10/14/42 Camp Gordon, GA. Pvt., Co. A, on LST 690 8/9/44. Pfc., Co. A, 2nd Platoon. WIA (light – premature muzzleburst), Bischweiler, France (Alsace) 2/18/45. Pfc., Co. A, 5/8/45 Innsbruck, Austria. d. 11/26/1987 Pulaski, Scott Co., MS.

STEWART, William C. Pvt., Co. B, KIA, 12/8/43 San Pietro, Italy.

ST GEMME, Harold L. b. 1919 MO. Res. St. Louis Co., MO. High School Drop-Out. Tug Boat Deck Hand. Worked on an iron ore freighter on the Great Lakes. Worked for an aircraft manufacturer. Enl. 1/3/44 Jefferson Barracks, MO. Ser. No. 37631950. Joined the 83rd CMB in France as a replacement in the Fall of 1944. France, Germany, Austria. Pfc., Co. B, 5/8/45 Innsbruck, Austria. Occupational Duty, Vienna, Austria after German surrender. Dischd. 5/13/46. Earned a University Bachelor & Master's degree. Entered Southern Baptist Christian Ministry. Ten years as Minister to students at Univ. of Mississippi schools of Medicine & Nursing. Chaplain, Baptist Medical Center, Little Rock, AR. Res. Little Rock, AR 2009.

STIEFVATER [Stiefvatvater], Joseph C. ["Steve"]. 2nd Lt., CWS, assigned to Co. A, Camp Gordon, GA 8/3/42. Transf. Co. D, Camp Gordon, GA 10/1/42. Assigned Co. C, Camp Gordon, GA 10/21/42. 2nd. Lt., transf. Co. A, Camp Gordon, GA, 12/16/42. 2nd Lt., Co. D, WIA (shell fragment), Sicily 7/10/43 Gela, Sicily. WIA (light), 7/11/43 Gela, Sicily. Purple Heart [presented 9/27/43 in Sicily]. Ed Trey said he had extremely thick lensed glasses and was very witty. Said the last time the 83rd saw him he was with a smoke generator outfit.

ST LOUIS, (Roger) Napoleon G. ("Blackie"). b. 1923 MI. Res. Chippewa Co., MI. Enl. 3/5/42 Ft. Brady, Sault St. Marie, MI. Ser. No. 16025746. Pvt., Co. D, WIA (light injure – truck over-turned on road between Pozzuoli & Minturno), 3/25 or 26/44 Italy. Retuned to duty 3/27/44. Pvt. WIA (injured in glider crash) 8/15/44 Le Muy, France. Pvt., WIA (light) 8/17/44 France – Purple Heart. Pfc., Med. Det., 5/8/45 Innsbruck, Austria.

STODDARD, Ralph W. b. 1924 MT. Res. Cache Co., UT. Enl. 5/4/43 Salt Lake City, UT. Ser. No. 39913523. Pvt., Co. D, WIA (light – enemy shell fragment), 5/24/44 Anzio, Italy – Purple Heart. Pfc., Co. A, 1st Platoon. WIA (slight – defective shell aerial burst), France (Alsace) 2/17/45. Pfc., Co. A, 5/8/45 Innsbruck, Austria. [also listed as Stoddart].

STOGNER, Kenneth L. b. 1/16/1921 MS. Res. Lafayette Co., MS. Enl. 9/22/42 Camp Shelby, MS. Ser. No. 34426552. Pvt. Co. A, 10/14/42 Camp Gordon, GA. d. 6/15/2006.

STOKES, ----------. Shot a Lt. In the head (graze). Information provided by Kelso Thompson.

STONE, Bernardo B. [probably same man as Bernard Stone, 2nd Lt., Co. B, Camp Gordon, GA 3/6/43]. 2nd Lt., Co. B, WIA (light – fragment in arm), 12/8/43 San Pietro, Italy. 1st Lt. Silver Star – presented 1/19/44. Lt., Co. B, slightly injured in jeep accident near Pierrepont, France 10/12/44. Capt., HQ Co., 5/8/45 Innsbruck, Austria. Capt. Assigned 65th Inf. Div. 7/23/45. Res. Glencoe, IL May 1954.

STOREY, Cy. Company Clerk, Co. D. Lawrenceville, GA. [may be the same as Miles Storey].

STOREY, Milus (Miles) K. b. 1920 GA. Res. Harris Co., GA. Enl. 10/3/42 Ft. McPherson, Atlanta, GA. Ser. No. 14139568. Pvt., Co. D, Camp Gordon, GA 10/9/42. Pvt., Co. D correspondent, Smokescreen, Camp Gordon, GA Feb. 1943. Corp. HQ Co. Company Clerk. [may be the same as Cy Storey].

STOUT, Thomas D. Pvt., Co. B, KIA (fell from his truck), 1/29/44 Caserta, Italy.

STRACK, Robert E. b. 7/22/1923 IN. Enl. 1/28/43 Toledo, OH. Ser. No. 35544601. Jeep driver for Wofford Jackson in Southern France. Pvt., Co. D, promo. T/5 (temp.), 11/1/44. T/5, Co. A, 5/8/45 Innsbruck, Austria. Postwar res. Ft. Wayne, IN. d. 9/1/1997.

STRAKA, George J. b. 8/1/1915 PA. Enl. 12/15/42 Pittsburgh, PA. Ser. No. 33405653. Pvt., Co. B, Camp Gordon, GA 4/10/43. Pvt., Co. B, WIA (light), 12/8/43 Italy. Returned to duty 12/9/43. d. Aug. 1974 PA.

STRANTZ, William R. b. 1920 IL. Res. Peoria Co., IL. Enl. 3/6/42 Peoria, IL. Ser. No. 16054574. Pvt. Attached to Co. C 5/28/42 Edge-

wood Arsenal, MD. Auto Rifleman (Pvt.).

STRAUSSER, Edwin C. b. 1924. Res. Berks Co., PA. Enl. 3/4/43 Allentown, PA. Ser. No. 33618423. Pfc., Co. D, MIA, 1/26/44, Italy (Anzio) SR Cem. Body recovered 1/26/44 by YMS 34 & buried at sea same day.

STRELOW, Robert W. b. 1917 MT. Res. Hennepin Co., MN. Enl. 1/30/42 Ft. Snelling, MN. Ser. No. 17048539. Pvt. Attached to Co. E 5/28/42 Edgewood Arsenal, MD. Platoon Sgt. (S/Sgt.). Pvt., Co. B transf. Co. A, Camp Gordon, GA 6/15/42. Cpl. (temp.), Co. A, promo. Sgt. (temp.), Camp Gordon, GA 9/23/42. Transf. Co. D, Camp Gordon, GA 10/21/42.

STRICKLAND, Seth W. b. 1922 NC. Res. Fair Bluff, Columbus Co., NC. Enl. 9/5/40 Ft. Bragg, NC. Field Artillery. Ser. No. 14018030. Pvt., Co. D, LST 422 Survivor, 1/26/44 Italy (Anzio) – Purple Heart.

STRICKLER, Clair M. b. 8/7/1922 Craley, PA. William Penn High School. Pre-war Occupation: Inspector. Res. York Co., PA. Enl. 10/5/42 Harrisburg, PA. Ser. No. 13093246. Pvt., HQ & HQ Co., Camp Gordon, GA 10/9/42. Pfc., HQ Co., 5/8/45 Innsbruck, Austria. Military Occupation: Supply Clerk. Also served in Co. A. Good Conduct Medal. EAME Service Medal with 6 Bronze Stars & 1 Bronze Arrowhead.. World War II Victory Medal. Dischd. 9/28/45. Res. York, PA May 1954. Attended 1954 Reunion. d. 1/16/2004 York, York Co., PA. Bur. Canadochly Evangelical & Reformed Church, Prospect Rd., York, PA.

STRINGER, Preston. b. 3/31/1921 MS. Res. Smith Co., MS. Enl. 9/22/42 Camp Shelby, MS. Ser. No. 34426399. Pvt. Co. A, 10/14/42 Camp Gordon, GA. Transf. Co. C, Camp Gordon, GA, 12/16/42. d. Aug. 1972.

STROCK, Zachariah W., Jr. Pvt., Co. D, Camp Gordon, GA 3/18/43. Ser. No. 33526999. Res. VA. Pfc., Co. D, MIA, 1/26/44, Italy (Anzio) SR Cem.

STUTTS, Hershel T. b. 1920 MS. Res. Corinth, Lafayette Co., MS. Enl. 9/22/42 Camp Shelby, MS. Ser. No. 34426544. Pvt. Co. A, 10/14/42 Camp Gordon, GA. T/5, Co. A on *LST 690* 8/9/44. T/5, HQ Co., 5/8/45 Innsbruck, Austria.

SUAREZ, ----------. Pvt., Co. C. In a photo taken April 1944 at Minturno including Lloyd Fiscus & Norman Brann. Fiscus said he was a "Latino from Louisiana."

SUBICK, Albert M. b. 9/7/1921 PA. Enl. 9/22/42 Philadelphia, PA. Ser. No. 33335594. Pvt., Co. A, Camp Gordon, GA 10/9/42. d. 5/2/1993 Philadelphia, PA.

SUHRKE, Robert V. b. 1/20/1920 WI. Res. Sheboygan Co., WI. Enl. 2/17/42 Milwaukee, WI. Ser. No. 16049347. Pvt. Attached to Co. H 5/28/42 Edgewood Arsenal, MD. Squad Leader (Sgt.). Pvt., Co. C transf. Co. D, Camp Gordon, GA 6/15/42. Sgt. (temp.), promo. S/Sgt. (temp.), Camp Gordon, GA 8/1/42. d. 7/26/1990 WI.

SULLIVAN, Herbert. b. 1921 VA. Res. Spotsylvania Co., VA. Enl. 9/21/42 Richmond, VA. Ser. No. 33225293. Pvt. Co. D, 10/11/42 Camp Gordon GA. Pvt., Co. D, WIA (light - injured by fall during debarkation in Sicily Invasion), 7/10/43 Gela, Sicily.

SULLIVAN, William E. Res. NY. Ser. No. 32782701. Pvt., Co. D, MIA, 1/26/44, Italy (Anzio) SR Cem. Body recovered 1/26/44 by YMS 34 & buried at sea same day. Next of kin: Jennie Sullivan, Staten Island, NY.

SULLIVAN, William M. b. 1906 NJ. Res. Bergen Co., NJ. Enl. 7/9/42 Newark, NJ. Ser. No. 32390581. Pvt., HQ & HQ Co., Camp Gordon, GA 7/28/42. Pvt., HQ Co., Camp Gordon, GA 10/21/42. Present HQ Co., Camp Gordon, GA, 1/9/43.

SUTLIC, Edward J. b. 1922 PA. Enl. 9/26/42 Pittsburgh, PA. Pvt., Ser. No. 33305748. Pvt. Co. C, 10/15/42 Camp Gordon GA. BAR man. Pfc. Co. C, KIA (drowned in a pond), 8/23/43, Castelvetrano, Sicily, SR Cem.

SUTPHIN, Thomas J. b. 8/3/1911 VA. Enl. 9/26/42 Baltimore, MD. Ser. No. 33377251. Pvt. HQ & HQ Co., 10/15/42 Camp Gordon GA. d. 9/1/1988 Crozier, Goochland Co., VA.

SWAIN, Robert H. b. 1923 OK. Res. Lane Co., OR. Enl. 2/5/43 Fresno, CA. Ser. No. 39693342. Pvt., Co. D, MIA, 1/26/44, Italy (Anzio) SR Cem.

SWAYZE, Douglas A. b. 1920 MS. Res. Yazoo Co., MS. Enl. 9/23/42 Camp Shelby, MS. Ser. No. 34426674. Pvt. Co. A, 10/14/42 Camp Gordon, GA. Transf. Co. B, Camp Gordon, GA, 12/16/42. Co. A. Purple Heart. Promo. T/4, HQ Co., July 1944. T/4, Med. Det., 5/8/45 Innsbruck, Austria. Dischd. Dec. 1945. Men's Shop, Yazoo City, MS. Mentioned in the May 1954 Directory. Retired 1977. Contributed to MFP 1997. Relative of actor Patrick Swayze.

SWEET, John. 1st. Lt., Co. C, 6/22/45 Innsbruck, Austria.

SWEETING, George R. b. 1918 MD. Enl. 9/28/42 Baltimore, MD. Ser. No. 13103987. Pvt. Co. D, 10/11/42 Camp Gordon GA. Pfc., Co. D, MIA, 1/26/44, Italy (Anzio) SR Cem.

SWETLAND, George L. Ser. No. 06251943. Res. OR. Pfc., Co. D, KIA, 1/26/44, Italy (Anzio), SR Cem.

SWIGER, William Ray. b. 7/7 or 11/1902 Fairmont or Folsom, Harrison Co., WV. Res. Haywood, Harrison Co., WV. Enl. 9/21/42 Baltimore, MD. Ser. No. 33376354. Pvt. Co. D, 10/11/42 Camp Gordon GA. Pvt. FA. Dischd. 3/20/43 (Essn. War Ind.). d. 2/10/ 1971 Mannington, Marion Co., WV. Bur. Mannington Memorial Park.

SWIFT, James L. Res. MN. Pvt., attached to Co. B 5/28/42 Edgewood Arsenal, MD. Squad Leader (Sgt.). Ser. No. 37165438. Cpl., Co. D, MIA, 1/26/44, Italy (Anzio) SR Cem. Body recovered 1/26/44 by YMS 34 & buried at sea same day. Next of kin: H. M. Swift, St. Paul, MN.

SWIFTON, ----------. Mentioned by Robert M. ("John") Chamblee, Co. D, as having jumped off LST 422 with him [Possibly same man as James L. Swift].

SZKSCINSKI [Sekscinski], Victor, Sr. b. 3/24/1905 PA. Res. Westmoreland Co., PA. Enl. 12/22/42 Greensburg, PA. Ser. No. 33413376. Pvt., Co. C, Camp Gordon, GA 3/18/43. d. 3/6/1992 PA.

SZYMANSKI, Frank J. b. 1917 NJ. Res. Bergen Co., NJ. Enl. 7/9/42 Newark, NJ. Ser. No. 32390623. Pvt., HQ & HQ Co., Camp Gordon, GA 7/28/42. Pvt., HQ & HQ Co., Camp Gordon, GA 9/25/42. T/5, HQ Co., 5/8/45 Innsbruck, Austria.

TAFF, Bruce G. b. 1/13/1915 TX. Enl. 2/3/42 Ft. Bliss, El Paso, TX. Ser. No. 38071551. d. 1/5/2001 Rio Frio, Real Co., TX.

TAMPORI, Salvatore F. b. 1906 NY. Res. New York Co., NY. Enl. 10/6/42 Ft. Jay, Governors Island, NY. Ser. No. 32521047. Pvt., Co. D, Camp Gordon, GA 4/10/43.

TANNER, Willie R. b. 9/17/1921 GA. Res. Wadley, Jefferson Co., GA. Enl. 9/19/42 Ft. McPherson, Atlanta, GA. Ser. No. 34442965. Pvt., Co. D, Camp Gordon, GA 10/9/42. Transf. Co. A, Camp Gordon, GA, 12/16/42. Pfc., Co. D transf. To Motor Pool, Camp Gordon, GA 1/25/43. S/Sgt.,Co. A, 5/8/45 Innsbruck, Austria. d. Feb. 1977 GA.

TAPP, John A. b. 7/13/1921 GA. Res. Hall Co., GA. Enl. 9/18/42 Ft. McPerson, Atlanta, GA. Ser. No. 34442609. Pvt., Co. A, Camp Gordon, GA 10/9/42. d. Oct. 1973.

TARASEK, George E. b. 1923. Res. Wiles Barre, Luzerne Co., PA. Enl. 4/28/43 Wilkes Barre, PA. Ser. No. 33604466. Pfc., Co. D, LST 422 Survivor, 1/26/44 Italy (Anzio) – Purple Heart. Rescued by USS Pilot. Cpl., WIA (serious – shell burst in barrel – lost leg below knee), 1/9/45 France.

TARASZEWSKI, Stanley E. b. 1915 PA. Res. Westmoreland Co., PA. Pvt. HQ & HQ Co., 10/15/42 Camp Gordon GA. T/4, HQ Co., 5/8/45 Innsbruck, Austria. Served in Panama Canal Zone 1946 [?].

TAUNTON, J. T. b. 5/10/1921 Tallassee, AL. Pepperell Grammar. Opelika High. Pre-war Occupation: Textile Worker. Res. Lee Co., AL. Enl. 9/19/42 Ft. McClellan, AL. Ser. No. 34391801. Pvt., Co. A, Camp Gordon, GA 10/8/42. Transf. Co. B, Camp Gordon, GA, 12/16/42. Cpl., Co. A, on *LST 690* 8/9/44. Sgt., Co. B, 5/8/45 Innsbruck, Austria. 103rd Inf. Div. June 1945 – Sept. 1945. Res. Opelika, AL 2009.

TAYLOR, Cecil M. b. 4/28/1902 VA. Res. Tazewell Co., VA. Enl. 10/3/42 Abingdon, VA. Ser. No. 33214381. Pvt. Co. D, 10/11/42 Camp Gordon GA. d. Feb. 1981 North Tazewell, Tazewell Co., VA.

TAYLOR, Lowell T. b. 3/5/1921 MS. Res. Itawamba Co., MS. Enl. 9/23/42 Camp Shelby, MS. Ser. No. 34426794. Pvt. Co. C, 10/14/42 Camp Gordon, GA. Transf. Co. A, Camp Gordon, GA, 12/16/42. Driver in Co. C. Mentioned in the 8/20/43 entry in the diary of Capt. Rupert Burford as having "shot himself in the foot with a .45 pistol during our absence . . . and [I] preferred charges against Taylor." d. 2/6/1999 Tupelo, Lee Co., MS.

TAYLOR, John M. 1st. Lt., Co. D, KIA, 10/22/44, France. Body recovered 10/25/44 by the Medics of the 143rd Infantry in a French coffin in Les Poulieres, France.

TAYLOR, Randall C. b. 1920 MS. Res. New Site, Prentiss Co., MS. Enl. 9/18/42 Camp Shelby, MS. Ser. No. 34425753. Pvt. Co. B, 10/14/42 Camp Gordon, GA. Pvt., Co. B, WIA, 5/24/44 Italy – Purple Heart. Returned to duty 6/19/44. Pfc., Co. B, 5/8/45 Innsbruck, Austria.

TAYLOR, Robert Sigafoos. b. 3/29/1917 Doylestown, PA. Doylestown High School. Pre-war Occupation: Plumber/Pipe-fitter. Res. Bucks Co., PA. Enl. 3/2/42 Ft. George Meade, MD. Ser. No. 33171368. Pvt. Attached to Co. B 5/28/42 Edgewood Arsenal, MD. Mechanic General (Pvt.). Pfc., Co. A, (Gen. Mech.), promo. T/5 (temp.), Camp Gordon, GA 7/15/42. T/5, Co. A, promo. Cpl. (temp.), Camp Gordon, GA 8/19/42. Silver Star. Purple Heart. Bronze Star. Good Conduct Medal. EAME Medal with 7 Bronze Campaign Stars & 1 Bronze Arrowhead. S/Sgt.,Co. A, 5/8/45 Innsbruck, Austria. Attended 1958 & 1960 Reunions as res. Doylestown, PA. d. 3/23/1998.

TAYLOR, Rollin D. b. 1914 GA. Res. Union Point, Greene Co., GA. Enl. 9/17/42 Ft. McPherson, Atlanta, GA. Ser. No. 34442534. Pvt., Co. D, Camp Gordon, GA 10/8/42. Pfc., Co. D, LST 422 Survivor, 1/26/44 Italy (Anzio) – Purple Heart. Cpl. WIA (injured in glider crash) 8/15/44 Le Muy, France. Cpl., HQ Co., 5/8/45 Innsbruck, Austria. Res. Union Point, GA May 1954. Attended 1954 reunion.

TEAL, Edward F. b. 1925 NY. Pre-war Occupation: R. P. I. Dormitories. Res. Rennselaer Co., NY. Enl. 4/14/43 Albany, NY. Ser. No. 32856663. Pvt., Co. D, MIA, 1/26/44, Italy (Anzio) SR Cem. Next of kin: Mrs. Katherine Teal.

TEENO, Michael, Jr. b. 1918 PA. Enl. 9/24/42 Allentown, PA. Ser. No. 33367844. Pvt. Co. B, 10/15/42 Camp Gordon GA. Transf. Co. A, Camp Gordon, GA, 12/16/42. Pfc., Co. B, arrived Salemi, Sicily from North Africa 8/2/43. Sgt., Co. B, KIA (enemy 240mm shell), 2/18/44, Anzio, Italy, SR Cem.

TEMPLIN, William B. b. 1914 PA. Res. Kenosha, WI. Enl. 5/4/42 Milwaukee, WI. Ser. No. 36224620. Pfc., Co. D, WIA, (light – machine gun bullet), 5/31/44 or 6/1/44, Italy – Purple Heart. Pfc., WIA (light-shrapnel in forearm & elbow), 8/17/44 France [on the 16th according to Co. D Journal].

TEN BRINK, Albert. b. 1919 MI. Res. Kent Co., MI. Enl. 11/27/42 Kalamazoo, MI. Ser. No. 36412249. Cpl., Co. B, promo. Sgt. (temp.) 9/15/45.

TERRES, Harry Y., Jr. b. 5/12/1906 PA. Enl. 10/5/42 Philadelphia, PA. Ser. No. 13124589. Pvt., Co. D, Camp Gordon, GA 10/9/42. Pvt., Co. D, Camp Gordon, GA 12/15/42. Present, Co. D, in hospital with broken wrist, Camp Gordon, GA, 1/9/43. Attended 1966 Reunion. d. Nov. 1971 Riverton, Burlington Co., NJ. (Muzzleblasts says d. 1984).

TERRIBILE, Louis. Pfc., Co. A, Camp Gordon, GA 4/16/43. Pvt., Co. A, on *LST 690* 8/9/44.

TESTA, Carmen. b. 1920 PA. Enl. 9/22/42 Philadelphia, PA. Ser. No. 33335433. Pvt., Co. D, Camp Gordon, GA 10/9/42. Present at Camp Gordon, GA. In Dan Shields' photo album.

TEWELL, Orville D. b. 1918 OH. Res. Hancock Co., OH. Enl. 12/21/42 Toledo, OH. Ser. No. 35538136. Pvt., Co. D, Camp Gordon, GA 4/10/43. Present at Camp Gordon, GA Nov. 1942. Pfc., Co. D. MIA 1/26/44 Italy (Anzio). Res. Dunkirk, OH. Next of kin: Evelyn Tewell, wife.

THACH, Julian L. b. 1919 NC. Res. Norfolk, VA. Enl. 4/29/42 Richmond, VA. Ser. No. 06943803. Pvt., Co. B, 5/8/45 Innsbruck, Austria.

THEIRRIEN, Alfred O. b. 1918 MA. Res. Worcester Co., MA. Enl. 2/4/42 Ft. Devens, MA. Ser. No. 31061299. Injured when enemy bombed vehicle while stationed in Italy. Pfc., Co. A, 5/8/45 Innsbruck, Austria. Res. Grafton, MA.

THOMAS, James D, Jr. b. 1919 OK. Res. Knox Co., TN. Enl. 9/7/40 Charlotte, NC. Ser. No. 14009946. Enl. For Philippine Dept. Pvt., Field Artillery. T/5, Co. B, WIA (serious), 11/28/44 Struth, France.

THOMAS, Kenneth N. b. 1921 KY. Res. Cumberland Co., KY. Enl. 7/20/42 Ft. Benjamin Harrison, IN. Ser. No. 35505267. Pvt., Co. C, Camp Gordon, GA 4/16/43. Pfc., MIA, Co. C, 1/26/44, Italy (Anzio) SR Cem.

THOMAS, Leonard R. b. 1918 OH. Res. Wayne Co., MI. Enl. 2/14/42 Ft. Custer, MI. Ser. No. 36172153. Pvt. Attached to Co. F 5/28/42 Edgewood Arsenal, MD. Gunner (Pvt.). Co. D, photo taken Sept. 20, 1944 Nice, France. Reportedly KIA the following day.

THOMAS, Louie F. b. 1906 NE. Res. Lancaster Co., NE. Enl. 4/27/42 Ft. Crook, NE. Ser. No. 37122210. Pvt., HQ & HQ Co., Camp Gordon, GA 3/18/43.

THOMAS, William. In a group photo of Co. C taken 1943 at Amalfi, Italy.

THOMPSON, Earl E. b. 1923 IA. Res. Page Co., IA. Enl. 5/31/44 Camp Dodge, Herrold, IA. Ser. No. 37697761. Sgt., Co. A, reduced to Private without prejudice 7/23/45.

THOMPSON, Edward M. Pfc., Co. B, 5/8/45 Innsbruck, Austria.

THOMPSON, Glen C. b. 1913 IA. Res. Onawa, Monona Co., IA. Enl. 12/19/42 Camp Dodge, Herrold, IA. Ser. No. 37651450. Pvt., Co. C, Camp Gordon, GA 4/10/43. T/5, Co. C, LST 422 Survivor, 1/26/44 Italy (Anzio) – Purple Heart with Oak Leaf Cluster. T/4, Silver Star, 1944. T/4, Soldier's Medal, 1944. Purple Heart with two Oak Leaf Clusters. ETO Ribbon with five stars. Good Conduct Ribbon. T/4, Co. C, 6/22/45 Innsbruck, Austria.

THOMPSON, James C. b. 1899 PA. Enl. 9/22/42 Philadelphia, PA. Ser. No. 33335586. Pvt., HQ & HQ Co., Camp Gordon, GA 10/9/42.

THOMPSON, John H. b. 1921 PA. Enl. 10/9/42 Greensburg, PA. Ser. No. 33292411. Pvt. Co. B, 10/15/42 Camp Gordon GA.

THOMPSON, Kelso Carthell ("Red"). b. 7/11/1924 McAllister, OK. Attended school at Stuart, OK. Pre-war Occupation: Auto Mechanic. Enl. 5/17/43. Served in Field Artillery. Joined 83rd CMB at Pozzouli. WIA (white phosphorous – back was on fire), on roof of a house at Anzio, Italy. Co. D, T/5 WIA (hit in leg by mortar shell during glider crash), Le Muy, France 8/15/44. T/5, Co. A, 5/8/45 Innsbruck, Austria. Res. Corte Madera, CA May 1954. Carpenter Foreman Stateside, American President Lines. Res. Corte Madera, CA 2009.

THOMSEN, Walter P. H. b. 1922 IA. Res. Crawford Co., IA. Enl. 12/21/42 Camp Dodge, Herrold, IA. Ser. No. 37651579. Pvt., Co. C, Camp Gordon, GA 4/10/43. Pfc., Co. C, MIA, 1/26/44, Italy (Anzio) SR Cem.

THOMSON, Frank J. b. 6/18/1923 MA. Res. Suffolk Co., MA. Enl. 3/10/43 Boston, MA. Ser. No. 31302767. Co. D, present in Southern France. d. December 1981 San Diego Co., CA.

THORNE, Edwin H. b. 1916 NH. Res. Ocean Co., NJ. Enl. 9/21/42 Ft. Myer, VA. Ser. No. 33197648. Pvt., Co. C, Camp Gordon, GA 10/11/42.

THORNE, Darwin K. b. 1920 PA. Res. Butler Co., PA. Enl. 9/25/42 Pittsburgh, PA. Ser. No. 33305675. Pvt. Co. B, 10/15/42 Camp Gordon GA. Pvt., Co. B & Sports Editor, Smokescreen, Camp Gordon, GA Nov. 1942. Pvt., Sports Editor, Smokescreen, Camp Gordon, GA 1/9/43. Pfc., Co. B, sent to hospital (56th Medical, Trapani) 8/5/43. Returned to duty 8/12/43. Pfc., HQ Co., 5/8/45 Innsbruck, Austria. d. ca. 1992.

THORNTON, Herman L. Res. OK. Ser. No. 06593461. Pvt., Co. D, MIA, 1/26/44, Italy (Anzio) SR Cem.

THORNTON, John A. b. 1901 MS. Res. Panola Co., MS. Enl. 9/22/42 Camp Shelby. MS. Ser. No. 34426127. Pvt. Co. A, 10/14/42 Camp Gordon, GA. Transf. Co. D, Camp Gordon, GA, 12/16/42.

THORP, Thomas R. b. 1910 NY. Res. Otsego Co., NY. Enl. 7/21/42 Albany, NY. Ser. No. 12096584. Pvt., HQ & HQ Co., Camp Gordon, GA 7/28/42. Pfc., HQ & HQ Co., promo. Cpl. (temp.), Camp Gordon, GA 10/13/42. Promo. Sgt. (temp.), Camp Gordon, GA 10/28/42 Promo. S/Sgt., Camp Gordon, GA 12/21/42. 1st. Sgt., Co. C, 6/22/45 Innsbruck, Austria. Postwar NY State Electric & Gas. Insurance. Res. Lexington, KY May 1954. Contracts Administrator, Irving Air Chute Co. [also spelled Thorpe].

THORPE, Robert F. b. 3/24/1925 Mt. Savage, MD. Pre-war Occupation: Sold Newspapers. Pvt., HQ Co./C Co. Radio-Man, F.O., Pvt., Co. C, MIA, 8/29/44 Briançon, France. POW Stalag 7A Moosburg, Bavaria. Liberated 6/8/45. POW Medal. Postwar: Took course in

air-conditioning & refrigeration. Mechanicsburg Naval Supply Co., PA. Air Conditioning Service. d. 3/28/2002 FL. [Muzzleblasts says d. 1992].

THORSON, Clyde L. b. 3/9/1916 IL. Res. Morris, Grundy Co., IL. Enl. 3/2/42 Camp Grant, IL. Ser. No. 36322612. Pvt. Attached to Co. H 5/28/42 Edgewood Arsenal, MD. Motor Sgt. (S/Sgt.). Pvt., HQ & HQ Co. transf. Co. D, Camp Gordon, GA 6/15/42. Sgt. (temp.), Co. D, promo. S/Sgt. (temp.), Camp Gordon, GA 9/12/42. S/Sgt., Co. D, transf. HQ & HQ Co. & promo. T/Sgt. (temp.), Camp Gordon, GA 10/6/42. M/Sgt., HQ & HQ Co., LST 422 Survivor, 1/26/44 Italy (Anzio) – Purple Heart. Reported safe on 1/30/44 Morning Report. M/Sgt., HQ Co., 5/8/45 Innsbruck, Austria. d. 7/7/1995 Morris, Grundy Co., IL.

THURLOW, Walter Irvin ("Walt"). b. 2/19/1923 Surry, ME. Res. Franklin Co., ME. Enl. 4/15/1943 Portland, ME. Ser. No. 31321767. Co. D, 83rd CMB. Pfc., Co. A, 5/8/45 Innsbruck, Austria. Res. Ridlonville, ME May 1954. Parts Manager, Turner Motor Sales Ford Garage, Mexico, ME for 36 years. Ripley and Fletcher, South Paris, ME. Part Time Police Work (Mexico Fire and Police Dept.). Attended 1958 Reunon as res. Mexico, ME. Retired 1979. Owned lawn care business. d. 7/8/1999 South Paris, ME.

THWEATT, Boyce L. b. 1921 MS. Res. Lafayette Co., MS. Enl. 9/22/42 Camp Shelby, MS. Ser. No. 34425531. Pvt. Co. A, 10/14/42 Camp Gordon, GA.

TICE, William P. b. 9/24/1913 NY. Res. Greene Co., NY. Enl. 5/15/42 Albany, NY. Ser. No. 32294362. 1st Lt., assigned Med. Det. & designated Assistant Battalion Surgeon, Camp Gordon, GA 4/15/43. 1st Lt., Med Det. Present Sicily 1943. d. 9/9/1994 Catskill, Greene Co., NY. Curtis Williams said he was nicknamed "The Coal Doctor" as Tice was a pre-med student working for the coal mines. Williams also said he became a neuro-surgeon after the war.

TICHENOR, Sinclair J. Res. NJ. Ser. No. 32772456. Pvt., Co. D, KIA, 1/26/44, Italy, FL Cem.

TILL, Wilbert E. b. 6/25/1920 NY. Res. Chautauqua Co., NY. Enl. 3/5/1942 Ft. Niagara, Youngstown, NY. Ser. No. 32251862. Pvt. Attached to Co. B 5/28/42 Edgewood Arsenal, MD. Telephone Lineman (Pvt.). Pfc., Co. B, arrived Gela, Sicily, from the rear echelon 7/11/43. T/5, Co. B, 5/8/45 Innsbruck, Austria. d. Nov. 1977 Jamestown, Chautauqua Co., NY.

TILLMAN, Lemuel Russell. b. 6/21/1921 Nashville, Davidson Co., TN. Res. Donelson, TN. Ross School – East High School. Res. Donelson, Davidson Co., TN. Pre-war Occupation: Salesman – Anthony Pure Milk Co. Enl. 9/18/42 Ft. Oglethorpe, GA. Ser. No. 34371807. Sgt., Co. C, LST 422 Survivor, 1/26/44 Italy (Anzio) – Purple Heart. Bronze Star 5/8/44 at Padiglione, Italy. Escaped from Briançon, France 8/29/44. S/Sgt., Co. C, 6/22/45 Innsbruck, Austria. Res. Nashville, TN 2009.

TILTON, William H. b. 1907 PA. Enl. 12/14/42 Philadelphia, PA. Ser. No. 33475500. Pvt., Co. D, Camp Gordon, GA 3/18/43.

TOALDO, Arthur C. b. 1921 NJ. Res. Bergen Co., NJ. Enl. 7/9/42 Newark, NJ. Ser. No. 32390574. Pvt., HQ & HQ Co., Camp Gordon, GA 7/28/42. Pvt., HQ & HQ CO., Camp Gordon, GA 9/25/42. T/5, HQ Co., MIA, 1/26/44, Italy (Anzio) SR Cem.

TOBIAS, Alvin J. b. 1924 TX. Res. Fayette Co., TX. Enl. 6/22/43 Ft. Sam Houston, TX. Ser. No. 38553144. Pvt., Co. A, on *LST 690* 8/9/44. Cook in Co. A 11/17/44 photo provided by Lawrence Ertzberger. T/5, Co. A, 5/8/45 Innsbruck, Austria.

TOMBERG, Tony. b. NJ. Res. Essex Co., NJ. Enl. 7/9/42 Newark, NJ. Ser. No. 32390373. Pvt., HQ & HQ Co., Camp Gordon, GA 7/28/42. Pvt., HQ Co., Camp Gordon, GA 10/21/42.

TOMBOLINI, Fred. b. 1922 CA. Res. San Anselmo, Marin Co., CA. Enl. 11/11/42 San Francisco, CA. Ser. No. 39113211. Pfc., Co. D, Camp Gordon, GA 3/18/43/. Corp., Co. C, LST 422 Survivor, 1/26/44 Italy (Anzio) – Purple Heart & Purple Heart with Oak Leaf Cluster. Cpl., Co. C, WIA (light – S-mine), Minturno, Italy 3/26/44. Not hospitalized. Cpl., Co. C, 6/22/45 Innsbruck, Austria.

TONIOLO, Reno L. b. 11/8/1921 PA. Enl. 9/25/42 Greensburg, PA. Ser. No. 33294842. Pvt. Co. A, 10/15/42 Camp Gordon GA. Bronze Star. Sgt., Co. A, on *LST 690* 8/9/44. S/Sgt., Co. A, 5/8/45 Innsbruck, Austria. Platoon Sgt. Dischd. Oct. 1945. Res. Jeanette, PA May 1954. Garage Business. Guitarist. Partner, Auto Parts Business. Attended 1958, 1960, 1962 & 1966 Reunions as res. Jeanette, PA. Contributed to MFP 1997. d. 4/26/2000 Jeanette, Westmoreland Co., PA.

TOWELL, Orville D. Pfc., KIA, 1/26/44, Italy (Anzio).

TOWLER, Allen G. b. 1911 VA. Res. Lunenberg Co., VA. Enl. 12/15/42 Richmond, VA. Ser. No. 33519029. Pvt., Co. D, Camp Gordon, GA 3/18/43. Pvt., Co. A, on *LST 690* 8/9/44.

TRACEY, George G. b. 6/21/1902 MD. Res. Baltimore Co., MD. Enl. 9/26/42 Baltimore, MD. Ser. No. 33377204. Pvt. Co. C, 10/15/42 Camp Gordon GA. d. 10/14/1998 Albany, Dougherty Co., GA.

TRAFICANTE, Biagio J. b. 1924 RI. Res. West Warwick, Kent Co., RI. Enl. 4/9/43 Providence, RI. Ser. No. 31292660. Pvt., Co. D, LST 422 Survivor, 1/26/44 Italy (Anzio) – Purple Heart.

TRAMMEL, ----------. Pvt. In the photo album of Dan Shields. At Camp Gordon, GA.

TRANCHITELLA, Peter A. b. 8/11/1914 PA. Res. Wildwood Village, Cape May Co., NJ. Enl. 2/27/42 Ft. Dix, NJ. Ser. No. 32243007. Pvt. Assigned to Co. G 5/28/42 Edgewood Arsenal, MD, Mess Sgt. (S/Sgt.). Pvt., Co. A, promo. T/4 (temp.), Camp Gordon, GA 6/16/42. T/4 (temp.), (Mess Sgt.), promo. S/Sgt. (temp.), Camp Gordon, GA 7/15/42. S/Sgt., Co. A, (light injure in action), LST 422 Survivor, 1/26/44 Italy (Anzio) – Purple Heart. Mess Sgt., Co. A., 1944. Transf. 2nd. Replacement Depot Oct. 1944. Joseph Cannetti; said: "Pete was a good Mess Sgt., he always fed us on the line with his two Italian prisoners." d. 6/3/1994.

TRAPNELL, William L. b. 9/9/1918 GA. Res. Bulloch Co., GA. Enl. 7/1/41 Ft. McPherson, Atlanta, GA. Ser. No. 34084665. Present with 83rd CMB 10/13/44. 1st. Lt., Co. C, 6/22/45 Innsbruck, Austria. Bronze Star, Sept., 1945. Present with 83rd CMB 11/10/45. d. 6/20/2000 Portal, Bulloch Co., GA.

TRASK, Stanley H. b. 6/26/1923 NY. Res. Otsego Co., NY. Enl. 7/6/42 Albany, NY. Ser. No. 12096584. Pvt., HQ & HQ Co., Camp Gordon, GA 7/28/42. d. Sept. 1978 Oneonta, Otsego Co., NY.

TRAUTMAN, Carlos R. b. 7/21/1922 Tower City, PA. High School. Res. Delaware Co., PA. Enl. 10/5/1942 Philadelphia, PA. Ser. No. 13124665. Pvt., HQ & HQ Co., Camp Gordon, GA 10/9/42. Co. A. Forward Observer. Distinguished in action Bischweiler, France, 3/7-8/45 - Bronze Star. Civil Service. National Guard 1948-53 Ft. Meade, MD. Re-enl. PA National Guard 1953-1982. Attended first A bomb explosion in Nevada 1951. Korean War. Res. Tower City, PA May 1954. Thompson Products. Attended 1954, 1958 & 1962 Reunions as res. Tower City, PA. Retired from National Guard May 1982. Res. Tower City, PA 2009.

TREGO, Charles A. b. 3/30/1924 OH. Res. Pickaway Co., OH. Enl. 2/22/43 Columbus, OH. Ser. No. 35630147. Pfc., HQ Co., 5/8/45 Innsbruck, Austria. d. 4/27/2004 Stoutsville, Fairfield Co., OH.

TREY, Edward Leon. ("Bulldog" / "Bulldog Drummond" / "Terrible Trey"). b. 2/23/1916 Grand Rapids, MI. Grand Rapids Technical High School. Lawrence Technological University. Pre-war Occupation: Traffic Management. Res. Grand Rapids, MI. Enl. Feb. 1941 as a Pvt. Comm. 2nd Lt. 4/4/42, Chemical Warfare Reserve, 1st CWS OCS, Edgewood Arsenal, MD. 2nd Lt., C.W.S., 5/28/42 Edgewood Arsenal, MD May 28, 1942. Co. B. Designated Bn. S-4, HQ & HQ Co., 6/12/42. Present as S-4 11/26/43. 1st Lt., CWS, LST 422 Survivor, 1/26/44 Italy (Anzio) – Purple Heart. Reported safe 1/30/44 Morning Report. Still present as S-4 3/24/44. Present as S-4, 5/8/44. Present as Capt. & S-4 8/2/44. Capt., Bronze Star [Presented 11/20/44]. Capt., HQ Co., 5/8/45 Innsbruck, Austria. Capt., assigned 65th Inf. Div. 7/23/45. Retired as Lt. Col., Reserves. Res. Elkridge, MD May 1954. Attended 1954, 1956, 1958, 1960 &1962 Reunions as res. Frederick, MD. Contributed to MFP 1997. Res. Frederick, MD 2009.

TRIGG, Edgar L. b. 2/13/1899 MS. Res. Jones Co., MS. Enl. 9/21/42 Camp Shelby, MS. Ser. No. 34426304. Pvt. Co. A, 10/14/42 Camp Gordon, GA. d. May 1965 MS.

TROIA, Paul. b. 11/1/1923 NY. Res. Queens Co., NY. Enl. 2/10/43 New York City, NY. Ser. No. 32799797. Co. D. Shared a foxhole in Vosges with Sam Kweskin. Pfc., Co. C, 6/22/45 Innsbruck, Austria. d. 3/9/1988 Levitwon, Nassau Co., NY.

TROTTA, Raymond A. ("Bugs"). b. 1923 MD. Enl. 1/29/43 Baltimore, MD. Ser. No. 33553522. Pfc., Co. B, 5/8/45 Innsbruck, Austria. Mentioned in the May 1954 Directory. Postwar res. NY.

TRUITT, Edward G. b. 1920 WI. Res. Menominee Co., MI. Enl. 3/18/42 Ft. Sheridan, IL. Ser. No. 36238264. Pvt., MWIA, 6/6 or

7/44, Italy, SR Cem. (ABMC) or 1/26/44 (Muzzleblasts for Dec. 12, 1960)

TRUMBLAK, John, Jr. b. 1907 OK. Res. Cuyahoga Co., OH. Enl. 3/3/42 Camp Perry, Lacarne, OH. Ser. No. 35287111. Pvt. Attached to Co. H 5/28/42 Edgewood Arsenal, MD. Gunner (Pvt.). Pfc., Co. A, promo. T/5 (temp.), Camp Gordon, GA 8/26/42. Pfc., Co. A, on *LST 690* 8/9/44. Cpl., Co. B, 5/8/45 Innsbruck, Austria. Res. Cleveland, OH.

TUCK, Clay. b. 1906 KY. Res. Beaver Co., PA. Enl. 9/25/42 Pittsburgh, PA. Ser. No. 33305621. Pvt., Co. D, WIA (light – shrapnel in hand), 11/17/43 Venafro, Italy. Pfc., Co. D, KIA, 1/26/44, Italy, (Anzio).

TUCKER, George F. b. 12/14/1923 MI. Res. Ingham Co., MI. Enl. 3/10/42 Detroit, MI. Ser. No. 16062981. In a Co. D group photo. T/5, Co. D, Bronze Star, at Zellenberg, France 12/17/44. d. 6/5/2000 Naubinway, Mackinac Co., MI.

TURAN, Leonard W. b. 7/30/1921 Saucier, MS [incorrectly listed as 7/3/21 on discharge]. Pre-war Occupation: Sales Person – Men's & Boy's Clothing, M. Salloum Dept. Store, Gulfport, MS. Res. Harrison Co., MS. Enl. 9/21/42 Camp Shelby, MS. Ser. No. 34426205. Pvt. Co. A, 10/14/42 Camp Gordon, GA. Departed U.S. 4/29/43. Pfc., distinguished in action 7/10/43 Sicily. Also served at Naples – Foggia, Rome – Arno, Southern France, Rhineland, Central Europe. Sgt., Co. C, WIA (light – enemy shell), 1/11/45 France -Purple Heart. Hospitalized. Good Conduct Medal. EAMETO Medal. Bronze Indian Arrowhead. Sgt., Co. C, 6/22/45 Innsbruck, Austria. As a Heavy Mortar Crewman he "supervised mortar crew setting up, aiming & firing weapon from ground mount to play high explosive & white phosphorous shells on enemy positions. Sighted in with compass, when sighted base plate with aiming stake. Was responsible for control, coordination & tactical employment of crew." Sgt., Co. H, 410th Inf. 1945. Dischd. 9/28/45. Salesman, United Gas (Entex). d. 11/4/1994 Saucier, MS. bur. Hickory Grove Cem., Laurel, MS.

TURCO, Philip J. b. 2/11/1922 MA. Res. Suffolk Co., MA. Enl. 2/18/43 Boston, MA. Ser. No. 31298163. Pvt., Co. D WIA (enemy shell - serious), 9/16/43 Vietre sul Mare, Italy. d. Sept. 1979 Somerville, Middlesex Co., MA.

TUREK, Adam G. b. 2/23/1921 PA. Res. Patton, PA. Enl. 10/5/42 Altoona, PA. Ser. No. 13084655. Pvt., HQ & HQ Co., Camp Gordon, GA 10/9/42. Pfc., Co. A, WIA (light), 2/18/44 Anzio, Italy. Hospitalized. Pfc., Co. A, on *LST 690* 8/9/44. T/5, Co. C, 6/22/45 Innsbruck, Austria. d. 9/18/2005 Bronx, NY.

TURMELLE, Roland E. b. 1924 NH. Res. Rochester, Strafford Co., NH. Enl. 4/23/43 Manchester, NH. Ser. No. 31269230. Pfc., Co. D, LST 422 Survivor, 1/26/44 Italy (Anzio) – Purple Heart. Cpl., Co. A, 5/8/45 Innsbruck, Austria. Postwar res. Rochester, NH.

TURNER, Horace A. b. 1920 GA. Res. Heard Co., GA. [also listed as res. Atlanta, GA]. Enl. 9/21/42 Ft. McPherson, Atlanta, GA. Ser. No. 34443301. Pvt., Co. A, Camp Gordon, GA 10/9/42. T/5, Co. A, on

LST 690 8/9/44. T/5, HQ Co., 5/8/45 Innsbruck, Austria.

TURNER, I. B. b. 1921 GA. Res. Spaulding Co., GA. Enl. 9/21/42 Ft. McPherson, Atlanta, GA. Ser. No. 34443197. Pvt., Co. B, Camp Gordon, GA 10/9/42. Served in North Africa, Sicily, Anzio, and the lower Alps until 1945. Postwar res. Dallas, GA.

TURNER, Ralph A., Jr. Assigned from 65th Inf. Division as Capt., HQ & HQ Co. (Asst. S-3) 7/23/45. Relsd. as battalion S-2 & Commanding Officer & apptd. battalion S-3 on 9/15/45.

TURNER, Vester Lamar ("Uncle Phil"). b. 7/1/1918 Groesbeck, TX. Baylor University: BA/Chemistry. Texas A&M: Masters/Chemistry. Res. McLennan Co., TX. Enl. 8/19/41 Ft. Sam Houston, TX. Grad. CWS, Edgewood Arsenal, MD 1942. 2nd Lt., CWS, assigned Co. B, Camp Gordon, GA 7/3/42. Transf. Co. A, Camp Gordon, GA, 12/16/42. 2nd Lt., sent to hospital (56th Medical, Trapani) 8/5/43. Returned to duty 8/13/43. Promo. 1st Lt. Sept. 1943. 1st. Lt., Co. B., KIA (caught in the middle of a mine field – no rescue sent), 12/20/43, near Ceppagna, Italy. Silver Star (posthumous) – presented 1/19/44.

TURY, John R. b. 1/3/1924. Res. Allegheny Co., PA. Enl. 3/1/43 Pittsburgh, PA. Ser. No. 33439229. Pfc., Co. A, 5/8/45 Innsbruck, Austria. d. 7/22/1996 Braddock, Allegheny Co., PA.

TYMA, George. b. 2/3/1922 Revloc, PA. Ambridge Area High School. Pre-war Occupation: Steel Mill/Rivet Catcher. Enl. 9/25/1942 Pittsburgh, PA. Ser. No. 33305602. Pvt. Co. A, 10/15/42 Camp Gordon GA. With Co. A at Anzio. Pfc., Co. A, on *LST 690* 8/9/44. d. 8/18/2005. Military funeral.

UCCELLO, Salvatore M. b. 1922 MA. Res. Cumberland Co., ME. Enl. 3/8/43 Portland, ME. Ser. No. 31320216. Pfc., Co. D, MIA, 1/26/44, Italy (Anzio) SR Cem.

ULIZIO, Bramo A. b. 1922 OH. Res. Ambridge, Beaver Co., PA. Enl. 9/25/42 Pittsburgh, PA. Ser. No. 33305600. Pvt. HQ & HQ Co., 10/15/42 Camp Gordon GA. Pvt., Co. D, LST 422 Survivor, 1/26/44 Italy (Anzio) – Purple Heart. Res. Salem, OH.

ULM, Will K. b. 2/26/1913 AL. Res. Crenshaw Co., AL. Enl. 2/15/42 Ft. McPherson, Atlanta, GA. Ser. No. 34199681. Pfc., Purple Heart, 1944. Pfc., Co. C, 6/22/45 Innsbruck, Austria. d. July 1983.

ULMER, William T. b. 10/14/1921 KY. Res. Jefferson Co., KY. Enl. 2/28/42 Ft. Benjamin Harrison, IN. Ser. No. 15099823. Pvt. Attached to Co. H 5/28/42 Edgewood Arsenal, MD. Ammunition Sgt. (S/Sgt.). Pfc., HQ & HQ Co., (Ammo. Sgt.), promo. Cpl. (temp.), Camp Gordon, GA 7/15/42. Sgt. (temp.), HQ Co., promo. S/Sgt. (temp.), Camp Gordon, GA 12/5/42. In command of a supply detail at Termini Immerse, Sicily 10/23/43. Ammunition Sgt., Venafro, Italy 11/18/43. Mentioned in a 1/20/44 letter from Hutchinson to Cunin as under consideration for a Silver Star for helping to put out a fire in the battalion ammo dump. Silver Star 1944. d. Aug. 1984, Louisville, Jefferson Co., KY.

UNDERWOOD, Ellis L. b. 2/15/1921 MS. Res. Itawamba Co., MS. Enl. 9/23/42 Camp Shelby, MS. Ser. No. 34426728. Pvt. Co. A, 10/14/42 Camp Gordon, GA. d. June 1977, Fullton, Itawamba Co., MS.

UNDERWOOD, Harlis V. b. 1922 MS. Res. Itawamba Co., MS. Enl. 9/23/42 Camp Shelby, MS. Ser. No. 34426768. Pvt. Co. A, 10/14/42 Camp Gordon, GA. Transf. Co. C, Camp Gordon, GA, 12/16/42. Pfc., Co. A, WIA (serious – anti-tank mine), 5/24/44 Anzio, Italy – Purple Heart. Returned to duty 6/19/44. Cpl., Co. A, on *LST 690* 8/9/44. Cpl., Co. A, 5/8/45 Innsbruck, Austria.

UPCHURCH, Cohen R. b. 12/21/1921 TN. Res. Little Crab, Fentress Co., TN. Enl. 9/15/42 Ft. Oglethorpe, GA. Ser. No. 34370909. Pfc., Co. C, LST 422 Survivor, 1/26/44 Italy (Anzio) – Purple Heart. Pfc., Co. C, 6/22/45 Innsbruck, Austria. d. 12/26/2003.

URSO, Nathaniel L. b. 1916 PA. Res. Wash., D.C. Enl. 12/16/42 Ft. Myer, VA. Ser. No. 33450479. Pvt., Co. C, Camp Gordon, GA 4/10/43. Pvt., Co. C, MIA, 1/26/44, Italy (Anzio) SR Cem.

USHER, Arthur J. b. 5/22/1916 IL. Res. Cook Co., IL. Enl. 3/13/42 Camp Grant, IL. Ser. No. 36324513. Pvt. Attached to Co. A 5/28/42 Edgewood Arsenal, MD. Clerk (Cpl. & Pvt.). Pfc., Co. B, (Pres. Clerk), promo. Cpl. (temp.), Camp Gordon, GA 7/15/42. Cpl., Co. D, Camp Gordon, GA 12/12/42. Sgt. (temp.), HQ Co. promo. S/Sgt. (temp.), Camp Gordon, GA 1/25/43. S/Sgt., apptd. T/Sgt., HQ & HQ Co. 3/13/43. Battalion Personnel Adjutant 7/11/44. CWO, HQ Co., 5/8/45 Innsbruck, Austria. Assigned to 41st Cav. Rcn. Sq. Mecz. 7/23/45. Res. Chicago, IL May 1954. Hotel Business. Attended 1954, 1956, 1958, 1960 & 1966 Reunions as res. Chicago, IL. d. Apr. 1982 Homewood, Cook Co., IL.

VAIL, George. b. 1917 OH. Enl. 12/3/42 Cincinnati, OH. Ser. No. 35675742. Pvt., Co. C, WIA, (light – enemy mortar shell), 5/8/44 Anzio, Italy.

VALENTINE, Hilmon Robert. b. 6/17/1921 MS. Res. McGee, Smith Co., MS. Enl. 9/22/42 Camp Shelby, MS. Ser. No. 34426414. Pvt. Co. A, 10/14/42 Camp Gordon, GA. Distinguished in action 7/12/43 Gela, Sicily. Sgt., WIA (light), 1/21/45 France. Sgt. Co., A, 5/8/45 Innsbruck, Austria. Weapons instructor and squad leader. Res. Taylorsville, MS. d. 3/9/2002 Mendenhall, Simpson Co., MS (Another source says d. 2005).

VANASSA, Patsy. Pvt., HQ & HQ Co., Camp Gordon, GA 10/9/42. Ser. No. 33296790.

VANCE, Charles ("Pants"). b. 1919 PA. Res. Philadelphia Co., PA. Enl. 9/22/42 Philadelphia, PA. Ser. No. 33335499. Pvt., Co. D, Camp Gordon, GA 10/9/42. Pfc., Co. D, MIA, 1/26/44, Italy (Anzio) SR Cem.

VANDERZELL, John H. b. 1924 NY. Res. Monroe Co., NY. Enl. 7/14/43 Rochester, NY. Ser. No. 32938641. Pfc., Co. B, promo. Cpl. (temp.) 9/15/45.

VAN DYKE, Charles M. Pfc. Ser. No. 36549764. Transf. 2nd CMB 7/25/45.

VAN ELKAN, William J. b. 1922 NY. Res. Queens Co., NY. Enl. 5/29/43 New York City, NY. Ser. No. 32963029. Pfc., Co. B, 5/8/45 Innsbruck, Austria.

VAN VALKENBURG, Edgar W. b. 1924 OR. Res. King Co., WA. Enl. 3/17/43 Seattle, WA. Ser. No. 39204265. Sgt., Co. A, promo. S/Sgt. (temp.) 9/15/45.

VERFIN, John. b. 12/11/1910 PA. Enl. 10/5/42 Wilkes Barre, PA. Ser. No. 06810624. Pvt., Co. D, Camp Gordon, GA 10/9/42. Transf. Co. A, Camp Gordon, GA, 12/16/42. Pfc., Co. D, WIA (serious), 7/11/43 Gela, Sicily. d. May 1974, Hunlock Creek, Luzerne Co., PA.

VERNON, Anthony E. b. 6/2/1911 VA. Res. Greene Co., VA. Enl. 2/18/42 Camp Lee, VA. Ser. No. 33133036. Pfc., Co. C, 6/22/45 Innsbruck, Austria. d. 12/30/2003 Dyke, Greene Co., VA.

VICKERS, James W. b. 1/17/1915 AL. Res. Wadley, Randolph Co., AL. Ser. No. 34585586. Pvt., Co. D, Camp Gordon, GA 4/10/43. Pfc., Co. D, LST 422 Survivor, 1/26/44 Italy (Anzio) – Purple Heart. T/5, Co. A, 5/8/45 Innsbruck, Austria. d. May 1980 Lafayette, Chambers Co., AL.

VINTSON, Jack. Pvt., Co. C, captured six prisoners near Catignac, France 8/20/44. Pvt., Co. C, 6/22/45 Innsbruck, Austria.

VIRGEN, Isidro P. b. 1923 TX. Res. Sutton Co., TX. Enl. 2/8/43 Ft. Sam Houston, TX. Ser. No. 38367800. Pvt., Co. D, MIA, 1/26/44, Italy (Anzio) SR Cem.

VITOLO, Giro. b. 1921 CT. Res, New Haven Co., CT. Enl. 12/14/42 Hartford, CT. Ser. No. 31274386. Pvt., HQ & HQ Co., Camp Gordon, GA 4/10/43. Pfc., Co. C, MIA, 1/26/44, Italy (Anzio)

"VITTS" or **"VITTO"** - Italian worker with Co. A mentioned in a diary 8/7/43.

VOGEL, Julius D. b. 1921 PA. Res. Sewickley, Allegheny Co., PA. Ser. No. 33392412. Pvt. Co. C, 10/15/42 Camp Gordon GA. Cpl., Co. C, LST 422 Survivor, 1/26/44 Italy (Anzio) – Purple Heart with Oak Leaf Cluster. Rescued by USS Pilot. Reported MIA 8/29/44 Briançon, France. Returned 8/31/44. Pfc., Co. C, 6/22/45 Innsbruck, Austria. Re-enlisted 1946.

VOGT, Carl H. b. 8/13/1911 OH. Res. Hamilton Co., OH. Enl. 3/7/42 Ft. Thomas, Newport, KY. Ser. No. 35132966. Pvt. Attached to Co. C 5/28/42 Edgewood Arsenal, MD. Auto Rifleman (Pvt.). Cpl. (temp.), Co. B, promo. Sgt. (temp.), Camp Gordon, GA 12/12/42. Cpl., Co. B, 5/8/45 Innsbruck, Austria. [Spelled Vogt 5/28/42 Edgewood Arsenal, MD]. Res. Cincinnati, OH May 1954. Fireman. d. Mar. 1984 Cincinnati, Hamilton Co., OH.

VOITHOFER, Joseph C. b. 1918 PA. Enl. 1/29/42 New Cumberland, PA. Ser. No. 33146545. Pvt., Co. B, 5/8/45 Innsbruck, Austria.

VUKSON, Stephen William. b. 9/25/1921 Torrance, PA. Derry Twp. High School. Robert Morris University. Enl. 9/24/42 Greensburg, PA. Ser. No. 33294796. Ft. George G. Meade, MD 10/8/42. Pvt. Co. B, 10/15/42 Camp Gordon GA. 4.2" Mortar Squad, Co. B, 83rd CMB Oct. 1942, Camp Gordon, GA. Pvt., Co. B correspondent, Smokescreen, Camp Gordon, GA Nov. 1942. Promo. Pfc. & Motor Pool, Assistant Dispatcher 2/22/43. Motor Pool, Dispatcher 3/28/43. Promo. Cpl. & transf. HQ Co. 4/3/43.. Battalion Motor Section, Parts & Supplies Apr. 1943 to end of war & Germany Occupation. Promo. Sgt. 6/10/44 Tarquinia, Italy. T/4, HQ Co., 5/8/45 Innsbruck, Austria. 928th Field Artillery, 103rd Div. 7/7/45 – 10/6/45. Debarked Hampton Roads – Newport, VA 9/22/45. Dischd. 10/6/45. EAME Medal with six bronze Stars & a Bronze Arrowhead. WW II Victory Medal. Good Conduct medal. Res. Trafford, PA May 1954. Accountant, Westinghouse Corp. City Auditor. Res. Trafford, PA 2009.

WACLAWSKI, Joseph S. b. 1916. Enl. 4/14/43 Philadelphia, PA. Ser. No. 33600345. Pvt., Co. D, KIA, 1/26/44, Italy (Anzio) SR Cem.

WAGGY, Stanley William. b. 11/9/1921 Sugar Grove, WV. Pre-war Occupation: Short Order Cook. Res. Rockingham Co., VA. / Res. Fayetteville, PA. Enl. 12/16/42 Ft. Hayes, OH. Ser. No. 35746316. Heavy Mortar Crewman. Pvt., Co. C, Camp Gordon, GA 4/10/43. WIA, 12/6/43 Italy Pvt., Co. C, WIA (light injure), LST 422 Survivor, 1/26/44 Italy (Anzio) – Purple Heart with Oak Leaf Cluster. Returned to duty 2/2/44. Sgt., Co. C, 6/22/45 Innsbruck, Austria. EAME Service Ribbon. Good Conduct Medal. Bronze Arrowhead to EAME Ribbon. Dischd. 10/19/45. Re-enlisted 1946. Shenandoah Pride 35 years. Retired 1984. Harrisonburg Auto Auction (part time). d. 1/7/1989 Harrisonburg, VA. Bur. Eastlawn Memorial Gardens.

WAHOSKY, Norman A. b. 5/18/1921 PA. Res. Shamokin, PA. Enl. 9/21/42 Harrisburg, PA. Ser. No. 33240921. Pvt., Co. C, Camp Gordon, GA 10/9/42. Cpl., Co. C, LST 422 Survivor, 1/26/44 Italy (Anzio) – Purple Heart. Sgt., Co. C, 6/22/45 Innsbruck, Austria. d. Aug. 1984 PA.

WALDEMARSON, Donald L. b. 1924 PA. Enl. 6/4/43 Erie, PA. Ser. No. 33680577. Infantryman. European Campaign, Marsailles to Brenner Pass. Cpl., Co. C, Bronze Star, Sept. 1945.

WALDEN, Lamar. b. 1905 MS. Res. Lee Co., MS. Enl. 9/22/42 Camp Shelby, MS. Ser. No. 34426588. Pvt. Co. A, 10/14/42 Camp Gordon, GA. Transf. Co. D, Camp Gordon, GA, 12/16/42.

WALDREP, Royce H., Jr. ("Leroy"). b. 3/8/1924 WA. Res. Pierce Co., WA. Enl. 8/30/43 Seattle, WA. Ser. No. 39213869. Pvt., Co. D, WIA (light), 6/2/44 Italy. Pfc., Co. A, 5/8/45 Innsbruck, Austria. d. 2/15/1997.

WALKER, Marion A. b. 1918 AL. Res. Talladega Co., AL. Ser. No. 34580492. Assigned from HQ 2nd Replacement Depot 11/17/44 as Pvt., Co. B. Pfc., Co. C, 6/22/45 Innsbruck, Austria. Re-enlisted 1945.

WALKER, Raymond C., Jr. b. 1920 NJ. Res. Essex Co., NJ. Enl. 7/8/42 Newark, NJ. Ser. No. 32389804. Pvt., Co. C, Camp Gordon, GA 7/28/42. Pvt., Co. C, Camp Gordon, GA 10/1/42. Pfc., promo. Cpl. (temp.), Camp Gordon, GA 10/21/42. Art Editor, Smokescreen, Camp Gordon, GA Nov. 1942. Sgt., Art Editor, Smokescreen, Camp Gordon, GA 1/9/43.

WALKER, Samuel C. Pvt., HQ & HQ Co., Camp Gordon, GA 10/9/42. Ser. No. 33296810.

WALLACE, Hilery H. b. 1902 TN. Res. Maury Co., TN. Enl. 9/17/42 Ft. Oglethorpe, GA. Ser. No. 34371660. Present Co. D, Camp Gordon, GA, 12/31/42. Pvt., Co. D, Camp Gordon, GA, 1/9/43.

WALLED, Jack H. Res. Gilbert, MN. Enl. 5/30/42. Served in Normandy, Northern France. Pfc., Co B (Medical Detachment). Ardennes. Rhineland. Central Europe. Good Conduct Medal. American Campaign Medal. EAME Campaign Medal with five bronze stars. World War II Victory Medal. Dischd. 12/7/45.

WALLIS, John S. b. 1916 MI. Res. Dickinson Co., MI. Enl. 5/14/42 Marquette, MI. Ser. No. 36198757. Cpl., HQ Co., promo. T/4 (temp.) 9/15/45.

WALOSKI, ----------. In a group photo provided by Sam Kweskin. [Possibly Wahosky].

WALSH, Michael W. b. 1905 Irish Free State. Res. Philadelphia Co., PA. Enl. 12/14/42 Philadelphia, PA. Ser. No. 33475170. Pvt., Co. D, Camp Gordon, GA 3/18/43. Pvt., Co. D, WIA (broken leg – sent to hospital), 7/21/43 Porto Empedocle, Sicily.

WALTERS, ----------. Lt. present at Minturno 4/6/44.

WALTERS, David L. Pvt., KIA, 1/26/44, Italy (Anzio). [See David L. Waters].

WALTERS, Emerson R. b. 1920 PA. Res. New Castle, Lawrence Co., PA. Enl. 8/13/42 Erie, PA. Ser. No. 33295029. Pfc., Co. C, WIA 5/1/44 Italy – Purple Heart. T/5, Bronze Star, 1944. T/5, Med. Det., MIA, 8/29/44 Briançon, France. POW Stalag 7A Moosburg, Bavaria. Liberated 8/10/45.

WALTON, Chester. Pfc., Co. B, 5/8/45 Innsbruck, Austria.

WALTON, Lawrence W. b. 2/28/1921 MS. Res. Darry, Itawamba Co., MS. Enl. 9/23/42 Camp Shelby, MS. Ser. No. 34426773. Pvt. Co. A, 10/14/42 Camp Gordon, GA. Pvt., Co. A, on *LST 690* 8/9/44. Pfc., Co. A, 5/8/45 Innsbruck, Austria. d. 5/31/2002 Itawamba Co., MS.

WAPNITSKY, Samuel. Mortar squad leader. Cpl., Co. D, WIA (light), LST 422 Survivor, 1/26/44 Italy (Anzio). Cpl., Co. A, 5/8/45 Innsbruck, Austria. EAME, Glider Badge, Silver Service Star, Bronze Star, Good Conduct Medal, & Purple Heart. Res. Bayside, NY.

WARE, Roswell C. b. 1914 MD. Res. New Castle Co., Res. DE. Enl. 11/22/43 Camden, NJ. Ser. #42080955. Assigned from 65th Inf. Division as 2nd Lt., Co. A, 7/23/45.

WARBERG, ----------. [possibly John W. Berg]. Present at Anzio 1/22/44.

WARGO, John W. Pvt. Attached to Co. H 5/28/42 Edgewood Arsenal, MD. Intelligence Sgt. (S/Sgt.).

WARING, Paul James. b. 2/19/1911 PA. Enl. 10/5/42 Altoona, PA. Ser. No. 13084640. Pvt., HQ & HQ Co., Camp Gordon, GA 11/21/42. To Radio Operators School, Ft. Benning, GA Dec. 1942. T/5, apptd. T/4, HQ & HQ Co. 4/15/43. [Possibly the Waring listed in Charles Rollings diary as AWOL 1/17/44-7/14/44]. T/4, WIA (light injure – truck ran off road), 8/17/44 France. Spent time in hospital in Richmond, VA. Res. Altoona, PA May 1954. Buyer for Department Stores. 2/12/1993 Altoona, Blair Co., PA.

WARNER, Louis J. b. 1919 OH. Res. Hamilton Co., OH. Enl. 11/18/41 Ft. Thomas, Newport, KY. Ser. No. 35132373. Cpl. Assigned to Co. G 5/28/42 Edgewood Arsenal, MD. 1st Sgt. Cpl. (temp.), HQ & HQ Co., promo. Sgt. (temp.), Camp Gordon, GA 6/16/42. Sgt. (temp.), (1st Sgt.), promo. S/Sgt., Camp Gordon, GA 7/15/42. S/Sgt. (temp.), promo. 1st Sgt. (temp.), Camp Gordon, GA 8/1/42. Transf. OCS Edgewood Arsenal, MD Nov. 1942.

WARNING, Loyd C. b. 1921 MS. Res. Jones Co., MS. Enl. 9/21/42 Camp Shelby, MS. Ser. No. 34426255. Pvt. Co. A, 10/14/42 Camp Gordon, GA.

WARREN, Howard W. b. 2/5/1920 GA. Res. Floyd Co., GA. Enl. 9/16/42 Ft. McPherson, Atlanta, GA. Ser. No. 34442408. Pvt. Co. A, Camp Gordon, GA 10/9/42. d. Dec. 1985, GA.

WATERMAN, William R., Jr. S/Sgt., HQ Co., presented Bronze Star & Purple Heart 8/25/45.

WATERS, David L. Res. MS. Ser. No. 07006838. Pvt., Co. C, MIA, 1/26/44, Italy (Anzio) SR Cem.

WATSON, Richard F. b. 1920 IL. Res. Adams Co., IL. Enl. 3/11/42 Camp Grant, IL. Ser. No. 36324389. Pvt., Co. B, WIA (light), 11/30/44 France. Returned to duty 2/11/45. Pfc., HQ Co., 5/8/45 Innsbruck, Austria.

WAUFLE, Gordon D. b. 9/16/1911 NY. Res. Ilion, Herkimer Co., NY. Enl. 4/20/43 Utica, NY. Ser. No. 32857196. Pvt., Co. D, LST 422 Survivor, 1/26/44 Italy (Anzio) – Purple Heart. Pfc., Co. A, 5/8/45 Innsbruck, Austria. d. Apr. 1979 Herkimer, Herkimer Co., PA.

WAXBURG, Saul. Pvt., Co. B, Camp Gordon, GA 4/10/43.

WAY, Ralph T. b. 3/27/1925 KY. Res. Los Angeles Co., CA. Enl. 7/28/43 Los Angeles, CA. Ser. No. 39706473. Pfc., Co. A, 5/8/45 Innsbruck, Austria. d. 1/29/2005 Canyon Country, Los Angeles Co., CA.

WEAKS, Lexie P. Pfc., Co. A, promo. T/5 (temp.) 7/24/45. Ser. No. 14132614. Promo. Sgt. (temp.) 9/15/45..

WEATHERFORD, George O. B. 3/25/1921 VA. Res. Rockingham Co., NC. Enl. 9/21/42 Roanoke, VA. Ser. No. 33213382. Pvt. Co. D, 10/11/42 Camp Gordon GA. Pvt., Co. D, WIA (serious – shell fragment), 9/10/43 Vietre sul Mare, Italy. d. Oct. 1980.

WEATHERLY, Benjamin G. b. 8/15/1912 GA. Res. Zebulon, Pike Co., GA. Enl. 9/21/42 Ft. McPherson, Atlanta, GA. Ser. No. 34443186. Pvt., Co. A, Camp Gordon, GA 10/9/42. Transf. Co. C, Camp Gordon, GA, 12/16/42. Pvt., Co. A, WIA (light – anti-tank mine), 5/23/44 Anzio, Italy – Purple Heart. Not hospitalized. Pfc., Co. A, 5/8/45 Innsbruck, Austria. d. 12///23/1992 Griffin, Spaulding Co., GA.

WEAVER, Charlie L. b. 1920 MS. Res. Itawamba Co., MS. Enl. 9/22/1942 Camp Shelby, MS. Ser. No. 34426792. Pvt. Co. A, 10/14/42 Camp Gordon, GA. Pvt., Co. A, on *LST 690* 8/9/44. Pfc., Co. C, 6/22/45 Innsbruck, Austria.

WEAVER, Fred C. Pvt., Co. B, assigned Med. Det., Camp Gordon, GA 11/14/42. Ser. No. 33296801. Pvt., Co. B, Camp Gordon, GA 10/9/42. Cpl., Co. B, MIA, 12/12/44, Riquewihr, France. POW. Stalag 7A Moosburg Bavaria. Liberated 10/22/45.

WEBB, Mack Clifton. b. 1922 GA. Res. Demorest, Habersham Co., GA. Enl. 12/15/42 Ft. McPherson, Atlanta, GA. Ser. No. 34578183. Pvt., Co. C, Camp Gordon, GA 4/10/43. Pfc., Co. C, LST 422 Survivor, 1/26/44 Italy (Anzio) – Purple Heart. Rescued by YMS 43. Pfc., Soldiers Medal [Presented 11/20/44]. Pfc., Co. C, 6/22/45 Innsbruck, Austria.

WEBSTER [Wobser], Clarence C. b. 1912 CA. Res. San Bernardino Co., CA. Enl. 12/1/42 Los Angeles, CA. Ser. No. 39268449. HQ 2nd CMB, assigned Pfc., HQ & HQ Co., 83rd CMB 7/25/45.

WEBSTER, Walter R. b. 1920 SC. Res. Cherokee Co., SC. Enl. 11/4/41 Ft. Jackson, Columbia, SC. Ser. No. 34098557. Pvt., Co. D, KIA, 1/26/44, Italy (Anzio).

WEHRHEIM, Robert J. b. 5/16/1911 IA. Res. Clarion, Wright Co., IA. Enl. 12/21/42 Camp Dodge, Herrold, IA. Ser. No. 37651552. Pvt., Co. D, Camp Gordon, GA 4/10/43. Pfc., Co. D, LST 422 Survivor, 1/26/44 Italy (Anzio) – Purple Heart. James M. Lester said Wehrheim's truck was 'blown up' at Anzio. Pfc., Co. A, 5/8/45 Innsbruck, Austria. d. Sept. 1965 IA.

WEIGEL, Robert W. Pvt., Co. B, Camp Gordon, GA 3/18/43. Ser. No. 37005892.

WEIKEL, Paul E. b. 1921 PA. Res. OH. Enl. 9/21/42 Harrisburg, PA. Ser. No. 33240918. Pvt., Co. C, Camp Gordon, GA 10/9/42. Cpl., Co. C – Silver Star (presented 12/5/43). Cpl., Co. C, KIA, 1/26/44, Italy (Anzio) SR Cem.

WEIKEL, Wilmer C. b. 3/8/1921 PA. Enl. 9/21/42 Harrisburg, PA. Ser. No. 33240958. Pvt., Co. B, Camp Gordon, GA 10/9/42. Pfc., Co. B, 5/8/45 Innsbruck, Austria. d. 8/9/1991 PA.

WELLS, Gerald ("The California Kid"). b. 1906 Montana. Res. Los Angeles Co., CA. Enl. 7/9/1942 Ft. MacArthur, San Pedro, CA. Ser. No. 39019476. Pvt. Attached to Co. F 5/28/42 Edgewood Arsenal, MD. Mechanic Auto (Pvt.). Pvt., HQ & HQ Co. transf. Co. B, Camp Gordon, GA 6/15/42. Pfc., (Auto Mech.), promo. T/5 (temp.), Camp Gordon, GA 7/15/42. T/5, Co. B, promo. T/4 (temp.), Camp Gordon, GA 9/12/42. T/4, Co. B, arrived Salemi, Sicily from North Africa 8/1/43. S/Sgt., Co. B, 5/8/45 Innsbruck, Austria.

WELLS, Jessie. b. 7/13/1920 MS. Res. Lafayette Co., MS. Enl. 9/22/42 Camp Shelby, MS. Ser. No. 34426563. Pvt. Co. A, 10/14/42 Camp Gordon, GA. Transf. Co. B, Camp Gordon, GA, 12/16/42. d. Nov. 1963.

WEST, Floyd A. b. 1911 MN. Res. St. Louis Co., MN. Enl. 3/3/1942 Ft. Sheridan, IL. Ser. No. 36236731. Attached to Co. H 5/28/42 Edgewood Arsenal, MD. Telephone Operator (Pvt.). Pfc., Co. C, promo. Cpl. (temp.), Camp Gordon, GA 9/3/42. Cpl. (temp.) Co. C, to Sgt. (temp.) Camp Gordon, GA 10/14/42.

WEST, George F. b. 1909 PA. Enl. 12/12/1942 Altoona, PA. Ser. No. 33567100. Pvt., Co. C, Camp Gordon, GA 4/10/43.

WHEELER, Jimmie J. b. 1923 TX. Res. Throckmorton Co., TX. Enl. 2/11/43 Abilene, TX. Ser. No. 38370985. Pfc., Co. C, 6/22/45 Innsbruck, Austria.

WHEELER, L. H. b. 2/27/1920 TX. Res. TX. Enl. 6/4/42 Houston, TX. Ser. No. 38162588. Pvt., Co. D, MIA, 1/26/44, Italy (Anzio) SR Cem. Bur. Wake Field Cem., Trinity, TX.

WHEELER, Paul F. Pfc., Co. A, 5/8/45 Innsbruck, Austria.

WHEELER, Paul R. (F.). b. 1921 MS. Res. Itawamba Co., MS. Enl. 9/23/42 Camp Shelby, MS. Ser. No. 34426781. Pvt. Co. D, 10/14/42 Camp Gordon, GA. Pfc. Co. D, WIA 11/21/43 Venafro, Italy. Pfc., Co. D, KIA, 1/26/44 Italy (Anzio), SR Cem.

WHEELER, Wiley B. b. 1916 MS. Res. Itawamba Co., MS. Enl. 9/23/42 Camp Shelby, MS. Ser. No. 34426737. Pvt. Co. D, 10/14/42 Camp Gordon, GA. Pfc. Co. D, MIA, 1/26/44, Italy (Anzio) SR Cem.

WHELAN, Andrew ("Andy") J. b. 1920 PA. Enl. 9/22/42 Philadelphia, PA. Ser. No. 33335560. Pvt., Co. D, Camp Gordon, GA 10/9/42. Transf. Co. A, Camp Gordon, GA, 12/16/42. Pfc., Co. D, MIA, 1/26/44, Italy (Anzio) SR Cem.

WHETSELL, George J. Pvt. Attached to Co. K 5/28/42 Edgewood Arsenal, MD. Telephone Operator (Pvt.). Pfc., Co. D, promo. Cpl. (temp.), Camp Gordon, GA 9/26/42. Promo. Sgt. (temp.), Camp Gordon, GA 10/21/42. Co. D, promo. S/Sgt.(temp.), Camp Gordon, GA 12/2/42. S/Sgt., HQ Co., 5/8/45 Innsbruck, Austria. Res. Dravasburg, PA May 1954. Strip Finisher, 5 Stand Rolling Mill. Attended 1954 &

1958 Reunions as res. Dravasburg, PA.

WHITE, Allen A., Jr. b. 1913 NJ. Res. Hamilton Co., OH. Enl. 3/3/42 Ft. Thomas, Newport, KY. Ser. No. 35269564. Pvt. Attached to Co. H 5/28/42 Edgewood Arsenal, MD. Squad Leader (Sgt.). Pfc., Co. C, promo. Cpl. (temp.), Camp Gordon, GA 12/15/42.

WHITE, Earl H. Pfc., Co. B, 5/8/45 Innsbruck, Austria.

WHITE, Earl N. b. 1920 GA. Res Cobb Co., GA. Enl. 9/11/42 Ft. McPherson, Atlanta, GA. Ser. No. 34441443. Pvt., Co. A, Camp Gordon, GA 10/8/42. Transf. Co. B, Camp Gordon, GA, 12/16/42.

WHITE, James N. b. 1921 MS. Res. Lafayette Co., MS. Enl. 9/22/42 Camp Shelby, MS. Ser. No. 34426560. Pvt. Co. A, 10/14/42 Camp Gordon, GA. Transf. Co. D, Camp Gordon, GA, 12/16/42.

WHITE, Lee R. Pfc., HQ Co., 5/8/45 Innsbruck, Austria.

WHITE, Warren C. Pvt., Co. D, WIA (light), 6/1/44 Italy – Purple Heart.. Pfc., Co. A, 5/8/45 Innsbruck, Austria. Evacuated to hospital. Res. Niagra Falls, NY, 2009.

WHITE, Woodrow W. b. 1913 MA. Res. Franklin Co., MA. Enl. 9/12/42 Springfield, MA. Pvt. Attached to Co. F 5/28/42 Edgewood Arsenal, MD. Motor Sgt. (S/Sgt.). Pvt., HQ & HQ Co. transf. Co. B, Camp Gordon, GA 6/15/42. Pfc., (Motor Sgt.), promo. Cpl. (temp.), Camp Gordon, GA. T/4 (temp.), Co. B, promo. S/Sgt. (temp.), Camp Gordon, GA 10/6/42. Jeep driver for Capt. Gordon Mindrum. Ser. No. 11061652. S/Sgt., Co. B, MIA, 1/26/44, Italy (Anzio) SR Cem.

WHITKUS, Stanley D. b. 3/20/1918 PA. Res. Passaic Co., NJ. Enl. 7/9/42 Newark, NJ. Ser. No. 32396630 Pvt., HQ & HQ Co., Camp Gordon, GA 7/28/42. T/4, Co. C, 6/22/45 Innsbruck, Austria. d. 3/6/1996 Passaic, Passaic Co., NJ.

WHITLEDGE, Kenneth R. b. 1925 IN. Enl. 1/20/44 Evansville, IN. Ser. No. 35813763. Pfc., Co. B, promo. Corp. (temp.) 9/15/45.

WHITT, Rudolph. b. 6/8/1921 VA. Res. Bear Wallow, Buchanan Co., VA. Pre-war Occupation: Coal Miner. Enl. 10/3/42 Abingdon, VA. Ser. No. 33214372. Pvt., Co. C, Camp Gordon, GA 10/11/42. Pvt., Co. C, WIA (light injure), LST 422 Survivor, 1/26/44 Italy (Anzio) – Purple Heart [belatedly awarded 2005]. Rescued by USS Pilot. Spent 21 days in a hospital. Pfc, Co. C, 6/22/45 Innsbruck, Austria. 103rd Inf. Div. During entire time in 83rd CMB served in 2nd Platoon, Co. C, in Communications as Radio Operator. Res. Cedar Bluff, VA, 2009.

WHITTAKER, Corbet. b. 1921 WV. Res. McDowell Co., WV. Enl. 10/10/42 Huntington, WV. Ser. No. 35449033. Pvt., Co. C, KIA (enemy shell), 9/16/43, Vietre sul Mare, Italy, SR Cem.

WHITTAKER, L. D. b. 1919 TN. Res. White Co., TN. Enl. 9/18/42 Ft. Oglethorpe, GA. Ser. No. 34371798. Present at B & C (cooking) school, Ft. Jackson, SC, 1/3/43 - 2/26/43. T/5, Co. D, WIA (shell fragment), 9/25/43, Italy. Hospitalized. Res. St. James City, FL.

WHITTLE, Jesse C. b. 5/3/1911 MS. Tunica Co., MS. Enl. 9/23/42 Camp Shelby, MS. Ser. No. 34426915. Pvt. Co. D, 10/14/42 Camp Gordon, GA. d. Jan. 1969.

WIAN, Harry P. b. 9/21/1920 PA. Enl. 9/20/42 Greensburg, PA. Ser. No. 33294884. Pvt. Co. B, 10/15/42 Camp Gordon GA. Pfc., Co. B, sent to hospital (120th Collecting Bn.) 8/4/43. Returned to duty 8/7/43. Pfc., Co. B, 5/8/45 Innsbruck, Austria. d. Nov. 1984 Youngwood, Westmoreland Co., PA.

WICKS, Clarence L. b. 1/18/1912 PA. Enl. 9/21/42 Harrisburg, PA. Ser. No. 33240898. Pvt., Co. B, Camp Gordon, GA 10/9/42. Pfc., Co. B, 5/8/45 Innsbruck, Austria. Attended 1954 & 1958 Reunions as res. Williamsport, PA. d. 12/17/1990 PA.

WIDING, Howard B. Res. St. Paul, MN. Ser. No. 37165437. Pvt. Attached to Co. C 5/28/42 Edgewood Arsenal, MD. Cook (Pvt.). Pfc., Co. C, (Cook), promo. T/5 (temp.), Camp Gordon, GA 71/15/42. T/5 (temp.), Co. C, promo. T/4 (temp.), Camp Gordon, GA 9/3/42. S/Sgt., Co. C, LST 422 Survivor, 1/26/44 Italy (Anzio) – Purple Heart with Oak Leaf Cluster. S/Sgt., Co. C, 6/22/45 Innsbruck, Austria.

WIEDMAN, Robert W. b. 4/2/1913 NJ. Res. Morris Co., NJ. Enl. 7/9/42 Newark, NJ. Ser. No. 32390378. Pvt., Co. A, Camp Gordon, GA 7/28/42. Pvt., Co. A, special duty to Chaplain, Camp Gordon, GA 8/26/42. Transf. HQ & HQ Co., Camp Gordon, GA 10/10/42. Pfc., promo. T/5 (temp.), Camp Gordon, GA 11/24/42. Pfc., HQ Co. correspondent, Smokescreen, Camp Gordon, GA Nov. 1942. T/4 HQ correspondent, Smokescreen, Camp Gordon, GA 1/9/43. d. 12/9/2001 Morris Co., NJ.

WIGGINS, L. W. b. 9/6/1921 GA. Res. Millen, Jenkins Co., GA. Enl. 9/18/42 Ft. McPherson, Atlanta, GA. Ser. No. 34442792. Pvt., Co. C, Camp Gordon, GA 10/8/42. Transf. Co. A, Camp Gordon, GA, 12/16/42. T/5, Co. C, LST 422 Survivor, 1/26/44 Italy (Anzio) – Purple Heart. Rescued by USS Pilot. T/5, Co. C, WIA (light), 6/6 or 7/44 Italy. T/5, Bronze Star [Presented 11/20/44]. T/5, Co. C, 6/22/45 Innsbruck, Austria. d. Apr. 1985 Millen, Jenkins Co., GA.

WIGGINS, Thomas W. Res. MS. Ser. No. 07006655. Pvt. Co. D, MIA, 1/26/44, Italy (Anzio) SR Cem.

WILDER, Lynn B. b. 1/1/1899 GA. Res. Mitchell Co., GA. Enl. 9/19/42 Ft. McPherson, Atlanta, GA. Ser. No. 34442985. Pvt., HQ & HQ Co., Camp Gordon, GA 10/9/42. Prom. To Pfc., HQ Co. in the 12/12/42 issue of Smokescreen. d. Feb. 1985, Valdosta, Lowndes Co., GA.

WILKERSON, Earl R. b. 1920 TN. Res. Clay Co., TN. Enl. 9/16/42 Ft. Oglethorpe, GA. Ser. No. 34371335. Pvt., Co. B, Camp Gordon, GA 10/7/42. Pfc., Co. D, WIA (light injure) LST 422 Survivor, 1/26/44 Italy (Anzio). According to Wilkerson he was WIA in Germany. Dischd. 1945. Spent two years in a VA hospital in NC. Returned home 1947.

WILKINSON, Malcolm Doyle ("Wilkie"). b. 8/27/1922 Gloster, MS. University of Texas, Austin, TX. Pre-war Occupation: Clerk at Swift & Co., Memphis, TN. Res. Neshoba Co., MS. Enl. 10/7/42 Camp Shelby, MS. Ser. No. 14150917. Pvt. Co. A, 10/14/42 Camp Gordon, GA. Co. A, Camp Gordon, GA. Transf. Co. B after LST 422 (not on ship). Sgt., Co. A, on *LST 690* 8/9/44. Transf. HQ Co., Dec. 1944. Sgt., Co. B, 5/8/45 Innsbruck, Austria. Honorable Discharge at Camp Shelby, MS. Postwar: Pharmacy School. Res. Corpus Christi, TX 2009.

WILLARD, (Williard), Tillmon. b. 1916 TN. Res. Cannon Co., TN. Enl. 4/4/41 Ft. Oglethorpe, GA. Ser. No. 34040877. Pvt., Co. D, KIA, 1/26/44, Italy (Anzio) SR Cem.

WILLARD, Hughel. b. 1920 TN. Res. Rutherford Co., TN. Enl. 9/17/42 Ft. Oglethorpe, GA. Ser. No. 34371587. Pvt., Co. B, sent to hospital (120th Collecting Bn.) 8/4/43. Returned to duty 8/8/43. Pfc., Co. B, WIA (serious), 11/30/44 France. Pfc., Co. B, 5/8/45 Innsbruck, Austria.

WILLIAMS, Bill. b. 1919 AL. Res. Houston Co., AL. Enl. 9/18/42 Ft. McClellan, AL. Ser. No.34391624. Pvt., Co. A, Camp Gordon, GA 10/8/42.

WILLIAMS, Carlton. b. August 3, 1912 GA. Res. Johnson Co., GA. Enl. 9/19/42 Ft. McPherson, Atlanta, GA. Ser. No. 34442890. Pvt., Co. B, Camp Gordon, GA 10/9/42. Heavy mortar crewman, setup, aimed and fired mortar from ground mount. Served in Sicily, Naples-Foggia, Rome, Souther France, Rhineland, and Central Europe. Postwar res. Kite, GA. d. Jan. 1968.

WILLIAMS, Clovis L. b. 8/27/1915 MS. Res. Monroe Co., MS. Enl. 9/23/42 Camp Shelby, MS. Ser. No. 34426741. Pvt. Co. A, 10/14/42 Camp Gordon, GA. d. 4/21/2005 Tupelo, Lee Co., MS.

WILLIAMS, Curtis Albert. b. 5/21/1921 Salisbury, TN. Res. Marks, Quitman Co., MS. Enl. 9/23/42 Camp Shelby, MS. Ser. No. 34426925. Pvt. Co. B, 10/14/42 Camp Gordon, GA. Pvt., Co. B, assigned Med. Det., Camp Gordon, GA 11/30/42. Pvt., Co. D, distinguished in action for giving aid to wounded while under heavy fire 7/11/43 Sicily. WIA (German soldier stuck knife in back) on Cassino front. Silver Star – presented 1/14/44 for gallantry at Sicily. Pfc., Med. Det., LST 422 Survivor, 1/26/44 Italy (Anzio) – Purple Heart with Oak Leaf Cluster. Rescued by USS Pilot. WIA (gash on left arm), Anzio, Italy. Res. Memphis, TN 2009.

WILLIAMS, Duvard H. b. 1922 AL. Res. Americus, GA. Enl. 9/25/42 Ft. McPherson, Atlanta, GA. Ser. No. 34444144. Pvt. HQ & HQ Co. 10/14/42 Camp Gordon, GA. Pfc., Co. D, MIA, 1/26/44, Italy (Anzio) SR Cem.

WILLIAMS, Earl J. b. 1904 MS. Res. Tangipahoa Co., LA. Enl. 9/18/42 Camp Shelby, MS. Ser. No. 34425597. Pvt. Co. C, 10/14/42 Camp Gordon, GA.

WILLIAMS, Elvin B. b. 1904 UT. Res. Los Angeles Co., CA. Enl. 2/28/42 Ft. MacArthur, San Pedro, CA. Ser. No. 39021201. Pvt. Attached to Co. B 5/28/42 Edgewood Arsenal, MD. Telephone Operator (Pvt.).

WILLIAMS, Harold A. b. 1920 PA. Res. Camden Co., NJ. Enl. 7/9/42 Camden, NJ. Ser. No. 32271781. Pvt., Co. C, Camp Gordon, GA 7/28/42.

WILLIAMS, Jim. Pfc., Co. C, 6/22/45 Innsbruck, Austria.

WILLIAMS, Lawrence Loyd. b. 5/2/1921 Itawamba Co., MS. I. A. High School – ICC – Mississippi State University. Pre-war Occupation: Home Work & School. Enl. 9/23/42 Camp Shelby, MS. Camp Gordon, GA. Pvt. Co. D, 10/14/42 Camp Gordon, GA. Pfc. Co. D, admitted to hospital for exhaustion 11/24/43 Venafro, Italy. Co. D, 83rd CMB (original member) to Anzio.

WILLIAMS, Monroe J. b. 1906 GA. Res. Jefferson Co., GA. Enl. 9/18/42 Ft. McPherson, Atlanta, GA. Ser. No. 34442769. Pvt., Co. D, Camp Gordon, GA 10/8/42.

WILLIAMS, Robert E. Pfc., Co. C, 6/22/45 Innsbruck, Austria.

WILLIAMSON, Glen Y. ("Smoky"). Capt., CWS, assigned HQ & HQ Co., & designated Assistant Battalion Operations & Training Officer, Camp Gordon, GA 10/26/42. Released as Asst. Operations & Training Officer & transf. Co. B, Camp Gordon, GA 11/4/42. Maj., HQ 63rd Inf. Div., Camp Van Dorn, MI 1/25/44. As Chemical Officer with the 63rd Inf. Div. he planned and largely executed the historic and pivoted crossing of the Siegfried Line. Res. San Marino, CA.

WILLIAMSON, Gordon L. b. 1919 OR. Res. Multnomah Co., OR. Enl. 3/11/42 Ft. Lewis, WA. Ser. No. 39388886. Pvt. Attached to Co. A 5/28/42 Edgewood Arsenal, MD. Platoon Sgt. (S/Sgt.). Pfc., Co. B, (Platoon Leader), promo. Cpl. (temp.), Camp Gordon, GA 7/15/42. Sgt. (temp.), promo. S/Sgt. (temp.), Camp Gordon, GA 8/1/42.

WILLIAMSON, Joseph A. b. 12/27/1921 Wilkes Barre, PA. Barringer High School, Newark, NJ. Atlantic City High. Rutgers University. Off Campus Center, Atlantic City, NJ. Res. Atlantic City, Camden Co., NJ. Enl. 7/9/42 Camden, NJ. Ser. No. 32271797. Pvt., Co. C, Camp Gordon, GA 7/28/42. Pfc., Co. C correspondent, Smokescreen, Nov. 1942. Cpl., Features Staff & Co. C correspondent, Smokescreen, Camp Gordon, GA Feb. 1943. Cpl., Co. C, WIA (shrapnel - temple), 5/29/44 Anzio, Italy – Purple Heart. 382nd Field Art. Battalion Sept. 1945 for demobilization. Army Reserve Corps 1945-47. Res. Margate City, NJ 2005. d. 2/28/2007 Margate City, NJ.

WILLINGHAM, Albert J., Sr. b. 1902 GA. Res. Jefferson Co., AL. Enl. 9/19/42 Ft. McClellan, AL. Ser. No. 34391838. Pvt., Co. B, Camp Gordon, GA 10/8/42.

WILLINGHAM, James F. b. 8/17/1915 GA. Res. Floyd Co., GA. Enl. 9/16/42 Ft. McPherson, Atlanta, GA. Ser. No. 34442296. Pvt., Co. C, Camp Gordon, GA 10/9/42. d. 6/1/2001 Centre, Cherokee Co., AL.

WILLS, Jerry. b. 1906 Germany. Res. Windham Co., CT. Enl. 12/21/1943 New Haven, CT. Ser. No. 31408939.

WILSON, Frank R. b. 1913 VA. Res. Tazewell Co., VA. Enl. 10/3/42 Abingdon, VA. Ser. No. 33214347. Pvt., Co. C, Camp Gordon, GA 10/11/42. Pfc., Co. C, MIA, 1/26/44, Italy (Anzio) SR Cem.

WILSON, Harry W. b. 1917 PA. (grave says 8/8/1920). Res. Philadelphia Co., PA. Enl. 9/22/42 Philadelphia, PA. Se. No. 33335624. Pvt., Co. D, Camp Gordon, GA 10/9/42. Pvt., Co. D, KIA, 1/26/44 Italy (Anzio). Body recovered 1/26/44 by USS YMS 226 and turned over to Graves Registration at Anzio 1/27/44. Next of kin: Sarah Wilson, Philadelphia, PA. Re-interred 8/8/48 at Beverly Nat. Cem., Beverly, NJ.

WILSON, John. b. 1917 VA. Res. Bedford Co., VA. Enl. 9/21/42 Roanoke, VA. Ser. No. 33213381. Pvt. Co. D, 10/11/42 Camp Gordon GA.

WILSON, Stewart R. b. 1903 PA. Enl. 10/9/42 Pittsburgh, PA. Ser. No. 33307690. Pvt. HQ & HQ Co., 10/15/42 Camp Gordon GA.

WILT, Henry B. b. 10/6/1918 PA. Res. York Co., PA. Enl. 2/24/42 Ft. George Meade, MD. Ser. No. 33169888. Pvt. Attached to Co. G 5/28/42 Edgewood Arsenal, MD. Squad Leader (Sgt.). Cpl. (temp.), Co. B, promo. Sgt. (temp.), Camp Gordon, GA 9/7/42. Sgt. Co. B, transf. Co. A, Camp Gordon, GA, 12/16/42. S/Sgt., Co. B, 5/8/45 Innsbruck, Austria. Res. York, PA May 1954. Attended 1954, 1956, 1958 & 1960 Reunions as res. York, PA. d. Nov. 1983 York, York Co., PA.

WIMS, ----------. Transf. To 10th Mountain Div. Had a brother named James Wims in the 179th Inf. & a brother called Louis "Cody" Wims in the 45th Div. Mentioned in an oral history with Louis Wims on the Internet.

WINCHESTER, Henry T. b. 1/15/1911 MI. Res. Allegan Co., MI. Enl. 3/17/42 Ft. Custer, MI. Ser. No. 36175947. Pvt. Attached to Co. A 5/28/42 Edgewood Arsenal, MD. Squad Leader (Sgt.). d. 1/18/1997.

WINDSOR, Albert O. b. 5/2/1911 MD. Enl. 3/9/44 Ft. George Meade, MD. Ser. No. 33844041. Pvt., HQ Co., 5/8/45 Innsbruck, Austria. Pvt., transf. 2nd CMB 7/25/45. d. Dec. 1977 MD.

WINKLER, John Henry. Pvt., Co. D, WIA (enemy shell - light), 9/16/43 Vietre sul Mare, Italy. Returned to duty 9/18/43. Pfc., Co. A, 5/8/45 Innsbruck, Austria. Res. Greenwood, SC May 1954. Doffer, Spinning Dept., Textile Plant.

WITT, William C. b. 4/1/1906 VA. Res. Bedford Co., VA. Enl. 9/21/42 Roanoke, VA. Ser. No. 33213353. Pvt. Co. D, 10/11/42 Camp Gordon GA. d. Aug. 1983 Bedford, VA.

WIX, Robert N. b. 1922 TN. Res. Macon Co., TN. Enl. 8/16/42 Ft. Oglethorpe, GA Ser. No. 34371373. Pvt., Co. B, Camp Gordon, GA 10/7/42. Pvt., Co. D, MIA, 1/26/44, Italy (Anzio) SR Cem.

WOBSER, Clarence C. [see entry for Clarence C. Webster].

WOJTYNA, John A. b. 1922 PA. Enl. 10/24/42 Pittsburgh. PA. Pvt., Co. C, Camp Gordon, GA 11/1/42. Ser. No. 13131888. Pfc., Co. C, MIA, 1/26/44, Italy (Anzio) SR Cem.

WOLCOTT, Henry W. Pvt. Attached to Co. H 5/28/42 Edgewood Arsenal, MD. Squad Leader (Sgt.).

WOLDMAN, Isadore. b. 1/11/1914 PA. Res. Camden Co., NJ. Enl. 7/7/42 Camden, NJ. Ser. No. 32271575. Pvt., Co. C, Camp Gordon, GA 7/28/42. d. 12/9/1991 NJ.

WOLFE, George W. b. 11/29/1919 PA. Res. Blair Co., PA. Enl. 3/3/42 New Cumberland, PA. Ser. No. 33160254. Pvt. Attached to Co. B 5/28/42 Edgewood Arsenal, MD. Telephone Operator (Pvt.). Pfc., Co. C, promo. Cpl. (temp.), Camp Gordon, GA 8/17/42. Sgt., Co. C, WIA, 9/24/43, Maiori, Italy. S/Sgt., Co. B, WIA (light – shrapnel in leg), 11/17/43 Venafro, Italy. d. June 1987 Hollidaysburg, Blair Co., PA.

WOLFE, Robert D. b. 1913 OH. Res. Blair Co., PA. Enl. 3/3/42 New Cumberland, PA. Ser. No. 33160308. Pvt. Attached to Co. H 5/28/42 Edgewood Arsenal, MD. Squad Leader (Sgt.). Sgt. (temp.), Co. D, promo. S/Sgt. (temp.), Camp Gordon, GA 10/6/42. Transf. OCS, Edgewood Arsenal, MD Nov. 1942.

WOLTERS, Theodore E. Pvt. Ser. No. 37137691. Attached to Co. A 5/28/42 Edgewood Arsenal, MD. Telephone Operator (Pvt.). Pfc., Co. D (temp.), T/5 Camp Gordon, GA 8/1/42. T/5, Camp Gordon, GA 11/21/42. [Possibly same as Theodore H. Wolters. b. 1916 WI. Res. Milwaukee Co., WI. Enl. 8/25/1941 Milwaukee, WI. Ser. No. 36218083].

WOOD, Milton F. ("Woody"). b. 1917 Indian Mills, NJ. Served in England, Africa, Italy & France. Owner & Operator of Seaboard Air Conditioning Company of Atlantic City, NJ for over 60 years. d. 12/7/2007 bur. Head of the River Cemetery (Estelle Manor).

WOOD, Robert E. Pvt., Co. B, Camp Gordon, GA 4/10/43. Ser. No. 36718580. Pvt., Co. B, sent to hospital 8/18/43. Pfc., Co. B, MIA, 12/12/44, Riquewihr, France. POW. Stalag 7A Moosburg, Bavaria. Liberated 6/30/45.

WOOD[S], Walter S. Claimed to be a member of the 83rd CMB while in the U.S. In a 1958 letter in Muzzleblasts. Res. East St. Louis, MO.

WOODIN [Woddin], Harry W., Jr. b. 3/15/1918 MA. Res. Franklin Co., MA. Enl. 3/14/42 Ft. Devens, MA. Pvt. Attached to Co. A 5/28/42 Edgewood Arsenal, MD. Squad Leader (Sgt.). Pvt., Co. C, WIA (injured by tank trap) 7/14/43 Gela, Sicily. Ser. No. 31073024. Sgt., Co. C, MIA, 1/26/44, Italy (Anzio) SR Cem. Brother of John O. Woodin. Bur. St. Marys Cem., Turners Falls, MA.

WOODIN, John O. b. 1920 MA. Res. Franklin Co., MA. Enl. 3/14/42 Ft. Devens, MA. Ser. No. 31073056. Pvt. Attached to Co. A 5/28/42 Edgewood Arsenal, MD. Squad Leader (Sgt.). Pfc., Co. C, detailed Dental Officer, Camp Gordon, GA 8/3/42. Pvt., Co. B transf. Co. C, Camp Gordon, GA 6/15/42. Returned to Co. duty, Camp Gordon,

GA 8/10/42. Survivor, LST 422, 1/26/44 Italy (Anzio). Taken to 93rd Evac. Hosp. Brother of Harry W. Woodin, Jr.

WOODWARD, Milton T. b. 12/20/1912 MS. Res. Neshoba Co., MS. Enl. 9/22/42 Camp Shelby, MS. Ser. No. 34426449. Pvt. Co. A, 10/14/42 Camp Gordon, GA. Transf. Co. C, Camp Gordon, GA, 12/16/42. d. 3/27/1988 Philadelphia, Neshoba Co., MS.

WOOMER, Justin Gerald. ("Jerry") b. 10/5/1909 PA. School Teacher 1934. Res. Yeagerstown, PA. Enl. 6/29/42 Altoona, PA. Ser. No. 33246755. 2nd. Lt., relvd. from assignment at the Officers Replacement Pool & assgnd Inspection Office, Office Chief, Edgewood Arsenal, MD. Joined 83rd CMB Sept. 1943 at Sicily & assgnd. HQ Co. Transf. Co. D at Salerno. 2nd Lt., CWS, LST 422 Survivor, 1/26/44 Italy (Anzio) – Purple Heart. Rescued by USS YMS 226. Taken to 93rd Evac. Hosp. 1st Lt., Silver Star [presented 11/20/44]. Acting CO, Co. D 2/2/44. 1st Lt., WIA (light), 2/5/45 France. Also served in Co. A as platoon commander. 1st. Lt., Co. B, 5/8/45 Innsbruck, Austria. In command of Co. B at end of war. 1st Lt. Assigned 65th Inf. Div. 7/23/45. Res. Milroy, PA May 1954. Attended 1954, 1956, 1958, 1960, 1962 & 1966 Reunions as res. Milroy, PA. d. 11/19/1973.

WORRALL, George E. b. 1915 PA. Enl. 9/3/42 Harrisburg, PA. Ser. No. 33239792. Pvt., HQ & HQ Co., Camp Gordon, GA 10/9/42. Pfc., Co. D, KIA, 1/26/44 Italy, (Anzio). [Army serial no. incorrectly gives name as Worra].

WRAY, Tom. Mentioned in 1956 Muzzleblasts.

WRIGHT, Carroll W. 2nd Lt., CWS-AUS, assigned Co. A, Camp Gordon, GA 10/30/42. Detached service, Columbia, SC Dec. 1942.

WRIGHT, Jackson R. Pfc., Co. C, 6/22/45 Innsbruck, Austria.

WRIGHT, John W. b. 1899 GA. Res. Montgomery Co., GA. Enl. 9/1942 Ft. McPherson, Atlanta, GA. Ser. No. 34442991. Pvt., Co. C, Camp Gordon, GA 10/9/42.

YAGER, Allen G. b. 1916 NY. Res. Bronx Co., NY. Enl. 7/9/42 Ft. Jay, Governors Island, NY. Ser. No. 32402143. Pvt., Co. A, Camp Gordon, GA 7/28/42. Pvt., Co. A, Camp Gordon, GA 9/25/42.

YAKUBISIN, George S. ("Yak"/"Jumbo"). b. 5/18/1921 PA. Enl. 9/25/42 Greensburg, PA. Ser. No. 33294862. Cpl., Co. D, LST 422 Survivor, 1/26/44 Italy (Anzio) – Purple Heart. Sgt. Co. A, 5/8/45 Innsbruck, Austria. Postwar res. Greensburg, PA. Res. Youngwood, PA May 1954. Attended 1954, 1956, 1958, 1960, 1962 & 1966 Reunions as res. Youngwood, PA. Yakubisin's nephew, Rich Rollins, played first base for the Baltimore Orioles. d. 10/30/1988 Youngwood, Westmoreland Co., PA.

YATES, Thomas E. Res. Irwin, PA. b. 1921 PA. Enl. 9/24/42 Greensburg, PA. Ser. No. 33294788. Pvt. Co. C, 10/15/42 Camp Gordon GA. Reported MIA 8/29/44 Briançon, France. Returned 8/31/44. Pvt., Co. C, Purple Heart [Presented 11/20/44]. Pfc., Co. C 6/22/45 Innsbruck, Austria.

YEAGER, Robert Henry. b. 1920 MD. Res. Wrightsville, York Co., PA. Enl. 10/5/42 Harrisburg, PA. Ser. No.13093266. Pvt., Co. D, Camp Gordon, GA 10/9/42. Pfc., Co. D, MIA, 1/26/44, Italy (Anzio) SR Cem.

YEATTS [Yeats], Carroll Vincent. b. 1921 VA. Res. Pittsylvania Co., VA. Enl. 9/21/42 Roanoke, VA. Ser. No. 33213393. Pvt., Co. C, Camp Gordon, GA 10/11/42. Pfc., Co. C, LST 422 Survivor, 1/26/44 Italy (Anzio). Rescued by USS YMS 226. Taken to 93rd Evac. Hosp. Sgt., Co. C, 6/22/45 Innsbruck, Austria.

YOST, Lawrence E. ("Larry"). b. 1911 IA. Res. Polk Co. IA. Enl. 6/23/42 Ft. Des Moines, IA. Ser. No. 37420413. Ammo Detail, Bronze Star for 5/28/44 near Lanuvio, Italy. Pvt./ Pfc., Bronze Star, [Presented 11/20/44]. Pfc., Co. D, WIA (light), 12/5/44 Zellenberg, France. Returned to duty 1/13/45. Pfc., Co. B, 5/8/45 Innsbruck, Austria. [Steedle's Squad, 2nd Platoon, Co. B].

YOUNG, Clark S. b. 1917 NJ. Res. Hunterdon Co., NJ. Enl. 1/7/42 Ft. Dix, NJ. Ser. No. 32188940. Pvt. Attached to Co. E 5/28/42 Edgewood Arsenal, MD. Platoon Sgt. (S/Sgt.). Pfc., Co. A, (Platoon Sgt.), promo. Cpl. (temp.), Camp Gordon, GA 7/15/42. Cpl. (temp.), Co. A promo. Sgt. (temp.), Camp Gordon, GA 7/27/42. Sgt. (temp.), promo. S/Sgt. (temp.), Camp Gordon, GA 8/1/42. Transf. OCS, Edgewood Arsenal, MD Nov. 1942.

YOUNG, George C. Pfc., KIA, 1/26/44, Italy (Anzio)

YOUNG, George G. b. 1922 AL.. Res. Mobile, Mobile Co., AL. Enl. 10/3/42 Ft. McClellan, AL. Sgt., Ser. No. 14163440. Pvt., Co. D, Camp Gordon, GA 10/9/42. Cpl., Co. D, LST 422 Survivor, 1/26/44 Italy (Anzio) – Purple Heart with Oak Leaf Cluster. Sgt., Co. D, KIA (shell exploded in barrel), 12/7/44, France, LO Cem.

YOUNG, Liss. Pvt., Co. A, Camp Gordon, GA 4/16/43.

YOUNG, William C. b. 1922 PA. Res. Westmoreland Co., PA. Enl. 9/25/42 Greensburg, PA. Ser. No. 33294885. Pvt. Co. C, 10/15/42 Camp Gordon GA. In a photo of Co. C taken 1943 at Amalfi, Italy. d. ca. 1993.

ZAMBRANO, Bernard B. b. 8/5/1922 CT. Res. New Haven Co., CT. Enl. 12/14/42 Hartford, CT. Ser. No. 31274256. Pvt., Co. C, Camp Gordon, GA 4/10/43. Pvt., Co. C, WIA (light - shell fragment), 7/10/43 Gela, Sicily. Purple Heart. d. 1/11/2001 New Haven Co., CT.

ZEPP, Llewellyn L. b. 3/5/1912 PA. Res. York Co., PA. Enl. 2/24/42 Ft. George Meade, MD. Ser. No. 33169951. Pvt. Attached to Co. G 5/28/42 Edgewood Arsenal, MD. Mess Sgt. (S/Sgt.). Pvt., Co. C transf. Co. D, Camp Gordon, GA 6/15/42. Pvt., promo. T/4 (temp.), Camp Gordon, GA 6/16/42. T/4 (temp.), (Mess), promo. S/Sgt. (temp.), Camp Gordon, GA 7/15/42. Served in Sicily & Italy. Present at 95th Evac., Naples, and left for Africa 10/23/43. Suffered a hearing loss. Removed from Anzio due to hearing loss. Present in hospital 5/15/44. Present at Camp Butner, SC, 8/7/44. Present at Indiantown Gap, Grantville, PA, temp. duty, 9/3/44-11/4/44. Sent to Camp Pickett, VA. PX clerk canteen. Discharged 11/30/44 Ft. George Meade, MD. d. Jan. 1979 PA.

ZICKLER, Horst R. b. Germany. Said his grandfather painted china in Dresden. Came to America at an early age. Res. St. Louis, MO. Joined the 83rd at Venafro. "First day in combat volunteered to carry rations to the OP and was baptized by small arms fire." Pvt., Co. D, LST 422 Survivor, 1/26/44 Italy (Anzio) – Purple Heart. Rescued by USS YMS 226. Taken to 93rd Evac. Hosp. Pfc. Sgt. Co. A, 5/8/45 Innsbruck, Austria. Res. St. Louis, MO May 1954. Trolley Conductor/Bus Operator, St. Louis Public Service Transit Co. Attended 1956, 1958, 1960, 1962 & 1966 Reunions as res. St. Louis, MO.

ZOLLER, Louis J. b. 1922 PA. Res. Aliquippa, Beaver Co., PA. Enl. 9/26/42 Pittsburgh, PA. Ser. No. 33305772. Pvt. HQ & HQ Co., 10/15/42 Camp Gordon GA. Pvt., Co. D, LST 422 Survivor, 1/26/44 Italy (Anzio) – Purple Heart. Rescued by USS YMS 226. Taken to 93rd Evac. Hosp.

ZUKOWSKI, John. b. 1908 PA. Enl. 5/11/42 Pittsburgh, PA. Ser. No. 33266095. 54th Chem. Imperg. Co. Pvt., attached to Co. B, 83rd CMB, Camp Gordon, GA 4/15/43. Pvt., Co. B, WIA (serious - by 75 mm shell), 7/10/43 Gela, Sicily. Evacuated. Purple Heart.

ZVINGIS, Stephan [Stephen] L. b. 8/26/1920 NY. Res. Kings Co., NY. Enl. 7/9/42 Ft. Jay, Governors Island, NY. Ser. No. 32402222. Pvt., Co. A, Camp Gordon, GA 7/28/42. Pvt., Co. A, Camp Gordon, GA 10/30/42. Transf. 2nd. Replacement Depot Oct. 1944. d. Aug. 1983 Ridgewood, Queens Co., NY.

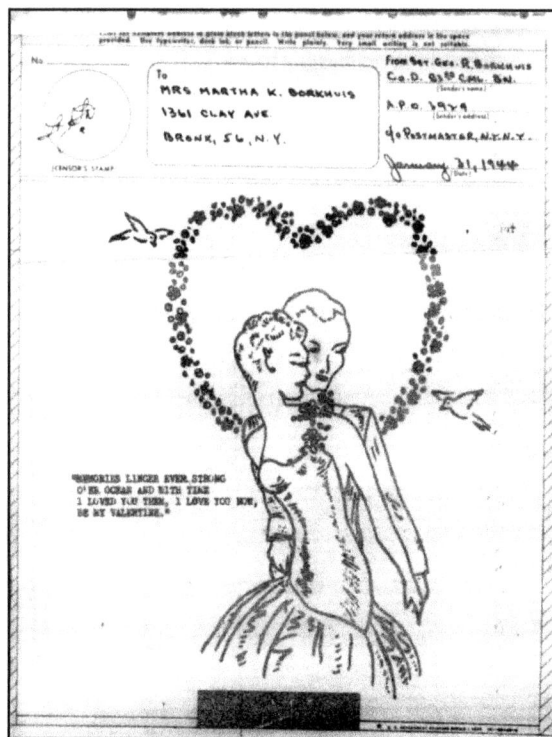

A Valentine's Day V-Mail from George Borkhuis
Borkhuis Collection

L-R: Lt. Robert Bundy, Layton Moore, Steve Sperian, and Mitchell Stanley.

From the Scrapbook of Eugene Pirani

Dugout used by some of the 83rd.

Back row, L-R: Eugene Pirani, Clay, and Robert Taylor; front row, L-R: Frank and Elmer, two children "adopted" by the 83rd.

Joe, the Italian prisoner, who made really good spaghetti.

"Heil Hitler"

James Kane sitting in chair and George S. Yakubisin standing.

Endnotes

[The correspondence of George R. Borkhuis and Jim C. Myers was received shortly before publication but too late to be included in the endnotes. Any quotes attributed to these two persons can be found in their collections which are noted in the bibliography.]

Chapter One

1. Officer Candidate School, *Chemical Warfare Service: Edgewood Arsenal*, Maryland, (The Horn-Shafer Co., Baltimore, MD, 1944).

2. Edwin Pike, *Military Papers of Edwin G. Pike 1940 – 1942*, (Courtesy Marcia Bunker).

3. *Ibid.*

4. *Ibid.*

5. *Ibid.*

6. *Ibid.*

7. Roster of Enlisted Cadre of the 83rd Chemical Battalion at Edgewood Arsenal, MD (Courtesy Eugene Plassmann & Dale Blank).

8. Michele (Mike) Codega, *Speech Given To the 1999 Reunion of the 83rd Chemical Mortar Battalion*, (Mike Codega Collection – Courtesy Sam Kweskin).

9. Russell H. Peterson, *Personal Papers of Russell H. Peterson, Co. D, 83rd Chemical Mortar Battalion, 1942 – 1944*, (Courtesy Marcia [Peterson] Daoust, Huntington, WV and Neal and Bruton Peterson); Robert E. Edwards, *V-Mail & Correspondence of Robert E. Edwards, HQ Co, 83rd Chemical Mortar Battalion*, (Courtesy Wendy Edwards).

10. Pike, op. cit.

11. Edwards, op. cit.; Peterson, op. cit.

12. Eighty-Third (83rd) Chemical Mortar Battalion. *General Orders #1 - #91 (1942) – Camp Gordon, GA* – Edgewood Arsenal Archives.

13. *Ibid.*

14. Pike, op. cit.

15. Eighty-Third (83rd) Chemical Mortar Battalion. *Unit Journal, May 10, 1942-July 13, 1943, National Archives*, College Park, MD.

16. Jerome A. Muschinske. *Correspondence With Terry Lowry.* Author's Collection.

17. Phone interview, 2008, between Edward Trey & author.

18. Rupert O. Burford, *Foreign Service Memoirs – Diary of Rupert O. Burford* [Co. C - 83rd CMB]. (Unpublished), Charleston, WV, n.d., Author's Collection, (Used by permission of Mrs. Rupert O. Burford); Edwin Pike, *V-Mail & Correspondence of Capt. Edwin G. Pike 1941 - 1945 - Co. D, 83rd Chemical Mortar Battalion*, (Courtesy Marcia Bunker); John P. McEvoy, *Correspondence With Terry Lowry.* Author's Collection; Obituary of Kenneth A. Cunin.

19. Academic Record, William S. Doughten, Jr., Class of 1941, Massachusetts Institute of Technology: *Muzzleblasts* – Official newsletter of the 83rd Chemical Mortar Battalion 1944 – present.

20. Edwin Pike, *Military Papers of Edwin G. Pike 1940 – 1942*, (Courtesy Marcia Bunker); Edwin Pike, *V-Mail & Correspondence of Capt. Edwin G. Pike 1941 - 1945 - Co. D, 83rd Chemical Mortar Battalion*, (Courtesy Marcia Bunker).

21. Charleston High School Yearbook 1927; West Virginia University Yearbook 1933; Military Discharge Paper of Rupert O. Burford; Obituary of Rupert O. Burford.

22. Personal Interviews with Edward L. Trey & author; *Trainee Tribune* – Official newsletter of the trainee men in the CWS at Edgewood Arsenal, MD 1942 – [Copies provided by Lorraine M. Salvi]; *Edwin Pike, V-Mail & Correspondence of Capt. Edwin G. Pike 1941 - 1945 - Co. D, 83rd Chemical Mortar Battalion*, (Courtesy Marcia Bunker).

23. *Trainee Tribune* – Official newsletter of the trainee men in the CWS at Edgewood Arsenal, MD 1942 – [Copies provided by Lorraine M. Salvi]; Eldredge, Walter J., *Finding My Father's War: A Baby Boomer and the 2nd Chemical Mortar Battalion in World War II*, (PageFree Publishing, Inc., Ostego, MI, 2004); Obituary of David W. Meyerson.

24. Edgewood Arsenal Order of May 28th, 1942, (Edgewood Arsenal Archives).

25. Eighty-Third (83rd) Chemical Mortar Battalion. *Unit Journal, May 10, 1942-July 13, 1943, National Archives*, College Park, MD.

26. *Ibid.*

Chapter Two

1. Eighty-Third (83rd) Chemical Mortar Battalion. *General Orders #1 - #91 (1942)* – Camp Gordon, GA; Eighty-Third (83rd) Chemical Mortar Battalion Journals, Battle Reports, Morning Reports: June 1943 – Nov. 1945.

2. James Marion Lester, *James Marion Lester's Story*, (unpublished manuscript interview), by Vicki S. Hibma, June 26, 1984; Correspondence with James & Iris Lester (Author's Collection).

3. Correspondence with Lee Steedle (Author's Collection).

4. Eighty-Third (83rd) Chemical Mortar Battalion. *General Orders #1 - #91 (1942)* – Camp Gordon, GA; Eighty-Third (83rd) Chemical Mortar Battalion Journals, Battle Reports, Morning Reports: June 1943 – Nov. 1945; Russell H. Peterson, *Personal Papers of Russell H. Peterson, Co. D, 83rd Chemical Mortar Battalion, 1942 – 1944*, (Courtesy Marcia [Peterson] Daoust, Huntington, WV and Neal and Bruton Peterson).

5. Eighty-Third (83rd) Chemical Mortar Battalion Journals, Battle Reports, Morning Reports: June 1943 – Nov. 1945.

6. Correspondence with Malcolm Doyle Wilkinson (Author's Collection).

7. *Muzzleblasts* – Official newsletter of the 83rd Chemical Mortar Battalion 1944 – present.

8. Wilkinson, op. cit.

9. Karl Garrett, *Memories 1942-1945*, (HQ Co., 83rd Chemical Mortar Battalion), [n.d.], [Courtesy Karl Garrett, Richmond, VA].

10. Loy J. Marshall, *Assorted Personal Experiences in the War*, (Courtesy Tricia Bridges).

11. Waitt, Brig. Gen. Alden H., *Gas Warfare: The Chemical Weapon, It's Use, and Protection Against It*, (J. J. Little & Ives Co., NY - 1942), P. 96-99.

12. John P. McEvoy, *Genesis of the 4.2 Mortar,* (unpublished), Nov. 1990; *Col. John P. McEvoy, 83rd Chemical Mortar Battalion* – Taped discussion of the 4.2 mortar, command structure of chemical battalions, some history of the 83rd Chemical Mortar Battalion – taped 2005 by McEvoy (Author's Collection).

13. Lester, op. cit.

14. Wilkinson, op. cit.

15. Steedle, op. cit.

16. Louis "Cody" Wims. Oral History (www.45thdivision.org/Veterans/Wims157.htm.).

17. Hale H. Hepler, *Hale Hunter Hepler – World War II Veteran*, (dictated to his daughter Pam Pace June 2005) [Courtesy Hale H. Hepler & Pam Pace].

18. Jerome A. Muschinske, *Correspondence With Terry Lowry*. (Author's Collection).

19. Stephen W. Vukson, Miscellaneous Notes on Service With the 83rd Chemical Mortar Battalion (Motor Pool)- (Courtesy Stephen W. Vukson).

20. Correspondence with Elizabeth Daly Regarding Kenneth Laundre, (Author's Collection).

21. John P. McEvoy, *Many Years Later*, (unpublished speech), n.d., (Author's Collection).

22. Michele (Mike) Codega, *Speech Given To the 1999 Reunion of the 83rd Chemical Mortar Battalion*, (Mike Codega Collection – Courtesy Sam Kweskin).

23. Eugene A. Plassmann, *Rounds Away*, Computer Reproduction (September 2004) - (Courtesy Eugene A. Plassmann).

24. Vukson, op. cit.

25. Military Discharge Paper of Charlie Lowry, 83rd Chemical Mortar Battalion, (Author's Collection).

26. McEvoy, op. cit.

27. Eighty-Third (83rd) Chemical Mortar Battalion. *General Orders #1 - #91 (1942)* – Camp Gordon, GA; Eighty-Third (83rd) Chemical Mortar Battalion Journals, Battle Reports, Morning Reports: June 1943 – Nov. 1945.

28. *Smoke Screen*- Official newsletter of the 83rd Chemical Battalion at Camp Gordon, Georgia 1942 – 1943.

29. Eighty-Third (83rd) Chemical Mortar Battalion. *General Orders #1 - #91 (1942)* – Camp Gordon, GA.

30. James G. Helsel, *Diary of James G. Helsel, Co. A, 83rd Chemical Mortar Battalion*, (Courtesy Joyce Berry, Lebanon, TN).

31. Eighty-Third (83rd) Chemical Mortar Battalion. *General Orders #1 - #91 (1942)* – Camp Gordon, GA; Eighty-Third (83rd) Chemical Mortar Battalion Journals, Battle Reports, Morning Reports: June 1943 – Nov. 1945.

32. *Smoke Screen*, op. cit.

33. *Ibid.*

34. *Ibid.*

35. *Ibid.*

36. Eighty-Third (83rd) Chemical Mortar Battalion Journals, Battle Reports, Morning Reports: June 1943 – Nov. 1945.

37. Daniel J. Shields, *Diary of Daniel J. Shields, Co. D & HQ Co., 83rd Chemical Mortar Battalion, 1942-1945*, (Courtesy Jean Decky).

38. Hayes, Veryl R., "Psych A – For Platoon Leaders", *Chemical Warfare Service Bulletin*, Vol. 30 – No. 5 (Nov. - Dec. 1944).

39. *Smoke Screen*, op. cit.

40. Eighty-Third (83rd) Chemical Mortar Battalion. *General Orders #1 - #91 (1942)* – Camp Gordon, GA.

41. Helsel, op. cit.

42. *Ibid.*

43. *Ibid.*

44. Codega, op. cit.

45. *Smoke Screen*, op. cit.

46. Shields, op. cit.

47. *Ibid.*

48. Michael J. Rebick, *V-Mail & Correspondence of Michael J. Rebick, Co. D, 83rd Chemical Mortar Battalion*, [Courtesy Linda Whalen].

49. Helsel, op. cit.

50. Eighty-Third (83rd) Chemical Mortar Battalion Journals, Battle Reports, Morning Reports: June 1943 – Nov. 1945.

51. *Ibid.*

52. Shields, op. cit.

53. Helsel, op. cit.

54. Shields, op. cit.

55. Helsel, op. cit.

56. *Ibid.*

57. Eighty-Third (83rd) Chemical Mortar Battalion Journals, Battle Reports, Morning Reports: June 1943 – Nov. 1945.

58. *Smoke Screen*, op. cit.

59. Eighty-Third (83rd) Chemical Mortar Battalion Journals, Battle Reports, Morning Reports: June 1943 – Nov. 1945.

60. Helsel, op. cit.

61. Rebick, op. cit.

62. *Smoke Screen*, op. cit.

63. *Ibid; Muzzleblasts*, op. cit.

64. *Smoke Screen*, op. cit.

65. Eighty-Third (83rd) Chemical Mortar Battalion. *General Orders #1 - #91 (1942)* – Camp Gordon, GA.

66. Rebick, op. cit.; Eighty-Third (83rd) Chemical Mortar Battalion. *General Orders #1 - #91 (1942)* – Camp Gordon, GA.

67. Eighty-Third (83rd) Chemical Mortar Battalion Journals, Battle Reports, Morning Reports: June 1943 – Nov. 1945; Shields, op. cit.

68. *Muzzleblasts*, op. cit.

69. Eighty-Third (83rd) Chemical Mortar Battalion Journals, Battle Reports, Morning Reports: June 1943 – Nov. 1945.

70. Vukson, op. cit.; *Smoke Screen*, op. cit.

71. Eighty-Third (83rd) Chemical Mortar Battalion Journals, Battle Reports, Morning Reports: June 1943 – Nov. 1945.

72. Richard A. Bridge, *V-Mail Letters of Richard A. Bridge, Co. D, 83rd Chemical Mortar Battalion*, [Courtesy Linda Whalen].

73. *Smoke Screen*, op. cit.; Report of Lt. Col. Kenneth Cunin, HQ, 83rd Chemical Battalion, September 12th, 1943. National Archives, College Park, MD.

74. Eighty-Third (83rd) Chemical Mortar Battalion Journals, Battle Reports, Morning Reports: June 1943 – Nov. 1945.

75. Codega, op. cit.

76. Rupert O. Burford, *Foreign Service Memoirs – Diary of Rupert O. Burford* [Co. C - 83rd CMB]. (Unpublished), Charleston, WV, n.d., Author's Collection, (Used by permission of Mrs. Rupert O. Burford).

Chapter Three

1. Rupert O. Burford, *Foreign Service Memoirs – Diary of Rupert O. Burford* [Co. C - 83rd CMB]. (Unpublished), Charleston, WV, n.d., Author's Collection, (Used by permission of Mrs. Rupert O. Burford).

2. Schneider, Dick (ed.). *Harold E. Hughes: The Man From Ida Grove*. Chosen Books Pub., 1979, pg. 51.

3. Eugene A. Plassmann, *Rounds Away*, Computer Reproduction (September 2004) - (Courtesy Eugene A. Plassmann).

4. Karl Garrett, *Memories 1942-1945*, (HQ Co., 83rd Chemical Mortar Battalion), [n.d.], [Courtesy Karl Garrett, Richmond, VA].

5. Burford, op. cit.; Schneider, Dick (ed.), *Harold E. Hughes: The Man From Ida Grove*, (Chosen Books Pub., 1979), pg. 51.

6. Burford, op. cit.; Eighty-Third (83rd) Chemical Mortar Battalion Journals, Battle Reports, Morning Reports: June 1943 – Nov. 1945; Eighty-Third (83rd) Chemical Mortar Battalion. General Orders #1 - #41 (1943) – Camp Gordon, GA; Eighty-Third (83rd) Chemical Mortar Battalion. Assorted Correspondence on Lineage and Honors of the 83rd Chemical Mortar Battalion 1942-1962.

7. Eighty-Third (83rd) Chemical Mortar Battalion. Co. D. Morning Reports/Unit Journal 1942-1944, (Courtesy Mike Codega and Sam Kweskin).

8. Burford, op. cit.

9. Jerome A. Muschinske, *Correspondence With Terry Lowry*. Author's Collection; James G. Helsel, *Diary of James G. Helsel, Co. A, 83rd Chemical Mortar Battalion*, (Courtesy Joyce Berry, Lebanon, TN).

10. James O. Beasley, *V-Mail & Correspondence of Lt. James O. Beasley, Co. D, 83rd Chemical Mortar Battalion*, (Courtesy John Beasley).

11. Michele (Mike) Codega, *Speech Given To the 1999 Reunion of the 83rd Chemical Mortar Battalion*, (Mike Codega Collection – Courtesy Sam Kweskin).

12. Beasley, op. cit.

13. Beasley, *Ibid.*

14. Burford, op. cit.

15. Samuel M. Bundy, Jr., *Co. A - 83rd Cml. Mortar Bn.*, (diary & record of events kept by Samuel Bundy from Camp Gordon through Sept. 22, 1945) – (approved by Samuel M. Bundy, Jr. 1984) - [Courtesy Lee Steedle].

16. Burford, op. cit.

17. Burford, *Ibid*; Bundy, op. cit.

18. Plassmann, op. cit.

19. Helsel, op. cit.; Beasley, op. cit.

20. Burford, op. cit.

21. Loy J. Marshall, *Assorted Personal Experiences in the War*, (Courtesy Tricia Bridges).

22. Burford, op. cit.; Plassmann, op. cit.; Bundy, op. cit.; Helsel, op. cit.

23. Bundy, op. cit.

24. Schneider, op. cit., pp. 51-52; *Muzzleblasts* – official newsletter of the 83rd Chemical Mortar Battalion 1944 – present. William Garner entry.

25. *U. S. S. Monticello*, Deck Log/War Diary/Business Records, National Archives, College Park, MD.

26. Leech, Dewey C., and William D. McCain (ed.), *The WW II Experiences of Andrew Candler Leech 1943-1945*, (Hattiesburg, MS, 1985), pg. 8; *U. S. S. Monticello*, op. cit.

27. Henry J. Gregorio (memoir), 85th Engineer Heavy Pontoon Battalion. Internet site. Unit home site 2008.

28. Eighty-Third (83rd) Chemical Mortar Battalion. General Orders #1 - #41 (1943) – Camp Gordon, GA; Burford, op. cit.; Eighty-Third (83rd) Chemical Mortar Battalion. Co. D. Morning Reports/Unit Journal 1942-1944, op. cit.

29. Daniel J. Shields, *Diary of Daniel J. Shields, Co. D & HQ Co., 83rd Chemical Mortar Battalion, 1942-1945*, (Courtesy Jean Decky).

30. Leech, op. cit.; Burford, op. cit.; Helsel, op. cit; Bundy, op. cit.

31. Burford, op. cit.

Chapter Four

1. Eighty-Third (83rd) Chemical Mortar Battalion. General Orders #1 - #41 (1943) – Camp Gordon, GA – Edgewood Arsenal Archives.

2. Edward L. Trey, Personal Correspondence and Interviews with Terry Lowry 2003-2008, (Author's Collection).

3. *U. S. S. Monticello*, Deck Log/War Diary/Business Records, National Archives, College Park, MD; Commander Task Force 67, *Report of Escort of Convoy UGF-8 and GUF-8, 29 April - 31 May, 1943*, Action Report, RG 38 - Box 242, National Archives, College Park, MD.

4. Leech, Dewey C., and William D. McCain (ed.), *The WW II Experiences of Andrew Candler Leech 1943-1945*, (Hattiesburg, MS, 1985), pg. 7.

5. *U. S. S. Monticello*, op. cit.; Commander Task Force 67, op. cit.

6. *Ibid.*

7. *Ibid.*; Rupert O. Burford, *Foreign Service Memoirs – Diary of Rupert O. Burford* [Co. C - 83rd CMB]. (Unpublished), Charleston, WV, n.d., Author's Collection.

8. Burford, op. cit.

9. *U. S. S. Monticello*, op. cit.; Commander Task Force 67, op. cit.

10. Hale H. Hepler, *Hale Hunter Hepler – World War II Veteran*, (dictated to his daughter Pam Pace June 2005) [Courtesy Hale H. Hepler & Pam Pace].

11. Charlie Lowry, *V-Mail & Correspondence 1943-45 - Co. D / Co. A, 83rd Chemical Mortar Battalion*, (Author's Collection).

12. Loy J. Marshall, *Assorted Personal Experiences in the War*, (Courtesy Tricia Bridges).

13. Karl Garrett, *Memories 1942-1945*, (HQ Co., 83rd Chemical Mortar Battalion), [n.d.], [Courtesy Karl Garrett, Richmond, VA].

14. *U. S. S. Monticello*, op. cit.; Commander Task Force 67, op. cit.

15. *Ibid.*

16. Burford, op. cit.

17. Henry J. Gregorio (memoir), 85*th* Engineer Heavy Pontoon Battalion, Internet Site. Unit Home Site.

18. Burford, op. cit.

19. Trey, op. cit.

20. Burford, op. cit.

21. Edwin Pike, *V-Mail & Correspondence of Capt. Edwin G. Pike 1941 - 1945 - Co. D, 83rd Chemical Mortar Battalion*, (Courtesy Marcia Bunker).

22. Burford, op. cit.

23. Pike, op. cit.

24. *Ibid.*

25. Burford, op. cit.

26. Pike, op. cit.

27. *U. S. S. Monticello*, op. cit.; Commander Task Force 67, op. cit.

28. *Ibid.*

29. James O. Beasley, *V-Mail & Correspondence of Lt. James O. Beasley, Co. D, 83rd Chemical Mortar Battalion*, (Courtesy John Beasley).

30. *U. S. S. Monticello*, op. cit.; Commander Task Force 67, op. cit.

31. *Ibid.*

32. Pike, op. cit.

33. *U. S. S. Monticello*, op. cit.; Commander Task Force 67, op. cit.

34. Pike, op. cit.; *U. S. S. Monticello*, op. cit.; Commander Task Force 67, op. cit.

35. Hepler, op. cit.

36. *U. S. S. Monticello*, op. cit.; Commander Task Force 67, op. cit.

37. Beasley, op. cit.

38. *U. S. S. Monticello*, op. cit.; Commander Task Force 67, op. cit.

39. Samuel M. Bundy, Jr., *Co. A - 83rd Cml. Mortar Bn.*, (diary & record of events kept by Samuel Bundy from Camp Gordon through Sept. 22, 1945) – (approved by Samuel M. Bundy, Jr. 1984); Ford, William Clifford, *Never Forget – A Soldier's Battlefield Memoirs*, (Network Printing, New Albany, MS, 2005) – [Co. C, 83rd Chemical Mortar Battalion], pg. 8; James G. Helsel, *Diary of James G. Helsel, Co. A, 83rd Chemical Mortar Battalion*.

40. *U. S. S. Monticello*, op. cit.; Commander Task Force 67, op. cit.

41. Ford, op. cit.

42. Eugene A. Plassmann, *Rounds Away*, Computer Reproduction (September 2004) - (Courtesy Eugene A. Plassmann).

43. Trey, op. cit.

44. Burford, op. cit.

45. Pike, op. cit.

46. *U. S. S. Monticello*, op. cit.; Commander Task Force 67, op. cit.

47. Bundy, op. cit.

48. Pike, op. cit.; Helsel, op. cit.

49. *U. S. S. Monticello*, op. cit.; Commander Task Force 67, op. cit.

50. *Muzzleblasts* – official newsletter of the 83rd Chemical Mortar Battalion 1944 – present. Martin Feerick entry.

51. Bundy, op. cit.

52. Pike, op. cit.

53. *U. S. S. Monticello*, op. cit.; Commander Task Force 67, op. cit.

54. *Ibid*; Schneider, Dick (ed.), *Harold E. Hughes: The Man From Ida Grove*, (Chosen Books Pub., 1979), pg. 52.

55. John P. McEvoy, *Many Years Later*, (unpublished speech), n.d.

56. *U. S. S. Monticello*, op. cit.; Commander Task Force 67, op. cit.

57. Leonard A. Merrill, Jr., Excerpts from the V-Mail of Leonard A. Merrill, Jr., (Courtesy Robert L. Merrill).

58. *U. S. S. Monticello*, op. cit.; Commander Task Force 67, op. cit.

59. *Muzzleblasts* – official newsletter of the 83rd Chemical Mortar Battalion 1944 – present [Gallagher].

60. *Muzzleblasts*, op. cit. George A. Barrett entry.

Chapter Five

1. Eighty-Third (83rd) Chemical Mortar Battalion Journals, Battle Reports, Morning Reports: June 1943 – Nov. 1945. Chemical Corps Museum Archives, Ft. Leonard Wood, MO, Edgewood Arsenal Archive, and National Archives, College Park, MD; Edwin Pike, *V-Mail & Correspondence of Capt. Edwin G. Pike 1941 - 1945 - Co. D, 83rd Chemical Mortar Battalion*, (Courtesy Marcia Bunker).

2. Rupert O. Burford, *Foreign Service Memoirs – Diary of Rupert O. Burford* [Co. C - 83rd CMB]. (Unpublished), Charleston, WV, n.d., Author's Collection.

3. James G. Helsel, *Diary of James G. Helsel, Co. A, 83rd Chemical Mortar Battalion*, (Courtesy Joyce Berry, Lebanon, TN).

4. Brashear, Alton D., *From Lee To Bari: The History of the 45th General Hospital*, (Whittet & Shepperson, Richmond, VA, 1957), pg. 151.

5. Eighty-Third (83rd) Chemical Mortar Battalion Journals, Battle Reports, Morning Reports: June 1943 – Nov. 1945; Burford, op. cit.

6. James O. Beasley, *V-Mail & Correspondence of Lt. James O. Beasley, Co. D, 83rd Chemical Mortar Battalion*, (Courtesy John Beasley).

7. Eighty-Third (83rd) Chemical Mortar Battalion Journals, Battle Reports, Morning Reports: June 1943 – Nov. 1945; Pike, op. cit.; Burford, op. cit.

8. Loy J. Marshall, *Assorted Personal Experiences in the War*, (Courtesy Tricia Bridges).

9. Burford, op. cit.

10. *Ibid.*

11. Samuel M. Bundy, Jr., *Co. A - 83rd Cml. Mortar Bn.*, (diary & record of events kept by Samuel Bundy from Camp Gordon through Sept. 22, 1945).

12. Helsel, op. cit.

13. Beasley, op. cit.; Edward L. Trey, Personal Correspondence and Interviews with Terry Lowry 2003-2008, (Author's Collection); Russell H. Peterson, *Personal Papers of Russell H. Peterson, Co. D, 83rd Chemical Mortar Battalion, 1942 – 1944*, (Courtesy Marcia [Peterson] Daoust, Huntington, WV and Neal and Bruton Peterson); Charlie Lowry, *V-Mail & Correspondence 1943-45 - Co. D / Co. A, 83rd Chemical Mortar Battalion*, (Author's Collection).

14. Pike, op. cit.

15. Bundy, op. cit.

16. Schneider, Dick (ed.), *Harold E. Hughes: The Man From Ida Grove*, (Chosen Books Pub., 1979), pg. 52; Robert L. Sorensen, (Medical Detachment, 83rd Chemical Mortar Battalion), Letter to Sam Kweskin Describing Harold Hughes, Oct. 25, 1996, (Courtesy Tricia Bridges).

17. Michael J. Rebick, *V-Mail & Correspondence of Michael J. Rebick, Co. D, 83rd Chemical Mortar Battalion*, [Courtesy Linda Whalen].

18. Author's Personal Conversations and Correspondence with Carl McNabb and Curtis Williams, 2003-2006.

19. Beasley, op. cit.

20. Robert E. Edwards, *V-Mail & Correspondence of Robert E. Edwards, HQ Co, 83rd Chemical Mortar Battalion*, (Courtesy Wendy Edwards).

21. Beasley, op. cit.

22. Eighty-Third (83rd) Chemical Mortar Battalion Journals, Battle Reports, Morning Reports: June 1943 – Nov. 1945; Burford, op. cit.

23. Eighty-Third (83rd) Chemical Mortar Battalion. Co. D. Morning Reports/Unit Journal 1942-1944, (Courtesy Mike Codega and Sam Kweskin); Edwin Pike, *Miscellaneous Materials Relating to the 83rd Chemical Mortar Battalion*, (Courtesy Marcia Bunker); Burford, op. cit.

24. Bundy, op. cit.

25. Burford, op. cit.

26. Bundy, op. cit.

27. Helsel, op. cit.

28. Richard A. Bridge, *V-Mail Letters of Richard A. Bridge, Co. D, 83rd Chemical Mortar Battalion*, [Courtesy Linda Whalen].

29. Bundy, op. cit.

30. Helsel, op. cit.

31. Pike, op. cit.

32. Rebick, op. cit.

33. Beasley, op. cit.

34. *U. S. S. Thurston*, War Diary, May - July, 1943, National Archives, College Park, MD.

35. Burford, op. cit.

36. Marshal, op. cit.

37. Hale H. Hepler, *Hale Hunter Hepler – World War II Veteran*, (dictated to his daughter Pam Pace June 2005) [Courtesy Hale H. Hepler & Pam Pace].

38. Michele (Mike) Codega, *Speech Given To the 1999 Reunion of the 83rd Chemical Mortar Battalion*, (Mike Codega Collection – Courtesy Sam Kweskin).

39. *U. S. S. Thurston*, op. cit.

40. Pike, op. cit.

41. Eighty-Third (83rd) Chemical Mortar Battalion Journals, Battle Reports, Morning Reports: June 1943 – Nov. 1945; Burford, op. cit.

42. Eighty-Third (83rd) Chemical Mortar Battalion. Co. D. Morning Reports/Unit Journal 1942-1944, (Courtesy Mike Codega and Sam Kweskin); Edwin Pike, *Miscellaneous Materials Relating to the 83rd Chemical Mortar Battalion*, (Courtesy Marcia Bunker); Edwin Pike, *V-Mail & Correspondence of Capt. Edwin G. Pike 1941 - 1945 - Co. D, 83rd Chemical Mortar Battalion*, (Courtesy Marcia Bunker).

43. Daniel J. Shields, *Diary of Daniel J. Shields, Co. D & HQ Co., 83rd Chemical Mortar Battalion, 1942-1945*, (Courtesy Jean Decky).

44. Pike, op. cit.

45. Eighty-Third (83rd) Chemical Mortar Battalion Journals, Battle Reports, Morning Reports: June 1943 – Nov. 1945.

46. Beasley, op. cit.

47. Eighty-Third (83ʳᵈ) Chemical Mortar Battalion Journals, Battle Reports, Morning Reports: June 1943 – Nov. 1945.

48. Darby, William O., with William H. Baumer, *Darby's Rangers - We Led the Way*, (Random House Publishing, NY,1980); Jeffers, H. Paul, *Onward We Charge - The Heroic Story of Darby's Rangers in World War II*, (NAL Caliber, July 2007).

49. Burford, op. cit.; Pike, op. cit.

50. Author's Personal Conversation with Edward L. Trey, 2007.

51. Burford, op. cit.

52. Eighty-Third (83ʳᵈ) Chemical Mortar Battalion Journals, Battle Reports, Morning Reports: June 1943 – Nov. 1945.

53. Photo Album of Daniel Shields, Co. D, 83ʳᵈ Chemical Mortar Battalion (Courtesy Jean Decky).

54. Eighty-Third (83ʳᵈ) Chemical Mortar Battalion Journals, Battle Reports, Morning Reports: June 1943 – Nov. 1945.

55. Pike, op. cit.

56. Karl Garrett, *Memories 1942-1945*, (HQ Co., 83ʳᵈ Chemical Mortar Battalion), [n.d.], [Courtesy Karl Garrett, Richmond, VA].

57. Eighty-Third (83ʳᵈ) Chemical Mortar Battalion Journals, Battle Reports, Morning Reports: June 1943 – Nov. 1945; *U.S.S. Lyon*, War Diary, June 10-12, 1943 & Deck Log Aug. 1944, National Archives, College Park, MD; Bundy, op. cit.

58. Eighty-Third (83ʳᵈ) Chemical Mortar Battalion Journals, Battle Reports, Morning Reports: June 1943 – Nov. 1945; Eighty-Third (83ʳᵈ) Chemical Mortar Battalion. Co. D. Morning Reports/Unit Journal 1942-1944, (Courtesy Mike Codega and Sam Kweskin); *U. S. S. Thurston*, op. cit.

59. *U. S. S. Thurston*, op. cit.

60. Eighty-Third (83ʳᵈ) Chemical Mortar Battalion. Co. D. Morning Reports/Unit Journal 1942-1944, (Courtesy Mike Codega and Sam Kweskin); Edwin Pike, *Miscellaneous Materials Relating to the 83ʳᵈ Chemical Mortar Battalion*, (Courtesy Marcia Bunker).

61. Burford, op. cit.; Bundy, op. cit.

62. Burford, op. cit.

63. *Ibid.*

64. Beasley, op. cit.

65. Helsel, op. cit.

66. Pike, op. cit.

67. Beasley, op. cit.

68. Jerome A. Muschinske. *Correspondence With Terry Lowry*. Author's Collection.

69. Helsel, op. cit.

70. Beasley, op. cit.

71. Edwin Pike, *Miscellaneous Materials Relating to the 83ʳᵈ Chemical Mortar Battalion*, (Courtesy Marcia Bunker); *U. S. S. Thurston*, op. cit.

72. Rebick, op. cit.

73. Eighty-Third (83ʳᵈ) Chemical Mortar Battalion Journals, Battle Reports, Morning Reports: June 1943 – Nov. 1945; *U. S. S. LCI 189*, War Diary, RG 38 - Box 1038, National Archives, College Park, MD; *U. S. S. Dickman*, Deck Log, National Archives, College Park, MD.

74. Burford, op. cit.

75. *Ibid.*

76. Edwin Pike, *Miscellaneous Materials Relating to the 83ʳᵈ Chemical Mortar Battalion*, (Courtesy Marcia Bunker.)

77. Edwin Pike, *V-Mail & Correspondence of Capt. Edwin G. Pike 1941 - 1945 - Co. D, 83ʳᵈ Chemical Mortar Battalion*, (Courtesy Marcia Bunker).

78. Burford, op. cit.; *U. S. S. LCI 189*, op. cit.

79. Pike, op. cit.

80. *U. S. S. LCI 189*, op. cit.; Burford, op. cit.

81. Bundy, op. cit.; Burford, op. cit.; *U. S. S. Dickman*, op. cit.

82. Pike, op. cit.

83. *Ibid.*

Chapter Six

1. First (1ˢᵗ), Third (3ʳᵈ), and Fourth (4ᵗʰ) Ranger Battalions. After Action Reports / Unit Journals. National Archives, College Park, MD.

2. Sixteenth (16ᵗʰ) Infantry - Records - *Ship Assignments & Loading: June 1943*: Co. D, 83ʳᵈ Chemical Battalion, National Archives, College Park, MD

3. *Ibid*; *U. S. S. Thurston*, War Diary, May - July, 1943, National Archives, College Park, MD.

4. James G. Helsel. Diary of James G. Helsel, Co. A, 83ʳᵈ Chemical Mortar Battalion. Courtesy Joyce Berry, Lebanon, TN.

5. *U. S. S. Thurston*, op. cit.; Edwin Pike, *V-Mail & Correspondence of Capt. Edwin G. Pike 1941 - 1945 - Co. D, 83ʳᵈ Chemical Mortar Battalion*, (Courtesy Marcia Bunker); Richard A. Bridge, *V-Mail Letters of Richard A. Bridge, Co. D, 83ʳᵈ Chemical Mortar Battalion*, [Courtesy Linda Whalen].

6. Eighty-Third (83ʳᵈ) Chemical Mortar Battalion Journals, Battle Reports, Morning Reports: June 1943 – Nov. 1945; Ford, William Clifford, *Never Forget – A Soldier's Battlefield Memoirs*, (Network Printing, New Albany, MS, 2005) – [Co. C, 83ʳᵈ Chemical Mortar Battalion], pg. 19; Rupert O. Burford, *Foreign Service Memoirs – Diary of Rupert O. Burford* [Co. C - 83ʳᵈ CMB]. (Unpublished), Charleston, WV, n.d., Author's Collection.

7. Samuel M. Bundy, Jr., *Co. A - 83ʳᵈ Cml. Mortar Bn.*, (diary & record of events kept by Samuel Bundy from Camp Gordon through Sept. 22, 1945); James G. Helsel, *Diary of James G. Helsel, Co. A, 83ʳᵈ Chemical Mortar Battalion*, (Courtesy Joyce Berry, Lebanon, TN).

8. Leonard A. Merrill, Jr., Excerpts from the V-Mail of Leonard A. Merrill, Jr., (Courtesy Robert L. Merrill).

9. *Final Troop & Ship Assignment and Landing Chart* (Force 343), National Archives, College Park, MD; *U. S. S. LCI 189*, War Diary, RG 38 - Box 1038, National Archives, College Park, MD; *U. S. S. Dickman*, Deck Log, National Archives, College Park, MD.

10. Nutter, Thomas E., *Operation Husky: The Allied Invasion of Sicily, 1943*, (2003); *Final Troop & Ship Assignment and Landing Chart* (Force 343), op. cit.; *U. S. S. LCI 189*, op. cit.

11. Pike, op. cit.

12. Nutter, op. cit.; Burford, op. cit.

13. Burford, op. cit.; Leech, Dewey C., and William D. McCain (ed.), *The WW II Experiences of Andrew Candler Leech 1943-1945*, (Hattiesburg, MS, 1985), pg. 11.

14. Bundy, op. cit.; Lawrence H. Powell, *Lest We Forget*, (brief memoir of Lawrence H. Powell, Co. A, 83rd CMB) – [Courtesy Lawrence H. Powell]; Helsel, op. cit.; *U. S. S. LCI 189*, op. cit.

15. Karl Garrett, *Memories 1942-1945*, (HQ Co., 83rd Chemical Mortar Battalion), [n.d.], [Courtesy Karl Garrett, Richmond, VA]; *U. S. S. Thurston*, op. cit.; Pike, op. cit.

16. *U. S. S. LCI 189*, op. cit.

17. John P. McEvoy, *Many Years Later*, (unpublished speech), n.d., (Author's Collection).

18. Personal Interviews with Edward L. Trey & author; *Muzzleblasts* – Official newsletter of the 83rd Chemical Mortar Battalion 1944 – present.

19. Personal Interview with Nolan McCraine & author, 2007.

20. Company A, 83rd Chemical Mortar Battalion History, National Archives, College Park, MD; Burford, op. cit.; *U. S. S. Dickman*, op. cit.

21. Burford, op. cit.; Jerome A. Muschinske. *Correspondence With Terry Lowry*. Author's Collection.

22. Muschinske, op. cit.

23. *Ibid.*

24. Company C, 83rd Chemical Mortar Battalion History, National Archives, College Park, MD.

25. Company A, 83rd Chemical Mortar Battalion History, op. cit.; Steedle, Lee (ed.), *Mark Freedom Paid: A Combat Anthology*, (Jeanette, PA: 83rd Chemical Mortar Battalion Veterans Association, 1997) (Illustrated by Sam Kweskin), pg. 11.

26. *Ibid*; General Orders, 1st U.S. Division, July 1943, National Archives, College Park, MD.

27. *Mark Freedom Paid: A Combat Anthology*, pp. 11 & 19 (Powell & Edwards); *Muzzleblasts*, op. cit. (Krebs).

28. Garrett, op. cit.; Helsel, op. cit.

29. Company A, 83rd Chemical Mortar Battalion History, op. cit.; *Mark Freedom Paid: A Combat Anthology*, pg. 20.

30. Company B, 83rd Chemical Mortar Battalion History, National Archives, College Park, MD.

31. Company B, 83rd Chemical Mortar Battalion History, op. cit.; Personal Interviews with Edward L. Trey & author, op. cit.; Leech, Dewey C., and William D. McCain (ed.), *The WW II Experiences of Andrew Candler Leech 1943-1945*, pg. 11.

32. Company B, 83rd Chemical Mortar Battalion History, op. cit.; Leech, op. cit., pp. 11-12.

33. *Ibid.*

34. Leech, op. cit.

35. Correspondence with Malcolm Doyle Wilkinson (Author's Collection).

36. *U. S. S. LCI 189*, op. cit.

37. *Ibid.*

38. Hale H. Hepler, *Hale Hunter Hepler – World War II Veteran*, (dictated to his daughter Pam Pace June 2005) [Courtesy Hale H. Hepler & Pam Pace]; Ford, op. cit., pg. 20.

39. Loy J. Marshall, *Assorted Personal Experiences in the War*, (Courtesy Tricia Bridges).

40. Burford, op. cit.

41. Company C, 83rd Chemical Mortar Battalion History, op. cit.

42. *Ibid.*

43. Burford, op. cit.; Report of Lt. Col. Kenneth Cunin, HQ, 83rd Chemical Battalion, September 12th, 1943. National Archives, College Park, MD; Company C, 83rd Chemical Mortar Battalion History, op. cit.

44. Muschinske, op. cit.

45. Marshall, op. cit.; Ford, op. cit., pp. 20-21; Burford, op. cit.

46. McEvoy, op. cit.; Company B, 83rd Chemical Mortar Battalion History, op. cit.

47. Steedle, Lee (ed.), *Mark Freedom Paid: A Combat Anthology*, op. cit., pg. 19.

48. Helsel, op. cit.; *Muzzleblasts*, op. cit. (Krebs); Company A, 83rd Chemical Mortar Battalion History, op. cit.; General Orders, 1st U.S. Division, July 1943, National Archives, College Park, MD.

49. Robert E. Edwards, *V-Mail & Correspondence of Robert E. Edwards, HQ Co, 83rd Chemical Mortar Battalion*, (Courtesy Wendy Edwards).

50. Eighty-Third (83rd) Chemical Mortar Battalion Journals, Battle Reports, Morning Reports: June 1943 – Nov. 1945.

51. Pike, op. cit.; Eighty-Third (83rd) Chemical Mortar Battalion Journals, Battle Reports, Morning Reports: June 1943 – Nov. 1945; Schneider, Dick (ed.), *Harold E. Hughes: The Man From Ida Grove*, (Chosen Books Pub., 1979), pg. 54 [hereafter cited as Hughes].

52. Pike, op. cit.

53. Eighty-Third (83rd) Chemical Mortar Battalion. Co. D. Morning Reports/Unit Journal 1942-1944, (Courtesy Mike Codega and Sam Kweskin); *Muzzleblasts*, op. cit. (Kiedrowski); *Mark Freedom Paid: A Combat Anthology*, op. cit., pg. 14; Edwin Pike, *Miscellaneous Materials Relating to the 83rd Chemical Mortar Battalion*, (Courtesy Marcia Bunker); Burford, op. cit.

54. Hughes, op. cit., pp. 54-55; , 83rd Chemical Mortar Battalion History, National Archives, College Park, MD.

55. Eighty-Third (83rd) Chemical Mortar Battalion. Co. D. Morning Reports/Unit Journal 1942-1944; Beasley, op. cit.

56. James H. Gallahan, Sr., *Military Service of James H. Gallahan, Sr. - World War II*, [Courtesy Roger Gallahan, Quinton, VA].

57. Richard A. Bridge, *V-Mail Letters of Richard A. Bridge, Co. D, 83rd Chemical Mortar Battalion*, [Courtesy Linda Whalen].

58. Brimm, Robert, *Rounds Away: Two Years of Combat With The Eighty-Third Chemical Mortar Battalion*, (Innsbruck, Austria, 1945) (Illustrated by Sam Kweskin - maps by Eugene Plassmann); Helsel, op. cit.; *Muzzleblasts*, op. cit. (Powell).

59. Ford, op. cit., pg. 23.

60. *Muzzleblasts*, op. cit. (Trey); Company B, 83rd Chemical Mortar Battalion History, op. cit.; Sgt. Mack Morris, *Rangers Come Home*, Yank Magazine, Aug, 4, 1944.

61. Pike, op. cit.; Daniel J. Shields, *Diary of Daniel J. Shields, Co. D & HQ Co., 83rd Chemical Mortar Battalion, 1942-1945*, (Courtesy Jean Decky).

62. McEvoy, op. cit.

63. Burford, op. cit.

64. Hepler, op. cit.; Burford, op. cit.

65. *U. S. S. Dickman*, op. cit.; Helsel, op. cit.; Bundy, op. cit.

66. Company B, 83rd Chemical Mortar Battalion History, op. cit.

67. Steedle, Lee (ed.), *Mark Freedom Paid: A Combat Anthology*, op. cit., pg. 15.

68. Trey, op. cit.; Brimm, op. cit.; Leech, op. cit., pg. 13.

69. Burford, op. cit.

70. *Ibid*; Hepler, op. cit.

71. Burford, op. cit.; Brimm, op. cit.

72. *Ibid*.

73. *Ibid*.

74. Eighty-Third (83rd) Chemical Mortar Battalion. Co. D. Morning Reports/Unit Journal 1942-1944, op. cit.

75. *Ibid*; Shields, op. cit.

76. Beasley, op. cit.

77. General Orders, 1st U.S. Division, July 1943., National Archives, College Park, MD; , 83rd Chemical Mortar Battalion History; General Orders, 1st U.S. Division, July 1943, op. cit.

78. Pike, op. cit.

79. Hughes, op. cit., pg. 55.

80. Pike, op. cit.

81. Hughes, op. cit., pg. 56.

82. Personal Interview with Curtis A. Williams and Terry Lowry, 2006; General Orders, 1st U.S. Division, July 1943, op. cit.

83. Pike, op. cit.; General Orders, 1st U.S. Division, July 1943, op. cit.

84. Company A, 83rd Chemical Mortar Battalion History, op. cit.

85. *Ibid*.

86. Helsel, op. cit.

87. Company A, 83rd Chemical Mortar Battalion History, op. cit.

88. *Ibid*.

89. Brimm, op. cit.; General Orders, 1st U.S. Division, July 1943, op. cit.; Unknown author, *"Lieut. Colonel Cunin Is In Thick of Sicilian Fighting"*, unknown newspaper clipping from files of Ed Trey.

90. Company A, 83rd Chemical Mortar Battalion History, op. cit.

91. *Ibid*; Helsel, op. cit.

92. Company B, 83rd Chemical Mortar Battalion History, op. cit.; Company C, 83rd Chemical Mortar Battalion History, op. cit.; Burford, op. cit.; Hepler, op. cit.

93. Eighty-Third (83rd) Chemical Mortar Battalion. Co. D. Morning Reports/Unit Journal 1942-1944, op. cit.; Earl Kann, *Personal Account of Gela*, (Courtesy Earl Kann), Author's Collection.; Personal Conversations of Sgt. Clark Riddle, Co. D, and Terry Lowry, 2007.

94. 83rd Chemical Mortar Battalion History, op. cit.; Shields, op. cit.

95. Pike, op. cit.

96. Helsel, op. cit.

97. Burford, op. cit.

98. Sixteenth (16th) Infantry, *S-1 Journal: July 1943*, National Archives, College Park, MD; Pike, op. cit.; Burford, op. cit.

99. Helsel, op. cit.

100. Company C, 83rd Chemical Mortar Battalion History, op. cit.; Company B, 83rd Chemical Mortar Battalion History, op. cit.; , 83rd Chemical Mortar Battalion History, op. cit.

101. Helsel, op. cit.; Burford, op. cit.

102. Leech, op. cit., pg. 15.

103. Burford, op. cit.

104. *Ibid*.

105. Various 83rd CMB Company Reports and Journals.

106. Pike, op. cit.; Burford, op. cit.; Trey, op. cit.; *Muzzleblasts*, op. cit.

107. Leech, op. cit., pg. 15; Garrett, op. cit.

108. Helsel, op. cit.; Burford, op. cit.

109. Beasley, op. cit.

110. Rebick, op. cit.

111. *Ibid*; Edwards, op. cit.

112. Beasley, op. cit.

113. *Ibid.*

114. Burford, op. cit.

115. One Hundred and Twentieth (120th) Medical Battalion, 45th Infantry Division, July-August 1943, Unit History (National Archives, College Park, MD).

116. Helsel, op. cit.; Beasley, op. cit.

117. Byron H. Jordan, *V-Mail of Byron H. Jordan 1943-1945*, (Courtesy Byron H. Jordan).

118. Burford, op. cit.

119. Merrill, op. cit.; Garrett, op. cit.; Hughes, op. cit., pg. 56; *Edwin Pike, Diary of Capt. Edwin G. Pike, 83rd Chemical Mortar Battalion, Co. D*, (unpublished – covers period from Apr. 27, 1943 through Italy), (Courtesy Marcia Bunker).

120. Helsel, op. cit.; Charles Rolling, *Diary of the 83rd Chemical Mortar Battalion, Company A (In Action)*. (Courtesy Gini Lemoine and Elizabeth Daly).

121. Beasley, op. cit.

122. Pike, op. cit.; Beasley, op. cit.; Rebick, op. cit.

123. Helsel, op. cit.

124. Beasley, op. cit.

125. *Ibid.*

126. Burford, op. cit.

127. *Ibid.*

128. Beasley, op. cit.

129. Extracts from Training Notes from the Sicilian Campaign, Nov. 6, 1943. National Archives, College Park, MD.

130. Report of Lt. Col. Kenneth Cunin, HQ 83rd Chemical Battalion, September 12, 1943. National Archives, College Park, MD.

131. Rebick, op. cit.

132. Burford, op. cit.

133. Leech, op. cit., pg. 16.

134. Pike, op. cit.; Beasley, op. cit.

135. Beasley, op. cit.

136. *Ibid.*

137. Pike, op. cit.

138. Garrett, op. cit.

139. Burford, op. cit.

140. Marshall, op. cit.

141. Burford, op. cit.

142. Helsel, op. cit.

143. Merrill, op. cit.; Pike, op. cit.

144. Beasley, op. cit.

145. George D. Gould, *Field Modification of Sight, 4.2" Chemical Mortar, Inspected at Co. C, 83rd Cml. Bn.*, Aug. 23, 1943. National Archives, College Park, MD.

146. William C. Hammond, Jr., *Tactical Use of Chemical Munitions*, Aug. 23, 1943. 45th Infantry Division, 7th Army. National Archives, College Park, MD.

147. Chemical Warfare Service Conference, HQ 7th Army, Aug. 1943. Records of the 7th Army, Chemical Warfare Section. National Archives, College Park, MD.

148. *Ibid.*

149. *Ibid.*

150. Pike, op. cit.

151. Burford, op. cit.

152. Beasley, op. cit.; Pike, op. cit.

Chapter Seven

1. Eighty- Third (83rd) Chemical Mortar Battalion Journals, Battle Reports, Morning Reports: June 1943 – Nov. 1945; Loy J. Marshall, *Assorted Personal Experiences in the War*, (Courtesy Tricia Bridges); Schneider, Dick (ed.), *Harold E. Hughes: The Man From Ida Grove*, (Chosen Books Pub., 1979), pg. 57 [hereafter cited as Hughes]; Russell H. Peterson, *Personal Papers of Russell H. Peterson, Co. D, 83rd Chemical Mortar Battalion, 1942 – 1944*, (Courtesy Marcia Daoust, Huntington, WV and Neal and Bruton Peterson).

2. Rupert O. Burford, *Foreign Service Memoirs – Diary of Rupert O. Burford* [Co. C - 83rd CMB]. (Unpublished), Charleston, WV, n.d., Author's Collection.

3. First (1st), Third (3rd), and Fourth (4th) Ranger Battalions. After Action Reports / Unit Journals. National Archives, College Park, MD.

4. James O. Beasley, *V-Mail & Correspondence of Lt. James O. Beasley, Co. D, 83rd Chemical Mortar Battalion*, (Courtesy John Beasley); Peterson, op. cit.

5. Michael J. Rebick, *V-Mail & Correspondence of Michael J. Rebick, Co. D, 83rd Chemical Mortar Battalion*, [Courtesy Linda Whalen]; Beasley, op. cit.

6. Beasley, op. cit. Samuel M. Bundy, Jr., *Co. A - 83rd Cml. Mortar Bn.*, (diary & record of events kept by Samuel Bundy from Camp Gordon through Sept. 22, 1945) – (approved by Samuel M. Bundy, Jr. 1984).

7. Burford, op. cit.; *U. S. S. LCI 35*, Deck Log / Action Report Sept. 1943, National Archives, College Park, MD; Marshall, op. cit.; Edwin Pike,

V-Mail & Correspondence of Capt. Edwin G. Pike 1941 - 1945 - Co. D, 83rd Chemical Mortar Battalion, (Courtesy Marcia Bunker).

8. Burford, op. cit.; *U. S. S. LCI 35*, op. cit.

9. *U. S. S. LCI 216*, Action Report, Sept. 10, 1943, RG 38, National Archives, College Park, MD.; Marshall, op. cit. Co. D. Morning Reports/ Unit Journal 1942-1944, (Courtesy Mike Codega and Sam Kweskin).

10. Burford, op. cit.

11. *LCI 35*, op. cit.; Burford, op. cit.; Ford, William Clifford, *Never Forget – A Soldier's Battlefield Memoirs*, (Network Printing, New Albany, MS, 2005) – [Co. C, 83rd Chemical Mortar Battalion], pg. 32.

12. Burford, op. cit.; Marshall, op. cit.

13. *U. S. S. LCI 216*; Pike, op. cit.

14. Co. D. Morning Reports/Unit Journal 1942-1944, op. cit.; John Beasley, *The Action at Vietri, September, 1943*, [James Beasley], (compiled May 24, 2003 – modified June 21, 2004) – [Courtesy John Beasley]; Hughes, op. cit., pg. 58; Daniel J. Shields, *Diary of Daniel J. Shields, Co. D & HQ Co., 83rd Chemical Mortar Battalion, 1942-1945*, (Courtesy Jean Decky).

15. Bundy, op. cit.

16. Burford, op. cit.; Co. D. Morning Reports/Unit Journal 1942-1944, op. cit.

17. Pike, op. cit.

18. *Mark Freedom Paid: A Combat Anthology*, (Jeanette, PA: 83rd Chemical Mortar Battalion Veterans Association, 1997) (Illustrated by Sam Kweskin), pg. 29.

19. Hughes, op. cit., pg. 59; Co. D. Morning Reports/Unit Journal 1942-1944, op. cit.

20. Burford, op. cit.; Ford, op. cit, pg. 34; First (1st), Third (3rd), and Fourth (4th) Ranger Battalions. After Action Reports / Unit Journals. National Archives, College Park, MD.

21. Co. D. Morning Reports/Unit Journal 1942-1944, op. cit.; Rebick, op. cit.

22. Burford, op. cit.

23. Marshall, op. cit.

24. Personal phone conversation between Hale H. Hepler and author, 2008; Correspondence between Don Harp, Panama City, FL, brother of Carlos Harp, and author, 2008.

25. Co. D. Morning Reports/Unit Journal 1942-1944, op. cit.; *The Action at Vietri, September, 1943*, [James Beasley], (compiled May 24, 2003 – modified June 21, 2004) – [Courtesy John Beasley].

26. John Beasley, op. cit.

27. Pike, op. cit.

28. John Beasley, op. cit.

29. Mangelsdorf, P. C., "James Otis Beasley", Science Magazine, (Vol. 99, No. 2577 - May 19, 1944): John Beasley, op. cit.; Correspondence with James & Iris Lester (Author's Collection); Pike, op. cit.

30. Shields, op. cit.; Report of Lt. Col. Kenneth Cunin, HQ, 83rd Chemical Battalion, September 12, 1943. National Archives, College Park, MD.

31. Burford, op. cit.; Co. D. Morning Reports/Unit Journal 1942-1944, op. cit.; Shields, op. cit.

32. Burford, op. cit.

33. Burford, op. cit.; Co. D. Morning Reports/Unit Journal 1942-1944, op. cit.

34. Burford, op. cit.

35. *Ibid.*

36. Co. D. Morning Reports/Unit Journal 1942-1944, op. cit.; *Muzzleblasts* – Official newsletter of the 83rd Chemical Mortar Battalion 1944 – present; Shields, op. cit.

37. Burford, op. cit.; Personal phone conversation between Hale H. Hepler and author, 2008.

38. Jerome A. Muschinske. *Correspondence With Terry Lowry*. Author's Collection.

39. Co. D. Morning Reports/Unit Journal 1942-1944, op. cit.; Hughes, op. cit., pg. 59.

40. Burford, op. cit.; Co. D. Morning Reports/Unit Journal 1942-1944, op. cit.; Shields, op. cit.

41. William S. Hutchinson, *Interview With Col. William S. Hutchinson*, CWS, Edgewood Arsenal, MD – Jan. 26, 1945. Edgewood Arsenal Archives; Hutchinson, William S., Jr., "The Forgotten Front", Chemical Warfare Service Bulletin #31, (Jan.- Feb. 1945).

42. Burford, op. cit.; Co. D. Morning Reports/Unit Journal 1942-1944, op. cit.; Shields, op. cit.

43. Burford, op. cit.; Co. D. Morning Reports/Unit Journal 1942-1944, op. cit.

44. Burford, op. cit.; Co. D. Morning Reports/Unit Journal 1942-1944, op. cit.; Hughes, op. cit., pg. 60.

45. Burford, op. cit.; Co. D. Morning Reports/Unit Journal 1942-1944, op. cit.

46. *Ibid.*

47. Burford, op. cit.

48. Burford, op. cit.; Co. D. Morning Reports/Unit Journal 1942-1944, op. cit.

49. Burford, op. cit.

50. Burford, op. cit.; Co. D. Morning Reports/Unit Journal 1942-1944, op. cit.

51. Burford, op. cit.

52. Obituary for William S. Hutchinson; Records of the Chemical Warfare Service, National Archives, College Park, MD; *General Orders #1 - #91 (1942)* – Camp Gordon, GA – Edgewood Arsenal Archives; First (1st) Infantry Division, *General Orders 1943*, National Archives, College Park, MD; Tregaskis, Richard, *Invasion Diary*, (New York, Random House, 1944), pg. 222; John P. McEvoy, *Correspondence With Terry Lowry*. Author's Collection.

53. Pike, op. cit.

54. Burford, op. cit.; Co. D. Morning Reports/Unit Journal 1942-1944, op. cit.

55. *Ibid.*

56. Burford, op. cit.; Shields, op. cit.

57. Burford, op. cit.; Chemical Warfare Service, HQ 7th Army, Records of the 7th Army, Chemical Warfare Section. National Archives, College Park, MD.

58. Chemical Warfare Service, HQ 7th Army, Records of the 7th Army, Chemical Warfare Section, op. cit.; William S. Hutchinson. *Interview With Col. William S. Hutchinson*, CWS, Edgewood Arsenal, MD – Jan. 26, 1945. Edgewood Arsenal Archives.

59. Eighty- Third (83rd) Chemical Mortar Battalion Journals, Battle Reports, Morning Reports: June 1943 – Nov. 1945.

60. Shields, op. cit.; Robert E. Edwards, *V-Mail & Correspondence of Robert E. Edwards, HQ Co, 83rd Chemical Mortar Battalion*, (Courtesy Wendy Edwards); Pike, op. cit.

61. Eighty-Third (83rd) Chemical Mortar Battalion Journals, Battle Reports, Morning Reports: June 1943 – Nov. 1945.

62. Eighty-Third (83rd) Chemical Mortar Battalion Journals, Battle Reports, Morning Reports: June 1943 – Nov. 1945; Co. D. Morning Reports/Unit Journal 1942-1944, op. cit.

63. *Ibid.*

64. Burford, op. cit.; Co. D. Morning Reports/Unit Journal 1942-1944, op. cit.; Charlie Lowry, *V-Mail & Correspondence 1943-45 - Co. D / Co. A, 83rd Chemical Mortar Battalion*, (Author's Collection); Pike, op. cit.

65. Burford, op. cit; Pike, op. cit.

66. William S. Hutchinson. *Personal Correspondence from Col. William S. Hutchinson to Kenneth A. Cunin 1943 -1944*. Fifteen Letters. Chemical Corps Museum Archives, Ft. Leonard Wood, MO.

67. *Ibid.*

68. *Ibid.*

69. *Ibid.*

70. *Ibid.*

71. James G. Helsel, *Diary of James G. Helsel, Co. A, 83rd Chemical Mortar Battalion*, (Courtesy Joyce Berry, Lebanon, TN).

72. Leech, Dewey C., and William D. McCain (ed.), *The WW II Experiences of Andrew Candler Leech 1943-1945*, (Hattiesburg, MS, 1985), pg. 17.

73. Pike, op. cit.

74. *Ibid*; Russell H. Peterson, *Personal Papers of Russell H. Peterson, Co. D, 83rd Chemical Mortar Battalion, 1942 – 1944*

75. Burford, op. cit.; Pike, op. cit.

76. Eighty-Third (83rd) Chemical Mortar Battalion Journals, Battle Reports, Morning Reports: June 1943 – Nov. 1945.

77. Burford, op. cit.

78. Pike, op. cit.

79. Helsel, op. cit.; Pike, op. cit.

80. Burford, op. cit.

81. Helsel, op. cit.

82. Eighty-Third (83rd) Chemical Mortar Battalion Journals, Battle Reports, Morning Reports: June 1943 – Nov. 1945.

83. Helsel, op. cit.; Shields, op. cit.; Leech, op. cit, pg. 18.

84. William S. Hutchinson. *Personal Correspondence from Col. William S. Hutchinson to Kenneth A. Cunin 1943 -1944*; William S. Hutchinson, Jr., *"The Forgotten Front"*, Chemical Warfare Service Bulletin #31, (Jan.- Feb. 1945), pg. 7.

85. Gordon M. Mindrum, *Personal Papers of Dr. Gordon M. Mindrum*, Cincinnati, OH [loaned to the author 2006]; Personal Conversations between Gordon Mindrum and author, 2005-2006.

86. Mindrum, op. cit.; Leech, op. cit, pg. 18.

87. Ford, op. cit., pg. 43; Newman, Bruce, *"Always in midst of battle"*, San Jose Mercury News, (May 26, 2008) - Interview with Vicente De Leon, Medic, Co. C, 83rd Chemical Mortar Battalion.

88. William S. Hutchinson. *Personal Correspondence from Col. William S. Hutchinson to Kenneth A. Cunin 1943 -1944*, op. cit.; Shields, op. cit; Pike, op. cit.

89. Eighty-Third (83rd) Chemical Mortar Battalion Journals, Battle Reports, Morning Reports: June 1943 – Nov. 1945.

90. *Ibid.*

91. *Ibid.*

92. Eighty-Third (83rd) Chemical Mortar Battalion Journals, Battle Reports, Morning Reports: June 1943 – Nov. 1945; Co. D. Morning Reports/Unit Journal 1942-1944, op. cit.

93. Eighty-Third (83rd) Chemical Mortar Battalion Journals, Battle Reports, Morning Reports: June 1943 – Nov. 1945; Co. D. Morning Reports/Unit Journal 1942-1944, op. cit.; James Marion Lester, *James Marion Lester's Story*, (unpublished manuscript interview), by Vicki S. Hibma, June 26, 1984.

94. Eighty-Third (83rd) Chemical Mortar Battalion Journals, Battle Reports, Morning Reports: June 1943 – Nov. 1945; Eighty-Fourth (84th) Chemical Mortar Battalion, Unit Journals, National Archives, College Park, MD.

95. Pike, op. cit.

96. *Ibid.*

97. Flamm, Capt. Paul F. (ed.), Combat History of the 84th Chemical Mortar Battalion, n.d., copy located in files of 84th Chemical Mortar Battalion, [Co. B section by Sgt. Dean O. Haley], National Archives, College Park, MD.

98. Eighty-Fourth (84th) Chemical Mortar Battalion, Unit Journals, op. cit.

99. William S. Hutchinson. *Personal Correspondence from Col. William S. Hutchinson to Kenneth A. Cunin 1943 -1944*, op. cit.; Rebick, op. cit.;

First (1st), Third (3rd), and Fourth (4th) Ranger Battalions. After Action Reports / Unit Journals, op. cit.; *Muzzleblasts* – Official newsletter of the 83rd Chemical Mortar Battalion 1944 – present, op. cit.

100. Karl Garrett, *Memories 1942-1945*, (HQ Co., 83rd Chemical Mortar Battalion), [n.d.], [Courtesy Karl Garrett, Richmond, VA]; Eighty-Fourth (84th) Chemical Mortar Battalion, Unit Journals, op. cit.; Rebick, op. cit.

101. Brashear, Alton D., *From Lee To Bari: The History of the 45th General Hospital*, (Whittet & Shepperson, Richmond, VA, 1957); Capt. (Dr.) Julius C. Hulcher, *Diary of Capt. Julius C. Hulcher 1943 - 1945, Medical Detachment*, 83rd Chemical Mortar Battalion, [Courtesy Charles Hulcher, Glen Allen, VA] [hereafter cited as Hulcher]; *Capt. (Dr.) Julius C. Hulcher – WW II – May 1942 to December 1945* – [DVD of color film footage taken during World War II by Capt. Julius C. "Doc" Hulcher, Medical Detachment, 83rd Chemical Mortar Battalion – approximately one and a half hour in length – Camp Lee, Rabat, Italy, France, Austria, etc. - Courtesy of Charles "Chuck" Hulcher, Richmond, VA]; Edward L. Trey, Personal Correspondence and Interviews with Terry Lowry 2003-2008, (Author's Collection); *Muzzleblasts* – Official newsletter of the 83rd Chemical Mortar Battalion 1944 – present, op. cit.

102. Eighty-Third (83rd) Chemical Mortar Battalion Journals, Battle Reports, Morning Reports: June 1943 – Nov. 1945.

103. Hulcher, op. cit.; Leech, op. cit, pg. 21.

104. Obituary of David W. Meyerson; Edgewood Arsenal Archives; *Trainee Tribune* – Official newsletter of the trainee men in the CWS at Edgewood Arsenal, MD 1942 – [Copies provided by Lorraine M. Salvi]; Eighty-Third (83rd) Chemical Mortar Battalion. *General Orders #1 - #91 (1942)* – Camp Gordon, GA, op. cit; Trey, op. cit; John P. McEvoy, *Correspondence With Terry Lowry*. Author's Collection; William S. Hutchinson. *Personal Correspondence from Col. William S. Hutchinson to Kenneth A. Cunin 1943 -1944*, op. cit.

105. Eldredge, Walter J., *Finding My Father's War: A Baby Boomer and the 2nd Chemical Mortar Battalion in World War II*, (PageFree Publishing, Inc., Ostego, MI, 2004).

106. Eighty-Fourth (84th) Chemical Mortar Battalion, Unit Journals, op. cit.; William S. Hutchinson. *Personal Correspondence from Col. William S. Hutchinson to Kenneth A. Cunin 1943 -1944*, op. cit.

107. Hulcher, op. cit.

108. Eighty-Third (83rd) Chemical Mortar Battalion Journals, Battle Reports, Morning Reports: June 1943 – Nov. 1945, op. cit.; Eighty-Fourth (84th) Chemical Mortar Battalion, Unit Journals, op. cit.

109. Hulcher, op. cit.; Rebick, op. cit.; Charlie Lowry, op. cit.

110. Company B, 83rd Chemical Mortar Battalion History, National Archives, College Park, MD; *Muzzleblasts* – Official newsletter of the 83rd Chemical Mortar Battalion 1944 – present, op. cit.

111. Helsel, op. cit.; Eighty-Fourth (84th) Chemical Mortar Battalion, Unit Journals, op. cit.

112. Eighty-Fourth (84th) Chemical Mortar Battalion, Unit Journals, op. cit.; Hulcher, op. cit.

113. Ford, op. cit., pp. 41-42.

114. Garrett, op. cit.

115. Hulcher, op. cit.

116. Report of Investigation, 4.2" Chemical Mortar, Jan., 1944 for the Period Dec. 11 - 15, 1943. National Archives, College Park, MD.

117. Hulcher, op. cit.; Curtis Williams, *Telephone Interviews with Terry Lowry, 2006*, Medical Detachment, 83rd Chemical Mortar Battalion.

118. Helsel, op. cit.

119. Burford, op. cit.; Helsel, op. cit.

120. Eighty-Third (83rd) Chemical Mortar Battalion Journals, Battle Reports, Morning Reports: June 1943 – Nov. 1945, op. cit.

121. *Ibid.*

122. *Ibid.*

123. Mindrum, op. cit.; Nolan McCraine, *Telephone Interview with Terry Lowry, 2006*, (Co. B, 83rd Chemical Mortar Battalion); Shields, op. cit.

124. Hulcher, op. cit.; Stephen W. Vukson, *Diary of Stephen W. Vukson*, HQ Co., 83rd Chemical Mortar Battalion - Dec. 1943 - 1945, (Courtesy Stephen W. Vukson).

125. Charlie Lowry, op. cit.; William S. Hutchinson. *Personal Correspondence from Col. William S. Hutchinson to Kenneth A. Cunin 1943 -1944*, op. cit.

126. Helsel, op. cit.; Pike, op. cit.; Hulcher, op. cit; Vukson, op. cit.

127. Hulcher, op. cit.; William S. Hutchinson. *Personal Correspondence from Col. William S. Hutchinson to Kenneth A. Cunin 1943 -1944*, op. cit.

128. Helsel, op. cit.; Burford, op. cit.; Shields, op. cit.; Charlie Lowry, *V-Mail & Correspondence 1943-45 - Co. D / Co. A, 83rd Chemical Mortar Battalion*, (Author's Collection); *Muzzleblasts* – Official newsletter of the 83rd Chemical Mortar Battalion 1944 – present, op. cit.; Vukson, op. cit.

129. Pike, op. cit.; Hulcher, op. cit.

130. Hulcher, op. cit.; Charlie Lowry, op. cit.

131. Pike, op. cit.

132. Eighty-Third (83rd) Chemical Mortar Battalion Journals, Battle Reports, Morning Reports: June 1943 – Nov. 1945, op. cit.

Chapter Eight

1. Eighty-Third (83rd) Chemical Mortar Battalion Journals, Battle Reports, Morning Reports: June 1943 – Nov. 1945, National Archives, College Park, MD; Co. D. Morning Reports/Unit Journal 1942-1944, (Courtesy Mike Codega and Sam Kweskin); Daniel J. Shields, *Diary of Daniel J. Shields, Co. D & HQ Co., 83rd Chemical Mortar Battalion, 1942-1945*, (Courtesy Jean Decky); Michael J. Rebick, *V-Mail & Correspondence of Michael J. Rebick, Co. D, 83rd Chemical Mortar Battalion*, [Courtesy Linda Whalen]; Capt. (Dr.) Julius C. Hulcher, *Diary of Capt. Julius C. Hulcher 1943 - 1945, Medical Detachment*, 83rd Chemical Mortar Battalion, [Courtesy Charles Hulcher, Glen Allen, VA] [hereafter cited as Hulcher]; *Muzzleblasts* – Official newsletter of the 83rd Chemical Mortar Battalion 1944 – present.

2. *Ibid.*

3. Rupert O. Burford, *Foreign Service Memoirs – Diary of Rupert O. Burford* [Co. C - 83rd CMB]. (Unpublished), Charleston, WV, n.d., Author's Collection, (Used by permission of Mrs. Rupert O. Burford).

4. Samuel M. Bundy, Jr., *Co. A - 83rd Cml. Mortar Bn.*, (diary & record of events kept by Samuel Bundy from Camp Gordon through Sept. 22, 1945) – (approved by Samuel M. Bundy, Jr. 1984) - [Courtesy Lee Steedle]; Hulcher, op. cit.; U. S. S. LST 379, Action Report / War Diary Jan. - Apr. 1944, National Archives, College Park, MD; Burford, op. cit.

5. Edwin Pike, *V-Mail & Correspondence of Capt. Edwin G. Pike 1941 - 1945 - Co. D, 83rd Chemical Mortar Battalion*, (Courtesy Marcia Bunker); Russell H. Peterson, *Personal Papers of Russell H. Peterson, Co. D, 83rd Chemical Mortar Battalion, 1942 – 1944*, (Courtesy Marcia Daoust, Huntington, WV and Neal and Bruton Peterson); Charlie Lowry, *V-Mail & Correspondence 1943-45 - Co. D / Co. A, 83rd Chemical Mortar Battalion*, (Author's Collection).

6. Eighty-Third (83rd) Chemical Mortar Battalion Journals, Battle Reports, Morning Reports: June 1943 – Nov. 1945, op. cit.

7. Rebick, op. cit.

8. First (1st), Third (3rd), and Fourth (4th) Ranger Battalions. After Action Reports / Unit Journals. National Archives, College Park, MD.

9. *Ibid.*

10. *Ibid.*

11. *Ibid.*

12. First (1st), Third (3rd), and Fourth (4th) Ranger Battalions. After Action Reports / Unit Journals, op. cit.; Burford, op. cit.; James G. Helsel, *Diary of James G. Helsel, Co. A, 83rd Chemical Mortar Battalion*, (Courtesy Joyce Berry, Lebanon, TN).

13. Pike, op. cit.; Rebick, op. cit.; Lowry, op. cit.; Helsel, op. cit.

14. William S. Hutchinson. *Personal Correspondence from Col. William S. Hutchinson to Kenneth A. Cunin 1943 -1944.* Fifteen Letters. Chemical Corps Museum Archives, Ft. Leonard Wood, MO.; Pike, op. cit.

15. Stephen W. Vukson, *Diary of Stephen W. Vukson*, HQ Co., 83rd Chemical Mortar Battalion - Dec. 1943 - 1945, (Courtesy Stephen W. Vukson); Hulcher, op. cit.

16. Hulcher, op. cit.; Vukson, op. cit.

17. Burford, op. cit.

18. Eighty-Third (83rd) Chemical Mortar Battalion Journals, Battle Reports, Morning Reports: June 1943 – Nov. 1945, op. cit.; First (1st), Third (3rd), and Fourth (4th) Ranger Battalions. After Action Reports / Unit Journals, op. cit.

19. Vukson, op. cit.; Burford, op. cit.

20. Joseph E. Cannetti, *War Experiences of Joseph E. Cannetti, Co. A, 83rd Chemical Mortar Battalion*, (Courtesy Joseph E. Cannetti); Bundy, op. cit.

21. Vukson, op. cit.

22. Helsel, op. cit.

23. Eighty-Third (83rd) Chemical Mortar Battalion Journals, Battle Reports, Morning Reports: June 1943 – Nov. 1945, op. cit.; First (1st), Third (3rd), and Fourth (4th) Ranger Battalions. After Action Reports / Unit Journals, op. cit.

24. Leech, Dewey C., and William D. McCain (ed.), *The WW II Experiences of Andrew Candler Leech 1943-1945*, (Hattiesburg, MS, 1985), pg. 23 [hereafter cited as Leech].

25. Hayes, Veryl R., "*Psych A – For Platoon Leaders*", Chemical Warfare Service Bulletin, Vol. 30 – No. 5 (Nov. - Dec. 1944), pg. 28.

26. Eighty-Third (83rd) Chemical Mortar Battalion Journals, Battle Reports, Morning Reports: June 1943 – Nov. 1945, op. cit.

27. Cannetti, op. cit.; Leech, op. cit. pg. 23; *Muzzleblasts* – Official newsletter of the 83rd Chemical Mortar Battalion 1944 – present, op. cit.

28. Vukson, op. cit.

29. First (1st), Third (3rd), and Fourth (4th) Ranger Battalions. After Action Reports / Unit Journals, op. cit.; Burford, op. cit.; Shields, op. cit.

30. Hulcher, op. cit.

31. Hulcher, op. cit.; Vukson, op. cit.; First (1st), Third (3rd), and Fourth (4th) Ranger Battalions. After Action Reports / Unit Journals, op. cit.

32. Shields, op. cit.; Byron H. Jordan, *V-Mail of Byron H. Jordan 1943-1945*, Co. D / Co. B, 83rd Chemical Mortar Battalion and Correspondence and Interview Between Byron Jordan and Terry Lowry, (Courtesy Byron H. Jordan).

33. Bundy, op. cit.

34. Vukson, op. cit.; Hulcher, op. cit.; First (1st), Third (3rd), and Fourth (4th) Ranger Battalions. After Action Reports / Unit Journals, op. cit.

35. Shields, op. cit.

36. Navy Source Online: Amphibious Photo Archives. *LST 422.* Information on Broadhurst courtesy Peter Berg.

37. *Muzzleblasts* – Official newsletter of the 83rd Chemical Mortar Battalion 1944 – present, op. cit. [Shaw & Whitt]; Shields, op. cit.; Trey, op. cit.

38. Sixty-Eighth (68th) Coastal Artillery, Unit Journals, National Archives, College Park, MD; Colin Lowe Broadhurst, Lt. Commander, Royal Navy Reserves, *Official Report of LST 422*, (Courtesy Peter Berg); Eighty-Third (83rd) Chemical Mortar Battalion Journals, Battle Reports, Morning Reports: June 1943 – Nov. 1945, op. cit.

39. George Rhoads, Letter to Gini Lemoine Regarding *LST 422*, (Courtesy Gini Lemoine); Charlie Lowry, op. cit.; James Marion Lester, *James Marion Lester's Story*, (unpublished manuscript interview), by Vicki S. Hibma, June 26, 1984.

40. Broadhurst, op. cit.

41. Eighty-Third (83rd) Chemical Mortar Battalion Journals, Battle Reports, Morning Reports: June 1943 – Nov. 1945, op. cit.; Vukson, op. cit.

42. Hale H. Hepler, *Hale Hunter Hepler – World War II Veteran*, (dictated to his daughter Pam Pace June 2005) [Courtesy Hale H. Hepler & Pam Pace]; Nearly every craft involved in the *LST 422* disaster gave a slightly varying location of the ship; Broadhurst, op. cit.; Eighty-Third (83rd) Chemical Mortar Battalion Journals, Battle Reports, Morning Reports: June 1943 – Nov. 1945, op. cit.; *Muzzleblasts* – Official newsletter of the 83rd Chemical Mortar Battalion 1944 – present, op. cit. [Woomer].

43. *U. S. S. YMS 226*, War Diary /Action Report, Jan. 1944, National Archives, College Park, MD; *U. S. S. Pilot*, Deck Log/War Diary/Action

Report Jan. 1944, National Archives, College Park, MD; Broadhurst, op. cit.

44. Commander Task Group 81.4, *Report of Amphibious Operations During Landings Near Cape D'Anzio, Italy Participated In By Task Group 81.4, Jan. 20 - Feb. 1, 1944, Action Report*, National Archives, College Park, MD [Report of *H.M.S. Ulster Queen*]; *U. S. S. LCI 32*, Action Report Jan. 1944 & Casualty Report File. National Archives, College Park, MD; Commander Task Group 81.14 (Return Convoy Group) & Commander Task Group 81.11 (Salvage Group), Jan . 22-30, 1944 - *Action Report - March 1, 1944* - National Archives, College Park, MD.

45. Commander Task Group 81.4, *Report of Amphibious Operations During Landings Near Cape D'Anzio, Italy Participated In By Task Group 81.4, Jan. 20 - Feb. 1, 1944*, Action Report, National Archives, College Park, MD [SC 649]; *U. S. S. YMS 62*, Action Report Jan. 1944, National Archives, College Park, MD; Commander Task Group 81.7, Commander Task Unit 81.7.1, Commander Mine Squadron 6 - Sweeper Operations Operation Shingle Jan. 21-30, 1944 - *Action Report - Feb. 8, 1944*, National Archives, College Park, MD; Eighty-Third (83rd) Chemical Mortar Battalion Journals, Battle Reports, Morning Reports: June 1943 – Nov. 1945, op. cit.

46. Broadhurst, op. cit.; Navy Mine Warfare Veterans Association Reunion, Cincinnati, OH Oct. 1998 – Reunion of YMS – 43 crew members and two soldiers [Eugene A. Plassmann & Claude Shaw] they saved from *LST 422* – tape and edited transcript provided by Eugene A. Plassmann.

47. Broadhurst, op. cit.

48. *Ibid.*

49. Eighty-Third (83rd) Chemical Mortar Battalion Journals, Battle Reports, Morning Reports: June 1943 – Nov. 1945, op. cit.; Michele (Mike) Codega, *Letter to Mrs. L. A. Merrill Describing the Sinking of LST 422 at Anzio*, (Courtesy Robert L. Merrill).

50. Eighty-Third (83rd) Chemical Mortar Battalion Journals, Battle Reports, Morning Reports: June 1943 – Nov. 1945, op. cit.; Awards and Citations for the 83rd Chemical Battalion (General Orders by Division), National Archives, College Park, MD.

51. Author's Correspondence with Bengie Foley, New Albany, MS (Author's Collection).

52. Eighty-Third (83rd) Chemical Mortar Battalion Journals, Battle Reports, Morning Reports: June 1943 – Nov. 1945, op. cit.; Edward L. Trey, Personal Correspondence and Interviews with Terry Lowry 2003-2008, (Author's Collection); David W. Meyerson, *V-Mail Letter to Mrs. L. A. Merrill Describing the Death of Lt. Leonard A. Merrill, Jr. on LST 422 at Anzio*, (Courtesy Robert L. Merrill); Unknown clipping, *"Lieut. L. A. Merrill Missing In Action"*, (Courtesy Robert L. Merrill); Unknown clipping, *"Lieut. Merrill of Petersborough Missing"*, (Courtesy Robert L. Merrill).

53. Broadhurst, op. cit.; Ford, William Clifford, *Never Forget – A Soldier's Battlefield Memoirs*, (Network Printing, New Albany, MS, 2005) – [Co. C, 83rd Chemical Mortar Battalion], pg. 49; *Muzzleblasts* – Official newsletter of the 83rd Chemical Mortar Battalion 1944 – present, op. cit.; William C. Ford, *Lest We Forget*, (Memoir by Staff Sgt. William C. Ford, Co. C, 83rd CMB), [Courtesy Gini Lemoine].

54. *YMS 226*, op. cit.; *U. S. S. YMS 69*, War Diary /Action Report / Deck Log, Jan. 1944, National Archives, College Park, MD.

55. Norm Holt, *Diary of Norm Holt – USN – YMS – 43*, Billy Rhoads Collection, (Courtesy Norm Holt and Gini Lemoine); Navy Mine Warfare Veterans Association Reunion, op. cit.

56. *Muzzleblasts* – Official newsletter of the 83rd Chemical Mortar Battalion 1944 – present, op. cit. [Woomer].

57. *Muzzleblasts* – Official newsletter of the 83rd Chemical Mortar Battalion 1944 – present, op. cit. [Kann].

58. Navy Mine Warfare Veterans Association Reunion, op. cit.

59. *Ibid.*

60. *Mark Freedom Paid: A Combat Anthology*, (Jeanette, PA: 83rd Chemical Mortar Battalion Veterans Association, 1997) (Illustrated by Sam Kweskin), pg. 52; *Muzzleblasts* – Official newsletter of the 83rd Chemical Mortar Battalion 1944 – present, op. cit. [Hoover].

61. Author's Correspondence with Dave Dougherty, Ft. Collins, CO, Regarding James Dougherty, Co. D, 83rd Chemical Mortar Battalion (Author's Collection).

62. Personal Interview with Curtis A. Williams and Terry Lowry, 2006.

63. Duvall, Bobbe J., *Robert Marlin "John" Chamblee, War Story*, (2000); *Muzzleblasts* – Official newsletter of the 83rd Chemical Mortar Battalion 1944 – present, op. cit. [Riddle].

64. *Ibid.*

65. Hale H. Hepler, *Hale Hunter Hepler – World War II Veteran*, op. cit.

66. *Muzzleblasts* – Official newsletter of the 83rd Chemical Mortar Battalion 1944 – present, op. cit. [Miller].

67. Lemuel R. Tillman, Personal Correspondence With Terry Lowry, (Co. C, 83rd Chemical Mortar Battalion); *Muzzleblasts* – Official newsletter of the 83rd Chemical Mortar Battalion 1944 – present, op. cit. [Tillman].

68. Duvall, Bobbe J., *Robert Marlin "John" Chamblee, War Story*, op. cit.; Correspondence with James & Iris Lester (Author's Collection).

69. *Mark Freedom Paid: A Combat Anthology*, (Jeanette, PA: 83rd Chemical Mortar Battalion Veterans Association, 1997) (Illustrated by Sam Kweskin), pg. 53-55.

70. *Muzzleblasts* – Official newsletter of the 83rd Chemical Mortar Battalion 1944 – present, op. cit. [Whitt].

71. *Mark Freedom Paid: A Combat Anthology*, (Jeanette, PA: 83rd Chemical Mortar Battalion Veterans Association, 1997) (Illustrated by Sam Kweskin), pg. 46-47.

72. Codega, op. cit.; Awards and Citations for the 83rd Chemical Battalion (General Orders by Division), National Archives, College Park, MD; *Muzzleblasts* – Official newsletter of the 83rd Chemical Mortar Battalion 1944 – present, op. cit.: Kann, op. cit.; *Mark Freedom Paid: A Combat Anthology*, (Jeanette, PA: 83rd Chemical Mortar Battalion Veterans Association, 1997) (Illustrated by Sam Kweskin), pg. 49-50; Audie Pierce, Personal interview with author, 2003.

73. Marshall, op. cit.

74. Shields, op. cit.; James H. Gallahan, Sr., *Military Service of James H. Gallahan, Sr.* - World War II, [Courtesy Roger Gallahan, Quinton, VA].

75. *Mark Freedom Paid: A Combat Anthology*, pg. 53-54.

76. *Ibid*, pg. 46-48.

77. *Muzzleblasts* – Official newsletter of the 83rd Chemical Mortar Battalion 1944 – present, op. cit. [Riddle].

78. Duvall, Bobbe J., *Robert Marlin "John" Chamblee, War Story,* op. cit.; *Muzzleblasts* – Official newsletter of the 83ʳᵈ Chemical Mortar Battalion 1944 – present, op. cit.; Pierce, op. cit.; Lester, op. cit.; Author's correspondence with Edward Kirk Atton, 83ʳᵈ Chemical Mortar Battalion, 2004-2008.
79. *U. S. S. Pilot,* op. cit.; *U. S. S. YMS 3,* Deck Log /Action Report Jan. 1944, National Archives, College Park, MD; Commander Mine Squadron 6 - Sweeper Operations, op. cit.; *U. S. S. YMS 207,* War Diary / Action Report / Deck Log, Jan. 1944, National Archives, College Park, MD; *U. S. S. YMS 83,* War Diary /Action Report / Deck Log, Jan. 1944, National Archives, College Park, MD.
80. *U. S. S. YMS 226,* op. cit.; *U. S. S. LCI 32,* op. cit.
81. *U.S.S. LCI 209,* Action Report Jan. 1944, National Archives, College Park, MD; *U. S. S. YMS 36,* Action Report Jan. 1944, National Archives, College Park, MD; *U. S. S. YMS 62,* op. cit.; Commander Task Group 81.4, *Report of Amphibious Operations During Landings Near Cape D'Anzio, Italy Participated In By Task Group 81.4, Jan. 20 - Feb. 1, 1944,* Action Report, National Archives, College Park, MD [SC 649], op. cit.
82. *U. S. S. LST 16,* Deck Log /Action Report Jan. 1944, National Archives, College Park, MD; Broadhurst, op. cit.; *U. S. S. YMS 226,* op. cit.; *U. S. S. YMS 3,* op. cit.
83. *U. S. S. LST 16,* op. cit.; United States Coast Guard, *Book of Valor - A Fact Book on Medals and Decorations,* Prepared by Public Relations Division, Washington, D.C.
84. Commander Mine Squadron 6 - Sweeper Operations, op. cit. [includes reports of YMS 13 and YMS 28].
85. *U. S. S. LCI 32,* op. cit.; Commander Task Group 81.14 (Return Convoy Group) & Commander Task Group 81.11 (Salvage Group), Jan . 22-30, 1944 - *Action Report - March 1, 1944;* Galik, Stanley, *LCI 35 – World War II Experiences* (website).
86. *U. S. S. LCI 32,* op. cit.; Galik, Stanley, *LCI 35 – World War II Experiences* (website), op. cit.
87. Author's personal interview with Walter Bielski, 83ʳᵈ Chemical Mortar Battalion, 2003.
88. *U. S. S. LCI 32,* op. cit.
89. *LST 422* website and correspondence of George Rhoads.
90. *U. S. S. YMS 226,* op. cit.; *U. S. S. LCI 32,* op. cit.
91. *U. S. S. YMS 226,* op. cit.
92. *H. M. S. LST 301,* Deck/Log/Action Report, Royal Navy Archives.
93. *U. S. S. PC 1227,* War Diary, National Archives, College Park, MD; *U.S. S. LCI 209,* op. cit.
94. Duvall, Bobbe J., *Robert Marlin "John" Chamblee, War Story,* op. cit.; *U. S. S. Dextrous,* Action Report Jan. 1944, National Archives, College Park, MD; *U. S. S. YMS 83,* op. cit.; *U. S. S. Herbert C. Jones,* Deck Log, War Diary, Action Report Jan. 1944, National Archives, College Park, MD.
95. Holt, op. cit.; *U. S. S. YMS 58,* War Diary /Action Report / Deck Log, Jan. 1944, National Archives, College Park, MD; *U.S.S. YMS 34,* Action Report, Jan. 1944, National Archives, College Park, MD; *U. S. S. Pilot,* op. cit.; *U. S. S. YMS 83,* op. cit.
96. *U. S. S. PC 1227,* op. cit.; *U. S. S. YMS 83,* op. cit.
97. *LCI 196,* Action Report, National Archives, College Park, MD; Broadhurst, op. cit.
98. Sixty-Eighth (68ᵗʰ) Coastal Artillery, Unit Journals, National Archives, College Park, MD; *U. S. S. Strive,* Deck Log/War Diary/Action Report Jan. 1944, National Archives, College Park, MD.
99. Broadhurst, op. cit.; Personal Interviews with Edward L. Trey & author; *Muzzleblasts* – Official newsletter of the 83ʳᵈ Chemical Mortar Battalion 1944 – present.
100. *U. S. S. YMS 58,* op. cit.; *U. S. S. PC 1227,* op. cit.; *U. S. S. YMS 62,* op. cit.
101. *U. S. S. YMS 3,* op. cit.
102. *Mark Freedom Paid: A Combat Anthology,* pg. 47-49.
103. *U. S. S. Strive,* op. cit.; *U. S. S. YMS 43,* War Diary /Action Report Jan. 1944, National Archives, College Park, MD; Holt, op. cit.; Commander Mine Squadron 6 - Sweeper Operations, op. cit.
104. *Muzzleblasts* – Official newsletter of the 83ʳᵈ Chemical Mortar Battalion 1944 – present, op. cit. [Woomer].
105. *U. S. S. YMS 29,* War Diary /Action Report / Deck Log, Jan. 1944, National Archives, College Park, MD; *U. S. S. Pilot,* op. cit.
106. *U. S. S. SC 638,* Action Report / Deck Log / War Diary, Jan. 1944, National Archives, College Park, MD; Unknown clipping, *"Lieut. L. A. Merrill Missing In Action",* (Courtesy Robert L. Merrill; Unknown clipping, *"Lieut. Merrill of Petersborough Missing",* (Courtesy Robert L. Merrill); Commander Task Group 81.4, *Report of Amphibious Operations During Landings Near Cape D'Anzio, Italy Participated In By Task Group 81.4, Jan. 20 - Feb. 1, 1944,* Action Report, op. cit.
107. *U. S. S. YMS 43,* op. cit.; Holt, op. cit.; Navy Mine Warfare Veterans Association Reunion, op. cit.
108. *Ibid.*
109. *Ibid.*
110. *Ibid.*
111. *Ibid.*
112. Shields, op. cit.
113. *U. S. S. YMS 69,* op. cit.; Commander Task Group 81.4, *Report of Amphibious Operations During Landings Near Cape D'Anzio, Italy Participated In By Task Group 81.4, Jan. 20 - Feb. 1, 1944,* Action Report, op. cit.; *U. S. S. Strive,* op. cit.; *U. S. S. YMS 36,* op. cit.; Author's personal interview and correspondence with Frank Kloxin, 2007-2008.
114. *LCI 196,* op. cit.; *U. S. S. Dextrous,* op. cit.; *U. S. S. Herbert C. Jones,* op. cit.; *U. S. S. Pilot,* op. cit.; Commander Mine Squadron 6 - Sweeper Operations, op. cit.; *U. S. S. YMS 69,* op. cit.
115. Ford, William Clifford, *Never Forget – A Soldier's Battlefield Memoirs,* op. cit., pg. 50-51.
116. Personal Interview with Curtis A. Williams and Terry Lowry, 2006; Personal correspondence of Rudolph Whitt and author; *Muzzleblasts* – Official newsletter of the 83ʳᵈ Chemical Mortar Battalion 1944 – present, op. cit. [Whitt].

117. *U. S. S. Pilot*, op. cit.

118. *U. S. S. YMS 58*, op. cit.; *SC 625*, Action Report, National Archives, College Park, MD; *LCI 10*, Action Report, National Archives, College Park, MD; *U. S. S. Strive*, op. cit.; *U. S. S. LCI 32*, op. cit.

119. *U. S. S. LCI 32*, op. cit.; *U. S. S. Strive*, op. cit.

120. *U. S. S. PC 1227*, op. cit.; *Mark Freedom Paid: A Combat Anthology*, pg. 53-55.

121. *Muzzleblasts – Official newsletter of the 83rd Chemical Mortar Battalion 1944 – present*, op. cit. [Riddle].

122. *U. S. S. YMS 207*, op. cit.; *U. S. S. YMS 83*, op. cit.

123. *U. S. S. YMS 43*, op. cit.; *U.S.S. YMS 34*, op. cit.; Commander Task Group 81.4, *Report of Amphibious Operations During Landings Near Cape D'Anzio, Italy Participated In By Task Group 81.4, Jan. 20 - Feb. 1, 1944*, Action Report, National Archives, College Park, MD [Report of *H.M.S. Ulster Queen*], op. cit.; Tillman, op. cit.; *LCI 10*, op. cit.; *YMS 226*, op. cit.; *U. S. S. Strive*, op. cit.; *U. S. S. YMS 58*, op. cit.

124. *U. S. S. Strive*, op. cit.

125. Hepler, op. cit.

126. *LCI 196*, op. cit.; *U. S. S. YMS 58*, op. cit.; Commander Mine Squadron 6 - Sweeper Operations, op. cit.

127. *YMS 226*, op. cit.; Pierce, op. cit.; Hurd, Beth, *"Town Turns Out to Honor the Purple Heart"*, Nov. 15, 2007 [article on Antonio Rabaiotti, Co. D, 83rd CMB]; Telephone interview of Antonio Rabaiotti and author, 2007.

128. Holt, op. cit.; Navy Mine Warfare Veterans Association Reunion, op. cit.; *U. S. S. YMS 29*, op. cit.: *U. S. S. YMS 43*, op. cit.; *U. S. S. YMS 58*, op. cit.

129. *YMS 226*, op. cit.; Commander Mine Squadron 6 - Sweeper Operations, op. cit.; *LCI 196*, op. cit.; *U. S. S. YMS 83*, op. cit.

130. Commander Mine Squadron 6 - Sweeper Operations, op. cit.; *U.S.S. YMS 34*, op. cit.; George Rhoads, *Billy Rhoads: Brave Soldier*, (n.d.), [Copy provided by Sam Kweskin].

131. Marshall, op. cit.

132. Robert E. Edwards, *V-Mail & Correspondence of Robert E. Edwards, HQ Co, 83rd Chemical Mortar Battalion*, (Courtesy Wendy Edwards).

133. Sixty-Eighth (68th) Coastal Artillery, op. cit.; *U. S. S. YMS 226*, op. cit.; *U. S. S. YMS 69*, op. cit.; *U. S. S. YMS 43*, op. cit.

134. *U. S. S. YMS 36*, op. cit.; Commander Mine Squadron 6 - Sweeper Operations, op. cit.; Commander Task Group 81.7, Commander Task Unit 81.7.1, Commander Mine Squadron 6 - Sweeper Operations Operation Shingle Jan. 21-30, 1944 - *Action Report - Feb. 8, 1944*, op. cit.

135. *U.S.S. YMS 34*, op. cit.; *U. S. S. YMS 207*, op. cit.; *U.S.S. YMS 34*, op. cit.; *U. S. S. YMS 62*, op. cit.

136. *U. S. S. YMS 226*, op. cit.; *LCI 10*, op. cit.

137. *LCI 10*, op. cit.; *U. S. S. YMS 62*, op. cit.; *U. S. S. YMS 36*, op. cit.

138. Broadhurst, op. cit.; Rhoads correspondence, op. cit.; *U. S. S. YMS 36*, op. cit.

139. *U.S.S. YMS 34*, op. cit.; *U. S. S. YMS 58*, op. cit.; *U. S. S. YMS 226*, op. cit.; *H. M. LST 425*, Action Report, Royal Navy Archives.

140. *U. S. S. YMS 3*, op. cit.; *U. S. S. YMS 58*, op. cit.; *U. S. S. LST 16*, op. cit.; *U. S. S. YMS 62*, op. cit.

141. Commander Mine Squadron 6 - Sweeper Operations Operation Shingle Jan. 21-30, 1944 - *Action Report - Feb. 8, 1944*, op. cit.; *U.S.S. YMS 34*, op. cit.; *U. S. S. YMS 207*, op. cit.; *U. S. S. YMS 226*, op. cit.; *U. S. S. YMS 58*, op. cit.

142. Eighty-Third (83rd) Chemical Mortar Battalion Journals, Battle Reports, Morning Reports: June 1943 – Nov. 1945.

143. *Ibid.*

144. *Ibid.*; Helsel, op. cit.

145. Eighty-Third (83rd) Chemical Mortar Battalion Journals, Battle Reports, Morning Reports: June 1943 – Nov. 1945, op. cit.; *U. S. S. YMS 226*, op. cit.; Cannetti, op. cit.; Charles Rolling, *Diary of the 83rd Chemical Mortar Battalion, Company A (In Action)*. (Courtesy Gini Lemoine and Elizabeth Daly); Hulcher, op. cit.; Helsel, op. cit.; *Mark Freedom Paid: A Combat Anthology*, pg. 63.

146. *U. S. S. YMS 207*, op. cit.; *U. S. S. PC 1227*, op. cit.; *U. S. S. YMS 29*, op. cit.; *U. S. S. YMS 83*, op. cit.; *U. S. S. SC 638*, op. cit.

147. First (1st), Third (3rd), and Fourth (4th) Ranger Battalions, op. cit.; Eighty-Third (83rd) Chemical Mortar Battalion Journals, Battle Reports, Morning Reports: June 1943 – Nov. 1945, op. cit.; *U. S. S. YMS 226*, op. cit.; Commander Mine Squadron 6 - Sweeper Operations Operation Shingle Jan. 21-30, 1944 - *Action Report - Feb. 8, 1944*, op. cit.

148. *U.S.S. YMS 34*, op. cit.; *YMS 226*, op. cit.

149. *U. S. S. Pilot*, op. cit.

150. Eighty-Third (83rd) Chemical Mortar Battalion Journals, Battle Reports, Morning Reports: June 1943 – Nov. 1945, op. cit.; *Muzzleblasts – Official newsletter of the 83rd Chemical Mortar Battalion 1944 – present*, op. cit.

151. Compiled from numerous casualty lists provided by the respective vessels and units. National Archives, College Park, MD.

152. *U. S. S. YMS 43*, op. cit.; *U. S. S. Strive*, op. cit.

153. *U. S. S. Pilot*, op. cit.

154. Eighty-Third (83rd) Chemical Mortar Battalion Journals, Battle Reports, Morning Reports: June 1943 – Nov. 1945, op. cit.; *H. M. LST 425*, op. cit.

155. *U.S.S. LCI 209*, op. cit.; *U. S. S. YMS 43*, op. cit.; *U. S. S. Strive*, op. cit.; *U. S. S. YMS 3*, op. cit.; *YMS 226*, op. cit.; *U. S. S. LST 383*, Deck Log, Jan. 1944, National Archives, College Park, MD; *U. S. S. YMS 62*, op. cit.; *U. S. S. YMS 43*, op. cit.

156. *U. S. S. YMS 3*, op. cit.; *U. S. S. YMS 36*, op. cit.; *U. S. S. Pilot*, op. cit.; *U. S. S. SC 522*, Action Report / Deck Log, Jan. 1944, National Archives, College Park, MD; *YMS 226*, op. cit.

157. *U. S. S. YMS 3*, op. cit.; *U. S. S. YMS 62*, op. cit.; *U. S. S. YMS 43*, op. cit.; Navy Mine Warfare Veterans Association Reunion, op. cit.; *LCI 10*, op. cit.; *U. S. S. Strive*, op. cit.; *U. S. S. LCI 32*, op. cit.; *MS 226*, op. cit.; *U. S. S. SC 522*, op. cit.; *U. S. S. YMS 69*, op. cit.; Shields, op. cit.; *U. S. S. LST 16*, op. cit.; *U. S. S. YMS 69*, op. cit.

158. *Muzzleblasts – Official newsletter of the 83rd Chemical Mortar Battalion 1944 – present*, op. cit. [Powell].

159. Eighty-Third (83rd) Chemical Mortar Battalion Journals, Battle Reports, Morning Reports: June 1943 – Nov. 1945, op. cit.; First (1st), Third (3rd), and Fourth (4th) Ranger Battalions, After Action Reports / Unit Journals, op. cit.; Helsel, op. cit.

160. Eighty-Third (83rd) Chemical Mortar Battalion Journals, Battle Reports, Morning Reports: June 1943 – Nov. 1945, op. cit.; Helsel, op. cit.

161. Eighty-Third (83rd) Chemical Mortar Battalion Journals, Battle Reports, Morning Reports: June 1943 – Nov. 1945, op. cit.; First (1st), Third (3rd), and Fourth (4th) Ranger Battalions. After Action Reports / Unit Journals, op. cit.; Hulcher, op. cit.

162. Eighty-Third (83rd) Chemical Mortar Battalion Journals, Battle Reports, Morning Reports: June 1943 – Nov. 1945, op. cit.; First (1st), Third (3rd), and Fourth (4th) Ranger Battalions. After Action Reports / Unit Journals, op. cit.

Chapter Nine

1. Eighty-Third (83rd) Chemical Mortar Battalion Journals, Battle Reports, Morning Reports: June 1943 – Nov. 1945, National Archives, College Park, MD; James G. Helsel, *Diary of James G. Helsel, Co. A, 83rd Chemical Mortar Battalion*, (Courtesy Joyce Berry, Lebanon, TN).

2. First (1st), Third (3rd), and Fourth (4th) Ranger Battalions. After Action Reports / Unit Journals. National Archives, College Park, MD; Eighty-Third (83rd) Chemical Mortar Battalion Journals, Battle Reports, Morning Reports: June 1943 – Nov. 1945, op. cit.; Helsel, op. cit.

3. Rupert O. Burford, *Foreign Service Memoirs – Diary of Rupert O. Burford* [Co. C - 83rd CMB]. (Unpublished), Charleston, WV, n.d., Author's Collection, (Used by permission of Mrs. Rupert O. Burford).

4. Eighty-Third (83rd) Chemical Mortar Battalion Journals, Battle Reports, Morning Reports: June 1943 – Nov. 1945, op. cit.

5. First (1st), Third (3rd), and Fourth (4th) Ranger Battalions. After Action Reports / Unit Journals, op. cit.; Eighty-Third (83rd) Chemical Mortar Battalion Journals, Battle Reports, Morning Reports: June 1943 – Nov. 1945, op. cit.; Samuel M. Bundy, Jr., *Co. A - 83rd Cml. Mortar Bn.*, (diary & record of events kept by Samuel Bundy from Camp Gordon through Sept. 22, 1945) – (approved by Samuel M. Bundy, Jr. 1984) - [Courtesy Lee Steedle].

6. Eighty-Third (83rd) Chemical Mortar Battalion Journals, Battle Reports, Morning Reports: June 1943 – Nov. 1945, op. cit.; Bundy, op. cit.; Joseph E. Cannetti, *War Experiences of Joseph E. Cannetti, Co. A, 83rd Chemical Mortar Battalion*, (Courtesy Joseph E. Cannetti).

7. Correspondence with Malcolm Doyle Wilkinson (Author's Collection).

8. Leech, Dewey C., and William D. McCain (ed.), *The WW II Experiences of Andrew Candler Leech 1943-1945*, (Hattiesburg, MS, 1985), pg. 24.

9. Eighty-Third (83rd) Chemical Mortar Battalion Journals, Battle Reports, Morning Reports: June 1943 – Nov. 1945, op. cit.; . First (1st), Third (3rd), and Fourth (4th) Ranger Battalions. After Action Reports / Unit Journals, op. cit.; Charles Rolling, *Diary of the 83rd Chemical Mortar Battalion, Company A (In Action)*. (Courtesy Gini Lemoine and Elizabeth Daly).

10. Leech, op. cit.; Eighty-Third (83rd) Chemical Mortar Battalion Journals, Battle Reports, Morning Reports: June 1943 – Nov. 1945, op. cit.

11. Eighty-Third (83rd) Chemical Mortar Battalion Journals, Battle Reports, Morning Reports: June 1943 – Nov. 1945, op. cit.; . First (1st), Third (3rd), and Fourth (4th) Ranger Battalions. After Action Reports / Unit Journals, op. cit.

12. *Ibid.*

13. Eighty-Third (83rd) Chemical Mortar Battalion Journals, Battle Reports, Morning Reports: June 1943 – Nov. 1945, op. cit.

14. Capt. (Dr.) Julius C. Hulcher, *Diary of Capt. Julius C. Hulcher 1943 - 1945, Medical Detachment*, 83rd Chemical Mortar Battalion, [Courtesy Charles Hulcher, Glen Allen, VA] [hereafter cited as Hulcher].

15. Eighty-Third (83rd) Chemical Mortar Battalion Journals, Battle Reports, Morning Reports: June 1943 – Nov. 1945, op. cit.

16. Eighty-Third (83rd) Chemical Mortar Battalion Journals, Battle Reports, Morning Reports: June 1943 – Nov. 1945, op. cit.; Robert E. Edwards, *V-Mail & Correspondence of Robert E. Edwards, HQ Co, 83rd Chemical Mortar Battalion*, (Courtesy Wendy Edwards).

17. Edwin Pike, *V-Mail & Correspondence of Capt. Edwin G. Pike 1941 - 1945 - Co. D, 83rd Chemical Mortar Battalion*, (Courtesy Marcia Bunker).

18. Eighty-Third (83rd) Chemical Mortar Battalion Journals, Battle Reports, Morning Reports: June 1943 – Nov. 1945, op. cit.

19. Edward L. Trey, Personal Correspondence and Interviews with Terry Lowry 2003-2008, (Author's Collection).

20. Pike, op. cit.

21. Burford, op. cit.; Hulcher, op. cit.

22. Burford, op. cit.

23. Helsel, op. cit.; Leech, op. cit., pg. 25; Hulcher, op. cit.

24. Helsel, op. cit; Cannetti, op. cit.

25. Hulcher, op. cit.

26. Pike, op. cit.

27. Eighty-Third (83rd) Chemical Mortar Battalion Journals, Battle Reports, Morning Reports: June 1943 – Nov. 1945, op. cit.

28. Stephen W. Vukson, *Diary of Stephen W. Vukson*, HQ Co., 83rd Chemical Mortar Battalion - Dec. 1943 - 1945, (Courtesy Stephen W. Vukson).

29. Pike, op. cit.

30. Vukson, op. cit.; Charlie Lowry, *V-Mail & Correspondence 1943-45 - Co. D / Co. A, 83rd Chemical Mortar Battalion*, (Author's Collection); Edwards, op. cit.

31. Eighty-Third (83rd) Chemical Mortar Battalion Journals, Battle Reports, Morning Reports: June 1943 – Nov. 1945, op. cit.; Burford, op. cit.

32. Eighty-Third (83rd) Chemical Mortar Battalion Journals, Battle Reports, Morning Reports: June 1943 – Nov. 1945, op. cit

33. Helsel. op. cit.

34. Leech, op. cit., pg. 26.

35. Eighty-Third (83rd) Chemical Mortar Battalion Journals, Battle Reports, Morning Reports: June 1943 – Nov. 1945, op. cit.; Pike, op. cit.; Personal Conversations between Gordon Mindrum and author, 2005-2006; Personal Interview with Nolan McCraine & author, 2007.

36. Leech, op. cit., pg. 26.

37. Eighty-Third (83rd) Chemical Mortar Battalion Journals, Battle Reports, Morning Reports: June 1943 – Nov. 1945, op. cit.

38. Bundy, op. cit.

39. Eighty-Third (83rd) Chemical Mortar Battalion Journals, Battle Reports, Morning Reports: June 1943 – Nov. 1945, op. cit.

40. Hayes, Veryl R., "*Psych A – For Platoon Leaders*", Chemical Warfare Service Bulletin, Vol. 30 – No. 5 (Nov. - Dec. 1944).

41. Bundy, op. cit.; William S. Hutchinson, *Interview With Col. William S. Hutchinson*, CWS, Edgewood Arsenal, MD – Jan. 26, 1945. Edgewood Arsenal Archives; Hutchinson, William S., Jr., "*The Forgotten Front*", Chemical Warfare Service Bulletin #31, (Jan.- Feb. 1945).

42. Eighty-Third (83rd) Chemical Mortar Battalion Journals, Battle Reports, Morning Reports: June 1943 – Nov. 1945, op. cit.

43. Leech, op. cit., pg. 27; Eighty-Third (83rd) Chemical Mortar Battalion Journals, Battle Reports, Morning Reports: June 1943 – Nov. 1945, op. cit.

44. Brimm, Robert, *Rounds Away: Two Years of Combat With The Eighty-Third Chemical Mortar Battalion*, (Innsbruck, Austria, 1945) (Illustrated by Sam Kweskin - maps by Eugene Plassmann); Helsel, op. cit.

45. Hulcher, op. cit.

46. Eighty-Third (83rd) Chemical Mortar Battalion Journals, Battle Reports, Morning Reports: June 1943 – Nov. 1945, op. cit.

47. *Ibid.*

48. *Ibid.*

49. Eighty-Third (83rd) Chemical Mortar Battalion Journals, Battle Reports, Morning Reports: June 1943 – Nov. 1945, op. cit.; Lowry, op. cit.

50. Pike, op. cit.

51. Burford, op. cit.; Edwards, op. cit.; Lowry, op. cit.

52. Helsel, op. cit.

53. Burford, op. cit.; Vukson, op. cit.

54. Eighty-Third (83rd) Chemical Mortar Battalion Journals, Battle Reports, Morning Reports: June 1943 – Nov. 1945, op. cit.

55. Hays, op. cit.

56. Burford, op. cit.; Vukson, op. cit.

57. Vukson, op. cit.

58. Pike, op. cit.

59. Burford, op. cit.; Vukson, op. cit.

60. Vukson, op. cit.

61. William S. Hutchinson. *Personal Correspondence from Col. William S. Hutchinson to Kenneth A. Cunin 1943 -1944*. Fifteen Letters. Chemical Corps Museum Archives, Ft. Leonard Wood, MO.

62. Lowry, op. cit.; Hotchner, A. E., *Sophia: Living and Loving: Her Own Story*, (William Morrow and Company, Inc., 1979), pp. 46-47; James Marion Lester, *James Marion Lester's Story*, (unpublished manuscript interview), by Vicki S. Hibma, June 26, 1984; Correspondence with James & Iris Lester (Author's Collection); Lowry, op. cit.

63. Pike, op. cit.; Burford, op. cit.; Hotchner, op. cit.

64. Burford, op. cit.

65. Wilkinson, op. cit.

66. Burford, op. cit.; Eighty-Third (83rd) Chemical Mortar Battalion Journals, Battle Reports, Morning Reports: June 1943 – Nov. 1945, op. cit.

67. Bernard Bernhardt (Co. C, 83rd Chemical Mortar Battalion), *Correspondence With Terry Lowry*, (Author's Collection); William J. Gagliardi (Co. A, 83rd Chemical Mortar Battalion), *Correspondence With Terry Lowry*, (Author's Collection); Lester, op. cit.

68. Vukson, op. cit.; Pike, op. cit.

69. Helsel, op. cit.

70. Hulcher, op. cit.

71. *Ibid.*

72. Burford, op. cit.; Vukson, op. cit.

73. Eighty-Third (83rd) Chemical Mortar Battalion Journals, Battle Reports, Morning Reports: June 1943 – Nov. 1945, op. cit.; Gagliardi, op. cit.

74. Edwards, op. cit.

75. Hulcher, op. cit.

76. Pike, op. cit.

77. Eighty-Third (83rd) Chemical Mortar Battalion Journals, Battle Reports, Morning Reports: June 1943 – Nov. 1945, op. cit.

78. Hulcher, op. cit.; Helsel, op. cit.; Correspondence with Bryan Turan regarding his father, Leonard Turan, (Author's Collection).

79. Hotchner, op. cit.

80. Eighty-Third (83rd) Chemical Mortar Battalion Journals, Battle Reports, Morning Reports: June 1943 – Nov. 1945, op. cit.; Lester, op. cit.

81. Hale H. Hepler, *Hale Hunter Hepler – World War II Veteran*, (dictated to his daughter Pam Pace June 2005) [Courtesy Hale H. Hepler & Pam Pace]; Kelly Seibels. *A Wartime Log* (Minturno to Briançon, Co. C, 83rd Chemical Mortar Battalion), (Courtesy Kelly Seibels and Kelly Seibels, Jr.).

82. Lee Steedle, *Nights and Days With the 83rd Chemical Mortar Battalion* (Unpublished Memoir), Oakdale, NY, 1990, Author's Collection, (Used by permission of Lee Steedle); Steedle, Lee (ed.), *Mark Freedom Paid: A Combat Anthology*, (Jeanette, PA: 83rd Chemical Mortar Battalion Veterans Association, 1997) (Illustrated by Sam Kweskin), pg. 41.

83. Seibels, op. cit.; Bernhardt, op. cit. *Mark Freedom Paid: A Combat Anthology*, op. cit.

84. *Mark Freedom Paid: A Combat Anthology*, op. cit.

85. Eighty-Third (83rd) Chemical Mortar Battalion Journals, Battle Reports, Morning Reports: June 1943 – Nov. 1945, op. cit.

86. Schneider, Dick (ed.), *Harold E. Hughes: The Man From Ida Grove*, (Chosen Books Pub., 1979), pg. 62.

87. Personal Interview with Curtis A. Williams and Terry Lowry, 2006.

88. Hulcher, op. cit.; Pike, op. cit.; Helsel, op. cit.

89. Hulcher, op. cit.; Steedle, op. cit.

90. Burford, op. cit.; Edwards, op. cit.; Trey, op. cit.

91. Lowry, op. cit.; Lawrence Ertzberger, *Correspondence With Terry Lowry*, (Author's Collection); 83rd Chemical Mortar Bn. Veterans Association, *Rounds Away: World War II Experiences As Told By Fifteen Combat Veterans of the 83rd Chemical Mortar Battalion*, (Jeanette, PA 1999 – compiled by Lee Steedle and Sam Kweskin) – [interview with Lawrence Ertzberger].

92. Hulcher, op. cit.; Bundy, op. cit.

93. Eighty-Third (83rd) Chemical Mortar Battalion Journals, Battle Reports, Morning Reports: June 1943 – Nov. 1945, op. cit.

94. Signal Corps Photo Collection, National Archives, College Park, MD; Hulcher, op. cit.

95. Hulcher, op. cit.; Hays, op. cit.

96. Eighty-Third (83rd) Chemical Mortar Battalion Journals, Battle Reports, Morning Reports: June 1943 – Nov. 1945, op. cit.

97. Hulcher, op. cit.; Pike, op. cit.

98. Annette Smith (ed.), *Rounds Away: Letters From World War II and the 83rd Chemical Mortar Battalion*, [Letters of Capt. Robert B. Smith, Co. C, 83rd Chemical Mortar Battalion] – Truth or Consequences, NM: 1987 – limited printing; Byron H. Jordan, *V-Mail of Byron H. Jordan 1943-1945*, (Courtesy Byron H. Jordan).

99. Eighty-Third (83rd) Chemical Mortar Battalion Journals, Battle Reports, Morning Reports: June 1943 – Nov. 1945, op. cit.; Steedle, op. cit.

100. Hulcher, op. cit.; Seibels, op. cit.; Vukson, op. cit.

101. Hulcher, op. cit.; Mario Ricci, Personal Experiences In Letter to Terry Lowry, San Mateo, CA, June 2004; Mario Ricci, Personal Experiences Written for Silvano Casaldi, Nettuno, Italy, July 1998, San Mateo, CA.

102. Daniel J. Shields, *Diary of Daniel J. Shields, Co. D & HQ Co., 83rd Chemical Mortar Battalion, 1942-1945*, (Courtesy Jean Decky); Paul S. Giles, *Correspondence With Terry Lowry*, (Author's Collection); Ricci, op. cit.; Bernhardt, op. cit.

103. Lester, op. cit.

104. Ricci, op. cit.

105. Lester, op. cit.

106. Shields, op. cit.; Hulcher, op. cit.

107. Eldredge, Walter J., *Finding My Father's War: A Baby Boomer and the 2nd Chemical Mortar Battalion in World War II*, (PageFree Publishing, Inc., Ostego, MI, 2004), pp. 162-163.

108. *Ibid.*

109. *Ibid.*

110. *Ibid.*

111. Pike, op. cit.

112. Hulcher, op. cit.; Eighty-Third (83rd) Chemical Mortar Battalion Journals, Battle Reports, Morning Reports: June 1943 – Nov. 1945, op. cit.

113. Hulcher, op. cit.; Eighty-Third (83rd) Chemical Mortar Battalion. Co. D. Morning Reports/Unit Journal 1942-1944, (Courtesy Mike Codega and Sam Kweskin).

114. Smith, op. cit.

115. Lee Steedle, *Collection (V-Mail)*, Oakdale, NY, (Used by permission of Lee Steedle).

116. Hulcher, op. cit.; Hutchinson, op. cit.

117. Steedle, op. cit.; Smith, op. cit.

118. Hulcher, op. cit.; Pike, op. cit.; Lowry, op. cit.

119. Pike, op. cit.; Eighty-Third (83rd) Chemical Mortar Battalion Journals, Battle Reports, Morning Reports: June 1943 – Nov. 1945, op. cit.; Burford, op. cit.

120. Martin J. Moloney, *Correspondence With Terry Lowry*, (Author's Collection); Hulcher, op. cit.

121. Eighty-Third (83rd) Chemical Mortar Battalion Journals, Battle Reports, Morning Reports: June 1943 – Nov. 1945, op. cit.; Shields, op. cit.; Hulcher, op. cit.

122. Hulcher, op. cit.

123. Smith, op. cit.; Dale C. Blank (Co. C, 83rd Chemical Mortar Battalion), *Correspondence With Terry Lowry*, (Author's Collection).

124. Blank, op. cit.

125. Eighty-Third (83rd) Chemical Mortar Battalion Journals, Battle Reports, Morning Reports: June 1943 – Nov. 1945, op. cit.

126. *Ibid.*

127. Eighty-Third (83rd) Chemical Mortar Battalion Journals, Battle Reports, Morning Reports: June 1943 – Nov. 1945, op. cit.; Giles, op. cit.

128. Eighty-Third (83rd) Chemical Mortar Battalion Journals, Battle Reports, Morning Reports: June 1943 – Nov. 1945, op. cit.

129. Ricci, op. cit.

130. Bernhardt, op. cit.

131. Kelso (Red) Thompson, (Co. D/Co. A, 83rd Chemical Mortar Battalion), Personal Interviews and Correspondence, (Author's Collection); Personal Conversation with Charlie Lowry, 83rd Chemical Mortar Battalion, (Author's Collection).

132. Eighty-Third (83rd) Chemical Mortar Battalion Journals, Battle Reports, Morning Reports: June 1943 – Nov. 1945, op. cit.

133. Hulcher, op. cit.; Pike, op. cit.

134. Hulcher, op. cit.; Robert Bush, *Army Officer's Notebook* (diary) & Photograph Collection. Courtesy Lt. Robert Bush, Co. A, 83rd Chemical Mortar Battalion.

135. Hulcher, op. cit.; Eighty-Third (83rd) Chemical Mortar Battalion Journals, Battle Reports, Morning Reports: June 1943 – Nov. 1945, op. cit.

136. Smith, op. cit.; Hulcher, op. cit.

137. *Muzzleblasts* – Official newsletter of the 83rd Chemical Mortar Battalion 1944 – present [Rice].

138. Helsel, op. cit.; Tillman, op. cit.; Hulcher, op. cit.

139. Pike, op. cit.

140. Smith, op. cit.

141. Eighty-Third (83rd) Chemical Mortar Battalion Journals, Battle Reports, Morning Reports: June 1943 – Nov. 1945, op. cit.

142. Eighty-Third (83rd) Chemical Mortar Battalion Journals, Battle Reports, Morning Reports: June 1943 – Nov. 1945, op. cit.; Smith, op. cit.

143. Eighty-Third (83rd) Chemical Mortar Battalion Journals, Battle Reports, Morning Reports: June 1943 – Nov. 1945, op. cit.; Eighty-Third (83rd) Chemical Mortar Battalion. Co. D. Morning Reports/Unit Journal 1942-1944, op. cit.

144. Pike, op. cit.

145. Vukson, op. cit.

146. Steedle, op. cit.

147. Smith, op. cit.; Ford, William Clifford, *Never Forget – A Soldier's Battlefield Memoirs*, op. cit., pg. 63; *Muzzleblasts* – Official newsletter of the 83rd Chemical Mortar Battalion 1944 – present [Barrett]; Steedle, op. cit.

148. Eighty-Third (83rd) Chemical Mortar Battalion. Co. D. Morning Reports/Unit Journal 1942-1944, op. cit.; Ford, op. cit., pg. 64.

149. *Ibid.*

150. Hulcher, op. cit.

151. Loy J. Marshall, *Assorted Personal Experiences in the War*, (Courtesy Tricia Bridges).

152. Hulcher, op. cit.

153. *Ibid.*

154. Pike, op. cit.

155. Pike, op. cit.; Hulcher, op. cit.; Joseph A. Williamson, *Personal Interview with Joseph A. Williamson and Son*, Co. C, 83rd Chemical Mortar Battalion, (Author's Collection).

156. Helsel, op. cit.

157. Vukson, op. cit.

158. *Ibid.*

159. Eighty-Third (83rd) Chemical Mortar Battalion Journals, Battle Reports, Morning Reports: June 1943 – Nov. 1945, op. cit.

160. *Ibid.*

161. *Ibid.*

162. Hulcher, op. cit.

163. *Ibid.*

164. Helsel, op. cit.

165. Hulcher, op. cit.; McCraine, op. cit.

166. Hulcher, op. cit.

167. John P. McEvoy, *Many Years Later*, (unpublished speech), n.d., (Author's Collection).

168. Leech, op. cit., pg. 29.

169. Cannetti, op. cit.

170. McEvoy, op. cit.

171. Interview with Vicente De Leon, Medic, Co. C, 83rd Chemical Mortar Battalion; Hulcher, op. cit.; Seibels, op. cit.; Blank, op. cit.

172. Eighty-Third (83rd) Chemical Mortar Battalion Journals, Battle Reports, Morning Reports: June 1943 – Nov. 1945, op. cit.; Hulcher, op. cit.

173. Hulcher, op. cit.; Pike, op. cit.; Seibels, op. cit.

174. Eighty-Third (83rd) Chemical Mortar Battalion Journals, Battle Reports, Morning Reports: June 1943 – Nov. 1945, op. cit.

175. Vukson, op. cit.

176. Moloney, op. cit.

177. Author's Correspondence with Dave Dougherty, Ft. Collins, CO, Regarding James Dougherty, Co. D, 83rd Chemical Mortar Battalion (Author's Collection); Pike, op. cit.; Hulcher, op. cit.

178. Thompson, op. cit.

179. Hulcher, op. cit.; Smith, op. cit.

180. Hulcher, op. cit.

181. Pike, op. cit.

182. *Ibid.*

183. Hulcher, op. cit.; Smith, op. cit.; Bush, op. cit.; Jordan, op. cit.; Lowry, op. cit.

184. Hulcher, op. cit.

185. Eighty-Third (83rd) Chemical Mortar Battalion Journals, Battle Reports, Morning Reports: June 1943 – Nov. 1945, op. cit.

186. Bush, op. cit.

187. Eighty-Third (83rd) Chemical Mortar Battalion Journals, Battle Reports, Morning Reports: June 1943 – Nov. 1945, op. cit.

188. Blank, op. cit.

189. Obituary for Sam Efnor, Jr., *Salt Lake Tribune*, Aug. 2002; Eldredge, Walter J., *Finding My Father's War: A Baby Boomer and the 2nd Chemical Mortar Battalion in World War II*, (PageFree Publishing, Inc., Ostego, MI, 2004); John P. McEvoy, *Correspondence With Terry Lowry*. Author's Collection; William S. Hutchinson, *Personal Correspondence from Col. William S. Hutchinson to Kenneth A. Cunin 1943 -1944*. Fifteen Letters. Chemical Corps Museum Archives, Ft. Leonard Wood, MO; Edward L. Trey, Personal Correspondence and Interviews with Terry Lowry 2003-2008, (Author's Collection); Pike, op. cit. Hulcher, op. cit.

190. Eighty-Third (83rd) Chemical Mortar Battalion Journals, Battle Reports, Morning Reports: June 1943 – Nov. 1945, op. cit.

191. Hutchinson, op. cit.

192. Hulcher, op. cit.; Cannetti, op. cit.; Vukson, op. cit.

193. Smith, op. cit.

194. Hulcher, op. cit.; Pike, op. cit.; Smith, op. cit.

195. Eighty-Third (83rd) Chemical Mortar Battalion Journals, Battle Reports, Morning Reports: June 1943 – Nov. 1945, op. cit.

196. Smith, op. cit.

197. Lee Steedle, *Collection (V-Mail)*, Oakdale, NY, (Used by permission of Lee Steedle).

198. Hulcher, op. cit.; Rolling, op. cit.

199. Andrew C, Leech, *V-Mail Letter of July 12, 1944*, Co. B, 83rd Chemical Mortar Battalion, (Courtesy Alice Hartley).

200. Eighty-Third (83rd) Chemical Mortar Battalion Journals, Battle Reports, Morning Reports: June 1943 – Nov. 1945, op. cit.; First (1st) Airborne Task Force - Records - National Archives, College Park, MD; Raymond J. Lakey. *Report: 4.2 Inch Mortar Airborne Company*, Oct. 15, 1944. Edgewood Arsenal Archives; Devlin, Gerard M., *Silent Wings: The Saga of the U.S. Army and Marine Combat Glider Pilots During World War II*, (St. Martin's Press, New York, NY: 1985); *Mark Freedom Paid: A Combat Anthology*, op. cit., pp. 71-72 (Rice).

201. Seibels, op. cit.; Pike, op. cit.

202. Pike, op. cit.

203. *Ibid.*

204. Smith, op. cit.

205. Eighty-Third (83rd) Chemical Mortar Battalion Journals, Battle Reports, Morning Reports: June 1943 – Nov. 1945, op. cit.

Chapter Ten

1. Eighty-Third (83rd) Chemical Mortar Battalion Journals, Battle Reports, Morning Reports: June 1943 – Nov. 1945, National Archives, College Park, MD; Annette Smith (ed.), *Rounds Away: Letters From World War II and the 83rd Chemical Mortar Battalion*, [Letters of Capt. Robert B. Smith, Co. C, 83rd Chemical Mortar Battalion] – Truth or Consequences, NM: 1987 – limited printing.

2. Eighty-Third (83rd) Chemical Mortar Battalion Journals, Battle Reports, Morning Reports: June 1943 – Nov. 1945, op. cit.; Edwin Pike, *V-Mail & Correspondence of Capt. Edwin G. Pike 1941 - 1945 - Co. D, 83rd Chemical Mortar Battalion*, (Courtesy Marcia Bunker).

3. Lee Steedle (ed.), *Mark Freedom Paid: A Combat Anthology*, (Jeanette, PA: 83rd Chemical Mortar Battalion Veterans Association, 1997) (Illustrated by Sam Kweskin), pg. 72 (Lee Steedle); *Muzzleblasts* – Official newsletter of the 83rd Chemical Mortar Battalion 1944 – present [Zickler]; Robert Bush, *Army Officer's Notebook* (diary) & Photograph Collection. Courtesy Lt. Robert Bush, Co. A, 83rd Chemical Mortar Battalion; James G. Helsel, *Diary of James G. Helsel, Co. A, 83rd Chemical Mortar Battalion*, (Courtesy Joyce Berry, Lebanon, TN).

4. Eighty-Third (83rd) Chemical Mortar Battalion Journals, Battle Reports, Morning Reports: June 1943 – Nov. 1945, op. cit.; *U.S.S. Lyon*, War Diary, June 10-12, 1943 & Deck Log Aug. 1944, National Archives, College Park, MD; Helsel, op. cit; Ford, William Clifford, *Never Forget – A Soldier's Battlefield Memoirs*, (Network Printing, New Albany, MS, 2005) – [Co. C, 83rd Chemical Mortar Battalion], pg. 65.

5. *LST 690* - Deck Log - Passenger List - Co. A, 83rd Chemical Battalion - Aug. 9, 1944 - National Archives, College Park, MD; Capt. (Dr.) Julius C. Hulcher, *Diary of Capt. Julius C. Hulcher 1943 - 1945*, Medical Detachment, 83rd Chemical Mortar Battalion, [Courtesy Charles Hulcher, Glen Allen, VA] [hereafter cited as Hulcher].

6. First (1st) Airborne Task Force - Records - National Archives, College Park, MD.

7. Kelly Seibels. *A Wartime Log* (Minturno to Briançon, Co. C, 83rd Chemical Mortar Battalion), (Courtesy Kelly Seibels and Kelly Seibels, Jr.); Bush, op. cit.; Charles Rolling, *Diary of the 83rd Chemical Mortar Battalion, Company A (In Action)*. (Courtesy Gini Lemoine and Elizabeth Daly); Co. D. Morning Reports/Unit Journal 1942-1944, (Courtesy Mike Codega and Sam Kweskin).

8. Eighty-Third (83rd) Chemical Mortar Battalion Journals, Battle Reports, Morning Reports: June 1943 – Nov. 1945, op. cit.; Edward L. Trey, Personal Correspondence and Interviews with Terry Lowry 2003-2008, (Author's Collection).

9. Co. D. Morning Reports/Unit Journal 1942-1944, op. cit.; Five-Hundred and Seventeenth (517th) Parachute Inf. RCT, Operations Report, Aug. 1944, National Archives, College Park, MD; Lee Steedle, *Nights and Days With the 83rd Chemical Mortar Battalion* (Unpublished Memoir), Oakdale, NY, 1990, Author's Collection, (Used by permission of Lee Steedle); Steedle, Lee (ed.), *Mark Freedom Paid: A Combat Anthology*, op. cit., pg. 73.

10. Devlin, Gerard M., *Silent Wings: The Saga of the U.S. Army and Marine Combat Glider Pilots During World War II*, (St. Martin's Press, New York, NY: 1985), pg. 218; Karl Garrett, *Memories 1942-1945*, (HQ Co., 83rd Chemical Mortar Battalion), [n.d.], [Courtesy Karl Garrett, Richmond, VA].

11. Eighty-Third (83rd) Chemical Mortar Battalion Journals, Battle Reports, Morning Reports: June 1943 – Nov. 1945, op. cit.

12. Leech, Dewey C., and William D. McCain (ed.), *The WW II Experiences of Andrew Candler Leech 1943-1945*, (Hattiesburg, MS, 1985), pg. 33.

13. Samuel M. Bundy, Jr., *Co. A - 83rd Cml. Mortar Bn.*, (diary & record of events kept by Samuel Bundy from Camp Gordon through Sept. 22, 1945) – (approved by Samuel M. Bundy, Jr. 1984) - [Courtesy Lee Steedle].

14. First (1st) Airborne Task Force – Records, op. cit.; Raymond J. Lakey. *Report: 4.2 Inch Mortar Airborne Company*, Oct. 15, 1944. Edgewood Arsenal Archives; Devlin, Gerard M., *Silent Wings: The Saga of the U.S. Army and Marine Combat Glider Pilots During World War II*, op. cit.; Five-Hundred and Seventeenth (517th) Parachute Inf. RCT, Operations Report, Aug. 1944, op. cit.

15. First (1st) Airborne Task Force – Records, op. cit.; Devlin, Gerard M., *Silent Wings: The Saga of the U.S. Army and Marine Combat Glider Pilots During World War II*, op. cit., pg. 218.

16. Co. D. Morning Reports/Unit Journal 1942-1944, op. cit.; First (1st) Airborne Task Force – Records, op. cit.; *Muzzleblasts* – Official newsletter of the 83rd Chemical Mortar Battalion 1944 – present [Kelso Thompson]; Author's Interview and Correspondence with Lee Steedle 2003-2008 (Author's Collection); Steedle, Lee (ed.), *Mark Freedom Paid: A Combat Anthology*, op. cit., pg. 73.

17. Eighty-Third (83rd) Chemical Mortar Battalion Journals, Battle Reports, Morning Reports: June 1943 – Nov. 1945, op. cit.; William C. Ford, *Lest We Forget*, (Memoir by Staff Sgt. William C. Ford, Co. C, 83rd CMB), [Courtesy Gini Lemoine]: Seibels, op. cit.

18. Author's Interviews and Correspondence with Robert J. Bush 2003-2006 (Author's Collection);

19. Steedle, Lee (ed.), *Mark Freedom Paid: A Combat Anthology*, op. cit., pg. 73; Joseph E. Cannetti, *War Experiences of Joseph E. Cannetti, Co. A, 83rd Chemical Mortar Battalion*, (Courtesy Joseph E. Cannetti).

20. Steedle, Lee (ed.), *Mark Freedom Paid: A Combat Anthology*, op. cit., pg. 75.

21. Eighty-Third (83rd) Chemical Mortar Battalion Journals, Battle Reports, Morning Reports: June 1943 – Nov. 1945, op. cit.; Co. D. Morning Reports/Unit Journal 1942-1944, op. cit.

22. Steedle, Lee (ed.), *Mark Freedom Paid: A Combat Anthology*, op. cit., pp. 75-78.

23. James H. Gallahan, Sr., *Military Service of James H. Gallahan, Sr.* - World War II, [Courtesy Roger Gallahan, Quinton, VA].

24. Kelso (Red) Thompson, (Co. D/Co. A, 83rd Chemical Mortar Battalion), Personal Interviews and Correspondence, (Author's Collection); Correspondence with James & Iris Lester (Author's Collection); Author's Correspondence with Kenneth Hopkins 2005-2008 (Author's Collection).

25. Devlin, Gerard M., *Silent Wings: The Saga of the U.S. Army and Marine Combat Glider Pilots During World War II*, op. cit., pg. 226.

26. First (1st) Airborne Task Force – Records, op. cit.

27. *Ibid.*

28. Co. D. Morning Reports/Unit Journal 1942-1944, op. cit.

29. Eighty-Third (83rd) Chemical Mortar Battalion Journals, Battle Reports, Morning Reports: June 1943 – Nov. 1945, op. cit.; Ford, William Clifford, *Never Forget – A Soldier's Battlefield Memoirs*, op. cit., pg. 71.

30. Co. D. Morning Reports/Unit Journal 1942-1944, op. cit.; Steedle, Lee (ed.), *Mark Freedom Paid: A Combat Anthology*, op. cit., pg. 78.

31. First (1st) Airborne Task Force – Records, op. cit.; *Muzzleblasts* – Official newsletter of the 83rd Chemical Mortar Battalion 1944 – present [Kelso Thompson].

32. Eighty-Third (83rd) Chemical Mortar Battalion Journals, Battle Reports, Morning Reports: June 1943 – Nov. 1945, op. cit.; Bundy, op. cit.; Rolling, op. cit.; Helsel, op. cit.

33. Eighty-Third (83rd) Chemical Mortar Battalion Journals, Battle Reports, Morning Reports: June 1943 – Nov. 1945, op. cit.; Co. D. Morning Reports/Unit Journal 1942-1944, op. cit.

34. *Ibid.*

35. *Ibid.*

36. Eighty-Third (83rd) Chemical Mortar Battalion Journals, Battle Reports, Morning Reports: June 1943 – Nov. 1945, op. cit.; Leech, Dewey C., and William D. McCain (ed.), *The WW II Experiences of Andrew Candler Leech 1943-1945*, op. cit., pg. 84; *Muzzleblasts* – Official newsletter of the 83rd Chemical Mortar Battalion 1944 – present [Endlein]; Author's Correspondence with David Bishop 2003-2008 (Author's Collection).

37. Eighty-Third (83rd) Chemical Mortar Battalion Journals, Battle Reports, Morning Reports: June 1943 – Nov. 1945, op. cit.; Eleventh (11th) Chemical Maintenance Company, Unit Journals, National Archives, College Park, MD; Edward L. Trey, Personal Correspondence and Interviews with Terry Lowry 2003-2008, op. cit.

38. Eighty-Third (83rd) Chemical Mortar Battalion Journals, Battle Reports, Morning Reports: June 1943 – Nov. 1945, op. cit.

39. *Ibid.*

40. Smith, op. cit.

41. Eighty-Third (83rd) Chemical Mortar Battalion Journals, Battle Reports, Morning Reports: June 1943 – Nov. 1945, op. cit.

42. *Ibid.*

43. *Ibid.*

44. *Ibid.*

45. Task Force Bibo, Aug. 27 - Sept. 2, 1944. Records of the 6th Corps. National Archives, College Park, MD; Eighty-Third (83rd) Chemical Mortar Battalion Journals, Battle Reports, Morning Reports: June 1943 – Nov. 1945, op. cit.

46. Bundy, op. cit.

47. Eighty-Third (83rd) Chemical Mortar Battalion Journals, Battle Reports, Morning Reports: June 1943 – Nov. 1945, op. cit.; Leech, op. cit, pg. 34; Seibels, op. cit.

48. Co. D. Morning Reports/Unit Journal 1942-1944, op. cit.

49. Eighty-Third (83rd) Chemical Mortar Battalion Journals, Battle Reports, Morning Reports: June 1943 – Nov. 1945, op. cit.

50. Task Force Bibo, Aug. 27 - Sept. 2, 1944. Records of the 6th Corps, op. cit.; Eighty-Third (83rd) Chemical Mortar Battalion Journals, Battle Reports, Morning Reports: June 1943 – Nov. 1945, op. cit.; Paul Bailey, *From Rookie to Kriegie 1943 - 1945*, (180th Infantry, AT Squad). Personal Memoir. (Courtesy Paul Bailey). Dale C. Blank, *The True Story of Briançon*, [written 2006 by Dale C. Blank, Co. C, 83rd Chemical Mortar Battalion - original copy in author's collection]; Seibels, op. cit.

51. Jean Pierre Combe [Honorary Member, Co. C, 83rd Chemical Mortar Battalion], Personal Correspondence With Terry Lowry 2003-2007 (Author's Collection).

52. Ford, William Clifford, *Never Forget – A Soldier's Battlefield Memoirs*, op. cit., pg. 73; Steedle, Lee (ed.), *Mark Freedom Paid: A Combat Anthology*, op. cit., pg. 83.

53. Combe, op. cit.

54. John L. Boyd, *Recollections of Briançon*, (with report written Sept. 14, 1944), [John L. Boyd, Co. C, 83rd Chemical Mortar Battalion - June 29, 1994 – Courtesy Gini Lemoine].

55. Task Force Bibo, Aug. 27 - Sept. 2, 1944. Records of the 6th Corps, op. cit.; Eighty-Third (83rd) Chemical Mortar Battalion Journals, Battle Reports, Morning Reports: June 1943 – Nov. 1945, op. cit.

56. Paul S. Giles, *Correspondence With Terry Lowry*, (Author's Collection).

57. Steedle, Lee (ed.), *Mark Freedom Paid: A Combat Anthology*, op. cit., pg. 85; Seibels, op. cit.; Bailey, op. cit.

58. Ford, William Clifford, *Never Forget – A Soldier's Battlefield Memoirs*, op. cit., pp. 73-78; Steedle, Lee (ed.), *Mark Freedom Paid: A Combat Anthology*, op. cit., pp. 88-91.

59. Mario Ricci, Personal Experiences In Letter to Terry Lowry, San Mateo, CA, June 2004; Mario Ricci, Personal Experiences Written for Silvano Casaldi, Nettuno, Italy, July 1998, San Mateo, CA.

60. Task Force Bibo, Aug. 27 - Sept. 2, 1944. Records of the 6th Corps, op. cit.; Ford, William Clifford, *Never Forget – A Soldier's Battlefield Memoirs*, op. cit., pp. 73-78; Bailey, op. cit.; Steedle, Lee (ed.), *Mark Freedom Paid: A Combat Anthology*, op. cit., pg. 85 and pp. 88-91.

61. Ford, op. cit.

62. Ford, op. cit.; Blank, op. cit.

63. Task Force Bibo, Aug. 27 - Sept. 2, 1944. Records of the 6th Corps, op. cit.; Blank, op. cit.; Ricci, op. cit.; Seibels, op. cit.; Bailey, op. cit.

64. Steedle, Lee (ed.), *Mark Freedom Paid: A Combat Anthology*, op. cit., pg. 85.

65. Ford, op. cit.

66. Eighty-Third (83rd) Chemical Mortar Battalion Journals, Battle Reports, Morning Reports: June 1943 – Nov. 1945, op. cit.; Steedle, Lee (ed.), *Mark Freedom Paid: A Combat Anthology*, op. cit., pg. 83; Smith, op. cit.

67. Smith, op. cit.; "From Sicily With the 83rd", *Beachhead News*, Dec. 3, 1944; Bailey, op. cit.

68. Task Force Bibo, Aug. 27 - Sept. 2, 1944. Records of the 6th Corps, op. cit.; Boyd, op. cit.

69. M. Daerrebe, Report On The Events That Happened In Briançon From 8-29-44 To 9-4-44, Made Out by M. Daerrebe, Solicitor Voluntary Administrator Of The Town During That Period, [Courtesy George Rhoads & Gini Lemoine].

70. Task Force Bibo, Aug. 27 - Sept. 2, 1944. Records of the 6th Corps, op. cit.

71. Blank, op. cit.

72. Steedle, Lee (ed.), *Mark Freedom Paid: A Combat Anthology*, op. cit., pp. 86-87.

73. Seibels, op. cit.; "From Sicily With the 83rd", *Beachhead News*, Dec. 3, 1944.

74. Task Force Bibo, Aug. 27 - Sept. 2, 1944. Records of the 6th Corps, op. cit.; Loy J. Marshall, *Assorted Personal Experiences in the War*, (Courtesy Tricia Bridges); Bailey, op. cit.

75. Daerrebe, op. cit.

76. Task Force Bibo, Aug. 27 - Sept. 2, 1944. Records of the 6th Corps, op. cit.

77. *Ibid.*

78. Combe, op. cit.

79. Ford, op. cit.

80. Lemuel R. Tillman, Personal Correspondence With Terry Lowry, (Co. C, 83rd Chemical Mortar Battalion); Marshall, op. cit.

81. Combe, op. cit.

82. Vicente De Leon [Co C, Medic, 83rd Chemical Mortar Battalion], Personal Account of Briançon, 2008 (Courtesy Vicente De Leon).

83. Ricci, op. cit.; Steedle, Lee (ed.), *Mark Freedom Paid: A Combat Anthology*, op. cit., pg. 93.

84. Bailey, op. cit.; Blank, op. cit.

85. Steedle, Lee (ed.), *Mark Freedom Paid: A Combat Anthology*, op. cit., pg. 87.

86. *Ibid*, pg. 85.

87. Task Force Bibo, Aug. 27 - Sept. 2, 1944. Records of the 6th Corps, op. cit.; Daerrebe, op. cit.

88. Task Force Bibo, Aug. 27 - Sept. 2, 1944. Records of the 6th Corps, op. cit.; Boyd, op. cit.

89. Eighty-Third (83rd) Chemical Mortar Battalion Journals, Battle Reports, Morning Reports: June 1943 – Nov. 1945, op. cit.; Task Force Bibo, Aug. 27 - Sept. 2, 1944. Records of the 6th Corps, op. cit.

90. *Ibid.*

91. *Ibid.*

92. Bundy, op. cit.; Helsel, op. cit.

93. Blank, op. cit.; Personal Conversations between Gordon Mindrum and author, 2005-2006; Smith, op. cit.; Bailey, op. cit.

94. Daerrebe, op. cit.

95. William S. Hutchinson, *Personal Correspondence from Col. William S. Hutchinson to Kenneth A. Cunin 1943 -1944.* Fifteen Letters. Chemical Corps Museum Archives, Ft. Leonard Wood, MO.

96. Eighty-Third (83rd) Chemical Mortar Battalion Journals, Battle Reports, Morning Reports: June 1943 – Nov. 1945, op. cit.

97. Eighty-Third (83rd) Chemical Mortar Battalion Journals, Battle Reports, Morning Reports: June 1943 – Nov. 1945, op. cit.; Task Force Bibo, Aug. 27 - Sept. 2, 1944. Records of the 6th Corps, op. cit.

98. Daerrebe, op. cit.

99. Eighty-Third (83rd) Chemical Mortar Battalion Journals, Battle Reports, Morning Reports: June 1943 – Nov. 1945, op. cit.; Stephen W. Vukson, *Diary of Stephen W. Vukson*, HQ Co., 83rd Chemical Mortar Battalion - Dec. 1943 - 1945, (Courtesy Stephen W. Vukson).

100. Eighty-Third (83rd) Chemical Mortar Battalion Journals, Battle Reports, Morning Reports: June 1943 – Nov. 1945, op. cit.; Task Force Bibo, Aug. 27 - Sept. 2, 1944. Records of the 6th Corps, op. cit.

101. *Ibid*; Leech, op. cit., pg. 35.

102. Eighty- Third (83rd) Chemical Mortar Battalion Journals, Battle Reports, Morning Reports: June 1943 – Nov. 1945, op. cit.

103. *Ibid.*

104. *Ibid.*

105. Daniel J. Shields, *Diary of Daniel J. Shields, Co. D & HQ Co., 83rd Chemical Mortar Battalion, 1942-1945*, (Courtesy Jean Decky); Hulcher, op. cit.

106. Eighty- Third (83rd) Chemical Mortar Battalion Journals, Battle Reports, Morning Reports: June 1943 – Nov. 1945, op. cit.

107. Smith, op. cit.

108. Eighty- Third (83rd) Chemical Mortar Battalion Journals, Battle Reports, Morning Reports: June 1943 – Nov. 1945, op. cit.; Eleventh (11th) Chemical Maintenance Company, Unit Journals, op. cit.

109. Vukson, op. cit.

110. Eighty- Third (83rd) Chemical Mortar Battalion Journals, Battle Reports, Morning Reports: June 1943 – Nov. 1945, op. cit.; Shields, op. cit.; Hulcher, op. cit.

111. Eighty- Third (83rd) Chemical Mortar Battalion Journals, Battle Reports, Morning Reports: June 1943 – Nov. 1945, op. cit.; Eleventh (11th) Chemical Maintenance Company, Unit Journals, op. cit.

112. Eighty- Third (83rd) Chemical Mortar Battalion Journals, Battle Reports, Morning Reports: June 1943 – Nov. 1945, op. cit.

113. *Ibid.*

114. Robert E. Edwards, *V-Mail & Correspondence of Robert E. Edwards, HQ Co, 83rd Chemical Mortar Battalion*, (Courtesy Wendy Edwards).

115. Eighty- Third (83rd) Chemical Mortar Battalion Journals, Battle Reports, Morning Reports: June 1943 – Nov. 1945, op. cit.; Eleventh (11th) Chemical Maintenance Company, Unit Journals, op. cit.; Hulcher, op. cit.

116. *Ibid.*

117. *Ibid.*

118. Eighty- Third (83rd) Chemical Mortar Battalion Journals, Battle Reports, Morning Reports: June 1943 – Nov. 1945, op. cit.; Eleventh (11th) Chemical Maintenance Company, Unit Journals, op. cit.; Hulcher, op. cit.; Alfred E. Green, Jr. [Co. D, 83rd Chemical Mortar Battalion], Correspondence and Interviews with Terry Lowry, 2003-2008, (Author's Collection).

119. *Muzzleblasts* – Official newsletter of the 83rd Chemical Mortar Battalion 1944 – present [Ertzberger].

120. Eighty- Third (83rd) Chemical Mortar Battalion Journals, Battle Reports, Morning Reports: June 1943 – Nov. 1945, op. cit.

121. Smith, op. cit.

122. Green, op. cit.; Smith, op. cit.; Edwards, op. cit.; Eleventh (11th) Chemical Maintenance Company, Unit Journals, op. cit.

123. Eighty- Third (83rd) Chemical Mortar Battalion Journals, Battle Reports, Morning Reports: June 1943 – Nov. 1945, op. cit.

124. Hulcher, op. cit.; Sam Kweskin, *Let Me Tell You A Story*, (Unpublished Memoir), July 1994, Author's Collection, Boca Raton, FL, (Used by permission of Sam Kweskin).

125. Eighty- Third (83rd) Chemical Mortar Battalion Journals, Battle Reports, Morning Reports: June 1943 – Nov. 1945, op. cit.; Eleventh (11th) Chemical Maintenance Company, Unit Journals, op. cit.; Leech, op. cit, pg. 36.

126. Eighty- Third (83rd) Chemical Mortar Battalion Journals, Battle Reports, Morning Reports: June 1943 – Nov. 1945, op. cit.

127. *Ibid*; Ford, op. cit., pg. 82; Hulcher, op. cit.

128. Hulcher, op. cit.; Edwards, op. cit.

129. Eighty- Third (83rd) Chemical Mortar Battalion Journals, Battle Reports, Morning Reports: June 1943 – Nov. 1945, op. cit.; Smith, op. cit.

130. Eighty- Third (83rd) Chemical Mortar Battalion Journals, Battle Reports, Morning Reports: June 1943 – Nov. 1945, op. cit.; Bush, op. cit.

131. Eighty- Third (83rd) Chemical Mortar Battalion Journals, Battle Reports, Morning Reports: June 1943 – Nov. 1945, op. cit.; Eleventh (11th) Chemical Maintenance Company, Unit Journals, op. cit.

Chapter Eleven

1. Eighty- Third (83rd) Chemical Mortar Battalion Journals, Battle Reports, Morning Reports: June 1943 – Nov. 1945, National Archives, College Park, MD.

2. *Ibid*; Robert E. Edwards, *V-Mail & Correspondence of Robert E. Edwards, HQ Co, 83rd Chemical Mortar Battalion*, (Courtesy Wendy Edwards).

3. Eighty- Third (83rd) Chemical Mortar Battalion Journals, Battle Reports, Morning Reports: June 1943 – Nov. 1945, op. cit.

4. Lee Steedle (ed.), *Mark Freedom Paid: A Combat Anthology*, (Jeanette, PA: 83rd Chemical Mortar Battalion Veterans Association, 1997) (Illustrated by Sam Kweskin), pp. 114-115; Author's Personal Conversations and Interviews with William Gallagher (Author's Collection).

5. Eighty- Third (83rd) Chemical Mortar Battalion Journals, Battle Reports, Morning Reports: June 1943 – Nov. 1945, op. cit.

6. *Ibid*; Edward L. Trey, Personal Correspondence and Interviews with Terry Lowry 2003-2008, (Author's Collection).

7. Eighty- Third (83rd) Chemical Mortar Battalion Journals, Battle Reports, Morning Reports: June 1943 – Nov. 1945, op. cit.

8. *Ibid.*

9. *Ibid*; Capt. (Dr.) Julius C. Hulcher, *Diary of Capt. Julius C. Hulcher 1943 - 1945, Medical Detachment*, 83rd Chemical Mortar Battalion, [Courtesy Charles Hulcher, Glen Allen, VA] [hereafter cited as Hulcher].

10. Eighty- Third (83rd) Chemical Mortar Battalion Journals, Battle Reports, Morning Reports: June 1943 – Nov. 1945, op. cit.

11. Task Force Bibo, Aug. 27 - Sept. 2, 1944. Records of the 6th Corps. National Archives, College Park, MD.

12. Eighty- Third (83rd) Chemical Mortar Battalion Journals, Battle Reports, Morning Reports: June 1943 – Nov. 1945, op. cit.

13. *Ibid*; Eleventh (11th) Chemical Maintenance Company, Unit Journals, National Archives, College Park, MD.

14. Eighty- Third (83rd) Chemical Mortar Battalion Journals, Battle Reports, Morning Reports: June 1943 – Nov. 1945, op. cit.

15. *Ibid.*

16. *Ibid*; Annette Smith (ed.), *Rounds Away: Letters From World War II and the 83rd Chemical Mortar Battalion*, [Letters of Capt. Robert B. Smith, Co. C, 83rd Chemical Mortar Battalion] – Truth or Consequences, NM: 1987 – limited printing.

17. *Ibid*; Charlie Lowry, *V-Mail & Correspondence 1943-45 - Co. D / Co. A, 83rd Chemical Mortar Battalion*, (Author's Collection); Ford, William Clifford, *Never Forget – A Soldier's Battlefield Memoirs*, (Network Printing, New Albany, MS, 2005) – [Co. C, 83rd Chemical Mortar Battalion], pg. 85.

18. Eighty- Third (83rd) Chemical Mortar Battalion Journals, Battle Reports, Morning Reports: June 1943 – Nov. 1945, op. cit.

19. *Ibid*; Eleventh (11th) Chemical Maintenance Company, Unit Journals, op. cit.

20. William S. Hutchinson, *Personal Correspondence from Col. William S. Hutchinson to Kenneth A. Cunin 1943 -1944.* Fifteen Letters. Chemical Corps Museum Archives, Ft. Leonard Wood, MO.

21. Eighty- Third (83rd) Chemical Mortar Battalion Journals, Battle Reports, Morning Reports: June 1943 – Nov. 1945, op. cit.; James G. Helsel, *Diary of James G. Helsel, Co. A, 83rd Chemical Mortar Battalion,* (Courtesy Joyce Berry, Lebanon, TN).

22. *Ibid.*

23. Eighty- Third (83rd) Chemical Mortar Battalion Journals, Battle Reports, Morning Reports: June 1943 – Nov. 1945, op. cit.

24. Eighty- Third (83rd) Chemical Mortar Battalion Journals, Battle Reports, Morning Reports: June 1943 – Nov. 1945, op. cit.; Sam Kweskin, *Let Me Tell You A Story,* (Unpublished Memoir), July 1994, Author's Collection, Boca Raton, FL, (Used by permission of Sam Kweskin); Correspondence with Lee Steedle (Author's Collection); Lee Steedle (ed.), *Mark Freedom Paid: A Combat Anthology,* op. cit., pp. 97-98.

25. Eighty-Third (83rd) Chemical Mortar Battalion Journals, Battle Reports, Morning Reports: June 1943 – Nov. 1945. Chemical Corps Museum Archives, Ft. Leonard Wood, MO, Edgewood Arsenal Archive, and National Archives, College Park, MD.

26. *Ibid.*

27. Eighty- Third (83rd) Chemical Mortar Battalion Journals, Battle Reports, Morning Reports: June 1943 – Nov. 1945, op. cit.; Hulcher, op. cit.; Charles Rolling, *Diary of the 83rd Chemical Mortar Battalion, Company A (In Action).* (Courtesy Gini Lemoine and Elizabeth Daly); Eleventh (11th) Chemical Maintenance Company, Unit Journals, op. cit.

28. Lee Steedle (ed.), *Mark Freedom Paid: A Combat Anthology,* op. cit., pp. 98-99; Sam Kweskin, *Let Me Tell You A Story,* op. cit.; Lee Steedle, *Nights and Days With the 83rd Chemical Mortar Battalion* (Unpublished Memoir), Oakdale, NY, 1990, Author's Collection, (Used by permission of Lee Steedle).

29. Eighty- Third (83rd) Chemical Mortar Battalion Journals, Battle Reports, Morning Reports: June 1943 – Nov. 1945, op. cit.; Sam Kweskin, *Let Me Tell You A Story,* op. cit.; Robert Bush, *Army Officer's Notebook* (diary) & Photograph Collection. Courtesy Lt. Robert Bush, Co. A, 83rd Chemical Mortar Battalion.

30. Eighty- Third (83rd) Chemical Mortar Battalion Journals, Battle Reports, Morning Reports: June 1943 – Nov. 1945, op. cit.; Hulcher, op. cit.

31. Eighty- Third (83rd) Chemical Mortar Battalion Journals, Battle Reports, Morning Reports: June 1943 – Nov. 1945, op. cit.

32. *Ibid.*

33. *Ibid.*

34. Eighty- Third (83rd) Chemical Mortar Battalion Journals, Battle Reports, Morning Reports: June 1943 – Nov. 1945, op. cit.; Eleventh (11th) Chemical Maintenance Company, Unit Journals, op. cit.

35. Eighty- Third (83rd) Chemical Mortar Battalion Journals, Battle Reports, Morning Reports: June 1943 – Nov. 1945, op. cit.; Helsel, op. cit.; Daniel J. Shields, *Diary of Daniel J. Shields, Co. D & HQ Co., 83rd Chemical Mortar Battalion, 1942-1945,* (Courtesy Jean Decky); Hulcher, op. cit.; Bush, op. cit.

36. Eighty- Third (83rd) Chemical Mortar Battalion Journals, Battle Reports, Morning Reports: June 1943 – Nov. 1945, op. cit.; Co. D. Morning Reports/Unit Journal 1942-1944, (Courtesy Mike Codega and Sam Kweskin).

37. Eighty- Third (83rd) Chemical Mortar Battalion Journals, Battle Reports, Morning Reports: June 1943 – Nov. 1945, op. cit.

38. *Ibid.*

39. *Ibid*; Sam Kweskin, *Let Me Tell You A Story,* op. cit.; Author's Personal Correspondence with Sam Kweskin, 2003-2006, (Author's Collection).

40. Kweskin, op. cit.; Hulcher, op. cit.; Smith, op. cit.

41. Eighty- Third (83rd) Chemical Mortar Battalion Journals, Battle Reports, Morning Reports: June 1943 – Nov. 1945, op. cit.; Kweskin, op. cit.

42. Smith, op. cit.; Eighty- Third (83rd) Chemical Mortar Battalion Journals, Battle Reports, Morning Reports: June 1943 – Nov. 1945, op. cit.

43. Ford, op. cit., pg. 87; Eighty- Third (83rd) Chemical Mortar Battalion Journals, Battle Reports, Morning Reports: June 1943 – Nov. 1945, op. cit.

44. Eighty- Third (83rd) Chemical Mortar Battalion Journals, Battle Reports, Morning Reports: June 1943 – Nov. 1945, op. cit.

45. *Ibid.*

46. *Ibid.*

47. *Ibid*; Hulcher, op. cit.

48. Samuel M. Bundy, Jr., *Co. A - 83rd Cml. Mortar Bn.,* (diary & record of events kept by Samuel Bundy from Camp Gordon through Sept. 22, 1945) – (approved by Samuel M. Bundy, Jr. 1984) - [Courtesy Lee Steedle].

49. Eighty- Third (83rd) Chemical Mortar Battalion Journals, Battle Reports, Morning Reports: June 1943 – Nov. 1945, op. cit.; Thirty-Sixth (36th) Infantry Division - *G-4 Journal: Nov.- Dec. 1944,* National Archives, College Park, MD; Eleventh (11th) Chemical Maintenance Company, Unit Journals, op. cit.

50. Shields, op. cit.; Kweskin, op. cit.; Rolling, op. cit.; Helsel, op. cit.; Bush, op. cit.

51. Hulcher, op. cit.; *Muzzleblasts* – Official newsletter of the 83rd Chemical Mortar Battalion 1944 – present [Rand]; Bush, op. cit.

52. Eighty- Third (83rd) Chemical Mortar Battalion Journals, Battle Reports, Morning Reports: June 1943 – Nov. 1945, op. cit.; Eleventh (11th) Chemical Maintenance Company, Unit Journals, op. cit.

53. Smith, op. cit.; Eighty- Third (83rd) Chemical Mortar Battalion Journals, Battle Reports, Morning Reports: June 1943 – Nov. 1945, op. cit.

54. Eighty- Third (83rd) Chemical Mortar Battalion Journals, Battle Reports, Morning Reports: June 1943 – Nov. 1945, op. cit.

55. Eighty- Third (83rd) Chemical Mortar Battalion Journals, Battle Reports, Morning Reports: June 1943 – Nov. 1945, op. cit.; Eleventh (11th) Chemical Maintenance Company, Unit Journals, op. cit. ; Hulcher, op. cit.

56. Helsel, op. cit.; Bundy, op. cit.; Rolling, op. cit.; Smith, op. cit.

57. Sam Kweskin, *Let Me Tell You A Story,* op. cit.; Author's Personal Correspondence with Sam Kweskin, 2003-2006, (Author's Collection);

Lee Steedle (ed.), *Mark Freedom Paid: A Combat Anthology*, op. cit., pp. 105-108; Edward L. Trey, Personal Correspondence and Interviews with Terry Lowry 2003-2008, (Author's Collection).

58. *Ibid.*

59. *Ibid.*

60. Edward L. Trey, Personal Correspondence and Interviews with Terry Lowry 2003-2008, (Author's Collection); Author's Interview with Marsha (Henry) Goff, daughter of Lt. Lester L. Henry, 2008; Mario Ricci, Personal Experiences In Letter to Terry Lowry, San Mateo, CA, June 2004; Mario Ricci, Personal Experiences Written for Silvano Casaldi, Nettuno, Italy, July 1998, San Mateo, CA.

61. Kweskin, op. cit.

62. Eighty- Third (83rd) Chemical Mortar Battalion Journals, Battle Reports, Morning Reports: June 1943 – Nov. 1945, op. cit.

63. *Ibid*; Eleventh (11th) Chemical Maintenance Company, Unit Journals, op. cit.

64.Eighty- Third (83rd) Chemical Mortar Battalion Journals, Battle Reports, Morning Reports: June 1943 – Nov. 1945, op. cit.; Helsel, op. cit.

65. Eighty- Third (83rd) Chemical Mortar Battalion Journals, Battle Reports, Morning Reports: June 1943 – Nov. 1945, op. cit.; Smith, op. cit.

66. Eighty- Third (83rd) Chemical Mortar Battalion Journals, Battle Reports, Morning Reports: June 1943 – Nov. 1945, op. cit.

67. Author Interview and Correspondence with Clovis Birdwell, Co. A, 83rd Chemical Mortar Battalion, 2003-2008, (Author's Collection); Eighty-Third (83rd) Chemical Mortar Battalion Journals, Battle Reports, Morning Reports: June 1943 – Nov. 1945, op. cit.

68. Thirty-Sixth (36th) Infantry Division - *Ordnance Journal: December 1944*, National Archives, College Park, MD; Eighty-Third (83rd) Chemical Mortar Battalion Journals, Battle Reports, Morning Reports: June 1943 – Nov. 1945, op. cit.

69. Kweskin, op. cit.; Eighty-Third (83rd) Chemical Mortar Battalion Journals, Battle Reports, Morning Reports: June 1943 – Nov. 1945, op. cit.

70. Alfred E. Green, Jr. [Co. D, 83rd Chemical Mortar Battalion], Correspondence and Interviews with Terry Lowry, 2003-2008, (Author's Collection).

71. Lee Steedle (ed.), *Mark Freedom Paid: A Combat Anthology*, op. cit., pp. 123-127; Lee Steedle, Nights and Days With the 83rd Chemical Mortar Battalion, op. cit.; Author's Personal Correspondence with Lee Steedle, 2003-2008, (Author's Collection).

72. Steedle, op. cit.

73. Eighty-Third (83rd) Chemical Mortar Battalion Journals, Battle Reports, Morning Reports: June 1943 – Nov. 1945, op. cit.

74. *Ibid.*

75. Eighty-Third (83rd) Chemical Mortar Battalion Journals, Battle Reports, Morning Reports: June 1943 – Nov. 1945, op. cit.

74. *Ibid.*

75. Eighty-Third (83rd) Chemical Mortar Battalion Journals, Battle Reports, Morning Reports: June 1943 – Nov. 1945, op. cit.; Rolling, op. cit.

76. Eighty-Third (83rd) Chemical Mortar Battalion Journals, Battle Reports, Morning Reports: June 1943 – Nov. 1945, op. cit.; Hulcher, op. cit.

77. Thirty-Sixth (36th) Infantry Division - *G-4 Journal: Nov.- Dec. 1944*, op. cit.

78. Eighty-Third (83rd) Chemical Mortar Battalion Journals, Battle Reports, Morning Reports: June 1943 – Nov. 1945, op. cit.

79. *Ibid.*

80. *Ibid.*

81. Leech, Dewey C., and William D. McCain (ed.), *The WW II Experiences of Andrew Candler Leech 1943-1945*, (Hattiesburg, MS, 1985), pg. 37; Eighty-Third (83rd) Chemical Mortar Battalion Journals, Battle Reports, Morning Reports: June 1943 – Nov. 1945, op. cit.

82. Information on Richard Griffin was provided by Susannah Powell, Fletcher, NC and his official commendation; *Muzzleblasts* – Official newsletter of the 83rd Chemical Mortar Battalion 1944 – present [Feerick].

83. Eighty-Third (83rd) Chemical Mortar Battalion Journals, Battle Reports, Morning Reports: June 1943 – Nov. 1945, op. cit.

84. Eighty-Third (83rd) Chemical Mortar Battalion Journals, Battle Reports, Morning Reports: June 1943 – Nov. 1945, op. cit.; Leech, op. cit.

85. Eighty-Third (83rd) Chemical Mortar Battalion Journals, Battle Reports, Morning Reports: June 1943 – Nov. 1945, op. cit.; Personal Interview with Nolan McCraine & author, 2007; Author's Personal Interview with Edward Stanley Davidson, 2007; *Muzzleblasts* – Official newsletter of the 83rd Chemical Mortar Battalion 1944 – present [Davidson].

86. Kritzer, Cy, "Bison Slugger Rapp, Pinned By German Fire, Vowed He'd Learn to Hit Lefties If Spared", *The Sporting News*, (Aug. 28, 1946).

87. Davidson, op. cit.; Kweskin, op. cit.

88. Leech, op. cit., pg. 37; One Hundred and Forty -First (141st) Infantry, Unit Journal, December 1944, National Archives, College Park, MD; Shields, op. cit.

89. Eighty-Third (83rd) Chemical Mortar Battalion Journals, Battle Reports, Morning Reports: June 1943 – Nov. 1945, op. cit.

90. Eighty-Third (83rd) Chemical Mortar Battalion Journals, Battle Reports, Morning Reports: June 1943 – Nov. 1945, op. cit.; Davidson, op. cit.; Kweskin, op. cit.; Hulcher, op. cit.; Thomas A. Cascio (Co. B, 83rd Chemical Mortar Battalion), Personal *Correspondence With Terry Lowry*, (Author's Collection).

91. Correspondence with Malcolm Doyle Wilkinson (Author's Collection); Eighty-Third (83rd) Chemical Mortar Battalion Journals, Battle Reports, Morning Reports: June 1943 – Nov. 1945, op. cit.

92. Eighty-Third (83rd) Chemical Mortar Battalion Journals, Battle Reports, Morning Reports: June 1943 – Nov. 1945, op. cit.; Bundy, op. cit.

93. Hulcher, op. cit.; Eighty-Third (83rd) Chemical Mortar Battalion Journals, Battle Reports, Morning Reports: June 1943 – Nov. 1945, op. cit.; Smith, op. cit.

94. Eighty-Third (83rd) Chemical Mortar Battalion Journals, Battle Reports, Morning Reports: June 1943 – Nov. 1945, op. cit.

95. *Muzzleblasts* – Official newsletter of the 83rd Chemical Mortar Battalion 1944 – present [Connolly].

96. Eighty-Third (83rd) Chemical Mortar Battalion Journals, Battle Reports, Morning Reports: June 1943 – Nov. 1945, op. cit.

97. *Ibid.*

98. *Ibid.*

99. *Ibid*; Eleventh (11th) Chemical Maintenance Company, Unit Journals, op. cit.

100. Bonn, Keith E., *When the Odds Were Even: The Vosges Mountains Campaign - October 1944 - January 1945*, (Random Press [Presidio], New

York, 1994).

101. Rolling, op. cit.; Eighty-Third (83rd) Chemical Mortar Battalion Journals, Battle Reports, Morning Reports: June 1943 – Nov. 1945, op. cit.

102. Eighty-Third (83rd) Chemical Mortar Battalion Journals, Battle Reports, Morning Reports: June 1943 – Nov. 1945, op. cit.

103. Eighty-Third (83rd) Chemical Mortar Battalion Journals, Battle Reports, Morning Reports: June 1943 – Nov. 1945, op. cit.; Eleventh (11th) Chemical Maintenance Company, Unit Journals, op. cit.; Paul S. Giles, *Correspondence With Terry Lowry*, (Author's Collection); Bonn, Keith E., *When the Odds Were Even: The Vosges Mountains Campaign - October 1944 - January 1945*, op. cit.

104. Bonn, Keith E., *When the Odds Were Even: The Vosges Mountains Campaign - October 1944 - January 1945*, op. cit.; Smith, op. cit.

105. Lee Steedle (ed.), *Mark Freedom Paid: A Combat Anthology*, op. cit., pp. 132-133.

106. Eighty-Third (83rd) Chemical Mortar Battalion Journals, Battle Reports, Morning Reports: June 1943 – Nov. 1945, op. cit.; Lee Steedle (ed.), *Mark Freedom Paid: A Combat Anthology*, op. cit., pp. 132-133; Shields, op. cit.; Hulcher, op. cit.; Lowry, op. cit.

107. Eighty-Third (83rd) Chemical Mortar Battalion Journals, Battle Reports, Morning Reports: June 1943 – Nov. 1945, op. cit.; Eleventh (11th) Chemical Maintenance Company, Unit Journals, op. cit.; Smith, op. cit.

108. Smith, op. cit.

109. *Ibid.*

110. Eighty-Third (83rd) Chemical Mortar Battalion Journals, Battle Reports, Morning Reports: June 1943 – Nov. 1945, op. cit.

111. *Ibid*; Shields, op. cit.; Hulcher, op. cit.; Helsel. op. cit.; Joseph H. Garsson, (Co. A, 83rd Chemical Mortar Battalion), Personal Correspondence and Interviews with Terry Lowry, 2005-2007, (Author's Collection).

112. Lawrence Ertzberger, *Correspondence With Terry Lowry*, (Author's Collection).

113. Lee Steedle (ed.), *Mark Freedom Paid: A Combat Anthology*, op. cit., pg. 134; Lee Steedle, *Nights and Days With the 83rd Chemical Mortar Battalion*, op. cit.; Author's Personal Correspondence with Lee Steedle, 2003-2008, (Author's Collection).

114. *Ibid.*

115. *Ibid.*

116. *Ibid.*

117. Eighty-Third (83rd) Chemical Mortar Battalion Journals, Battle Reports, Morning Reports: June 1943 – Nov. 1945, op. cit.; Eleventh (11th) Chemical Maintenance Company, Unit Journals, op. cit.

Chapter Twelve

1. Eighty-Third (83rd) Chemical Mortar Battalion Journals, Battle Reports, Morning Reports: June 1943 – Nov. 1945, National Archives, College Park, MD.

2. *Ibid.*

3. *Ibid*; Leech, Dewey C., and William D. McCain (ed.), *The WW II Experiences of Andrew Candler Leech 1943-1945*, (Hattiesburg, MS, 1985), pg. 39.

4. Lee Steedle, *Nights and Days With the 83rd Chemical Mortar Battalion* (Unpublished Memoir), Oakdale, NY, 1990, Author's Collection, (Used by permission of Lee Steedle); Steedle, Lee (ed.), *Mark Freedom Paid: A Combat Anthology*, (Jeanette, PA: 83rd Chemical Mortar Battalion Veterans Association, 1997) (Illustrated by Sam Kweskin), pg. 134; Author's Personal Correspondence with Lee Steedle, 2003-2008, (Author's Collection).

5. Samuel M. Bundy, Jr., *Co. A - 83rd Cml. Mortar Bn.*, (diary & record of events kept by Samuel Bundy from Camp Gordon through Sept. 22, 1945) – (approved by Samuel M. Bundy, Jr. 1984) - [Courtesy Lee Steedle].

6. Eighty-Third (83rd) Chemical Mortar Battalion Journals, Battle Reports, Morning Reports: June 1943 – Nov. 1945, op. cit.; Eleventh (11th) Chemical Maintenance Company, Unit Journals, National Archives, College Park, MD; *Muzzleblasts* – Official newsletter of the 83rd Chemical Mortar Battalion 1944 – present [Wayne M. Moser]; Leech, op. cit., pg. 39; Charles Rolling, *Diary of the 83rd Chemical Mortar Battalion, Company A (In Action)*. (Courtesy Gini Lemoine and Elizabeth Daly).

7. Sam Kweskin, *Let Me Tell You A Story*, (Unpublished Memoir), July 1994, Author's Collection, Boca Raton, FL, (Used by permission of Sam Kweskin); Daniel J. Shields, *Diary of Daniel J. Shields, Co. D & HQ Co., 83rd Chemical Mortar Battalion, 1942-1945*, (Courtesy Jean Decky); Robert Bush, *Army Officer's Notebook* (diary) & Photograph Collection. Courtesy Lt. Robert Bush, Co. A, 83rd Chemical Mortar Battalion; Annette Smith (ed.), *Rounds Away: Letters From World War II and the 83rd Chemical Mortar Battalion*, [Letters of Capt. Robert B. Smith, Co. C, 83rd Chemical Mortar Battalion] – Truth or Consequences, NM: 1987 - limited printing.

8. Eighty-Third (83rd) Chemical Mortar Battalion Journals, Battle Reports, Morning Reports: June 1943 – Nov. 1945, op. cit.; Eleventh (11th) Chemical Maintenance Company, Unit Journals, op. cit.; Kweskin, op. cit.; Capt. (Dr.) Julius C. Hulcher, *Diary of Capt. Julius C. Hulcher 1943 - 1945, Medical Detachment*, 83rd Chemical Mortar Battalion, [Courtesy Charles Hulcher, Glen Allen, VA] [hereafter cited as Hulcher]; James G. Helsel, *Diary of James G. Helsel, Co. A, 83rd Chemical Mortar Battalion*, (Courtesy Joyce Berry, Lebanon, TN).

9. Eighty-Third (83rd) Chemical Mortar Battalion Journals, Battle Reports, Morning Reports: June 1943 – Nov. 1945, op. cit.; Leech, op. cit., pg. 38; Rolling, op. cit.

10. Joseph H. Garsson, (Co. A, 83rd Chemical Mortar Battalion), Personal Correspondence and Interviews with Terry Lowry, 2005-2007, (Author's Collection); Unknown clipping, *"Didn't Coddle Capt. Garsson"*, [Courtesy Gordon Mindrum; Unknown author and newspaper, *"Garsson's Son Tells of Favors"*, n.d., from files of Sam Kweskin; John P. McEvoy, *Correspondence With Terry Lowry*. Author's Collection; Author's Personal Interviews and Correspondence with Sam Kweskin, Co. D/HQ Co., 83rd Chemical Mortar Battalion, (Author's Collection); Author's Personal Interview and Correspondence with Robert Bush (Co. A, 83rd Chemical Mortar Battalion, (Author's Collection).

11. Jean Pierre Combe [Honorary Member, Co. C, 83rd Chemical Mortar Battalion], Personal *Correspondence With Terry Lowry* 2003-2007 (Author's Collection).

12. Eighty-Third (83rd) Chemical Mortar Battalion Journals, Battle Reports, Morning Reports: June 1943 – Nov. 1945, op. cit.

13. Helsel, op. cit.

14. Robert Bush, *Army Officer's Notebook* (diary) & Photograph Collection. Courtesy Lt. Robert Bush, Co. A, 83rd Chemical Mortar Battalion; William Clifford Ford, *Never Forget – A Soldier's Battlefield Memoirs*, (Network Printing, New Albany, MS, 2005) – [Co. C, 83rd Chemical Mortar Battalion], pg. 92.

15. Eighty-Third (83rd) Chemical Mortar Battalion Journals, Battle Reports, Morning Reports: June 1943 – Nov. 1945, op. cit.

16. Lee Steedle, *Nights and Days With the 83rd Chemical Mortar Battalion* (Unpublished Memoir), op. cit.

17. Eighty-Third (83rd) Chemical Mortar Battalion Journals, Battle Reports, Morning Reports: June 1943 – Nov. 1945, op. cit.

18. *Ibid*; Rolling, op. cit.

19. Ford, op. cit, pg. 100.

20. Eighty-Third (83rd) Chemical Mortar Battalion Journals, Battle Reports, Morning Reports: June 1943 – Nov. 1945, op. cit.

21. *Ibid.*

22. Lester L. Henry, *V-Mail of Lt. Lester L. Henry, Co. A, 83rd Chemical Mortar Battalion*, (Courtesy Marsha Goff Henry).

23. Eighty-Third (83rd) Chemical Mortar Battalion Journals, Battle Reports, Morning Reports: June 1943 – Nov. 1945, op. cit.; Ford, op. cit., pg. 101.

24. Eighty-Third (83rd) Chemical Mortar Battalion Journals, Battle Reports, Morning Reports: June 1943 – Nov. 1945, op. cit.

25. *Muzzleblasts* – Official newsletter of the 83rd Chemical Mortar Battalion 1944 – present.

26. Joseph H. Garsson, (Co. A, 83rd Chemical Mortar Battalion), Personal Correspondence and Interviews with Terry Lowry, 2005-2007, op. cit.; Unknown clipping; *"Garsson's Son Tells of Favors"*, n.d., from files of Sam Kweskin; Author's Personal Interviews and Correspondence with Sam Kweskin, Co. D/HQ Co., 83rd Chemical Mortar Battalion, (Author's Collection); Author's Personal Interview and Correspondence with Robert Bush (Co. A, 83rd Chemical Mortar Battalion, (Author's Collection); Moore, William, *"Untitled Article on Trial of Joseph Garsson"*, Chicago Tribune, n.d.; One Hundred and Forty-Third (143rd) Infantry, Unit Journal, February 1945, National Archives, College Park, MD.

27. One Hundred and Forty-Third (143rd) Infantry, Unit Journal, February 1945, op. cit.

28. Kweskin, op. cit.

29. Bush, op. cit.

30. Helsel, op. cit.

31. Eighty-Third (83rd) Chemical Mortar Battalion Journals, Battle Reports, Morning Reports: June 1943 – Nov. 1945, op. cit.

32. *Ibid*; Eleventh (11th) Chemical Maintenance Company, Unit Journals, op. cit.

33. Eighty-Third (83rd) Chemical Mortar Battalion Journals, Battle Reports, Morning Reports: June 1943 – Nov. 1945, op. cit.; Kweskin, op. cit.; Smith, op. cit.

34. Eighty-Third (83rd) Chemical Mortar Battalion Journals, Battle Reports, Morning Reports: June 1943 – Nov. 1945, op. cit.

35. Robert Bush, *Army Officer's Notebook* (diary) & Photograph Collection, op. cit.; Helsel, op. cit.; Author's Correspondence with Dave Dougherty, Ft. Collins, CO, Regarding James Dougherty, Co. D, 83rd Chemical Mortar Battalion (Author's Collection); Smith, op. cit.

36. Eighty-Third (83rd) Chemical Mortar Battalion Journals, Battle Reports, Morning Reports: June 1943 – Nov. 1945, op. cit.; Smith, op. cit.

37. Eleventh (11th) Chemical Maintenance Company, Unit Journals, op. cit.; Eighty-Third (83rd) Chemical Mortar Battalion Journals, Battle Reports, Morning Reports: June 1943 – Nov. 1945, op. cit.

38. Eighty-Third (83rd) Chemical Mortar Battalion Journals, Battle Reports, Morning Reports: June 1943 – Nov. 1945, op. cit.

39. Author's Personal Conversations and Interviews with William Gallagher (Author's Collection); Martin, Ralph G., *"How Far Are They Now?"*, Stars and Stripes, (Feb. 2, 1945).

40. Eighty-Third (83rd) Chemical Mortar Battalion Journals, Battle Reports, Morning Reports: June 1943 – Nov. 1945, op. cit.; Smith, op. cit.

41. Elwood "Long John" Guthrie, Letter to Lt. Lester Lew Henry, Dec. 22, 1945, [Courtesy Marsha (Henry) Goff]; Helsel, op. cit.; Smith, op. cit.

42. Eighty-Third (83rd) Chemical Mortar Battalion Journals, Battle Reports, Morning Reports: June 1943 – Nov. 1945, op. cit.; Charlie Lowry, *V-Mail & Correspondence 1943-45 - Co. D / Co. A, 83rd Chemical Mortar Battalion*, (Author's Collection).

43. *Ibid.*

44. *Ibid*; Eleventh (11th) Chemical Maintenance Company, Unit Journals, op. cit.

45. Bundy, op. cit.; Smith, op. cit.

46. Eighty-Third (83rd) Chemical Mortar Battalion Journals, Battle Reports, Morning Reports: June 1943 – Nov. 1945, op. cit.; Lee Steedle, *Nights and Days With the 83rd Chemical Mortar Battalion* (Unpublished Memoir), op. cit.

47. Eighty-Third (83rd) Chemical Mortar Battalion Journals, Battle Reports, Morning Reports: June 1943 – Nov. 1945, op. cit.

48. *Mark Freedom Paid: A Combat Anthology*, (Jeanette, PA: 83rd Chemical Mortar Battalion Veterans Association, 1997) (Illustrated by Sam Kweskin), pg. 113; Bundy, op. cit.; Helsel, op. cit.; Hulcher, op. cit.

49. Eighty-Third (83rd) Chemical Mortar Battalion Journals, Battle Reports, Morning Reports: June 1943 – Nov. 1945, op. cit.

50. *Ibid*; Smith, op. cit.

51. Eleventh (11th) Chemical Maintenance Company, Unit Journals, op. cit.; Eighty-Third (83rd) Chemical Mortar Battalion Journals, Battle Reports, Morning Reports: June 1943 – Nov. 1945, op. cit.

52. Eighty-Third (83rd) Chemical Mortar Battalion Journals, Battle Reports, Morning Reports: June 1943 – Nov. 1945, op. cit.

53. *Ibid*; Robert E. Bundy, (Co. A/HQ Co., 83rd Chemical Mortar Battalion), Personal Correspondence With Terry Lowry, 2003-2008, (Author's Collection); Henry, op. cit.; Hulcher, op. cit.

54. Eighty-Third (83rd) Chemical Mortar Battalion Journals, Battle Reports, Morning Reports: June 1943 – Nov. 1945, op. cit.

55. *Ibid*; Carlos R. Trautman, (Co. A, 83rd Chemical Mortar Battalion), Personal Interviews and *Correspondence With Terry Lowry*, 2008, (Author's Collection); Smith, op. cit.

56. Trautman, op. cit.

57. Eighty-Third (83rd) Chemical Mortar Battalion Journals, Battle Reports, Morning Reports: June 1943 – Nov. 1945, op. cit.

58. *Ibid.*

59. *Ibid.*

60. *Ibid*; Smith, op. cit.

61. *Ibid*; Smith, op. cit.

62. *Ibid*; Smith, op. cit.

63. Eighty-Third (83rd) Chemical Mortar Battalion Journals, Battle Reports, Morning Reports: June 1943 – Nov. 1945, op. cit.; Hulcher, op. cit.

64. Eighty-Third (83rd) Chemical Mortar Battalion Journals, Battle Reports, Morning Reports: June 1943 – Nov. 1945, op. cit.; Eleventh (11th) Chemical Maintenance Company, Unit Journals, op. cit.

65. *Ibid.*

66. Eighty-Third (83rd) Chemical Mortar Battalion Journals, Battle Reports, Morning Reports: June 1943 – Nov. 1945, op. cit.

67. *Ibid.*

68. *Ibid*; Shields, op. cit.; Stephen W. Vukson, *Diary of Stephen W. Vukson*, HQ Co., 83rd Chemical Mortar Battalion - Dec. 1943 - 1945, (Courtesy Stephen W. Vukson).

69. Helsel, op. cit.; Hulcher, op. cit.; Eighty-Third (83rd) Chemical Mortar Battalion Journals, Battle Reports, Morning Reports: June 1943 – Nov. 1945, op. cit.; Eleventh (11th) Chemical Maintenance Company, Unit Journals, op. cit.

70. *Ibid*; Mario Ricci, Personal Experiences In Letter to Terry Lowry, San Mateo, CA, June 2004, (Author's Collection).

71. Eighty-Third (83rd) Chemical Mortar Battalion Journals, Battle Reports, Morning Reports: June 1943 – Nov. 1945, op. cit.; Eleventh (11th) Chemical Maintenance Company, Unit Journals, op. cit.

72. Sam Kweskin, *Let Me Tell You A Story*, (Unpublished Memoir), op. cit.

73. Eighty-Third (83rd) Chemical Mortar Battalion Journals, Battle Reports, Morning Reports: June 1943 – Nov. 1945, op. cit.

74. Hulcher, op. cit.; Smith, op. cit.

75. Brimm, Robert, *Rounds Away: Two Years of Combat With The Eighty-Third Chemical Mortar Battalion*, (Innsbruck, Austria, 1945) (Illustrated by Sam Kweskin - maps by Eugene Plassmann); Eighty-Third (83rd) Chemical Mortar Battalion Journals, Battle Reports, Morning Reports: June 1943 – Nov. 1945, op. cit.; Kweskin, op. cit.

76. Eighty-Third (83rd) Chemical Mortar Battalion Journals, Battle Reports, Morning Reports: June 1943 – Nov. 1945, op. cit.; Vukson, op. cit.; *Chemical Warfare Service Personnel Who Died During World War II - 7 December 1941 Through 30 June 1946 (CFN-140)*, National Archives, College Park, MD; Shields, op. cit.; Bundy, op. cit.

77. Eighty-Third (83rd) Chemical Mortar Battalion Journals, Battle Reports, Morning Reports: June 1943 – Nov. 1945, op. cit.; Eleventh (11th) Chemical Maintenance Company, Unit Journals, op. cit.

78. *Muzzleblasts* – Official newsletter of the 83rd Chemical Mortar Battalion 1944 – present; Kweskin, op. cit.

79. Eighty-Third (83rd) Chemical Mortar Battalion Journals, Battle Reports, Morning Reports: June 1943 – Nov. 1945, op. cit.; Eleventh (11th) Chemical Maintenance Company, Unit Journals, op. cit.

80. Eighty-Third (83rd) Chemical Mortar Battalion Journals, Battle Reports, Morning Reports: June 1943 – Nov. 1945, op. cit.; Hulcher, op. cit.; Smith, op. cit.

81. Ricci, op. cit.; Bush, op. cit.

82. Eighty-Third (83rd) Chemical Mortar Battalion Journals, Battle Reports, Morning Reports: June 1943 – Nov. 1945, op. cit.; Eleventh (11th) Chemical Maintenance Company, Unit Journals, op. cit.; Rolling, op. cit.; Hulcher, op. cit.; Kweskin, op. cit.

83. Eighty-Third (83rd) Chemical Mortar Battalion Journals, Battle Reports, Morning Reports: June 1943 – Nov. 1945, op. cit.; Ford, op. cit., pg. 115; Eleventh (11th) Chemical Maintenance Company, Unit Journals, op. cit.; Hulcher, op. cit.; Smith, op. cit.

84. Eighty-Third (83rd) Chemical Mortar Battalion Journals, Battle Reports, Morning Reports: June 1943 – Nov. 1945, op. cit.; Robert E. Bundy, (Co. A/HQ Co., 83rd Chemical Mortar Battalion), Personal Correspondence With Terry Lowry, 2003-2008, (Author's Collection); Three Hundred & Eighty-Fourth (384th) Field Artillery Battalion, Unit Journal & History, April 1945, National Archives, College Park, MD.

85. Rolling, op. cit.; Helsel, op. cit.

86. Eighty-Third (83rd) Chemical Mortar Battalion Journals, Battle Reports, Morning Reports: June 1943 – Nov. 1945, op. cit.; Eleventh (11th) Chemical Maintenance Company, Unit Journals, op. cit.

87. *Ibid.*

88. Hulcher, op. cit.

89. Loy J. Marshall, *Assorted Personal Experiences in the War*, (Courtesy Tricia Bridges).

90. Eighty-Third (83rd) Chemical Mortar Battalion Journals, Battle Reports, Morning Reports: June 1943 – Nov. 1945, op. cit.; Kweskin, op. cit.

91. Eighty-Third (83rd) Chemical Mortar Battalion Journals, Battle Reports, Morning Reports: June 1943 – Nov. 1945, op. cit.; Eleventh (11th) Chemical Maintenance Company, Unit Journals, op. cit.

92. Hulcher, op. cit.

93. Smith, op. cit.

94. Eighty-Third (83rd) Chemical Mortar Battalion Journals, Battle Reports, Morning Reports: June 1943 – Nov. 1945, op. cit.; Eleventh (11th) Chemical Maintenance Company, Unit Journals, op. cit.; Samuel M. Bundy, Jr., *Co. A - 83rd Cml. Mortar Bn.*, (diary & record of events kept by Samuel Bundy from Camp Gordon through Sept. 22, 1945) – (approved by Samuel M. Bundy, Jr. 1984) - [Courtesy Lee Steedle]; Shields, op. cit.

95. Ford, op. cit., pg. 117; *Muzzleblasts* – Official newsletter of the 83rd Chemical Mortar Battalion 1944 – present [Rand];

96. Ford, op. cit.; Robert E. Bundy, (Co. A/HQ Co., 83rd Chemical Mortar Battalion), Personal Correspondence With Terry Lowry, 2003-2008, (Author's Collection); James Marion Lester, *James Marion Lester's Story*, (unpublished manuscript interview), by Vicki S. Hibma, June 26, 1984; Ricci, op. cit.

97. Leech, op. cit., pg. 43.

98. Eighty-Third (83rd) Chemical Mortar Battalion Journals, Battle Reports, Morning Reports: June 1943 – Nov. 1945, op. cit.; Ford, op. cit., pg. 119; Hulcher, op. cit.

99. Bush, op. cit.; Robert E. Bundy, (Co. A/HQ Co., 83rd Chemical Mortar Battalion), Personal Correspondence With Terry Lowry, 2003-2008, (Author's Collection).

100. Leech, op. cit., pg. 43.

101. Harold St. Gemme, (Co. B, 83rd Chemical Mortar Battalion), Correspondence With Terry Lowry (Author's Collection).

102. Eighty-Third (83rd) Chemical Mortar Battalion Journals, Battle Reports, Morning Reports: June 1943 – Nov. 1945, op. cit.; Eleventh (11th) Chemical Maintenance Company, Unit Journals, op. cit.

103. Bundy, op. cit.

104. Eighty-Third (83rd) Chemical Mortar Battalion Journals, Battle Reports, Morning Reports: June 1943 – Nov. 1945, op. cit.; Smith, op. cit.

105. Bundy, op. cit.

106. *Muzzleblasts* – Official newsletter of the 83rd Chemical Mortar Battalion 1944 – present [Rand]; Kweskin, op. cit.

107. Paul S. Giles, Correspondence With Terry Lowry, (Author's Collection); Hulcher, op. cit.

108. Eighty-Third (83rd) Chemical Mortar Battalion Journals, Battle Reports, Morning Reports: June 1943 – Nov. 1945, op. cit.; Steedle, op. cit.; *Muzzleblasts* – Official newsletter of the 83rd Chemical Mortar Battalion 1944 – present [Rand].

109. Dougherty, op. cit.

110. Joseph H. Garsson, (Co. A, 83rd Chemical Mortar Battalion), Personal Correspondence and Interviews with Terry Lowry, 2005-2007, op. cit.; Unknown clipping; *"Garsson's Son Tells of Favors"*, n.d., from files of Sam Kweskin; Author's Personal Interviews and Correspondence with Sam Kweskin, Co. D/HQ Co., 83rd Chemical Mortar Battalion, (Author's Collection); Author's Personal Interview and Correspondence with Robert Bush (Co. A, 83rd Chemical Mortar Battalion, (Author's Collection); Moore, William, *"Untitled Article on Trial of Joseph Garsson"*, Chicago Tribune, n.d.; One Hundred and Forty-Third (143rd) Infantry, Unit Journal, February 1945, National Archives, College Park, MD; Gordon M. Mindrum, *Personal Papers of Dr. Gordon M. Mindrum*, Cincinnati, OH [loaned to the author 2006].

111. Sam Bundy, op. cit.; Rolling, op. cit.; Smith, op. cit.

112. Kweskin, op. cit.; *Muzzleblasts* – Official newsletter of the 83rd Chemical Mortar Battalion 1944 – present [McNeil].

113. Combe, op. cit.

Chapter Thirteen

1. Brimm, Robert, *Rounds Away: Two Years of Combat With The Eighty-Third Chemical Mortar Battalion*, (Innsbruck, Austria, 1945) (Illustrated by Sam Kweskin - maps by Eugene Plassmann).

2. Eighty-Third (83rd) Chemical Mortar Battalion Journals, Battle Reports, Morning Reports: June 1943 – Nov. 1945, National Archives, College Park, MD; Author's Personal Interviews and Correspondence with Sam Kweskin, Co. D/HQ Co., 83rd Chemical Mortar Battalion, (Author's Collection); Sam Kweskin, *Let Me Tell You A Story*, (Unpublished Memoir).

3. Eighty-Third (83rd) Chemical Mortar Battalion Journals, Battle Reports, Morning Reports: June 1943 – Nov. 1945, op. cit.; Charles Rolling, *Diary of the 83rd Chemical Mortar Battalion, Company A (In Action)*. (Courtesy Gini Lemoine and Elizabeth Daly); Dale C. Blank (Co. C, 83rd Chemical Mortar Battalion), *Correspondence With Terry Lowry*, (Author's Collection).

4. Annette Smith (ed.), *Rounds Away: Letters From World War II and the 83rd Chemical Mortar Battalion*, [Letters of Capt. Robert B. Smith, Co. C, 83rd Chemical Mortar Battalion] – Truth or Consequences, NM: 1987 – limited printing.

5. *Ibid.*

6. Eighty-Third (83rd) Chemical Mortar Battalion Journals, Battle Reports, Morning Reports: June 1943 – Nov. 1945, op. cit.; Smith, op. cit.; Kweskin, op. cit.

7. Eighty-Third (83rd) Chemical Mortar Battalion Journals, Battle Reports, Morning Reports: June 1943 – Nov. 1945, op. cit.; Jean Pierre Combe [Honorary Member, Co. C, 83rd Chemical Mortar Battalion], Personal *Correspondence With Terry Lowry* 2003-2007 (Author's Collection).

8. Samuel M. Bundy, Jr., *Co. A - 83rd Cml. Mortar Bn.*, (diary & record of events kept by Samuel Bundy from Camp Gordon through Sept. 22, 1945) – (approved by Samuel M. Bundy, Jr. 1984) - [Courtesy Lee Steedle]; Byron H. Jordan, *V-Mail of Byron H. Jordan 1943-1945*, (Courtesy Byron H. Jordan).

9. Eighty-Third (83rd) Chemical Mortar Battalion Journals, Battle Reports, Morning Reports: June 1943 – Nov. 1945, op. cit.; James G. Helsel, *Diary of James G. Helsel, Co. A, 83rd Chemical Mortar Battalion*, (Courtesy Joyce Berry, Lebanon, TN).

10. Eighty-Third (83rd) Chemical Mortar Battalion Journals, Battle Reports, Morning Reports: June 1943 – Nov. 1945, op. cit.; John P. McEvoy, *Many Years Later*, (unpublished speech), n.d., (Author's Collection).

11. Eighty-Third (83rd) Chemical Mortar Battalion Journals, Battle Reports, Morning Reports: June 1943 – Nov. 1945, op. cit.; Bundy, op. cit.; Smith, op. cit.

12. Smith, op. cit.

13. Bundy, op. cit.; Helsel, op. cit.; *Muzzleblasts* – Official newsletter of the 83rd Chemical Mortar Battalion 1944 – present [Barrett]; Combe, op. cit.

14. Robert E. Bundy, (Co. A/HQ Co., 83rd Chemical Mortar Battalion), Personal Correspondence With Terry Lowry, 2003-2008, (Author's Collection).

15. Eighty-Third (83rd) Chemical Mortar Battalion Journals, Battle Reports, Morning Reports: June 1943 – Nov. 1945, op. cit.; Smith, op. cit.; Bundy, op. cit.

16. *Ibid.*

17. Eighty-Third (83rd) Chemical Mortar Battalion Journals, Battle Reports, Morning Reports: June 1943 – Nov. 1945, op. cit.

18. Smith, op. cit.; Personal Conversations between Gordon Mindrum and author, 2005-2006; Robert E. Bundy, op. cit.; Burdge, Evan &

Penny, *Guardians of Freedom: Fred Kohl (Interview)*, (2001) – website.

19. Efnor, Sam (Lt. Col.), Drawn Shell for the 4.2" Chemical Mortar, Nov. 27, 1945. Chemical Warfare Service. National Archives, College Park, MD.

20. Eighty- Third (83rd) Chemical Mortar Battalion Journals, Battle Reports, Morning Reports: June 1943 – Nov. 1945, op. cit.

21. *Ibid.*

22. Gordon M. Mindrum, *Personal Papers of Dr. Gordon M. Mindrum*, Cincinnati, OH [loaned to the author 2006].

23. Smith, op. cit.; Eighty- Third (83rd) Chemical Mortar Battalion Journals, Battle Reports, Morning Reports: June 1943 – Nov. 1945, op. cit.

24. Smith, op. cit.; Eighty- Third (83rd) Chemical Mortar Battalion Journals, Battle Reports, Morning Reports: June 1943 – Nov. 1945, op. cit.; *Muzzleblasts* – Official newsletter of the 83rd Chemical Mortar Battalion 1944 – present [Barrett].

25. Eighty- Third (83rd) Chemical Mortar Battalion Journals, Battle Reports, Morning Reports: June 1943 – Nov. 1945, op. cit.; Smith, op. cit.

26. *Ibid.*

27. Ford Hopkins, *V-Mail Letters of Ford Hopkins, Co. A, 83rd Chemical Mortar Battalion*, (Courtesy Kenneth Hopkins).

28. Smith, op. cit.; James Marion Lester, *James Marion Lester's Story*, (unpublished manuscript interview), by Vicki S. Hibma, June 26, 1984; Robert Bundy, op. cit

29. Kohl, op. cit.; Combe, op. cit.

30. Eighty- Third (83rd) Chemical Mortar Battalion Journals, Battle Reports, Morning Reports: June 1943 – Nov. 1945, op. cit.; Combe, op. cit.; One Hundred and First (101st) Infantry, Unit Journals, National Archives, College Park, MD.

31. Eighty- Third (83rd) Chemical Mortar Battalion Journals, Battle Reports, Morning Reports: June 1943 – Nov. 1945, op. cit.; Combe, op. cit.

32. Hopkins, op. cit.

33. Robert Bundy, op. cit.; Joseph E. Cannetti, *War Experiences of Joseph E. Cannetti, Co. A, 83rd Chemical Mortar Battalion*, (Courtesy Joseph E. Cannetti).

34. Robert Bundy, op. cit.

35. Eighty- Third (83rd) Chemical Mortar Battalion Journals, Battle Reports, Morning Reports: June 1943 – Nov. 1945, op. cit.; Smith, op. cit.; Hopkins, op. cit.

36. One Hundred and First (101st) Infantry, Unit Journals, op. cit.; Hopkins, op. cit.; Smith, op. cit.

37. Eighty-Third (83rd) Chemical Mortar Battalion Journals, Battle Reports, Morning Reports: June 1943 – Nov. 1945, op. cit.; Personal Conversations between Gordon Mindrum and author, 2005-2006; Smith, op. cit.; One Hundred and First (101st) Infantry, Unit Journals, op. cit.

38. Smith, op. cit.

39. *Ibid.*

40. *Ibid.*

41. *Ibid.*

42. Smith, op. cit.; Combe, op. cit.

43. Robert Bundy, op. cit.

44. Kweskin, op. cit.; Author's personal interview with Walter Bielski, 83rd Chemical Mortar Battalion, 2003.

45. Combe, op. cit.

46. Smith, op. cit.; United States Government. *Historical Data On the 83rd Chemical Mortar Battalion 1942-1945.* Edgewood Arsenal Archives; Elwood "Long John" Guthrie, Letter to Lt. Lester Lew Henry, Dec. 12, 1945, [Courtesy Marsha (Henry) Goff].

Epilogue

1. Correspondence with Malcolm Doyle Wilkinson (Author's Collection).

2. Various biographical information on John Baer, Joe Bova, Earl Rapp. Carl McNabb, Harold Hughes, and Sam Kweskin.

3. Joseph H. Garsson, (Co. A, 83rd Chemical Mortar Battalion), Personal Correspondence and Interviews with Terry Lowry, 2005-2007, op. cit.; Unknown clipping; *"Garsson's Son Tells of Favors"*, n.d., from files of Sam Kweskin; Author's Personal Interviews and Correspondence with Sam Kweskin, Co. D/HQ Co., 83rd Chemical Mortar Battalion, (Author's Collection); Author's Personal Interview and Correspondence with Robert Bush (Co. A, 83rd Chemical Mortar Battalion, (Author's Collection); Moore, William, *"Untitled Article on Trial of Joseph Garsson"*, Chicago Tribune, n.d.; One Hundred and Forty-Three (143rd) Infantry, Unit Journal, February 1945, National Archives, College Park, MD; Gordon M. Mindrum, *Personal Papers of Dr. Gordon M. Mindrum*, Cincinnati, OH [loaned to the author 2006]; John Hamilton Dryden, *The Garsson-May Connection: An Account of War Profiteering In Batavia, Illinois*, (Thesis - History 491 - Northern Illinois University - April 28, 1992); Unknown author and newspaper, *"Garsson's Son Tells of Favors"*, n.d., from files of Sam Kweskin; Moore, William, *"Untitled Article on Trial of Joseph Garsson"*, Chicago Tribune, n.d.; *"Garsson Firms Reported Cleared In Defective Shell Deaths of 38"*, Stars and Stripes, (Sept. 7, 1946); Davis, J. W., *"Indict May, Garssons on Fraud Charge"*, [Unknown and undated newspaper clipping courtesy Gordon Mindrum]; Bancroft, Griffing, *"Probe Told Garsson Paid Bills of Generals and May at Gay Party"*, Chicago Sun, n.d., from files of Sam Kweskin; Brophy, Leo P. & Wyndam D. Miles & Rexmond C. Cochrane, *The Technical Services: The Chemical Warfare Service: From Laboratory to Field*, (Washington: U.S. Government Printing Office: 1959), pp. 361-366.

4. *Ibid.*

5. *Ibid*; *All My Sons*, 1947 play by Arthur Miller. Made into a 1948 film and a 1986 made-for-TV movie.

BIBLIOGRAPHY

Manuscripts & Personal Interviews

Paul Bailey. *From Rookie to Kriegie 1943 - 1945*, (180th Infantry, AT Squad). Personal Memoir. Courtesy Paul Bailey.

Baseplate Support Experiment Note, Feb. 1, 1945. National Archives, College Park, MD.

James O. Beasley. V-Mail & Correspondence of Lt. James O. Beasley, Co. D, 83rd Chemical Mortar Battalion. Courtesy John Beasley

John Beasley. *The Action at Vietri, September, 1943*, [James Beasley], (compiled May 24, 2003 – modified June 21, 2004) – [Courtesy John Beasley].

Bernard Bernhardt (Co. C, 83rd Chemical Mortar Battalion). Correspondence with Terry Lowry. Author's Collection.

Dale C. Blank. *The True Story of Briançon*. Written 2006 by Dale C. Blank, Co. C, 83rd Chemical Mortar Battalion. Original copy in author's collection.

Dale C. Blank (Co. C, 83rd Chemical Mortar Battalion). Correspondence with Terry Lowry. Author's Collection.

George R. Borkhuis. Letters and Correspondence of George R. Borkhuis, Co. D-HQ Co., 83rd Chemical Mortar Battalion, 1942-1945. Courtesy Fred Thompson, NY, and Thomasina Edwards, FL.

John L. Boyd. *Recollections of Briançon* (with report written Sept. 14, 1944). John L. Boyd, Co. C, 83rd Chemical Mortar Battalion - June 29, 1994. Courtesy Gini Lemoine.

Richard A. Bridge. V-Mail Letters of Richard A. Bridge, Co. D, 83rd Chemical Mortar Battalion. Courtesy Linda Whalen.

Colin Lowe Broadhurst, Lt. Commander, Royal Navy Reserves. *Official Report of LST 422*. Courtesy Peter Berg.

Robert E. Bundy (Co. A/HQ Co., 83rd Chemical Mortar Battalion). Personal Correspondence with Terry Lowry, 2003-2008. Author's Collection.

Samuel M. Bundy, Jr. *Co. A - 83rd Cml. Mortar Bn.* (diary & record of events kept by Samuel Bundy from Camp Gordon through Sept. 22, 1945) – (approved by Samuel M. Bundy, Jr. 1984) - Courtesy Lee Steedle.

Samuel M. Bundy, Jr. [A transcription of the above listed item which omits the first and last portion of the diary as well as portions of entries) – Courtesy Lee Steedle.

Bureau of Ships, (includes repairs and construction records of *LST 422*), RG 19, National Archives. College Park, MD.

Rupert O. Burford. *Foreign Service Memoirs – Diary of Rupert O. Burford* [Co. C - 83rd CMB]. (Unpublished), Charleston, WV, n.d. Author's Collection. Used by permission of Mrs. Rupert O. Burford.

Robert Bush. *Army Officer's Notebook* (diary) & Photograph Collection. Courtesy Lt. Robert Bush, Co. A, 83rd Chemical Mortar Battalion.

Robert Bush. Extracts from the V-Mail of Lt. Robert J. Bush. Courtesy Carole Beller.

Joseph E. Cannetti. *War Experiences of Joseph E. Cannetti, Co. A, 83rd Chemical Mortar Battalion*. Courtesy Joseph E. Cannetti.

Thomas A. Cascio (Co. B, 83rd Chemical Mortar Battalion). Personal Correspondence with Terry Lowry. Author's Collection.

Chemical Warfare Service RG 175. Boxes 1-24, 230-241, 1421-1445. National Archives, College Park, MD.

Chemical Warfare Service Conference, HQ, 7th Army, Aug. 1943. Records of the 7th Army, Chemical Warfare Section. National Archives, College Park, MD.

Chemical Warfare Service Personnel Who Died During World War II - 7 December 1941 Through 30 June 1946 (CFN-140). National Archives, College Park, MD.

Michele (Mike) Codega. Letter to Mrs. L. A. Merrill Describing the Sinking of *LST 422* at Anzio. Courtesy Robert L. Merrill.

Michele (Mike) Codega. *Soldier's Pay Record*. Courtesy Lee Steedle.

Michele (Mike) Codega. Speech Given To the 1999 Reunion of the 83rd Chemical Mortar Battalion. Mike Codega Collection – Courtesy Sam Kweskin.

Harry Cohen. Letter Describing Capt. Robert B. Smith, Co. C, 83rd Chemical Mortar Battalion Dec. 20, 1959. Courtesy Annette Smith.

Jean Pierre Combe [Honorary Member, Co. C, 83rd Chemical Mortar Battalion]. Personal Correspondence with Terry Lowry 2003-2007. Author's Collection.

Commander Task Force 67, *Report of Escort of Convoy UGF-8 and GUF-8, 29 April - 31 May, 1943*, Action Report, RG 38 - Box 242. National Archives, College Park, MD.

Commander Task Group 81.4, *Report of Amphibious Operations During Landings Near Cape D'Anzio, Italy Participated In By Task Group 81.4, Jan. 20 - Feb. 1, 1944*, Action Report. National Archives, College Park, MD.

Commander Task Group 81.7, Commander Task Unit 81.7.1, Commander Mine Squadron 6 - Sweeper Operations Operation Shingle Jan. 21-30, 1944 - *Action Report - Feb. 8, 1944*. National Archives, College Park, MD.

Commander Task Group 81.14 (Return Convoy Group) & Commander Task Group 81.11 (Salvage Group), Jan . 22-30, 1944 - *Action Report - March 1, 1944*. National Archives, College Park, MD.

Kenneth A. Cunin. Correspondence with Ed Trey 1993 – 94. Courtesy Ed Trey.

S. Daerrebe. *Report On The Events That Happened In Briançon From 8-29-44 To 9-4-44, Made Out by S. Daerrebe, Solicitor Voluntary Administrator Of The Town During That Period*. Courtesy George Rhoads & Gini Lemoine.

C. M. Dalrymple-Hay, Royal Navy, Commander, 2nd LST Flotilla & Assistant Commander H.M. LST 425. *Operation Shingle Official Report*. Courtesy Peter Berg.

Decorations & Medals, Northwest African Waters, Naval RG 24. National Archives, College Park, MD.

Vicente De Leon [Co C, Medic, 83rd Chemical Mortar Battalion]. *Personal Account of Briançon*, 2008. Courtesy Vicente De Leon.

John Hamilton Dryden. *The Garsson-May Connection: An Account of War Profiteering In Batavia, Illinois*. Thesis - History 491 - Northern Illinois University - April 28, 1992.

Robert E. Edwards. V-Mail & Correspondence of Robert E. Edwards. HQ Co, 83rd Chemical Mortar Battalion. Courtesy Wendy Edwards.

Sam Efnor (Lt. Col.). *Drawn Shell for the 4.2" Chemical Mortar*, Nov. 27, 1945. Chemical Warfare Service. National Archives, College Park, MD.

Eighty-Third (83rd) Chemical Mortar Battalion. Assorted Correspondence on Lineage and Honors of the 83rd Chemical Mortar Battalion 1942-1962. Edgewood Arsenal Archives.

Eighty-Third (83rd) Chemical Mortar Battalion. Co. D. Morning Reports/Unit Journal 1942-1944. Courtesy Mike Codega and Sam Kweskin.

Eighty-Third (83rd) Chemical Mortar Battalion. General Orders #1 - #41 (1943) – Camp Gordon, GA – Edgewood Arsenal Archives.

Eighty-Third (83rd) Chemical Mortar Battalion. General Orders #1 - #91 (1942) – Camp Gordon, GA – Edgewood Arsenal Archives.

Eighty-Third (83rd) Chemical Mortar Battalion. Miscellaneous Papers. Edgewood Arsenal Archives and Chemical Corps Museum Archives, Ft. Leonard Wood, MO.

Eighty-Third (83rd) Chemical Mortar Battalion. Morning Reports for Jan. 29 & 31, 1944. National Personnel Records Center, St. Louis, MO.

Eighty-Third (83rd) Chemical Mortar Battalion. Pay Roll (Roster), HQ & HQ Co., 83rd Chemical Mortar Battalion - May 1 - 31, 1943. National Personnel Records Center, St. Louis, MO.

Eighty-Third (83rd) Chemical Mortar Battalion Journals, Battle Reports, Morning Reports: June 1943 – Nov. 1945. Chemical Corps Museum Archives, Ft. Leonard Wood, MO, Edgewood Arsenal Archive, and National Archives, College Park, MD.

Eighty-Fourth (84th) Chemical Mortar Battalion, Unit Journals. National Archives, College Park, MD.

Eleventh (11th) Chemical Maintenance Company, Unit Journals. National Archives, College Park, MD.

Lawrence Ertzberger. Correspondence with Terry Lowry. Author's Collection.

Extracts from Training Notes from the Sicilian Campaign, Nov. 6, 1943. National Archives, College Park, MD.

First (1st) Airborne Task Force Records. National Archives, College Park, MD.

First (1st) Airborne Task Force Glider Loading Charts, August 1944. National Archives, College Park, MD.

First (1st) Infantry Division. General Orders 1943. National Archives, College Park, MD.

First (1st), Third (3rd), and Fourth (4th) Ranger Battalions. After Action Reports / Unit Journals. National Archives, College Park, MD.

Five-Hundred and Seventeenth (517th) Parachute Inf. RCT. Operations Report, Aug. 1944. National Archives, College Park, MD.

William C. Ford. *Lest We Forget*. Memoir by Staff Sgt. William C. Ford, Co. C, 83rd CMB. Courtesy Gini Lemoine.

William J. Gagliardi (Co. A, 83rd Chemical Mortar Battalion). Correspondence with Terry Lowry. Author's Collection.

James H. Gallahan, Sr. Military Service of James H. Gallahan, Sr. - World War II. Courtesy Roger Gallahan, Quinton, VA.

Karl Garrett. *Memories 1942-1945*, (HQ Co., 83rd Chemical Mortar Battalion), n.d. Courtesy Karl Garrett, Richmond, VA.

Joseph H. Garsson, (Co. A, 83rd Chemical Mortar Battalion). Personal Correspondence and Interviews with Terry Lowry, 2005-2007. Author's Collection.

Paul S. Giles. Correspondence with Terry Lowry. Author's Collection.

George D. Gould. *Field Modification of Sight, 4.2" Chemical Mortar, Inspected at Co. C, 83rd Cml. Bn.*, Aug. 23, 1943. National Archives, College Park, MD.

Alfred E. Green, Jr. [Co. D, 83rd Chemical Mortar Battalion]. Correspondence and Interviews with Terry Lowry, 2003-2008. Author's Collection.

Elwood "Long John" Guthrie. Letter to Lt. Lester Lew Henry, Dec. 22, 1945. Courtesy Marsha (Henry) Goff.

H. M. S. LST 301. Deck/Log/Action Report. Royal Navy Archives, England.

William C. Hammond, Jr. *Tactical Use of Chemical Munitions*, Aug. 23, 1943. 45th Infantry Division, 7th Army. National Archives, College Park, MD.

James G. Helsel. Diary of James G. Helsel, Co. A, 83rd Chemical Mortar Battalion. Courtesy Joyce Berry, Lebanon, TN.

Lester L. Henry. Letters 1945. Courtesy Marsha (Henry) Goff.

Hale H. Hepler. *Hale Hunter Hepler – World War II Veteran*, (dictated to his daughter Pam Pace June 2005). Courtesy Hale H. Hepler & Pam Pace.

Norman Holt. Diary of Norm Holt – USN – YMS – 43. Billy Rhoads Collection. Courtesy Norm Holt and Gini Lemoine.

Ford E. Hopkins, (Co. A - D CMB). Letters & V-Mail. Courtesy Kenneth Hopkins.

Capt. (Dr.) Julius C. Hulcher. Diary of Capt. Julius C. Hulcher 1943 - 1945. Medical Detachment, 83rd Chemical Mortar Battalion. Courtesy Charles Hulcher, Glen Allen, VA.

William S. Hutchinson. *Interview With Col. William S. Hutchinson*, CWS, Edgewood Arsenal, MD – Jan. 26, 1945. Edgewood Arsenal Archives.

William S. Hutchinson. Personal Correspondence from Col. William S. Hutchinson to Kenneth A. Cunin 1943 -1944. Fifteen Letters. Chemical Corps Museum Archives, Ft. Leonard Wood, MO.

Byron H. Jordan. V-Mail of Byron H. Jordan 1943-1945, Co. D / Co. B, 83rd Chemical Mortar Battalion and Correspondence and Interview Between Byron Jordan and Terry Lowry. Courtesy Byron H. Jordan and Terry Lowry.

Earl Kann. *Personal Account of Gela*. Courtesy Earl Kann. Author's Collection.

Sam Kweskin. *Let Me Tell You A Story* (Unpublished Memoir), July 1994. Author's Collection. Boca Raton, FL, Used by permission of Sam Kweskin.

Raymond J. Lakey. *Report: 4.2 Inch Mortar Airborne Company*, Oct. 15, 1944. Edgewood Arsenal Archives.

Andrew C. Leech. V-Mail Letter of July 12, 1944, Co. B, 83rd Chemical Mortar Battalion. Courtesy Alice Hartley.

James Marion Lester. *James Marion Lester's Story*, (unpublished manuscript interview), by Vicki S. Hibma, June 26, 1984. Courtesy Sally and Vicki Hibma.

Charlie Lowry. Collection, (83rd Chemical Mortar Battalion). Author's Collection.

Charlie Lowry. Letters from Germany 1945-48. Author's Collection.

Charlie Lowry. V-Mail & Correspondence 1943-45 - Co. D / Co. A, 83rd Chemical Mortar Battalion. Author's Collection.

LST 690 Deck Log - Passenger List - Co. A, 83rd Chemical Battalion - Aug. 9, 1944. National Archives, College Park, MD.

Loy J. Marshall. *Assorted Personal Experiences in the War*. Courtesy Tricia Bridges.

Nolan McCraine. Telephone Interview with Terry Lowry, 2006, (Co. B, 83rd Chemical Mortar Battalion). Author's Collection.

John P. McEvoy. Correspondence With Terry Lowry. Author's Collection.

John P. McEvoy. *First Action*. (Unpublished), Oct. 2, 1996. Copy provided by L. R. Tillman.

John P. McEvoy. *Genesis of the 4.2 Mortar*, (unpublished), Nov. 1990.

John P. McEvoy. *Many Years Later*, (unpublished speech), n.d.

Leonard A. Merrill, Jr. Excerpts from the V-Mail of Leonard A. Merrill, Jr. Courtesy Robert L. Merrill.

David W. Meyerson. V-Mail Letter to Mrs. L. A. Merrill Describing the Death of Lt. Leonard A. Merrill, Jr. on *LST 422* at Anzio. Courtesy Robert L. Merrill.

Gordon M. Mindrum. 83rd Chemical Mortar Battalion Display. Cincinnati VA Medical Center - Nov. 2006.

Gordon M. Mindrum. Letter To Mrs. Ed Trey, Feb. 6, 1944. Courtesy Ed Trey.

Gordon M. Mindrum. Personal Papers of Dr. Gordon M. Mindrum. Cincinnati, OH. Loaned to the author by Gordon M. Mindrum 2006.

Martin J. Moloney. Correspondence with Terry Lowry. Author's Collection.

Jerome A. Muschinske. Correspondence With Terry Lowry and his Account of Service with Co. C, 83rd Chemical Mortar Battalion. Author's Collection.

Jim C. Myers. Correspondence of Jim C. Myers, Co. C, 83rd Chemical Mortar Battalion. Courtesy Delores "Kitten" Rice.

One Hundred and Forty -First (141st) Infantry. Unit Journal, December 1944. National Archives, College Park, MD.

One Hundred and Forty-Second (142nd) Infantry. Unit Journal, February 1945. National Archives, College Park, MD.

One Hundred and Forty-Third (143rd) Infantry. Unit Journal, February 1945. National Archives, College Park, MD.

One Hundred and Twentieth (120th) Medical Battalion, 45th Infantry Division, July-August 1943. Unit History. National Archives, College Park, MD.

Russell H. Peterson. Personal Papers of Russell H. Peterson, Co. D, 83rd Chemical Mortar Battalion, 1942 – 1944. Courtesy Marcia (Peterson) Daoust, Huntington, WV and Neal and Bruton Peterson.

Edwin Pike. Diary of Capt. Edwin G. Pike, 83rd Chemical Mortar Battalion, Co. D, (unpublished – covers period from Apr. 27, 1943 through Italy). Courtesy Marcia Bunker.

Edwin Pike. Korean War Correspondence - Chemical Warfare Service. Courtesy Marcia Bunker.

Edwin Pike. Military Papers of Edwin G. Pike 1940 – 1942. Courtesy Marcia Bunker.

Edwin Pike. Miscellaneous Materials Relating to the 83rd Chemical Mortar Battalion. Courtesy Marcia Bunker.

Edwin Pike. V-Mail & Correspondence of Capt. Edwin G. Pike 1941 - 1945 - Co. D, 83rd Chemical Mortar Battalion. Courtesy Marcia Bunker.

Eugene A. Plassmann. *Rounds Away*, Computer Reproduction (September 2004). Courtesy Eugene A. Plassmann.

Lawrence H. Powell. *Lest We Forget*, (brief memoir of Lawrence H. Powell, Co. A, 83rd CMB). Courtesy Lawrence H. Powell.

Fred G. Rand. Letter to Gini and George Dec. 20, 2002.

Michael J. Rebick. V-Mail & Correspondence of Michael J. Rebick, Co. D, 83rd Chemical Mortar Battalion. Courtesy Linda Whalen.

Report of Investigation, 4.2" Chemical Mortar, Jan., 1944 for the Period Dec. 11 - 15, 1943. National Archives, College Park, MD.

Report of Lt. Col. Kenneth Cunin, HQ, 83rd Chemical Battalion, September 12, 1943. National Archives, College Park, MD.

George Rhoads. *Billy Rhoads: Brave Soldier*, (n.d.). Copy provided by Sam Kweskin.

George Rhoads. Letter to Gini Lemoine Regarding *LST 422*. Courtesy Gini Lemoine.

George Rhoads. Various Correspondence & Materials on Billy Rhoads. Courtesy Gini Lemoine.

Mario Ricci. Personal Experiences In Letter to Terry Lowry, San Mateo, CA, June 2004.

Mario Ricci. Personal Experiences Written for Silvano Casaldi, Nettuno, Italy, July 1998, San Mateo, CA.

Mario Ricci. Wartime Sketches, San Mateo, CA.

Perry Rice. Conversations with Perry Rice, Co. D/Co. B, 83rd Chemical Mortar Battalion.

Charles Rolling. *Diary of the 83rd Chemical Mortar Battalion, Company A (In Action)*. Courtesy Gini Lemoine and Elizabeth Daly.

Kelly Seibels. *A Wartime Log* (Minturno to Briançon, Co. C, 83rd Chemical Mortar Battalion). Courtesy Kelly Seibels and Kelly Seibels, Jr.

Daniel J. Shields. Diary of Daniel J. Shields, Co. D & HQ Co., 83rd Chemical Mortar Battalion, 1942-1945. Courtesy Jean Decky.

Sixteenth (16th) Infantry. Records - *Ship Assignments & Loading: June 1943: Co. D, 83rd Chemical Battalion*. National Archives, College Park, MD.

Sixteenth (16th) Infantry. *S-1 Journal: July 1943*. National Archives, College Park, MD

Sixty-Eighth (68th) Coastal Artillery. Unit Journals. National Archives, College Park, MD.

Annette Smith (ed.). *Rounds Away: Letters From World War II and the 83rd Chemical Mortar Battalion*. [Letters of Capt. Robert B. Smith, Co. C, 83rd Chemical Mortar Battalion] Truth or Consequences, NM: 1987 – limited printing.

Robert L. Sorensen, (Medical Detachment, 83rd Chemical Mortar Battalion). Letter to Sam Kweskin Describing Harold Hughes, Oct. 25, 1996. Courtesy Tricia Bridges.

Lee Steedle. Collection (V-Mail). Oakdale, NY. Used by permission of Lee Steedle.

Lee Steedle. *Nights and Days With the 83rd Chemical Mortar Battalion*. Unpublished Memoir, Oakdale, NY, 1990. Author's Collection. Used by permission of Lee Steedle.

Task Force Bibo, Aug. 27 - Sept. 2, 1944. Records of the 6th Corps. National Archives, College Park, MD.

Thirty-Sixth (36th) Infantry Division. *G-4 Journal: Nov.- Dec. 1944*. National Archives, College Park, MD.

Thirty-Sixth (36th) Infantry Division. *Ordnance Journal: December 1944*. National Archives, College Park, MD.

Kelso (Red) Thompson, (Co. D/Co. A, 83rd Chemical Mortar Battalion). Personal Interviews and Correspondence. Author's Collection.

Three Hundred and Eighty-Fourth (384th) Field Artillery Battalion, Unit Journal & History, April 1945. National Archives, College Park, MD.

Three Hundred and Forty-Ninth (349th) Infantry. Unit Journals, March-April 1944. National Archives, College Park, MD.

Three Hundred and Ninety-Seventh (397th) Infantry. Unit Journal, November 1944. National Archives, College Park, MD.

Lemuel R. Tillman, (Co. C, 83rd Chemical Mortar Battalion). Personal Correspondence with Terry Lowry.

Carlos R. Trautman, (Co. A, 83rd Chemical Mortar Battalion). Personal Interviews and Correspondence with Terry Lowry, 2008. Author's Collection.

Edward L. Trey. Personal Correspondence and Interviews with Terry Lowry 2003-2008. Author's Collection.

Leonard Turan. Address Notebook Carried By Leonard Turan. Courtesy Bryan Turan.

Leonard Turan. Pocket Notebook of Leonard Turan. Courtesy Bryan Turan.

Twelfth (12th) Armored Division. Records - January 1945. National Archives, College Park, MD.

Twenty-Sixth Infantry (26th) Division. Operation Reports - 1945 *Journal of the 101st Infantry*. National Archives, College Park, MD.

U. S. S. *Dextrous*. Action Report Jan. 1944. National Archives, College Park, MD.

U. S. S. *Herbert C. Jones*. Deck Log. War Diary, Action Report Jan. 1944. National Archives, College Park, MD.

U. S. S. *LCI 19*. Action Report / War Diary Jan. 1944. National Archives, College Park, MD.

U. S. S. *LCI 32*. Action Report Jan. 1944 & Casualty Report File. National Archives, College Park, MD.

U. S. S. *LCI 35*. Deck Log / Action Report Sept. 1943. National Archives, College Park, MD.

U. S. S. *LCI 189*. War Diary, RG 38 - Box 1038, National Archives. College Park, MD.

U. S. S. *LCI 209*. Action Report Jan. 1944. National Archives, College Park, MD.

U. S. S. *LCI 216*. Action Report, Sept. 10, 1943, RG 38. National Archives, College Park, MD.

U. S. S. *LST 16*. Deck Log /Action Report Jan. 1944. National Archives, College Park, MD.

U. S. S. *LST 379*. Action Report / War Diary Jan. - Apr. 1944. National Archives, College Park, MD.

U. S. S. *LST 383*. Deck Log, Jan. 1944. National Archives, College Park, MD.

U. S. S. *Lyon*. War Diary, June 10-12, 1943 & Deck Log Aug. 1944. National Archives, College Park, MD.

U. S. S. *Monticello*. Deck Log/War Diary/Business Records. National Archives, College Park, MD.

U. S. S. *PC 1227*. War Diary. National Archives, College Park, MD.

U. S. S. *Dickman*. Deck Log. National Archives, College Park, MD.

U. S. S. *Pilot*. Deck Log/War Diary/Action Report Jan. 1944. National Archives, College Park, MD.

U. S. S. *SC 522*. Action Report / Deck Log, Jan. 1944. National Archives, College Park, MD.

U. S. S. *SC 638*. Action Report / Deck Log / War Diary, Jan. 1944. National Archives, College Park, MD.

U. S. S. *Strive*. Deck Log/War Diary/Action Report Jan. 1944. National Archives, College Park, MD.

U. S. S. *Thurston*. War Diary, May - July, 1943. National Archives, College Park, MD.

U. S. S. *YMS 3*. Deck Log /Action Report Jan. 1944. National Archives, College Park, MD.

U. S. S. *YMS 29*. War Diary /Action Report / Deck Log, Jan. 1944. National Archives, College Park, MD.

U. S. S *YMS 30*. Action Report, Jan. 1944. National Archives, College Park, MD.

U. S. S. *YMS 34*. Action Report, Jan. 1944. National Archives, College Park, MD.

U. S. S. *YMS 36*. Action Report Jan. 1944. National Archives, College Park, MD.

U. S. S. *YMS 43*. War Diary /Action Report Jan. 1944. National Archives, College Park, MD.

U. S. S. *YMS 58*. War Diary /Action Report / Deck Log, Jan. 1944. National Archives, College Park, MD.

U. S. S. *YMS 62*. Action Report Jan. 1944. National Archives, College Park, MD.

U. S. S. *YMS 69*. War Diary /Action Report / Deck Log, Jan. 1944. National Archives, College Park, MD.

U. S. S. *YMS 83*. War Diary /Action Report / Deck Log, Jan. 1944. National Archives, College Park, MD.

U. S. S. *YMS 207*. War Diary / Action Report / Deck Log, Jan. 1944. National Archives, College Park, MD.

U. S. S. *YMS 226*. War Diary /Action Report, Jan. 1944. National Archives, College Park, MD.

United States Government. *Historical Data On the 83rd Chemical Mortar Battalion 1942-1945*. Edgewood Arsenal Archives

Stephen W. Vukson. Diary of Stephen W. Vukson, HQ Co., 83rd Chemical Mortar Battalion - Dec. 1943 - 1945. Courtesy Stephen W. Vukson.

Stephen W. Vukson. Miscellaneous Notes on Service With the 83rd Chemical Mortar Battalion (Motor Pool).

Stephen W. Vukson. *My Anzio Diary*, n.d. Used by permission of Stephen W. Vukson, HQ Co., 83rd Chemical Mortar Battalion.

Norman A. Wahosky. Letter Sent Mar. 14, 1944 by Sgt. Norman A. Wahosky, Co. C, 83rd Chemical Mortar Battalion, To Family of Edward Carothers and additional information on *LST 422* provided to the family. Courtesy Richard Carothers.

Col. George L. Watson. *"You're On Your Own - An Address by Col. George L. Watson Before Graduating Class – Battalion 'Officers' Course."* CWS, Edgewood Arsenal, MD – Feb. 12, 1944. Edgewood Arsenal Archives.

Curtis Williams. Telephone Interviews with Terry Lowry, 2006. Medical Detachment, 83rd Chemical Mortar Battalion.

Joseph A. Williamson. Personal Interview with Joseph A. Williamson and Son, Co. C, 83rd Chemical Mortar Battalion. Author's Collection.

Books and Pamphlets

Black, Robert W. *Rangers in World War II*. New York: Random House Publishing, 1992.

Blumenson, Martin. *Sicily: Whose Victory?*. New York, NY: Ballantine Books Inc., 1969.

-------------- . *The Mediterranean Theater of Operations: Salerno to Cassino*. Washington: U.S. Government Printing Office, 1969.

Bonn, Keith E. *When the Odds Were Even: The Vosges Mountains Campaign - October 1944 - January 1945*. New York: Random Press [Presidio], 1994.

Brashear, Alton D. *From Lee To Bari: The History of the 45th General Hospital*. Richmond, VA: Whittet & Shepperson, Richmond, VA, 1957.

Brimm, Robert. *Rounds Away: Two Years of Combat With The Eighty-Third Chemical Mortar Battalion*. Innsbruck, Austria, 1945. Illustrated by Sam Kweskin - maps by Eugene Plassmann.

Brinkley, Douglas (ed.). *The World War II Memorial: A Grateful Nation Remembers*. New Voyage Communications, Inc., 2004.

Brophy, Leo P. , Wyndam D. Miles, & Rexmond C. Cochrane. *The Technical Services: The Chemical Warfare Service: From Laboratory to Field*. Washington: U.S. Government Printing Office, 1959.

Brophy, Leo P., & George J. B. Fisher. *The Technical Services: The Chemical Warfare Service: Organizing for War*. Washington: U.S. Government Printing Office, 1959.

Chemical Corps Association. *The Chemical Warfare Service In World War II: A Report of Accomplishments*. New York: Reinhold Publishing Corporation.

Chemical Publishing Co. *Medical Manual of Chemical Warfare*. New York, NY: Doray Press, 1942.

Chemical Warfare School. *Study Guide – Chemical Warfare: Questions, Answers and Practical Exercises; Pamphlet No. 2*. Chemical Warfare Center, Edgewood Arsenal, MD, Oct. 1942.

Chemical Warfare Service. *Introducing – the Chemical Warfare Service Enlisted Replacement Training Center, Edgewood Arsenal, MD*. [n.d. - probably ca. 1942-43].

Clarke, Jeffrey J., and Robert R. Smith. *Riviera to the Rhine: The European Theater of Operations*. University Press of the Pacific, Honolulu, Hawaii, 2005 - reprint of 1993 edition.

Darby, William O., with William H. Baumer. *Darby's Rangers - We Led the Way*. New York: Random House Publishing,1980).

Devlin, Gerard M. *Silent Wings: The Saga of the U.S. Army and Marine Combat Glider Pilots During World War II*. New York, NY: St. Martin's Press, 1985.

Eldredge, Walter J. *Finding My Father's War: A Baby Boomer and the 2nd Chemical Mortar Battalion in World War II*. Ostego, MI: PageFree Publishing, Inc., 2004.

Fisher, Ernest F., Jr. *The Mediterranean Theater of Operations: Cassino to the Alps*. Washington: U.S. Government Printing Office, 1977.

Fisher, George A. *The Story of the 180th Infantry Regiment*. San Angelo, TX: Newsfoto Publishing Co., 1947.

Flamm, Capt. Paul F. (ed.). *Combat History of the 84th Chemical Mortar Battalion*, n.d., copy located in files of 84th Chemical Mortar Battalion. [Co. B section by Sgt. Dean O. Haley], National Archives, College Park, MD.

Ford, William Clifford. *Never Forget – A Soldier's Battlefield Memoirs*. New Albany, MS: Network Printing, 2005 – [Co. C, 83rd Chemical Mortar Battalion].

Garland, Albert N., & Howard McGaw Smith. *The Mediterranean Theater of Operations: Sicily and the Surrender of Italy*. Washington: U.S. Government Printing Office, 1965.

Gleim, Albert F., and George B. Harris III. *Distinguished Service Cross Awards For World War II*. Ft. Myer, VA: Planchet Press, 1991.

Goff, Marsha Henry. *A Gathering of Heroes - Ranger Battalions Association WW II National Reunion, Lawrence, Kansas - 2006*. Lawrence , KS: Willow Sun Publishing, 2006. [Marsha Henry Goff is the daughter of Lester Lew Henry of the 83rd Chemical Mortar Battalion]

Headquarters, 5th Army. *Road To Rome: Salerno - Naples - Volturno - Cassino - Anzio - Rome*, (n.d.).

Hibbert, Christopher. *Anzio: The Bid for Rome*. New York, NY: Ballantine Books, Inc., 1970.

History of the 157th Infantry Regiment (Rifle). Baton Rouge, LA: Army & Navy Publishing Co., 1946.

Hotchner, A. E. *Sophia: Living and Loving: Her Own Story*. William Morrow and Company, Inc., 1979.

Hoyt, Edwin P. *The GI's War: American Soldiers In Europe During World War II*.

Huff, Sgt. Richard (ed.). *A Pictorial History of the 36th "Texas" Infantry Division*. Austin, Texas: The 36th Division Association.

Jeffers, H. Paul. *Onward We Charge - The Heroic Story of Darby's Rangers in World War II*. NAL Caliber, July 2007.

Kinlaw, Howard M., Edward A. Johnson & James L. Rusk. *From Bruyeres To Brenner: The Combat Story of the Fighting 411th*. Innsbruck, Austria, May 1945.

Kleber, Brooks E. & Dale Birdsell. *The Technical Services: The Chemical Warfare Service: Chemicals In Combat*. Washington: U.S. Government Printing Office, 1966.

Kloxin, Frank. *Hey Kid*. Garretson, SD: Sanders Printing Company, Garretson, 2007.

Kweskin, Sam. *Rounds Away: One Year's Combat With a 4.2" Mortar Battalion Through Sicily and Italy: The Story of the Eighty Third Chemical Battalion*. Passed for Publication – DDS – Field Press Censors – Nov. 18, 1944.

Leech, Dewey C., and William D. McCain (ed.). *The WW II Experiences of Andrew Candler Leech 1943-1945*. Hattiesburg, MS, 1985.

MacDermott, Brian. *Ships Without Names - The Story of the Royal Navy's Tank Landing Ships of World War II*. England: Arms & Armour, May 1993.

Marshall, Charles F. *A Ramble Through My War: Anzio and Other Joys*. Baton Rouge: Louisiana State University Press, 1998.

Munsell, Warren P., Jr. *The Story of a Regiment: A History of the 179th Regimental Combat Team*. New York City, NY, 1946.

Naval Historical Center. *The Sicilian Campaign 10 July – 17 August 1943*. Washington, D.C.:Naval Historical Center, Dept. of the Navy, 1993.

Pack, S. W. C. *Operation Husky: The Allied Invasion of Sicily*. New York, NY: Hippocrene Books, Inc., 1977.

Schneider, Dick (ed.). *Harold E. Hughes: The Man From Ida Grove*. Chosen Books Pub., 1979.

Steedle, Lee (ed.). *Mark Freedom Paid: A Combat Anthology*. Jeanette, PA: 83rd Chemical Mortar Battalion Veterans Association, 1997. (Illustrated by Sam Kweskin)

Sylvia, Stephen W. & Michael J. O'Donnell. *Uniforms, Weapons and Equipment of the World War II G.I.* Orange, VA: Moss Publications, 1982.

Tregaskis, Richard. *Invasion Diary*. New York, Random House, 1944.

United States Coast Guard. *Book of Valor - A Fact Book on Medals and Decorations*. Prepared by Public Relations Division, Washington, D.C.

United States Congress. *Congressional Record: Proceedings and Debates of the 79th Congress Second Session*. Vol. 92 - Part 8, July 19, 1946 to August 2, 1946. Washington, D.C.: U. S. Government Printing Office.

United States War Department. *Chemical Warfare Service Field Manual: Tactics of Chemical Warfare: July 20, 1942*. Washington: U.S. Government Printing Office, 1942.

_____ . *Basic Field Manual: Defense Against Chemical Attack: Sept. 7, 1942*. Washington: U.S. Government Printing Office, 1942.

_____ . *Driver's Manual: Technical Manual No. 10-460*. Washington: U.S. Government Printing Office, May 6, 1942.

_____ . *4.2 – Inch Recoilless Chemical Mortar E34R1*. Washington: U.S. Government Printing Office, Dec. 21, 1944.

_____ . *Anzio Beachhead: January 22 – May 25, 1944*. Washington, D.C.: Historical Division, War Department: Center of Military History, U.S. Army, 1990.

Maryland & Delaware. *Young American Patriots: World War II: Maryland – Delaware*, Richmond, VA: National Publishers, 1950.

Officer Candidate School. *Chemical Warfare Service: Edgewood Arsenal, Maryland*. Baltimore, MD: The Horn-Shafer Co., 1944.

Ohio. *Young American Patriots: World War II: Ohio*. Richmond, VA: National Publishing Co., n.d.

Pennsylvania. *Young American Patriots: World War II: Pennsylvania*. Richmond, VA: National Publishing Co., n.d.

Report of Accomplishments: The Chemical Warfare Service in World War II. Washington, D.C.: Reinhold Publishing Corporation, NY for the Chemical Corps Association, 1948.

Virginia. *Young American Patriots: World War II: Virginia*. Richmond, VA: National Publishing Co., 1945.

Waitt, Brig. Gen. Alden H. *Gas Warfare: The Chemical Weapon, It's Use, and Protection Against It*. New York: J. J. Little & Ives Co., 1942.

West Virginia. *Young American Patriots: World War II: West Virginia*. Richmond, VA: National Publishing Co., n.d.

_____ . *Young American Patriots: World War II: West Virginia: Vol. II*. Richmond, VA: National Publishing Co., n.d.

Whitlock, Flint. *The Rock of Anzio: From Sicily to Dachau: A History of the 45th Infantry Division*. Boulder, CO: Westview Press, Boulder, 1998.

Magazines and Newspaper Articles

Anderson, James K. "Saga of the 4.2 Mortar." *VFW Magazine* (Feb. 1970).

Arms, Angie. "SVCC Breakfast Honors Veterans." *The Richlands News Press* (Nov. 8, 2005) - [Rudolph Whitt, Co. C, 83rd CMB].

Bancroft, Griffing. "Probe Told Garsson Paid Bills of Generals and May at Gay Party." *Chicago Sun* n.d., from files of Sam Kweskin.

Bingham, Rob. "Veterans Gather, Swap war Stories." *The Tennessean* (June 21, 1986) - [83rd CMB 1986 Reunion].

Bluemel, Corey. "A Voice From The Past." [Claude Scovill], *Emory County Progress* (Aug. 12, 2003).

Caraccilo, Dominic J. "Assault On Anzio." *VFW Magazine* (Jan. 1994).

_____ . "Operation Husky: The Capture of Sicily." *VFW Magazine* (June/July 1993).

Colley, David. "Operation Northwind: Greatest Defensive Battle." *VFW Magazine* (Jan. 1995).

Davis, J. W. "Indict May, Garssons on Fraud Charge." Unidentified newspaper clipping courtesy Gordon Mindrum.

Deppen, John. "Bought With Blood, Sold for Cash." *The Daily Item* (July 24, 2005).

Eldredge, Walter J. "Firing Smoke and Conventional Shells, the 4.2 Inch Chemical Mortar Earned Respect On the Battlefield." *World War II Magazine* (Feb. 1999).

"Faulty Shells Killed GI's, Chief Testifies." *The Bluefield (West Virginia) Daily Telegraph* (July 24, 1946).

Foisie, Jack. "How Chemical Mortar Shells Were Lobbed In Sicily." *Chemical Warfare Service Bulletin*.

"Garsson Firms Reported Cleared In Defective Shell Deaths of 38." *Stars and Stripes* (Sept. 7, 1946).

"From Sicily With the 83rd." *Beachhead News* (Dec. 3, 1944).

Gray, Pvt. Justin. "Security Mission." Unidentified article about the 3rd Ranger Battalion in Sicily and Italy.

Hayes, Veryl R. "Psych A – For Platoon Leaders." *Chemical Warfare Service Bulletin*, Vol. 30 – No. 5 (Nov. - Dec. 1944).

Hobbs, Caye. "Army Buddies Reunite." *The Panolian* (May 28, 1999).

Hurd, Beth. "Town Turns Out to Honor the Purple Heart." (Nov. 15, 2007) [article on Antonio Rabaiotti, Co. D, 83rd CMB].

Huso, Deborah. "Veterans Share Memories of World War II." *The Recorder* (May 23, 2003) [Includes interview with Hale H. Hepler - 83rd CMB - of Millboro, VA).

Hutchinson, William S., Jr. "The Forgotten Front." *Chemical Warfare Service Bulletin* #31 (Jan.-Feb. 1945).

_____ . "Use of the 4.2 Inch Chemical Mortar In the Invasion of Italy." *Military Review* #23 (Nov. 1943) [Also in *Chemical Warfare Service Bulletin*, Vol. 29 – No. 8 (Dec. 1943 – Jan. 1944).

Kitchen, Carr P. "From Arzew To Messina." *Chemical Warfare Service Bulletin*, Vol. 29 – No. 6 (Oct. 1943).

Knight, Rex A. "Fighting Engineers On Sicily." *World War II Magazine* (Sept. 1999).

Korman, Seymour. "This Chicagoan Knows His Oaks, Finds Phony One." *The Chicago Tribune* (1945).

Kritzer, Cy. "Bison Slugger Rapp, Pinned By German Fire, Vowed He'd Learn to Hit Lefties If Spared." *The Sporting News* (Aug. 28, 1946).

Kweskin, Sam (artist). [Front Cover], *VFW Magazine* (June/July 2001).

Lakey, R. J. "4.2 By Air Express." *Chemical Warfare Service Bulletin*, Vol. 31 – No. 3 (June – Aug. 1945).

Lewis, Andy J. "U.S. Army Battalion Honors Three World War II Veterans." *The Woodville Republican* (May 1, 2008).

Lt. W. R. W. "Lost Battalion." *Stars and Stripes* (Nov. 30, 1944).

Luz, Lia. "Doctor, 83, Goes Back to Class as a VA Fellow." [Gordon M. Mindrum], *The Cincinnati Post* (Apr. 5, 2003).

Mangelsdorf, P. C. "James Otis Beasley." *Science Magazine* (Vol. 99, No. 2577 - May 19, 1944).

Martin, Ralph G. "How Far Are They Now?". *Stars and Stripes* (Feb. 2, 1945).

_____ . "Biggest Russian Fans Are In 'Foxhole Row'." *Stars and Stripes* (Feb. 5, 1945).

McKenzie, Paul. "The Gas House Gang - A Fighting Song of the CWS." *Chemical Warfare Service Bulletin*, Vol. 29 – No. 5 (Sept. 1943).

Moore, William. "Untitled Article on Trial of Joseph Garsson." *Chicago Tribune*, n.d.

Newman, Bruce. "Always in midst of battle." *San Jose Mercury News* (May 26, 2008) - Interview with Vicente De Leon, Medic, Co. C, 83rd Chemical Mortar Battalion.

Pearl, Jack. "How We Goofed And Won Sicily." *Climax: Exciting Stories For Men* (Oct. 1962).

Pittman, Bob. "Nolan McCraine Is Part of Our Greatest Generation." *The Times* (Mississippi Newspaper) (June 15, 2000)

"Posthumous DSC Given 83rd Officer." (Andre Laus) - possibly from *Stars and Stripes*, n.d., from files of Mike Codega.

Pyle, Ernie. "Beachhead Organization A Marvel of Speed." Unidentified Boston newspaper, courtesy John P. McEvoy.

Schwab, Howard [Co. C, 83rd Chemical Mortar Battalion]. "Pair of Clerks Remove Krauts From Gal's Room." Unidentified newspaper clipping.
Smith, Capt. Robert B. "Case of the Rifled Mortar." *True Magazine*, n.d. [Letter from Capt. Robert B. Smith, Co. C, 83rd Chemical Mortar Battalion] - Courtesy Annette Smith.
"Roll Of Honor." *Chemical Warfare Service Bulletin* (1942 – 1945).
Unidentified article and author. *Yank Magazine*, Aug. 4 (no year given) [article about Gela].
Unidentified author and newspaper. "Garsson's Son Tells of Favors." From files of Sam Kweskin.
Unidentified author. "Lieut. Colonel Cunin Is In Thick of Sicilian Fighting. "From files of Ed Trey.
Unidentified clipping. "Lieutenant Leaves Estate of $6700." From the files of William Gallagher [article about Lt. William S. Doughten, Jr.].
Unidentified clipping. "Lieut. L. A. Merrill Missing In Action." Courtesy Robert L. Merrill.
Unidentified clipping. "Lieut. Merrill of Petersborough Missing." Courtesy Robert L. Merrill.
Unidentified clipping. "Symphony Man's Son Decorated." Courtesy Robert L. Merrill [regarding Lt. Andre N. Laus].
Unidentified clipping. "Robert E. Wilson Home On Leave." Courtesy Robert L. Merrill [describes rescue of *LST 422* survivors by *U.S.S. P.C. 1227* at Anzio].
Unidentified clipping. "Didn't Coddle Capt. Garsson." Courtesy Gordon Mindrum.
Unidentified author. "Army's Smoke Throwers." *Popular Science Magazine* (1941).
Unidentified author. "Observers Wouldn't Play This Nazi Game." Courtesy Ed Trey.
Van Gieson, Paul. "Recalling the Nurses of Anzio." *The Purple Heart* (July - Aug. 1992).
"Vets Defend 4.2 Mortars As 'Above Attack.'" *Stars and Stripes* (Sept. 10, 1946).
Vukson, Stephen W. "83rd Mortar Battalion Distinguished In WW II." Unidentified 2004 Trafford, PA newspaper.
"War Profits Committee Hears Reports Of Deaths From Faulty Mortar Shells." *Stars and Stripes* (July 26, 1946).
Whitt, Rudolph. "Fighting Through WW II: In Combat With the 83rd" Unidentified newspaper clipping, Courtesy Gini Lemoine.
Wren, Christopher S. "Gone, and Mostly Forgotten, Veterans Lament." *The New York Times Metro* (June 1, 1999 – (Interview with Murray Gaille - 83rd CMB). Courtesy Gini Lemoine.

Audio Recordings

83rd Chemical Mortar Bn. Veterans Association, *Rounds Away: World War II Experiences As Told By Fifteen Combat Veterans of the 83rd Chemical Mortar Battalion*, (Jeanette, PA 1999 – compiled by Lee Steedle and Sam Kweskin)
Col. John P. McEvoy, 83rd Chemical Mortar Battalion – Discussion of the 4.2 mortar, command structure of chemical battalions, some history of the 83rd Chemical Mortar Battalion – taped 2005 by McEvoy for Terry Lowry – copy in possession of Terry Lowry
Navy Mine Warfare Veterans Association Reunion, Cincinnati, OH Oct. 1998 – Reunion of YMS – 43 crew members and two soldiers [Eugene A. Plassmann & Claude Shaw] they saved from *LST 422* – tape and edited transcript provided by Eugene A. Plassmann

Newsletters

Trainee Tribune. Official newsletter of the trainee men in the CWS at Edgewood Arsenal, MD 1942, copies provided by Lorraine M. Salvi.
Smoke Screen. Official newsletter of the 83rd Chemical Battalion at Camp Gordon, Georgia 1942 – 1943. Copies provided by Chemical Corps Museum & Archives, Ft. Leonard Wood, MO; Edgewood Arsenal Archives, MD; Jerry Muschinske, St. Francis, WI; and Marcia Daoust, Huntington, WV.
Muzzleblasts. Official newsletter of the 83rd Chemical Mortar Battalion 1944 – present. Copies provided by Sam Kweskin (deceased), Earl Kann (deceased), Ed Trey, Charlie Lowry (deceased), James Fitzgerald, Chemical Corps Museum, Edgewood Arsenal Archives, MD.
Home-Run. Official newsletter of the *U.S.A.T. Thomas H. Barry*, Sept. 17, 1945. Farewell issue for the 103rd Infantry Division. Courtesy Dave Dougherty, Fort Collins, CO.
The Polecat Review. Official newsletter of the 11th Chemical Maintenance Company, January 1945. Vol. 1, No. 1. Copy in records of the 11th Chemical Maintenance Company (RG 400), National Archives, College Park, MD.

Moving Images

Capt. (Dr.) Julius C. Hulcher – WW II – May 1942 to December 1945 – [DVD of color film footage taken during World War II by Capt. Julius C. "Doc" Hulcher, Medical Detachment, 83rd Chemical Mortar Battalion – approximately one and a half hour in length – Camp Lee, Rabat, Italy, France, Austria, etc. - Courtesy of Charles "Chuck" Hulcher, Richmond, VA]
All My Sons, 1947 play by Arthur Miller. Made into a 1948 film and a 1986 made-for-TV movie.

Internet Sites/Articles

Bedingfield, Gary, *Baseball In Wartime*, (www.baseballinwartime.co.uk).
Burdge, Evan & Penny, *Guardians of Freedom: Fred Kohl (Interview)*, (2001)(http://connections.smsd.org/veterans/fred_kohl.htm).
Correll, Jim (Webmaster), *488th Port Battalion* (www.488thportbattalion.org).
Duvall, Bobbe J., *Robert Marlin "John" Chamblee, War Story*, (2000)
Galik, Stanley, *LCI 35 – World War II Experiences* (www.galik.com/stanleygalik1922/lci/lci09.htm).
Gregorio, Henry J. (memoir), *85th Engineer Heavy Pontoon Battalion*, Internet Site. Unit Home Site. (2008). (http://my.att.net/p/s/community.dll?ep=16&groupid=890668&ck=).

Kindell, Don, *Men and Women of the Royal Navy Lost 1922-2007*, (dkindell1@woh.rr.com).

King, Dr. Michael J., *Rangers: Selected Combat Operations of World War II*, (Combat Studies Institute: Leavenworth, KS, June 1985) (http://usacac.army.mil/CAC2/CSI/index.asp).

Nutter, Thomas E., *Operation Husky: The Allied Invasion of Sicily, 1943*, (2003) (www.militaryhistoryonline.com/wwii/husky/postlandings.aspx).

Brenner Pass, on way to Bolzano, Italy
Pirani Collection

Other 83rd Media & Publications

Rounds Away!

Experiences in the Second World War as told in their own words by

Rounds Away - a cassette tape of the WWII experiences of 15 veterans of the 83rd CMB (1999)

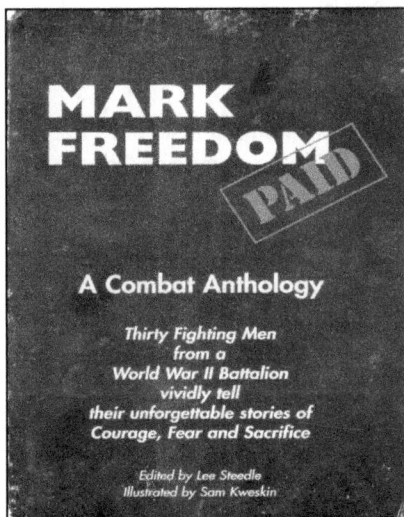

Mark Freedom Paid - A Combat Anthology, (1st Printing 1997)

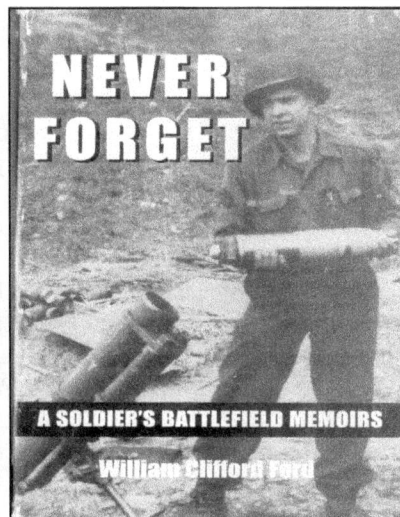

Never Forget - A Soldier's Battlefield Memoirs, by William Clifford Ford, Co. C, 83rd CMB (Published 2005)

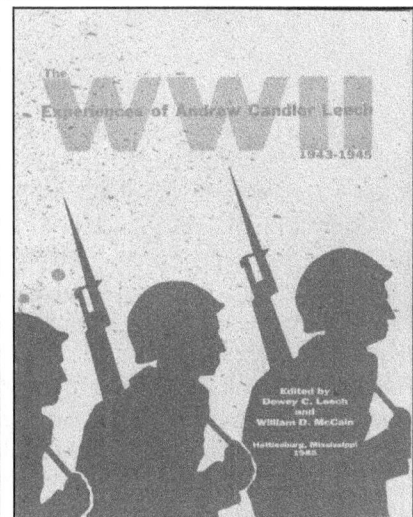

The WWII Experiences of Andrew Candler Leech, Co. B, 83rd CMB (Published 1985)

Terrance David Lowry

Photo: Joetta McCallister Kuhn

Born in Charleston, West Virginia, in 1949, Lowry is a 1967 graduate of South Charleston High School where he worked on the school newspaper. He graduated in 1974 with a B. A. in History from West Virginia State College and studied Civil War History at Marshall University Graduate School.

A professional musician, he was contributing music editor for *The Charleston Gazette* 1970-75 and music editor 1977-78. Lowry spent two years with the Circulation Department of *The Atlanta Journal*. Lowry was employed for 20 years with the circulation department of Charleston Newspapers, Inc. Lowry published his first book, *The Battle of Scary Creek: Military Operations in the Kanawha Valley, April-July 1861*, in July of 1982. He also published *September Blood: The Battle of Carnifex Ferry* (1985); two volumes in the Virginia Regimental Series, *22nd Virginia Infantry* (1988) and *26th (Edgar's) Battalion Virginia Infantry* (1991); and *Last Sleep: The Battle of Droop Mountain November 6, 1863* (1996). He co-authored with Stan Cohen *Images of the Civil War in West Virginia* (2000). Additionally his Civil War articles have been published in *North South Trader, Wonderful West Virginia,* and *Confederate Veteran* magazines, as well as the *West Virginia Hillbilly*. He has also been a contributor to the *Time-Life* series of books and remains an avid collector of Civil War memorabilia. He was historian/curator of the Craik-Patton House, Charleston, West Virginia, for two years and since 2001 has been a historian at the West Virginia State Archives, Charleston, West Virginia.

The author can be reached at 237 Kenna Drive, South Charleston, WV 25309 or by e-mail: TLSnoop@aol.com

www.ingramcontent.com/pod-product-compliance
Lightning Source LLC
Chambersburg PA
CBHW062019090426

42811CB00005B/904